Americans Traveling Abroad: What You Should Know Before You Go

By Gladson I. Nwanna, Ph.D

Second edition, completely revised

World Travel Institute
Baltimore, Maryland

910.2
NWAN

Library of Congress Cataloging-in-Publication Data

Nwanna, Gladson I.
        Americans traveling abroad : what you should know before you go /
by Gladson I. Nwanna. -- 2nd ed., completely rev.
        p.   cm.
        Includes bibliographical references (p.   -   ) and index.
        ISBN 0-9623820-7-8 (alk. paper)
        1. Travel--Handbooks, manuals, etc. I. Title.
G151.N93 1996
910'.2'02--dc20   95-49933
                                                     CIP

ISSN: 1070-3365

Cover Design by Lamont W. Harvey

Printed in the United States of America

Acknowledgement

A lot of people have helped me with the first edition of this book, and continued to do so with this revised edition, giving me everything from encouragement and typesetting to editorial advice and help. I would like to thank, especially, Mrs. Phyllis Desbordes, Dr. Sydney E. Onyeberechi and Mr. Thomas J. Wilcox for their relentless assistance in editing parts of the chapters, and for other valuable suggestions, and Ms. Deborah G. Brown for her assistance in numerous ways.

A special thanks goes to the various agencies of the government whose research and publications have been reproduced in this book, including the employees of the U.S. State Department, Consumer Affairs Division, who put up with my numerous questions and constant requests for one brochure or another. There is no doubt that this book, liked the revised edition would not have materialized within the time it took to put it together without the assistance of the United States Departments of State, Commerce (Customs), Transportation, Treasury, Agriculture, Health and Human Resources whose publications make up a substantial portion of this book

My gratitude and indebtedness also go to the numerous organizations and firms that gave me permission to reproduce some of their proprietary works. These include:

Agora, Inc.: The material was excerpted from The World Catalog, price $12.95 and from International Living, one year subscription price is $29; both publications by Agora Inc., 824 E. Baltimore St., Baltimore, MD 21202; (410) 234-0515. Reprinted by permission. [Reference Code Used in the text **IL**]

Official Airline Guides: Reprinted by permission, Official Airline Guides. [Reference Code used in the text **OG**]

The Putnam Berkley Group, Inc.: Reprinted from Overcoming Jetlag by Charles Ehret and Lynne Scanlon, © 1983. Reprinted by permission, The Berkley Publishing Group, Inc. [Reference Code used in text **PB**]

SPRINT: Reprinted by permission. All rights reserved by SPRINT. .[Reference Code used in the text **ST**]

Runzheimer International: Reprinted by permission. All rights reserved by Runzheimer International. [Reference Code used in the text **RI**]

Airport Association Council International (AACI): Reprinted by permission. All rights reserved by AACI. [Reference Code used in the text **AI**]

Thomas Cook: Reprinted by permission. All rights reserved by Thomas Cook. [Reference Code used in the text **TC**]

Society for the Advancement of Travel for the Handicapped (SATH): Reprinted by permission. All rights reserved by SATH. [Reference Code used in the text **SH**]

Suburban Publishing of Connecticut, Inc. (SPCI): Reprinted by permission. All rights reserved by SPCI. AT&T Green Pages. [Reference Code used in the text **SP**]

Air Transport Association of America (ATAA): Reprinted by permission. [Reference Code used in the text **AT**]

Major Long Distance Telephone Carriers whose information and cooperation contributed immensely in the writing of Chapter 44: AT&T, MCI, SPRINT, RCI, METROMEDIA

Finally, I thank the thousands of travelers whose lives and trips have been enriched by information they found in the maiden edition of this book, particularly, to the hundreds of you who either called or wrote us, with praises for the content and coverage. Your encouragement and inspiration remains a driving force towards the completion of this edition.

Preface

International travel can be very safe, enriching and exciting with careful and adequate preparations. On the other hand, it can become wasteful, expensive, boring, embarrassing and a nightmare if the traveler is misinformed or not adequately informed.

The key to a successful trip overseas, however, will depend, to a large part, on how well you invest in preparing for such trips; particularly, familiarizing yourself with a variety of conditions, laws, rules, regulations and requirements, both at home and abroad that will affect your trip. Learning as much as you can about the host countries is very important and should be considered a vital aspect of your trip overseas. Such a learning exercise is invaluable and will cut down on the potential for costly and avoidable mistakes. Above all, it will add more fun to your trip, rather than hurt your trip.

The key to having a successful trip abroad is to start preparing for the trip not on the day you plan to take off, but weeks or months earlier. Your preparation should start from home and not when you are already in transit or when you are already overseas. Plans should include pre-flight preparations and considerations, as well as on-flight and post-flight considerations.

Admittedly, investment in pre-vacation planning aimed at ensuring a successful and enjoyable trip overseas can be time-consuming, expensive, and many times, confusing and frustrating to both seasoned and non-seasoned overseas travelers alike.

For most overseas travelers and intending travelers, a major difficulty is having access to relevant and reliable information and resources in a timely, direct, comprehensive and simplified form to maximize time, energy and knowledge. These goals have been met in this book.

The driving motive of the author is to compile a book that is truly informative, comprehensive in form and, at the same time, reliable and authoritative as a source. It is a one-stop source for the numerous, but fragmented and little publicized overseas travel information and resources. Further, it provides answers and sources of reference for the frequently asked questions, issues and concerns often sought after by Americans traveling abroad.

This book is, indeed, comprehensive and has several unique features that separate it from the numerous tour and travel books and guides available on the market. This book contains information:

■ covering **over 170** countries;

- including most of the available information directed to Americans traveling abroad prepared by agencies of the United States Government such as the Departments of State, Health and Human Resources, Customs, Transportation, Commerce and the Treasury;

- covering every continent or region of the world that Americans travel;

- including passports and current visa, vaccination and other entry/exit requirements for most countries of the world;

- for Americans residing abroad;

- first time as well as seasoned travelers;

- for business travelers;

- for disabled travelers, older travelers, student travelers, and for minors traveling unaccompanied;

- including safety, money, shopping, security, and health tips;

- including tips on getting financial and other forms of assistance overseas;

- including information on foreign adoptions, international child abduction and hostage situations;

- including up-to-date information on the new democracies of Eastern Europe and the former Soviet republics, now the Commonwealth of Independent States.

    Importantly, in this second edition of the book, readers will find additional unique features including:

- completely updated and revised information;

- tips for business travelers;

- tips for traveling and transporting pets;

- U.S. Customs tips for returning U.S. Government Personnel.

The Appendix section is filled with valuable addresses and telephone numbers of numerous organizations, institutions and agencies often sought after, but very often not readily accessible to Americans traveling abroad, together with country by country information, ranging from tipping, telephone codes, electricity requirements, commercial holidays and currencies to local weights and measures.

The book includes tips and advice on a variety of issues, questions and concerns of travelers to almost any part of the globe. The information will benefit the first time traveler, seasoned travelers, travel agencies, tour operators, tourists and those going on business trips; it contains security information for both American citizens and American businesses operating overseas. It also includes tips and guidelines on cultural **Do's and Don'ts** for several countries, and provides a unique perspective, considering that a large portion of the information is directly from the United States Government through its various agencies and directed particularly to Americans traveling abroad.

An additional and unique feature of this book is its wide appeal. Most of the information should be useful and beneficial to every international traveler, irrespective of the country of origin and/or country of departure. Several of the topics discussed and tips provided have no boundaries, and are applicable to anyone traveling to a foreign country.

There are, of course, a number of helpful travel books readily found in bookstores, including those published by the major publishers referenced in Chapter 46 of this book. Although these guides are useful, most of them tell you what you need to know while you are already abroad, leaving out the more important things that you should know **BEFORE YOU GO**: things that could determine how well you enjoy your trip and how successful it will be. This book provides you precisely with those important pieces of information you need to know **BEFORE YOU GO** and more. It covers more countries and provides more region and country-specific detailed information that you will need **While Abroad**.

It is my expectation that the information contained in this revised edition will continue to make a big difference, particularly in ensuring a safe, enjoyable, rewarding and hitch-free trip for millions of Americans and overseas-bound travelers. We hope that your expectations will be met, and when they are, we will appreciate hearing from you. Should we fall short in meeting your expectations or in addressing adequately your overseas travel concerns, we would certainly like to hear from you, so that an effort can be made to improve future editions. Suggestions and letters should be mailed to Public Relations Department, WTI, P.O. Box 32674, Baltimore, Maryland 21208.

Editor's Note:

[1]   Perhaps, little is known about the numerous publications and services for Americans traveling abroad, made available by the United States Government through its various agencies. A good number is also available from several non-governmental agencies and organizations. Unfortunately, many needy overseas travelers are not aware of these resources. In this book, an effort has been made to fill in that gap by reproducing most of those publications with adequate references to other useful services and resources available to overseas travelers. Similarly, a variety of valuable expert advice and answers to questions of potential interest to travelers is available in the media, but are often limited to a few subscribers to travel newsletters and magazines. This book provides these sources by incorporating the advice of experts in the field. To all these sources, we must say THANKS for facilitating the process of preparing this book.

[2]   The publisher has made a determined effort to reproduce all the borrowed materials verbatim and in their entirety. For the most part, this objective was accomplished. Only in a few instances in the book, was it necessary to make minor alterations in order to facilitate reading and to ensure consistency and uniformity. This is particularly the case with pagination, cross referencing and, also, with the use of chapter, section and text in the place of brochure, publication, bulletin, pamphlet and leaflet as used in the original documents. We must also point out an important but deliberate feature of the book that could easily become obvious to a meticulous reader; that is, a seeming repetition of titles, topics, ideas, paragraphs and sections. This is a deliberate action, due in part, to our determination to represent, as much as possible, borrowed materials in their original forms and structure. It is, in addition, partly, due to our desire and resolve to ensure that important tips and advice are not missed by those travelers or readers who, under the pressures of daily life, may not have the time to read the entire book and/or might only concentrate on a few select chapters. Furthermore, where repetition appears to be the case, it underscores our own belief in the importance of the information being conveyed. While it is realistic to assume that some readers and travelers may be pressed for time and, thus, may not be able to go through the entire book, we do encourage them (without prejudice) to include in their reading, Chapters 1, 4, 5 and 43. These chapters contain information that is more general than most of the other chapters.

[3]   We believe you will agree with us that we live in changing times, which include changing political, social, cultural and economic climates, both at home and abroad, that, invariably, may impact on international travels. Whereas most of the information contained in this book will remain valid perhaps through the ages, some is bound to change. We have anticipated that to be the case; hence, we have provided you with relevant references, including addresses and phone numbers of government and non-government agencies and organizations that will keep you up-to-date.

Not the least of interest for readers of this type of book will be that relating to information on prices of publications quoted here and addresses and phone numbers of various organizations cited throughout the book. Similarly, for a book of this size, even with all the carefulness and diligence on the part of the publisher, errors and omissions are bound to occur and we have acknowledged that. We urge you to inform us whenever you find such errors and omissions, so that we may correct them in the next edition. Whereas, at the time this book went to press, we did our best to ensure that all of the prices and references are accurate, we must, however, make this explicit disclaimer:

DISCLAIMER:

Neither the publisher nor the author can accept responsibility for errors or omissions that may occur, nor will they be held responsible for the experiences of readers while they are traveling. The information contained in this book is meant to serve only as a guide and to assist you in your travel plans. This information is neither all inclusive, exhaustive nor cast in bronze. Similarly, we warn that neither the author nor the publisher recommends or attests to the legal status, reliability and quality of services and products provided by any of the agencies, organizations, and business firms mentioned in this book. Independent verification and assessment are strongly recommended, including checking with your local government's Consumer Affairs Office and the Better Business Bureau

TABLE OF CONTENTS

CHAPTER 7: KNOW BEFORE YOU GO: US CUSTOMS HINTS (including customs duties) 73

CHAPTER 8: U.S. CUSTOMS HIGHLIGHTS FOR GOVERNMENT PERSONNEL (Civilian & Military) 89

CHAPTER 9: HEALTH INFORMATION FOR INTERNATIONAL TRAVELS 99

CHAPTER 10: TIPS FOR AMERICANS RESIDING ABROAD 151

CHAPTER 11: TRAVEL TIPS FOR OLDER AMERICANS 161

CHAPTER 12: TRAVEL TIPS FOR THE DISABLED 167

CHAPTER 13: TIPS FOR STUDENTS TRAVELING ABROAD 173

CHAPTER 14: TIPS FOR TRAVELERS TO THE CARIBBEAN 177

CHAPTER 15: TIPS FOR TRAVELERS TO CENTRAL AND SOUTH AMERICA 185

CHAPTER 16: TIPS FOR TRAVELERS TO THE PEOPLE'S REPUBLIC OF CHINA 191

CHAPTER 17: TIPS FOR TRAVELERS TO EASTERN EUROPE 197

CHAPTER 18: TIPS FOR TRAVELERS TO MEXICO 207

CHAPTER 19: TIPS FOR TRAVELERS TO THE MIDDLE EAST AND NORTH AFRICA 217

CHAPTER 20: TIPS FOR TRAVELERS TO RUSSIA AND THE NEWLY INDEPENDENT STATES 231

CHAPTER 21: TIPS FOR TRAVELERS TO SOUTH ASIA 245

CHAPTER 22: TIPS FOR TRAVELERS TO SUB-SAHARAN AFRICA 249

CHAPTER 23: TIPS FOR TRAVELERS TO WESTERN EUROPE AND AUSTRALIA 263

CHAPTER 24: TIPS FOR BUSINESS TRAVELERS 271

CHAPTER 25: DUAL NATIONALITY 275

CHAPTER 26: GETTING HELP ABROAD FROM US CONSULS 277

CHAPTER 33: TIPS ON BRINGING FOOD, PLANT, AND ANIMAL PRODUCTS INTO THE US 305

CHAPTER 34: BUYING A CAR OVERSEAS? BEWARE! 311

CHAPTER 35: IMPORTING A CAR/PLEASURE BOAT 315

CHAPTER 36: GENERALIZED SYSTEM OF PREFERENCE AND THE TRAVELER 327

CHAPTER 37: US CUSTOMS: INTERNATIONAL MAIL IMPORTS 331

CHAPTER 38:
INTERNATIONAL PARENTAL CHILD ABDUCTION 337

CHAPTER 39:
INTERNATIONAL ADOPTIONS 357

CHAPTER 40: FLY RIGHTS: YOUR RIGHTS AND RESPONSIBILITIES AS AN AIR TRAVELER 365

CHAPTER 41: AVOIDING JET LAG 387

CHAPTER 42: COMMUNICATING TO AND FROM OVERSEAS 391

CHAPTER 43: CLIMATES OF THE WORLD 397

CHAPTER 44: UNDECIDED ON WHICH COUNTRY TO VISIT? 421

APPENDICES

Chapter 1

Your Trip Abroad (Before, During and After)

[The information in this chapter is reprinted verbatim from a bulletin issued by the U.S. State Department, Bureau of Consular Affairs. It is intended to serve as advice to Americans traveling abroad.]

- - - -

FOREWORD

Whether you are traveling overseas for business, pleasure or study, the best way to insure a carefree and relaxing trip is to prevent problems before they happen. The more you learn about passports, visas, customs, immunizations, and other travel basics, the less likely you are to have difficulties on the road.

We have written this guide to help you organize and take a pleasant, trouble-free trip. In the back of the book, we refer you to other sources of travel information covering such matters as customs regulations, agricultural restrictions, visa requirements, U.S. embassy addresses, foreign country information, and more. For your convenience, U.S. passport agencies are listed at the end of the pamphlet.

The Department of State in Washington, D. C., and its more than 250 U.S. embassies and consulates worldwide, as well as other U.S. Government agencies, are ready and pleased to offer assistance whenever possible. This is your trip. Make it a good one.

Elizabeth M. Tamposi
Assistant Secretary
Bureau of Consular Affairs

Before You Go

There is a lot you can do to prepare for your trip, depending upon where, how long and why you are going. Get organized--you can use this chapter's Table of Contents as a checklist.

Learn About the Places You Will Visit

Here are some good sources:

A travel agent can provide brochures and tourist information about the countries you plan to visit.Your travel agent should also be able to provide you with the Department of State travel advisory for any country you plan to visit, if an advisory has been issued for the country. If your travel agent cannot provide travel advisories, you can obtain them 24-hours a day by calling (202) 647-

5225 (see below for details). Look in your local bookstore and public library for books on foreign travel.

Many countries have tourist information offices in large cities[1] that can give you brochures and, in some cases, maps, international airlines[2] may also supply you with travel brochures on the countries they serve.

Foreign embassies or consulates in the United States can provide up-to-date information on their countries. Addresses and telephone numbers of the embassies of foreign governments are listed in the Congressional Directory[3], available at most public libraries. In addition to their embassies, some countries also have consulates in major U.S. cities. Look for their addresses in your local telephone directory, or find them in the publication, Foreign Consular Offices in the United States, available in many public libraries.

Check on Travel Advisories

The Department of State issues travel advisories to alert U.S. citizens to conditions overseas that may affect them adversely. There are three types of travel advisories:[4]

Warning: recommends deferral of travel to all or part of a country.

Caution: advises about unusual security conditions, including the potential for unexpected detention, unstable political conditions, or serious health problems. It is not intended to deter travel to a country.

Notice: provides information on situations that do not present a broad scale risk, but which could result in inconvenience or difficulty for traveling Americans.

Travel advisories are posted at U.S. passport agencies, Department of Commerce field offices, and at U.S. embassies and consulates around the world. They are distributed to the travel and airline industry and can be found through airline computer reservation systems. If

1

you plan travel to an area or country where there is some concern about existing conditions, find out if there is a travel advisory by contacting the nearest passport agency or your travel agent or airline. You may also listen to recorded travel advisories, 24-hours a day. Call the Department of State's Citizens Emergency Center[5] on 202-647-5225.

Things to Be Sure You Have
Travel document requirements vary from country to country, but you will need the following: a passport or other proof of citizenship, plus a visa or a tourist card. You may also need evidence that you have enough money for your trip and/or have ongoing or return transportation tickets.

A Valid Passport
[The Information on Passports slotted for this section is reproduced in the chapter entitled "Passports". Check the Table of Contents for location.]

Obtain Visas
A visa is an endorsement or stamp placed in your passport by a foreign government that permits you to visit that country for a specified purpose and a limited time - for example, a 3-month tourist visa. It is advisable to obtain visas before you leave the United States because you will not be able to obtain visas for some countries once you have departed. Apply directly to the embassy or nearest consulate of each country you plan to visit, or consult a travel agent. **Passport agencies cannot help you obtain visas.**

"Foreign Entry Requirements"
Department of State publication M-264, Foreign Entry Requirements[6], gives entry requirements for every country and tells where and how to apply for visas and tourist cards. It can be ordered for $0.50 from the Consumer Information Center, Pueblo, Colorado 81009. Note: The publication is updated annually but may not reflect the most current requirements. It is advisable to verify the latest visa requirements with the embassy or consulate of each country you plan to visit.

Because a visa is stamped directly onto a blank page in your passport, you will need to give your passport to an official of each foreign embassy or consulate. You will also need to fill out a form, and you may need one or more photographs. Many visas require a fee. The process may take several weeks for each visa, so apply well in advance of your trip.

Tourist Card
If the country you plan to visit only requires a tourist card, obtain one from the country's embassy or consulate, from an airline serving the country, or at the port of entry. There is a fee for some tourist cards.

Proof of Citizenship
Check with the embassy or consulate of each country you plan to visit to learn what proof of citizenship is required of visitors. Even if a country does not require a visitor to have a passport, it will require some proof of citizenship and identity. Remember that no matter what proof of citizenship a foreign country requires. U.S. Immigration has strict requirements for your reentry into the United States. See page 19 for U.S. Immigration entry requirements.

Immunizations
Under international health regulations adopted by the World Health Organization, a country may require international certificates of vaccination against yellow fever and cholera. Typhoid vaccinations are not required for international travel, but are recommended for areas where there is risk of exposure. Smallpox vaccinations are no longer given. Check your health care records to insure that your measles, mumps, rubella, polio, diphtheria, tetanus, and pertussis immunizations are up-to-date. Medications to deter malaria and other preventive measures are advisable for certain areas. No immunizations are needed to return to the United States.

Information on immunization requirements, U.S. Public Health Service recommendations, and other health hints are included in the book, Health Information for International Travel[7], available for $6.50 from the U.S. Government Printing Office, Washington, D.C. 20402. You may also obtain such information from local and state health departments or physicians.

This information is also available on the Centers for Disease Control 24-hour hotline: 404-639-2572.

It is not necessary to be vaccinated against a disease you will not be exposed to and few countries refuse to admit you if you arrive without the necessary vaccinations. Officials will either vaccinate you, give you a medical follow-up card, or, in rare circumstances, put you in isolation for the incubation period of the disease you were not vaccinated against. Check requirements before you depart.

If vaccinations are required, they must be recorded on approved forms, such as those in the booklet PHS-731, International Certificates of Vaccination as Approved by the World Health Organization. If your doctor or public health office does not have this booklet, it can be obtained for $2 from the Superintendent of Documents, U.S. Government Printing Office, Washington, D.C. 20402 or Government Printing Office Bookstores.

Keep it with your passport.

Some countries require certification from long-term visitors that they are free of the human immuno-deficiency virus (HIV). Generally, this has little bearing on tourists and short-term visitors. Check with the embassy or consultant of the countries you will visit for the latest information.

Health Insurance

For travelers who become seriously ill or injured overseas, obtaining medical treatment and hospital care can be costly. **The Social Security Medicare program does not cover hospital and medical services outside the United States.** Before you leave the United States, learn what medical services your health insurance will cover abroad.

If your health insurance policy does not cover you abroad, you are urged to purchase a temporary health policy that does. There are short-term health and emergency assistance policies designed for travelers.

You can find the names of such companies from your travel agent, your health insurance company, or from advertisements in travel publications[4]. In addition to health insurance, many policies include trip cancellation, baggage loss, and travel accident insurance in the same package. Some travelers check companies have protection policies available for those who purchase travelers checks.

Medical Evacuation

One of the chief advantages of health and emergency assistance policies is that they often include coverage for medical evacuation to the United States. Medical evacuation can easily cost $5,000 depending upon your location and medical condition. Even if your regular health insurance covers you for emergencies abroad, consider purchasing a supplemental insurance policy to cover medical evacuation.

Whichever health insurance coverage you choose for overseas, remember to bring your policy identity card and claim forms with you.

How to Bring Money

Travelers Checks

Do not carry large amounts of cash. Take most of your money in travelers checks and remember to record the serial number, denomination and the date and location of the issuing bank or agency. Keep this information in a safe and separate place so if you lose your travelers checks you can get replacements quickly.

Credit Cards

Some credit cards can be used world-wide, even for cash advances. Keep track of your credit card purchases so as not to exceed your limit. Travelers have been arrested overseas for mistakenly exceeding their credit limit! Leave all unnecessary credit cards at home. Record the numbers of the credit cards that you do bring and keep the list in a separate place from the cards.

Always report the loss or theft of your credit cards or travelers checks immediately to the companies and notify the local police. If you will stay in one place for some time, consider opening an account for check cashing and other transactions at a U.S. bank that has an overseas affiliate. U.S. embassies and consulates cannot cash checks for you.

Prepare for Emergency Funds

Keep the telephone number for your bank in the United States with you in the event you run out of cash and need to transfer money. In some countries, major banks and certain travel agencies can help you arrange a transfer of funds from your account to a foreign bank. If you do not have a bank account from which you can obtain emergency funds, make arrangements in advance with a relative or friend to send you emergency funds should it become necessary. If you find yourself destitute, contact the nearest U.S. embassy or consulate for assistance in arranging a money wire transfer from a relative or friend in the United States.

Foreign Currency

Before departing, you may wish to purchase small amounts of foreign currency to use for buses, taxis, phones, or tips when you first arrive. Foreign exchange facilities at airports may be closed when your flight arrives. You can purchase foreign currency at some U.S. banks, at foreign exchange firms, or at foreign exchange windows or even vending machines at many international airports in the United States.

Some countries regulate the amount of local currency you can bring into or take out of the country; others require that you exchange a minimum amount of currency. For currency regulations, check with a bank, foreign exchange firm, your travel agent, or the embassy or consulate of the countries you plan to visit.

If you leave or enter the United States with more than $10,000 in monetary instruments of any kind, you must file a report, Customs Form 4790, with U.S. Customs at the time. Failure to comply can result in civil and criminal proceedings.

3

Valuables-Don't Bring Them!

Do not bring anything on your trip that you would hate to lose such as expensive jewelry, family photographs, or objects of sentimental value. If you bring jewelry, wear it discreetly to help avoid grab-and-run robbery.

Other Things to Arrange Ahead

Lodging

Reserve in Advance

Many travelers wait until they reach their destination before making hotel reservations. Some train stations and airports have travel desks to assist you in finding lodging. However, when you arrive, you may be tired and unfamiliar with your surroundings, and could have difficulty locating a hotel to meet your needs. Therefore, when possible, reserve your lodging in advance and reconfirm your reservations along the way. During peak tourist season, it is important have a hotel reservation for at least the first night you arrive in a foreign city.

An alternative to hotels and pensions is the youth hostel system, offering travelers of all ages clean, inexpensive, overnight accommodations in more than 6,000 locations in over 70 countries worldwide. Hostels provide dormitory-style accommodations with separate facilities for males and females. Some hostels have family rooms that can be reserved in advance. Curfews are often imposed and membership is often required. You may write to: American Youth Hostels, P.O. Box 37613, Washington, D.C. 20013-7613.

Organized Programs

The majority of private programs for vacation, study of work abroad are reputable and financially sound. However, some charge exorbitant fees, use deliberately false "educational" claims, and provide working conditions far different from those advertised. Even programs of legitimate organizations can be poorly administered. Be cautious. **Before committing yourself of your finances, find out about the organization and what it offers.**

Student Travelers

Students can save money on transportation and accommodations, and obtain other discounts if they have an International Student Identity Card. This card is available with proof of student status and a small fee from: Council on International Educational Exchange; 205 East 42nd Street; New York, New York 10017. Membership also provides some accident and health insurance while abroad.

Transportation

At the time of publication, U.S. citizens traveling abroad are required to pay a $12 federal inspection fee and a $6 federal departure tax that are included in the price of the air ticket.

Charter Flights and Airlines

There have been occasions when airlines or companies that sell charter flights or tour packages have gone out of business with little warning, stranding passengers overseas. If you know from the media or from your travel agent or the airline what recourse you would have if the airline ceased to operate. Some airlines may honor the tickets of a defunct airline, but they usually do so with restrictions.

Before you purchase a charter flight or tour package, read the contract carefully. Unless it guarantees they will deliver services promised or give a full refund, consider purchasing trip insurance. If you are unsure of the reputation of a charter company or tour operator, consult your local Better Business Bureau or the American Society of Travel Agents at 1101 King Street, Alexandria, VA 22314 Tel. (703) 739-2782, to learn if the company has a complaint record.

Driver's License/Auto Insurance

If you intend to drive overseas, check with the embassy or consulate of the countries you will visit to learn their driver's license, road permit, and auto insurance requirements. If possible, obtain road maps before you go.

Many countries do not recognize a U.S. driver's license. Most, however, accept an international driver's permit. Before departure, obtain one at a local office of an automobile association.[9] You must be at least age 18, and you will need two passport-sized photographs and your valid U.S. license. Certain countries require road permits instead of tolls to use their divided highways and will fine drivers without a permit.

Car rental agencies overseas usually provide auto insurance, but in some countries, the required coverage is minimal. A good rule of thumb when renting a car overseas is to purchase insurance coverage that is at least equivalent to that which you carry at home.

In general, your U.S. auto insurance does not cover you abroad. However, your policy may apply when you drive to countries that neighbor the United States. Check with your insurer to see if your policy covers you in Canada, Mexico, or countries south of Mexico. Even if your policy is valid in one of these countries, it may not meet its minimum requirements. For instance, in most of Canada, you must carry at least $200,000 in liability insurance, and Mexico requires that if vehicles do not carry theft, third party liability, and comprehensive insurance, the owner must post a bond that could be as high as 50% of the value of the vehicle. If you are under-insured for a country, auto insurance can usually be purchased on either side of the border.

U.S. Custom Pre-registration
Learn about U.S. Customs regulations. Foreign-made personal articles taken abroad are subject to duty and tax unless you have proof of prior possession such as a receipt, bill of sale, an insurance policy, or a jeweler's appraisal. If you do not have proof of prior possession, items such as foreign-made watches, cameras, or tape recorders that can be identified by serial number or permanent markings may be taken to the Customs office nearest you or at the port of departure for registration before departing the Unites States. The certificate of registration provided can expedite free entry of these items when you return.

Documentation for Medications
If you go abroad with preexisting medical problems, carry a letter from your doctor describing your condition, including information on any prescription medicines you must take. You should also have the generic names of the drugs. Leave medicines in their original, labeled containers. These precautions make customs processing easier. A doctor's certificate, however, may not suffice as authorization to transport all prescription drugs to all foreign countries. Travelers have innocently been arrested for drug violations when carrying items not considered to be narcotics in the United States. To ensure you do not violate the drug laws of the countries you visit, consult the embassy or consulate of those countries for precise information before leaving the United States.

If you have allergies, reactions to certain medicines, or other unique medical problems, consider wearing a medical alert bracelet or carrying a similar warning.

Several private organizations provide listings of physicians to international travelers. Membership in these organizations is generally free, although a donation may be requested. Membership entitles the traveler to a number of traveler's medical aids, including a directory of physicians with their overseas locations, telephone numbers and doctors' fee schedules. The physicians are generally English-speaking and provide medical assistance 24 hours a day. The addresses of these medical organizations are in travel magazines or may be available from your travel agent.[10]

Places to Receive Mail
If you are traveling for an extended period, you may want to arrange to pick up mail or messages. Some banks and international credit card companies handle mail for customers at their overseas branches. General Delivery (Poste Restante) services at post offices in most countries will hold mail for you. **U.S. embassies and consulates do not handle private mail.**

Learn About Dual Nationality
Whether you are a U.S. Citizen from birth or were naturalized as a U.S. citizen, a foreign country may claim you as its citizen if:

- You were born there.
- Your parent is or was a citizen of that country.
- You are married to a citizen of that country.

If any of the possibilities for dual nationality applies to you, check on your status (including military obligations) with the embassy or consulate of the country that might claim you as citizen. In particular, Americans may have problems with dual nationality in certain countries in the Middle East, in South America, and in Africa. Some foreign countries refuse to recognize a dual national's U.S. citizenship and do not allow U.S. officials access to arrested Americans.

Some Things to Leave Behind

Your Itinerary - Leave a Paper Trail
Leave a detailed itinerary (with names, addresses, and phone numbers of persons and places to be visited) with relatives or friends in the United States so you can be reached in an emergency. Also include a photocopy of your passport information page.

Other Important Numbers
It is a good idea to make a list of all important numbers - your passport information as well as your credit card, travelers checks, and airline ticket numbers. Leave a copy at home and carry a copy with you, separate from your valuables.

While You Are Overseas

How to Deal With the Unexpected
If you change your travel plans, miss your return flight, or extend your trip, be sure to notify relatives or friends back home. Should you find yourself in an area of civil unrest or natural disaster, let them know as soon as you can that you are safe. In addition, contact the nearest U.S. embassy or consulate to register your

presence and to keep the U.S. consul informed of your whereabouts.

Safety Tips

Protect Your Passport

Your passport is the most valuable document you will carry abroad. It confirms your U.S. citizenship. Guard it carefully. Do not use it as collateral for a loan or lend it to anyone. It is your best form of identification. You will need it when you pick up mail or check into hotel, embassies or consulates.

When entering some countries or registering at hotels, you may be asked to fill out a police card listing your name, passport number, destination, local address, and reason for traveling. You may be required to leave your passport at the hotel reception desk overnight so it may be checked by local police officials. These are normal procedures required by local laws. If your passport is not returned the following morning, immediately report the impoundment to local police authorities and the nearest U.S. embassy or consulate.

Passport Fraud

Law enforcement records show that U.S. passports are sometimes used for illegal entry into the United States or by criminals abroad seeking to establish another identity. This can cause embarrassment to innocent citizens whose names become associated with illegal activities. To protect the integrity of the U.S. passport and the security of the person bearing it, consular officers overseas have found it necessary to take precautions in processing lost passport cases. These precautions may involve some delay before a new passport is issued.

Safeguard Your Passport

Carelessness is the main cause for losing a passport or having it stolen. You may find that you have to carry your passport with you because either you need to show it when you cash travelers checks or the country you are in requires you to carry it as an identity document. When you must carry your passport, hide it securely on your person. Do not leave it in a handbag or an exposed pocket. Whenever possible, leave your passport in the hotel safe, not in an empty hotel room or packed in your luggage. One family members should not carry all the passports for the entire family.

Guard Against Thieves

Coat pockets, handbags, and hip pockets are particularly susceptible to theft. Thieves will use all kinds of ploys to divert your attention just long enough to pick your pocket and grab your purse or wallet.

These ploys include creating a disturbance, spilling something on your clothing, or even handing you a baby to hold!

Prevent theft by carrying your belongings in a secure manner. Consider not carrying a purse or wallet when going on crowed street. Women who carry a shoulder bag should keep it tucker under the arm and held securely by the strap. Men should put their wallets in their front trouser pockets or use money belts instead of hip pockets. A wallet wrapped in rubber bands is more difficult to remove undetected.

Be especially cautious in a large crowd - in the subway, marketplace, at a festival, or if surrounded by groups of vagrant children. Do not make it easy for thieves!

Financial and Shopping Tips

Currency

Local banks usually offer better rates of exchange than hotels, restaurants, or stores. Rates are often posted in windows. Above all, avoid private currency transactions. In some countries, you risk more than being swindled or stuck with counterfeit currency - you risk arrest. Avoid the black market - learn and obey the local currency laws wherever you go.

Shopping

Mail Small Items

When you purchase small items, it is a good idea to mail them personally to your home or to carry them in your luggage. This will help prevent misdirected packages, nonreceipt of merchandise, or receipt of wrong merchandise. When you mail purchases, be sure to ask about insurance.

American embassies and consulates abroad cannot serve as post offices. They cannot accept, hold, or forward mail for U.S. citizens abroad.

The Value Added Tax

Some European countries levy a value added tax (VAT) on the items you buy. In some places, if you ship your purchase home, the VAT can be waived. Other places may require you to pay the VAT, but have a system to refund it to you by mail. Ask the store clerk for an application to apply for the refund. The VAT refund is only for items you can ship or carry with you. It does not apply to food, hotel bills, or other services. Because the rules for VAT refunds vary from country to country, check with the country's tourist office to learn the local requirements.

Things to Beware of Purchasing

Wildlife Souvenirs

Be careful when you buy articles made from animals and plants or purchase live wild animals to bring back as pets. Some items, such as those made from elephant ivory, sea turtles, crocodile leather, or fur from endangered cats, and many species of live animals cannot be brought into the United States legally. Your wildlife souvenirs could be confiscated by government inspectors, and you could face other penalties for attempting to bring them into the United States. **Do not buy wildlife or wildlife products unless you are certain they are legal for import into the United States.** For more information, see page 10.

Glazed Ceramics

Beware of purchasing glazed ceramic ware abroad. It is possible to suffer lead poisoning if you consume food or beverages that are stored or served in improperly glazed ceramics. Unless the ceramics are made by a firm with an international reputation, there is not immediate way to be certain a particular item is safe. The U.S. Food and Drug Administration recommends that ceramic tableware purchased abroad be tested for lead release by a commercial laboratory on your return or be used for decorative purposes only. For more information, see page 10.

Antiques

Some countries consider antiques to be national treasures and the "inalienable property of the nation". In some countries, customs authorities seize illegally purchased antiques without compensation and may also levy fines on the purchaser. Americans have been arrested and prosecuted for purchasing antiques. Americans have even been arrested for purchasing reproductions of antiques from street vendors because a local authority believed the purchase was a national treasure.

Protect yourself. In countries where antiques are important, document your purchases as reproductions if that is the case, or if they are authentic, secure the necessary export permit. The documentation or export permit may be available through the country's national museum. A reputable dealer may provide the export permit or information on how to secure one.

If you have questions about purchasing antiques, the country's tourist office can guide you. If you still have doubts, consult the Consular Section of the nearest U.S. embassy or consulate. In places where Americans have had problems because of purchasing antiques, the Consular Section is well aware of the situation. They can tell you about the local laws and the correct procedures to follow.

Customs

Keep all receipts for items you buy overseas. They will be

helpful in making your U.S. Customs declaration when you return.

Legal Tips

Obey Foreign Laws

When you are in a foreign country, you are subject to its laws. Learn about local laws and regulations and obey them. Avoid areas of unrest and disturbance. Deal only with authorized outlets when exchanging money or buying airline tickets and travelers checks. Do not deliver a package for anyone unless you know the person well and are certain the package does not contain drugs or other contraband.

Before you sell personal effects, such as clothing, cameras, or jewelry, learn the local regulations regarding such sales. Adhere strictly to local laws because the penalties you risk are severe.

Some countries are particularly sensitive about photographs. In general, refrain from photographing police and military installations and personnel; industrial structures including harbor, rail, and airport facilities; border areas; and scenes of civil disorder or other public disturbance. Taking such photographs may result in your detention, in the confiscation of your camera and films, and the imposition of fines. For information on photograph restrictions, check with the country's tourist office or its embassy or consulate in the United States. Once abroad, check with local authorities or at the Consular Section of the nearest U.S. embassy or consulate.

Drug Arrests

About 3000 Americans are arrested abroad each year. Of these, approximately one-third are held on drug charges. Despite repeated warnings, drug arrests and convictions are still a common occurrence. Many countries have stiff penalties for drug violations and strictly enforce drug laws. You are subject to foreign, not U.S. laws overseas, and you will find, if arrested, that:

- Few countries provide a jury trail.
- Most countries do not accept bail.
- Pretrial detention, often in solitary confinement, may last months.
- Prisons may lack even minimal

comforts - beds, toilet, wash basin.

- Diets are often inadequate and require supplements from relatives and friends.
- Officials may not speak English.
- Physical abuse, confiscation of personal property, degrading or inhumane treatment, and extortion are possible.

If you are convicted, you face a possible sentence of:

- 2 - 10 years in many countries.
- A minimum of 6 years hard labor and a stiff fine in some countries.
- The death penalty in some countries.

Do not get involved will illegal drugs overseas. It can spoil more than your vacation. It can ruin you life!

Legal Aid

Because you are subject to local laws abroad, there is little that a U.S. consul can do for you if you encounter legal difficulties. For example, a consular officer cannot get you out of jail. What American officials can do is limited by both foreign and U.S. laws. The U.S. Government has neither funds nor authority to pay your legal fees or related expenses.

Although U.S. consular officers cannot serve as attorney or give legal advice, they can provide a list of local attorneys and help you find adequate legal representation. The lists of attorneys are carefully compiled from local bar association lists and responses to questionnaires, but neither the Department of State nor U.S. embassies or consulates abroad can assume responsibility for the caliber, competence, or professional integrity of the attorneys.

If you are arrested, ask the authorities to notify a consular officer at the nearest U.S. embassy or consulate. **Under international agreements and practice, you have the right to talk the U.S. consul.** If you are denied this right, be persistent and try to have someone get in touch for you.

When alerted, U.S. officials will visit you, advise you of your rights according to local laws, and contact your family and friends if you wish. They will do whatever they can to protect your legitimate interests and to ensure you are not discriminated against under local law. Consuls can transfer money, food, and clothing to the prison authorities from your family or friends. They will try to get relief if you are held under inhumane or unhealthy conditions or treated less favorably than others in the same situation.

Help From American Consuls Abroad

When to Register With the U.S. Embassy

Register at the Consular Section of the nearest U.S. embassy or consulate:

- If you find yourself in a country or area that is experiencing civil unrest, has an unstable political climate, or is undergoing a natural disaster, such as an earthquake or hurricane.

- If you plan to go to a country where there are no U.S. officials. In such cases, register in an adjacent country, leave an itinerary, and ask about conditions in the country you will visit and what third country may represent U.S. interest there.

- If you plan to stay in a country for longer than one month.

Registration makes your presence and whereabouts known in case it is necessary for a consular employee to contact you in an emergency. During a disaster overseas, American consular officers offer assistance to Americans and can even assist in evacuation when that becomes necessary. But they cannot assists you if they do not know where you are. Registration also makes it easier to apply for a replacement passport if yours is lost or stolen.

If you are traveling with an escorted tour to areas experiencing political uncertainty or other problems, find out if registration is being done for you by your tour operator. If it is not, or if you are traveling on your own, leave a copy of your itinerary at the nearest U.S. embassy or consulate soon after arrival.

What U.S. Consuls Can Do

U.S. consular officers are located at U.S. embassies and consulates in most countries overseas. They are available to advise and help you if you are in any serious trouble.

Destitution

If you become destitute abroad, the U.S. consul can help you get in touch with you family, friends, bank, or employer and tell you how to arrange for them to send fund for you. These funds can sometimes be wired to you through the Department of State.

If Ill or Injured

Should you become ill while abroad, contact the nearest

U.S. embassy or consulate for a list of local doctors, dentists, medical specialists, clinics and hospitals. If your illness or injury is serious, the consul can help you find medical assistance from that list and, at your request, will inform your family or friends of your condition. If necessary, a consul can assist in the transfer of funds from the United States. Payment of hospital and other expenses is your responsibility. Consular officers cannot supply you with medication.

In an emergency when you are unable to communicate, the consul will check your passport for the name and address of any relative, friend, or legal representative whom you wish to have notified. Because the U.S. Government cannot pay for medical evacuations, it is advisable to have private medical insurance to cover this.

Marriage Abroad

U.S. diplomatic and consular officials do not have the authority to perform marriages overseas. Marriage abroad must be performed in accordance with local law. There are always documentary requirements, and in some countries, there is a lengthy residence requirement before a marriage may take place.

Before traveling, ask the embassy or consulate of the country in which you plan to marry about their regulations and how to prepare to marry abroad. Once abroad, the Consular Section of the nearest U.S. embassy or consulate may be able to answer some of your question, but it is your responsibility to deal with local civil authorities.

Birth Abroad

A child born abroad to a U.S. citizen parent or parents generally acquires U.S. citizenship at birth. The U.S. parent or parents should contact the nearest U.S. embassy or consulate to have a Report of Birth Abroad of a Citizen of the United States of America prepared. This document serves as proof of acquisition of U.S. citizenship and is acceptable evidence for obtaining a U.S. passport and for most other purposes where one must show a birth certificate or proof of citizenship.

Adoption Abroad

The Department of State and its embassies and consulates abroad have become increasingly concern and about international adoptions because of an increase in illegal activities by some intermediaries and adoption agencies. Illegal adoption practices can cause great difficulty, financial strain, and emotional upheaval for adopting parents. If your are a prospective adopting parent, beware of any agency or attorney claiming to be able to streamline established producers. Because of irregular activities, foreign governments sometimes

determine that an adoption in process is illegal and refuse to finalize the adoption.

For more information, you may write for a free pamphlet, International Adoptions. Send a self-addressed, triple-stamped 9"x12" envelope to: Citizens Consular Services (CA/OCS/CCS), Room 4817, Department of State, Washington, D.C. 20520-4818. If you are planning to adopt from a particular country, mention that in your request, because Citizens Consular Services has specific information on the adoption process in certain countries.

Death Abroad

When a U.S. citizen dies abroad, the consular officer reports the death to the next kin or legal representative and arranges to obtain from them the necessary private funds for local burial or return of the body to the United States. Before you begin your trip, complete the address page in the front of your passport. Provide the name, address and telephone number of someone to be contacted in an emergency. Do not give the names of your traveling companions in case the entire party is involved in the same accident.

Because the U.S. Government cannot pay for local burial or shipment of remains to the United States, it is worthwhile to have insurance to cover this. Following a death, a Report of the Death of An American Citizen (Optional Form 180) is prepared by the consular officer to provide the facts concerning the death and the custody of the personal estate of the deceased Under certain circumstances, a consular officer becomes the provisional conservator of a deceased American's estate and arranges for the disposition of those effects.

A Variety of Nonemergency Services

Consular employees provide nonemergency services as well. These include information on Selective Service registration, travel advisories, absentee voting, and the acquisition or loss of U.S. citizenship. They arrange for the transfer of Social Security and other federal benefits to beneficiaries residing abroad, provide U.S. tax forms, and notarize documents. Consuls can also provide information on how to obtain foreign public documents.

What U.S. Consuls Cannot Do

Consular officers will do their best to assist U.S. nationals abroad. However, they must devote priority time and energies to those Americans who find themselves in the most serious legal, medical, or financial difficulties.

Because of limited resources, consuls cannot provide routine or commercial-type services. They cannot act as travel agents, information bureaus, banks, or law enforcement officers. U.S. federal law forbids a consular officer from acting as your lawyer. Consular officers cannot: find you employment; get you visas, residence permits or driving permits; act as interpreters; search for missing luggage; call your credit card company or bank; replace stolen travelers checks; or settle disputes with hotel managers. They can, however, tell you how to get assistance on these and other matters.

When You Return

Return Transportation
Reconfirm your return reservation at least 72 hours before departure. Whenever possible, obtain a written confirmation. If you do it by phone, record the time, day, and the agent's name who took the call. If your name does not appear on the reservations list, you have no recourse and may find yourself stranded.

Departure Tax
Some countries levy an airport departure tax on travelers that can be as high as $50. Ask the airline or a travel agent about this. **Make certain to have enough money at the end of your trip to be able to get on the plane.**

Immigration and Customs
If a passport was required for your trip, have it ready when you go through Immigration and Customs. If you took other documents with you, such an International Certificate of Vaccination, a medical letter, or a Customs certificate of registration for foreign-made personal articles, have them ready also. Have your receipts handy in case you need to support your customs declaration. When returning to the United States by car from Mexico or Canada have your certificate of vehicle registration handy. It is a good idea to pack your baggage in a way to make inspection easier. For example, pack the articles you acquired abroad separately.

U.S. Customs currently allows each U.S. citizen to bring back $400 worth of merchandise duty free, provided the traveler has been outside the United States for at least 48 hours, has not already used this exemption within 30 days, and provided the traveler can present the purchases upon his or her arrival at the port of entry. The next $100 worth of items brought back for personal use or gifts is subject to duty at a flat rate of 10%.

There are two groups of destinations from which the duty-free exemption is higher. These are a group of 24 countries and dependencies in the Caribbean and Central America from which the exemption is $600 and a group of U.S. insular possessions (the U.S. Virgin Island, American Samoa, and Guam) from which the exemption is $1,200. For details, consult your travel agent or the U.S. Customs Service publication, *Know Before You Go,* listed directly below.

Additional Sources of Information

Customs
Know Before You Go, Customs Hints for Returning U.S. Residents[11] contains information on key U.S. Customs regulations and procedures, including duty rates. Single copies are free from any local Customs office or write: U.S. Customs Service, P.O. Box 7407, Washington, D.C. 20044.

Agricultural Products
*Travelers Tips on Bringing Food, Plant, and Animal Products Into the United States*** lists entry requirements for these items from most parts of the world. Fresh fruit and vegetables, meat, potted plants, pet birds, and other items are prohibited or restricted from entry into the United States. The publication is available from the U.S. Department of Agriculture, 613 Federal Bldg., 6505 Belcrest Road, Hyattsville, MD 20782.

Wildlife and Wildlife Products
Buyer Beware![12] provides general guidelines governing restrictions on imports of wildlife and wildlife products into the United States. For a free copy, write to the Publication Unit, U.S. Fish and Wildlife Service, Department of the Interior, Washington, DC 20240. Additional information on importing wildlife and wildlife products can be obtained through TRAFFIC USA, World Wildlife Fund, 1250 24th Street, N.W. Washington, DC 20037.

Glazed Ceramic Purchases
The article, *An Unwanted Souvenir, Lead in Ceramic Ware*, explains the danger of lead poisoning from some glazed ceramic ware sold abroad. For a free copy, write: U.S. Food and Drug Administration, HFI- 0, Rockville, MD, 20857.

Foreign Country Information
Background Notes are brief, factual pamphlets describing the countries of the world. There are about 170 Notes containing the most current information on each country's people, culture, geography, history, government, economy, and political conditions. Background Notes also include a reading list, travel notes, and maps. Single copies are available from the U.S. Government Printing Office for about $2 each. Confirm price by calling 202-783-3238.

Tips for Travelers[13] provide advice prepared by the Bureau of Consular Affairs on travel to specific areas of the world. Depending on the particular region being discussed, a brochure might cover such topics as currency and customs regulations, entry requirements, dual nationality, import and export controls, vaccination requirements, restrictions on use of photography, and warnings on the use of drugs. Single copies of the following publications are for sale for $1 from the U.S. Government Printing Office:

- *Tips for Travelers to the Caribbean*
- *Tips for Travelers to Central and South America*
- *Tips for Travelers to Mexico*
- *Tips for Travelers to the Middle East and North Africa*
- *Tips for Travelers to the People's Republic Of China*
- *Tips for Travelers to South Asia*
- *Tips for Travelers to Sub-Saharan Africa*
- *Tips for Travelers to the Russia*

U.S. Embassy Addresses
Key Officers of Foreign Service Posts gives the names of key officers and the addresses for all U.S. embassies, consulates, and missions abroad. This publication is updated three times a year. The single copy price is $3.75. To obtain a copy, write to:

Superintendent of Documents
U.S. Government Printing Office
Washington, D.C. 20402.

You may also order by telephone: 202-783-3238.

Older Americans
Travel Tips for Older Americans[12] provides information on passports, visas, health, currency, and suggestions for older Americans planning a trip abroad. Copies are available for $1 from the U.S. Government Printing Office (see Chapter 46 for ordering information)

Safe Travel
A Safe Trip Abroad[12] contains helpful precautions to minimize the chance of becoming a victim of terrorism and also provides other safety tips. To obtain copy for $1, write to the U.S. Government Printing Office (address on page 473).

Passport Agencies
[For a listing of U.S. Government Passport Agencies, **See Appendix J.**]

**Brochures on Consular Services
for Americans Abroad**
Single copies of the following brochures can be obtained free by sending a self-addressed, stamped envelope (SASE) to: CA/PA, room 5807; Department of State: Washington, D.C. 20520-4818.

Crisis Abroad - What the State Department Does[12] summarizes the work of the State Department during a crisis. For example, for concerned relatives and friends in the U.S., the Department attempts to obtain information from local authorities abroad Americans located in the disaster area.

The Citizens Emergency Center gives information about the assistance the Center provides to American citizens in four major categories: deaths, arrests, welfare/whereabouts inquires, and financial/medical emergencies.

US consuls Help Americans Abroad[12] explains the emergency and nonemergency services that consular officers abroad provide to U.S. citizens.

Other Information Sheets on Consular Matters

The Department of State has information on other subjects of interest to traveling Americans. Single copies of the following information sheets are free. Please send a SASE to: CA/OCS/CCS, Room 4817; Department of State; Washington, D.C. 20520-4818. Ask for any of the following:

- *Dual Nationality (U.S./Other)*
- *Loss of U.S. Citizenship*
- *Marriage Abroad*
- *Foreign Military Service*
- *Claims to Inheritance Abroad*
- *Estates Abroad*
- *Tourist and Trade Complaints*

~ ~ ENDNOTES ~ ~

1. A complete listing of Foreign Government Tourist Offices is provided in **Appendix L.**

2. See **Appendix P** for a listing.

3. See **Appendix B** for a list of foreign embassies in the U.S., including their addresses and telephone numbers.

4. For more on the State Department travel advisories, See **Chapter 29.**

11

5.   See **Chapter 28** for more information on the Citizens Emergency Center and its activities.

6.   This publication which details the visa and other entry requirements of foreign governments is reprinted in **Chapter 3** of this book.

7.   A large portion of this booklet has been reproduced verbatim elsewhere in this book, including a country by country listing of vaccination requirements. Check the Table of Contents for location.

8.   See **Appendix 13M** for a list of travel insurance providers.

9.   See **Appendix M** for additional information on how to apply for an International driver's permit.

10.   See **Appendix 14N** for a listing of some of these organizations.

11.   This publication is reprinted elsewhere in this book. See Table of Contents for location.

12.   This publication is reprinted elsewhere in this book. Check the Table of Contents for location.

13.   All current **Tips For Travelers** are reproduced elsewhere in this book. Check the Table of Contents for location.

Chapter 2

Passports

[The Information in this chapter is reprinted verbatim from a bulletin issued by the U.S. State Department, Bureau of Consular Affairs. It is intended to serve as advice to Americans applying for passport.]

— — — —

[Applying For Them The Easy Way]

Applying for Your U.S. Passport

The Department of State's Bureau of Consular Affairs has prepared this publication to assist you in applying for your U. S. passport. This guide will give you information on where to apply, how to apply, and the best time to apply.

****

Other Than Passport Agencies, Where Can I Apply for a Passport?

You can apply for a passport at many Federal and state courts, probate courts, and some post offices.

Over 2500 courts and 900 post offices in the United States accept passport applications. Courts and post offices are usually more convenient because they are near your home or your place of business. You save time and money by not having to travel to one of the 13 major U.S. cities where passport agencies are located.

When Do I Have to Apply in Person?

You must always apply in person if you are 13 or older, and if you do not meet the requirements for applying by mail (see section "May I Apply for a Passport by Mail?").

Usually, for children under 13, **only** a parent or legal guardian need appear to execute a passport application.

What Do I Need to Do to Apply for a Passport at a Courthouse or Post Office? Go to a courthouse or post office authorized to accept passport applications and complete the DSP-11 application form, but do not sign it until instructed to do so.
You must present:

1. **PROOF OF U.S. CITIZENSHIP**
    That is...

    · a previous U.S. passport, or

    · if you were born in the U.S., a certified copy of your birth certificate issued by the state, city, or county of your birth (a certified copy will have a registrar's raised, embossed, impressed, or multicolored seal and the date the certificate was filed with the registrar's office).

    If you have neither a passport nor a certified birth certificate...

    · bring a notice from the registrar of the state where you were born that no birth record exists;

    · also, bring as many as possible of the following: a baptismal certificate, hospital birth record, early census, school record, or family Bible record. (To be considered, these documents must show your full name and date and place of birth.);

    · also, bring a notarized affidavit completed by an older blood relative who has personal knowledge of your birth.

    · If you were born abroad, bring a Certificate of Naturalization, Certificate of Citizenship, Report of Birth Abroad of a U.S. Citizen, or a Certification of Birth (Form FS-545 or DS1350). If you do not have these documents, check with the acceptance office agent for documents that can be used in their place.

2. **TWO PHOTOGRAPHS**
    · The photos must be recent (taken within the past six months), identical, 2x2 inches, and either color or black/white;

    · They must show a front view, full face, on a plain, light (white or off-white) background. (Vending machine photographs are not acceptable.)

3. PROOF OF IDENTITY
That is...

· a previous U.S. passport, a Certificate of Naturalization or Citizenship, a valid driver's license, government or military ID, or corporate ID.

4. FEES
· $65 for a ten-year passport;

· $40 for a five-year passport for persons under 18 (these amounts include a $10 execution fee.)

Make your check or money order payable to Passport Services. Post offices (and passport agencies) accept cash, but courts are not required to do so.

5. SOCIAL SECURITY NUMBER

Although a Social Security number is not required for issuance of a passport, Section 603E of the Internal Revenue Code of 1986 requires passport applicants to provide this information. Passport Services will provide this information to the Internal Revenue Service (IRS) routinely. Any applicant who fails to provide the information is subject to a $500 penalty enforced by the IRS. All questions on this matter should be referred to the nearest IRS office.

May I Apply for a Passport by Mail?
Yes, if you already have a passport and that passport is your most recent passport, and it was issued within the past 12 years, and if you were over 18 years old at the time it was issued.

Ask the court, post office, or your travel agent for a DSP-82 "Application For Passport By Mail." Fill it out, sign it, and date it.

Attach to it:
· your most recent passport;

· two identical passport photographs (see previous section on passport photographs);

· and a $55 fee; make your check or money order payable to Passport Services. (The $10 execution fee is waived for those eligible to apply by mail.)

If your name has been changed, enclose the Court Order, Adoption Decree or Marriage Certificate, or Divorce Decree specifying another name for you to use. (Photocopies will not be accepted.) If your name has

changed by any other means, you must apply in person.

Mail the completed DSP-82 application and attachments to:
National Passport Center
P.O. Box 371971
Pittsburgh, PA 15250-7971.

Your previous passport will be returned to you with your new passport.

If you need faster service, you can use an overnight delivery service. If the service of your choice will not deliver to a post office box, send It to:
Mellon Bank
Attn: Passport Supervisor 371971
3 Mellon Bank Center, Rm. 153-2723
Pittsburgh. PA 15259-0001.

Include the appropriate fee for overnight return of your passport.

[Note: If the passport has been mutilated, altered or damaged in any manner, you cannot apply by mail. You must apply in person and use Form DSP-11, present evidence of U.S. citizens and acceptable identification.]

When Should I Apply for a Passport? Apply for your passport several months in advance of your planned departure. If you will need visas from foreign embassies, allow additional time.

What Happens to My Passport Application After I Submit It?
If you apply at a passport acceptance facility, the day you apply your application will be forwarded to the passport agency that services the acceptance office, or, in the case of mail-in applications, they are forwarded to the National Passport Center.

Applications are processed according to the departure date indicated on the application form. If you give no departure date, the passport agency will assume you are not planning any immediate travel. Your passport will be returned to you by mail at the address you provided on your application.

What Should I Do if My Passport Is Lost or Stolen?
If your passport is lost or stolen in the U.S., report the loss or theft in writing to Passport Services, 1425 K Street, N.W., Department of State, Washington, D.C. 20522-1705, or to the nearest passport agency. If you are abroad, report the loss immediately to local police authorities and contact the nearest U.S. embassy or consulate.

What Else Should I Know About Passports?
All persons, including new born infants, are required to obtain passports in their own name.

If you need to get a valid passport amended because of a name change, use Form DSP-19.

Before traveling abroad, make a copy of the identification page to make It easier to get a new one should it be necessary.

If you require additional visa pages before your passport expires, submit your passport with a signed request for extra pages to one of the passport agencies listed in Appendix J. (Please allow time for the processing of the request.) If you travel abroad frequently, you may request a 48-page passport at the time of application.

Some countries require that your passport be valid at least 6 months beyond the dates of your trip. If your passport is expiring in less than the required validity, you will need to get a new one. Check with the nearest embassy or consulate of the countries you plan to visit to find out their entry requirements.

In addition to foreign entry requirements, U.S. law must also be considered. With certain exceptions, it is against U.S. law to enter or leave the country without a valid passport. Generally for tourists, the exceptions refer to direct travel within U.S. territories or between North, South, or Central America (except Cuba).

[Note: If you mutilate or alter your U.S. passport, you may render it invalid and expose yourself to possible prosecution under the law (Section 1543 of Title 22 of the U.S. Code).]

What If I Need a Passport in a Hurry?
If you are leaving on an emergency trip within five working days, apply in person at the nearest passport agency and present your tickets or travel itinerary from an airline, as well as the other required items. Or, apply at a court or post office and have the application sent to the passport agency through an overnight delivery service of your choice (you should include a self addressed, pre-paid envelope for the return of the passport). Be sure to include your dates of departure and travel plans on your application.

15

UNITED STATES DEPARTMENT OF STATE

APPLICATION FOR ☐ PASSPORT ☐ REGISTRATION

SEE INSTRUCTIONS—TYPE OR PRINT IN INK IN WHITE AREAS

1. NAME FIRST NAME   MIDDLE NAME

LAST NAME

2. MAILING ADDRESS

STREET

CITY, STATE, ZIP CODE

COUNTRY   IN CARE OF

☐ 5 Yr. ☐ 10 Yr.   Issue
R   D   O   DP   Date _____
End. # _____   Exp. _____

3. SEX   **4. PLACE OF BIRTH** City, State or Province, Country

Male   Female

5. DATE OF BIRTH
Mo.   Day   Year

6. SEE FEDERAL TAX LAW NOTICE ON REVERSE SIDE   SOCIAL SECURITY NUMBER

7. HEIGHT   **8. COLOR OF HAIR**   **9. COLOR OF EYES**   **10. (Area Code) HOME PHONE**   **11. (Area Code) BUSINESS PHONE**

Feet Inches   **12. PERMANENT ADDRESS (Street, City, State, ZIP Code)**   **13. OCCUPATION**

FOLD

14. FATHER'S NAME	BIRTHPLACE	BIRTH DATE	U.S. CITIZEN ☐ YES ☐ NO
15. MOTHER'S MAIDEN NAME	BIRTHPLACE	BIRTH DATE	U.S. CITIZEN ☐ YES ☐ NO

16. TRAVEL PLANS *(Not Mandatory)*
COUNTRIES   DEPARTURE DATE
LENGTH OF STAY

17. HAVE YOU EVER BEEN ISSUED A U.S. PASSPORT? YES ☐ NO ☐   IF YES, SUBMIT PASSPORT IF AVAILABLE. ☐ Submitted

IF UNABLE TO SUBMIT MOST RECENT PASSPORT, STATE ITS DISPOSITION: COMPLETE NEXT LINE

NAME IN WHICH ISSUED   PASSPORT NUMBER   ISSUE DATE (Mo., Day, Yr.)   DISPOSITION

SUBMIT TWO RECENT IDENTICAL PHOTOS

FROM 1" TO 1-3/8"

2" × 2"

18. HAVE YOU EVER BEEN MARRIED? ☐ YES ☐ NO   DATE OF MOST RECENT MARRIAGE Mo. Day Year

WIDOWED/DIVORCED? ☐ YES ☐ NO   IF YES, GIVE DATE Mo. Day Year

SPOUSE'S FULL BIRTH NAME   SPOUSE'S BIRTHPLACE

19. IN CASE OF EMERGENCY, NOTIFY *(Person Not Traveling With You)*   RELATIONSHIP
(Not Mandatory)
FULL NAME
ADDRESS   (Area Code) PHONE NUMBER

FOLD

20. TO BE COMPLETED BY AN APPLICANT WHO BECAME A CITIZEN THROUGH NATURALIZATION

I IMMIGRATED TO THE U.S. (Month, Year)   I RESIDED CONTINUOUSLY IN THE U.S. From (Mo., Yr.) To (Mo., Yr.)   DATE NATURALIZED (Mo., Day, Yr.)   PLACE

21. DO NOT SIGN APPLICATION UNTIL REQUESTED TO DO SO BY PERSON ADMINISTERING OATH

I have not, since acquiring United States citizenship, performed any of the acts listed under "Acts or Conditions" on the reverse of this application form (unless explanatory statement is attached). I solemnly swear (or affirm) that the statements made on this application are true and the photograph attached is a true likeness of me.

Subscribed and sworn to (affirmed) before me   (SEAL)   X

Month   Day   Year

☐ Clerk of Court or
☐ PASSPORT Agent
☐ Postal Employee
☐ (Vice) Consul USA At _____

(Sign in presence of person authorized to accept application)

(Signature of person authorized to accept application)

22. APPLICANT'S IDENTIFYING DOCUMENTS ☐ PASSPORT ☐ DRIVER'S LICENSE ☐ OTHER (Specify)   No.

ISSUE DATE   EXPIRATION DATE   PLACE OF ISSUE   ISSUED IN THE NAME OF
Month Day Year   Month Day Year

23. FOR ISSUING OFFICE USE ONLY (Applicant's evidence of citizenship)

☐ Birth Cert.   SR   CR   City   Filed/Issued:
☐ Passport   Bearer's Name:
☐ Report of Birth
☐ Naturalization/Citizenship Cert.   No.:
☐ Other:
☐ Seen & Returned
☐ Attached

APPLICATION APPROVAL
Examiner Name
Office, Date

24.

FEE _____ EXEC. _____ POST _____

FORM DSP-11 (12-87)   (SEE INSTRUCTIONS ON REVERSE)   Form Approved OMB No. 1405-0004 (Exp. 8/1/89)

16

UNITED STATES DEPARTMENT OF STATE

APPLICATION FOR PASSPORT BY MAIL

IMPORTANT:
- READ INSTRUCTIONS ON BACK OF FORM
- TYPE OR PRINT IN INK IN WHITE AREAS ONLY

IDENTIFYING INFORMATION

1. NAME   FIRST NAME   MIDDLE NAME

LAST NAME

2. MAILING ADDRESS

STREET

CITY, STATE, ZIP CODE

COUNTRY   IN CARE OF

R   D   O   DP   Issue Date _____

End.# _____   Exp. _____

FOLD

3. SEX	4. PLACE OF BIRTH	5. DATE OF BIRTH	6. SEE FEDERAL TAX LAW NOTICE ON REVERSE SIDE	SOCIAL SECURITY NUMBER
Male Female	City, State or Province, Country	Month Day Year		

7. HEIGHT	8. COLOR OF HAIR	9. COLOR OF EYES	10. (Area Code) HOME PHONE	11. (Area Code) BUSINESS PHONE
Feet Inches				

NOTE: MOST RECENT PASSPORT ISSUED ON OR AFTER YOUR 16TH BIRTHDAY AND ISSUED WITHIN THE PAST 12 YEARS MUST BE ATTACHED.

12. PASSPORT NUMBER	13. ISSUE DATE	14. OCCUPATION	15. DEPARTURE DATE
	Month Day Year		

16. PERMANENT ADDRESS (Street, City, State, ZIP Code)

SUBMIT TWO RECENT IDENTICAL PHOTOS

2" X 2"   FROM 1" TO   1-3/8"

17. TRAVEL PLANS (Not Mandatory)

COUNTRIES

LENGTH OF STAY

18. IN CASE OF EMERGENCY, NOTIFY (Person Not Traveling With You) (Not Mandatory)

FULL NAME

ADDRESS
STREET

CITY, STATE, ZIP CODE

(Area Code) PHONE NUMBER   RELATIONSHIP

19. OATH AND SIGNATURE (If any of the below-mentioned acts or conditions have been performed by or apply to the applicant, the portion which applies should be lined out, and a supplementary explanatory statement should be attached, signed, and made a part of this application.)

I have not, since acquiring United States citizenship, been naturalized as a citizen of a foreign state; taken an oath, or made an affirmation or other formal declaration of allegiance to a foreign state; entered or served in the armed forces of a foreign state; accepted or performed the duties of any office, post, or employment under the Government of a foreign state or political subdivision thereof; made a formal renunciation of nationality either in the United States or before a diplomatic or consular officer of the United States in a foreign state; or been convicted by a court or court martial of competent jurisdiction of committing any act of treason against, or attempting by force to overthrow, or bearing arms against the United States, or conspiring to overthrow, put down or destroy by force the Government of the United States.

WARNING: False statements made knowingly and willfully in passport applications or affidavits or other supporting documents are punishable by fine and/or imprisonment under the provisions of 18 USC 1001 and/or 18 USC 1542. The alteration or mutilation of a passport issued pursuant to this application is punishable by fine and/or imprisonment under 18 USC 1543. The use of a passport in violation of the restrictions therein is punishable by fine and/or imprisonment under 18 USC 1544.

DECLARATION: I declare that the statements made in this application are true and complete to the best of my knowledge and belief, that the attached photographs are a true likeness of me, and that I have not been issued or included in a passport issued subsequent to the one submitted herein.

FOLD

X

(Date)   Signature of Applicant (Must be signed by applicant)

FOLLOW INSTRUCTIONS CAREFULLY—INCOMPLETE OR UNACCEPTABLE APPLICATIONS WILL DELAY THE ISSUANCE OF YOUR PASSPORT.

20. FOR ISSUING OFFICE USE ONLY RECORD: Type of Document(s), Number, Date Filed/Issued, Court/Place, Bearer's Name as Appropriate.

☐ Passport   ☐ Evidence of Name Change   ☐ Other: ☐ Seen & Returned

Bearer's Name:

APPLICATION APPROVAL

Examiner Name

Office, Date

No.: _____

Place: _____

21.

FEE _____

POST _____

FORM DSP-82 (11-90)   (SEE INSTRUCTIONS ON REVERSE)   OMB No. 1405-0020 (Exp. 8/31/92) Estimated Burden - 5 Minutes*

17

Chapter 3

Visa and Other Entry Requirements of Foreign Governments

[The Information in this chapter is reprinted verbatim from a bulletin issued by the U.S. State Department, Bureau of Consular Affairs. It is intended to serve as advice to Americans traveling abroad.]

- - - -

(Foreign Entry Requirements)
This listing is for U.S. citizens traveling on tourism/business and does not apply to persons planning to emigrate to foreign countries. Persons traveling on official business for the U.S. Government should obtain visa information from the agency sponsoring their travel. For purposes of this publication, a visa is an endorsement or stamp placed by officials of a foreign country on a U.S. passport that allows the bearer to visit that foreign country. Note: Wherever you see the words 'photo(s) required' in this publication it means that you will need to submit passport-size photographs- IMPORTANT: THIS LISTING IS PREPARED FROM INFORMATION OBTAINED FROM FOREIGN EMBASSIES PRIOR TO MARCH 1995. THIS INFORMATION IS SUBJECT TO CHANGE. CHECK ENTRY REQUIREMENTS WITH THE CONSULAR OFFICIALS OF THE COUNTRIES TO BE VISITED WELL IN ADVANCE.

PASSPORTS: U.S.citizens who travel to a country where a valid passport is not required will need documentary evidence of their U.S. citizenship and identity. Proof of U.S. citizenship includes an expired passport, a certified (original) birth certificate, Certificate of Naturalization, Certificate of Citizenship, or Report of Birth Abroad of a Citizen of the United States. To prove identity, a valid drivers license or government identification card are acceptable provided they identify you by physical description or photograph. However, for travel overseas and to facilitate reentry into the U.S., a valid U.S. passport is the best documentation available and it unquestionably proves your U.S. citizenship.

Some countries require that your passport be valid at least six months beyond the dates of your trip. *If your passport expires before the required validity, you will have to apply for a new one. Please check with the embassy or nearest consulate of the country you plan to visit for their requirements.*

Some Arab or African countries will not issue visas or allow entry if your passport indicates travel to Israel or South Africa. Consult the nearest U S. passport agency for guidance if this applies to you.

VISAS SHOULD BE OBTAINED BEFORE PROCEEDING ABROAD. Allow sufficient time for processing your visa application, especially if you are applying by mail. Most foreign consular representatives are located in principal cities, and in many instances, a traveler may be required to obtain visas from the consular office in the area of his/her residence. The addresses of foreign consular offices in the United States may be obtained by consulting the *Congressional Directory* in the library. IT IS THE RESPONSIBILITY OF THE TRAVELER TO OBTAIN VISAS, WHERE REQUIRED, FROM THE APPROPRIATE EMBASSY OR NEAREST CONSULATE OF THE COUNTRY YOU ARE PLANNING TO VISIT.

IMMUNIZATIONS: Under the international Health Regulations adopted by the World Health Organization, a country may require International Certificates of I Vaccination against yellow fever. A cholera immunization may be required if you are traveling from an infected area. Check with health care providers or your records to ensure other immunizations (e.g.tetanus and polio) are up-to-date. Prophylactic medication for malaria and certain other preventive measures are advisable for travel to some countries. No immunizations are required to return to the United States. Detailed health information is included in *Health Information for International Travel,* available from the U.S. Government Printing Office (address on page 473) for $7 or may be obtained from your locAl health department or physician or by calling the Centers for Disease Control on 404/ 332-4559.

An increasing number of countries have established regulations regarding AIDS testing, particularly for long-term visitors. Although many are listed here, check with the embassy or consulate of the country you plan to visit to verify if this is a requirement for entry.

19

All international flights are subject to U.S. Immigration and U.S. Customs fees paid in advance as part of your ticket. In addition, many countries have departure fees that are sometimes collected at the time of ticket purchase.

AFGHANISTAN - Passport and visa required. No tourist or business visas are being issued at this time. For further information contact Embassy of the Republic of Afghanistan, 2341 Wyoming Ave., N.W., Washington, D.C. 20008 (202/ 234-3770/1).

ALBANIA - Passport required. Visa not required for tourist stay of up to 3 months. Departure tax $10. For further information contact the Embassy of the Republic of Albania at 1150 18th Street N.W., Washington, D.C. 20036 (202/2234942).

ALGERIA - Passport and visa required. Obtain visa before arrival. Visa valid up to 90 days, requires 2 application forms, 2 photos, and $12 fee (money order or certified check). Company letter (+ 1 copy) required for business visa. Visa not granted to passports showing Israeli visas. Enclose prepaid self-addressed envelope for return of passport by registered, certified or express mail. For currency regulations and other information contact the Consular Section of the Embassy of the Democratic and Popular Republic of Algeria, 2137 Wyoming Ave., N.W., Washington, D.C. 20008 (202/265-2800).

ANDORRA - (See France.)

ANGOLA - Passport and visa required. Tourist/business visas require an application form, letter stating purpose of travel, and 2 recent photos. Applications by mail require prepaid return envelope. Yellow fever and cholera immunizations required. For additional information contact Embassy of Angola, 1819 L Street, N.W., Suite 400, Washington, D.C. 20036 (202/785-1156) or the Permanent Mission of the Republic of Angola to the U.N., 125 East 73rd Street, New York, NY 10021 (212/861-5656).

ANTIGUA AND BARBUDA -Passport or proof of U.S. citizenship required, return/onward ticket and/or proof of funds needed for tourist stay up to 6 months. Check Embassy of Antigua and Barbuda, Suite 4M, 3400 International Drive, N.W., Washington, D.C. 20008 (202/362-5122/5166/5211) for further information.

ARGENTINA - Passport required. Visa not required for tourist stay up to 3 months. Business visa requires company letter detailing purpose of trip and length of stay. For more information contact Argentine

Embassy, 1600 New Hampshire Ave., N.W., Washington, D.C. 20009 (202/939-6400) or the nearest Consulate: CA (213/739-5959 and 415/982-3050), FL (305/373-1889), IL (312/263-7435), LA (504/523-2823), NY (212/603-0415),PR (8091754-6500) or TX (713/871-8935).

ARMENIA - Passport and visa required. Visa for stay of up to 21 days, requires I application form, 1 photo and $50 fee. For stays longer than 21 days, an official invitation from a qualifying entity in Armenia is required. If applying by mail, enclose a SASE or prepaid air bill indicating type of mail service (i.e. Federal Express, etc). For more information contact the Consular Section of the Embassy of the Republic of Armenia, 1660 L Street, N.W., Suite 210, Washington, D.C. 20036 (202/ 393-5983).

ARUBA - Passport or proof of U.S. citizenship required. Visa not required for stay up to 14 days, extendable to 90 days after arrival. Proof of onward/return ticket or sufficient funds for stay may be required. Departure tax $9.50. For further information consult Embassy of the Netherlands (202/244-5300), or nearest Consulate General: CA (212/380-3440), IL (314/8561429), NY (212/246-1429) or TX (713/622-8000).

AUSTRALIA - Passport, visa and onward/return transportation required. Transit visa not necessary for up to 8-hour stay at airport. Visitor visa valid 1 year for multiple entries up to 3 months, no charge, requires 1 application and 1 photo. Applications for a stay of longer than 3 months or with a validity longer than 1 year, require fee of $24 (U.S.). Need company letter for business visa. Departure tax, $20 (Australian), paid at airport. Minors not accompanied by parent require notarized copy of the child's birth certificate and notarized written parental consent from both parents. AIDS test required for permanent resident visa applicants age 15 and over; U.S. test accepted. Send prepaid envelope for return of passport by mail. Allow 3 to 4 weeks for processing. For further information contact the Embassy of Australia, 1601 Mass. Ave., N.W., Washington, D.C. 20036 (1-800-242-2878,202/797-3145) or the nearest Consulate General: CA (213/469-4300 or 415362-6160), HI (808/524-5050), NY (212/245-4000) or TX (713/629-9131).

AUSTRIA - Passport required. Tourist visa not required for stay of up to 3 months as a tourist. For information concerning longer stays, employment, or other types of visas check with the Embassy of Austria, 3524 International Court, N.W., Washington, D.C. 20008 (202/895-6767) or nearest Consulate General: Los Angeles (310/444-9310), Chicago (312/ 222-1515) or New York (212/737-6400).

AZERBAIJAN - Passport and visa required. Visa (no charge) requires 1 application form, 1 photo, and a letter of invitation. Please include SASE or prepaid airbill for return of documents. For additional information contact the Embassy of the Republic of Azerbaijan, 927 15th Street, N.W., Suite 700, Washington, D.C. 20005 (202/842-0001).

AZORES - (See Portugal.)

BAHAMAS - Proof of U.S. citizenship, photo ID and onward/ return ticket required for stay up to 8 months. Passport and residence work permit needed for residence and business. Permit required for firearms and to import pets. Departure tax of $15 must be paid at airport. For further information call Embassy of the Commonwealth of the Bahamas, 2220 Massachusetts Ave., N.W., Washington, D.C. 20008 (202/3192660) or nearest Consulate: Miami (305/373-6295) or New York (212/421-6420).

BAHRAIN - Passport and visa required. No tourist visas issued at this time. Transit visa available upon arrival for stay up to 72 hours, must have return/onward ticket. Business, work, or resident visas valid for 3 months, single-entry, require 1 application form, 1 photo, letter from company or No Objection Certificate (NOC) from Immigration Dept. in Bahrain and $30 fee ($20 for bearer of NOC). Yellow fever vaccination needed if arriving from infected area. Send SASE for return of passport by mail. For departure tax and other information, contact Embassy of the State of Bahrain, 3502 International Drive, N.W., Washington, D.C. 20008 (202/342-0741); or the Permanent Mission to the U.N., 2 United Nations Plaza, East 44th Street, Now York, NY 10017 (212/223-6200).

BANGLADESH - Passport, visa, and onward/return ticket required. Tourist/business visa requires 2 application forms, 2 photos and $21 fee. Business visa also requires company letter. For longer stays and more information consult Embassy of the People's Republic of Bangladesh, 2201 Wisconsin Ave., N.W., Washington, D.C. 20007 (202/342-8373).

BARBADOS - U.S. tourists traveling directly from the U.S. to Barbados may enter for up to 3 months stay with proof of U.S. citizenship (original or certified copy of birth certificate), photo ID and onward/return ticket. Passport required for longer visits and other types of travel. Business visas $25, single entry and $30 multiple-entry (may require work permit). Departure tax of $12.50 US ($25 BDS) is paid at airport. Check information with Embassy of Barbados, 2144

Wyoming Ave., N.W., Washington, D.C. 20008 (202/939-9200) or Consulate General in New York (212/867-8435).

BELARUS - Passport and visa required. Visa requires 1 application form, 1 photo, letter of invitation from a citizen of Belarus or a Belarus organization, company or agency. Tourist visa (for stay of up to 2 days) requires 1 application form, 1 photo, confirmation from receiving tourist organization in Belarus. The visa processing fee is $30 for 7 working days, $60 for next day, and $1 00 for same day processing. Transit visa is required when traveling through Belarus ($20). For additional information contact Embassy of Belarus, 1619 New Hampshire Ave., N.W., Washington, D.C. 20009 (202/9861604), Consulate General, 708 3rd Ave., Suite 1802, New York, NY 10017 (212/682-5392).

BELGIUM - Passport required. Visa not required for business/tourist stay up to 90 days. Temporary residence permit required for longer stays. For residence authorization, consult Embassy of Belgium, 3330 Garfield St., N.W., Washington, D.C. 20008 (202/333-6900) or nearest Consulate General: Los Angeles (213/857-1244), Atlanta (404/659-2150), Chicago (312/263-6624) or New York (212/586-51 1 0).

BELIZE - Passport, return/onward ticket and sufficient funds required. Visa not required for stay up to 30 days. If visit exceeds 1 month, a stay permit must be obtained from the Immigration Authorities in Belize. AIDS test required for those staying more than 3 months; U.S. test accepted if within 3 months of visit. For longer stays and other information contact Embassy of Belize, 2535 Massachusetts Ave., N.W., Washington, D.C. 20008 (202/332-9636) or the Belize Mission in New York at (212/599-0233).

BENIN-Passport and visa required. Entry/transit visa for stay up to 90 days, requires $20 fee (money orders only), 2 application forms, 2 photos, vaccination certificates for yellow fever and cholera, proof of return/onward transportation (guarantee from travel agency or photocopy of round trip ticket) and letter of guarantee from employer. Send prepaid envelope for return of passport by certified or express mail. Apply at Embassy of the Republic of Benin, 2737 Cathedral Ave., N.W., Washington, D.C. 20008 (202/232-6656).

BERMUDA - Passport (or proof of U.S. citizenship with photo ID) and onward/return ticket required for tourist stay up to 3 months. Departure tax of $1 0 is paid at airport. For further information consult British

Embassy (202/986-0205).

BHUTAN - Passport and visa required. Visa requires $20 fee, 1 application and 2 photos. Tourist visas arranged by Tourism Department and issued at entry checkpoints in Bhutan. Apply 2 months in advance. Yellow fever vaccination required if traveling from an infected area. For further information call the Consulate of the Kingdom of Bhutan in New York (212/ 826-1919).

BOLIVIA -Passport required. Visa not required for tourist stay up to 30 days. Business visa requires $50 fee and company letter explaining purpose of trip. Send SASE for return of passport by mail. AIDS test required. A "Defined Purpose Vise must be obtained for those wishing to obtain permanent residency, $50 fee. For more information contact Embassy of Bolivia (Consular Section), 3014 Mass. Ave., N.W., Washington, D.C. 20008 (202/232-4828 or 483-441 0) or nearest Consulate General: San Francisco (415/495-5173), Miami (305/358-3450), New York (212/687-0530) or Houston (713/ 780-8001). (Check special requirements for pets.)

BOSNIA AND HERZEGOVINA - Passport required. At the time of publication, Bosnia-Herzegovina entry permission is being granted at the border on a case by-case basis.

BOTSWANA - Passport required. Visa not required for stay up to 90 days. For further information contact Embassy of the Republic of Botswana, Suite 7M, 3400 International Drive, N.W., Washington, D.C. 20008 (202/244-4990/1) or nearest Honorary Consulate: Los Angeles (213/626-8484), San Francisco (415/346-4435) or Houston (713/622-1 900).

BRAZIL - Passport and visa required. Passport must be valid for at least six months at the time of first entry in Brazil. Visas are issued within 24 hours if submitted in person by the applicant. Multiple-entry visa valid for a stay of 90 days (renewable in Brazil for an equal period), requires 1 application form, 1 passport size photo, proof of onward/return transportation, and yellow fever vaccination if arriving from infected area. Tourist visas are granted free of charge if applications are submitted in person or by next of kin. There is a $10 service fee for applications sent by mail (money orders, certified check or company check only). Provide SASE for return of passport by mail. For travel with children or business visa contact Brazilian Embassy (Consular Section), 3009 Whitehaven St., N.W., Washington, D.C. 20008 (202/745-2828) or nearest Consulate: CA (213/651-2664 or 415/981-8170), FL (305/285-6200), IL (312/464-0245), MA

(617/542-4000), NY (212/757-3080), PR (809/754-7983) or TX (713/961-3063).

BRUNEI - Passport required. Visa not required for tourist/ business stay up to 90 days. Yellow fever vaccination needed if arriving from infected area. For more information, contact Embassy of the State of Brunei Darussalam, Suite 300,2600 Virginia Ave., N.W., Washington, D.C. 20037 (202/342-0159) or Brunei Permanent Mission to the U.N., 866 United Nations Plaza, Rm. 248, New York, NY 10017 (212/838-1600).

BULGARIA - Passport required. Tourist visa not required for stay up to 30 days. AIDS test may be required for those staying more than 1 month. For longer stays, business visas and other information contact Embassy of the Republic of Bulgaria, 1621 22nd St., N.W., Washington, D.C. 20008 (202/ 387-7969).

BURKINA FASO - Passport and visa required. Single-entry visa valid 3 months for visit up to 1 month, extendable, requires $80 fee, 2 application forms, 2 photos and yellow fever vaccination (cholera immunization recommended). Send passport by registered mail and include postage or prepaid envelope for return by mail. Payment accepted in cash or money order only. For further information call Embassy of Burkina Faso, 2340 Mass. Ave., N.W., Washington, D.C. 20008 (202/332-5577) or Honorary Consulate in Decatur, GA (404/378-7278), Los Angeles, CA (213/824-51 00) or New Orleans, LA (504/945-3152).

BURMA - (See Myanmar.)

BURUNDI - Passport and visa required. Obtain visa before arrival to avoid long airport delay. Multi-entry visa valid for 2 months (must be used within 2 months of date of issue) requires $11 fee, 3 application forms, 3 photos, yellow fever and cholera immunizations, return/onward ticket, and detailed itinerary (meningitis immunization recommended). Company letter needed for business travel. Send U.S. postal money order only and SASE for return of passport by mail. For further information consult Embassy of the Republic of Burundi, Suite 212, 2233 Wisconsin Ave., N.W., Washington, D.C. 20007 (202/342-2574) or Permanent Mission of Burundi to the U.N. (212/687-1180).

CAMBODIA (formerly Kampuchea) - Passport and visa required. Visa valid for a 1 month stay. Visa available through the Permanent Mission to the U.N. or upon arrival in Cambodia from the Ministry of National Security; requires 3 photos, 3 copies of applications and $20 fee. For further information please consult the

22

Cambodian Permanent Mission to the U.N. at 866 U.N. Plaza, Room 420, New York, New York 10017 (212/421-7626)

CAMEROON - Passport and visa required. Obtain visa before arrival to avoid difficulty at airport. Multiple-entry tourist visa for stay up to 90 days, requires $65.22 fee, 2 application forms, 2 photos, yellow fever and cholera immunizations, proof of onward/return transportation and bank statement. If invited by family or friends, visa available for up to 3 months, may be extended 1 month. Invitation must be signed by authorities in Cameroon. Multiple-entry business visa, valid 12 months, requires company letter to guarantee financial and legal responsibility; include exact dates of travel. Enclose prepaid envelope for return of passport by registered, certified or express mail. For additional information contact Embassy of the Republic of Cameroon, 2349 Mass. Ave., N.W., Washington, D.C. 20008 (202/265-8790 to 8794).

CANADA - Proof of U.S. citizenship and photo ID required. Minors (under 16) traveling alone or in someone else's custody, must present written authorization signed before a notary from the parent(s) or guardian. Visa not required for U.S. tourists entering from the U.S. for a stay up to 180 days. Anyone with a criminal record (including a DWI charge) should contact the Canadian Embassy or nearest Consulate General before travel. U.S. citizens entering Canada from a third country must have a valid passport. For student or business travel, check with the Canadian Embassy, 501 Pennsylvania Ave., N.W., Washington, D.C. 20001 (202/682-1740) or nearest Consulate General: CA (213/687-7412), Ml (313/567-2085), NY (212/596-1700 or 716/852-1252), or WA (206/4431377).

CAPE VERDE - Passport and visa required. Single-entry tourist visa (must be used within 120 days of issue), requires $11 fee, 1 application form, 1 photo and yellow fever immunization if arriving from infected area. Include SASE. for return of passport by mail. For further information contact the Embassy of the Republic of Cape Verde, 3415 Mass. Ave., N.W., Washington, D.C. 20007 (202/965-6820) or Consulate General, 535 Boylston St., 2nd Floor, Boston, MA 02116 (617/353-0014).

CAYMAN ISLANDS - (See West Indies, British.)

CENTRAL AFRICAN REPUBLIC - Passport and visa required. Visa must be obtained before arrival and are available for less than 90 days, $60 fee; and over 90 days, $150 fee. Requirements: 2 application forms, 2 recent photos, yellow fever immunization,

onward/return ticket, and SASE for return of passport by mail. Company letter needed for business visa. For further information contact Embassy of Central African Republic, 1618 22nd St.,N.W.,Washington, D.C.20008(202/ 483-7800 or 7801).

CHAD - Passport and visa required. Transit visa valid for up to 1 week, requires onward ticket. Single-entry visa valid 2 months for tourist/business stay up to 30 days (extendable), requires $25 fee (no personal checks), yellow fever and cholera vaccinations, 3 application forms and 3 photos. For business visa need company letter stating purpose of trip. Send prepaid envelope for registered/certified return of passport. Apply Embassy of the Republic of Chad, 2002 R St., N.W., Washington, D.C. 20009 (202/462-4009), and check specific requirements.

CHILE - Passport required. Visa not required for stay up to 3 months, may be extended. For other information consult Embassy of Chile, 1732 Mass. Ave., N.W., Washington, D.C. 20036 (202/785-3159) or nearest Consulate General: CA (310/785-0113 and 415/982-7662),FL (305/373-8623),IL (312/654-8780), PA (215/829-9520),NY (212/980-3366), TX (713/621-5853) or PR (809/725-6365).

CHINA, PEOPLE'S REPUBLIC OF - Passport and visa required. Transit visa required for any stop (even if you do not exit the plane or train) in China. Visitors must show hotel reservation and "letter of confirmation" from the China International Travel Service (CITS) or an invitation from an individual or institution in China. Business travelers are required to obtain informal invitation from Chinese business contact. CITS tours may be booked through several travel agencies and airlines in the United States and abroad and are often advertised in newspapers and magazines. Visas for tour group members are usually obtained by the travel agent as part of the tour package. Visa requires $30 fee (no personal checks), 2 application forms and 2 photos. Allow at least 10 days processing time. Medical examination required for those staying 1 year or longer. AIDS test required for those staying more than 6 months. For further information contact Chinese Embassy, 2300 Connecticut Avenue, N.W., Washington, D.C. 20008 (202/328-2517) or nearest Consulate General: Chicago (312/346-0287), Houston (713/524-431 1), Los Angeles (213/380-2506), New York (212/330-7409)or San Francisco (415/ 563-4857).

COLOMBIA - Passport, proof of onward/return ticket, and entry permit required for tourist stay. Entry permits are granted by the immigration authorities at the port of entry, for an initial stay of up to 90 days, extendable for multiple additional periods. Minors (under 18) traveling alone, with one parent or in someone else's custody, must present written authorization signed before a notary and authenticated by the Colombian Consulate from the absent parent(s) or guardian. Persons suspected of being HIV-positive may be denied entry. For information about longer stays, business and official travel contact Embassy of Colombia (Consulate), 1825 Conn. Ave., N.W., Suite 218, Washington, D.C. 20009 (202/ 332-7476) or nearest Consulate General: CA (213/382-1137 or 415/495-7191), FL (305/448-5558), GA (404/237-1045), IL (312/923-1196), LA (504/525-5580), MA (617/536-6222), MN (612/933-2408), MO (314/991-3636), OH (216/943-1200 ext. 2530), NY (212/949-9898), PR (809/754-6885), TX (713/5278919), or WV (304/234-8561).

COMOROS ISLANDS - Passport and onward/return ticket required. Visa for up to 3 weeks (extendable) issued at airport upon arrival. Anti-malarial suppressants suggested. For further information consult Embassy of the Federal and Islamic Republic of Comoros, 336 East 45th St., 2nd Floor, New York, NY 10017 (212/972-8010).

CONGO - Passport and visa required. Single-entry $30 or multiple-entry $50, for tourist/business stay up to 3 months, requires yellow fever and cholera immunizations and onward/ return ticket. First-time applicants need 2 application forms and 2 photos, returning visitors need only 2. For business visa must have company letter stating reason for trip. Include SASE for return of passport by mail. Letter of introduction stating reason for trip, 2 applications and 2 photos required. Apply Embassy of the Republic of the Congo, 4891 Colorado Ave., N.W., Washington, D.C. 20011 (202/726-5500) or the Permanent Mission of the Congo to the UN, 14 East 65th St. New York, NY 10021 (212/744-7840).

COOK ISLANDS - Passport and onward/return ticket required. Visa not needed for visit up to 31 days. For longer stays and further information contact Consulate for the Cook Islands, Kamehameha Schools, #16, Kapalama Heights, Honolulu, Hi 96817 (808/847-6377).

COSTA RICA - Passport required. Travelers are sometimes admitted with (original) certified U.S. birth certificate and photo ID for tourist stay of up to 90 days. Tourist card issued upon arrival at airport upon presentation of aforementioned documents for approximately $20. U.S. citizens must have onward/return ticket. For stays over 90 days, you must apply for an extension (within the first week of visit) with Costa Rican Immigration and, after 90 days, obtain exit visa and possess a valid U.S. passport. For travel with pets and other information contact the Consular Section of the Embassy of Costa Rica, 2112 S St. N.W. , Washington, D.C. 20008 (202/3286628) or nearest Consulate General: CA (415/392-8488), GA (404/951-7025), FL (305/371-7485), IL (312/263-2772), LA (504/887-8131), NY (212/425-2620) or TX (713/266-1527).

COTE D'IVOIRE (formerly Ivory Coast) - Passport required. Visa not required for stay up to 90,days. Visa $33, requires 4 application forms, 4 photos, yellow fever vaccination, onward/ return ticket and financial guarantee. Include postage for return of passport by registered mail. For further information contact Embassy of the Republic of Cote D'Ivoire, 2424 Mass. Ave., N.W., Washington,'D.C. 20008 (202/797-0300) or Honorary Consulate: CA (415/391-0176).

CROATIA-Passport and visa required. Visa can be obtained at port of entry but obtaining it in advance may prevent potential complications at the border. There is no charge for business or tourist visa. Please provide SASE or prepaid airbill for return of documents. For further information consult the Embassy of Croatia, 236 Massachusetts Ave., N.E., Washington, D.C. 20002 (202/588-5899).

CUBA - Passport and visa required. Tourist visa $26, business visa $50, valid up to 6 months, requires 1 application and photo. Send money order only and SASE for return of passport. Apply Cuban Interests Section, 2639 16th Street, N.W., Washington, D.C. 20009 (202/797-8609 or 8518). AIDS test required for those staying longer than 90 days. Attention: U.S. citizens need a Treasury Dept. license in order to engage in any transactions related to travel to and within Cuba. Before planning any travel to Cuba, U.S. citizens should contact the Licensing Division, Office of Foreign Assets Control, Department of the Treasury, 1331 G St., N.W., Washington, D.C. 20220 (202/622-2480).

CURACAO - (See Netherlands Antilles.)

CYPRUS - Passport required. Visa not required for tourist/ business up to 3 months. For employment and other travel, visa required and must be obtained in advance. AIDS test required for certain entertainers; U.S. test accepted. For additional information consult Embassy of the Republic of Cyprus, 2211 R St., N.W., Washington, D.C. 20008 (202/4625772) or nearest Consulate: AR (602/264-9701), CA (310/397-

0771,510/286-1831),GA (404/941-3764),IN (219/481-6897), LA (504/388-8701), MA (617/497-0219), MI (513/582141 1), NY (212/686-6016),OR (503/227-141 1), PA (215/9284290), or TX (713/928-2264) .

CZECH REPUBLIC - Passport required. Visa not required for stay up to 30 days. All visitors staying longer than 30 days must register with the appropriate authorities within 3 days after their arrival. For more information contact Embassy of the Czech Republic, 3900 Spring of Freedom Street., N.W., Washington, D.C. 20008 (202/363-6308).

DENMARK (including GREENLAND) - Passport required. Tourist/business visa issued on arrival for stay up to 3 months. Period begins when entering Scandinavian area: Finland, Iceland, Norway, Sweden. Special rules apply for entry into the U.S.-operated defense area in Greenland. For further information contact the Royal Danish Embassy, 3200 Whitehaven St., N.W., Washington, D.C. 20008 (202/2344300) or nearest Consulate General: CA (213/387-4277), Chicago (312/787-8780) or New York (212/223-4545).

DJIBOUTI - Passport and visa required. Visas must be obtained before arrival. Single-entry visa valid for 30 days, extendable, requires $30 fee, 2 applications, 2 photos, yellow fever immunization, onward/return ticket and sufficient funds. Company letter needed for business visa. Send prepaid envelope for return of passport by registered, certified, or express mail. Apply Embassy of the Republic of Djibouti, 1 156 15th St., N.W., Suite 515, Washington, D.C. 20005 (202/331 0270) or the Djibouti Mission to the U.N., 866 United Nations Plaza, Suite 401 1, New York, NY 1001 7 (2121753-3163).

DOMINICA - Proof of U.S. citizenship, photo ID and return/ onward ticket required for tourist stay up to 6 months. For longer stays and other information consult Consulate of the Commonwealth of Dominica, 820 2nd Ave., Suite 900, New York, NY 10017 (212/599-8478).

DOMINICAN REPUBLIC - Passport or proof of U.S. citizenship and tourist card or visa required. Tourist card for stay up to 2 months, available from Consulate or from airline serving the Dominican Republic, $1 0 fee. Visa issued by Consulate, valid up to 5 years, no charge. All persons must pay $10 airport departure fee. AIDS test required for residence permit. U.S.test not accepted. For business travel and other information call the Embassy of the Dominican Republic, 1715 22nd St., N.W.,Washington, D.C. 20008 (202/332-6280) or nearest Consulate General: CA (415/982-5144), FL (305/358-3221), IL (3121772-6363), LA

(504/522-1843), MA (617/482-8121), NY (212/768-2480), PA (215/923-3006), PR (809/725-9550), or TX (713/266-0165).

ECUADOR - Passport and return/onward ticket required for stay up to 3 months. For additional information contact the Embassy of Ecuador, 2535 15th St., N.W., Washington, D.C. 20009 (202/234-7166) or nearest Consulate General: CA (213/628-3014 or 415/957-5921), FL (305/539-8214), IL (312/ 329-0266), LA (504/523-3229), MA (617/523-2700), MD (41 O/ 889-4435), MI (313/332-7356), NJ (201/642-0208), NV (702/735-8193),NY (212/808-0170171),PR (809/781-4408), or TX (713/622-8105).

EGYPT - Passport and visa required. Transit visa for stay up to 48 hours available. Tourist visa, valid 3 months, requires $15 fee (cash or money order), 1 application form and 1 photo. Visa may be issued at airport upon arrival for fee of $20. For business travel, need company letter stating purpose of trip. Enclose prepaid envelope for return of passport by certified mail. Proof of yellow fever immunization required if arriving from infected area. AIDS test required for workers and students staying over 30 days. Register with local authorities or at hotel within 7 days of arrival. Travelers must declare foreign currency on Form 'D' on arrival and show Form 'D' and bank receipts upon departure. Maximum Egyptian currency allowed into and out of Egypt is LE20. For additional information consult Embassy of the Arab Republic of Egypt, 3521 International Court, N.W., Washington, D.C. 20008 (202/966-6342/48) or nearest Consulate General: CA (415/ 346-9700), IL (312/828-9162), NY (212/759-7120) or Houston (713/961-4915).

EL SALVADOR - Passport and visa required. (Length of validity of visa will be determined by Consulate). Requires 1 application form and 2 photos. Allow 3 working days for processing. Send SASE for return of passport by mail. AIDS test required for permanent residence permit. U.S. test not accepted. Apply Consulate General of El Salvador, 101 0 16th St., N.W., 3rd Floor, Washington, D.C. 20036 (202/331-4032) or nearest Consulate: CA (213/383-5776 or 4151781-7924),FL (305/371-8850),IL (312/322-1393), LA (504/522-4266), NY (212/889-3608) or TX (713/270-6239).

ENGLAND - (See United Kingdom.)

EQUATORIAL GUINEA - Passport and visa required. Obtain visa in advance. For further information contact the residence of the Ambassador of Equatorial Guinea at 57 Magnolia Ave., Mount Vernon, NY (914/667-9664).

ERITREA - Passport and visa required. Tourist/business visa valid for a stay of up to 6 months, requires 1 application, 1 photo, $25 fee (no personal checks). Business visa can be extended up to 1 year, requires company letter stating purpose of travel. Include SASE for return of passport by mail. Allow 3 working days for processing. For more information contact the Embassy of Eritrea, 910 17th St., NW, Suite 400, Washington, D.C. 20006 (202/429-1991).

ESTONIA - Passport required. Visas not required for stay of up to 90 days. AIDS test required for residency and work permits. U.S. test sometimes accepted. For further information contact the Consulate General of Estonia, 630 Fifth Avenue, Suite 2415, New York, NY 10020 (212/247-2131).

ETHIOPIA - Passport and visa required. Tourist/business visa valid for stay up to 2 years, fee $70 or transit visa for 48 hours, $40, requires 1 application, 1 photo and yellow fever immunization. Business visa requires company letter. Send $2 postage for return of passport or $15.30 for Federal Express and $9.95 for Express Mail service. (Money orders only.) Allow 3-4 working days for processing. Exit visas are required of all visitors remaining in Ethiopia for more than 30 days. For longer stays and other information contact Embassy of Ethiopia, 2134 Kalorama Rd., N.W., Washington, D.C. 20008 (202/234-2281/2).

FIJI - Passport, proof of sufficient funds and onward/return ticket required. Visa issued on arrival for stay up to 30 days and may be extended up to 6 months. For further information contact Embassy of Fiji, 2233 Wisconsin Ave., N.W., #240, Washington, D.C. 20007 (202/337-8320) or Mission to the U.N., One United Nations Plaza, '26th Floor, New York, NY 10017 (212/355-7316).

FINLAND - Passport required. Tourist/business visa not required for stay up to 90 days. (90 day period begins when entering Scandinavian area: Sweden, Norway, Denmark, Iceland.) Check Embassy of Finland, 3301 Massachusetts Ave., N.W., Washington, D.C. 20008 (202/298-5800) or nearest Consulate General: Los Angeles (310/203-9903) or New York (212/750-4400).

FRANCE - Passport required to visit France, Andorra, Monaco, Corsica and French Polynesia. Visa not required for tourist/business stay up to 3 months in France, Andorra, Monaco and Corsica, and 1 month in French Polynesia. Journalists on assignment, ship or plane crew members, and students are required to obtain a visa in advance. For further information consult Embassy of France, 41 01 Reservoir Rd., N.W., Washington, D.C. 20007 (202/944-600016200) or nearest Consulate: CA(310/479-4426 or 4l5/397-4330),FL(305/ 372-9798), GA (404/522-4226), HI (808/599-4458), IL (312/ 787-5359), LA (504/523-5774), MA (617/482-3650), NY (212/ 606-3600), PR (809/753-1700) or TX (713/528-2181).

FRENCH GUIANA - Proof of U.S. citizenship and photo ID required for visit up to 3 weeks. (For stays longer than 3 weeks, a passport is required.) No visa required for stay up to 3 months. For further information consult Embassy of France, 4101 Reservoir Rd., N.W., Washington, D.C. 20007 (202/ 944-6000/6200).

FRENCH POLYNESIA - Includes Society Islands, French Southern and Antarctic Lands, Tuamotu, Gambier, French Austral, Marquesas, Kerguelen, Crozet, New Caledonia, Tahiti, Wallis and Furtuna Islands. Passport required. Visa not required for visit up to 1 month. For longer stays and further information consult Embassy of France (202/944-6000/6200).

GABON - Passport and visa required. Visas must be obtained before arrival. Single-entry visa valid up to 1 month, multiple entry visa valid for 1-4 months. Both visas require 2 application forms, 2 photos, yellow fever vaccinations, and $50 fee (no personal checks accepted). Also need detailed travel arrangements, including flight numbers, arrival and departure dates, accommodations and next destination. A certificate of accommodation issued by the host family or institution in Gabon is required. Business visa requires company letter stating purpose of trip and contacts in Gabon. Accompanying family must be included in letter. For longer stays and other information call Embassy of the Gabonese Republic, 2034 20th St., N.W., Washington, D.C. 20009 (2021797-1000) or the Permanent Mission of the Gabonese . Republic to the UN, 18 East 41st St., 6th Floor, New York, NY 1001 7 (212/6869720).

GALAPAGOS ISLANDS - Passport and onward/return ticket required for visits up to 3 months. For further information consult Embassy of Ecuador (202/234-7166).

GAMBIA - Passport and visa required. Tourist/business visa for a stay of up to 12 months, requires 1 application, and 1 photo. For business visa, you also need company letter stating purpose of visit and itinerary. Allow at least 2 working days for processing. Include prepaid envelope for return of passport by mail. Apply Embassy of the Gambia, 1155 15th St., N.W., Washington, D.C. 20005 (202/785-

1399) or Permanent Mission of The Gambia to the U.N., 820 2nd Ave., 9th floor, New York, NY 10017 (212/949-6640).

GEORGIA - Passport, visa and.letter of invitation required. Visa requires 1 application, 1 photo, itinerary and processing fee. Please provide SASE or prepaid airbill for return of documents. For additional information contact the Embassy of the Republic of Georgia, Suite 424, 1511 K St., N.W., Washington, D.C. 20005 (202/393-6060).

GERMANY - Passport required. Tourist/business visa not required for stay up to 3 months. For longer stays (e.g. employment, students) obtain temporary residence permit upon arrival. Applicants of residence permits staying over 90 days may be asked to undergo a medical examination. Every foreign national entering Germany is required to provide proof of sufficient health insurance and funds. For further information contact the Embassy of the Federal Republic of Germany, 4645 Reservoir Rd., N.W., Washington, D.C. 20007 (202/ 298-4000) or nearest Consulate General: CA (415/775-1061, 213/930-2703), FL (305/358-0290), GA (404/659-4760), IL (312/580-1199), MA (617/536-4414), MI (313/962-6526), NY (212/308-8700), TX (713/627-7770), or WA (206/682-4312).

GHANA - Passport and visa required. Passport must be valid for at least six months at time of entry. Tourist visa required for stay up to 30 days (extendable). Requires 1 application form, 4 photos, photocopy of onward/return ticket, bank statement or pay stub and yellow fever immunization. Single-entry visa requires $20 fee, multiple-entry $50. Allow 3 working days for processing. Include prepaid envelope for return of passport by certified mail. For additional information contact Embassy of Ghana, 3512 International Drive, N.W., Washington, D.C. 20008 (202/686-4520) or Consulate General, 19 East 47th St., New York, NY 10017 (212/832-1300).

GIBRALTAR - Passport required. Visa not required for tourist stay up to 3 months. For further information consult British Embassy (202/986-0205).

GILBERT ISLANDS - (See Kiribati.)

GREAT BRITAIN AND NORTHERN IRELAND - (See United Kingdom.)

GREECE - Passport required. Visa not required for tourist/ business stay up to 3 months. AIDS test required for performing artists and students on Greek scholarships; U.S. test accepted. For additional

information consult Consular Section of the Embassy of Greece, 2211 Mass. Ave., N.W., Washington, D.C. 20008 (202/232-8222) or nearest Consulate: CA (213/385-1447 or 4151775-2102), GA (404/261-3313),IL (312/372-5356), LA (504/523-1167), MA (617/542-3240),NY (212/988-5500) or TX (713/840-7522).

GREENLAND - (See Denmark.)

GRENADA - Passport is recommended, but tourists may enter with birth certificate and photo ID. Visa not required for tourist stay up to 3 months, may be extended to maximum of 6 months. For additional information consult Embassy of Grenada, 1701 New Hampshire Ave., N.W., Washington, D.C. 20009 (202/265-2561)or Permanent Mission of Grenada to the U.N. (212/599-0301).

GUADELOUPE - (See West Indies, French.)

GUATEMALA - Passport and visa or tourist card required. Visa is valid for 3 years with multiple entries of 30 days each. Requires passport and 1 application form. Tourist card of 30 days stay (extendable). Requires passport and $5 fee. Provide SASE for return of passport by mail. For travel by minors and general information about contact the Embassy of Guatemala, 2220 R St., N.W., Washington, D.C. 20008-4081 (202/745-4952), or nearest Consulate: CA (213/365-9251/2 or 415/788-5651), FL (305/443-4828/29), IL (312/332-3170), NY (212/686-3837) or TX (713/953-9531).

GUIANA, FRENCH - (See French Guiana.)

GUINEA - Passport and visa required. Tourist/business visa for stay up to three months, requires 3 application forms, 3 photos, yellow fever immunization and $25 fee (cash or money order only). Malaria suppressants are recommended. For business visa need company letter stating purpose of trip and letter of invitation from company in Guinea. Provide SASE for return of passport by mail. For more information contact the Embassy of the Republic of Guinea, 2112 Leroy PI., N.W., Washington, D.C. 20008 (202/483-9420).

GUINEA-BISSAU - Passport and visa required. Visa must be obtained in advance. Visa valid up to 90 days, requires 2 application forms, 2 photos, financial guarantee to cover stay, letter staying purpose of travel and $12 fee (payment by money order only). Include prepaid envelope for return of passport by express mail. Apply Embassy of Guinea-Bissau, 918 16th St., N.W., Mezzanine Suite, Washington, D.C. 20006 (202/872-

4222).

GUYANA - Passport required. For more information consult Embassy of Guyana, 2490 Tracy Pl., N.W., Washington, D.C. 20008 (202/265-6900/03) or Consulate General, 866 U.N. Plaza, 3rd Floor. New York, NY 1001 7 (212/527-3215).

HAITI - Passport required. For further information consult Embassy of Haiti, 2311 Mass. Ave., N.W., Washington, D.C. 20008 (202/332-4090) or nearest Consulate: FL (305/8592003), MA (617/266-36601), NY (212/697-9767), PR (809/ 764-1392), or IL (312/922-4004).

HOLY SEE, APOSTOLIC NUNCIATURE OF THE - Passport required (for entry into Italy). For further information consult Apostolic Nunciature of the Holy See, 3339 Mass. Ave., N.W., Washington, D.C. 20008 (202/333-7121) or call Embassy of Italy (202/328-5500).

HONDURAS - Passport and onward/return ticket required. For additional information contact Embassy of Honduras (Consular Section), Suite 310, 1612 K Street., N.W., Washington, D.C. 20006 (202/223-0185) or nearest Consulate: CA (213/383-9244 and 415/392-0076), FL (305/447-8927), IL (312/772-7090), LA (504/522-3118), NY (212/269-361 1) or TX (713/622-4572).

HONG KONG - Passport and onward/return transportation by sea/air required. Visa not required for tourist stay up to 30 days, may be extended to 3 months. Confirmed hotel and flight reservations recommended during peak travel months. Departure tax 150 Hong Kong dollars (approx. $20 U.S.) paid at airport. Visa required for work or study. For other types of travel consult British Embassy (202/986-0205). HUNGARY - Passport required. Visa not required for stay up to 90 days. For business travel and other information check Embassy of the Republic of Hungary, 391 0 Shoe maker Street, N.W., Washington, D.C. 20008 (202/362-6730) or Consulate General, 8 East 75th Street, New York, NY 10021 (212/8794127).

ICELAND - Passport required. Visa not required for stay up to 3 months. Period begins when entering Scandinavian area: Denmark, Finland, Norway, Sweden. For additional information call Embassy of Iceland, 1156 15th Street, N.W., Suite 1200, Washington, D.C. 20005 (202/265-6653-5) or Consulate General in New York (212/686-41 00).

INDIA - Passport and visa required. Obtain visa in advance. Transit visa valid for stay up to 15 days,

requires 25 e. Visas are available up to 3 months for $40, up to 6 months for $60, 1 year for $70, and a 5 yr. visa for $120 but given only on a strict basis. 1 application form, 2 photos, onward/return ticket and proof of sufficient funds. Visa must be obtained before arrival. Business visa requires $70 fee, 1 application form, 2 photos and company letter stating purpose of trip and itinerary. Include prepaid envelope for return of passport by certified mail. Allow 1 weeks for processing if sent by mail. Yellow fever immunization needed if arriving from infected area. AIDS test required for all students and anyone over 18 staying more than 1 year; U.S. test from well known lab accepted. Check requirements with Embassy of India, 2536 Mass. Ave., N.W., Washington, D.C. 20008 (202/939-9839/ 9849) or nearest Consulate General: Chicago (312/7186280), New York (212/879-7805/6) or San Francisco (415/ 668-0683).

INDONESIA - Valid passport and onward/return ticket required. Visa not required for tourist stay up to 2 months (nonextendable). For longer stays and additional information consult Embassy of the Republic of Indonesia, 2020 Mass. Ave., N.W., Washington, D.C. 20036 (202/775-5200) or nearest Consulate: CA (213/383-5126 or 415/474-9571), IL (312/ 938-0101), NY (212/879-0600) or TX (713/785-1691).

IRAN - Passport and visa required. The United States does not maintain diplomatic or consular relations with Iran. Travel by U.S. citizens is not recommended. For visa information contact Embassy of Pakistan, Iranian Interests Section, 2209 Wisconsin Ave., N.W., Washington, D.C. 20007 (202/9654990).

IRAQ-Passport and visa required. AIDS test required for stay over 5 days. The United States suspended diplomatic and consular operations in Iraq in 1990. Since February 1991, U.S. passports are not valid for travel in, to, or through Iraq without authorization from the Department of State. Application for exemptions to this restriction should be submitted in writing to Passport Services, U.S. Department of State, 1111 19th St., N.W., Washington, D.C. 20524, Attn.: CA/PPT/C. Attention: U.S. citizens need a Treasury Dept. license in order to engage in any transactions related to travel to and within Iraq. Before planning any travel to Iraq, U.S. citizens should contact the Licensing Division, Office of Foreign Assets Control, Department of the Treasury, 1331 G St., N.W., Washington, D.C. 20220 (202/622-2480). For visa information contact a country that maintains diplomatic relations with Iraq.

IRELAND - Passport required. Tourists are not required to obtain visas for stays under 90 days, but may be asked to show onward/return ticket. For further information consult Embassy of Ireland, 2234 Mass. Ave., N.W., Washington, D.C. 20008 (202/462-3939) or nearest Consulate General: CA (415/392-4214), IL (312/337-1868), MA (617/267-9330) or NY (212/319-2555).

ISRAEL - Passport, onward/return ticket and proof of sufficient funds required. Tourist visa issued upon arrival valid for 3 months, but can be renewed. Consult Embassy of Israel, 3514 International Dr., N.W., Washington, D.C. 20008 (202/ 364-5500) or nearest Consulate General: CA (213/651-5700 and 415/398-8885), FL (305/358-8111), GA (404/875-7851), IL (312/565-3300), MA (617/542-0041), NY (212/351-5200), PA (215/546-5556) or TX (713/627-3780).

ITALY - Passport required. Visa not required for tourist stay up to 3 months. For longer stays, employment or study, obtain visa in advance. For additional information consult Embassy of Italy, 1601 Fuller St., N.W., Washington, D.C. 20009 (202/ 328-5500) or nearest Consulate General: CA (310/820-0622 or 415/931-4924), FL (305/374-6322), IL (312/467-1550), LA (504/524-2272), MA (617/542-0483/4), MI (313/963-8560), NJ (201/643-1448), NY (2121737-9100), PA (215/592-7329) or TX (713/850-7520).

IVORY COAST - (See Cote d'Ivoire.)

JAMAICA - Passport (or original birth certificate and photo ID), onward/return ticket and proof of sufficient funds required. (Photo ID is not required for U.S. citizens under 16 using birth certificate.) Tourist card issued on arrival for stay up to 6 months; must be returned to immigration authorities on departure. For business or study, visa must be obtained in advance, no charge. Departure tax $15 paid at airport. Check information with Embassy of Jamaica, 1520 New Hampshire Ave., N.W., Washington, D.C. 20036 (202/452-0660) or nearest Consulate: CA (310/559-3822 or 510/886-6061), FL (305/ 374-8431), GA (404/593-1500), IL (312/663-0023), NY (212/ 935-9000), or MA (617/266-8604).

JAPAN - Passport and onward/return ticket required. Visa not required for tourist/business stay up to 90days. Departure tax $20 (2,000 yen) paid at airport. For specific information consult Embassy of Japan, 2526 Mass. Ave., N.W., Washington, D.C. 20008 (202/939-6800) or nearest Consulate: AK (907/279-8428), CA (213/617-6700 or 415/777-3533), FL (305/530-9090), GA (404/892-2700), Guam (671/646-1290), HI (808/536-2226), IL (312/280-0400), LA (504/529-2101), MA (617/973-9772), MI (313/567-

0120), MO (816/471 -011 1), NY (212/371-8222), OR (503/221-181 1), TX (713/652-2977) or WA (206/682-9107).

JORDAN - Passport required. Visa required in advance only if entering Jordan via the King Hussein Bridge. For details consult the Embassy of the Hashemite Kingdom of Jordan, 3504 International Dr., N.W., Washington, D.C. 20008 (202/ 966-2664).

KAZAKHSTAN - Passport and visa required. Visa requires 1 application, 1 photo, original passport or travel document, a letter of invitation clearly stating dates of visit and itinerary, and confirmation of accommodations. Requirements for business travel include confirmation from inviting organization, registration with the Ministry of Foreign Affairs of Kazakhstan by inviting organization, cover letter from your company, and prepaid airbill or SASE. Visa fees should be paid by company check or money order, $30 for 1 week processing, $60 for three day processing, $1 00 for same day processing, and $120 for multi-entry processing. For home stay or other additional information contact the Embassy of Kazakhstan, 3421 Mass. Ave., N.W., Washington, D.C. 20007 (202/3334507).

KENYA - Passport and visa required. Visa must be obtained in advance. Single-entry visa for tourist/business stay up to 6 months, $30 (money order or cashier's check only); requires 1 application form, 2 photos and onward/return ticket. Yellow fever immunization is recommend. Anti-malarial pills are recommended for those travelling to the western or coastal regions. Multiple-entry business visa valid for up to 1 year, $50 Payment by cashiers check or money order only. Airport departure tax is $20. Consult the Embassy of Kenya, 2249 R St., N.W., Washington, D.C. 20008 (202/387-61 01) or Consulate General: Los Angeles (310/274-6635) or New York (212/ 486-1300).

KIRIBATI (formerly Gilbert Islands) - Passport and visa required. For additional information consult British Embassy (202/462-1340).

KOREA, DEMOCRATIC PEOPLE'S REPUBLIC OF (North Korea) - The United States does not maintain diplomatic or consular relations with North Korea and has no third country representing U.S. interests there. Attention: U.S. citizens need a Treasury Dept. license in order to engage in any transactions related to travel to and within North Korea. Before planning any travel to North Korea, U.S. citizens should contact the Licensing Division, Office of Foreign Assets Control, Department of the Treasury, 1331 G St., N.W., Washington, D.C. 20220 (202/622-

2480). Visa information must be obtained from a consulate in a country that maintains diplomatic relations with North Korea.

KOREA, REPUBLIC OF (South Korea) -Passport required. Visa not required for a tourist stay up to 15 days. For longer stays and other types of travel, visa must be obtained in advance, $20 fee. Tourist visa for longer stay requires 1 application form and 1 photo. Business visa requires 1 application form, 1 photo and company letter. Fine imposed for overstaying visa and for long-term visa holders not registered within 60 days after entry. If applying by mail, enclose SASE or prepaid airbill. Vaccination certificate required if coming from infected area within 14 days of arrival in Korea. For further information check Embassy of the Republic of Korea, (Consular Division), 2320 Massachusetts Ave., N.W., Washington, D.C. 20008 (202/939-5660/63) or nearest Consulate General: AK (907/561-5488), CA (213/385-9300 and 415/921-2251/3), FL (305/372-1555), GA (404/522-1611/3), Guam (671/472-6109), Hi (808/595-6109), IL (312/822-9485), MA (617/348-3660), NY (212/752-1700), TX (713/961-0186) or WA (206/441-1011/4).

KUWAIT-Passport and visa required. AIDS test required for work visa; U.S. test accepted. For further information contact the Embassy of the State of Kuwait, 2940 Tilden St., N.W., Washington, D.C. 20008 (202/966-0702) or Consulate, 321 East 44th St., New York, NY 1001 7 (212/973-4318).

KYRGYZ REPUBLIC (Kyrgyzstan) - Passport and visa required. Visa requires 1 application form, 2 photos and detailed itinerary. Visa valid for 60 days after date of issuance. Multi entry visa $100 (no personal checks). Include SASE for return of passport by mail (or proper fee for express mail service). For additional information contact the Embassy of the Kyrgyz Republic, 1511 K St., N.W., Suite 707, Washington, D.C. 20005 (202/628-0433).

LAOS - Passport and visa required. Visa requires $35 fee, 3 application forms, 3 photos, onward/return transportation, sufficient funds, cholera immunization and SASE for return of passport by mail. Transit visas for stay up to 5 days requires onward/return ticket and visa for next destination. Period of stay: maximum 5 days in Vietiane only. Visitor visa are issued for 1 entry and must be used within 3 months of issue date. Period of stay: 1 month, can be extended for another 30 days (visitor visa application must be accompanied by letter from relative or friends in Laos). Tourist visas are issued only to those who apply through a tourist agency. Period of stay: 15 days which may be

extended for another 15 days. Business visa requires letter from counterpart in Laos and is valid for 1 entry and must be used within 3 months of issue date. Period of stay: 1 month, can be extended for another 30 days. For more information, check with the Embassy of the Lao People's Democratic Republic, 2222 S St., N.W., Washington, D.C. 20008 (202/332-6416/7).

LATVIA - Passport and visa required. Tourist/business visa issued at Embassy. Require 1 application form, 1 photo, and $5 fee. Please provide SASE or prepaid airbill for return of documents. For further information contact Embassy of Latvia, 4325 17th St., N.W., Washington, D.C. 20011 (202/ 726-8213).

LEBANON - Passport and visa required. AIDS test required for those seeking residence permits; U.S. test accepted. Since January 1987, U.S. passports are not valid for travel in, to, or through Lebanon without authorization from the Department of State. Application for exemptions to this restriction should be submitted in writing to Passport Services, U.S. Department of State, 1111 19th St., N.W., Washington, D.C. 20524, Attn.: CA/PPT/C. For further visa information contact Embassy of Lebanon, 2560 28th St., N.W., Washington, D.C. 20008 (202/939-6300) or nearest Consulate General: Los Angeles (213/467-1253), Detroit (313/567-0233) or New York (212/744-7905).

LEEWARD ISLANDS - (See Virgin Islands, British.)

LESOTHO- Passport and visa required. Visa requires 1 form. Single-entry visa requires $7.50 fee and multiple-entry $15. For more information, check Embassy of the Kingdom of Lesotho, 2511 Mass. Ave., N.W., Washington, D.C. 20008 (202/797-5533).

LIBERIA - Passport and visa required. Transit visitors with onward ticket can remain at airport up to 48 hours. Other travelers must have round trip ticket and obtain visas before arrival. Tourist/business entry visa valid 3 months, no fee, requires 2 application forms, 2 photos, cholera and yellow fever vaccinations and medical certificate to confirm that traveler is in good health and free of any communicable disease. Company letter needed for business visa. Include SASE for return of passport by mail. Obtain exit permit from immigration authorities upon arrival, 1 photo required. For business requirements call Embassy of the Republic of Liberia, 5303 Colorado Ave., N.W., Washington, D.C. 20011 (202/ 723-0437) or nearest Consulate: CA (213/277-7692), GA (404/753-4754), IL (312/643-8635), LA (504/523-7784), MI (313/342-3900) or NY (212/687-1025).

LIBYA - Passport and visa required. AIDS test required for those seeking residence permits; U.S. test accepted. Since December 1981, U.S.passports are not valid for travel into, or through Libya without authorization from the Department of State. Application for exemptions to this restriction should be submitted in writing to Passport Services, U.S. Department of State, 1111 19th St., N.W., Washington, D.C. 20524, Attn.: CAIPPT/C. Attention: U.S. citizens need a Treasury Dept. license in order to engage in any transactions related to travel to and within Libya. Before planning any travel to Libya, U.S. citizens should contact the Licensing Division, Office of Foreign Assets Control, Department of the Treasury, 1331 G St., N.W., Washington, D.C. 20220 (202/622-2480). Application and inquiries for visas must be made through a country that maintains diplomatic relations with Libya.

LIECHTENSTEIN - Passport required. Visa not required for tourist/business stay up to 3 months. For further information consult the Swiss Embassy (202/745-7900).

LITHUANIA - Passport required. For further information contact Embassy of Lithuania, 2622 16th St., N.W., Washington, D.C. 20009 (202/234-5860).

LUXEMBOURG - Passport required. Visa not required for tourist/business stay up to 3 months. For additional information contact Embassy of Luxembourg, 2200 Mass. Ave., N.W., Washington, D.C. 20008 (202/265-4171) or the nearest Consulate: CA (415/788-0816), FL (305/373-1300), GA (404/ 668-981 1), IL (312/726-0355), MN (612/644-0942), MO (816/ 792-0841), NY (212/888-6664) or OH (513/422-4697).

MACAU - Passport required. Visa not required for visits up to 60 days. For further information consult nearest Portuguese Consulate: Washington, D.C. (202/332-3007), San Francisco (415/346-3400), New Bedford (508/997-6151), Newark (201/622-7300), NY (212/246-4580), Providence (401/2722003) or Portuguese Consulate in Hong Kong (231-338).

MACEDONIA, FORMER YUGOSLAV REPUBLIC OF - Entry permission can be obtained at border points. Macedonia does not currently maintain an embassy in the U.S. For more information check with the Office of Macedonia, 3050 K St., N.W., Suite 210 20007 (202/337-3063).

MADAGASCAR - Passport and visa required. Visa allows entry in Madagascar within 6 months from the date of issue. Short term visa valid for single-entry up to 90 days, $22.50; or double-entries,$44.15(no personal checks). Requires 4 blue application forms, 4 photos, yellow fever and cholera immunizations if arriving from infected areas, proof of onward/return transportation, and sufficient funds for stay. For business visa, the aforementioned is required including company letter. Include a prepaid envelope for return of passport by registered mail. For longer stays and additional information contact Embassy of the Democratic Republic of Madagascar, 2374 Mass. Ave., N.W., Washington, D.C. 20008 (202/265-5525/6) or nearest Consulate: NY (212/986-9491), PA (215/8933067) or CA (1 -800/856-2721 .

MALAWI - Passport required. Visa not required for stay up to 1 year. No dress codes apply for anyone visiting Malawi. For further information contact the Embassy of Malawi, 2408 Mass. Ave., N.W., Washington, D.C. 20008 (202/797-1007) or Malawi Mission to the U.N., 600 3rd Ave., New York, NY 10016 (212/949-0180).

MALAYSIA (and the Borneo States, Sarawak and Sabah) - Passport required. Visa not required for stay up to 3 months. Yellow fever and cholera immunizations necessary if arriving from infected areas. AIDS test required for work permits. U.S. test sometimes accepted. For entry of pets or other types of visits, consult Embassy of Malaysia, 2401 Mass. Ave., N.W., Washington, D.C. 20008 (202/328-2700) or nearest Consulate: Los Angeles (213/621-2991) or New York (212/4902722).

MALDIVES - Passport required. Tourist visa issued upon arrival for 30 days validity, no charge. Visitors must have proof of onward/return transportation and sufficient funds (minimum of $25 per person per day). Yellow fever vaccination certificate is required for those arriving from infected areas. Check with the Maldives Mission to the U.N. in New York (212/5996195) for further information.

MALI - Passport and visa required. Visa must be obtained in advance. Tourist/business visa for stay up to 4 weeks, may be extended after arrival, requires $17 fee (cash or money order), 2 application forms, 2 photos, proof of onward/return transportation and yellow fever vaccination. (Cholera immunization is recommended.)For business travel, must have company letter stating Purpose of trip. Send SASE for return of passport if applying by mail. Apply Embassy of the Republic of Mali, 2130 R St., N.W., Washington, D.C. 20008 (202/3322249).

MALTA - Passport required. Visa not required for stay up to 3 months (extension must be applied for prior to end of 3 month period or expiration of original

31

visa). Visa requires 3 application forms, 2 photos, proof of onward/return transportation and $46 fee (check or money order). Transit visa available for $31. For additional information consult Embassy of Malta, 2017 Conn. Ave., N.W., Washington, D.C. 20008 (202/462-3611/2) or nearest Consulate: CA (213/939-5011 and 415/468-4321), FL (305/942-2491), MA (617/259-1391), MI (313/525-9777), MO (816/833-0033), MN (612/699-3433), NY (212/725-2345), PA (412/279-6170) or TX (713/497-21 00 or 713/999-1812).

MARSHALL ISLANDS, REPUBLIC OF THE - Proof of U.S. citizenship, sufficient funds for stay and onward/return ticket required for stay up to 30 days (extendable up to 90 days from date of entry). Entry permit not needed to bring in sea-going vessel. Obtain necessary forms from airline or shipping agent serving Marshall Islands. Departure fee $15 (those over age 60 exempt). Health certificate required if arriving from infected areas. AIDS test may be required for visits over 30 days; U.S. test accepted. Check information with Embassy of Marshall Islands, 2433 Massachusetts Avenue, N.W., Washington, 220 East 42nd St., New York, NY 10017 (211/983-3040 or the nearest Consulate General: CA (714/474-0331) or Hi (808/942-4422).

MARTINIQUE - (See West Indies, French.)

MAURITANIA - Passport and visa required. Obtain visa before arrival. Visa valid 3 months, requires $10 fee (money order only), 2 application forms, 4 photos, yellow fever and cholera immunizations and proof of onward/return transportation. Business travelers must have proof of sufficient funds (bank statement) or letter from sponsoring company. For further information contact Embassy of the Republic of Mauritania, 2129 Leroy PI., N.W., Washington, D.C. 20008 (202/232-5700/01) or Permanent Mission to the U.N., 211 East 43rd Street, Suite 2000, New York, NY 10017 (212/9867963).

MAURITIUS - Passport, sufficient funds for stay and onward/ return ticket required. Visa not required for tourist/business stay up to 3 months. AIDS test required for permanent residence and work permits. U.S. test sometimes accepted. For further information consult Embassy of Mauritius, Suite 441, 4301 Conn. Ave., N.W., Washington, D.C. 20008 (202/ 244-1491/2) or Honorary Consulate in Los Angeles (818/788-3720).

MAYOTTE ISLAND - (See France.)

MEXICO - Passport and visa not required of U.S.

citizens for tourist/transit stay up to 90 days. Tourist card is required. Tourist card valid 3 months for single entry up to 180 days, no charge, requires proof of U.S. citizenship, photo ID and proof of sufficient funds. Tourist cards may be obtained in advance from Consulate, Tourism Office, and most airlines serving Mexico upon arrival. Departure tax $10 is paid at airport. Notarized consent from parent(s) required for children travelling alone, with one parent or in someone else's custody. (This permit is not necessary when a minor is in possession of a valid passport.) For other types of travel and details, check Embassy of Mexico's Consular Section, 2827 16th St., N.W., Washington, DC 20009-4260 (2021736-1 000) or nearest Consulate General: CA (213/351-6800, 415/392-5554 and 619/231-8414), CO (303/830-0601), FL (305/716-4977), IL (312/ 855-1380), LA (504/522-3596), NY (212/689-0460), PR (809/ 764-0258) or TX (214/631-7772, 713/542-2300, 512/7739255 and 915/533-3644).

MICRONESIA, FEDERATED STATES OF (Kosrae, Yap, Ponape,and Truk)-Proof of citizenship, sufficient funds, and onward/return ticket required for tourist visit up to 6 months, extendable (up to 12 months from date of entry) after arrival in Micronesia. Entry permit may be needed for other types of travel; obtain forms from airline. Departure fee $5 (U.S.). Health certificate may be required if traveling from infected area. Typhoid and tetanus immunizations are recommended. AIDS test required if staying over 1 year. U.S. test is accepted. For further information contact Embassy of the Federated States of Micronesia, 1725 N St., N.W., Washington, D.C. 20036 (202/223-4383) or nearest Consulate: Hawaii (8081 836-4775) or Guam (671/646-9154).

MIQUELON ISLAND - Proof of U.S. citizenship and photo ID required for visit up to 3 months. For further information consult Embassy of France (202/944-6000).

MOLDOVA - Passport and visa required. Visas are issued at the Embassy of Moldova. Visas can not be issued at the entry points along the Romanian and Ukrainian borders. Visa requirements: 1 application form and 1 photo. For additional information consult Embassy of the Republic of Moldova, 1533 K Street, N.W., Suits 333, Washington, D.C. 20005, (202/783-4218).

MONACO - Passport required. Visa not required for visit up to 3 months. For further information consult French Embassy (202/944-6000) or nearest Honorary Consulate of the Principality of Monaco: CA (213/655-8970 or 415/362-5050), IL (312/642-1242), LA (504/522-5700), NY (212/759-5227) or PR (809/721-

4215).

MONGOLIA - Passport and visa required. Multiple-entry visa valid for period of 6 months may be issued for $65. Transit visa for stay up to 48 hours requires copy of onward ticket, visa for next destination and $15 fee ($30 for double transit). Tourist visa for up to 90 days requires confirmation from Mongolian Travel Agency (Zhuulchin) and $25 fee. Business visa requires letter from company stating purpose of trip and invitation from Mongolian organization and $25 fee. Submit 1 application form, 1 photo, itinerary and prepaid envelope for return of passport by certified or special delivery mail. AIDS test required for students and anyone staying longer than 3 months; U.S. test accepted. All foreigners are required to be registered with the Civil Registration Information Center Police Department in Mongolia Upon arrival regardless of duration of stay and are warned to do so in order to avoid any inconveniences they may face upon departure. For additional information contact Embassy of Mongolia, 2833 M Street, N.W., Washington, D.C. 20007 (202/333-7117). or the UN Mission of Mongolia, 6 East 77th St., New York, NY 10021 (212/861-9460).

MOROCCO - Passport required. Passport must have 6 months validity. Visa not required for stay up to 3 months, extendable. For additional information consult Embassy of Morocco, 1601 21 St., N.W., Washington, D.C. 20009 (202/ 462-7979 to 7982) or Consulate General in New York (212/ 213-9644).

MOZAMBIQUE - Passport and visa required. Visa must be obtained in advance. Entry visa valid 30 days from date of issuance, requires 2 application forms, 2 photos, immunization for yellow fever and cholera, $20 fee and letter (from company or individual) giving detailed itinerary. Visitors may have to exchange $25 at point of entry and declare all foreign currency. Apply Embassy of the Republic of Mozambique, Suite 570,1990 M St., N.W., Washington, D.C. 20036 (202/ 293-7146).

MYANMAR (formerly Burma) - Passport and visa required. Single-entry visas, for stay up to 28 days, requires $18 fee, 2 application forms, 3 photos and itinerary. Single-entry business visa, for stay. up to 28 days, requires $30 fee, 3 application forms and 4 photos. Tourists visas are issued for package or group tours as well as Foreign Independent Travelers (FITs). FITs holding tourist visas must change a minimum of $300 (U.S.) upon arrival. Business visa requires company letter and invitation from a Myanmarian company. Overland travel into and out of Myanmar is only permitted at certain points (check with Embassy).

Enclose prepaid envelope for return of passport by registered/certified mail. Allow 24 hours for processing. For further information contact Embassy of the Union of Myanmar, 2300 S St., N.W., Washington, D.C. 20008 (202/332-9044-5) or the Permanent Mission of Myanmar to the U.N., 1 0 East 77th St., New York, NY 10021 (212/ 535-1311).

NAMIBIA - Passport, onward/return ticket and proof of sufficient funds required. Visa not required for tourist or business stay up to 90 days. Consult Embassy of Namibia, 1605 New Hampshire Ave., N.W., Washington, D.C. 20009 (202/9860540) for further information on entry requirements.

NAURU - Passport, visa, onward/return ticket and sponsorship from a resident in Nauru required. For more information contact Consulate of the Republic of Nauru in Guam, P.O. Box Am, Agana, Guam 96910 (671/649-8300).

NEPAL - Passport and visa required. Tourist visa extendable to a maximum period of 150 days in one visa year (January to December). Single-entry visa for 15 days, $15; single entry visa for 30 days, $25; double entry visa for 30 days, $40; and multiple entry visa with a validity for 60 days, $60; requires 1 application form and 1 photo. Entry visas are valid for entry into Nepal within six months from the date of issue. Tourist visacan also be obtained from Immigration Office at Kathmandu Airport and other specified ports of entry. Trekking permit is required for trekking purposes. For additional information contact Royal Nepalese Embassy, 2131 Leroy Pl., N.W., Washington, D.C. 20008 (202/667-4550) or Consulate General in New York (212/370-4188).

NETHERLANDS - Passport required. Visa not required for tourist/business visit up to 90 days. Tourists may be asked to show onward/return ticket or proof of sufficient funds for stay. For further information contact Embassy of the Netherlands, 4200 Wisconsin Ave., N.W., Washington, D.C. 20016 (202/ 244-5300) or nearest Consulate General: CA 310/268-1598), IL (312/856-01 1 0), NY (212/246-1429) or TX (713/ 622-8000).

NETHERLANDS ANTILLES - Islands include Bonaire, Curacao, Saba, Statia, St. Maarten. Passport or proof of U.S. citizenship (i.e. certified birth certificate or voter registration card with photo I.D.) required. Visa not required for stay up to 14 days, extendable to 90 days after arrival. Tourists may be asked to show onward/return ticket or proof of sufficient funds for stay. Departure tax $10 when leaving Bonaire and Curacao, $4 in Statia, $10 in St. Maarten. For further information consult Embassy of the Netherlands (202/244-5300), or nearest Consulate General: CA (213/380-3440), IL (312/85601 1 0), NY (212/246-1429) or TX (713/622-8000).

NEW CALEDONIA - (See French Polynesia.)

NEW ZEALAND - Passport and visitor's card (to be completed upon arrival) required. Passport must be valid until at least 3 months past the date you plan to leave New Zealand. Visa not required for tourist stay of up to 3 months, must have onward/return ticket, visa for next destination and proof of sufficient funds. For business or additional information contact Embassy of New Zealand, 37 Observatory Circle, N.W., Washington, D.C. 20008 (202/328-4800) or the Consulate General, Los Angeles (310/207-1605).

NICARAGUA - Passport valid 6 months beyond duration of stay and onward/return ticket required. For further information, travelers may contact the Consulate of Nicaragua, 1627 New Hampshire Ave., N.W., Washington, D.C. 20009 (202/ 939-6531/32) or the nearest Consulate in CA (213/252-1170 or 415/765-6821), FL (305/220-6900), LA (504/523-1507), NY (212/983-1981), or TX (713/272-9628).

NIGER - Passport and visa required. Visa must be used within 3 months of issuance. All visas types require 3 application forms, 3 photos, yellow fever vaccination (cholera vaccination is recommended, but not required), proof of onward/return transportation and $25.20 fee. Transit visas required for those travelers continuing through Niger. General requirements apply plus 2 copies of round trip ticket and/or 2 copies of itinerary, or letter from travel agent certifying round trip ticket has been purchased. For tourist visa the general requirements apply as well as 2 copies of bank statement certifying that traveler has at least $500 in their bank account. Business visas require general requirements as well as 2 copies of a letter from the company that is being represented stating the purpose, activities, duration, and source of financial responsibility for the trip. Please provide SASE or prepaid airbill for return of documents. For further information and fees contact Embassy of the Republic of Niger, 2204 R St., N.W., Washington, D.C. 20008 (202/483-4224).

NIGERIA - Passport and visa required. Single-entry visa $20 fee and multiple entry visa - $40 fee, both valid for 12 months, requires 1 photo, yellow fever vaccination, proof of onward/return transportation, and detailed itinerary. Business visa requires letter from counterpart in Nigeria and letter of introduction from

U.S. company. For further information contact Embassy of the Republic of Nigeria, 2201 M St., N.W., Washington, D.C. 20037 (202/822-1500 or 1522) or the Consulate General in New York (212/715-7200).

NIUE - Passport, onward/return ticket and confirmed hotel accommodations required. Visa not required for stay up to 30 days. For additional information consult Embassy of New Zealand (202/328-4800).

NORFOLK ISLAND - Passport and visa required. Visa issued upon arrival for visit up to 30 days, extendable, requires confirmed accommodations and onward/return ticket. Australian transit visa must also be obtained in advance for travel to Norfolk Island. For both visas consult Australian Embassy (202/797-3000).

NORWAY - Passport required. Visa not required for stay up to 3 months. Period begins when entering Scandinavian area: Finland, Sweden, Denmark, Iceland. For further information contact Royal Norwegian Embassy, 2720 34th St., N.W., Washington, D.C. 20008 (202/333-6000) or nearest Consulate General: CA (415/986-0766 to 7168 and 213/933-7717), MN (612/332-3338), NY (212/421-7333) or TX (713/521 - 2900).

OMAN - Passport and visa required. Tourist/business visas for multiple-entry issued for stay up to 6 months and valid for 2 years. Requires $21 fee, 1 application form and cholera immunization if arriving from infected area. AIDS test required for work permits. U.S test not accepted. Allow 1 week to 1 0 days for processing. For transit and road travel check Embassy of the Sultanate of Oman, 2535 Belmont Rd.. N.W., Washington, D.C. 20008 (202/387-1980-2).

PAKISTAN - Passport and visa required. Visa must be obtained before arrival. Tourist visa requires 1 application form, 1 photo and proof of onward/return transportation. Validity depends on length of visit, multiple entries, $20 fee. Need company cover letter and invitation for business visa. Include prepaid envelope for return of passport by registered mail. AIDS test required for stays over 1 year. For applications and inquiries in Washington area, contact Consular Section of the Embassy of Pakistan, 2315 Mass. Ave., N.W., Washington, D.C. 20008 (202/939-6295/61), or CA (310/441-5114), or NY (212/879-5800).

PALAU, THE REPUBLIC OF - Passport required. Onward/ return ticket required. Obtain forms for entry permit from airline or shipping agent serving Palau.

For further information consult with Representative Office, 444 N. Capitol St., Suite 619, Washington, D.C. 20001 (202/624-7793).

PANAMA - Passport, tourist card or visa and onward/return ticket required. Tourist card valid 30 days, available from airline serving Panama for $5 fee. For longer stays and additional information regarding travel other than via a commercial airline, contact Embassy of Panama, 2862 McGill Terrace, N.W., Washington, D.C. 20008 (202/483-1407).

PAPUA NEW GUINEA - Passport, onward/return ticket and proof of sufficient funds required. Tourist visa for a stay of up to 30 days may be issued upon arrival. Business visa requires passport validity at least one year from the date visa is issued, 2 application forms, 2 photos, company letter, bio-data, recent annual report of parent company and $10.25 fee (single entry) or $154.00 (multiple entry). Single entry business visa is good for 3 weeks maximum stay. Multiple entry visa is valid for 1 year, with 8 weeks maximum stay each visit. AIDS test required for work and residency permits; U.S. test accepted. Please provide SASE or prepaid airbill for return of documents. For longer stays and further information contact Embassy of Papua New Guinea, Suite 300,1615 New Hampshire Ave., N.W., Washington, D.C. 20009 (2021745-3680).

PARAGUAY- Passport required. Visa not required for tourist/business stay upto 9O days (extendable). AIDS test required for resident visas. U.S. test sometimes accepted. For additional information consult Embassy of Paraguay, 2400 Mass. Ave., N.W., Washington, D.C. 20008 (202/483-6960).

PERU - Passport required. Visa not required for tourist stay up to 90 days, extendable after arrival. Tourists may need onward/return ticket. Business visa requires company letter stating purpose of trip and $27 fee. For further information contact Embassy of Peru, 1700 Mass. Ave., N.W., Washington, D.C. 20036 (202/833-9860-9) or nearest Consulate: CA (213/383-9896 and 415/362-5185), FL (305/374-1407), IL (312/853-6173), NY (212/644-2850), PR (809/763-0679) or TX (713/781-5000).

PHILIPPINES - Passport and onward/return ticket required. For entry by Manila International Airport, visa not required for transit/tourist stay up to 21 days. Visa required for longer stay, maximum of 59 days, 1 application form, 1 photo, $25 fee for single entry. Company letter needed for business visa. AIDS test required for permanent residency; U.S. test accepted. For longer stays or more information contact the Embassy of the Philippines, 1600 Mass. Ave., N.W.,

Washington, D.C. 20036 (202/467-9300) or nearest Consulate General: CA (213/387-5321 and 415/433-6666), Hi (808/595-6316), IL (312/332-6458), NY (2121764-1330), or Guam (671/646-4620).

POLAND - Passport (must be valid at least 12 months past date of entry) required. Visa not required for stay up to 90 days. Visitors must register at hotel or with local authorities within 48 hours after arrival. Check with the Embassy of the Republic of Poland (Consular Division), 2224 Wyoming Ave., N.W., Washington, D.C. 20008 (202/232-4517) or nearest Consulate General: Chicago, IL, 1530 Lakeshore Dr., 6061 0 (312/337-8816), Los Angeles, CA, 12400 Wilshire Blvd., Suite 555, 90025 (310/442-8500) or New York, NY, 233 Madison Ave., 10016 (212/889-8360).

PORTUGAL - (Includes travel to the Azores and Madeira Islands.) Passport required. Passport must be valid for at least 3 months beyond the limit of allowed stay in Portugal. Visa not required for visit up to 60 days (extendable). For travel with pets and other information consult nearest Consulate: Washington, D.C. (202/332-3007, CA (415/346-3400), MA (617/536-8740 and 508/997-6151), NJ (201/622-7300), NY (212/246-4580) or RI (401/272-2003).

QATAR - Passport and visa required. Business persons, tourists, those attending scientific or cultural symposia, and medical visitors are granted a 10 year multiple entry visa at the Embassy in Washington, D.C. A non-refundable application fee of $22 is required. Please provide a SASE for return of passport by mail. AIDS test required for work and student visas; U.S. test accepted if within 3 months of visit. For specific information contact Embassy of the State of Qatar, Suite 1180, 600 New Hampshire Ave., N.W., Washington, D.C. 20037 (202/338-0111).

REUNION - (See France.)

ROMANIA - Passport and visa required. Transit and tourist visa may be obtained at border in Romania or from the Romanian Embassy or Consulate before departure. Transit visa for stay up to 4 days, single-entry $21 or double-entry $31. Tourist/business visa, single-entry valid 6 months for stay up to 60 days, $31 (multiple-entry $68). No application or photos needed. Provide SASE for return of passport by mail. Allow 1 to 3 days for processing. For additional information consult Embassy of Romania, 1607 23rd St., N.W., Washington, D.C. 20008 (202/232-4747-9) or the Consulate General, New York (212/682-9120, 9121, 9122),

RUSSIA - Passport and visa required. Tourist visa

requires 1 application form, 3 photos, confirmation from tourist agency in Russia and processing fee. Business visa requires 1 application, 3 photos, and letter of invitation from a Russian counterpart and visa processing fee. Visa processing fee for business and tourist visas is $20 for 2 weeks, $30 for one week and$60 for four working days processing time. Multiple-entry business visa (needs confirmation through the Russian MFA) - $120 processing fee. Fee paid by money order or company check only. Provide SASE for return of passport by mail. AIDS test required for anyone staying over 3 months; U.S. test accepted. For additional information contact the Consular Section of the Embassy of Russia, 1825 Phelps Pl., N.W., Washington, D.C. 20008 (202/939-8907,8913 or 8918) or the nearest Consulate General: NY (212/348-0926,0955,0626),CA (415/928-6878) or WA (206/728-191 0).

RWANDA - Passport and visa required. Multiple-entry visa for stay up to 3 months (extendable) requires, $30 fee, 2 application forms, 2 photos and immunizations for yellow fever. Exact date of entry and departure to and from Rwanda required with application. Include prepaid envelope or postage for return of passport by certified mail. Apply at one of the following: Embassy of the Republic of Rwanda, 1714 New Hampshire Ave., N.W., Washington, D.C. 20009 (202/2322882), Permanent Mission of Rwanda to the U.N., 124 East 39th Street, New York, NY 10016 (212/696-0644/45/46), the Consulate General in Chicago (708/205-1188), or Denver (303/321-2400).

SAINT KITTS AND NEVIS - Proof of U.S. citizenship, photo ID and onward/return ticket required for stay up to 6 months. AIDS test required for work permit, residency or student visas; U.S. test is accepted. For further information consult Embassy of St. Kitts and Nevis, OECS Building, 3216 New Mexico Ave., N.W., Washington, D.C. 20016 (202/686-2636) or Permanent Mission to the U.N., 414 East 75th St., Fifth Floor, New York, NY 10021 (212/535-1234).

SAINT LUCIA - Passport (or proof of U.S. citizenship and photo ID) and return/onward ticket required for stay up to 6 months. For additional information contact Embassy of Saint Lucia, 3216 New Mexico Ave., Washington, D.C. 20016 (202/ 364-6792) or Permanent Mission to the U.N., 820 Second Ave., Suite 900E, New York, NY 10017 (2121697-9360).

ST. MARTIN (St. Maarten*) - (See West Indies, French or 'Netherlands Antilles.)

ST. PIERRE - Proof of U.S. citizenship and photo ID required for visit up to 3 months. For specific information consult Embassy of France (202/944-6000).

SAINT VINCENT AND THE GRENADINES - Proof of U.S. citizenship, photo ID, and onward/return ticket and/or proof of sufficient funds required for tourist stay up to 6 months. For more information consult the Embassy of Saint Vincent and the Grenadines, 3216 New Mexico Ave., Washington, D.C. 20016 (202/342-6734) or Consulate, 801 Second Ave., 21 st Floor, New York, NY 10017 (212/687-4490).

SAN MARINO - Passport required. Visa not required for tourist stay up to 3 months. For additional information contact the nearest Honorary Consulate of the Republic of San Marino: Washington, D.C. (1899 L St., N.W., Suite 500, Washington, D.C. 20036, 202/223-3517), Detroit (313/5281 1 90) or New York (516/242-2212).

SAO TOME AND PRINCIPE - Passport and visa required. Tourist/business visa for single entry up to 3 months ($25) or multiple entry up to 6 months ($30), requires 2 application forms, 2 photos and yellow fever immunization card, and letter stating purpose of travel. Fees are to be paid by money order only. Company letter is required for a business visa. Enclose prepaid envelope or postage for return of passport by certified or special delivery mail. Apply Permanent Mission of Sao Tome and Principe to the U.N., 122 East 42nd Street, Suite 1604, New York, NY 10 1 68 (212/697-421 1).

SAUDI ARABIA - Passport and visa required. (Tourist visas are not available for travel to Saudi Arabia.) Transit visa valid 24 hours for stay in airport, need onward/return ticket, 1 application form, no fee. Business visa requires $54 fee (money order only), 1 application form, 1 photo, company letter stating purpose of visit, invitation from Foreign Ministry in Saudi Arabia and SASE for return of passport by mail. Meningitis and cholera vaccinations are highly recommended. Medical report, including AIDS test, required for work permits; U.S. test accepted. For details and requirements for family visits, contact The Royal Embassy of Saudi Arabia, 601 New Hampshire Ave., N.W., Washington, D.C. 20037 (202/3423800) or nearest Consulate General: Los Angeles (213/208-6566), New York (212/752-2740)or Houston (713/785-5577).

SCOTLAND - (See United Kingdom.)

SENEGAL - Passport required. Visa not needed for stay up to 90 days. U.S. citizens need onward/return ticket and yellow fever vaccination (if you are arriving from an infected area). For further information contact Embassy of the Republic of Senegal, 2112 Wyoming Ave., N.W., Washington, D.C. 20008 (202/234-0540).

SERBIA AND MONTENEGRO - Passport and visa required. Required for tourist visa is 1 application form. No photograph is needed. For business visas an official letter is required stating the nature of business, name of the institution to be visited and its location, as well as the approximate duration of the visit. Please provide SASE or prepaid airbill for return of documents of applying by mail. For further information check with the Embassy of the Former Federal Republic of Yugoslavia (Serbia & Montenegro), 2410 California St., N.W., Washington, D.C. 20008 (202/462-6566) Attention: U.S. citizens need a Treasury Dept. license in order to engage in any commercial transactions within Serbia & Montenegro. Before planning any travel to Serbia & Montenegro, U.S. citizens should contact the Licensing Division, Office of Foreign Assets Control, Department of the Treasury, 1331 G St., N.W., Washington, D.C. 20220 (202/622-2480).

SEYCHELLES - passport, onward/return ticket and proof of sufficient funds required. Visa issued upon arrival for stay up to 1 month, no charge, extendable up to 1 year. Consult Permanent Mission of Seychelles to the U.N., 820 Second Ave., Suite 900F, New York, NY 10017 (212/687-9766) for further information.

SIERRA LEONE - Passport and visa required. Single-entry visa valid 3 months, requires 1 application form, 1 photo, return/onward ticket, proof of financial support from bank or employer and $20 fee (cash or money order only). Cholera and yellow fever immunizations required and malarial suppressants recommended. Provide SASE or prepaid airbill for return of documentation. For business and additional information consult Embassy of Sierra Leone, 1701 19th St., N.W., Washington, D.C. 20009 (202/939-9261).

SINGAPORE - Passport and onward/return ticket required. Visa not required for tourist/business stay up to 2 weeks, extendable to 3 months maximum. AIDS test required for some work visas. U.S. test is not accepted. For additional information contact Embassy of Singapore, 3501 Int'l Place, N.W., Washington, D.C. 20008 (202/537-31 00).

SLOVAK REPUBLIC - Passport required. Visa not required for stay up to 30 days. , For longer stays and other types of travel contact Embassy of the Slovak Republic, 2201 Wisconsin Ave., N.W., Suite 380, Washington, D.C. 20007 (202/965-5164).

SLOVENIA - Passport required. Visa not required for stay of up to 90 days. Additional information can be obtained from the Embassy of the Republic of Slovenia, 1525 New Hampshire Ave., N.W., Washington, D.C. 20036 (202/667-5363).

SOLOMON ISLANDS - Passport, onward/return ticket and proof of sufficient funds required. Visitors permit issued on arrival for stay up to 2 months in 1 -year period. For further information consult British Embassy (202/986-0205).

SOMALIA - Passport required. For further information contact Consulate of the Somali Democratic Republic in New York (212/688-9410).

SOUTH AFRICA - Passport required. Tourist or business visa not required for stay up to 90 days. Yellow fever immunization needed if arriving from infected area. Malarial suppressants are recommended. For more information con-tact:Embassy of South Africa, Attn.: Consular Office, 3201 New Mexico Ave., N.W., Washington, D.C. 20016 (202/9661650) or nearest Consulate in CA (310/657-9200), IL (312/939-7929), or NY (212/213-4880).

SPAIN - Passport required. Visa not required for tourist or business stay up to 3 months. For additional information check with Embassy of Spain, 2375 Pennsylvania Ave., N.W., Washington, D.C. 20037 (202/425-0100 and 728-2330) or nearest Consulate General in CA (415/922-2995 and 213/ 658-6050), FL (305/446-551 1). IL (312/782-4588), LA (504/ 525-4951), MA (617/536-2506), NY (212/355-4080), PR (809/ 758-6090) or TX (713/783-6200).

SRI LANKA - Passport, onward/return ticket and proof of sufficient funds ($15 per day) required. Tourist visa not required for stay up to 90 days (extendable in Sri Lanka). For business travel visa required and must be obtained in advance. Business visa valid 1 month, requires 1 application form, 2 photos, a company letter, a letter from sponsoring agency in Sri Lanka and employing company in U.S., a copy of an onward/return ticket, and $5 fee. Include $6 postage for return of passport by registered mail. Yellow fever and cholera immunizations needed if arriving from infected area. For further information contact Embassy of Sri Lanka, 2148 Wyoming Ave., N.W., Washington, D.C. 20008 (202/483-4025) or nearest Consulate: CA (805/323-8975 and 504/362-3232), HI (808/373-2040), NJ (201/627-7855) or NY (212/986-7040).

SUDAN - Passport and visa required. Visa must be obtained in advance. Transit visa valid up to 7 days, requires $50 fee (cash or money order), onward/return ticket and visa for next destination, if appropriate. Tourist/business visa for single entry up to 3 months (extendable), requires $50 fee, 1 application form, 1 photo, proof of sufficient funds for stay and SASE for return passport. Business visa requires company letter stating purpose of visit and invitation from Sudanese officials. Malarial suppressants and vaccinations for yellow fever, cholera, and meningitis recommended. Visas not granted to passports showing Israeli visas. Allow 4 weeks for processing. Travelers must declare currency upon arrival and departure. Check additional currency regulations for stays longer than 2 months. Contact Embassy of the Republic of the Sudan, 2210 Mass. Ave., N.W., Washington, D.C. 20008 (202/338-8565 to 8570) or Consulate General, 21 0 East 49th St., New York, NY 10017 (212/573-6035).

SURINAME - Passport and visa required. Multiple Entry visa requires 2 application forms and 2 photos. Business visa requires letter from sponsoring company. At the Johan Adolf Pengel International Airport the equivalent in convertible currency of NF 300.00 = three hundred Dutch guilders shall have to be changed at the airport bank, on the presentation of the completed H/A form, passport and ticket. Children younger than two years are exempted. The above mentioned amount shall be reduced by half for children between the ages of two and twelve. For the application of these regulations, the exchange rate will be SF 6 = six Surinamese guilders to NF 1 = one Dutch guilder. Hotel bills in Suriname shall be paid in convertible currencies. For return of passport by maii, send $5 for registered mail or $9.95f or Express Mail, or enclose SASE. Allow ten working days for processing. For additional requirements contact Embassy of the Republic of Suriname, Suite 108,4301 Conn. Ave., N.W., Washington, D.C. 20008 (202/ 244-7488 and 7490) or the Consulate in Miami (305/5932163).

SWAZILAND - Passport required. Visa not required for stay up to 60 days. Temporary residence permit available in Mbabane for longer stay. Visitors must report to immigration authorities or police station within 48 hours unless lodging in a hotel. Yellow fever and cholera immunizations required if arriving from infected area and anti-malarial treatment recommended. For further information consult Embassy of the Kingdom of Swaziland, 3400 International Dr., N.W., Suite 3M, Washington, D.C. (202/362-6683).

SWEDEN - Valid passport required. Visa not required for stay up to 3 months. Period begins when entering Scandinavian area: Finland, Norway, Denmark, Iceland. For further information consult the Embassy of Sweden, 1501 M St., N.W., Washington, D.C.

20005-1702 (202/467-2600) or nearest Consulate General: Los Angeles (310/575-3383) or New York (212/751-5900).

SWITZERLAND - Passport required. Visa not required for tourist/business stay up to 3 months. For further information contact Embassy of Switzerland, 2900 Cathedral Ave., N.W., Washington, D.C. 20008 (202/745-7900) or nearest Consulate General: CA (310/575-1145 or 415/788-2272), GA (404/ 870-2000), IL (312/915-0061), NY (212/758-2560) or TX (713/650-0000).

SYRIA - Passport and visa required. Obtain visa in advance. Single-entry visa valid 6 months or double-entry for 3 months, $15; multiple-entry visa valid 6 months, $30. Submit 2 application forms, 2 photos (signed) and fee (payment must be money order only). Enclose prepaid envelope (with correct postage) for return of passport by mail. AIDS test required for students and others staying over 1 year; U.S. test sometimes accepted. For group visas and other information contact Embassy of the Syrian Arab Republic, 2215 Wyoming Ave., N.W., Washington, D.C. 20008 (202/232-6313).

TAHITI - (See French Polynesia.)

TAIWAN - Passport required. Visa not required for stay up to 14 days. AIDS test mandatory for anyone staying over 3 months; U.S. test sometimes accepted. Visitors must hold passports valid for at least 6 months from the date of entry into Taiwan. For business travel, longer stays or other information contact Taipei Economic and Cultural Representative Office, 4201 Wisconsin Avenue, N.W., Washington, D.C. 20016-2137 (202/895-1800) or Taipaii Economic and Cultural Office in Atlanta (404/872-0123), Boston (617/737-2050), Chicago (312/616-0100), Guam (671/472-5865), Honolulu (808/5956347), Houston (713/626-7445), Kansas City (816/531-1298, Los Angeles (213/389-1215), Miami (305/443-8917), New York (213/370-6600), San Francisco (415-362-7680), and Seattle (206/441-4586).

TAJIKISTAN - Passport and visa required. At the time of publication, visa issuances are being handled by the Russian Consulate. The visa process must be initiated in Tajikistan by the sponsoring agency or by the travel agent involved; no visa request is initiated at the Russian Consulate. Visas are not issued until an approval cable arrives from the Ministry of Foreign Affairs in Tajikistan to the Russian Consulate.

TANZANIA - Passport and visa required. Obtain visa before departure. Visas for mainland Tanzania are

AMERICANS TRAVELING ABROAD: WHAT YOU SHOULD KNOW BEFORE YOU GO

valid for Zanzibar. Tourist visa (valid 6 months from date of issuance) for 1 entry up to 30 days, may be extended after arrival. Requires 1 application, 1 form and $10.50 fee (no personal checks). Enclose prepaid envelope for return of passport by certified or registered mail. Yellow fever and cholera immunizations recommended (required if arriving from infected area) and malarial suppressants advised. Allow 1 month for processing. For business visa and other information, consult Embassy of the United Republic of Tanzania, 2139 R St., N.W., Washington, D.C. 20008 (202/939-6125) or Tanzanian Permanent Mission to the U.N. 205 East 42nd St., 13th Floor, New York, NY 10017 (212/972-9160).

THAILAND - Passport and onward/return ticket required. Visa not needed for stay up to 15 days. For longer stays obtain a visa in advance. Transit visa, for stay up to 30 days, $10 fee; or tourist visa for stay up to 6O days, $15 fee. For business visa valid up to 90 days, need $20 fee and company letter stating purpose of visit. Submit 1 application form, 2 photos and postage for return of passport by mail. Apply Embassy of Thailand, 1024 Wisconsin Ave., N.W., Washington, D.C. 20007 (202/944-3608) or nearest Consulate General: CA (213/937-1894), IL (312/236-2447) or NY (212/754-1770).

TOGO - Passport required. Visa not required for stay up to 3 months. Yellow fever and cholera vaccinations are required. Check further information, with Embassy of the Republic of Togo, 2208 Mass. Ave., N.W., Washington, D.C. 20008 (202/ 234-4212/3).

TONGA - Passport and onward/return ticket required. Visa not required for stay up to 30 days. For additional information consult the Consulate General of Tonga, 360 Post St., Suite 604, San Francisco, CA 94108 (415/781-0365).

TRINIDAD AND TOBAGO - Passport required. Visa not required for tourist/business stay up to 3 months. Business visa requires passport and company letter. For further information consult Embassy of Trinidad and Tobago, 1708 Mass. Ave., N.W., Washington, D.C. 20036 (202/467-6490) or nearest Consulate in New York (212/682-7272).

TUNISIA - Passport and onward/return ticket required. Visas not required for tourist/business stay up to 4 months. For further information consult Embassy of Tunisia, 1515 Mass. Ave., N.W., Washington, D.C. 20005 (202/862-1850) or nearest Consulate: San Francisco (415/922-9222) or New York (212/272-6962).

TURKEY - Passport required and visa required U.S. citizens with conventional passports may obtain visas at Turkish border crossing points for tourist/business visits up to three months or through overseas Turkish consular offices (1 application form required). Visa must be obtained in advance for visits lasting longer than the three month period, for study/ research purposes, or for employment purposes. A visa fee of $20 is charged (cash or money order only). For further information contact Embassy of the Republic of Turkey, 1714 Massachusetts Ave., N.W., Washington, D.C. 20036 (202-1 659-0742) or nearest Consulate: CA (213/937-0118), IL (312/ 263-0644), NY (212/949-0160) or TX (713/622-5849).

TURKMENISTAN - Passport and visa required. Visa requires 1 application, 1 photo, and letter of invitation. Ordinary visas are available in a variety of time periods: up to 1 0 days (fee $10), up to 20 days ($20), up to 1 month ($30), from 1 to 3 months ($30 per month), and from 3 to 12 months ($20 per month). Multiple entry visas are available for 1 month ($50), for 1 to 3 months ($50 per month), and for 3 to 12 months ($30 per month). Transit visas are $10. Extensions are also available. Fees are payable by check or money order. Please provide SASE or prepaid airbill for document return. For further information consult the Embassy of Turkmenistan, 1511 K Street, N.W., Suite 412, Washington, D.C. 20005 (202/737-4800).

TURKS AND CAICOS - (See West Indies, British.)

TUVALU - Passport and onward/return ticket and proof of sufficient funds required. Visitors permit issued on arrival. For further information consult British Embassy (202/986-0205).

UGANDA-Passport required. Immunization certificates for yellow fever and cholera are required (typhoid and malarial suppressants recommended). For other information contact Embassy of the Republic of Uganda, 5909 16th St., N.W., Washington, D.C. 20011 (202/726-7100-02) or Permanent Mission to the U.N. (212/949-0110).

UKRAINE - Passport and visa required. Visas may be obtained at the Ukraine Embassy in the U.S. (visas limited to 3 days may be obtained at airports in Ukraine, or at any border crossing point). Visa requires 1 form, 1 photo and $30-100 fee, depending upon processing time (cash, company check, or money order only). An invitation/confirmation letter from receiving party in Ukraine is required for business, tourist, or private trips. Multiple entry visas are being issued to business visitors who met specific requirements. For additional information contact

39

Embassy of Ukraine, 3350 M St., N.W., Washington, D.C. 20007 (202/333-7507,08,09) or the nearest Consulate: IL (312/642-4388) or NY (212/371-5690).

UNITED ARAB EMIRATES - Passport and visa required. Tourist visa must be obtained by a hotel, relative, or sponsor in UAE, and sponsor must meet visitor at airport. Business visas issued only by Embassy, and require company letter and sponsor in UAE to send a fax or telex to Embassy confirming trip and accepting financial responsibility. Single entry visa valid within 2 months from the date of issuance for tay up to 30 days, $30 fee. Multiple-entry visa (for business only), valid 6 months from date of issue for maximum stay of 30 days per entry, $225 fee, paid by cash, money order or certified check. Transit visas may be issued at the airport, and should be confirmed before departure, valid for stay of 15 days provided you are met at the airport by sponsor or relative. Submit 2 application forms, 2 photo and prepaid envelope for return of passport by certified/registered mail (typed not hand written). For further information contact Embassy of the United Arab Emirates, 3000 K St., N.W., Washington, D.C. 20007 (202/338-6500).

UNITED KINGDOM (England, Northern Ireland, Scotland, and Wales) - Passport required. Visa not required for stay up to 6 months. For additional information consult the Consular Section of the British Embassy, 1 9 Observatory Circle, N.W., Washington, D.C. 20008 (202/986-0205) or nearest Consulate General: CA (310/477-3322), GA (404/524-5856), IL (312/346-1810), MA (617/248-9555), NY (212/745-0200), OH (216/621-7674) or TX (713/659-6270).

URUGUAY - Passport required. Visa not required for stay up to 3 months. For additional information consult Embassy of Uruguay, 1918 F St., N.W., Washington, D.C. 20008 (202/ 331-1313-6) or nearest Consulate: CA (213/394-5777), FL (305/358-9350), IL (31 2/236-3366), LA (504/525-8354) or NY (212/753-8191/2).

UZBEKISTAN - Passport and visa required. Apply Uzbekistan Consulate, 866 United Nations Plaza, Suite 326, New York, NY 10017 (212/486-7570).

VANUATU - Passport and onward/return ticket required. Visa not required for stay up to 30 days. For further information consult the British Embassy (202/986-0205).

VATICAN - (See Holy See.)

VENEZUELA - Passport and tourist card required. Tourist card can be obtained from airlines serving Venezuela, no charge, valid 90 days, cannot be extended. Multiple-entry visa valid up to 1 year, extendable, available from any Venezuelan Consulate, requires $30 fee (money order or company check), 1 application form, 1 photo, onward/return ticket, proof of sufficient funds and certification of employment. For business visa, need letter from company stating purpose of trip, responsibility for traveler, name and address of companies to be visited in Venezuela and $60 fee. All travelers must pay departure tax ($12) at airport. Business travelers must present a Declaration of Income Tax in the Ministerio de Hacienda (Treasury Department). For additional information contact the Consular Section of the Embassy of Venezuela, 1099 30th Street, N.W., Washington, DC 20007 (202/342-2214) or the nearest Consulate: CA (415/512-8340), FL (305/ 577-3834), IL (312/236-9655), LA (504/522-3284), MA (617/ 266-9355), NY (212-/826-1660), PR (809/766-4250/1) or TX (713/961-5141).

VIETNAM - Passport and visa required. Tourist visa, valid 3 months, requires 2 application forms, 3 photos, invitation and $25 fee for single entry visa. Allow at least 2 to 3 weeks for processing for first time visitors. Tourist visas can be issued only after the Liaison Office receives visa approvals directly from Vietnam or through a travel agency. Business visas will be processed through the Liaison Office. Requires purpose of trip, names of agencies/companies, and names of business contacts including standard visa application. Provide SASE or prepaid airbill for return of documents. For more information contact the Chancery of the Vietnam Liaison Office at 1233 20th St., N.W., Suite 501, Washington, D.C. 20036 (202/ 861-0737) or Vietnamese Permanent Mission to the U.N., 20 Waterside Plaza, New York, NY 1001 0 (212/679-3779).

VIRGIN ISLANDS, British - Islands include Anegarda, Jost van Dyke, Tortola and Virgin Gorda. Proof of U.S. citizenship, photo ID, onward/return ticket and sufficient funds required for tourist stay up to 6 months. Consult British Embassy for further information (202/986-0205).

WALES - (See United Kingdom.)

WEST INDIES, British - Islands include Anguilla, Montserrat, Cayman Islands, Turks and Caicos. Proof of U.S. citizenship, photo ID, onward/return ticket and sufficient funds required for tourist stay up to 6 months. Consult British Embassy for further information (202/986-0205).

WEST INDIES, French - Islands include Guadeloupe, Isles des Saintes, La Desirade, Marie Galante, Saint Barthelemy, St. Martin and Martinique. Proof of U.S.

citizenship and photo ID required for visit up to 3 weeks. (For stays longer than 3 weeks a passport is required.) No visa required for stay up to 3 months. For further information consult Embassy of France (202/944-6200/6215).

WESTERN SAMOA - Passport and onward/return ticket required. Visa not required for stay up to 3O days. For longer stays contact the Western Samoa Mission to the U.N., 820 2nd Avenue, Suite 800, New York, NY (212/599-6196) or the Honorary Consul HI (808/677-7197).

YEMEN, REPUBLIC OF- Passport and visa required. Visa valid 30 days from date of issuance for single entry, requires 1 application form and 2 photos. For tourist visa need proof of onward/return transportation and employment and $30 fee. Visitors visa requires letter of invitation and $30 fee. Business visa requires $30, company letter stating purpose of trip. Payment by money order only and include postage for return of passport by registered mail. Entry not granted to passports showing Israeli visas. Yellow fever and cholera vaccinations and malarial suppressants recommended. For more information contact the Embassy of the Republic of Yemen , Suite 705,2600 Virginia Ave., N.W., Washington, D.C. 20037 (202/965-4760) or Yemen Mission to the U.N., 866 United Nations Plaza, Rm. 435, New York, NY 10017 (212/355-1730).

ZAIRE - Passport and visa required. Visa must be obtained before arrival. Transit visa for stay up to 8 days, single-entry $45; double-entry $70. Tourist/business visa, valid 1 month $75-120, 2 months $140-180, 3 months $190-220 and 6 months $264-360, requires 3 photos, 3 applications, yellow fever immunization and onward/return ticket. Business visa also requires company letter accepting financial responsibility for traveler. No personal checks, send money order and enclose SASE for return of passport by mail. Apply Embassy of the Republic of Zaire, 1800 New Hampshire Ave., N.W., Washington, D.C. 20009 (202/234-7690/1) or Permanent Mission to the U.N., 747 Third Ave., New York, NY 10017 (212/754-1966).

ZAMBIA - Passport and visa required. Obtain visa in advance. Multiple entry visa valid up to 12 months, requires $20 fee (no personal checks), 2 application forms and 2 photos. Business visa also requires company letter. Yellow fever and cholera immunizations recommended. Apply Embassy of the Republic of Zambia, 2419 Mass. Ave., N.W., Washington, D.C. 20008 (202/265-9717 to 19).

ZANZIBAR - (See Tanzania.)

ZIMBABWE - Passport, onward/return ticket and proof of sufficient funds required. Visitors must declare currency upon arrival. For regulations check with Embassy of Zimbabwe, 1608 New Hampshire Ave., N.W., Washington, D.C. 20009 (202/332-7100).

NOTES.

- SASE is self-addressed, stamped envelope.

- If applying in person, remember to call about office hours. Many consulates are only open in the morning.

-This booklet is updated yearly and is available from the Consumer Information Center, Pueblo, CO 81009 for 50 cents.

OTHER INFORMATION,

The State Department issues *Consular Information Sheets* for every country in the world. They include such information as the location of the U.S. embassy or consulate in the subject country, health conditions, political disturbances, unusual currency and entry regulations, crime and security information, and drug penalties.

The State Department also issues *Travel Warnings*. *Travel* Warnings are issued when the State Department decides, based on all relevant information, to recommend that Americans avoid travel to a certain country. Countries where avoidance of travel is recommended will have *Travel Warnings* as well as *Consular Information Sheets.*

Consular Information Sheets and Travel Warnings may be heard anytime by dialing (202) 647-5225 from a touchtone phone. They are also available at any of the 13 regional U.S. passport agencies, at U.S. embassies and consulates abroad, and through the airline computer reservation systems, or, by writing and sending a self-addressed, stamped business size envelope to the Overseas Citizens Services, Bureau of Consular Affairs, Room 481 1, U.S. Department of State, Washington, D.C. 20520-4818.

If you have a personal computer, modem and communications software, you can access them, and other consular handouts and publications through the Consular Affairs Bulletin Board (CABB). This service is free of charge.

To access CABB, dial the modem number: (202) 647-

9225; set modem speed (will accommodate 300,1200, 2400, 9600 or 14400 bps); and terminal communications program to
N-8-1 (parity, 8 bits, 1 stop bit).

Or you can have Information Sheets, Warnings and publications faxed to you via the Consular Affairs automated fax system by dialing from your fax phone (202) 647-3000.

PUBLICATIONS:

Available for $1.25 from the Superintendent of Documents, U.S. Government Printing Office, Washington, DC 20402 (2021783-3238):

Your Trip Abroad
- offers tips on obtaining passport, considerations in preparing for your trip and traveling, and other sources of information.

Also available for $1 each from the U.S. Government Printing Office:

Safe Trip Abroad
- contains helpful precautions one can take to minimize the chance of becoming a victim of terrorism or crime and other safety tips.

Tips for Americans Residing Abroad
- offers information for U.S. citizens living abroad on dual citizenship, tax regulations, voting, and other overseas consular services.

Travel Tips for Older Americans
- contains special health, safety and travel information for older Americans. Available for $1 each from the U.S. Government Printing Office are the following travel tips which contain information on currency regulations, customs, and dual nationality for specific areas of the world:

Tips for Travelers to the Caribbean
Tips for Travelers to Central & South America
Tips for Travelers to Mexico
Tips for Travelers to the People's Republic of China
Tips for Travelers to Russia
Tips for Travelers to South Asia
Tips for Travelers to Sub-Saharan Africa

Also available for $1.25:

Tips for Travelers to the Middle *East and North* Africa

Passports-Applying for them the EASY *WAY,* gives detailed information on how and where to apply for

your U.S. passport. It is available for 50 cents from the Consumer Information Center, Pueblo, CO 81 009.

Background Notes are brief, factual pamphlets describing the countries of the world. They contain the most current information on each country's people, culture, geography, history, government, economy and political conditions. Single copies are available from the U.S. Government Printing Office for about $1 each. Yearly subscription for updated copies is available. Confirm price by calling (202) 783-3238.

Key Officers of Foreign Service Posts provides names of key officers and addresses for all U.S. embassies, consulates, and missions abroad. This publication is updated biannually and is available from the U.S. Government Printing Office. Single copy purchase price is $3.75; subscription is $5/year.

Health Information for International Travel contains detailed information on international health requirements and is available from the U.S. Government Printing Office for $7.

Chapter 4

A Safe Trip Abroad

[The information in this chapter is reprinted verbatim from a bulletin issued
by the U.S. State Department, Bureau of Consular Affairs. It is intended to serve as advice
to Americans traveling abroad.]

- - - -

Foreword

Millions of U.S. citizens travel abroad each year and use their U.S. passport. When you travel abroad, the odds are in your favor that you will have a safe and incident-free trip. Even if you do come into difficulty abroad, the odds are still in your favor that you will not be a victim of crime or violence.

But crime and violence, as well as unexpected difficulties, do befall U.S. citizens in all parts of the world. No one is better able to tell you this than U.S. consular officers who work in the more than 250 U.S. embassies and consulates around the world. Every day of the year U.S. embassies and consulates receive calls from American citizens in distress.

Fortunately, most problems can be solved over the telephone or by a visit of the U.S. citizens to the Consular Section of the nearest U.S. embassy or consulate. But there are less fortunate occasions when U.S. consular officers are called on to meet U.S. citizens at foreign police stations, hospitals, prisons, and even at morgues. In these cases, the assistance that consular officers can offer is specific, but **limited.** For a description of consular assistance abroad, see pages 8-9.

In the hope of helping you avoid unhappy meetings when you go abroad, we have prepared the following travel tips. **Please have a safe trip abroad.**

Before You Go

What to Bring

Safety begins when you pack. To avoid being a target, dress conservatively. A flashy wardrobe or one that is too casual can mark you as a tourist. As much as possible, avoid the appearance of affluence.

Always try to travel light. If you do, you can move more quickly and will be more likely to have a free hand. You will also be less tired and less likely to set your luggage down, leaving it unattended.

Carry the minimum amount of valuables necessary for your trip and plan a place or places to conceal them. Your passport, cash and credit cards are safest when locked in a hotel safe. When you have to carry them on your person, you may wish to conceal them in several places rather than putting them in one wallet or pouch. Avoid hand bags, fanny packs and outside pockets which are easy targets for thieves. Inside pockets and a sturdy shoulder bag with the strap worn across your chest are somewhat safer. The safest place to carry valuables is probably a pouch or money belt that you wear under your clothing.

If you wear glasses, pack an extra pair. Carry them and any medicines you need in your carry-on luggage.

To avoid problems when passing through customs, keep medicines in their original, labeled containers. Bring a copy of your prescriptions and the generic names for the drugs. If a medication is unusual or contains narcotics, carry a letter from your doctor attesting to your need to take the drug. If you have any doubt about the legality of carrying a certain drug into a country, consult the embassy or consulate of that country first.

Bring travelers checks and one or two major credit cards instead of cash.

Pack an extra set of passport photos along with a photocopy of your passport information page to make replacement of your passport easier in case it is lost or stolen.

Put your name, address and telephone numbers inside and outside of each piece of luggage. Use covered luggage tags to avoid casual observation of your identity or nationality. Last of all, lock your luggage.

What to Leave Behind

Don't bring anything you would hate to lose.
Leave at home:

-            expensive or expensive-looking jewelry

- irreplaceable family objects,
- all unnecessary credit cards.

Leave a copy of your itinerary with family or friends at home in case they need to contact you in an emergency.

A Few Things, to Bring and Leave Behind

Make photocopies of your passport identification page, airline tickets, driver's license, and the credit cards that you bring with you. Make two copies. Leave one with family or friends at home; pack the other in a place separate from where you carry your valuables.

Leave a copy of the serial numbers of your travelers checks at home. Carry your copy with you in a separate place and, as you cash the checks, cross them off the list.

What to Learn About Before You Go

Security. The Department of State's Consular Information Sheets are available for every country of the world. They describe unusual entry or currency regulations, unusual health conditions, the crime and security situation, political disturbances, areas of instability, and drug penalties. They also provide addresses and emergency telephone numbers for US. embassies and consulates. In general, the sheets do not give advice. Instead, they describe conditions so travelers can make informed decisions about their trips.

In some dangerous situations, however, the Department of State recommends that Americans defer travel to a country. In such a case, a Travel Warning is issued for the country in addition to its Consular information Sheet.

Consular Information Sheets and Travel Warnings are available at the 13 regional passport agencies; at U.S. embassies and consulates abroad; or by sending a self-addressed, stamped envelope to: Overseas Citizens Services, Room 4811, Department of State, Washington, DC 20520-4818. They are also available through airline computer reservation systems when you or your travel agent make your international air reservations.

In addition, you can access Consular Information Sheets and Travel Warnings **24-hours a day** from three different electronic systems. To listen to them, call (202) 647-5225 from a touchtone phone. To receive them by fax, dial (202) 647-3000 from a fax machine and follow the prompts that you will hear on the machine's telephone receiver. To view or download the documents through a computer and modem, dial the Consular Affairs Bulletin Board (CABB) on (202) 647-9225, setting your software to N-8-1. There is no charge to use these systems other than normal long distance charges.

Local Laws and Customs. When you leave the United States, you are subject to the laws of the country where you are. Therefore, before you go, leave as much as you can about the local laws and customs of the places you plan to visit. Good resources are your library, your travel agent, and the embassies, consulates or tourist bureaus of the countries you will visit. In addition, keep track of what is being reported in the media about recent developments in those countries.

Things to Arrange Before You Go

Your Itinerary. As much as possible, plan to stay in larger hotels that have more elaborate security. The safest floor to book a room may be from the second to seventh floors - above ground level to deter easy entrance from outside, but low enough for fire equipment to reach-Because take-off and landing are the most dangerous times of a fight, book non-stop flights when possible. When there is a choice of airport or airline, ask your travel agent about comparative safety records. There are differences.

Legal Document. Have your affairs at home in order. If you leave an up-to-date win, insurance documents, and a power of attorney with your family or a friend, you can feel safe about traveling and will be prepared for any emergency that may occur while you are away. If you have minor children, consider making guardianship arrangements for them.

Credit. Make a note of the credit limit on each credit card that you bring. Make certain not to charge over that amount on your trip. In some countries, Americans have been arrested for innocently exceeding their credit limit. Ask your credit card company how to report the loss of your card from abroad. 800 numbers do not work from abroad, but your company will have a number that you can call.

Insurance. Find out if your personal property insurance covers you for loss or theft abroad. Even more important, check if your health insurance will cover you abroad. Social Security Medicare does not provide payment for medical care outside the U.S. Even if your health insurance will reimburse you for medical care that you pay for abroad, normal health insurance does not pay for medical evacuation from a remote area or from a country where medical facilities are inadequate. Consider purchasing one of the short-term health and emergency assistance policies designed for travelers that includes medical evacuation in the event of an accident or serious illness.

Precautions to Take While Traveling

Safety on the Street

Use the same common sense traveling overseas that you would at home. Be especially cautious in, or avoid areas where you are likely to be victimized. These include crowded subways, train stations, elevators, tourist sites, market places, festivals and marginal areas of cities.

Don't use short cuts, narrow alleys or poorly-lit streets. Try not to travel alone at night.

Avoid public demonstrations and other civil disturbances.

Keep a low profile and avoid loud conversations or arguments. Do not discuss travel plans or other personal matters with strangers.

To avoid scam artists, beware of strangers who approach you, offering bargains or to be your guide.

Beware of pickpockets. They often have an accomplice who will:

- jostle you,
- ask you for directions or the time,
- point to something spilled on your clothing,
- or distract you by creating a disturbance.

A child or even a woman carrying a baby can be a pickpocket. Beware- of groups of vagrant children.

Wear the shoulder strap of your bag across your chest and walk with the bag away from the curb to avoid drive-by purse snatcher's.

Try to seem purposeful when you move about.

Even if you are lost, act as if you know where you are going. When possible, ask directions only from individuals in authority.

Know how to use a pay telephone and have the proper change or token on hand.

Learn a few phrases in the local language so you can signal your need for help, the police, or a doctor.

Make note of emergency telephone numbers you may need: police, fire, your hotel, and the nearest US. embassy or consulate.

If confronted by superior force, don't fight attackers - give up valuables.

Safety in Your Hotel

Keep your hotel door locked at all times. Meet visitors in the lobby.

Do not leave money and other valuables in your hotel room while you are out. Use the hotel safe.

Let someone know when you expect to return, especially if out late at night.

If you are alone, do not get on an elevator if there is a suspicious-looking person inside.

Read the **fire safety** instructions in your hotel room. Know how to report a fire. Be sure you know where the nearest fire exit and an alternate are. Count the doors between your room and the nearest exit - this could be a life-saver if you have to crawl through a smoke-filled corridor.

Safety on Public Transport

In countries where there is a pattern of tourists being targeted by animals on public transport, this information is mentioned in Consular Information Sheets (see chapter 29).

Taxis. Only take taxis clearly identified with official markings. Beware of irregular cabs.

Trains. Well organized, systematic robbery of passengers on trains along popular tourists routes is a serious problem. It is more common at right and especially on overnight trains.

If you see your way blocked by someone and another person is pressing you from behind, move away. This can happen in the corridor of the train or on the platform or station.

Do not accept food or drink from strangers. Criminals have been known to drug passengers by offering them food or drink. Criminals may also spray sleeping gas in train compartments.

Where possible, lock your compartment. If it cannot be locked securely, take turns with your traveling companions sleeping in shifts. If that is not possible, stay awake. If you must sleep unprotected, tie down your luggage, strap your valuables to you and sleep on top of them as much as possible.

Do not be afraid to alert authorities if you feel threatened in any way. Extra police are often assigned to ride trains on routes where crime is a serious problem.

Buses. The same type of criminal activity found on trains can be found on public buses on popular tourist routes. For example, tourists have been drugged and robbed while sleeping on buses or in bus stations. In some countries whole bus loads of passengers have been held up and robbed by gangs of bandits.

Safety When You Drive

When you rent a car, don't go for the exotic; choose a " commonly available locally. Where possible, ask that markings that identify it as a rental car be removed. Make certain it is in good repair. If available, choose a car with universal door locks and power windows, features that give the driver better control of access to the car,

An air conditioner, when available, is also a safety feature, allowing you to drive with windows closed. Thieves can and do snatch purses through open windows of moving cars.

Keep car doors locked at all times. Wear seat belts.

As much as possible, avoid driving at night.

Don't leave valuables in the car. If you must carry things with you, keep them out of sight in the trunk.

Don't park your car on the street overnight. If the hotel or municipality does not have a parking garage or other secure area, select a well lit area.

Never pick up hitchhikers.

Don't get out of the car if there are suspicious individuals nearby. Drive away.

Patterns of Crime Against Motorists

In many places frequented by tourists, including areas of southern Europe, victimization of motorists has been refined to an art. Where it is a problem, U.S. embassies are aware of it and consular officers try to work with local authorities to warn the public about the dangers. In some locations, these efforts at public awareness have paid off, reducing the frequency of incidents. Ask your rental car agency for advice on avoiding robbery. Where it is a problem, they are well aware of it and should tell you how best to protect yourself.

Carjackers and thieves operate at gas stations, parking lots, in city traffic, and along the highway. Be suspicious of anyone who hails you or tries to get your attention when you are in or near your car.

Criminals use ingenious ploys. They may masquerade

as good Samaritans, offering help for tires that they claim are flat or that they have made flat. Or they may flag down a motorist, ask for assistance, and then steal the rescuer's luggage or car. Usually they work in groups, one person carrying on the pretense while the others rob you.

Other criminals get your attention with abuse, either trying to drive you off the road, or causing an "accident' by rear-ending you or creating a "fender bender."

In some urban areas, thieves don't waste time on ploys, they simply smash car windows at traffic lights, grab your valuables or your car and get away. In cities around the world, "defensive driving" has come to mean more than avoiding auto accidents; it means keeping an eye out for potentially criminal pedestrians, cyclists, and scooter riders.

How to Handle Money Safely

To avoid carrying large amounts of cash, change your travelers checks only as you need currency. Counter sign travelers checks only in front of the person who will cash them.

Do not flash large amounts of money when paying a bill. Make sure your credit card is returned to you after each transaction.

Deal only with authorized agents when you exchange money, buy airline tickets, or purchase souvenirs. Do not change money on the black market.

If your possessions are lost or stolen, report the loss immediately to the local police. Keep a copy of the police report for insurance claims and as an explanation of your plight.

After reporting lost items to the police, report the loss of:

- travelers checks to the nearest agent of the issuing company.
- credit cards to the issuing company (see page 44).
- airline tickets to the airline or travel agent.
- passport to the nearest U.S. embassy or consulate.

How to Avoid Legal Difficulties

When you are in a foreign country, you are subject to its laws and are under its protection - not the protection of the U.S. Constitution.

You can be arrested overseas for actions that may be

46

either legal or considered minor infractions in the United States. Be aware of what is considered criminal in the country where you are. Consular Information Sheets (see page 285-289) include information on unusual patterns of arrests in various countries.

Some of the offenses for which U.S. citizens have been arrested abroad are:

Drug Violations. More than 1/3 of U.S. citizens incarcerated abroad are held on drug charges. Some countries do not distinguish between possession and trafficking; many have mandatory sentences - even for a small amount of marijuana or cocaine. Although we know of no U.S. citizens who have been arrested abroad for prescription drugs purchased **in the United States for personal use and carried in original labeled containers,** a number of Americans have been arrested for possessing prescription drugs, particularly tranquilizers and amphetamines, that they purchased legally in certain Asian countries and took to some countries in the Middle East where they are illegal. Other U.S. citizens have been arrested for purchasing prescription drugs abroad in quantities that local authorities suspected were for commercial use. If in doubt about foreign drug laws, ask local authorities or the nearest U.S. embassy or consulate.

Possession of Firearms. The places where U.S. citizens most often come into difficulties for illegal possession of firearms are nearby - Mexico, Canada and the Caribbean. Sentences for possession of firearms in Mexico can be up to 30 years.

In general, firearms, even those legally registered in the U.S., cannot be brought into a country unless a permit is first obtained from the embassy or a consulate of that country. (Note: If you take firearms or ammunition to another country, you cannot bring them back into the U.S. unless you register them with U.S. Customs before you leave the U.S.)

Photography. In many countries you can be harassed or detained for photographing such things as police and military installations, government buildings, border areas, and transportation facilities. If in doubt, ask permission before taking photographs.

Purchasing Antiques. Americans have been arrested for purchasing souvenirs that were, or looked like, antiques and which local customs authorities believed were national treasures. Some of the countries where this has happened were Turkey, Egypt, and Mexico. In countries where antiques are important, document your purchases as reproductions if that is the case, or if they are authentic, secure the necessary export permit

(usually from the national museum).

Protection Against Terrorism

Terrorist acts occur at random and unpredictably, making it impossible to protect oneself absolutely. The first and best protection is to avoid travel to unsafe areas where there has been a persistent record of terrorist attacks or kidnapping. The vast majority of foreign states have good records of maintaining public order and protecting residents and visitors within their borders from terrorism.

Most terrorist attacks are the result of long and careful planning. Just as a car-thief will first be attracted to an unlocked car with the key in the ignition, terrorists are looking for defenseless, easily accessible targets who follow predictable patterns. The chances that a tourist, traveling with an unpublished program or itinerary, would be the victim of terrorism are slight - no more than the random possibility of being in the wrong place at the wrong time. In addition, many terrorist groups, seeking publicity for political causes within their own country or region, are not looking for American targets.

Nevertheless, the pointers below may help you avoid becoming a "target of opportunity." They should be considered as adjuncts to the tips listed in the previous sections on how to protect yourself against the far greater likelihood of being a victim of ordinary crime. These precautions may provide some degree of protection, and can serve as practical and psychological deterrents to would-be terrorists.

-       Schedule direct flights if possible and avoid stops in high-risk airports or areas. Consider other options for travel, such as trains.

-       Be aware of what you discuss with strangers, or what may be overheard by others.

-       Try to minimize the time spent in the public area of an airport, which is a less protected area. Move quickly from the check-in counter to the secured areas. on **arrival,** leave the airport as soon as possible.

-       As much as possible, avoid luggage tags, dress, and behavior which may identify you as an American.

-       Keep an eye out for suspicious abandoned packages or briefcases. Report them to airport security or other authorities and leave the area promptly.

- Avoid obvious terrorist targets such as places where Americans and Westerners are known to congregate.

Travel to High-Risk Areas

If you must travel in an area where there has been a history of terrorist attacks or kidnappings make it a habit to:

- Discuss with your family what they would do in case of an emergency, in addition to making sure your affairs are in order before leaving home.

- Register with the U.S. embassy or consulate upon arrival.

- Remain friendly, but be cautious about discussing personal matters, your itinerary or program.

- Leave no personal or business papers in your hotel room.

- Watch for people following you or "loiterers" observing your comings and goings.

- Keep a mental note of safe havens, such as police stations, hotels, hospitals.

- Let someone else know what your travel plans are. Keep them informed if you change your plans.

- Avoid predictable times and routes of travel, and report any suspicious activity to local police, and the neatest U.S. embassy or consulate.

- Select your own taxi cabs at random - don't take a cab that is not clearly identified as a taxi. Compare the face of the driver with the one posted on his or her license.

- If possible, travel with others.

- Be sure of the identity of visitors before opening the door of your hotel room. Don't meet strangers at unknown or remote locations.

- Refuse unexpected packages.

- Formulate a plan of action for what you will do if a bomb explodes or there is gunfire nearby.

- Check for loose wires or other suspicious activity around your car.

- Be sure your vehicle is in good operating condition in case you need to resort to high-speed or evasive driving.

- Drive with car windows closed in crowded streets; bombs can be thrown through open windows.

- If you are ever in a situation where somebody starts shooting, drop to the floor or get down as low as possible. Don't move until you are sure the danger has passed. Do not attempt to help rescuers and do not pick up a weapon. If possible, shield yourself behind or under a solid object. If you must move, crawl on your stomach.

Hijacking/Hostage Situations

While every hostage situation is different and the chance of becoming a hostage is remote, some considerations are important.

The US. government's policy not to negotiate with terrorists is **firm -** to do so would only increase the risk of further hostage-taking. When Americans are abducted overseas, we look to the host government to exercise its responsibility under international law to protect all persons within its territories and to bring about the safe release of hostages. We work closely with these governments from the outset of a hostage-taking incident to ensure that our citizens and other innocent victim are released as quickly and safely as possible.

Normally, the most dangerous phases of a hijacking or hostage situation are the beginning and, if there is a rescue attempt, the end. At the outset, the terrorists typically are tense, high-strung and may behave irrationally. It is extremely important that you remain calm and alert and manage your own behavior.

- Avoid resistance, sudden or threatening movements. Do not struggle or try to escape unless you are certain of being successful.

- Make a concerted effort to relax. Breathe deeply and prepare yourself mentally, physically and emotionally for the possibility of a long ordeal.

- Try to remain inconspicuous, avoid direct eye contact and the appearance of observing your captors' actions.

- Avoid alcoholic beverages. Consume little food and drink.

- Consciously put yourself in a mode of passive cooperation. Talk normally. Do not complain, avoid belligerency, and comply with all orders and instructions.

- If questioned, keep your answers short. Don't volunteer information or make unnecessary overtures.

- Don't try to be a hero, endangering yourself and others.

- Maintain your sense of personal dignity, a gradually increase your requests for personal comforts. Make these requests in a reasonable low-key manner.

- If you are involved in a lengthier, drawn-out situation, try to establish a rapport with your captors, avoiding political discussions or other confrontation

- Establish a daily program of mental and physical activity. Don't be afraid to ask for anything you need or want - medicines, books, pencils, paper.

- Eat what they give you, even if it does not look or taste appetizing. A loss of appetite and weight is normal.

- Think positively; avoid a sense of despair. Rely on your inner resources. Remember that you are valuable commodity to your captors. It is important to them

Assistance Abroad

If you plan to stay more than two weeks in one place, if you are in an area experiencing civil unrest or a natural disaster, or if you are planning travel to a remote area, it is advisable to register at the Consular Section of the nearest U.S. embassy or consulate. The will make it easier if someone at home needs to locate you urgently or in the unlikely event that you need to be evacuated in an emergency. It will also facilitate the issuance of new passport should yours be lost or stolen.

Another reason to contact the Consular Section is to obtain updated information on the security situation in a country.

If you are ill or injured, contact the nearest U.S. embassy or consulate for a list of local physicians and medical facilities. If the illness is serious, consular officers can help you find medical assistance from this list and, at your request, will inform your family or friends. If necessary, a consul can assist in the transfer of funds from the United States. Payment of hospital and other medical expenses is your responsibility.

If you become destitute overseas, consular officers can help you get in touch with your family, friends, bank, or employer and inform them how to wire funds to you.

Should you find yourself in legal difficulty, contact a consular officer immediately. Consular officers cannot serve as attorneys, give legal advice, or get you out of jail. What they can do is provide a list of local attorneys who speak English and who may have had experience in representing U.S. citizens. If you are arrested, consular officials will visit you, advise you of your rights under local laws, and ensure that you are held under humane conditions and are treated fairly under local law. A consular officer will also contact your family or friends if you desire. When necessary, consuls can transfer money from home for you and will try to get relief for you, including food and clothing in countries where this is a problem. **If you are detained remember that under international agreements and practice, you have the right to talk to the U.S. consul.** If you are denied this right, be persistent; try to have someone get in touch for you.

[Thank you for taking the time to become an informed traveler. We wish you a safe and wonderful journey.]

49

Chapter 5

Know Before You Go: U.S. State Department Hints for Americans Traveling Abroad

[The information in this chapter is an excerpt from a bulletin issued by the U.S. State Department, Bureau of Consular Affairs. It is intended to serve as advice to Americans traveling abroad.]

- - - -

Soon you'll be experiencing the joys of international travel--meeting new people, exploring foreign lands, and discovering different cultures.

And whether you're a seasoned traveler or making your first trip abroad, you want your foreign experience to be as relaxing and enjoyable as possible.

That's why you should take the time to learn about the country you'll be visiting before you go, and use this brochure to help plan and guide you through your journey.

Inside you'll find up-to-date information on passports, foreign laws and customs, personal safety, and helpful travel tips.

Remember, the more you know before you go, the less likely you are to encounter difficulties while you're away.

I GETTING READY

(a)   PASSPORTS AND VISA

Imagine the freedom a passport can give you--taking off to an exotic country on a moment's notice. Every American citizen who anticipates traveling abroad should have a valid U.S. passport. It's easy to get a passport or renew one. It is the best documentation you can have while traveling overseas, and it is usually required to depart or enter the United States and most foreign countries. For detailed information on Passports **See Chapter 2.**

TIP:

If you plan to travel during the peak vacation season (March-June), you should apply as soon as possible.

Allow several weeks for delivery to avoid unnecessary delays.

WILL I NEED A VISA?

Many countries require a visa--an official authorization stamped within the passport that permits travel within a country for a specified purpose and a limited time.

To find out if you need a visa:

*   Contact the country's embassy or consulate here in the United States for the most up-to-date information on visa requirements

*   Ask your travel agent

For written information on visa requirements, write to:

> Foreign Entry Requirements[1]
> Consumer Information Center
> Pueblo, CO 81009

> Be sure to enclose 50 cents with your request for Foreign Entry Requirements.

(b)   CASH, TRAVELER'S CHECKS AND CREDIT CARDS

Don't take chances carrying large amounts of cash when you travel. Protect yourself from loss and theft by using traveler's checks and credit cards.

Traveler's checks are the preferred alternative to cash. Buy them at your bank and use them as you would cash. When using traveler's checks, always remember to record the serial number, denominations, date and location of where they were purchased. Keep this information in a separate place so replacement checks can be issued quickly if they are lost or stolen. For convenience, carry $10 and $20 denominations with you.

It's helpful to know that most major credit cards are accepted abroad. If you plan to use credit cards on your trip, verify your available credit limit **before you leave the United States.** Avoid the potential embarrassment of overdrawing, having your card

51

confiscated, or possibly being arrested. Many travelers mistakenly exceed their limit by overcharging and making cash withdrawals. Be sure to keep track of **all** your transactions. Take only those credit cards that can be used overseas; leave the rest at home.

BEFORE YOU GO...

• Photocopy your passport descriptive data page and the contents of your wallet (credit cards, licenses, and insurance numbers). Keep this record in a separate place so if documents are lost or stolen, you can speed the replacement process.

• Purchase a small amount of foreign currency for taxis, telephone calls, tips, etc. Most international airports have 24-hour currency exchange windows.

• If you are bringing more than $10,000 out of the United States in coins, currency, or traveler's checks, you **must** file a report with U.S. Customs Service.

TIP:

Bring along a pocket calculator to help convert currencies.

(c) MEDICAL CARE, MEDICINES, IMMUNIZATIONS

Some foreign countries may require international certificates of vaccination. Depending on the areas you'll be visiting, you may be advised to carry special medication or follow other preventive steps to ensure your well-being. Be sure to ask your doctor or the local public health department for vaccination requirements of specific countries. Or, call the Centers for Disease Control in Atlanta at (404) 639-2572. [See **Chapter 9** for a list of country by country recommended vaccinations.]

GET A HEALTHY START ON YOUR TRIP WHILE YOU'RE STILL IN THE STATES.

Take precautions to prevent yourself from becoming ill while you are abroad. Get a medical and dental checkup before your trip and make sure you are up-to-date with the following immunizations:

[] Measles   [] Mumps
[] Rubella [] Diphtheria
[] Polio   [] Tetanus
[] Whooping Cough

BE PREPARED

If you have allergies or other medical conditions, be sure to take along an ample supply of medication, and keep it in a carry-on bag. Don't make the common

mistake of packing all your medications in your suitcase, which can get lost or stolen. Before you go, you may obtain a list of English-speaking doctors for the areas you plan to visit. Contact the International Association for Medical Assistance to Travelers for such a list at (716) 754-4883. [A listing of other Medical Assistance Organizations is provided in **Appendix 14N.**

BE AWARE

If you are planning to take any prescription drugs on your trip, check with your doctor, or the embassies of the countries you are visiting to ensure you do not violate foreign laws. Many travelers have been innocently arrested for possessing drugs not considered to be narcotic in the United States, but that are illegal in other countries, You can ask your doctor for a certificate attesting to your need to make customs processing easier. Note, however, that this may not be enough authorization to transport drugs into some foreign countries.

IMPORTANT TIPS TO REMEMBER...

• Always leave medicines in original labeled containers. Ask your pharmacists for the generic name of any prescribed drug in case you need to refill the prescription. Brand names differ in other countries.

• If you are allergic to certain medication, insect or snake bites wear a medical alert bracelet and carry a similar warning in your wallet.

• If you wear glasses or contact lenses, bring an extra pair along with your lens prescription and ample supplies of lens solution and cleaner.

• If you become injured or seriously ill abroad, a U.S. consular officer can help you find a physician. He or she can arrange the transfer of funds from your family or friends in the United States to pay for your treatment.

• Carry a summary of your medical records. Be sure to include past illnesses and blood type.

• An increasing number of countries are establishing entry regulations for AIDS, particularly for students and other long-term residents. Check with the embassy or consulate of the individual country to see if this applies to you.

INSURANCE

Enjoying yourself abroad means having your worries at home. That's why you should check with your insurance company to make sure your policy provides adequate medical coverage for you and your family. Did you know that Medicare programs do not provide payment for hospitals or medical services outside the United States? Check with your state insurance association for information on available protection plans for international travelers. The State Department recommends that you purchase the full available automobile insurance policy if you plan to drive. If you plan to rent a car while abroad, consider hiring a driver. In many countries the driver is detained in an accident until settlement is made.

Here are some important questions you should ask your insurance agent, travel agent, and automobile insurance agent:

● Am I protected against trip cancellation, interruption, and baggage loss?

● Will my medical expenses be covered if I incur an . . injury or illness while traveling abroad?

● Will I be reimbursed for my flight if I have to curtail my trip due to an emergency?

● Do I need additional automobile coverage if I am . . going to be driving abroad?

● Will I need additional life insurance coverage while overseas?

● Will I need a driver's license?

TIP:
> If you plan to drive an automobile while in a foreign country, check with the Automobile Association of America (AAA) to see if you'll need an international driver's license and to find out where you can purchase supplemental insurance coverage, as needed. [For information on how to obtain an International Drivers License as well as where to purchase travel insurance **See Appendices M & 13M** respectively.]

BEFORE YOU GO

Protecting Yourself

Sometimes peace of mind can be just a phone call away. If you have any concerns or questions about local conditions or your destination, call the Department of State's Citizens Emergency Center as (202) 647-5225 for 24-hour-a-day recordings of all current travel advisories. You can also obtain travel advisories from U.S. passport agencies, or U.S. Embassies and consulates abroad. The Citizens Emergency Center also provides information on emergency services to U.S. citizens overseas. [See **Chapter 28** for additional information.]

TIP:
> Once you've reached your destination, if you have problems or concerns, visit the American Embassy to register. Let them know where you are staying, the areas you plan to visit, and when you will be returning to the United States.

II WHILE YOU'RE ABROAD

(a) BE SMART!

When you're having a wonderful time in a new environment it's easy to let your guard down. That's why you need to use your common sense and be extra conscious of you actions so you do not become and easy target for crime.

Here are some precautions to take while traveling in a foreign country:

> **Keep a low profile**. This means leaving your valuables, expensive jewelry, and luggage at home. These items might mark you as a wealthy or important American.

> **Avoid dangerous areas.** Don't use short-cuts or . . walk down narrow alleys or poorly lit streets.

> **Never travel alone after dark.** Always let someone know where you are going, and what time you expect to return, especially at night.

> **Meet visitors in the lobby of your hotel.** Don't give out your room number. Always keep your hotel and car doors locked.

> **Carry belongings in a secure manner.** Women . . should wear handbags tucked under their arm and hold the strap. Men should put their wallets in their front trouser pocket or wear a money belt.

> **Don't carry valuables in coat pockets, handbags, or hip pockets** which are particularly susceptible to theft.

> **Avoid using "gypsy" taxis that pick up more that one person per cab.** Use a hotel or airport

taxi. If there is no meter, always agree on the fare in advance.

Be wary of street vendors. While one has your . . attention selling you goods, someone else may be picking your pocket.

Book hotel rooms between the second and seventh floors to prevent easy entrance from the outside, but low enough for fire equipment to reach. Check out the fire safety instructions and the exits.

If you have a problem, the local police department is the best place to go for help.

Learn a few important phrases in the local language so you can signal for fire, the police, the doctor, or the nearest bathroom.

Avoid displaying company name or logos on luggage and tags.

BE ALERT!
(b) GETTING TO KNOW FOREIGN LAWS
Be a Considerate Guest
Visiting a foreign country exposes you to different customs and different laws. That's why you should familiarize yourself with the local regulations before you go. Don't assume that what is acceptable in the United States is acceptable abroad. For example, some countries are particularly sensitive about photographs. It's best to refrain from taking pictures of police, military installations and personnel, or industrial structures unless you know for certain that it will not offend anyone, or break any laws. Check around to see what is considered appropriate clothing. What's acceptable in the United States may offensive elsewhere. And before you decide to sell personal effects such as clothing, cameras, or jewelry. make sure that the local law permits you to do so.

(c) BE INFORMED!
On the average, 2700 Americans are arrested abroad each year. About one-third are held on drug charges. **Do Not Get Involved With Illegal Drugs.** The consequences are serious. If arrested, you will be subject to local, not U.S. laws.

KNOW THE LAWS ABOUT ARREST LAWS!
Many countries do not provide a jury trial or accept bail, which means you may endure lengthy pretrial detention.

• Prison conditions overseas can be harsh. Some lack minimal comforts, such as beds, toilets, and wash basins.

• Officials may not speak English.

• Diets are often inadequate. Payment for food and . amenities may be expected.

• Inhumane treatment and extortion are possible.

• Depending upon your offense, if convicted of a drug charge, you could face up to 10 years in prison with a minimum of 6 years of hard labor, and stiff fines in some countries. The death penalty is possible in others.

(D) GETTING LEGAL AID ABROAD
If you are arrested, the U.S. Embassy or consulate will do what it can to protect your legitimate interests and ensure you are not discriminated against, but cannot pay your legal fees or get you out of jail. A list of local attorneys can be provided by a U.S. consular officer. However, neither the state Department nor the U.S. consular officer can act as your attorney or assume responsibility for the professional competence of local attorneys.

(e) DO'S AND DON'TS AT THE AIRPORT
Traveling abroad means you'll be spending time in foreign airports--going through customs, exchanging money and waiting for flights. That's why you should take a moment to review these practical tactics.

DO
Proceed to boarding gate as soon as possible.

Secure belongings.

Keep your distance from unattended luggage.

Keep a low profile, behave quietly and inconspicuously.

Be alert. Survey your surroundings and check out . . emergency exits.

DON'T
Discuss travel plans indiscriminately.

Leave bags unattended, even for a minute.

Carry any bags or packages for strangers or friends unless you are certain of what is inside.

Carry all your money in one place.

(f) WHEN EXCHANGING YOUR CURRENCY

- Deal only with authorized outlets when you exchange money, or buy airline tickets or traveler's checks. Shop around for the best exchange rate.

- If your passport, credit cards, or traveler's checks are   stolen or lost, notify the **local police** at once! Apply for   replacement passport at the nearest U.S. Embassy or consulate as soon a possible. If credit cards or traveler's checks are lost, contact the issuing companies promptly.

(g) WHAT TO DO IF THERE IS AN INCIDENT:

- Try to remain calm and inconspicuous. Do not move until the   situation is under control. Be passive, yet remain alert.

- Avoid confrontation. Do not engage in political . . discussions or volunteer information.

- Comply with requests. If you must surrender personal belongings, do so without a struggle.

- Make any requests you may have in short, simple . . sentences.

- If there is a rescue attempt, stay as close to the ground as possible.

- Do not try to be a hero.

(h) TRAVEL CHECKLIST

Let's review some important details to consider before you leave the country. Take a moment to go through this checklist.

1. Is your passport valid?   Will it be valid throughout the duration of your trip abroad? Do you have the necessary visas?

2. Are all your travel plans set--from tickets to seating arrangements to hotels to itinerary?

3. Does your family or a close friend know your specific travel plans? Did you leave a copy of your passport, credit cards and traveler's checks numbers?

4. Is your attire appropriate for your destination, that is, comfortable and conservative without indicating your nationality or religion?

5. Do you know the local conditions of your destination? Are there travel advisories for the areas you'll be visiting?

6. Are you aware of the cultural and political differences of the areas you are visiting to avoid any misunderstandings and potential difficulties? For instance, in some Middle East countries, high fashion magazines are considered pornography!

7. Have you reviewed with a family member or close friend what is to be done in case of an emergency?

TIP:

If you are planning to bring valuables on your trip (watch, jewelry, cameras) check with U.S. Customs regarding registration requirements and proper proof of ownership. **Always** obtain a receipt before buying any foreign item, especially antiques.

AMERICAN CHILDREN ABROAD

If you plan to bring your children overseas, it is important that they become familiar with the local laws and customs. Foreign languages, symbols, and signs can be very confusing to young children. Be sure to prepare them well in advance for the differences they will encounter. Here are some common sense issues to discuss with your children before leaving the United States and once you have reached your destinations.

1. Make sure young children know the name and the address of the place where they are staying. A sample child I.D. a Form/Card has been provided. It should be filled out on both sides by an adult and kept in a safe place on your child at all times.

2. Using a foreign telephone can be confusing to a child. Show your child how to use the telephone, and be sure he or she has enough money to make several calls if needed.

3. Go over with your child who to call or approach in an emergency situation. These numbers and addresses should be kept on his or her I.D. card and, if possible, memorized. Point out a local, uniformed police officer to your child so he ore she will be able to recognize one.

4. Discuss traffic rules with your child. Red lights don't always necessarily mean stop.

5. Make sure your child is aware of the dangers of electrical outlets, appliances, and TVs that operate on strong current overseas.

6. Do not let your child go anywhere alone. Enforce the "Buddy System" and explain the importance of

always being aware of his or her surroundings.

7. In crowded places such as open market, busy streets, and airports, keep your child close by. Always have a designated spot to meet in case you get separated.

RESOURCES FOR OVERSEAS TRAVELERS

Background Notes.
If you are looking for more detailed information about a particular foreign country, you might want to send away for **Background Notes**. Background Notes are concise, authoritative pamphlets containing information on some 170 countries and geographic areas around the world. Each pamphlet describes the country's people, culture, geography, history, government, economy and political conditions. To receive Background Notes, just send $2.00 for each country to:

Background Notes
Superintendent of Documents
U.S. Government Printing Office
Washington, DC 20402

● Be sure to include the specific country or area you'll be traveling to with your request.

Key Officers of Foreign Service Posts. This publication contains information (including names, addresses, and telephone numbers) on all the American Embassies, consulates, and missions in foreign countries, send $3.75 with your request to:

(Same address as Background Notes **or** call (202) 783-3238)

THE BUREAU OF CONSULAR AFFAIRS PUBLISHES A VARIETY OF INTERNATIONAL TRAVEL BROCHURES. THEY INCLUDE:[2]

■ Tips for Americans Residing Abroad.

■ A Safe Trip Abroad (covers security and health issues)

■ Your Trip Abroad (general travel information)

■ Tips for Travelers to:
    The Caribbean
    Mexico
    The Middle East and North Africa
    The People's Republic of China
    South Asia
    The USSR
    Sub-Saharan Africa
    Central and South Africa

■ Travel Tips for Older Americans

[See **Chapter 46** for information on ordering any of the publications mentioned here.]

~ ~ ENDNOTES ~ ~

1. This publication is reprinted in chapter 3 of this book.

2. These publications including all current issues of **Tips for Travelers** are reproduced elsewhere in this book. Check the Table of Contents for location.

Chapter 6

Security Awareness Overseas

[The information in this chapter is reprinted verbatim from a bulletin issued by the U.S. State Department, Bureau of Diplomatic Security. It is intended to serve as advice to Americans traveling abroad.]

- - - -

FORWARD

The Overseas Security Advisory Council (OSAC) was established by the Department of State in 1985 to foster the exchange of information between American companies with overseas operations and the U.S. Government. Since then, OSAC has become an outstanding joint venture and effective vehicle for security cooperation.

Among their other accomplishments, government and business representatives have joined to use OSAC as a forum for producing a series of publications providing guidance, suggestions and planning techniques on a variety of security related issues, including terrorism and crime.

Personal security abroad is a major concern of individuals and companies and thus, a natural forum for an OSAC publication. This booklet, along with such previous OSAC publications as Security Guidelines for American Families Living Abroad, will surely find a wide audience and make a strong contribution to the security and well-being of American citizens who live and work abroad.

James A. Baker, III

Preface

The Overseas Security Advisory Council (OSAC) of the U.S. Department of State consists of representatives from 21 private sector organizations and four from U.S. Government departments and agencies.

As part of its security program, OSAC has prepared publications containing suggested security and emergency planning guidelines for American private sector personnel and enterprises abroad. A listing of current OSAC publications is contained under the subtitle *Publications* on page 71.

This publication is intended as a guideline for business persons in the private sector who travel or reside abroad. It was written by the Committee on Security Awareness, consisting of Robert R. Burke, Monsanto Company, Chairman; Oliver Wainwright, American

International Group, Inc.; Bernard C. Dowling, U.S. Information Agency; Craig Beek, Deere & Company; Winston Griffin, McDonald's Corporation; and John MacDonald, McDonnell Douglas Corp.

We are grateful to Lee Lacy, Director of the Overseas Briefing Center of the Foreign Service Institute for her assistance with this publication. Much of the information contained here is based on the SOS: *Security Overseas Seminar Handbook,* produced and edited by Barbara Hoganson, Coordinator of the Security Overseas Seminar, Department of State; designed and written by Helen Strother Fouche of The Washington Editorial Services, Inc. As with previous booklets, this publication is printed and distributed by the Bureau of Diplomatic Security, U.S. Department of State.

A rapidly changing political world has not lessened the attention one should pay to personal security when overseas. Natural disasters will continue, as will acts of terrorism. Indeed, one might expect increased incidents of civil unrest, some directed against Americans, as political situations remain unresolved. The guidelines which follow are suggested to assist American companies and their personnel abroad in planning to meet their individual needs and circumstances. Individuals should ensure, however, that any approach chosen is best suited to their individual situation.

Take the time to think through your upcoming travel and to use this booklet to plan for emergencies and other special contingencies. Hopefully, you will never be required to act upon your plan, but if an emergency does develop, the time spent planning may ensure your safety and that of your family.

Introduction

We gain a great sense of security and self confidence knowing we are prepared for potential crises. This booklet provides assistance in preparing us to face those emergencies we may encounter while living or traveling overseas. Many potential overseas crises may be eased or averted by taking the time to read and study the information that follows.

Cultural misunderstandings and inadequate local support services often make crises abroad more intense than similar situations in the United States. Overseas, we must assume greater responsibility for our own safety.

Information and suggestions in this booklet have been collected from several government and private sources. Personal experiences of those who have been through particular crises abroad have added substantially to the store of ideas and advice. The experience of each-whether hostage, crime victim, evacuee, or other-is distinct. Yet there are common threads that provide guidelines on how to handle crises successfully. We hope, in this booklet, to pass those guidelines on to you.

Although we have attempted to organize tips and information according to whether your stay will be temporary or permanent, most apply to either situation.

Preparing To Travel

Have Your Affairs in Order
Many hostages have expressed regret that their affairs were not left in better order for their families. An evacuation, illness, or death can often place a family in a similar situation. Three actions, taken before you depart, will alleviate this potential problem:

- Discuss and plan with your family what should be done in the case of any emergency separation. All adult family members should be aware of these plans.

- Supply family and close friends with the emergency notification numbers found on this page. They serve both to notify you while you are overseas in the event of an illness or death in your family in the United States and to provide your family in the U.S. with information about you in case of a crisis abroad.

- See that all important papers are up-to-date. List papers and leave originals with a family member or attorney in the United States. Carry only copies to your overseas assignment. Safe deposit boxes and bank accounts are very useful but may be sealed on the death of an owner. Therefore, make sure your representative has joint right of access.

Important Papers
Your collection of important papers might include:
- Will
- Birth and marriage certificates
- Guardianship or adoption papers for children
- Power of attorney for spouse or relative

- Naturalization papers
- Deeds, mortgages, stocks and bonds, car titles
- Insurance papers-car, home, life, personal effects, medical
- Tax records
- Proof of termination of previous marriage(s)
- Child support/alimony agreements Proof of membership in any organization or union that entitles the estate to any benefits

Useful Information

An Information List might include:
- Bank account numbers and addresses
- Passport numbers
- Duplicate passport pictures in case passport needs to be replaced due to loss
- U.S. and local driver's license numbers
- Insurance policy numbers and names of carriers
- Social Security numbers
- Credit card numbers
- Travelers check numbers and issuing bank
- Medical and dental information, distinguishing marks and scars, and medicine and eyeglass prescriptions
- Assets and debts
- Names and addresses of business and professional contacts
- Updated inventory of household and personal possessions with pictures/videos
- Employment records for each family member; resumes, references, commendations
- Personal address list
- Fingerprints, current photos/videos, voice recording, known handwriting samples of family members

Emergency Notification
While abroad, you may need to be notified of an emergency involving someone in the United States. And during a political, social, or natural crisis abroad, your family in the United States will be anxious to get news of you.

The appropriate telephone numbers below should be given to your family for such purposes.
- U.S. Embassy/consulate
    (Day)
    (Night)
- U.S. Corporate HQ
    (Day)
    (Night)
- Corporate Security
- Local Legal Counsel
- Local Police
- Airline(s)

- Red Cross
- Department of State
- Host Country Embassy, Washington, D.C.
- Local Company Office
- Residence
- International Operator
- Relatives

Before initiating calls, the caller in the United States should have the following information available:

- Your name, company, and current location
- Name and relationship of family member
- In case of death-Date of death
- In case of illness-Name, address, and telephone number of attending physician or hospital

Miscellaneous Tips

The corporate traveler should also consider the following, which will assist and possibly protect him/her during the actual journey:

- Obtain International Driving Permit.
- Prepare a wallet card identifying your blood type, known allergies, required medications, insurance company, and name of person to contact in case of emergency.
- Remove from wallet all credit cards and other items not necessary for trip.
- Remove unessential papers, such as reserve, military, or humorous cards, e.g., "Honorary Sheriff."
- Put a plain cover on your passport (covers available in stationery stores);
- Use hard, lockable luggage.
- Be sure luggage tags contain your name, phone number, and full street address; that information is concealed from casual observation; and that company logos are not displayed on luggage.
- Inform family member or friend of specific travel plans. Give your office a complete itinerary. Be sure to notify the local company manager of your travel plans.
- Obtain the name(s) and address(es) of your local office(s).
- Obtain small amount of local currency if possible.
- Be aware of airline safety records when booking vacation trips while overseas; do not include company name in reservation.
- When possible, mail personal papers to yourself at the local overseas office.

Stay informed! Check for any travel advisories pertinent to countries you plan to visit. Call the Department of State's Citizens Emergency Center (see Chapter 28), or your company's Corporate Security Department.

In Transit

Most of the following suggestions apply to any travel; several are specifically directed at surviving a terrorist situation. It is recognized that the level of risk varies from country to country and time to time, so that you may need to choose among the suggested options or modify the concepts to meet your needs.

If you plan to stay in one country any length of time while traveling, especially in a country that is in a period of civil unrest, register with the embassy or consulate and provide a copy of your itinerary. Registration makes it easier to contact you in case of an emergency and to evacuate you if necessary.

On the Plane

Carry-on luggage should contain a supply of any regularly taken prescription medicines (in original containers labeled with the pharmacy name and prescribing physician), an extra pair of eyeglasses, passport, and carefully chosen personal documents (copies only!).

Dress inconspicuously to blend into the international environment.

Consider wearing no jewelry.

On foreign carriers, avoid speaking English as much as possible. Do not discuss business or travel plans with fellow passengers, crew, or even traveling companions.

Select a window seat in the coach section. This position is less accessible by hijackers inflicting indiscriminate violence.

Memorize your passport number so you do not have to reveal your passport when filling out landing cards.

At an Overseas Airport

Maintain a low profile, and avoid public areas as much as possible. Check in quickly and do not delay in the main terminal area. Do not discuss travel plans indiscriminately.

Stay away from unattended baggage. Verify baggage claim checks before and after flight. Always maintain custody of your carry-on bag.

Survey surroundings, noting exits and safe areas.

If an incident occurs, survival may depend on your ability to remain calm and alert. During a terrorist attack or rescue operation, you do not want to be confused with the terrorists and shot. Avoid sudden moves; hide behind something and drop to floor.

Car Rentals

Ideally, choose a conservative model car with locking trunk, hood, and gas cap; power brakes and steering; seat belts; quick accelerating engine; heavy duty bumpers; smooth interior locks. In a hot climate, choose air conditioning. Keep the gas tank at least half full.

Before getting into the car, examine it for strange objects or wires inside, around, or underneath it. If found, do not touch; clear the area and call police.

When driving, lock the doors, keep windows rolled up, avoid being boxed in by other cars. Vary routes. Check for suspicious individuals before getting out of the car.

Lock the car when unattended. Never let anyone place a package inside or enter the car unless you are present.

Public Transportation

Stay on your guard against pickpockets and petty thieves while in a bus/train terminal or at a taxi stop. Avoid carrying a wallet in your hip or easily accessible coat pocket. Carry a purse/handbag that you may firmly grip or secure to your body. Beware of people jostling you at busy stations.

Take only licensed taxis. Generally those found in front of terminals and the better hotels are the safest. You may pay a bit more, but the companies are reputable and normally the drivers have been screened. Be sure the photo on displayed license is of the driver. Have the address of your destination written out in local language and carry it with you. Get a map and learn the route to your destination; note if taxi driver takes you a different or longer way.

Try not to travel alone in a taxi, and never get out in deserted areas. If the door doesn't lock, sit near the middle of the seat so you will thwart thieves who might open the door to grab a purse, briefcase, or wallet.

On subways, choose a middle car but never an empty car. On buses, sit in an aisle seat near the driver. Stand back from the curb while waiting for a bus.

Avoid arriving anywhere at night and using dim or vacant entrances to stations or terminals. Utilize only busy, well-lit stations.

Take as little luggage as possible; ideally, no more than you can comfortably carry.

In-Transit Accommodations

Accommodations in many countries differ considerably from those found in North America and Western Europe. Safety features required in U.S. hotels, such as sprinkler systems, fire stairwells, and emergency lighting, often are either lacking or inoperable. The following measures will enable you to better plan for unforeseen contingencies in hotels.

Hotel Crime

Stay alert in your hotel. Put the "do not disturb" sign on your door to give the impression that the room is occupied. Call the maid when you are ready for the room to be cleaned. Consider leaving the light or TV on when you are out of the room. Carry the room key with you instead of leaving it at front desk. Do not use your name when answering the phone. Do not accept packages or open the door to workmen without verification from the front desk.

When walking, remain on wide, well-lit streets. Know where you are going when you leave the hotel-if on a tour, enlist a reputable guide. Generally, the hotel will recommend or procure one. Do not take shortcuts through alleys or off the beaten path. If alone, be back in the hotel by dark. Never resist armed robbery; it could lead to violence. Always carry some cash to appease muggers who may resort to violence at finding no reward for their efforts.

Civil Unrest

In some areas of the world, civil unrest or violence directed against Americans and other foreigners is common. Travelers should be alert to indicators of civil unrest and take the following precautions in the event of such situations:

- If in your hotel, stay there. Contact the U.S. Embassy, consulate or other friendly embassy. Hire someone to take a note to them if phones are out of order.

- Contact your local office representative.

- Do not watch activity from your window, and try to sleep in an inside room which provides greater protection from gunfire, rocks, grenades, etc.

- If you are caught outside in the middle of a riot or unrest, do not take sides or attempt to gather information. Play the tourist who just wants to get home to his/her family.

Hotel Fires

Many hotels abroad are not as fire-resistant as those in the United States. Interior materials are often extremely flammable. Escape routes may not be posted in hallways and exits may be few or sealed. Fire fighting equipment and water supplies may be limited. There may be no fast method for

alerting a fire department. Sprinkler systems and smoke detectors may be nonexistent.

You must aggressively take responsibility for the safety of yourself and your family. Think "contingency plan" and discuss it with your dependents. Begin planning your escape from a fire as soon as you check in to a hotel. When a fire occurs, you can then act without panic and without wasting time.

Stay in the most modern hotel; consider a U.S. chain. Request a lower floor, ideally the second or third. Selecting a room no higher than the second floor enables you to jump to safety. Although most fire departments can reach above the second floor, they may not get to you in time or position a fire truck on your side of the building.

Locate exits and stairways as soon as you check in; be sure the doors open. Count the number of doors between your room and exit or stairway. In a smoke-filled hallway, you could have to "feel" your way to an exit. Form a mental map of your escape route.

If the hotel has a fire alarm system, find the nearest alarm. Be sure you know how to use it. You may have to activate it in the dark or in dense smoke.

Ensure that your room windows open and that you know how the latches work. Look out the window and mentally rehearse your escape through it. Make note of any ledges or decks that will aid escape.

Check the smoke detector by pushing the test button. If it does not work, have it fixed or move to another room. Better yet, carry your own portable smoke detector (with the battery removed while traveling). Place it in your room by the hall door near the ceiling.

Keep the room key and a flashlight on the bedside table so that you may locate the key quickly if you have to leave your room.

If a Fire Starts

If you awake to find smoke in your room, grab your key and crawl to the door on your hands and knees. Don't stand-smoke and deadly gases rise while the fresher air will be near the floor.

Before you open the door, feel it with the palm of your hand. If the door or knob is hot, the fire may be right outside. Open the door slowly. Be ready to slam it shut

if the fire is close by. If your exit path is clear, crawl into the hallway. Be sure to close the door behind you to keep smoke out in case you have to return to your room. Take your key, as most hotel doors lock automatically. Stay close to the wall to avoid being trampled.

Do not use elevators during a fire. They may malfunction, or if they have heat-activated call buttons, they may take you directly to the fire floor.

As you make your way to the fire exit, stay on the same side as the exit door. Count the doors to the exit.

When you reach the exit, walk down the stairs to the first floor. Hold onto the handrail for guidance and protection from being knocked down by other occupants.

If you encounter heavy smoke in the stairwell, don't try to run through it. You may not make it. Instead, turn around and walk up to the roof fire exit. Prop the door open to ventilate the stairwell and to keep from being locked out. Find the windward side of the roof, sit down, and wait for fire fighters to find you.

If all exits are blocked or if there is heavy smoke in the hallway, you'll be better off staying in your room. If there is smoke in your room, open a window and turn on the bathroom vent. Don't break the window unless it can't be opened. You might want to close the window later to keep smoke out, and broken glass could injure you or people below.

If your phone works, call the desk to tell someone where you are, or call the fire department to report your location in the building. Hang a bed sheet out the window as a signal.

Fill the bathtub with water to use for fire fighting. Bail water onto your door or any hot walls with an ice bucket or waste basket. Stuff wet towels into cracks under and around doors where smoke can enter. Tie a wet towel over your mouth and nose to help filter out smoke. If there is fire outside your window, take down the drapes and move everything combustible away from the window.

If you are above the second floor, you probably will be better off fighting the fire in your room than jumping. A jump from above the third floor may result in severe injury or death.

Remember that panic and a fire's byproducts, such as super-heated gases and smoke, present a greater danger than the fire itself. If you know your plan of escape in

61

advance, you will be less likely to panic and more likely to survive.

Terrorism

Although for most of us it is not a probability, terrorism is a fact. The likelihood of terrorist incidents varies according to country or area of the world, generally depending on the

stability of the local government and the degree of frustration felt by indigenous groups or individuals.

Although the number of incidents worldwide has increased at the rate of 10 percent per year, less than a quarter of these have been directed against American businesses or their employees. Most acts of terrorism are directed against citizens of the country where they occur.

When an act of terrorism does occur, it often has dire consequences: murder, hostage taking, property destruction. Much has been learned about the mentality of terrorists, their methods of operation, and the behavior patterns of both victims and perpetrators.

Alert individuals, prepared for possible terrorist acts, can minimize the likelihood that these acts will be successfully carried out against them. While there is no absolute protection against terrorism, there are a number of reasonable precautions that can provide some degree of individual protection.

U.S. Policy

U.S. policy is firmly committed to resisting terrorist blackmail.

The U.S. Government will not pay ransom for the release of hostages. It will not support the freeing of prisoners from incarceration in response to terrorist demands. The U.S. Government will not negotiate with terrorists on the substance of their demands, but it does not rule out contact and dialogue with hostage takers if this will promote the safe release of hostages.

In terrorist incidents abroad affecting Americans, our government looks to the host government to provide for the safety of U.S. citizens in accordance with international agreements.

The U.S. Government is prepared to offer terrorist experts, specialized assistance, military equipment, and personnel should the foreign government decide such assistance could be useful.

Terrorist Demands

U.S. Government policy is to make no concessions to

terrorist demands. However, such a decision on the part of private individuals or companies is a personal one and in some special circumstances may be made by the family or company of the victim. Whatever the decision, it should conform to local law.

Terrorist Surveillance

Terrorists may shadow an intended victim at length and with infinite patience before an actual abduction or assassination is attempted. Initial surveillance efforts may be clumsy and could be spotted by an alert target. In most cases, more than one individual is a likely candidate for the terrorist act. Usually the choice is based on the probability of success. In one documented instance, both an American and another country's representative were under surveillance. Though the American was the first choice of the terrorists, their surveillance showed that it would be more difficult to kidnap him. Consequently, the other individual was abducted and spent a long period in captivity.

Precise risks of surveillance and popular local tactics can be explained by your company's security representative. However, you must also learn to cultivate a "sixth sense" about your surroundings.

Know what is normal in your neighborhood and along your commute routes, especially at choke points. If you know what is ordinary, you will notice anything extraordinary-people who are in the wrong place or dressed inappropriately, or cars parked in strange locations.

Be particularly observant whenever you leave your home or office. Look up and down the street for suspicious vehicles, motorcycles, mopeds, etc. Note people near your home who appear to be repair personnel, utility crew teams, even peddlers. Ask yourself if they appear genuine.

Become familiar with vehicle makes and models; learn to memorize license numbers. Determine if a pattern is developing with specific vehicles. See if cars suddenly pull out of parking places or side streets when you pass. Cars with extra mirrors or large mirrors are suspicious.

Be aware of the types of surveillance: stationary (at residence, along route, at work); following (on foot, by car); monitoring (of telephone, mail); searching (of luggage, personal effects, even trash); and eavesdropping (electronic and personal). An elaborate system involving several people and cars might be used.

Make their job tougher by not being predictable. Eat at different times and places. Stagger professional and social activities; don't play tennis "every Wednesday at three," for example.

Know the choke points on your routes and be aware of other vehicles, vans, or motorcycles as you enter those bottleneck areas. Search out safe havens that you can pull into along the route.

Drive with windows rolled up to within 2 inches of the top and lock all doors. Report any suspicious activity promptly to law enforcement.

Avoid using unlicensed cabs or cabs that appear out of nowhere. Do not permit taxi drivers to deviate from desired route.

Be circumspect with members of the press, as terrorists often pose as journalists. Do not submit to interviews or allow photographs to be made in or of your home.

Always speak guardedly and caution children to do the same. Never discuss travel or business plans within hearing of servants. Surveillants consider children and servants to be a prime source of information. Always assume that your telephone is tapped.

In elevators, watch for anyone who waits for you to select your floor, then pushes a button for the one just above or below yours.

If you become aware of surveillance, don't let those watching you know you are onto them. And certainly never confront them. Immediately notify your appropriate company representative. Memorize emergency numbers, and carry change for phone calls.

Hijackings
The experience of others will be helpful to you if you are the victim of a hijacking. Blend in with the other airline passengers. Avoid eye contact with your captors. Remember there may be other hijackers covertly mixed among the regular passengers.

Although captors may appear calm, they cannot be trusted to behave reasonably or rationally at all times. Stay alert, but do not challenge them physically or verbally. Comply with their instructions.

If interrogated, keep answers short and limited to nonpolitical topics. Carry a family photo; at some point you may be able to appeal to captors' family feelings.

Minimize the importance of your job. Give innocuous reasons for traveling. Never admit to any accusations.

Armed Assault on the Ground
Hostages taken by ground assault are in a situation similar to hijacking except that it occurs within buildings. Business offices, banks, embassies, and trains have been targets. The same advice for dealing with hijackers applies to ground assaults. Should shooting occur, seek cover or lie flat on the floor.

Kidnappings
Kidnapping is a terrifying experience, but you possess more personal resources than you may be aware of to cope with the situation. Remember, you are only of value to them alive, and they want to keep you that way.

The common hostage responses of fear, denial, and withdrawal are all experienced in varying degrees. You may be blindfolded, drugged, handled roughly, or even stuffed in the trunk of a car. If drugs are administered, don't resist. Their purpose will be to sedate you and make you more manageable; these same drugs may actually help you to get control of your emotions, which should be your immediate goal. If conscious, follow your captors' instructions.

Captivity
A hostage-taking situation is at its worst at the onset. The terrorists are nervous and unsure, easily irritated, often irrational. It is a psychologically traumatic moment for the hostage. Violence may be used even if the hostage remains passive, but resistance could result in death.

If taken hostage, your best defense is passive cooperation. You may be terrified, but try to regain your composure as soon as possible and to organize your thoughts. Being able to behave rationally increases your chances for survival. The more time that passes, the better your chances of being released alive.

Behavior Suggestions
Each captivity is different, but some behavior suggestions apply to most:

- Try to establish some kind of rapport with your captors. Family is a universal subject. Avoid political dialogues, but listen attentively to their point of view. If you know their language, listen and observe; and if addressed, use it.

- Plan on a lengthy stay, and determine to keep track of the passage of time. Captors may attempt to confuse your sense of time by taking your watch, keeping you in a windowless cell, or serving meals at odd hours. However, you can approximate time by noting, for example, changes in temperatures between night and day; the frequency and intensity of outside noises-traffic, whistles, birds; and by observing the alertness of guards.

- Maintain your dignity and self respect at all times.

- Manage your time by setting up schedules for simple tasks, exercises, daydreaming, housekeeping.

- Build relations with fellow captives and with the terrorists. If hostages are held apart, devise ways to communicate with one another. Where hostages are moved back and forth, to bathrooms for example, messages can be written and left. However, do not jeopardize your safety or the safety or treatment of others if attempting to communicate with fellow captives seems too risky.

- Maintain your physical and mental health; it is critical to exercise body and mind. Eat food provided without complaint; keep up your strength. Request medical treatment or special medicines if required.

- Establish exercise and relaxation programs. Exercise produces a healthy tiredness and gives you a sense of accomplishment. If space is confined, do isometrics. Relaxation reduces stress. Techniques include meditation, prayer, daydreaming.

- Keep your mind active; read anything available. Write, even if you are not allowed to retain your writings. If materials are not available, mentally compose poetry or fiction, try to recall Scripture, design a house, even "play tennis" (as one hostage did).

- Take note of the characteristics of your captors and surroundings: their habits, speech, contacts; exterior noises (typical of city or country); and other distinctive sounds. This information could prove very valuable later.

- If selected for early release, consider it an opportunity to help remaining hostages. Details you have observed on the terrorists and the general situation can assist authorities with a rescue.

You can expect to be accused of working for the government's intelligence service, to be interrogated extensively, and to lose weight. You may be put in isolation; your captives may try to disorient you. It is important that you mentally maintain control.

Avoidance of Capture or Escape

Efforts to avoid capture or to attempt escape have in most cases been futile. The decision, however, is a personal one, although it could affect fellow hostages by placing them in jeopardy. Several other considerations should be weighed.

To have any chance of success, you should be in excellent physical condition and mentally prepared to react before the terrorists have consolidated their position. This, also, is the riskiest psychological time. You would need to have a plan in mind, and possibly have been trained in special driving tactics or other survival skills.

If you are held in a country in which you would stand out because of race or other physical characteristics, if you know nothing of the language or your location, or if you are held in a country where anti-American or anti-Western attitudes prevail, you should consider the consequences of your escape before attempting it.

If you conclude that an escape attempt is worthwhile, take terrorists by surprise and you may make it. If their organization has a poor track record of hostage safety, it may be worth the risk.

Rescue

The termination of any terrorist incident is extremely tense. If an assault force attempts a rescue, it is imperative that you remain calm and out of the way. Make no sudden moves or take any action by which you could be mistaken for a terrorist and risk being injured or killed.

Even in a voluntary release or surrender by the terrorists, tensions are charged and tempers volatile. Very precise instructions will be given to the hostages, either by the captors or the police. Follow instructions precisely. You may be asked to exit with hands in the air, and you may be searched by the rescue team. You may experience rough treatment until you are identified and the situation has stabilized.

Finally, it's worth keeping in mind three facts about terrorism:

- The overwhelming majority of victims have been abducted from their vehicles on the way to or from work.

- A large number of people taken hostage ignored the most basic security precautions.

- Terrorist tactics are not static. As precautions prove effective, they change their methods. There is a brief "window of vulnerability" while we learn to counter their new styles.

Additional Precautions

Do not settle into a routine. Vary times and routes to and from work or social engagements.

Remember, there is safety in numbers. Avoid going out alone. When traveling long distances by automobile, go in a convoy. Avoid back country roads and dangerous areas of the city.

A privately owned car generally offers the best security. Avoid luxury or ostentatious cars. Keep your automobile in good repair and the gas tank at least half full. Driving in the center lane of a multiple lane highway makes it difficult for the car to be forced off the road.

Overseas Crisis Planning

Culture Shock

Culture shock is the physiological and psychological stress experienced when a traveler is suddenly deprived of old, familiar cues-language, customs, etc. Both the seasoned traveler and the first-timer, whether in transit or taking up residence, are susceptible. The sensation may be severe or mild, last months or only hours, strike in a remote village or in a modern European city, in one country, but not another-or not at all.

Culture shock is most prevalent in the second or third month after arrival when the novelty of the new country fades. Symptoms typically disappear by the fourth to sixth month, when the family has settled in and a sense of equilibrium is restored.

Traveler disorientation is a form of culture shock. You may encounter so many strange sounds, sights, and smells upon arrival in a country new to you that you may be more vulnerable to accidents or crime. You may experience this disorientation on a fast-paced business trip to several different cultures.

You can combat traveler disorientation by gathering, in advance, information of a practical nature-knowing the routine at the airport, which taxis are recommended, knowing the exchange rate, etc. Pay particular attention to any host nation cultural behavior which may affect your security or safety.

As with any type of stress, culture shock may manifest itself both physically and emotionally. If you should experience it at a time when you need to be alert to security concerns, your awareness could be impaired. But if you understand it, you can successfully deal with

it.

Symptoms

In children, you may notice a drop in school work and disruptive or regressive behavior. Teens may rebel with drugs or sex.

Symptoms to watch for in adults and children include:
- Sleepiness, apathy, depression
- Compulsive eating or drinking
- Exaggerated homesickness
- Decline in efficiency
- Negative stereotyping of nationals
- Recurrent minor illnesses

Successful Handling

The trauma of culture shock is most successfully dealt with if you:
- Realize that operating in a new setting with strange sights, sounds, smells, and possibly a new language, is a different experience for each person in the family.

- Communicate with each other; have patience and understanding; be sensitive to each others' feelings and difficulties.

- Exercise! Lack of proper rest, diet, and exercise aggravate culture shock stress symptoms. Establish a daily exercise schedule quickly.

- Use the support system of experienced associates at first. Begin to participate in the life of the new country to whatever extent possible. There are many possibilities for family or individual activities within the American and international communities and in the new country. Sightsee, join a tennis club, enroll at the university, join a church, go to a concert, volunteer with the Red Cross, join Rotary.

We never build up an absolute immunity to culture shock. Yet that same sensitivity to change also means that we have the capacity to be enriched by the new experience travel brings us. Remember, each positive effort at stepping into the local culture usually opens yet another door of opportunity and diminishes the effects of culture shock.

If severe culture shock symptoms persist past six months, seek professional help.

Helping Children Adjust

Before the Move

Set the stage with children before the transfer process

begins. Discuss the contents of this booklet with them and share what you have learned about the new country. Keep discussions informal. Bring up selected subjects during routine activities-dinner or a weekend hike. Be careful not to be apologetic about any restrictions that living overseas may place on them.

Talk to them about:

- Cultural restrictions: Teens need to understand any dress or behavior restrictions ahead of time. Help children accept the local mores rather than resent them. Make your guidelines clear.

- Health precautions: It may be the first time children have not been able to drink tap water or eat the local fruits, vegetables, and meats. They may require shots or pills to prevent the onset of local diseases.

- Stress factors: Discuss with them the stress placed on a family by such a move and how they can relieve it. Many children instinctively reduce stress through play with others or a pet or by spending hours on the phone with friends. Still, they may express anger at relocation and anxiety about what the future holds. Flashbacks and nightmares are not uncommon in these situations.

Relocation Crisis

Children are creatures of habit. Settling them into a daily routine helps them adjust more successfully to any situation-whether it's a normal move, an evacuation, a separation, or a catastrophic disaster that has affected the whole community.

Give them information on the crisis appropriate to their age level. Listen to them. Talk to them. Let them express their anxieties. Acknowledge their feelings.

Encourage them to be physically active. Little ones can play games, teenagers can help with community needs related to the crisis, such as organizing activities for younger children or cleaning up earthquake damage. Vigorous exercise and sports are good for everyone during periods of high stress.

Make opportunities for them to be with peers. The older the child the more important this is, but most need to interact with children their own age. Insist they attend school, as this is the center of life with peers.

Let them feel that they have complete parental support. In times of crisis, children regress to earlier developmental stages. Young children can become almost infantile, forget toilet training, cling to parents. School-age children may refuse to go to school, be

disruptive. Even teens, who have begun to break away from parents, may need reassurance that they are still securely within the family circle.

Stress During Crisis
A crisis is best handled collectively. Parents, teachers, family, and friends can play a part in helping any child handle a crisis. Adults should support each other in guiding children through the crisis; there is no need to feel you're in this alone. Play groups or support groups may be formed.

Parents and teachers are models. If they handle a crisis calmly, children will be less anxious.

Children "borrow" strengths from adults around them. Help them put labels on their reactions; encourage them to verbalize feelings. Play is a natural form of communication for children; it will discharge bottled-up feelings. If allowed to work through their fears, most children will emerge strengthened from a crisis.

Children need to see you express your feelings of fear and grief, too. By example, parents and other adults can show children how these feelings are handled. It's important that they see not only the expression of grief and sadness, but that they understand that the feeling will pass.

Some parents attempt to protect children by not allowing discussion about a crisis. The healthy route is to let them discuss it until they can get some psychological distance from it. Verbal repetition is a natural cathartic process.

Give them information-real details in language appropriate to their ages. Children are more painfully aware of what's going on than adults realize. And, if it's not discussed, what they do know, or think they know, can become unpleasantly distorted in their minds.

If a child requires medical attention, someone from the immediate family should stay with him or her. See that the procedures that are to be done are explained to the child.

Security for Children

Rules for Children
Children must be taught:
- To keep a parent in sight in public places and to go to a store clerk if lost and in need of help.
- Not to go anywhere with anyone without a parent's permission.
  A password known only to family and close

friends.
- Not to accept packages or letters from people you don't now.
- To know at least key phrases in the local language.
- To let someone know their location and plans.

Rules for Parents

Parents need to:
- Teach your child never to get into a car or go into a house without your permission. Don't leave your child alone in a public place, even for a moment.

- Teach your child your home address and telephone number. Children should know how to use public phones. Keep a list of emergency numbers by your phone and make children aware of them.

- Train children not to give personal information over the phone, even though the caller purports to be a friend. "Personal information" includes whether family members are away, travel plans, where parents work, or recreation and school routines.

- Explain the importance of never divulging any information in front of strangers.

- Caution children to always keep doors locked, and never to unlock a door to a stranger without adult approval.

- Listen when your child tells you he or she does not want to be with someone; there may be a reason. Have the child present when you interview a servant who will be caring for him or her; observe their reactions.

Child-Watch Checklist

Post an information list by each phone. Your sitter should be familiar with every item.
- Family name
- Address
- Phone number
- Fire
- Police
- Medical
- Poison
- Neighbor's name
- Neighbor's address
- Neighbor's phone
- Nearest fire call box
- Miscellaneous information of importance

Checklist for Babysitters
- Ensure all doors and windows are locked and that doors are not opened to anyone.

- Do not give out any information over the telephone. Simply state that Mr./Mrs. X cannot come to the phone right now. Take a message.

- Never leave the children alone, even for a minute.

- Know the dangers to children of matches, gasoline, stoves, deep water, poisons, falls.

- Know the locations of all exits (stairs, doors, windows, fire escapes) and phones in case of emergency.

- List the names and ages of children.

Evacuation
Many evacuations have taken place in past years for reasons of political instability, acts of terrorism, and natural disasters. In a number of cases, people have gone back to their new home after a short time; in others they have not returned at all. Notification times can range from a couple of hours to several weeks.

No two evacuations are the same. But there are common threads that run through all; knowing them can make an evacuation easier. What we have learned, both as a government and from individuals who have been evacuated, is distilled here for you.

Preparation
Be prepared. Assume an evacuation could occur at any point and have everything in place to execute it. It is better to be ready and not need it, than to need it and be unprepared.

Determine the "who and where" with your family. Who should be contacted and where your family would go in case of an extended evacuation. This is especially important for single parents; employees could be required to stay in the new country while children must leave. Parents should make arrangements for emergency child care before leaving the United States.

Establish a line of credit to cover emergencies. Obtain individual credit cards for you and your spouse. Open two checking accounts; use one as an active account, and keep the other in reserve. If possible, arrange for your paycheck to be deposited in a U.S. bank. Keep only a small account in a local bank for currency exchange or local purchases.

Know the emergency evacuation plan of the school. If

there is none, be an active parent organizer and ensure that one is instituted. Join or start a safety network of parents.

Keep a small bag packed with essentials-clothing changes, snack food (dry, nonperishable), bottled water, medications. Small means small; anything over 10 pounds is not small.

In your residence, group important papers together along with checkbooks, U.S. credit cards, some traveler's checks, a small amount of cash, and U.S. driver's licenses. Maintain a basic emergency supply of food, water, gasoline, and first-aid supplies.

Meet your neighbors. Learn the location of the nearest hospital, police station, and friendly embassy or consulate.

Remember pets; have inoculations current and arrange for a suitable home in case they must be left behind.

If Evacuated
In the event an evacuation order is given, it is crucial for parents to discuss with children what is going to happen. Even if there is very little time before a departure, talk with them about the parent who will be staying. Reassure them; explain what will take place in the evacuation. They also need to know that the same rules and routines that structured their lives during normal times will continue.

Establish a daily routine with the children as soon as possible after evacuation and relocation. Be sure to incorporate family rituals-bedtime stories, family meals, church, pancakes on Saturday morning, whatever! Accentuate any advantages of the alternate location museums, amusement park, proximity to grandma and grandpa.

Minimize separation from the remaining parent as much as possible. Try not to use day care for a while. The child's fear of abandonment will be intense for a time.

Residential Fire Safety
Although fire does not sound as dramatic as terrorism, in fact it kills far more people each year than does terrorist activity overseas. In many countries fire regulations do not exist, fire fighting equipment is antiquated, water sources are inadequate, and buildings are constructed with minimum standards.

Each year thousands of people die in home fires, half of them killed in their sleep by the toxic gases and smoke. Many who do survive spend months in hospitals and suffer lifelong physical and emotional scars.

Children are often killed because they panic and try to hide from fire under beds and in closets.

Most of this devastation can be prevented. In only a few years, the use of smoke detectors in the United States has cut in half the number of annual fire fatalities. Fire prevention education is gradually making the odds even better.

Take these basic steps to protect your family from fire, whether you are in the United States or overseas:
* Use smoke detectors in your home.
* Prepare a fire escape plan with your family.
* Conduct a fire drill at least once every six months.

Smoke Detectors
If fire occurs in your home, you may never awaken; smoke and toxic gases kill quietly and quickly. Yet you can be saved by the same smoke that can kill you-if it activates a smoke detector.

A smoke detector sounds a warning before you can even smell the smoke or see any flames. Smoke detectors should be installed, on each floor of the residence. If you have only one, place it on the ceiling outside the sleeping area.

Smoke detectors must be tested once a month and whenever you return from vacation. Never paint them. Once a year they should be vacuumed to remove any dust or cobwebs inside that would interfere with their functioning. Be sure everyone in the family recognizes the sound of the alert; test it with all members in the bedrooms with doors closed to be sure that they can hear it.

Fire Escape Plan
Since fire and smoke travel quickly, you have, at most, only minutes to escape. It is imperative that each member of the family knows what to do, automatically.

A fire escape plan is your best bet. With your family, draw a floor plan of your house marking all possible exits. Since fire could block any exit, always have an alternative way to escape. Know in advance where to go. Double check exits to be sure they open and that children can handle doors or windows by themselves.

Show all windows, doors, and outdoor features. Note escape aids such as a tree or balcony; check to ensure that they would work. Locate the nearest fire alarm box or the neighbor's house. Teach your children how to report a fire.
Designate a meeting place outside the house. You must know immediately who may be trapped inside.

Tape a copy of the floor plan by the telephone. Advise household employees and babysitters (see page 67).

Fire Drills

Practice your plan! Regular fire drills assure that everyone knows what to do. Change the imaginary situation from drill to drill. Decide where the "fire" is and what exits are blocked. When small children learn what to do by rote, they will be less likely to panic in real life situations.

Pets cannot be considered. The dangers of a fire are overwhelming, and the primary consideration is saving human lives. Often pets will escape before you do, anyway.

Fire Extinguishers

Every home should have at least one fire extinguisher and one smoke detector. Be sure that the extinguisher works and that you know how to operate it.

Portable fire extinguishers can be effective on a small, confined fire, such as a cooking fire. But if a fire is large and spreading, using an extinguisher may be unsafe; you risk the dangers of inhaling toxic smoke and having your escape route cut off.

Use a fire extinguisher only after you:
- Are sure everyone else is out of the building.
- Have called the fire department.
- Are certain you can approach the fire safely.

Use of Window Escapes

Before using a window escape, be sure that the door to the room is closed; otherwise, a draft from the open window could draw smoke and fire into the room.

Use an escape ladder or balcony if possible. If there is none, don't jump, wait for rescue as long as you can. Open a window a few inches at the top and bottom while you wait; gases will go out through the top and fresher air will enter through the bottom.

Children must know that it is all right to break a window. Discuss how to do it, using a baseball bat or a chair. Stand aside to avoid flying glass shards. Place a rug or blanket over the sill before crawling out.

Lower small children from the window. Don't leave first and expect them to follow. If they panic and refuse to jump, you will be unable to get them.

A Summary of Fire Safety Reminders

After a smoke detector warns you of a fire, you have only a few moments to escape.

Even concrete buildings are not fireproof. Virtually all the contents of your home or office will burn very quickly and produce toxic gases that can overpower you.

Sleep with bedroom doors closed. A closed door can hamper the spread of a fire, and the chances of a fire starting in a bedroom are remote.

To escape, keep low and crawl on hands and knees. A safety zone of cleaner air exists nearer the floor.

Once out, no one should be permitted to re-enter a burning house for any reason. Hold on to children who may impulsively run back inside. Children panic in fire and tend to attempt hiding as a means of escape. Train them to react correctly. As you escape, try to close every door behind you. It may slow the fire's progress.

Feel every door before you open it. If it is hot, don't open it. If it is cool, brace yourself against the door and open it slowly, checking for fire. A fire that has died down due to lack of oxygen could flare up once the door is open. If that happens, close the door immediately. Never waste time getting dressed or grabbing valuables.

If clothes catch fire, drop to the ground and roll to extinguish flames, or smother the fire with a blanket or rug. Never run. Teach children to stop, drop, and roll.

The Final Word

Fires are preventable. The major causes of home fires are:
- Carelessness with cigarettes. Never smoke in bed; poisonous gases from a smoldering mattress can kill long before there are flames. After a party, look under cushions for smoldering cigarettes.

- Faulty electrical wiring. Many homes in lesser developed countries are wired insufficiently to handle the simultaneous use of many electrical appliances. Don't overload circuits. Limit appliances plugged into the same extension cord. Major appliances should have their own heavy-duty circuit. Know where the fuse box is and instruct older children and household employees on how to shut off power in case of an electrical fire. Household current and plugs/sockets in many countries are different than in the United States. Transformers may be required to adapt U.S. appliances to the local current. Be sure your appliance, transformer, and the local current are compatible before using.

- Faulty lighting equipment. Check electrical cords

for cracks, broken plugs, poor connections. Use correct size bulbs in lamps, and be sure shades are not too close to bulbs.

- Carelessness with cooking and heating appliances. Don't leave food cooking unattended. Have heating system and fireplaces inspected professionally once a year.

- Children playing with matches. Teach children fire safety; keep matches and combustibles out of their reach.

Community Participation in Security

Safety in Numbers
As you consider the issues of safety and security, remember you are not alone. Overseas, you have the support and guidance of your company, the U.S. Embassy, colleagues, and their families. The best security results from information and support flowing between these entities.

Remember, you also have a responsibility to them. Do your part to contribute to the safety and security of the community.

What You Can Do
Keep abreast of current events, not only in the country, but internationally. Know what's going on in the country and in the world that could affect that country. Watch TV news programs, read newspapers, attend embassy security briefings periodically. It is your responsibility to keep current.

Locate yourself in relation to emergency services and places of refuge. Assist newcomers to do the same.

Other Useful Steps
- Assemble a list of telephone numbers.
- Maintain a set of local maps.
- Meet neighbors and friendly people in your neighborhood.
- Locate fire department and police stations.
- Pinpoint nearest hospitals and clinics.
- Know how to reach friendly diplomatic missions.
- Know how to get accurate information.
- Don't repeat rumors.
- Establish an I.D. system for children.
- Establish and participate in a neighborhood warden plan and a buddy system.
- Prepare and keep current a telephone notification system.
- Identify an alternative notification system in the event telephone service is lost.
- Be a good listener. Be sensitive to special needs in

your community. Single parents and employed couples may need help arranging security for their children. People who are ill, pregnant, or have new babies may have limited mobility. Elderly, dependent parents are a growing concern. Those who are isolated may need help in getting information. You can refer those with needs to the appropriate person.

Resources

Government Resources in the U.S.

Bureau of Consular Affairs, Citizens Emergency Center
Focal point of liaison between concerned families, friends and U.S. Consular posts and citizens overseas; may render assistance in the areas of passports, visas, inoculations; maintains and issues travel advisories.
Phone: (202) 647-5225 (24 hours)

Department of State Operations Center
Primary point of contact between U.S. citizens residing in the United States and American embassies and consulates overseas. Phone: (202) 647-1512 (24 hours)

Department of State Task Forces
Ad hoc groups formed to deal with civil disturbances, coups, natural disasters, etc., which occur overseas.
Phone: Contact through Department of State Operations Center

Foreign Commercial Service
Primary U.S. Government liaison with U.S. firms operating overseas.
Phone: (202) 377-5351 (6:30 a.m.-6:30 p.m. EST)

OSAC/Private Sector Liaison Staff, Department of State
Departmental point of contact for interface between Diplomatic Security and the private sector.
Phone: (703) 204-6185 (8:00-5:00 EST)

Overseas Resources

U.S. Embassy/Consulate Personnel
The Chief of Mission (with the title of Ambassador, Minister, or Charge d'Affaires) and the Deputy Chief of Mission head each U.S. diplomatic mission overseas. These officers are responsible for all components of the U.S. Mission within a country, including consular posts.

Commercial Officers, at larger posts, represent U.S. commercial interests within their country of assignment.

They specialize in U.S. export promotion and will provide assistance to American business in furtherance of that effort. Economic/Commercial Officers fulfill these functions at smaller posts. Consular Officers extend the protection of the U.S. Government to U.S. citizens and their property abroad. They maintain lists of local attorneys, act as liaison with police and other officials, and have the authority to notarize documents. Business representatives residing overseas should register with the Consular Officer. In troubled areas, even travelers are advised to register.

Regional Security Officers are responsible for providing physical, procedural, and personal security services to U.S. diplomatic facilities and personnel. Their responsibilities extend to providing incountry security briefings and threat assessments to business executives.

Publications
The Department of State publication Key Officers of Foreign Service Posts; Guide for Business Representatives contains essential information pertaining to telephone numbers, FAX numbers, addresses, and assigned personnel for all U.S. diplomatic posts abroad. It is available for a small price from the Superintendent of Documents, U.S. Government Printing Office, Washington, D.C. 20402.

Under the aegis of the State Department, current OSAC publications include the following:

"Security Guidelines for American Families Living Abroad"
"Security Guidelines for American Enterprises Abroad"
"Emergency Planning Guidelines for American Businesses Abroad"

These are available, as supplies last, through the Overseas Security Advisory Council, Bureau of Diplomatic Security, U.S. Department of State. Additional copies of some OSAC publications are also available at the U.S. Government Printing Office

Conclusion
Although this booklet contains many tips for successful travel and residence abroad, it is by no means all inclusive. Additional information is available from a variety of sources, ranging from travel brochures, magazines, and books, to conversations with persons who have lived or traveled to your assigned country.

You can never know too much about what you're getting into. Prior organization and preparation will significantly reduce your anxieties, lessen the shock of adjustment, and enable you to settle in with relative ease to a safe and enjoyable experience abroad.

Chapter 7

Know Before You Go: U.S. Customs Hints for Returning Residents

[The information in this chapter is reprinted verbatim from a bulletin issued by the Department of the Treasury, U.S. Customs Service. It is intended to serve as advice to Americans traveling abroad.]

- - - -

On behalf of U.S. Customs, let me wish you a wonderful trip. We know you will be anxious to reach your destination upon your return, so we want to do everything we can to facilitate your entry into the United States. You are our customers, and we hope to serve you well by making your Customs clearance as pleasant and unobtrusive as possible.

I hope this booklet will help you understand our mission to protect your interests. Please read it carefully and don't hesitate to contact us if there is anything you would like clarified.

With your help, we can protect our borders and the interests of all citizens of this great nation. The Customs Service has an effect on nearly every aspect of American life. We protect industry, trademarks, and products; interdict illicit drugs; support the American farmer and the environment by guarding against contaminated products and foodstuffs; and for every dollar provided to this agency, we return approximately $20 directly to the U.S. Treasury.

I am proud of this agency's heritage and its continued commitment to serving and protecting you. If you have any suggestions, questions, or problems with the Customs Service, do not hesitate to contact me: Commissioner, U.S. Customs Service, 1301 Constitution Avenue, NW, Washington, D.C. 20229. I will be glad to hear from you.
Thank you for your support.

GEORGE J. WEISE
Commissioner
U.S. Customs Service

Your Declaration

You must declare all articles acquired abroad and in session at the time of your return. This includes:

- Articles that you purchased.

- Gifts presented to you while abroad, such as wedding or birthday presents.

- Articles purchased in duty-free shops.

- Repairs or alterations made to any articles taken abroad and returned, whether or not repairs or alterations were free of charge.

- Items you have been requested to bring home for another person.

- Any articles you intend to sell or use in your business.

In addition, you must declare any articles acquired in the U.S. Virgin Islands, American Samoa, or Guam and not accompanying you at the time of your return.

The price actually paid for each article must be stated on your declaration in U.S. currency or its equivalent in country of acquisition. If the article was not purchased, obtain an estimate of its fair retail value in the country in which it was acquired.

Note: The wearing or use of any article acquired abroad does not exempt it from duty. It must be declared at the price you paid for it. The Customs officer will make an appropriate reduction in its value for significant wear and use.

Oral Declaration

Customs declaration forms are distributed on vessels and planes and should be prepared in advance of arrival for presentation to the Immigration and Customs inspectors. Fill out the identification portion of the declaration form. You may declare orally to the Customs inspector the articles you acquired abroad if the articles are accompanying you and you have not exceeded the duty-free exemption allowed (see pages 74-75). A Customs officer may, however, ask you to prepare a written list if it is necessary.

73

Written Declaration

A written declaration will be necessary when:

- The total fair retail value of articles acquired abroad exceeds your personal exemption (see pages 74-75).

- More than one liter (33.8 fl. oz.) of alcoholic beverages, 200 cigarettes (one carton), or 100 cigars are included.

- Some of the items are not intended for your personal or household use, such as commercial samples, items for sale or use in your business, or articles you are bringing home for another person.

- Articles acquired in the U.S. Virgin Islands, American Samoa, or Guam are being sent to the U.S.

- A customs duty or internal revenue tax is collectible on any article in your possession.

- A Customs officer requests a written list.

- If you have used your exemption in the last 30 days.

Family Declaration

The head of a family may make a joint declaration for all members residing in the same household and returning together to the United States. Family members making a joint declaration may combine their personal exemptions (see pages 74-75), even if the articles acquired by one member of the family exceeds the personal exemption allowed.

Infants and children returning to the United States are entitled to the same exemptions as adults (except for alcoholic beverages). Children born abroad, who have never resided in the United States, are entitled to the customs exemptions granted nonresidents.

Visitors to the United States should obtain the leaflet *Customs Hints for Visitors* (Nonresidents).

Military and civilian personnel of the U.S. Government should obtain the leaflet *Customs Highlights for Government Personnel* for information about their customs exemptions when returning from an extended duty assignment abroad.

warning!

If you understate the value of an article you declare, or if you otherwise misrepresent an article in your declaration, you may have to pay a penalty in addition to payment of duty. Under certain circumstances, the article could be seized and forfeited if the penalty is not paid.

It is well known that some merchants abroad offer travelers invoices or bills of sale showing false or understated values. This practice not only delays your customs examination, but can prove very costly.

If you fail to declare an article acquired abroad, not only is the article subject to seizure and forfeiture, but you will be liable for a personal penalty in an amount equal to the value of the article in the United States. In addition, you may also be liable to criminal prosecution.

Don't rely on advice given by persons outside the Customs Service. It may be bad advice which could lead you to violate the customs laws and incur costly penalties.

If in doubt about whether an article should be declared, always declare it first and then direct your question to the Customs inspector. If in doubt about the value of an article, declare the article at the actual price paid (transaction value).

Customs inspectors handle tourist items day after day and become acquainted with the normal foreign values. Moreover, current commercial prices of foreign items are available at all times and on-the-spot comparisons of these values can be made.

Play It safe-avoid customs penalties

Your Exemptions

In clearing U.S. Customs, a traveler is considered either a "returning resident of the United States" or a "nonresident."

Generally speaking, if you leave the United States for purposes of traveling, working or studying abroad and return to resume residency in the United States, you are considered a returning resident by Customs.

However, U.S. residents living abroad temporarily are entitled to be classified as nonresidents, and thus receive more liberal Customs exemptions, on short visits to the United States, provided they export any foreign-acquired items at the completion of their visit.

Residents of American Samoa, Guam, or the U.S. Virgin Islands, who are American citizens, are also considered as returning U.S. residents.

Articles acquired abroad and brought into the United States are subject to applicable duty and internal revenue tax, but as a returning resident you are allowed certain exemptions from paying duty on items obtained while abroad.

$400 Exemption

Articles totaling $400 (based on the fair retail value of each item in the country where acquired) may be entered free of duty, subject to the limitations on liquors, cigarettes, and cigars, if:

- Articles were acquired as an incident of your trip for your personal or household use.

- You bring the articles with you at the time of your return to the United States and they are properly declared to Customs. *Articles purchased and left for alterations or other reasons cannot be applied to your $400 exemption when shipped to follow at a later date. The 10% flat rate of duty does not apply to mailed articles (See page 85). Duty is assessed when received.*

- You are returning from a stay abroad of at least 48 hours. Example: A resident who leaves United States territory at 1:30 p.m. on June 1st would complete the required 48-hour period at 1:30 p.m. on June 3rd. This time limitation does not apply if you are returning from Mexico or the Virgin Islands of the U.S.

- You have not used this $400 exemption, or any part of it, within the preceding 30-day period. Also, your exemption is not cumulative. If you use a portion of your exemption on entering the United States, then you must wait for 30 days before you are entitled to another exemption other than a $25 exemption. (See details below.)

- Articles are not prohibited or restricted. See page 80.

Cigars and Cigarettes: Not more than 100 cigars and 200 cigarettes (one carton) may be included in your exemption. Products of Cuban tobacco may be included if purchased in Cuba. This exemption is available to each person regardless of age. Your cigarettes, however, may be subject to a tax imposed by state and local authorities.

Liquor: One liter (33.8 fl. oz.) of alcoholic beverages may be included in this exemption if:

- You are 21 years of age or older.
- It is for your own use or for use as a gift.
- It is not in violation of the laws of the state in which you arrive.

Note: Most states restrict the quantity of alcoholic beverages you may import, and you must meet state alcoholic beverage laws in addition to federal ones. If the state in which you arrive permits less liquor than you have legally brought into the United States, that state's laws prevail.

Information about state restrictions and taxes should be obtained from the state government as laws vary from state to state.

Alcoholic beverages in excess of the one-liter limitation are subject to duty and Internal revenue tax.

Shipping of alcoholic beverages by mail is prohibited by United States postal laws. Alcoholic beverages include wine and beer as well as distilled spirits.

$600 and $1200 Exemptions

If you return directly or indirectly from a U.S. insular possession-American Samoa, Guam, or the U.S. Virgin Islands-you may receive a customs exemption of $1200 (based upon the transaction value of the articles in the country where acquired). You may also bring in 1,000 cigarettes, but only 200 of them may have been acquired elsewhere.

If you are returning from any of the following 24 beneficiary countries, your customs exemption is $600, based upon fair market value:

Antigua and Grenada
Panama
Barbuda
Guatemala
St.Christopher/Kitts and Nevis
Aruba
Guyana
Bahamas
Haiti
Saint Lucia
Barbados
Honduras
Saint Vincent and the Grenadines
Belize
Jamaica
Costa Rica
Montserrat
Trinidad and Tobago
Dominica
Virgin Islands, British
Netherlands Antilles
Dominican Rep.
El Salvador
Nicaragua

75

In the case of the $1200 exemption, up to $600 worth of the merchandise may have been obtained in any of the beneficiary countries listed above, or up to $400 in any other country. For example, if you traveled to the U.S. Virgin Islands and Jamaica and then returned home, you would be entitled to bring in $1200 worth of merchandise duty-free. Of this amount, $600 worth may have been acquired in Jamaica.

In the case of the $600 exemption, up to $400 worth of merchandise may have been acquired in other foreign countries. For instance, if you travel to England and the Bahamas, and then return home, your exemption is $600, $400 of which may have been acquired in England.

$25 Exemption

If you cannot claim the $400, $600, or $1200 exemptions, because of the 30-day or 48-hour minimum limitations, you may bring in free of duty and tax articles acquired abroad for your personal or household use if the total fair retail value does not exceed $25. This is an individual exemption and may not be grouped with other members of a family on one customs declaration.

You may include any of the following: 50 cigarettes, 10 cigars, 150 milliliters (4 fl. oz.) of alcoholic beverages, or 150 milliliters (4 fl. oz.) of alcoholic perfume. Cuban tobacco products brought directly from Cuba may be included. Alcoholic beverages cannot be mailed into the United States. Customs enforces the liquor laws of the state in which you arrive. Because state laws vary greatly as to the quantity of alcoholic beverages which can be brought in, we suggest you consult the appropriate state authorities.

If any article brought with you is subject to duty or tax, or if the total value of all dutiable articles exceeds $25, no article may be exempted from duty or tax.

Gifts

Bona fide gifts of not more than $50 in fair retail value where shipped can be received by friends and relations in the United States free of duty and tax, if the same person does not receive more than $50 in gift shipments in one day. The "day" in reference is the day in which the parcel(s) are received for customs processing. This amount is increased to $100 if shipped from the U.S. Virgin islands, American Samoa, or Guam. You do not declare these upon your return to the States.

NOTE: Gift exemption of $50 per day will increase to $200 per day on July 28, 1994.

Gifts accompanying you are considered to be for your personal use and may be included within your exemption. This includes gifts given to you by others while abroad and those you intend to give to others after you return. Gifts intended for business, promotional or other commercial purposes may not be included.

Perfume containing alcohol valued at more than $5 retail, tobacco products, and alcoholic beverages are excluded from the gift provision.

Gifts intended for more than one person may be consolidated in the same package provided they are individually wrapped and labeled with the name of the recipient.

Be sure that the outer wrapping of the package is marked 1) unsolicited gift, 2) nature of the gift, and 3) its fair retail value. In addition, a consolidated gift parcel should be marked as such on the outside with the names of the recipients listed and the value of each gift. This will facilitate customs clearance of your package.

If any article imported in the gift parcel is subject to duty and tax, or if the total value of all articles exceeds the bona fide gift allowance, no article may be exempt from duty or tax.

If a parcel is subject to duty, the United States Postal Service will collect the duty plus a handling charge in the form of "Postage Due" stamps. Duty cannot be prepaid.

You, as a traveler, cannot send a "gift" parcel to yourself nor can persons traveling together send "gifts" to each other. Gifts ordered by mail from the United States do not qualify under this duty-free gift provision and are subject to duty.

Other Articles: free of duty or dutiable

Duty preferences are granted to certain developing countries under the Generalized System of Preferences (GSP). Some products from these countries have been exempted from duty which would otherwise be collected if imported from any other country. For details, obtain the leaflet *GSP & The Traveler*[2] from your nearest Customs office. Many products of certain Caribbean and Andean countries are also exempt from duty under the Caribbean Basin Initiative and Andean Trade Preference Act. Most products of Israel may enter the United States either free of duty or at a reduced duty rate. Check with customs.

The North American Free Trade Agreement was

implemented on January 1, 1994. U.S. returning residents arriving directly or indirectly from Canada or Mexico are eligible for free or reduced duty rates as applicable, on goods originating in Canada or Mexico as defined in the Agreement.

Personal belongings of United States origin are entitled to entry free of duty. Personal belongings taken abroad, such as worn clothing, etc., may be sent home by mail before you return and receive free entry provided they have not been altered or repaired while abroad. These packages should be marked *"American Goods Returned."* When a claim of United States origin is made, marking on the article to so indicate facilitates customs processing.

Foreign made personal article taken abroad are dutiable each time they are brought into our country unless you have acceptable proof of prior possession. Documents which fully describe the article, such as a bill of sale, insurance policy, jeweler's appraisal, or receipt for purchase, may be considered reasonable proof of prior possession.

Items such as watches, cameras, tape recorders, or other articles which may be readily identified by serial number or permanently affixed markings, may be taken to the Customs office nearest you and registered before your departure. The Certificate of Registration provided will expedite free entry of these items when you return. Keep the certificate as it is valid

for any future trips as long as the information on it remains legible.

Registration cannot be accomplished by telephone nor can blank registration forms be given or mailed to you to be filled out at a later time.

Automobiles, boats, planes, etc., or other vehicles taken abroad for noncommercial use may be returned duty free by proving to the Customs officer that you took them out of the United States. This proof may be the state registration card for an automobile, the Federal Aviation Administration certificate for an aircraft, a yacht license or motorboat identification certificate for a pleasure boat, or a customs certificate of registration obtained before departure.

Dutiable repairs or accessories acquired abroad for articles taken out of the United States must be declared on your return.

Warning: Catalytic-equipped vehicles (1976 or later model years) driven outside the United States, Canada, or Mexico will not, in most cases, meet EPA standards

when brought back to the U.S. As unleaded fuel generally is not available in other countries, the catalytic converter will become inoperative and must be replaced. Contact Environmental Protection Agency, Washington, D.C. 20460, for details and exceptions. (See page 81.)

Your local Customs office has the following leaflets which will be of interest-*Importing a Car and Pleasure Boats[3]*. You may purchase *Customs Guide for Private Flyers* from your local Government Printing Office bookstore. Consult your local telephone book under "U.S. Government."

Household effects and tools of trade or occupation which you take out of the United States are duty free at the time you return if properly declared and entered.

All furniture, carpets, paintings, tableware, linens, and similar household furnishings acquired abroad may be imported free of duty, if:

- They are not imported for another person or for sale.

- They have been used abroad by you for not less than one year or were available for use in a household in which you were resident member for one year. This privilege does not include articles placed in storage outside the home. The year of use need not be continuous nor does it need to be the year immediately preceding the date of importation. Shipping time may not be included when you compute the "one year of use". For information on freight shipments, see page 85.

Items such as wearing apparel, jewelry, photograph equipment, tape recorders, stereo components, and vehicles are considered as personal articles and cannot be passed free of duty as household effects.

Articles imported in excess of your customs exemption will be subject to duty unless the items are entitled to free entry or prohibited.

The inspector will place the items having the highest rate of duty under your exemption, and duty will be assessed on the lower-rated items.

After deducting your exemptions and the value of any articles duty free, a flat 10% rate of duty will be applied to the next $1,000 worth (fair retail value) of merchandise. Any dollar amount of an article or articles over $1,000 will be dutiable at the various rates of duty applicable to the articles.

Articles to which the flat rate of duty is applied must be for your personal use or for use as gifts and you cannot receive this flat rate provision more than once every 30 days, excluding the day of your last arrival.

The flat rate of duty is 5% for articles purchased in the U.S. Virgin Islands, American Samoa, or Guam, whether the articles accompany you or are shipped.

Example: You acquire goods valued at $2,500 from:

U.S. insular possessions:

Personal exemption (free of duty) . .up to $1,200
Flat duty rate at 5%. . . . . next $1,000 Various rates of duty.. . .remaining $300
Total $2,500

Caribbean Basin Economic Recovery or Andean Tract Act countries:

Personal exemption (free of duty). . up to $600
Flat duty rate at 10% . . . . . . next $1,000
Various rates of duty .. . .remaining $900
Total $2,500
Other countries or locations:
Personal exemption (free of duty) .. .up to $400
Flat duty rate at 10%.. . . . next $1,000
Various rates of duty . . .remaining $1,100
Total $2,500

The flat rate of duty will apply to any articles which are dutiable and cannot be included in your personal exemption, even if you have not exceeded the dollar amount of your exemption. Example: you are returning from Europe with $200 worth of articles which includes 2 liters of liquor. One liter will be free of duty under your exemption, the other dutiable at 10%, plus any internal revenue tax.

Members of a family residing in one household traveling together on their return to the U.S. will group articles for application of the flat duty rate no matter which member of the family may be the owner of the articles.

Payment of duty, required at the time of your arrival on articles accompanying you, may be made by any of the following ways:

- U.S. currency (foreign currency is not acceptable).

- Personal check in the exact amount of duty, drawn on a national or state bank or trust company of the United States, made payable to

the "U.S. Customs Service."

- Government check, money orders or traveler's checks are acceptable if they do not exceed the amount of the duty by more than $50. [Second endorsements are not acceptable. Identification must be presented; e.g. traveler's passport or driver's license].

- In some locations you may pay duty with credit cards from Discover, Mastercard and VISA.

Goods covered by an ATA Carnet: Residents returning to the U.S. with goods covered by an ATA carnet are reminded to report to a Customs inspector upon their arrival. The inspector will examine the covered goods against the carnet and certify the appropriate reimportation counterfoil and voucher. The carnet will serve as the customs control registration document and no entry or payment of duty will be necessary as long as the goods qualify as U.S. goods returned and are being brought back into the United States within the validity period of the carnet.

Rates of Duty

Various rates of duty for some of the more popular items imported by tourists are provided for use as an advisory guide only. If you have dutiable articles not subject to a flat rate of duty, the Customs officer examining your baggage will determine the rates of duty.

Rates of duty on imported goods are provided for in the Harmonized Tariff Schedule of the United States. There are two duty rates for each item, known as "column 1" and "column 2". Column 1 rates are those applicable to most favored nations. Column 2 rates are higher and apply to products from the following countries: Afghanistan, Azerbaijan, Cuba*, Kampuchea, Laos, North Korea*, Vietnam.
*(*Goods from, or products of these countries are subject to foreign asets controls)*

NOTE: The tariff duty status accorded these countries is subject to change. Please check with customs for updated information.

Products of the above-listed column 2 countries are dutiable at the column 2 rates of duty, even if purchased in or sent from another country. Example: A crystal vase made in Azerbaijan and purchased in Switzerland would be dutiable at the column 2 rate. If the article accompanies you, however, it may be entered under your duty-free personal exemption or the flat rate of duty allowance.

*Goods from, or products of, these countries are subject to foreign assets controls, see page 83.

ALCOHOLIC BEVERAGES

(Subject to federal excise taxes, which greatly exceed Customs duties. These taxes vary from approximately 15 cents per liter for beer to more than $3.50 per proof liter for distilled spirits, liquors, and cordials.)

Distilled Spirits
per proof liter

Brandy	10.6cents to 89.8cents
Gin	13.2cents
Liqueurs	13.2cents
Rum	37cents
Tequila	33cents to 60cents
Vodka	13.2cents to 67.6cents
Scotch	5.3cents
Other whiskeys	6.6cents

Wine per liter
(33.814 fluid ounces)

Sparkling	30.9cents
Still	8.3cents to 26.4cents
Beer	1.6cents

ANTIQUES produced prior to 100 years before date of entry are admitted duty-free. Get proof of antiquity obtained from seller.

	Free

AUTOMOBILES

Passenger	2.5%

BAGS

Hand, leather	5.3% to 10%

BEADS

Glass beads	4.7%
imitation precious and	
semi-precious stone (not glass)	2.8%
Ivory*	4.7%

BINOCULARS (PRISM),
OPERA AND FIELD GLASSES   Free

BOOKS   Free

CAMERAS

Motion picture	4.5%	
Still, over $10 each		3.0%
Cases * *, leather		8%
Lenses, mounted		6.6%

CANDY

Sweetened chocolate bars	5.0%
Other	7.0%

CHESS SETS   4.64%

CHINA, other than tableware

Bone	6.6%
Non-bone	2.5% to 9%

CHINA TABLEWARE

Bone	8%
Non-bone, valued up to $56 per set	26%
Non-bone, valued more than $56 per set	8%

CIGARETTE LIGHTERS

Pocket	7.2% to 10%
Table	4.8%

CLOCKS

Valued over $5 each	45cents + 6.4%

CRYSTAL   6% to 20%

DOLLS

Stuffed	Check with
Customs	
Other	12%

DRAWINGS

Done-by-hand	Free

FIGURINES, china   9%
(By professional
sculptor)   3.1%

FILM

Unexposed	3.7%
Exposed	Free

** *Cases imported with camera are classifiable with the camera*

* *Ivory beads made from elephant ivory are prohibited. See page 84.*

FUR*

Wearing apparel	5.8%
Other	3.4%

FURNITURE

Wood chairs	3.4% to 5.3%
Wood furniture other than chairs	2.5%
Bentwood	6.6%

GOLF BALLS	2.4%
GLOVES	
Fur	5.8%
Horsehide or	
cowhide	14%
HANDKERCHIEFS,	
linen, hemmed	10.7%
IVORY*, manufactured	4.2%

Note: May be prohibited. See page 84, Wildlife and Fish.

JADE AND OTHER SEMI-PRECIOUS STONES
    Cut, but not set,

suitable for jewelry	2.1%

    Other articles of jade or semi-precious stone   21%

JEWELRY, precious metal
    Silver chief value, valued

not over $18 a doz.	27.5%
Other	6 . 5 %
LEATHER	
Flatgoods, wallets	4.7% to 8%
Other manufactures of	Free to 5.6%
MUSIC BOXES	3.2%

PAINTINGS, done
    entirely by hand   Free

PEARLS
    Loose or temporarily strung without clasp:

Natural	Free
Cultured	2.1%
Imitation	8%

    Permanently strung or temporarily strung, with clasp attached or separate
    . .   6.5% to 11%

PERFUME**	5%
POSTAGE STAMPS	Free
PRINTED MATTER	Free to 5.3%
RADIOS, solid state	
radio receivers	6%
RECORDS (PHONOGRAPH)	3.7%

    May be prohibited. See p. 81, Wildlife and Fish.
    **Subject to federal excise tax of $3.566322 per liter.*

SHAVERS, ELECTRIC	4.4%
SHELL ARTICLES*	3.4%
SHOES, Leather	2.5% to 20%
SKIS AND SKI EQUIPMENT	3.5% to 5.5%
SOUND RECORDINGS	Free
STONES, Cut but not set Diamonds	Free
Others	Free to 21%
SWEATERS-wool	7.5% to 17%
TAPE RECORDERS	3.7% to 4.9%
TOYS	Free to 68%

WATCHES
    Mechanical type (depending on jewels) plus

Gold case	6.25%
Gold bracelet	14%
Digital type	3.9%

WEARING APPAREL

Cotton, not knit	3% to 32%
Cotton, knit	7.9% to 21%
Linen, not knit	3% to 12%
Manmade fiber, knit	16.2% to 34.6%
Manmade fiber, not	
knit	7.6% to 52.9cents/Kg. + 21%
Silk, not knit	3% to 7.5%
Wool, knit	6% to 77.2cts/Kg.
. .	+ 20%
Wool, not knit	9.8% to 30.4%

WOOD, CARVINGS AND
ARTICLES OF   5.1%

    May be prohibited. See p. 81, Wildlife and Fish.

NOTE: Duty rates are subject to change without notice by statute. For further information call your nearest Customs District office.

Prohibited and Restricted Articles

Because Customs inspectors are stationed at ports of entry and along our land and sea borders, they are often called upon to enforce laws and requirements of other Government agencies. For example, the Department of Agriculture is responsible for preventing the entry of injurious pest, plant, and animal diseases into the United States. The Customs officer cannot ignore the

80

Agriculture requirements-the risk of costly damage to our crops, poultry and livestock industry is too great.

Certain articles considered injurious or detrimental to the general welfare of the United States are prohibited entry by law. *Among these are absinthe, liquor-filled candy (where prohibited by state law), lottery tickets, narcotics and dangerous drugs, obscene articles and publications, seditious and treasonable materials, hazardous articles (e.g., fireworks, dangerous toys, toxic or poisonous substances), and switch-blade knives (however, a one-armed person may import a switchblade knife for personal use.)*

Other items must meet special requirements before they can be released. You will be given a receipt for any articles retained by Customs.

Automobiles

Automobiles imported into the United States must conform to Environmental Protection Agency (EPA) emission standards and Department of Transportation (DOT) safety, bumper and theft prevention standards.

Automobiles that do not meet EPA emission standards can only be imported by holders of conformity certificates from EPA. These certificate holders are known as independent Commercial Importers (ICI). Individuals contemplating purchasing a nonconforming vehicle should first make arrangements with an ICI for importing and modifying the vehicle to U.S. specifications.

All motor vehicles less than 25 years old (including trailers and motorcycles of all sizes) must comply with all applicable Federal motor vehicle safety standards of the DOT. In addition, passenger cars must comply with bumper and theft prevention standards as applicable. If your vehicle does not bear conformity certification label permanently affixed by the original manufacturer, you will have to obtain a contract with a Registered Importer and a DOT bond of one and one-half times its entered value in order to complete the US Customs entry. If the model and model year of your vehicle have not been determined to be eligible for importation prior to entry, your Registered Importer must petition such eligibility in addition to the other DOT requirements.

Prospective purchasers should be aware that almost all automobiles purchased overseas are not manufactured to comply with U.S. standards and will require modification. Vehicles imported conditionally to be modified to U.S. specifications, and not modified, or not modified acceptably, must either be exported or destroyed under Customs supervision.

Also, vehicles that were originally manufactured to meet EPA emission requirements may, depending upon what countries the car was driven in, be subject to additional EPA requirements or require a bond upon entry. You are advised to call the EPA for further assistance.

Information on importing vehicles may be obtained from the Environmental Protection Agency Attn: 6405J, Washington, D.C. 20460, telephone (202) 233-9660, and the Department of Transportation, Office of Vehicle Safety Compliance (NEF 32), Washington, D.C. 20590. Copies of the Customs pamphlet *Importing a Car* and EPA's *Automotive Imports Factsheet* and may be obtained by writing, respectively, the U.S. Customs Service, P.O. Box 7407, Washington, D.C. 20044, or the Environmental Protection Agency, Washington, D.C. 20460.

Biological Materials

Biological materials of public health or veterinary importance (disease organisms and vectors for research and educational purposes) require import permits. Write to the Foreign Quarantine Program, U.S. Public Health Service, Center for Disease Control, Atlanta, Ga. 30333.

Books, Records, Computer Programs and Cassettes

Pirated copies of copyrighted articles-unlawfully made articles produced without the authorization of the copyright owner-are prohibited from importation into the United States. Pirated copies will be seized and destroyed, unless the importer can demonstrate that he had no reasonable grounds for believing his actions violated the law. Then, they may only be returned to the country of export.

Ceramic Tableware

Some ceramic tableware sold abroad contains dangerous levels of lead in the glaze that can leach into certain foods and beverages served in them. The Food and Drug Administration recommends that ceramic tableware, especially when purchased in Mexico, Hong Kong or India, be tested for lead release on your return or be used for decorative purposes only.

Cultural Property (Objects/Artifacts)

U.S. law prohibits the importation of pre-Columbian monumental and architectural sculpture and murals from Mexico and from certain countries in Central and South America. These importations are prohibited no matter where the artifacts are shipped from, be it the country of origin or elsewhere.

Federal law and international treaties prohibit the importation of any articles of stolen cultural property from museums, religious, or secular public monuments. Would-be buyers of such property should be aware that, unlike purchases of customary tourist merchandise, purchases of cultural objects do not confer ownership should such an object be found to be stolen.

Imports of certain archeological and ethnographic material (e.g., masks or textiles) from Bolivia, El Salvador, Guatemala, Peru, and Mali are restricted and require export certificates from the country of origin. Purveyors of such merchandise have been known to offer phony export certificates, and again, prospective buyers should be aware that Customs inspectors are expert at spotting fraudulent export certificates that accompany cultural property. Additional restrictions are expected to be imposed on material from countries in Europe, Asia, Africa, and Central America. These restrictions are aimed at providing international access to cultural objects to all members of the public for legitimate scientific, cultural, and educational purposes. For more information, contact the United States Information Agency, Washington, D.C., (202) 619-6612.

Drug Paraphernalia
The importation, exportation, manufacture, sale, and transportation of drug paraphernalia are prohibited. Persons convicted of these offenses are subject to fines and imprisonment. As importations contrary to law, drug paraphernalia may be seized by U.S. Customs.

Firearms and Ammunition
Firearms and ammunition are subject to restrictions and import permits approved by the Bureau of Alcohol, Tobacco and Firearms (ATF). Applications to import may be made only by or through a licensed importer, dealer, or manufacturer. Weapons, ammunition, or other devices prohibited by the National Firearms Act will not be admitted into the United States unless specifically authorized by ATF.

No import permit is required when it is proven that the firearms or ammunition were previously taken out of the United States by the person who is returning with such firearms or ammunition. To facilitate reentry, persons may have them registered before departing from the United States at any Customs office or ATF field office. Exports are subject to export licensing requirements of the Office of Defence Trade Controls, Department of State, Washington, D.C. 20520, (202) 927-8320).

For further information, contact the Bureau of Alcohol, Tobacco and Firearms, Department of the Treasury, Washington, D.C. 20226.

Residents of the United States carrying firearms or ammunition with them to other countries should consult in advance the customs officials or the respective embassies of those countries as to their regulations.

Food Products

Bakery items and all cured cheeses are admissible. The USDA Animal and Plant Health Inspection Service leaflet, *Travelers' Tips,*[4] provides detailed information on bringing food, plant, and animal products into the U.S.[3] Imported foods are also subject to requirements of the Food and Drug Administration.

Fruits and Vegetables
Most fruits and vegetables are either prohibited from entering the country or require an import permit. Every fruit or vegetable must be declared to the Customs officer and must be presented for inspection, no matter how free of pests it appears to be. Most canned or processed items are admissible.

Applications for import permits or requests for information should be addressed to Quarantines, USDA-APHIS-PPQ, Federal Bldg., Hyattsville, Md. 20782, or ccall (301) 436-8645.

Gold
Gold coins, medals, and bullion, formerly prohibited, may be brought into the U.S.However, under regulations administered by the office of Foreign Assets Control, such items originating or bought from Cuba, Haiti, Iran, Iraq, Libya, North Korea, and Yugoslavia (Serbia and Montenegro) are prohibited entry. Copies of gold coins are prohibited if not properly marked by country of issuance.

Meats, Livestock, Poultry
Meats, livestock, poultry, and their by-products (such as sausage, pate), are either prohibited or restricted from entering the United States, depending on the animal disease condition in country of origin. Fresh meat is generally prohibited from most countries. Canned meat is permitted if the inspector can determine that it is commercially canned, cooked in the container, hermetically sealed, and can be kept without refrigeration. Other canned, cured, or dried meat is severely restricted from most countries.

All prohibited importations will be seized and destroyed unless the importer returns them immediately to their country of origin.

You should contact USDA-APHIS-PPQ, Federal Building, 6505 Belcrest Road, Hyattsville, Maryland 20782, for detailed requirements or call (301)

436-7885.

Medicine/Narcotics

Narcotics and dangerous drugs, including anabolic steroids, are prohibited entry and there are severe penalties if imported. A traveler requiring medicines containing habit-forming drugs or narcotics (e.g., cough medicines, diuretics, heart drugs, tranquilizers, sleeping pills, depressants, stimulants, etc.) should:

● Have all drugs, medicinals, and similar products properly identified;

● Carry only such quantity as might normally be carried by an individual having some sort of health problem;

● Have either a prescription or written statement from your personal physician that the medicinals are being used under a doctor's direction and are necessary for your physical well-being while traveling.

Warning

The Food and Drug Administration prohibits the importation, by mail or in person, of fraudulent prescription and non-prescription drugs and medical devices. These may include unorthodox "cures" for medical conditions including cancer, AIDS, and multiple sclerosis. While these drugs and devices may be completely legal elsewhere, they may not have been approved for use in the United States, even under a prescription issued by a foreign physician. They may not legally enter the United States and may be confiscated should they be sent through the mail.

For additional information, contact your nearest FDA office or write:

Food and Drug Administration
Division of Import Operations and Policy Unit,
Room 12-8 (HFC-170)
5600 Fishers Lane
Rockville, MD 20857

Merchandise

The importation of merchandise or goods that contain components from the following countries is generally prohibited under regulations administered by the Office of Foreign Assets Control: Cambodia, Cuba, Iran, Iraq, Haiti, Libya, North Korea, and Yugoslavia (Serbia and Montenegro). Importation of all merchandise produced, grown, manufactured, marketed, or exported by any public or quasi-governmental South African agency is prohibited. In addition, agricultural commodities, derivatives, and articles suitable for human consumption, textiles, gold, and Krugerrands from South Africa are also prohibited imports.

These prescriptions do not apply to informational materials such as pamphlets, books, tapes, films, or recordings.

Specific licenses from Office of Foreign Assets Control are required to bring prohibited merchandise into the United States; but they are rarely granted. Foreign visitors to the United States, may be permitted to bring in small articles for personal use as accompanied baggage, depending upon the goods' country of origin. A limited number of specific licenses are being issued for articles assembled or processed in Haiti using parts or materials previously exported from the United States.

Travelers should be aware that there are severe restrictions on travel and transportation transactions involving Libya and Iraq. Spending money on travel-related transactions involving Cuba and North Korea is also closely controlled and monitored. Because of the strict enforcement of prohibitions, anyone considering travel to any of the countries listed above should contact the Office of Foreign Assets Control, Department of the Treasury, 1500 Pennsylvania Avenue, N.W., Washington, Washington D.C. 20220 or call 202/622-2500.

Money and Other Monetary Instruments

There is no limitation in terms of total amount of monetary instruments which may be brought into or taken out of the United States nor is it illegal to do so. However, if you transport or cause to be transported (including by mail or other means) more than $10,000 in monetary instruments on any occasion into or out of the United States, or if you receive more than that amount, you must file a report (Customs Form 4790) with U.S. Customs (Currency & Foreign Transactions Reporting Act, 31 U.S.C. 1101, et seq.). Failure to comply can result in civil and criminal penalties. Monetary instruments include U.S. or foreign coin in current circulation, currency, traveler's checks in any form, money orders, and negotiable instruments or investment securities in bearer form.

Pets

There are controls, restrictions, and prohibitions on entry of animals, birds, turtles, wildlife, and endangered species. Cats and dogs must be free of evidence of diseases communicable to man. Vaccination against rabies is not required for cats or dogs arriving from rabies-free countries. Personally owned pet birds may be entered (limit of two if of the psittacine family), but APHIS and Public Health Service requirements must be met, including quarantine at any APHIS facility at specified locations, at the owner's expense. Advance reservations are required. Non-human primates, such as monkeys, apes and similar animals, may not be imported. If you plan to take your pet abroad or import one on your return, obtain a copy of the leaflet, *Pets, Wildlife, U.S. Customs.*[5]

You should check with state, county and municipal authorities about any restrictions and prohibitions they may have before importing a pet.

Plants

Plants, cuttings, seeds, unprocessed plant products and certain endangered species either require an import permit or are prohibited from entering the United States. Endangered or threatened species of plants and plant products, if importation is not prohibited, will require an export permit from the country of origin. Every single plant or plant product must be declared to the Customs officer and must be presented for inspection, no matter how free of pests it appears to be. Applications for import permits or requests for information should be addressed to: Quarantines, USDA-APHIS-PPQ, Federal Building, 6505 Belcrest Road, Hyattsville, MD. 20782. (303) 436-8645.

Textiles

Textile and apparel items which accompany you and which you have acquired abroad for personal use or as gifts are generally not subject to quantitative restrictions. However, unaccompanied textile and apparel items may be subject to certain quantitative restrictions (quotas) which require a document called a "visa" or "export license" or exempt certificate as appropriate from the country of production. Check with Customs before you depart on your trip.

Trademarked Articles

Foreign-made trademarked articles may be limited as to the quantity which may be brought into the United States if the registered trademark has been recorded with Customs by an American trademark owner.

The types of articles usually of interest to tourists are 1) lenses, cameras, binoculars, optical goods; 2) tape recorders, musical instruments; 3) jewelry, precious metalware; 4) perfumes; 5) watches, clocks.

Persons arriving in the United States with a trademarked article are allowed an exemption, usually one article of a type bearing a protected trademark. An exempted trademark article must accompany you, and you can claim this exemption for the same type of article only once each 30 days. The article must be for your personal use and not for sale. If an exempted article is sold within one year following importation, the article or its value is subject to forfeiture.

If the trademark owner allows a quantity in excess of the aforementioned exemption for its particular trademarked article, the total of those trademarked articles authorized may be entered. Articles bearing counterfeit trademarks, if the amount of such articles exceeds the traveler's personal exemption, are subject to seizure and forfeiture.

Wildlife and Fish

Wildlife and fish are subject to certain import and export restrictions, prohibitions, permits or certificates, and quarantine requirements. This includes:

- Wild birds, mammals including marine mammals, reptiles, crustaceans, fish, and mollusks and invertebrates.

- Any part or product, such as skins, feathers, eggs.

- Products and articles manufactured from wildlife and fish.

Endangered species of wildlife and products made from them are prohibited from being imported or exported. All ivory and ivory products made from elephant or marine mammal ivory are also generally prohibited from being imported. Antiques containing wildlife parts may be imported if accompanied by documentation providing that they are at least 100 years old. (Certain other requirements for antiques may apply.) If you contemplate purchasing articles made from wildlife, such as tortoise shell jewelry, leather goods, or other articles made from whalebone, ivory, skins, or fur, please contact-before you go-the U.S. Fish and Wildlife Service, Division of law Enforcement, P.O. Box 3247, Arlington, VA 22203-3247. Information on the limit for migratory game birds for import and export can also be obtained from this office. Ask for their pamphlet *"Fish and Wildlife."*

If you plan to import fish or wildlife, or any product, article or part, check with Customs or Fish and Wildlife Service first, as only certain ports are designated to handle these entries. Additional information is contained in our leaflet *Pets, Wildlife, U.S. Customs.*

Federal regulations do not authorize the importation of any wildlife or fish into any state of the United States if the state's laws or regulations are more restrictive than any applicable Federal treatment. Wild mammals or birds taken, killed, sold, possessed, or exported to the United States in violation of any foreign laws are not allowed entry into the United States.

Customs Pointers
Traveling Back and Forth Across Border
After you have crossed the United States boundary at one point and you swing back into the United States to travel to another point in the foreign country, you run the risk of losing your customs exemption unless you meet certain requirements. If you make a "swing back," don't risk your exemptions-ask the nearest Customs officer about these requirements.

"Duty-Free" Shops
Articles bought in "duty-free" shops in foreign countries are subject to U.S. customs duty and restrictions but may be included in your personal exemption.

Articles purchased in U.S. "duty-free" shops are subject to U.S. customs duty if reentered into the U.S. Example: Liquor bought in a "duty-free" shop before entering Canada and brought back into the United States will be subject to duty and internal revenue tax.

Note: Many travelers are confused by the term "duty-free" as it relates to shops. Articles sold in duty-free shops are free of duty and taxes only for the country in which that shop is located. Articles sold in duty-free shops are intended for export and are not to be returned to the country of purchase. Thus, for example, if you were to buy a Hermes scarf in Orly Airport's duty-free shop, the price you pay will not include the tax you would have to pay if you bought that same scarf at Hermes in Faubourg St. Honore. So if your purchases exceed your personal exemption, that scarf may not be duty free for you.

Keep Your Sales Slips
You will find your sales slips, invoices, or other evidence of purchase not only helpful when making out your declaration, but necessary if you have unaccompanied articles being sent from the U.S. Virgin Islands, American Samoa, Guam or any of the Caribbean Basin Countries listed p. 73.

Packing Your Baggage
Pack your baggage in a manner that will make inspection easy. Do your best to pack separately the articles you have acquired abroad. When the Customs officer asks you to open your luggage or the trunk of your car, please do so without hesitation.

Photographic Film
All imported photographic films, which accompany a traveler, if not for commercial purpose, may be released without examination by Customs unless there is reason to believe they contain objectionable matter. Films prohibited from entry are those that contain obscene matter, advocate treason or insurrection against the United States, advocate forcible resistance to any law of the United States, or those that threaten the life of or infliction of bodily harm upon any person in the United States.

Developed or undeveloped U.S. film exposed abroad (except motion-picture film to be used for commercial purposes) may enter free of duty and need not be included in your customs exemption.

Foreign film purchased abroad and prints made abroad are dutiable but may be included in your customs exemption.

Shipping Hints
Merchandise acquired abroad may be sent home by you or by the store where purchased. *As these items do not accompany you on your return, they cannot be included in your customs exemption and are subject to duty when received in the United States. Duty cannot be prepaid.* There are, however, special procedures to follow for merchandise acquired in and sent from the U.S. Virgin Islands, American Samoa, Guam or Caribbean Basin countries. See page 75.

All incoming shipments must be cleared through U.S. Customs. Customs employees cannot, by law, perform entry tasks for the importing public, but they will advise and give information to importers about customs requirements.

Customs collects customs duty (if any) as provided for in the tariff schedule, certain Internal Revenue taxes and sometimes a user fee. Any other charges paid on import shipments are for handling by freight forwarders, commercial brokers, or for other delivery services. Some carriers may add other clearance charges that have nothing to do with Customs duties.

Note: Customs brokers are not U.S. Customs employees. Brokers fees are based on the amount of work done, not on the value of the personal effects or tourist purchases you shipped. The fee may seem excessive to you in relation to the value of the shipment. The most cost-effective thing to do is to take your purchases with you if at all possible .

"Mail Shipments (including parcel post) are generally cost-effective. Parcels must meet the mail requirements of the exporting country as to weight, size, or measurement.

The U.S. Postal Service sends all incoming foreign mail shipments to Customs for examination. Packages free of customs duty are returned to the Postal Service for delivery to you by your home post office without additional postage, handling costs, or other fees.

For packages containing dutiable articles, the Customs officer will attach a mail entry showing the amount of duty to be paid and return the parcel to the Postal Service. The duty and a postal handling fee will be collected when the package is delivered. In addition, there is a $5 Customs processing fee on dutiable packages.

Formal entry may be required for some shipments (some textiles, wearing apparel and small leather goods) regardless of value. Customs employees cannot prepare this type of entry for you. Only you or a licensed customs broker may prepare a formal entry.

If you pay the duty on a package but feel that the duty was not correct, you may file a protest. This protest can be acted on only by the Customs office which issued the mail entry receipt-Customs Form 3419A-attached to your package. Send a copy of this form with your protest letter to the Customs office at the location and address shown on the left side of the form. That office will review the duty assessment based on the information furnished in your letter and, if appropriate, authorize a refund.

Another procedure would be to not accept the parcel. You would then have to provide, within five days, a written statement of your objections to the Postmaster where the parcel is being held. Your letter will be forwarded to the issuing Customs office. The shipment will be detained at the post office until a reply is received.

Express shipments may be sent to the United States from anywhere in the world. The express company usually provides or arranges for customs clearance of the merchandise for you. A fee is charged for this service.

Freight shipments, whether or not they are free of duty at the time of importation, must clear Customs at the first port of arrival into the United States, or, if you choose, the merchandise may be forwarded in Customs custody (in bond) from the port of arrival to another Customs port of entry for customs clearance.

All arrangements for customs clearance and forwarding in bond must be made by you or someone you designate to act for you. Frequently, a freight forwarder in a foreign country will handle all the necessary arrangements, including the clearance through Customs in the United States by a customs broker. A fee is charged for this service. This fee is not a Customs charge. If a foreign seller consigns a shipment to a broker or agent in the United States, the freight charge is usually paid only to the first port of arrival in the United States. This means there will be additional inland transportation or freight forwarding charges, brokers fees, insurance, and other items.

An individual may also effect the customs clearance of a single, noncommercial shipment not requiring formal entry for you, if it is not possible for you to personally secure the release of the goods. You must authorize and empower the individual in writing to execute the customs declaration and the entry for you as your unpaid agent. The written authority provided to the individual should be addressed to the "Officer in Charge of Customs" at the port of entry.

Unaccompanied tourist purchases acquired in and sent directly from the U.S. Virgin Islands, American Samoa, Guam, or a Caribbean Basin country, may be entered, if properly declared and processed, as follows:

- Up to $1200 free of duty under your personal exemption if from an insular possession; $600 if from a Caribbean Basin country. Remember that if up to $400 of this amount was acquired elsewhere than these countries, those articles must accompany you at the time of your return in order to claim duty-free entry under your personal exemption.

- An additional $1,000 worth of articles, dutiable at a flat five percent rate if from an insular possession, or a flat 10 percent rate if the merchandise is from a Caribbean Basin country.
- Any amount over the above, dutiable at various rates of duty.

The procedure outlined below must be followed:

Step 1. You will: a) list all articles acquired abroad on your baggage declaration (Customs Form 6059B) except those sent under the $50 or the $100 bona fide gift provision described on p. 74 to friends and relatives in the U.S.; b) indicate which articles are unaccompanied; c) fill out a Declaration of Unaccompanied Articles (Customs Form 255) for each package or container to be sent. This form may be obtained when you clear Customs if it was not available where you made your purchase.

Step 2. Customs at the time of your return will: a) collect duty and tax if owed on goods accompanying you; b) verify your unaccompanied articles against sales slips, invoices, etc.; c) validate Form 255 as to whether goods are free of duty under your personal exemption or subject to a flat rate of duty. Two copies of the three-part form will be returned to you.

Step 3. You will return the yellow copy of the form to the shopkeeper (or vendor) holding your purchase and keep the other copy for your records. You are responsible for advising the shopkeeper at the time you make your purchase that your package is not to be sent until this form is received.

Step 4. The shopkeeper will place the form in an envelope and attach the envelope securely to the outside of the package or container, which must be clearly *"Unaccompanied Tourist Purchase."* **Please note that a form must be placed on each box or container.** This is the most important step to be followed in order for you to receive the benefits allowed under this procedure.

Step 5. The Postal Service will deliver the package, if sent by mail, to you after Customs clearance. Any duty owed will be collected by the Postal Service plus a postal handling fee; or

You will be notified by the carrier as to the arrival of your shipment at which time you will go to the Customs office processing your shipment and make entry. Any duty or tax owed will be paid at that time. You may employ a customs broker to do this for you. A fee will be charged by the broker.

Storage charges. Freight and express packages delivered before you return (without prior arrangements for acceptance) will be placed in storage by Customs after five days, at the expense and risk of the owner. If not claimed within one year, the items will be sold.

Mail parcels not claimed within 30 days will be returned to the sender unless a duty assessment is being protested.

Notice to California Residents:
California residents should know that merchandise purchased abroad and brought back to California may be subject to "use tax." On October 1, 1990, California began to assess a use tax on these purchases, using information from Customs declarations completed by returning travelers at ports of entry. The use-tax rate is the same as the sales-tax rate in the traveler's California county of residence.

For more information about the use-tax program, contact the California Board of Equalization's Occasional Sales Use Tax Unit, (916) 445-9524.

For Further Information
Every effort has been made to indicate essential requirements; however, all regulations of Customs and other agencies cannot be covered in full.

Customs offices will be glad to advise you of any changes in regulations which may have occurred since publication of this leaflet.

[See **Appendices E, F, and G** for the location and telephone numbers of the U.S. Customs District Offices, U.S. Customs Foreign Offices, and International Mail Branches.]

Frequently, We Are Asked Questions which are not Customs matters. If you want to know about . . .

Passports. Contact the Passport Agency nearest you. [A listing of these agencies is provided in **Appendix J.**] See **Chapter 2** for more on passports.

Baggage Allowance. Ask the airline or steamship line you are traveling on about this.

Currency of Other Nations. Your local bank can be of assistance.

Foreign Countries. For information about the country you will visit or about what articles may be taken into that country, contact the appropriate Embassy, consular office, or tourist information office.

Report Drug Smuggling to U.S. Customs Service
1 (800) BE-ALERT

~ ~ ENDNOTES ~ ~

1, 2, 3, 4, 5, These publications are reproduced elsewhere in this book. Check the Table of Contents for location.

Chapter 8

U.S. Customs Highlights For Government personnel

[The information in this chapter is an excerpt from a bulletin issued by the
Department of the Treasury, U.S. Customs Service.
It is intended to serve as advice to U.S. Government Personnel traveling abroad.]

- - - -

Welcome Home

This leaflet provides customs information for civilian employees and military personnel of the U.S. Government when returning to the States with personal and household effects after an extended tour of duty abroad or when returning on leave or TDY.

Every effort has been made to make the information in this pamphlet as accurate as possible and to cover the subjects which are of most general interest and concern. It is not possible, however, to cover all matters in detail and regulations do change from time to time.

Military personnel may also refer to Department Defense Regulation DOD 5030.49-R, Customs Inspection, which contains detailed procedures and information regarding the military customs inspection program.

If you need additional information, our Customs Advisors assigned overseas will be happy to advise you. They are located in the following areas:
Korea-HQS/UNC/USFK/EUSA
Philippines-CINCPACREPHIL
Germany-Hq. 42nd Military Police Group
Panama-Hq., Southern

You may also write to the U.S. Customs Service, Washington, D.C. 20229, if you need a definitive ruling on any customs subject.

This leaflet, as well as others mentioned, such as *U.S. Customs Trademark Information and Importing a Car,* have been provided to the Army, Navy, and Air Force. Copies, if not available at your base or post, may be requisitioned from your Stateside distribution center.

A resident of a foreign country married to a U.S. resident and children born abroad will be considered as nonresidents when coming into this country for the first time.

Military and civilian Government employees stationed

or working in the United States and going to foreign countries on temporary duty or travel are considered returning U.S. residents for customs purposes on their return.

Returning on PCS

The U.S. Customs Service is responsible for clearing all merchandise entering the United States. All imported goods are subject to a customs duty unless specifically exempted from this duty by law.

Persons arriving in the United States from foreign countries are classified for customs purposes as either residents of the United States or nonresidents. Certain exemptions from payment of duty on the articles brought with them are provided.

A special provision allows U.S. Government personnel (military and civilian) to enter their personal and household effects without payment of duty and tax when returning from an extended duty assignment overseas. Should they return to the United States for purposes of leave

or TDY before their overseas assignment is concluded, they may claim the customs status of either a returning resident or nonresident. Members of their family residing with them may also claim either status when returning for a short visit.

The classification and rates of duty, or exemptions therefrom, on imported goods are governed by the Harmonized Tariff Schedule of the United States (HTSUS). Under item 9805.00.50 of the Tariff Schedules, personal and household effects of any person (military or civilian) employed by the U.S. Government, and members of his family residing with him at his post or station, may be entered free of duty unless items are restricted, prohibited, or limited as in the case of liquor and tobacco.

To claim this exemption, the person in the service of the United States must be returning to the States under

Government orders upon termination of an assignment to extended duty outside the Customs territory of the United States.

An assignment to extended duty abroad must be of at least 140 days duration, except as noted for Navy personnel. Military and civilian personnel are entitled to free entry privileges if:

They are returning, at any time, upon termination of an assignment of extended duty; or

They are under permanent change of station orders to another post or station abroad, necessitating return of their personal and household effects to the United States.

Navy personnel serving aboard a United States naval vessel or supporting naval vessel when it departs from the United States on an intended deployment of 120 days or more outside the country and who continue to serve on the vessel until it returns to the United States

Free entry of accompanied and unaccompanied effects of family members who have resided with the employee cannot be claimed under item 9805.00.50 HTSUS when imported before the employee's receipt of orders terminating his extended duty assignment.

Persons not entitled to this exemption:
* Employees of private business and commercial organizations working under contract for the U.S. Government.
* Persons under research fellowships granted by the United States Government.
* Peace Corps Volunteers or employees of UNICEF.
* Persons going abroad under the Fulbright-Hays Act of 1961 or under the Mutual Educational and Cultural Exchange Act of 1961. Item 9805.00.50 applies, however, to any person evacuated to the United States under U S. Government orders or instructions.

Customs Declarations

Accompanied Baggage
Articles which accompany you upon your return to the United States on PCS orders should be declared on Customs form CF 6059B, "Customs Declaration," if you travel on a commercial carrier. If you travel on a carrier owned or operated by the U.S. Government, including charter aircraft, you will execute Department of Defense form DD 1854, 'Customs Accompanied

Baggage Declaration," or CF 6059B. Be prepared to show Customs a copy of your travel orders.

Unaccompanied Baggage
If you are a DOD civilian or military member returning to the U.S. from extended duty overseas, you should execute DD Form 1252, "U.S. Customs Declaration for Personal Property Shipments,' to facilitate the entry of your unaccompanied baggage and/or household goods into the U.S. A copy of your PCS orders, terminating your assignment to extended duty abroad, should accompany DD Form 1252. This form is also used by a DOD sponsored or directed individual or employee of a nonappropriated fund agency which is an integral part of the military services. All other Government employees should complete "Declaration for Free Entry of Unaccompanied Articles," CF 3299, and attach a copy to their orders.

By these declarations you certify that the shipment consists of personal and household effects which were in your direct personal possession while abroad and the articles are not imported for the account of another person or intended for sale.

Employees completing CF 3299 must list restricted articles (e.g., trademarked items, firearms), and goods not subject to their exemption (e.g., excess liquor, articles carried for other persons) on the declaration and show the actual prices paid. DOD employees and military members whose shipment of personal and household effects are cleared by a military customs inspector (MCI) will indicate to the MCI any articles which are restricted or subject to customs duty. A notation will be made by the MCI on DD form 1252 and the shipment will be examined by U.S. Customs upon its arrival in the U.S. Shipments from areas where MCIs are not assigned will be cleared upon arrival in the U.S.

Effects sent by mail are eligible for duty-free entry if the articles were in the returnee's possession prior to leaving the duty station. A copy of the Government orders terminating the assignment must accompany the articles in a sealed envelope securely affixed to the outer wrapper of the parcel. The parcel should also be marked clearly on the outside 'Returned Personal Effects-Orders Enclosed."

Articles taken with you from the United States need not be listed on your declaration. If such articles were repaired in a foreign country, list the cost of repairs. If the repaired or altered article is changed sufficiently to become a different article, it must be declared at its full value.

Effects sent home before your orders are issued, or purchased overseas and not delivered to you abroad but sent to your address in the States, do not qualify for free entry.

Merchandise of foreign origin purchased in overseas Post or Base Exchanges is subject to customs treatment and other import requirements and regulations, including trademark restrictions.

Limitations

Tobacco
Not more than 100 cigars may be imported free of duty as personal effects. You may import a reasonable number of cigarettes. Products of Cuban tobacco are prohibited to arriving U.S. citizens and residents, unless acquired in Cuba. See 'Merchandise" on page 94.

Liquor
Not more than 4 liters (1 35.2 fluid ounces) of alcoholic beverages, of which 3 liters must be bottled in the United States and of U.S. manufacture, may be imported free of duty as personal effects, if:

· It accompanies the employee or the member of his family making claim for entry at the time that person arrives in the United States.

· The member of the employee's family claiming the exemption is 21 years of age or over. (U.S.civilian or military personnel are exempt from the age requirement.)

· The person requesting free entry does not claim the customs exemption for alcoholic beverages as a returning U.S. resident or nonresident.

No alcoholic beverages may be imported into the U.S. by mail nor can Customs release liquor in violation of the laws of the State where it is entered. As laws vary from State to State, this information may be obtained from State liquor authorities.

Any person in the United States may receive bona fide gifts through the mail from persons in foreign countries free of customs duty provided the fair retail value (country of shipment) of all shipments received for that person for customs processing in one day doe not exceed $ 50 (or $ 100 if sent from American Samoa U.S. Virgin Islands, or Guam). Each package of article sent as a gift should be clearly marked on the outside: (1) UNSOLICITED GIFT; (2) name of donor; (3) fair retail value. These gifts need not be included in the baggage declaration of the donor when he returns to the United States.

Gifts which exceed the $50 or $100 retail value will be subject to customs duty based on the entire value. There is no deduction. Alcoholic beverages, cigars, an cigarettes are not included in this exemption from duty nor are alcoholic perfumes in the shipment if valued a more than $5.

Gifts intended for more than one person and meeting the above requirements may be consolidated in the same package provided they are individually wrapped and labeled with the name of the recipient.

Gifts for relatives and friends which accompany you on your return to the United States must be declared to Customs but may be included under item 9805.00.50

Automobiles
A foreign-made automobile may be included as part of your personal effects. However, an automobile purchased abroad and sent home before your Government orders are issued, or *a* car purchased and not in your possession before you leave (merely ordered but not delivered to you), will not be entitled to free entry as a personal or household effect under 9805.00.50. The vehicle would be subject to customs duty. Autos made in Canada by a Canadian manufacturer are free of duty.

Auto undercarriage must be free from foreign soil before it can be entered into the United States. This may be done by steam spray or thorough cleaning before embarking.

Motor Vehicle Standards
It is important for you to know that any imported vehicle, new or used, must comply with U.S. safety, cost savings, and air pollution control standards. If an imported vehicle does not conform to these standards, it must be brought into conformity; otherwise it must be destroyed or exported.

Both the Department of Transportation (DOT) and the Environmental Protection Agency (EPA) advise that although a nonconforming car may be conditionally admitted, modifications may be impractical, impossible, or require such extensive engineering that the labor and material cost may be prohibitive. Moreover, after June 30, 1988, EPA will not permit some nonconforming vehicle models to be imported into the U.S., and most of those that are permitted entry must be imported by a business that holds a currently valid EPA certificate of conformity. Effective July 1, 1988, EPA will no longer have the one-time exception for cars five or more model years old.

91

Nonconforming vehicles must be entered by either a company that is both a DOT Registered Importer (RI) and an EPA Independent Commercial Importer (ICI) or the owner, if the owner can show a contract with both an RI and ICI.

Bonds required may be up to three times the value of the car, and it may be difficult to find a broker who will post a bond. In addition, the broker may require that the person who imports the car post more than half the bond with his own money.

Effective January 31, 1990, Customs will require a formal entry, regardless of value, for all importations of nonconforming vehicles unless the nonresident exemption is claimed.

If you do not have a copy of our leaflet *Importing a Car¹* DOT and EPA standards are briefly described below for your information. EPA also publishes a brochure entitled 'Buying A Car Overseas? Beware!' which describes its new program for vehicles imported after June 30, 1988. (See Table of contents)

Safety Standards

Automobiles, new or used, and certain automobile equipment manufactured on or after January 1, 1968 must conform to applicable Federal motor vehicle safety and cost savings standards. The original manufacturer is required to affix a label certifying that the standards have been met and a declaration, DOT form HS-7, must be filed by the importer.

If the car has been brought into conformity after manufacture and prior to importation, the car must be entered under bond.

A nonconforming automobile admitted under bond (cash or surety) must be brought into conformity with 120 days after importation, unless an extension is granted by DOT. In either case, the conforming statement must be provided to Customs within 180 days. The importer should determine from the dealer or manufacturer what modifications are necessary.

Trailers, motorcycles, including mopeds, and certain equipment are also subject to DOT standards.

Inquiries regarding motor vehicle safety and cost savings standards should be addressed to: U.S. Department of Transportation, Office of Vehicle Safety Compliance, Enforcement (NEF 32), Washington, D.C. 20590.

Emission Standards

The following passenger cars, light-trucks and motorcycles are subject to Federal emission standards:

Gasoline-fueled cars and light-trucks originally manufactured after December 31, 1967.

- Diesel-fueled cars originally manufactured after December 31, 1974.
- Diesel-fueled light-trucks originally manufactured after December 31, 1975.
- Motorcycles with a displacement of more than 49 cubic centimeters originally manufactured after December 31, 1977.

For those vehicles that are subject to U.S. emission standards, the following must be complied with upon entry into the U.S.:

Passenger Cars or Trucks Originally Manufactured to Meet U.S. Emission Standards

1971 and later model cars or trucks in this category can be identified by a label in a readily visible position in the engine compartment. This label will indicate that the vehicle was originally manufactured to comply with U.S. emission standards. For pre-1971 models, you should verify the original compliance of the vehicle with the vehicle manufacturer. Vehicles originally equipped with a catalyst or oxygen sensor will be subject to EPA's retrofit requirements. If the catalyst was removed from your vehicle before shipment overseas, the catalyst must accompany the vehicle and must be reinstalled upon reentry of the vehicle into the U.S. If the catalyst was not removed before shipment overseas, it must be replaced. The oxygen sensor must be changed in accordance with the manufacturer's instruction. An entry must be filed and a bond posted if you choose to have the catalyst reinstalled or replaced or the oxygen sensor replaced other than at the port of entry.

Passenger Cars or Trucks Not originally Manufactured to Meet U.S. Emission Standards

For vehicles imported prior to July 1, 1988, you must post a bond and subsequently modify and/or test the vehicle to show that, as modified, the vehicle complies with U.S. emission standards. Information regarding the modification and/or test process may be obtained from EPA.

For vehicles imported on or after July 1, 1988, you must import your vehicle through a currently qualified EPA certificate holder. A list of these certificate holders are available at the port of entry or from EPA. The certificate holder will be responsible for ensuring that your vehicle complies with all U.S. emission requirements. Note that not all vehicle models will be allowed entry into the U.S. Should you possess a model that is not permitted entry, you must either export or destroy the vehicle. You may contact EPA for a list of models that are permitted entry.

Inquiries regarding emission requirements should be addressed to the Investigation/imports Section (EN-340F), U.S. EPA, Washington, D.C. 20460; (202) 382-2504.

Shipping Arrangements
In many cases, shipping regulations of the employing agency (DOD, Department of State, etc.) prohibit packing personal belongings in an automobile being shipped to the U.S. at government expense.

Additionally, the practice of shipping personal belongings packed in an automobile is discouraged for the following reasons:

*   Theft or pilferage of your personal belongings while waiting to be loaded on the carrier, while being transported to the U.S., or after being unloaded in the U.S.
*   The carrier is required to list the automobile and its contents on the ship's manifest. if the contents are not listed, the carrier is subject to fines or penalties.
*   The vehicle and its contents may be subject to seizure and you may be subject to fines or penalties if the complete contents of the vehicle are not declared by you or your agent at the time the automobile is examined by U.S. Customs.

Prohibited & Restricted Importations
The importation of certain classes of merchandise is prohibited or restricted to protect community health, to preserve domestic plant and animal life, and for other reasons.

Among articles prohibited are absinthe, liquor-filled candy, lottery tickets, narcotics and dangerous drugs, pornographic articles and publications, seditious and treasonable materials, hazardous articles (e.g., fireworks, dangerous toys, toxic or poisonous substances), and switchblade knives.

Merchandise that is prohibited from entry into the United States will be seized. Merchandise that is restricted from entry into the United States will be released after inspection by the Government agency which imposed the restrictions, or detained until the conditions attached to the restrictions are met. The importer of merchandise which is prohibited or restricted entry may be liable for a personal penalty, and the merchandise may be confiscated.

Biological Materials
Biological materials of public health or veterinary importance (disease organisms and vectors for research and educational purposes) require import permits.

Write to Foreign Quarantine Program, U.S. Public Health Service, Center for Disease Control, Atlanta, Ga. 30333.

Books
"Infringing" copies of copyrighted books-those produced without the authorization of the copyright owner-are prohibited, such as unauthorized photo-offset copies of American bestsellers and expensive textbooks produced and sold in the Far East for a fraction of what their cost would be if produced in the U.S

Cultural Property
An export certificate may be required by certain Latin American countries in order to import pre-Columbian monumental and architectural sculpture or murals whether they are shipped directly or indirectly from the country of origin into the U.S.

Firearms and Ammunition
Generally, all other firearms and ammunition acquired abroad may be imported only under permit upon compliance with regulations of the Bureau of Alcohol, Tobacco and Firearms, (ATF), Department of the Treasury, Washington, D.C. 20226. That agency will furnish permit applications and answer inquiries about the Gun Control Act of 1968.

The Department of Defense and the U.S. Postal Service prohibit acceptance by military post offices of war trophy firearms, ammunition, and handguns for shipment through an APO or FPO of the military post system.

Military members (under certain conditions) may import not more than three nonautomatic long guns (rifles or shotguns) and 1,000 rounds of ammunition therefor, without presentation of an approved firearm import permit to U.S. Customs. Surplus military firearms of any description are prohibited entry.

Military personnel should ask installation transportation officers or military customs inspectors for additional information and necessary forms for import permits and mailing by postal channels.

Firearms and ammunition previously taken out of and returned to the United States by the same person may be released upon presentation to U.S. Customs of adequate proof of prior possession, i.e., bill of sale, household goods inventory showing serial number,

Customs registration Forms 4455 or 4457.

Food Products

Bakery items and all cured cheeses are admissible. The USDA Animal and Plant Health Inspection Service (APHIS) leaflet, *Travelers' Tips*[2], provides detailed information on bringing food, plant, and animal products into the U.S. Imported foods are also subject (FDA). Foods not approved by the FDA may not be entered into the United States. (See Chapter 33).

Fruits, Plants, Vegetables

Fruits, plants, vegetables, cuttings, seeds, unprocessed plant products and certain endangered species of plants are either prohibited from entering the country or require an import permit. Canned or processed items are admissible.

Gold

Gold coins, medals, and bullion, formerly prohibited, may be brought into the U.S.; however, copies of gold coins are prohibited if not properly marked.

Meats, Livestock, Poultry

Meats, livestock, poultry, and their by-products such as pate and sausage are either prohibited or restricted from entering the United States, depending on *animal* disease condition in country of origin. This includes fresh, frozen, dried, cured, cooked or canned items. Commercially labeled, cooked, canned meats, not requiring refrigeration and hermetically sealed, may be brought into the U.S.

Medicine/Narcotics

Narcotics and dangerous drugs are prohibited entry and there are severe penalties if imported. A traveler requiring medicines containing habit-forming drugs o narcotics (e.g., cough medicines, tranquilizers, sleeping pills, depressants, stimulants, etc.) should:

* have all drugs, medicinals, and similar products properly identified;
* carry only such quantity as might normally be carried by an individual having some sort of health problem
* have either a prescription or written statement from his personal physician that the medicinals are being used under a doctor's direction and are necessary the traveler's physical well-being while traveling.

Drugs not approved by the Food and Drug Administration may not be entered into the United States.

Merchandise

Merchandise originating in Cambodia (Kampuchea

Cuba (and all goods containing Cuban components), Haiti, Iraq, Iran, Libya, North Korea, and Vietnam ar prohibited from being imported without a Treasury license under regulations of the Office of Foreign Assets Control (FAC).

Under a general license issued by FAC, travelers visiting North Korea, Libya, or Vietnam may purchase and bring into the United States $100 worth of articles (based on retail value). These articles must be for personal use, not for resale, and must accompany the traveler. The allowance may only be used once everr 6 months.

Money

There is no limitation in terms of total amount monetary instruments which may be brought int taken out of the United States nor is it illegal to do so. However, if you transport or cause to be transported (including by mail or other means), more than $10,000 in monetary instruments on any occasion into or out of the United States, or if you receive more than that amount, you must file a report (Customs Form 4790) with U.S. Customs (Currency & Foreign Transactions Reporting Act, 31 U.S.C. 1101, et seq.). Failure to comply can result in civil and criminal penalties. Monetary instruments include U.S. or foreign coin, currency, traveler's checks, money orders, and negotiable instruments or investment securities in bearer form.

Pets

There are controls, restrictions, and prohibitions on entry of animals, birds, turtles, wildlife, and endangered species. Cats and dogs must be free of evidence of diseases communicable to man. Vaccination against rabies is not required for cats or for dogs arriving from rabies-free countries. Personally owned pet birds may be entered (limit of two if of the Psittacine family), but APHIS and Public Health Service requirements must be met, including quarantine at any APHIS facility at specified locations, at the owner's expense. Advance reservations are required. Non-human primates, such as monkeys, apes, and similar animals, may not be imported. If you plan to take your pet abroad or import one on your return, obtain a copy of our leaflet, *Pets, Wildlife, U.S. Customs*[3]

Trademarked Articles

The importation of goods violating the copyright laws or bearing counterfeit or confusingly similar trademarks is prohibited by the U.S. Customs Service. The importation of some goods bearing genuine trademarks is also prohibited. Information on the restricted status of genuine trademarked merchandise is published in the

Customs Bulletin beginning with the July 17, 1991, edition. That edition contains a listing of all trademarks receiving protection against the importation of genuine goods ('gray market" protection) as of that date. The *Bulletin* is published every week and trademark recordation information is updated in the *Bulletin* about once a month. The *Customs Bulletin is* available from the U.S. Government Printing Office at (202) 512-2457.

The types of articles usually of interest to tourists are 1) lenses, cameras, binoculars, optical goods; 2) tape recorders, musical instruments; 3) jewelry, precious metalware; 4) perfumery; 5) watches, clocks.

Persons arriving in the U.S. with a trademarked article are allowed an exemption, usually one article of a type bearing a protected trademark. An exempted trademark article must accompany you, and you can claim this exemption for the same type of article only once each 30 days. The article must be for your personal use and not for sale. If an exempted article is sold within I year following importation, the article or its value is subject to forfeiture. If the trademark owner allows a quantity in excess of the aforementioned exemption for its particular trademarked article, the total of those trademarked articles authorized may be entered.

Wildlife, Fish, and Plants

Wildlife, fish, and plants are subject to certain import and export restrictions, prohibitions, permits or certificates, and quarantine requirements. This includes:

* wild birds, mammals including marine mammals, reptiles, crustaceans, fish, and mollusks;

* any part or product, such as skins, feathers, eggs; and

* products and articles manufactured from wildlife and fish.

Endangered species of wildlife and plants including products made from them are prohibited from being imported or exported. if you contemplate purchasing articles made from wildlife, such as tortoise shell jewelry, leather goods, articles made from whalebone, ivory, skins, or fur, contact the U.S. Fish and Wildlife Service, Department of the Interior, Washington, D.C. 20240, for additional information.

Returning Prior to PCS

Civilian and military personnel of the U.S. Government and members of their family returning to the United States for a short visit, on TDY, voluntarily on leave, or for other personal reasons, with or without orders before termination of the employee's assignment to extended duty may claim customs status as either a returning U.S. resident or a nonresident. The head of a family may make a joint declaration for all members residing in the same household and returning together *to the United States*. Exemptions are explained below. To be entitled to these exemptions all articles must accompany the returnee. Liquor is subject to the laws of the State in which it is entered. U.S. Customs inspectors cannot release alcoholic beverages in excess of State restrictions. Restricted and prohibited importations covered on pages 93-95, apply at all times. See page 91 for restrictions on Cuban tobacco.

$400 Residents' Exemption for articles acquired abroad for own use:

* $400 based on the aggregate fair retail value of the articles in the country of acquisition upon arrival from abroad other than from American Samoa, Guam, and the Virgin Islands of the United States.

* Not more than 200 cigarettes, 100 cigars, and one liter of alcoholic beverages per person over 21 years of age.

. Returnee must have remained beyond territorial limits of the United States not less than 48 hours (exception-arrival from Mexico), and not used the exemption within the 30 days immediately preceding his arrival.

$600 Residents' Exemption allowed if you are returning directly from any of the 24 beneficiary countries. Articles acquired in these islands may either accompany you or may be sent directly to the United States and entered under the exemption allowed:

Antigua and Grenada		Panama
Barbuda Guatemala		SaintChristopher/Kitts
Aruba	Guyana	and Nevis
Bahamas Haiti	Saint Lucia	
Barbados Honduras	Saint Vincent and	
Belize	Jamaica	the Grenadines
Costa Rica	Montserrat	Trinidad and
Tobago		
Dominica Netherlands		Virgin Islands,
Dominican	Antilles	British
Republic Nicaragua		
El Salvador		

* Alcoholic beverages: not over 2 liters per person 21 years of age or over, provided not more than one liter of the amount is acquired elsewhere than in such beneficiary countries.

95

* Not more than $400 of articles acquired abroad may have been acquired elsewhere than in such beneficiary countries. You may not bring more than 100 cigars and 200 cigarettes.

$1200 Residents' Exemption allowed if you return directly or indirectly from a U.S. insular possession- American Samoa, Guam, or the U.S. Virgin Islands. Articles acquired in these islands may either accompany you or may be sent to the United States and entered under the exemption allowed:

* Alcoholic beverages: not over 4 liters per person 21 years of age or over, provided not more than one liter of the amount is acquired elsewhere than in such insular possessions.

* Not more than $400 of articles acquired abroad may have been acquired elsewhere than in such insular possessions. You may bring 100 cigars and 1,000 cigarettes, but only 200 of the cigarettes may be from outside the islands.

* 48-hour minimum time limitation not required on arrivals from the United States Virgin Islands.

Nonresidents' Exemption allows the following articles to be brought in free of duty and internal revenue taxes:

Personal effects for one's own use while traveling, but not intended for another person, sale, or gift (e.g., wearing apparel, toilet articles). 50 cigars or 200 cigarettes or 2 kilograms of smoking tobacco, or proportionate amounts of each. Not over one liter of alcoholic beverage for personal consumption.

$100 of articles for use as bona fide gifts for other persons. You may include in this gift exemption not more than 100 cigars. These articles, however, must accompany you; you have not used this gift exemption in the past six months; and you will be in the United States for at least 72 hours. Alcoholic beverages are excluded from this gift exemption. Foreign-made car, for personal use.

All articles (except gifts and articles consumed during your visit) must be exported by you on your departure from the United States.

A Customs officer may ask you to list imported articles of substantial value and to note the expected duration of your visit. He will furnish you with a duplicate copy of this listing which must be presented to a Customs officer at the time you depart from the United States at the end of your visit.

If for any reason you do not return abroad, you must immediately notify the District Director of Customs for the area where you entered. None of the returning residents' exemptions apply if you are permitted the "nonresident" exemptions on your short visit to the United States.

$25 Administrative Exemption is allowed if you are not entitled to the $400, $600 or $1200 exemption because of the 30-day or 48-hour minimum limitations. You may bring in free of duty and tax articles acquired abroad for your personal or household use if their aggregate fair retail value does not exceed $25. This is an individual exemption and may not be grouped with other members of a family on one customs declaration. You may not exceed any of the following: 50 cigarettes, 10 cigars, 1 50 milliliters of alcoholic beverages, or 150 milliliters of alcoholic perfume. If any article brought with you is subject to duty or tax, or if the total value of all articles exceeds $25, no article may be exempted from duty or tax.

A nonresident is entitled to the $25 exemption if the $100 gift exemption is not applicable.

Articles imported in excess of your customs exemption will be subject to duty unless the items are entitled to free entry or prohibited.

The inspector will place the items having the highest rate of duty under your exemption and duty will be assessed upon the lower rated items.

After deducting your exemptions and the value of any articles duty free, a flat rate of duty will be applied to the next $1000 worth (fair retail value) of merchandise. Any dollar amount of an article or articles over $1000 will be dutiable at the various rates of duty applicable to the articles.

Articles to which the flat rate of duty is applied must be for your personal use or for use as gifts and you cannot receive this flat rate provision more than once every 30 days, excluding the day of your last arrival.

The flat rate of duty is 10% based on fair retail value in the country of acquisition including Communist countries, and *articles must accompany you.*

The flat rate of duty is 5% for articles purchased in the U.S. Virgin Islands, American Samoa, or Guam whether the articles accompany you or are shipped.

Some Products from certain developing countries may enter the United States free of duty under the Generalized System of Preferences (GSP). For further details, obtain the leaflet *GSP and The Traveler*[4] from your nearest Customs office. Many products of certain Caribbean countries are also exempt from duty under the Caribbean Basin Initiative (CBI). Most products of Israel may enter the United States either free of duty or at a reduced duty rate. Check with Customs.

Articles bought in "duty-free" shops in foreign countries are subject to U.S. Customs duty and restrictions but may be included in your personal exemption.

~ ~ ENDNOTES ~ ~

1, 2, 3, 4,   These publications are reproduced elsewhere in this book. Check the Table of Contents for location.

Chapter 8

Health Information For International Travels

[The information in this chapter is an excerpt from a bulletin issued by the
U.S. Department of Health and Human Services, Centers for Disease Control.
It is intended to serve as advice to Americans traveling abroad.]

- - - -

Health Information for International Travel is published annually by the Division of Quarantine, Center for Prevention Services, Centers for Disease Control (CDC), for use as a reference by health departments, physicians, travel agencies, international air lines, shipping companies, and other private and public agencies that advise international travelers concerning the risks they might encounter when visiting other countries. It specifies the vaccinations required by different countries and includes information on measures for travelers to take to protect their health and facilitate their travel.

The purpose of the International Health Regulations (IHR) adopted by the World Health Organization (WHO) is to ensure maximum security against the international spread of diseases with minimum interference with world traffic. In addition to the quarantinable diseases (cholera, yellow fever, and plague), covered by the IHR, there are other conditions of importance to travelers, their families, and to the community when the travelers return home.

Because some countries require vaccination against yellow fever only if a traveler arrives from a country infected with this disease, it is essential that current information regarding infected areas be taken into consideration in determining whether vaccinations are required. The Division of Quarantine publishes a biweekly "Summary of Health Information for International Travel" (also known as the Blue Sheet) to show where cholera and yellow fever are being reported. These supplemental publications are available upon request.

Official changes in individual country vaccination requirements reported by WHO are published in the Blue Sheet and also in the Morbidity and Mortality Weekly Report (MMWR) under "International Notes: Quarantine Measures". These changes should be entered in the Vaccination Certificate Requirements section of this chapter to keep information on vaccination requirements current. The information in this chapter when kept up-to-date with changes in individual vaccination requirements, and utilized in conjunction with the Blue Sheet provides accurate information on vaccinations required for international travel.

Occasionally, the Division of Quarantine issues an Advisory Memorandum containing special recommendations or information about newly identified health problems associated with international travel. International travelers are advised to contact their local health department, physician, or private or public agency that advises international travelers at least 6 weeks prior to departure to obtain current health information on countries they plan to visit. They may also call the Centers for Disease Control automated travelers' hotline accessible from a touchtone phone 24 hours-a-day, 7 days-a-week at (404) 332-4559. This system provides information on requirements and recommendations for the international traveler and is updated as needed. This information is also available by facsimile at (404) 332-4565.

VACCINATION INFORMATION

EXEMPTION FROM VACCINATION

Age: Some countries do not require an International Certificate of Vaccination for infants under 6 months or 1 year of age. Check the individual country requirements for age exemptions.

Medical grounds: If a physician thinks that a particular vaccination should not be performed for medical reasons, the traveler should be given a signed, dated statement of the reasons on the physician's letterhead stationery.

There are no other acceptable reasons for exemption from vaccination.

UNVACCINATED PERSONS
Travelers who do not have the required vaccinations

upon entering a country may be subject to vaccination, medical follow-up, and/or isolation. In a few countries, unvaccinated travelers are denied entry.

TRAVEL ON MILITARY ORDERS
Since military requirements may exceed the requirements indicated in this booklet, any person who plans to travel on military orders (civilians and military personnel) should contact the nearest military medical facility to determine the requirements for the trip.

PERSONS AUTHORIZED TO VACCINATE AND TO VALIDATE THE INTERNATIONAL CERTIFICATE OF VACCINATION
Yellow fever vaccinations must be given at official Yellow Fever Vaccination Centers as designated by respective State health departments, and the certificate must be validated by the center that administers the vaccine. Other vaccinations may be given under the supervision of any licensed physician. Validation of the certificate can be obtained at most city, county, and State health departments, or from vaccinating physicians who possess a "Uniform Stamp." State health departments are responsible for designating non-Federal Yellow Fever Vaccination Centers and issuing Uniform Stamps to be used to validate the International Certificate of Vaccination. Information regarding the location and hours of Yellow Fever Vaccination Centers may be obtained by contacting local or State health departments. Physicians administering vaccine to travelers should emphasize that an International Certificate of Vaccination must be validated to be acceptable to quarantine authorities. Failure to secure validation may cause a traveler to be revaccinated, quarantined, or denied entry.

PERSONS AUTHORIZED TO SIGN THE CERTIFICATE
The International Certificate of Vaccination must be signed by a licensed physician or by a person designated by the physician to sign the certificate. A signature stamp is not acceptable.

An International Certificate of Vaccination must be complete in every detail; if incomplete or inaccurate, it is not valid.

MODEL OF A CORRECTLY COMPLETED CERTIFICATE
The International Certificate of Vaccination, PHS-731 may be purchased from the Superintendent of Documents, U.S. Government Printing Office, Washington, D.C. 20402, telephone: 202-783-3238. The stock number is 017-001-00483-9 and the price is $1.00 each or $15.00 per 100.

VACCINATION CERTIFICATE REQUIREMENTS
Under the International Health Regulations adopted by the World Health Organization, a country under certain conditions may require an International Certificate of Vaccination against Yellow Fever from international travelers. Smallpox was deleted from the diseases subject to the Regulations effective January 1, 1982. Smallpox vaccination should not be given. No country requires a certificate of cholera immunization. Vaccination against cholera cannot prevent the introduction into the country. The World Health Assembly therefore amended the International Health Regulations in 1973 so that cholera vaccination should no longer be required of any traveler. Information on vaccination requirements included in this booklet has been furnished WHO by the countries.

TABLE 1. Summary of Vaccinations That May Be Required by International Health Regulations (WHO)

Type	Doses	Comments
Cholera		No longer required
Yellow Fever	1	Certificate valid for 10 years beginning 10 days after primary vaccination or on the date of revaccination if within 10 years of first injection.

Vaccination Certificate Requirements for Direct Travel from the United States to Other Countries

For direct travel from the United States, only the following countries require an International Certificate of Vaccination:

Cholera
None

Yellow fever
Benin
Liberia
Burkina Faso
Mali
Cameroon
Mauritania (for stay of > 2 week
Central African Republic
Niger
Congo
Rwanda
Cote d'Ivoire

Sao Tome and
French Guiana (for stay of > 2 weeks)
Gabon
Togo
Ghana
Liberia
Zaire

For travel to and between other countries, check the individual country requirements.

Return to the United States
No vaccinations are required to return to the United States.

HOW TO USE INFORMATION IN THIS CHAPTER TO DETERMINE VACCINATIONS REQUIRED OR RECOMMENDED
It is important to note that the Vaccinations Required section of this chapter lists the vaccinations required by the countries; the biweekly "Summary of Health Information for International Travel" (also known as the Blue Sheet) published by the CDC lists countries that currently have areas infected with quarantinable diseases. Both must be checked to determine vaccinations required.

The following steps are suggested to determine vaccinations required:

1. List the traveler's itinerary in the sequence in which the countries will be visited. Consider the length of stay in each country. For the purpose of the International Health Regulations, the incubation periods of the quarantinable diseases are:

   Cholera-5 days Plague-6 days
   Yellow Fever 6-days

2. Check the current biweekly Blue Sheet to determine if any country on the itinerary is currently infected with cholera or yellow fever. This is essential because some countries require vaccination only if a traveler arrives from an infected area.

3. Use the "Vaccinations Required" section of this chapter to determine the vaccinations required by each country (consider the sequence of travel). Read the code by each disease first, then read all notes carefully. The codes are explained below. If code I appears, vaccination against that disease is required of travelers arriving from ALL COUNTRIES. If code II appears,

vaccination against that disease is required only of travelers ARRIVING FROM INFECTED AREAS, except as indicated in notes for individual countries. If code III appears, vaccination against that disease is required of travelers arriving from a COUNTRY ANY PART OF WHICH IS INFECTED, except as indicated in notes for individual countries. INFECTED COUNTRIES and INFECTED AREAS are reported in the biweekly "Summary of Health Information for International Travel" (Blue Sheet). READ BOTH OF THESE RESOURCES CAREFULLY, since many countries have exceptions to these codes.

Some immunizations are not required under the International Health Regulations but are recommended to protect the health of the travelers. Check with your physician to find out additional immunizations you may need.

EXPLANATION OF VACCINATION CODES:

I   Vaccination certificate is required of travelers arriving from ALL COUNTRIES, except as indicated in notes for individual countries.

II   Vaccination certificate is required of travelers arriving from INFECTED AREAS, except as indicated in notes for individual countries. INFECTED AREAS are reported in the biweekly "Summary of Health Information for International Travel" (also known as the Blue Sheet).

III Vaccination certificate is required of travelers arriving from a COUNTRY ANY PART OF WHICH IS INFECTED, except as indicated in notes for individual countries. INFECTED COUNTRIES are reported in the biweekly "Summary of Health Information for International Travel" (also known as the Blue Sheet).

*CDC recommends yellow fever vaccination for travelers > 9 months of age who go outside urban areas.

> Required only of travelers of age indicated or older.

EXPLANATION OF MALARIA PROPHYLAXIS REGIMEN CODES

REGIMEN A--Routine Weekly Prophylaxis with

chloroquine alone

REGIMEN B--Prophylaxis with Mefloquine

( )   Letters in parenthesis after country name denote
        recommended regimen for travelers to areas of
        risk. (See Codes)

VACCINATIONS REQUIRED AND INFORMATION ON MALARIA RISK AND PROPHYLAXIS, BY
COUNTRY.

	Information on Malaria Prophylaxis	
Vaccination Required by the country (Read all notes carefully)	Areas of risk within country	Chloroquine resistance
Afghanistan (B)	All	confirmed
Yellow Fever - II		
Albania	None	
Yellow Fever - II > 1 yr		
Algeria	Very limited risk in Sahara Region.	None
Yellow Fever - II > 1 yr		
Andorra	None	
No vaccinations are required.		
Angola (B)	All	Confirmed
Yellow Fever* - II > 1 yr		
Antigua and Barbuda Yellow Fever - II > 1 yr	None	
Argentina (A)	Rural areas near Bolivian	None
No vaccinations are required.	border, i.e., Salta and Jujuy	
Yellow Fever*†	Provinces.	
Australia Yellow Fever-III > 1 yr A certificate is also required of travelers who have within the previous 6 days been in a country infected with yellow fever.	None	

Note: Australia is not bound by the
International Health Regulations

Azerbaijan (B)   None
Follow former USSR regulations   Exists in some
until further notice   very small Southern
   . .   border areas.

Austria   None
No vaccinations are required.

Azores (Portugal)   None
Yellow Fever - II > 1 yr Except
that NO certificate is required
from travelers in transit at Santa
Maria.

Bahamas   None
Yellow Fever - II > 1 yr

Bahrain   None
Yellow Fever - II > 1 yr

Bangladesh (B)   All areas,   widespread in
                                        except no   areas along
Yellow Fever - III   risk in   the northern
A certificate is required ALSO   city of   and eastern
from travelers arriving from   Dhaka.   border.
or transiting:
Africa: Angola; Benin;
            Botswana; Burkina
            Faso; Burundi;
            Cameroon; Central
            African Republic;
            Chad; Congo; Cote
            d'Ivoire; Equatorial
            Guinea; Ethiopia;
            Gabon; Gambia,
            Ghana; Guinea;
            Guinea-Bissau; Kenya;
            Liberia; Malawi; Mali;
            Mauritania; Niger;
            Nigeria; Rwanda; Sao
            Tome and Principe;
            Senegal; Sierra Leone;
            Somalia; Sudan (south
            of 15⁰N): Tanzania,
            United Republic of;
            Togo; Uganda; Zaire;
            Zambia.

            Americas: Belize; Bolivia;
            Brazil: Colombia;
            Costa Rica;
            Ecuador; French

103

Guiana;
Guatemala;
Guyana;
Honduras;
Nicaragua;
Panama; Peru;
Suriname;
Venezuela.

Caribbean:Trinidad and Tobago.

Any person (including infants)
arriving by air or sea without
a certificate within 6 days of
departure from or transit through
an infected area will be isolated
up to 6 days.

Barbados   None
Yellow Fever - II > 1 yr

Belgium   None
No vaccinations are required.

Belize (A)   Rural areas,   None
(formerly Br. Honduras)   (including forest
Yellow Fever - II   preserves and
     . .   offshore islands,
     . .   including the resort
     . .   areas) except no
                              risk in central
                              coastal District
                              of Belize.

Benin (B)   All   Confirmed
(formerly Dahomey)

Yellow fever* - I > 1 yr

Bermuda (U.K.)   None
No vaccinations are required.

Bhutan (B)   Rural areas   Confirmed
                              in districts
Yellow Fever - II   bordering
                              India.

Bolivia   (B)   Rural areas   Confirmed
                              only except
Yellow Fever* - II   no risk in
Bolivia recommends   highland areas,
vaccination for all   i.e., Oruro Dept.
travelers from   and Prov. of
non-infected areas.   Ingavi, Los
                              Andes, Omasuyos, and Pacajes,
                              (La Paz Dept)

104

and southern and
central Potosi
Department.

Bosnia/Herzegovina   None
Follow Yugoslavia regulations
until further notice

Botswana (B)   Northern part   Confirmed
                                                of country
No vaccinations are required.   (North of 21°S).

Brazil (B)   Acre and   Confirmed
Yellow Fever*-II >9 mo,   Rondonia States,
unless they are in possession   Terr. of Amapa
of a waiver stating that   and Roraima
immunization is contraindicated   and in part
on medical grounds   of rural areas,
A certificate is ALSO required   Amazonas,
from travelers arriving from: Maranhao, Mato Grosso,
Africa: Angola, Gambia   Para and and Tocantins States.[1]
         Ghana, Guinea, Mali
         Nigeria, Sudan, Zaire
Americas: Bolivia, Colombia,
         Peru
Brazil recommends vaccination for
travel to rural areas in Acre,
Amazonas, Goias, Maranhao, Mato
Grosso, Mato Grosso do Sul, Para
and Rondonia States and Territories
of Amapa and Roraima.

Brunei Darussalam   None
Yellow Fever - II > 1 yr
A certificate is required ALSO
from travelers transiting endemic
zones within the preceding 6 days
(see p. 115).

Bulgaria   None
No vaccinations are required.

Burkina Faso (B)   All   Confirmed
(formerly Upper Volta)

Yellow Fever* - I > 1 yr

Burma (see Myanmar)

Burundi (B)   All   Confirmed
Yellow Fever* - II > 1 yr

Cambodia (B)   All, except no   Confirmed
    . .   risk in Phenom Penh
Yellow Fever -II

105

Cameroon (B) Yellow Fever* - I > 1 yr	All	Confirmed
Canada No vaccinations are required.	None	
Canary Islands (Spain)	None	
Cape Verde (None) Yellow Fever - III > 1 yr. Required from travelers coming from countries having reported cases in the last 6 years.	Limited to Island of Sao Tiago	None
Cayman Islands (U.K.) No vaccinations are required.	None	
Central African Republic (B) Yellow Fever* - I > 1 yr	All	Confirmed
Chad (B) Yellow Fever* - No vaccination is required, however, Chad recommends vaccination for all travelers >1 yr of age.	All	Confirmed
Chile No vaccinations are required.	None	
China (A/B)[2] Yellow Fever - II	Rural areas only except no risk in northern provinces bordering Mongolia and in the western provinces of Heilungkiang, Kirin, Ningsia Hui Tibet and Tsinghai, North of 33°N latitude transmission occurs July to November; between 33° and 25°N latitude transmission occurs May to December; south of 25°N latitude transmission occurs	Confirmed in Southern China; Hainan Island, and provinces bordering Myanmar (formerly Burma), Lao People's Demo- cratic Republic and VietNam

. .   year-round.

Christmas Island (Australia)   None
Yellow Fever - III > 1 yr A certificate
is also required of travelers who have
within the previous 6 days been in a
country infected with yellow fever.

Note: Christmas Island is not bound
by the International Health Regulations.

Columbia (B)   Rural areas   Confirmed
                                      only, except
Yellow Fever* -   no risk in
No vaccination required, how-   Bogota and
ever, Colombia recommends   vicinity.[3]
vaccination for travelers to the
middle valley of the Magdalena River,
eastern and western foothills of
the Cordillera Oriental from the
frontier with Ecuador to that with
Venezuela, Uraba, foothills of the
Sierra Nevada, eastern plains
(Orinoquia) and Amazonia.

Comoros (B)   All   Confirmed
No vaccinations are required.

Congo (B)   All   Confirmed
Yellow Fever* - I > 1 yr

Cook Islands (New Zealand)   None
No vaccinations are required.

Costa Rica (A)   None
                                      Rural areas only,
No vaccinations are required.   except there is no
                                      risk in central
                                      highlands, i.e.,
                                      Cartago and
                                      San Jose
                                      Provinces.

Cote d'Ivoire (B)   All   Confirmed
(formerly Ivory Coast)

Yellow Fever* - I > 1 yr

Croatia   None
No vaccinations are required

Cuba   None
No vaccinations are required.

Cyprus   None

No vaccinations are required.

Czech Republic No vaccinations are required.	None	
Denmark No vaccinations are required.	None	
Djibouti (B) Yellow Fever - II > 1 yr	All	Confirmed
Dominica Yellow Fever - II > 1 yr	None	
Dominican Republic (A) No vaccinations are required.	All rural areas except no risk in tourist resorts. Highest risk in provinces bordering Haiti.	None
Ecuador (B) Yellow Fever* - II > 1 yr	All areas in the provinces along the eastern border and the pacific coast, i.e., Esmeraldas, El Oro, Guayas (including Guayaquil), Los Rios, Manabi, Morona-Santiago, Napo, Pastaza, Pichincha, and Zamora-Chinchipe provinces.[4]	Confirmed
Egypt (A) Yellow Fever - II > 1 yr A certificate is required ALSO from travelers arriving from or transiting:	Rural areas of Nile Delta, El Faiyum area, the oases, and part of southern (upper) Egypt[5].	None

Africa: Angola; Benin;
          Botswana; Burkina
          Faso; Burundi;
          Cameroon; Central
          African Republic;
          Chad; Congo; Cote d'
          Ivoire; Equatorial
          Guinea; Ethiopia,
          Gabon; Gambia;
          Ghana; Guinea;
          Guinea-Bissau; Kenya;
          Liberia; Malawi; Mali;
          Mauritania; Niger;
..   Nigeria; Rwanda;

108

.. Sao Tome and Principe;
.. Senegal; Sierra Leone;
.. Somalia; Sudan
.. (south of 15°N):
.. Tanzania, United Rep.
.. of; Togo; Uganda;
.. Zaire; Zambia.

Americas: Belize, Bolivia; Brazil; Colombia; Costa Rica; Ecuador, French Guiana; Guatemala; Guyana; Honduras; Nicaragua; Panama; Peru; Suriname; Venezuela.

Caribbean: Trinidad and Tobago.

Air passengers in transit coming from these countries or areas without a certificate will be detained in the precincts of the airport until they resume their journey. All travelers arriving from Sudan are required to possess a vaccination certificate or a location certificate issued by a Sudanese official center stating that they have not been in that part of Sudan south of 15°N latitude within the preceding 6 days.

El Salvador (A)	Rural areas only.	None
Yellow Fever - II > 6 mo		
Equatorial Guinea (B) Yellow Fever* - II	All	Confirmed
Estonia Follow former USSR regulations until further notice	None	
Ethiopia (B) Yellow Fever* - II > 1 yr	All areas except no risk in Addis above 2,000 meters	Confirmed
Falkland Islands (U.K.) No vaccinations are required.	None	
Faroe Islands (Denmark) No vaccinations are required.	None	

109

Fiji Yellow Fever - II > 1 yr	None	
Finland No vaccinations are required.	None	
France No vaccinations are required.	None	
French Guiana (B) Yellow Fever* - I > 1 yr	All	Confirmed
French Polynesia (Tahiti) Yellow Fever - II > 1 yr	None	
Gabon (B) Yellow Fever* - I > 1 yr	All	Confirmed
Gambia (B) Yellow Fever* - II > 1 yr A certificate is required ALSO from travelers arriving from countries in the endemic zones (p.115).	All	Confirmed
Georgia Follow former USSR regulations until further notice	None	
Germany No vaccinations are required.	None	
Ghana (B) Yellow Fever* - I	All	Confirmed
Gibraltar (U.K.) No vaccinations are required.	None	
Greece Yellow Fever - II > 6 mo	None	
Greenland (Denmark) No vaccinations are required.	None	
Grenada Yellow Fever - II	None	
Guadeloupe (France) Yellow Fever - II > 1 yr	None	
Guam (U.S.) No vaccinations are required.	None	
Guatemala (A)	Rural areas only, except	None

110

Yellow Fever - III > 1 yr	no risk in central highlands.	
Guinea (B) Yellow Fever* - II > 1 yr	All	Confirmed
Guinea-Bissau (B) Yellow Fever* - II > 1 yr	All	Confirmed

A certificate is required ALSO
from travelers arriving from:
Africa; Angola; Benin;
        Burkina Faso;
        Burundi; Cape Verde;
        Central African
        Republic; Chad;
        Congo; Cote d'Ivoire;
        Djibouti; Equatorial
        Guinea; Ethiopia;
        Gabon; Gambia;
        Ghana; Guinea;
        Kenya; Liberia;
        Madagascar; Mali;
        Mauritania;
        Mozambique; Niger;
        Nigeria; Rwanda; Sao
        Tome and Principe;
        Senegal; Sierra Leone;
        Somalia; Tanzania;
        United Republic of;
  . .   Togo; Uganda; Zaire;
        Zambia.

Americas: Bolivia; Brazil;
        Colombia;
        Ecuador; French
        Guiana; Guyana;
        Panama; Peru;
        Suriname;
        Venezuela.

Guyana (B) Yellow Fever* - II	Rural areas in the southern interior and northwest coast, i.e., Rupununi and North West Regions.	Confirmed

A certificate is required ALSO
from travelers arriving from:
Africa: Angola; Benin;
        Burkina Faso;
        Burundi, Cameroon;
        Central African
        Republic; Chad;
        Congo; Cote
        d'Ivoire; Gabon;

> Gambia; Ghana;
> Guinea; Guinea-
> Bissau; Kenya;
> Liberia; Mali; Niger;
> Nigeria; Rwanda;
> Sao Tome and Principe;
> Senegal;
> Sierra Leone;
> Somalia; Tanzania,
> United Republic of;
> Togo; Uganda; Zaire.

Americas: Belize; Bolivia;
> Brazil; Colombia;
> Costa Rica;
> Ecuador; French Guiana;
> Guatemala;
> Honduras;
> Nicaragua; Panama;
> Peru; Suriname;
> Venezuela.

Haiti (A)   All   None
Yellow Fever - II

Honduras (A)   Rural areas   None
                                              only.

Yellow Fever - II

Hong Kong (U.K.)   None
No vaccinations are required.

Hungary   None
No vaccinations are required.

Iceland   None
No vaccinations are required.

India (B)   All areas, including   Confirmed
                                              the cities of Delhi
Cholera-A Certificate is   and Bombay except no
required ONLY from travelers   risk in parts of the
proceeding to countries which   States of Himechel
require a certificate.   Pradesh, Jammu
                                              and Kashmir
Yellow Fever - III   and Sikkim
A certificate is required ALSO
from travelers arriving from or
transiting:
> Africa: Angola; Benin;
> Burkina Faso;
> Burundi; Cameroon;
> Central African
> Republic; Chad;
> Congo; Cote d'Ivoire;
> Equatorial Guinea;
> Ethiopia; Gabon;

112

Gambia; Ghana;
Guinea; Guinea-Bissau;
Kenya
Liberia: Mali; Niger;
Nigeria; Rwanda; Sao
Tome and Principe;
Senegal; Sierra Leone;
Somalia; Sudan;
Tanzania, United
Republic of Togo;
Uganda; Zaire;
Zambia.
Americas:Bolivia; Brazil;
Colombia; Ecuador;
French Guiana;
Guyana; Panama;
Peru; Suriname;
Venezuela.

Caribbean:Trinidad and Tobago.

Any person (except infants up to the age of 6 mos.) arriving without a certificate within 6 days of departure from or transit through an infected area will be isolated up to 6 days.

Indonesia (B)[6] Yellow Fever - II A certificate is required ALSO from travelers arriving from countries in the endemic zones (see p. 115).	In general, rural areas only, except high risk in all areas of Irian Jaya (western half of island of New Guinea). No risk in big cities of Java and Sumatra and no risk for main resort areas of Java and Bali.	Confirmed
Iran (Islamic Republic of) (B) Yellow Fever - II > 1 yr A certificate is required ALSO from travelers arriving from countries in the endemic zones (see p. 115).	Rural areas only in the provinces of Sistan-Baluchestan and Hormozgan, the southern parts of Fars, Kohgiluyeh-Boyar, Lorestan, and Chahar Mahal-Bakhtiari, and the north of Khuzestan.	Confirmed
Iraq (A)	All areas	None

113

Yellow Fever - II	in northern region, i.e., Duhok, Erbil, Kirkuk, Ninawa, Sulaimaniya Provinces.	
Ireland No vaccinations are required.	None	
Israel No vaccinations are required.	None	
Italy No vaccinations are required.	None	
Jamaica Yellow Fever - II > 1 yr	None	
Japan No vaccinations are required.	None	
Jordan Yellow Fever A certificate is required from travelers arriving from countries in the endemic zone in Africa (See page 126).	None	
Kazakhstan Follow former USSR regulations until further notice.	None	
Kenya (B) Yellow Fever*†† - II > 1 yr	All areas (including game parks), except no risk in Nairobi, and areas above 2,500 meters.	Confirmed
Kiribati **(formerly Gilbert Islands)** Yellow Fever - II > 1 yr	None	
Korea, Democratic People's Republic of (North) No vaccinations are required.	None	
Korea, Republic of (South) No vaccinations are required.	None	
Kuwait No vaccinations are required.	None	

Kyrgyzstan Follow USSR regulations until furthet notice	None	
Lao People's (B) **Democratic Republic** Yellow Fever - II	All areas except no risk in city of Vientiane.	Confirmed
Latvia . Follow USSR regulations until further notice	None	
Lebanon Yellow Fever - II	None	
Lesotho Yellow Fever - II	None	
Liberia (B) Yellow Fever* - I > 1 yr	All	Confirmed
Libyan Arab Jamahiriya (None) Yellow Fever - II > 1 yr	Very limited risk in two small foci in southwest of country.	None
Liechtenstein No vaccinations are required.	None	
Luxembourg No vaccinations are required.	None	
Macao (Portugal) No vaccinations are required.	None	
Madagascar (B) . . Yellow Fever - II Requirement ALSO includes transiting travelers.	All, highest risk in coastal areas .	Confirmed
Madeira (Portugal) Yellow Fever - II > 1 yr Except that NO certificate is required from travelers in transit at Funchal and Porto Santo.	None	
Malawi (B) Yellow Fever - II	All	Confirmed

Malaysia (B[7]) Yellow Fever - II > 1 yr A certificate is required ALSO from travelers arriving from countries in the endemic zones see p. 115).	Peninsular Malaysia and Sarawak (NW Borneo) malaria is limited to the rural hinterland; urban and coastal areas are malaria free. Sabah (NE Borneo) has malaria throughout.	Confirmed
Maldives Yellow Fever - II	None	
Mali (B) Yellow Fever* - I > 1 yr	All	Confirmed
Malta Yellow Fever - II > 6 mo Children under 6 months of age arriving from an infected area may be subject to isolation or surveillance.	None	
Martinique (France) Yellow Fever - II > 1 yr	None	
Mauritania (B) Yellow Fever - I > 1 yr Except that NO certificate is required from travelers who arrive from a non-infected area and stay less than 2 weeks.	All areas, except no risk in the northern region, i.e.. Dakhlet- Nouadhibou, Inchiri, Adrar, and Tiris-Zemour.	Probable
Mauritius (A) Yellow Fever - II > 1 yr A certificate is required ALSO from travelers arriving from countries in the endemic zones (see p. 115).	Rural areas only, except no risk on Rodriguez Island.	None
Mayotte (French territorial **collectivity) (B)** No Vaccinations are required.	All	Confirmed
Mexico (A) Yellow Fever - II > 6 mos. . .	Malaria exists in some rural areas of the following states: Oaxaca Chiapas, Guerrero Campeche, Quintana Roo, Sinaloa, Mich- oacan, Nayarit, Colima	None

Tabasco.[8]

Monaco
No vaccinations are required.

None

Mongolia
No vaccinations are required.

None

Montserrat (U.K.)
Yellow Fever - II > 1 yr

None

Morocco (None)

. .
No vaccinations are required.

Very limited
risk in rural
areas of coastal
provinces.

None

Mozambique (B)
Yellow Fever - II > 1 yr

All

Confirmed

Myanmar (formerly Burma) (B)[9]

Yellow Fever - II
A certificate is required ALSO
from nationals and residents of
Myanmar departing for an infected area.

Rural areas
only.

Confirmed

Namibia (B)

Yellow Fever - II > 1 yr
A certificate is required ALSO
from travelers arriving from
countries in the endemic zone
in Africa and South America
(see p. 115). A certificate
is required ALSO from travelers
on unscheduled flights which use
airports other than those used by
scheduled airlines. Children under
one year of age may be subject to
surveillance.

All areas of
Ovamboland,
and Caprivi Strip.

Confirmed

Nauru
Yellow Fever - II > 1 yr

None

Nepal (B)

Yellow Fever - II

Rural areas
in Terai Dist.
and Hill
Districts below
1,200 meters.
There is no risk
in Katmandu.

Confirmed

Netherlands
No vaccinations are required.

None

Netherlands Antilles   None
Yellow Fever - II > 6 mo

New Caledonia (France)   None
Cholera-
Vaccination is not required,
however, travelers from infected
areas are required to complete a
form for the use of the Health Service.

Yellow Fever - II > 1 yr

New Zealand   None
No vaccinations are required.

Nicaragua (A)   Rural areas
                                             only, however,
Yellow Fever - II > 1 yr   risk exists
                                             in outskirts of
                                             Chinandega,
                                             Leon, Granada,
                                             Managua, Nandaime,
                                             Puerto Cabeza, Rosita,
                                             Siuna and Tipitapa.

Niger (B)   All   Confirmed
Yellow Fever* - I > 1 yr
Niger ALSO recommends vaccination
for travelers leaving the country.

Nigeria (B)   All   Confirmed
Yellow Fever* - II > 1 yr

New (New Zealand)   None
Yellow Fever - II > 1 yr

Northern Mariana Islands   None
U.S.)
No vaccinations are required.

Norway   None
No vaccinations are required.

Oman (B)   All   Confiremd
Yellow Fever - II

Pacific Islands, Trust   None
Territory of the U.S.A.
No vaccinations are required.

Pakistan (B)   All   Confirmed
Yellow Fever - III
A certificate is required ALSO
from travelers arriving from
countries in the endemic zones
(see p. 115). A certificate

118

is not required of infants less
than 6 months of age if the mother's
certificate shows she was vaccinated
prior to the birth of the child.

Panama (A/B)[10]

Yellow Fever* -
No vaccination required,
however, Panama recommends
vaccination for travelers
who are destined for the
province of Darien.

Rural areas
of the eastern
provinces
(Darien and
San Blas) and
the northwest-
ern provinces
(Boca del Toro
and Veraguas).
Lake Boyana area
and Lake Gatun

Confirmed in
areas east of
Canal Zone
including San
Blas Islands

Papua New Guinea (B)
Yellow Fever - II > 1 yr

All

Confirmed

Paraguay (A)

Yellow Fever* - II > 6 mo
A certificate is required ALSO
from travelers arriving from
countries in the endemic zones
(see p. 115).

Rural areas
bordering
Brazil.

None

Peru (A/B)[12]

Yellow Fever* - II > 6 mo
Peru also recommends vaccination
for those who intend to visit
any rural areas of the country.

Rural areas.[10]

Confirmed in
northern provinces
bordering Brazil

Philippines (A/B)[13]

Yellow Fever - II > 1 yr
Children under one year of age
arriving from infected areas
are subject to isolation or
surveillance.

Rural areas
only, except
there is no risk
in Provinces
of Bohol,
Catanduanes,
Cebu, and
Leyte.

Confirmed in
Islands of Luzon,
Basilan, Mindoro
Palawan, and
Mindanao; and Sulu
Archipelago

Pitcairn (U.K.)
Yellow Fever - II > 1 yr

None

Poland
No vaccinations are required.

None

Portugal
Yellow Fever -
A certificate is required ONLY
from travelers over 1 year of
age arriving from infected areas
who are destined for the Azores

None

119

and Madeira. However, no certi
-ficate is required from passengers
in transit at Funchal, Porto Santo,
and Santa Maria.

Puerto Rico (U.S.)   None
No vaccinations are required.

Qatar   None
Yellow Fever - II > 1 yr

Republic of Moldova   None
Follow former USSR
regulations until further notice.

Reunion (France)   None

Yellow Fever - II > 1 yr

Romania   None
No vaccinations are required.

Russian Federation   None
Follow former USSR
regulations until further notice.

Rwanda (B)   All   Confirmed
Yellow Fever* - I > 1 yr

Saint Christopher   None
(Saint Kitts) and Nevis (U.K.)
Yellow Fever - II > 1 yr

Saint Helena (U.K.)   None
No vaccinations are required.

Saint Lucia   None
Yellow Fever - II > 1 yr

Saint Pierre &   None
Miquelon (France)
No vaccinations are required.

Saint Vincent and   None
the Grenadines
Yellow Fever - II > 1 yr

Samoa (formerly   None
Western Samoa)
Yellow Fever - II > 1 yr

Samoa, American (U.S.)   None
Yellow Fever - II > 1 yr

San Marino   None
No vaccinations are required.

Sao Tome and Principe (B) Yellow Fever - I > 1 yr Except that NO certificate is required from travelers who arrive from a non-infected area and stay less than 2 weeks.	All	Confirmed
Saudi Arabia (A) Yellow Fever - III	All areas in the western provinces except no risk in the high altitude areas of Asir Province (Yemen border), and the urban areas of Jeddah, Mecca, Medina, and Taif.	Suspected
Senegal (B) Yellow Fever* - II > 1 yr A certificate is required ALSO from travelers arriving from countries in the endemic zones (see p. 115).	All	Confirmed
Serbia/Montenegro Follow Yugoslavia regulations until further notice.	None	
Seychelles No vaccinations are required.	None	
Sierra Leone (B) Yellow Fever* - II	All	Confirmed
Singapore Yellow Fever - III > 1 yr A certificate is required ALSO from travelers arriving from or transiting countries in the endemic zones (see p. 115).	None	
Slovak Republic No vaccinations are required.	None	
Slovenia No vaccinations are required.	None	
Solomon Islands (B) Yellow Fever - II	All	Confirmed
Somalia (B) Yellow Fever - II	All	Confirmed

121

South Africa (B) Yellow Fever - III A certificate is required ALSO from travelers arriving from countries in the endemic zone in Africa (see p. 115). A certificate is required ALSO from travelers on unscheduled flights which use airports other than those used by scheduled airlines.	Rural areas (including game parks) in the north, east, and western low altitude areas of Transvaal and in the Natal coastal areas north of 28⁰S.	Confirmed
Spain No vaccinations are required.	None	
Sri Lanka (B) Yellow Fever - II > 1 yr	All areas except Colombo. [14]	Confirmed
Sudan (All) Yellow Fever* - II > 1 yr A certificate is required ALSO from travelers arriving from countries in the endemic zones \(see p. 115). A certificate may be required from travelers leaving Sudan.	All	Confirmed
Suriname (B) Yellow Fever* - II	Rural areas only, except no risk in Paramaribo District and coastal areas north of 5⁰N.	Confirmed
Swaziland (B) Yellow Fever - II	All lowland areas.	Confirmed
Sweden No vaccinations are required.	None	
Switzerland No vaccinations are required.	None	
Syrian Arab Republic (A) Yellow Fever - II	Rural areas only, except no risk in the southern and western Districts of Deir-es-zor, and Sweida.	None

Taiwan Yellow Fever - II	None	
Tajikistan (A) Follow USSR regulations until further notice.	Exists in Southern border areas.	Suspected
Tanzania, United Republic of (B) Yellow Fever*†† - II > 1 yr A certificate is required ALSO from travelers arriving from countries in the endemic zones (see p. 115).	All	Confirmed
Thailand [15] Yellow Fever - II > 1 yr A certificate is required ALSO from travelers arriving from countries in the endemic zones (see p. 115).	Limited risk	Confirmed
Togo (B) Yellow Fever* - I > 1 yr	All	Confirmed
Tonga Yellow Fever - II > 1 yr	None	
Trinidad and Tobago Yellow Fever* - II > 1 yr	None	
Tunisia Yellow Fever - II > 1 yr	None	
Turkey (A) No vaccinations are required.	Southeast Anatolia from coastal city of Mersin to the Iraqi border (Cukorova/ Amikova areas).	None
Turkmenistan Follow former USSR regulations until further notice.	None	
Tuvalu Yellow Fever - II > 1 yr	None	
Uganda (B) Yellow Fever* - II > 1 yr A certificate is required ALSO from travelers arriving from countries in the endemic zones (p. 115).	All	Confirmed

123

Ukraine
Follow former USSR regulations
until further notice.

None

**(Former)Union of Soviet
Socialist Republics**
No vaccinations are required
(Editor's Note: Presume requirements
will remain the same for Russia and
other newly indepemdent states.
You may check with respective
embassies to be certain.

See individual
countries

United Arab Emirates (A)

No vaccinations are required.

Northern Emirates,
except no risk in
cities of Dubai,
Sharjah, Ajman, Umm
al Qaiwan, and Emirate
of Abu Dhabi.

None

**United Kingdom (with
Channel Islands and
the Isle of Man)**
No vaccinations are required.

None

United States of America
No vaccinations are required.

None

Uruguay
No vaccinations are required.

None

Uzbekistan
Follow former USSR regulations
until further notice.

None

**Vanuatu (formerly
New Hebrides) (B)**

No vaccinations are required.

All areas
except no
risk on
Fortuna island.

Confirmed

Venezuela (B)

No vaccinations are required.

Yellow Fever*

Rural areas of
all border states
and territories
and the south-
eastern states of
Barinas, Merida,
and Portuguesa.

Confirmed

Viet Nam (B)

Yellow Fever - II > 1 yr

Rural areas
only, except no
risk in the Red
and Mekong
Deltas.

Confirmed

Virgin Islands, British

None

124

No vaccinations are required.

Virgin Islands, U.S.   None
No vaccinations are required.

Wake Island (U.S.)   None
No vaccinations are required.

Yemen (B)   All areas,   Confirmed
                                            except no
Yellow Fever - II > 1 yr   risk in Aden
                                            and arport perimenter

Yugoslavia   None
No vaccinations are required.
(Editor's note: Presume requirements
will remain the same for the newly
independent states. Youmay check
with respective embassies to be certain.

Zaire (B)   All   Confirmed
Yellow Fever* -
A certificate is required ONLY
from travelers over 1 year of
age coming from infected areas
and arriving in or destined for
that part of Zaire south of 10'S.

Typhoid -
Zaire recommends vaccination.

Zambia (B)   All   Confirmed
Yellow Fever*† - II > 1 yr

Zimbabwe (formerly   All areas,   Confirmed
Rhodesia) (B)   except no
                                            risk in city
Yellow Fever - II   of Harare.

YELLOW FEVER ENDEMIC ZONES

IN AFRICA

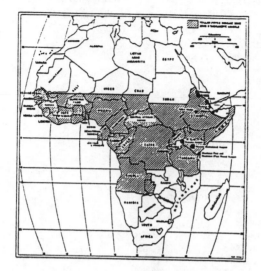

NOTE: Although the "yellow fever endemic zones" are no longer included in the International Health Regulations, a number of countries (most of them being not bound by the Regulations or bound with reservations) consider these zones as infected areas and require an International Certificate of Vaccination against Yellow Fever from travelers arriving from those areas. The above map based on information from WHO is therefore included in this publication for practical reasons.

YELLOW FEVER ENDEMIC ZONES

IN THE AMERICAS

NOTE: Although the "yellow fever endemic zones" are no longer included in the International Health Regulations, a number of countries (most of them being not bound by the Regulations or bound with reservations) consider these zones as infected areas and require an International Certificate of Vaccination against Yellow Fever from travelers arriving from those areas. The above map based on information from WHO is therefore included in this publication for practical reasons.
In addition to areas shaded (WHO, 1988) CDC recommends vaccination for entire state of Mato Grosso in Brazil.

GEOGRAPHICAL DISTRIBUTION OF POTENTIAL HEALTH HAZARDS TO TRAVELERS*

*[*This chapter has been reprinted from International Travel and Health: Vaccination Requirements and Health Advice-Situation as on 1 January 1994, published by World Health Organization.]*

This section is intended to give a broad indication of the health risks to which travelers may be exposed in various areas of the world and which they may not encounter in their usual place of residence.

In practice, to identify areas accurately and define the degree of risk likely in each of them is extremely difficult, if not impossible. For example, viral hepatitis A is ubiquitous but the risk of infection varies not only according to area but also according to eating habits; hence, there may be more risk from communal eating in an area of low incidence than from eating in a private home in an area of high incidence. Generalizations may therefore be misleading.

Another factor is that tourism is an important source of income for many countries and to label specific areas as being of high risk for a disease may be misinterpreted. However, this does not absolve national health administrations from their responsibility to provide an accurate picture of the risks from communicable diseases that may be encountered in various parts of their countries.

AFRICA

Northern Africa (Algeria, Egypt, Libyan Arab Jamahiriya, Morocco, and Tunisia) is characterized by a generally fertile coastal area and a desert hinterland with oases that are often foci of infections.

Arthropod-borne diseases are unlikely to be a major problem to the traveler, although dengue fever, filariasis (focally in the Nile Delta), leishmaniasis, malaria, relapsing fever, Rift Valley fever, sandfly fever, typhus, and West Nile fever do occur. Small foci of plague have been reported in the Libyan Arab Jamahiriya.

Foodborne and waterborne diseases are endemic; the dysenteries and other diarrheal diseases are particularly common. Typhoid fever and viral hepatitis A are common in some areas. Schistosomiasis (bilharziasis) is very prevalent in the Nile Delta area in Egypt and in the Nile valley; it occurs focally in other countries in the area. Alimentary helminthic infections, brucellosis, and giardiasis are common. Echinococcosis (hydatid disease) may occur. Sporadic cases of cholera occur.

Other hazards include poliomyelitis, trachoma, rabies, scorpion stings, and snake bites. However, no cases of poliomyelities have been reported from Algeria since 1990, from Libyan Arab Jamahiriya since 1991 or from Morocco since 1989

Sub-Saharan Africa (Angola, Benin, Burkina Faso, Burundi, Cameroon, Cape Verde, Central African Republic, Chad, Comoros, Congo, Cote d'Ivoire, Djibouti, Equatorial Guinea, Ethiopia, Gabon, Gambia, Ghana, Guinea, Guinea-Bissau, Kenya, Liberia, Madagascar, Malawi, Mali, Mauritania, Mauritius, Mozambique, Niger, Nigeria, Reunion. Rwanda, Sao Tome and Principe, Senegal, Seychelles, Sierra Leone, Somalia, Sudan, Togo, Uganda, United Republic of Tanzania, Zaire, Zambia, and Zimbabwe). In this area, entirely within the tropics, the vegetation varies from the tropical rain forests of the west and center to the wooded steppes of the east, and from the desert of the north through the Sahel and Sudan savannas to the moist orchard savanna and woodlands north and south of the equator.

Many of the diseases listed below occur in localized rural foci. They are mentioned so that the international traveler and the medical practitioner concerned may be aware of the diseases that may occur.

Arthropod-borne diseases are a major cause of morbidity. Malaria in the severe falciparum (malignant) form occurs throughout the area, except at over 3,000 meters altitude and in the islands of Cape Verde, Mauritius, Reunion, and Seychelles. Various forms of filariasis are widespread; endemic foci of onchocerciasis (river blindness) exist in all the countries listed except in the greater part of Kenya and in Djibouti, Gambia, Mauritania, Mozambique, Somalia, Zambia, Zimbabwe, and the island countries of the Atlantic and Indian Oceans. However, onchocerciasis exists in the island of Bioko, Equatorial Guinea. Both cutaneous and visceral leishmaniasis may be found, particularly in the drier areas. Visceral leishmaniasis is on the increase in Sudan. Human trypanosomiasis (sleeping-sickness), mainly in small isolated foci, is reported from all countries except Djibouti, Gambia, Mauritania, Somalia, and the island countries of the Atlantic and Indian Oceans. Relapsing fever and louse-, flea-, and tick-borne typhus occur. Natural foci of plague have been reported from Kenya, Madagascar, Mozambique, Uganda, the United Republic of Tanzania, and Zaire. Tungiasis is widespread in western Africa. Many viral diseases, some presenting as severe hemorrhagic fevers, are transmitted by mosquitos, ticks, sandflies, etc., which are found throughout this region. Large outbreaks of yellow fever occur periodically in the unvaccinated population.

127

Foodborne and waterborne diseases are highly endemic. Schistosomiasis (bilharziasis) is present throughout the area except in Cape Verde, Comoras, Djibouti, Reunion, and the Seychelles. Alimentary helminthic infections, the dysenteries and diarrheal diseases, including cholera, giardiasis, typhoid fever, and viral hepatitis are widespread. Guinea-worm infection occurs in isolated foci. Paragonimiasis (oriental long fluke) has been reported from Cameroon, Gabon, Liberia and most recently from Equatorial Guinea.

Other diseases. Herpatities B is hyperendemic. Poliomyelitis is endemic in most countries except in Cape Verde, Comoros, Mauritius, Reunion, and the Seychelles. Trachoma is widespread. Among other diseases, certain, frequently fatal, arenavirus haemorrhagic fevers have attained notoriety. Lassa fever has a virus reservoir in a commonly found multimammate rat. Studies have shown that an appreciable reservoir exists in some rural areas of West Africa; people visiting these areas should take particular care to avoid rat-contaminated food or food containers, but the extent of the disease should not be exaggerated. The Ebola and Marburg hemorrhagic fevers are present but reported only infrequently. Echinococcosis (hydatid disease) is widespread in animal-breeding areas.

Epidemics of meningococcoccal meningitis may occur throughout tropical Africa, particularly in the savanna areas during the dry season. Other hazards include rabies and snake bites.

Southern Africa (Botswana, Lesotho, Namibia, St. Helena, South Africa, and Swaziland) varies physically from the Namib and Kalahari deserts to fertile plateaux and plains and to the more temperate climate of the southern coast.

Arthropod-borne diseases such as Crimean-Congo hemorrhagic fever, malaria, plague, relapsing fever, Rift Valley fever, tick-bite fever, and typhus-mainly tick-borne - have been reported from most of this area except St. Helena, but except for malaria in certain areas, they are not likely to be a major health problem for the traveler. Trypanosomiasis (sleeping sickness) may occur in Botswana and Namibia.

Foodborne and waterborne diseases are common in some areas, particularly amebiasis and typhoid fever. Schistosomiasis (bilharziasis) is endemic in Botswana, Namibia, Swaziland and South Africa.

Other hazards. No cases of poliomyelitis have been reported from these countries since 1988. Hepatities B is hyperendemic. Snakes may be a hazard in some areas.

THE AMERICAS
Available data suggest that transmission of the poliomyelitis virus in the Region of the Americas may have been interruped or is , at the very least, rapidly approaching this point. Wild virus transmission in 1991 was documented only in Colombia and Peru. However, in 1993 wild virus was detected in Canada, although, no paralytic cases have been found despite intensive surveillance.

North America (Bermuda, Canada, Greenland, St. Pierre and Miquelon, and the United States of America with [Hawaii]) extends from the Arctic to the subtropical cays of the southern USA.

The incidence of communicable diseases is such that, they are unlikely to prove a hazard for international travelers greater than that found in their own country. There are, of course, health risks but in general, the precautions required are minimal. Plague, rabies in wildlife including bats, Rocky Mountain spotted fever, tularemia, and arthropod-borne encephalitis occasionally occur. Lyme disease is endemic in the northeastern United States and the upper Midwest. During recent years, the incidence of certain food-borne diseases, e.g. salmonellosis, has increased in some reagions. Other hazards include poisonous snakes, poison ivy, and poison oak. In the north, a serious hazard is the very low temperature in the winter.

In the USA, proof of immunization against diphtheria, measles, poliomyelitis, and rubella is now universally required for entry into school. In addition, the school entry requirements of most States include immunization against tetanus (49 States), pertussis (44 States), and mumps (43 States).

Mainland Middle America (Belize, Costa Rica, El Salvador, Guatemala, Honduras, Mexico, Nicaragua, and Panama) ranges from the deserts of the north to the tropical rain forests of the southeast.

Of the arthropod-borne diseases, malaria exists in all eight countries, but in Costa Rica and Panama it is confined to a few areas and in Mexico, mainly to the west coast. Visceral leishmaniasis occurs in El Salvador, Guatemala, Honduras and Mexico. Onchocerciasis (river blindness) is found in two small foci in the south of Mexico and four dispersed foci in Guatemala. American trypanosomiasis (Chagas' disease) has been reported to occur in localized foci in rural areas in all eight countries. Bancroftian filariasis is present in Costa Rica. Dengue fever and Venezuelan equine encephalitis may occur in all countries.

The foodborne and waterborne diseases, including

amebic and bacillary dysenteries and other diarrheal diseases, and typhoid fever are very common throughout the area. [All countries have reported cases of cholera since mid-1991]. Viral hepatitis occurs throughout the area. Helminthic infections are common. Paragonimiasis (oriental lung fluke) has been reported in Costa Rica, Honduras and Panama. Brucellosis occurs in the northern part of the area. Many Salmonella typhi infections from Mexico and Shigella dysenteriae type 1 infections from mainland Middle America as a whole have been caused by drug-resistant enterobacteria.

Other diseases. Rabies in animals (usually dogs and bats) is widespread throughout the area. Snakes may be a hazard in some areas.

Caribbean Middle America (Antigua and Barbuda, Aruba, Bahamas, Barbados, British Virgin Islands, Cayman Islands, Cuba, Dominica, Dominican Republic, Grenada, Guadeloupe, Haiti, Jamaica, Martinique, Montserrat, Netherlands Antilles, Puerto Rico, St. Christopher and Nevis, Saint Lucia, Saint Vincent and the Grenadines, Trinidad and Tobago, Turks and Caicos Islands, and the Virgin Islands (USA)). The islands, a number of them mountainous with peaks 1000-2500 m high, have an equable tropical climate with heavy rain storms and high winds at certain times of the year.

Of the arthropod-borne diseases, malaria occurs in endemic form only in Haiti and in parts of the Dominican Republic; elsewhere it has been eradicated. Diffuse cutaneous leishmaniasis was recently discovered in the Dominican Republic. Bancroftian filariasis occurs in Haiti and some other islands and other filariases may occasionally be found. Human fascioliasis due to Fasciola hepatica is endemic in Cuba. Outbreaks of dengue fever occur in the area, and dengue hemorrhagic fever has also occurred. Tularemia has been reported from Haiti.

Of the foodborne and waterborne diseases, bacillary and amebic dysenteries are common and hepatitis A is reported, particularly in the northern islands. No cases of cholera had been reported in the Caribbean at the time of printing. Schistosomiasis (bilharziasis) is endemic in the Dominican Republic, Guadeloupe, Martinique, Puerto Rico, and Saint Lucia, in each of which control operations are in progress, and it may also occur sporadically in other islands.

Other diseases: Other hazards may occur from spiny sea urchins and coelenterates (coral and jellyfish) and snakes. Animal rabies, particularly in the mongoose, is reported from several islands (see pp. 131-132).

Tropical South America (Bolivia, Brazil, Colombia, Ecuador, French Guiana, Guyana, Paraguay, Peru, Suriname, and Venezuela) covers the narrow coastal strip on the Pacific Ocean, the high Andean range with numerous peaks 5000-7000 m high, and the tropical rain forests of the Amazon basin, bordered to the north and south by savanna zones and dry tropical forest or scrub.

Arthropod-borne diseases are an important cause of ill health in rural areas. Malaria (in the falciparum, malariae and vivax forms) occurs in all ten countries or areas, as do American trypanosomiasis (Chagas disease), and cutaneous and mucocutaneous leishmaniasis. There has been an increase of the latter in Brazil and Paraguay. Visceral leishmaniasis is frequent in north-east Brazil, with foci in other parts of Brazil, less frequent in Colombia, and Venezuela, rare in Bolivia and Paraguay, and unknown in Peru. Endemic onchocerciasis occurs in isolated foci in rural areas in Ecuador, Venezuela, and northern Brazil. The bites of blackflies, the vectors of onchocerciasis, may also transmit other filarial parasites or cause unpleasant and sometimes severe hemorrhagic reactions. Bancroftian filariasis is endemic in parts of Brazil, Guyana and Suriname. Plague has been reported in natural foci in Bolivia, Brazil, Ecuador, and Peru. Among the arthropod-borne viral diseases, jungle yellow fever may be found in forest areas in all countries except Paraguay and areas east of the Andes; in Brazil it is confined to the northern and western states. Epidemics of viral encephalitis and dengue fever occur in some countries of this area. Bartonellosis, or Oroya fever, a sandfly-borne disease, occurs in arid river valleys on the western slopes of the Andes up to 3,000 meters. Louse-borne typhus is often found in mountain areas of Colombia and Peru.

Foodborne and waterborne diseases are common and include amebiasis, cholera, diarrheal diseases, helminthic infections, and hepatitis A. The intestinal form of schistosomiasis (bilharziasis) is found in Brazil, Suriname, and north-central Venezuela. Paragonimiasis (oriental lung fluke) has been reported from Ecuador, Peru and Venezuela. Brucellosis is common and echinococcosis (hydatid disease) occurs, particularly in Peru. All countries except Paraguay reported cases of cholera in 1992. Bolivia, Ecuador, Peru continue to be affected by the epidemic wave which originated in the latter country in 1991. Risk of cholera transmission is low to moderate in other countries.

Other diseases include rodent-borne arenavirus hemorrhagic fever in Bolivia. Hepetaitis B & D (delta hepatitis) are highly endemic in the Amazon basin. Poliomyelitis is reported from all areas, but at a low incidence from French Guiana, Guyana, and Suriname. Rabies has been reported from many of the countries in this area. Meningococcal meningitis occurs in epidemic outbreaks in Brazil.

Snakes and leeches may be a hazard in some areas.

Temperate South America (Argentina, Chile, Falkland Islands (Malvinas), and Uruguay). The mainland ranges from the Mediterranean climatic area of the western coastal strip over the Andes divide on to the steppes and desert of Patagonia in the south and to the prairies of the northeast.

The arthropod-borne diseases are relatively unimportant except for the widespread occurrence of American trypanosomiasis (Chagas disease). Outbreaks of malaria occur in northwestern Argentina, and cutaneous leishmaniasis is also reported from the northeastern part of the country.

Of the foodborne and waterborne diseases, gastroenteritis (mainly salmonellosis) is relatively common in Argentina, especially in suburban areas and among children under 5 years of age. Cases of cholera have occured in the northern provinces of Argentina and few cases have been reported from Chile. No cases of cholera have been reported from Uruguay. Typhoid fever is not very common in Argentina but viral hepatitis and intestinal parasitosis are widespread, the latter especially in the coastal region. Taeniasis (tapeworm), typhoid fever, viral hepatitis, and echinococcosis (hydatid disease) are reported from the other countries.

Anthrax is an occupational hazard in the mainland countries. Animal rabies is endemic in Argentina; it has increased in the last five years but is confined mainly to urban and suburban areas. Rodent-borne hemorrhagic fever is endemic in a limited zone of the pampas and in the center of the country.

Anthrax is an occupational hazard in the three mainland countries. Animal rabies is endemic in Argentina; it has increased in the last five years but is confined mainly to urban and suburban areas. Rodent-borne hemorrhagic fever is endemic in a limited zone of the pampas and in the center of the country.

ASIA

East Asia (China, the Democratic People's Republic of Korea, Hong Kong, Japan, Macao, Mongolia, and the Republic of Korea). The area includes the high mountain complexes, the desert and the steppes of the west, the various forest zones of the east, down to the subtropical forests of the southeast.

Among the arthropod-borne diseases, malaria now occurs only in China. Although reduced in distribution and prevalence, bancroftian and brugian filariasis are still reported in southern China. A resurgence of viceral leishmaniasis is occuring in China and plague may be found in China. Cutaneous leishmaniasis has recently been reported from Xinjiang, Uygur Auotonomous Region. Hemorrhagic fever with renal syndrome-rodent-borne, Korean hemorrhagic fever-is endemic, and epidemics of dengue fever and Japanese encephalitis may occur in this area. Mite-borne or scrub typhus may be found in scrub areas in southern China, certain river valleys in Japan, and in the Republic of Korea.

Foodborne and waterborne diseases such as diarrheal diseases and hepatitis A are common in most countries. hepatitis E is prevalent in western China. The present endemic area of schistosomiasis (bilharziasis) is in the central Chang Jiang (Yangtze) river basin; active foci no longer occur in Japan. Clonorchiasis (oriental liver fluke) and paragonimiasis (oriental lung fluke) are reported in China, Japan, Macao and the Republic of Korea, and fasciolopsiasis (giant intestinal fluke) in China. Brucellosis occurs in China.

Other diseases. Hepatitis B is highly endemic. Poliomyelitis continues to be reported. Trachoma, and leptospirosis occur in China.

Eastern South Asia (Brunei Darussalam, Cambodia, Indonesia, Lao People's Democratic Republic, Malaysia, Myanmar (formerly Burma), the Philippines,Singapore, Thailand, and Viet Nam). From the tropical rain and monsoon forests of the north-west, the area extends through the savanna and the dry tropical forests of Indochina peninsula, returning to the tropical rain and monsoon forests of the lands bordering the South China Sea.

The arthropod-borne diseases are an important cause of morbidity throughout area. Malaria and filariasis are endemic in many parts of the rural areas of all the countries or areas-except for malaria in Brunei Darussalam, and Singapore, where only imported cases occur. Foci of plague exist in Myanmar. Plague also occurs in Viet Nam. Japanese encephalitis, dengue and dengue hemorrhagic fever can occur in epidemics in both urban and rural areas. Mite-borne typhus has been reported in deforested areas in most countries.

Foodborne and waterborne diseases are common. Cholera and other watery diarrheas, amebic and bacillary dysentery, typhoid fever, and hepatitis A & E

130

may occur in all countries in the area. Schistosomiasis (bilharziasis) is endemic in the Southern Philippines and in central Sulawesi (Indonesia) and occurs in small foci in the Mekong delta. Among other helminthic infections, fasciolopsiasis (giant intestinal fluke) may be acquired in most countries in the area; clonorchiasis (oriental liver fluke) in the Indochina peninsula; opisthorchiasis (cat liver fluke) in the Indochina peninsula, the Philippines, and Thailand; and paragonimiasis in most countries. Melioidosis can occur sporadically throughout the area.

Other diseases. Poliomyelitis is reported throughout the area, but the incidence is low in Malaysia and it has been eliminated in Brunei Darussalam and Singapore. Trachoma exists in Indonesia, Myanmar, Thailand, and Viet Nam.

Other hazards include rabies, snake bites, and leeches.

Middle South Asia (Afghanistan, Armenia, Azerbaijan, Bangladesh, Bhutan, India, Islamic Republic of Iran, Kazakhstan, Kyrgyzstan, Maldives, Nepal, Pakistan, and Sri Lanka, Tajikistan, Turkmenistan and Uzbekistan). Bordered for the most part by high mountain ranges in the north, the area extends from steppes and desert in the west to monsoon and tropical rain forests in the east and south.

Arthropod-borne diseases are endemic in all these countries except for malaria in the Maldives. There are small foci of malaria in Azerbaijan and Tajikistan. In some of the other countries, malaria occurs in urban as well as rural areas. Filariasis is common in Bangladesh and India, and the southwestern coastal belt of Sri Lanka. Sandfly fever are on the increase. A sharp rise in the incidence of viceral leishmaniasis has been observed in Bangladesh, India and Nepal. In Pakistan, it is mainly reported from the north (Baltisan) Cutaneous leishmaniasis occurs in Afghanistan, India (Rajasthan), the Islamic Republic of Iran, and Pakistan. There are very small foci of cutaneous and viceral leishmaniasis in Azerbaijan and Tajikistan. Tick-borne relapsing fever is reported from Afghanistan, India, and the Islamic Republic of Iran, and typhus occurs in Afghanistan and India. Epidemics of dengue fever may occur in Bangladesh, India, Pakistan, and Sri Lanka and the hemorrhagic form has been reported from eastern India and Sri Lanka. Japanese encephalitis has been reported from the eastern part of the area and Crimean-Congo hemorrhagic fever from the western part. Another tick-borne hemorrhagic fever has been reported in forest areas of Karnataka State in India and in a rural area of Rawalpindi District in Pakistan.

Foodborne and waterborne diseases are common

throughout the area, in particular cholera and other watery diarrheas, the dysenteries, typhoid fever, hepatitis A & E, and helminthic infections. Large epidemics of hepatitis E can occur. Giardiasis is said to be common in the Islamic Republic of Iran. A focus of urinary schistosomiasis (bilharziasis) exists in the southwest of the Islamic Republic of Iran. Foci of dracunculiasis (guinea-worm) infection occur in India and in Pakistan. Brucellosis and echinococcosis (hydatid disease) are found in many countries in the area.

Other diseases. Hepatitis B is endemic. Outbreaks of meningococcal meningitis have been reported in India and Nepal. Poliomyelitis is widespread except in Bhutan and the Maldives. Trachoma is common in Afghanistan, India, the Islamic Republic of Iran, Nepal, and Pakistan. Snakes and the presence of rabies in animals are hazards in most of the countries in the area.

Western South Asia-Bahrain, Cyprus, Iraq, Israel, Jordan, Kuwait, Lebanon, Oman, Qatar, Saudi Arabia, Syrian Arab Republic, Turkey, the United Arab Emirates, and Yemen). The area ranges from the mountains and steppes of the north-west to the large deserts and dry tropical scrub of the south.

The arthropod-borne diseases, except for malaria in certain areas, are not a major hazard for the traveler. Malaria does not exist in Kuwait and no longer occurs in Bahrain, Cyprus, Israel, Jordan, Lebanon, or Qatar. Its incidence in the Syrian Arab Republic is low, but elsewhere is endemic in certain rural areas. Cutaneous leishmaniasis is reported throughout the area; visceral leishmaniasis, although rare throughout most of the area, is common in central Iraq, in the southeast of Saudi Arabia, in the north of the Syrian Arab Republic, in Turkey and in the west of Yemen. Murine and tick-borne typhus can occur in most countries. Tick-borne relapsing fever may occur. Crimean-Congo hemorrhagic fever has been reported from Iraq. Limited foci of onchocerciasis are reported in Yemen.

The **foodborne and waterborne** diseases are a major hazard in most countries. The typhoid fever and hepatitis A exist in all countries and cases of cholera has been reported from Iraq. Schistosomiasis (bilharziasis) occurs in Iraq, Saudi Arabia, the Syrian Arab Republic, and Yemen. Dracunculiasis (Guinea-worm) infection is found in some of these countries. Taeniasis (tapeworm) is reported from many of the countries. Brucellosis is widespread and there are foci of echinococcosis (hydatid disease).

Other diseases. No cases of poliomyelitis have been reported from Bahrain since 1981, from Kuwait since 1986, from Quatar since 1985 or from Israel since

1989, but is endemic in other countries. Trachoma and animal rabies are found in many countries in the area. The greatest hazards to pilgrims to Mecca and Medina are heat and water depletion if the period of the Hajj coincides with the hot season.

EUROPE

Northern Europe (Belgium, Czech Republic, Denmark (with the Faroe Islands), Finland, Germany, Iceland, Ireland, Latvia, Lithuania, Luxembourg, Netherlands, Norway, Poland, Republic of Moldova, Russian federation, Slovakia, Sweden, Ukraine and the United Kingdom (with the Channel Islands and the Isle of Man). The area encompassed by these countries extends from the broadleaf forests and the plains of the west to the boreal and mixed forest to be found as far as the Pacific Ocean.

The incidence of communicable diseases in most countries is such that they are unlikely to prove a hazard to international travelers greater than that found in their own country. There are, of course, health risks but in most areas very few precautions are required.

Of the arthropod-borne diseases, there are very small foci of malaria and cutaneous and visceral leishmaniasis in southern USSR, and tick-borne typhus in east and central Siberia. Tick-borne encephalitis, for which a vaccine exists, Lyme disease, and Crimean-Congo hemorrhagic fever may occur throughout Northern Europe. Rodent-borne hemorrhagic fever with renal syndrome is now recognized as occurring at low endemic levels in this area.

The foodborne and waterborne diseases reported, other than the ubiquitous diarrheal diseases, are taeniasis (tapeworm) and trichinellosis in parts of northern Europe, diphyllobothriasis (fish tapeworm) from the freshwater fish around the Baltic Sea area. Fasciola hepatica infection can occur. The incidence of certain food-borne diseases, e.g., salmonellosis and campylobacterioses, is increasing significantly in some of these countries.

Other diseases. Rabies is endemic in wild animals (particularly foxes) in rural areas of northern Europe except Finland, Iceland, Ireland, Norway, Sweden, and the United Kingdom.

A climatic hazard in part of northern Europe is the extreme cold in winter.

Southern Europe (Albania, Andorra, Austria, Bulgaria, France, Gibraltar, Greece, Hungary, Italy, Liechtenstein, Malta, Monaco, Portugal (with the

Azores and Madeira), Romania, San Marino, Spain (with the Canary Islands), Switzerland, and Yugoslavia). The area extends from the-broad-leaf forests in the north-west and the mountains of the Alps to the prairies and, in the south and south-east, the scrub vegetation of the Mediterranean.

Among the arthropod-borne diseases, sporadic cases of murine and tick-borne typhus and mosquito-borne West Nile fever occur in some countries bordering the Mediterranean littoral. Cutaneous and visceral leishmaniasis and sandfly fever are also reported from this area. Tickborne encephalitis, for which a vaccine exists, Lyme disease, and rodent-borne hemorrhagic fever with renal syndrome may occur in the eastern and southern parts of the area.

The foodborne and waterborne diseases-bacillary dysentery and other diarrheas, and typhoid fever-are more common in the summer and autumn months, with a high incidence in the southeastern and southwestern parts of the area. Brucellosis can occur in the extreme southwest and southeast and echinococcosis (hydatid disease) in the southeast. Fasciola hepatica infection has been reported from different countries in the area. The incidence of certain food-borne diseases e.g., salmonellosis and campylobacteriosis, is increasing significantly in some of these areas.

Other diseases. Poliomyelitis is reported from Croatia and Yugoslavia, hepatitis B is endemic in the southern part of Eastern europe (Albania, Bulgaria and Romania). Rabies in animals exists in most countries of southern Europe except Gibraltar, Malta, Monaco, Portugal and Spain.

OCEANIA
Australia, New Zealand and the Antarctic. In Australia the mainland has tropical monsoon forests in the north and east, dry tropical forests, savanna and deserts in the center, and Mediterranean scrub and subtropical forests in the south. New Zealand has a temperate climate with the North Island characterized by subtropical forests and the South Island by steppe vegetation and hardwood forests.

International travelers to Australia and New Zealand, will, in general, not be subjected to the hazards of communicable diseases to an extent greater than that found in their own country.
Arthropod-borne diseases (mosquito-borne epidemic polyarthritis and viral encephalitis) may occur in some rural areas of Australia.
Among the foodborne and waterborne diseases, amebic meningoencephalitis has been reported.

Other hazards. Coelenterates (corals and jellyfish) may prove a hazard to the sea-bather, and heat is a hazard in the northern and central parts of Australia.

Melanesia and Micronesia-Polynesia (American Samoa, Cook Islands, Easter Island, Fiji, French Polynesia, Guam, Kiribati, Nauru, New Caledonia, New, Palau, Papua New Guinea, Samoa, Solomon Islands, Tokelau, Tonga, Trust Territory of the Pacific Islands, Tuvalu, Vanuatu, and the Wallis and Futuna Islands). The area covers an enormous expanse of ocean with the larger, mountainous, tropical and monsoon rain forest-covered islands of the west giving way to the smaller, originally volcanic peaks and coral islands of the east.

Anrthropod-borne diseases occur in the majority of the islands. Malaria is endemic in Papua New Guinea and is found as far east and south as Vanuatu. Neither malaria nor anopheline vectors are found in Fiji or the islands to the north and as far as French Polynesia and Easter Island in the east, nor in New Caledonia to the south. Filariais is widespread but its prevalence varies. Mite-borne typhus has been reported from Papua New Guinea, Dengue fever, including its hemorrhagic form, can occur in epidemics in most islands.

Foodborne and waterborne diseases such as the diarrheal diseases, typhoid fever and helminthic infections are commonly reported. Biointoxication may occur from raw or cooked fish and shellfish. Hepatitis A occurs in this area.

Other diseases. Hepatitis B is endemic. Poliomyelitis occurs in Papua New Guinea and trachoma in parts of Melanesia.

Hazards to bathers are coelenterates, poisonous fish, a   n   d   s   e   a snakes.

HEALTH HINTS FOR THE INTERNATIONAL TRAVELER

INTRODUCTION
This section includes practical information on how to avoid potential health problems. Some of these recommendations are common-sense precautions; others have been scientifically documented.

Personal and specific preventive measures against certain diseases may require advance planning and advice from a physician concerning immunization and prophylaxis. If more specific information is needed, travelers should contact their local health department or physician.

Travelers who take prescription medications should carry an adequate supply accompanied by a signed and dated statement from a physician: the statement should indicate the major health problems and dosage of such medications, to provide information for medical authorities in case of emergency. The traveler should take an extra pair of glasses or lens prescription, and a card, tag, or bracelet that identifies any physical condition that may require emergency care.

IF MEDICAL CARE IS NEEDED ABROAD
If medical care is needed abroad, travel agents or the American Embassy or Consulate can usually provide names of hospitals, physicians, or emergency medical service agencies. Prior to departure, travelers should contact their own insurance companies concerning their coverage.

WHO Blood Transfusion Guidelines for International Travelers
There is a growing public awareness of the AIDS epidemic, and a resulting concern about acquiring the AIDS virus through blood transfusion. Systematic screening of blood donations is not yet feasible in all developing countries. Requests have been made by persons planning international travels, to have their own blood, or blood from their home country, available to them in case of urgent need. These requests raise logistic, technical and ethical issues which are not easy to resolve. Ultimately, the safety of blood for such persons will depend upon the quality of blood transfusion services in the host country. The strengthening of these services is of the highest priority. While efforts are being made to achieve this end, other approaches are also needed.

Basic Principles:
1. Unexpected, emergency blood transfusion is rarely required. It is needed only in situations of massive hemorrhage like severe trauma, gynecologic and obstetric emergency, or gastrointestinal bleeding.

2. In many cases, resuscitation can be achieved by use of colloid or crystalloid plasma expanders* instead of blood.

3. Blood transfusion is not free of risk, even in the best of conditions. In most developing countries, the risk is increased by limited technical resources for screening blood donors for HIV infection and other diseases transmissible by blood.

See World Health Organization documents LAR/81.5: "Use of plasma volume substitutes and plasma in developing countries," for further details, and

133

WHO/GPA/INF/88.5 "Guidelines for Treatment of Acute Blood Loss;" or standard medical or surgical textbooks.

4. The international shipment of blood for transfusion is practical only when handled by agreement between two responsible organizations, such as national blood transfusion services. This mechanism is not useful for emergency needs of individual patients and should not be attempted by private individuals or organizations not operating recognized blood programs.

Therefore:
1. There are no medical indications for travelers to take blood with them from their home country.

2. The limited storage period of blood and the need for special equipment negate the feasibility of independent blood banking for individual travelers or small groups.

3. Blood should be transfused only when absolutely indicated. This applies even more forcefully in those countries where screening of blood for transmissible diseases is not yet widely performed.

Proposed Options:
1. When urgent resuscitation is necessary, the use of plasma expanders rather than blood should always be considered.

2. In case of emergency need of blood, use of plasma expanders and urgent evacuation home may be the actions of choice.

3. When blood transfusion cannot be avoided, the attending physician should make every effort to ensure that the blood has been screened for transmissible diseases, including HIV.

4. International travelers should:
a. take active steps to minimize the risk of injury;
b. establish a plan for dealing with medical emergencies;
c. support the development within countries of safe and adequate blood supplies.

This information is taken from the WHO publication "World Health Organization Global Program on AIDS: Blood Transfusion Guidelines for International Travelers."

MOTION SICKNESS
Travelers with a history of motion sickness or sea sickness can attempt to avoid symptoms by taking anti-motion-sickness pills or antihistaminics before departure.

PROTECTION AGAINST MOSQUITOES AND OTHER ARTHROPOD VECTORS
Although vaccines or chemoprophylactic drugs are available against important vector-borne diseases such as yellow fever and malaria, for various reasons, travelers still should avail themselves of repellents and other general protective measures against arthropods. The effectiveness of malaria chemoprophylaxis is variable, depending on patterns of resistance and compliance with medication, and for many vector-borne diseases, no specific preventatives are available.

General preventative measures
The principal approach to prevention of vector-borne diseases is avoidance. Tick and mite-borne infections characteristically are diseases of "place"; whenever possible, known foci of disease transmission should be avoided. Although many vector-borne infections can be prevented by avoiding rural locations, certain mosquito- and midge-bome arboviral and parasitic infections are transmitted around human residences and in urban locations. Most vector-borne infections are transmitted seasonally and simple changes in itinerary may greatly reduce risk for acquiring certain infections.

Exposure to arthropod bites can be minimized by modifying patterns of activity or behavior. Some vector mosquitoes are most active in twilight periods at dawn and dusk or in the evening. Avoidance of outdoor activity in these periods may reduce risk of exposure. Wearing long-sleeved shirts, long pants and hats will minimize areas of exposed skin. Shirts should be tucked in. Repellents applied to clothing, shoes, tents, mosquito nets and other gear will enhance protection.

When exposure to ticks or mites are a possibility, pants should be tucked into socks and boots should be worn; sandals should be avoided. Permethrin-based repellents applied as directed (se belo) will enhance protection. During outdoor activity and at the end of the day, travelers should inspect themselves and clothing for ticks. Ticks are detected more easily on light colored or white clothing. Prompt removal of attached ticks may prevent infection.

When accommodations are not adequately screened or air-conditioned, bednets are essential to provide protection and comfort. Bednets should be tucked under mattresses and can be sprayed with repellent. Aerosol insecticides and mosquito coils may help to clear rooms of mosquitoes; however, some coils contain DDT and should be used with caution.

Repellents
Permethrin-containing repellents (Permanone)* are recommended for use on clothing, shoes, bednets and

camping gear. Permethrin is highly effective as an insecticide and as a repellent. Permethrin-treated clothing repels and kills ticks, mosquitoes and other arthropods and retains this effect after repeated laundering. There appears to be little potential for toxicity from permethrin-treated clothing.

Permethrin-containing shampoo (Nix)* and cream (Elimite)*, marketed for use against head lice and scabies infestations, potentially could be extremely effective as repellents when applied on the hair and skin. However, they are approved only to treat existing conditions. Most authorities recommend repellents containing deet (diethylmethylbenzamide) as an active ingredient. Deet repels mosquitoes, ticks, and other arthropods when applied to skin or clothing. Formulations containing <30% deet are recommended because the additional gain in repellent effect with higher concentrations is not significant when weighed against the potential for toxicity. A microencapsulated formulation (Skeedadle)* may have a longer period of activity than liquid formulations. Deet is toxic when ingested. High concentrations applied to skin may cause blistering. Rare cases of encephalopathy in children, some fatal, have been reported after cutaneous exposure. Other neurologic side effects also have been reported. Toxicity did not appear to be dose-related in many cases and these may have been idiosyncratic reactions in predisposed individuals. However, a dose-related effect leading to irritability and impaired concentration and memory has been reported. Recommendations and precautions on the use of repellents are given in Table 2.

[Use of trade names is for identification only and does not imply endorsement by the Public Health Service or the U.S. Department of Health and Human Services].

TABLE 2. Precautions to Minimize Potential for Adverse Reactions from Repellents

- Apply repellent sparingly only to exposed skin or clothing.

- Avoid applying high-concentration (>30% DEET) products to the skin, particularly of children.

- Do not inhale or ingest repellents or get them into the eyes.

- Wear long sleeves and long pants, when possible, and apply repellents (e.g. permethrin) to clothing to reduce cutaneous exposure.

- Avoid applying repellents to portions of children's hands that are likely to have contact with eyes or mouth.

- Pregnant and nursing women should minimize use of repellents.

- Never use repellents on wounds or irritated skin.

- Use repellent sparingly; one application will last approximately 4 hours. Saturation does not increase efficacy.

- Wash repellent-treated skin after coming indoors.

- If a suspected reaction to insect repellents occurs, wash treated skin, and call a physician. Take the repellent container to the physician.

PREGNANT WOMEN TRAVELING ABROAD

The problems that a pregnant woman might encounter during international travel are basically the same problems that other international travelers have. These have to do with exposure to infectious diseases and availability of good medical care. There is the additional potential problem that air travel late in pregnancy might precipitate labor.

Potential health problems vary from country to country; therefore, if the traveler has specific questions, she should be advised to check with the embassy or local consulate general office of the country in question before traveling.

DISABLED TRAVELERS

The United States (U.S.) Architectural and Transportation Barriers Compliance Board produces or distributes a variety of publications, at no cost. U.S. air carriers must comply with the U.S. laws or regulations regarding access. Up-to-date information regarding access abroad is more difficult to ascertain. A booklet *Access Travel: Airports,* is available free from the Consumer Information Center in Pueblo, Colorado 81009. It lists accessibility features at 553 airports worldwide. U.S. companies or entities conducting programs or tours on cruise ships also have some obligations for access, even if the ship itself is foreign flagged. Write or call, ATBCB, 1111 18th Street, N.W., Suite 501, Washington, D.C. 20036-3894, 1-800-USA-ABLE (voice/TDD) for a list of its publications.

RISKS FROM FOOD AND DRINK

Contaminated food and drink are common sources for the introduction of infection into the body. Among the more common infections that travelers may acquire from contaminated food and drink are Escherichia coli infections, shigellosis or bacillary dysentery, giardiasis, cryptosporidiosis, and hepatitis A. Other less common infectious disease risks for travelers include typhoid

135

fever and other salmonelloses, cholera, infections caused by rotaviruses and Norwalk-like viruses, and a variety of protozoan and helminth parasites (other than those that cause giardiasis and cryptosporidiosis). Many of the infectious diseases transmitted in food and water can also be acquired directly through the fecal-oral route.

Water

Water that has been adequately chlorinated, using minimum recommended water-works standards as practiced in the United States, will afford significant protection against viral and bacterial waterborne diseases. However, chlorine treatment alone, as used in the routine disinfection of water, may not kill some enteric viruses and the parasitic organisms that cause giardiasis and amebiasis. In areas where chlorinated tap water is not available, or where hygiene and sanitation are poor, travelers should be advised that only the following may be safe to drink:

1. Beverages, such as tea and coffee, made with boiled water.
2. Canned or bottled carbonated beverages, including carbonated bottled water and soft drinks.
3. Beer and wine.

Where water may be contaminated, ice (or containers for drinking) also should be considered contaminated. Thus, in these areas ice should not be used in beverages. If ice has been in contact with containers used for drinking, the containers should be thoroughly cleaned, preferably with soap and hot water, after the ice has been discarded.

It is safer to drink directly from a can or bottle of a beverage than from a questionable container. However, water on the outside of cans or bottles of beverages might be contaminated. Therefore, wet cans or bottles should be dried before being opened, and surfaces which are contacted directly by the mouth in drinking should first be wiped clean. Where water may be contaminated, travelers should avoid brushing their teeth with tap water.

Treatment of water

Boiling is by far the most reliable method to make water of uncertain purity safe for drinking. Water should be brought to a vigorous boil and allowed to cool to room temperature-do not add ice. At very high altitudes, for an extra margin of safety, boil for several minutes or use chemical disinfection. Adding a pinch of alt to each quart, or pouring the water several times from one container to another will improve the taste.

Chemical disinfection with iodine is an alternative method of water treatment when it is not feasible to boil

water. Two well-tested methods for disinfection with iodine are the use of tincture of iodine (Table 3), and the use of tetraglycine hydroperiodide tablets (Globaline, Potable-Aqua, Coghlan's*, etc.). The tablets are available from pharmacies and sporting goods stores. The manufacturer's instructions should be followed. If water is cloudy, the number of tablets should be doubled, if water is extremely cold, an attempt should be made to warm the water, and the recommended contact time should be increased to achieve reliable disinfection. Cloudy water should be strained through a clean cloth into a container to remove any sediment or floating matter, and then the water should be treated with heat or iodine. Chlorine, in various forms, has also been used for chemical disinfection. However, its germicidal activity varies greatly with pH, temperature, and organic content of the water to be purified, and is less reliable than iodine.

There are a variety of portable filters currently on the market which according to the manufacturers' data will provide safe drinking water. Although the iodide-impregnated resins and the microstrainer type filters will kill and/or remove many microorganisms, very few published reports in the scientific literature deal both with the methods used and the results of the tests employed to evaluate the efficacy of these filters against water-borne pathogens. Until there is sufficient independent verification of the efficacy of these filters, CDC makes no recommendation regarding their use.

As a last resort, if no source of safe drinking water is available or can be obtained, tap water that is uncomfortably hot to touch may be safer than cold tap water, however proper sisinfection or boiling is still advised.

TABLE 3. Treatment of Water With Tincture of Iodine

Tincture of Iodine (from medicine chest or first aid kit)		Drops* to be added per quart or liter
	Clear water water**	Cold or cloudy
2%	5	10

*1 drop = 0.05 ml
Let stand for 30 minutes.
Water is safe to use.

**Very turbid or very cold water may require prolonged contact time; let stand up to several hours prior to use, if possible.

Food

To avoid illness, food should be selected with care. All raw food is subject to contamination. Particularly in areas where hygiene and sanitation are inadequate, the traveler should be advised to avoid salads, uncooked vegetables, unpasteurized milk and milk products such as cheese, and to eat only food that has been cooked and is still hot, or fruit that has been peeled by the traveler. Undercooked and raw meat, fish, and shellfish may carry various intestinal pathogens. Cooked food that has been allowed to stand for several hours in ambient temperature may provide a fertile medium for bacterial growth and should be thoroughly reheated before serving

The easiest way to guarantee a safe food source for an infant less than 6 months of age is to have the child breast-feed. If the infant has already been weaned from the breast, formula prepared from commercial powder and boiled water is the safest and most practical food.

Some species of fish and shellfish can contain poisonous biotoxins, even when well cooked. The most common type of fish poisoning in travelers is ciguatera fish poisoning. Barracuda is the most toxic fish and should always be avoided. Red. Snapper, grouper, amberjack, sea bass, and a wide range or tropical reef fish contain the toxin at unpredictable times. The potential for ciguatera poisoning exists in all subtropical and tropical insular areas of the West Indies, Pacific and Indian Oceans where the implicated fish species are consumed.

Recently, cholera cases have occurred among persons who ate crab brought back from Latin America by travelers. Travelers should not bring perishable seafoods with them when they return.

TRAVELERS' DIARRHEA

Epidemiology

Travelers' diarrhea (TD) is a syndrome characterized by a twofold or greater increase in the frequency of unformed bowel movements. Commonly associated symptoms include abdominal cramps, nausea, bloating, urgency, fever, and malaise. Episodes of TD usually begin abruptly, occur during travel or soon after returning home, and are generally self-limited. The most important determinant of risk is the destination of the traveler. Attack rates in the range of 20 to 50 percent are commonly reported. High-risk destinations include most of the developing countries of Latin America , Africa, the Middle East, and Asia. Intermediate risk destinations include most of the Southern European countries and a few Caribbean islands. Low risk destinations include Canada, Northern Europe, Australia, New Zealand, the United States and a number of the Caribbean islands.

TD is slightly more common in young adults than in older people. The reasons for this difference are unclear, but may include a lack of acquired immunity, more adventurous travel styles, and different eating habits. Attack rates are similar in men and women. The onset of TD is usually within the first week, but may occur at any time during the visit, and even after returning home.

TD is acquired through ingestion of fecally contaminated food and/or water. Both cooked and uncooked foods may be implicated if improperly handled. Especially risky foods include raw meat, raw seafood, and raw fruits and vegetables. Tap water ice, and unpasteurized milk and dairy products may be associated with increased risk of TD; safe beverages include bottled carbonated beverages (especially flavored beverages), beer, wine, hot coffee or tea, or water boiled or appropriately treated with iodine or chlorine.

The place food is prepared appears to be an important variable; with private homes, restaurants, and street vendors listed in order of increasing risk.

TD typically results in four to five loose or watery stools per day. The median duration of diarrhea is 3 to 4 days. Ten percent of the cases persist longer than 1 week, approximately 2 percent longer than 1 month, and less than 1 percent longer than 3 months. Persistent diarrhea is thus quite uncommon and may differ considerably from acute TD with respect to etiology and risk factors. Travelers may experience more than one attack of TD during a single trip. Approximately 15 percent experience vomiting, and 2 to 10 percent may have diarrhea accompanied by fever or bloody stools, or both. Rarely is TD life-threatening.

Etiology

Infectious agents are the primary cause of TD. Travelers from industrialized countries to developing countries frequently develop a rapid, dramatic change in the type of organisms in their gastrointestinal tract. These new organisms often include potential enteric pathogens. Those who develop diarrhea have ingested an inoculum of virulent organisms sufficiently large to overcome individual defense mechanisms, resulting in symptoms.Enteric Bacterial Pathogens

Enterotoxigenic Escherichia coli (ETEC) are the most common causative agents of TD in all countries where surveys have been conducted. ETEC produce a watery diarrhea associated with cramps and a low-grade or no fever.
Salmonella gastroenteritis is a well-known disease that occurs throughout the world. In the industrialized nations, this large group of organisms is the most common cause of outbreaks of food-associated diarrhea.

In the developing countries, the proportion of cases of TD caused by salmonellae varies but is not high. Salmonellae also can cause dysentery characterized by bloody mucus-containing small-volume stools.

Shigellae are well known as the cause of bacillary dysentery. However, few of the infected travelers have dysentery, but most have watery diarrhea often with fever and cramps. The shigellae are the cause of TD in from 0 to about 20 percent of travelers to developing countries.

Campylobacter jejuni is a common cause of diarrhea throughout the world, and is responsible for a small percentage of the reported cases of TD, some with bloody diarrhea. Additional studies are needed to determine how frequently it causes TD.

Vibrio parahaemolyticus is associated with ingestion of raw or poorly cooked seafood and has caused TD in passengers on Caribbean cruise ships and in Japanese people traveling in Asia. How frequently it causes disease in other areas of the world is unknown.

Other potential bacterial pathogens include Aeromonas hydrophila, Yersinia enterocolitica, Plesiomonas shigelloides, Vibrio cholerae (non-01), and Vibrio fluvialis.

Viral Enteric Pathogens-Rotavirus and Norwalk-like Virus

Along with the newly acquired bacteria, the traveler may also acquire many viruses. In six studies, for example, 0 to 36 percent of diarrheal illnesses (median 22 percent) were associated with rotaviruses in the stools. However, a comparable number of asymptomatic travelers also had rotaviruses, and up to 50 percent of symptomatic persons with rotavirus infections also had nonviral pathogens. Ten to fifteen percent of travelers develop serologic evidence of infection with Norwalk-like viruses. The roles of adenoviruses, astroviruses, coronaviruses, enteroviruses, or other viral agents in causing TD are even less clear. Although viruses are commonly acquired by travelers, they do not appear to be frequent causes of TD in adults.

Parasitic Enteric Pathogens

The few studies that have included an examination for parasites reveal that 0 to 6 percent have Giardia lamblia and 0 to 6 percent have Entamoeba histolytica. Cryptosporidium has recently been recognized in sporadic cases of TD.

Dientamoeba fragilis, Isospora belli, Balantidium coli, or Strongyloides stercoralis may cause occasional cases of TD. While not major causes of acute TD, these parasites should be sought in persisting, unexplained cases.

Unknown Causes

No data have been presented to support noninfectious causes of TD such as changes in diet, jet lag, altitude, and fatigue. Current evidence indicates that in all but a few instances, e.g., drug-induced or preexisting gastrointestinal disorders, an infectious agent or agents cause diarrhea in tourists. However, even with the application of the best current methods for detecting bacteria, viruses, and parasites, 20 to 50 percent of cases of TD remain without recognized etiologies.

Prevention

There are four possible approaches to prevention of TD. They include instruction regarding food and beverage preparation, immunization, use of nonantimicrobial medications, and prophylactic antimicrobial drugs.

Data indicate that meticulous attention to food and beverage preparation, as mentioned above, can decrease the likelihood of developing TD. Most travelers, however, encounter great difficulty in observing the requisite dietary restrictions.

No available vaccines and none that are expected to be available in the next 5 years are effective against TD.

Several nonantimicrobial agents have been advocated for prevention of TD. Available controlled studies indicate that prophylactic use of difenoxine, the active metabolite of diphenoxylate (Lomotil*), actually increases the incidence of TD in addition to producing other undesirable side effects. No antiperistaltic agents, e.g., Lomotil* and Imodium* are effective in preventing TD. No data support the prophylactic use of activated charcoal.

Bismuth subsalicylate, taken as the active ingredient of Pepto-Bismol* (2 oz four times daily, or 2 tablets four times daily), has decreased the incidence of diarrhea by about 60 percent in several placebo-controlled studies. Side effects include temporary blackening of tongue and stools, occasional nausea and constipation, and rarely, tinnitus. Available data are not extensive enough to exclude a risk to the traveler from the use of such large doses of bismuth subsalicylate for a period of more than three weeks. Bismuth subsalicylate should be avoided by persons with aspirin-allergy or gout, those who are on anticoagulant therapy, or persons taking probenecid or methotrexate. In patients already taking salicylates for arthritis, large concurrent doses of bismuth subsalicylate can produce toxic serum concentrations of salicylate. Caution should be used in giving bismuth subsalicylate to adolescents and children with chicken pox or flu because of potential risk of Reye's syndrome. Bismuth subsaliclate has not been approved for children under three years old. Bismuth subsalicylate appears to be an effective prophylactic agent for TD, but is not recommended for prophylaxis of TD for periods of more than three weeks. Further studies of the efficacy and side effects of lower dose regimensare needed.

Controlled data are available on the prophylactic value of several other nonantimicrobial drugs. Enterovioform* and related halogenated hydroxyquinoline derivatives e.g., clioquinol, iodoquinol, Mexaform*, Intestopan*, and others, are not helpful in preventing TD, may have serious neurological side effects, and should never be used for prophylaxis of TD.

Controlled studies have indicated that a variety of antibiotics, including doxycycline, trimethoprim/sulfamethoxazole (TMP/SMX), trimethoprim alone, and the fluoroquinolone agents ciprofloxacin and norfloxacin, when taken prophylactically have been 52-95% effective in preventing traveler's diarrhea in several areas of the developing world. The effectiveness of these agents, however, depends upon the antibiotic resistance patterns of the pathogenic bacteria in each area of travel, and such information is seldom available. Resistance to the fluoroquinolones is the least common, but this may change as the use of these agents increases worldwide.

While effective in preventing bacterial causes of diarrhea, antibiotics have no effect on the acquisition of various viral and parasitic diseases. Prophylactic antibiotics may give travelers a false sense of security about the risk associated with consuming certain local foods and beverages.

The benefits of widespread prophylactic use of doxycycline, quinolones, TMP/ SMX or TMP alone in several million travelers must be weighed against the potential drawbacks. The known risks include allergic and other side effects (such as common skin rashes, photosensitivity of the skin, blood disorders, Stevens-Johnson syndrome and staining of the teeth in children) as well as other infections that may be induced by antimicrobial therapy (such as antibiotic-associated colitis, Candida vaginitis, and *Salmonella* enteritis). Because of the uncertain risk of widespread administration of these antimicrobial agents, their prophylactic use is not recommended. While it seems reasonable to use prophylactic antibiotics in certain high risk groups, such as travelers with immunosuppression or immunodeficiency, there are no data which directly support this practice. There is little evidence that other disease entities are worsened sufficiently by an episode of TD to risk the rare undesirable side effects of prophylactic antimicrobial drugs. **Therefore, prophylactic antimicrobial agents are not recommended for travelers.** Instead, available data support the recommendation that travelers be instructed in sensible dietary practices as a prophylactic measure. This recommendation is justified by the excellent results of early treatment of TD as outlined below. Some travelers may wish to consult with their physician and may elect to use prophylactic antimicrobial agents for travel under special circumstances, once the risks and benefits are clearly understood.

Treatment
Individuals with TD have two major complaints for which they desire relief-abdominal cramps and diarrhea. Many agents have been proposed to control these symptoms, but few have been demonstrated to be effective by rigorous clinical trials.

Nonspecific Agents
A variety of "adsorbents" have been used in treating diarrhea. For example, activated charcoal has been found to be ineffective in the treatment of diarrhea. Kaolin and pectin have been widely used for diarrhea. The combination appears to give the stools more consistency but has not been shown to decrease cramps and frequency of stools nor to shorten the course of infectious diarrhea.

Lactobacillus preparations and yogurt have also been advocated, but no evidence supports use of these treatments for TD.

Bismuth subsalicylate preparation (1 oz of liquid or 2 262.5 mg tablets every 30 minutes for eight doses) decreased the rate of stooling and shortened the duration of illness in several placebo-controlled studies. Treatment was limited to 48 hours at most, with no more than 8 doses in a 24-hour period. There is concern about taking, without supervision, large amounts of bismuth and salicylate, especially in individuals who may be intolerant to salicylates, who have renal insufficiency, or who take salicylates for other reasons.

Antimotility Agents
Antimotility agents are widely used in treating diarrhea of all types. Natural opiates (paregoric, deodorized tincture of opium, and codeine) have long been used to control diarrhea and cramps. Synthetic agents, diphenoxylate and loperamide, come in convenient dosage forms and provide prompt symptomatic but

temporary relief of uncomplicated TD. However, they should not be used in patients with high fever or with blood in the stool. These drugs should be discontinued if symptoms persist beyond 48 hours. Diphenoxylate and loperamide should not be used in children under the age of 2.

Antimicrobial Treatment
Travelers who develop diarrhea with three or more loose stools in an 8-hour period, especially if associated with nausea, vomiting, abdominal cramps, fever, or blood in the stools, may benefit from antimicrobial treatment. A typical 3- to 5-day illness can often be shortened to 1 to 1 1/2 days by effective antimicrobial agents. Those best studied to date are daily TMP/SMX (160 mg TMP and 800 mg SMX) or TMP alone, 200 mg taken twice daily. Other fluoroquinolones such as fleroxacin, norfloxacine and ofloxacin may be equally effective as ciprofloxacin. Fewer side effects and less widespread resistance has been reported with the fluoroquinolones than with TMP/SMX. Three days of treatment is recommended, although 2 days or fewer may be sufficient. Nausea and vomiting without diarrhea should not be treated with antimicrobial drugs.

Travelers should consult a physician, rather than attempt self-medication, if the diarrhea is severe or does not resolve within several days; if there is blood and/or mucus in the stool, if fever occurs with shaking chills; or if there is dehydration with persistent diarrhea.

Oral fluids
Most cases of diarrhea are self-limited and require only simple replacement of fluids and salts lost in diarrheal stools. This is best achieved by use of an oral rehydration solution such as World Health Organization Oral Rehydration Salts (ORS) solution (Table 4). This solution is appropriate for treating as well as preventing dehydration. ORS packets are available at stores or pharmacies in almost all developing countries. ORS is prepared by adding one packet to boiled or treated water. Packet instructions should be checked carefully to ensure that the salts are added to the correct volume of water. ORS solution should be consumed or discarded within 12 hours if held at room temperature, or 24 hours if held refrigerated.

Iced drinks and noncarbonated bottled fluids made from water of uncertain quality should be avoided. Dairy products aggravate diarrhea in some people and should be avoided.

TABLE 4. Composition of World Health Organization Oral Rehydration Solution (ORS) for diarrheal illness

Ingredient	Amount
Sodium chloride	3.5 grams/liter
Potassium chloride	1.5 grams/liter
Glucose	20.0 grams/liter
Trisodium citrate*	2.9 grams/liter

**An earlier formulation used sodium bicarbonate 2.5 grams/liter had a shorter shelf-life, but was physiologically equivalent, and may still be produced in some countries.

Infants with Diarrhea
Children aged 0-2 years are at high risk of acquiring traveler's diarrhea. The greatest risk to the infant with diarrhea is dehydration. Dehydration is best prevented by use of WHO ORS solution in addition to the infant's usual food. ORS packets are available at stores or pharmacies in almost all developing countries. ORS is prepared by adding one packet to boiled or treated water. Packet instructions should be checked carefully to ensure that the salts are added to the correct volume of water. ORS solution should be consumed or discarded within 12 hours if held at room temperature, or 24 hours if held refrigerated. The dehydrated child will drink ORS avidly; ORS is given *ad lib* to the child as long as the dehydration persists. The infant who vomits the ORS will usually keep it down if the ORS is offered by spoon in frequent small sips. Breast-fed infants should continue nursing on demand. For bottle-fed infants, full strength lactose-free, or lactose-reduced formulas should be administered. Older children receiving semi-solid or solid foods should continue to receive their usual diet during diarrhea. Recommended foods include starches, cereals, yogurt, fruits, and vegetables.

Immediate medical attention is required for the infant with diarrhea who develops signs of moderate to severe dehydration (Table 23), bloody diarrhea, fever of greater than 102°F, or persistent vomiting. While medical attention is being obtained, the infant should be offered ORS.

More information is available from CDC in a publication entitled, "The management of acute diarrhea in children: oral rehydration, maintenance, and nutritional therapy." (MMWR No. RR- 16, October 16, 1992). ORS packets are available in the United States from Jianas Brothers Packaging Company, Kansas City, Missouri (telephone:(816)421-2880).

Precautions in Children and Pregnant Women
Although children do not make up a large proportion of travelers to high-risk areas, some children do accompany their families. Teenagers should follow the advice given to adults, with possible adjustment of doses of medication. Physicians should be aware of the

risks of tetracyclines to children under 12 years of age. There are few data available about usage of antidiarrheal drugs in children. Drugs should be prescribed with caution for pregnant women and nursing mothers.

TABLE 5. Assessment of the Dehydration Levels in Infants

Signs

. .	Mild	Moderate	Severe
General Condition	Thirsty,	Thirsty	Withdrawn,
. . restless,	restless	somnolent,	
agitated.	irritable.	or comatose.	
Pulse	normal	Rapid and weak	Rapid
. .			and weak
Anterior fontanelle	Normal	Sunken	Very sunken
Eyes . .	Normal	Sunken	Very sunken
Tears	Present	Absent	Absent
Urine	Normal	Reduced and	None
. .		concentrated	for
. .		several	
. . hours			
Weight loss	4-5%	6-9%	10% or more

CRUISE SHIP SANITATION

The Centers for Disease Control and Prevention (CDC) established the Vessel Sanitation Program (VSP) in 1975 as a cooperative activity with the cruise ship industry as a result of several major disease outbreaks on cruise vessels. This joint program strives to achieve and maintain a level of sanitation on passenger vessels that will lower the risk of gastrointestinal disease outbreaks and provide a healthful environment. The program goals are addressed through encouraging industry to establish and maintain a comprehensive sanitation program and oversight of its success through an inspections process. Every vessel with a foreign itinerary that carries 13 or more passengers is subject to twice yearly inspections and when necessary reinspection. Inspections are only conducted at those ports under U.S. control and cover such environmental aspects as:

1. Water supply, storage, distribution, backflow protection and disinfection.
2. Food preparation during storage, preparation, and service and product temperature control.
3. Potential contamination of food, water, and ice.
4. Employee practices and personal hygiene.
5. General cleanliness, facility repair, and vector control.

A score of 86 or higher at the time of the inspection indicates that the ship is providing an accepted standard of sanitation. In general, the lower the score the lower the level of sanitation; however, a low score does not necessarily imply an imminent risk of an outbreak of gastrointestinal disease. CDC reserves the right to recommend that a ship not sail when circumstances so dictate. This may include but is not restricted to, contamination of the potable water supply, inadequate treatment of the potable water supply, or food temperature violations. A copy of the most recent sanitation inspection report on an individual vessel or a copy of *The Summary of Sanitation Inspections of International Cruise Ships* may be obtained by writing to: Chief, Vessel Sanitation Program, National Center for Environmental Health, 1015 North America Way, Suite 107, Miami, Florida 33132.

DISINSECTION OF AIRCRAFT

International travelers should be aware that some countries require disinsection of certain passenger aircraft in order to prevent the importation of insects such as mosquitos. Disinsection procedures may include the spraying of the aircraft passenger compartment with insecticide while passengers are present. While the recommended disinsection procedures have been determined to be safe by the World Health Organization, they may aggravate certain health conditions (i.e, allergies). Travelers with such conditions or who are otherwise interested in determining what disinsection procedures may be performed on a particular flight should contact their travel agent or airline.

ENVIRONMENTAL EFFECTS

International travelers may be subject to certain stresses that may lower resistance to disease, such as crowding, disruption of usual eating and drinking habits, and time changes with "jet lag" contributing to a disturbed pattern of the sleep and wakefulness cycle. These conditions of stress can lead to nausea, indigestion, fatigue, or insomnia. Complete adaptation depends on the number of time zones crossed but may take a week or more.

Heat and cold can be directly or indirectly responsible for some diseases and can give rise to serious skin conditions. Dermatophytoses such as athlete's foot are often made worse by warm, humid conditions.

Excessive heat and humidity alone, or immoderate activity under those conditions, may lead to heat exhaustion due to salt and water deficiency and to the more serious heat stroke or hyperthermia. The ultraviolet rays of the sun can cause severe and very debilitating sunburn in lighter-skinned persons.

Excessive cold affects persons who may be inadequately dressed and particularly the elderly; it can lead to hypothermia and to frost-bite of exposed parts of the body.

Breathing and swallowing dust when traveling on unpaved roads or in and areas may be followed by nausea and malaise, and may cause increased susceptibility to infections of the upper respiratory tract.

Traveling in high altitudes may lead to insomnia, headache, nausea, and altitude sickness, even in young and healthy persons, and can cause distress to those with cardiac or pulmonary conditions. Individual susceptibility to acute mountain sickness is highly variable. Travelers who are at greatest risk are those who ascend rapidly to tourist sites in the Andes and the Himalayas. Acetazolamide has been shown, under both simulated and actual climbing conditions, to hasten the process of acclimatization to high altitudes. The recommended dosage to prevent acute mountain sickness is 250 mg every 8-12 hours, with medication initiated 24-48 hours before, and continued during ascent. Acetazolamide should not be taken by individuals who are allergic to sulfonamides.

CHERNOBYL

Effects of the radiological release at Chernobyl
The Chernobyl Nuclear Power station, located in the Ukraine Republic about 100 kilometers (62 miles) north-west of Kiev and 3 10 kilometers (193 miles) south-east of Minsk (in Belarus), experienced an uncontrolled release of radioactive material in April, 1986. This event seems to have resulted in the largest short term release of radioactive materials to the atmosphere ever recorded. The radiological contamination primarily affected three Republics: the Ukraine, Belarus, and Russia. The highest areas of radioactive ground contamination occurred within 30 km (19 miles) of Chernobyl.

Area Considerations
Short term international travelers to the republics of Ukraine, Belarus, and Russia (i.e., those who plan to stay in the region less than a few months) should not be concerned about residing in areas that are not controlled (i.e., marked with signs or fenced). However, we do caution longer term visitors that there are some non-controlled areas where an individual could receive a radiation dose from the radioactive ground contamination in excess of the international radiological health standards recommended for most members of the public. Long term visitors should investigate the local conditions prior to choosing a long-term residence. (For example, ground contamination that exceeds 5 curies per square kilometer (5 Ci/km2) of cesium- 137 could result in a radiation dose greater than the recommended standards.)

Food and Water Considerations
Officials of the three republics attempt to monitor all food stuffs sold in the public markets for levels of radioactivity. Radioactive concentration limits have been established for various classes of food, e.g., milk, meat, and vegetables. These limits are comparable to standards used by many western nations including the European Economic Community. Food with contamination levels in excess of these limits is not allowed to be sold in the market. Private farmers regularly make food available for sale outside the official market system. This food is not monitored for radioactivity and it is recommended that travelers not consume this food. Likewise, it is recommended that travelers not consume any wild berries, wild mushrooms or wild game from these regions. And, it is also recommended that travelers drink only bottled water.

Age and Health Considerations
Young children, unborn babies, and nursing infants are potentially at greater risk from exposure to radiation than adults. Pregnant or nursing mothers should pay extra attention in acquiring and consuming food from reliable well-monitored sources.

INJURIES
The major causes of serious disability or loss of life are not infectious. Trauma caused by injuries, principally that suffered in motor vehicle crashes, is the leading cause of death and disability in both developed and developing countries worldwide. Motor vehicle crashes result from a variety of factors, including inadequate roadway design, hazardous poor vehicle conditions, lack of appropriate vehicles and vehicle maintenance, unskilled or inexperienced drivers, inattention to pedestrians and pedalcyclists, or impairment due to alcohol or drug use; all these factors are preventable or can be abated. Defensive driving is an important preventive measure. When driving or riding, insist on a vehicle equipped with safety belts and where available, use them. When available, also insist on a vehicle equipped with airbags and anti-lock brakes. As a high proportion of crashes occur at night when returning from "social events," avoid non-essential night driving, alcohol, and riding with persons who are under the influence of alcohol or drugs. Pedestrian, bicycle, and motorcycle travel are often dangerous, and helmet use is imperative for bicycle and motorcycle travel.

Fire injuries are also a significant cause of injuries and

142

death-inquire about whether hotels have smoke detectors and sprinkler systems, and do not smoke in bed. Travelers may wish to bring their own smoke detectors with them. Always look for a primary and alternate escape route in rooms in which you are meeting or staying. Look for improperly vented heating devices which may cause carbon monoxide poisoning. Remember to escape a fire by crawling low under smoke.

Other major causes of injury trauma include drowning (see swimming precautions p. 173) and drug reactions. Protection against potentially hazardous drugs is nonexistent in some countries. Do not buy medications "over the counter" unless you are familiar with the product.

Travelers should also be aware of the potential for violence-related injuries. Risk for assault or terrorist attack varies from country to country; heed advice from residents and tour guides about areas to be avoided, going out at night, and going out alone. Do not fight attackers. If confronted, give up your valuables. For more information, contact the U.S. Department of State. Overseas Citizens Emergency Center, at (202) 647-5225.

ANIMAL-ASSOCIATED HAZARDS

Animals in general tend to avoid human beings, but they can attack, particularly if they are with young. In areas of endemic rabies, domestic dogs, cats, or other animals should not be petted. Wild animals should be avoided.

The bites, stings, and contact of some insects cause unpleasant reactions. Medical attention should be sought if an insect bite or sting causes redness, swelling, bruising, or persistent pain. Many insects also transmit communicable diseases. Some insects can bite and transmit disease without the person being aware of the bite, particularly when camping or staying in rustic or primitive accommodations. Insect repellents, protective clothing, and mosquito netting are advisable in many parts of the world (See p.158, Protection Against Mosquitoes and Other Arthropod Vectors).

Poisonous snakes are hazards in many parts of the world, although deaths from snake bites are relatively rare. The Australian brown snake, Russell's viper and cobras in southern Asia, carpet vipers in the Middle East, and coral and rattlesnakes in the Americas are particularly dangerous. Most snakebites are the direct result of handling or harassing snakes, which bite as a defensive reaction. Attempts to kill snakes are dangerous, often leading to bites on the fingers. The

venom of a small or immature snakes may be even more concentrated than that of a larger individual, therefore all snakes should be left strictly alone.

Less than half of all snake bite wounds actually contain venom, but medical attention should be sought anytime a bite wound breaks the skin. A pressure bandage, ice (if available), and immobilization of the affected limb are recommended first aid measures while the victim is moved as quickly as possible to a medical facility. Specific therapy for snakebite is controversial, and should be left to the judgement of local emergency medical personnel. Snakes tend to be active at night and in warm weather. As a precaution, boots and long pants may be worn when walking outdoors at night in snake-infested regions. Bites from scorpions may be painful but seldom are dangerous except possibly in infants. In general, exposure to bites can be avoided by sleeping under mosquito nets and by shaking clothing and shoes before putting them on, particularly in the morning. Snakes and scorpions tend to rest in shoes and clothing.

ANTHRAX-CONTAMINATED GOATSKIN HANDICRAFTS

Anthrax is a disease caused by a bacterial organism that produces spores that are highway resistant to disinfection. These infectious spores may persist on a contaminated item for many years. Anthrax spores have been found on goatskin handicrafts from Haiti.

Travelers to Caribbean countries are advised not to purchase Haitian goatskin handicrafts. Because of the risk, importation of goatskin handicrafts from Haiti will not be permitted at U.S. ports of entry; they will be confiscated and destroyed.

SWIMMING PRECAUTIONS

Swimming in contaminated water may result in skin, eye, ear, and certain intestinal infections, particularly if the swimmer's head is submerged. Generally only pools that contain chlorinated water can be considered safe places to swim. In certain areas, fatal primary amebic meningoencephalitis has occurred following swimming in warm dirty water. Swimmers should avoid beaches that might be contaminated with human sewage, or with dog feces. Wading or swimming should be avoided in freshwater streams, canals, and lakes liable to be infested with the snail hosts of schistosomiasis (bilharziasis) or contaminated with urine from animals infected with *Leptospira*. Biting and stinging fish and corals and jelly fish may provide a hazard to the swimmer. Never swim alone or when under the influence of alcohol or drugs, and never dive head first into an unfamiliar body of water.

THE POST-TRAVEL PERIOD
Some diseases may not manifest themselves immediately. If travelers become ill after they return home, they should tell their physician where they have traveled. Most persons who acquire viral, bacterial, or parasitic infections abroad become ill within 6 weeks after returning from international travel. However, some diseases may not manifest themselves immediately, e.g., malaria may not cause symptoms for as long as 6 months to a year after the traveler returns to the United States. It is recommended that a traveler always advise a physician of the countries visited within the 12 months preceding onset of illness. Knowledge of such travel and the possibility the patient may be ill with a disease the physician rarely encounters will help the physician arrive at a correct diagnosis.

IMPORTATION OR EXPORTATION OF HUMAN REMAINS
There are no federal restrictions on the importation of human remains unless the death was the result of one of the following communicable diseases: cholera or suspected cholera, diphtheria, infectious tuberculosis, plague, suspected smallpox, yellow fever, suspected viral hemorrhagic fevers (Lassa, Marburg, Ebola, Congo Crimean and others not yet isolated or named). If the death was the result of one of these diseases, the remains must he cremated or properly embalmed and place hermetically sealed casket, and be accompanied by a death certificate, translate English, which states the cause of death. Following importation, the local mortician will be subject to the regulations of the State and local health authorities for interstate or intrastate shipment.

The United States has no requirements for the exportation of human remains; however, the requirements of the country of destination must be met. Information regarding these requirements may be obtained from the appropriate embassy or local consulate general.

IMPORTATION OR REENTRY OF PETS
Pets which are transported internationally should be free of communicable diseases that may be transmissible to humans. U.S. Public Health Service regulations place the following restrictions on the importation of dogs, cats, nonhuman primates and turtles:

DOGS-Dogs older than 3 months presented for importation from count rabies is known to occur (See Table 16), must be accompanied by a vaccination certificate which includes the following information:

1. The breed, sex, age, color, markings, and other identifying information

2. Vaccination date at least 30 days prior to importation (See below)
3. Vaccination expiration date. If not shown, the date of vaccinate within 12 months prior to the importation, and
4. Signature of a licensed veterinarian.

Dogs not accompanied by the above described certificate may be admitted provided the importer completes a confinement agreement. Such dogs must be kept in confinement during transit to, and be vaccinated within 4 days after arrival destination. Such dogs must remain in confinement for at least 30 days after the date of vaccination.

Dogs less than 3 months of age may be admitted, provided the importer complete a confinement agreement. Such dogs must be kept in confinement during transit and at the U.S. destination until vaccinated at 3 months of age and for at least 30 days after vaccination.

Routine rabies vaccination of dogs is recommended in the U.S. and is required most State and local health authorities.

CATS--While proof of rabies vaccination is not required for cats, routine rabies vaccination of cats is recommended in the U.S. and is required by most State local health authorities.

TURTLES-Turtles may transmit salmonellosis to humans, and because small turtles are often kept as pets, restrictions apply to their importation. Live turtles with carapace (shell) length of less than 4 inches and viable turtle eggs may be imported into the United States if the importation is not for commercial purposes. The Public Health Service has no restrictions on the importation of live turtles with a carapace length of more than 4 inches.

MONKEYS AND OTHER NONHUMAN PRIMATES-
Nonhuman primates may transmit a variety of serious diseases to humans. Live monkeys and other nonhuman primates may be imported into the United States only by importers registered with CDC and only for scientific, educational, or exhibition purposes. Monkeys and other nonhuman primates may not be imported for use as pets.

MEASURES AT PORT OF ENTRY
U.S. Public Health Service regulations provide for the examination of admissible dogs, cats, nonhuman primates and turtles presented for importation into the U.S. Animals with evidence of disease that may be

144

transmissible to humans may be subject to additional disease control measures.

GENERAL

For additional information regarding importation of these animals, contact the Centers for Disease Control and Prevention, Attention: National Center for Prevention Services, Division of Quarantine, Mailstop E03, Atlanta, Georgia 30333, Telephone (404) 639-8107.

Persons planning to import horses, ruminants, swine, poultry, birds, and dogs used in handling livestock should contact the U.S. Department of Agriculture regarding additional requirements, Telephone (301) 436-8170.

Persons planning to import fish, reptiles, spiders, wild birds, rabbits, bears, wild members of the cat family, or other wild or endangered animals should contact the U.S. Department of the Interior, Fish and Wildlife Service, Telephone (202) 342-9242.

Travelers planning to take a pet to a foreign country are advised to meet entry requirements of the country of destination. To obtain this information write to or call the country's embassy in Washington, D.C. or to the consulate nearest you.

TABLE 6. Countries Reporting No cases or Rabies*

The following countries and political units stated that rabies was not present:

REGION COUNTRIES

AFRICA: Mauritius**; Libya**.

AMERICAS: North: Bermuda; St. Pierre
                          and Miquelon.

Caribbean: Anguilla; Antigua and Barbuda; Bahamas; Barbados; Cayman Islands, Dominica; Guadeloupe; Jamaica; Martinique; Montserrat; Netherlands Antilles (Aruba, Bonaire, Curacao, Saba, St. Maarten, and St. Eustatius), Redonda; St. Christopher (St. Kitts) and Nevis; St. Lucia: St. Martin; St. Vincent; Turks and Caicos Islands; Virgin Islands (U.K. and U.S.).

South: Uruguay.**

ASIA: Bahrain; Brunei Darussalam**; Japan; Republic of Korea; Kuwait; Malaysia (Malaysia-Sabah**), Maldives**; Oman**; Singapore; Taiwan.

EUROPE: Bulgaria**; Cyprus; Faroe Islands, Gibraltar; Greece; Iceland; Ireland; Malta; Norway (mainland); Portugal***; Sweden; United Kingdom.

OCEANIA:*** American Samoa; Australia; Belau (Palau); Cook Islands; Federated States of Micronesia (Kosrae, Ponape, Truk, and Yap); Fiji; French Polynesia; Guam; Kiribati; New Caledonia; New Zealand; New; Northern Mariana Islands; Papua New Guinea; Samoa; Solomon Islands; Tonga; Vanuatu.

Most of Pacific Oceania is "rabies-free." For information on specific islands not listed above, contact the Centers for Disease Control, Division of Quarantine.

Bat rabies should be considered separately.

**Countries that have only recently reported no cases of rabies; these classifications should be considered provisional.*

***Most of Pacific Oceania is free of rabies.*

This list is based on data from the following publications and information provided to the Centers for Disease Control (CDC):

(1) World Health Organization: World Survey of Rabies XXI (for years 1986/87); Veterinary Public Health Unit, Division of Communicable Diseases, WHO, Geneva, 1989.

(2) WHO Collaborating Center for Rabies Surveillance and Research: Rabies Bulletin Europe, 1991;15(1):3.

(3) Pan American Zoonoses Center (PAHO/WHO): Epidemiological Surveillance Rabies for the Americas, 1989;21:(1-6).

UNITED STATES PUBLIC HEALTH SERVICE RECOMMENDATIONS

INTRODUCTION

Recommendations for individuals engaging in international travel apply primarily to vaccinations and prophylactic measures not required by countries but generally advisable for U.S. travelers planning to spend time in areas of the world where diseases such as measles, poliomyelitis, typhoid fever, viral hepatitis, and malaria occur either in endemic form or epidemic form and, therefore, pose a threat to their health. In addition, some countries require an International Certificate of Vaccination against cholera and/or yellow fever as a condition for entry. The majority of U.S. international travelers probably do not need any additional immunizations or prophylaxis, provided their routine immunization status is up-to-date according to the standards of the Public Health Service Immunization Practices Advisory Committee (ACIP).

The extent to which advisory statements can be made

145

specific for each country and each disease is limited by the lack of reliable data. Although data on the occurrence of many of these diseases are published regularly by WHO, these Figures represent only a small percentage of the total number of cases that actually occur-in fact, many countries do not report these diseases at all. Furthermore, communicable diseases are not well reported by practicing physicians, and in some countries where the number of physicians is inadequate, many cases never come to medical attention. For these reasons, any recommendations must be interpreted with care.

In general, the risk of acquiring illness when engaging in international travel depends on the areas of the world to be visited-travelers in developing countries are at greater risk than those traveling in developed areas. In most developed countries, Canada, Australia, New Zealand, Japan, and the continent of Europe, the risk to the general health of the traveler will be no greater than that incurred throughout the United States; however, there may be a higher risk of measles, mumps, and rubella. In many developed countries such as the Federal Republic of Germany, Ireland, Italy, Spain, Sweden, and the United Kingdom, pertussis immunization is not as widely practiced as in the United States, and the risk of acquiring pertussis is greater. In the countries in Africa, Asia, South America, Central America, Mexico, the South Pacific, Middle East, and Far East, living conditions and standards of sanitation and hygiene vary considerably, and immunization coverage levels may be low. There the risk of acquiring disease also can vary greatly. Travelers visiting primarily tourist areas on itineraries that do not include travel or visits in rural areas have less risk of exposure to food or water of questionable quality. Travelers who visit smaller cities off the usual tourist routes and those who spend time in small villages or rural areas for extended periods or who expect to have extended contact with children are at greater risk of acquiring infectious diseases, because of exposure to water and food of uncertain quality and closer contact with local residents who may harbor the organisms that cause such diseases. Consequently, the added protection of booster or additional doses of certain vaccines and prophylaxis is recommended for these persons.

GENERAL RECOMMENDATIONS ON HUMAN IMMUNODEFICIENCY VIRUS (HIV) INFECTION AND ACQUIRED IMMUNODEFICIENCY SYNDROME (AIDS)

Acquired immunodeficiency syndrome (AIDS) is a severe, often life-threatening, illness caused by the human immunodeficiency virus (HIV). The incubation period for AIDS may be very long, ranging from a few months to many years. Some individuals infected with

HIV have remained asymptomatic for 10 years or longer. Currently, there is no vaccine to protect against infection with HIV. Although there is no cure for AIDS, treatments for HIV infection and prophylaxis for opportunistic diseases that characterize AIDS are becoming available as a result of intense international research efforts.

HIV infection and AIDS have been reported worldwide. Comprehensive surveillance systems are lacking in many countries, so that the true number of cases is likely to be far greater than the numbers officially reported from some non-industrialized nations. The number of persons infected with HIV is estimated by WHO to be in the range of 8-10 million worldwide. Because HIV infection and AIDS are globally distributed, the risk to international travelers is determined less by their geographic destination than by their individual behavior.

The global epidemic of HIV infection and AIDS has raised several issues regarding HIV infection and international travel. The first is the need of information for international travelers regarding HIV transmission and how HIV infection can be prevented.

HIV infection is preventable. HIV is transmitted through sexual intercourse, needlesharing, by blood or blood components, and perinatally from an infected mother. HIV is not transmitted through casual contact; air, food, or water routes; contact with inanimate objects; or through mosquitoes or other arthropod vectors. The use of any public conveyance (e.g., airplane, automobile, boat, bus, train) by persons with AIDS or HIV infection does not pose a risk of infection for other passengers.

Travelers are at risk if they:
-have sexual intercourse (homosexual or heterosexual) with an infected person;

-use or allow the use of contaminated, unsterilized syringes or needles for any injections or other skin-piercing procedures including acupuncture, use of illicit drugs, steroid injections, medical/dental procedures, ear piercing, or tattooing;

- use infected blood, blood components, or clotting factor concentrates. HIV infection by this route is a rare occurrence in those countries or cities where donated blood/plasma is screened for HIV antibody.
Travelers should avoid sexual encounters with a person who is infected with HIV or whose HIV-infection status is unknown. This includes avoiding sexual activity with intravenous drug users and persons with multiple sexual

partners, such as male or female prostitutes. Condoms decrease, but do not entirely eliminate, the risk of transmission of HIV. Persons who engage in vaginal, anal, or oral-genital intercourse with anyone who is infected with HIV or whose infection status is unknown should use condoms. Use of spermicides with condoms may provide additional protection and is recommended.

In many countries, needle sharing by IV drug users is a major source of HIV transmission and other infections such as hepatitis B. Do not use drugs intravenously or share needles for any purpose.

In the United States, Australia, New Zealand, Canada, Japan, and western European countries, the risk of infection of transfusion-associated HIV infection is greatly reduced through required testing of all donated blood for antibodies to HIV. If produced in the United States according to procedures approved by the Food and Drug Administration, immune globulin preparations (such as these used for the prevention of hepatitis A and B) and hepatitis B virus vaccine undergo processes that are known to inactivate HIV and therefore these products should be used as indicated.

In less-developed nations, there may not be a formal program for testing blood or biological products for antibody to HIV. In these countries, use of locally-produced blood clotting factor concentrates should be avoided (when medically prudent). If transfusion is necessary, the blood should be tested, if at all possible, for HIV antibodies by appropriately-trained laboratory technicians using a reliable test. For WHO blood transfusion guidelines for international travelers, see p. 122. Needles used to draw blood or administer injections should be sterile, preferably of the single-use disposable type, and prepackaged in a sealed container. Insulin-dependent diabetics or other persons who require routine or frequent injections should carry a supply of syringes and needles sufficient to last their entire stay abroad.

International travelers should be aware that some countries serologically screen incoming travelers (primarily those with extended visits, such as for work or study) and exclude persons with AIDS and those whose test results indicate infection with HIV. Persons who are intending to visit a country for a prolonged period should be informed of the policies and requirements of the particular country. This information is usually available from consular officials of individual nations.

Medical Information for Americans Traveling Abroad

If an American becomes seriously ill or injured abroad, a U. S. consular officer, when notified of the problem, can assist in locating appropriate medical services and help in informing the next-of-kin, family or friends. If necessary, a consular officer can also assist in the transfer of funds from the United States, but payment of hospital and other expenses is your responsibility.

Before going abroad, learn what medical services your health insurance will cover overseas. If your health insurance policy provides coverage outside the United States, REMEMBER to carry both your insurance policy identity card as proof of such insurance and a claim form. Although many health insurance companies will pay "customary and reasonable" hospital costs abroad, very few will pay for your medical evacuation back to the United States which can easily cost $5,000 and up, depending on your location and medical condition. THE SOCIAL SECURITY MEDICARE PROGRAM DOES NOT PROVIDE FOR PAYMENT OF HOSPITAL OR MEDICAL SERVICES OUTSIDE THE U.S.A.

The American Association of Retired Persons offers foreign medical care coverage at no extra charge with its Medicare supplement plans. This coverage is restricted to treatments considered eligible under Medicare. In general, it covers 80% of the "customary and reasonable" charges, subject to a $50 deductible for the covered care during the first 60 days. There is a ceiling of $25,000 per trip. This is a reimbursement plan so you must pay the bills first and obtain receipts for submission to the plan.

To facilitate identification in case of an accident, complete the information page on the inside of your passport, providing the name, address and telephone number of someone to be contacted in an emergency. The name given should not be the same its your traveling companions in case the entire party is involved in the same accident.

Travelers going abroad with any preexisting medical problems should carry a letter from their attending physician. 'Me letter should describe their condition and include information on any prescription medications, including the generic name of any prescribed drugs, that they need to take. Any medications being carried overseas should be left in their original containers and be clearly labeled. Travelers should check with the foreign embassy' of the country they are visiting to make sure any required medications are not considered to be illegal narcotics.

A listing of addresses and telephone numbers of U.S. embassies and consulates abroad is contained in "Key

Officers of Foreign Service Posts" (Publication No. 7877, $1.75 each). This booklet may be obtained through the Superintendent of Documents, U.S. Government Printing Office, Washington, DC 20402. "Health Information for International Travelers" by the Centers for Disease Control (Publication No. HHS-CDC 90-8280, $7.00 each) is an annual global rundown of disease and immunization advice and other health guidance, including risks in particular countries that may also be obtained from the Government Printing Office. For additional

health information, the Centers for Disease Control in Atlanta maintains the international travelers hotline at 404-332-4559.

For detailed information on physicians abroad, the authoritative reference is the "Directory of Medical Specialists" published for the American Board of Medical Specialists and its 22 certifying member boards. This publication should be available in your local library. If abroad. A list of hospitals and physicians can be obtained from the nearest American embassy or consulate.

A number of countries require foreign visitors to be tested for the AIDS virus as a requirement for entry. This applies mostly to those planning to reside overseas, Before traveling, check the latest entry requirements with the foreign embassy of the country to be visited. A listing of "Foreign Entry Requirements" is available for 50 cents from the Consumer Information Center, Pueblo, CO 81009. The Citizens Emergency Center maintains a travel notice on HIV/AIDS entry requirements. Call 202-647-5225 to obtain these requirements.

DEFINITIONS

Active immunization-The production of immunity in response to the administration of a vaccine or a toxoid.
Antigen(s)-Substances inducing the formation of an immune response.

Antitoxin-A solution of antibodies derived from the serum of animals immunized with specific antigens used to achieve passive immunity or to effect a treatment.

"Blue Sheet"-Summary of Health Information for International Travel, published biweekly by CDC.

CDC-Centers for Disease Control.

Direct transit area-A special area established in an airport, approved and supervised directly by the health

administration concerned, for segregating passengers and crews breaking their air voyage without leaving the airport.

Diseases subject to International Health

Regulations-Cholera, yellow fever, and plague.

Endemic-The usual frequency of occurrence of a disease, including possible seasonal variations, in a human population.

Enzootic-The usual frequency of occurrence of a disease, including possible seasonal variations, in an animal population.

Epidemic-More than the expected number of cases of disease which would occur in a community or region during a given time period.

Epizootic-The occurrence of a disease in a defined animal population at a higher than expected rate.

Immune globulin (IG)-A sterile solution containing antibody from human blood. It is primarily indicated for routine maintenance of certain immunodeficient persons, and for passive immunization against measles and hepatitis A.

Immunization-The process of inducing or providing immunity artificially by administering an immunobiologic. Immunization can be active or passive.

Imported case-A person who acquired an infection outside of a specified area.

Infected area-An area which harbors a particular agent of infection and which because of population characteristics, density, and mobility, and/or vector and animal reservoir potential could support transmission of disease(s) identified there. It is defined on epidemiologic principles by the health administration reporting the disease and need not correspond to administrative boundaries.
International Certificate of Vaccination-The official certificate used to document the vaccinations a traveler has received, when and where received, and who administered them.

Isolation-The separation of a person or group of persons from others (except the health staff on duty) to prevent the spread of infection.

Motion sickness-A functional disorder thought to be brought on by repetitive motion and characterized by nausea or vomiting.

MMWR-Morbidity and Mortality Weekly Report, published by CDC.

Parasitic disease-A disease caused by an organism that lives in or on another organism.

Passive immunization-The provision of temporary immunity by the administration of preformed antitoxin or antibodies.

Quarantine-That state or condition during which measures are applied by a health administration to a ship, an aircraft, a train, road vehicle, other means of transport or container, or individuals to prevent the spread of disease from the object of quarantine to reservoirs, vectors of disease, or other individuals.

Quarantinable diseases-Cholera, yellow fever, and plague.

Recommended vaccination-Vaccination not required by International Health Regulations but suggested for travelers visiting or living in certain countries.

Required vaccination-Vaccination the traveler must have for entry into or exit from a country. The traveler must present a validated International Certificate of Vaccination which documents the vaccination(s) received.

Specific immune globulin-Special preparations obtained from donor pools preselected for a high antibody content against a specific disease.

Toxoid-A modified bacterial toxin that has been rendered nontoxic but that retains the ability to stimulate the formation of antitoxin.

Travelers' diarrhea-A syndrome characterized by a twofold or greater increase in the frequency of unformed bowel movements. Commonly associated symptoms include abdominal cramps, nausea, bloating, urgency, fever, and malaise. Episodes of traveler' diarrhea usually begin abruptly, occur during travel or soon after returning home, and are generally self-limited.

Uniform Stamp-An official validation stamp which may be issued in the United States by the State health departments to local health departments and physicians licensed by the State.

Vaccination-The administration of any vaccine or toxoid without regard to whether the recipient is successfully made immune.

Vaccine-A suspension of attenuated live or killed microorganisms, or fractions thereof administered to induce immunity and thereby prevent infectious disease.

Validation-Application of an official stamp or seal to the International Certificate of Vaccination by the health department or other appropriate agency. Approved validation stamps and seals in the United States are: (1) The Department of Defense Stamp, (2) the Department of State Seal, (3) the Public Health Service Seal, (4) the National Aeronautics and Space Administration Stamp, and (5) the Uniform Stamp.

Valid certificate-An International Certificate of Vaccination that has been fully completed, signed, and validated with an official stamp or seal.

WHO-World Health Organization.

Yellow Fever Vaccination Center-A center designated under the authority of the health administration of a country to administer yellow fever vaccine.

~ ~ ENDNOTES ~ ~

1. Travelers who will only visit the coastal States from the horn to the Uruguay border are not at risk and need no prophylaxis.

2. Travelers visiting cities and popular rural sites on usual tourist routes are generally not at risk, and chemoprophylaxis is, therefore, not recommended. Travelers on special scientific, educational, or recreational visits should check whether their itineraries include evening or nighttime exposure in areas of risk, or in areas of chloroquine resistance. Travelers to most areas of. risk within China should follow Regimen A; travelers to areas of chloroquine resistance should follow Regimen B.

3. Risk exists in rural areas of Uraba (Antioquia Dept.), Bajo Cauca-Nechi (Cauca and Antioquia Dept.), Magdalena Medio, Caqueta (Caqueta Intendencia), Sarare (Arauca Intendencia). Catatumbo (Norte de Santander Dept.). Pacifico Central and Sur, Putumayo (Putumayo Intendencia), Ariari (Meta Dept.), Alto Vaupes (Vaupes Comisaria), Amazonas, and Guainia (Comisarias).

4. Travelers who will only visit Quito and vicinity, the central highland tourist areas, or the Galapagos Is. are not at risk and need no prophylaxis.

5. Travelers who will only visit the main tourist areas, including the cruises, are not at risk and need no prophylaxis.

6. Malaria transmission in Indonesia (except for Irian Jaya) is largely confined to rural areas not visited by most travelers; most travel to rural areas of Indonesia is during daytime hours when there is minimal risk of exposure. Chemoprophylaxis is recommended only for those travelers who will have outdoor exposure during evening and nighttime hours in rural areas.

7. Malaria transmission in Malaysia (except Sabah) is largely confined to rural areas not visited by most travelers; most travel to rural areas is during daytime hours when there is minimal risk of exposure.

Chemoprophylaxis is recommended only for those travelers who will have outdoor exposure during evening and nighttime hours in rural areas.

8. Although chemoprophylaxis is not recommended for travel to the major resort areas on the Pacific and Gulf Coasts, all travelers should be advised to use insect repellants and other personal protection measures.

9. Malaria transmission in Myanmar (Burma) is largely confined to rural areas not visited by most travelers; most travel to rural areas of Myanmar is during daytime hours when there is minimal risk of exposure.

10. There is no risk in the Canal Zone or in Panama City and vicinity. Travelers to rural areas west of the Canal Zone should follow Regimen A; travelers to areas east of the Canal Zone (including the San Blas Islands) should follow Regimen B.

11. Travelers who will only visit Lima and vicinity, coastal area south of Lima, or the highland tourist areas (Cuzco, Machu Picchu, Lake Titicaca) are not at risk and need no prophylaxis. Risk exists in rural areas of Departments of Amazonas, Cajamarca (except Hualgayoc Province), La Libertad (except Otuzco, Santiago de Chuco Provinces), Lambayeque, Loreto, Piura (except Talara Province). San Martin and Tumbes, Provinces of Santa (Ancash Dept.); parts of La Convension (Cuzco Dept.), Tayacaja (Huancavelica Dept.), Satipo (Junin Dept.).

12. Travelers to most areas of risk within Peru should follow Regimen A; travelers to the northern provinces bordering Brazil who will have rural exposure during evening and nighttime hours should follow Regimen B.

13. Malaria transmission in the Philippines is largely confined to rural areas not visited by most travelers: most travel to rural areas in the Philippines is during daytime hours when there is minimal risk of exposure. Chemoprophylaxis is recommended only for those travelers who will have outdoor exposure during evening and nighttime hours in rural areas. Travelers at risk should use Regimen A, unless they will be at risk in areas of chloroquine resistance, in which case, they should follow Regimen B.

14. Risk exists in districts of Amparai, Anuradhapura, Badulla (part). Batticaloa, Hambantota, Jaffna, Kandy, Kegalle, Kurungala, Mannar, Matale, Matara, Moneragala, Polonnaruwa, Puttalam, Ratnapura, Trincomalee, and Vavuniya.

15. Malaria transmission in Thailand is largely confined to forested rural areas principally along the borders with Cambodia and Myanmar (formerly Burma) not visited by most travelers; most travel to rural areas in Thailand is during daytime hours when there is minimal risk of exposure. Doxycycline is the drug of choice for travelers who overnight in the few areas with risk of malaria.

----

† Risk in northeastern forest areas only.
†† Risk in northwestern forest areas only.

*   Use of trade names in this chapter is for identification only and does not imply endorsement by the Public Health Service or the U.S. Department of Health and Human Services.

Chapter 10

Tips for Americans Residing Abroad

[The information in this chapter is reprinted verbatim from a bulletin issued by the U.S. State Department, Bureau of Consular Affairs. It is intended to serve as advice to Americans traveling abroad.]

— — — —

FOREWORD

The Department of State's Bureau of Consular Affairs has prepared this publication for Americans considering residence abroad as well as for those U.S. citizens who are currently residing in a foreign country. Our primary goal is to provide assistance to and protect the welfare of American citizens who live abroad.

Before taking up a foreign residence, there are many details that you will need to consider. This brochure will acquaint you with the wide range of services provided to American citizens by U.S. embassies and consulates worldwide. We are committed to providing prompt, courteous, and effective assistance.

There are approximately two million private U.S. citizens living overseas worldwide. We strongly recommend this publication to all Americans living or planning to reside abroad. Any additional guidance not specifically addressed in this publication may be obtained from the Bureau of Consular Affairs in the Department of State or from the nearest U.S. embassy or consulate if you are living overseas.

BEFORE YOU GO

LEARN ABOUT THE HOST COUNTRY

Read as much as possible about the country where you plan to reside. Learning about a nation's culture, customs, people, and history will make your stay more meaningful. Libraries, bookstores and tourist bureaus are good resources for this information. Keep abreast as well of the international news for the latest political developments in the country where you will live. Although English is spoken in many countries, learning the language of the nation in which you plan to reside will make the transition to your new environment easier.

One of the best ways to learn about living in a foreign country is to get advice from U.S. citizens already residing there. Countries with large numbers of U.S. expatriates often have U.S. Chamber of Commerce, a bicultural organization, or an American women's club that could give you information on living in that country. In countries with fewer U.S. residents, you may be able to meet fellow expatriates through a local international club. The consular section of the U.S. embassy or consulate may be able to assist you in finding these organizations.

Background Notes

The Department of State publishes *Background Notes* on countries around the world. These are brief, factual pamphlets with information on each country's people, culture, geography, history, government, economy, and political conditions. They are available for about 170 countries worldwide and often include a reading list, travel notes, and maps. Single copies are $2. A 1-year subscription for all updated issues is also available. To obtain copies write to the Superintendent of Documents, U.S. Government Printing Office, Washington, D.C. 20402 or call (202) 783-3238.

Travel Advisories*

The Department of State issues travel advisories to alert U.S. citizens traveling or residing overseas to potential problems that could adversely affect them. The advisories are available through U.S. passport agencies, travel agents' computer reservation systems, major airlines, and American embassies and consulates abroad. If you are contemplating establishing residence in a country where there may be concern about existing conditions, contact the nearest U.S. passport agency or the Department of State's Citizens Emergency Center, Room 4800, Washington, D.C. 20520 at (202)647-5225 to learn if there is a travel advisory in effect. You can call this number 24 hours a day to hear recorded travel advisories.

Tips for Travelers

The Department of State publishes a series of pamphlets on travel to specific regions of the world. The brochures cover topics such as entry requirements, currency and customs regulations, import and export controls, dual nationality, and photography restrictions. The following publications are available from the Superintendent of Documents, U.S. Government Printing Office, Washington, D.C. 20402.

[All current issues of TIPS FOR TRAVELERS are reproduced elsewhere in this book. Check the Table of Contents for location]

REQUIRED DOCUMENTS

Passports

[The information on PASSPORTS originally slotted for this section is provided in detail in **Chapter 2**]

Health Insurance

The Social Security Medicare Program does not cover hospital or medical services outside the United States. The Department of Veterans Affairs will only pay for hospital and medical service outside the United States if you are a veteran with a service-related disability.

When considering medical insurance, first find out how citizens of the country where you will reside pay their medical bills and if the same coverage is available to resident foreigners. Some countries have government-sponsored health insurance that may also provide coverage to foreign residents, while others have a dual system with national health supplemented by private insurance. In countries where many American expatriates reside, such as mexico, you may find that local private international health insurance companies will offer coverage to U.S. citizen residents. Once you arrive, check with organized groups in the American community to learn about these companies. Wherever possible, try to get the best medical insurance available. If good coverage is not available where you will live, you may have to rely on a U.S. medical insurance company. Before taking up residence abroad, learn which U.S. medical services or health insurance plans provide coverage for Americans living overseas. Check with the insurance company on whether the coverage offered abroad includes both routine and emergency medical treatment, hospitalization, and medical evacuation should it be necessary. Once you obtain health insurance, remember to carry your policy's identity card and to keep a supply of insurance claim forms handy. The U.S. Government cannot pay for hospital or medical services for Americans overseas and cannot pay to evacuate you for treatment in the United States.

There are a number of emergency medical assistance companies operating internationally who offer urgent medical treatment for their member travelers. Although the service is designed primarily for tourists who encounter a medical or personal emergency while on vacation, some companies offer yearly memberships which may be available to Americans residing overseas. To learn about these emergency assistance companies contact a travel agent.[1]

Medication

For your protection, leave all medicines in their original, labeled containers. If you require medication containing habit-forming drugs or narcotics, carry a copy of the doctor's prescription attesting to that fact. These precautions will make customs processing easier and also will ensure you do not violate the laws of the country in which you live.

If you have allergies, reactions to certain medicines, or other unique medical problems, consider wearing a medical alert bracelet or carrying a similar warning at all times.

Immunizations

Under the International Health Regulations adopted by the World Health Organization, some countries require International Certificates of vaccination against yellow fever from international travelers. A few countries still require a certificate of cholera immunization as well. A helpful guide to immunizations and preventive measures for international travel is the booklet, *Health Information for International Travel*.[2] It is available for $6.50 from the Superintendent of Documents, U.S. Government Printing Office, Washington, D.C. 20402. Specific information may also be obtained from local and state health departments, physicians, or travel clinics that advise international travelers. You may also call the U.S. Public Health Service's Quarantine division on (404) 639-2572 for immunization recommendations.

AIDS Testing

Many countries require long-term foreign residents and students to submit proof that they are free of the HIV virus. Some of the countries that require this proof may accept certified test results from the United States. Consult the embassy of the country you will be residing in on whether an AIDS test is required and if test results from the United states are accepted. If not, check on the type of test to be performed and if it is permissible to supply your own disposable needle. If you are overseas, consult the nearest U.S. embassy or consulate for information and advice, keeping in mind that you are in a foreign country and are subject to its laws and requirements.

PRACTICAL MATTERS

Federal Benefits
If you are receiving monthly benefits from a Federal or state agency (Social Security, Department of Veterans Affairs, Office of Personnel Management, etc.), contact the appropriate agency prior to your departure from the United States to advise them of your residence abroad and to inquire about the procedures for having your benefits checks sent overseas.

Customs Hints
The pamphlet *Know Before You Go*[3] contains information about U.S. Customs regulations and procedures. Single copies are available from any U.S. Customs office abroad or by writing to U.S. Customs, P.O. Box 7407, Washington, D.C. 20044.

Taking A Pet Overseas
If you decide to bring your pet with you overseas, check specific requirements with the country's embassy. Many countries have strict health, quarantine, agriculture, wildlife, and customs requirements and prohibitions.

LIVING OVERSEAS

HELP FROM THE U.S. GOVERNMENT

Assistance From American Consuls
U.S. consular officers are located in over 250 foreign service posts abroad. They are available to advise and help you, especially if you are in any kind of serious trouble. In addition, consular agents in approximately 35 foreign cities without U.S. consulates provide a limited range of emergency and other consular services.

Consular officers are responsive to the needs of Americans traveling or residing abroad. However, the majority of their time is devoted to assisting Americans who are in serious legal, medical, or financial difficulties. They can provide the names of local doctors, dentists, medical specialists, and attorneys, and give you information about travel advisories. Consular officers also perform non-emergency services, including information on absentee voting, selective service registration, and acquisition and loss of U.S. citizenship. They can arrange for the transfer of Social Security and other U.S. Government benefits to beneficiaries residing abroad, provide U.S. tax forms, and notarize documents. They may also provide information on how to obtain foreign public documents.

Because of the limited number of consular officers and the growing number of U.S. tourists and residents abroad, consuls cannot provide tourism or commercial services. For example, consuls cannot perform the work of travel agencies, lawyers, information bureaus, banks, or the police. They cannot find you jobs, get residence or driving permits, act as interpreters, search for missing luggage, or settle commercial disputes.

Registration at U.S. Embassies or Consulates
As soon as you arrive abroad, you should register in person or by telephone with the nearest U.S. embassy or consulate. Registration will make your presence and whereabouts known in case it is necessary to contact you in an emergency. In accordance with the Privacy Act, information on your welfare or whereabouts may not be released to inquirers without your express authorization. If you register in person, you should bring your U.S. passport with you. Your passport data will be recorded at the embassy or consulate, thereby making it easier for you to apply for a replacement passport should it be lost or stolen.

Missing Persons
When a U.S. citizen abroad loses contact with friends or relatives in the United States, the U.S. consul is often requested to give information about that individual's welfare and whereabouts. Similar requests often come from American private and official welfare organizations attempting, for example, to track down an errant parent who failed to make child support payments. The U.S. consul tries to comply with such requests after determining carefully the reasons for the inquiry. If the consul has the address of the U.S. citizen about whom the inquiry is being made, the consul will inform the American of the inquirer's interest in getting in touch with them and pass on any urgent messages. Consistent with the Privacy Act, the consul then reports back to the inquirer the results of their search efforts. Except in emergency situations, the consul will not release any details about a U.S. citizen's welfare and whereabouts without the citizen's expressed consent.

Arrests

Legal Aid for Americans Arrested Abroad
When living abroad, you are subject to local - i.e. foreign-laws. If you experience difficulties with the local authorities, remember American officials are limited by foreign laws, U.S. regulations, and geography as to what they can do to assist you. The U.S. Government cannot fund your legal fees or other related expenses. Should you find yourself in a dispute that may lead to police or legal action, consult the nearest U.S. consular officer. Although consular

officers cannot get you out of jail, serve as your attorneys or give legal advice, they can provide lists of local attorneys and help you find legal representation. However, neither the Department of State nor U.S. embassies or consulates can assume any responsibility for the caliber, competence, or professional integrity of these attorneys.

If you are arrested, immediately ask to speak to the consular officer at the nearest U.S. embassy or consulate. Under international agreements and practice, you have a right to get in touch with the U.S. consul. If you are turned down, keep asking-politely, but persistently. If unsuccessful, try to have someone get in touch for you.

Consular officers will do whatever they can to protect your legitimate interests and ensure that you are not discriminated against under local law. Upon learning of your arrest, a U.S. consular officer will visit you, provide a list of local attorneys and, if requested, contact family and friends. In cases of arrest, consuls can help transfer money, food, and clothing from your family and friends to you. They also try to get relief if you are held under inhumane or unhealthful conditions or being treated less equitably than others in the same situation.

Drug Arrests

Despite repeated warnings, drug arrests and convictions of American citizens are still a problem. If you are caught with any type of narcotics overseas, you are subject to local-not U.S. laws. Penalties for possession or trafficking are often the same. If you are arrested, you will find the following:

- Few countries provide a jury trial.

- Most countries do not accept bail.

- Pre-trial detention, often in solitary confinement, may last many months.

- Prisons may lack even minimal comforts-bed, toilet, wash basin.

- Diets are often inadequate and require supplements from relatives and friends.

- Officials may not speak English.

- Physical abuse, confiscation of personal property, degrading or inhumane treatment, and extortion are possible.

If you are convicted, you may face one of the following sentences:

- Two to ten years in most countries. A minimum of six year's hard labor and a stiff fine.

- The death sentence in some countries.

Learn what the local laws are and obey them.

Marriage Abroad

Consular officers abroad cannot perform a marriage for you. Marriages abroad are generally performed by local civil or religious officials. Once your marriage is performed overseas, U.S. consular officers can authenticate your foreign marriage documents for a fee (currently $36). A marriage which is valid under the laws of the country where the marriage was performed is generally recognized by most states in the United States. If you are married abroad and need confirmation that your marriage will be recognized in the United States, consult the Attorney General of your state of residence in the United States.

Marriages abroad are subject to the residency requirements of the country where the marriage is performed. There is almost always a lengthy waiting period. Some countries require that the civil documents which are presented to the marriage registrar abroad be translated and authenticated by a foreign consular official in the United States. This process can be time consuming and expensive. Unlike in the United States, civil law countries require proof of legal capacity to enter into a marriage contract. If it is necessary to obtain this proof overseas, you can execute an affidavit of eligibility to marry at a U.S. embassy or consulate for a small fee (currently $4). There are also individual requirements which vary from country to country, i.e. parental consent and blood tests. Before going abroad, check with the embassy or tourist information bureau of the country where you plan to marry to learn of any specific requirements. In addition, the Office of Citizens Consular Services, Room 4817, Department of State, Washington, D.C. 20520 has some general information on marriage in a number of countries overseas. If you are already abroad, consult with the nearest U.S. embassy or consulate.

Divorce Abroad

The validity of divorces obtained overseas will vary according to the requirements of an individual's state of residence. Consult the authorities of your state of residence in the United States for these requirements.

Birth Abroad of a U.S. Citizen

Most children born abroad to a U.S. citizen parent or parents acquire U.S. citizenship at birth. As soon as possible after the birth, the U.S. citizen parent should contact the nearest American embassy or consulate.

When it is determined that the child has acquired U.S. citizenship, a consular officer prepares a *Report of Birth Abroad of a Citizen of the United States of America*. This document is recognized by U.S. law as proof of acquisition of U.S. citizenship and is acceptable evidence of citizenship for obtaining a passport, entering school, and most other purposes.

Death of a U.S. Citizen Abroad

When a U.S. citizen dies abroad, the nearest U.S. embassy or consulate should be notified as soon as possible. Upon notification, the consular officer, in accordance with local laws, may do the following:

- Require proof of the decedent's citizenship (for example, U.S. passport, birth certificate, or naturalization certificate).

- Report the death to the next of kin or legal representative.

- Obtain instructions and funds from the family to make arrangements for local burial or return of the body to the United States. Obtain the local death certificate and prepare a *Report of Death of an American Citizen Abroad* (Form OF-180) to forward to the next of kin or legal representative. (This document may be used in U.S. courts to settle estate matters.)

- Serve as provisional conservator of a deceased American's estate and arrange for disposition of those effects.

Because the costs for local burial or transporting a deceased body back to the United States can be quite expensive, you may wish to obtain insurance to cover this cost. Otherwise, your relative or next of kin must bear these expenses. The U.S. Government cannot pay to have your body buried overseas or returned to the United States.

Federal Benefits Services Abroad

Federal agency monthly benefits checks are generally sent from the Department of the Treasury to the U.S. embassies or consulates in the countries where the beneficiaries are residing. When you move overseas, report your change of residence to the nearest U.S. embassy or consulate. The usual procedure is for the embassy or consulate to then forward the check through the local mail system to you. It may be possible to make arrangements to have your check deposited directly into a bank account located in the United States or in the country where you reside. Check with the benefits paying agency or the nearest U.S. embassy or consulate for further information.

If your check does not arrive or you have other questions about your benefits, contact the nearest U.S. embassy or consulate. If they cannot answer your inquiry, they will contact the appropriate paying agency, such as the Social Security Administration, and make inquiries on your behalf. If you move, notify the nearest U.S. embassy or consulate at least 60 days before the move. This will enable the Federal agency to update its records so your checks are sent to the correct address.

Assistance In Voting in U.S. Elections

Americans who reside abroad are usually eligible to vote by absentee ballot in all Federal elections and may also be eligible to vote in many state and local U.S. elections. Eligibility depends upon the laws and regulations of your state of residence in the United States. To vote absentee, you must meet state voter registration requirements and apply for the ballot as early as possible from the state of your last domicile. Should your state ballot not arrive in sufficient time, you may be eligible to use a Federal write-in ballot known as a F.W.A.B. You should consult the nearest U.S. embassy or consulate for additional information.

Selective Service Registration

Section I-202 of the Presidential Proclamation of July 2, 1980, reinstituting registration under the Military Selective Service Act, states:

Citizens of the United States who are to be registered and who are not in the United States on any of the days set aside for their registration, shall present themselves at a U.S. embassy or consulate for registration before a diplomatic or consular officer of the United States or before a registrar duly appointed by a diplomatic or consular officer of the United States.

FAMILY MATTERS

Adopting A Child Overseas

If you plan to adopt a child overseas, you should be aware that the U.S. Government considers foreign adoptions to be a private legal matter within the judicial sovereignty of the nation where the child is residing. U.S. authorities have no right to intervene on behalf of American citizens in the courts in the country where the adoption takes place. However, there are a number of ways that U.S. embassies and consulates can assist prospective parents.

The U.S. embassy or consulate can provide you with information on the adoption process in the country where you reside. Consular officers can make inquiries on your behalf regarding the status of your case in the

155

foreign court and will assist in clarifying documentary requirements if necessary. Embassies and consulates will also ensure that as an American you are not being discriminated against by foreign courts and will provide you with information on the visa application process for your adopted child. Because children in foreign adoptions are considered to be nationals of the country of origin, prospective parents must comply with local laws. One way to achieve this is by dealing only with a reputable international adoption agency experienced in handling adoptions in the country where you are living. In the case of a private adoption, you should hire a local attorney with expertise in adoptions. Because of the potential for fraud in international adoptions, you need to be aware of the pitfalls. The U.S. embassy or consulate can offer you advice on what problems you might encounter.

Foreign children adopted overseas by U.S. citizens can gain U.S. citizenship if the adoptive parents apply for the child's naturalization after they return to the United States. In most cases, the adoptive parents would merely apply for a Certificate of Citizenship from the Immigration and Naturalization Service (INS) after the adoption. However, until they return to the United States, the adopted child remains a national of their country of origin. Before returning to the United States with your adopted child, you will need to petition the INS for your child's immigrant visa. For further information on adoption procedures, obtain INS Form M-249 entitled, *The Immigration of Adopted and Prospective Adoptive Children*. You can also contact the Department of State, Office of Citizens Consular Services, Washington, D.C. 20520 to learn more about U.S. citizenship requirements and adoption procedures.

International Child Custody Disputes

For parents involved in a child custody dispute, there are limits on the assistance that U.S. authorities can provide. In cases where an American child is abducted overseas by a parent, the U.S. Government's role is confined to helping the remaining parent locate the child, monitoring the child's welfare, and providing general information about child custody laws and procedures in the country where the abduction took place. Consular officers overseas can issue a U.S. passport to a child involved in a custody dispute if the child appears in person at the U.S. embassy or consulate and there is no court order issued by the foreign court of that country which bars the child's departure from the country.

U.S. consuls cannot take custody of a child, force the child's return to the United States, or attempt to influence child custody proceedings in foreign courts. If the parents cannot work out an amicable settlement of

a child custody dispute, the only recourse is usually court action in the country where the child is residing. A custody decree originating in the United States is not automatically recognized overseas. On the contrary, foreign courts will decide custody in accordance with the laws of that country. If you are involved in a custody dispute, you will need to obtain a foreign attorney to represent you in court. You can obtain a list of such attorneys from the U.S. embassy or consulate in the country where your child has been taken.

If you are a parent involved in a custody battle overseas find out whether the country you are in is a party to the Hague Convention on the Civil Aspects of International Child Abduction. Under the Hague Convention, a child who has been wrongfully removed may be returned to his or her place of habitual residence. For further information on the Hague Convention contact the Office of Citizens Consular Services, Bureau of Consular Affairs, Department of State, Room 4817 Washington, D.C. 20520. That office also has copies of the booklet *International Parental Child Abduction* which contains helpful information on what U.S. citizen parents can do to prevent their child from becoming a victim of parental child abduction. If you are overseas and would like information on this subject, contact the nearest U.S. embassy or consulate for guidance.

PRECAUTIONS

Safeguarding Your Passport

Your passport is a valuable document which should be carefully safeguarded. When living overseas, the Department of State recommends that you keep your passport at home in a safe, secure place. Although a passport kept at an available storage facility outside the home might offer maximum security, keep in mind that an emergency requiring immediate travel may make it difficult or impossible to obtain your passport before departure. In such a case, it may not be possible to obtain a replacement or temporary passport in time to make the intended travel.

Lost or Theft of a U.S. Passport

If your passport is lost or stolen abroad, report the loss immediately to the nearest foreign service post and to local police authorities. If you can provide the consular officer with the information in the passport, it will facilitate issuance of a new passport. Therefore, you should photocopy the data page of your passport and keep it in a separate place where it can be easily retrieved.

Passport Fraud

Multiple and fraudulent U.S. passports are used in many types of criminal activity, including illegal entry into the United States. In processing lost passport cases, the Department of State must take special precautions that may delay the issuance of a new passport. If you suspect a U.S. passport is being used fraudulently, do not hesitate to contact the nearest passport agency in the United States or American foreign service post overseas.

Glazed Ceramic Purchases
Be careful when purchasing ceramic tableware and clay pottery while overseas. The U.S. Food and Drug Administration has determined that there are dangerous levels of lead found in the glazes of some ceramic dinnerware and pottery sold abroad. Because there is no way of knowing whether a particular item is safe, the Food and Drug Administration recommends that you use such wares for decorative purposes only.

CITIZENSHIP AND NATIONALITY

U.S. Citizenship and Residence Abroad
U.S. citizens who take up residence abroad or who are contemplating doing so frequently ask whether this will have any effect on their citizenship. Residence abroad, in and of itself, has no effect on U.S. citizenship. However, a person who becomes a U.S. citizen through naturalization and then takes up a permanent residence abroad within 1 year thereafter is subject to possible revocation of naturalization on the grounds that he/she did not intend to reside permanently in the United States when the petition for naturalization was filed. Each particular case is judged on its own merits. Clearly, some persons may have intended to reside in the United States but due to unexpected circumstances, it became necessary for them to take up residence abroad. Revocation of naturalization is the responsibility of the court where the naturalization occurred. The initial steps leading to revocation are taken by the Departments of State and justice. Contact the nearest U.S. embassy or consulate if you have any questions about nationality.

Acquisition and Loss of Citizenship
U.S. citizenship may be acquired by birth in the United States or by birth abroad to a U.S. citizen parent or parents. However, there are certain residency or physical presence requirements that U.S. citizens may need to fulfill before the child's birth in order to transmit citizenship to their child born overseas. A child born abroad in wedlock to one citizen parent and one alien parent acquires U.S. citizenship only if the citizen parent was physically present in the United States for 5 years prior to the child's birth, at least 2 years of which were after the age of 14. Living abroad in military service or U.S. Government employment, or as an unmarried dependent in the household of someone so employed, can be considered as presence in the United States. A child born out of wedlock to a U.S. citizen mother acquires citizenship if the mother was physically present in the United States for 1 year. A child born out of wedlock to a U.S. citizen father must establish a legal relationship to the father before age 18 or be legitimated before reaching age 21, depending on the date of birth, if he/she is to acquire U.S. citizenship through the father. For further information on these legal requirements, consult the nearest foreign service post. Citizenship may also be acquired subsequent to birth through the process of naturalization (see details elsewhere on this page).

Loss of citizenship can occur only as the result of a citizen's voluntarily performing an act of expatriation as set forth in the immigration and Nationality Act with the intent to relinquish citizenship. Such acts most frequently performed include the following:

- Naturalization in a foreign state;

- Taking an oath or making an affirmation of allegiance to a foreign state;

- Service in the armed forces of a foreign state;

- Employment with a foreign government; or

- Taking a formal oath of renunciation of allegiance before a U.S. consular or diplomatic officer.

If you have any question about any aspect of loss of nationality, contact the nearest foreign service post or the Office of Citizens Consular Services, Bureau of Consular Affairs, Room 4817, Department of State, Washington, D.C. 20520.

Dual Nationality
A foreign country might claim you as a citizen of that country if:
- You were born there.

- Your parent or parents are or were citizens of that country.

- You are a naturalized U.S. Citizen but are still considered a citizen under that country's laws.

If you are in any of the above categories, consult the embassy of the country where you are planning to reside or are presently living. While recognizing the existence of dual nationality, the U.S. Government does not encourage it as a matter of policy because of the problems it may cause. Claims of other countries upon dual-national U.S. citizens often place them in situations

157

where their obligations to one country are in conflict with U.S. law. Dual nationality may hamper efforts by the U.S. Government to provide diplomatic and consular protection to individuals overseas. When a U.S. citizen is in the other country of their dual nationality, that country has a predominant claim on the person. If you have any question about dual nationality, contact the nearest foreign service post or the Office of Citizens Consular Services at the address on the previous page.

FINANCIAL AND BUSINESS MATTERS

U.S. Taxes

U.S. citizens must report their worldwide income on their Federal income tax returns. Living or earning income outside the United States does not relieve a U.S. citizen of responsibility for filing tax returns. However, U.S. citizens living and/or working abroad may be entitled to various deductions, exclusions, and credits under U.S. tax laws, as well as under international tax treaties and conventions between the United States and a number of foreign countries. Consult the Internal Revenue Service (IRS) for further information.

For information on taxes and locations of IRS offices overseas, contact any office of the IRS or write to the Forms Distribution Center, Post Office Box 25866, Richmond, Virginia 23289. That office also has copies of Publication 54, *Tax Guide for U.S. Citizens and Resident Aliens Abroad,* Publication 901, *U.S. Tax Treaties,* Publication 514, *Foreign Tax Credit for Individuals* and Publication 520, *Scholarships and Fellowships.* The IRS has also put together a package of forms and instructions (Publication 776) for U.S. citizens living abroad. You can get the package by writing to the Forms Distribution Center at the address shown above. During the filing period, you can usually obtain the necessary Federal income tax forms from the nearest U.S. embassy or consulate.

Foreign Country Taxes

If you earn any income while you are overseas, you may be required to pay tax on that income. You should check the rules and regulations with that country's embassy or consulate before you leave the United States, or consult the nearest U.S. embassy or consulate abroad.

Bank Accounts

Some countries will permit you to maintain a local bank account denominated in dollars or in another foreign currency of your choice. This may be a good idea if the U.S. dollar is strong and the local currency in the country you reside in is weak. If that country does not permit you to maintain U.S. dollar bank accounts, another idea would be to keep your dollars in a bank in the United States. That way you could convert them to the local currency as you need them rather than all at once. This would protect you in the event that the country you are living in devalues its currency.

Wills

To avoid the risk of running afoul of foreign laws, if you own property or other assets both in the United States and overseas, consider the idea of having two wills drawn up. One should cover your assets in your adopted country and the other your U.S. assets. Each will should mention the other.

Having two wills should ensure that your foreign property is disposed of in accordance with your wishes in the event of your death.

Property Investment

A major decision that you will have to face when you live abroad is whether or not to purchase a home or property. Because prices in many foreign countries may seem like a bargain compared to the United States, there may be some merit to investing in real estate. However, you will need to keep several things in mind. First, check to see whether the country where you plan to invest permits foreigners to own property. Many foreign countries do not permit foreigners without immigrant status to buy real estate. Also, there may be restrictions on areas in which you may buy property and on the total number of foreigners who may purchase property in any one year.

One way for a foreigner to purchase real estate overseas may be to set up a bank trust and then lease the property. For your protection, you should first consult with a local real estate agent and then hire a reputable attorney. Check with the U.S. embassy or consulate in the country where you plan to purchase property to obtain a list of lawyers. A good lawyer will provide you with information about having your real estate contract notarized, registered, and if necessary, translated. Your attorney should also be able to advise you on protection against unscrupulous land deals.

Before you make a real estate purchase, learn the customs and laws of the foreign government with regard to real estate. In the event of a dispute, you will have to abide by local and not U.S. laws. A good rule to follow is that before you invest in any real estate take the same precautions which you normally would take before you make a sizeable investment in the United States.

RETURNING TO THE U.S.
U.S. IMMIGRATION AND CUSTOMS

If you leave the U.S. for purposes of traveling, working, or studying abroad, and return to resume U.S. residence, you are considered a returning U.S. resident by the U.S. Customs Service. When you go through immigration and customs at the port of entry, have your passport ready. Where possible, pack separately the articles you have acquired abroad to make inspection easy. Have your receipts handy in case you need to support your customs declaration. If you took other documents with you, such as an International Certification of Vaccination, a medical certificate, or a customs certificate of registration for foreign-made personal articles, have them ready also. If you are returning to the U.S. by car from either Mexico or Canada, a certificate of vehicle registration should be available.

Articles acquired abroad and brought back with you are subject to duty and internal revenue tax. As a returning U.S. resident, you are allowed to bring back $400 worth of merchandise duty free. However, you must have been outside the United States for at least 48 hours, and you must not have used this exemption within the preceding 30-day period. The next $1,000 worth of items you bring back with you for personal use or gifts are dutiable at a flat 10% rate.

Restriction on Products Entering the U.S.

Fresh fruit, meat, vegetables, plants in soil, and many other agricultural products are prohibited from entering the United States because they may carry foreign insects and diseases that could damage U.S. crops, forests, gardens, and livestock. Other items may also be restricted, so be sure to obtain details of regulations before departing for your trip back to the U.S. These restrictions also apply to mailed products. Prohibited items confiscated and destroyed at U.S. international postal facilities have almost doubled in recent years. For more information and to request the pamphlet, *Travelers Tips on Prohibited Agricultural Products* contact the agricultural affairs office at the nearest U.S. embassy or consulate, or write to the Animal and Plant Health Inspection Service, U.S. Department of Agriculture, 613 Federal Building, 6505 Belcrest Road, Hyattsville, Maryland 20782.

Importing A Car

If you plan to bring a car back with you, before purchasing it, make sure it conforms to U.S. emission standards established by the Environmental Protection Agency (EPA). If your vehicle does not conform to standards, it may be banned from entering the country. For further information, obtain the pamphlet, *Buying a Car Overseas? Beware!*[5] from the U.S. Environmental Protection Agency, Public Information Center, PM-211B, 401 M Street, S.W., Washington, D.C. 20460.

Wildlife and Wildlife Products

While you were overseas, if you purchased any articles made from endangered animals and plants or any five wild animals to bring back as pets, you need to be aware that U.S. laws and international treaties make it a crime to bring many wildlife souvenirs into the United States. Some prohibited items include those made from sea turtle shell, most reptile skins, crocodile leather, ivory, furs from endangered cat species, and those from coral reefs. Do not buy wildlife souvenirs if you are unsure of being able to bring them legally into the United States. The penalties you risk are severe and your purchases could be confiscated. To learn more about endangered wildlife and guidelines governing restrictions on imports into the United States, you can obtain the pamphlet, *"Buyer Beware!"*[5] For a free copy, contact the Publications Unit, U.S. Fish and Wildlife Service, Department of the Interior, Washington, D.C. 20240. Additional information on the import of wildlife and wildlife products can be obtained through TRAFFIC (U.S.A.), World Wildlife Fund-U.S., 1250 24th Street, N.W., Washington, D.C. 20037.

ADDITIONAL INFORMATION

U.S. Embassies and Consulates

Key Officers of Foreign Service Posts: Guide for Business Representatives has names of key officers and addresses for U.S. embassies, consulates, and missions abroad.[6] Updated 3 times a year; a 1-year subscription is $5. Order from the Superintendent of Documents, U.S. Government Printing Office, Washington, D.C. 20402.

Older Americans

Travel Tips for Older Americans[4] provides general information on passports, visas, health, currency, and other travel tidbits for elderly U.S. citizens planning to travel overseas. Copies are available for $1 from the U.S. Government Printing Office.

Safe Travel

A Safe Trip Abroad[5] contains helpful precautions to minimize the chance of becoming a victim of terrorism and also provides other safety tips for Americans traveling overseas. To obtain a copy, send $1 to the U.S. Government Printing Office.

Crisis Abroad

Crisis Abroad-What the State Department Does[5] summarizes the work by the State Department during a crisis and its efforts to obtain reliable information from local authorities abroad for concerned relatives and friends of Americans located in the disaster area. Copies are free from CA/PA, Room 5807, Department of State, Washington, D,C. 20520.

The Citizens Emergency Center

The Citizens Emergency Center[5] contains information about the assistance that office provides in four major categories: deaths, arrests, welfare/whereabouts inquiries, and financial-medical emergencies. The leaflet is free from CA/PA at the address above.

~ ~ ENDNOTES ~ ~

1. A list of Medical Assistance Organizations is provided in **Appendix 14N.**

2. A large portion of this booklet has been reproduced verbatim elsewhere in this book, including a country by country listing of vaccination requirements. Check the Table of Contents for location.

3. This publication is reprinted elsewhere in this book. See Table of Contents for location.

4. This publication is reprinted verbatim elsewhere in this book. See Table of Contents for location.

5. This publication is reprinted elsewhere in this book. See Table of Contents for location.

6. See **Appendix A** for complete listing of U.S. embassies and consulated abroad, including their addresses, telephone, fax and telex numbers.

7. This publication is reprinted elsewhere in this book. Check the Table of Contents.

Chapter 11

Tips for Older Americans

[The information in this chapter is reprinted verbatim from a bulletin issued by the U.S. State Department, Bureau of Consular Affairs. It is intended to serve as advice to Americans traveling abroad.]

- - - -

International travel can be a rich and rewarding adventure. Whether you have waited a lifetime to take the perfect trip or are an experienced world traveler, we would like to offer some advice to help you plan a safe and healthy trip.

American consuls at U.S. embassies and consulates abroad are there to help if you encounter serious difficulties in your travels. They are happy to meet you if you come in to register your passport at the consular section of the U.S. embassy or consulate. But it is also their duty to assist American citizens abroad in times of emergency-at hospitals or police stations, for instance. This pamphlet is written in the hopes that it will help you to prevent such emergencies from arising.

Preparation for Your Trip

Start Early. Apply for your passport as soon as possible. Three months before your departure date should give you plenty of time. See the section "Passports and Visas" on page 163 for details on how to apply.

Learn About the Countries You Plan to Visit. The countries you visit will seem like old friends if, before you go, you read up on their culture, people, and history. Bookstores and libraries are good resources. Travel magazines and the travel sections of major newspapers tell about places to visit and also give advice on everything from discount airfares to international health insurance. Many travel agents and foreign tourist bureaus provide free information on travel abroad.

Travel Advisories. The Department of State issues travel advisories concerning serious health or security conditions that may affect U.S. citizens. If you are traveling to an area where there may be problems, you may contact the nearest U.S. passport agency or the Department of State's Citizens Emergency Center on (202) 647-5225 to learn whether there are travel advisories in effect for the countries you plan to visit.

Charter Flights. Before you pay for a charter flight or travel package, read your contract carefully and see what guarantee it gives that the company will deliver the services that it is trying to sell you. Tour operators sometimes go out of business in the middle of a season, leaving passengers stranded, holding unusable return tickets and unable to obtain a refund for the unused portion of their trip. Unless you are certain a company is reputable, check its credentials with your local Better Business Bureau (BBB). The BBB maintains complaint files for a year. You can also check with the consumer affairs office of the American Society of Travel Agents, 1101 King Street, Alexandria, VA 22314, tel. (703) 739-2782 to learn if a travel company has a complaint record.

Trip Insurance. One sure way to ruin a vacation is to lose money because an emergency forces you to postpone or cancel your trip. Except for tickets on regularly scheduled airlines, almost any travel package you purchase will have a penalty for cancellation, and some companies will give no refund at all. Regularly scheduled airlines usually give a refund if an illness or death in the family forces you to cancel. They require a note from the doctor or a death certificate. Take careful note of the cancellation penalty for any other large travel purchase you make, such as a tour package, charter flight, or cruise. If you invest in trip insurance, make sure your policy covers all reasonable possibilities for your having to cancel. For instance, if an emergency with a family member would force you to cancel, insure against that as well.

Some trip insurance policies will also give a refund if the company goes out of business or otherwise does not make good on its offering. The best insurance against company default is to choose a reputable company that guarantees a refund if they do not deliver the goods. If, however, you are tempted to purchase a tour at a great bargain price and you can't find a guarantee of delivery in the fine print, protect yourself by purchasing trip insurance that covers company default.

Shop around for the trip insurance policy that offers the

161

most benefits. Some credit card and traveler's check companies

offer travel protection packages for an additional fee. Benefits may even include accident and illness coverage while traveling.

Health Insurance. The Social Security Medicare program does not provide for payment of hospital or medical services obtained outside the U.S. However, some Medicare supplement plans offer foreign medical care coverage at no extra cost for treatments considered eligible under Medicare. These are reimbursement plans. You must pay the bills first and obtain receipts in order to submit them later for compensation. Many of these plans have a dollar ceiling per trip.

Review your health insurance policy. Obtaining medical treatment and hospital care abroad can be expensive. If your Medicare supplement or other medical insurance does not provide protection while traveling outside the United States, we strongly urge you to buy coverage that does. There are short-term health and emergency assistance policies called medical assistance programs that are designed specifically for travelers.

Medical Assistance Programs. One strong advantage of medical assistance programs is that they also cover the exorbitant cost of medical evacuation in the event of an accident or serious illness. As part of the coverage, these companies usually offer emergency consultation by telephone. They may refer you to the nearest hospital or call directly for help for you. If you need an interpreter, they may translate your instructions to a health care worker on the scene. Another benefit that is normally part of such coverage is payment for the return of remains to the United States in case of death.

If your regular health insurance already covers you for medical expenses abroad, you can buy a medical assistance program that offers all the consultative and evacuation services listed above, except for the health insurance itself. The cost of medical assistance coverage can be as low as $25 for a 2-week trip without health insurance coverage or $49 for the complete medical assistance program, including health insurance. Without this insurance medical evacuation can cost thousands of dollars.

If your travel agent cannot direct you to a medical assistance company, look for information on such services in travel magazines.[1] Once you have adequate coverage, carry your insurance policy identity cards and claim forms with you when you travel.

Medication. If you require medication, bring an ample supply in its original containers. Because of strict laws concerning narcotics throughout the world, bring along copies of your prescriptions and, if you have an unusual prescription, carry a letter from your physician explaining your need for the drug. As an extra precaution, carry the generic names of your medications with you, because pharmaceutical companies overseas may use different names from those used in the United States. If you wear eyeglasses, take an extra pair with you. Pack medicines and extra eyeglasses in your hand luggage so they will be available in case your checked luggage is lost. To be extra secure, pack a backup supply of medicines and a third pair of eyeglasses in your checked luggage. If you have allergies, reactions to certain medications, foods, or insect bites, or other unique medical problems, consider wearing a "medical alert" bracelet. You may also wish to carry a letter from your physician explaining desired treatment should you become ill.

Immunizations. Information on immunizations and health precautions for travelers can be obtained from local health departments, the U.S. Public Health Service, private doctors, or travel clinics. General guidance can also be found in the U.S. Public Health Service book *Health Information for International Travel.*[2]

Passport. Pack an "emergency kit" to help you get a replacement passport in case yours is lost or stolen. To make a kit, photocopy the data page at the front of your passport; write down the addresses and telephone numbers of the U.S. embassies and consulates in the countries you plan to visit; and put this information, along with two passport-sized photographs, in a place separate from your passport.

Leave a Detailed Itinerary. Give a friend or relative your travel schedule. Include names, addresses, and telephone numbers of persons and places to be visited; your passport number and the date and place it was issued; and credit card, traveler's check, and airline ticket numbers. Keep a copy of this information for yourself in a separate place from your purse or wallet. If you change your travel plans-for example, if you miss your return flight to the United States or extend your trip-be sure to notify relatives or friends at home.

Don't Overprogram. Allow time to relax and really enjoy yourself. Even if this is your once-in-a-lifetime trip, don't feel you have to fill every available minute.

If you are visiting a country such as China, where physical activity can be quite strenuous and sudden changes in diet and climate can have serious health consequences for the unprepared traveler, consult your physician before you depart.

What to Pack. Carefully consider the clothing you take. Don't pack more than you need and end up lugging around heavy suitcases. Wash-and-wear clothing and sturdy walking shoes are good ideas. Consider the climate and season in the countries you will visit and bring an extra outfit for unexpectedly warm or cool weather. A sweater or shawl is always useful for cooler evenings and air-conditioned planes and hotels. Dress conservatively-a wardrobe that is flashy or too causal may attract the attention of thieves or con artists.

Include a change of clothing in your carry-on luggage. Otherwise, if your bags are lost, you could be wearing the same clothes you were traveling in during the entire time it takes to locate your luggage-an average of 72 hours.

Do not pack anything that you would hate to lose, such as valuable jewelry, family photographs, or objects of sentimental value.

Passports and Visas

Passports. It is a good idea to apply 3 months before you plan to travel. If you also need visas, allow more time, as you must have a valid passport before applying for a visa.

[See Chapter 2 for more information on passports.]

When you receive your passport, be sure to sign it on page 1 and to pencil in on page 4 the requested information. This will help us notify your family or friends in case of an accident or other emergency. Do not designate your traveling companion as the person to be notified in case of an emergency.

Visas. Many countries require a visa-an endorsement or stamp placed in your passport by a foreign government-that permits you to visit that country for a specified purpose and a limited time. Many countries require you to obtain a visa from their consular office nearest to your residence. The addresses of foreign consular offices can be found in telephone directories of large cities or in the *Congressional Directory,* available in most libraries; or you may write or call the appropriate embassy in Washington, D.C. Apply for your visa directly to the embassy or consulate of each country you plan to visit or ask your travel agent to assist you with visas. U.S. passport agencies cannot obtain visas for you. For more information on visas, you may order the publication *Foreign Entry Requirements.*[3]

An increasing number of countries are establishing entry requirements regarding AIDS testing, particularly for long-term residents and students. Check with the embassy or consulate of the countries you plan to visit for the latest information.

Money and Valuables

Don't Take Your Money in Cash. Bring most of your money in traveler's checks. Have a reasonable amount of cash with you, but not more than you will need for a day or two. Convert your traveler's checks to local currency as you use them rather than all at once.

You may also wish to bring at least one internationally recognized credit card. Before you leave, find out what your credit card limit is and do not exceed it. In some countries, travelers who have innocently exceeded their limit have been arrested for fraud. Leave unneeded credit cards at home.

If you must take jewelry or other valuables, use hotel security vaults to store them. It is wise to register such items with U.S. Customs before leaving the United States to make customs processing easier when you return.

It is a violation of law in some countries to enter or exit with that country's currency. Check with a travel agent or the embassy or consulate of the countries you plan to visit to learn their currency restrictions. Before departing from the U.S., you may wish, if allowed, to purchase small amounts of foreign currency and coins to use for buses, taxis, telephone calls, and other incidentals when you first arrive in a country. You may purchase foreign currency from some banks or from foreign exchange dealers. Most international airports also have money exchange facilities.

Once you are abroad, local banks generally give more favorable rates of exchange than hotels, restaurants, or stores for converting your U.S. dollars and traveler's checks into foreign currency.

Your Trip

Driving. U.S. auto insurance is usually not valid outside of the United States and Canada. When you drive in any other country, be sure to buy adequate auto insurance in that country. When renting a car abroad, make certain that adequate insurance is part of your contract; otherwise, purchase additional coverage in an amount similar to that which you carry at home.

Flying. On long flights, break up long periods of

sitting. Leave your seat from time to time and also do in-place exercises. This will help prevent your arriving tired and stiff-jointed. Also, get some exercise after a long flight. For example, take a walk or use your hotel's exercise room.

Reconfirm. Upon arrival at each stopover, reconfirm your onward reservations. When possible, obtain a written confirmation. International flights generally require confirmation 72 hours in advance. If your name does not appear on the reservation list, you could find yourself stranded.

Register. If you plan to be in a location for 2 weeks or more or in an area where there is civil unrest or any other emergency situation, register with the nearest U.S. embassy or consulate. This will help in locating you, should someone in the United States wish to confirm your safety and welfare or need to contact you urgently.

Practical Safety Tips

Respect the Local Laws and Customs. While abroad, you are subject to the laws and regulations of your host country and are not protected by the U.S. Constitution. If you should be detained by local authorities, ask to talk to a U.S. consular officer. Under international agreements and practice, you have a right to contact an American consul. Although U.S. consuls cannot act as your attorney or get you out of jail, they can provide you with a list of local attorneys and inform you of your rights under local laws. They will also monitor the status of detained Americans and make sure they are treated fairly under local laws.

Guard Your Passport. Your passport is the most valuable document you carry abroad. It confirms that you are an American citizen. Do not carry your passport in the same place as your money, use it as collateral for a loan, or pack it in your luggage. Remember to keep your passport number in a separate location in case it is lost or stolen. In some countries, you may be required to leave your passport overnight or for several days with the hotel management. This may be local practice-do not be concerned unless the passport is not retained as promised. If your passport is lost or stolen abroad, immediately report it to the local police; obtain a copy of the report, and contact the nearest U.S. embassy or consulate to apply for a new passport.

Be Alert. Move purposefully and confidently. If you should find yourself in a crowded area, such as in an elevator, subway, marketplace, or at a parade, exercise special caution to avoid theft.

Robbery. Help prevent theft by carrying your belongings securely. Carry purses tucked under an arm and not dangling by a strap. Carry valuables in an inside front pocket or in a money belt, not in a hip pocket. You may wish to wrap your wallet with rubber bands to make it more difficult for someone to slip it from your pocket unnoticed. Money belts or pouches that fit around your shoulder or waist are available through travel magazines and at some luggage shops and department stores.

Assistance From U.S. Embassies and Consulates

Emergencies. If you encounter serious legal, medical, or financial difficulties or other problems abroad, contact the nearest U.S. embassy or consulate for assistance. Although, as mentioned above, consular officers cannot serve as attorneys, they can help you find legal assistance. Consular offices cannot cash checks, tend money, or act as travel agents. However, in an emergency, they can help you get in touch with your family back home to inform them on how to wire funds to you and to let them know of your situation. They can also provide you with the latest travel advisories to alert you to adverse conditions abroad.

Nonemergencies. Consular officers can also provide nonemergency services such as information on absentee voting and acquisition or loss of U.S. citizenship. They can arrange for the transfer of Social Security and other benefits to Americans residing abroad, provide U.S. tax forms, notarize documents, and advise U.S. citizens on property claims.

Safeguarding Your Health. If you are injured or become seriously ill abroad, a U.S. consular officer will assist you in finding a physician or other medical services, and, with your permission, will inform your family members or friends of your condition. If needed, consular officers can assist your family in transferring money to the foreign country to pay for your treatment.

Death Abroad. Each year, about 6,000 Americans die abroad. Two-thirds of them are Americans who live overseas, but approximately 2,000 Americans per year die while traveling abroad. Consular officers will contact the next of kin in the United States and will explain the local requirements. It is a worthwhile precaution to have insurance that covers the cost of local burial or shipment of remains home to the United States (see information on medical assistance programs on page 162). Otherwise, this cost must be borne by next of kin and can be extremely expensive. The U.S. Government cannot pay for shipment of remains to the United States.

Shopping-Some Things To Avoid

Beware of purchasing souvenirs made from endangered wildlife. Much wildlife and wildlife products are prohibited either by U.S. or foreign laws from import into the United States. You risk confiscation and a possible fine if you attempt to import such things. Watch out for and avoid purchasing the following prohibited items:

- All products made from sea turtles.
- All ivory, both Asian and African.
- Furs from spotted cats.
- Furs from marine mammals.
- Feathers and feather products from wild birds.
- All live or stuffed birds from Australia, Brazil, Columbia, Costa Rica, Ecuador, Guatemala, Mexico, Paraguay, Venezuela, and some Caribbean countries.
- Most crocodile and caiman leather.
- Most coral, whether in chunks or in jewelry.

When You Return

Be Prepared. On arrival in the United States, have your passport ready when you go through immigration and customs controls.

Keep receipts for any items you purchased abroad. U.S. citizens may bring back and orally declare $400 worth of merchandise duty free. The next $1,000 is taxed at a flat rate of 10%. Check with U.S. Customs for further information.

Currency. There is no limit on the amount of money or negotiable instruments which can be brought into or taken out of the United States. However, any amount over $10,000 must be reported to U.S. Customs on Customs Form 4790 when you depart from or enter into the United States.

Don't bring home any fresh fruits or vegetables. Such items will be confiscated.

Passport Agencies. See Appendix J.

ADDITIONAL INFORMATION FROM THE EDITOR:

As You Go Do not Forget to:

- take your medications with you

- take your glasses with you

- take a copy of your medical history with you

- some proof of age (e.g. passport, drivers license...)

- get travel insurance

- request for senior discounts when making purchases and reservations

- travel light

- get plenty of rest before, during and after your trips

- have fun

[For more of the things you may not want to forget, turn to the travel checklist provided elsewhere in this book]

USEFUL PUBLICATIONS

You will find the following publications helpful.

- *Get Up and Go: A Guide for the Mature Traveler,* by Gene and Adele Malott. (Gateway Books, San Rafael, CA) (415) 451-5215

- *The International Health Guide for Senior Travelers,* and *The Senior Citizen's Guide to Budget Travel in Europe.* These books are, distributed by Pilot Books. 103 Cooper St Babylon, New York (576) 422-2225

- *101 Tips for Mature Travelers,* available free of charge from Grand Circle Travel, (Boston, MA) (617) 350-7500

- *Travel Easy: The Practical Guide for People Over 50.* Available from AARP Books, 1865 Miner St., Des Plains, IL 60016. (800) 238-2300.

- *The Discount Guide for Travelers over 55* by Caroline and Walter Weinz, published by Dutton

- *Travel and Retirement Edens Abroad* by Peter A. Dickins. Available from ARRP/Scott Foresman and CO., 1865 Miner Street, Desplaines, IL 60016

- *Mature Outlook* (a travel magazine) available by subscription from, 6601 North Clark Street, Chicago, IL 60660; (800) 336-6330

HELPING HANDS:

The following organizations are useful sources for a variety of services and products available to seniors, including money-saving bargains. Write and request for a catalog.

When you contact these agencies do inquire from them what other services and consideration such as, discounts, are available to seniors. You may qualify for some of them. And while overseas, do not forget to ask hotels, museums, airlines, rail authorities, and large department stores if there are discounts available to seniors.

- **American Association of Retired Persons** (AARP) 1900 K St. NW. Washington, D.C. 20049 (800) 441-7575 or (202) 662-4850

- **AARP Purchase Privilege Program.** Contact AARP at the above address.

- **AARP Travel Services,** (800) 927-0111

- **AARP Motoring Plan,** P.O. Box 9049, Des Moines, IA 50369.

- **National Council of Senior Citizens, 1331** F St. NW, Washington, D.C. 20004 (202) 347-8800

- **National Association of Senior Citizens** 925 15th St. NW, Washington DC 20005. (202) 347-8800.

- **Grand Travel,** 6900 Wisconsin Ave. Suite 706, Chevy Chase, MD 20815, (800) 247-7651 or (301) 986-0790.

- **Gadabout Tours,** 700 E. Tahquitz, Palm Springs, CA 92262. (800) 952-5068.

- **Insight International Tours,** 745 Atlantic Ave., Boston MA 02111. (800) 582-8380 or (617) 482-2000.

- **Saga International Holidays,** 120 Boylston St., Boston MA, 02116. (800) 343-0273 or (617) 451-6808.

- **Sun Holidays** 26 6th Street, Stanford CT 06905 (800) 243-2057; (203) 323-1166

- **September Days Club,** 2751 Buford Hwy., NE, Atlanta Georgia, 30324, Tel. (404) 728-4405

- **AARP Experience (from American Express)** P.O. Box 37580 Louisville KY 50233 (800) 927-0111 or (800) 745-4567 or (800) 659-5678 TDD or TTY

- **Partners-in-Travel;** P.O. Box 491145, Los Angeles, CA 90049 (213) 476-4869

- **Travel Companion Exchange** P.O. Box 833-F, Amityville, NY. 11701 (516) 454-0880

- **Grand Circle Travel,** 555 Madison Ave., New York, NY 10022; 347 Congress St. Suite 3A, Boston MA 02210. (617) 350-7500 or (800) 221-2610

- **Elderhostel,** 75 Federal St., 3rd flr., Boston MA 02110 (617) 426-7788.

- **Golden Companions,** P.O. Box 754, Pullman, WA 99163 (208) 883- 5052

Keep in mind that medicare and U.S. medical insurance is not always valid outside the United States. Additional insurance should be considered.

To assist you further, a list of medical assistance organization is provided in Appendix 14N.

Additional Travel Publications

See Chapter 46 for a listing of resources available to the general traveler from the U.S. Departments of State, Customs, Transportation, Health and various government and non-government organizations. All of the available International travel-related pamphlets, brochures and publications issued by the U.S. Department of State and by U.S. Customs have been reproduced in full in this book. See Table of Contents for location.

~ ~ ENDNOTES ~ ~

1. A list of Medical Assistance Organizations is provided in **Appendix 14N.**

2. A large portion of this booklet has been reproduced verbatim elsewhere in this book, including a country by country listing of vaccination requirements. Check the Table of Contents for location.

3. This publication is reprinted in **Chapter 3** of this book.

Chapter 12

Travel Tips for the Disabled

*[The information in this chapter is intended to serve as advice
to disabled travelers.]*

- - - -

Suggestions for Convenient Travel

Over 43 million people in the U.S. with some kind of a disability need to use air transportation for business or pleasure. With the passage of the Air Carrier Access Act of 1986 and the Americans with Disabilities Act of 1990, air transportation providers have made great strides to increase accessible services for people with disabilities.

The following suggestions offer tips to help travelers with disabilities and older people to experience a trouble-free trip:

Advance Reservations

It will be helpful to give the airline ample time to supply any special equipment or services you may need. This procedure will allow the reservation agent to program your request into the airline computer system and distribute it to other airline representatives who you may encounter on your trip.

> Request information about the airline's special services for people who are disabled and/or older, as well as any other customer service requests such as: special meals, braille briefing procedures, open-captions on videos, visual displays at gate areas, procedures for packaging battery-powered wheelchairs, and special senior fares.

> Request written confirmation after you make your reservation. Ask the reservation or travel agent to repeat your request to make sure they have recorded it correctly.
> Deadlines for purchasing reservations will vary according to the airline and type of fares you are investigating. Make sure you confirm the deadline for purchasing your ticket(s) with the reservation agent.

If you are hearing impaired, inform the reservation or travel agent of a relay telephone number, as well as your TDD number, in case they need to reach you.

Inform the airline as to whether you wish to transport your own wheelchair and if so, whether it is battery-powered and the type of battery it has so the airline can provide appropriate packaging. Be sure you understand the airline's procedure for transporting battery-powered wheelchairs.

Make sure a baggage destination tag and a personal I.D. tag are attached to your wheelchair before you check it in.

Inform the airline/travel agent if you will be traveling with a service animal or will need special equipment during the flight such as portable oxygen, on board wheelchair, or a stretcher, among other items.

Upon request, airlines, by law, will provide assistance for boarding, exiting the aircraft, flight connections, and for transportation between gates.

Advance Check-In

> It is helpful to check in early, at least (1) hour before departure to provide enough time for the airline to accommodate your wishes.

> If paying by check, make sure you have the proper identification-a drivers license, major credit card, etc.
> When checking in be sure to give the final destination and not the city where you might connect to go to another flight.

> Make sure your tickets have the correct originating city, connecting city, and final destination.

> Make sure your claim ticket and luggage tag matches your final destination.

> Carry on luggage is limited to two pieces of luggage that will fit underneath the passengers seat, in the overhead bin or closet of the aircraft. Assistive devices such as canes, TDDs, wheelchairs, crutches, prosthetic devices etc., are not counted as

carry on baggage according to the Air Carrier Access Act of 1986.

Many airports provide printed access guides which outline accessible services available in the airport. These brochures may be found at travelers aid stations, information counters, and airport administration offices. Airport authorities will be happy to send you a copy of their brochure if requested in advance.

Procedures for Boarding, In-Flight and Deplaning

Airlines must offer the opportunity for you to pre-board upon request. Be prepared to provide instructions on how to best help you. If you are hearing impaired, ask the agent to let you know when it is time to board. Confirm the flight number and destination before boarding, and sit facing the boarding station if possible.

If you are unable to hear announcements in-flight, request that they be communicated to you, in person, by the flight attendant.

Federal Aviation Regulations require in-flight crews to brief passengers on evacuation procedures. It may be necessary to provide you with an independent briefing. Ask the attendant for print or braille instructions to facilitate the briefing.

If you need assistance leaving the plane upon arrival, advise the in-flight crew during the flight to make arrangements with ground crew personnel.

Medical Traveling Tips

According to the American Academy of Otolaryngology Head and Neck Surgery, ear problems are the most common medical complaint of airplane travelers. Many people experience a sensation of fullness in the ears or popping when in-flight. During an airplane descent babies often cry due to this discomfort.

A fullness or blocked sensation can be experienced when the middle ear pressure cannot be equalized. The Eustachian tube must open frequently and widely enough to equalize the changes in pressure. Since air travelers can experience rapid changes in air pressure, the following tips can help to equalize the pressure in the middle ear.

Swallow frequently when you are in-flight, especially before descent. Chewing gum or allowing mints to melt in your mouth will create a need for you to swallow more often.

Avoid sleeping during descent, because you may not be swallowing often enough to keep up with pressure changes.

If yawning or swallowing is not effective, use the 'valsalva' maneuver:

- Pinch your nostrils shut.

- Breathe in a mouthful of air.

- Using only your cheek and throat muscles, create pressure and force the air into the back of your nose as if you were trying to blow your thumb and fingers off your nostrils.

- Be very gentle and blow in short successive attempts. When you hear or feel a pop in your ears, you have succeeded.

Never use force from your chest (lungs) or abdomen (diaphragm) which can create pressures that are too intense.

If travelling with a baby, allow the baby to suck on a pacifier or bottle, and do not allow the baby to sleep during descent.

If you have a cold, a sinus infection or allergy attack, postpone the airplane trip if at all possible.

Decongestant tablets and nasal sprays can be used an hour or so before descent. Travelers with allergy problems should take their medication at the beginning of the flight. Decongestant tablets and sprays should be avoided by persons with heart disease, high blood pressure, irregular heart rhythms, thyroid diseases or excessive nervousness. Pregnant women should consult their physicians first before using these over the counter medications.

After landing you may continue the pressure equalizing techniques, but if your ears fail to open or pain persists, seek the help of a physician who has experience in the care of ear disorders.

Do not put medication or glasses in checked bags; always bring them with you in carry-on bags. Bring a copy of your prescriptions for medication, glasses, and a statement from your physician explaining any special medical problems

ADVICE TO TRAVEL AGENTS AND HANDICAPPED TRAVELLERS ON ALERTING AIR CARRIERS TO SPECIAL NEEDS[SH]

It concerns the use of SSR (Special Services Request) and OSI (Other Service Information) codes which are used to alert the airlines to the individual client's special needs. Entered in the PNR (Passenger Name Record) the SSR "sends an action message to the airline and station that will provide the service and product. "while the OSI merely alerts boarding agents or inflight personnel of some special condition. Following is a list of special services, some provided as a matter of course others requiring action on the agent's part.

Advance boarding: This is standard procedure and requires no advance notification. The passenger should, however, be advised to check in early if they desire it.

Blind passengers - There is no restriction on the number of guide dogs per flight, but they must be properly harnessed.

Canes and Cruches - FAA regulations allow these in the cabin but require them to be secured at least during take-off and landing.

Deaf passengers: Hearing dogs are also not restricted, but must be properly harnessed.

Special Meal Requirement: An SSR must specify the type of meal, e.g. diabetic. low cholesterol, low sodium, vegetarian and must be entered at least 24 hours before the flight. Escort Service: An SSR to "meet and assist" can be sent for the disabled or elderly.

Inability to sit upright: If a reclining seat is needed even during take-off and landing, special arrangements must be made. Some carriers will not allow this, while others will do so only for seats in front of the bulkhead or if the row behind can be closed off.

Mentally handicapped: Those who are self-sufficient can travel alone. An SSR to "meet and assist" will help ensure that all goes smoothly. Those who require an attendant must also have a physician's statement that they can travel without causing inconvenience or injury to themselves or others. The carrier must be notified in advance and sent the doctor's release. Early check-in is necessary to allow for pre-boarding.

Obesity: Those who require it can travel as a "passenger occupying two seats". Usually this allows them to reserve two adjacent seats for one and a half fares. and entitles them to twice the normal free baggage allowance.

Oxygen: Therapeutic inflight oxygen is provided by many carriers but requires advance notification. The traveller must have a doctor's certificate which gives the maximum oxygen usage per hour and the flow rate per minute. For reasons of safety, the patient's own equipment normally must be checked as cargo, packed and labeled as required for hazardous materials. The charge for inflight oxygen varies by carrier.

Pregnancy: In order to be checked in, expectant mothers in their ninth month must have a doctor's release no more than three days old and which gives the estimated delivery date. To avoid inconvenience, those with visibly advanced pregnancies but not yet in their ninth month may want to have a certificate as well.

Prosthetic devices and walkers: Carried at no charge, but may have to be transported as checked baggage. Consult the carrier and request special assistance if needed.

Seating restrictions: The standard policy is that handicapped persons not be seated in emergency exit rows. SATH feels that the physically handicapped should, if anything, be seated so that they can get to exits without undue hinderance. In general, the handicapped should be allowed to sit where they choose: they do not constitute a safety problem.

Wheelchairs: airline owned: Send an SSR to all stations on the passenger itinerary so that a wheelchair is available for each departure and arrival. The three types of wheelchair requests are as follows: WCHC - completely immobile, WCHR - Can ascend/descend stairs, WCHS - Cannot ascend/descend stairs, can walk in cabin.

Wheelchairs: passenger owned: Carried at no charge as checked baggage on a last on first off basis, (this ensures that it is immediately available on landings, On electric chairs, batteries are frequently disconnected in flight for safety reasons. Reconnecting them after arrival and making sure the chair is working should be the airline's responsibility. Advise the passenger to label all detachable parts of the wheelchair (surgical tape works well) with his/her name, destination address, and how long he/she will be there so that the part can be forwarded if it gets lost. However if possible he/she should remove them and keep them with him/her if possible. Also advise the passenger to get wheelchair insurance: airline insurance policies are restricted to

169

$600.00 maximum at time of writing.

OTHER HELPFUL RESOURCES AND REFERENCES

A Guide to Recreation, Leisure and Travel for the Handicapped, vol., 2: **Travel and Transportation**. This reference manual is available (for a price), from Resource Directories, Toledo, Ohio, (419)-536-5353

A Travel Guide for the Disabled: Western Europe by Mary Meister. This book is available (for a price), from Van Nostrand Reinhold Co. Inc. 135, W. 50th Street, New York, N.Y. 10020.

A World of Options for the 1990's A Guide to International Educational Exchange, Community Service and Travel for Persons With Disabilities published by Mobility International, Eugene Oregon. (503) 343-1284

Access to the World: A travel guide for the Handicapped, by Louise Weiss. Available from Facts on File, Inc. 460 Park Avenues South, New York, NY 10016 (212) 683-2244.

Access Travel: *A Guide to Accessibility of Airport Terminals* Available free of charge from Consumer Information Center, Pueblo Colorado, 81009. and from Airport Operators Councils International Inc., 1220 19th Street, N.W. Suite 200, Washington D.C. 20036, Fax: (202) 331-1362

Airline Seating Guide, Available from Carlson Publishing Company, 3535 Farguhar Ave., P.O. Box 888 Los Alamitos CA 90720.

Dialysis World-Wide, published by N.A.P.H.T. 7628 Densmore Ave., Van Nuys, CA 91406, Tel. (818) 782-7328.

Directory of Travel Agencies for the Disabled; Travel for the Disabled and *Wheelchair Vagabond* published by Twin Peaks Press, P.O. Box 129, Vancouver, WA 98666 (800) 637-2256 or (206) 694-2462. Twin Peaks also publish travel information on accommodations, as well as provide travel hints and advice directed to travelers who are disabled.

Frommer's A Guide For The Disabled Traveler by Frances Barish Published by Frommer/Pasmantler Publishers, A Division of Simon & Schuster 1230 Avenue of The Americas, New York, NY 10020

Handi-Travel A Resource Book for Disabled & Elderly Travellers by Cinnie Noble Published by the Canadian

Rehabilitation Council for the Disabled One Yonge Street, Ste. 2110, Toronto, Ontario M5E IE3

Incapacitated Passengers Handling Guide, T.A.T.A. Travel Services, Director, International Air Transport association, 1000 Sherbrooke Street, West Montreal, Quebec, Canada, H3A 2R4

International Directory of Access Guides, Travel Survey Rehabilitation International U.S.A. 20 West 40th St. New York, NY 10018

Moss Rehabilitation Hospital (Travel Information Service), 1200 W. Tabor Road. Philadelphia PA 19141 (215) 456-9602

Ten Questions and Answers About Air Travel for Wheel Chair Users. This booklet is available free from Eastern Paralyzed Veterans Association, Jackson heights, N.Y. (718) 803-3782.

The Guide to Recreation, Leisure & Travel for The Handicapped, Vol.2 Travel & Transportation by Rod W. Durgin, PH.D. Resource Directories 3103 Executive Parkway Toledo, OH 43606

The Handicapped Traveller: A Guide for Travel Counsellors by Cinnie Noble Published by the Canadian Institutes of Travel Counsellors/Instituts Canadiens des Conseillers de Voyages 2333 Dundas St. W Ste 302 Toronto, Ontario M6R 3A6

The Real Guide, Able To Travel. True Stories by and for People with Disabilities edited by Allison Walsh with Jodi Abbott and Peg L.Smith.Published by Prentice Hall Travel, New York .

The Physically Disabled Traveler's Guide is also available from Resource Directories, Toledo, Ohio, (419) 536-5353.

The *Handicapped Driver's Mobility Guide* published by the American Automobile Association. This guide is free to AAA members. or write to the Traffic Safety Department, 8111 Gatehouse Road, Falls Church VA 22047.

The Itinerary (a bimonthly magazine) For subscription write to Box 2012, Bayonne NJ 07002; (201) 858-3400

The Braille Institute Press, Braille Institute, 741 N. Vermont Ave., Los Angeles CA 90020; (213) 663-1111. The Braille Institute publishes a number of travel books in Braille.

Travel Tips for People with Arthritis, published by the Arthrities Foundation. For a free copy call the foundation. Washington, D.C. Chapter at (202) 276-7555, or (800) 242-9945.

Travel Ability by Lois Reamy, Macmillan Publishing Co, Inc 866 Third Avenue New York, NY 10022. Collier Macmillan Canada Ltd

Travel For The Disabled: A Handbook of Travel Resources & 500 Worldwide Access Guide by Helen Hecker R.N. Published by Twin Peaks Press, P.O. Box 8097, Portland, OR 97207

Additional information could be obtained from:
* The airport, rail, and other transportation authorities.

* The airline(s) you plan to use in your travels. (See Appendix L for a listing).

* The tourist offices or tourist boards of foreign governments located here in the U.S. (See Appendix P for a listing).

Once you have decide on the countries to visit, check Appendix L for addresses and phone numbers of that country's tourist office.

When making inquiries find out what services and considerations if any, are given to disabled persons. Request for brochures, addresses and telephone number if available.

SERVICES
Write or call these organizations and request for their catalogue as well on any other services they offer to disabled persons or disabled international travelers.

TOUR COMPANIES FOR THE DISABLED

Accessible Journeys, 412 S. 45th St, Philadelphia, PA 19104, Tel. (215) 747-0171.

Dialysis & Sea Cruises/Unique Reservations Inc., 611 Barry Place, Indian Rocks Beach, FL 34635, Tel. (800) 544-7604 or (813) 596-7604.

Dialysis Travel Services, 9301 East Shea Blvd., Scottsdale, AZ, Tel. (800) 832-5445.

Dialysis in Wonderland, 1130 West Center St., North Salt Lake city, UT 84054, Tel. (800) 777-5727.

Evergreen Travel Services (Wings on Wheels), 4114

198th Ave. Lynnwood WA 98036. (800) 435-2288 or (206) 776-1184.

Flying Wheels Travel, 143 West Bridge St, P.O. Box 382, Owatonna, MN 55060. (800) 535-6790) or (507) 451-5005.

Interpret Tours, 1730 Citronia Street, North Ridge CA 91325 Telephone:TTY (818) 885-6921; In California dial (800) 342-5833

Med Escort International, Inc., ABE International Airport, P.O. Box 8766, Allentown, PA 18105, Tel. (800) 255-7182 or (215) 791-3111.

The Guided Tour Inc. 613 Cheltenham Ave, St. 200 Melrose Park, PA 19126. (215) 782-1370.

Travel Care Health Services, 630-21 10405 Jasper Avenue, Edmonton, Alberta, T5J 3S2, Canada, Tel. (403) 429-2323.

U.S. Travel, 11 East 44th Street, New York, NY 10017, Tel. (800) 487 8787 or (212) 883-5687.

Whole Person Tours, P.O. Box 1084 Bayonne New Jersey 07002. (201) 858-3400

HELPING HANDS (Also See Appendix 14N)

American Foundation for the Blind, 15 West 16th St., New York (800)232-5463 or (212) 620-2159.

Directions Unlimited, 720 N. Bedford Rd., Bedford Hills, NY 10507 (800) 533-5343

Medic Alert Foundation International, P.O. Box 1009, Turlock California 95831. (800)432-5378. Medic Alert manufactures and distributes the Medic Alert Identification Tag, a useful device for those overseas travelers with special medical conditions.

Opening Door, Rte. 2, Box 1805, Woodford, VA 22580, Tel. (804) 633-6752

Mobility International P.O. Box 3551, Eugene, OR 97403 (503) 343-1284 (voice and TDD).

Society for the Advancement of Travel for the Handicapped, 347 Fifth Ave., Suite 610, New York, NY 10016 (212) 447-7284 fax (212) 725-8253. Membership required.

The American Diabetes Association 1660 Duke St. Alexandria, VA 2324 (800) 232-3472.

The Information Center for Individuals with Disabilities, Fort Point Pl., Worm wood St., Boston MA 02210 (617) 727-5540

The Access Foundation for the Disabled, Malverne, New York (516)887-5798

Travel Industry and Disabled Exchange, 5435 Donna Ave., Tarzana CA 91356. (818) 368-5648

Traveling Nurses Network, P.O. Box 129, Vancouver, Washington, (202) 694-2462

Chapter 13

Tips For Students Traveling Abroad

- - - -

Introduction

So you are a student and you are preparing to travel abroad. You are not alone. Every year tens of thousands of American students travel overseas either unaccompanied by or in the company of their parents, friends or guardians. The purpose of these travels vary. Whereas some of the students go abroad to continue their education, in which case they take up semi-permanent residence; others go in search of summer jobs or as volunteers.

Whatever the reasons or motives for your trip, you will inevitably be exposed to the same type of problems often experienced by the majority of non-student Americans who travel abroad. This means that you should engage yourself in the same type of preparation and take the same general precautions suggested throughout this book, particularly in Chapters 1, 4, 5 and 43. Like the rest of the population of Americans traveling abroad, you are concerned with security issues, health issues, time, as well as money saving opportunities. Ultimately, you want to have an exciting, safe and incident-free trip.

This book addresses precisely those issues aimed at enabling you to make a successful trip and, enabling to learn in particular, the things you need to know before you go. This theme has been echoed in several chapters throughout this book. I suggest, therefore, that you refer to the relevant chapters for those aspects of international travel that you may be interested in, that have not been addressed in this chapter.

In the course of my research and travels, I have come to appreciate the importance of a number of subjects of real interest to international student travelers. Few, if any, have matched the wishes of these students to learn about cost-saving opportunities to finance their trip. Of course, students are not alone in this category; except to say that a number of such opportunities, specifically limited to students, do exist, and student travelers should know about them and take advantage of them.

First and foremost, you should avail yourself of the services of the Council on International Education Exchange (CIEE).

Founded in 1947, CIEE is a world-renowned organization known for its active promotion and sponsorship of International Education Exchange.

Today, CIEE services the interest of students, youths and teachers, assisting them in a variety of ways with study, hospitality and travel programs. In cooperation with member institutions world-wide, CIEE administers several study programs, including language programs, voluntary service opportunities for American students in Europe, and a variety of work camps for American and non-American youths, as well as exchange programs between secondary schools in the U.S. and in several countries of the world.

The budget-conscious student traveler may want to explore CIEE's international travel programs. CIEE distinguishes itself as a clearing house for information and services relating to all aspects of student travel. They arrange low cost transportation for individuals and groups, including students flights to Europe, Asia and various destinations in Latin America. Furthermore, CIEE provides information on low-cost hotel accommodations available to students overseas.

International Identification Cards

Further, CIEE issues a number of identification cards, including the International Student Identity Cards (ISIC), the International Teachers Identification (ITIC), and the Federation of International Youth Organization Cards (FIYTO). These cards are available from CIEE and other centers listed in the section of this chapter entitled "Helping Hands". They usually have a one year expiration date, the cost is less than $20.00 each and they often require a passport photo 1 1/2 x 2 inches and some form of identification, such as a letter from your school, your grade report or transcript.

ADVANTAGES OF THE ISIC:

Although you may be able to receive just about the same services with your standard university or college I.D. card as those available to ISIC holders, the ISIC has the unique feature of being the most widely recognized proof of student status all over the world. As a holder of the ISIC, you will have access to a variety of money-saving discount opportunities and services, from airfare, bus, ferry and train rides to accommodations to museums and theaters. These money saving opportunities may not be advertised and may not be available in every country. Therefore, always initiate the request. Ask your travel or ticket agent if there are discounts available to students. If one exists, request to receive such discounts or considerations. Remember, "If You Don't Ask, You Don't Receive!" Do not forget to be polite and courteous; it could make the difference.

The other advantage of the ISIC is that, if bought in the United States, it also provides you with some amount of accident and health insurance, an important asset for every traveler going abroad.

Not the least of the ISIC advantages is its unique 'classy look'. Besides, the card serves as an important piece of identification, one that could become very useful in the event of an incident. That is the primary reason you should carry it with you at all times.

LODGING:

Finding suitable lodging overseas has not always been a problem, particularly if you have lots of money to spend. However for those on a limited budget this may not be so. Some avenues, nevertheless, exist for the budget-conscious student traveler. Some of these avenues may require some flexibility and tolerance on your part, while others may require long-term planning.

An alternative to hotels and pensions are the youth hostels. These hostels offer travelers of all ages clean, inexpensive, overnight accommodations in more than 6000 locations in over 70 countries world wide. Hostels provide dormitory-style accommodations with separate facilities for males and females. Some hostels have family rooms that can be reserved in advance. Curfews are often imposed, and membership is often required. For more information contact the American Youth Hostels, P.O. Box 37613, Washington, D.C. 20013-7613 or call (202) 783-4943. Some of the other agencies listed below in the section "Helping Hands" would be willing to assist you in finding inexpensive lodging. Should you, on the other hand, wish to use instead, a hotel or pension for lodging, present your ISIC or school I.D. card and request a discount. Who knows, they might be able to give you one.

The other alternative available to student budget travelers is to identify in the countries they plan to visit, a university or college with boarding facilities for its students, preferably, one located closest to your intended destination. Write to the "President of the Student Union/Organization/Council" of that institution requesting accommodations on campus, if possible.

Your letter should explain briefly who you are, your school affiliation, your intended travel plans to that country (not your detailed day-to-day itinerary), the length of time for which you seek accommodation, and more important, that you are writing because you are traveling on a budget and do not have enough funds to cover your lodgings. Of course, you must have some funds, sufficient to subsist on for a few days in a hotel, but you do not want to include that in your request. If you succeed, that might provide you with a token gift to leave with your host or hostess. When carefully done, success with this plan has quite a number of advantages. Besides saving you money on lodging, you may be lucky enough to get free or discounted meals. As a special guest, you may have the opportunity to visit and explore many more exciting places than you probably would see in the absence of this type of accommodation.

The camaraderie created between you and your host/hostess, and their friends and relatives may provide just another opportunity for future trips at even cheaper costs.

Alternatively, you may consider renting a room in a nearby college or university (University Hostels). Several institutions abroad do have room and board facilities that are rented out to students and non-student travelers, during vacation time. The rates charged to students are usually lower than rates charged non-students. Inquiries should be directed to the Director of Housing at the respective institutions

There are, of course, several, other less conventional and cheap lodging facilities available to the international traveler. They include, farms, camps, road-side shelters and parks

Not withstanding which plans you chose, or which countries you visit, remember you are in a foreign country and that all of the precautions emphasized elsewhere in this book should be followed to safeguard your valuables, health and safety.

It is important, as with every American traveling abroad, to register immediately your presence with the Consular Section of the American Embassy immediately upon arrival. The usefulness of such registration has been stated and emphasized in Chapters 1 and 45 of this book.

For a country-by-country listing of foreign universities and other institutions of higher learning, including their addresses, consult your college or local public library.

174

USEFUL PUBLICATIONS

You will find the following publications helpful *Work, Study, Travel Abroad: The Whole World Handbook; The Teenager's Guide to Study, Travel and Adventure Abroad; The Student Travel Catalog* and *Volunteer*. These publications are produced by CIEE. The first two publications are available from CIEE and at many bookstores. The student travel catalog which is updated annually is offered free of charge. CIEE also distributes directories and brochures on foreign travel and study programs.

- LET'S GO SERIES of travel books published by Harvard Student Agencies, Inc. Cambridge, MA. (671) 495-9695. These travel books are widely available in bookstores across the country. Also check your local libraries.

Study Abroad, Published by UNESCO (1989) and *The World of Learning,* published by Europe Publications Ltd: These and other sources should be available in your local public or school library. You may, also, contact the respective education departments of the Embassies for a complete listing and location of institutions of higher learning with boarding facilities in their country.

HELPING HANDS (National and International Student Organizations)

The following organizations have a reputation for catering to the needs of students, youths and teachers traveling abroad.

They provide a wide range of services and products including bargain fares, discount travel guides, insurance, accommodation, international rail passes, and identification cards (ISIC, ITIC & FIYTO Cards). Write and request for information on their services.

Council on International Education Exchange (CIEE) 205 E. 42nd St., New York NY. 10017 (212) 661-1414. OTHER CIEE OFFICES are located in the following cities: Boston: 729 Boylston St., Boston, MA 02116. (617) 266-1926; Los Angeles: 1093 Broxton Ave., Los Angeles, CA 90024, (213) 208-3551; Chigago: 1153 N. Dearborn St., Chicago, IL 60610 (312) 951-0585; San Francisco: 919 Irvin St., San Francisco, CA 94122, (415) 566-9222, Austin : 2000 Guadelupe St. Austin TX 78705, (512) 472-4931.:The ISIC, ITIC and the YIYTO cards are administered by CIEE and are available from any of their offices.

Education Travel Center (ETC) 438 North Frances St. Madison, Wisconsin (608) 256-5551.

International Student Exchange Flights (ISE), 5010 East Shea Blvd. Suite A 104, Scottsdale, Arizona 85254. (602) 951-1177.

Let's Go Travel Services, Harvard Student Agencies Inc. Thayer Hall, B. Harvard University, Cambridge MA. 02138 (617) 495-9649.

Council Travel (is a subsidiary of CIEE. See CIEE **STA Travel,** 17 East 45th St. New York, NY 10017 (800) 777-0112 or (212) 986-9470.

American Youth Hostels, P.O.Box 37613 Washington, D.C. 20013 (202) 783-4943.

Institute For Foreign Study (AIFS), 102 Greenwich Ave., Greenwich, CT 06830. (800) 727 AIFS or (203) 869-9090 or (203) 863-6087

Experiment in International Living, Kipling Rd., Brattleboro, VT. 05302, (800) 345-2929, or (802) 257-7751.

Institute of International Education, 809 United Nations Plaza, New York NY 10017, (800) 883-8200

* **Your Student Office:** Check with the student office of your institution. They may have valuable information, references and contacts that may save you both time and money. Some student offices do issue the ISIC card.

Chapter 14

Tips for Travelers to the Caribbean

[The information in this chapter is reprinted verbatim from a bulletin issued by the U.S. State Department, Bureau of Consular Affairs. It is intended to serve as advice to Americans traveling abroad.]

- - - -

Anguilla, Antigua, Aruba, Bahamas, Barbados, Barbuda, Bermuda, Bimini, Bonaire, British Virgin.Is., Caicos, Cayman Islands, Cuba, Curacao, Dominica, Dominican Republic, Grenada, Grenadines, Guadeloupe, Haiti, Jamaica, Martinique, Montserrat, Netherlands Antilles,St. Kitts, St. Lucia, St Vincent, Trinidad and Tobago, U.S. Virgin Is.

Originally named the West Indies by explorers seeking a sea route to India, the Caribbean is the region of tropical islands in the Caribbean Sea situated between North and South America and east of Central America. The islands extend for nearly 1,700 miles from Cuba in the west to Barbados in the east.

Note: There are special conditions relating to travel to Cuba, including U.S. Treasury restrictions. See page 182 for details.

Travel to Mexico and to Central and South America is covered in separate chapter. See table of contents for location.

If you plan to visit the most popular islands during high tourist season (from mid December to mid-April), confirm your hotel reservations two to three months in advance. There are, however, lesser-known islands where you may be able to book first class accommodations on short notice. In addition, you can usually book reservations with ease during the off - season, but be aware of hurricane season which runs from June to November.

Most of the islands in the Caribbean belong to one of 13 independent countries. In addition, several islands and groups of islands in the Caribbean are part of or dependent upon France, the Netherlands, the United Kingdom, or the United States. A directory of the major islands is on page 181.

Consular Information Sheets and Travel Warnings
Consular Information Sheets and Travel Warnings have replaced the old travel advisory system. There is a

Consular Information Sheet for every country in the world. They cover entry regulations, health conditions, the crime and security situation, political disturbances, areas of instability, and drug penalties. A Travel Warning advises travelers not to 90 to a country because of dangerous conditions and/or because the ability to assist a U.S. citizen in distress there is severely limited.

Consular Information Sheets for the Caribbean are available at the 13 regional U.S. passport agencies; from U.S. embassies and consulates abroad; or by sending a self-addressed, stamped envelope to: Overseas Citizens Services, Room 4811, Department of State, Washington, DC 20520-4818. On the envelope, write the name of the country or countries needed in the lower left corner.

In addition, there are three electronic methods to access Consular Information Sheets and Travel Warnings 24-hours a day. To listen to a recording of them, call 202-647-5225 from a touchtone phone. To receive them by fax, dial 202-647-3000 from a fax machine and follow the prompts from the machine's telephone receiver. To view or download the documents from a computer and modem, dial the Consular Affairs Bulletin Board (CABB) on 202-647-9225, setting your software to N-8-1. There is no charge to use these systems.

As you travel, keep abreast of local news coverage. If you are in an area experiencing civil unrest or a natural disaster, will be staying more than two weeks in an area, or if you are going to a place where communications are poor, you are encouraged to register with the nearest U.S. embassy or consulate. (See Appendix A.) Registration takes only a few moments, and it may be invaluable in case of an emergency. Remember to leave a detailed itinerary and the numbers of your passport or other citizenship documents with a friend or relative in the United States.

Entry and Exit Requirements
Going: Every island in the Caribbean has entry

requirements. Most countries allow you to visit for up to two or three months if you show proof of citizenship and a return or onward ticket. Some countries, such as Trinidad and Tobago, require that you have a valid passport. Haiti requires children under 18 to have a valid passport. If you are arriving from an area infected with yellow fever, many Caribbean countries require you to have a certificate of vaccination against yellow fever. Some countries have an airport departure tax of up to $25. For authoritative information on a country's entry and exit requirements and on its customs and currency regulations, contact its embassy, consulate, or tourist office in the United States. (See Appendix L.)

Returning - Caution! Make certain that you can return to the United States with the proof of citizenship that you take with you. Although some Caribbean countries may allow you to enter with only a voter's registration card or a birth certificate to indicate citizenship, U.S. Immigration requires that you document both your U.S. citizenship and identity when you re-enter the United States.

The best document to prove your U.S. citizenship is a valid U.S. passport. Other documents of U.S. citizenship include an expired U.S. passport, a certified copy of your birth certificate, a Certificate of Naturalization, a Certificate of Citizenship, or a Report of Birth Abroad of a Citizen of the United States. To prove your identity, either a valid driver's license or a government identification card that includes a photo or a physical description is acceptable.

The loss or theft of a U.S. passport overseas should be reported to the local police and the nearest U.S. embassy or consulate. A lost or stolen birth certificate or driver's license cannot be replaced outside of the United States. There are several countries, most notably Barbados, the Dominican Republic, Grenada, and Jamaica, where airlines have refused to board American citizens with insufficient proof of U.S. citizenship. The resulting delays can be inconvenient as well as expensive.

Bringing Your Own Boat or Plane
If you plan to arrive in the Caribbean in your own boat or plane, contact the embassy, consulate, or tourist office of each country you plan to visit to learn what is required for entry and exit. Besides title of ownership, most ports of entry will require proof of insurance coverage for the country you are entering. Some countries require a temporary import permit for your boat or plane.

Authorities in the Caribbean are familiar with U.S.

regulations for documentation of air and sea craft. They will detain improperly documented craft that enter their territory. In some countries, authorities will confiscate **firearms** found on a boat or plane unless the owner or master can show proof that U.S. licensing and export procedures have been followed. In addition, some countries impose stiff prison terms for the importation of illegal firearms.

Customs, Firearms, and Currency Regulations
Customs formalities are generally simple in the Caribbean. As a rule, one carton of cigarettes and one quart of liquor are permitted duty free into the islands. Most countries tax additional quantities at a high rate. In general, tourists are permitted to enter with other commodities required for personal use. If you wish to bring firearms into any country, inquire at the country's embassy or consulate about the permit required. **As noted above, some countries in the Caribbean impose a stiff prison term for importing illegal firearms.**

Currency regulations vary. Inquire about them when you check on entry requirements. In some countries, you must declare all currency and are not allowed to take out more money than you brought in. Other countries limit the amount of their own currency that can be brought in or taken out.

Check with your travel agent about extra fees and taxes that may be overlooked in the tourist literature. Examples are hotel taxes, obligatory restaurant gratuities, and airport departure taxes.

When you convert your money to local currency, retain receipts. You will need to show them if you wish to reconvert money upon departure. It is usually advantageous to reconvert local currency before departure. Although U.S. currency is used along with local currency in some places, such as the Bahamas and Haiti, there may be an advantage to using local currency.

Health
Information on health precautions for travelers can be obtained from local health departments, private doctors, or travel clinics. You may also call the Centers for Disease Control's 24-hour hotline on (404) 332-4559 for information on immunizations and health risks worldwide. Immunizations are recommended against diphtheria, hepatitis A, polio, and tetanus. Typhoid immunization is also recommended if you go to remote areas of Haiti or Jamaica. Polio is endemic in Haiti and in the Dominican Republic.

Malaria is prevalent in Haiti and in the rural, non-tourist areas of the Dominican Republic that border

Haiti. If you are going to a malaria area, take a weekly dose of chloroquine, beginning two weeks before your trip. In addition, take precautions to avoid being bitten by mosquitoes because malaria can break through any preventative drug.

Review your health insurance policy. U.S. medical insurance is often not valid outside the United States. Social Security Medicare does not provide payment for medical services obtained outside the U.S. In addition to medical insurance, consider obtaining insurance to cover evacuation in the event of an accident or serious illness. Air evacuation to the United States can easily cost $15,000 if you are not insured. There are short-term health and emergency assistance policies designed for travelers. Ask your travel agent about them or look for ads in travel publications.

If you need medical attention during your trip, your hotel may be able to recommend the nearest clinic, hospital or doctor, or you can obtain a list of local medical services from the nearest U.S. embassy or consulate. In a medical emergency, a U.S. consul can help you locate medical treatment.

The most prevalent health hazard in the Caribbean is one you can avoid - overexposure to the sun. Use sunscreen and bring a shirt to wear over your bathing suit, especially if you plan to snorkel.

Where the quality of drinking water is questionable, bottled water is recommended. Travelers to remote areas should boil or chemically treat drinking water.

Safety Tips
Crime. The Caribbean has a somewhat slower pace than at home. However, thievery, purse snatching, and pick pocketing do happen, particularly in towns and at beaches. There has also been an increase in violent crimes such as rape and assault against tourists. In some places, U.S. passports and identity documents are especially attractive to thieves. Robbery of yachts is a problem in some marinas.

Here are some precautions to keep in mind:

- Safety begins when you pack. Leave expensive jewelry, unnecessary credit cards, and anything you would hate to lose at home.

- Use a concealed money pouch or belt for passports, cash, and other valuables.

- To facilitate replacing a lost or stolen passport, carry two extra passport photos

and a photocopy of your passport information page and other identity documents with you in a separate place from those items.

- Do not take valuables to the beach. When possible, use the hotel safe when you go to the beach or to town.

- When you enter a marina, register with the local government authorities.

Water Safety. Make certain that sports equipment, including scuba equipment, that you rent or buy meets international safety standards.

If you use a pool or beach without a lifeguard, exercise extreme caution. The surf on the Atlantic side of an island can be rough; the Caribbean side is usually calmer. Drowning is one of the leading causes of death for Americans in the Caribbean.

Do not dive into unknown bodies of water because hidden rocks or shallow depths can cause serious injury or death. In some places, you may need to wear sneakers in the water for protection against sea urchins.

Drug Offenses
Most countries in the Caribbean have strict laws against the use, possession, or sale of narcotics. Foreigners arrested for possession of even small amounts of marijuana, cocaine or other illegal drugs are often charged and tried as international traffickers. The penalty for carrying narcotics into or out of the country can be 20 years imprisonment. There are usually expensive fines as well. In some places, there is no bail and there are long judicial delays where you can spend more than two years awaiting trial. Conditions in most Caribbean prisons do not meet even minimum U.S. standards.

If you carry prescription drugs, keep them in their original container, clearly labeled with the doctor's name, pharmacy, and contents.

Judicial Systems
When you travel abroad, you are subject to the laws of the country you are in. If you find yourself in serious difficulty while abroad, contact a consular officer at the nearest U.S. embassy o, consulate. U.S. consuls cannot serve as attorneys or give legal assistance, and they cannot get you out of jail. They can, however, provide lists of local attorneys and advise you of your rights under local law. If you are detained, a consul can monitor your case and make sure you are treated fairly under local law.

Driving in the Caribbean

If you plan to rent a car, be aware that most jurisdictions of the Caribbean drive on the left. The only places where you drive on the right are Aruba, Cuba, Dominican Republic, Guadaloupe, Haiti, Martinique, and the Netherlands Antillies. In the other places, if you are not used to driving on the left, proceed slowly and with utmost caution. You may wish to ride as a passenger for a while before trying to drive yourself.

Driving Conditions and local driving patterns are different from the U.S. Many roads are narrow or winding, signs may not be in English, and in some places, domestic animals roam freely. Defensive driving is a must.

Shopping: Avoid Wildlife Products

Beware of purchasing a live animal or plant or an item made from one. Many such items are prohibited from international traffic. You risk confiscation and a possible fine by U.S. Customs if you attempt to import certain wildlife or wildlife products. In particular, watch out for and avoid:

- All products made from sea turtles, including turtle leather boots, tortoise-shell jewelry, and sea turtle oil cosmetics.

- Fur from spotted cats.

- Feathers and feather products from wild birds.

- Birds, stuffed or alive, such as parrots or parakeets.

- Crocodile and caiman leather.

- Black coral and most other coral, whether in chunks or in jewelry.

Residence or Investments in the Caribbean

You will need a passport and visas to reside in or go into business in the Caribbean. Although some Caribbean countries welcome retirees or others of independent means as long-term residents, requests for work permits are rarely granted. Before you travel, apply to a country's embassy or consulate in the United States to obtain a visa if you wish to reside, go into business, or work in the country.

U.S. -citizens who wish to invest in the Caribbean, such as in real estate or a business, should first thoroughly investigate the company making the offer and, in addition, learn about the investment climate in the country. A good resource is the Trade Information Center of the U.S. Department of Commerce, telephone 1-800 USA-TRADE. The Center can tell you how to access the National Trade Data Bank. Among the things you can learn, are how to find out if the company is registered with local authorities and how to get in touch with local trade associations.

Directory of Islands	Political Status (see code below)	U.S. Embassy with Consular Jurisdiction (See Appendix A for addresses)
Anguilla	UK	St.John's, Antigua
Antigua and Barbuda	I	St.John's, Antigua
Aruba	N	Curacao, Netherlands Antilles*
Bahamas	I	Nassau, Bahamas
Barbados	I	Bridgetown, Barbados
Barbuda	part of Antigua and Barbuda	
Bermuda(in Atlantic)	UK	Hamilton, Bermuda*
Bimini	part of Bahamas	
Bonaire	part of Netherlands Antilles	
British Virgin Islands	UK	St.John's, Antigua
Caicos	part of Turks and Caicos	
Cayman Islands	UK	Kingston, Jamaica
Cuba	I	U.S. Interests Section, Swiss Embassy, Havana Cuba
Curacao	part of Netherlands Antilles	
Dominica	I	Bridgetown, Barbados
Dominican Republic	I	Santo Domingo, Dominican Republic
Eleuthera;Exuma	part of Bahamas	
Grenada	I	St. Georges's, Grenada
Grenadines	part of St.Vincent/Grenadines	
Guadeloupe	F	Fort-de-France, Martinique*
Haiti	I	Port-au-Prince, Haiti
Jamaica	I	Kingston, Jamaica
Marie-Galante	part of Guadeloupe	
Martinique	F	Fort-de-France, Martinique*
Montserrat	UK	St.John's, Antigua
Netherlands Antilles	N	Curacao, Netherlands Antilles*
Nevis	part of St.Kitts and Nevis	
Puerto Rico	US	(not applicable, U.S. commonwealth)
Saba	part of Netherlands Antilles	
St. Barthelemy (St. Barts)	part of Guadeloupe	
St. Croix	part of U.S. Virgin Is.	
St. Eustatius (Statia)	part of Netherlands Antilles	
St. John	part of U.S. Virgin Is.	
St.Kitts(St. Christopher) and Nevis	I	St.John's, Antigua
St.Lucia	I	Bridgetown, Barbados
St. Marteen	part of Netherlands Antilles	
St. Martin	part of Guadeloupe	
St. Thomas	part of U.S. Virgin Is.	
St.Vincent and the Grenadines	I	Bridgetown, Barbados
San Salvador	part of Bahamas	
Tortola	part of British Virgin Is.	
Trinidad and Tobago	I	Port of Spain, Trinidad
Turks and Caicos	UK	Nassau, Bahamas
U.S. Virgin Islands	US	(not applicable, U.S territory)
Virgin Gorda	part of British Virgin Is.	

Code: F=Overseas department of France; I =independent country; N=commonwealth of the Netherlands; U.K =dependency of the United Kingdom; US =commonwealth or territory of the United States; * =U.S. Consulate General

181

Additional Country Information

Criminal penalties for possession of or trafficking in drugs in the Bahamas are severe. The Bahamian court system has a heavy volume of pending cases, and U.S. citizens arrested for drugs or other offenses are often held in prison for months while awaiting trial.

In the Bahamas, be sure to budget for a hotel room tax, an energy surtax, a 15% obligatory gratuity in restaurants, and a departure tax of up to $15.

CAYMAN ISLANDS

Persons wearing their hair in dreadlocks have occasionally been refused entry to the Cayman Islands. Cayman authorities say they may "refuse entry to any person whose mode of dress or behavior, or unkempt appearance, may cause offense to the Caymanian community." The authorities emphasize that "this policy does not automatically exclude from entry persons wearing their hair in any particular manner. However, if such persons are also unkempt and slovenly in their attire and behavior, it is possible they could then be refused entry."

CUBA

Financial Restrictions. The Cuban Assets Control Regulations of the U.S. Department of the Treasury require that transactions incident to the travel to and within Cuba of U.S. citizens or residents be licensed. A general license needs no application. Transactions under a general license are authorized only for the following categories of travelers:

- U.S. and foreign government officials, including representatives of international organizations of which the U.S. is a member, traveling on official business;

- persons gathering news or making news or documentary films;

- persons visiting close relatives who reside in Cuba;

- and full-time professionals engaging in fulltime research in their professional areas, where the research is specifically related to Cuba, is largely academic in nature, and there is substantial likelihood the product of research will be disseminated.

U.S. persons whose transactions are not authorized by general or specific license may not buy goods (a meal at a hotel or restaurant, for example) or services (an airline ticket or hotel room) related to Cuban travel.

WARNING

Transactions relating to travel to Cuba for tourism or business purposes are not authorized by a general license, nor would they be authorized in response to an application for a specific license. This restriction includes transactions related to tourist and business travel from or through a third country such as Canada or Mexico.

Under U.S. Treasury regulations, **authorized** travelers may spend no more than $100 per day for living expenses in Cuba, and, except for informational materials which are not limited, may bring back to the U.S. no more than $100 total worth of Cuban goods. **Failure to comply with U.S. Treasury regulations could result in prosecution upon return to the United States.**

Dual Nationals. For all practical purposes, the government of Cuba considers Cuban-born U.S. citizens to be solely Cuban citizens. The Cuban government does not recognize the right or obligation of the U.S. government to protect dual U.S.-Cuban citizens. Cuban authorities have consistently denied U.S. consular officers the right to visit incarcerated dual nationals and to ascertain their welfare and proper treatment under Cuban law. Dual U.S.-Cuban nationals may be subject to a range of restrictions and obligations, including military service.

Other Information for Authorized Visitors. Street crime, including purse snatching, is a growing problem in Havana. Authorized visitors should exercise caution and keep a close eye on personal belongings while in tourist areas. Credit cards issued by U.S. financial institutions are not valid in Cuba. Hotels will not accept American Express and other U.S. travelers checks regardless of where they are issued.

U.S. Interests Section. U.S. travelers in Cuba should register in person, in writing, or by telephone during business hours at the U.S. Interests Section which is part of the Embassy of Switzerland. See address on Appendix A. Further information is available in the Consular Information Sheet for Cuba, see page 177.

DOMINICAN REPUBLIC

Drug laws are severe and strictly enforced in the Dominican Republic. Penalties for possession of less than 20 grams of marijuana or 20 milligrams of cocaine range from six months to two years imprisonment, plus fines. For quantities of narcotic substances that meet the definition of trafficker, the penalty is a five to 20-year prison term, plus fines.

No more than $5000 may be taken from the Dominican Republic upon departure. The peso is the only legal currency in the Dominican Republic, and it should be purchased only at authorized hotels and banks. In crackdowns on black market activity, U.S. tourists have sometimes been arrested for even minor illegal currency transactions.

The Dominican Republic is among the places where U.S. passports and other identity documents are frequently stolen.

There may be restrictions on minor children being allowed to leave the Dominican Republic without their parent(s). A child without a U.S. passport may be particularly vulnerable to being denied permission to travel alone or with only one parent. If this applies to you, check with the Embassy of the Dominican Republic about their requirements for the travel of unaccompanied children.

Visitors to Haiti should exercise caution. Although, at time of publication, there does not appear to be a specific threat to American citizens, the potential exists for civil disturbances and isolated serious criminal acts. Avoid crowds and areas of unrest.

Although U.S. dollars can be used as currency in Haiti, it is usually to the traveler's advantage to use Haitian dollars. Haiti's $25 airport departure tax must be paid in cash in U.S. currency. It cannot be paid as part of the airline ticket.

JAMAICA
Crime is a serious problem in and around Kingston, Jamaica's capital. Visitors should exercise prudence, not walk around at night, and should use licensed taxis or hotel recommended transportation. In the north coast tourist areas, care should be taken at isolated villas and small establishments.

TRINIDAD AND TOBAGO
Drug laws are severe and strictly enforced in Trinidad and Tobago. Possession of even small amounts of narcotics can result in lengthy jail sentences and expensive fines. The penalty for carrying narcotics into or out of the country is five to 15 years with no possibility of parole.

U.S. Consular Agents
To supplement the consular services available to American citizens at U.S. embassies and consulates, resident consular agents have been designated in two locations in the Caribbean. You may contact the consulate agent directly or through the U.S. embassy in the country where he or she is located.

American Consular Agent
51 Beller Street
Puerto Plata, Dominican Republic
Tel: (809) 586-4204

American Consular Agent
St. James Place, Second Floor
Glocester Avenue
Montego Bay, Jamaica
Tel: (809) 952-0160

Note: As we go to press, it is expected that a consular agent will be designated in the Cayman Islands in the near future. To learn the address, contact the U.S. Embassy in Kingston, Jamaica.

Chapter 15

Tips for Travelers to Central and South America

[The information in this chapter is reprinted verbatim from a bulletin issued by the
U.S. State Department, Bureau of Consular Affairs. It is intended to serve as advice
to Americans traveling abroad.]

- - - -

Argentina, Belize, Bolivia, Brazil, Chile, Colombia, Costa Rica, Ecuador, El Salvador, French Guiana, Guatemala, Guyana, Honduras, Nicaragua, Panama, Paraguay, Peru, Suriname, Uruguay, and Venezuela.

Travelers to Central and South America are usually welcomed with courtesy and warmth. There is great diversity in the region-you can visit some of the largest cities in the world as well as some of the most unspoiled primitive environments. You can have a wonderful trip; however, there are some precautions to take.

Please note that travel to Mexico and the Caribbean is covered in separate publications. [Check the Table of Contents for location.]

Travel Advisories
The Department of State issues travel advisories concerning serious health or security conditions that may affect U.S. citizens. Current advisories are available at the 13 regional passport agencies in the United States and from the Citizens Emergency Center, Room 4811, Department of State, Washington, DC 20520, (202) 647-5225. Advisories are also available at U.S. embassies and consulates abroad.

At the time of publication, travel advisories are in effect for Columbia, El Salvador, Guatemala, Honduras, Nicaragua, Panama, Peru, and Suriname. Some of the dangers covered in these advisories are guerrilla or terrorist activity, banditry, and areas under control of narcotics producers. If you plan to travel to one of these countries, check with the Citizens Emergency Center or the nearest passport agency to see if a travel advisory is still in effect.

As you travel, keep abreast of local news coverage. If you plan more than a short stay in one place, expect to travel to an area where communications are poor, or if you are in an area experiencing civil unrest or natural disaster, you are encouraged to register with the nearest U.S. embassy or consulate. Registration takes only a few moments, and it may be invaluable in case of an emergency. Remember also to leave a detailed itinerary and the number of your passport with a friend or relative in the United States.

Getting In and Out
U.S. citizens must have a valid U.S. passport to travel to all countries in Central or South America, except for Costa Rica. (Costa Rica requires proof of U.S. citizenship, such as a birth certificate, and proof of identity.) Visa requirements for U.S. citizens vary from country to country: some countries do not require a visa for a tourist stay of 90 days or less; for some you need to obtain a tourist card from the airline office or the destination airport; for other countries you must obtain a visa in advance from the country's embassy or consulate. Some countries have additional entry requirements such as proof of sufficient funds or proof of onward or return tickets.

In addition, all South American countries and most Central American countries require a departure tax. If you are departing to a neighboring country, the tax may be small, but, if you are returning to the U.S., the tax could be as high as $50 per person. **Be sure to have enough money at the end of your trip to be able to get on the plane.**

For authoritative information on a country's entry and exit requirements, contact its embassy or consulate (Check the Appendix for a listing of foreign embassies in the U.S.). When you make your inquiries, ask about:

■   Where to obtain a tourist card or visa.

■   Visa price, length of validity, and number of entries.

■   Financial requirements-proof of sufficient funds, proof of onward or return ticket.

■   Special requirements for children traveling alone or with only one parent (see below).

■   Yellow fever immunization or other health

185

requirements.

■ Currency regulations-how much local or dollar currency can be brought in or out.

■ Export/import restrictions.

■ Departure tax.

Restrictions on Minors

Many countries impose restrictions on minor children who travel alone, with only one parent, or with someone who is not their parent. A child must present written authorization for travel from the absent parent, parents, or legal guardian. If the parent or guardian traveling with the child is the sole custodian, the court order granting custody may, in some cases, serve as the authorization document. If any of this applies to you, inquire about the following at the embassy or consulate of the country your child plans to visit:

■ The age of majority at which the restriction no longer applies (e.g., age 15 in Argentina, age 18 in Brazil).

■ The type of document that can overcome the restriction (e.g., court order, statement of absent parent or parents).

■ Whether notarizing the document is sufficient or if it must also be authenticated by the country's embassy or consulate.

■ Whether the document must be translated.

Note: In Brazil, a child may travel with its father without authorization from the mother, but, if traveling alone or with its mother, must have notarized authorization from its father. A woman may authorize a child's travel in Brazil only when she is the sole legal parent or guardian.

Bringing Your Own Car, Plane, or Boat

If you plan to drive to Central or South America or arrive in a private plane or boat, contact the embassy or consulate of each country you plan to visit to learn what is required for entry and exit. You may not be able to enter certain countries unless you have had your vehicle documented at the embassy or consulate of the country before you left your country of residence.

Besides title of ownership, at most borders, you will need to show insurance coverage effective for the country you are entering. If your U.S. auto insurance does not cover you abroad, you can usually purchase insurance when you enter a country. In some countries,

if you are involved in an accident that causes injury, you will automatically be taken into police custody until it can be determined who is liable and whether you have the insurance or financial ability to pay any judgment. Criminal liability may also be assigned if the injuries or damages are serious.

If you are a visitor, you will not ordinarily have to pay import duty on your car or other vehicle. You may, however, have to post a bond or otherwise satisfy customs officials that you will not sell or dispose of the vehicle in the country.

Health

Information on health precautions for travelers can be obtained from local health departments, the U.S. Public Health Service, private doctors, or travel clinics. General guidance can also be found in the U.S. Public Health Service book, *Health Information for International Travel*[1], available for $6.00 from the U.S. Government Printing Office, Washington, DC 20402.

Review your health insurance policy. If it does not cover you abroad, consider purchasing insurance that does. Also consider obtaining insurance to cover the very high cost of medical evacuation in event of accident or serious illness.

Depending on your destination, immunization may be recommended against diphtheria, tetanus, hepatitis, polio, rabies, typhoid, and yellow fever.

Malaria is found in rural areas of every country in the region, except Chile and Uruguay. Malaria prophylaxis and mosquito avoidance measures are recommended. When possible, avoid contact with mosquitoes from dusk to dawn by wearing long clothing and using insect repellent on exposed skin. Use a flying insect spray and a bed net in living quarters. Prophylaxis should begin 2 weeks before going to an area where malaria is endemic and should continue for at least 4 weeks after leaving. Chloroquine is the malaria prophylaxis most easily tolerated by the body. However, malaria resistant to chloroquine has been reported in an area beginning east of the Panama Canal and extending through northern South America as far south as the Amazon Basin. If you plan to visit this area, consult a medical expert to work out an additional prophylaxis, At times, however, malaria may break through any drug or drug combination.

If you develop chills, fever, and headaches while taking a malaria prophylaxis, seek medical attention promptly. Early treatment of malaria can be effective, but delaying therapy could have serious consequences.

Mosquito avoidance measures, if used day and night, may also help prevent other less prevalent insect-borne diseases found in parts of Central and South America such as Chagas' disease, dengue fever, leishmaniasis, and yellow fever.

Throughout most of Central and South America, fruits and vegetables should be washed with care and meats and fish thoroughly cooked. Problems of food contamination are less prevalent in Argentina, Chile, and Uruguay, and tap water is potable in those countries. Elsewhere water is generally not potable and should be boiled or chemically treated. Diarrhea caused by contaminated food is potentially serious. If it persists, seek medical attention. Certain beaches in the region, including some at or near Lima, Montevideo, Rio de Janeiro, and Valparaiso are dangerously polluted. Avoid swimming at beaches that might be contaminated with human sewage or dog feces. Avoid swimming in fresh water in areas where schistosomiasis is found: Brazil, Suriname, and north-central Venezuela.

Visitors in the Andes may experience symptoms of altitude sickness such as insomnia, headache, and nausea. If you become sick, wait until your symptoms disappear before you attempt to go higher. Mountaineers should learn about the symptoms of high altitude pulmonary edema, a condition that is fatal unless remedied by immediate descent.

Another hazard of high altitudes is sunburn. Exposure to ultraviolet radiation increases not only as you approach the equator, but also as you ascend in altitude. Sunscreens may help prevent this.

Safety Tips-Crime

Like many large cities throughout the world, major cities in Central and South America experience assaults, robberies, and thefts. Visitors should take common sense precautions:

- **Safety begins when you pack.** Leave expensive jewelry behind. Dress conservatively; a flashy wardrobe or one that is too casual can mark you as a tourist. Use travelers checks, not cash. Leave photocopies of your passport personal information page and of your airline tickets with someone at home and carry an extra set of copies with you.

- **Use a money belt** or a concealed money pouch for passports, cash, and other valuables.

- **In a car,** keep doors locked, windows rolled up, and valuables out of sight. A common trick is for a thief to reach through a car window and grab a watch from a person's wrist or a purse or package from the seat while you are driving slowly or stopped in traffic.

- **When you leave your car,** try to find a guarded parking lot, lock the car, and keep valuables out of sight.

- **When walking,** avoid dark alleys, crowds, and marginal areas of cities. Do not stop if you are approached on the street by strangers, including street vendors and beggars. Be aware that women and small children, as well as men, can be pickpockets or purse snatchers. Keep your billfold in an inner front pocket, carry your purse tucked securely under your arm, and wear the shoulder strap of your camera or bag across your chest. To guard against thieves on motorcycles, walk away from the curb, carrying your purse away from the street.

- **Whenever possible, do not travel alone.** If you travel in isolated areas, go with a group or a reputable guide.

- **Avoid travel at night.**

- **Do not take valuables to the beach.**

Any U.S. citizen who is criminally assaulted should report the incident to the local police and to the nearest U.S. embassy or consulate (Check the Appendix Section for a listing).

Safety Tips-Civil Unrest

Several countries in Central and South America have areas of instability or war zones that are off-limits to visitors without special permits. Others have similar areas that are open but surrounded by security check points where travelers must show their passport or tourist card. Always carry your papers with you, and do not overstay the validity of your visa or tourist card.

Avoid public demonstrations. American citizens have been arrested when local authorities have thought they were participating in civil demonstrations. If you are detained or arrested for this or any reason, ask to speak with a U.S. consular officer.

Drug Offenses

Most Central and South American countries strictly

187

enforce laws against the use, possession, and sale of narcotics. Foreigners arrested for possession of even small amounts of narcotics are generally charged and tried as international traffickers. There is no bail, judicial delays are lengthy, and you can spend 2 to 4 years in prison awaiting trial and sentencing. If you carry prescription drugs, keep them in their original container, clearly labeled with the doctor's name, pharmacy, and contents. You may wish to check with the embassy of the country you plan to visit for specific customs requirements for prescription drugs.

Photography
Be cautious when taking pictures. Local authorities in Central and South American countries consider all airports, police stations, military locations, oil installations, harbors, mines, and bridges to be security-related. Photography of demonstrations or civil disturbances is also usually prohibited. Tourists have had their film confiscated and have been detained for trying to take these types of pictures. When in doubt about whether you can take a picture, ask first.

U.S. Wildlife Regulations
Endangered species and products made from them may not be brought into the United States. The penalty is confiscation and a possible fine. These items are prohibited from import: virtually all birds originating in Brazil, Ecuador, Paraguay, and Venezuela; furs from spotted cats; most lizard-skin products from Brazil and Paraguay; many snake-skin products from Brazil, Ecuador, and Paraguay; skins from the Orinoco crocodile; and all sea turtle products.

Shopping for Antiques
Most countries in Central and South America control the export of objects from their pre-Columbian and colonial heritage. Some countries claim ownership of all such material and consider the export of antiques, without the permission of the government, to be an act of theft. In addition, under U.S. law, importers of all pre-Columbian monumental and architectural sculpture, murals, and certain archaeological and ethnological materials are required to provide proof to the U.S. Customs Service that these artifacts are legally exported from the country of origin. Beware of purchasing artifacts unless they are accompanied by an export permit issued by the government of origin.

Dual Nationality
Some countries in Central and South America do not recognize acquisition of U.S. citizenship unless the naturalized U.S. citizen renounces his or her original nationality at an embassy or consulate of the country of origin. A person born in the United States of a parent or parents who were citizens of another country may also be considered by that country to be their national. If arrested, a dual national may be denied the right to communicate with the U.S. embassy or consulate. Dual nationals may also be forced to serve in the military of their former country, or they may not be allowed to depart the country when their visit is over.

If you are a naturalized U.S. citizen, a dual national, or have any reason to believe another country may consider you its national, check with the embassy of that country as to your citizenship status and any obligations you may have while visiting there. When you research your citizenship status, bear in mind that the purpose of your planned trip can affect your status. Your acquired U.S. citizenship may be recognized by your former country if you only visit there. If, however, you take up residence, the country may consider you as having resumed your former nationality. This can happen even if the embassy of the country has stamped a visa in your U.S. passport.

Dual nationals should also be aware that they may be required to use a passport from their country of origin in order to enter or leave that country. The U.S. Government does not object to the use of a foreign passport in such situations. U.S. citizens may not, however, use a foreign passport to enter or leave the United States. If you have any questions about dual nationality, contact the Office of Citizens Consular Services, Room 4817, Department of State, Washington, DC 20520, (202) 647-3712.

Adopting a Child Abroad
Because of scandals over the illegal activities of some adoption agencies and attorneys both in the United States and abroad, U.S. citizens have recently experienced difficulties when attempting to adopt children from Central or South America. Several countries in the region have either outlawed adoptions by foreigners or passed a law requiring formal court adoption of the child in the country before the child is permitted to emigrate to the United States. Although this has resulted in adoptions less likely to be challenged from a legal standpoint, it has made the process more difficult and time consuming.

U.S. citizens interested in adopting a child from a country in Central or South America are encouraged to contact the U.S. embassy or consulate in the country involved, or, in the United States, the Department of State's Office of Citizen Consular Services, Inter-American Division, (202) 647-3712, to obtain information on the adoption process in that country.

Additional Information for Certain Countries

Belize

Belize enforces a strict policy of refusing admittance to persons who an immigration officer suspects of drug use.

Brazil

Obtain your visa in advance. Brazilian immigration authorities do not hesitate to require a traveler without a visa to leave on the next available flight.

Street crime can be a major problem in large cities in Brazil. Guard against it- see "Safety Tips" on page 179. In Sao Paulo, if you encounter difficulties or need emergency assistance, dial 190, radio police patrol, from any public telephone. No coin or token is needed for the call.

Chile

Anyone considering scientific, technical, or mountaineering expeditions to regions in Chile classified as frontier areas or to Antarctica must apply for authorization to a Chilean embassy or consulate a minimum of 90 days prior to the beginning of the expedition. The application will be forwarded to the Chilean government for decision. Chilean authorities reserve the right to request Chilean participation in foreign expeditions and require the submission of a post-expedition report on the activities undertaken and the results obtained.

Costa Rica

Although U.S. citizens do not need a passport to enter Costa Rica, it is a good idea that you have one, particularly if you plan to stay more than 30 days. Some Americans have experienced difficulties in cashing travelers checks without a passport. Costa Rica strictly enforces immigration rules. If you need to extend your visa, do so promptly with local authorities.

Ecuador

Travelers to the Galapagos Islands should be aware that there are few medical facilities on the islands and cruise ships may also offer only limited medical care. Moving about the islands in the equatorial heat requires physical exertion and may be debilitating to someone in poor health. Before traveling, you may wish to consult the U.S. Consulate General in Guayaquil for more information.

To travel to the Galapagos by private yacht, you must have a license from the Ecuadorian Ministry of Defense. You may apply through an Ecuadorian embassy or consulate, but do so well in advance because approval can take from 1 to 3 months.

El Salvador

Pre-Hispanic artifacts from the Cara Sucia archaeological region are prohibited entry into the United States unless accompanied by proof that they were exported with the permission of the government of El Salvador.

Nicaragua

Upon entry, tourists may need to show $200 as proof of sufficient funds for their stay. They must exchange $60 upon arrival at the airport.

Panama

As of April 1989, a U.S. citizen must have a passport and a visa to enter Panama. Tourist cards may no longer be used by U.S. citizens. Travelers should bring cash and a major credit card because travelers checks may be difficult or impossible to cash.

Suriname

Visitors must buy 500 Suriname guilders (approximately $283) at the port of entry.

Foreign Embassies in the United States

[For a complete listing of foreign embassies in the United States including their address, telephone, fax and telex numbers see **Appendix B**].

U.S. Embassies and Consulates Abroad

[For a complete listing of U.S. embassies and consulates abroad see **Appendix A**].

Planning Another Trip?

See Chapter 46 for a listing of resources available to the general traveler from the U.S. Departments of State, Customs, Transportation, Health and various government and non-government organizations. All of the available International travel-related pamphlets, brochures and publications issued by the U.S. Department of State and by U.S. Customs have been reproduced in full in this book. See Table of Contents for location.

~ ~ ENDNOTES ~ ~

1.   A large portion of this booklet has been reproduced verbatim elsewhere in this book, including a country by country listing of vaccination requirements.

Chapter 16

Tips for Travelers to the People's Republic of China

[The information in this chapter is reprinted verbatim from a bulletin issued by the
U.S. State Department, Bureau of Consular Affairs. It is intended to serve as advice
to Americans traveling abroad.]

- - - -

U.S. citizens planning to visit the People's Republic of China (P.R.C.) should be aware of the following information in order to avoid inconvenience or serious difficulty while traveling.

Visa Requirements

To enter the People's Republic of China, a U.S. citizen must have a visa. China receives tens of thousands of visa requests annually from U.S citizens but cannot accommodate all of them because the number of hotels, interpreter-guides, and other facilities, although increasing, is still limited.

Business visas are issued on the basis of an invitation from one of the Chinese foreign trade organizations. If you wish to visit for business purposes, you must first correspond directly with the appropriate organization in China (e.g., China National Machinery Import-Export Corporation, etc.).

Visas for tour group members are usually obtained by the travel agent as part of the tour package. China International Travel Service (CITS) has exclusive responsibility for all foreign tourism in China. You may book a CITS tour through a number of travel agencies and airlines in the United States and abroad. You can find advertisements for these tours in newspapers or magazines, or you may contact the China National Tourist Office at: 60 E. 42nd Street, Suite 3126; New York, NY 10165; (212) 867-0271.

Tourist visas for individuals were formerly difficult to obtain, but official policy toward individual travel has relaxed, facilities have increased, and a well-planned private trip is now feasible. Over 500 major Chinese urban and tourist centers are now open to unrestricted travel. Unless you speak Chinese, however, you should plan to visit only the most popular tourist areas. To qualify for a visa to visit China on an individual or special interest group basis, you must have an invitation from an individual or institution in China, or a "letter of confirmation" from CITS in China. Write to: China International Travel Service, 6 East Changang Avenue, Beijing, People's Republic of China (telex: 22350 CITSHCN). In your request, include your name, date

of birth, nationality, passport number, the dates and destinations of your trip, and your reason for the trip. Remember, however, that CITS may not be able to accommodate all requests for individual or special interest tours. You may have better luck in obtaining confirmation if you avoid the high seasons: April to June and September to October.

Once you have your invitation or letter, apply for a visa at the Chinese Embassy in Washington, D.C., or at a Chinese consulate in Chicago, Houston, Los Angeles, New York, or San Francisco. (Addresses are listed at the end of this pamphlet.) The current cost of a visa for China is $10. To apply, each person must send an application form, a valid passport, two photographs, and the fee. U.S. citizens applying for visas outside the United States may be requested to fill out visa application forms both in English and in Chinese.

If you wish to travel independently and do not want to make the arrangements yourself, some of the travel agents that arrange group tours will also arrange an FIT (Foreign Independent Travel) tour for you and, for an additional fee, will get your visa.

Whether you visit on your own or with a tour, allow at least 3 weeks for visa processing. The Chinese Embassy and consulates in the United States require at least 10 working days to process visas.

In addition to the requirements above, long-term visitors to China must have an AIDS test. The test is required for students, teachers, and visiting scholars who plan to stay more than 9 months and for business persons who plan to stay over a year. If this applies to you, you may have the test done in the United States. However, the results of the test must indicate the test was given by a government facility such as your state's health department; or, if done at a private health facility, the results must be notarized by a notary public.

For individuals visiting Hong Kong en route, tours to China depart regularly from that city and may be

191

booked through China Travel Service, LTD., 77 Queens Road, Central, Hong Kong (tel. 5-259-121) or 27-33 Nathan Road, Kowloon, Hong Kong (tel. 3-721-1331). (Cable address: TRAVEL BANK.) For a handling fee, individual visas for travel originating in Hong Kong may be obtained through these agencies in 2 working days. If you have made travel arrangements and wish to obtain your visa on your own, apply to the visa office of the Ministry of Foreign Affairs of the People's Republic of China, 5th Floor, Low Block, 26 Harbour Road, Wanchai, Hong Kong.

Note: All travelers transiting China, regardless of whether or not they are required to pass through customs and immigration, must have a transit visa or they will be fined $1,000.

Travel Arrangements Within China

Packaged tours can be at least double the cost of self-arranged tours. A packaged tour will, however, insulate you from some of the difficulties of booking travel by air or rail in China. Because transportation systems have not expanded as fast as the number of tourists has increased, travelers should be prepared for delays as long as several days. Planes and trains are often overbooked or are canceled because of mechanical problems.

The Civil Aviation Administration of China (CAAC) is responsible for all civilian aviation in China and operates both international and domestic flights. Air travel within China on international flights may only be booked as part of an international ticket. Once you are in China, you cannot book domestic air travel on the within-country segments of a CAAC or any other international flight; you may only book travel on domestic CAAC flights.

Round trip reservations and tickets are not available on CAAC flights. Onward arrangements must be made at each stop. Thus, passengers may arrive with reservations from Tokyo to Beijing, to Shanghai, to Hong Kong, and find that the flights after Beijing are nonexistent, or exist, but are fully booked.

Local CAAC agents issue tickets only for travel originating in their own cities. To confirm a reservation on a CAAC ticket purchased outside of China, present your ticket and passport to the local CAAC office at least 3 working days (Monday-Friday) before departure. Hotels, for a fee, will sometimes assist in making reservations and purchasing tickets on CAAC flights if you make the request in advance. Plane reservations to the most popular tourist cities must often be made a month in advance.

Train travel is similarly difficult to reserve and trains are often overbooked. Round trip rail tickets are not sold. Beware of counterfeit train tickets. Unethical entrepreneurs have been caught manufacturing and selling such tickets at railway stations.

Restricted Areas

Visitors to China should be aware that Chinese regulations strictly prohibit travel in certain areas without special permission. However, over 500 cities and areas in China are open to visitors without special travel permits, including most major scenic and historical sites. If you need to know if an area is open to travel without a permit, seek advice from the nearest Chinese embassy or consulate, or, if you are already in China, from the U.S. Embassy in Beijing or the nearest American consulate. (See addresses in **Appendix A**.)

Travel to Tibet

Americans visiting Tibet, whether individually or in tour groups, should be aware that all areas of the region are closed to foreign travel except for Lhasa, Shigatze (Xigaze), Naqu, Zedong, Zhang Muxkhasa, and the main roads between these points. Special permission to visit any of the closed areas must be obtained from the region's public security bureau. At time of publication, there is a ban on individual travel anywhere within Tibet. Occasionally, visitors have been refused admission or had difficulty entering Tibet from Nepal. In addition, the Kathmandu/Lhasa highway that connects Nepal and Tibet can be washed out in the monsoon season, from June through September. Avoid this road during the monsoon.

Virtually all of the Tibetan autonomous region, much of Qinghai and Xinjiang, and parts of Sichuan, Yannan, and Gansu are above 13,000 feet (4,000 meters) in altitude. Some main roads in Tibet, Qinghai, and Xinjiang go above 17,000 feet (5,200 meters), where available oxygen is only half of that at sea level. Conditions in Tibet are primitive, and travel there can be particularly arduous. Medical facilities are practically nonexistent. Many otherwise healthy visitors to the high altitude areas may suffer severe headaches, nausea, dizziness, shortness of breath, or a dry cough. These symptoms usually disappear after a few days of acclimatization. However, if symptoms persist, sufferers should descend to a lower altitude, or seek medical assistance. Visitors with respiratory or cardiac problems should avoid such high attitudes. Consult a physician before making the trip.

Travel on the Trans-Siberian Express

If you wish to take the Trans-Siberian railway from Beijing to Berlin, you must obtain visas from Mongolia and Poland before the Soviet Union will issue a transit visa. Plan ahead, because the Mongolian Consulate in Beijing is only open a few hours per week and those hours may vary.

Customs

Foreign visitors to the P.R.C. are allowed to import 4 bottles of wine and 600 cigarettes with their personal belongings. Any items of value, such as watches, radios, calculators, and still, movie, or video cameras must be declared. They may be imported duty free for personal use but may not be transferred or sold to others. Gifts and articles carried on behalf of others must be declared to the customs inspector and are subject to duty.

Chinese customs regulations prohibit the import or export of the following items:

(a)   arms, ammunition, and explosives;
(b)   radio transmitter-receivers and principal parts;
(c)   Chinese currency *(renminbi)*;
(d)   *books, films, records, tapes, etc., which are "detrimental to China's politics, economy, culture, and ethics";*
(e)   *poisonous drugs and narcotics;*
(f)   *infected animal or plant products; and*
(g)   *infected foodstuffs.*

Note: Videotapes will be seized by customs to determine that they do not violate prohibitions noted in item (d), above. Tapes are sometimes held for several months before being returned.

Export of the following items is also prohibited:

(a)   valuable cultural relics and rare books relating to the Chinese revolution, history, culture, and art;

(b)   rare animals, rare plants and their seeds; and

(c)   precious metals and diamonds and articles made from them.

Antiques which are approved for export are marked with a red wax seal.

According to the U.S. Food and Drug Administration, improper glazing of some dinnerware for sale in China can cause lead contamination in food. Therefore, unless you have proof of its safety, dinnerware purchased in China should be used for decorative purposes only. Chinese commercial shipments of dinnerware to the United States are tested to conform to U.S. safety standards.

If you seek to enter China with religious materials, such as Bibles, in a quantity greater than what is considered needed for personal use, you could be detained and fined.

Currency Regulations

Chinese currency is called *yuan* or, more commonly, *renminbi* (RMB). The official rate of exchange of RMB to the U.S. dollar was 5.55 as of November 1992. The import of Chinese currency is prohibited, except in the form of RMB traveler's checks, which are available from the Bank of China in Hong Kong. Although there is no limit on the amount of foreign currency which may be brought into China, all foreign currency must be declared to customs upon entry.

The only legal place where foreign currency (cash or traveler's cheeks) may be exchanged for Chinese currency is an exchange facility of the Bank of China. Foreign currency is exchanged for Foreign Exchange Certificates in RMB denominations. The certificates are used just as ordinary RMB is used and are required for all transactions made by foreigners. Keep your exchange receipts to show as evidence if you need to convert Chinese currency back to foreign currency when you depart China. Buying regular RMB on the black market is illegal, dangerous, and, moreover, impractical-there is almost no place that will accept regular RMB from a foreigner, and it cannot be converted to foreign currency when you leave.

Money exchange facilities are also available at the airports, hotels, and "friendship stores." Major brands of traveler's checks and credit cards are selectively accepted by various facilities in China, and a nominal service charge is usually added to the latter. Consult with your bank before departing the United States to be sure that your brand of check or credit card will be accepted.

Health

Information on health precautions for travelers can be obtained in the United States from local health departments, the U.S. Public Health Service, private doctors, and travel clinics. For China, immunizations are recommended for diphtheria, tetanus, and polio. A gamma globulin shot may offer protection against hepatitis A. In addition, immunization for Japanese B encephalitis (JE) is recommended during the epidemic summer months for visitors planning to stay longer than 2 or 3 weeks. At present, no vaccine for JE is available in the United States, but it can be obtained in Japan or Hong Kong. Malaria occurs in China, particularly in rural areas and in southern China. Depending on the

193

season and your destination, you may need to take antimalarial drugs, use insect repellant, and take other measures to reduce contact with mosquitoes.

Few cities in China have Western-style pharmacies stocked with drugs common in the United States. Therefore, carry medications in your hand luggage to avoid emergencies should your checked luggage go astray.

Foreign visitors who become ill in China are provided with the best medical care available in the country. Generally speaking, the doctors and nurses are qualified and competent, but hospital accommodations are Spartan, and medical technology is not up-to-date.

Hospital costs for non-Chinese visitors are similar to those charged for similar services in the United States. Prospective travelers should review their health insurance policies. If your policy does not provide coverage overseas, consider buying coverage that does. In addition, insurance covering medical evacuation is highly recommended. Although several private companies offer evacuation service in the P.R.C., the cost can be extremely high. For example, the estimated cost of evacuation, using a stretcher and with a medical escort, from Beijing to San Francisco is between $16,000 and $22,000.

Tourist travel in China can be extremely strenuous and may be especially debilitating to someone in poor health. Tours often involve walking long distances and up steep hills. All visitors, especially those with a history of coronary/pulmonary problems, should have a complete medical checkup before making final travel plans. Plans should include rest time and avoiding overly full schedules that could lead to exhaustion or illness. China discourages travel by persons who are ill, pregnant, or of advanced age. Visa applicants over 60 usually are required to complete a health questionnaire. If medical problems exist, a letter from your physician in the United States explaining treatment and, if relevant, copies of your most recent electrocardiograms would be helpful in case a medical emergency occurs in China.

Air pollution in the large cities is often severe, particularly in winter when soft coal is burned in the northern cities. It is common for tourists to become afflicted with respiratory ailments. Visitors are advised not to drink the tapwater in China. Hotels almost always supply boiled water that is safe to drink. Bottled water and carbonated drinks are sold in stores. Carry water purification tablets to use when neither boiled water nor bottled water are available.

Dual Nationality

The status of American citizens who might also be considered Chinese citizens under Chinese law was addressed in the agreement on consular relations between the United States and the People's Republic of China, signed in Washington, D.C., on January 31, 1979. The agreement states that U.S. citizens entering the P.R.C. on a U.S. passport containing a Chinese visa will be considered by Chinese authorities to be U.S. nationals for the purpose of consular protection, and that such persons shall have the right of departure from the P.R.C. without further documentation, regardless of whether they might also be regarded as Chinese citizens.

A U.S. citizen must enter and leave the United States on a U.S. passport. If you are a dual national and wish to use a Chinese passport to enter and travel in China, you may do so, but be aware that you will be considered and treated as a Chinese national by Chinese authorities.

While You Are in China

All American citizens visiting China for a month or more, or who expect to receive communications from the United States, are encouraged to register with the American Embassy in Beijing or the nearest American consulate. Registration will assist our posts in China in locating you in the event of an emergency at home or in replacing a lost or stolen passport. You should also photocopy the data page of your passport and keep it in a separate place from your passport. In the event your passport is lost, stolen, or in the possession of foreign government officials, you will have the requisite information available.

American citizens should be aware that foreign visitors and residents in China have sometimes been detained and heavily fined for having improper sexual relations with Chinese citizens. In most of these cases, the foreigners involved had invited Chinese citizens to their hotel rooms. Any U.S. citizen who is detained by Chinese authorities for questioning regarding this or any other violation of Chinese law or regulations should notify the American Embassy or nearest consulate as soon as possible.

Chinese Embassy and Consulates in the United States

[For a complete listing of foreign embassies in the United States see **Appendix B**].

U.S. Embassy and Consulates Abroad

[For a complete listing of United States embassies and consulates abroad, including their addresses, telephone, fax, and telex numbers see **Appendix A**].

Planning Another Trip?

See Chapter 46 for a listing of resources available to the general traveler from the U.S. Departments of State, Customs, Transportation, Health and various government and non-government organizations. All of the available International travel-related pamphlets, brochures and publications issued by the U.S. Department of State and by U.S. Customs have been reproduced in full in this book. See Table of Contents for location.

195

Chapter 17

Tips for Travelers to Eastern Europe

*[The information in this chapter is excepted from a bulletin issued by the
U.S. State Department, Bureau of Consular Affairs. It is intended to serve as advice
to Americans traveling abroad.]*

- - - -

Albania, Bulgaria, Croatia, Czech Republic, Hungary, Poland, Serbia and Montenegro, Slovak Republic, Slovenia, Romania. Eastern Europe also includes the western part of the former Soviet Union. For travel information on the former Soviet Union, see Tips for Travelers to RUSSIA[1].

Conditions in Eastern European countries are unlike those in Western European countries. Americans traveling to any of the countries of the former Eastern Block need to take the utmost precaution, particularly, during this period. Most of the countries, although moderately developed, are undergoing profound economic and political changes. Tourist facilities are not highly developed and many of the goods and services taken for granted in Western European countries are not yet available.

With the easing of entry and exit requirements, the opportunity to travel to Eastern Europe has gained popularity with U.S. citizens. In visiting the countries in Eastern Europe, you will see many of the changes that have taken place since the crumbling of the Berlin Wall.

This is a truly exciting time in history to visit Eastern Europe. Nevertheless, there are a few cautionary measures you can take to ensure a pleasant and rewarding stay. The Department of State's Bureau of Consular Affairs has prepared this pamphlet to acquaint you with the services we provide to Americans traveling or residing in Eastern Europe.

Any additional guidance not covered here may be obtained from the Bureau of Consular Affairs in the Department of State or from the nearest U.S. embassy or consulate in Eastern Europe at one of the addresses listed in **Appendix A.**

The countries of Eastern Europe are rich in history with civilizations and traditions dating back to the beginning of recorded European history. These countries are in a period of transition, and their rules for visitors are changing. Before you go, contact the embassy of each country you plan to visit for the latest information on visa requirements, customs and currency regulations.

Although tourist facilities are expanding to meet the rapid increase in tourism to Eastern Europe, in most of the region they are quite limited. In many places, you will have to be patient with scarce or inadequate hotels, rental cars, and other facilities. To be certain of accommodations, make reservations for hotels and transportation, and make them well in advance. If you cannot get a hotel reservation, check with the country's tourist office, because many cities have a bureau that arranges accommodations in small hotels or private homes.

The Department of State issues travel advisories concerning serious health or security conditions that may affect U.S. citizens. Travel advisories are available in the 13 regional passport agencies, or by calling or writing the Citizens Emergency Center,

Entry Requirements
U.S. citizens should travel to Eastern Europe with a valid U.S. passport and with appropriate visas when necessary. Visa regulations change, so check with each embassy's consular section for current information.

Remember to leave a detailed itinerary and your passport information with a friend or relative in the United States in case of an emergency. If you are a national of both the United States and an Eastern European country, see the section on dual nationality in this chapter (and in Chapter 25) before you travel to Eastern Europe.

Customs
Customs regulations in some Eastern European countries are strict. U.S. citizens should comply fully. Generally, you should carry only those articles that you need for your trip and personal use.

When obtaining your visa, declare to the country's embassy in the United States anything manufactured before 1945 (considered antique in some countries) and

197

any precious metals, including gold jewelry, that you plan to bring with you. Ask for customs information when you apply for your visa.

If you are asked to declare valuables and currency when you enter a country, include pocket calculators, digital watches, or other electronic devices that may be rare or more expensive in Eastern European than at home. Failure to declare items could result in their confiscation upon departure. Carry a copy of your declaration with you. You may need it when you depart the country.

Do not carry parcels or letters on behalf of third persons. It is highly dangerous to carry something if you do not know its contents.

Currency
Some Eastern European governments restrict the import and export of their currencies. In general, do not transport these currencies across international borders. Currency regulations in Eastern Europe change frequently. Some countries have a dual exchange rate. For example, hotel bills and credit card purchases may have to be paid at a rate that is higher than a "tourist" rate. Before you go, learn the most advantageous way to handle your purchases by inquiring about exchange rates and currency regulations from your travel agent or the embassies of the countries you plan to visit.

Unlimited amounts of U.S. dollars and other freely convertible or "hard" currencies usually may be carried into and out of Eastern European countries. Travelers may be asked to declare the amount and kind of currency they carry. Purchase currencies only at officially authorized exchange facilities in the country of issue and retain your receipts. Do not engage in private currency transactions or sell personal property. While U.S. dollars may be exchanged for Eastern European currencies, it is difficult or impossible to reconvert those currencies to dollars or another hard currency. Therefore, do not exchange more money than you plan to spend.

Western travelers are frequently required to settle hotel, auto rental, train, airplane, medical, and other bills in hard currency. Keep sufficient hard currency for this purpose.

Credit Cards
Most major credit cards may be used in place of hard currency to cover purchases at major hotels or stores in Eastern Europe. However, in general, credit cards, travelers checks, and personal checks cannot be used to obtain hard currency in the region.

A few major credit card companies offer services, such as cash advances in local currency and card replacement, to travelers in a few places in Eastern Europe, most notably in Czech Republic and Hungary. In addition, some travelers check companies offer replacement for lost or stolen travelers checks in some places in the region. Check with your credit card company and with the company that sells you travelers checks to learn what services they now offer in the cities you plan to visit.

Driving
Except in major cities and on super highways, avoid driving at night in Eastern Europe. Night driving can be hazardous because some roads are narrow and winding, and horse-drawn vehicles and bicycles may be encountered at any time on any road.

Traffic regulations, especially those related to driving under the influence of alcohol, are very strict. An international driver's license is usually accepted and, in some cases required by Eastern European governments. You may obtain an international driver's license from an automobile association.

Political Statements or Acts
In countries where there is political unrest, refrain from political comments and activities that might be construed as interference in the internal affairs of the host country. Avoid photographing or otherwise becoming involved in demonstrations.

There are restrictions on photography in Eastern Europe. In general, refrain from photographing military and police installations and personnel as well as scenes of civil disorder or other public disturbances. In some countries, also avoid photographing border areas and industrial structures, including harbors, bridges, rail and airport facilities. For detailed information, consult local authorities or the U.S. embassy or consulate in the country concerned.

Crime
One result of the changes taking place in Eastern Europe is an increase in street crime in almost every major city in the region. Car break-ins have become a problem. Some cities have groups of pickpockets that use various gimmicks to distract their victims. Be especially careful on public transportation, in crowded shopping areas, and in all places frequented by tourists. Watch your purse, passport, wallet, travel documents, and other valuables.

Loss of a passport in some locations can mean a wait of a day or more while local authorities process a new exit permit, without which it is impossible to leave the country. It is therefore strongly recommended that you make every effort to safeguard your U.S. passport from loss or theft. Carry a copy of your passport data page with you in a location separate from your passport.

Registration

Foreigners are required by the authorities in some Eastern European countries to register with the local police. This is usually taken care of by your hotel. You may have to turn your passport over to the hotel for a period of up to 24 hours. If you stay with relatives or a private family, ask your hosts or consult the U.S. embassy or consulate about how to meet the registration requirement.

If you plan more than a short stay in one place, or if you are in an area experiencing civil unrest or some natural disaster, you are strongly encouraged to register with the nearest U.S. embassy or consulate. Addresses and telephone numbers are listed in Appendix A.

Dual Nationality

U.S. citizens who were born in Eastern Europe, or who were once citizens of an Eastern European country, or are the children of such persons may be dual nationals. The concept of dual nationality has recently come to be accepted by most governments in Eastern Europe. U.S. citizens who have dual nationality with Bulgaria, Czech Republic, Hungary, Poland, or Romania have not experienced difficulties in the recent past when traveling to those countries. However, if you are a U.S. citizen with Eastern European dual nationality, you may wish to seek clarification of your citizenship status from the embassy of your other country before you travel there.

A dual national with a background of political activity in an Eastern European country should seek the Department of State's advice if contemplating travel to any of these countries.

As a general rule, if a U.S. citizen receives a visa from an Eastern European country in his or her U.S. passport, it may be inferred that the government concerned does not have an objection to the visit. There have been a few cases, however, in which dual nationals have received visas and then encountered difficulties, including being detained after arrival in their country of origin. These cases normally have involved the following:

(a)   persons who were charged with illegal acts prior to departure from their country of origin;

(b)   persons who were charged with acts against the country after departure (usually in

connection with emigre political activity);

(c)   persons who, during their visits, committed acts forbidden to citizens of the country concerned and who were prosecuted as local citizens regardless of their U.S. citizenship; and

(d)   persons who were conscripted into the military service of their country of origin.

The United States has consular conventions in effect with Bulgaria, Czech Republic, Hungary, Poland and Romania. These conventions guarantee the right of consular officials to be notified promptly of the detention of any U.S. citizen and to visit the individual within a few days of detention. The citizen must ask to see a U.S. consul.

If you are unable to clarify your status as a dual national from the embassy of your other country, or if you have unanswered questions about dual nationality, you may call or write the Office of Citizens Consular Services, Room 4811, Department of State, Washington, D.C. 20520-4818, (202) 647-3444.

Generally, travelers to Eastern Europe should take about the same level of precaution and make about the same level of preparation as they would ordinarily do when traveling to major U.S. cities. A little more preparation and precaution would not hurt, however, since your present or upcoming trip involves traveling out of the United States to a country with its own set of laws, rules and regulations that are different from those of the U.S., and where U.S. government protection may be of little assistance. See chapters 1, 4, 5, 6 and 45 for useful tips and other information on guarding your valuables and protecting personal security while traveling abroad.

A recommended habit for Americans traveling abroad is to register their presence in the country with the consular section of the U.S. Embassy in that country. This should be your very first task upon arrival in a foreign country. Very often, this important step is forgotten or not taken seriously until the traveler is faced with a crisis. One immediate advantage is that you will be able to access current in-country information ranging from crime and terrorism activities to health conditions, currency regulations and areas of instability. Besides, it offers you the most objective and reliable source for last minute information and answers to any questions you may have once you are already in the country.

Americans traveling to Eastern Europe   must be

familiar with a variety of important issues relevant to their country of destination, particularly the official, host government position on such issues as, dual citizenship and crime. Travelers must also be up to date with prevailing, health conditions, political situation and potential areas of risk and instability.

These issues are addressed below for each country.

ALBANIA
Country Description: Albania has undergone profound political change and continues to see significant economic change. The government has restored stability and public order. Facilities for tourism are not highly developed, and many of the goods and services taken for granted in other European countries are not yet available.

Medical Facilities: Medical facilities are limited and medicine is in short supply. Doctors and hospitals often expect immediate cash payment for health services.

Crime Information: Albania has a low rate of Crime. However, crime against tourists (robbery, mugging, and pickpocketing) do occur, especially on city streets after dark.

Currency Regulations: Credit cards, personal checks, and travelers checks are rarely accepted in Albania. In addition, hotel accommodations are very limited, and even confirmed reservations are sometimes not honored.

Other Information: On March 19, 1992, the Albanian government suspended the adoption process until further notice. The Albanian government has passed new legislation governing the international adoption process. However, this legislation is not expected to be implemented until January 1995.

BOSNIA-HERZEGOVINA
Warning: The Department of State warns U.S. citizens not to travel to the Republic of Bosnia-Herzegovina because of increased hostilities. All U.S. citizens presently In Bosnia-Herzegovina are urged to leave. The recent hostage-taking by Bosnian Serb militia suggests that foreigners, Including U.S. citizens, are at risk of being taken hostage. At the same time, the ability of the American Embassy in Sarajevo to assist citizens, even in emergencies, is severely limited by the increased military activity.

Country Description: The Republic of Bosnia and Herzegovina, formerly one of the Yugoslav republics, is currently in a state of war. The resulting deaths,

destruction, food shortages and travel disruptions affecting roads, airports and railways, make travel to all parts of Bosnia and Herzegovina extremely hazardous. The popular religious shrine at Medjugorje is located within Bosnia and Herzegovina's borders.

Areas of Instability: Over 70% of Bosnia is under the control of Bosnian Serb military forces. These rebel forces have taken hostages, both military and civilian. The Bosnian government and federation-controlled regions, while currently stable, are subject to possible deterioration of civilian security.

Medical Facilities: Health facilities are, minimal or non-existent. Most medicines are unobtainable. Further information on health matters can be obtained from the Centers for Disease Control's international traveler's hotline at (404) 332-4559.

Crime Information: General lawlessness and deteriorating economic conditions have brought an increase in crime. Adequate police response in the event of an emergency is doubtful. Anti-American sentiments run high in many parts of the country, particularly in Serb-dominated areas.

Currency Information: It is impossible to use credit cards or to cash traveler's checks. German deutsche marks are the currency of favor at present.

Other Information: Roadblocks manned by local militias are numerous. These militia groups frequently confiscate relief goods and trucks, and may otherwise behave unprofessionally. U.S. citizens are reminded that they are subject to the laws of the country in which they are traveling.

BULGARIA
Country Description: Bulgaria is a moderately developed European nation undergoing profound political and economic changes. Tourist facilities are widely available, but conditions vary considerably and some facilities are not up to Western standards. Goods and services taken for granted in other European countries are still not available in many areas of Bulgaria.

Medical Facilities: Although Bulgarian physicians are trained to a very high standard, hospitals and clinics are generally not equipped and maintained at U.S. or West European levels. Basic medical supplies are widely available, but specialized treatments may not be. Visitors must pay cash for medical and health services.

Crime Information: There has been a recent rise in street crime, much of which is directed against foreigners. Pickpocketing and purse snatching are frequent occurrences as is theft from automobiles, where thieves smash windows to remove valuables left in sight. There have been a number of incidents in which tourists have accepted offers of "help from friendly people" met by chance at the airport, bus stations or train stations and have been drugged or assaulted and robbed. Taxi drivers at Sofia Airport are notoriously dishonest and refuse to run their meters. Travelers who insist upon a pre-agreed fare can avoid the more outrageous overcharging. Automobile theft is also a frequent problem, with four-wheel drive vehicles and late model European sedans the most popular targets. Very few vehicles are recovered.

CROATIA

Warning: The United States Department of State warns U.S. citizens to avoid travel to Croatia until further notice. U.S. citizens residing in Croatia are encouraged to depart. Because of missile attacks on Zagreb in early May, U.S. Embassy non-essential personnel and dependents were ordered to depart from Zagreb. A threat of continued attacks remains. The Zagreb airport should be avoided as it has been the target of direct attacks.

Despite unsettled conditions in the remainder of Croatia, the city of Rijeka and the Istrian Peninsula in western Croatia remain beyond the range of Serb shells and are largely unaffected by the fighting. This area is accessible by road from Slovenia or ferry from Italy.

Country Description: Croatia is an independent nation, formerly a constituent republic of Yugoslavia. Facilities for tourism are fully developed although not always accessible in the unstable areas of the country.

Areas of instability: Rebel Serb forces control about one-quarter of Croatia. These Serb-controlled regions and adjacent areas, known as United Nations Sectors, may experience shelling. gunfire, or other military activity. Travel to these regions or any travel which may entail crossing through Serb lines or checkpoints is dangerous. Assistance to U.S. citizens in these areas is severely limited by the difficulty of gaining access to them.

Serb forces launched rocket attacks on Zagreb in September 1993 and May 1995; however, Zagreb and other areas controlled by the Croatian government are usually calm. Similar attacks could occur in connection with further outbreaks of fighting. Zagreb airport has been a specific target and should be avoided during periods of tension.

The city of Rijeka and the Istrian Peninsula in western Croatia are beyond the range of Serb shells. This area is accessible by road from Slovenia or by ferry from Italy, visitors who stay abreast of developments and familiarize themselves with local protective shelters, police stations, and hospitals reduce the risk to their safety.

Medical Facilities: Health facilities in Croatia, although generally of Western caliber, are under severe-strain. Some medicines are in short supply.

Currency Information: Credit cards and traveler's checks are more widely used than previously but still are not accepted everywhere In Croatia.

Terrorist Activities: There have been isolated terrorist bombing incidents in Zagreb in recent years, but these seldom resulted in personal injuries. Though no major incidents were reported in the last year, some crude, small-scale bombs have been used against property in incidents that police suspect are linked to crime or ethnic tensions.

Other Information: If stopped at a check point, travelers are expected to be courteous and follow instructions. Many parts of the UN protected areas are under the control of undisciplined militia groups with which the U.S. Embassy has little contact or influence.

CZECH REPUBLIC

Country Description: The Czech Republic is a moderated developed European nation. It is undergoing profound economic and political changes. Tourist facilities are not as developed as those found in Western Europe, and some of the goods and services taken for granted in other European countries are not yet available.

Medical Facilities: Medical facilities are available. Some facilities, particularly in remote areas, may be limited. Doctors and hospitals often expect cash payment for health services.

Crime Information: The Czech Republic has a low rate of violent crime. However, there has been an increase in street crime such as pickpocketing, especially at night near major tourist sites.

HUNGARY

Country Description: Hungary is a moderately developed European nation which has had a smooth transition to democratic rule but is still undergoing significant economic change. Tourist facilities outside Budapest are not as developed as those found in Western Europe, and many of the goods and services taken for granted in other western countries's are not yet available outside the capital.

Medical facilities: Adequate to excellent medical treatment is available in Hungary, although hospital facilities and staffing are not always comparable to those In the U.S. or Western Europe. Doctors and hospitals often expect Immediate cash payments for health services.

Crime Information: Hungary has a low rate of violent crime. However. street crime, which occasionally involves violence, has increased especially at night near major hotels and

FORMER YUGOSLAV REPUBLIC OF MACEDONIA

Country Description: The Former Yugoslav Republic of Macedonia (FYROM) is a developing nation. Facilities for tourism are not fully developed. The use of the name "The Former Yugoslav Republic of Macedonia" is provisional and subject to review.

Entry Requirements: U.S. citizens need a passport and can obtain entry permission at border points of entry. The FYROM does not have an embassy or consulate in the United States, but has a representative office at 1015 15th Street NW, Suite 402, Washington, DC 20005, telephone (202) 682-0519, where further information can be obtained.

Medical Facilities: Health facilities in the Former Yugoslav Republic of Macedonia are limited.

Medicines are in short supply. Doctors and hospitals usually expect immediate cash payment for health-services.

Crime Information: Theft and other petty crimes are on the rise in the FYROM, but are still low by U.S. standards. Emergency police assistance can be obtained by dialing 92. Response time varies, but is generally considered to be effective.

Other information: Westerners who travel to the Former Yugoslav Republic of Macedonia can expect shortages of fuel, and in some cases, long waits for processing at the border. To date, the war in Bosnia-Herzegovina and tensions in parts of Serbia-Montenegro have not otherwise significantly affected the FYROM.

Registration: U.S. citizens who register at the U.S. Embassy in Belgrade, Serbia-Montenegro or the U.S. Embassy in Sofia, Bulgaria can obtain updated information on travel and security in the Former Yugoslav Republic of Macedonia.

Embassy Location: The Former Yugoslav Republic of Macedonia has been recognized as an independent country by the United States along with several other Western nations. However, although officially recognized by the United States, no full diplomatic relations between the FYROM and the United States have been established. In December 1993, the United States opened a liaison office in Skopje, which provides only emergency services to American citizens.

The U.S. Liaison Office is located at 27 Mart Street. No 5, Skopje, Macedonia. The telephone number is (389-91) 116-180, and the fax is (389-91) 117-103.

U.S. citizens seeking non-emergency assistance can contact the U.S. Embassy in Sofia. Bulgaria or the U.S. Embassy in Belgrade, Serbia-Montenegro. The U.S. Embassy in Sofia, Bulgaria is located at 1 Saborna, telephone (359-2) 88-48-01 through 88-48-05. The Consular Section of the U.S. Embassy Is located at 1 Kapitan Andreev Street, the telephone numbers are the same. The U.S. Embassy in Belgrade is located at Kneza Milosa 50; telephone (381-11) 645-655. It provides limited assistance to U.S. citizens because of conflict in the general area and reduced U.S. Embassy Staffing.

POLAND

Country Description: Poland is a moderately developed European nation working to build a new political system and a market economy. Tourist facilities are not highly developed in all areas, and many of the goods and services taken for granted in other European countries can be difficult to find.

Medical Facilities: Adequate medical care is available in Poland, but generally does not meet western standards. Doctors and hospitals often expect immediate cash payment for health services.

Crime Information: Crimes a serious problem throughout Poland and is on the rise, particularly in large cities such as Warsaw. Krakow, Poznan, Wroclaw and Gdansk. Organized groups of thieves and pickpockets appear to be operating in the train stations, and on trains, trams, and buses in major cities. A number of thefts have occurred on the overnight trains, including thefts from passengers in closed compartments. In Warsaw, car thefts and break-ins, street crime, and residential burglaries are increasingly prevalent. There have also been incidents of harassment and threats of violence directed against African-Americans by so-called "skinheads" in several Polish cities.

Currency Information: Polish law prohibits the import or export of Polish currency (zlotys). Upon entry into Poland visitors must declare in writing all money and valuable items they are bringing in. The declaration form should be stamped by Polish customs and retained by the traveler for presentation on departure. Undeclared cash may be confiscated upon departure if the customs declaration is unavailable. Throughout Poland, particularly outside Warsaw, it is difficult to cash traveler's checks or obtain cash advances on credit cards.

SERBIA AND MONTENEGRO

Warning: The U.S. Department of State warns U.S. citizens not to travel to Serbia and Montenegro because of the potential for rapid changes in the security situation there, and the threat of potential repercussions from the ongoing conflict in Bosnia and Herzegovina.

Country Description: The former Yugoslav republics of Serbia and Montenegro are currently under stringent United Nations economic sanctions; however, international commercial air traffic has been reestablished after a two year hiatus. Belgrade airport is open for civilian passengers but cargo is still prohibited. There may be long delays at the border when entering the country by car or bus. Internal air travel is possible, but schedules are unreliable. Trains continue to operate, but are often overbooked, unreliable. and unsafe. There have been incidents of assaults and robberies on the trains. Travelers should be aware that essential supplies, including basic food items and medicines, often are unavailable, and that traveler's checks and credit cards are not valid. Rapid changes in the value of local currency occur as hyperinflation continues and travelers may experience power outages and heating irregularities. Although automobile travel is generally possible, there is a shortage of spare parts and gasoline. and it is wise to make certain that sufficient fuel is available before undertaking such travel. Travel after dark on many roads is hazardous because of the presence of slow, poorly marked vehicles, horse-drawn carts, and worn or nonexistent median lines and shoulder markings. In addition, traffic signs may be poorly marked and new signs are likely to be written in the cyrillic alphabet in some areas of Serbia. The road between Zagreb and Belgrade is closed and it is impossible to enter Croatia from Serbia.

There are checkpoints throughout the country which are manned generally by policemen (militia), but occasionally by undisciplined, untrained reserve militia groups. Travelers are expected to provide identification and cooperate fully at these checkpoints. Travelers are prohibited from photographing police, buildings under police or military guard, border' crossings, demonstrations, riots, and military personnel, convoys, maneuvers and bases. There are marked areas where all photography is prohibited.

Areas of Instability: U.S. Embassy personnel, may not enter the following areas without prior U.S. government permission: the border areas with Croatia and Bosnia-Herzegovina, the Sandzak region, and Kosovo.

The Border with Croatia: Sporadic violence, which can become intense, continues in areas of Croatia along this boundary.

The Border with Bosnia-Herzegovina: The ongoing war in Bosnia-Herzegovina makes this area very dangerous. The danger is especially acute in the Drina River valley of both Bosnia-Herzegovina and Serbia.

Sandzak Region: Heightened ethnic tensions and sporadic acts of violence (particularly near the border with Bosnia-Herzegovina), as well as the presence in some areas of paramilitary forces, makes travel to this region of Serbia and Montenegro potentially dangerous. Travel in the border regions may be especially perilous.

Kosovo: Ethnic tensions are especially acute in this southern Serbian province (called Kosovo Metohija by Serbian authorities). Demonstrations, sometimes violent, can occur without warning. In recent months, there have been several armed attacks on Serbian police, resulting in death and injury. Security forces are at a high state of alert and police check points are widespread. Travelers are routinely subject to police search and interrogation.

Danube River: Them have been recent Incidents of both cargo and passenger ships on the Danube transiting Serbia being delayed for several days by purported private organizations protesting U.N. sanctions. Persons traveling on the Danube through Serbia should be prepared for delays and alterations to their plans.

The Remainder of Serbia and Montenegro: While this area is generally calm, in some areas, for example, Vojvodina, tensions are high as a result of bombings, other acts of intimidation and threats by armed paramilitary groups. The potential for violent incidents exists and will probably increase as a result of the political situation and worsening economic conditions. For example, a bomb was detonated in front of the U.S. Embassy in Belgrade in 1993, causing some damage.

Medical Facilities: Medical facilities are limited. Many medicines and basic medical supplies as well as X-ray film often are unavailable. Hospitals usually require payment in hard-currency for all services. U.S. medical Insurance is not always valid outside the United States. The travelers have found that supplemental medical insurance with specific overseas coverage has proven to be useful, they may be forced to pay first and then seek reimbursement. Further information on health matters can be obtained from the Centers for Disease Control's international travelers' hotline. telephone (404) 332-4559.

Crime Information: There is a continuing trend toward lawlessness and disorder. Murder has increased dramatically with many incidents in broad daylight and some at popular public places. Crime has increased markedly in the cities. particularly near railroad and bus stations and on trains. The possession of firearms has proliferated greatly and it is estimated that 20 percent of the citizens are now armed. Police protection is almost non-existent.

Commercial Regulations: United Nations economic sanctions on Serbia and Montenegro, enforced by the United States, prohibit imports. exports and all other commercial transactions. Humanitarian transactions require waivers from the U.N. Security Council's Yugoslavia Sanctions Committee. Further information regarding waivers can be obtained from the U.S. Department of Treasury. Travel is permitted for personal, non-commercial reasons only. Credit cards, travelers' checks and personal checks are not accepted locally and their use is prohibited. The only medium of exchange is hard currency, for example, U.S. dollars or German marks. It is illegal to exchange currency at other than official banks and institutions. For further information, travelers can contact the Office of Foreign Assets Control at the U.S. Treasury Department in Washington, D.C.

Drug Penalties: U.S. citizens are subject to the laws of the country in which they are traveling. Penalties for possession, use or trafficking in illegal drugs are strict, and convicted offenders can expect jail sentences and fines.

Other Information: In compliance with a U.N. resolution mandating the reduction of Embassy staffs' the Department of State has reduced the size of its mission in Belgrade. Assistance to U.S. citizens may therefore be limited.

SLOVAK REPUBLIC
Country Description: The Slovak Republic is a moderately developed European nation undergoing profound economic and political changes. Tourist facilities are not as developed as those found in Western Europe and many of the goods and services taken for granted in other European countries are not yet available.

Medical Facilities: Medical facilities are available, however only a limited number of doctors are English speakers. Doctors and hospitals expect cash payment for health services unless the patient can present an insurance number from the Slovak National Insurance Company.

Information on Crime: The Slovak Republic has a low rate of violent crime. However' there has been an increase in street crime such as pickpocketing, especially at night near major tourist sites. The loss or theft abroad of a U.S. passport should be reported immediately to the local police and the nearest U.S. embassy or consulate.

SLOVENIA
Country Description: Slovenia, independent from Yugoslavia since 1991, is a moderately developed European nation which enjoys the highest per capita GNP of the former Communist countries. Essentially unaffected by the war in Bosnia-Herzegovina, tourist facilities are available but may be limited, especially in the more rural parts of the country.

Medical Facilities: Adequate medical care is readily available. Doctors and hospitals often expect immediate payment in cash for health services.

Crime Information: Crime in Slovenia is rare, but has increased since the onset of civil unrest in neighboring countries. As in any country, travelers, especially those who appear affluent. can become targets of pickpockets and purse snatchers, especially at railroad stations and airports.

ROMANIA
Country Description: Romania has undergone profound political and economic changes since the 1989 revolution and is in a period of economic transition. Most tourist facilities. while being upgraded, have not yet reached Western European standards.

Medical Facilities: Medical care in Romania is limited.

Crime Information: Crimes against tourists (robbery, mugging. Pickpocketing, and confidence scams perpetrated by black-market money changers) are a growing problem in Romania. Presently thefts are most likely to occur on trains and at railroad stations.

Currency Information: Credit cards and travelers checks are of limited utility in Romania.

Adoptions: Recent changes in the U.S. Immigration and Naturalization Service's definition of an orphan are having a widespread effect on international adoptions. Before traveling to Romania, prospective parents may wish to obtain information about both American visa requirements and Romanian adoption law from the U.S. Embassy in Bucharest. Romanian adoption law mandates criminal penalties for offering money or goods to obtain the release of children for adoption. An information packet on Romanian adoptions is available by writing the Office of Overseas Citizens Services, Room 4817. Department of State, Washington. D.C. 20520. or by telephoning (202) 647-3444.

Other Information: Customs regulations prohibit the export of some items from Romania. At the time of departure, tourists may need all receipts for presentation to customs authorities. Persons who participate in or photograph demonstrations risk arrest.

U.S. Embassies and Consulates Abroad

See **Appendix A for** a complete listing of United States embassies and consulates abroad, including their addresses, telephone, fax, and telex numbers.

Foreign Embassies in the United states

See **Appendix B for** a complete listing of foreign embassies in the United States.

Planning Another Trip?

See Chapter 46 for a listing of resources available to the general traveler from the U.S. Departments of State, Customs, Transportation, Health and various government and non-government organizations. All of the available International travel-related pamphlets, brochures and publications issued by the U.S. Department of State and by U.S. Customs have been reproduced in full in this book. See Table of Contents for location.

~ ~ ENDNOTES ~ ~

1.   This publication is reprinted elsewhere in this book. See Table of Contents for location.

Chapter 18

Tips for Travelers to Mexico

[The information in this chapter is reprinted verbatim from a bulletin issued by the U.S. State Department, Bureau of Consular Affairs. It is intended to serve as advice to Americans traveling abroad.]

- - - -

Between 6 and 7 million U.S. citizens visit Mexico each year, while more than 400,000 Americans reside there. Although the majority thoroughly enjoy their stay, some experience difficulties and serious inconvenience. The Department of State and its Foreign Service posts in Mexico offer a wide range of services to assist U.S. citizens in distress. U.S. consular officials meet regularly with Mexican authorities to promote the safety of U.S. citizens in Mexico. To keep you among the happy majority who do not experience difficulties, here are some precautions you can take.

Note: Entry requirements for Mexico are on page 211.

How To Have a Safe and Healthy Trip

Before You Go
Give your family or friends in the United States a copy of your proposed itinerary-and keep them informed if your travel plans change. This will help them find you in an emergency. Carry a photo identification with you and include with it the name of a person to contact in the event of serious illness or other emergency.

Safety begins before you leave home. Do not bring anything you would hate to lose. Leave things like unnecessary credit cards and expensive jewelry at home. Bring travelers checks, not cash. Use a money belt or concealed pouch for passport, cash, and other valuables.

It is also wise to photocopy your airline or other tickets and your list of travelers checks. Leave a copy with someone at home, and carry an extra copy with you.

If you plan to drive, learn about your route from an auto club, guide book, or a Mexican government tourist office. Some routes have heavy truck and bus traffic, others have poor or nonexistent shoulders, and many have animals on the loose, Also, some of the new roads have very few restaurants, motels, gas stations, or auto repair shops.

You may not be able to avoid all problems, but at least you will know what to expect if you have done some research.

Caution: See page 208 for routes to avoid because of highway crime.
Also: Be sure to read page 212 for more information on driving your car in Mexico.

For your safety, have your vehicle serviced and in optimum condition before you leave for Mexico. It is wise to bring an extra fan belt, fuses, and other spare parts. (See page 212 for information on bringing spare parts through Mexican customs.) Pack a basic first-aid kit and carry an emergency water supply in your vehicle. Be aware that unleaded gasoline is generally not available, especially after you leave the main highways. Bring a flexible funnel to fill your gas tank because some gas stations have nozzles too large to fit unleaded gas tanks.

After You Arrive-Emergency Help

In an emergency, call [91] (5) 250-0123, the 24-hour hotline of the Mexican Ministry of Tourism.

Note on telephones: If you are calling long distance within Mexico, use the prefix 91, plus the city code. When calling from the U.S., dial 52 in place of 91.

The hotline is for immediate assistance, but it can give you general, non-emergency guidance as well. It is an important number to keep with you. If necessary, in an emergency, you may also call the U.S. Embassy or the nearest U.S. consulate or consular agency. (See addresses in Appendix A.)

If you have an emergency while driving, call the Ministry of Tourism's hotline to obtain help from the "Green Angels," a fleet of radio-dispatched trucks with bilingual crews that operate daily. Services include protection, medical first aid, mechanical aid for your car, and basic supplies. You will not be charged for services, only for parts, gas and oil. The Green Angels patrol daily, from dawn until sunset. If you are unable to call them, pull well off the road and lift the hood of your car; chances are good that they will find you.

Safety Tips

As a visitor to Mexico, be alert to your new surroundings. Hazards in Mexico may be different from those you are used to, and safety regulations and their enforcement are generally not equivalent to U.S. standards.

On Foot. Watch out for irregular pavement and open manholes.

In large cities, take the same precautions against assault, robbery, or pickpockets that you would take in any large U.S. city. Avoid dark alleys, crowds, and marginal areas. Be aware that women and small children, as well as men, can be pickpockets or purse snatchers. Keep your billfold in an inner front pocket; carry your purse tucked securely under your arm; and wear the shoulder strap of your camera or bag across your chest. To guard against thieves on motorcycles, walk away from the curb and carry your purse away from the street.

By Car. Avoid excessive speed and, if at all possible, do not drive at night. Loose livestock can appear at any time. Construction sites or stranded vehicles are often unmarked by flares or other warning signals. Sometimes cars have only one headlight; bicycles seldom have lights or reflectors. Be prepared for a sudden stop at any time. Mexican driving conditions are such that, for your safety, you must drive more slowly than you do at home.

Learn local driving signals. In Mexico, a blinking left turn signal on the vehicle in front of you could mean that it is clear ahead and you may pass, or it could mean the driver is making a left turn. An outstretched left arm may mean an invitation for you to pass. When in doubt, do not pass.

An oncoming vehicle flashing its headlights is a warning for you to slow down or pull over because you are both approaching a narrow bridge or place in the road. The custom is that the first vehicle to flash has the right of way and the other must yield.

When it begins to rain, immediately slow down to a crawl. Freshly wet roads are dangerous because oil and road dust mix with water and form a lubricant. Until this mixture washes away, driving is extremely hazardous. Beware of sudden rains. Stop, or go extremely slowly, until conditions improve.

To avoid highway crime, try not to drive at night and never drive alone at night. Never sleep in vehicles along the road. If your vehicle breaks down, stay with it and wait for the

police or the Green Angels. Do not, under any circumstances, pick up hitchhikers who not only pose a threat to your physical safety, but also put you in danger of being arrested for unwittingly transporting narcotics or narcotics traffickers in your vehicle. Your vehicle can be confiscated if you are transporting marijuana or other narcotics. There are checkpoints and temporary road-blocks where vehicles are checked.

Beware of Highway 15 in the state of Sinaloa and of Highway 40 between the city of Durango and the Pacific coast, areas that are particularly dangerous and where a number of criminal assaults have occurred. Avoid express Highway 1 (limited access) in Sinaloa altogether - even in daytime - because it is remote and subject to bandits.

On Public Transport. Be vigilant in bus and train stations and on public transport. Do not accept beverages from other passengers. In the past, tourists have occasionally been drugged and robbed while they slept.

On Streets and Highways. Be aware of persons representing themselves as Mexican police or other local officials. Some Americans have been the victims of harassment, mistreatment, and extortion by criminals masquerading as officials. Mexican authorities are concerned about these incidents and have cooperated in investigating such cases. You must, however, have the officer's name, badge number, and patrol car number to pursue a complaint. Make a note of this information if you are ever involved with police or other officials.

Do not be surprised if you encounter several types of police in Mexico. The Preventive Police, the Transit Police, and the Federal Highway Police all wear uniforms. The Judicial Police who work for the public prosecutor are not uniformed.

At the Pool or Beach. Do not leave your belongings on the beach while you are swimming. Keep your passport and other valuables in the hotel safe.

Carefully assess the risk potential of recreational activities. Sports equipment that you rent or buy may not meet the safety standards to which you are accustomed. For example, unless you are certain that scuba diving equipment is up to standard, do not use it. Inexperienced scuba divers should beware of dive shops that promise to "certify" you after a few hours instruction. Safe diving requires lengthy training.

If you are interested in the parachute rides offered at many Mexican beach resorts, be aware that, by putting your name on the passenger list, you are relieving the boat operator and owner of responsibility for your safety.

Do not use pools or beaches without lifeguards, or, if you do, exercise extreme caution. Do not dive into unknown bodies of water because hidden rocks or shallow depths can cause serious injury or death. Some Mexican beaches, such as those in Cancun, have warning signs about undertow; take them seriously. Be aware that the newer resorts may lack comprehensive medical facilities.

Reporting a Crime

If You Are in Danger. Call the Mexican Ministry of Tourism's emergency hotline, [91](5) 250-0123, for immediate assistance. Or, in Mexico City, dial 06 for police assistance.

If You Have Been the Victim of a Crime. Immediately contact the U.S. Embassy or the nearest U.S. consulate or consular agency. For addresses and telephone numbers, see Appendix A. You should also report the crime to the local police immediately. If you have difficulty filing this report, the Mexican police have a complement to the Green Angels, called the Silver Angels. This group helps tourists who are victims of crime file a police report. Call the Silver Angels on [91](5) 588-5100.

Avoiding Legal Problems

While traveling in Mexico, you are subject to Mexican laws and not U.S. laws. Tourists who commit illegal acts have no special privileges and are subject to full prosecution under the Mexican judicial system.

First and Foremost, Avoid Drug Offenses. Mexico rigorously prosecutes drug cases. Under Mexican law, possession of and trafficking in illegal drugs are federal offenses. For drug trafficking, bail does not exist. Mexican law does not differentiate between types of narcotics: heroin, marijuana, and amphetamines, for example, are treated the same. Offenders found guilty of possessing more than a token amount of any narcotic substance are subject to a minimum sentence of 10 years, and it is not uncommon for persons charged with drug offenses to be detained for up to 1 year before a verdict is reached.

Remember, if narcotics are found in your vehicle, you are subject to arrest and your vehicle can be confiscated.

Avoid Public Drunkenness. It is against the law in Mexico. Certain border towns have become impatient with teenaged (and older) Americans who cross the border to drink and carouse. This behavior can lead to fights, arrests, traffic accidents, and even death.

Do not bring firearms or ammunition of any kind into Mexico unless you have first obtained a consular firearms certificate from a Mexican consulate. To hunt in Mexico, you must obtain a hunting permit, also available from the consulate. Travelers carrying guns or ammunition into Mexico without a Mexican certificate have been arrested, detained, and sentenced to stiff fines and lengthy prison terms. The sentence for clandestine importation of firearms is up to 6 years. If the weapon is greater than .38 caliber, it is considered of military type, and the sentence is from 5 to 30 years. When you enter Mexico, make certain that Mexican customs officials check both the firearms and your certificate. When you reach your destination, register your firearms with the appropriate military zone headquarters.

Be aware that, even when you enter Mexican waters on your private boat, you are subject to the ban on importing firearms.
Note: Before you leave the United States, you must register your firearms and ammunition with U.S. Customs if you wish to bring them back with you.

In some areas of Mexico, it is not wise to carry anything that might be construed as a weapon. Some cities, such as Nuevo Laredo, have ordinances prohibiting the possession of knives and similar weapons. Tourists have even been arrested for possessing souvenir knives. Most arrests for knife possession occur in connection with some other infraction, such as drunk and disorderly behavior.

Failure to pay hotel bills or for other services rendered is considered fraud under Mexican law. Those accused of these offenses are subject to arrest and conviction with stiff fines and jail sentences.

Be Cautious When Purchasing Real Estate. There are various restrictions on foreigners purchasing property in Mexico. Before you invest money, be certain that you are in compliance with Mexican law and that you are dealing with a reputable developer, time-share company, or real estate agent. For information and for names of Mexican lawyers, contact the American Society of Mexico or the American Chamber of Commerce. You may also obtain a list of Mexican lawyers from the U.S. Embassy or a U.S. consulate or from the Office of Citizens Consular Services, Inter-American Division, Room 4817, Department of State, Washington, DC 20520, (202) 647-3712. If your investment in Mexican property is illegal, you risk confiscation by the government of Mexico.

Be aware that most time-share condo companies are not registered in the U.S. and do not abide by U.S. rules. For instance, there is no day or two "remorse period" in which you can change your mind and back out of a contract that you have signed.

To Avoid Disputes With Merchants, Be a Careful Shopper. Make sure the goods you buy are in good condition and always get a receipt. There is a federal consumer protection office, the Procuraduria Federal del Consumidor, to assist you if you have a major problem with a faulty product or service. However, if the problem is with a service of the tourist industry, you should bring the matter to the Mexican Government Tourist Office (Secretaria de Turismo).

Staying Healthy

Review Your Health Insurance Policy. In some places, particularly at resorts, medical costs can be as high or higher than in the United States. If your insurance policy does not cover you in Mexico, it is strongly recommended that you purchase a policy that does. There are short-term health insurance policies designed specifically to cover travel.

Medical facilities in Mexico differ from those in the United States, and treatment for some types of illnesses or injuries may be only remedial. Some remote areas or coastal islands may have few or no medical facilities. For these reasons, in addition to medical insurance that you can use in Mexico, consider obtaining insurance or joining a medical assistance program to cover the exorbitant cost of medical evacuation in the event of an accident or serious illness. As part of the coverage, these programs usually offer emergency consultation by telephone. They may refer you to the nearest hospital or call for help on your behalf; they may translate your instructions to a health care worker on the scene. The cost of medical evacuation coverage can be as low as $50 for a trip of 30 days. Without this insurance, medical evacuation can cost thousands of dollars.

If your travel agent cannot direct you to a medical assistance company, look for information on them in travel magazines. The U.S. Government cannot pay to have you medically evacuated to the United States.

Immunizations are recommended against diphtheria, tetanus, polio, typhoid, and hepatitis A. For visitors coming directly from the United States, no vaccinations are required to enter Mexico. If you are traveling from an area known to be infected with yellow fever, a vaccination certificate is required.

Malaria is found in some rural areas of Mexico, particularly those near the southwest coast. Travelers to malarial areas should consult their physician or the U.S. Public Health Service and take the recommended dosage of chloroquine. Although chloroquine is not considered necessary for travelers to the major resort areas on the Pacific and Gulf coasts, travelers to those areas should use insect repellent and take other personal protection measures to reduce contact with mosquitoes, particularly from dusk to dawn when malaria transmission is most likely.

Drink Only Bottled Water or Water That Has Been Boiled for 20 Minutes. Avoid ice cubes. Vegetables and fruits should be peeled or washed in a purifying solution. A good rule of thumb is, if you can't peel it or cook it, don't eat it. Medication to prevent travelers' diarrhea is not recommended. If symptoms present themselves and persist, seek medical attention because diarrhea is potentially dangerous.

Air pollution in Mexico City is severe. It is the most dangerous during thermal inversions which occur most often from December to May. Air pollution plus Mexico City's high altitude are a particular health risk for the elderly and persons with high blood pressure, anemia, or respiratory or cardiac problems. If this applies to you, consult your doctor before traveling to Mexico City.

In high altitude areas, such as Mexico City, most people need a short adjustment period. Spend the first few days in a leisurely manner, with a light diet and reduced intake of alcohol. Avoid strenuous activity-this includes everything from sports to rushing up the stairs. Reaction signs to high altitude are lack of energy, a tendency to tire easily, shortness of breath, occasional dizziness, and insomnia.

U.S. Assistance in Mexico

Where To Turn If You Have Serious Legal, Medical, or Financial Difficulties

Legal Problems. If you find yourself in serious difficulty while in Mexico, contact a consular officer at the U.S. Embassy or the nearest U.S. consulate for assistance. U.S. consuls cannot serve as attorneys or give legal assistance. They can, however, provide lists of local attorneys and advise you of your rights under Mexican laws.

Worldwide, Mexico has the highest number of arrests of Americans abroad-over 2,000 per year-and the highest prison population of U.S. citizens outside of the United States-about 425 at any one time. If you are arrested, ask permission to notify the U.S. Embassy or nearest U.S. consulate. Under international agreements and practice, you have the right to talk with an American consul. Although U.S. consuls are limited in what they can do to assist you in legal difficulties, they can monitor the status of detained U.S. Citizens and make sure they are treated fairly under local laws. They will also notify your relatives or friends upon your request.

An individual is guaranteed certain rights under the Mexican constitution, but those rights differ significantly from U.S. constitutional guarantees. The Mexican judicial system is based on Roman and Napoleonic law and presumes a person accused of a crime to be guilty until proven innocent. There is no trial by jury nor writ of habeas corpus in the Anglo-American sense. Trial under the Mexican system is a prolonged process based largely on documents examined on a fixed date in court by prosecution and defense counsel. Sentencing usually takes 6 to 10 months. Bail can be granted after sentencing if the sentence is less than 5 years. Pre-trial bail exists but is never granted when the possible sentence upon conviction is greater than 5 years.

Medical or Financial Problems. If you become seriously ill, U.S. consular officers can assist in finding a doctor and in notifying your family and friends about your condition. Consular officers can also help arrange the transfer of emergency funds to you if you become destitute as a result of robbery, accident, or other emergency.

Advice on Dual Nationality
U.S. law recognizes that Americans may also be citizens of other countries.

Under Mexican law, an individual born in Mexico of an American parent or parents may acquire both nationalities at birth. Also, a U.S. citizen born in the United States of a Mexican father-or after December 26, 1969, of a Mexican mother-may have dual nationality.

If you are a U.S.-Mexican dual national, you must have evidence of your U.S. Citizenship with you when you travel between the United States and Mexico. Such evidence can be a U.S. passport, naturalization certificate, consular report of birth abroad, certificate of citizenship, or a certified copy of your U.S. birth certificate.

If you are a dual national, be aware that you could lose your U.S. nationality if you obtain a Certificate of Mexican Nationality. The Mexican Government recognizes a child's dual nationality from birth to age 18 without requiring an oath of allegiance. Starting at age 18, in order to obtain a Mexican passport or to obtain other benefits, such as the right to own property in a restricted zone, to pay a favorable resident tuition rate at a Mexican university, or to vote in a Mexican election, a dual national is required by Mexican law to obtain a Certificate of Mexican Nationality (CMN). To obtain a CMN, a person must complete an application in which he or she subscribes to an oath of allegiance to Mexico and renounces any other nationality that he or she might possess. Under U.S. law, subscribing to this oath and obtaining a CMN normally results in the loss of U.S. nationality. If you contemplate obtaining a CMN, it is strongly recommended that you first consult the U.S. Embassy or the nearest U.S. consulate.

A Guide to Entry and Exit Regulations

Getting Into Mexico
U.S. citizens visiting Mexico for no more than 72 hours and remaining within 20 kilometers of the border do not need a permit to enter. Those transiting Mexico to another country need a transit visa which costs a nominal fee and is valid for up to 30 days.

Tourist Cards. All U.S. citizens visiting Mexico for tourism or study for up to 180 days need a document, called a tourist card in English or FMT in Spanish, to enter and leave Mexico. The tourist card is free and may be obtained from Mexican consulates, Mexican tourism offices, Mexican border crossing points, and from most airlines serving Mexico. If you fly to Mexico, you must obtain your tourist card before boarding your flight; it cannot be obtained upon arrival at an airport in Mexico.

The tourist card is issued upon presentation of proof of citizenship, such as a U.S. passport or a U.S. birth certificate, plus a photo I.D., such as a driver's license. Tourist cards are issued for up to 90 days with a single entry, or if you present proof of sufficient funds, for 180 days with multiple entries.

Upon entering Mexico, retain and safeguard the pink copy of your tourist card so you may surrender it to Mexican immigration when you depart. You must leave Mexico before your tourist card expires or you are subject to a fine. A tourist card for less than 180 days may be revalidated in Mexico by the Mexican immigration service (Direccion General de Servicios Migratorios).

Visas. If you wish to stay longer than 180 days, or if you wish to do business or conduct religious work in Mexico, contact the Mexican Embassy or the nearest Mexican consulate to obtain a visa or permit. Persons conducting religious work on a tourist card are subject to arrest and deportation.

Residing or Retiring in Mexico. If you plan to live or retire in Mexico, consult a Mexican consulate on the type of long-term visa you will need. As soon as possible after you arrive in the place you will live, it is a good idea to register with the U.S. Embassy or the nearest U.S. consulate or consular agent. Bring your passport or other identification with you. Registration makes it easier to contact you in an emergency. (Registration information is confidential and will not be released to inquirers without your express authorization.)

Travel Requirements for Children
A child under age 18 traveling with only one parent must have written, notarized consent from the other parent to travel, or must carry, if applicable, a decree of sole custody for the accompanying parent or a death certificate for the other parent. A child traveling alone or in someone else's custody must have notarized consent from both parents to travel, or if applicable, notarized consent from a single parent plus documentation that the parent is the only custodial parent.

Driving Your Car to Mexico

Permits. When you drive to Mexico, you must obtain a temporary vehicle import permit. You must show: your proof of ownership or notarized authorization from the owner to bring the car into Mexico, a valid driver's license, proof of auto liability insurance, and current registration and plates. The permit is issued free at border entry points and should be valid for the same period of time as your tourist card (up to 180 days). Verify that your permit is valid for as long a period as your tourist card. You must remove your motor vehicle from Mexico before the permit expires or have the permit extended by the Temporary Importation Department of a Mexican customs office. If you do not do so, your motor vehicle may be confiscated.

You may not sell, transfer, or otherwise dispose of a motor vehicle brought into Mexico on a temporary importation permit, nor may you leave Mexico without the vehicle. In case of emergency, or following an accident where the vehicle cannot be removed, the owner may request permission to depart Mexico without the vehicle through the Mexican Customs Office in Mexico City, or the local office of the Treasury

Department (Hacienda) in other cities.

If you bring spare auto parts to Mexico, declare them when you enter the country. When you leave, be prepared to show that you are taking the unused parts with you or that you have had them installed in Mexico. Save your repair receipts for this purpose.

If you wish to authorize another person to drive your car, record the authorization with Mexican officials when you enter Mexico-even if you expect to be a passenger when the other person drives. Do not, under any circumstances, allow an unauthorized person to drive your vehicle when you are not in the car. Such a person could have to pay a fine amounting to a substantial percentage of the vehicles's value, or your vehicle could be confiscated.

Insurance. Mexican auto insurance is sold in most cities and towns on both sides of the border. U.S. automobile liability insurance is not valid in Mexico nor is most collision and comprehensive coverage issued by U.S. companies. Therefore, when you cross the border, purchase auto insurance adequate for your needs in Mexico. A good rule of thumb is to buy coverage equivalent to that which you carry in the United States.

Motor vehicle insurance is invalid in Mexico if the driver is found to be under the influence of alcohol or drugs. Regardless of whether you have insurance, if you are involved in an accident, you will be taken into police custody until it can be determined who is liable and whether you have the ability to pay any judgment. If you do not have Mexican liability insurance, you are almost certain to spend some time in jail until all parties are satisfied that responsibility has been assigned and adequate financial satisfaction received. There may also be criminal liability assigned if the injuries or damages are serious.

Rental Cars

Renting in the United States. Many car rental companies in the United States have clauses in their contracts prohibiting drivers from traveling out of the country. The Mexican police are aware of these regulations, and will sometimes impound rental vehicles driven from the United States. When renting a vehicle in the United States, check with the company to see if your contract allows you to drive it into Mexico.

Renting a Car in Mexico. The standard insurance included with many car rental contracts in Mexico provides only nominal liability coverage, often as little as the equivalent of $200. Because Mexican law permits the jailing of drivers after an accident until they have

212

met their obligations to third parties and to the rental company, renters should read their contracts carefully and purchase additional liability and comprehensive insurance if necessary.

Bringing Your Own Plane or Boat to Mexico

Private aircraft and boats are subject to the same Mexican customs regulations as are motor vehicles. When you arrive at a Mexican port in your private boat, you can obtain a temporary import permit for it similar to the one given for motor vehicles.

Flying your own plane to Mexico, however, is more complicated. Well before your trip, inquire about private aircraft regulations and procedures from a Mexican consulate or Mexican Government Tourist Office.

Operation of Citizen's Band (CB) Equipment

American tourists are permitted to operate CB radios in Mexico. You must, however, obtain a 180 day permit for a nominal fee by presenting your U.S. citizen's band radio authorization at a Mexican consulate or Mexican Government Tourist Office. This permit cannot be obtained at the border.

Transmissions on CB equipment are allowed only on channels 9, 10, and 11, and only for personal communication and emergency road assistance. Any device which increases transmission power to over 5 watts is prohibited. CB equipment may not be used near radio installations of the aeronautical and marine services.

What You May Bring Into Mexico

Customs Regulations. Tourists should enter Mexico with only the items needed for their trip. Entering with large quantities of an item a tourist might not normally be expected to have, particularly expensive appliances, such as televisions, stereos, or other items, may lead to suspicion of smuggling and possible confiscation of the items and arrest of the individual.

Unless you prepare ahead, you may have difficulty bringing computers or other expensive electronic equipment into Mexico for your personal use. To prevent being charged an import tax, write a statement about your intention to use the equipment for personal use and to remove it from Mexico when you leave. Have this statement signed and certified at a Mexican consulate in the United States and present it to Mexican customs as you enter Mexico.

Land travelers should verify from Mexican customs at the border that all items in their possession may be legally brought into Mexico. You will be subject to a second immigration and customs inspection south of the Mexican border where unlawful items may be seized, and you could be prosecuted regardless of whether or not the items passed through the initial customs inspection.

Firearms. Do not bring firearms or ammunition into Mexico without first obtaining a permit from a Mexican consulate in the United States. See page 209 for more on importing firearms.

Currency. In 1982, the Mexican government lifted currency controls and modified its exchange rate system, permitting tourists to exchange dollars for pesos at the fluctuating free market rate. There are no restrictions on the import or export of bank notes and none on the export of reasonable quantities of ordinary Mexican coins. However, gold or silver Mexican coins may not be exported.

Take travelers checks with you because personal U.S. checks are rarely accepted by Mexican hotels or banks. Major credit cards are accepted in many hotels, shops, and restaurants. An exchange office (casa de cambios) usually gives a better rate of exchange than do stores, hotels, or restaurants.

Pets. U.S. visitors to Mexico may bring a dog, cat, or up to four canaries by presenting the following certificates at the border:

(1)   a pet health certificate signed by a registered veterinarian in the United States and issued not more than 72 hours before the animal enters Mexico; and

(2)   a pet vaccination certificate showing that the animal has been treated for rabies, hepatitis, pip, and leptospirosis.

Certification by Mexican consular authorities is not required for the health or vaccination certificate. A permit fee is charged at the time of entry into Mexico.

Shopping-Some Things To Beware of Buying

Wildlife and Wildlife Products. Beware of purchasing souvenirs made from endangered wildlife. Mexican markets and stores abound with wildlife, most of it prohibited from international traffic. You risk confiscation and a possible fine by U.S. Customs if you attempt to import virtually any wildlife from Mexico. In particular, watch out for and avoid:

■   All products made from sea turtles,

including such items as turtle leather boots, tortoise-shell jewelry, and sea turtle oil cosmetics.

- Fur from spotted cats.

- Mexican birds, stuffed or alive, such as parrots, parakeets, or birds of prey.

- Crocodile and caiman leather.

- Black coral jewelry.

- Wildlife curios, such as stuffed iguanas.

When driving across state lines within Mexico, you can expect to be stopped at agricultural livestock inspection stations.

Antiques. Mexico considers all pre-Columbian objects to be the "inalienable property of the Nation" and that the unauthorized export of such objects is theft and is punishable by arrest, detention, and judicial prosecution. Under U.S. law, to import pre-Columbian monumental and architectural sculpture and murals, you must present proof that they were legally exported from the country of origin. U.S. law does not prohibit the import of non-monumental or non-architectural artifacts from Mexico.

Glazed Ceramics. According to the U.S. Food and Drug Administration, it is possible to suffer lead poisoning if you consume food or beverages that have been stored or served in improperly glazed ceramic ware. Analysis of many ceramic pieces from Mexico has shown them to contain dangerous levels of lead. Unless you have proof of their safety, use glazed ceramics purchased in Mexico for decorative purposes only.

Returning to the United States
You must present the pink copy of your tourist card at your point of departure from Mexico. If you are returning by motor vehicle, you will need to show your vehicle import permit when you cross the border. At the time of publication, the airport departure tax is $10 or the equivalent in Mexican currency for those returning by commercial airline.

The U.S. Customs Service currently permits U.S. citizens returning from international travel to bring back $400 worth of merchandise, including 1 liter of alcohol, duty free. The next $1,000 worth of items brought back is subject to a duty of 10%.

In addition to U.S. customs regulations, be aware that

some U.S. border states (most notably, Texas) have imposed state restrictions on liquor, wine, and beer imports from Mexico. If you are planning to bring back alcoholic beverages, inquire about these restrictions from the liquor control office of the state through which you plan to return.

Useful Addresses and Telephone/Telex Numbers

Note: For calls from the United States, dial the country code for Mexico, 52. For long distance within Mexico, dial 91 instead of 52. Telephones listed below without the [52] prefix are U.S. long distance numbers, not international numbers.

American Embassy
Paseo de la Reforma 305
Mexico 06500, D.F.
Tel [52] (5) 211-0042
Telex 017-73-091 and 017-75-685

U.S. Export Development Office/U.S. Trade Center
31 Liverpool
Mexico 06600, D.F.
Tel [52] (5) 591-0155
Telex 017-73-471

Consulates General and Consulates
American Consulate General
Avenue Lopez Mateos 924-N
Ciudad Juarez, Chihuahua
Tel: [52] (16) 134-048
After hours (emergencies): (915) 525-6066
Telex 033-840

American Consulate General
Progreso 175
Guadalajara, Jalisco
Tel [52] (36) 25-2998, or 25-2700
Telex 068-2-860 ACDMC

American Consulate
Calle Monterrey 141, Poniente
Hermosillo, Sonora
Tel [52] (621) 723-75
After hours (emergencies): [52] (621) 725-85
Telex 058-829 ACHEME

American Consulate
Ave. Primera No. 2002
Matamoros, Tamaulipas
Tel [52] (891) 2-52-50, or 2-52-51
After hours (emergencies): (512) 546-1611
Telex 035-827 ACMTME

American Consulate

Circunvalacion No. 120 Centro
Mazatlan, Sinaloa
Tel [52] (678) 5-2205
Telex 066-883 ACMZME

American Consulate
Paseo Montejo 453,
Merida, Yucatan
Tel [52] (99) 25-5011
After hours (emergencies): (52) (99) 25-5409
Telex 0753885 ACMEME
American Consulate General
Avenida Constitucion 411 Poniente
Monterrey, Nuevo Leon
Tel [52] (83) 45-2120
Telex 0382853 ACMYME

American Consulate
Avenida Allende 3330, Col. Jardin
Nuevo Laredo, Tamaulipas
Tel [52] (871) 4-0696, 4-9616, or 4-0512
After hours (emergencies): (512) 727-9661
Telex 036-849 ACMLME

American Consulate General
Tapachula 96
Tijuana, Baja California
Tel [52] (66) 81-7400 or (706) 681-7400
After hours (emergencies): (619) 585-2000
Telex 056-6836 ACTJMEX

Consular Agents
Resident consular agents have been designated in 10
other locations in Mexico to assist U.S. citizens in
serious emergencies. Each consular agent is supervised
by one of the above-listed offices and may be contacted
through it or by calling the consular agent's direct
number. The following list gives each consular agent's
city and state, direct phone number, and the name of its
supervisory office.

Acapulco, Guerrero; [52] (748) 5-7207 ext. 273;
U.S. Embassy, Mexico City
Cancun, Quintana Roo, [52] (988) 4-63-99;
U.S. Consulate, Merida
Durango, Durango; [52] (181) 1-2217;
U.S. Consulate General, Monterrey
Mulege, Baja California Sur; [52] (68) 5-3-0111;
U.S. Consulate General, Tijuana
Oaxaca, Oaxaca; [52] (951) 6-0654;
U.S. Embassy, Mexico City
Puerto Vallarta, Jalisco; [52] (322) 2-0069;
U.S. Consulate General Guadalajara
San Luis Potosi, San Luis Potosi;
[52] (481) 7-2501;
U.S. Consulate General, Monterrey

San Miguel de Allende, Guanajuato;
[52] (465) 2-2357;
U.S. Consulate General, Guadalajara
Tampico, Tamaulipas; [52] (121) 3-2217
U.S. Embassy, Mexico City
Vera Cruz, Vera Cruz;
U.S. Embassy, Mexico City

Planning another Trip?

See Chapter 46 for a listing of resources available to
the general traveler from the U.S. Departments of
State, Customs, Transportation, Health and various
government and non-government organizations. All of
the available International travel-related pamphlets,
brochures and publications issued by the U.S.
Department of State and by U.S. Customs have been
reproduced in full in this book. See Table of Contents
for location.

Chapter 19

Tips for Travelers to The Middle East and North Africa

[The information in this chapter is reprinted verbatim from a bulletin issued by the U.S. State Department, Bureau of Consular Affairs. It is intended to serve as advice to Americans traveling abroad.]

- - - -

Algeria, Bahrain, Egypt, Iran, Iraq, Israel, Jordan, Kuwait, Lebanon, Libya, Morocco, Oman, Quatar, Saudi Arabia, Syria, Tunisia, United Arab Emirates, Yemen

How to Prepare for a Safe Trip
The policies of the countries in the Middle East and North Africa toward foreign visitors vary greatly from country to country. Some countries encourage tourism and put very few restrictions on visitors. Other countries do not allow tourism and carefully regulate business travel. Some areas in the region have experienced military conflict over an extended period of time.

A little planning and knowledge will go a long way toward making your trip to the Middle East and North Africa go smoothly. If you learn about the countries you will visit and obey the laws and respect the customs of those places, you can make your stay as pleasant and incident-free as possible.

Consular Information Sheets
For travel information on any country, see the Department of State's Consular Information Sheet for the country. Consular Information Sheets cover such matters as health conditions, unusual currency and entry regulations crime and security conditions drug penalties, and areas of instability. In addition, there are a number of Travel Warnings which advise Americans to defer travel because of unsafe conditions. Regulations may also prohibit the use of U.S. passports to visit certain countries. This prohibition will be included in the Travel Warnings issued for affected countries. Travel Warnings are under continuous review by the Department of State. Before you depart for a country that has a Travel Warning, make certain that you have the most recent revision of the Warning. The Department of State also issues Public Announcements. Public Announcements are issued as a means to disseminate information quickly about terrorist threats and other relatively short-term and/or transnational condition which would pose significant risks to the security of American travelers.

There are several ways to access Consular Information Sheets, Travel Warnings and Public Announcements. You can listen to them 24-hours a day by calling 202-647-5225 from a touchtone phone. You can receive copies of them by sending a self-addressed, stamped envelope to the Overseas Citizens Services, Room 4800, Department of State, Washington, DC 20520-4818. (Write the name of the requested country or countries on the outside of the envelope.) You can also find Consular Information Sheets and Travel Warnings at the 13 regional passport agencies and at U.S. embassies and consulates abroad. They can also be accessed through an airline or travel agent's computer reservation system, the Bureau of Consular Affairs' 24-hour automated fax system at 202/647-3000, or through many computer bulletin boards, including the Consular Affairs Bulletin Board (CABB). You may call the CABB on modem number 202-647-9225. Set your communications software to: no parity, 8 bits, one stop bit (N-8-1).

Registration
As you travel, keep abreast of local news coverage. If you plan more than a short stay in one place, or if you are in an area experiencing civil unrest or a natural disaster, you are encouraged to register with the nearest U.S. embassy or consulate. Remember to leave a detailed itinerary with a friend or relative in the United States in case of an emergency.

Your U.S. Passport
Make a record or photocopy of the data from your passport's identification page and from your visas, Also make a copy of the addresses and telephone numbers of the U.S. embassy and consulates in the countries you will visit (see Appendix A). Put this information along with two passport photos in a place separate from your passport to be available in case of loss or theft of your passport.

217

Visa and Other Entry Requirements

A U.S. passport is required for travel to all countries in the region. U.S. citizens are not required to have visas for tourist or business travel to Israel, Morocco, or Tunisia, but may need to supply proof of sufficient funds for the trip and proof of onward or round trip travel arrangements. All other countries in the Middle East and North Africa require U.S. citizens to have visas.

If you plan to travel extensively in the region, entry and exit stamps could quickly fill the pages of your passport. Before you go, you may wish to ask the nearest passport agency to add extra pages to your passport. Or, if applying for a new passport, you can request one with 48 pages instead of the usual 24.

Each country has its own set of entry requirements. For authoritative visa information, contact the embassy or consulate of the country you plan to visit. See Appendix B for a list of foreign embassies in the United States.

When you make inquiries, ask about the following:

- Visa price, length of validity, number of entries.

- Financial requirements--proof of sufficient funds and proof of onward/return ticket.

- Immunization requirements. Yellow fever immunization is often required if arriving from a yellow-fever- infected area.

- Currency regulations.

- Import/export restrictions and limitations. Several countries prohibit the import and consumption of alcoholic beverages.

- Departure tax. Be sure to keep enough local currency to be able to depart as planned.

Some Arab countries will not allow travelers to enter if their passports show any evidence of previous or expected travel to Israel. Other Arab countries apply the ban inconsistently, sometimes refusing and at other times allowing entry.when a passport shows evidence of travel to Israel. The U.S. government has informed the members of the Arab League that it objects to restrictive policies regarding U.S. passports containing **Israeli** markings. If passport restrictions imposed by other countries may be a problem for you, contact the nearest U.S. passport agency, embassy, or consulate for guidance.

Several Arab countries ask visa applicants to state their religious affiliation. The U.S. government is opposed to the use of this information to discriminate against visa applicants, and has made its views known to the governments concerned. In turn, the United States has received assurances that visa applications are not denied on the basis of religious affiliation.

Special Entry Requirements for Countries That Permit No Tourists

Kuwait, Oman, Qatar, and Saudi Arabia do not permit tourism. All business visitors must be sponsored by a company in the country to be visited. Private visitors must be sponsored by a relative or friend native to the country. To visit a foreigner working in a country where tourism is not permitted, you must be sponsored by the same local company that sponsors the person you are visiting. Entry is by visa or the non-objection certificate (NOC) system. An NOC is obtained by a visitor's sponsor and filed with the appropriate foreign government authorities before the planned visit. For more information see the individual country sections beginning on page 220.

Exit Permits

Countries that require visitors to be sponsored usually also require them to obtain exit permits from their sponsors. U.S. citizens can have difficulty obtaining exit permits if they are involved in business disputes. A U.S. citizen who is the wife or child of the local sponsor needs the sponsor's permission to leave the country. Do not accept sponsorship to visit a country unless you are certain you will also be able to obtain an exit permit.

U.S. Citizens Married to Foreign Nationals

In many Islamic countries, even those that give tourist visas and do not require sponsorship, a woman needs the permission of her husband, and children need the permission of their father, to leave the country. If you travel or allow your children to travel, be aware of the laws of the country you plan to visit. The Department of State is aware of many American citizen children who have been abducted to, or wrongfully retained in countries of the Middle East and North Africa notwithstanding a U.S. custody order. Although some of these children were taken abroad illegally by one of their parents, many originally traveled abroad with the consent of both parents. Do not visit or allow your children to visit unless you are completely confident that you and they will be allowed to leave. Once overseas, you are subject to the laws of the country where you are; U.S. law cannot protect you.

Dual Nationality

Some countries in the Middle East and North Africa do

not recognize acquisition of U.S. citizenship by their nationals. Unless the naturalized U.S. citizen renounces his or her original nationality at an embassy or consulate of the country of origin, he or she may still be considered a citizen of that country. A person born in the United States with a parent who was a citizen of another country may also be considered a citizen of that country. The laws of some countries provide for automatic acquisition of citizenship when a person marries a national of that country.

If arrested, a dual national may be denied the right to communicate with the U.S. embassy or consulate. Another consequence could be having to serve in the military of one's former country. If you are a naturalized U.S. citizen, a dual national, or have any reason to believe another country may claim you as their national, check with the embassy of that country as to your citizenship status and any obligations you may have while visiting. Dual nationals who have not researched their citizenship status before traveling have sometimes, to their surprise, encountered difficulties, such as not being allowed to depart.

Even countries that recognize acquired U.S. citizenship may consider their former citizens as having resumed original citizenship if they take up residence in their country of origin. This can happen even if the embassy of the country of origin stamps a visa in the U.S. passport of its former citizen.

Dual nationals may find that they are required to use a passport from their country of origin in order to enter or leave that country. The U.S. government does not object to the use of a foreign passport by a dual national to enter or depart a foreign country in compliance with the requirements of that country. U.S. regulations require, however, that U.S. citizens, including dual nationals, use a U.S. passport to depart from and enter the United States.

If you have any questions about dual nationality or the use of foreign passports, contact Overseas Citizens Services, Room 4817, Department of State, Washington, D.C. 20520-4818, (202-647-3926) before you travel. Recorded information on dual nationality and other citizenship matters is available 24-hours a day by calling 202-647-3444.

Currency and Customs Regulations

Some countries in the region have no restrictions on currency imports or exports. Some prohibit Israeli currency. Most countries in the Middle East and North Africa, however, have detailed currency regulations, including a requirement to declare all currency, including travelers checks, upon entry. In those countries, the export of foreign currency is limited to the amount that was imported and declared. Be sure to make the required currency declaration, have it validated, and retain it for use at departure. Buy local currency only at banks or other authorized exchange places and retain your receipts for use at departure. Currency not accounted for may be confiscated.

Several countries prohibit the import and consumption of alcoholic beverages. Most countries restrict the entry of products containing pork, as well as any literature, videotapes, and cassette tapes deemed pornographic. Also, some countries will not permit the import of books or other goods from Israel.

Shopping--Be Wary of Antiques

Americans have been arrested in some countries in the region for the unauthorized purchase of antiques or other important cultural artifacts. If you purchase such items, always insist that the seller provide a receipt and the official museum export certificate required by law. Travelers have also been detained at customs for possessing reproductions of antiques. The safest policy is to purchase copies of antiques from reputable stores and have them documented as such. **Obtain receipts for all such purchases.**

Health

Immunizations

Information on immunizations and health precautions for travelers can be obtained in the United States from local health departments, private doctors, or travel clinics. Information is also available from the Centers for Disease Control's 24-hour hotline on 404-332-4559 and from the U.S. Public Health Service book, *Health Information for International Travel'*, available for $7.00 from the Superintendent of Documents, U.S. Government Printing Office, Washington, D.C. 20402. Depending on your destination, immunization may be recommended against diphtheria, tetanus, polio, typhoid, and hepatitis A. Chloroquine prophylaxis against malaria is recommended for travel to some areas of the region.

An increasing number of countries have established regulations regarding AIDS testing, particularly for long-term residents and students. Check with the embassy or consulate of the country you plan to visit for the latest information.

Review Your Health Insurance Policy

If your health insurance does not provide coverage overseas, consider buying temporary insurance that does. In addition, consider obtaining insurance to cover the exorbitant cost of medical evacuation in the event of an illness or for the return of remains in case of death. Insurance companies and some credit card and travelers check companies offer short-term health and emergency assistance policies designed for travelers. Medical facilities vary in the region; in some countries they are similar to U.S. standards. U.S. embassies or consulates can furnish you with a list of local hospitals and English-speaking physicians.

Precautions
In the hot and dry climates that prevail in the Middle East and North Africa, it is important to avoid water depletion and heat stroke. Safe tap water is available in many areas. In some places, however, it is highly saline and should be avoided by persons on sodium-restricted diets. In many rural and some urban areas, tap water is not potable, and travelers should drink only boiled or chemically treated water or bottled carbonated drinks. In these areas, avoid fresh vegetables and fruits unless they are washed in a purifying solution and peeled. Diarrhea is potentially serious. If it persists, seek medical attention.

Schistosomiasis (or bilharzia) is present in the area of the Nile and in several other areas in North Africa and the Middle East. These parasites are best avoided by not swimming or wading in fresh water in endemic areas.

Drug Offenses
Drug enforcement policies in the region are strict. Possession of even small amounts of narcotics, including substances such as marijuana, LSD, or amphetamines, can lead to arrest. If found guilty, drug offenders are subject to lengthy prison sentences. Because what is considered to be 'narcotics' varies from country to country, learn and obey the laws in the places you will visit. Keep all prescription drugs in their original containers clearly labeled with the doctor's name, pharmacy and contents. In addition, if you take an unusual prescription drug, carry a letter from your doctor explaining your need for the drug and a copy of the prescription.

Dress and Local Customs

Islam
Islam is the pre-eminent influence on local laws and customs in much of the Middle East and North Africa. The extent of this influence varies. Some Arab countries have secular governments, but in certain other countries, particularly those in the Arabian peninsula, Islam dictates a total way of life. It prescribes the behavior for individuals and society, codifying law, fancily relations, business etiquette, dress, food, personal hygiene, and much more. Among the

important values is a family-centered way of life, including a protected role for women and clear limits on their participation in public life. In traditional societies, Muslims believe open social relations between the sexes result in the breakdown of family life. Contact between men and women, therefore, is rigidly controlled in traditional societies.

Travel during Ramadan, the holiest time in the Islamic year, can prove to be very difficult. Business is rarely conducted during this time and nonobservance of the Ramadan tradition of fasting during daylight hours can carry penalties in some countries.

In the traditional societies of the region, it is considered rude to face the soles of one's feet toward other people. At traditional meals, the left hand is not used for eating.

Apparel
Conservative Western street clothing (except for shorts) is appropriate in most areas. In more traditional societies, however, attire for women should be more conservative, garments should have sleeves, and dress length should be below the knee. On the other hand, in some areas of the region visited by many tourists - for example, the beaches of Israel and Morocco - attire similar to that worn in the United States is acceptable.

The Workweek
In many countries in the Middle East and North Africa, the weekend is either Thursday/Friday or Friday/Saturday. Workweek information is included in the list of Appendices.

Country Information

Algeria
Travelers to Algeria are warned that due to political, social, and economic problems a climate of violent unrest has occurred. A number of terrorist attacks have been carried out against foreigners. Terrorists have also threatened to kill all foreigners who are in Algeria. A state of emergency has been in effect since early 1992.

Crime is also a major problem in Algeria. Crimes include car break-ins, theft of auto parts from parked cars, theft of items (even those of moderate value) left in hotel rooms, home burglary, and pickpocketing and purse snatching near hotels and on trains and buses. Some tactics that residents of Algeria use to avoid being victimized include carrying only a minimum amount of cash and concealing it well and parking only in guarded locations. The police can be reached in Algerian cities by dialing 17. In rural areas, contact the *gendarmerie nationals*.

220

Algeria does not give visas to persons whose passports indicate travel to Israel. Some hotels accept some credit cards. Before traveling, ask your credit card company if your card will be accepted in Algeria, and if not, bring travelers checks to cover your expenses.

Algerian currency and customs regulations are strictly enforced. All currency must be declared upon entering the country, and completely accounted for when departing. Non-residents are required to change the equivalent of approximately $200 into Algerian dinars at the official exchange rate while in Algeria. You will need to present evidence of this currency exchange before you are allowed to depart the country. All hotel bills must be paid in hard currency such as U.S. dollars. Paid hotel receipts may be used as evidence of currency exchange.

Bahrain
Business representatives, conference and exhibition delegates, and holders of diplomatic and official passports may obtain a visitors visa, valid for up to three months, from the Bahrain Embassy in Washington, DC, or the UN Mission for Bahrain in New York. Persons in the above categories may also be able to obtain either a 7-day visa or a 72 hour transit visa at the Bahrain airport upon arrival if they present a confirmed return or onward air ticket. Single women who have no sponsor or family ties in Bahrain may have difficulty in obtaining an airport visa. In addition to an onward ticket, they may wish to secure in advance a sponsorship from a hotel that will arrange to have an airport visa waiting for them. The 72-hour airport visa can be extended, on a case by case basis, for up to one week if a Bahraini sponsor applies to the Immigration Director stating the purpose for the extension.

A 7-day visa is possible for members of tourist groups, provided arrangements are made with the Directorate of Tourism and Archaeology in the Ministry of Information or through a private agency in Bahrain, such as a hotel, travel agent, or tour group organizer.

Journalists planning travel to Bahrain should contact the Ministry of Information providing travel details at least one week in advance of arrival. The Ministry will then authorize airport officials to issue a 72-hour or a 7-day visa upon arrival. Failure to notify the Ministry may result in delay at the airport or denial of permission to enter the country. The Ministry's address is: P.O. Box 253, State of Bahrain; telephone: (973) 689-099; FAX (973) 780-345; telex: 8399 inform BN. Office hours:0700-1400 Saturday through Wednesday.

Water is drinkable though often highly saline. Conservative dress is recommended. Bahrain prohibits the import of pornography, firearms, ammunition, or of items such as knives, swords, or daggers that are capable of being used as weapons. Videotapes may be screened by customs in Bahrain and either confiscated or held until the traveler departs the country.

Consumption of alcohol is allowed in most bars and restaurants, except during the month of Ramadan. If there is any indication that a driver has consumed alcohol, authorities will regard that as evidence of driving under the influence of alcohol. The penalty for drunken driving may be incarceration or a fine of 500 Bahraini dinars, the equivalent of $1,300. This fine can be increased to up to double that amount, depending on the circumstances of the case and the judge's decision. Under Bahraini law, convicted drug traffickers may receive the death penalty.

Egypt
There are no currency declaration requirements for travelers. Travelers may carry a maximum of 100 Egyptian pounds into or out of Egypt. Excess Egyptian currency found on a traveler entering Egypt will be confiscated.

There are strict duties on the importation of expensive photographic and video equipment. This includes most types of equipment typically carried by tourists to Egypt, including all video and autofocus cameras. Travelers who wish to take such equipment with them on a temporary visit have the following options with customs authorities: (A) They may have it by model and serial number in their passports, so that the equipment can be cross-checked upon the traveler's departure from Egypt. In this instance no duty will be collected. (B) They have the equipment placed in storage for the duration of stay, in which case a storage fee may be collected. (C) Long term visitors or residents will pay a standard duty fee for importing the items and be issued a receipt (at the time of departure, the fee will be refunded upon presentation of the receipt).

All persons entering Egypt from cholera or yellow fever areas must produce evidence of up-to-date immunizations. Immunization must have been administered before arrival-cholera at least 6 days before arrival and yellow fever at least 10 days. Travelers without evidence of required immunizations may not enter unless they are vaccinated and detained in quarantine for 6 or 10 days, respectively.

Foreigners are required to register with the police within 7 days of arrival. Hotels usually take care of this. All hotel bills must be paid in foreign currency or in Egyptian pounds exchanged at the official bank rate,

221

as evidenced by a bank receipt.

All travelers to Egypt should be aware that Egyptian authorities strictly enforce drug laws. The death penalty may be imposed on anyone convicted of smuggling or selling marijuana, hashish, opium, or other narcotics.

Iran

U.S. citizens are advised to avoid all travel to Iran. Travel to Iran continues to be dangerous because of the generally anti-American atmosphere and Iranian government hostility to the U.S. government. U.S. citizens traveling to Iran have been detained without charge, arrested, and harassed by Iranian authorities. Persons who violate Iranian laws, such as those concerning proper dress, may face penalties that are, at times, severe.

U.S./Iranian dual nationals often have their U.S. passports confiscated, have been denied permission to leave Iran, have been compelled to serve in the Iranian armed forces, or have encountered other problems while in Iran. U.S. citizens who are the spouse or child of an Iranian citizen are also considered Iranian citizens and may be required to enter Iran using an Iranian passport. The wife and minor children of an Iranian citizen will not be allowed to leave Iran without the written permission of the husband or father. Before planning a trip to Iran, Americans who also possess Iranian nationality are advised to contact Overseas Citizens Services at 202-647-3926.

The United States does not have diplomatic relations with Iran. U.S. interests in Iran are currently served by the Embassy of Switzerland. Iranian officials have often prevented Swiss officials from providing even minimal protective services to U.S. citizens.

Iraq

U.S. citizens are warned to avoid all travel to Iraq. Conditions in Iraq remain unsettled and dangerous and travel is extremely hazardous, particularly for U.S. citizens.

On February 8,1991, U.S. passports ceased to be valid for travel to, in, or through Iraq unless a special validation has been obtained. An automatic exemption to the restriction is granted to Americans residing in Iraq as of February 8, 1991, and to professional journalists on assignment. The categories of individuals eligible for consideration for special passport validation are representatives of the American or International Red Cross, persons with compelling humanitarian consider- ations, or applicants whose travel is determined to be in the national interest. Exceptions will be scrutinized

carefully on a case-by-case basis. Requests for exceptions should be forwarded in writing to:

Office of Citizenship Appeals and Legal Assistance
U.S. Department of State
1111 19th Street, N.W., Suite 260
Washington, DC 20522-1705.
Telephone: 202-955-0232 or 955-0231

The request must be accompanied by substantiating documentation according to the category under which an exception is sought. It must also include the prospective traveler's name, date and place of birth, and passport number.

In addition, the Department of the Treasury prohibits all travel-related transactions by U.S. persons intending to visit Iraq, unless specifically licensed by the Office of Foreign Assets Control. The only exceptions are for persons engaged in journalism or in official U.S. government or U.N. business. Questions on U.S. Treasury restrictions should be directed to:

Licensing Section
Office of Foreign Assets Control
U.S. Department of the Treasury
Washington, DC 20220
Telephone: 202-622-2480.

Travelers granted exceptions to travel to Iraq should be aware that normal protection by U.S. diplomatic and consular representatives cannot be provided. U.S. interests in Iraq are represented by the government of Poland which can provide only limited emergency services to U.S. citizens. All travelers to Iraq are required to submit certification or be tested upon arrival for AIDS.

Israel, the Gaza Strip, Jericho Area, and the Territories Occupied and Administered by Israel U.S. citizens do not need a visa to visit Israel, the West Bank, the Golan Heights, or the Gaza Strip and Jericho area In the Gaza Strip and Jericho area, a transfer of certain powers and responsibilities to the Palestinian Authority has taken place pursuant to the September 13,1993 Israel-PLO Declaration of Principles on Interim Self-Governing Arrangements and the May 4,1994 Cairo Agreement. Upon arrival in Israel, a U.S. citizen is issued a tourist visa that is valid for 3 months and is renewable. Anyone, however, who has been refused entry to Israel or experienced difficulties with their visa status during a previous visit should contact the nearest Israeli embassy or consulate before attempting to return to Israel. At ports of entry, Israeli officials determine a U.S. citizen's eligibility to enter Israel. Applicants may be questioned in detail and/or required to post a departure bond.

Entering Israel

American citizens have, on occasion, had their U.S. passports taken as a guarantee of their departure. If this should happen to you, contact a U.S. consular officer and report the seizure of your passport. Any U.S. citizen experiencing difficulties at points of entry, to Israel or the Gaza Strip, should ask to telephone the U.S. Embassy in Tel Aviv on 03-5174338 (weekends: 03-5174347). Those experiencing difficulties attempting to enter from Jordan or who encounter difficulties in the Jericho area should ask to contact the U.S. Consulate General in Jerusalem on 02-253-288 (weekends 02-253-201). Although they will be pleased to assist you, neither the U.S. Embassy nor the Consulate General can guarantee the admission into Israel, the West Bank, Gaza Strip and Jericho area, or the Golan Heights of any traveler.

Visitors to Israel will experience strict security screening. They may be subject to prolonged questioning, detailed searches of their personal effects and, in some cases, body searches. Anything that cannot be readily examined, such as tubes of toothpaste, cans of shaving cream, computers, cameras, and other electronic or video equipment may be refused entity and may be confiscated and destroyed. If you plan to bring electronic, video, or other high-tech equipment to Israel, check with an Israeli embassy or consulate as to whether it could pass through security. Cameras should be empty when going through security so they can be opened for inspection. American citizens with Arab surnames, and in particular those seeking to enter Israel at the Allenby Bridge from Jordan, may encounter extra delays, including greater difficulty in bringing cameras and electronic equipment into the country,

Western dress is appropriate in Israel. At religious sites, attire should be modest. Religious holidays in Israel and Jerusalem are determined according to the Hebrew calendar and fall on different dates each year. It is likely that religious holidays in the Gaza Strip and Jericho area will be determined by the Moslem calendar, and also will fall on different dates each year. Because hotels are usually heavily booked before and during religious holidays, tourists should check holiday schedules with their travel agent or with the Embassy of Israel in Washington, D.C. Travelers should make reservations for holiday periods well in advance.

Dangerous Areas

On June 22,1994, the Department of State issued a public announcement advising U.S. citizens to avoid travel to the Gaza Strip and West Bank, except for daylight visits to Bethlehem, Jericho, Highway 1 from Jerusalem to the Dead Sea , Route 90 through the Jordan Valley, and tourist sites along these routes, because of continuing disturbances in those areas. Should you decide to travel to the West Bank despite the public announcement, register with the U.S. Consulate General in Jerusalem. In the case of travel to Gaza or the Golan Heights, register with the U.S. Embassy in Tel Aviv. The situation in East Jerusalem, including the old city, is unpredictable and Americans should check with the U.S. Consulate General in Jerusalem for an update on conditions. Avoid demonstrations and other situations that have the potential to lead to violence and remember to carry your U.S. passport with you at all times.

Persons who need to cross into Jordan via the West Bank can use the Allenby Bridge crossing near the city of Jericho or the Arava crossing located near Eilat in the southern part of the country. A new land crossing in the north, near the former location of the Sheik Hussein Bridge. is expected to open before the end of 1994.

Travelers wishing to cross via the Allenby Bridge need a bridge crossing permit and a visa. Neither of these is obtainable in Israel. Some travelers arrange the papers through contacts in Jordan or use travel agents in East Jerusalem who specialize in this service. It takes several weeks to get the crossing permits and visas in order. Visas are not available at the bridge. They must be obtained ahead of time. The Allenby Bridge is open from 0800 to 1200 Sunday through Thursday and from 0800 to 1000 on Friday. It is closed on Saturday and on many Israeli holidays.

Persons travelling on a U.S. passport who wish to travel via the Arava crossing do not need to have a previously obtained crossing permit or visa. Jordanian visas can be obtained at this crossing point for a fee of approximately $20 (U.S.). Israeli dual nationals with third country passports may use their other (e.g., U.S.) passport to obtain Israeli permission to exit Israel and apply for a Jordanian entry visa. Normally, all Israelis, including dual nationals, must use their Israeli passports to enter and exit Israel. Travelers are not allowed to bring their personal vehicles across the border unless the vehicles are registered in another country. The Arava crossing is open Sunday-Thursday from 0800 to 1600. Procedures for the Sheik Hussein

Bridge crossing when it becomes operable are expected to be similar to those for the **Arava** crossing.

A few areas in Israel are off-limits to unauthorized persons for military reasons. American visitors are expected to observe those off-limits restrictions.

Conditions along Israel's cease-fire lines, including the Lebanese border, change frequently. U.S. travelers planning a visit close to the lines should first consult the U.S. Embassy in Tel Aviv.

Dual Nationality
It is our understanding that Israeli citizens who are naturalized in the United States retain their Israeli citizenship, and their children are considered Israeli citizens as well. In addition, children born in the United States to Israeli parents acquire both U.S. citizenship and Israeli nationality at birth. Israeli citizens, including dual nationals, are subject to Israeli laws requiring service in Israel's armed forces. Dual nationals of military age who do not wish to serve in the Israeli armed forces should contact the Israeli Embassy to obtain proof of exemption or deferment from Israeli military service before traveling to Israel.

Departing Israel
Persons leaving Israel by air are subject to lengthy and detailed security questioning. Travelers should arrive at the airport several hours before flight time.

There is no departure tax when leaving Israel.

Jordan
Travelers wishing to cross the Allenby-King Hussein Bridge from Jordan into the West Bank territories occupied by Israel must obtain written authorization by submitting their passport and one photo, in person, to the Jordanian Ministry of Interior three working days before the crossing date. The permit allows you to cross the bridge and to make a return crossing within 30 days. The bridge is open from 0800 to 1200 Sunday through Thursday and from 0800 to 1000 on Friday. The bridge is closed Saturdays and on many Israeli holidays. Travelers should arrive at the bridge at least one hour before closing time.

Conservative dress is recommended for Jordan. Travelers with dual U.S. and Jordanian nationality should be aware that the Jordanian government may require them to enter and leave Jordan on a Jordanian passport. Males between the ages of 18 and 40 who possess dual nationality may need to prove that they have met their military service obligation. For further information, see the section on dual nationality on page 218.

Kuwait
Those traveling on a temporary or visitor visa to Kuwait must observe the length of stay permitted in their visas. Currently, most visitor visas are valid for one year, multiple entries, and stays of up to one month. Fines are charged for each day overstayed; the fine is currently 10 Kuwait dinars per day, per person (approximately $34 U.S.).

Visitors to Kuwait should be aware of the danger of unexploded land mines, bombs, and shells throughout the country. Stay on main roads, do not travel on unpaved roads, and avoid open areas and beaches.

The crime rate in Kuwait has increased from prewar levels and women have been objects of increased harassment. Woman should take precautions as they would in any large city, remaining alert to the possibility of being followed, whether they are walking or driving. They should not respond to any approach from strangers and should avoid travel alone in unfamiliar or isolated parts of the city, especially at night. Conservative dress is recommended for both men and women. Garments should fit loosely and cover elbows and knees.

No alcohol, pork products, or pornographic materials may be imported into or used in Kuwait. If customs official discover prohibited items in a traveler's effects, he or she may be arrested and prosecuted.

U.S. citizens should not go near the border with Iraq, and should be very careful when traveling north or west of Kuwait City. In recent years, a number of foreigners traveling near the border have been taken into custody by Iraqi officials and some have received lengthy prison sentences. Anyone who must travel or work near the demilitarized zone is strongly advised to contact the U.S. Embassy for further advice before their travel begins.

Lebanon
As of January 31, 1987, U.S. passports became invalid for travel to, in, or through Lebanon. U.S. citizens are advised to avoid all travel to Lebanon. The situation in the country is so dangerous that no U.S. citizen can be considered safe from terrorist acts. To avoid the possibility of transiting Lebanon, U.S. citizens should make certain that any international flight they book in the region does not make an intermediate stop in Beirut. Such stops are not always announced.

Individuals in the following categories are eligible for consideration for special passport validation: professional journalists, representatives of the American or International Red Cross, persons with compelling humanitarian considerations, or persons whose travel is determined to be in the national interest. Applications for exceptions to the U.S. passport restriction may be made following the procedures outlined on page 222 in the section on Iraq.

224

U.S. dual nationals do not violate U.S. law if they use a foreign passport for travel to Lebanon, but they are required to use their U.S. passport when they depart from and return to the United States. There are no U.S. Treasury restrictions on travel to Lebanon.

Travelers who are granted passport exceptions to travel to Lebanon should be aware that normal protection of U.S. diplomatic and consular representatives cannot be provided. The U.S. Embassy in Beirut is not fully staffed and its personnel operate under exceptionally tight security conditions. Local telephone service is unreliable, and it is extremely difficult to contact the U.S. Embassy or place a local call from most of the country.

Libya
On December 10, 1981, U.S. passports ceased to be valid for travel to, in, or through Libya unless a special validation has been obtained, and on January 8,1986, U.S. economic sanctions were imposed on Libya. In addition, on March 31,1992, United Nations sanctions were imposed. These sanctions include an air embargo which took effect April 15,1992. The categories of individuals eligible for consideration for special passport validation are professional journalists, representatives of the American or International Red Cross, persons with compelling humanitarian consider-ations, or persons whose travel is determined to be in the national interest.

All financial and commercial transactions with Libya are prohibited, unless licensed by the Office of Foreign Assets Control, U.S. Treasury Department. For the addresses to which applications can be made to overcome both the U.S. passport and the U.S. Treasury restrictions, see the section on Iraq, page 222.

Those persons granted exceptions to travel to Libya should be aware that there is no U.S. mission in Libya and U.S. interests are represented by the government of Belgium which can provide only limited protection for U.S. citizens.

Morocco
U.S. citizens do not require a visa for a tourist or business visit of up to 3 months.

Oman
There are no tourist visas to Orian, and visa requirements for business travelers are stringent. **Anyone arriving in Oman without a visa is subject to arrest.** A business visitor must contact an Omani sponsor, either a businessman or firm, for assistance in procuring a non-objection certificate (NOC). The sponsor should begin application procedures several weeks ahead of expected travel. American firms new to Oman may receive guidance on Omani sponsorship from the commercial office of the U.S. Embassy in Muscat. They should send a telex (TLX 3785 AMEMBMUS ON) describing their company's activities and what they expect to accomplish in Oman.

Relatives of Omanis may be sponsored for a short visit using the NOC procedure. Although Oman imposes stringent entry requirements for all visitors, it does not require exit permits. Conservative dress is recommended for Oman. No alcohol, firearms, pornography or fresh food may be imported.

Qatar
U.S. citizens must have a visa to enter Qatar. To receive a visa, an applicant must be sponsored by a resident of Qatar, a local business, or by the hotel at which he or she will be staying. After obtaining a sponsor, travelers may apply for visas at a Qatari embassy or consulate.

A sponsor can arrange to have a visa waiting for the U.S. traveler upon his or her **arrival** at Doha's International Airport. However, a traveler should ask his or her sponsor for written confirmation that an airport visa has been approved prior to departing for Qatar.

Passengers may transit Qatar without a visa if they continue their journey within 24 hours and have confirmed reservations on the same or the next available flight. Transit passengers may not leave the transit lounge of Doha Airport.

Qatar is a traditional Muslim country. Conservative dress and behavior are strongly recommended for all visitors. Travelers to Qatar may not bring in narcotics, weapons, items deemed pornographic, or pork products. Luggage is subject to careful inspection by customs officials.

Qatar's population is approximately 400,000, of whom an estimated 100,000 are Qataris. Serious crime is virtually unknown and medical facilities are adequate. Although Arabic is the official language, English is widely spoken.

Saudi Arabia
Nearly 36% of the inhabitants of Saudi Arabia are resident foreigners. This includes approximately 30,000 American citizens. English is acknowledged as a second language and is taught in the secondary schools.

Islam dominates all aspects of life in Saudi Arabia-

225

government policy, cultural norms, and social behavior. Islam is the only official religion of the country, and public observance of any other religion is forbidden. The Saudi government considers it a sacred duty to safeguard two of the greatest shrines of Islam, the holy mosques located in the cities of Mecca and Medina. Travel to Mecca and Medina is forbidden to non-Muslims. Muslims throughout the world turn to Mecca five times a day for prayer. Restaurants, stores, and other public places close for approximately a halfhour upon hearing the call to prayer, and Muslims stop their activities to pray during that time. Government and business activities are noticeably curtailed during the month of Ramadan, during the celebrations at the end of Ramadan, and during the time of the annual pilgrimage to Mecca, the Hajj. Travel facilities into, out of, and within Saudi Arabia are crowded during these periods.

Saudi Arabian Social Norms. U.S. citizens are advised that Saudi Arabia is a conservative country with a rigorous code of public behavior that everyone, including foreigners, is fully expected to observe. In particular, Westerners need to be aware of the standards of appropriate attire and the prohibition of mingling of the sexes in public places.

Dress. Although Westerners have some leeway in dress and social contacts within company residential compounds, both men and women should dress conservatively in public. Women's clothing should be loose fitting and concealing, with high necks, skirts worn well below the knee, and sleeves below the elbow. It is recommended that women not wear pants.

Social Behavior in Public. Females are prohibited from driving vehicles or riding bicycles on public roads, or in places where they might be observed. Males and females beyond childhood are not free to congregate together in most public places, and a man may be arrested for being seen with, walking with, traveling with, or driving a woman other than his wife or immediate relative. In Saudi Arabia, playing of music or dancing in public, mixed bathing, public showing of movies, and consumption of alcoholic beverages are forbidden.

Saudi religious police, known as Mutawwa, have been empowered to enforce the conservative interpretation of Islamic codes of dress and behavior for women, and may rebuke or harass women who do not cover their heads or whose clothing is insufficiently concealing. In addition, in more conservative areas, there have been incidents of private Saudi citizens stoning, accosting, or pursuing foreigners, including U.S. citizens, for perceived dress code or other infractions. While most

such incidents have resulted in little more than inconvenience or embarrassment for the individual targeted, there have been incidents where Westerners were physically harmed.

U.S. citizens in Saudi Arabia should be aware of Saudi social practices, and that any infractions may be dealt with aggressively. If you are accosted by Saudi authorities, cooperate fully in accordance with local customs and regulations. U.S. citizens who are harassed by private Saudi citizens or Saudi authorities should report the incidents immediately to the U.S. Embassy in Riyadh or the U.S. Consulate General either in Dhahran or in Jeddah.

Entry Visas and Requirements. The Saudi government **does not issue tourist visas.** It issues two types of entry visas: one for temporary business visits or to visit relatives, the other for individuals entering Saudi Arabia on an employment contract.

Temporary Visits. All applicants for temporary visitor visas for the purpose of business consultations must have a Saudi company **or** individual sponsor their applications. Individuals who wish to visit non-Saudi relatives must have their relatives' Saudi sponsor request authorization of their applications through the Saudi Foreign Ministry. **Persons present in Saudi Arabia** on **temporary visitor visas should not surrender their passports to the Saudi sponsor.** The passport and visa are the only evidence of the bearer's legal right to be present in the country. If an individual is present in the Kingdom on a temporary visitor visa and has obtained Saudi sponsorship for employment, he or she must exit Saudi Arabia to obtain an entry visa for employment. This visa need not be issued in the individual's country of origin, but the applicant must be physically present to apply for the visa.

Employment and Residence. Visas for employment and residence are obtained the same way as visas for temporary visits. Documentation, such as a letter from the sponsoring company, a copy of your signed contract, or a notarized copy of the your university degree may also be required. Before you sign a contract with a Saudi company, it is extremely important you obtain an independent English translation of the contract. The official and binding version of the contract that you sign is the Arabic text. Some Americans have signed contracts that in fact did not include all of the benefits they believed they were acquiring.

The employee's dependents (spouse and children under the age of 18) may be brought into Saudi Arabia only with the concurrence of the Saudi sponsor and authorization of the Foreign Ministry. Ordinarily, only managers and professionals (holders of college degrees) may bring their families. Children over age 18 are likely to be refused residence.

Exit Visas. Persons entering Saudi Arabia for the purpose of employment are issued residence permits (iqamas). These permits are evidence of legal residence in Saudi Arabia and must be retained at all times. Foreign residents are not permitted to travel between different major regions of Saudi Arabia unless permission is noted in their permits. A resident in Saudi Arabia may not depart the country under any circumstances, however exigent, without obtaining an exit visa. Exit visas are issued only upon request of the Saudi sponsor. US. consular officials are not able to 'sponsor' exit visas for Americans resident in Saudi Arabia under any circumstances. In a genuine emergency, however, consular officials will attempt to facilitate the Saudi sponsor's request for the exit visa.

Residents in Saudi Arabia are almost always required to surrender their passports, and those of their dependents, to the Saudi sponsor. This practice is specifically authorized in the Saudi employment law. If an urgent need for travel exists and if the Saudi sponsor will not release the first passport, the U.S. Embassy or Consulate can issue a replacement passport. The issuance of a replacement passport does not guarantee, however, that a person will be able to depart, since the replacement passport would not contain a Saudi residence permit or exit visa.

Mixed Marriages. A married woman residing with her Saudi husband should be aware that she, must have her husband's permission to depart or have their children depart from Saudi Arabia. This is true even if the woman or children are U.S. citizens. The husband is the sponsor of his foreign wife and of his children, and is, as such, the only individual who can request an exit visa for the wife or children.

Commercial and Business Disputes. Disputes between parties who do not have a signed formal contract must be settled through mutual agreement or through an appeal to the local governor (amir) for judgment. Such disputes usually involve business representatives on temporary visitor visas. Some Saudi business sponsors have gained possession of the passports of their visitors to use as leverage in disputes, but this is not authorized under Saudi law.

Commercial disputes between parties who have a formal contract can be brought to the Commercial Arbitration Board of the Saudi Chamber of Commerce or to the

Committee for the Settlement of Commercial Disputes in the Ministry of Commerce. Disputes involving a government agency may be brought before the Grievance Board, an autonomous court body under the Office of the King. Employer/employee disputes may be brought before the Committee for the Settlement of Labor Disputes in the Ministry of Labor. An amicable out-of court settlement is always the best and least expensive way to resolve a dispute, since referring matters to commercial or labor tribunals can be costly and time consuming.

Ultimate responsibility for obtaining private legal counsel and resolving a dispute through the Saudi legal system lies with the parties involved. Consular officers will offer lists of local attorneys to help settle such disputes. Business visitors should be, aware that if the Saudi party in a commercial dispute files a complaint with the authorities, Saudi law permits barring the exit of the foreign party until the dispute is completely settled, including payment of any damages.

Saudi law is applied exclusively in all commercial and contract dispute cases, even if the contract was drawn up and/or signed outside Saudi Arabia. Remember that the Arabic text of the contract or agreement is the text that is considered binding.

Customs Clearance. Customs clearance procedures in Saudi Arabia are formal, thorough, and lengthy and may involve a full search of every piece of luggage. Transit passengers who wish to leave the transit area of the airport are subject to the same strict searches as arriving passengers.

Vaccinations. Travelers to Saudi Arabia may wish to get a meningococcal vaccine prior to departure, and may be required to have one during the Hajj. Before traveling, consult the Centers for Disease Control for updated recommendations on this and other vaccines.

AIDS Clearance. All persons going to Saudi Arabia for purposes of employment are required to present a certification stating that they are free of the Acquired Immune Deficiency Syndrome virus. The test should be included as part of the global medical examination which is given to those who enter Saudi Arabia on a work permit. It is not required of travelers entering Saudi Arabia on a temporary visitor visa.

Photography. Visitors should not photograph mosques, people who are praying, military or government installations, and key industrial, communications, or transportation facilities. If you have any doubts about what you may photograph, request permission first

227

Alcohol and Drugs. Import, manufacture, possession, and consumption of alcoholic beverages or drugs are strictly forbidden. Saudi officials make no exceptions. Americans have spent up to a year in Saudi prisons for alcohol-related offenses. Americans have also been sentenced to receive 75 or more lashes in lieu of prison for failing a blood test for alcohol. Travelers should also exercise extreme care and discretion when consuming alcohol on flights landing in the Kingdom. Persons obviously inebriated are subject to arrest or deportation,

Many drugs sold with or without prescription in other countries may be illegal in Saudi Arabia. For instance, captagon (fenetylline hydrochloride), a drug used to treat exhaustion which is available without a prescription in some countries in Asia, is considered an illegal substance in Saudi Arabia. Americans in Saudi Arabia have received prison sentences of up to 2 1/2 months and 70 lashes for possession of captagon.

The attempted importation of drugs or controlled substances, even in very small amounts, is a serious offense under Saudi law. The traveler will be arrested and tried for carrying drugs into the country. Americans have served prisons sentences for drug possession or use. The death penalty for drug smugglers and traffickers convicted of a second offense underscores the gravity with which authorities treat drug offenses in the Kingdom. Customs authorities are now using dogs to detect drugs at Saudi airports.

Prescription drugs in small quantities, clearly labeled with the travelers name, doctor's name, pharmacy, and contents on the original container, should cause no problem. It is wise to carry a copy of the prescription as well. The importation of drugs in large amounts, however, can be done legally only through the Ministry of Health.

Other Forbidden Items. Items considered pornographic by Saudi standards, including magazines and video cassettes, are strictly forbidden. It is also illegal to import firearms of any type, ammunition, related items such as gunsights and gun magazines, food items, and banned books.

Personal religious items such as a Bible or a rosary are usually permitted, but travelers should be aware that on occasion, these items have been seized at entry and not returned to the traveler.

Pets. Most pets, except dogs, may be brought into the country provided they are accompanied by a health certificate authenticated by the Saudi consulate in the country of origin. Dogs are banned with the exception of guard dogs, hunting dogs, and seeing-eye dogs. Dogs in these excepted categories must be accompanied by a health certificate and a certificate authenticated by the Saudi consulate in the country of origin that attests that the dog fits into one of the exempt categories.

Syria

All visitors to Syria must have a valid Syrian visa on arrival in the country. Although airport visas are technically available, they are virtually unattainable.

Syrian law does not recognize the U.S. citizenship of a naturalized Syrian unless the Syrian government has given that person permission to renounce Syrian nationality. U.S.-Syrian dual nationals who have not received that permission are considered Syrian when they enter Syria even when they enter on their U.S. passports. A Syrian male cannot leave the country until he has satisfied the requirement for military service. (Syrian-American males who have not completed the obligatory military service, but who wish to visit Syria should contact the Syria Embassy in Washington for more information.) This does not apply to a man who is the only son in a family, but it applies to all other men of normal military service age or older. Any person, male or female, who is considered Syrian may take no more than $2,000 worth of convertible currency out of Syria, no matter how much they may have brought into the country. U.S. citizens of Syrian origin may experience difficulties if they remain in Syria after the expiration of their visas. If you are a dual national, check with the Syrian Embassy on the obligations of Syrian citizenship before you visit Syria.

Travelers may bring any amount of currency into Syria. Syrian law does not require currency to be declared unless the total is more than $5,000. It is wise, however, to declare any currency you have, because you can not take currency out of Syria unless it has been declared upon arrival. There are two rates of exchange in Syria. In addition to the official rate, Syrian pounds may be purchased at the more favorable 'neighboring country rate' at the Syrian Commercial Bank or at a major hotel if you have convertible currency in cash or travelers checks. Hotel bills must be paid in convertible currency or with Syrian pounds obtained at the official rate from the Commercial Bank of Syria (receipt required). Meals and all other purchases can be paid for with Syrian pounds and do not require official rate certification. Credit card charges may be figured at either the official rate or the neighboring country rate. Travelers should check which rate will apply before making any credit card purchase.

Syrian pounds cannot be taken out of Syria. Travelers

cannot convert Syrian pounds back into convertible currency, and should therefore not purchase more of the currency than they expect to spend in Syria.

Conservative dress is recommended for Syria. Travelers should exercise caution when photographing historic sites. Photographs may be taken of regular tourist attractions, such as ancient ruins and temples, but warnings are issued against photographing government buildings, government property, and anything other than tourist sites.

Tunisia

U.S. citizens do not need a visa for a tourist or business visit of up to four months, but must possess return or onward tickets. No local currency may be imported or exported.

As of August 1991, naturalized U.S. citizens of Tunisian origin are no longer required to have a Tunisian travel document in order to depart from Tunisia. They may enter and depart Tunisia on their U.S. passport.

United Arab Emirates

The United Arab Emirates (U.A.E.) is a federation of seven independent emirates. Visitors to the U.A.E. must obtain a visa before arrival. Some of the Emirates allow hotels or airlines to sponsor persons entering for short visits. Persons who overstay their visas are subject to fines and/or imprisonment. Both penalties have been imposed on U.S. citizens.

The U.A.E. prohibits the import of pornography controlled substances, firearms, ammunition, or items capable of being used as weapons. Videotapes will be screened by customs officials, an often lengthy process, and may be confiscated. Non-Muslims may consume alcohol in licensed **Bars or restaurants**.

Visitors may apply for a temporary U.A.E. driver's licence upon presentation of a valid U.S. license. There are strict penalties for persons involved in traffic accidents while under the influence of alcohol, including lashings for Muslims.

Women residing in the U.A.E. do not require their husband's permission to travel abroad, but a husband may block his wife's departure by submitting her name to immigration authorities. The U.A.E. does not recognize dual nationality, and U.A.E. citizenship is transmitted through the father regardless of the child's place of birth. Dual national children generally must enter and depart the U.A.E. using their U.A.E. passports.

Yemen

Conditions in Yemen remain unsettled due to to recent end of Yemen's civil war. Ordnance such mines, left over from the war, may pose a hazard to travelers. U.S. citizens should exercise caution in Yemen and avoid travel in remote areas. Local tribal disputes have occasionally led to violence Westerners, including U.S. citizens, have been kidnapped as a result of such local disputes, an vehicles have been hijacked. Urban violence and crime is a growing problem in Yemen, including within the capital, Sanaa.

Visitor visas, which are usually valid for entry up to one month, are required. Entry to Yemen may be denied to persons with passports showing Israeli visas or entry/exit stamps.

Because of the 7200 feet altitude of Sanaa and the lack of adequate medical facilities, travelers may wish to consult their physicians before visiting Yemen. Independent travel in Yemen is difficult it is advisable to arrange your trip though a travel agent. Photography of military installations, equipment, or troops is forbidden.

Foreign Embassies in the United States

[For a complete listing of foreign embassies in the United States see **Appendix B**.]

U.S. Embassies and Consulates Abroad

[For a complete listing of United States embassies and consulates abroad, including their addresses, telephone, fax, and telex numbers see **Appendix A**].

Planning Another Trip?

See Chapter 46 for a listing of resources available to the general traveler from the U.S. Departments of State, Customs, Transportation, Health and various government and non-government organizations. All of the available International travel-related pamphlets, brochures and publications issued by the U.S. Department of State and by U.S. Customs have been reproduced in full in this book. See Table of Contents for location.

~ ~ ENDNOTES ~ ~

1.   A large portion of this booklet has been reproduced verbatim elsewhere in this book, including a country by country listing of vaccination requirements.

Chapter 20

Tips for Travelers to Russia and the Independent States

[The information in this chapter is reprinted verbatim from a bulletin issued by the
U.S. State Department, Bureau of Consular Affairs. It is intended to serve as advice
to Americans traveling abroad.]

- - - -

Armenia, Azerbaijan, Belarus, Estonia, Georgia, Latvia, Lithuania, Moldova, Kazakhstan, Kyrgyzstan, Russia, Tajikistan, Turkmenistan, Ukraine, Uzbekistan.

FOREWORD
You have chosen a challenging and exciting time to visit Russia or any of the other countries of the former Soviet Union. Because travel conditions are changing rapidly in these countries, you will need to research and plan your visit carefully and, in addition, be patient and flexible once you are underway in order to have a successful and pleasurable trip.

We have prepared this text to help acquaint you with the areas you will visit. Because so much is changing in the region, some of our information may be obsolete by the time you read this. To assist you further, we also have more up-to-date information-see the section beow to learn how to access the Consular Information Sheet for any of the countries you plan to visit.

We wish you an enjoyable trip. Remember that if you have difficulties abroad on your trip, contact the U.S consul at the nearest U.S embassy or consulate.

Introduction
In December 1991, the Soviet Union was dissolved. In its place emerged 12 independent countries: Armenia, Azerbaijan, Belarus, Georgia, Kazakhstan, Kyrgyzstan, Moldova, Russia, Tajikistan, Turkmenistan, Ukraine, and Uzbekistan. The information in this pamphlet is mainly on Russia. However, much of the information and particularly the sections on health, safety, and travel planning is applicable to the other former Soviet republics.

Consular Information Sheets
To find specific travel information for any country you plan to visit, see the Department of State Consular Information Sheet for the country. Consular Information Sheets contain information on such matters as the location and telephone number of the nearest U.S. embassy, crime problems, and health or security

problems that may affect travel.

In addition to Consular Information Sheets, Travel Warnings may also be issued about certain countries. Travel Warnings advise Americans to defer travel to all or part of a country. There are several ways to access Consular Information Sheets and Travel Warnings. You can listen to them 24 hours a day by calling 202-647-5225 from a touchtone phone. You can receive

copies of them by sending a self-addressed, stamped envelope to the Citizens Emergency Center, Room 4800, Department of State Washington, D.C. 20520-4818. (Write the name of the requested country or countries on the outside of the envelope.)

You can also find Consular Information Sheets and Travel Warnings posted at the 13 regional passport agencies and at American embassies and consulates abroad. They can also be accessed through an airline or travel agent's computer reservation system or by computer through many electronic bulletin boards.

Geography
Russia is the largest country that emerged from the former U.S.S.R. It stretches from the Baltic Sea, across the northern Eurasian landmass, to the Bering Strait where a Russian island lies only three miles from an island that is part of Alaska. Russia and the other republics of the former Soviet Union are going through profound political and economic changes. At present, the tourism industry, like other industries that were strictly regulated in the former USSR, is undergoing a transformation that can be confusing to customers as well as to the industry itself. Throughout the entire former Soviet region, major structures of civil authority and service organizations are either being replaced by new bodies or are withering away without replacement. In addition to Consular Information Sheets, a good source of information on current conditions is Intourist, telephone 212-757-3884. Before 1991, Intourist was the official and only Soviet tour operator. It is now a non-governmental body and is still by far the largest tour operator in Russia and the other 11 former Soviet republics. Intourist has contracts with a large network

of hotels and restaurants, but it must now compete with other Russian tour operators such as Sputnik and Intratours. There are also a number of specialized tour operators. For example, the Host Family Association and Wild World specialize in, respectively, stays with families and adventure tours. You can book travel with Russian tour operators through U.S. travel agents.

Before You Go

Visas
A U.S. citizen must have a valid U.S. passport and a visa to travel to any country of the former USSR. At present, only Russia and Ukraine are issuing visas. At the time of publication, the other countries of the former USSR had either not established embassies in the United States or, in the case of Armenia and Belarus, had opened embassies but were not yet issuing visas. To travel to a country of the former USSR that is not yet issuing visas, a Russian visa is still required, and it is valid for all such countries. At present, travel between countries that require a Russian visa is still considered internal travel by local authorities, and passports are not normally checked upon arrival or departure.

You may obtain a visa for Ukraine from the Ukrainian Embassy (see **Appendix B**). All of the following visa information pertains to Russian visas. Travelers arriving without a visa in a country that requires a Russian visa cannot register at a hotel and must leave the country immediately by the same route they entered. Even for a brief transit, you must have a visa. If possible, obtain your Russian visa in the United States, because a Russian visa can be difficult and time-consuming to obtain abroad. In some countries like Ukraine, Estonia, and Lithuania, you cannot obtain a Russian visa.

Visas are valid for specific dates. Before starting on your trip, be sure your visa is valid for the dates of your planned entry and departure. Delays caused by illness or changes in plans must be approved in advance by the office that issued your visa. The categories of Russian visa that a U.S. citizen can apply for are transit, tourist, business, or, for a private visit to friends or relatives, a visitor or 'homestay' visa.

Tourist, Business, and Transit Visas
Most travelers to Russia and the other countries of the former USSR arrange for their visas and accommodations through an American travel agent. A business visa requires a letter of invitation from your foreign business contact. A transit visa requires a copy of your confirmed ticket and visa (if required) to your onward destination.

Visitor or 'Homestay' Visas
Visas for private trips to stay in a private home are issued by the consular division of either the Russian Embassy in Washington, DC or the Russian Consulate general in either San Francisco or New York. You may request application forms by mail. The person you wish to visit must also apply for permission well in advance of your visit. In larger cities, your host can apply at the local visa office (called OVIR, an acronym for Otdel Viz i Registratsii). In smaller towns, your host can apply to the local police. OVIR or police consideration of these applications can be a slow process. Upon approval of your application, your host will be issued a notification of permission (izveshcheniye) for your visit. Your host should send this notification to you.

Private Visits During Group Tours
An American traveling on a group tour may request permission to visit local acquaintances or take short individual excursions away from the group itinerary to places of personal interest. Arrangements for side trips should be made through your American travel agent and, if possible, before you leave the United States. On your visa application, include the names and addresses of those citizens of countries of the former USSR whom you hope to visit.

How to Obtain Visa Information
You can obtain visa information from your travel agent. However, authoritative information on visas can only be obtained from the embassies or consulates of the countries you plan to visit. Whatever your source, make certain that your visa information is up to date, because, during this period of transition, visa requirements will change frequently. When you inquire about visas, ask about price, length of validity, and the number of entries that are permitted.

Your U.S. Passport

Theft of U.S. passports continues to increase rapidly. Stolen passports are reportedly sold for large sums of hard currency. The theft or loss of a passport, particularly when the nearest U.S. consular office is hundreds or thousands of miles away, is a major source of inconvenience and expense to travelers in Russia and the other countries of the former USSR. Before starting your trip, make a record or photocopy of the data from your passport's identification page and from your visa(s). Also make a copy of the addresses and telephone numbers of the U.S. embassies and consulates in the countries you will visit (see **Appendix A**). Put this information along with two passport photos in a place separate from your passport to be available in case of loss or theft.

Leave a second copy of your passport information and your itinerary with a relative or friend in the U.S. Complete the address page of your passport in pencil and update it as necessary.

While in the former Soviet Union, you may be asked to turn over your passport to hotel personnel or a tour leader for short periods of time for registration with police or for other purposes. Your passport should be returned within two or three days. Be sure to safeguard your passport at all other times, as its loss can cause you delays and problems. If your passport is lost or stolen, you must apply for a replacement passport at a U.S. embassy or consulate and then obtain a new or duplicate visa from the nearest visa office (OVIR). If you are with a tour, your guide can assist you with the visa.

Planning Your Trip
Many geographic names throughout the region are being changed. Try to obtain maps before your trip, but keep in mind that some names of places may be out of date. You may need to correct city names and even some street names. In these countries, if your street sign does not agree with your map, you may not be lost, you may just be dealing with a new name.

Previously, in the former Soviet Union, departure and arrival times for planes, trains, and boats were quoted in Moscow time. In the post-Soviet period, that practice has changed, and timetables for travel in and between former Soviet countries usually use local time. Within Russia itself, however, you may still find Moscow time in use--regardless of which of the 11 time zones you are in. Whenever you make reservations or purchase tickets, learn which time zones the schedule refers to and, as you travel, confirm all departure and arrival times.

Air Travel Within Russia
Aeroflot still dominates air travel in Russia and the region. Although many international airlines have flights to Russia and the other former Soviet republics, and some, like Turkish Airlines, even have flights between a few of the countries, the **domestic service** of Aeroflot is still the major carrier in and **between** the countries of the former USSR. Since late 1991, domestic Aeroflot flights have been delayed for hours or days and sometimes canceled because of jet fuel shortages. Travelers should be prepared for long waits or for the possibility that their itineraries will have to be changed with little or no advance notice.

In the United States, booking domestic Aeroflot flights can be difficult. You may discover, once you are in Russia or

another country of the former USSR, that a domestic Aeroflot flight you booked does not exist, or at least does not exist on the day you are confirmed to go. Or, before you leave the U.S., you may be told flights do not exist to a certain city, when in fact they do. Because of the difficulty in using Aeroflot's domestic service, it is advisable to use international carriers, including Aeroflot, wherever possible when planning your itinerary. While Aeroflot is in transition to meet international standards, flexibility and patience are the keys to successful air travel in Russia and all countries of the former USSR.

Overland Travel
It is a good idea when traveling by train or automobile in former Soviet countries to bring food and water with you.

If you travel overland between Central European countries and countries of the former USSR, be certain that you have visas for all countries through which you will pass. For example, the train from Warsaw, Poland to Vilnius, Lithuania passes through Grodno, Belarus, and transit visas are not available on the train. On occasion, Americans have been required to leave the train in Grodno and return to their point of departure to obtain a Russian visa for Belarus. (There is a direct rail route, however, that does not pass through Belarus. It goes to Sestokai, Lithuania via Suwalki, Poland.)

Auto Travel
Driving conditions in Russia and the other former Soviet republics are more rugged than in Western Europe, service stations are few, and fuel may be scarce at those stations. Adhere to all local driving regulations. They are strictly enforced and violators are subject to legal penalties. All tourists entering Russia by automobile are required to sign an obligation guaranteeing the re-export of their automobiles. This obligation also applies to damaged vehicles.

Auto Insurance
Your automobile should be fully insured under a policy valid for Russia and for any other country you will enter. Insurance policies may be purchased from Lloyds of London or from In-**gosstrakh,** Kuybyshev Street 11/10, Moscow, a Russian organization that insures foreigners. Auto insurance obtained in Russia is still accepted in some of the other former Soviet republics. Be aware that Russian law allows the company to refuse compensation for damage if a driver is pronounced by the authorities to be under the influence of alcohol at the time of an accident. Such determinations can be made without the benefit of any tests.

233

HEALTH

Precautions

Travel in the former USSR can be strenuous, particularly for the elderly and individuals with special health problems. When you plan your trip, be careful not to overschedule; leave time for rest and relaxation. **Tourists in frail health are strongly advised not to visit.**

Immunizations

No immunizations are required for travelers to the former Soviet Union. However, diphtheria, tetanus, polio, typhoid, and gamma globulin are recommended for the region and in particular for the Central Asian countries.

Review Your Health Insurance Policy

If your insurance does not cover you abroad, consider purchasing temporary insurance that does. In addition to medical insurance, consider obtaining insurance to cover evacuation in the event of an accident or serious illness. Because conditions in many hospitals are not adequate to ensure recovery, medical evacuation is frequently necessary for illnesses or injuries which could be treated locally in other countries. Minimum cost from Moscow to New York on a stretcher is more than $10,000. Medical evacuation by hospital aircraft on the same route approaches $100,000. Insurance companies as well as some credit card and travelers check companies offer short-term health and emergency assistance policies designed for travelers. Ask your travel agent about them or look for ads in travel publications.

Bring Your Own Medicines

Bring with you any necessary medications and keep them in their **original, labeled** containers in your hand luggage. Because of strict laws on narcotics, carry a letter from your physician explaining your need for any prescription drugs in your possession. Also bring along any toiletries and personal hygiene items that you will need. These items can be difficult to find in major cities and even more scarce elsewhere.

About Medical Care in the Region

Medical care in the former Soviet Union does not meet Western standards. There is a severe shortage of basic medical supplies, including disposable needles, anesthetics, common medications, and antibiotics. X-rays are of poor quality, and advanced diagnostic equipment, such as CAT scan machines, is not widely available. Patient support services, including basic hygiene measures, are inadequate, and travelers may expect the length of hospitalization to exceed the duration of stay they would expect in Western facilities.

In addition, full, frank, and empathic discussions between doctor and patient are hampered by language barriers as well as the lack of a tradition of patient rights. If you need medical care, ask your hotel or tour guide to direct you to an appropriate facility. You may also contact the nearest U.S. embassy or consulate for a list of local medical services.

Drinking Water

The U.S. Public Health Service warns that many U.S. visitors to Russia, particularly to St. Petersburg, have returned to the United States infected with the intestinal parasite Giardia lamblia. This infection is probably contracted by drinking tap water. Some travelers to Russia and surrounding countries bring drinking water with them in their luggage. If you cannot import your drinking water, drink only bottled carbonated drinks or beverages that have been boiled for at least five minutes. Avoid ice cubes, use bottled water for brushing teeth, and avoid salads or uncooked vegetables and fruits which cannot be peeled. In addition, carry iodine tablets to disinfect drinking water. Travelers returning from the region who develop a diarrheal illness lasting more than five days should consult a physician and have a stool specimen examined for parasites.

The Chernobyl Nuclear Accident of April 1986

Recent tap water samples from Moscow, St. Petersburg, and Kiev show no detectable radiation. Background radiation levels in areas outside the immediate accident site and fallout path have been tested periodically and are considered to be within acceptable ranges. Access to the Chernobyl zone is strictly controlled by Ukrainian authorities.

Currency

Russia, like the other 11 countries of the former Soviet Union, has a cash-only economy. During periodic cash shortages, it can be difficult to impossible to cash travelers checks for dollars, for other convertible (hard) currency, or even for rubles. The fee to cash travelers checks may be high (for example, 5%). In Moscow, cash may be available at Dialogbank or American Express. In St. Petersburg, rubles may be available but not hard currency. In Kiev, cash may be available at the Agroprombank, Export/Import Bank, or Bank Ukraina.

Some travelers avoid a number of the difficulties of the currency shortage by taking a prepaid tour that includes all meals and hotels. Travelers find it useful to bring major credit cards because they are accepted at some hotels and restaurants, particularly those in Moscow. Most travelers, however, solve the problem of the currency shortage by coming to Russia and the other former Soviet republics with a sufficient supply of hard currency to cover their obligations in the country. Some hotel restaurants and shops will accept payment **only in dollars or other hard currency. Beware! Make it your practice to keep your excess cash in the hotel safe.**

Before you leave home, check with your credit card and travelers check companies to learn where these instruments can be used in the former Soviet Union.

Customs and currency laws are strict. When you arrive, make an accurate and complete customs declaration of all money, travelers checks, and valuables in your possession. Include all personal jewelry, such as wedding rings and watches. Have your customs declaration stamped by the authorities and keep it with you until you leave the country. Keep your exchange receipts in order to account for your expenditures. Without these records, customs officials could confiscate your cash and valuables upon departure.

The Russian ruble is still the currency of the 12 former Soviet republics. In Ukraine, 'coupons' have been introduced in preparation for issuing a national currency. The coupons are used in Ukraine along with the Russian ruble, but cannot be used outside of the country.

Customs Regulations
Attempts to bring any of the following articles into the former Soviet Union have caused difficulties for U.S. citizens in the past:

Narcotics - Drug laws are strict. U.S. citizens have received long sentences for trying to enter or transit with illegal narcotics.

Pornography - Magazines with sexually explicit photographs, that may be considered commonplace in Western countries, may be regarded as pornography and are often confiscated.

Gifts for Persons in the Former USSR - A high rate of customs duty may be assessed on gifts that you bring into a foreign country. U.S. citizens have had to abandon gifts at the airport because they lacked funds to pay the customs duty.

Video Cassettes - Customs regulations allow for the import and re-export of a limited number of blank or commercially recorded video cassettes for personal use. Some travelers with a large number of cassettes have had them confiscated upon departure. Travelers are advised to leave blank video cassettes sealed in their wrappers when entering a country.

Customs regulations prohibit the import or export, of personally recorded video cassettes. To avoid confiscation of valuable travel memories, travelers should either leave those cassettes some place, outside of the country to be picked up later or mail them home before entering the country.

Legal Matters

Dual Nationality
Russia's new citizenship law that went into effect February 6, 1992, recognizes dual nationality only if there is an agreement between the two countries that covers dual nationality. At this time, the United States and Russia do not have a dual nationality agreement. This means that if you are a dual national and encounter problems in Russia, you may not be permitted to leave and the ability of a U.S. consul to assist you may be limited.

The U.S. government has notified the governments of the Soviet successor states that the U.S. government considers the U.S.-USSR consular convention of 1968 to be still in force. The United States recognizes as an established principle of international law that every sovereign state has the right to decide under the provisions of its own laws who is and who is not its citizen. The Department of State maintains the following:

- U.S. citizens, whether by birth or naturalization, possess full American citizenship and its accompanying benefits and responsibilities despite any additional entitlement to other citizenship.

- A U.S. citizen entering a country of the former USSR with a U.S. passport and a valid visa is to be regarded as a U.S. citizen by that country for purposes of the visit, regardless of whether the foreign government might also consider them to be their citizen.

- U.S. citizens cannot lose their U.S. citizenship because of automatic acquisition of foreign citizenship. However, if a U.S. citizen contemplates voluntarily accepting dual nationality in connection with assuming duties as a government official in one of the Soviet successor states, he or she should first consult with the Department of State's Office of Citizens Consular Services on (202) 647-3445 or with the nearest U.S. embassy or consulate.

The countries of the former USSR generally do not prevent a U.S. citizen possessing a U.S. passport and appropriate visas from visiting those countries and returning to the United States, or to his or her country of permanent residence, even if under foreign laws he or she is considered a citizen of a Soviet successor state. **Any dual national U.S. citizen traveling in Russia or any other country of the former Soviet Union should contact the nearest U.S. embassy or consulate immediately if any question arises about his or her U.S. or foreign citizenship.**

To avoid any possible inconvenience or uncertainty, the Department of State urges any U.S. citizen who is or believes they may be a citizen of a country of the former USSR to consider formally renouncing that citizenship before visiting any of the former Soviet republics. For information on how to renounce foreign citizenship, contact, in the United States, the embassy or consulate of the country concerned before traveling.

In any case, possible dual nationals who travel to Russia or any of the other countries of the former Soviet Union should register upon arrival in writing or in person at the Consular Section of the nearest U.S. embassy or consulate. Give your full name, passport number, date and place of birth, occupation, hotel and room number, phone number, purpose and dates of your visit, home address, and the name, address, and telephone number of any relatives that you have in the countries of the former Soviet Union.

Permanent legal U.S. residents should travel with appropriate documentation of their legal permanent residence status in the U.S. Those who are citizens of a country of the former Soviet Union should ensure that they have the correct entry/exit permission from the Russian or other appropriate embassy in the United States before they travel.

Adopting A child Abroad

Current law allows adoptions in Russia and Ukraine, although U.S. citizens report the process in these republics to be long and difficult. The status of adoptions in Armenia, Azerbaijan, Belarus, Georgia, Kazakhstan, Kyrgyzstan, Moldova, Tajikistan, Turkmenistan, and Uzbekistan remains uncertain.

Russia has established a quasi-governmental bureaucratic structure in an attempt to regulate foreign adoptions. The agency, "Rights of the Child" (Pravo Rebyonka), was formed to coordinate international adoptions, ensure that Russian legal procedures are followed, and establish a centralized data bank for information on Russian children adoptable by foreigners.

U.S. citizens interested in adopting a child from one of the countries of the former Soviet Union are encouraged to contact the U.S. embassy or consulate in that country, or, in the United States, the Department of State's Office of Citizens Consular Services on 202 647-3444 to obtain information on the adoption process in that country.

While You Are Abroad

Registration

All U.S. citizens who visit Russia or any of the other countries of the former Soviet Union are ,encouraged to register in writing or in person at the nearest U.S. embassy or consulate (see **Appendix A** for a listing). Registration is especially important if you are in an area experiencing civil unrest or a natural disaster, if you are going to a place where communications are poor, or if you plan to stay for any length of time. Registration takes only a few moments, and it may be invaluable in case of an emergency. If your passport is lost or stolen, having previously registered at an embassy or consulate can make it easier to issue you a new passport without a delay.

Safety Tips Against Crime

In Russia and much of the rest of the former USSR, crimes such as robbery, mugging, and pickpocketing are an increasing problem for tourists, particularly in cities and around major tourist sites.

Crimes are perpetrated not only by adults, but also by adolescents or even children, often operating in groups.

Crime aboard trains has also increased. For example, travelers have been drugged without their knowledge and robbed on the train from Moscow to St. Petersburg. Crime is also a problem on trains between Moscow and Warsaw and armed robberies have occurred on the trains, between Moscow and Ulaanbaatar, Mongolia. On some trains, thieves have been able to open locked compartment doors.

Although officials in Russia have expressed willingness to cooperate with U.S. officials in emergencies involving U.S. citizens, communications and transportation can be slow and difficult, and the nearest U.S. embassy or consulate may be more than a day's travel away. To reduce the risk of becoming a victim of crime, exercise the same precautions that you would in any large city and follow these tips:

■ Safety begins when you pack. Leave expensive jewelry, unnecessary credit cards, and anything you would hate to lose at home.

- Never display large sums of money when paying a bill. Conceal your passport, cash, and other valuables on your person. Do not trust waist packs or fanny packs because pickpockets have learned that is where the valuables are.

- Do not leave valuables in your hotel room, have them locked in the hotel safe.

- Be vigilant on public transport and at tourist sites, food markets, flea markets, art exhibitions, and all places where crowds gather.

- Even slight intoxication is noted by professional thieves. Therefore, if you drink in a public place, do so only with a trusted friend who has agreed to remain sober.

- If you are the victim of crime, report it immediately to the local police and to the nearest U.S. embassy or consulate. It is worthwhile to report a theft, because stolen items are sometimes retrieved.

Russian Law

How to Avoid Legal Problems

While in a foreign country, a U.S. citizen is subject to its laws and regulations. Laws in the countries of the former Soviet Union can differ significantly from those in the United States and do not afford the protections available to the individual under U.S. law. Exercise caution and carefully obey local laws. Penalties for breaking the law can be more severe than in the United States for similar offenses. Persons violating the law, even unknowingly, may have difficulties with the authorities and may be expelled and forced to forfeit the unused part of a pre-purchased tour. Serious transgressions of the law can lead to arrest and imprisonment.

Under Article 12 of the U.S.-USSR Consular Convention of 1968 (which the U.S. considers to still be in force, see pages 235-236), government authorities in the Soviet successor states are required to immediately inform the U.S. Embassy or consulate of the arrest or detention of a U.S. citizen and to permit, without delay, communication with the detained citizen. If you are detained by authorities, ask that a U.S. consular officer be informed and that you be allowed to meet with a U.S. consular officer without delay.

Avoid breaking the law. Never take 'souvenirs' from local hotels, no matter how insignificant in value they may appear. Pay for your souvenirs, handicrafts, or artwork in local currency, because most vendors do not have permission to accept dollars or other hard currency. Travelers have been arrested by plainclothes police after paying for a souvenir with hard currency. The traveler is usually released after several hours of detention, but both the hard currency and the item purchased are usually confiscated. Only special tourist stores, usually found in large hotels, are permitted to accept hard currency.

Marriage Abroad

Americans contemplating marriage to a citizen of the former Soviet Union should contact the Consular Section of the nearest American embassy or consulate before the marriage takes place. Consular officers cannot perform marriages, but can provide information about local regulations concerning marriage.

Photography Restrictions

Regulations on photography are strict, particularly regarding military installations. Because of unwitting violations of these regulations, U.S. citizens have had film confiscated, have been temporarily detained or interrogated, and have even been asked to leave the country. Be sure that your photographs do not contain forbidden subjects, not even in the background. When in doubt, ask your tour guide or someone else in authority.

1. Photographs are permitted of architectural monuments; cultural, educational, and medical buildings; theaters; museums; parks; stadiums; streets and squares; and living quarters and landscape scenes which do not include subjects listed below under item 3.

2. If prior permission is obtained from officials of the institution concerned, photographs may be taken of industrial enterprises which manufacture non-military products, farms, railroad stations, airports, river ports, and governmental, educational, and social organizations.

3. All photographs are prohibited within the 25 kilometer-wide border zones, except in those portions not closed to foreigners. Photographs of the following are forbidden: all military objects, institutions, and personnel; storage facilities for combustibles; seaports; hydroelectric installations (sluices); pumping stations; dams; railroad junctions; railroad and highway bridges; industrial, scientific, and research establishments; electric, telephone, and telegraph stations; and radio facilities. Photographs from airplanes and panoramic shots of industrial cities are prohibited.

4. Foreigners may not mail exposed film out of Russia.

Shopping-- Be Wary of antiques
Artwork, souvenirs, and handicrafts purchased at special stores for tourists may be taken out of Russia and the other former Soviet republics. However, antiques (defined as virtually anything which may be deemed of historical or cultural value) and artifacts, including samovars, purchased at regular stores and secondhand shops often may not be taken out of these countries without inspection by local cultural authorities and payment of substantial export duty. This procedure is almost prohibitively cumbersome and time consuming. Samovars not purchased at tourist stores and not cleared by cultural authorities are normally confiscated at pre-departure customs inspections.

Areas of Instability, The political situation remains particularly unsettled in Russia's Caucasus area, which is located in Southern Russia along its border with Georgia and Azerbaijan. Travel to this area is considered dangerous. Travel to the Chechen Republic, in particular, is considered extremely dangerous, due to ongoing armed conflict between Russian military forces and Chechen nationalists. The Ingush Republic and the North Ossetian Republic have also experienced continued armed violence and have a state of emergency and curfew in effect. Street demonstrations. which sometimes turn violent, may occur without warning, though announcements of demonstrations in Moscow are usually carried on local English-language radio news programs.

Medical Facilities: Medical care in Russia is usually far below Western standards, with severe shortages of basic medical supplies. Access to the few quality facilities that exist in major cities usually requires payment in cash at western rates upon admission. The U.S. Embassy and consulates maintain lists of such facilities and English-speaking doctors. Many resident Americans travel to the West for virtually all their medical needs; such travel can be very expensive if undertaken under emergency conditions. Travelers may wish to check their insurance coverage and consider supplemental coverage for medical evacuation. Elderly travelers and those with existing health problems may be at particular risk.

Health Concerns: Outbreaks of diphtheria have been reported in Moscow, St. Petersburg, and other parts of Russia. The Centers for Disease Control recommend up-to-date diphtheria immunizations before traveling to Russia. Typhoid can be a concern for those who plan to travel extensively in Russia. Drinking only boiled or bottled water will help guard against cholera, which has been reported, as well as other diseases. More complete and updated information on health matters can be obtained from the Centers for Disease Control's international travelers hotline, tel: (404) 332-4559.

Crime Information: Crime against foreigners in Russia continues to increase. especially in major cities. Pickpocketings, assaults and robberies occur both day and night, and most frequently on city streets, in underground walkways and the subway, on intercity trains, especially the Moscow - St. Petersburg overnight train; in train stations and airports; at markets, tourist attractions and restaurants, and in hotel rooms and residences, even when locked or occupied. Members of religious and missionary groups have been robbed by people pretending to be interested in their beliefs. Groups of children are known to assault and rob foreigners on city streets or underground walkways. Foreigners who have been drinking alcohol are especially vulnerable to assault and robbery in or around night clubs or bars, or on their way home. Robberies may occur in taxis shared with strangers. Traffic police sometimes stop motorists to extract cash "fines" and bandits prey on travelers on the highway between St. Petersburg and Vyborg. Travelers have found it safer to travel in groups organized by reputable tour agencies as solo travelers are more vulnerable to crime.

Crime Against Foreign Businesses: Extortion and corruption permeate the business environment in Russia. Organized criminal groups target foreign businesses in many Russian cities and reportedly demand protection money under threat of serious violence. Many western companies hire security services, but this has not always proven effective in avoiding armed extortion attempts.

Currency Exchange: Travelers checks and credit cards are not widely accepted in Russia; credit cards are only accepted at establishments catering to Westerners. Old, or very worn dollar bills are often not accepted, even at banks. Major hotels or the American Express offices in Moscow or St. Petersburg may be able to suggest locations for cashing travelers checks or obtaining cash advances on credit cards. Western Union has agents in Moscow, St. Petersburg, and some other large cities which can disburse money wired from the U.S.

Customs Regulations: Russian custom laws and regulations are in a state of flux and are not consistently enforced. A 600 percent duty is required to export any item with a value greater than 300,000 rubles. All items which may appear to have historical or cultural value -- icons, art, rugs, antiques, etc. -- may be taken out of Russia only with prior written approval of the Ministry of Culture and payment of 100 percent duty.

Caviar may only be taken out of Russia with a receipt indicating it was bought in a store licensed to sell to foreigners. Failure to, follow the customs regulations may result in confiscation of the property in question.

Air Travel: Air travel within Russia is often unreliable, with unpredictable schedules and difficult conditions including deterioration of airplane maintenance and quality of service. The U.S. Federal Aviation Administration and Russian Civil Air Authorities recently concluded a joint safety evaluation of Russia's civil aviation. As a result of their findings, the U.S. Embassy in Moscow removed restrictions on travel by U.S. government personnel on certain Russian airlines. Travel by U.S. government personnel is now permitted on airlines certified for international air service by the Russian Department of Air Transport. Airlines certified to operate internationally meet higher standards than domestic only air carriers yet also fly to most domestic destinations. The Russian Department of Air Transport has provided a list, which is available from the U.S. Embassy in Moscow, of those airlines certified by Russia for international operations. Travelers should note that safety certification of the airlines on this list is provided solely by the Russian Department of Air Transport. The Federal Aviation Administration only provides safety certification of U.S. airlines.

A FINAL NOTE FOR TRAVELERS TO THE INDEPENDENT STATES

The majority of countries in the former Soviet Union now the Commonwealth of Independent States (C.I.S.), are undergoing profound political and economic changes. Several of these countries are presently engaged in a variety of internal and external conflicts, ranging from boundary disputes to long, outstanding ethnic and religious disputes. As a result, street demonstrations and other disturbances may occur without warnings. At the time this book went to press, some of the states continued to face shortages of fuel, food and medical supplies. Other problems include frequent interruptions in electrical power, and disruptions to internal travels, especially by air. Although it is expected that some of these problems will get resolved with time, travelers to the C.I.S. must consider the potential effect of the present economic and political state of these countries with respect to their trip objectives. Travel to the C.I.S., at this time without doubt, does provide a unique learning opportunity to those U.S. travelers who are truly adventurous, physically fit, and flexible with their plans and who, above all, are patient and tolerant.

Tourism:
With the exception of Russia, tourist facilities for the countries of the C.I.S. are not highly developed. Many of the goods and services taken for granted in the West and other European countries are not yet available.

Medical Facilities:
Americans traveling to the C.I.S. must be particularly aware of the state of medical facilities. Medical care is limited. There is a severe shortage of basic medical supplies, including disposable needles, anesthetics and antibiotics. Elderly travelers and persons with existing health problems may be at risk due to inadequate medical facilities. Doctors and hospitals often expect immediate cash payment for health services. Since U.S. medical insurance is not always valid outside the United States, travelers to the C.I.S. should consider purchasing supplemental medical insurance with specific overseas coverage. Subscribing to the services of one of the medical assistance organizations listed in **Appendix 14N** may be a good idea.

Currency Information:
The majority of countries of the C.I.S. continue to use the ruble, in addition to their newly instituted. The countries of the C.I.S. operate now, for the most part, on a cash only basis. Travelers checks and credit cards are rarely accepted.

Even in Russia, these instruments of payment are not widely accepted in most hotels and restaurants. Because of increasing difficulties in exchanging travelers checks for U.S. dollars or even exchanging funds to local currency at banks or other facilities, travelers should consider carrying an adequate amount of cash with them. Alternatively, you should consider traveling to the C.I.S. as part of a tour group, in which case you should have your expenses, particularly those for meals and hotels, pre-paid.

Crime:
The rate of violent crime is relatively low in the C.I.S. Recently, however, there has been a surge in street crimes, especially at night and near major hotels and restaurants. Part of the recent crime wave has been attributed to the disintegration of local economic conditions, widespread unemployment and a less than effective police force. At the time this book went to press, robberies on trains and in train stations continued to be reported in several countries of the C.I.S. including widespread violent crimes in many cities. In some of these criminal incidents, foreigners (not necessarily Americans) have fallen victims or have been the targets of such criminal behaviour. For useful information on guarding your valuables and protecting personal security while traveling abroad, see Chapters 1, 4, 5, and 45.

ARMENIA

Crime Information: Armenia has a low rate of violent crime, but common street crime has increased especially at night.

Areas of instability: Since 1988, armed conflict has taken place in and around the enclave of Nagorno-Karabakh (located within Azerbaidjan). There is frequent shelling along many areas of the Armenian-Azerbaijani border. A ceasefire has been in effect since May 1994, though there have been some reports of minor violations.

Internal Travel: Travelers flying Armenia Airlines should be prepared to cope with frequent delays, unexpected refueling stops, and poor service. Other modes of transportation may be unreliable and uncomfortable. Train service to neighboring Georgia is subject to frequent disruptions and delays, and crime on board is an increasing problem.

AZERBAIJAN

Crime Information: Although Azerbaijan has a low rate of violent crime, incidents of street crime and assaults on foreigners are increasing.

Areas of Instability: Following a political crisis in Azerbaijan in mid-March 1995, the situation in the capital, Baku, remains unsettled. Government tanks and armed troops continue to patrol certain areas of the city, in particular around the parliament and presidency buildings. A state of emergency and midnight to 5:00 a.m. curfew first established in October 1994 remains in effect for Baku. There are numerous roadblocks and checkpoints throughout the capital. Visitors to Azerbaijan are encouraged to exercise extreme caution. Armed conflict is taking place in and around the Armenian-populated area of Nagorno-Karabakh located inside Azerbaijan and along the borders with Armenia and Iran. Travelers may be stopped at roadblocks while vehicles and travel documents are inspected. Internal travel to several regions is restricted; travelers must obtain special permission from the Ministry of the Interior to visit these areas.

Travel Information: Train travel in the Caucasus region is not secure. Travelers on airlines between the countries of the former Soviet Union may experience prolonged delays and sudden cancellations of flights. Air travel to Azerbaijan on international carriers via Turkey is generally more reliable.

BELARUS

Crime Information: Belarus has a medium rate of violent crime, but common street crime is continuing to increase, especially at night and in or near hotels frequented by foreigners. Foreigner's and particularly foreign cars tend to be targets of crime.

ESTONIA

Crime Information: Estonian police authorities have advised the U.S. Embassy of significant crime problems, and the rate of violent crime is increasing. It is unadvisable for foreigners who are not in large groups to be on the streets of Tallinn after-dark, especially if they have been drinking. Street muggings, car vandalism and car thefts are not uncommon. Robberies have occurred on trains, in train stations, in hotel rooms, in bars and restaurants, and on the street even during the day. The police force suffers from a lack of manpower, resources and equipment and is not capable of responding to these problems. Local police officers are not likely to speak English, and It can be difficult to obtain police assistance. The emergency telephone number in Estonia for police assistance is 445266. It is wise for travelers to exercise the same precautions with regard to personal safety and protection of valuables in Tallinn that they would in any major U.S. city.

GEORGIA

Crime Information: Georgia has a high rate of crime. Petty thefts and pickpocketing occur, particularly in crowded open-air markets. Violent crimes are not uncommon, occurring most -frequently at night. Sporadic gunfire, often celebratory in nature, can be dangerous to bystanders. Travelers on the metro system in Tbilisi are particularly susceptible to criminal acts. Police authority has improved slightly in the past few months. However, security conditions can change rapidly, especially outside the capital city of Tbilisi.

Areas of Instability: Despite the nominal end of the war in Abkhazia, travel in that region is still hazardous. High crime rates in South Ossetia make unofficial and unescorted travel there risky. The security situation in Tbilisi has improved slightly, but crime rates are still high. The security of overland travel inside Georgia is minimal. Trains destined for Armenia have occasionally been targeted by terrorists, and all train and vehicular traffic is vulnerable to robbery by bandits.

Terrorist Activities: Some terrorist incidents have occurred in the country in connection with regional conflicts. Passenger trains traveling between Georgia and Armenia have been the targets of bombings.

KAZAKHSTAN

Crime Information: Common street crime has increased, especially at night, and some robbery victims have been assaulted. Robbers congregate around hotels that cater to foreigners. Walking in a group or utilizing an official metered taxi with door to door service is the best way to traverse the cities after sunset.

KYRYGYZSTAN

Crime Information: Kyrgyzstan has a moderate rate of violent crime. Recently. common street crimes and burglaries have increased, especially at night. Members of the foreign community have been singled out as targets. Traveling in a group, especially at night, can improve security. Some incidents of muggings have occurred outside hotels that cater to foreigners. The government is taking steps to reduce the crime level, and has initiated walking militia patrols throughout the city. More specific information is available at the consular section of the U.S. Embassy.

Air Travel: With the breakup of Aeroflot into many small airlines, air travel in the former Soviet Union is often unreliable. Travelers must often cope with unpredictable schedules and difficult conditions including deterioration of quality of service and overloading. At present, no airline provides dependable regularly scheduled international air service into Bishkek. Most international air travelers fly to Almaty and then travel overland (approx. 3 hours) to Bishkek. Train travel in Central Asia is irregular and arduous.

LATVIA

Crime Information: Latvia has a relatively high rate of crime. Street crime has increased, especially at night. Robberies have occurred on trains and in train stations. Burglaries of apartments and houses are common. The same precautions taken in an unfamiliar U.S. urban center are useful in Latvia as well.

LITHUANIA

Crime Information: Street crime, including purse snatchings and muggings, can occur, especially at night near major tourist hotels and restaurants. Auto theft and auto vandalism is common. Robberies have occurred on trains, in train stations, and in hotel rooms. Police forces suffer from a lack of manpower, resources and equipment. Local police are not likely to speak English, and it may be difficult to obtain police assistance.

MOLDOVA

Country Description: Moldova is a nation under-going profound political and economic change. It is a newly Independent nation still in the process of stabilizing its relations with neighboring countries. Tourist facilities are not highly developed, and many of the goods and services taken for granted in other countries are not yet available. Internal travel, especially by air, may be disrupted by fuel shortages and other problems.

Areas of Instability. The U.S. Embassy in Chisinau advises that only essential travel should be undertaken into or through the Transnistria region. There are frequent checkpoints in Transnistria, manned by armed, young and inexperienced paramilitary units who are not under the control of the Moldovan government and whose members rarely understand English. Tourists and truckers may be subject to extortion or robbery at checkpoints.

Medical Facilities: Medical care in Moldova is limited. There is a severe shortage of basic medical supplies, including disposable needles, anesthetics, antibiotics. and vaccines. Elderly travelers and those with existing health problems may be at risk due to inadequate medical facilities. The U.S. Embassy maintains a fist of English speaking physicians.

Doctor's and hospitals often expect immediate cash payment for health services. U.S. medical insurance is not always valid outside the United States so travelers have found supplemental medical insurance with specific overseas coverage has proven useful. Rabies vaccinations may be useful as casual exposure to stray dogs is common throughout Chisinau. The Centers for Disease Control (CDC) recommend Hepatitis B series for certain travelers. Further information on health matters can be obtained from the CDC's international travelers' hotline, tel: (404) 332-4559.

Crime Information: Moldova has a low rate of crime. but foreigners have been increasingly targeted for both violent crime and common street crime, especially after dark

Internal Travel: Only Air Moldova and Tarom (Romania's national airline) regularly fly to Moldova. Air Moldova service is well below Western standards. Aircraft appear to be old and cabin areas are in poor condition. Train service is also below Western standards and an increasing number of Americans have been victimized while traveling on international trains to and from Moldova.

Currency Regulations: Moldova is a cash only economy. Traveler's checks and credit cards are rarely accepted.

TAJIKISTAN

Warning: U.S. citizens are warned against travel to Tajikistan. Although a cease-fire is in effect between warring factions and peaceful elections were recently held, sporadic fighting continues along the Tajikistan-Afghanistan border. In addition. unsettled conditions exist in some areas of the countryside, particularly in parts of the Gharm Valley and Gorno-Badakhshan.

There is a potential for terrorist actions in the capital, Dushanbe, primarily targeted against Russians. The U.S. Embassy provides a full range of consular services, but is extremely limited in the services it can provide outside Dushanbe.

Crime Information: Tajikistan is a country with a disintegrating economy and widespread unemployment, which has resulted in an increase in street crime. Criminal gangs are most prevalent on the streets of Dushanbe at night.

Areas of Instability: Travelers can expect to find checkpoints and, occasionally, unsettled conditions in many parts of the country. Travel within 15 miles of the Tajikistan-Afghanistan border is tightly controlled and potentially dangerous due to occasional armed clashes.

Internal Travel: Travel to, from and within Tajikistan is difficult and unreliable. The only regular international air travel to and from Dushanbe are connections to Moscow and St. Petersburg via Air Tajikistan (Aeroflot). These flights may be cancelled due to lack of fuel. There are infrequent and irregular charter flights to other destinations. International train connections are extremely dangerous because of criminals operating on board. Travelers to other central Asian republics or Russia must have the appropriate visa, often not available in Tajikistan.

TURKMENISTAN
Crime Information: Turkmenistan has a low rate of violent crime, but common street crime has increased, especially at night.

UKRAINE
Crime Information: The deteriorated state of the Ukrainian economy has led to an increase in economically motivated crimes. Inflation, unemployment, and the breakdown of the country's social fabric have contributed to an ever increasing and violent crime rate. Westerners and their residences are increasingly being viewed by the local criminal element as a target-rich environment.

Internal Travel: Roads in Ukraine are in generally poor condition. Gasoline and diesel fuel may be very difficult to obtain and repair services are often unsatisfactory. Many Westerners who choose to travel by automobile often rent a car and driver, although some self-drive rental cars are available. A few isolated cases of car jackings of Western-made or foreign-registered cars in particular have been reported in western Ukraine near the Polish border. Recently, there has been an increase in the number of documented reports of criminal acts occurring on Ukrainian trains: these acts include gassings and robberies. Make sure passenger compartment doors are shut at night.

Ukraine Registration: All foreigners visiting Ukraine are required to register their passports with local law enforcement authorities. Visitors who do not register may experience delays when leaving Ukraine, or difficulty when trying to extend visas. The registration requirement is automatically met when foreigners stay in hotels, or when resident business persons register their businesses, or, when students register under established exchange programs. Private visitors must have their hosts, relatives or landlords register their U.S. passport at the local "Visas, Permits and Passport Department" office of the Ministry of Internal Affairs (VVIR) office. Foreigners staying three working days or less need not register. A fee of 10 U.S. dollars or the Ukrainian equivalent is usually charged for visa extensions or passport registration. Since December, 1993, foreign missionaries with expired Ukrainian visas may only renew them with the support of the committee on religious affairs of the city administration of the city in which their sponsoring organization is registered.

UZBEKISTAN
Crime Information: Uzbekistan has a low rate of violent crime, but common street crime has increased, especially at night. Wearing jewelry or carrying valuables can be risky.

Medical Facilities: Medical care in Uzbekistan is limited. There is a severe shortage of basic medical supplies, including disposable needles, anesthetics, antibiotics, and vaccines. Diseases contracted by foreigners in Uzbekistan include salmonella, hepatitis A and B, typhoid rabies and meningitis. Other food and waterborne diseases are common. The government of Uzbekistan officially requires visitors to carry a medical certificate proving they are not HIV infected, but this is only sporadically enforced and generally only for long-term visitors. Further information on health matters can be obtained from the Centers for Disease Control's international travelers' hotline, tel: (404) 332-4559.

General Standards of Conduct.- Uzbekistan is an Islamic nation. Although many people in Tashkent wear Western-style clothing, women outside the capital dress in ankle-length dresses, and do not wear trousers in public. Women not in appropriate attire face a risk of harassment about their clothing.

REGISTRATION:
Americans who register at the Consular Section of the U.S. Embassy can obtain updated information on travel

and security within any of the countries of C.I.S. However, before you go, call for recorded state department travel information at 202-647-5225 for up to date travel warnings and advisories.

U.S. Embassies and Consulates Abroad

[For a complete listing of United States embassies and consulates abroad, including their addresses, telephone, fax, and telex numbers see **Appendix A**].

Foreign Embassies and Consulates in the United States

[For a complete listing of foreign embassies in the United States see **Appendix B**].

Planning Another Trip?

See Chapter 46 for a listing of resources available to the general traveler from the U.S. Departments of State, Customs, Transportation, Health and various government and non-government organizations. All of the available International travel-related pamphlets, brochures and publications issued by the U.S. Department of State and by U.S. Customs have been reproduced in full in this book. See Table of Contents for location.

Chapter 21

Tips for Travelers to South Asia

[The information in this chapter is reprinted verbatim from a bulletin issued by the U.S. State Department, Bureau of Consular Affairs. It is intended to serve as advice to Americans traveling abroad.]

- - - -

Afghanistan, Bangladesh, Bhutan, India, Maldives, Nepal, Pakistan, and Sri Lanka

General Information
Your trip to South Asia can be a rich and rewarding experience. There are ancient cultures and artistic traditions to appreciate and a wealth of natural wonders-all coexisting with modern societies. However, the customs and local conditions can be as distant from home as the miles, and travelers should plan their trip carefully.

The Department of State issues travel advisories concerning serious health or security conditions which may affect U.S. citizens. Current advisories are available at the 13 regional passport agencies in the United States, U.S. embassies and consulates abroad, and the Citizens Emergency Center, Room 4811, Department of State, Washington, DC 20520, telephone (202) 647-5225. Travelers to areas where conditions are unsettled or communication is poor are encouraged to consult advisories and to register at the nearest U.S. embassy or consulate (see **Appendix A** for a listing). All travelers are encouraged to leave a detailed itinerary and their passport numbers at home in case of an emergency.

Weather
If you have a choice, winter is the best time to visit most areas of South Asia. South of the Himalayas, South Asian weather is warm to very hot. Hot, humid regions like Bangladesh and central, eastern, and southern India are somewhat more comfortable December through February. Hot, dry regions like Pakistan and northern India have pleasant weather from October to March, with the winter months cool enough for light woolens. The worst weather in the dry regions, when heat and dust can make sightseeing or other outdoor activity a chore, is during the pre-monsoon period from approximately April through mid-July.

Visa and Other Entry Requirements
A U.S. passport is required for travel to all countries in the region. India, Pakistan, and most other South Asian countries also require entry visas. Travel to certain areas of some South Asian countries is restricted and special permits may be required for these areas in addition to an entry visa. Prospective travelers should contact the embassy or consulate of the country they plan to visit for specific information (see Appendix B for a list of foreign embassies in the U.S.).

All South Asian countries require travelers who have been in yellow-fever infected areas within the last 6 days to show valid yellow-fever immunization certificates. (Yellow fever is found in some African and Latin American countries.) If you plan to travel from Africa or Latin America directly to South Asia, check with the embassy of the South Asian country where you are going to see if a yellow-fever certificate will be required. If so, you will be refused entry without a certificate unless you are inoculated and kept in quarantine for up to 6 days.

Customs and Currency Regulations
Most South Asian countries require that foreign currency and valuables be declared upon entry because they have restrictions on the importation of items such as gold, electronic equipment, firearms, and prescription drugs. Failure to make an accurate declaration or other violations of these restrictions can lead to high fines and/or imprisonment. Although illegal narcotic drugs may be available in the South Asian country you visit, their use and/or possession can result in severe punishment.

Shopping for Antiques
Most South Asian countries have strict regulations against the unlicensed export of antiquities. Items that are antique, or even appear to be, may be confiscated by customs officials unless the traveler has proof of authorization from the appropriate government office to export the antique, or proof that the item is not an antique.

U.S. Wildlife Regulations

The United States prohibits importation of Asian ivory because Asian elephants are an endangered species. Most lizard-skin and many snake-skin products cannot be brought into the United States. The penalty for importing products derived from endangered species is seizure of the product and a substantial fine.

Health

In the United States, local health departments, the U.S. Public Health Service, private doctors, and travel clinics can provide information on health precautions for travelers to South Asia. Depending on your destination, immunization is recommended against cholera, diphtheria/tetanus, hepatitis, Japanese B encephalitis, meningitis, polio, and typhoid. Drug prophylaxis against malaria may also be necessary. General guidance can also be found in the U.S. Public Health Service booklet, "Health Information for International Travel,"[1] which is available for $6.00 from the U.S. Government Printing Office, Washington, DC 20402, or from local and state health departments.

Travelers should be careful to take precautions against mosquitos, to guard against overexertion at high altitudes, to drink only boiled water (or bottled drinks), and to avoid unpeeled fruits and vegetables as well as ice cubes in beverages. Trekkers and mountain climbers, in particular, should take precautions to avoid frostbite, hypothermia, and altitude sickness. The latter two can be fatal if not detected in time. Modern health facilities are not always available, particularly in rural areas. Prospective travelers should review their health insurance policies to see if they provide coverage while overseas, including medical evacuation service.

Afghanistan

All of Afghanistan is effectively a "war zone" in view of the continuing conflict between Soviet occupation forces and the Afghan resistance fighters. All U.S. citizens are urged to avoid travel to Afghanistan. The U.S. Embassy can provide only limited assistance to U.S. citizens in distress in the capital city of Kabul, and no assistance outside the Kabul city limits.

Bangladesh

No visa is required for a tourist stay of up to 2 weeks if you have an onward ticket; however, all business travelers must have visas. Bangladesh is an Islamic country, and visitors should dress modestly-shorts are considered inappropriate. Travelers should pay special attention to preventive health measures because medical facilities, especially in rural areas, are not always available. River ferries are necessary for travel throughout much of Bangladesh. However, travelers should exercise caution when using them, bearing in mind that accidents frequently occur from overcrowding and from hazardous navigation during poor weather. Trekkers may not go to the Chittagong Hill Tracts, which are off limits to foreigners.

Kingdom of Bhutan

While Bhutan and the United States do not have formal diplomatic relations, informal contact is maintained through the U.S. Embassy in New Delhi. Bhutan is a Buddhist mountain kingdom. Although visitors are welcome, tourism is carefully controlled in order to preserve the country's unique cultural heritage. Tourists are admitted only in groups by prearrangement with the Ministry of Tourism in Thimphu. Entry must be via India or Bangladesh; the border with China is closed. For information, contact the Bhutan Travel Service, 120 East 56 Street, New York, NY 10022, telephone (212) 838-6382.

India

India is the South Asian country most frequently visited by U.S. citizens. Visas must be obtained before arrival. Persons arriving without visas must leave on the next plane. If you plan to travel from India to Nepal or another country and return to India, be sure to request a multiple entry visa. Tourist visas are issued for a maximum of 90 days. Once in India, visitors who wish to extend their stay must apply to a Foreigners Regional Registration Office. Extensions, if granted, may not bring the total visit to more than 6 months. Customs regulations prohibiting the importation of gold or Indian currency, and regulating importation of electronics, foreign currency, and firearms are strictly enforced. Offenders of these regulations may be jailed, fined and/or charged duty at rates exceeding 300 percent of the item's value. Laws against drug smuggling carry heavy penalties, including a 10-year prison term.

Due to the threat of political or ethnic violence, unstable security conditions pose some danger in the State of Punjab, in Darjeeling, and in several other areas. Many areas of India have been declared off-limits to foreigners by Indian authorities. Permits are required for: Punjab, Sikkim, all of India east of West Bengal, all island territories, and parts of the states of Himachal Pradesh, Jammu and Kashmir, Uttar Pradesh, and West Bengal. Persons of Indian origin wishing to visit relatives, and businessmen planning to do business can usually obtain permits to visit restricted areas. Other visitors may be unable to obtain a permit or have to wait a long time for one. Before departing the United States, consult the latest Department of State travel advisory listing which areas are restricted. Consult the Embassy of India for permit requirements. Once in India, the U.S. Embassy or the nearest U.S. consulate can provide additional information on restricted areas and advice on obtaining permits to visit them. In planning your trip, you should keep in mind that India does not recognize U.S. consular jurisdiction in restricted areas and that consular officers may not be able to provide protection and assistance if you experience problems. With the exception of the Golden Temple in the Punjab, and Darjeeling in West Bengal, the popular tourist sites in India are outside of restricted areas.

Republic of Maldives

The islands of the Maldives have long been popular vacation sites. Diplomatic relations are maintained and consular services are provided through the U.S. Embassy in Colombo, Sri Lanka. In emergency situations there is a U.S. consular agent on the capital island of Male, who can help travelers communicate with the U.S. Embassy in Colombo. For the address of the consular agent, ask at a resort or hotel. A no-fee visa for a tourist visit of up to 30 days is issued upon arrival at the airport. Foreign currency may be taken in or out of the Maldives without restriction. Pork foodstuffs and alcohol may not be imported.

Nepal

Tourism to Nepal is increasing; over 20,000 Americans visit Nepal each year. A visa valid for 1 week can be obtained upon arrival at the Kathmandu airport or at any authorized border-crossing point. It can be renewed for an additional 3 weeks at the nearest immigration office. After that, tourists may renew their month-long visa two consecutive times, allowing a total 3-month visit. Departure from Nepal is mandatory at the end of a 3-month tourist visit. Travelers can avoid initial immigration-processing delays by obtaining a 30-day visa prior to arrival in Nepal. Nepalese customs laws, particularly those forbidding smuggling of drugs, gold, and foreign currency, are strictly enforced. The penalty for smuggling is a stiff fine and/or a prison sentence. Travelers should take adequate funds in the form of travelers checks. It is difficult to obtain additional funds through bank transfers and, except at major Kathmandu hotels, credit cards are rarely accepted.

Trekking is very popular in Nepal. Tourists are cautioned to obtain a trekking permit from the Central Immigration Office, to avoid trekking alone, to be alert for signs of altitude sickness, and to obtain a meningococcal vaccination if trekking outside the Kathmandu Valley. Those wishing to climb the high peaks should write for permission to the Ministry of Tourism, to the attention of the mountaineering division, well in advance of planned expeditions. Travelers should note that there are no forms of international communication in rural areas. In the event

of an emergency, the U.S. Embassy may assist Americans in contacting family or friends.

Americans planning to travel from Nepal to Tibet should be aware that Chinese authorities strictly regulate such trips. Additional information is contained in the Department of State's travel advisory on China and in *Tips for Travelers to the People's Republic of China*.[2]

Pakistan

A visa must be obtained before arrival in Pakistan. Pakistan is an Islamic country, and visitors must respect Islamic standards of behavior. Travelers (especially women) i.e., wear clothes with high necks and long sleeves; do not wear shorts. The import, manufacture, and consumption of alcohol or drugs are strictly forbidden. Major hotels have special rooms where non-Islamic foreigners may buy and drink alcoholic beverages.

A special permit is required for travel to the tribal areas bordering Afghanistan, including the Khyber Pass, and to transit the tribal area of Darra Adam Khel. Persons traveling to restricted areas without a permit are subject to arrest. Onward overland travel to India is difficult because border crossings are limited to certain days and because the only permitted crossing point is into a restricted area of India.

Major cities in Pakistan are safe for tourists, but travel to remote rural areas, especially in Baluchistan, Sind, and the Northwest Frontier Province is not recommended. Security conditions vary; some dangerous areas are considered safe for daytime travel in groups. Because the security situation can change with little warning, visitors should check at the nearest U.S. embassy or consulate for up-to-date travel information.

Sri Lanka

The insurgency of Tamil separatists against the government in Sri Lanka (formerly Ceylon) has caused tension and violence within the country. For this reason, U.S. citizens should avoid all travel to the northern and eastern provinces. This includes the cities of Jaffna, Batticaloa, and Trincomalee. There have been isolated incidents of violence in other parts of Sri Lanka, including Colombo. Because terrorists have often targeted public transportation, travel on trains and public buses should be avoided. Travel to the major tourist sites in the southern and western parts of the island has usually been safe. However, security conditions throughout the country can change with little warning, and travelers should get current information from the latest Department of State travel advisory or from the U.S. Embassy in Colombo. No visa is required for a tourist stay of up to 30 days.

Foreign Embassies in the United States
[For a complete listing of foreign embassies in the United States see **Appendix B**]

U.S Embassies and Consulates Abroad
For a complete listing of United States embassies and consulates abroad, including their addresses, telephone, fax, and telex numbers see **Appendix A**]

Planning Another Trip?
See Chapter 46 for a complete listing of resources available to the general traveler.

~ ~ ENDNOTES ~ ~

1.   A large portion of this booklet has been reproduced verbatim elsewhere in this book.

2.   This publication is reprinted elsewhere in this book. Check the Table of Contents for location.

Chapter 22

Tips for Travelers to Sub-Saharan Africa

*[The information in this chapter is reprinted verbatim from a bulletin issued by the
U.S. State Department, Bureau of Consular Affairs. It is intended to serve as advice
to Americans traveling abroad.]*

- - - -

Angola, Benin, Botswana, Burkina Faso, Burundi, Cameroon, Cape Verde, Central African Republic, Chad, Comoros, Cote D'Ivoire, Djibouti, Equatorial Guinea, Ethiopia, Gabon, Gambia, Ghana, Guinea, Guinea-Bissau, Kenya, Lesotho, Liberia, Madagascar, Malawi, MAli, Mauritania, Mauritius, Mozambique, Namibia, Niger, Nigeria, Rwanda, Sao Tome and Principe, Senegal, Seychelles, Sierra Leone, Somalia, South Africa, Sudan, Swaziland, Tanzania, Togo, Uganda, Zaire, Zambia, Zimbabwe.

General Information
Your trip to Africa will be an adventure off the beaten path. The estimated 325,000 U.S. citizens who travel to Africa each year are only a fraction of the more than 44 million Americans who go overseas annually.

The Department of State seeks to encourage international travel. Conditions and customs in sub Saharan Africa, however, can contrast sharply with what you are accustomed. These pages contain advice to help you avoid inconvenience and difficulties as you go. Take our advice seriously but do not let it keep you at home. Africans are happy to share not just their scenery, but their culture and traditions as well. This brochure should be used in conjunction with the Consular Information Sheets and Travel Warnings.

Before you go, learn as much as you can about your destination. Your travel agent, local bookstore, public library and the embassies of the countries you plan to visit are all useful sources of information. Another source is the Department of State's *Background Notes* series which include a pamphlet for each country in Africa. To obtain specific pamphlet prices and information, contact the Superintendent of Documents, U.S. Government Printing Office, Washington, D.C. 20402; tel: (202) 738-3238. You may also obtain select issues by fax by calling (202) 736-7720 from your fax machine.

This chapter covers all of Africa except the five nations bordering the Mediterranean. Sub Saharan Africa includes 48 nations. Forty two of these nations are on

the mainland. In addition, four island nations in the southwest Indian Ocean (Madagascar, Comoros, Mauritius, and Seychelles) and two island nations in the Atlantic Ocean (Cape Verde and Sao Tome and Principe) are considered part of Africa. For convenience, we will often use the word "Africa" to refer to the sub-Saharan region. For travel tips for the five northern African nations of Tunisia, Algeria, Morocco, Libya, and Egypt see *Tips for Travelers to the Middle East and North Africa.*[1]

Consular Information Program
Before traveling, obtain the Consular Information Sheet for the country or countries you plan to visit. You should also check to see if the Department of State has issued a Travel Warning for the country or countries you will be visiting. Warnings are issued when the State Department decides, based on all relevant information, to recommend that Americans avoid travel to a certain country. Consular Information Sheets are available for every country of the world. They include such information as the location of the U.S. embassy or consulate in the subject country, usual immigration practices, health conditions, minor political disturbances, unusual currency and entry regulations, crime and security information, and drug penalties. If an unstable condition exists in a country that is not severe enough to warrant a Warning, a description of the conditions may be included under an optional section entitled "Areas of Instability." On limited occasions, we also restate in this section any U.S. embassy advice given to official employees. Consular Information Sheets generally do not include advice, but present information on factual matters so travelers can make knowledgeable decisions concerning travel to a particular country. Countries where avoidance of travel is recommended will have Travel Warnings as well as Consular Information Sheets.

How to Access Consular Information Sheets and Travel Warnings
Consular Information Sheets and Travel Warnings may be heard any time by dialing the Citizens Emergency Center at (202) 647-5225 from a touchtone phone. The recording is updated as new information becomes

available. They are also available at any of the 13 regional passport agencies, field offices of the U.S. Department of Commerce, and U.S. embassies and consulates abroad, or, by writing or sending a self-addressed, stamped envelope to the Office of Overseas Citizens Services, Bureau of Consular Affairs, Room 4811, U.S. Department of State, Washington, D.C. 20520-4818.

By fax
From your fax machine, dial (202) 647-3000, using the handset as you would a regular telephone. The system will instruct you on how to proceed.

Consular Affairs Bulletin Board - CABB
If you have a personal computer, modem and communication software, you can access the Consular Affairs Bulletin Board (CABB). This service is free of charge.

To view or download the documents from a computer and modem, dial the CABB on (202)647-9225, setting your software to N-8-1.

As you travel, keep abreast of local news coverage. If you plan a long stay in one place or if you are in an area where communications are poor or that is experiencing civil unrest or some natural disaster, you are encouraged to register with the nearest U.S. embassy or consulate. Registration takes only a few moments, and it may be invaluable in case of an emergency. Remember to leave a detailed itinerary and the numbers of your passport or other citizenship documents with a friend or relative in the United States.

Health
Health problems affect more visitors to Africa than any other difficulty. Information on health precautions can be obtained from local health departments, private doctors, or travel clinics. General guidance can also be found in the U.S. Public Health Service book, *Health Information for International Travel*,[2] available for $7.00 from the Superintendent of Documents, U.S. Government Printing Office, Washington, D.C. 20402, or the Centers for Disease Control's international travelers hotline at (404) 3324559. Depending on your destination, immunization may be recommended against cholera, diphtheria, tetanus, hepatitis, meningitis, polio, typhoid, and yellow fever. These diseases are transmitted by insects, contaminated food and water, or close contact with infected people. Travelers should take the proper precautions before leaving for sub-Saharan Africa to reduce the risk of infection.

Diseases transmitted by insects
Many diseases are transmitted through the bite of infected insects such as mosquitoes, flies, fleas, ticks, and lice. Travelers must protect themselves from insect bites by wearing proper clothing, using bed nets, and applying the proper insect repellent. Mosquito activity is most prominent during the hours between dusk and dawn. *Malaria* is a serious parasitic infection transmitted to humans by the mosquito. Symptoms range from fever and flu-like symptoms, to chills, general achiness, and tiredness. Travelers at risk for malaria should take Mefloquine to prevent malaria. This drug should be taken one week before leaving, while in the malarious area, and for a period of four weeks after leaving the area. Travelers are advised to consult their personal physicians on the possible side effects of the malaria medication they choose. *Yellow Fever* is a viral disease transmitted to human by a mosquito bite. Symptoms range from fever, chills, headache, and vomiting to jaundice, internal bleeding, and kidney failure. Some sub-Saharan countries require yellow fever vaccination for entry. *Dengue Fever* is primarily an urban viral infection transmitted by mosquito bites. The illness is flu-like and characterized by the sudden onset of a high fever, severe headaches, joint and muscle pain, and rash. Prevention is important since no vaccine or specific treatment exists.

Diseases transmitted through food and water

Food and waterborne diseases are one of the major causes of illness to travelers, the most frequent being diarrhea. It can be caused by viruses, bacteria, or parasites which are found universally throughout the region. *Typhoid Fever* is a bacterial infection transmitted throughout contaminated food and/or water, or directly between people. Symptoms of typhoid include fever, headaches, tiredness, loss of appetite, and constipation more often then diarrhea. Typhoid fever can be treated effectively with antibiotics. Drinking only bottled or boiled water and eating only thoroughly cooked food reduces the risk of infection. *Cholera* is an acute intestinal infection caused by a bacterium. Infection is acquired by ingesting contaminated water or food. Symptoms include an abrupt onset of voluminous watery diarrhea, dehydration, vomiting, and muscle cramps. The best method of prevention is to follow the standard food and water precautions. Individuals with severe cases should receive medical attention immediately. *Hepatitis A* is a viral infection of the liver transmitted by the fecal oral; through direct person to person contact; from contaminated water, ice or shellfish; or from fruits or uncooked vegetables contaminated through handling. Symptoms include fatigue, fever, loss of appetite, nausea, dark urine, jaundice, vomiting, aches and pains, and light stools. No specific therapy is available. The virus is inactivated by boiling or cooking to 85 degrees centigrade for one minute. Travelers should eat thoroughly cooked foods and drink only treated water as a precaution.

Diseases transmitted through intimate contact with people

Human immunodeficiency (HIV) which causes acquired immunodeficiency syndrome or AIDS is found primarily in blood, semen, and vaginal secretions of an infected person. HIV is spread by contact with an infected person, by needle sharing among injecting drug users, and through transfusions of infected blood and blood clotting factors. Treatment has prolonged the survival of some HIV infected persons, but there is no known cure or vaccine available. International travelers should be aware that some countries serologically screen incoming travelers (primarily those with extended visits, such as for work or study) and deny entry to persons with AIDS and those whose test results indicate infection with HIV. Persons who are intending to visit a country for substantial periods or to work or study may wish to consult the embassy of that country concerning the policies and requirements on HIV testing. *Hepatitis B* is a viral infection of the liver. Primarily, Hepatitis B is transmitted through activities which result in the exchange of blood or blood derived fluids and/or through sexual activity with an infected person. The primary prevention consists of either vaccination and/or reducing intimate contact with those suspected of being infected. *Meningococcal Disease* (bacterial meningitis) is a bacterial infection in the lining of the brain or spinal cord. Early symptoms are headache, stiff neck, a rash, and fever. This is spread by repository droplets when an infected person sneezes or coughs on you. A one dose vaccine called Menomune is available.

Other diseases

Schistosomiasis is an infection that develops after the larvae of a flatworm have penetrated the skin. Water treated with chlorine or iodine is virtually safe, and salt water poses no risk. The risk is a function of the frequency and degree of contact with contaminated fresh water for bathing, wading, or swimming. It is often difficult to distinguish between infested and non-infested water; therefore, swimming in fresh water in rural areas should be avoided. *Rabies* is a viral infection that affects the central nervous system. The virus is introduced by an animal bite. The best prevention is not to handle animals. Any animal bite should receive prompt attention.

Some countries have shortages of medicines; bring an adequate supply of any prescription and over the-counter medicines that you are accustomed to taking. Keep all prescriptions in their original, labeled containers.

Medical facilities may be limited, particularly in rural areas. Should you become seriously ill or injured abroad, contact the nearest U.S. embassy or consulate. A U.S. consular officer can furnish you with a list of recommended local hospitals and English-speaking doctors. Consular officers can also inform your family or friends in the United States of your condition. Because medical coverage overseas can be quite expensive, prospective travelers should review their health insurance policies. Doctors and hospitals expect immediate payment in full for health services in many sub-Saharan countries. If your policy does not provide medical coverage overseas, consider buying supplemental insurance. It is also advisable to obtain insurance to cover the exorbitant cost of medical evacuation in the event of a medical emergency.

Except in first-class hotels, drink only boiled water or bottled beverages. Avoid ice cubes. Unless you are certain they are pasteurized, avoid dairy products. Vegetables and fruits should be peeled or washed in a purifying solution. A good rule of thumb is, "if you can't peel it or cook it, don't eat it."

Crime

Crime is a worldwide problem, particularly in urban populated areas. In places where crime is especially acute, we have noted this problem under the specific geographic country section. Travelers should, however, be alert to the increasing crime problem throughout sub-Saharan Africa.

Weather

Sub-Saharan Africa is tropical, except for the hi inland plateaus and the southern part of South Africa, Within 10 degrees of the Equator, the climate seldom varies and is generally hot and rainy. Further from the Equator, the seasons become more apparent, and if possible, you should plan your trip in the cooler months. If traveling to rural areas, avoid the rainy months which generally run from May through October north of the equator and November through April south of the equator. Roads may be washed out during these times.

Visa and Other Entry Requirements

A U.S. passport is required for travel to all countries in Africa. In addition, most countries in Sub Saharan Africa require U.S. citizens to have a visa. If visas are required, obtain them before you leave home. If you decide to visit additional countries en route, it may be difficult or impossible to obtain visas. In most African countries, you will not admitted into the country and will have to depart on the next plane, if you arrive without a visa. This can be inconvenient if the next plane does not arrive for several days, the airport hotel is full, the airport has no other sleeping accommodations. The best authority on a country's visa and other entry requirements is its embassy or consulate. The Department of State publication, *Foreign Entry Requirements[3]*, gives basic information on entry requirements and tells where and how to apply for visas. You can order a copy for $.50 from the Consumer Information Center, Pueblo, Colorado

Allow plenty of time to apply for visas. An average of two weeks for each visa is recommended. When you inquire, check the following:

- visa price, length of validity, and number of entries
- immunizations required; financial data required - proof of sufficient funds, proof of onward/return ticket;
- immunizations required;
- currency regulations;
- import/export restrictions; and
- departure tax. If required, be sure to keep sufficient hard currency so that you may leave count on schedule.
- HIV clearance certification. Some countries require travelers to submit certification or tested upon arrival for HIV.

In the past, some African countries refused to admit travelers who had South African visas or entry and exit stamps in their passports. The situation has improved.

Restricted Areas

A visa is good only for those parts of a count that are open to foreigners. Several countries Africa have areas of civil unrest or war zones that are off-limits to visitors without special permits Others have similar areas that are open but surrounded by security checkpoints where travelers must show their passport, complete valid visa. When traveling in such a country your passport with you at all times. No matter where you travel in Africa, do not overstay the validity of your visa; renew it if necessary.

If stopped at a roadblock, be courteous and responsive to questions asked by persons in authority. In areas of instability, however, try to avoid travel at night. If you must travel at night, turn on the interior light of the car. For information on restricted or risky areas, consult Department of State Consular Information Sheets or, if you are already in Africa, the nearest U.S. embassy or consulate.

In some areas, when U.S. citizens are arrested or detained, police or prison officials have failed to inform the U.S. embassy or consulate. If you are ever detained for any reason, it is your right to speak with a U.S. consular officer immediately.

U.S. Citizens Married to Foreign Nationals

Women who travel to Africa should be aware that in some countries, either by law or by custom, a woman and her children need the permission of her husband to leave the country. If you or your children travel, be aware of the laws and customs of the places you visit. Do not visit or allow your children to visit unless you are confident that you will be permitted to leave. Once overseas, you are subject to the laws of the country you visit; U.S. law cannot protect you.

Currency Regulations

The amount of money, including traveler's checks, which may be taken into or out of African countries varies. In general, visitors must declare all currency and travelers checks upon arrival. Do not exchange money on the black market. Use only banks and other authorized foreign exchange offices and retain receipts. You may need to present the receipts as well as your original currency declaration when you depart. Currency not accounted for may be confiscated, and you may be fined or detained. Many countries require that hotel bills be paid in hard currency. Some require that a minimum amount of hard currency be changed into the local currency upon arrival. Some countries prohibit the import or export of local currency. Also, some countries prohibit the destruction of local currency, no matter how small the denomination.

U.S. Wildlife Regulations

The United States prohibits the import of products from endangered species, including the furs of any spotted cats. Most African countries have enacted laws protecting wildlife, but poaching and illegal trafficking in wildlife are still commonplace. Importing products made from endangered species, may result in the seizure of the product and a possible fine. African ivory cannot generally be imported legally into the United States.

The import of most types of parrots and other wild birds from Africa is now restricted and subject to licensing and other controls. There are also restrictions which require the birds to be placed in quarantine upon arrival to ensure they are free from disease. For further information on the import of wildlife and related products, consult the U.S. Fish and Wildlife Service or TRAFFIC U.S.A., World Wildlife Fund-U.S., 1250 24th Street, N.W., Washington, D.C. 20037.

Air Travel

If you are flying to places in Africa other than the major tourist destinations, you may have difficulty securing and retaining reservations and experience long waits at airports for customs and immigration processing. If stranded, you may need proof of a confirmed reservation in order to obtain food and lodging vouchers from some airlines. Flights are often overbooked, delayed, or canceled and, when competing for space on a plane, you may be dealing with a surging crowd rather than a line. Traveling with a packaged tour may insulate you from some of these difficulties. All problems cannot be avoided, but you can:

- Learn the reputation of the airline and the airports you will use to forestall problems and avoid any unpleasant surprises.

- Reserve your return passage before you go; reconfirm immediately upon arrival.

- Ask for confirmation in writing, complete with file number or locator code, when you make or confirm a reservation.

- Arrive at the airport earlier than required in order to put yourself at the front of the line - or the crowd, as the case may be.

- Travel with funds sufficient for an extra week's subsistence in case you are stranded.

Photography

Africa is filled with photogenic scenery, and photography is generally encouraged. However, most governments prohibit photography of military installations or locations having military significance, including airports, bridges, tunnels, port facilities, and public buildings. Visitors can seek guidance on restrictions from local tourist offices or from the nearest U.S. embassy or consulate. Taking such photographs without prior permission can result in your arrest or the confiscation of your film and/or equipment.

Shortages, High Prices, and Other Problems

Consumer goods, gas, and food are in short supply in some African countries and prices for these commodities may be high by U.S. standards.

Shortages of hotel accommodations also exist so confirm reservations well in advance. Some countries experience disruptions in electricity and water supply or in services such as mail and telecommunications.

Local Transportation

Rental cars, where available, may be expensive. Hiring a taxi is often the easiest way to go sightseeing. Taxi fares should be negotiated in advance. Travel on rural roads can be slow and difficult in the dry season and disrupted by floods in the rainy season.

Country Information

Angola

Angola is a developing country which has experienced war and civil strife since before independence from Portugal in 1975. In 1993, the U.S. recognized the Angolan government and a U.S. Embassy was established in Luanda. Facilities for tourism are virtually nonexistent. Visas are required. Persons arriving without visas are subjected to possible arrest or deportation. Travel in many parts of the city is considered unsafe at night because of the increased incidence of armed robberies and carjackings. Violent crime exists throughout the country. Adequate medical facilities are scarce in Angola, and most medicine is not available. Travelers are advised to purchase medical evacuation insurance.

Benin

Benin is a developing West African country. Its capital is Porto Novo; however the adjoining city of Cotonou is the main port and site of most government and tourist activity. Tourist facilities in Cotonou are available, but are not fully developed elsewhere in Benin. U.S. citizens are required to have a visa. Because of security concerns in remote areas, especially the northern region of Atacora, travel can be dangerous. Medical facilities in Benin are limited. Crime rates are rising, particularly in Cotonou.

Botswana

Botswana is a developing southern African nation. Facilities for tourism are available. No visa is necessary for stays of less than 90 days. Medical facilities in Botswana are limited. Some petty crime, such as pickpocketing and purse snatching is common in the capital city of Gaborone. Travel by automobile outside of large towns may be dangerous. Although major roads are generally in good condition, the combination of long stretches of two-lane highway, high speed limits, and the occasional presence of large animals on the roads makes accidents a frequent occurrence.

Burkina Faso

Burkina Faso, previously known as Upper Volta, is a developing West African country which borders the Sahara Desert. The official language is French. Facilities for tourism are not widely available. A visa is required. Cholera and yellow fever immunizations is recommended. Medical facilities in Burkina Faso are limited and medicine is in short supply. Some petty crime occurs. There are restrictions on photography and a valid photo permit must be obtained from the Ministry of Tourism. The Ministry maintains a list of photo restrictions that are expected to be observed by visitors. The U.S. Embassy in Ouagadougou can provide information on specific photography regulations. Credit cards are rarely accepted. Travelers checks can be cashed at local banks. Local telephone service is excellent but expensive.

Burundi

Burundi is a small, inland African nation passing through a period of instability following a coup attempt in October 1993. Facilities for tourism, particularly in the interior, are limited. A passport is required. Medical facilities are limited. Street crime poses a high risk for visitors. Burundi has a good network of roads between the major towns and border posts. Travel on other roads is difficult, particularly in the rainy season. Public transportation to border points is often difficult and frequently unavailable. At the time of publication, the Department of State warned U.S. citizens to avoid travel due to continuing unstable conditions throughout the country.

Cameroon

Cameroon is a developing African country. Facilities for tourism are limited. A visa and proof of inoculation against yellow fever are required. Obtain a visa before arrival to avoid difficulty at the airport. Airport security is stringent and visitors may be subject to baggage searches. Medical facilities are limited. Armed banditry is an increasing problem in the extreme north and petty crime is common throughout the country. Persons traveling at night on rural highways are at extreme risk. While photography is not officially forbidden, security officials are extremely sensitive about the photographing of government buildings and military installations, many of which are unmarked. Photography of these subjects may result in seizure of photographic equipment by Cameroonian authorities.

Cape Verde

The Republic of Cape Verde consists of several rugged volcanic islands off the west coast of Africa. The climate is warm and dry. Tourist facilities are limited. A visa is required. Evidence of immunization against yellow fever (if arriving from an infected area) is required. Medical facilities in Cape Verde are extremely limited. Some petty theft is common.

Central African Republic

The Central African Republic is a developing African country. Facilities for tourism are limited. A passport

and visa are required. Medical facilities in the Central African Republic are limited. Petty crime such as pickpocketing can occur throughout the country, especially in the urban areas. Foreigners have been victims of assault on the streets of Bangui, the capital. Walking at night in Bangui is unsafe; caution should be displayed in the market areas at all times. Endemic banditry in the northern strip of the country which borders Chad sometimes affects foreign travelers. Taking photographs of police or military installations, as well as government buildings, is prohibited.

Chad

Chad is a developing country in north central Africa which has experienced sporadic armed disturbances over the past several years. Facilities for tourism are limited. Visitors to Chad must have a visa before arrival. Evidence of a yellow fever vaccination must be presented. Medical facilities are extremely limited. Medicines are in short supply. Pickpocketing and purse snatching are endemic in market and commercial areas. A permit is required for all photography. Even with a permit, there are prohibitions against taking pictures of military establishments and official buildings. At the time of publication, the U.S.

Embassy advised U.S. citizens that travel across the southwestern border into Cameroon was hazardous because of highway banditry and other violence in northern Cameroon.

Comoros

Comoros is a developing island nation located in the Indian Ocean, off the east coast of Africa. Facilities for tourism are limited. A visa is required. Visas for stays of three weeks or less can be issued at the airport upon arrival, provided an onward/return ticket is presented. Medical facilities in Comoros are limited. Petty thievery is common.

Congo

Congo is a developing nation in central Africa. Facilities for tourism are limited. A visa is required. Medical facilities in Congo are limited. Some medical supplies are in short supply. Street crime, including mugging and purse snatching, is common in Brazzaville, as well as in parts of the countryside. Driving may be hazardous, particularly at night, and travelers should be alert to possible roadblocks. Travelers may wish to contact the U.S. Embassy in Brazzaville for the latest information on conditions on the Congo.

Cote d'Ivoire

Cote d'Ivoire is also known as the Ivory Coast. it is a developing West African nation. Tourism facilities in the capital city of Abidjan include some luxury hotels. Other accommodations, especially outside the capital, may be limited in quality and availability. A visa is not required for a stay of up to 90 days. All travelers arriving in Cote D'Ivoire must be in possession of a World Health Organization (W.H.O.) vaccination card reflecting a current yellow fever inoculation. The W.H.O. card is inspected is inspected by Ivorian Health officials at the airport before admittance into the country.

Medical facilities are adequate in Abidjan but may be limited elsewhere. Not all medicines are available. Street crime of the "grab and run" variety, as well as pickpocketing in crowded areas, has increased. Automobile accidents are one of the greatest threats to Americans in Cote d'Ivoire. Night driving is particularly hazardous due to poorly lit roads and vehicles. Airline travel in Cote d'Ivoire and many other parts of West Africa is routinely overbooked; schedules are limited, and airline assistance is of varying quality.

Djibouti
Djibouti is a developing African country. Facilities for tourism are limited. Visitors to Djibouti must obtain a visa before arrival. Evidence of yellow fever immunization must be presented. Medical facilities are limited. Medicine is often unavailable. Petty crime occurs in Djibouti City and elsewhere in the country.

Equatorial Guinea
Equatorial Guinea is a developing country in West Africa. Tourism facilities are minimal. A visa is required and must be obtained in advance. Medical facilities are extremely limited. Many medicines are unavailable. Petty crime is common. The government of Equatorial Guinea has established stringent currency restrictions, applied both on arrival and departure from the country. Special permits may be needed for some types of photography. Permits are also required to visit certain areas of the country.

Eritrea
Eritrea is a poor but developing East African country. Formerly a province of Ethiopia, Eritrea became an independent country in 1993, following a 30-year long struggle for independence. Tourism facilities in Eritrea are very limited. A visa is required as well as evidence of yellow fever immunization. Airport visas are unavailable. Flights between Asmara and Addis Ababa, the capital of Ethiopia, are heavily booked and advance reservations are recommended. Medical facilities in Eritrea are extremely limited. Travelers must bring their own supplies of prescription drugs and preventative medicines. Street crime such as theft and robbery is on the increase, particularly in the capital of Asmara. While travel throughout Eritrea is relatively safe, visitors may wish to exercise normal safety precautions with regard to what valuables are carried and what environs are visited. The government of Eritrea continues to use the Ethiopian birr as a currency. Credit cards are not accepted in Eritrea. Foreigners must pay bills in U.S. dollars or U.S. dollar denomination travelers checks.

Ethiopia
Ethiopia is a developing East African country. Tourism facilities, although available in larger cities, are limited. A visa is required, as well as evidence of yellow fever immunization. Travelers must enter Ethiopia by air, either at Addis Ababa or Dire Dawa. Individuals entering overland risk being detained by immigration authorities and/or fined. Airport visas may be obtained if 48 hours advance notice has been provided by the traveler's sponsoring organization to proper authorities within Ethiopia. Visitors must declare hard currency upon arrival and may be required to present this declaration when applying for an exit visa. Upon departure, travelers should remember that antiquities and religious artifacts require export permission. There is a functioning black market for hard currency, although the official and unofficial exchange rates continue to converge. Black market exchanges remain illegal and visitors are encouraged to exchange funds at banks or hotels. Domestic and international air services generally operate on schedule, although flights between Addis Ababa and Asmara, Eritrea are heavily booked and may be canceled without prior warning. Internal travel is usually safe along major arteries. However, in rural areas and at night, bandit attacks are common. Additionally, not all land mines have been disabled and cleared, especially in rural and isolated areas. Pickpocketing is rampant, and there have been numerous reports of thieves snatching jewelry. Although physicians are well trained, medical facilities are minimal. Hospitals in Addis Ababa suffer from inadequate facilities, antiquated equipment and shortages of supplies, particularly medications. Certain buildings and public places may not be photographed.

Gabon
Gabon is a developing West African nation. French is the official language. Facilities for tourism are limited, especially outside the capital city. A visa is required. Evidence of a yellow fever vaccination must be submitted. Medical facilities in Gabon are limited. Some medicines are not available. Petty crime, such as robbery and mugging, is common, especially in urban areas.

255

Gambia

The Gambia is a developing West African nation. Facilities for tourists are among the most extensive in West Africa, including one five star hotel and several other hotels of acceptable quality near the coast. In inland areas there are few tourist facilities. Health facilities and services do not meet U.S. standards and there is a limited selections of medicines available. A visa is required. Malaria is common. Evidence of yellow fever immunization must be submitted with one's visa application. Petty street crime is common such as pickpocketing and purse snatching is common in some urban areas. All international travelers must pay $20 (U.S.) at the airport upon departure.

Ghana

Ghana is a developing country on the west coast of Africa. A visa is required. Evidence of immunization for yellow fever is also required. Medical facilities in Ghana are limited, particularly outside the capital city of Accra. Malaria is common, as are other tropical diseases. Petty crime, such as pickpocketing, is common. Robberies often occur in public places and at the beach. In order to comply with Ghanaian law, currency transactions must be conducted with banks or foreign exchange bureaus. Visitors arriving in Ghana with electronic equipment, particularly video cameras and laptop computers, may be required to pay a refundable deposit of 17.5 per cent of the value of the item prior to entry into the country. In some areas, possession of a camera is considered to be suspicious. Individuals have been arrested for taking pictures near sensitive installations. The government of Ghana does not recognize dual nationality except for minors under 21 years of age. The wearing of any military apparel, such as camouflage jackets or pants, or any clothing or items which may appear military in nature is strictly prohibited.

Guinea

Guinea is a developing coastal West African country. Facilities for tourism are minimal. A visa is required. Evidence of yellow fever immunization is required, and the Guinean government recommends taking of malarial suppressants. Medical facilities are limited. Diseases such as malaria, including cerebral malaria, hepatitis and intestinal hepatitis disorders are endemic. Street crime is very common. Criminals particularly target visitors at the airport in Conakry. Pickpockets or persons posing as officials sometimes offer assistance and then steal bags, purses or wallets. Travelers may wish to be met at the airport by travel agents, business contacts, family members or friends to avoid this possibility. Permission from the Guinean governmen's security personnel is required for photographing government buildings, airports, bridges or official looking buildings. Credit cards are rarely accepted in Guinea. Inter-bank fund transfers are frequently difficult, if not impossible, to accomplish. The communication system is poor. The limited telephone and fax lines are usually available only between 6:00 pm and 6:00 am local time.

Guinea-Bissau

Guinea-Bissau is a developing nation on the west coast of Africa. Portuguese is the official language; French is also widely spoken. Facilities for tourism are minimal, particularly outside the capital city of Bissau. A visa must be obtained in advance; recent visitors arriving without visas via land or air have been turned back. Visa applications must be accompanied by two photos and evidence of yellow fever immunization. Medical facilities in Guinea-Bissau are extremely limited. Medicines often are not available. Malaria is common, as are other tropical diseases. Petty thievery and pickpocketing are increasingly common, particularly at the airport, in markets and at public gatherings. Thieves have occasionally posed as officials and stolen bags and other personal items. Visitors should request permission from security personnel before photographing military or police installations. Small U.S. currency denominations are most useful for exchange into Guinea-Bissau pesos. Credit cards and travelers checks are rarely accepted in Guinea Bissau. Inter-bank fund transfers are frequently difficult and time-consuming to accomplish. Taking pesos out of the country is prohibited. Travelers may have difficulty finding public phones and receiving international calls. Telephone services are expensive.

Kenya

Kenya is a developing East African country known for the wildlife in its national park system. Tourist facilities are widely available in Nairobi, on the coast, and in the game park and reserves. A visa is required. Visas may be obtained in advance at any Kenyan embassy or consulate, or upon arrival at a Kenyan port of entry. Evidence of yellow fever immunization may be requested. Adequate medical services are available in Nairobi. There is a high rate of street crime against tourists in downtown Nairobi, Mombasa and at the coastal beach resorts. Pickpockets and thieves are also involved in "snatch and run" crimes near crowds. While traveling in wildlife areas, visitors should use reputable travel firms and knowledgeable guides and avoid camping alone. Water in Nairobi is potable. In other parts of the country, water must be boiled or bottled. Travel by passenger train in Kenya may be unsafe, particularly during the rainy season, because of the lack of routine maintenance and safety checks.

Lesotho

Lesotho is a developing country in southern Africa. Facilities for tourists are limited. Visas are required and should be obtained at a Lesotho diplomatic mission abroad. However, Americans have obtained visas without difficulties at the immigration office in Maseru after entering the country. Basic medical facilities are available, although many medicines are unavailable. Lesotho has experienced varying degrees of political and military instability since January 1994; during such periods the U.S. Embassy advises American citizens to avoid public demonstrations and travelling at night. Armed robberies, break-ins, and auto thefts are common in Maseru and can occur elsewhere in the country.

Liberia

Liberia is a West African country which has suffered internal strife for the past several years. Tourism facilities are poor, and in some cases, nonexistent. At the time of publication, U.S. citizens were warned to avoid travel due to unsettled security conditions. Travelers are required to have a visa prior to arrival. Evidence of yellow fever vaccinations are required. An exit permit must be obtained from Liberian immigration authorities upon arrival. Medical facilities have been disrupted. Medicines are scarce. Monrovia's crime rate is high. Foreigners have been targets of street crime. Lodging, water, electricity, fuel, transportation, telephone and postal services continue to be uneven in Monrovia.

Madagascar

Madagascar is an island nation off the east coast of Africa. Facilities for tourism are available, but vary in quality. Visas are required. Evidence of yellow fever immunizations must be submitted. Medical facilities are minimal. Many medicines are unavailable. Street crimes poses a risk for visitors, especially in the capital of Antananarivo. Reported incidents include muggings and purse snatching. These crimes generally occur in or near public mass transit systems, and against individuals walking at night in the Antananarivo city center. Foreigners who remain near or photograph political gatherings or demonstrations, especially in towns outside Antananarivo, may be at risk.

Malawi

Malawi is a developing African nation. In May 1994, it established its first democratically elected government in thirty years, following peaceful and universally supported elections. Facilities for tourists exist in major cities, resort areas, and game parks, but are limited and vary in quality. Visas are not required for a stay of up to three months. Medical facilities are limited and not up to U.S. standards. Medicines and medical equipment are in short supply. The dress code restrictions which applied to all visitors in Malawi (no slacks or short skirts for women and no long hair or flared slacks for men) are no longer in effect. Travelers may wear comfortable clothes, but may wish to dress modestly, especially when visiting remote areas. Lake Malawi is not bilharzia-free. Petty crime including pickpocketing and purse snatching occurs in urban areas. Residential crime and vehicle thefts are on the increase. Road travel at night, particularly outside the three major cities is not recommended due to the high number of serious road accidents. Hotel bills must be paid in U.S. currency, but major credit cards are generally accepted. It is forbidden to take more than 200 kwacha (Malawi currency) out of the country.

Mali

Mali is a West African nation with a new democratically elected system of government. Facilities for tourism are limited. A visa is required. Medical facilities are limited. Many medicines are unavailable. Petty crime, including pickpocketing and purse snatching, is common. Incidents of banditry and vehicle theft have been reported along major travel routes, near the principal cities and in smaller towns. Victims have included foreigners. The roads from Bamako to Mopti, Douentza, Koutiala, Sikasso, and Bougouni, and a few other roads are paved. Road conditions are poor, particularly in the rainy season from mid June to mid-September. Driving is hazardous after dark, and nighttime travel may be dangerous. Photography of military subjects is restricted. However, interpretation of what may be considered off limits varies. Other subjects may be considered sensitive from a cultural or religious viewpoint, and it is helpful to obtain permission before taking pictures. The Malian currency is the CFA franc which is exchangeable for French francs. Exchange of dollars in cash or travelers checks is slow and often involves out-of-date rates. Use of credit cards is limited to payments for services at only two hotels in Bamako. Cash advances on credit cards are performed by one bank in Mali, the BMCD Bank in Bamako, and only with a "VISA" credit card. International calls are expensive and difficult to make outside of Bamako. Collect calls cannot be made from Mali. Calls to the United States cost approximately ten dollars a minute.

Mauritania

Mauritania is located in northwestern Africa. A visa is required. Evidence of yellow fever immunization and proof of sufficient funds are required. Medical facilities in Mauritania are limited. Medicines are difficult to obtain. Petty crime exists. Local currency may not be imported or exported. Credit cards, other than American Express, are not acceptable in

Mauritania. American Express cards can only be used at a few hotels in Nouakchott and Nouadhibou. The land border with neighboring Senegal, closed as a result of a 1989 crisis, was reopened in 1992. Overland travel is now possible between the two countries.

Mauritius

The Republic of Mauritius has a stable government and growing economy. Facilities for tourism are largely available. Although the spoken languages are French and Creole, English is the official language. An onward/return ticket and evidence of sufficient funds are required for entrance to Mauritius. U.S. citizens do not need visas for a stay of three months or less for business or tourism. Petty crime is common in Mauritius.

Mozambique

Mozambique, a less developed country in southern Africa, ended a 17-year civil war in October 1992 with the signing of a peace agreement between the government and the rival rebel group. Facilities for tourism are severely limited outside of Maputo. Travel by road outside of the major urban areas is possible; however, road conditions vary greatly. A visa is required. Visas must be obtained in advance. Medical facilities are minimal. Many medicines are unavailable. Maputo's special clinic, which requires payment in hard currency, can provide general non-emergency services. Economic conditions in the country, spotty police protection, and years of war have caused an increase in violent and armed robberies, break-ins, and auto thefts. Victims, including members of the foreign community, have been killed. Traveling alone or at night is particularly risky. Currency can be converted at locations authorized by the Mozambican government. Currency conversions on the black market are illegal and very risky. Credit cards are not widely accepted in Mozambique. Some merchants prefer to be paid in U.S. dollars.

Namibia[4]

Namibia is a southern African country with a moderately developed economy. Facilities for tourism are available. An onward/return ticket and proof of sufficient funds are required for entrance into Namibia. A visa is not required for tourist or business visits. Medical facilities are relatively modem, especially in the city of Windhoek. Some petty crime occurs.

Niger

Niger is an inland African nation whose northern area includes a part of the Sahara Desert. Tourism facilities are minimal, particularly outside of Niamey. A visa is required to enter Niger. Visas are valid for a period of one week to three months from the date of issuance, depending on the type of visa and category of traveler. Yellow fever and cholera vaccinations are required for entry into Niger. Medical facilities are minimal in Niger, particularly outside the capital of Niamey. Some medicines are in short supply. Armed bandits operate in northern Niger, and a number of people have been killed. Thieves and pickpockets are especially active in tourist areas. Care must be taken in walking city streets anywhere at any time but especially at night. There have been incidents of groups of men assaulting women who are, or appear to be, African, and who are wearing garments other than the traditional ankle-length wrap known as "pagnes." Tourists are free to take pictures anywhere in Niger, except near military installations, radio and television stations, the Presidency Building, and the airport. There are no laws restricting currency transactions in Niger. Local currency (the CFA Franc) or foreign currency, up to the equivalent of $4,000 (U.S.), may be taken into or out of Niger. International telephones service to and from Niger is expensive and callers experience delays getting a line. Telefaxes are often garbled due to poor quality.

Nigeria

At the time of publication, Nigeria, with limited facilities for tourism, poses many risks for travelers. A visa is required for admission to the country, and no visas are issued at the airport. Evidence of yellow fever and cholera vaccination are also required. Violent crime is a serious problem, especially in Lagos and the southern half of the country. Foreigners in particular are vulnerable to armed robbery, assault, burglary, carjackings and extortion. Disease is widespread and the public is not always informed in a timely manner about outbreaks of typhoid, cholera an yellow fever. Malaria, including potentially fatal cerebral malaria, and hepatitis are endemic. Medical facilities are limited; not all medicines are available. Permission is required to take photographs of government buildings, airports, bridges or official looking buildings. Permission may be obtained from Nigerian security personnel.

Persons seeking to trade at lower rates on the "black market' could be arrested or shaken down. To avoid problems, dollars should be exchanged for naira (Nigerian currency) only at the official rate and at approved exchange facilities, including many major hotels. Credit cards are rarely accepted, and their use is generally ill advised because of the prevalence of credit card fraud in Nigeria and perpetrated by Nigerians in the United States. It is often necessary to bring travelers checks or currency in sufficient amounts to cover the trip. Interbank transfers are practically impossible to accomplish. Prospective visitors should consult the Consular Information Sheet for Nigeria. Because of the incidence of business scams and swindles, persons interested in doing business in Nigeria are advised to consult *Tips for Business Travelers to Nigeria* before providing any information or funds in response to an unverified business offer. This publication is available free of charge by sending a self addressed, stamped envelope to the Office of Overseas Citizens Services, Department of State, Washington, D.C. 20520-4818.

Rwanda

Rwanda is a central East African country torn by ethnic and political strife. A four year civil war resumed in April and ended in mid-July of 199 Much of the country's basic infrastructuretelephones, water distribution, electricity, etc. was destroyed in the war. Medical facilities are severely limited and extremely overburdened. Almost all medical facilities in the capital, Kigal were destroyed during the civil war. Looting a street crime are common. Civilian law enforcement authorities may be limited or non-existant. Clean water and food are unavailable on a regular basis, and only rudimentary lodging can be found. At the time of publication, the Department of State warned U.S. citizens to avoid travel due to the unsettled conditions following the aftermath of civil war.

Sao Tome and Principe

Sao Tome and Principe is a developing island nation off the west coast of Africa. Facilities for tourism are not widely available. A visa is required. Fees are charged for both business and tourist visas. Evidence of yellow fever immunization must be submitted. Medical facilities in Sao Tome and Principe are limited. Some crime occurs.

Senegal

Senegal is a French speaking West African country. Facilities for tourists are widely available although of varying quality. Visas are not required for stays of less than 90 days. Medical facilities are limited, particularly in areas outside the capital, Dakar. Street crime in Senegal poses moderate risks for visitors. Most reported incidents involve pickpockets, purse snatchers and street scam artists.

Seychelles

Seychelles is a tropical island nation in the Indian Ocean off the east coast of Africa. The principle island of Mahe has a population of about 50,000. The two other islands with significant permanent populations are Praslin and La Digue. Facilities for tourism are generally well developed. A visa is required and may be issued on arrival for a stay of up to one month. There is no charge. The visa may be extended for a period of up to one year. Medical facilities in Seychelles are limited, especially in the isolated outer islands, where doctors are often unavailable. Petty crime occurs, although violent crime against tourists is considered to be rare. Keep valuables in hotel safes; close and lock hotel windows at right, even while the room is occupied to minimize the risk of crime.

Sierra Leone

Sierra Leone is a developing country which has few facilities for tourism and poses considerable risks for travelers. Military activity and banditry affect large parts of the country outside Freetown. Telephone service is unreliable. A visa is required. Airport visas are not available upon arrival in Sierra Leone. Yellow fever immunizations are required. Malaria suppressants are recommended. Travelers must declare foreign currency being brought into Sierra Leone. Declaration is made on an exchange control form which must be certified and stamped at the port of entry. Medical facilities are limited and medicines are in short supply. Sterility of equipment is questionable, and treatment is often unreliable. Petty crime and theft of wallets and passports are common. Requests for payments at military roadblocks are common. Permission is required to photograph government buildings, airports, bridges or official-looking buildings. Areas forbidding photography are not marked or defined.

Somalia

At the time of publication, U.S. citizens were warned not to travel to Somalia. The Liaison Office in Mogodishu ceased operations in September 1994. No visas are required because there is no functioning government. Anyone entering Somalia must receive immunization against cholera, typhoid, and yellow fever, and obtain a doctor's advice regarding any other immunizations that might be necessary. There are virtually no health facilities or medicines available in Somalia. Looting, banditry, and all forms of violent crime are common in Somalia, particularly in the capital city of Mogodishu. Electricity, water, food, and lodging are unobtainable on a regular basis.

South Africa

Although South Africa is in many respects a developed country, much of its population, particularly in rural areas, lives in poverty. The political situation in South Africa remains unsettled as the country continues its transition to a non-racial democracy. There are adequate facilities in all urban centers, game parks and areas most commonly visited by tourists. Food and water are generally safe, and a wide variety of consumer goods and pharmaceutical are readily available. Road conditions are generally good, but there is a very high incidence of highway casualties, especially over holiday weekends. A passport valid for at least six months is required, but a visa is not required for visits for holiday, business or transit purposes. Visas are required, however, for extended stays, employment, study and for diplomatic and official passport holders. Evidence of a yellow fever vaccination is necessary if arriving from an infected area. Medical facilities are good in urban areas and in the vicinity of game parks and beaches, but may be limited elsewhere. There is continuing and significant street crime such as muggings, pickpocketing, and random street violence, which affects foreigners as well as local residents, especially in the center of major cities such as Johannesburg.

Sudan

Sudan is a large under-developed country in northeastern Africa. Tourism facilities are minimal. A visa is required to enter Sudan. The Sudanese government recommends that malarial suppressants be taken, and that yellow fever, cholera and meningitis vaccinations be in order. Visas are not granted in passports showing Israeli visas. Travelers are required to register with police headquarters within three days of arrival. Travelers must obtain police permission before moving to another location in Sudan and must register with police within 24 hours of arrival at the new location. The exchange of money at other than an authorized banking institution may result in arrest and loss of funds though unscrupulous black marketeers. A permit must be obtained before taking photographs anywhere in Khartoum, as well as in the interior of the country. Photographing military areas, bridges, drainage stations, broadcast stations, public utilities, and slum areas or beggars is prohibited. Disruption of water and electricity is frequent. Telecommunications are slow and often not possible. Unforeseen circumstances such as sandstorms and electrical outages may cause flight delays,

Swaziland

Swaziland is a small developing nation in southern Africa. Facilities for tourism are available. Visas are not required of tourists planning to stay less than 60 days. Temporary residence permits are issued in Mbabane, the capital. For longer stays, visitors must report to immigration authorities or to a police station within 48 hours of arrival, if they are not lodged in a hotel. Yellow fever and cholera immunizations are required for visitors arriving from an infected area. Anti-malarial treatment is recommended. Medical facilities are limited. Petty street crime, primarily theft of money and personal property occurs with some frequency.

Tanzania

Tanzania is an East African nation. Tourist facilities are adequate in major cities, but limited in remote areas. A visa is required for entrance into the country. Visas for mainland Tanzania are also valid for Zanzibar. Airport visas may be obtained only in Zanzibar; they are not available at mainland airports. Yellow fever and cholera immunizations are required if arriving from an affected area. Airport officials often require current immunizations records from travelers arriving from non-infected areas as well. Medical facilities are limited. Some medicines are in short supply or unavailable. Malaria is endemic in Tanzania and anti-malarial prophylaxis are advisable. Numerous cases of meningococcal meningitis and cholera have been reported throughout the country. Crime is a concern in both urban and rural areas of Tanzania. Incidents include muggings, vehicle thefts and residential break-ins. Valuables such as passports, travelers checks, cameras and jewelry are particular targets for thieves, and are easily stolen if left in luggage at airline check-ins or hotel lobbies. Photography of military installations is forbidden. Individuals have been detained and/ or had their cameras and film confiscated for taking pictures of hospitals, schools, bridges, industrial sites and airports.

Togo

Togo is a small West African nation with a developing economy. Tourism facilities are limited, especially outside the capital city. No visa is required for a stay of less than three months. Yellow fever immunizations are required. Medical facilities in Togo are limited under normal conditions and have degraded because of a long general strike, the departure of medical personnel and the closure or reduction of service in clinics and hospitals. Some medicines are available through local pharmacies. Petty crime, including pickpocketing, has increased.

Uganda

Uganda is an East African nation. Tourism facilities are adequate in Kampala; they are limited, but are improving in other areas. A visa is not required for U.S. citizens. Evidence of immunization for yellow fever, cholera and typhoid is often requested. Medical facilities in Uganda are limited. Medical supplies, equipment and medication are often in short supply or not available. Incidents of armed vehicle hijacking and armed highway robbery occur throughout the country with varying frequency. Many roads in Uganda are poor, and bandit activity in some areas is both frequent and unpredictable. Insurgent activities have made travel to the northern area of the country risky. Highway travel at night is particularly dangerous. Photographing security forces or government installations is prohibited.

Zaire

Zaire is the largest sub-Saharan African country. Although Zaire has substantial human and natural resources, in recent years, the country has suffered a profound political and economic crisis. This has resulted in the dramatic deterioration of the physical infrastructure of the country, insecurity and an increase in crime in urban areas (including occasional episodes of looting and murder in Kinshasa's streets). There have also been occasional official hostility to U.S. citizens and nationals of European countries, periodic shortages of basic needs such as gasoline, chronic shortages of medicine and supplies for some basic medical care, hyperinflation, and corruption. In some urban areas, malnutrition and starvation are acute. Tourism facilities are minimal. A visa and vaccination certificate showing valid yellow fever and cholera immunizations are required for entry. Medical facilities are extremely limited. Medicine is in short supply. Most intercity roads are difficult or impassable in the rainy season. While the U.S. dollar and travelers checks can, in theory, be exchanged for local currency (zaires) at banks in Kinshasa, banks often do not have sufficient new Zaire cash on hand to make transactions. Credit cards are generally not accepted, except by a few major hotels and restaurants. Photography of public buildings and/or military installations is forbidden, including photography of the banks of the Congo River. Offenders may to be arrested, held for a minimum of several hours, fined and the film and camera may also be confiscated.

Zambia

Zambia is a developing African country. Tourist facilities outside of well-known game parks are not fully developed. Visa are required prior to entering the country. Medical facilities are limited. Cholera and yellow fever are endemic. Crime is prevalent in Zambia. Muggings and petty theft are commonplace, especially in Lusaka in the vicinity of Cairo Road and in other commercial areas.

Zimbabwe

Zimbabwe is a landlocked southern African nation with extensive tourist facilities. Although no visa is required to enter Zimbabwe, immigration authorities require a firm itinerary, sufficient funds for the visit, and a return ticket to the United States. Onward tickets to non-U.S. destinations may not suffice. If these requirements are not met, immigration authorities may order departure by the next available flight. Medical facilities in Zimbabwe are limited. Some medicine is in short supply. Muggings, purse snatching and break-ins are an increasing problem in Harare, Bulawayo and tourist resorts areas. Thieves often operate in downtown Harare, especially in crowded areas, and on public transportation. Bus travel can be dangerous due to overloaded buses, inadequate maintenance, unskilled drivers and occasional cases of drivers operating buses while intoxicated. Zimbabwean authorities are extremely sensitive about photographing certain locations and buildings, including government offices, airports, military installations, official residences and embassies.

Foreign Embassies in the United States

[For a complete listing of foreign embassies in the United States see **Appendix B**].

United States Embassies and Consulates Abroad

[For a complete listing of United States embassies and consulates abroad, including their addresses, telephone, fax, and telex numbers see **Appendix A**].

Planning Another Trip?

See Chapter 46 for a listing of resources available to the general traveler from the U.S. Departments of State, Customs, Transportation, Health and various government and non-government organizations. All of the available International travel-related pamphlets, brochures and publications issued by the U.S. Department of State and by U.S. Customs have been reproduced in full in this book. See Table of Contents for location.

~ ~ ENDNOTES ~ ~

1.   This publication is reprinted elsewhere in this book. Check the Table of Contents for location.

2.   A large portion of this booklet has been reproduced verbatim elsewhere in this book, including a country by country listing of vaccination requirements.

3.   This publication is reprinted in **Chapter 3** of this book.

4.   **Editor's Note:** Namibia is presently an Independent country and is no longer under the administration of South Africa.

Chapter 23

Tips for Travelers to Western Europe and Australia

- - - -

Australia, Austria, Belgium, Cyprus, Denmark, Finland, France, Germany, Greece, Greenland, Iceland, Ireland, Italy, Luxembourg, Liechtensein, Monaco, Netherlands, New Zealand, Norway, Portugal, Spain, Sweden, Switzerland, Turkey, United Kingdom.

INTRODUCTION

Americans traveling to Western Europe and Australia, particularly to the major metropolitan areas, should expect a comparable level of conditions as available in the United States. Accessibility to primary services and other facilities are comparable, and so are the standards of delivery. In other words you should not have problems getting quality medical treatment or difficulty using your credit cards, communicating to home, shopping, dinning out; or finding a good, familiar menu. Obviously, there are always exceptions, but this should be more in terms of location within a particularly country than generally is the case.

On the whole, medical facilities and good medical care are widely available in Western European countries and in Australia. In some countries however, doctors and hospitals may expect immediate cash payment for health care services. This is particularly the case in Australia, Germany, Turkey and the United Kingdom. U.S. medical insurance is not always valid outside the United States. In some cases, supplemental medical insurance with specific overseas coverage has proved useful. Further information on health matters can be obtained from the Centers for Disease Control's International Traveler's Hotline at (404) 332-4559. Also, see Appendices 13M and 14N for a list of travel insurance providers and medical assistance organizations.

Generally, travelers to Europe and Australia should take about the same level of precaution and make about the same level of preparation as they would ordinarily do when traveling to major U.S. cities. A little more preparation and precaution would not hurt, however, since your present or upcoming trip involves traveling out of the United States to a country with its own set of laws, rules and regulations that are different from those

of the U.S., and where U.S. government protection may be of little assistance. See chapters 1, 4, 5, 6 and 45 for useful tips and other information on guarding your valuables and protecting personal security while traveling abroad.

By and large, all of the European countries and the Australian government are concerned about the very same issues as the U.S., such as crime, drugs, and drunk driving, and have their own laws, rules and regulations that their citizens and visitors are expected to follow. You must, however, bear in mind that, for the most part, punishment for those who break the law is not the same; it could be harsher and stiffer. Furthermore, there may be cultural differences that may be of importance to your host country, particularly as you travel deeper into the country sides. Therefore, it is important to familiarize yourself and to learn as much as you can about the countries you want to visit.

Obviously, language barriers remain a consideration for the traveler in some of these countries, even though you are more apt to find, particularly, in urban centers, English-speaking persons and tour guides in most of the countries such that you may not even feel the handicap. The one advantage you have as an American traveling to Australia and Europe, particularly to Western European countries, however, is the unique relationship of cooperation and reciprocity between these countries and the United States Government. This is particularly evident in a host of bilateral and multilateral agreements that they share or to which the United States Government is a signatory that provide you with some level of protection and assistance as a U.S. citizen. As you can readily find out elsewhere in this book, some of these countries do not require entry visas for U.S. citizens. In fact, entry requirements for U.S. citizens are less stringent than for citizens of other countries.

A recommended habit for Americans traveling abroad is to register their presence in the country with the consular section of the U.S. Embassy in that country. This should be your very first task upon arrival in a foreign country. Very often, this important step is forgotten or not taken seriously until the traveler is faced with a crisis. One immediate advantage is that you will be able to access current in-country information ranging from crime and terrorism activities to health conditions, currency regulations and areas of instability. Besides, it offers you the most objective and reliable source for last minute information and answers to any questions you may have once you are already in the country.

Americans traveling to Europe and Australia must be familiar with a variety of important issues relevant to their country of destination, particularly the official, host government position on such issues as, dual citizenship and crime.

These issues are addressed below for each country.

AUSTRALIA
Australia is a highly developed stable democracy with a federal-state system. Tourist facilities are widely available.

Crime Information: Australia has a relatively low crime rate in most regions.

AUSTRIA
Crime Information: Austria has a low crime rate, and violent crime is rare. Crimes involving theft of personal property, however, have been on the increase in recent years. Travelers can become targets of pickpockets and purse snatchers who operate where tourists tend to gather, favorite spots being Vienna's two largest train stations.

Other Information: Certain Air Austria flights between Austria and various Middle Eastern points (usually Damascus or Amman) make en route stops in Beirut. (The State Department warns U.S. citizen to avoid all travel to or through Lebanon).

BELGIUM
Crime Information: Belgium has a relatively low crime rate in most regions, but U.S. citizens visiting major cities can become targets for pickpockets and purse snatchers, especially while traveling by metro (subway) and at tourist attractions. Theft of and from vehicles is the most common crime in Belgium, and the usual precautions apply. The two largest cities, Brussels and Antwerp, both have areas best avoided by the prudent traveler and resident, particularly at night, because it is in these areas that the majority of crimes involving violence occur. In Brussels, the areas around the Botanical Gardens and the Westward Arc between the North and Midi train stations all have high incidence Of Crime. Additionally, Rogier and De Brouckere metro stations should be used with caution. In Antwerp, the area behind the central train station

including Statiesstraat, Breydelstraat and Deconinck Plein, as well as the Borgerhout District, are places to avoid. Although increased police surveillance has reduced petty crime around metro and train stations by about 40 percent over the past year, U.S. citizens should continue to be especially alert in these locales. Crime victims themselves must make the report to the police as third party notification of a crime is not accepted. As the police have a high recovery rate for stolen property, victims are encouraged to report all crimes.

Belgian law requires that everyone carry some form of official identification with them at all times which must be displayed upon request to any police official. A U.S. passport will suffice for this requirement, and the police are almost always satisfied if they see a photocopy of the information page of the passport.

CYPRUS
Cyprus is a developed Mediterranean island nation divided "de facto" into two areas. The government of the Republic of Cyprus is the internationally recognized authority on the island but, in practice, its control extends only to the Greek Cypriot southern part of the island. The northern area operates under an autonomous Turkish Cypriot administrative zone supported by Turkish troops. In 1983, this section declared itself the "Turkish Republic of Northern Cyprus", which is recognized only by Turkey. Facilities for tourism in the southern sector are highly developed: those in the northern Turkish-controlled zone, while adequate, tend to be smaller and less modern.

Crime Information: Cyprus has a low rate of crime.

Terrorist Activities: While civil disorder is uncommon Cyprus, demonstrations sometimes occur, and there have been occasional violent incidents along the "green line". Terrorist groups from the Middle East have occasionally used Cyprus as a site for carrying out acts of terrorism against third country targets.

Dual Nationality: U.S. citizen whom the Cypriot government considers to be Cypriot citizens could be subject to compulsory military service and other aspects of Cypriot law while in Cyprus. Those who may be affected can inquire at the Cypriot Embassy regarding their status. In some instances, dual nationality might hamper U.S. government efforts to provide protection abroad.

Other Information: Since 1974, the Cyprus government has designated Larnaca and Paphos international airports, and the seaports of Limassol, Larnaca, and Paphos as the only legal points of entry into and exit from Cyprus. These ports are all in the government-controlled southern part of the island. Entry or exit via any other air or seaport is not authorized by the Cyprus government. It is possible for visitors to arrive at non-designated air and seaports in the northern sector, but they should not expect to cross the United Nations-patrolled "green line" to the government controlled areas in the south. Such travel is not permitted by the government of Cyprus, even for transit purposes. Visitors arriving through designated ports of entry may be able to cross into the north for short day trips. The policy and procedures regarding such travel are subject to change. The U.S. Embassy in Nicosia can inform travellers of current requirements.

DENMARK

Crime Information: While Denmark has a low crime rate, travelers to Copenhagen and other major cities can become targets for pickpockets and sophisticated purse snatchers. Purses and luggage are particular targets for thieves in hotel lobbies, airports, and train stations.

Other Information: The nationwide police/fire/ambulance emergency telephone number is 112. Cyclists have the right-of-way over pedestrians and automobiles in Denmark

FINLAND

Medical Facilities: Medical facilities are widely available. The public hospital system will not honor foreign credit cards and/or U. S. insurance coverage. However, private hospitals and clinics which accept major credit cards are widely available. U.S. medical insurance is not always valid outside the United States. Travelers have found that in some cases, a letter from their carrier describing supplemental medical insurance with specific overseas coverage has proven to be useful. Further information on health matters can be obtained from the Centers for Disease Control's international travelers' hotline on (404)332-4559.

Crime Information: Finland has a low crime rate. The nationwide phone number for Police/emergency services in Finland is 112.

FRANCE

Crime Information: France has a relatively low rate of violent crime. Crimes involving larceny are becoming more common. Pickpocketing, theft of unattended baggage and theft from rental cars or vehicles with out-of-town or foreign license plates are daily occurrences. Criminals often operate around popular tourist attractions such as museums, monuments, restaurants, hotels, beaches. and on trains and subways. Americans in France should be particularly alert to pickpockets on trains and subways, as well as in train and subway

stations. Travelers are advised to carry only whatever cash and personal checks are absolutely necessary, leaving extra cash, credit cards, personal documents, and passport copies at home or in the hotel safe.

Dual Nationality: U.S. citizens who are considered to have also acquired French citizenship may be subject to compulsory military service and other aspects of French law while in France. Those who might be affected can inquire at a French Embassy or Consulate regarding their status. In some instances, dual nationality may hamper U.S. Government efforts to provide protection abroad.

Other Information: Certain Air France flights between France and various Middle Eastern points (usually Damascus or Amman) make en route stops in Beirut. U.S. passports are not valid for travel to, in, or through Lebanon unless special validation has been obtained from the Department of State.

Terrorist Activities: Civil disorder is rare in France. The Basque Separatist Party (ETA) and the National Front for the Liberation of Corsica (FLNC). however, are active in the south of France, and have occasionally bombed local government targets, tax offices, travel agencies. etc. These bombings usually occur late in the evening in an apparent attempt to limit or minimize casualties. Over the last year, terrorist groups have committed other terrorist acts, including a few closely targeted political killings and kidnappings, but no Americans have been affected.

GERMANY

Crime Information: Germany has a low rate of violent crime. Crimes such as burglary, petty theft, and narcotics trucking are increasing but not dramatically. Pickpocketing and purse snatching occur in urban areas, particularly on public transportation and in crowded department stores, train stations, and other areas frequented by tourists. Travelers should therefore take normal precautions to safeguard their valuables. money. and credit cards. Major cities have certain sections where crime rates are higher. These areas are normally easily identifiable, and can be avoided.

Extremist Activities: There are a small number of right- and left-wing extremist groups active in Germany. Right-wing groups have staged violent but isolated demonstrations and attacks, the majority of which have been directed against foreigners or ethnic minorities. Most such acts are perpetrated spontaneously, often by persons under the influence of alcohol. Extremists, often displaying unpredictable behavior, should be avoided. Although Americans have not generally been targets, they could become inadvertently involved in spontaneous demonstrations.

Terrorist Activities: Although Germany is a possible venue for transnational terrorism, present activities of various terrorist elements in Germany are not perceived to pose a direct threat to Americans at this time.

GREECE
Crime Information: Greece has a low rate of crime, but some pickpocketing, purse-snatching, and luggage theft does occur in Greece at popular tourist areas.

Terrorist Activities: Civil disorder is rare. However, there are several active terrorist groups, including the "17 November" organization, which at times has targeted U.S. government and U.S. commercial interests. Between 1975 and 1991. "17 November" assassinated four Americans assigned to U.S. diplomatic or military installations in Greece. Terrorists in Greece have seldom targeted tourists.

Drug Penalties: Penalties for possession, use, and trafficking in illegal drugs are strict, and convicted offenders can expect jail sentences and fines. Arrestee may spend up to 18 months in pre-trial confinement.

Dual Nationality: U.S. citizens who are also considered to be Greek citizens could be subject to compulsory military service and other aspects of Greek law while in Greece. Those who may by affected can inquire at a Greek Embassy or consulate to determine status. In some instances, dual nationality may hamper U.S. government efforts to provide protection abroad.

GREENLAND
Crime Information: Greenland has a low crime rate.

ICELAND
Crime Information: Iceland has a low crime rate. There is little violent crime. There has been a recent small increase in muggings and disturbances in the Reykjavik city center, an area frequented by large numbers of adolescent youths in late evening and early morning hours, particularly on weekends. The Reykjavik police emergency number is 11166. The fire/ambulance emergency number in Reykjavik is 11100.

IRELAND
Crime Information: Ireland has a low crime rate. However, in larger towns and cities, U.S. citizens and other foreign tourists have been victimized by pickpockets and purse snatchers. Petty theft, especially from hotel rooms, rental cars, and in the form of purse snatchings, has increased markedly in recent years.

Terrorist Activities: There is a history of sectarian terrorist violence related to the political situation in Northern Ireland, a part of the United Kingdom. U.S. citizens are not the target of this violence. Acts of violence can spill over into the Republic of Ireland, mainly along the border with Northern Ireland. where heightened security measures are practiced.

ITALY
Medical Facilities: Medical facilities in Italy are adequate for most emergencies. Many hospitals in major cities have at least some personnel who speak English. Public hospitals sometimes do not maintain the same standards as hospitals in the U.S., so travellers may wish to obtain insurance that would cover a stay in a private Italian hospital or crude. In public hospitals patients are billed sometime after discharge. Private hospitals usually require cash payment before discharge: neither credit cards nor foreign medical coverage is generally accepted, Travelers may wish to purchase supplemental medical insurance with specific overseas coverage. Further information on health matters can be obtained from the Centers for Disease Control's international travelers' hotline on (404) 332-4559.

Crime Information: Italy has a very low rate of violent crime, little of which is directed toward tourists. Petty cranes such as pickpocketing, theft from parked cars, and purse snatching, however, are serious problems, especially in large cities. Most reported thefts occur at crowded tourist sites, on public buses, or at the major railway stations, including Rome's Termini, Milan's Centrale. Florence's Santa Maria Novella, and the Centrale in Naples. Consular officers report cases of elderly tourists who sought to resist petty thieves on motor scooters and have suffered broken arms and collarbones. Carrying wallets or purses should be avoided when possible. When carried, shoulder bags should be held tightly under the arm with the clasp facing the body. Waist packs may be worn in the front, although they can unobtrusively be opened. Extra cash, credit cards and personal documents are better left in a hotel safe. Travelers should only carry what cash or checks are necessary. Copies of passports and financial documents should be carried separately from those items.

Thieves in Italy often work in groups or pairs. In most cases, one thief distracts a victim while an accomplice performs the robbery. Groups of street urchins are known to poke tourists with newspapers or pieces of cardboard to divert their attention so that another urchin can pickpocket them. In one popular routine, one thief throws trash or waste at a victim; a second thief assists the victim in cleaning up the mess; and the third discreetly takes the victim's belongings. Criminals on crowded public transportation slit the bottoms of purses or bags with a razor or sharp knife, then remove the contents through the bottom.

Theft of small items such as radios, luggage, cameras. briefcases, and even cigarettes from parked cars is a major problem. Robbers in southern Italy take items from cars at gas stations (often by smashing car windows). Tourists should immediately report thefts or other crimes to the local police station.

In a scam practiced on the highway running between Rome and Naples, one thief punctures the tire of a rental or out-of-town car. An accomplice signals the flat tire to the driver and encourages the driver to pull over. When the driver stops, one thief helps change the tire, while the other helps himself to the driver's belongings. Highway robberies have occurred on the super highway between Salerno and Reggio Calabria in Sicily. A U.S. citizen was lolled by gunshot during a random nighttime robbery attempt in 1994.

In a scam practiced on trains. primarily in northern Italy, one or more persons will befriend a traveller and offer a drink. The drink will be drugged, and the traveller awakens to find he has been robbed. Thieves have been known to impersonate police officers to gain the confidence of tourists. The thief shows the prospective victim a circular plastic sign with the words "police" or "International police." If this happens, the tourist should insist on seeing the officer's identification card (documents) as impersonators tend not to carry forged documents.

Terrorist Activities: In May 1993. bombs exploded on separate occasions in Rome and in Florence. The explosions resulted in the death of five people. more than 40 injuries, and extensive property damage. In July 1993 three separate car bombings, two in Rome and one in Milan, left five people dead and 28 "injured. In September 1993 a hand grenade was thrown and 12 shots were fired at the air base in Aviano. Between October 1993 and January 1994 four bombs exploded in public offices in Padova, and in February 1994 in Rome, the vehicle of a Spanish military officer exploded, causing light injuries to the driver. Most of the bombs were placed near public buildings (e.g. churches, museums) and all exploded during non-business hours. Officials of the Italian government have indicated their belief that the bombs are the work of criminal elements or international terrorists. U.S. citizens have not been the targets of these attacks.

Dual Nationality: U.S. citizens who are also considered to be Italian citizens may be subject to compulsory military service and other Italian laws while in Italy. Those who might be affected can inquire at an Italian Embassy or Consulate regarding their status. In some Instances, dual nationality may hamper U.S. Government efforts to provide protection abroad.

Other Information: U.S. citizens are reminded that certain Alitalia flights between Italy and various Middle Eastern Points (usually Damascus or Amman) make en route stops in Beirut. The State Department warns U.S. citizens to avoid all travel to or through Lebanon.

LUXEMBOURG
Medical Facilities: Medical Facilities are widely available.

Crime Information: Luxembourg has a low crime rate. However, during the tourist season, pickpocketing, theft or unattended baggage, and theft from vehicles can occur.

LIECHTENSTEIN
Liechtenstein is a stable democratically run constitutional monarchy with a modern economy. Tourist activities are widely available. There is no U.S. embassy or consulate in Liechtenstein. For assistance American citizens can contact the U.S. Consulate General in Zurich, Switzerland, telephone (41) (1) 422-2566

Medical Facilities: Good medical care is available. Doctors and hospitals often expect immediate cash payment for health services.

Information on Crime: Liechtenstein has low crime rate.

Registration: Americans who register at the Zurich Consulate General can obtain updated information on travel and security within the area.

MONACO
Monaco is a constitutional monarchy and is a highly developed European nation. Tourist facilities are widely available. There is no U.S. embassy or consulate in Monaco. For assistance American citizens can contact the U.S. Consulate General in Marseille, France, telephone (33) 91549200 or the U.S. Consulate Agent in Nice, France, telephone (33) 93888955

Medical Facilities: Medical care is available.

Crime Information: Monaco has a low crime rate. During the summer tourist season pickpocketing, theft of unattended baggage, and theft from vehicles with foreign, out-of-town, or rental licenses can occur.

Popular tourist attractions such as museums, monuments, restaurants, hotels, and transportation systems are often areas where criminals operate.

Registration: Americans who register with the Consulate General in Marseille or the Consular Agent in Nice and obtain updated information on travel and security in the area.

NETHERLANDS
Crime Information: The Netherlands has a low crime rate. Nevertheless, as in any country, crime does occur in city centers. Visitors to Amsterdam can become targets of pickpockets, bag snatchers, and thefts from autos in and around the central train station and in the adult entertainment district.

NEW ZEALAND
Information on Crime: Crime in New Zealand is comparatively low but has increased in recent years. Foreign visitors, including those from the U.S., are seldom victims of crime. The most prevalent incident is occasional theft or attempted theft.

NORWAY
Crime Information: Norway has a low crime rate. Violent crime is rare. Most crime involve theft of personal property in public areas or burglary. Weapons are rarely used.

Other Information: Mandatory jail sentences are also routine for any alcohol abuse while driving.

PORTUGAL
Country Description: Portugal is a moderately developed and stable democracy. Tourist facilities are widely available.

Medical Facilities: Medical facilities are available. Doctors and hospitals often expect immediate cash payment for health services.

Crime Information: Portugal has a low but increasing rate of violent crime. Travelers, especially those who appear to be affluent' may become targets of pickpockets and purse snatchers. Automobile break-ins, particularly from rental cars, and car thefts are common.

SPAIN
Crime Information: Spain has a very low rate of violent crime. Nevertheless, minor crimes such as pickpocketing, robbery, and theft from cars are a problem, and are often directed against unwary tourists. Thieves often attempt to distract their victims by squirting mustard on their clothing. asking directions on

the street, or otherwise diverting their attention from an accomplice. Thefts of small items like radios, luggage, cameras, briefcases. and even cigarettes from parked cars are a common problem. The American Embassy in Madrid has issued a notice to U.S. citizens stating that it frequently receives reports of roadside thieves posing as "good Samaritans" to persons experiencing car and tire problems. The thieves typically attempt to divert the driver's attention by pointing out a mechanical problem and then steal items from the vehicle while the driver is looking elsewhere. The problem is particularly acute with vehicles rented at Madrid's Barajas Airport. The Embassy notice advises drivers to be extremely cautious about accepting help from anyone other than a uniformed Spanish police officer or Civil Guard. Travelers who accept unofficial assistance are advised to protect their valuables by keeping them in sight or locking them in the vehicle.

Terrorist Activities: Civil disorder in Spain is rare. Although a few small terrorist groups, including ETA (Basque separatists) and GRAPO (a Marxist group). are occasionally active, their efforts are primarily directed against police, military, and other Spanish government targets. Americans have not been targets of these attacks.

SWEDEN
Crime Information: Sweden has a low crime rate. Violent crime is rare. Most crimes involve theft of personal property in public areas or burglary of vacant residences. However, travelers, especially those who appear affluent, can become targets of pickpockets and purse snatchers. The telephone number for police and other emergency services throughout the country is 90000.

Other Information: Driving regulations and signs differ from those in the U.S. Moving violations, especially speeding and driving under the influence of alcohol, are strictly enforced, and fines can be severe.

Other Information: Over the past year, there have been isolated incidents of violence directed against non-European immigrants.

SWITZERLAND
Crime Information: Switzerland has a low rate of violent crime. However, pickpocketing and purse-snatching do occur during peak tourist periods (such as summer and Christmas) and when major conferences, shows, or exhibits are scheduled in Geneva. Most crime is restricted to specific localities in major cities (areas frequented by drug users, the general vicinity of train and bus stations, and some public parks, for example) Countrywide emergency telephone numbers are police

117, fire 118, and ambulance 144.

Travelers should exercise caution on trains, especially when transiting neighboring countries is reports of thefts on trains in southern France and Italy indicate that even locked sleeping compartments can be entered surreptitiously by thieves who steal from passengers while they sleep.

Dual Nationality: U.S. citizens who are considered to also have Swiss citizenship may be subject to compulsory military service and other requirements while Switzerland. Those who might be affected can inquire at a Swiss embassy or consulate regarding their status. In some instances, dual nationality may hamper U.S. government efforts to provide protection abroad.

TURKEY
Areas of Instability: For at least ten years, urban and rural acts of terrorism throughout Turkey have caused injury and loss of life to government officials and civilians, including some foreign tourists. While most incidents have occurred in eastern Turkey, in 1993, one terrorist group. the Kurdistan Workers' Party (PKK) began to target tourist sites and tourist-oriented facilities in western Turkey in an effort to inflict economic harm on Turkey by discouraging tourism. Such attacks continued into 1994. During the summer of 1993, a series of bomb attacks in Antalya wounded 26 persons. including some tourists; in Istanbul, a grenade was thrown under a tour bus injuring eight persons, and a bomb was thrown at a group of tourists as they were sightseeing around the city walls, resulting in six injuries; a hand grenade was found buried on a beach southeast of Izmir and there were reports of similar incidents in other areas along the west coast. In 1994; PKK bomb attacks at some of Istanbul's most popular tourist attractions, including St. Sophia and the Covered Bazaar, resulted in the death of two foreign tourists. No group has claimed responsibility for three bomb attacks that wounded 23 persons in the Mediterranean resorts of Marmaris and Fethiye.

Intermittent terrorist bombings, not directed against tourists, have also occurred elsewhere, including Ankara, causing damage to property and loss of life. Due to PKK bombings on local intercity buses, travelers may be subject to security baggage screening by the Turkish National Police. Some terrorist groups have also targeted the personnel and property of organizations with official and commercial ties to the United States. The U.S. Embassy in Ankara has advised all Americans to be aware of their surroundings and report suspicious incidents to local authorities.

Eastern Provinces: With the exception of the Mediterranean and Black Sea coasts, travel to eastern Turkey is hazardous. Terrorist acts by the PKK continue throughout the eastern provinces. These attacks are not only against Turkish police and military installations but also against civilian targets including public ground transportation. While most attacks have been at night, day-time attacks are increasingly frequent. Over the past nine years, several thousand Turkish civilians and security personnel have been killed in terrorist attacks. In 1991, the PKK began kidnapping foreigners in eastern Turkey to generate media attention for their separatist cause. Over the past two years, a number of foreigners, including Americans, have been held by the PKK and eventually released. As recently as October 9, 1993, an American tourist was abducted by the PKK while traveling by bus on the main highway between Erzurum and Erzincan. Due to the tense security situation, the climbing of Mt. Ararat in eastern Turkey is extremely dangerous, even with the required Turkish government permits. In light of the dangerous security conditions for travelers in eastern Turkey, the U.S. military has advised its personnel to avoid all tourist travel to this region. U.S. Embassy and Consulate personnel travel to eastern Turkey only for essential U.S. Government business and only with prior approval. In instances where travel to cities in eastern Turkey is essential, air travel is considered safer than other forms of public transportation.

Medical Information: Medical facilities are available. but may be limited outside urban areas. Doctors and hospitals often expect immediate cash payment for health services.

Other Pertinent Information: Unauthorized purchase of or removal from Turkey of antiquities or other important cultural artifacts is strictly forbidden. Violation of this law may result in imprisonment. At the time of departure, travelers who purchase such items may be asked to present a receipt from the seller as well as the official museum export certificate required by law.

Crime Information: There is some crime against tourists, including pickpocketing, purse snatching and mugging. In Istanbul, incidents have been reported of tourists who have been drugged and robbed in nightclubs and bars. usually by other foreigners who speak English and French.

Public Safety: Travel by road after dark is hazardous throughout Turkey. Road and driving conditions off the main highways and in remote areas are particularly dangerous. In the eastern provinces, the incidence of terrorism poses additional risks for road travelers.

Turkish authorities expect travelers to cooperate with travel restrictions and other security measures Imposed in the cast.

Dual Nationality: U.S. citizens who are also considered to be Turkish citizens may be subject to compulsory military service and other aspects of Turkish law while in Turkey. Those who may be affected can inquire at a Turkish embassy or consulate to determine status. In some instances, dual nationality may hamper U.S. government efforts to provide protection abroad.

UNITED KINGDOM

Quarantine Requirements: The United Kingdom has particularly rigorous quarantine restrictions on the importation of pets and livestock. There is a six-month quarantine, for example, on importation of dogs and cats.

Crime Information: The incidence of criminal activity in the United Kingdom is generally low, though many major cities have areas where caution should be exercised. Visitors generally lock vehicles and guard their personal possessions. As in any developed country, the United Kingdom has higher incidents of criminal activity in urban areas than in the countryside. Incidents of violent crimes such as murder, armed robbery, and rape are minimal. Firearms are strictly controlled, making weapons-related offenses far less frequent than in large U.S. metropolitan areas. Large cities in England do have areas where the level of crime is significant.

Terrorist Activities: The United Kingdom is a stable, modem democracy. Political demonstrations in the United Kingdom are generally orderly and well policed. There is, however, a history of terrorist violence related to the political situation in Northern Ireland, a part of the United Kingdom. The ceasefire announced on August 31, 1994 by the Irish Republican Army (IRA) and the October 1994 ceasefire announced by "Loyalist" paramilitaries have greatly reduced the threat of violence, as both ceasefires have held.

Planning Another Trip?

See Chapter 46 for a listing of resources available to the general traveler from the U.S. Departments of State, Customs, Transportation, Health and various government and non-government organizations. All of the available International travel-related pamphlets, brochures and publications issued by the U.S. Department of State and by U.S. Customs have been reproduced in full in this book. See Table of Contents for location.

Chapter 24

Tips for Business Travelers

- - - -

A Guide for Business Travelers

Officials of companies that are successful in selling overseas often tell Business America that one of the keys to their success is frequent travel to overseas markets. As in domestic business, there is nothing like a face-to-face meeting with a client or customer. Business travel abroad can locate and cultivate new customers and improve relationships and communication with current foreign representatives and associates.

The following suggestions can help officials of U.S. companies prepare for a trip. By keeping in mind that even little things (such as forgetting to check foreign holiday schedules or neglecting to arrange for translator services) can cost time, opportunity, and money, a firm can get maximum value from its time spent abroad.

Planning the Itinerary

A well-planned itinerary enables a traveler to make the best possible use of time abroad. Although travel time is expensive, care must be taken not to overload the schedule. Two or three definite appointments, confirmed well in advance and spaced comfortably throughout one day, are more productive and enjoyable than a crowded agenda that forces the business person to rush from one meeting to the next before business is really concluded. If possible, an extra rest day to deal with jet lag should be planned before scheduled business appointments. The following travel tips should be kept in mind.

The travel plans should reflect what the company hopes to accomplish. The traveler should give some thought to the trip's goals and their relative priorities. The traveler should accomplish as much as possible before the trip begins by obtaining names of possible contacts, arranging appointments, checking transportation schedules, and so on. Important meetings should be confirmed before the traveler leaves the United States.

As a general rule, the business person should keep the schedule flexible enough to allow for both unexpected problems (such as transportation delays) and unexpected opportunities. For instance, accepting an unscheduled luncheon invitation from a prospective client should not make it necessary to miss the next scheduled meeting.

The traveler should check the normal work days and business hours in the countries to be visited. In many Middle Eastern regions, for instance, the work week typically runs from Saturday to Thursday. In many countries, lunch hours of two to four hours are customary. Along the same lines, take foreign holidays into account. Business America at year-end publishes a list of commercial holidays observed in countries around the world for the following year (See Appendix 8H). The potential U.S. traveler should also contact the local Commerce Department district office(See Appendix C). to learn what travel advisories the U.S. Department of State has issued for countries to be visited. Each district office maintains a file of current travel advisory cables, which alert travelers to potentially dangerous in-country situations. The Department of State also has a telephone number for recorded travel advisories, (202) 647-5225.

The U.S. business person should be aware that travel from one country to another may be restricted. For example, a passport containing an Israeli visa may disallow the traveler from entering certain countries in the middle East.

Other Considerations

Travel agents can frequently arrange for transportation and hotel reservations quickly and efficiently. They can also help plan the itinerary, obtain the best travel rates, explain which countries require visas, advise on hotel rates and locations, and provide other valuable services. Since travel agents' fees are paid by the hotels, airlines, and other carriers, this assistance and expertise may cost nothing.

The U.S. traveler should obtain the necessary travel documents two to three months before departure, especially if visas are needed. A travel agent can help make the arrangements. A valid U.S. passport is required for all travel outside the United States and Canada. If traveling on an old passport, the U.S. citizen should make sure that it remains valid for the entire duration of the trip.

Passports may be obtained through certain local post

271

offices and U.S. district courts. Application may be made in person or, in some cases, by mail. A separate passport is needed for each family member who will be traveling. The applicant must provide (1) proof of citizenship, (2) proof of identify, (3) two identical passport photos, (4) a completed application form, and (5) the appropriate fees. The cost is $55 per passport ($30 for travelers under 18) plus a $10 execution fee for first-time passports or travelers applying in person. The usual processing time for a passport (including time in the mail) is three weeks, but travelers should apply as early as possible, particularly if time is needed to obtain visas, international drivers licenses, or other documents. Additional information is available from the nearest local passport office or by calling the Office of Passport Services in Washington, D.C., (202) 647-0518. (also See Appendix J).

Visas, which are required by many countries, cannot be obtained through the Office of Passport Services. They are provided for a small fee by the foreign country's embassy or consulate in the United States. To obtain a visa, the traveler must have a current U.S. passport. In addition, many countries require a recent photo. The travelers should allow several weeks to obtain visas, especially if traveling to Eastern Europe or developing nations. Some countries that do not require visas for tourist travel do require them for business travel. Visa requirements may change from time to time. (See Chapter 3).

Requirements for vaccinations differ from country to country. A travel agent or airline can advise the travelers on various requirements. In some cases, vaccinations against typhus, typhoid, and other diseases are advisable even though they are not required. (Also See Chapter 9).

Business Preparations For International Travel
Before leaving the United States, the traveler should prepare to deal with language differences by learning whether individuals are to be met are comfortable speaking English. If not, plans should be made for an interpreter. Business language is generally more technical than the conversational speech with which many travelers are familiar; mistakes can be costly.

In some countries, exchanging business cards at any first meeting is considered a basic part of good business manner. As a matter of courtesy, it is best to carry business cards printed both in English and in the language of the country being visited. Some international airlines arrange this service.

The following travel checklist covers a number of considerations that apply equally to business travelers

and vacations. A travel agent or various travel publications can help take these considerations into account:

-      Seasonal weather conditions in the countries being visited.
-      Health care (e.g., what to eat abroad, special medical problems, and prescription drugs).
-      Electrical current (a transformer or plug adapter may be needed to use electrical appliances).
-      Money (e.g., exchanging currency and using credit cards and travelers checks).
-      Transportation and communication abroad.
-      Cultural differences.
-      Tipping (who is tipped and how much is appropriate).
-      U.S. Customs regulations on what can be brought home.

Assistance from U.S. Embassies and Consulates
Economic and commercial officers in U.S. embassies and consulates abroad can provide assistance to U.S. exporters, both through in-depth briefings and by arranging introductions to appropriate firms, individuals, or foreign government officials. Because of the value and low cost of these services, it is recommended that the exporter visit the U.S. embassy soon after arriving in a foreign country.

When planning a trip, business travelers can discuss their needs and the services available at particular embassies with the staff of the local Commerce district office. It is also advisable to write directly to the U.S. embassy or consulate in the countries to be visited at least two weeks before leaving the United States and to address any communication to the commercial section. The U.S. business traveler should identify his or her business affiliation and complete address and indicate the objective of the trip and the type of assistance required from the post. Also a description of the firm and the extent of its international experience would be helpful to the post. Addresses of U.S. embassies and consulates are provided in Key Officers of Foreign Service Posts, a publication available from the Superintendent of Documents, U.S. Government Printing Office, Washington, D.C. 20402-9371; telephone (202) 783-3238. The cost for this publication is $5 for one year, and it is issued twice a year. (See Chapter 46).

A program of special value to U.S. business travelers is the Department of Commerce's Gold Key Service, which is custom tailored to U.S. firms visiting overseas markets. This service combines several forms of Commerce assistance, including agent and distributor location, one-on-one business counseling, prescheduled appointments with key contacts, and U.S. embassy assistance with interpreters and translators, clerical support, office services, and so on. The service is not available in all markets and may be known under a different name in some countries (e.g., RepFind in Mexico). Further information and assistance are available from any Commerce district office.

Carnets

Foreign customs regulations vary widely from place to place, and the traveler is wise to learn in advance the regulations that apply to each country to be visited. If allowances for cigarettes, liquor, currency, and certain other items are not taken into account, they can be impounded at national borders. Business travelers who plan to carry product samples with them should be alert to import duties they may be required to pay. In some countries, duties and extensive customs procedures on sample products may be avoided by obtaining an ATA (Admission Temporoire) Carnet.

The ATA Carnet is a standardized international customs document used to obtain duty-free temporary admission of certain goods into the countries that are signatories to the ATA Convention. Under the ATA Convention, commercial and professional travelers may take commercial samples; tools of the trade; advertising material; and cinematographic, audiovisual, medical, scientific, or other professional equipment into member countries temporarily without paying customs duties and taxes or posting a bond at the border of each country to be visited.

Countries are continuously added to the ATA Carnet system. The traveler should contact the U.S. Council for International Business to determine if the country to be visited is a participant. Applications for carnets should be made to the same organization. A fee is charged, depending on the value of the goods to be covered. A bond, letter of credit, or bank guaranty of 40 percent of the value of the goods is also required to cover duties and taxes that would be due if goods imported into a foreign country by carnet were not reexported and the duties were not paid by the carnet holder. The carnets generally are valid for 12 months.

To obtain a Carnet, dial Carnet headquarters at (212) 354-4480; 1-800-CARNETS (for the office nearest your calling number); or 1-800-ATA-2900 (Carnet Helpline). The Roanoke Companies, an authorized issuing agent of the U.S. Council, has Carnet issuing facilities in New York, Los Angeles, Chicago, San Francisco, Boston, Baltimore, Miami, and Houston.

Cultural Factors

Business executives who hope to profit from their travel should learn about the history, culture, and customs of the countries to be visited. Flexibility and cultural adaptation should be the guiding principles for traveling abroad on business. Business manners and methods, religious customs, dietary practices, humor, and acceptable dress vary widely from country to country. For example, consider the following:

☐ Never touch the head of a Thai or pass an object over it; the head is considered sacred in Thailand.

☐ Avoid using triangular shapes in Hong Kong, Korea, and Taiwan; the triangle is considered a negative shape.

☐ The number 7 is considered bad luck in Kenya and good luck in the Czech Republic, and it has magical connotations in Benin. The number 10 is bad luck in Korea, and 4 means death in Japan.

☐ Red is a positive color in Denmark, but it represents witchcraft and death in many African countries.

☐ A nod of the head means no to a Bulgarian, and shaking the head from side to side means yes.

☐ The "okay" sign commonly used in the United States (thumb and index finger forming a circle and the other fingers raised) means zero in France, is a symbol for money in Japan, and carries a vulgar connotation in Brazil.

☐ The use of a palm-up hand and moving index finger signals "come here" in the United States and in some other countries, but it is considered vulgar in others.

☐ In Ethiopia, repeatedly opening and closing the palm-down hand means "come here."

Understanding and heeding cultural variables such as these is critical to success in international business travel and in international business itself. Lack of familiarity with the business practices, social customs, and etiquette of a country can weaken a company's position in the market, prevent it from accomplishing its objectives, and ultimately lead to failure.

Some of the cultural distinctions that U.S. firms most

273

often face include differences in business styles, attitudes toward development of business relationships, attitudes toward punctuality, negotiating styles, gift-giving customs, greetings, significance of gestures, meanings of colors and numbers, and customs regarding titles.

American firms must pay close attention to different styles of doing business and the degree of importance placed on developing business relationships. In some countries, business people have a very direct style, while in others they are much more subtle in style and value the personal relationship more than most Americans do in business. For example, in the Middle East, engaging in small talk before engaging in business is standard practice.

Attitudes toward punctuality vary greatly from one culture to another and, if misunderstood, can cause confusion and misunderstanding. Romanians, Japanese, and Germans are very punctual, whereas people in many of the Latin countries have a more relaxed attitude toward time. The Japanese consider it rude to be late for a business meeting, but acceptable, even fashionable, to be late for a social occasion. In Guatemala, on the other hand, one might arrive anytime from 10 minutes early to 45 minutes late for a luncheon appointment.

When cultural lines are being crossed, something as simple as a greeting can be misunderstood. Traditional greetings may be a handshake, a hug, a nose rub, a kiss, placing the hands in praying position, or various other gestures. Lack of awareness concerning the country's accepted form of greeting can lead to awkward encounters.

People around the world use body movements and gestures to convey specific messages. Sometimes the same gestures have very different meanings, however. Misunderstanding over gestures is a common occurrence in cross-cultural communication, and misinterpretation along these lines can lead to business complications and social embarrassment.

Proper use of names and titles is often a source of confusion in international business relations. In many countries (including the United Kingdom, France, and Denmark) it is appropriate to use titles until use of first names is suggested. First names are seldom used when doing business in Germany. Visiting business people should use the surname preceded by the title. Titles such as "Herr Direktor" are sometimes used to indicate prestige, status, and rank. Thais, on the other hand, address one other by first names and reserve last names for very formal occasions and written communications.

In Belgium it is important to address French-speaking business contacts as "Monsieur" or "Madame," while Dutch-speaking contacts should be addressed as ''Mr.'' or "Mrs." To confuse the two is a great insult.

Customs concerning gift giving are extremely important to understand. In some cultures gifts are expected and failure to present them is considered an insult, whereas in other countries offering a gift is considered offensive. Business executives also need to know when to present gifts-on the initial visit or afterwards; where to present gifts-in public or private; what type of gift to present; what color it should be; and how many to present.

Gift giving is an important part of doing business in Japan, where gifts are usually exchanged at the first meeting. In sharp contrast, gifts are rarely exchanged in Germany and are usually not appropriate. Gift giving is not a normal custom in Belgium or the United Kingdom either, although in both countries, flowers are a suitable gift when invited to someone's home.

Customs concerning the exchange of business cards vary, too. Although this point seems of minor importance, observing a country's customs for card giving is a key part of business protocol. In Japan, for example, the Western practice of accepting a business card and pocketing it immediately is considered rude. The proper approach is to carefully look at the card after accepting it, observe the title and organization, acknowledge with a nod that the information has been digested, and perhaps make a relevant comment or ask a police question.

Negotiating-a complex process even between parties from the same nation-is even more complicated in international transactions because of the added chance of misunderstandings stemming from cultural differences. It is essential to understand the importance of rank in the other country; to know who the decision-makers are; to be familiar with the business style of the foreign company; and to understand the nature of agreements in the country, the significance of gestures, and negotiating etiquette.

It is important to acquire, through reading or training, a basic knowledge of the business culture, management attitudes, business methods, and consumer habits of the country being visited. This does not mean that the traveler must go native when conducting business abroad. It does mean that the traveler should be sensitive to the customs and business procedures of the country being visited.

Chapter 25

Dual Nationality

[The information in this chapter is reprinted verbatim from a number of bulletins issued by the U.S. State Department, Bureau of Consular Affairs. It is intended to serve as advice to Americans traveling abroad.]

- - - -

What It Is: Dual nationality is the simultaneous possession of two citizenship. The Supreme Court of the United States has stated that dual nationality is "a status long recognized in the law" and that "a person may have and exercise rights of nationality in two countries and be subject to the responsibilities of both. The mere fact that he asserts the rights of one citizenship does not without more mean that he renounces the other", Kawakita v. U.S., 343 U.S. 717 (1952). The concepts discussed in this chapter apply also to persons who have more than two nationalities.

How Acquired: Dual nationality results from the fact that there is no uniform rule of international law relating to the acquisition of nationality. Each country has its own laws on the subject, and its nationality is conferred upon individuals on the basis of its own independent domestic policy. Individuals may have dual nationality not by choice but by automatic operation of these different and sometimes conflicting laws.

The laws of the United States, no less than those of other countries, contribute to the situation because they provide for acquisition of U.S. citizenship by birth in the United States and also by birth abroad to an American, regardless of the other nationalities which a person might acquire at birth. For example, a child born abroad to U.S. citizens may acquire at birth not only American citizenship but also the nationality of the country in which it was born. Similarly, a child born in the United States to foreigners may acquire at birth both U.S. citizenship and a foreign nationality.

The laws of some countries provide for automatic acquisition of citizenship after birth, for example, by marriage. In addition, some countries do not recognize naturalization in a foreign state as grounds for loss of citizenship. A person from one of those countries who is naturalized in the United States keeps the nationality of the country of origin despite the fact that one of the requirements for U.S. naturalization is a renunciation of other nationalities.

Current Law and Policy: The current nationality laws of the United States do not specifically refer to dual nationality. The automatic acquisition or retention of a foreign nationality does not affect U.S. citizenship; however, under limited circumstances, the acquisition of a foreign nationality upon one's own application or the application of a duly authorized agent may cause loss of U.S. citizenship under Section 349(9)(1) of the Immigration and Nationality Act [8 U.S.C. 1481(a)(1)]. In order for loss of nationality to occur under Section 34q(a)(1), it must be established that the naturalization was obtained voluntarily by a person eighteen years of age or older with the intention of relinquishing U.S. citizenship. Such an intention may be shown by the person's statements or conduct, Vance v. Terrazas, 444 U.S 252 (1980). but in most cases it is assumed that Americans who are naturalized in other countries intend to keep their U S. citizenship As a result, they have both nationalities.

United States law does not contain any provisions requiring U.S. citizens who are born with dual nationality to choose one nationality or the other when they become adults, Mandoli v. Acheson, 344 U.S. 133 (1952).

While recognizing the existence of dual nationality and permitting Americans to have other nationalities, the U.S. Government does not endorse dual nationality as a matter of policy because of the problems which it may cause. Claims of other countries upon dual-national U.S. citizens often place them in situations where their obligations to one country are in conflict with the laws of the other. In addition, their dual nationality may hamper efforts to provide diplomatic and consular protection to them when they are abroad.

Allegiance to Which Country: It generally is considered that while dual nationals are in the other country of which they are citizens that country has a predominant claim on them. Like Americans who possess only U.S. citizenship, dual national U.S. citizens owe allegiance to the United States and are obliged to obey its laws and regulations. Such persons usually have certain obligations to the foreign country as well. Although failure to fulfill such obligations may have no adverse effect on dual nationals while in the United States because the foreign country would have few means to force compliance under those circumstances, dual nationals might be forced to comply with those obligations or pay a penalty if they go to the foreign country. In cases where dual nationals encounter difficulty in a foreign country of which they are citizens, the ability of U.S. Foreign Service posts to provide assistance may be quite limited since many foreign countries may not recognize a dual national's claim to U.S. citizenship.

Which Passport to Use: Section 215 of the Immigration and Nationality Act [8 U.S.C. 1185] requires U.S. citizens to use U.S. passports when entering or leaving the United States unless one of the exceptions listed in Section 53.2 of Title 22 of the Code of Federal Regulations applies. Dual nationals may be required by the other country of which they are citizens to enter and leave that country using its passport, but do not endanger their U.S. citizenship by complying with such a requirement.

How to Give Up Dual Nationality: Most countries have laws which specify how a cit-izen may lose or divest citizenship. Generally, persons who do not wish to maintain dual nationality may renounce the citizenship which they do not want. Information on renouncing a foreign nationality may be obtained from the foreign country's Embassies and Consulates or from the appropriate governmental agency in that country. Americans may renounce their U.S. citizenship abroad pursuant to Section 349(a)(5) of the Immigration and Nationality Act [8 U.S.C. 1481(a)(5)]. Information on renouncing U.S. citizenship may be obtained from U.S. Embassies and Consulates and the Office of Citizens Consular Services, Department of State, Washington, D.C. 20520.

For further information on dual nationality, see Marjorie M. Whiteman's _Digest of International Law_ (Department of State Publication 8290, released September 1967), Volume 8, pages 64-84.

A Few words to the American Traveler:
A foreign country may claim you as a citizen of that country if:
*   You were born there.
*   Your parent is a citizen of that country.
*   You are married to a citizen of that country
*   You are a naturalized U.S. citizen but are still considered a citizen by your country of origin.
If you are in any of the above categories, before departing check your status (including military

obligations) with the embassy or consulate of the country that might claim you as a citizen. Countries in the Middle East and Eastern Europe, in particular, may regard you as one of their citizens. In some cases of dual nationality, foreign countries have refused to recognize an individual's american citizenship and have not allowed U.S. officials access to arrested American citizens. Some countries especially, in the Middle East, Africa, South America, Asia and Eastern Europe do not recognize acquisition of U.S. citizenship. Unless the naturalized U.S. citizen renounces his or her original nationality at an embassy or consulate of the country of origin, he or she may still be considered to be a citizen of that country. A person born in the United States of a parent or parents who were citizens of another country may also be considered by that country to be their national. If arrested, a dual national may be denied the right to communicate with the U.S. embassy or consulate. Dual nationals may also be forced to serve in the military of their former country, or they may not be allowed to depart the country when their visit is over. If you are a naturalized U.S. citizen, a dual national, or have any reason to believe another country may consider you its national, check with the embassy of that country as to your citizenship status and any obligations you may have while visiting there. When you research your citizenship status, bear in mind that the purpose of your planned trip can affect your status. Your acquired U.S. citizenship may be recognized by your former country if you only visit there. If, however, you take up residence, the country may consider you as having resumed your former nationality. This can happen even if the embassy of the country has stamped a visa in your U.S. passport.

Dual nationals should also be aware that they may be required to use a passport from their country of origin in order to enter or leave that country. The U.S. Government does not object to the use of a foreign passport in such situations. U.S. citizens may however, use a foreign passport to enter or leave the United States.

If you have any questions about dual nationality or the use of foreign passports, contact the Office of citizens consular services, room 4817, Department of state Washington, D.C., 20520, (202) 647-3926 before you travel.

If you have any questions about dual nationality or the use of foreign passports, contact the Office of Citizens Consular Services, Room 4817, Department of State, Washington, D.C. 20520-4818, (202- 647-3926) before you travel. Recorded information on dual nationality and other citizenship matters is available 24-hours a day by calling 202 647-3444.

Chapter 26

Getting Help Abroad from U.S. Consuls

*[The information in this chapter is reprinted verbatim from a bulletin issued by the
U.S. State Department, Bureau of Consular Affairs. It is intended to serve as advice
to Americans traveling abroad.]*

- - - -

U.S. Consuls Help Americans Abroad

There are U.S. embassies in 160 capital cities of the world. Each embassy has a consular section. Consular officers in consular sections of embassies do two things:

- they issue visas to foreigners;

- they help U.S. citizens abroad.

There are also consular officers at about 60 U.S. consulates general and 20 U.S. consulates around the world. (Consulates general and consulates are regional offices of embassies.)

U.S. consuls usually are assisted by local employees who are citizens of the host country. Because of the growing number of Americans traveling abroad, and the relatively small number of consuls, the expertise of local employees is invaluable.

In this chapter, we highlight ways in which consular officers can assist you while you are traveling or residing abroad.

To help us help you while you are abroad, register with the nearest U.S. embassy or consulate. This makes it easier for consular officers to reach you in an emergency or to replace a lost passport.

Consular officers provide a range of services - some emergency, some nonemergency.

EMERGENCY SERVICES

Replace A Passport - If you lose your passport, a consul can issue you a replacement, often within 24 hours. If you believe your passport has been stolen, first report the theft to the local police and get a police declaration.

Help Find Medical Assistance - If you get sick, you can contact a consular officer for a list of local doctors, dentists, and medical specialists, along with other medical information.

If you are injured or become seriously ill, a consul will help you find medical assistance and, at your request, inform your family or friends. (Consider getting private medical insurance before you travel, to cover the high cost of getting you back to the U.S. for hospital care in the event of a medical emergency.)

Help Get Funds - Should you lose all your money and other financial resources, consular officers can help you contact your family, bank, or employer to arrange for them to send you funds. In some cases, these funds can be wired to you through the Department of State.

Help In An Emergency - Your family may need to reach you because of an emergency at home or because they are worried about your welfare. They should call the State Department's Citizens Emergency Center (202) 647-5225. The State Department will relay the message to consular officers in the country in which you are traveling. Consular officers will attempt to locate you, pass on urgent messages, and, consistent with the Privacy Act, report back to your family.

Visit In Jail - If you are arrested, you should ask the authorities to notify a U.S. consul. Consuls cannot get you out of jail (when you are in a foreign country you are subject to its laws). However, they can work to protect your legitimate interests and ensure you are not discriminated against. They can provide a list of local attorneys, visit you, inform you generally about local laws, and contact your family and friends. Consular officers can transfer money, food, and clothing to the prison authorities from your family or friends. They can try to get relief if you are held under inhumane or unhealthful conditions.

Make Arrangements After The Death Of An American - When an American dies abroad, a consular officer notifies the American's family and informs them about options and costs for disposition of remains. Costs for preparing and returning a body to the U.S. may be high and must be paid by the family. Often, local laws and procedures make returning a body to the U.S. for burial a lengthy process. A consul prepares a Report of Death based on the local death certificate;

this is forwarded to the next of kin for use in estate and insurance matters.

Help in a Disaster/Evacuation - If you are caught up in a natural disaster or civil disturbance, you should let your relatives know as soon as possible that you are safe, or contact a U.S. consul who will pass that message to your family through the State Department. Be resourceful. U.S. officials will do everything they can to contact you and advise you. However, they must give priority to helping Americans who have been hurt or are in immediate danger. In a disaster, consuls face the same constraints you do - lack of electricity or fuel, interrupted phone lines, closed airports.

NONEMERGENCY SERVICES

Issue a Consular Report of Birth - A child born abroad to U.S. citizen parents usually acquires U.S. citizenship at birth. The parents should contact the nearest U.S. embassy or consulate to have a "Report of Birth Abroad of a U.S. Citizen" prepared. This is proof of citizenship for all purposes.

Issue a Passport - Consuls issue approximately 200,000 passports abroad each year. Many of these are issued to persons whose current passports have expired.

Distribute Federal Benefits Payments - Over a half-million people living overseas receive monthly federal benefit payments. In many countries, the checks are mailed to the U.S. embassy or consulate and distributed through the local postal service.

Assist in Child Custody Disputes - In an international custody dispute, a consul can try to locate a child abroad, monitor the child's welfare, and provide general information to the American parent about laws and procedures which may be used to effect the child's return to the United States. Consuls may not take custody of a child, or help a parent regain custody of a child illegally or by force or deception.

Help In Other Ways - Consuls handle personal estates of deceased U.S. citizens, assist with absentee voting and Selective Service registration, notarize documents, advise on property claims, and provide U.S. tax forms. They also perform such functions as adjudicating U.S. citizenship claims and assisting U.S. courts in legal matters.

WHAT CONSULAR OFFICERS CANNOT DO

In addition to the qualifications noted above, consular officers cannot act as travel agents, banks, lawyers, investigators, or law enforcement officers. Please do not expect them to find you employment, get you residence or driving permits, act as interpreters, search for missing luggage, or settle disputes with hotel managers. They can, however, tell you how to get help on these and other matters.

If you need to pick up mail or messages while traveling, some banks and international credit card companies handle mail for customers at their overseas branches. General Delivery (Poste Restante) services at post offices in most countries will hold mail for you.

PRIVACY ACT

The provisions of the Privacy Act are designed to protect the privacy rights of Americans. Occasionally they complicate a consul's efforts to assist Americans. As a general rule, consular officers may not reveal information regarding an individual American's location, welfare, intentions, or problems to anyone, including family members and Congressional representatives, without the expressed consent of that individual. Although sympathetic to the distress this can cause concerned families, consular officers must comply with the provisions of the Privacy Act.

For more information, contact Overseas Citizens Services, Department of State, Room 4800, Washington, D.C. 20520.

Chapter 27

Crises Abroad-What the State Department Does

*[The Information in this chapter is reprinted verbatim from a bulletin issued by the
U.S. State Department, Bureau of Consular Affairs. It is intended to serve as advice
to Americans traveling abroad.]*

- - - -

When Disaster Strikes Abroad . . .

What can the State Department's Bureau of Consular Affairs do for Americans caught in a disaster or a crisis abroad?

Earthquakes, hurricanes, political upheavals, acts of terrorism, and hijackings are only some of the events threatening the safety of Americans abroad. Each event is unique and poses its own special difficulties. However, for the State Department there are certain responsibilities and actions that apply in every disaster or crisis.

When a crisis occurs, the State Department sets up a task force or working group to bring together in one set of rooms all the people necessary to work on that event. Usually this Washington task force will be in touch by telephone 24 hours a day with our Ambassador and Foreign Service Officers at the embassy in the country affected.

In a task force, the immediate job of the State Department's Bureau of Consular Affairs is to respond to the thousands of concerned relatives and friends who begin to telephone the State Department immediately after the news of a disaster is broadcast.

Relatives want information on the welfare of their family members and on the disaster. The State Department relies for hard information on its embassies and consulates abroad. Often these installations are also affected by the disaster and lack electricity, phone lines, gasoline, etc. Nevertheless, foreign service officers work hard to get information back to Washington as quickly as possible. This is rarely as quickly as the press is able to relay information. Foreign Service Officers cannot speculate; their information must be accurate. Often this means getting important information from the local government, which may or may not be immediately responsive.

Welfare & Whereabouts

As concerned relatives call in, officers of the Bureau of Consular Affairs collect the names of the Americans possibly involved in the disaster and pass them to the embassy and consulates. Officers at post attempt to locate these Americans in order to report on their welfare. The officers work with local authorities and, depending on the circumstances, may personally search hotels, airports, hospitals, or even prisons. As they try to get the information, their first priority is Americans dead or injured.

Death

When an American dies abroad, the Bureau of Consular Affairs must locate and inform the next-of-kin. Sometimes discovering the next-of-kin is difficult. If the American's name is known, the Bureau's Office of Passport Services will search for his or her passport application. However, the information there may not be current.

The Bureau of Consular Affairs provides guidance to grieving family members on how to make arrangements for local burial or return of the remains to the U.S. The disposition of remains is affected by local laws, customs, and facilities which are often vastly different from those in the U.S. The Bureau of Consular Affairs relays the family's instructions and necessary private funds to cover the costs involved to the embassy or consulate. The Department of State has no funds to assist in the return of remains or ashes of American citizens who die abroad. Upon completion of all formalities, the consular officer abroad prepares an official Foreign Service Report of Death, based upon the local death certificate, and sends it to the next-of-kin or legal representative for use in U.S. courts to settle estate matters.

A U.S. consular officer overseas has statutory responsibility for the personal estate of an American who dies abroad if the deceased has no legal representative in the country where the death occurred. The consular officer takes possession of personal effects, such as convertible assets, apparel, jewelry, personal documents and paper. The officer prepares an inventory and then carries out instructions from members of the deceased's family concerning the effects. A final statement of the account is then sent to the next-of-kin. The Diplomatic Pouch cannot be used to ship personal items, including valuables, but legal documents and correspondence relating to the estate can be transmitted by pouch. In Washington, the Bureau of Consular Affairs gives next-of-kin guidance on procedures to follow in preparing Letters Testamentary, Letters of Administration, and Affidavits of Next-of-Kin as acceptable evidence of legal claim of an estate.

Injury

In the case of an injured American, the embassy or consulate abroad notifies the task force which notifies family members in the U.S. The Bureau of Consular Affairs can assist in sending private funds to the injured American; frequently it collects information on the individual's prior medical history and forwards it to the embassy or consulate. When necessary, the State Department assists in arranging the return of the injured American to the U.S. commercially, with appropriate medical escort, via commercial air ambulance or, occasionally, by U.S. Air Force medical evacuation aircraft. The use of Air Force facilities for a medical evacuation is authorized only under certain stringent conditions, and when commercial evacuation is not possible. The full expense must be borne by the injured American or his family.

Evacuation

Sometimes commercial transportation entering and leaving a country is disrupted during a political upheaval or natural disaster. If this happens, and if it appears unsafe for Americans to remain, the embassy and consulates will work with the task force in Washington to charter special air flights and ground transportation to help Americans to depart. The U.S. Government cannot order Americans to leave a foreign country. It can only advise and try to assist those who wish to leave.

Privacy Act

The provisions of the Privacy Act are designed to protect the privacy and rights of Americans, but occasionally they complicate our efforts to assist citizens abroad. As a rule, consular officers may not reveal information regarding an individual American's location, welfare, intentions, or problems to anyone, including family members and Congressional representatives, without the expressed consent of that individual. Although sympathetic to the distress this can cause concerned families, consular officers are forced to comply with the provisions of the Privacy Act.

Chapter 28

Overseas Citizens Services/The Citizens Emergency Center

[The information in this chapter is reprinted verbatim from a bulletin issued by the U.S. State Department, Bureau of Consular Affairs. It is intended to serve as advice to Americans both at home and abroad.]

- - - -

THE OFFICE OF OVERSEAS CITIZENS SERVICES

When You Need Help ...

Overseas Citizens Services

Overseas Citizens Services (OCS) in the State Department's Bureau of Consular Affairs is responsible for the welfare and whereabouts of U.S. citizens traveling and residing abroad. OCS has three offices: American Citizens Services and Crisis Management, the Office of Children's Issues and the Office of Policy Review and Interagency Liaison.

AMERICAN CITIZENS SERVICES AND CRISIS MANAGEMENT (ACS)

American Citizens Services and Crisis Management corresponds organizationally to American Citizens Services offices set up at U.S. embassies and consulates throughout the world. ACS has six geographical divisions with case officers who assist in all matters involving protective services for Americans abroad, including arrests, death cases, financial or medical emergencies, and welfare and whereabouts inquiries. The office also issues Travel Warnings and Consular Information Sheets and provides guidance on nationality and citizenship determination, document issuance, judicial and notarial services, estates and property claims, third-country representation, and disaster assistance.

Arrests
Over 2,500 Americans are arrested abroad annually. More than 30% of these arrests are drug related. Over 70% of drug related arrests involve marijuana or cocaine.

The rights an American enjoys in this country do not travel abroad. Each country is sovereign and its laws apply to everyone who enters regardless of nationality. The U.S. government cannot get Americans released from foreign jails. However, a U.S. consul will insist on prompt access to an arrested American, provide a list of attorneys, and provide information on the host country's legal system, offer to contact the arrested American's family or friends, visit on a regular basis, protest mistreatment, monitor jail conditions, provide dietary supplements, if needed, and keep the State Department informed.

ACS is the point of contact in the U.S. for family members and others who are concerned about a U.S. citizen arrested abroad.

Deaths
Approximately 6,000 Americans die outside of the U.S. each year. The majority of these are long-term residents of a foreign country. ACS assists with the return of remains for approximately 2,000 Americans annually.

When an American dies abroad, a consular officer notifies the next of kin about options and costs for disposition of remains. Costs for preparing and returning a body to the U.S. are high and are the responsibility of the family. Often local laws and procedures make returning a body to the U.S. for burial a lengthy process.

Financial Assistance
If destitute, Americans can turn to a U.S. consular officer abroad for help. ACS will help by contacting the destitute person's family, friends, or business associates to raise private funds, It will help transmit these funds to destitute Americans.

ACS transfers approximately 3 million dollars a year in private emergency funds. It can approve small government loans to destitute Americans abroad until private funds arrive.

ACS also approves repatriation loans to pay for destitute Americans' direct return to the U.S. Each year over $500,000 are loaned to destitute Americans.

Medical Assistance
ACS works with U.S. consuls abroad to assist

Americans who become physically or mentally ill while traveling. ACS locates family members, guardians, and friends in the U.S., assists in transmitting private funds, and, when necessary, assists in arranging the return of ill or injured Americans to the U.S. by commercial carrier.

Welfare and Whereabouts of U.S. Citizens
ACS receives approximately 12,000 inquiries a year concerning the welfare or whereabouts of an American abroad. Many inquiries are from worried relatives who have not heard from the traveler. Others are attempts to notify the traveler about a family crisis at home.

Most welfare/whereabouts inquiries are successfully resolved. However, occasionally, a person is truly missing. It is the responsibility of local authorities to investigate and U.S. consuls abroad will work to ensure their continued interest in cases involving Americans. Unfortunately, as in the U.S., sometimes missing persons are never found.

Consular Information Program
ACS issues fact sheets on every country in the world called Consular Information Sheets (CIS). The CIS contains information on entry requirements, crime and security conditions, areas of instability and other details relevant to travel in a particular country.

The Office also issues Travel Warnings. Travel Warnings are issued when the State Department recommends deferral of travel by Americans to a country because of civil unrest, dangerous conditions, terrorist activity and/or because the U.S. has no diplomatic relations with the country and cannot assist an American in distress.

Consular Information Sheets and Travel Warnings may be heard anytime, by dialing the Off ice of Overseas Citizens Services travelers' hotline at (202) 647-5225 from a touchtone phone. They are also available via Consular Affairs' automated fax system at (202) 647-3000, or at any of the 13 regional passport agencies, at U.S. embassies and consulates abroad, and through the airline computer reservation systems, or, by sending a self-addressed, stamped business size envelope to the Office of Overseas Citizens Services, Bureau of Consular Affairs, Room 4811, U.S. Department of State, Washington, D.C. 20520-4818

If you have a personal computer, modem and communications software, you can access them, and other consular handouts and publications through the Consular Affairs Bulletin Board (CABB). This service is free of charge. To access CABB, dial the modem number:(202) 647-9225; set modem speed (it will accommodate 300, 1200, 2400, 9600 or 14400 bps); and terminal communications program to N-8-1 (parity, 8 bits, 1 stop bit).

Disaster Assistance
ACS coordinates the Bureau's activities and efforts relating to international crises or emergency situations involving the welfare and safety of large numbers of Americans residing or traveling in a crisis area. Such crises can include plane crashes, hijackings, natural disasters, civil disorders, and political unrest.

CHILDREN'S ISSUES (CI)
The Office of Children's Issues (CI) formulates, develops and coordinates policies and programs, and provides direction to foreign service posts on international parental child abduction and international adoptions. It also fulfills U.S. treaty obligations relating to the abduction of children.

International adoptions
Coordinates policy and provides information on international adoption to the potential parents. In 1994, over 8,000 foreign born children where adopted by U.S. citizens. The Department of State cannot intervene on behalf of an individual in foreign courts because adoption is a private legal matter within the judicial sovereignty of the country where the child resides. This off ice can, however, offer general information and assistance regarding the adoption process in over 60 countries.

International Parental Child Abductions
In recent years, the Bureau of Consular Affairs has taken action in thousands of cases of international parental child abduction. The Bureau also provides information in response to thousands of additional inquiries pertaining to international child abduction, enforcement of visitation rights and abduction prevention techniques. Cl works closely with parents, attorneys, other government agencies, and private organizations in the U.S. to prevent international abductions.

The Hague Convention provides for the return of a child to his or her habitual place of residence if the child has been wrongfully removed or retained. Cl has been designated by Congress as the Central Authority to administer the Hague Convention in the United States.

POLICY REVIEW AND INTERAGENCY LIAISON (PRI)
The Office of Policy Review and Interagency Liaison (PRI) provides guidance concerning the administration and enforcement of laws on U.S. citizenship, and on

the documentation of Americans traveling and residing abroad. The Office also provides advice on matters involving treaties and agreements, legislative matters, including implementation of new laws, conducts reconsideration of acquisition and loss of U.S. citizenship in complex cases abroad, and administer overseas federal benefits program.

Consular Conventions and Treaties
PRI works closely with other offices in the State Department in the negotiation of consular conventions and treaties, including prisoner transfer treaties.

As a result of these prisoner transfer treaties, many U.S. citizens convicted of crimes and incarcerated abroad have returned to the U.S. to complete their sentences.

Federal Benefits
Over a half-million people receive monthly federal benefits payments outside the U.S. In many countries, the monthly benefits checks are mailed or pouched to the consular post and then distributed through the local postal service. In other countries, the checks are mailed directly into the beneficiaries' foreign bank accounts. Consular officers assist in the processing of individual benefits claims and problems; investigate claims on behalf of the agency concerned; and perform other tasks requested by the agencies or needed by the beneficiaries or survivors.

Legislation
PRI is involved with legislation affecting U.S. citizens abroad. The office participates in hearings and provides testimony to Congress on proposed legislation, particularly legislation relating to the citizenship and welfare of U.S. citizens, They also interpret laws and regulations pertaining to citizens consular services, including the administration of the Immigration and Nationality Act.

Privacy Act
PRI responds to inquires under the Privacy Act. The provisions of the Privacy Act are
designed to protect the privacy and rights of Americans but occasionally complicate efforts to assist U.S. citizens abroad. As a general rule, consular officers may not reveal information regarding an individual American's location, welfare, intentions, or problems to anyone, including family members and Congressional representatives, without the expressed consent of that individual. In all potential cases, consular officers explain Privacy Act restrictions and requirements so that all individuals involved in a case understand the Privacy Act's constraints.

Hours of Operation:

Monday-Friday 8:15 a.m.-10:00 p.m., and Saturday 9:00 a.m.-3:00 p.m.: (Telephone: **(202) 647-5225***

For after-hours emergencies, Sundays and Holidays, (Telephone: **(202) 647-4000** and request the OCS duty officer.

*Overseas Citizens Services has a 24-hours a day hotline at **(202) 647-5225**
for American Citizens Services (including travel and citizenship information).
Policy Review and Interagency Liaison can also be reached at this number.

The Office of Children's Issues can be reached by calling **(202) 736-7000.**

Hours:
Monday-Friday 8:15 a.m-10:00 p.m.,
and Saturday 9:00 a.m.-3:00 p.m.:
Telephone: (202) 647-5225.

After-hours, Sundays and Holidays:
Telephone: (202) 647-4000

Travel Advisory Information
24 hours a day, seven days a week:
Telephone: (202) 647-5225

Chapter 29

The State Department Travel Advisories

[The information in this chapter is reprinted verbatim from a number of bulletins issued by the
U.S. State Department, Bureau of Consular Affairs. It is intended to serve as advice
to Americans traveling abroad.]

- - - -

The State Department issues travel advisories to inform traveling Americans of conditions abroad which may affect them adversely. Travel advisories are generally about physical dangers, unexpected arrests or detentions, serious health hazards, and other conditions abroad with serious consequences for traveling Americans.

Travel advisories which describe a potential for violence and physical danger usually reflect a trend or pattern of violence over a period of time in which the government of the country involved is unwilling or unable to afford normal protection. For that reason, isolated international terrorist of criminal attacks - which can and do occur virtually anywhere at any time - do not generally trigger travel advisories.

Travel advisories are issued on the basis of objective evidence about emerging or existing circumstances and are modified or canceled when those circumstances change. Travel advisories are issued only after careful review of information from our diplomatic post in the affected country, and in coordination with various bureaus of the Department of State and other concerned federal agencies.

The Department of State has revised the travel advisory program to expand the type of information distributed to U.S. citizens traveling and residing abroad. The system changes the three general categories of travel advisories - warnings, cautions and notices - to two: Travel Warnings and Consular Information Sheets.

Under the previous three-tier system, **warnings** recommend deferral to all or part of the country, **cautions** describe unstable political conditions, possible detention, or health problems and **notices** describe inconveniences, such as crime or currency changes. Under the new system, when the State Department recommends deferral of all travel to a country, a Travel Warning will be issued for that country. Consular Information Sheets will be made available for every country of the world. In countries where avoidance of travel is recommended, both Travel Warnings and

Consular Information Sheets will be issued.

Consular Information Sheets will include such information as the location of the U.S. Embassy or Consulate in the subject country, unusual immigration practices, health conditions, minor political disturbances, unusual currency and entry regulations, crime and security information, and drug penalties. If an unstable condition exists in a country that is not severe enough to warrant a Warning, a description of the condition(s) may be included under an optional section entitled **"Areas of Instability."** Occasionally, we the State Department will also restate in this section any advice given by the U.S. Embassy to official employees. Consular Information Sheets generally do not include advice, but present information in a factual manner so travelers can make their own decisions concerning travel to particular countries.

USER GUIDE TO BUREAU OF CONSULAR AFFAIRS AUTOMATED FAX SYSTEM

The Consular Affairs automated fax system is available to anyone with a fax machine equipped with a telephone jack. The system offers all of the Bureau's Consular Information Sheets, Travel Warnings, Public Announcements, Tips for Travelers brochures, Visa Bulletins, and other consular information. The telephone number for all information is: (202) 647-3000. Callers must use the receiver on their fax machines to dial the automated fax service and will then be given a series of prompts to select the information they wish to receive on their fax machine. Callers should not hang up their fax receivers until completing all prompts. Callers outside of the metropolitan Washington, D.C. area can expect to be charged the cost of a long distance phone call, but there are no additional charges for this service.

For Consular Information Sheets and Travel Warnings

Dial (202) 647-3000 from the touchtone telephone connected to your fax machine. When instructed to do so, enter the first four letters of the country for which you wish to receive information, (if the telephone keypad on your fax does not have letters, you will need to either label the keys with standard telephone letters or order the index with the number codes for the sheets.) If the first four letters contain a Q, press 7 in place of the Q. If the first four letters contain a Z, press 9 in place of the Z. Once you have entered the first four letters, your selection will be verified along with the total number of pages to expect. Should you wish to receive additional Consular Information Sheets or Travel Warnings on the same telephone call, do not hang up the phone, simply enter the first four letters for the next country sheet you wish to order. After each selection, you will need to verify your choice (for Yes enter 9, for No enter 6). Once verified, press the 'pound' key, followed by the start or connect button on your fax, to begin the transmission. There is a limit of 9 documents that you can order in a single telephone call.

To receive all Consular Information Sheets and Travel Warnings issued within the last 7 days and any other new information entered in the automated fax database within the last 7 days:

Dial (202) 647-3000 from the touchtone telephone connected to your fax machine. When instructed to enter your choice, enter 'week' or 9335. You will be able to receive the lost 7 days' information in alphabetical segments. Select 'Weekly Update - Part I " for the first segment,"Weekly Update - Part 2" for the second segment and so on. You will need to verify your choice ("Y" for yes, "N" for no). Once verified, press the 'pound' key, followed by the start or connect button on your fax, to begin the transmission.

For Index
To receive an index of available publications and documents, dial (202) 647-3000. When instructed to do so, press the 'star' key and then press the start/connect button to receive the index.

Once you have the index, you may order up to 9 documents by entering the four or five-digit code(s) for the document(s) you wish to receive. After you have made your selection(s), the voice prompt will verify your choices and inform you of the number of pages being sent. You will then need to confirm your selection (for Yes enter 9, for No enter 6), push the 'pound' key, and push the start or connect button to receive your fax.

To obtain information provided by the Bureau of Public Affairs by fax, including press material, testimony, speeches, biographies and "Background Notes" on selected countries, call 202-736-7720.

CONSULAR INFORMATION PROGRAM
There are two categories of information. Travel Warnings and Consular Information Sheets. Warnings are issued when the State Department decides, based on all relevant information, to recommended that Americans avoid travel to a certain country. Countries where avoidance of travel is recommended will have Travel Warnings as well as Consular Information Sheets.

Consular Information Sheets are available for every country of the world. They include such information as location of the U.S. Embassy or Consulate in the subject country, unusual immigration practices, health conditions, minor political disturbances, unusual currency and entry regulations, crime and security information, and drug penalties. If an unstable condition exists in a country that is not severe enough to warrant a Warning, a description of the condition(s) may be included under an optional section entitled "Areas of Instability". On limited occasions, we also restate in this section any Embassy advice given to official employees. Consular Information Sheets generally do not include advice, but present information in a factual manner so the traveler can make his or her own decisions concerning travel to a particular country.

HOW TO ACCESS CONSULAR INFORMATION SHEETS AND TRAVEL WARNINGS
Consular Information Sheets and Travel Warnings may be heard anytime by dialing the Citizens Emergency Center at (202) 647-5225 from a touchtone phone. The recording is updated as new information becomes available. They are also available at any of the 13 regional passport agencies, field offices of the U.S. Department of Commerce, and U.S. embassies and consulates abroad, or, by writing and sending a self-addressed, stamped envelope to the Citizens Emergency Center, Bureau of Consular Affairs, Room 4811.

By Fax
From your fax machine, dial 202-647-3000, using the handset as you would a regular telephone. The system will instruct you on how to proceed.

Consular Affairs Bulletin Board - CABB
If you have a personal computer, modem and communications software, you can access the Consular Affairs Bulletin Board or CABB. This service is free of charge.

Modem Number. 202-647-9225

Modem Speed: Will accommodate 300, 1200, 2400, 9600 or 1440 bps.

Terminal Communications Program: Set to N-8-1 (No parity, 8 bits, 1 stop bit)

By Computer Network

If you have a personal computer and a modem, you can also access Consular Information Sheets and Travel Warnings through the Official Airlines Guide (OAG). The OAG provides the full text of Consular Information Sheets and Travel Warnings on many online computer services. To obtain information on accessing Consular Information Sheets and Travel Warnings through OAG on any of the following computer services, call the OAG Electronic Edition at 1-800-323-4000.

CompuServe
Dialcom
Dialog
Dow Jones News/Retrieval
General Videotex-Delphi
GEnie
iNet-America
iNet-Bell of Canada
NewsNet
IP Sharp
Telenet
Western Union-Easylink

Infosys America Inc. also provides the full text of Consular Information Sheets and Travel Warnings through Travel Online BBS on the SmartNet International Computer Network in the U.S. Canada and overseas. The (modem) telephone number for Infosys America is (314) 625-4054.

Interactive Office Services, Inc. offers online travel information in Travel+Plus through the networks listed below. For information on access, call Travel+Plus at (617) 876-5551 or 1-800-544-4005.

The Overseas Security Electronic Bulletin Board provides State Department Consular Information Sheets and Travel Warnings as a free service (purchase of necessary software required) for American firms doing business overseas. Apply to the Executive Director, Overseas Security Advisory Council (DS/OSAC), Department of State Washington, D.C. 20522-1003.

Access by Colleges and Universities: NAFSANET & INTER-I

NAFSANET is the term used to refer to all the members of NAFSA, an association of international educators who have access to electronic mail and are using it to communicate among themselves and with colleagues in other countries. INTER-L is a program which manages the distribution of e-mail to various lists of subscribers. To subscribe to INTER-L, you need an e-mail account on either Bitnet or Internet. Then, send a message to **LISTSERV@VTVM2.BINET**. You may leave the subject line blank. The text of the message should read **SUBSCRIBE INTER-L Your Name**. (Note: Some system require that you prefix listserv commands with TELL LISTERV. In that case, the message should read **TELL LISTSERV SUBSCRIBE INTER-L Your Name**). You may wish to consult your computer center on the correct format to use at your institution. Once subscribed to INTER-L, to receive Consular Information Sheets and Travel Warnings, send a request to **travel-advisories-REQUEST@stolaf.edu**.

For more information, contact one of the INTER-L co-managers:

Jim Graham
4301 Terry Lake Road
Fort Colline, CO. 80524
Phone: 303-493-0207
Fax: 303-491-5501
Bitnet: JGRAHAM@CSUGREEN.BITNET
Internet:
JGRAHAM@CSUGREEN.UCC.COLOSTATE.EDU

Bernard LaBerge, Graduate School
100 Sandy Hall, V.P.I. & S. U.
Blacksburg VA. 24060
Phone: 703-231-6271
Fax: 703-231-3714
Bitnet: GSBEL@VTVM1.BITNET
Internet: GSBEL@VTVM.1.CC.VT.EDU

By Computer Reservation System (CRS)

The following computer reservation systems (CRS) maintain State Department Consular Information Sheets and Travel Warnings. This Information can be accessed by entering the CRS codes listed below.

APOLLO - For the index, enter: S*BRF/TVLADV For the full text of Consular Information Sheets and Travel Warnings, enter: TD*DS/ADV

DATAS II - For full text of Consular Information Sheets and Travel Warnings, enter: G* (country)

PARS - For the index, enter: G/AAI/TVL

Travel Document Systems, Inc. provides the full text of Consular Information Sheets and Travel Warnings to the following reservation systems:

SABRE - Enter: N*/ADVISORY INDEX

SYSTEM ONE -   Enter: GG SUP TD ADV

IN Western Europe, SYSTEM ONE is accessed through the AMADEUS system and APOLLO through the GALLE System.

SAMPLES OF ACTUAL TRAVEL WARNINGS
Travel Warning

United States Department of State
Bureau of Consular Affairs
Washington, D.C. 20520

For recorded travel information call 202-647-5225.
To access the Consular Affairs Bulletin Board, call 202-647-9225.
For information by fax, call 202-647-3000 from your fax machine

Tajikistan--Warning

December 12, 1994

U.S. citizens are warned against travel to Tajikistan. Although a cease-fire is in effect between warring factions and peaceful elections were recently held, sporadic fighting continues along the Tajikistan-Afghanistan border. In addition, unsettled conditions exist in some areas of the countryside, particularly in parts of the Gharm Valley and Gorno-Badakhshan. There is a potential for terrorist actions in the capital, Dushanbe, primarily targeted agist Russians. The U.S. embassy provides a full range of consular services, but is extremely limited in the services it can provide outside Dushanbe.

No. 94-049

This replaces the Travel Warning for Tajikistan dated June 8, 1994, to update the present security situation.
October 7, 1992

Travel Warning

United States Department of State
Bureau of Consular Affairs
Washington, D.C. 20520

For recorded travel information call 202-647-5225.

To access the Consular Affairs Bulletin Board, call 202-647-9225.
For information by fax, call 202-647-3000 from your fax machine
----
Bosnia-Hercegovina--Warning

Bosnia-Hercegovina - Warning

May 31, 1995

The Department of State warns U.S. citizens not to travel to the Republic of Bosnia-Herzegovina are urged to leave. The recent hostage-taking by Bosnian Serb militia suggests that foreigners, including U.S. citizens, are at risk of being taken hostage. At the same time, the ability of the American Embassy in Sarajevo to assist citizens, even in emergencies, is severely limited by the increased military activity.

No.95-017

This replaces the Warning for Bosnia-Herzegovina dated May 17, 1995, to add the threat of hostage-taking.

TRAVEL WARNING LIST
(as of June 1995).

The U.S. Department of State has issued Travel Warnings for the countries listed below. To hear the full text of a Warning, or to request that a copy of a Warning be mailed to you, contact the Citizens Emergency Center at (202) 647-5225. Warnings are continually reviewed and revised, reissued or canceled as circumstances dictate. Therefore, over time, these warnings listed will change.

COUNTRY	DATE ISSUED
Afghanistan	1/12/94
Algeria	5/22/95
Angola	4/25/95
Bosnia-Herzegovina	5/31/95
Burundi	6/16/95
Croatia	8/16/95
Guatemala	4/18/95
Iran	8/31/93
Iraq	9/15/94
Lebanon	9/6/94
Lesotho	8/18/94
Liberia	10/27/94
Libya	12/22/94
Nigeria	6/5/95
North Korea	7/16/93
Peru	7/20/94
Rwanda	8/3/94
Serbia & Montenegro	4/29/94
Sierra Leone	2/1/95
Somalia	4/6/95
Sudan	1/30/95
Tajikistan	12/12/94

ACTUAL SAMPLE OF A CONSULAR INFORMATION SHEET

Austria--Consular Information Sheet

February 9, 1994

Country Description: Austria is a highly developed stable democracy with a modern economy. Tourist facilities are widely available.

Entry Requirements: A passport is required. A visa is not required for business or tourist stays up to three months. For information concerning longer stays or any other Austrian regulation, travelers can contact the Embassy of Austria at 3524 International Court N.W. Washington, D.C. 20008, tel: (202) 895-6750, or the nearest Austrian Consulate General in Chicago, Los Angeles, or New York.

Medical Facilities: Good medical care is widely available. U.S. medical insurance is not always valid out of the United States. Travelers have found that in some cases, supplemental medical insurance with specific overseas coverage has proved to be useful. Further information on health matters can be obtained from the Centers for Disease Control's international travelers hotline on (404) 332-4559.

Crime Information: Austria has a low crime rate, and violent crime is rare. Crimes involving theft of personal property, however, have been on the increase in recent years. Travelers can become targets of pickpockets and purse snatchers who operate where tourists tend to gather, favorite spots being Vienna's two largest train stations. U.S. citizens can refer to the Department of State's pamphlet "A Safe Trip Abroad" for ways to promote a more trouble-free voyage. The pamphlet is available from the Superintendent of Documents, U.S. Government Printing Office, Washington DC 20402.

Drug Penalties: Penalties for possession, use, or trafficking in illegal drugs are strict, and convicted offenders can expect jail sentences and fines.

Other Information: Certain Air Austria flights between Austria and various Middle Eastern points (usually Damascus or Amman) make en route stops in Beirut. (The State Department warns U.S. citizens to avoid all travel to or through Lebanon and that U.S. passports are not valid for such travel without special validation.)

Registration: Americans who register in the Consular Section of the Embassy or Consulate can obtain updated information on travel and security in Austria.

Embassy and Consulate Locations: The U.S. Embassy in Vienna is located at Boltzmanngasse 16 in the Ninth District. The Consular Section of the U.S. Embassy is located on the fourth floor of Gartenbaupromenade 2 in the First District. The telephone number for both the Embassy and the Consular Section is (43) (1) 339. There is also a Consular Agency in Salzburg at Herbert Von Karajan Platz 1, telephone (43-662) 84-87-76. Office hours for the Consular Agency are Monday, Wednesday, and Friday from 9:00 am to 12:00 noon. U.S. citizens in Salzburg who require emergency assistance after hours should contact the U.S. Embassy in Vienna.

94-010

This replaces the Consular Information Sheet dated April 29, 1993, to announce the opening of a Consular Agency in Salzburg.

Chapter 30

Travel Warnings on Drugs Abroad

[The Information in this chapter is reprinted verbatim from a bulletin issued by the U.S. State Department, Bureau of Consular Affairs. It is intended to serve as advice to Americans traveling abroad.]

- - - -

Things You Should Know Before You Go Abroad;

HARD FACTS

During 1991, 3,050 Americans were arrested in 105 foreign countries. Of these, 1,271 ended up in jails abroad because they assumed they couldn't get arrested for drug possession. From Asia to Africa, Europe to South America, Americans are finding out the hard way that drug possession or trafficking equals jail in foreign countries.

There is very little that anyone can do to help you if you are caught with drugs.

It is *your* responsibility to know what the drug laws are in a foreign country before you go, because "I *didn't know it was illegal"* will not get you out of jail.

In 1991, there was a 55 percent increase in the number of women arrested abroad. The rise is a result of women who serve as drug couriers or "mules" in the belief they can make quick money and have a vacation without getting caught. Instead of a vacation, they get a permanent residence in an overseas jail.

Of all Americans arrested abroad on drug charges in 1991, marijuana was involved in 77% of the cases. Many of these possessed one ounce or less of the substance. The risk of being put in jail for just one marijuana cigarette is not worth it.

Once you're arrested, the American consular officer **CANNOT** get you out!

You may say *"it couldn't happen to me"* but the fact is that it could happen to you if you find yourself saying any of the following:

... *"my family has enough money and influence to get me out of trouble."*

... *"if I only buy or carry a small amount, it won't be a problem."*

... *"As long as I'm an American citizen, no foreign government will put ME in THEIR jail.'*

If you are arrested on a drug charge it is important that you know what CAN and CANNOT be done.

The U.S. Consular Officer CAN

- visit you in jail after being notified of your arrest

- give you a list of local attorneys (the U.S. Government cannot assume responsibility for the professional ability or integrity of these individuals)

- notify your family and/or friends and relay requests for money or other aid - but only with your authorization

- intercede with local authorities to make sure that your rights under local law are fully observed and that you are treated humanely, according to internationally accepted standards

- protest mistreatment or abuse to the appropriate authorities

The U.S. Consular Officer CANNOT

- demand your immediate release or get you out of jail or the country!

- represent you at trial or give legal counsel

- pay legal fees and/or fines with U.S. Government funds

If you are caught buying, selling, carrying or using any type of drug - from hashish to heroin, marijuana to mescaline, cocaine to quaaludes -

291

IT CAN MEAN:

· **Interrogation and Delays Before Trial**
including mistreatment and solitary confinement for up to one year under very primitive conditions

· **Lengthy Trials**
conducted in a foreign language, with delays and postponements

· **Two Years to Life In Prison** some places include hard labor and heavy fines, if found guilty

· **The Death Penalty**
in a growing number of countries (e.g., Saudi Arabia, Malaysia, Turkey, Thailand)

Although drug laws may vary in each country you visit, it is important to realize, before you make the mistake of getting involved with drugs, that foreign countries do not react lightly to drug offenders. Anyone who is caught with even a very small quantity for personal use may be tried and receive the same sentence as the large scale trafficker.

[DON'T LET YOUR TRIP ABROAD BECOME A NIGHTMARE! *This information has been provided to inform you before it is too late. SO THINK FIRST!]*

* A number of countries, including Mexico, Jamaica, the Bahamas, and the Dominican Republic, have enacted more stringent drug laws which impose mandatory jail sentences for individuals convicted of possessing even small amounts of marijuana or cocaine for personal use

* Once you leave the United States, you are not covered by U.S. laws and constitutional rights

* Bail is not granted in many countries when drugs are involved

* The burden of proof in many countries is on the accused to prove his/her innocence

* In some countries, evidence obtained illegally by local authorities may be admissible in court

* Few countries offer drug offenders jury trials or even require the prisoner's presence at his/her trial

* Many countries have mandatory prison sentences of seven years or more without parole for drug violations

REMEMBER!

* If someone offers you a free trip and some quick and easy money just for bringing back a suitcase .... *SAY NO!*

* Don't carry a package for anyone, no matter how small it might seem

* The police will be waiting for you at the airport

* If it's in your suitcase, you will be caught

* You will go to jail for years and years and may even lose your family

* Don't make a jail sentence part of your trip abroad

The Citizens Emergency Center of the Bureau of Consular Affairs, Department of State, provides emergency services pertaining to the protection of Americans arrested or detained abroad, the search for U.S. citizens overseas, and the transmission of emergency messages to those citizens or their next of kin in the United States. Assistance at the Citizens Emergency Center is available Monday through Friday, 8:15 am to 10:00 pm at (202) 647-5525. For an emergency after hours or on weekends and holidays, ask for the Citizens Emergency Center duty officer at (202) 647-1512.

Chapter 31

Bringing Pets, Wildlife into the U.S.

*[The Information in this chapter is reprinted verbatim from a bulletin issued by the
U.S. Department of the Treasury, U.S. Customs Service. It is intended to serve as advice
to Americans traveling abroad.]*

- - - -

General Customs Information

Travelers frequently inquire about taking their pets with them to the United States. All importations are subject to health, quarantine, agriculture, wildlife, and customs requirements and prohibitions. Pets taken out of the United States and returned are subject to the same requirements as those entering for the first time.

As heartless as it may seem, pets excluded from entry into the United States must either be exported or destroyed. While awaiting disposition, the pet will be detained at the owner's expense at the port of arrival.

The U.S. Public Health Service requires that pets, particularly dogs, cats, and turtles-brought into this country be examined at the first port of entry for possible evidence of disease that can be transmitted to humans.

The Animal and Plant Health Inspection Service requires that animals and birds, both domestic and wild, be free from contagious, infectious, communicable diseases in order to protect our livestock and poultry industry. Certain animals are prohibited entry by law. Any ruminant (cud-chewing animal) or swine shipped from or transiting through an area where foot-and-mouth disease exists is prohibited from entry. Such prohibited animals must be sent out of the country on the same carrier on which they arrive, within a time fixed by the Department of Agriculture, or be destroyed.

The U.S. Fish and Wildlife Service is concerned with the importation, trade, sale, and taking of wildlife and protection of endangered species, both plant and animal. Some wildlife species of dogs, cats, turtles, reptiles, and birds, although imported as pets, may be listed as endangered. Endangered and threatened animal and plant wildlife, migratory birds, marine mammals, and certain injurious wildlife may not be imported without special Federal permits. Sportsmen will find the information under the section on wildlife of particular interest, as game birds and animals are subject to special entry requirements.

We also suggest that you check with state, county, and municipal authorities as to any local restrictions on importing a pet.

For information on requirements of the country into which you will take your pet, write to the respective Embassy in Washington, D.C., or the nearest consular office.

Animal Welfare Act

All birds and animals must be imported under humane and healthful conditions. USDA regulations require that careful arrangements be made with the carrier for suitable cages, space, ventilation, and protection from the elements. Cleaning, feeding, watering, and other necessary services must be provided. Under the Animal Welfare Act, the Department of Agriculture is responsible for setting standards concerning the transportation, handling care, and treatment of animals.

Every imported package or container of pets must be plainly marked, labeled, or tagged on the outside with the names and addresses of the shipper and consignee, along with an accurate invoice statement specifying the number of each species contained in the shipment.

Since hours of service and availability of inspectors of the agencies involved may vary from port to port, you are strongly urged to check with your anticipated port of arrival prior to importing a pet or other animal. This will assure expeditious processing and reduce the possibility of unnecessary delays.

customs duty

Dogs, cats, and turtles are free of duty. Other pets imported into the United States if subject to a customs duty may be included in your customs exemption if they accompany you and are imported for your personal use, not for sale.

purebred animals

Purebred animals, other than domesticated livestock,

293

imported for breeding purposes are free of duty under certain conditions. A declaration is required to show that the importer is a citizen of the United States; the animal is imported specifically for breeding purposes; the animal is identical with the description in the certificate of pedigree presented: and the animal is registered in a book of registry in the country of origin recognized by the U.S. Department of Agriculture.

An application to the Department of Agriculture on form VS 17-338 for a certificate of pure breeding must be furnished before the animal is examined at the designated port of entry. For complete information write to Animal and Plant Health Inspection Service.

birds

All birds, including those taken out of the country and being returned, are subject to controls and restrictions.

To prevent outbreaks of the exotic Newcastle disease, the following U.S. Department of Agriculture controls and restrictions became effective January 15, 1980.

- Birds must be quarantined upon arrival, for at least 30 days in a USDA-operated facility at the owners expense. These facilities are located in the following cities: New York, Laredo, Hidalgo, San Ysidro, Honolulu, Miami, and Los Angeles. The cost is $126.50 per bird or $155.40 if two birds share a cage; cost is subject to change.

- Quarantine space must be reserved in advance by submitting VS Form 17-23 with the full amount. The form is available from USDA offices, American consulates, and Embassies.

- A health certificate executed within 30 days prior to entry by the national veterinarian of the country of export must accompany the bird and affirm that the bird has been examined, shows no evidence of communicable disease and is being exported in accordance with the laws of that country. Health certificate on VS form 17-23 may be used.

- The bird must be removed from the quarantine facility within 5 days of notification of release. Arrangements for transportation and cost involved are the owner's responsibility.

- Bird(s) from Canada that have been in the owner's possession for 90 days or more

preceding the date of importation and found healthy upon veterinary inspection at one of the designated Canadian border ports of entry where veterinarians are stationed are exempt from the 30-day quarantine.

- Pet bird(s) originating in the United States may be reimported without being quarantined provided they are accompanied by a U.S. veterinary health certificate. This certificate must be obtained prior to departure from U.S. and include the same legband or tattoo number as the one on the health certificate.

- In addition, special Federal permits may be required by the U.S. Fish and Wildlife Service for the importation of live or dead migratory birds, including feathers, parts, and mounted specimens, and for certain live injurious or endangered birds.

cats

All domestic cats must be free of evidence of diseases communicable to man when examined at the port of entry. If the animal is not in apparent good health, further examination by a licensed veterinarian may be required at the expense of the owner.

dogs

Domestic dogs must be accompanied by a health certificate stating that they are free of evidence of diseases communicable to man. Dogs to be used with livestock must be examined for tapeworms at the port of entry and, if found infested, must be freed of tapeworms.

vaccination

Dogs and cats must be vaccinated against rabies at least 30 days prior to entry into the United States, except for puppies and kittens less than 3 months of age and for dogs and cats originating or located for 6 months or more in areas designated by the Public Health Service as being rabies free.

The following procedures pertain to dogs arriving from areas not free of rabies.

- A valid rabies vaccination certificate should accompany the dog. This certificate should identify the dog, specify the date of vaccination, date of expiration, and bear the signature of a licensed veterinarian. If no date of expiration is specified, the certificate is acceptable if the date of vaccination is no more than 12 months before the date of arrival.

■ If the vaccination has not been accomplished or the certificate is not valid, the dog may be admitted provided the owner has the dog confined and vaccinated within 4 days after arrival at destination but no more than 10 days after arrival at port of entry. It must be kept in confinement for at least 30 days after the date of vaccination.

■ If the vaccination was received less than one month before arrival, the animal may be admitted but shall be placed in confinement by the owner until at least 30 days have passed since the vaccination.

■ Young puppies must be confined at a place of the owner's choice until they are 3 months of age and then must be vaccinated. Vaccination must be followed by a confinement of 30 days.

■ Vaccination and inspection by the Public Health Service of wild dogs and wild cats is not required.

monkeys

All monkeys and other nonhuman primates, such as lemurs, baboons, and chimpanzees, may not be imported into the United States except for scientific, educational, or exhibition purposes by an importer registered with the Centers for Disease Control. *Under no circumstances may they be imported as pets.* In addition, permits may be required by the Fish and Wildlife Service for certain endangered species of nonhuman primates.

Remember, certain wildlife species of cats, dogs, birds, turtles, and reptiles are listed as endangered. Permits for importation may be required by the U.S. Fish and Wildlife Service.

turtles

A person may import live turtles with a carapace length of less than 4 inches and viable turtle eggs into the United States, provided that for each arrival, no more than one lot containing fewer than seven live turtles or fewer than seven viable turtle eggs, or any combination thereof totaling fewer than seven. There are no Public Health Service restrictions on the importation of live turtles with a carapace length of more than 4 inches. Turtles are subject to all requirements of the U.S. Fish and wildlife Service which are outlined below.

wildlife

Wildlife and fish are subject to certain prohibitions, restrictions, permit, and quarantine requirements. This includes:

■ Mammals, birds, amphibians, fish, insects, crustaceans, mollusks, and other invertebrates.

■ Any part or products, such as feathers, skins, eggs; and articles manufactured from wildlife.

Federal laws prohibit the importation and/or transportation of any wildlife or parts thereof, in violation of state or foreign laws.

Ports designated for entry of all fish and wildlife are Chicago, Dallas/Ft. Worth, Honolulu, Los Angeles, Miami, New Orleans, New York, San Francisco, and Seattle. All packages and containers must be marked, labeled or tagged to plainly indicate the name and address of the shipper and consignee, and the number and kind of the contents. Wildlife in any form, including pets, imported into the U.S. must be declared on U.S. Fish and Wildlife Form 3-177 (Declaration for Importation of Fish and Wildlife). Certain USDA restrictions apply. Contact the Animal and Plant Health Inspection Service, which is listed at the end of this chapter.

game birds and animals

Game birds and animals, other than endangered species, legally taken in a foreign country may be imported for non-commercial purposes at any Customs port of entry and declared on Customs Form 3777. Game must be accompanied by a valid hunting license, tags, stamps, or export document if such is required. Only U.S. residents may import game duty free. They may import only those migratory game birds legally killed. The U.S. Fish and Wildlife Service publishes the limits on migratory game birds prior to each hunting season. Hunters should familiarize themselves with the restrictions placed on migratory game birds lawfully taken during open season in other countries. Certain USDA restriction apply. Contact the Animal and Plant Health Inspection Service, which is listed below.

Many animals, game birds, products, and by-products from such animals and game birds are prohibited or restricted entry into the U.S. Specific requirements for the country from which you wish to import can be obtained by calling the U.S. Department of Agriculture (USDA), Animal and Plant Health Inspection Service (APHIS), the National Import-Export Center, Tel. (301) 436-7885, fax (301) 436-8226.

endangered species

The United States is a party to the Convention on International Trade in Endangered Species of Wild Fauna and Flora. This treaty regulates trade in endangered species of wildlife and plants and products thereof. International trade in species listed by the Convention is unlawful unless authorized by permit. This includes, for example, articles made from whale teeth, certain ivory, tortoise shell, reptile and fur skins. Permits to import into or export from the United States or re-export certificates are issued by the Office of Management, Authority of the U.S. Fish and Wildlife Service. Information on wildlife and plants, including lists of endangered species may be obtained from the Fish and Wildlife Service.

Although essential requirements are provided in this leaflet, all regulations cannot be covered in detail. If you have any questions, or are in doubt, write or call your local Customs office or the specific agency mentioned. Their addresses are:

U.S. Public Health Service
Centers for Disease Control
Division of Quarantine (E-03)
Atlanta, Georgia 30333
Tel. (404) 639-1437

Animal and Plant Health Inspection Service
U.S. Department of Agriculture
Hyattsville, Md. 20782
Tel. (301) 436-8590

U.S. Fish and Wildlife Service
Department of the Interior
Washington, D.C. 20240
Tel. 1-800-358-2104

Department of the Treasury
U.S. Customs Service
Washington, D.C. 20229
Customs Publication No. 509
Revised September 1992

Buyer Beware!

Some souvenirs you buy overseas could end up costing a lot more than you paid for them.

Going abroad? Think twice about the things you buy. If they're made from the hides, shells, feathers, or teeth of endangered species-and it's quite possible that they are-you risk their seizure by government inspectors and may face a substantial fine.

Seemingly innocuous products made from tortoise shell, coral, ivory, and reptile skin, for example, are available in marketplaces all over the world. But just because wildlife items are on sale in another country does not necessarily mean that they are legal to import to the United States. Travelers don't realize that several U.S. laws and an international treaty make it a crime to bring many of these wildlife souvenirs into our country.

At The Heart of the Issue: Protecting Endangered Wildlife

More and more species are declining in numbers because of destruction of their natural environment and increased exploitation. Modern transportation now makes it possible to provide exotic pets, pelts, and other wildlife products to a steadily growing worldwide market. To combat declines from excessive exploitation, most countries have adopted laws that regulate imports, exports, and sale of wildlife.

Ivory from elephant tusks is traditionally carved into products such as jewelry, figurines, and piano keys. Imports of ivory, including many antiques, from both Asian and African elephants are now generally prohibited. Purchase of ivory may provide an incentive to poachers and illegal traders and threaten the survival of the African elephant. Imports of ivory and scrimshaws from whales, walruses, and narwhals are also prohibited.

Furs from most larger spotted cats, such as jaguar, snow leopard, and tiger, and from most smaller cats, such as ocelot, margay, and tiger cat, cannot enter the United States legally, nor can furs of marine mammals, such as seals and polar bears.

Coral reefs are the building blocks of important marine communities and serve as natural barriers against beach erosion. Recognizing this, many countries in the Caribbean, the Pacific, and Southeast Asia prohibit the collection, sale, and export of corals, and international commercial trade is regulated. Yet corals, including precious and semiprecious, are often fashioned into jewelry and decorative ornaments and sold in enormous quantities. Coral collection is only one of several reasons for the destruction of coral ecosystems. So check for restrictions on coral trade before you buy.

Plants, like animals, are subject to illegal trade through laundering, smuggling, and improper documentation. As a result, many plant species are in danger of extinction and receive protection under United States law. Species prohibited from import into the U.S. include many orchids, cacti, and cycads. Whether endangered or not, all imported plants must undergo inspection by the Department of Agriculture and be accompanied by documents certifying they are free of disease and pests.

Guidelines To Follow
Wildlife is sometimes illegally killed or collected in one country, smuggled into another, and then exported with false permits to a third, making its origins hard to trace. If you're considering the purchase of any wildlife or wildlife product while abroad, you should first try to determine its origin and any U.S. restrictions on its import.

Reptile Skins and Leathers are most commonly used in watchbands, handbags, belts, and shoes. The legality of importing these products depends upon the species and the country of origin.

Prohibited imports include
· All sea turtle products

· Products made from black caiman, American crocodile, Orinoco crocodile, Philippine crocodile, and, in many cases, the common caiman.

· Most lizard-skin products originating in Brazil, Costa Rica, Ecuador, Peru, Venezuela, India, and Nepal.

· Many snakeskin products originating in Argentina, Brazil, Costa Rica, Ecuador, Guatemala, Mexico, Venezuela, and India.

Other Leather Products made from pangolin (sometimes labeled "anteater") skin originating in Thailand, Malaysia, and Indonesia may not be brought into the United States.

The survival of many **wild bird species** is threatened by habitat destruction and trade, and alarming numbers of birds die during capture, transit, and quarantine.

Prohibited from import are
· Many live birds, except as authorized by the Wild Bird ConserVation Act. This includes many parrots, macaws, cockatoos, and certain finches.

· Most wild-bird feathers, mounted birds, skins, and some skin products.

The Laws That Affect What You Buy
The regulations governing wildlife imports are complicated enough to make the U.S. consumer think twice before buying any wildlife overseas. If you are considering the purchase of a live animal or plant or a product made from one, you should be familiar with

certain laws:

Endangered Species Act-prohibits the importation and export of species listed as endangered and most species listed as threatened.

Lacey Act-prohibits the import of animal species that have been taken, possessed, transported, or sold in violation of foreign law. Many countries completely, ban or strictly limit wildlife trade.

CITES-a comprehensive wildlife treaty signed by over 115 countries, including the United States, that regulates and in many cases prohibits imports and exports of wild animal and plant species that are threatened by trade.

Marine Mammal Protection Act-prohibits the import of marine mammals and their parts and products. The se species include whales, walruses, narwhals, seals, sea lions, sea otters, and polar bears.

African Elephant Conservation Act-prohibits imports of ivory products from any country, and only permits non commercial import of whole tusks from elephants that have been legally hunted in certain African countries.

Wild Bird Conservation Act-regulates or prohibits the import of many exotic bird species.

The United States is the world's largest wildlife-consuming country. Despite strong prohibitions, a significant percentage of the international wildlife trade still involves protected or endangered species, but you can play a significant role in curbing this illegal trade by becoming a better-informed consumer and traveler.

Remember, when you are unsure of the regulations, check with the U.S. Fish and Wildlife Service or TRAFFIC USA, the wildlife trade monitoring program of WWF, well before you go, or, once there, with the local authorities or the U.S. embassy before making a purchase. **When in doubt, don't buy!** You may save yourself some frustration and the loss of your purchase.

For More information, contact:

World Wildlife Fund
1250 24th Street, NW
Washington, D.C. 20037

Division of Law Enforcement
U.S. Fish & Wildlife Service
P.O. Box 347
Arlington, VA 22203-3247

Sponsored By:
-U.S. Fish and Wildlife Service
-Department of the Interior
-National Fish and Wildlife Foundation
-American Society of Travel Agents
-U.S. Customs Service
-Department of the Treasury
-Wildlife and Marine Resources Section
-Land and Natural Resource Division
-U.S. Department of Justice

Chapter 32

Tips on Traveling and Transporting Your Pet

*[The information in this chapter is reprinted verbatim from bulletins issued by the
U.S. Department of Agriculture and Air Transport Association of America.
It is intended to serve as advice to Americans traveling abroad.]*

- - - -

Traveling By Air With Your Pet

Dogs, cats, and most other warm blooded animals transported by air are protected by the Animal Welfare Act. The Animal and Plant Health Inspection Service (APHIS)-an agency of the U.S. Department of Agriculture (USDA)-enforces this law.

APHIS' shipping regulations help assure that animals are treated humanely by airlines as well as animal dealers, exhibitors and research laboratories. Pet exhibitors owners, and other shippers also are affect by the regulations established to protect the well-being and safety of animals in transit.

Airline Procedures

Airlines transport animals in the cargo compartment of the plane, but some airlines allow passengers to transport small animals in the cabin as carryon luggage. The pet must be placed in a kennel that is comfortable yet small enough to fit under the passenger's seat. Carryon pets are not protected by the Animal Welfare Act. For specific airline requirements. contact the airline.

APHIS Requirements

Age

Dogs and cats must be at least 8 weeks old and must have been weaned before traveling with the airlines.

Kennels

Kennels must meet minimum standards for size strength, sanitation an ventilation.

- **Size and strength**-Kennels must be enclosed and allow room for the animal to stand, sit, breathe, and rest comfortably. They must be easy to open, strong enough to withstand the stress of shipping, and free objects that could injure the animal.

- **Sanitation**-Kennels must have a solid, leak-proof floor that is covered with litter or absorbent lining. Wire or other ventilated subfloors are generally allowed; pegboard flooring is prohibited. This provides the maximum cleanliness for the animal in travel.

- **Ventilation**-Kennels must be well ventilated with openings that make up at least **14** percent of the total wall space. At least one-third of the openings must be located in the top half of the kennel. Kennels also must have rims to prevent ventilation openings from being blocked by other shipments. These rims -usually placed on the sides of the kennel-must provide at least three-quarters of an inch clearance.

- **Grips and markings**-Kennels must have grips or handles for lifting to prevent cargo workers from being bitten. Kennels also must be labeled "live animals" or "wild animals" on the top and one side with directional arrows indicating the upright position of the kennel. Lettering must be at least 1 inch high.

- **Animals per kennel**-Each species must have its own kennel with the exception of compatible personal pets of similar size. Maximum numbers include 2 puppies or kittens under 6 months old and under 20 pounds each, 15 guinea pigs or rabbits, and 50

Feeding and Watering

Instructions for feeding, watering, and administering medication to the animal over a 24-hour period must be attached to the kennel. The 24-hour schedule will assist the airline in providing care for animals that are diverted from their scheduled destination. The shipper is required to document that the animal was given food and water within 4 hours of transport, and the certification must include the time and date of feeding.

Food and water dishes must be securely attached and be accessible without opening the kennel. Food and water must be provided to puppies and kittens every 12 hours if they are less than 16 weeks old. Mature animals must be fed every 24 hours and given water every 12 hours.

Health Certification

Airlines and State health officials generally require health certificates for all animals transported by air. Health certificates must be issued by a licensed veterinarian who examined the animal within 1 0 days of transport. Dealers, exhibitors, and others regulated under the Animal Welfare Act must provide a health certificate for each dog, cat, or nonhuman primate shipped.

Trips Outside the Continental United States

Foreign countries and Hawaii have quarantine or health requirements for arriving pets. For information about Hawaii's requirements, write to: Hawaii Quarantine Office, 99-770 Moanalua Road, Aiea, HI 96701. For information about international requirements, contact the appropriate embassy or consulate at least 4 weeks before the trip.

Airlines or a full-service travel agency can provide additional information about animal care requirements for international flights.

For more information about the Animal Welfare Act, write to:
Regulatory Enforcement and Animal Care
APHIS, USDA
Room 565, Federal Building
6505 Belcrest Road
Hyattsville, MD 20782-2058

Air Travel for Your Dog and Cat[AT]

Millions of animals travel safely aboard aircraft every year. Airline personnel make every effort to handle these animals with the care they deserve. The purpose of this section is to assist you with general information about transporting your dog or cat by air. For specific requirements of a particular airline, contact that airline directly. The cargo department is an especially good source of information.

The U.S. Department of Agriculture (USDA) regulates the transportation of animals such as dogs and cats. These regulations apply to you, the shipper, as well as to the airlines. If you decide that your dog or cat must travel by air, there are some points to check for compliance with applicable laws, and to assure the safest and most comfortable trip for your animal.

How to Ship by Air

Sometimes the terminology of an industry can create a false impression. The point is made because of the two most commonly accepted ways of transporting dogs and cats by air -- as accompanied baggage or as cargo. Despite the work-a-day sound of these terms, both describe humane means of shipping animals.

Baggage -- You may only transport your pet as accompanied baggage if you are a passenger traveling on the same flight to your pet's destination.

Cargo -- In the cargo system, the animal may travel unaccompanied, either through the regular cargo channels or via the special expedited delivery service that many airlines have developed. Many airline cargo departments have specialists in the movement of animals who can assist you with questions and handle your pet with knowledge, humane care, and experience.

Animals in the cargo system are transported in the same pressurized holds as those in the checked baggage system. (Some airlines may permit a small animal to be carried in the passenger cabin as carry-on luggage, provided the pet is small enough to fit comfortably in a kennel that is placed under the seat.)

Questions to Consider When Your Animal

Is your pet old enough? USDA says that your animal must be at least 8 weeks old and fully wean before traveling with the airlines.

Is your pet healthy? Check with a veterinarian to b sure that your animal is fit to travel. Some species -for example pug-nosed dogs -- simply do not fly well because they have difficulty breathing under normal conditions. You will need a health certificate in order to comply with the rules of most airlines, and your veterinarian will be able to supply this. In addition, State and Federal rules require a health certificate in many instances. To be valid for your trip on most airlines it should be issued no more than 10 days before departure. In some cases, the health certificate should be issued no more than 7 days before departure.

Have you selected your flight to make the trip as easy as possible? Whenever possible, book a direct, non-stop flight and avoid holiday or weekend travel. To be most fair to your pet, consider schedules that minimize temperature extremes -- for example, try to avoid travel during excessively hot or cold periods. Morning or evening flights are most preferable during the summer. In the cargo mode, it is possible to reserve space on a specific flight by paying for either priority or the special expedited delivery service.

Is your pet acclimated to low temperatures? If your pet is traveling in the winter and is used to low temperatures, you may be able to facilitate the journey by obtaining a certificate from your veterinarian stating that your dog or cat is acclimated to temperatures lower than 45°F (7.2°C). According to USDA regulations, this certificate must be issued no more than 10 days before departure.

Prepare in Advance

Do you have the right kennel? You and the airlines must follow USDA regulations on the size of kennel for your pet. The kennel must be sturdy properly ventilated, and large enough that the animal may freely stand, turn around, and lie down. The kennel must close securely with a mechanism that requires no special tools to operate. Prescribed kennels are available at pet stores and most airlines. Remember to check with the airline when in doubt, because the USDA assigns full responsibility for accepting the proper kennel to the airline. When your pet travels, the kennel should --

* contain no more than 1 adult dog or cat; or no more than 2 puppies or kittens younger than months and under 20 lbs.;

* display "LIVE ANIMALS" labels with letter least I inch high, placing labels on top and on least one side;

* certify with a signature the last time (within 4 hours before tendering the animal to the airline) that your dog or cat was offered food and water;

* indicate your name and address;

* indicate the top with arrows or "This End Up" marking;

* include food and water dishes (both empty) secured inside the kennel and accessible from outside;

* contain absorbent material or bedding, such as newspaper;

* show a food and water schedule;

* if any food is necessary, an ample supply should be attached in a bag to the outside of the kennel.

Is your animal comfortable in the travel kennel? As far in advance of the trip as possible, let your pet get to know the flight kennel, Veterinarians recommend leaving it open in the house with an old sock or other familiar object inside so that your pet will spend time in the kennel. It is important for your dog or cat to be as relaxed as possible during the flight.

Have you made advance arrangements for your pet? At the time you book a trip on which you will bring your pet, advise the airline directly that you will have an animal. Be sure to reconfirm with the airline 24-48 hours before departure that you will be bringing an animal. If you are shipping your pet as cargo, 24-48 hours' notice should be given to the airline. This is important since each airplane can transport only a limited number of animals.

Please note that advance arrangements are not guarantees that your animal will travel on a specific flight. To be as humane as possible, airlines reserve the right to refuse to handle an animal for such reasons as illness or poor kenneling of the animal, or extreme temperatures at origin, transfer or destination airports.

Is your trip outside the Continental United States? If you are flying abroad to a foreign country or even Hawaii, be sure to find out whether there are quarantine or other health requirements at the destination. For example, rules in the United Kingdom are very strict. It is essential to comply with such requirements. A full-service travel agency or pet travel service should be able to assist you with this information. You should contact the appropriate embassy or consulate at least 4 weeks before the trip.

For international flights, there are additional airline requirements. More kennel ventilation is required for international flights than for USD domestic rules. Labeling and a shipper's certificate are also parts of the international conventions. It is important to contact your airline if you contemplate an international trip for your pet.

Ready for the Flight

Food and Water, USDA requires that your pet be offered food and water within four hours before check-in with the airline, Do not overfeed your pet at this time. A full stomach is not good for a traveling pet. When you check in with the airline you must certify with a signature the time that your pet was last offered food and water. (Do not leave food or water in the dish in the kennel; it will only spill and make travel unpleasant for your animal.)

Use of Tranquilizers. Sedation is not advised since the effects of tranquilizers on animals at high altitudes are unpredictable. The decision to prescribe a tranquilizer for your pet should be made by your veterinarian. If you believe some form of sedation might be helpful, be sure to obtain and follow expert advice.

Arrival and Check-In. Get to the airport with plenty of time to spare, so that there will be no rush. If your animal is traveling as excess baggage or by the special expedited delivery service, check-in will usually be at the passenger terminal. If you are sending your pet through the cargo system, you will need to go to the air freight terminal, which is located in a separate part of the airport. Be sure to check with your airline for the acceptance cut-off time for your flight. Note that by regulation an animal may be tendered no more than 4 hours before flight time (6 hours by special arrangement).

Acceptance of Animals. Because they care about animals, no airline will guarantee acceptance of an animal it has not seen. This is to protect both the animal and the airline.

Important considerations for acceptance of animals include health and disposition of the animal, since an airline cannot transport an animal that is violent or dangerously ill. A health certificate will help to minimize questions. An airline must also determine whether all paperwork, kennel marking and sizing is in order. This is especially important, because USDA assigns airlines the final responsibility for safety and compliance of the kennels they accept.

Finally airlines must assure that facilities are able to handle animals at the airports of transfer or final destination. USDA has clear guidelines on allowable temperature limits for animal-holding areas, which airlines must obey.

Interline Transfer of Animals

When pets travel as accompanied baggage, it is very unlikely that one airline can check an animal through from its own system to a final destination served by another airline. Since each airline cares about and is responsible for the animals it accepts, airline agents will need to inspect the animal at the time of check-in. On a trip involving more than one airline, you will need to claim the animal at the connecting stop where you change airlines and check in your pet with the agents at the new airline. Be sure to plan adequate time for this transfer.

However, when your pet travels in the cargo system, an interline transfer is possible. Animals routed via more than one airline in the air cargo system will be transferred from one airline to the next. It is important

to recognize the need to schedule adequate time for transfers between aircraft. Be sure to consult the airlines involved since you will need to make advance arrangements with the connecting airline, and the minimum transfer times for cargo vary by airport and sometimes by airline.

Helpful Hints

- It is a good idea to carry a leash with you on a trip, so that you may walk your pet before check-in and after arrival. (Do not put the leash with the animal, either inside or attached to the outside of the kennel.)

- Do not take your pet out of its kennel inside the airport. In keeping with airport regulations and courtesy for other passengers, you should let your pet out only after you leave the terminal building.

- You should mark the kennel with your pet's name.

- In addition to showing your name and address, as required by USDA, you must mark the kennel with the telephone number of a person at the destination who can be contacted about your pet. This is especially important if you are sending your animal unaccompanied through the cargo system, because you will not be at the airport to claim your pet upon arrival. It may be helpful to contact a pet travel service to handle unaccompanied shipments since these services manage pick-up and delivery, and can advise on quarantine requirements for international travel.

- If you animal is traveling in the cargo system, remember that after arrival at destination there is a processing period for cargo, which may vary by airline and airport.

- If you have questions, be sure to contact your airline.

PLANNING THE FLIGHT
- ☐ Ship as baggage or cargo?
- ☐ Select flight scheduling to minimize distress?
- ☐ If there is a change of airplanes or airline on the trip, will scheduling accommodate your pet?
- ☐ Advance arrangements with the airline?
- ☐ Call passenger services if your pet will travel as baggage.

302

☐   Call cargo services if your pet will be unaccompanied.

PREPARING YOUR ANIMAL

☐   Is your pet old enough?

☐   Health certificate?

☐   Proper kennel of the right size?

☐   Labeled "LIVE ANIMALS" in letters at least one (1) inch high?

☐   Certified last time food and water were offered before check-in?

☐   Food and water schedule shown?

☐   Any necessary food attached?

☐   Are your name, address, date and signature shown?

Transportation Tips

PROTECTING ANIMALS DURING SHIPMENT IN AIRCRAFT BAGGAGE/CARGO HOLDS

This section provides general information and precautions to help assure humane transport and good arrival condition of animals shipped in the lower cargo compartments of airplanes. Many types of animals are shipped in the lower baggage/cargo compartments of aircraft. With a few exceptions, there is limited temperature control and very little ventilation in these lower cargo holds. Usually there is only enough ventilation capacity for a few household pets. If too many animals are loaded in a lower compartment, they may suffer or die from heat or cold stress or from suffocation.

In most cases, animal stress or loss can be averted by (1) a better understanding of the ventilation capabilities of aircraft cargo compartments, (2) knowledge of the heat output of various types of animals, and (3) improved ground handling and loading procedures.

Ventilation in Aircraft Baggage/Cargo Holds

There are several classes of lower aircraft compartments, but "class D" is most commonly used for baggage and live animal cargo. Class D compartments are designed with little or no positive ventilation, so that if a fire breaks out it will extinguish itself in a matter of seconds due to lack of oxygen.

Some airline literature and personnel will indicate that the baggage compartments are pressurized the same as passenger compartments. Although this is true, such compartments do not necessarily have their own ventilation systems. Usually the ventilation in class D compartments is limited to the migration of small amounts of air from the main deck to replace air that leaks from the cargo bay door seals. Some class D

compartments are heated with hot air or electric blankets in the walls. Few older models aircraft have thermostatic temperature control in their lower compartments.

Positive ventilation and temperature. control are standard equipment on some of the newer models of aircraft. These features also are optional on most aircraft at the time of manufacture or during factory overhaul ' However, unless assured otherwise by the carrier, shippers should assume that limited ventilation is available when animals are shipped in the lower compartments of airplanes.

Animal Heat Output

Lack of consideration for the amount of heat produced by live animals is a major factor leading to animal losses in baggage/cargo compartments of aircraft.

Generally, the smaller the animal, the greater the heat produced per unit of live weight. Many tragic losses have occurred because this factor was neglected when shipments were planned. 100 pounds of pigeons or pet birds for example, will produce more heat than a 1000-pound horse. On thousand pounds of pigeons, will produce, 38.000 Btu's of heat per hour--the equivalent of a small household furnace . Furthermore, approximately one third of the total heat produced by live animals is latent. This latent or evaporative heat--plus carbon dioxide-has to be ventilated in order for an animal's natural cooling mechanisms to work. For example, on a pound-for-pound basis, baby chicks require three times more air volume than humans to supply their oxygen needs. High heat production plus oxygen depletion in a small, practically air-tight compartment will lead to rapid suffocation, especially if an aircraft is on the ground in hot weather with the Cargo bay doors closed.

Preplan to Protect Your Animals During Air Shipment

Tell airline cargo personnel or your freight forwarder about any special requirements of your animals. Determine the type of aircraft in which your animals will travel and then determine the type of lower compartments available for live animals in that aircraft. If compartments are available with air conditioning and positive ventilation, ask that your animals be shipped in these compartments. Large shipments should be split or, preferably, shipped on the main deck of a freighter, especially if only class D compartments are available.

Try to schedule your shipment on a flight with as little ground layover time as possible. During extended layovers in hot weather, the cargo bay doors should be opened and ground air conditioning introduced.

In warm weather try to Schedule night or early morning departures and arrivals so the animals will be loaded and handled during periods of cool ambient temperatures and out of direct sunlight. In cold weather, keep the animals in draft-free and adequately heated areas in the cargo terminal. Handle animals expeditiously during loading.

Make sure the containers you use comply with applicable regulations and are designed to allow adequate ventilation for the animals inside. Container ventilation requirements for cats, dogs and laboratory animals are. specified by USDA's Animal and Plant Health Inspection Service (see the Code of Federal Regulations, Title 9, Animals and Animal Products, Parts 1 to 199). Container, boxes or crates carrying live animals should never be loaded inside enclosed airline containers or igloos.

Weight and balance requirements have priority during the loading of aircraft. However, to the extent possible, keep animal shipments away from the doors because these areas may be extremely cold and drafty during the flight. Also, do not load containers of animals, particularly baby chicks, directly against walls that may adsorb heat from the containers and chill the animals. Do not stack containers of animals tightly together or against other cargo. Always leave adequate space for ventilation around the containers. Do not ship animals in holds containing a large amount of cargo cooled with dry ice, since the carbon dioxide generated will reduce the oxygen level in the hold.

Airline Travel With Your Bird

- Five to seven days poor to a flight, take your bird for a veterinary check-up and ask the veterinarian to issue a health certificate. It is a good idea to have the bird's wings clipped as a precautionary measure, in case the bird escapes.

- If at all possible, reserve a direct, non-stop flight for your bird.

- Purchase a USDA-approved shipping crate.' Size is important The crate must be large enough so that the bird can stand up comfortably, but it should also limit movement so the bird cannot flap his wings and injure himself.

- Write the words "Live Animal' in letters no smaller than 1-inch high on the top and sides of the crate. Use arrows to indicate the upright position.

- On the top of the crate, write the name, address and telephone number of the bird's point of origin and destination in non-erasable ink.

- Line the crate with hay (available at most pet supply stores), and scatter dry seeds throughout the hay. Place pieces of juicy fruits (such as apples, oranges, pears) on top of the hay. [For **International** flights, you must use shredded, non-toxic, paper (such as brown food-wrapping paper) instead of hay.]

- When shipping in cool weather, place burlap or cloth on the open end of the

- We recommend that only canaries and finches travel with a perch.

- Do not lock the door of the crate. Make sure it is securely closed but not locked so that airline personnel can open the crate in an emergency.

- Upon arrival at his destination, keep the bird in a calm, quiet area and give him time to adjust to the new environment.

Wishing your bird a safe and comfortable journey!

For additional Information, contact:
ASPCA Education
424 East 92nd street
New York. NY 10128

304

Chapter 33

Tips on Bringing Food, Plant, and Animal Products into the U.S.

[The information in this chapter is reprinted verbatim from a bulletin issued by the U.S. Department of Agriculture, Animal and Plant Health Inspection Service. It is intended to serve as advice to Americans traveling abroad.]

— — — —

A Special Message for Travelers

Please take a few minutes to become familiar with restrictions on bringing agricultural products into the United States. This booklet lists acceptable agricultural products and tells you about other products that require permits or are prohibited.

The U.S. Department of Agriculture places limits on items brought to the United States from foreign countries as well as those brought to the mainland from Hawaii, Puerto Rico, and the U.S. Virgin Islands. Prohibited items can harbor foreign animal and plant pests and diseases that could seriously damage America's crops, livestock, pets, and the environment. Because of this threat, you are required to declare any meats, fruits, vegetables, plants, animals, and plant and animal products you are bringing. Your declaration must cover all items carried in your baggage and hand luggage or in your vehicle.

One Piece Can Spell Danger

Travelers often are surprised when told that their "one little piece of fruit or meat" can cause serious damage. In fact, one item carelessly discarded can wreak havoc in American crops. For example, it's quite likely that a traveler carried in the wormy fruit that brought Mediterranean fruit flies to California in 1979. The 3-year fight to eradicate this pest cost more than $100 million.

A single link of sausage contaminated with the dreaded virus of foot-and-mouth disease can do similar damage to the livestock business. Foot-and-mouth disease last struck the United States in 1929. Economists say that an outbreak today would cost farmers and consumers billions of dollars in lost production, higher food prices, and lost export markets.

Declarations Prevent Fines

The declaration you're required to make may be oral, written, or both. If you're traveling from abroad on a plane or ship, you will be given a Customs form on which to declare your agricultural products. You also will be asked to indicate whether you have visited a farm or ranch outside the United States.

Officers of USDA's Animal and Plant Health Inspection Service inspect passenger baggage for undeclared agricultural products. At some ports, they use beagle dogs to sniff out hidden items. At other ports, they use low-energy X-ray machines adapted to reveal fruits and meats.

Smugglers get caught. In an average month, 1,250 violations are uncovered. The traveler who fails to declare a prohibited item is fined on the spot (up to $50 or more), and the item is confiscated.

Fruits, Vegetables, and Plants

You may bring in some fruits, vegetables, and plants without advance permission, provided they are declared, inspected, and found free of pests. However, you must get a permit in advance to bring in certain plants and plant parts intended for growing.

For information and permit applications, write: Permit Unit, USDA, APHIS, PPQ, 6505 Belcrest Road, Hyattsville, MD 20782. To bring back endangered plant species, you also will need permits from the country of origin as well as the U.S. Fish and Wildlife Service (see page 307).

Meat and Animal Products

Regulations prohibit you from bringing in fresh, dried, and canned meats and meat products from most foreign countries. If any meat is used in preparing a product, it is prohibited. Commercially canned meat is allowed if the inspector can determine that the meat was cooked in the can after it was scaled to make it shelf-stable without refrigeration.

Hunting trophies, game-animal carcasses, and hides are severely restricted. If you intend to bring them in, write for applicable information and forms.

Address: Import/Export and Emergency Planning Staff,

305

USDA, APHIS, VS, 6505 Belcrest Road, Hyattsville, MD 20782.

Live Animals and Birds
Live animals and birds can enter only subject to certification, permits, inspection, and quarantine rules that vary with the animal and its origin. Dogs that have been in Central and South America pose a special health hazard if they have wounds infested with screwworms. If your dog has even a small wound, be sure that have it treated before you travel to the United States. The U.S. Public Health Service further restricts imports of dogs, cats, monkeys, and turtles (see page 307).

Pet birds you purchased abroad for your personal use can enter, subject to restrictions by some State departments of agriculture, if quarantined by USDA for 30 days. Make quarantine arrangements in advance because facilities are limited and available only at certain ports. For information and a permit application, write Import/Export and Emergency Planning at the address listed previously.

No Federal quarantine is required for personally owned U.S. pet birds returning to the United States. Bring along a valid U.S. veterinary health certificate that individually identifies each bird by referring to a leg band or tattoo. Be sure to keep your bird separated from other birds while out of the country. No Federal quarantine is required for pet birds originating in Canada.

Other Biological Materials

You must have a permit to bring in most organisms, cells and cultures, monoclonal antibodies, vaccines, and related substances, whether of plant or animal origin. This includes organisms and products used in the biotechnology industry. For information and a permit application, write Import/Export and Emergency Planning at the address listed previously.

Soil, Sand, Minerals, and Shells

Soil-borne organisms threaten both plants and animals. If you visited a farm or ranch overseas, agricultural inspectors may have to disinfect your shoes or clothes. Vehicles also must be cleaned of soil.

You may not bring in any soil, earth, or sand, although 1 ounce or less of decorative beach sand is allowed. Rocks, minerals, and shells are allowed, but all sand and soil must be cleaned off. Products grown in soil (like shamrocks and truffles) must be free of soil.

What You Can Bring Back

When you plan your trip abroad, check the lists of approved products. If you're unsure of what's allowed, call for help. Look in your phone book for the nearest office of the U.S. Department of Agriculture, Animal and Plant Health Inspection Service, Plant Protection and Quarantine: or call the central office at (301) 436-8645. The agricultural inspector at your U.S. port of departure also can answer many of your questions, as can some U.S. consulates abroad.

Note that agricultural products of U.S. origin taken out of the United States may not be allowed back into the country. Check with a U.S. border inspector before taking such goods across the border.

General List of Approved Products
This list covers products from all areas except Canada, Mexico, Hawaii, Puerto Rico, and the U.S. Virgin Islands.

Bamboo, dried poles only
Beads made of seeds (but not jequirity beans)
Breads, cakes, cookies and other bakery goods
Candies
Cheeses, fully cured (but not cottage cheeses)
Coconuts (but husks or milk must be removed)
Coffee, roasted beans only
Cones of trees, like pine cones
Dried foods, including polished rice, beans, and tea
Fish
Flower bulbs (but not gladiolus bulbs from Africa, Italy,   Malta, and Portugal)
Flowers, most fresh or dried kinds (but not with roots)
Fruits, canned or dried products only
Herbarium plants (but not witchweed)
Herbs, dried, for medicinal use
Meats, canned (for restrictions. see page. 305).
Mushrooms
Nuts (but not chestnuts or acorns or nuts with other husks)
Sauces, canned or processed
Seaweed
Seeds (but not avocado, bamboo, barberry, coconuts, corn, cotton, cucumber, currant, elm, hibiscus, lentil, mahonia, mango, melon, pearl millet, potato, pumpkin, rice, sorghum, squash, and wheat)
Shamrocks, without roots or soil
Soup and soup mixes (but not those containing meat)
Spices, dried (but not curry leaves)
Straw animals, hats, baskets, and other souvenirs (but not items stuffed with straw)
Vegetables, canned or processed.

Approved Products from Canada
Most products produced or grown in Canada are allowed. This includes vegetables: fruits other than

306

black currants; and meat and dressed poultry, if accompanied by proof of origin.

Approved Products from Mexico
Products must have been produced or grown in Mexico.

For meats proof of origin is required.

Acorns	Blackberries
Bananas	Cactus fruits
Cerimans	Melons
Coconuts (but husks	
or milk must	
be removed	Mexican jumping beans
	Nuts
Corn husks	Papayas
Dates	Pineapples
Dewberries	Strawberries
Grapes	Tamarind bean pods
Litchis	Vegetables (but not
potatoes,	

Meats (but not sweet potatoes, or yams).
pork or uncooked poultry)

Approved Products from Hawaii
Products must have been produced or grown in Hawaii.

Coconuts (but not for travelers	Pineapples
going to Florida)	insects, dried and
	preserved
Coffee (roasted only)	Meats
Flowers, including leis (but not	Nuts
mauna loas, gardenias, jade,	
vines, and roses)	
Seeds, including seed jewelry	
and leis	
Papayas (only if officially	
Sugar (but not sugarcane)	certified
Wood roses.	

Approved Products from Puerto Rico and the U.S. Virgin Islands
Products must have been produced or grown in Puerto Rico and the U.S. Virgin Islands.

Avocados	Herbs, dried, for medicinal
Bananas	purposes
Beans, fresh shelled	Leeks
Breadfruits	Meats
Breadnuts	Nuts
Cacao beans	Onions
Calabazas	Papayas
Chayotes	Peas
Citrus fruits (but not	Pineapples
for travelers going	
to ports South of	

Baltimore, Md.)

	Plantains
	Pumpkins
Coconuts (but not	Quenepas
going to Florida	
and Hawaii)	Root crops, most kinds
Coriander	Seeds, dried
Eggplant	Squash
Garlic	Strawberries
Ginger root	Tamarind bean pods.
Gourds	

Information on Other Federal Requirements

The U.S. Customs Service collects import duties (tax) and assists the U.S. Public Health Service in regulating the import of dogs, cats, monkeys, and birds. Publications: "Know Before You Go (Customs Hints for Returning Residents)"[1] and "Pets, Wildlife, U.S. Customs." Address: U.S. Customs Service, P.O. Box 7474, Washington, DC 20044.

The U.S. Department of State issues travel documents for U.S. citizens and visitors. Publication: "Your Trip Abroad.[2]" Contact: Passport agencies located in Boston, Chicago, Honolulu, Houston, Los Angeles, Miami, New Orleans, New York, Philadelphia, San Francisco, Seattle, Stanford, and Washington, D.C., or a U.S. consulate abroad.

The U.S. Fish and Wildlife Service restricts or prohibits wild animals and endangered animals and their products. Publications: "Facts About Federal Wildlife Laws" and "Buyer Beware Guide." Address: Federal Wildlife Permit Office, U.S. Fish and Wildlife Service, Washington, DC 20240.

SHIPPING FOREIGN PLANTS HOME

Shipping Plants Simplifies Importation
There is a simple way to import plants that you admired overseas: Secure a permit in advance and ship them home. This avoids delays at the port when you return from your trip and improves the chance that your plants will survive the trip and get a good start in their new location.

Protecting America's Animal Health
Many destructive plant pests now posing problems to U.S. producers originally were "foreigners" that entered on incoming plants. Pests like the alfalfa weevil, citrus bacterial canker, the golden nematode of potatoes, the Russian wheat aphid, and many others originally were imported. The plants or plant materials you import could be carrying more such foreign plant pests, making agricultural inspection of incoming plants an

important precaution. Not having these inspections could cause serious harm to U.S. agriculture.

To inspect the Plants you ship home, the U.S. Department of Agriculture (USDA) maintains 14 plant inspection stations at various ports of entry into the country. At these stations, specially trained inspectors in USDA's Animal and Plant Health Inspection Service (APHIS) carefully examine your plants for insects and diseases. Infested plants are either treated or destroyed.

Securing a Permit
All plants you import for growing or propagation require a permit. For some, you also may have to make arrangements for a postentry quarantine, requiring that you grow the plants subject to APHIS supervision and inspection.

Along with your permit, you can secure a "priority passport" for your plants, a green-and-yellow mailing label available from APHIS. A package with the distinctive label gets directed quickly to the plant inspection station and is forwarded soon after to its destination.

Some plant materials don't require permits. There's no advantage to mailing them, and you can carry them with you as personal baggage when you enter the country; you have to do nothing further than to include them in your Customs declaration and show them to a USDA inspector at the port of entry.

Other materials are prohibited, and there's no point in your even trying to ship them. See below for a list of commonly imported materials and their entry status.

To be sure whether you need a permit and to secure the proper form, labels, and instructions, write:

> Permit Unit
> Plant Protection and Quarantine
> Animal and Plant Health Inspection Service
> U.S. Department of Agriculture
> Federal Building
> Hyattsville, MD 20782

Here is a list of common plant materials and their entry status:

Flower bulbs-In general, admitted. Must be free of soil. Anemone bulbs from Germany and gladiolus bulbs from Africa, prohibited.

Flowers-Fresh cut or dried, generally admitted. Fresh camelia and gardenia, prohibited into Florida, treatment required in California. Chrysanthemums from

Venezuela and protea from South Africa and Swaziland, prohibited.

Plants-All plants in soil, prohibited. Most kinds of dried plants, flowers, and leaves for herbarium or decorative purposes, admitted. Live plants, shrubs, trees, and fresh cuttings, either prohibited or permit required. Postentry quarantine may be required.

Seeds-of flowers, shrubs, trees, and other plants, admitted in general. Tree and shrub seeds require a permit.

Packing materials-Peat moss, sphagnum moss, wood shavings, sawdust, paper, and excelsior, admitted. Grass, straw, and similar unprocessed plant materials, prohibited.

There are exceptions to the above list. For example, requirements may differ for materials brought in from Canada, Hawaii, Puerto Rico, and Mexico. Also, procedures may differ for large commercial shipments. Such exceptions emphasize the importance of checking with APHIS in advance.

Inspection Station Treatments
APHIS inspectors treat your plants with professional care, even though your materials are only a small proportion of the 247 million plants they examine in a year's time. Fumigation or other treatment is applied only when pests are found or when individual inspection is impractical. Every precaution is taken to minimize damage. Strict guidelines are followed and specific treatments are prescribed for different plant groups and pest types.

Every effort is made to expedite inspection and treatment of plants. Most shipments are released the same day they are received.

Tips for Buying, Handling, and Shipping
The general suggestions below can guide you in buying, handling, and shipping plants. They will help your plants survive the trip home, clear through APHIS inspection, and thrive in your collection. You can obtain further tips on shipping and transplanting from plant societies.

Buying. Be selective about the plants you buy. Plants that grow well in a foreign location may not do well in your garden or your greenhouse. For example, plants from a high altitude may not survive at sea level.

Buy from reputable dealers when you make your purchases overseas. APHIS inspectors find that some foreign dealers consistently sell pest-free plants; others sell plants that are always "buggy." Plants' collected from the wild and those not grown in the greenhouse are most likely to require treatment before being admitted into the United States.

Cleaning and inspection. Remove all soil, other growing media, or forest lifter from all parts of plants before you ship or bring them home. Plants arriving with sand, -soil, or earth will be refused entry. However, epiphytic plants (such as some orchids) established on tree-fern slabs or similar soil-free media may be admitted.

Inspect your plants carefully and discard those obviously diseased or infested with insects. Do not attempt to remove insects or disease symptoms in order to get the plants through APHIS inspection. The end result could be introduction of the insect or disease into your collection.

Do not treat plants yourself. Chemical residues can endanger the health of APHIS inspectors or camouflage a pest problem. Nonprofessional treatment may be ineffective and unnecessarily stress, weaken, or kill your plants. Plant inspection station treatments are given only when necessary and are specific for the pest to be controlled.

Packaging for shipment. Improper packaging is the most common cause of plant death or deterioration during shipment. APHIS inspectors frequently find plants jammed into small containers, turned to mush in plastic bags, or damaged by use of nonprotective containers.

Plants are best shipped while dormant. In this state, they can best withstand temperature extremes, dehydration, and other rigors of transit, and the effects of treatments at the inspection station.

Use a sturdy container for shipment. Wooden crates or native baskets are recommended. Cardboard boxes can be used but are more easily crushed. Pack the plants loosely, using crumpled newspaper or excelsior to protect them from bruising and to allow free air movement.

Never enclose the plants in plastic bags or in containers wrapped in or coated with a moisture barrier such as plastic or foil. Too much or too little moisture promotes rot or other deteriorating conditions.

Mailing. To minimize delay and expense, you may mail plant materials directly to an APHIS plant inspection station, preferably by air parcel post.

Some pointers:

- Use APHIS's green-and-yellow mailing label to assure prompt handling of your package.

- Mark the outside of the package to show its contents.

- Send the package early in the week to avoid postal delay on the weekend. Reducing transit time increases the likelihood that your plant will survive the trip.

- Enclose a sheet of paper with your name, home address, and permit number inside the package. After clearance, the package will be forwarded to you without additional cost. Import duties assessed will be collected at your local post office.

- Send the package to: U.S. Department of Agriculture, APHIS, PPO, at one of the following addresses:

ARIZONA

102 Terrace Ave., Rm. 116

Nogales, AZ 85621

CALIFORNIA

(Los Angeles Int'l Airport)

9650 S. La Cienega Blvd.

Inglewood, CA 90301

Jamaica, NY 11430

(San Francisco Int'l Airport)

P.O. Box 250009

San Francisco,

St., So., Room 4)

CA 94125-0009

San Juan, PR 00904

(U.S. Border Station)

P.O. Box 43-L

San Ysidro, CA 92073

Services Building)

P.O. Box 1500 E

FLORIDA

Brownsville, TX 78520

NEW JERSEY

209 River Street

Hoboken, NJ 07030

NEW YORK

(John F. Kennedy Int'l Airport)

Plant Inspection Station,

Cargo Building 80

PUERTO RICO

(Commercio

P.O. Box 3386

TEXAS

(Border

309

Plant Inspection Station
P.O. Box 592136   (Cordova
Border Station)
Miami, FL 33159   3600 East
Paisano, Room 172-A

El Paso, TX 79905
HAWAII
P.O. Box 50002   (1 0 0 0
Zaragoza St.)
Honolulu, Hi 96820   P.O. Box
277

Laredo, TX 78040
LOUISIANA
U.S. Custom House
WASHINGTON
423 Canal Street   F e d e r a l
Office Building,
New Orleans, LA 70130   Room 9014

Seattle, WA 98104

Products into the United States-PA 1083." Send your request to: "Travelers' Tips," U.S. Department of Agriculture, G-110 Federal Building, Hyaftsville, MD 20782.

"Custom Hints for Returning U.S. Residents-Know Before You Go". Send your request to the U.S. Customs Service, P.O. Box 7474, Washington, DC 20044.

~ ~ ENDNOTES ~ ~

1.   This publication is reprinted elsewhere in this book. See Table of Contents for location.

2.   This publication is reprinted elsewhere in this book. Check the Table of Contents.

Cooperation Makes Sense

Complying with import and permit requirements makes good sense. You safeguard your own plant collection while also protecting the Nation's crops, forests, lawns, gardens, and environment. Your cooperation is needed whether you are a collector, a hobbyist, a commercial grower, or a researcher.

You may think, "My one plant can't hurt," and try to smuggle plants through inspection. But just one plant can be the means of introducing a highly destructive insect, pest, or disease.

Customs and USDA inspectors are serious about enforcing the laws. Together, the two agencies look into the luggage and personal effects of incoming travelers, and in the process they catch thousands of smugglers. In a typical month, they impose about $30,000 in $25 or $50 fines for agricultural import violations.

Endangered Plants

Orchids and other rare and endangered plants are also subject to import restrictions under the Convention on International Trade in Endangered Species (CITES).

For further information, contact: U.S. Fish and Wildlife Service Office of Management Authority P.O. Box 27329, Central Station Washington, DC 20038-7329

Additional Publications

"Travelers'Tips On Bringing Food, Plant and Animal

Chapter 34

Buying a Car Overseas? Beware!

[The information in this chapter is reprinted verbatim from a bulletin issued by the U.S. Environmental Protection Agency. It is intended to serve as advice to Americans who buy cars from overseas.]

- - - -

Importing Motor Vehicles

Are you planning to buy a car in a foreign country and bring it back to the United States? Many vehicles manufactured outside the United States do not conform with air pollution control requirements under the Clean Air Act. Avoid unnecessary risks! Know the difficulties of importing a car and the rules for meeting vehicle emission standards before you go!

EPA has established new rules, effective for all vehicles imported after June 30, 1988, covering the importation of "nonconforming vehicles." A "nonconforming vehicle," as the term is used in this text, is any motor vehicle (car, truck, van, motorcycle, etc.) or heavy-duty engine not originally manufactured to meet U.S. emission standards. In addition, special rules apply to any motor vehicle which was originally manufactured with a catalytic converter, or a catalytic converter and oxygen (O_2) sensor, to meet U.S. emission standards, but has been driven outside the United States, Canada, Mexico, or Japan.

Questions Buyers Ask

Q I am a prospective buyer. Why should I be concerned with the new EPA importation rules?

A Knowledge of the rules can affect your buying decisions overseas. By knowing the rules beforehand, you can avoid unnecessary costs and headaches-or even the risk of having your nonconforming vehicle banned from entry into the United States.

Q Why has EPA changed the rules?

A EPA has changed the regulations in order to make sure that imported vehicles meet U.S. emission standards. The new rules require that if a nonconforming vehicle is allowed to enter the United States, it must be modified within 120 days to meet the same EPA emission standards that apply to vehicles built in the United States. This will mean cleaner air for everyone.

Q Will I still be allowed to import a five-year-old or older car that does not meet standards under a one-time special exemption from EPA's rules?

A No. The EPA policy permitting a first-time individual importer to import one nonconforming vehicle at least five model years old without modifying it to meet emission standards has been eliminated for all vehicles imported after June 30, 1988.

Q Are there certain older vehicles that do not need to comply with EPA's new importation rules?

A Yes. The following vehicles are not covered by the Clean Air Act and, therefore, are not subject to the new importation rules and may be imported by any individual:

- Gasoline-fueled light-duty vehicles and gasoline-fueled light-duty trucks originally manufactured before January 1, 1968.

- Diesel-fueled light-duty vehicles originally manufactured before January 1, 1975.

- Diesel-fueled light-duty trucks originally manufactured before January 1, 1976.

- Motorcycles originally manufactured before January 1, 1978.

- Gasoline-fueled and diesel-fueled heavy-duty engines originally manufactured before January 1, 1970.

Five New EPA Requirements

1. Only parties holding valid "certificates of conformity" issued by EPA are permitted to import nonconforming vehicles (with a few exceptions).

A "certificate of conformity" is a document issued by EPA to certify that a particular class of vehicles (like 1985 Mercedes-Benz 500, 5.0 liter engine) has been tested and shown to meet U.S. emissions standards. The party who receives the certificate (the "certificate holder") is thereby authorized to import nonconforming vehicles and modify them so that they are identical to the tested vehicle. Such certificate holders must meet all EPA requirements that apply to them as motor vehicle manufacturers.

If you are considering importing a car, you can no longer do so on your own after June 30, 1988. Instead, you must arrange for the importation-and other activities like modification and testing-through a certificate holder.

2.   Not all vehicles are eligible to be imported. Requirements vary with vehicle age and the qualifications of the certificate holder.

You need to determine whether your car is eligible to be imported by a certificate holder and make arrangements for importation before you buy! Even then, if the certificate holder is no longer in business when you are ready to import the vehicle, you may be unable to bring the car into the United States.

The following vehicles must comply with EPA standards and may be imported only by certificate holders:

● Vehicles less than six model years old. Whether a vehicle may be imported depends on several factors (including the year in which the vehicle will be imported and whether the certificate holder has a certificate for a vehicle like yours). Check with EPA before you buy!

● Vehicles six model years old or older: Any vehicle may be imported by a certificate holder if the holder is willing to be responsible for the modification and testing.

● Vehicles 21 model years old or older: Any vehicle may be imported and will be exempt from meeting U.S. emission standards. However, these vehicles must still be imported by a certificate holder unless they are not covered by the Clean Air Act. As explained above, vehicles that are not covered by the Clean Air Act may be imported by any individual.

Note: A vehicle's model year age is determined by subtracting the calendar year in which it was originally manufactured from the calendar year of importation. For example, a vehicle built by a European

manufacturer in 1986 and imported into the United States in 1988 would be two model years old.

3.   A certificate holder who imports your nonconforming vehicle is responsible for the following:

● Performing all modifications and emission testing within 120 days after the vehicle enters the United States.

● Ensuring that the vehicle contains an emission label and vacuum hose diagram, and providing you with prepaid emission warranties and maintenance instructions for the vehicle.

● Reporting the results of the modification and testing to EPA and holding the vehicle for 15 working days (or longer if EPA wishes to examine, the vehicle).

4.   Certificate holders who violate the rules may be penalized and in some cases may be prohibited from importing nonconforming vehicles.

Even if you have arranged ahead of time for a certificate holder to import your car, if EPA later prohibits the holder from importing cars, the holder will not be eligible to import your car when it arrives in the United States. You may then have trouble finding another certificate holder who is eligible to import your car.

● Vehicles which are equipped with a catalytic converter or a catalytic converter and O_2 sensor, and were originally built to meet U.S. emission standards (i.e., covered by a certificate of conformity) but have been driven outside of the United States, Canada, Mexico, or Japan, may be imported by individuals. However, these vehicles are subject to import restrictions.

The new rule requires that the catalytic converter, or catalytic converter and O_2 sensor, be replaced on vehicles which may have been contaminated with leaded gasoline overseas. This requirement is necessary because unleaded gasoline is still not widely available outside North America, and use of leaded fuel can damage these components. Therefore, these vehicles may be bonded with U.S. Customs at the time of entry to assure these components are replaced. Once the catalytic converter or the catalytic converter and O_2 sensor are replaced, EPA will recommend that Customs release the EPA portion of your bond.

The importation of vehicles equipped with a catalytic converter or a catalytic converter and O_2 sensor from countries other than Canada, Mexico, or Japan will be subject to the above requirements except in the following cases:

- Vehicles imported as part of a Department of State or Department of Defense shipment, and covered by the approved catalyst and O_2 sensor control program of either agency.
- Any vehicle which is equipped with a catalytic converter or catalytic converter and O_2 sensor and is included in a manufacturer's control program that has been approved by EPA. Such vehicles are identified by the statement "Catalyst Approved for Import," which may appear on or near the Department of Transportation door-post label, or on the engine emission control label.

Warning:This is to remind you that the EPA policy which permits a first-time individual importer to import one nonconforming vehicle at least five model years old without a need to meet Federal emission standards is eliminated for all vehicles imported after June 30, 1988.

Because of the expense and potential difficulties involved with importing a vehicle not originally built to meet U.S. emission standards, EPA strongly recommends that you buy a vehicle that is labeled by the manufacturer as meeting U.S. emission standards. If you are interested in purchasing such a car while travelling in Europe, many manufacturers provide a delivery plan that enables you to pick up your U.S.-certified vehicle in Europe. Please contact your local dealership for more information.

Other Requirements

- The new EPA rules do not change the federal safety requirements to which the vehicles must comply. For information on safety requirements, contact:
U.S. Department of Transportation
400 7th Street, SW.
Room 6115
Washington, DC 20590

- A "Gas Guzzler Tax" may need to be paid on your vehicle. These taxes range from $500 to $3,850 per vehicle. For more information, contact:
Internal Revenue Service
Public Affairs Office
1111 Constitution Avenue, NW.
Washington, DC 20224

- The State of California has its own program for regulating the importation of nonconforming vehicles that are sold, registered, or operated in California. For more information on California's requirements, contact:

State of California
Air Resources Board
Mobile Source Control Division
9528 Telstar Avenue
El Monte, CA 91731

- Your state may have its own requirements for nonconforming vehicles. For more information, contact your state Department of Motor Vehicles *before you buy!*

EPA Can Help

- For more information on EPA's rules and requirements concerning imported vehicles, contact:
U.S. Environmental Protection Agency
Manufacturers Operations Division
(EN-340F)

Investigation/Imports Section
401 M Street, SW.
Washington, DC 20460
(202) 382-2504

Chapter 35

Importing a Car/Pleasure Boat

[The information in this chapter is reprinted verbatim from a bulletin issued by the
U.S. Department of the Treasury, U.S. Customs Service. It is intended to serve as advice
to Americans importing cars into the U.S..]

▬ ▬ ▬ ▬

WARNING!

Imported motor vehicles are subject to safety standards under the Motor Vehicle Safety Act of 1966, revised under the Imported Vehicle Safety Act of 1988; to bumper standards under the Motor Vehicle Information and Cost Savings Act of 1972, which became effective in 1978; and to air pollution control standards under the Clean Air Act of 1968, as amended in 1977 and 1990.

Most vehicles manufactured abroad that conform with U.S. safety, bumper, and emissions standards are exported to be sold in the United States; *therefore, it is unlikely that a vehicle obtained abroad meets all relevant standards.* Be skeptical of claims by a foreign dealer or other seller that a vehicle meets these standards or can readily be *brought into compliance. Nonconforming vehicles entering the U.S. must be brought into compliance, exported, or destroyed.* See pages 317-318 for general requirements.

This chapter provides essential information for U.S. residents, military, or civilian government employees, and foreign nationals who are importing a vehicle into the U.S. It includes U.S. customs requirements and those of other agencies whose regulations we enforce. Since Environmental Protection Agency and Department of Transportation requirements are subject to frequent changes, we recommend that you contact these agencies before buying a vehicle abroad. Their addresses are listed eleswhere on this page and on page 317.

Our publications, *Know Before You Go (Customs Hints for Returning U.S. Residents[1])* and *Customs Hints for Visitors (Nonresidents),* contain general information for persons entering the U.S. Request them from your nearest Customs office or from U.S. Customs, P.O. Box 7407, Washington, D.C. 20044; or from embassies and consulates abroad.

The Environmental Protection Agency has a detailed fact sheet describing emission requirements for imported vehicles. You can get a copy of this fact sheet or other information about importing motor vehicles by calling EPA's Imports Hotline (202) 233 9660. You can also communicate by facsimile (FAX) at (202) 233-9596, or by writing to the U.S. Environmental Protection Agency, Manufacturers Operations Division (EN-340F), Investigation/ Imports Section, 401 M Street, S.W., Washington, D.C. 20460.

NOTE: Importations from Cuba, Haiti, Iran, Iraq, Libya, North Korea, Serbia/Montenegro, or Vietnam, or involving the governments of those countries are generally prohibited pursuant to regulations issued by the Treasury Department's Office of Foreign Assets Control. Prior to any attempt to make such an importation, information concerning the prohibitions and licensing policy should be obtained by contacting the Director, Office of Foreign Assets Control, U.S. Department of the Treasury, 2nd Floor ANX, 1500 Pennsylvania Avenue, N.W., washington, D.C. 20220, tel. (202) 622-2500, or FAX (202) 622-1657.

PRIOR ARRANGEMENTS

Arrangements for shipping a vehicle are made by the owner. Have your shipper or carrier notify you of the vehicle's arrival date so that Customs can clear it. Shipments are cleared at the first port of entry unless you arrange for a freight forwarder abroad to have the vehicle sent in bond to a Customs port more convenient to you.

Customs officers are prohibited by law from acting as agents or making entries for an importer. However, you may employ a commercial customhouse broker to handle your entry.

DOCUMENTATION

For Customs clearance you will need the shipper's or carrier's original bill of lading, the bill of sale, foreign registration, and any other documents covering the vehicle. You will also need written prior approval from EPA, which will be evident to the Customs inspector at the port of entry in the form of an approval letter from the EPA or a manufacturer's label affixed to the car stating that the vehicle meets all U.S. emission requirements. Or, you may make arrangements to import your vehicle with an Independent Commercial Importer (ICI). In this case, the ICI will import your vehicle and perform any EPA-required modifications and be responsible for assuring that all EPA requirements have been met. ICIs can only import certain vehicles, however, and in general, their fees are very high.

See page 317 for DOT requirements and page 318 for driver's license and tag requirements.

CLEANING UNDERCARRIAGE
To safeguard against importation of dangerous pests, the U.S. Department of Agriculture requires that the undercarriage of imported cars be free from foreign soil. Have your car steam sprayed or cleaned thoroughly before shipment.

YOUR CAR IS NOT A SHIPPING CONTAINER
For your own safety, security, and convenience, DO NOT use your car as a container for personal belongings.

- Your possessions are susceptible to pilferage while the vehicle is on the loading and unloading docks and in transit. Many shippers and carriers will not accept your vehicle if it contains personal belongings.

- The entire contents of your car must be declared to Customs on entry. Failure to do so can result in a fine and seizure of the car and its contents.

- Your vehicle may be subject to seizure, and you may incur a personal penalty, if anyone uses it as a conveyance for illegal narcotics.

DUTIABLE ENTRY

Foreign-made vehicles imported into the U.S., whether new or used, either for personal use or for sale, are dutiable at the following rates:

Autos	2.5%
Trucks valued at $1,000 or more	25%
Motorcycles up to 700cc	3.7%

Duty rates are based on price paid or invoice price. Most Canadian-made vehicles are duty-free.

As a returning U.S. resident, you may apply your $400 Customs exemption and those of accompanying family members toward the value of the vehicle if it:

- Accompanies you on your return

- Is imported for personal use

- Was acquired during the journey from which you are returning.

For Customs purposes, a returning U.S. resident is one who is returning from travel, work, or study abroad.

After the exemption has been applied, a flat duty rate of 10% is applied toward the next $1,000 of the vehicle's value. The remaining amount is dutiable at the regular duty rate.

FREE ENTRY
U.S. CITIZENS EMPLOYED ABROAD or government employees returning on TDY or voluntary leave may import a foreign-made car free of duty provided they enter the U.S. for a short visit, claim nonresident status, and export the vehicle when they leave.

MILITARY AND CIVILIAN EMPLOYEES of the U.S. government returning at the end of an assignment to extended duty outside the Customs territory of the U.S. may include a conforming vehicle among their duty-free personal and household effects. The auto must have been purchased abroad and be in its owner's possession prior to departure. Generally, extended duty is 140 days or more. Navy personnel serving aboard a U.S. naval vessel or supporting naval vessel from its departure from the U.S. to its return after an intended overseas deployment of 120 days or more are entitled to the extended duty exemption.

NONRESIDENTS may import a vehicle duty-free for personal use if the vehicle is imported in conjunction with the owner's arrival. Conforming vehicles so imported may remain in the U.S. indefinitely. Nonconforming vehicles must be exported within one year and may not be sold in the U.S. *There is no exemption or extension of the export requirement.* Conforming vehicles imported under duty-free exemption are dutiable if sold within one year of importation. Duty must be paid at the most convenient Customs office before the sale is completed. Conforming vehicles so imported may remain in the U.S. indefinitely once a formal entry is made for EPA purposes. (See page 317 "Emission Standards.")

CARS IMPORTED FOR OTHER PURPOSES
Nonresidents may import an automobile or motorcycle and its usual equipment free of duty for a temporary stay to take part in races or other specific purposes. However, prior written approval from EPA is required and such approval is granted only to those racing vehicles that EPA deems not capable of safe or practical use on streets and highways. If the contests are for other than money purposes, the car may be admitted for

90 days without formal entry or bond if the customs officer is satisfied as to the importer's identity and good faith. The vehicle becomes subject to forfeiture if it is not exported or if a bond is not given within 90 days of its importation. Prior authorization must be obtained from DOT if the vehicle does not conform to all applicable Federal motor vehicle safety standards.

SAFETY, BUMPER AND THEFT PREVENTION STANDARDS

Motor vehicles not more than 25 or more years old must conform to the DOT motor vehicle safety standards that were in effect when these vehicles or items were manufactured. Passenger cars manufactured after September 1, 1973 must also meet bumper standards. The importer must file form DOT HS-7 at the time of entry, indicating whether the vehicle conforms to applicable safety and bumper standards. The original manufacturer is required to affix a label to the vehicle certifying that these standards have been met. Vehicles that do not bear a certification label attached by the original manufacturer must be entered as a nonconforming vehicle under a DOT bond for one and a half times the vehicle's dutiable value. This is in addition to the regular Customs entry bond.

Unless specifically excepted, the importer must sign a contract with a DOT Registered Importer (RI), who will modify the vehicle to conform with all applicable safety and bumper standards and who can certify the modifications, just as the ICI can do for EPA-required modifications. A copy of the RI's contract must be attached to the DOT HS-7 form and furnished to the Customs Service with the DOT bond at the port of entry. A list of RIs is available from DOT and should be obtained before you decide to import a vehicle. Furthermore, DOT requires that the vehicle model and model year must, prior to entry, be determined eligible for importation. A DOT RI can advise you whether your vehicle is eligible; if it is not, the RI can submit a petition in your behalf to have your vehicle considered for eligibility, if you so desire. Understand, however, that substantial fees must be paid at the time such petitions are filed.

For additional information or details on these requirements, contact the U.S. Department of Transportation, National Highway Traffic Safety Administration, Director of the Office of Vehicle Safety Compliance (NEF-32), 400 Seventh Street, S.W., Washington, D.C. 20590, tel. (202) 366-5313 or FAX (202) 366-1024.

FEDERAL TAX

Certain imported automobiles may be subject to the gas-guzzler tax imposed by section 4064 of the Internal

Revenue Code. An individual who imports an automobile for personal use, or a commercial importer, may be considered an importer for purposes of the tax and thus liable for payment of the tax.

The amount of the tax is based on a combined urban/highway fuel economy (miles per gallon) rating assigned by the EPA for gas-guzzler tax purposes. This EPA rating may be different from fuel economy ratings indicated by the manufacturer.

If the EPA has not assigned a gas-guzzler fuel economy rating for the model automobile you import, a rating must be independently determined. No tax is imposed on 1986 or later model year automobiles that have a combined fuel economy rating of at least 22.5 miles per gallon.

Information on determining fuel economy ratings and liability for the tax are contained in section 4064 of the Code, Revenue Procedures 86-9, 1986-1 Cumulative Bulletin 530, Revenue Procedure 87-10, 1987-4 Internal Revenue Bulletin 29, and Revenue Ruling 86-20, 1986-1 C.B. 319.

The gas-guzzler tax is reported on Form 720, Quarterly Federal Excise Tax Return. Additional information may be obtained from your local district office of the Internal Revenue Service.

EMISSION STANDARDS

The following passenger cars, light-duty trucks, heavy-duty engines and motorcycles are subject to Federal emission standards:

- Gasoline-fueled cars and light-duty trucks originally manufactured after December 31, 31967.

- Diesel-fueled cars originally manufactured after December 31, 1974.

- Diesel-fueled light-duty trucks originally manufactured after December 31, 1975.

- Heavy-duty engines originally manufactured after December 31, 1969.

- Motorcycles with a displacement of more than 49 cubic centimeters originally manufactured after December 31, 1977.

Beginning with the 1974 model year, vehicles that were originally manufactured to meet U.S. emission requirements if driven outside the United States, Canada, Mexico, Japan, Australia, Taiwan or Grand

Bahamas Islands may be required to have their oxygen sensor and/or catalytic converter replaced. You may import your U.S. version vehicle under a Customs bond and have any qualified mechanism perform the necessary work. You should contact the EPA directly for detailed requirements and options before shipping your vehicle.

Nonconforming vehicles must be imported for you by a currently certified Independent Commercial Importer (ICI), a list of which is available from the EPA. This list should be obtained *before* you decide to import a car. The ICI will be responsible for assuring that your car complies with all U.S. emission requirements. (As of July 1, 1988, EPA no longer has the one-time exemption for vehicles five or more model-years old.) Be aware that EPA will deny entry to certain makes, models, and model-years if an ICI is not certified or is unwilling to accept responsibility for the vehicle(s) in question.

You can obtain additional information on emission control requirements or on ICIs from the U.S. EPA Manufacturers Operations Division (EN-340F), Investigation/Imports Section, Washington, D.C. 20460, tel. (202) 233-9660, FAX (202) 233-9596.

Individual state emission requirements may differ from those of the federal government. Proper registration of a vehicle in a state may depend upon satisfaction of its requirements, so you should contact the appropriate state authorities prior to importation. Be aware, however, that some state requirements may be less stringent than those of the federal government. EPA will not necessarily accept compliance with a state's emission requirements as satisfying EPA's.

A WORD OF CAUTION

Both the Department of Transportation and the Environmental Protection Agency advise that although a nonconforming car may be conditionally admitted, the modifications required to bring it into compliance may be so extensive and costly that it may be impractical and even impossible to achieve such compliance. Moreover, under Federal Regulations 49 CFR parts 591 through 594, effective January 31, 1990, some vehicle models are prohibited from importation. It is highly recommended that these prohibitions and modifications be investigated *before* a vehicle is purchased for importation.

EXCEPTIONS

The following vehicles need not conform to emission or safety requirements but may NOT be sold in the U.S. and may require EPA and DOT declarations.

- Those imported by nonresidents for personal use not exceeding one year. The vehicle must be exported at the end of that year-no exceptions or extensions. Those belonging to members of foreign armed forces, foreign diplomatic personnel, and members of public international organizations on assignment in the U.S. for whom free entry has been authorized by the Department of State.

- Those temporarily imported for research, demonstration or competition, provided they are not licensed for use, or driven, on public roads. Parties responsible for such vehicles must submit proper documents-that is, forms EPA 3520-1 and DOT HS-7-to Customs at the time entry is made. Also, applicable written approvals from these agencies must be obtained in advance and presented to Customs along with these forms. *Remember, the cost to return vehicles that have been refused prior approval can be very high and must be borne by the vehicles' owner(s).*

DRIVER'S PLATES AND PERMITS

Imported cars should bear the International Registration Marker. The International Driving Permit, issued in five languages, is a valuable asset. Consult an international automobile federation or your local automobile club about these documents.[4]

U.S. RESIDENTS importing a new or used car should consult the Department of Motor Vehicles in their state of residence about temporary license plates.

NATIONALS OF CENTRAL AND SOUTH AMERICAN countries that have ratified the Inter-American Convention of 1943 may drive their cars in the U.S. for touring purposes for one year or the validity of the documents, whichever is shorter, without U.S. license plates or U.S. driver's permits, provided the car carries the international Registration Marker and registration card, and the driver has the International Driving Permit.

MOTORISTS VISITING THE UNITED STATES as tourists from countries that have ratified the Convention on International Road Traffic of 1949 may drive in the U.S. for one year with their own national license plates (registration tags) on their cars and with their own personal driver's licenses.

MOTORISTS FROM CANADA AND MEXICO are permitted to tour in the U.S. without U.S. license plates or U.S. driver's permits, under agreements between the United States and these countries.

318

MOTORISTS FROM A COUNTRY NOT A PARTY to any of the above agreements must secure a driving permit in the U. S. after taking an examination.

FOREIGN NATIONALS employed in the U.S. may use their foreign license tags from the port of entry to their destination in the U.S.

IMPORTING A PLEASURE BOAT

When a pleasure boat or yacht (hereinafter referred to as "pleasure boats" or "boats") arrives in the United States, the first landing must be at a Customs port or designated place where Customs service is available. This section explains the Customs formalities involving pleasure boats to help you plan your importation and reporting requirements; explains overtime charges; and provides other information relating strictly to pleasure boats. Further details on any of the material in this publication may be obtained from the U.S. Customs Service, Washington, D.C. 20229 (ATTN: Carrier Rulings Branch). For information about location of reporting stations, contact the District Director in the area where you will be cruising.

HOW TO IMPORT YOUR BOAT

Shipping Arrangements
Arrangements for shipping a pleasure boat are made by the importer. He or his agent for customs purposes must arrange to be notified of the date the boat will arrive at the first port of entry in the United States so Customs procedures can be completed.

Customs officers are not permitted to act as agents or to make customs entries for an importer. Commercial brokers, known as customhouse brokers, are usually retained by importers who find it impractical to handle their own shipments or who are unfamiliar with customs formalities. The broker charges a fee for this service.

When your pleasure boat arrives, the original bill of lading from the shipper or carrier, bill of sale and foreign registration, if any, must be presented to effect release. In certain instances additional documents may be required.

Dutiable Value
The dutiable value of a new pleasure boat purchased just prior to its exportation to the United States will most probably equal the price actually paid for the boat. The value of a pleasure boat which is used for a period of time after its purchase abroad will be determined by adjusting the original purchase price of the boat downward to reflect reasonable depreciation. The extent of the adjustment will depend upon the age and condition of the boat at the time of importation.

Rates of Duty
All new and used pleasure boats are dutiable if owned by a resident or brought into the country for sale or charter to a resident. Any general offer to sell is considered evidence that the vessel was brought in for sale or charter to a resident. The duty on a pleasure boat is 1.5 percent of the value. (Boats used in trade, commerce, or intended to be used in travel or commerce, are not dutiable)

The rates of duty on non-self-propelled pleasure boats are now:

Wood or bark canoes and paddles	Free
Pneumatic craft	2.4 percent
Other	4 percent

> **Note:** The duty rates on pleasure boats imported from certain countries in the Sino-Soviet bloc are higher.

A pleasure boat owned by a foreign corporation whose principal asset is the pleasure boat or whose primary business relates to its use is considered owned by a resident of the United States if a substantial portion of the corporate stock is owned by one or more residents of the United States.

Virgin Island Exception
The Virgin Islands *(United States)* are not within the Customs territory of the United States and pleasure boats imported in the United States Virgin Islands are not dutiable under their laws. The boat is, however, subject to duty when it first is imported into the Customs territory of the United States, defined as the 50 states, the District of Columbia and Puerto Rico.

Parts, Kits and Repairs
Boat parts and kits may be dutiable. If a kit contains enough parts to form a complete boat, it is subject to the same duty as an assembled boat. The same is true of a partially completed boat with a hull capable of floating. Parts imported separately are dutiable according to the specific rate applicable to that part.

Repairs incidental to use of the pleasure boat abroad are not dutiable. Non-incidental repairs, alterations, and additions made abroad that improve the boat or otherwise add to its value are generally subject to the duty at the rate the pleasure boat itself would be dutiable if imported if imported in its newer, modified condition.

Emergencies

If it is necessary to make an emergency stop in the United States to preserve life or property, the master of the pleasure craft must report as soon as possible to the nearest Customs, Immigration, Agriculture, or Public Health officer. He should not permit any merchandise or baggage to be removed from the boat or passengers or crew to depart the place of arrival without official permission, unless necessary for the protection of life, health, or property.

PERSONAL EXEMPTIONS

Returning U.S. Residents

Customs determines if a person who has formerly resided in the United States is a returning resident by ascertaining whether, when the person departed, he intended to leave the United States permanently. In making this determination, Customs may consider the duration and purpose of the person's foreign stay and whether, while abroad, the person maintained a home in the United States.

A United States resident living or stationed abroad and entering the country for a short visit may import a foreign-built boat duty free if he claims on arrival and is accorded nonresident Customs status and exports the boat upon his departure from the United States. United States citizens employed abroad and Government employees returning on TDY or leave may be granted this status.

A returning United States resident may apply his personal Customs exemption toward the duty on a foreign-built pleasure boat under the following conditions:

- The boat is imported for his personal use or for use by members of his household.

- The boat was acquired abroad as an incident of the journey from which he is returning.

- The boat accompanies him at the time of his return.

The head of a family returning together may make a joint declaration for all members residing in the same household and pool their customs exemption toward the duty on the imported boat.

Government Employees

Any Government employee or person in the service of the United States stationed overseas may include his pleasure boat as part of his personal and household effects which are allowed free entry providing:

- He is returning home upon termination of an extended *duty* assignment at a location outside the Customs territory of the United States. Generally, *extended duty* means at least 140 days, or 120 days for naval personnel who continuously serve aboard a warship or supply vessel from the time of departure from the United States until it returns.

- The pleasure boat was purchased abroad and is in his possession--not merely on order to be delivered.

- The boat enters the United States within one year of issuance of order terminating his assignment abroad.

A copy of the Government order, issued prior to shipment and showing the person is returning because of termination of an extended duty assignment, should be presented to Customs when claim for free entry is made. In the absence of such order, other evidence must be presented.

Who is a Nonresident?

A nonresident for Customs purposes is a foreign visitor to the United States, a person emigrating to the United States, or a person who left the country with no intent to reestablish residency.

A nonresident entering the United States may import a pleasure boat free of duty for his personal use and for the transportation of his family and guests provided the boat is imported in connection with his arrival and owned by him or ordered prior to his departure.

A nonresident bringing a pleasure boat into the United States under a duty-free exemption must formally enter the boat and pay applicable Customs duty if he sells the boat or offers it for sale or charter within the U.S. within one year after the date of importation.

Temporary Stays/Entry Under Bond

A pleasure boat and its usual equipment may be entered duty free by a nonresident for a temporary stay to take part in races or other contests. If the contests are for other than money purses and the Customs officer is satisfied as to the importer's good faith, the boat may be admitted without formal entry or bond for a period of 90 days. A certificate identifying the boat will be issued to the importer and must be delivered with the vessel to the Customs office at the point of departure from the country.

If the boat is not exported nor a bond obtained within 90 days after the date of temporary importation, it

320

becomes subject to forfeiture. Bond is taken in an amount equal to twice the estimated duty. Cash may be deposited in lieu of surety on the bond and will be refunded if the boat is exported within the time limit and under Customs supervision.

Pleasure boats brought into the country for sale or for sale on approval will not be accepted for entry under bond.

Boats entered for alterations or repairs; as samples for taking orders; for experimental testing, review, or study purposes; for use by illustrators and photographers solely as models in their own establishments; or as professional equipment and tools of trade may be entered without payment of duty as temporary importations under bond. The length of stay in these circumstances is normally one year and may not exceed three years.

REPORTING ENTRY

American Pleasure Boats
American pleasure boats not documented by the United States Coast Guard but owned by citizens residing in the United States must comply with Federal laws relating to identification numbers issued by a State, Puerto Rico, the U.S. Virgin Islands, Guam, American Samoa, or the District of Columbia. The master of any American pleasure boat must report arrival from a foreign port or place to Customs immediately and must also report foreign merchandise aboard his boat that is subject to duty. The report may be made by any means of communication and should include the name of the boat, its nationality, name of the master, place of docking, and arrival time. If an inspection is required, the Customs officer will direct the vessel to an inspection area.

Notice:The operator of a pleasure boat whose intended destination is a point within the jurisdiction of the Miami (Florida) Customs District must make the report immediately upon arrival at one of 26 locations designated by the Miami Customs District. These 26 locations are at five areas within the district: Ft. Pierce, Ft. Lauderdale, Key West, Miami, and West Palm Beach. The locations are listed on page 323 and are marked with a double asterisk (**).

Pleasure boats which measure less than 5 net tons arriving from Canada or Mexico otherwise than by sea (e.g. Great Lakes, Rio Grande), if carrying baggage or merchandise, must immediately report arrival to the nearest Customs office. (A boat less than 30 feet in length will probably measure less than 5 net tons.)

American pleasure boats arriving in the United States from a foreign port or place are not required to make formal entry provided they are not engaged in trade, are not in violation of the Customs or navigation laws of the United States, and have not visited any vessel lying off the coast which is apparently there for illegal purposes.

No notification to Customs is required when the boats depart for foreign ports or places.

Cruising Licenses
Cruising licenses exempt pleasure boats of certain countries from formal entry and clearance procedures--filing manifests and obtaining permits to proceed, and from the payment of tonnage tax and entry and clearance fees--*at all but the first port of entry*. They can be obtained from the District Director of Customs at the first port of arrival in the United States. Normally issued for no more than a one-year period, a cruising license has no bearing on the dutiability of a pleasure boat.

NOTE: Under Customs policy, upon expiration of that vessel's cruising license, the pleasure vessel will not be issued another until it again arrives in the United States from a foreign port or place and more than 15 days have elapsed since the expiration of the vessel's previous cruising license. (Customs Directive 3100-006, November 7, 1988.) Vessels of the following countries (subject to change) are eligible for cruising licenses (these countries extend the same privileges to American pleasure boats):

Argentina, Australia, Austria, Bahama Islands, Belgium, Bermuda, Canada, Denmark, Federal Republic of Germany, France, Greece, Honduras, Ireland, Jamaica, Liberia, Netherlands, New Zealand, Norway Sweden, Switzerland, Turkey, Great Britain (including Turks and Caicos Islands, St. Vincent (including the territorial waters of the Northern Grenadine Islands), the Cayman Islands, the British Virgin Islands and the St. Christopher-Nevis-Anguilla Islands).

Foreign-Flag Pleasure Boats
The master of a foreign-flag or undocumented foreign pleasure boat must report arrivals to U.S. Customs immediately and make formal entry within 48 hours. In the absence of a cruising license, vessels in this category must obtain a permit before proceeding to each subsequent U.S. port. The boat must also clear Customs prior to departing for a foreign port. Navigation fees will be charged for the formal entry, the permit to proceed and the clearance of foreign-flag pleasure boats.

The following documents are required for Customs purposes: original register; original *Customs form 1300;* master's oath on entry on vessel; general declaration, *Customs form 1301;* ship stores declaration, *Customs form 1303;* crew's effects declaration, *Customs form 1304;* clearance from last foreign port; original crew list; original passenger list; and cargo declaration.

Restrictions on Foreign-Built or Foreign-Flag Vessels
Vessels that are foreign built or of foreign registry may be used in the United States for pleasure purposes or in the foreign trade of the United States. Federal law prohibits, however, the use of such vessels in the coastwide trade--the transportation of passengers or merchandise between points in the United States, including the carrying of fishing parties for hire. The documentation of foreign-built vessels is under the jurisdiction of the United States Coast Guard.

Boarding Charges and Overtime
There is no charge for Customs inspection during official business hours, 8 a.m.-5 p.m., Monday through Saturday, except holidays. After hours, Sundays, and holidays, inspection service will be provided at *pro rata* overtime rates, not to exceed $25 per boat. '

User Fees
Effective July 6, 1986, pleasure craft must pay an annual $25 user fee. Contact your local Customs office if you have any questions on this subject.

Immigration Requirements
U. S . citizens should carry proof of their citizenship, such as a passport, birth certificate or voter registration card.

Resident aliens should present their "green card" (Immigration Form I151 or I551) upon arrival. Non-resident aliens should present a valid passport with a valid non-immigration visa in it. Visas are normally obtained from a U.S. consulate or embassy. Contact the U.S. consulate or embassy in your country for further information on this subject. Immigration form I-94 should be filled out by all nonresident aliens. This form is for sale by the Superintendent of Documents, Government Printing Office, Washington, D.C. 20402.

Canadian citizens do not need a visa, but must present proof of their citizenship. If a Canadian citizen is arriving from a country outside the Western Hemisphere, he must present a valid Canadian passport.

Plant and Animal Restrictions
The importation of fruits, plants, meats, other plant or animal products, birds or other live organisms of any kind is regulated by the Department of Agriculture to prevent the introduction of pests and disease. Such items cannot be brought into the United States unless advance permission is granted by the Department of Agriculture or U.S. Customs.

Stay on Board
If your boat has anchored or tied up, you are considered to have entered the United States. No person shall board or leave the boat prior to completion of Customs processing without permission from the Customs officer in charge, except to report arrival.

If it is necessary for someone to leave the boat to report arrival to Customs, he must return to the boat after reporting and remain on board. No one who arrived on board the boat may leave until the Customs officer grants permission to go ashore. Violations may result in substantial penalties and forfeiture of the boat.

A Final Word...
The United States Coast Guard administers a number of safety and documentation laws applicable to pleasure boats. With certain exceptions, a pleasure boat manufactured after November 1, 1972 may not be imported unless the manufacturer has affixed a certification label with the words "This Boat Complies with U.S. Coast Guard Safety Standards in Effect on the Date of Certification." For further information on matters under Coast Guard jurisdiction, contact: Commandant, U.S. Coast Guard Headquarters, 2100 Second Street, SW, Washington, D.C. 20593.

Report your arrival in the United States to the U.S. Customs office nearest to your point of entry. Customs numbers follow below.

ALABAMA
Mobile
1. (205) 690-2111
2. (504) 589-3771*

ALASKA
Anchorage
I. (907) 248-3373
2. (907) 243-43 12
Juneau
(907) 586-7211*
Ketchikan
(907) 225-2254*
Sitka
(907) 747-3374*
Skagway
(907) 983-2325*
Valdez
(907) 835-2355*
Wrangell

(907) 874-3415

CALIFORNIA
Los Angeles
1. (310) 514-6013
2. (310) 514-6083
3. (310) 980-3300

Port Hueneme
(805) 488-8574*
San Diego
I . (6;9) 293-5370
2. (619) 428-7209*
San Francisco
1. (415) 705-4444
2. (415) 876-2812
San Luis Obispo
(805) 595-238 1 *

CONNECTICUT
Bridgeport
1. (203) 579-5606/07
2. (800) 743-7416*

DELAWARE
Dover
1. (302) 674-2205
2. (800) 743-7416*

Wilmington
1. (302) 573-6191
2. (800) 743-7416*

FLORIDA
Ft. Myers
1. (813) 768-4318
2. (813) 228-2385 after 5 p.m.
Jacksonville
I . (904) 291-2775*
Naples
Naples City Dock**
880 12 Ave. S.

Panama City
1. (904) 785-4688
2. (904) 291-2775*

Pensacola
I . (904) 432-681I
2. (904) 291-2775*
Pt. Canaveral
1. (407) 783-2066*
St. Petersburg
1. (813) 536-7311*
Tampa
1. (813) 228-2385*

Miami
Ft. Pierce Area Harbortown Marina**
25 N. Causeway Drive Ft. Pierce, FL.

Sailfish Marina** 3565 Southeast Street Stuart, FL.

Sebastian Inlet Marina** 2580 U.S. I Sebastian, FL.

Ft. Lauderdale Area Lauderdale Marina** 1800 S.E.
15th Street Ft. Lauderdale, FL.

Bahia Mar** 801 Sea Breeze Boulevard Ft. Lauderdale,
FL.

Lighthouse Point Marina** 2830 N.E. 29th Street
Pompano Beach, FL.

Delray Harbour Club Marina** 1035 South Federal
Highway Delray, FL.

Pier 66** 2301 S.E. 17th Street Ft. Lauderdale, FL.

Sands Harbor Marina** 125 N. Riverside Drive
Pompano Beach, FL.

Cove Marina** 1755 S.E. 3rd Court Deerfield Beach,
FL.

Key West Area Ocean Reef Club** Key Largo, FL.

Oceanside Marina** 5950 Maloney Avenue Key West,
FL.

Tavernier Creek Marina** Tavernier, FL.

A & B Marina** 700 Marina Street Key West, FL.

Boot Key Marina** 1000 15th Street Marathon, FL.
Dial: 1-800-432-1216

Holiday Isle Marina**
Mile Marker #85, U.S. I Islamorada, FL.

Miami Area

Phillips 66 Marina** 1050 MacArthur
Causeway-Watson Island Miami, FL.

Crandon Park Marina** Virginia Key Miami, FL.

Sunset Harbour Marina** 1982 Purdy Avenue Miami
Beach, FL.

Bakers Haulover Marina* * 10800 Collins Avenue
Miami Beach, FL.

323

Miamarina** 401 Biscayne Boulevard Bayside, Miami, FL.
Dial: 1-800-432-1216

West Palm Beach Area Sailfish Marina**
96 Lake Drive Palm Beach Shores, FL.
Jupiter Marina** 97 Lake Drive Jupiter, FL.

Spencers Boat Yard** 4000 Dixie Highway West Palm Beach, FL.

Lake Worth Boating Center (Palm Beach Yatch Club) ** 7848 South Federal Highway Hypoloxo, FL.

Marco Island
O'Shea's Restaurant**
1081 Bald Eagle Dr., Marco Island FL.

GEORGIA
Brunswick
1. (912) 262-6692*
Savannah
1. (912) 232-7507*
2. (912) 652-4400
3. (912) 966-0557

HAWAII
Hilo
1. (808) 935-6976
2. (808) 836-3613*

Honolulu
(808) 541-1717
(808) 836-3613*
Kauai
(808) 833-5521*
Maui
(808) 877-6013*

ILLINOIS
Chicago
(312) 894-2900

LOUISIANA
New Orleans
(504) 389-0261
(504) 589-3771*

Lake Charles
(318) 439-5512
(504) 589-3771*
Morgan City
(504) 384--6654
(504) 589-3771*
New Orleans
(504) 589-6804

(504) 589-3771*

MAINE
Portland
1. (207) 775-3131
2. (800) 343-2840*

MASSACHUSETTS
Boston
1. (617) 565-4657
   (800) 343-2840*

MICHIGAN
Detroit
(313) 226-3140
Grand Rapids
(616) 456-2515
Port Huron
(313) 985-9541
Sault Ste. Marie
(906) 632-2631

MINNESOTA
Crane Lake (218) 933-2321
Duluth (218) 720-5203
Ely (218) 365-3262

Grand Marais (218) 387-1750 (open 5-15/10-15
Grand Portage (218) 475-2244
International Falls (218) 283-2541
Lake of the Woods (Call Pembina, N.D.)

MISSISSIPPI
Gulfport
1. (601)864-1274
2. (504)589-3771*
Pascagoula
1. (601)762-7311
2. (504)589-3771*

MONTANA
Great Falls
(406)453-7631

NEW JERSEY
Newark
1. (201) 645-6561
2. (201)645-3762
3. (800)221-4265*
Perth Amboy
1. (908) 442-0415
2. (800)221-4265*
(If you arrive in New Jersey south of the Manasquan Inlet contact Customs' Philadelphia

324

Pa.office)

NEW YORK
New York City
1. (800) 522-5270*
2. (212) 466-5472*
3. (212) 466-5602 (6 World Trade Center)
4. (212) 399-2901 (Pier 92 North River)
5. (718) 816-0469 (Rosebank Staten Island)

Albany
1. (518) 472-3456
2. (800) 522-5270*
Buffalo
1. (800) 927-5015#
2. (716) 846-4311##
Ogdensburg
(800) 827-2851*

NORTH CAROLINA
Morehead City
1. (919) 726-5845
2. (919) 726-3651
3. (919) 726-2034
Wilmington
(919) 343-4616

NORTH DAKOTA
Pembina
(701) 825-6551

OHIO
Cleveland
(216) 267-3600

OREGON
Astoria
(503) 325-554
Coos Bay
(503) 267-6312
Longview
(206) 425-3710*
Newport
(503) 265-6456
Portland
(503) 221-2871*

PENNSYLVANIA
Philadelphia
1. (215) 597-4648
2. (800) 743-7416*

SOUTH CAROLINA
Charleston
1. (803) 723-1272

TEXAS
Brownsville
1. (210) 831-4121
2. (210) 548-2744**
Corpus Christi
1. (512) 888-3352
2. (800) 800-0294*
Freeport
1. (409) 233-3004
2. (800) 800-0294*
Galveston
1. (409) 766-3624
2. (800) 800-0294*
Houston
1. (409) 766-3624
2. (800) 800-0294*
Port Aransas
1. (512) 88-3352
2. (800) 800-0294*
Port Arthur
1. (409) 724-0087
2. (800) 800-0294*
Port Lavaca
1. (512) 888-3352
2. (800) 800-0294*
Port O'Connor
1. (512) 88-3352
2. (800) 800-0294*
Rockport
1. (512) 888-3352
2. (800) 800-0294*

VERMONT
St. Albans
1. (802) 524-6527
2. (800) 343-2840*
Lake Chaplain
(802) 866--2778
Lake Memphremagog
(802) 873-3219

VIRGINIA
Alexandria
1. (703) 557-1950
2. (301) 953-7454
3. (800) 767-4007*
4. (305) 536-5132*
Newport News
(804) 245-6470
Norfolk
(804) 441-6741*
Richmond
(804) 771-2552

WASHINGTON
Aberdeen

325

1. (206) 532-2030
2. (800) 562-5934*
Anacortes
1. (206) 293-2331
2. (800) 562-5943*
Bellingham
1. (206) 734-5463
2. (800) 562-5943*
Blaine
1. (206) 332-6318
2 . (800) 562-5943 *
Everett
1. (206) 259-0246
2. (800) 562-5934*
Friday/Roche Harbors
1. (206) 378-2080
2. (800) 562-5943*
Neah Bay
1. (206) 645-2236
2. (800) 562-5934
Olympia
1. (206) 593-6338
2. (800) 562-5934*
Point Roberts
1. (206) 945-2314
2 . (800) 562-5943 *
Port Angeles
1. (206) 457-4311
2. (800) 562-5934*
Port Townsend
1. (206) 385-3777
2. (800) 562-5934*
Seattle
(206) 442-4678*
Tacoma
I . (206) 593-6338
2. (800) 562-5934*

Vancouver
(503) 240-2171

WISCONSIN
Green Bay
(414) 433-3923
Milwaukee
(414) 297-8932
Racine
(414) 633-0286

PUERTO RICO
Fajardo
(809) 863-0950
Mayaguez
1. (809) 832-3342
2. (809) 832-3343
3. (809) 832-3345

Ponce
(809) 841-3130
2. (809) 841-3131
3. (809) 841-3132
San Juan
I . (809) 253-4533
2 . (809) 253-4534
3. (809) 253-4535

U.S. VIRGIN ISLANDS
St. Croix
(809) 773-1011
St. John
(809) 776-6741
St. Thomas
(809) 774-6755

---

* (24-Hours.)
** Designating reporting station
# Primary number during vessel arrival season.
If no answer at primary number or out of season.

~ ~ ENDNOTES ~ ~

1.   This publication is reprinted elsewhere in this book. See Table of Contents for location.

2.   See **Appendix M** for information on how to obtain an International Driver's permit

Chapter 36

Generalized Systems of Preferences & the Traveler

[The information in this chapter is reprinted verbatim from a bulletin issued by the
Department of the Treasury, U.S. Customs Service. It is intended to serve as advice
to Americans traveling abroad.]

- - - -

Please Note

Some products, although entitled to duty-free treatment under GSP may be restricted or prohibited from entering the United States. For example, endangered species of wildlife and plants, and products made from them, are protected by the Convention on International Trade in Endangered Species of Wild Fauna and Flora and are prohibited from being exported or imported. A ban on elephant ivory is presently in effect. Any elephant ivory brought into the United States is subject to seizure. If you contemplate purchasing articles made from ivory, skin, fur, etc., please contact the U.S. Fish and Wildlife Service, Department of Interior, or your nearest U.S. Customs Office, in advance of your trip.

Our publication Customs *Hints-Know Before You Go* provides information on Customs clearance, exemptions, and restricted or prohibited items.

This text has been prepared to serve only as an advisory guide for the traveling public for entry of non-commercial importations intended for personal use only. More specific and definitive advice in this regard should be obtained from one of the Customs field offices. Please also note that details or requirements for commercial importers are not included.

Questions & Answers

What is GSP?

GSP (Generalized System of Preferences) is a system used by many developed countries to help developing nations improve their financial or economic condition through export trade. In effect, it provides for the duty-free importation of a wide range of products from certain countries, which would otherwise be subject to customs duty.

When did GSP go into effect for the United States?

GSP went into effect on January 1, 1976. and will remain in effect until July 31, 1995.(The latter date may change. Check with the U.S. Department of the Treasury.)

How is GSP administered?

GSP is administered by the United States Trade Representative in consultation with the Secretary of State The duty suspensions are proclaimed by the President under the Trade Act of 1974 as amended. The U.S. Customs Service is responsible for determining eligibility for duty-free entry under GSP.

What products are eligible?

Approximately 4,284 items have been designated as eligible for duty-free treatment from beneficiary developing countries (BDCs). The eligible articles are identified in the Harmonized Tariff Schedule of the United States Annotated and the designated countries are also listed therein.

For the traveler's convenience, an advisory list of the most popular tourist items which, in general, have been accorded GSP status is included in this chapter.

Are certain items excluded?

Under the Trade Act, many items, such as most footwear, most textile articles (including clothing), watches, some electronic products, and certain glass and steel products are specifically excluded from GSP benefits.

What countries have been designated as BDCs?

Approximately 140 countries and territories have been designated, see page 329.

Are the articles and countries subject to change?

Yes.

Articles may be excluded by Executive Order if it is determined that their importation is harmful to domestic industry. Beneficiary countries may also be excluded from the GSP program at any time, due to other trade considerations.

In addition, some articles from specified countries may be excluded from GSP treatment, if during the preceding year:

- the level of imports of those articles exceeded a specific dollar limit indexed to the nominal growth of the U.S. gross national product since 1984).

- that country supplied 50 percent or more of the total U.S. imports of that product.

Are there any specific requirements or qualifications I must be aware of to be sure an article qualifies for duty-free treatment? In order to take advantage of GSP, you must have acquired the eligible article in the same beneficiary country where it was grown, manufactured, or produced. Articles may accompany you or may be shipped from the developing country *directly* to the United States.

What forms are required?
If shipped, the goods should be accompanied by a commercial invoice. No other forms are necessary unless it is a commercial importation.

What about merchandise acquired in duty-free shops?
Most items purchased in duty-free shops will not be eligible for GSP treatment unless the merchandise was produced in the country in which the duty-free shop is located.

What about Internal Revenue tax?
Such items as gin, liqueur, perfume, if designated as eligible articles, may be subject to Internal Revenue Service tax despite their GSP status.

What happens if I thought an article was eligible for duty-free entry and it is not?
When merchandise claimed to be free of duty under GSP is found to be dutiable, you may include it in your customs exemption. Articles imported in excess of your exemption will be subject to duty. If you feel your article should have been passed free of duty, you may write to the district Director of Customs where you entered, giving him the information concerning your entry. He will make a determination as to whether you are due a refund.

Am I still entitled to my basic customs exemption?
As a returning U.S. resident, you may still bring in free of duty $400 worth of articles (fair retail value) acquired abroad in addition to those items covered by GSP. This exemption is $1200 if you are returning from the U.S. Virgin Islands, American Samoa, or Guam and $600 if you are returning from certain Caribbean Basin or Andean nations. (See page 329 for this list. Remember that all articles acquired abroad, whether free of duty or not, including those entitled to GSP, must be declared to U.S. Customs on your return.

Visitors or nonresidents are entitled to bring in articles which are duty free under GSP in addition to their basic customs exemption.

Whom should I contact if I have any questions about GSP? Contact your nearest U.S. Customs office-there are almost 300 ports of entry throughout the United States. If you are overseas, the U.S. Embassy or consulate can be of assistance.

Popular Tourist Items
This listing is solely an advisory guide to items designated as eligible for duty-free treatment under GSP which may be of interest to travelers for their personal use. Note that certain items, if from a particular beneficiary country, may be excluded. Do not hesitate to check with your nearest Customs office or the American Embassy or consulate in the country you are visiting to verify the GSP status of any article you are considering bringing into the United States.

BASKETS or bags of bamboo, willow, or rattan.
CAMERAS, motion-picture and still; lenses; and other photographic equipment.
CANDY
CHINAWARE, bone: household ware; and other articles such as vases, statues, figurines; non-bone: articles other than household ware (except for non-bone chinaware or subporcelain).
CIGARETTE LIGHTERS, pocket and table.
CORK, manufactures of.
EARTHENWARE or stoneware except household ware available in sets.
FLOWERS, artificial of plastic or feathers.
FURNITURE of wood, rattan, or plastic.
GAMES, played on boards: chess, backgammon, darts, Mah-Jongg.
GOLF BALLS and EQUIPMENT
IVORY, beads; other manufactures of ivory.
JADE, cut but not set for use in jewelry and other articles of jade.
JEWELRY of precious metal, of precious stones, or of precious metal set with semi-precious stones, cameos, intaglios, amber, or coral: Silver, chief value, valued not over $18 per dozen. Necklaces and neck chains, almost wholly of gold: except rope from Israel and mixed link.
JEWELRY BOXES, unlined.
MUSIC BOXES and MUSICAL INSTRUMENTS
PAPER, manufactures of.
PEARLS, cultured or imitation, loose or temporarily strung and without clasp.
PERFUME
PRINTED MATTER
RADIO RECEIVERS, solid state (not for motor vehicles).
RECORDS, phonograph and tapes.

328

SHAVERS, electric
SHELL, manufactures of.
SILVER, tableware and flatware.
SKIS and SKI EQUIPMENT, ski boots not included.
STONES, cut but not set, suitable for use in jewelry.
Precious and semi-precious stones including marcasites;
coral and cameos.
TAPE RECORDERS
TOILET PREPARATIONS
TOYS
WIGS
WOOD, carvings.

Beneficiary Countries

The countries listed below have been designated as beneficiary developing countries in the U.S. Generalized System of Preferences.

Albania
Angola
Botswana
+Antigua and Barbuda
Brazil
Barbuda***
Burkina Faso
Argentina
Burma
Burundi
+Bahamas***
Cameroon
Bahrain
Bangladesh
Cape Verde
+Barbados***
Central African
+Belize***
Republic
BeninChad
Bhutan
+Colombia*
Bolivia*
Comoros
Bosnia-Hercegovina
Congo
Namibia
Mozambique
+Costa Rica
Nepal
Croatia
Cyprus
Czech Republic
Niger
Djibouti
Oman
+Dominica***
Pakistan

+Dominican Republic
Papua New Guinea
Ecuador*
Paraguay
Peru*
Egypt
Philippines**
Poland
+El Salvador
Rwanda
Estonia
Ethiopia
Equatorial Guinea+
Saint Kitts(Christopher) and Nevis
Fiji
Gambia+
Saint Lucia***
Ghana+
Saint Vincent and the Grenadines***
+Grenada***
+Guatemala
Sao Tome and Principe
Senegal
Seychelles
Guinea Bissau
+Guyana***
Sierra Leone
Slovakia
Slovenia
+Haiti
Solomon Islands
+Honduras
Hungary
Somalia
India
Sri Lanka
Indonesia**
Sudan
Israel
Surinam
Cote D'Ivoire
Swaziland
+Jamaica***
Jordan
Tanzania
Kenya
Thailand**
Kiribati
Togo
Lebanon
Tonga
Lithuania
Lesotho+
Trinidad and Tobago***
Tunisia
Madagascar

329

Turkey
Malawi
Tuvalu
Malaysia**
Uganda
Maldives
Uruguay
Mali
Vanuatu
Malta
Venezuela*
Western Samoa
Yemen Arab Rep.
Maritius
Mexico
Zaire
Zambia
Morocco
Zimbabwe

Wallis and Futuna
Western Sahara

*** Member countries of the Caribbean Common Market. (CARICOM)

+ $600 personal exemption
(Panama and Nicaragua are also eligible for this exemption

* Member countries of the Cartagena Agreement-Andean Group (treated as one country).

** Association of South East Asian Nationals-Nations (ASEAN) except Brunei, Dar es Salaam and Singapore (treated as one country).

*** Member countries of the Caribbean Common Market. (CARICOM)

Non-Independent Countries & Territories

Anguilla
Macau
+Aruba
British Indian Ocean Territory
+Montserrat***
+Netherlands Antilles
Cayman Islands
New Caledonia
Christmas Island (Australia)
Niue
Norfolk Island
Cocos (Keeling) Islands
Cook Islands
Saint Helena
Falkland Islands (Islas Malvinas)
Tokelau
Trust Territory of the Pacific Islands (Palau)
French Polynesia
Gibraltar
Turks and Caicos Islands
Greenland
+Virgin Islands, British
Heard Island and McDonald Islands

Chapter 37

U.S. Customs: International Mail Imports

*[The information in this chapter is reprinted verbatim from a bulletin issued by the
Department of the Treasury, U.S. Customs Service. It is intended to serve as advice
to Americans who ship or receive parcels by mail.]*

- - - -

Introduction

- I've ordered commemorative plates from Europe before and never paid duty. Why did I have to pay this time?

- I received a gift package from my aunt who was traveling abroad. Am I required to pay duty on a gift?

- I need to send a foreign-made watch to Switzerland for repair. Will I have to pay duty when it comes?

We get lots of questions like these, so we have prepared this leaflet to explain U.S. Customs procedures and requirements for parcels mailed to the United States from abroad. If you follow the suggestions offered here, you will get your packages through the customs process as efficiently as possible.

The fastest way to inquire about a particular mail shipment is to communicate directly with the Customs international mail branch that processed your shipment. You will find these mail branches, as well as Customs' district offices in the appendix section of this book. Should you need to contact Customs headquarters, you may write to: U.S. Customs Service, Office of Cargo Enforcement and Facilitation, Washington, D.C. 20229.

Mail parcels must meet United States and international postal requirements regarding weight size and measurement.

What mail is subject to Customs examination?

In general, all mail originating *outside* the Customs territory of the United States (the 50 states, the District of Columbia, and Puerto Rico), which is to be delivered *within* U.S. Customs territory, is subject to Customs examination. All mail arriving from outside the U.S. Virgin Islands that is to be delivered *inside* the U.S. Virgin Islands is also subject to Customs examination. The U.S. Postal Service sends all incoming foreign mail packages to Customs for examination and assessment of any applicable duty. This includes international (civilian) mail parcels and those originating at overseas

military postal facilities (APO/FPO).

Free of Duty

Packages that Customs has passed free of duty will be endorsed on the will be endorsed on the outer wrapper: **"Passed Free - U.S. Customs."** These packages receive minimal Customs handling and are returned immediately to the Postal Service for delivery by the local post office. In these cases, there will be no additional postage, handling costs or other fees required of the addressee.

Dutiable

Packages that require payment duty will have a Customs form CF 3419A attached to the outer wrapper. This form is the Customs mail entry, and it will have been filled out by the examining Customs officer indicating the tariff item number, rate of duty, processing fee, and total amount to be paid for that shipment.

The package is then returned to the Postal Service for local delivery and collection of both duty and a postal handling fee, which is assessed by the Postal Service. Some mail importations valued at more than $1,250 will require a formal entry by the importer, rather than the procedure just described.

The Postal Service fee will appear on the package in the form of postage-due stamps. This procedure has been authorized by international postal convention. An exception to this is made for dutiable material mailed from U.S. military post offices located abroad; in these cases, postal handling fees are not charged. A Customs processing fee of $5.00 will be assessed on all dutiable mail shipments.

What happens to my parcel if it is not claimed?

Mail parcels not claimed within 30 days will be returned to the sender unless a duty assessment is being protested.

How do I locate a missing or overdue mail parcel.

If your parcel is long overdue, or if you think it may be

lost in the mail, you should contact your local post office and request that a *parcel tracer action* be initiated to locate it. This is a matter over which Customs has no control.

If a parcel has been detained by Customs for a specific reason, such as the lack of a proper invoice, bill of sale, or other documentation; a possible trademark violation; or if a formal Customs entry is required, the Customs office holding your shipment will notify you immediately of the reason for detention and how you can obtain release of the shipment.

How do I protest the Customs duty on my mail package?

If you think the amount of duty has been assessed incorrectly, you may obtain a reconsideration of the duty in either of two ways:

(1)   Pay the assessed duty and take delivery of the merchandise. Then, send the *yellow copy of* the mail entry receipt, CF 3419A, which accompanied the parcel when it was delivered, to the *issuing Customs office* identified on the form. Include with the *yellow copy* a statement as to why you believe the assessment is incorrect and copies of any invoices, bills of sale, or other evidence you may have. Requests for an adjustment must be made within 90 days after you have received the package and paid the duty.

(2)   Decline to pay the duty and postpone acceptance of the shipment. Then, provide the postmaster, within five days of your refusal, a written statement of your objections to the duty assessment. The postmaster will forward your statement, along with the mail entry (form CF 3419A), any invoices, bills of sale, or other evidence you choose to furnish, to the international mail branch that issued the mail entry.

The postmaster retains custody of the shipment until informed by the international mail branch of the disposition to be made of your protest. No postal storage charges will accrue during this period.

If you are located near one of Customs' international mail branches, the postmaster may send the CF 3419A to that branch instead, along with your statement and evidence for reconsideration of duties or tariffs.

If consideration of your protest results in a refund, the refund check must be made payable to the addressee shown on the mail entry.

Will the same rate of duty apply on future shipments?

The rate of duty assessed on a mail entry is not binding for future importations. A binding ruling on tariff classification may be obtained by writing to the Commissioner of Customs, Attn: Office of Regulations and Rulings, Washington, D.C. 20229.

> **U.S. Postal Service Regulations prohibit sending alcoholic beverages through the mail (18 U.S.C. 1716(f)).**

Am I entitled to any exemptions from duty?

Bona fide gifts.

Bona fide, *unsolicited* gifts are allowed to enter duty free as long as their fair retail value does not exceed $50, and if the recipient does not receive more than $50 worth of such gifts in the same day. (See 19 CFR Section 10.152.) There is no duty exemption for shipments containing alcohol-based perfume, tobacco products or alcoholic beverages unless the entire shipment has a retail value of less than $5.00. On bona fide gifts sent to the United States from the U.S. Virgin Islands, Guam, and American Samoa, the limitation is $ 1 00 fair retail value. To qualify for a duty exemption under this provision, the gifts must be sent by persons already outside the United States to persons *in* the United States.

The gift exemption does *not* apply to gifts mailed to oneself or mail-ordered from the United States. It also *does not* apply where two or more persons traveling abroad together mail home gifts to each other.

Gifts intended for more than one person may be consolidated in the same package provided:
- They are individually wrapped,
- They are labeled with the name of the recipient, and
- The value of each gift does not exceed $50 ($100 if sent from the U.S. Virgin Islands, American Samoa, or Guam).

Following these simple instructions will insure quick Customs clearance of gift packages.

Gift Packages, including consolidated gift packages, should be clearly marked on the outside of the package: "Unsolicited Gifts" with 1) the name of the donor, 2) nature of the gifts, if there is more than one in a consolidated package, 3) the accurate fair retail value of each gift, 4) the name of each recipient.

Here is an example of the correct way to mark a consolidated package:

Christmas gifts:

· To John Jones-one belt, $20; one box of candy, $5; one tie, $5.

· To Bill Jones-two shirts, $25; one belt, $5; one pair of trousers, $15.

Customs duty will be collected on all improperly marked consolidated packages and individual gifts worth more than $50.

Should any single gift within a consolidated package exceed the $50 value limit, then all the gifts making up the consolidated package will be dutiable. Each gift shall be dutiable at the rate that would normally be assessed on it, unless the sender has not marked all gifts so that the quantity and value of each can be readily ascertained. In such a case, the duty rate shall be based on the highest rate of duty for any gift in the consolidated package.

All foreign-made merchandise that enters the United States, whether new or used, is subject to duty.

United States Products Returned.
Articles which are the growth, manufacture, or product of the United States and have not been processed or enhanced in value while abroad are not subject to duty upon their return to the United States. Packages containing only products of the United States should be clearly marked on the outside wrapper **"American Goods Returned."**

Personal and Household Effects.
The personal and household effects of any person (military or civilian) employed by the United States Government are eligible for duty-free entry if that person is returning to the United States after completing an assignment of extended duty abroad. The articles must have been in the returnee's possession prior to departure for the United States. A sealed envelope containing a copy of the Government orders terminating the assignment must accompany the articles. This envelope should be attached securely to the outer wrapper of the parcel. The parcel should also be clearly marked on the outside, **"Returned Personal Effects-Orders Enclosed."**

Articles ordered from military exchanges prior to departure for the United States and mailed from the exchange to a service member's home address after departure do not qualify under this exemption and *are dutiable. Goods of foreign origin are subject to duty, even if purchased in military exchanges* (PX, AAFEX, NEX).

Will articles acquired while traveling abroad and mailed home be duty-free under my personal exemption?

Travelers returning from abroad are allowed an exemption from Customs duty on $400 worth of foreign merchandise that *accompanies* them upon their return to the United States. Except as noted below under the $1,200 exemption, *all merchandise to be entered under the traveler's personal exemption must accompany that individual when reentering the United States.* Foreign-made articles purchased during a trip abroad and mailed home are subject to duty.

$1,200 Exemption
If you return directly or indirectly from the Virgin Islands of the U.S., American Samoa, or Guam, you may receive a Customs exemption of $1,200, based upon the fair retail value of the articles in the country where you acquired them. Of this $1,200, not more than $400 may be applied to merchandise not obtained in these islands. This duty-free exemption is increased to $600 if the merchandise was acquired in a Caribbean Basin Initiative beneficiary country.

Tourist purchases acquired in and sent directly from a U.S. insular possession to the United States may be entered free of duty under your $1,200 exemption if the items are properly declared and processed. *Articles acquired elsewhere must accompany you at the time of your return for duty-free entry* under your personal exemption.

An additional $1,000 worth of articles acquired in these islands may also be sent to the United States as unaccompanied tourist purchases and entered at a flat 5% rate of duty. Any amount over this will be dutiable at the various rates of duty applicable to the articles.

The procedures outlined below must be followed.

Step 1. At the time of your return: a) list all articles acquired abroad on your baggage declaration (CF 6059B) *except* those sent under the bona fide gift provision to friends and relatives in the United States; b) indicate which articles are unaccompanied; c) fill out a Declaration of Unaccompanied Articles (CF 255) for each package you are sending. This three-part form should be available where you make your purchase; if it is not, ask for a copy when you clear U.S. Customs.

Step 2. When you return to the United States, Customs will: a) collect duty and tax on goods accompanying you, if tax or duty is owed; b) verify your unaccompanied articles against sales slips, invoices, etc.; c) validate form 255 as to whether goods are free

333

of duty under your personal exemption or subject to a flat rate of duty. Two copies of the 255 (a yellow and a white) will be returned to, you.

Step 3. Return the yellow copy of the form to the shopkeeper or vendor holding your purchase and keep the other copy for your records. The traveler is responsible for informing the shopkeeper *at the time of purchase* not to send the merchandise until the shopkeeper has received this yellow copy.

Step 4. The shopkeeper then puts the yellow copy of the 255 into an envelope and attaches the envelope securely to the outside of the package. The merchant must also label the package, on the outside wrapper near the envelope if possible, "**Unaccompanied Tourist Purchase.**" NOTE: This is the most important step to follow in order to receive the benefits allowed under this procedure.

Step 5. The Postal Service will deliver your package after it has cleared Customs. The Postal Service will also collect any duty or other Customs fees that may be owed, along with package handling fees.

Are articles from the U.S. insular possessions dutiable other than tourist purchases mailed to the U.S.?

While the U.S. Virgin Islands, American Samoa, and Guam are insular possessions of the United States, they are outside the Customs territory of the United States. Articles imported into the United States from these insular possessions *are subject to duty.* However, articles which are the growth or product of these islands, and articles which are manufactured or produced there, are duty free if they: 1) do not contain foreign materials to the value of more than 50 percent of the appraised value of the manufactured article, as determined by Customs, 2) come directly to the Customs territory of the United States from these islands, and 3) are not prohibited by quota limitations or otherwise.

How do I return an article for repair or alteration?
If you are sending foreign-made merchandise abroad for repairs or alterations, you should register the item with Customs *before* mailing it in order to avoid paying duty twice. (Foreign-made merchandise is dutiable when entering the United States unless the owner has demonstrated prior ownership, and foreign-made repairs may also be dutiable.) You can get a Certificate of Registration, Customs form 4455, for this purpose at any local Customs office.

To export articles for repair, you should bring the merchandise to your nearest Customs office for

certification, which simply means that the Customs officer will verify that the article(s) described on the 4455 form are indeed those being shipped abroad. After doing so, the Customs officer will complete the CF 4455 in duplicate and will enter the *Date, Port,* and his or her *Signature* on the forms. The officer will then give both forms to you.

Enclose the original 4455 with the merchandise you are shipping abroad to facilitate Customs processing after the repaired merchandise has been mailed back to you. Keep the duplicate copy just in case something goes awry and you need to assure that you are liable only for duty on the repairs and not on the complete article. Also, be sure to instruct your foreign supplier to return the CF 4455 with the repaired article and to mark on the outside of the return package "**Repaired/Altered Merchandise CF 4455 Enclosed.**" Goods that have been repaired or altered free of charge may still be subject to Customs duty depending upon the Customs officer's determination after examining the return shipment.

The Customs Service has an arrangement with the U.S. Postal Service for those who live more than 20 miles from a Customs office. In such cases, you may bring your merchandise to the nearest post office, where the postmaster can certify the articles on the CF 4455 in the manner described above. It will still be necessary, however, to get copies CF 4455 from the Customs Service.

Are replacement articles dutiable?
Occasionally, merchandise from a foreign supplier is unsatisfactory; for example, it may be the wrong size, color, broken in transit, or simply not according to the order placed with the supplier. Recipients of these parcels generally return the item to the foreign firm and request a replacement free of charge.

The replacement article is *dutiable.* You may, however, request a refund of duty on the *original* package - the unsatisfactory one - by writing to the Customs international mail branch that first issued the mail entry (CF 3419A) for the unsatisfactory shipment. This branch will be found on the front of form 3419A. When you write to the mail branch requesting a refund on the original package, you must include with your letter: 1) a copy of the original mail entry (CF 3419A) and 2) a statement or other evidence from the post office from which you mailed it back to the supplier showing that the first article was, in fact, returned. You should also enclose any supporting correspondence to or from the foreign supplier concerning the exchange. Upon receipt of this information, the issuing Customs international mail branch will review the transaction and issue you a refund of duty, if appropriate.

How is a duty refund obtained on a damaged article?
Parcels in transit from abroad undergo much handling and processing by foreign and domestic post offices as well as by Customs. Customs has possession of a parcel for only a short time out of that entire period and has no control over the shipment during the remainder of its journey. If your parcel arrives so damaged that its contents are beyond repair, you may choose to simply abandon the shipment to the post office. If you do this and you have already paid the Customs duty, you should obtain a statement from the delivering post office that you have abandoned the shipment. Send a copy of that statement along with a copy of your mail entry receipt (CF 3419A) to the issuing Customs office shown on the front of the mail entry receipt and request a full refund of the duty and postal handling fee.

Why are clear and complete Customs declarations so important?
We realize that some of the foregoing paperwork requirements may sound cumbersome, but millions of parcels come through Customs international mail branches each year. Without readily accessible, easy-to-read Customs forms attached to the outer wrapping - especially forms 3419A and 4455 Customs officers would be forced to do time consuming, intrusive examinations of almost all packages, which would seriously delay the arrival of your merchandise.

When items are mailed from abroad, responsibility for completing and attaching the Customs declaration lies with the foreign sender, who must provide a full, accurate description of the package's contents and value. Complete, accurate Customs declarations attached to the outside wrapping allows the vast majority to pass Customs unopened, allowing Customs officers to make accurate duty assessments based strictly on the information supplied in the "dec."

Warning
The Food and Drug Administration prohibits the importation, by mail or in person, of fraudulent prescription and non-prescription drugs and medical devices. These may include unorthodox "cures" for medical conditions including cancer, AIDS and multiple sclerosis. While these drugs an devices may be completely legal elsewhere, they m not have been approved for use in the United States even under a prescription issued by a foreign physician or under the supervision of a domestic physician. They may not legally enter the United States and may be confiscated upon arrival by mail.

Ceramic tableware sold abroad may contain dangerous

levels of lead in the glaze which may be extracted by acid foods and beverages. The Food and Drug Administration recommends that ceramic tableware, especially when purchased in Mexico, Peoples Republic of China, Hong Kong or India, be tested for lead release by a commercial laboratory your return or be used for decorative purposes only.

For additional information, contact your nearest FDA office or write:
Food and Drug Administration
Division of Import Operations and Policy
Room 12-30, (HFC-170)
5600 Fishers Lane
Rockville, MD 20857

The United States Customs Service is authorized by law to prohibit the importation of goods that violate U.S.-registered intellectual property rights namely, trademarks and copyrights. This authority extends to articles imported into the United States through the international mail system. Goods imported in violation of intellectual property rights are subject to seizure and forfeiture. In addition, Customs may assess a monetary penalty, based on the domestic value of the articles, against the importer. Examples of unlawful merchandise include:

- Articles which bear counterfeit trademarks, such as "fake" designer or brand-name clothing or watches.
- Toys which are unlawful copies of copy-right-protected designs.
- Unauthorized reproductions of certain sound recordings.

The Customs Regulations governing intellectual property rights may be found in Title 19, Code of Federal Regulations, Part 133.

There are other categories of merchandise whose importation into the United States also is restricted or prohibited. These categories of merchandise include certain foodstuffs; certain domesticated and wild animals; products made from endangered species; narcotics and certain weapons. The consequences of the attempted entry of restricted or prohibited merchandise vary according to which law the importation violates.

The Customs Regulations governing these classes of merchandise may be found in Title 19, Code of Federal Regulations, Part 12.

For additional information on the above restrictions, please contact the nearest U.S. Customs Service office or write to the U.S. Customs Service, Office of

Regulations and Rulings, Washington, D.C. 20229.
ATTN: Intellectual Property Rights Branch.

Chapter 38

International Parental Child Abduction

[The information in this chapter is reprinted verbatim from a bulletin issued by the U.S. State Department, Bureau of Consular Affairs. It is intended to serve as advice to Americans at home and abroad.]

– – – –

INTRODUCTION

Parental child abduction is a tragedy. When a child is abducted across international borders, the difficulties are compounded for everyone involved. This pamphlet is addressed to the adult most directly affected by international child abduction, the left-behind parent.

The Department of State's Office of Children's Issues (CA/OCS/CI) deals with the victims of international parental child abduction every day. Since the late 1970's, we have been contacted in the cases of approximately 7,000 American children who were either abducted from the United States or prevented from returning to the United States by one of their parents. At the time of publication, we have over 1,200 active, unresolved cases on file.

You, as the deprived parent, must direct the search and recovery operation yourself. Because it can be a bewildering experience, we have prepared a checklist for you (see page 352). In this booklet, we tell you what the Department of State can and cannot do to help you (see page 339). In addition, because we are only part of the network of resources available to you, we mention other avenues to pursue when a child or children have been abducted across international borders. Your case is unique, and you will have to decide how much of the information here is useful and whether it can be applied to your particular needs to resolve your crisis.

If you have any further questions, please call us at 202-736-7000. You may also fax us at 202-647-2835, or write to us at:

Office of Children's Issues
CA/OCS/CI, Room 4811
Department of State
Washington, D.C. 20520-4818.

PART I- PREVENTION

HOW TO GUARD AGAINST INTERNATIONAL CHILD ABDUCTION

How Vulnerable is Your Child?

You and your child are most vulnerable when your relationship with the other parent is broken or troubled; the other parent has close ties to another country; and the other country has traditions or laws that may be prejudicial to a parent of your gender or to aliens in general.

Cross-cultural Marriages: Should You or Your Child Visit the Country of the Other Parent?

Many cases of international parental child abduction are actually cases in which the child traveled to a foreign country with the approval of both parents but was later prevented from returning to the United States. While these cases are not abductions, but wrongful retention, they are just as troubling to a child. Sometimes the marriage is neither broken nor troubled, but the foreign parent, upon returning to his or her country of origin, decides not to return to the U.S. or to allow the child to do so. A person who has assimilated a second culture may find a return to his or her roots traumatic and may feel a pull to shift loyalties back to the original culture. A person's personality may change when he or she returns to the place where he or she grew up.

In some traditional societies, children must have their father's permission and a woman must have her husband's permission to travel. If you are a woman, to prevent your own or your child's detention abroad, find out about the laws and traditions of the country you plan to visit or to allow your child to visit, and consider carefully the effect that a return to his roots might have on your husband. The Office of Children's Issues has several country flyers that provide some general information. For detailed advice in your specific case, you may wish to contact an attorney in that country. We can provide you with a list of attorneys practicing around the word.

Precautions That Any Vulnerable Parent Should Take

In international parental child abduction, an ounce of prevention is worth a pound of cure. Be alert to the possibility and be prepared-keep a list of the addresses and telephone numbers of the other parent's relatives, friends, and business associates both here and abroad. Keep a record of other important information on the other parent, including these numbers: passport, social security, bank account, driver's license, and auto license. In addition, keep a written description of your child, including hair and eye color, height, weight, and any special physical characteristics. Take color photographs of your child every six months. If your child should be abducted, this information could be vital in locating your child.

The National Center for Missing and Exploited Children (NCMEC at telephone 1-800-843-5678), in addition, suggests that you teach your child to use the telephone; practice making collect calls; and instruct him or her to call home immediately if anything unusual happens. If you feel your child is vulnerable to abduction, get professional counseling. Do not merely tell a friend about your fears.

The Importance of a Custody Decree
Under the laws of many American states and many foreign countries, **if there is no decree of custody prior to an abduction, both parents are considered to have equal legal custody of their child.** If you are contemplating divorce or separation, or are divorced or separated, or even if you were never legally married to the other parent, obtain a decree of sole custody or a decree that prohibits the travel of your child without your permission or that of the court as soon as possible. If you have or would prefer to have a joint custody decree, make certain that it prohibits your child from traveling abroad without your permission or that of the court.

How to Draft or Modify a Custody Decree
A well-written custody decree is an important line of defense against international parental child abduction. NCMEC, in its publication *Family Abduction: How to Prevent an Abduction and What to Do If Your Child is Abducted,* has several recommendations to help prevent the abduction of your child if your spouse is a legal permanent resident alien or a U.S. citizen with ties to a foreign country. For instance, it may be advisable to include court-ordered supervised visitation and/or prohibiting your child from traveling without your permission or that of the court. If the country to which your child might be taken is a member of the Hague Convention on International Child Abduction (see page 341), the custody decree should state that the parties agree that the terms of the Hague Convention apply should an abduction or wrongful retention occur. The ABA also suggests having the court require the alien parent or the parent with ties to a foreign country to post a bond. This may be useful both as a deterrent to

abduction and, if forfeited because of an abduction, as a source of revenue for you in your efforts to locate and recover your child. For further information, you may contact the NCMEC at the address on page 347.

How a Custody Decree Can Help
Obtain several *certified* copies of your custody decree from the court that issued it. Give a copy to your child's school and advise school personnel to whom your child may be released.

U.S. Passports
From the Department of State, you may learn whether your child has been issued a U.S. passport. You may also ask that your child's name be entered into the State Department's passport name check system. This will enable the Department to notify you or your attorney if an application for a U.S. passport for the child is received anywhere in the United States or at any U.S. embassy or consulate abroad. If you have a court order that either grants you sole custody or prohibits your child from traveling without your permission or the permission of the court, the Department may also refuse to issue a U.S. passport for your child. **The Department may not, however, revoke a passport that has already been issued to the child.**

To inquire about a U.S. passport or to have your child's name entered into the name check system, mail or fax your request to

Office of Passport Policy and Advisory Services
Passport Services, Suite 260
1111 19th Street, N.W.
Washington, D.C. 20522-1705
Tel. (202) 955-0377; Fax (202) 955-0230

With your request, include your child's full name or names, date of birth, place of birth, and the address and telephone number(s) where you may be contacted. If there is a court order relating to the custody or travel of the child, include a complete copy.

Foreign Passport-the Problem of Dual Nationality
Many U.S. citizen children who fall victim to international parental abduction possess dual nationality. While the Department of State will make every effort to avoid issuing a U.S. passport if the custodial parent has provided a custody decree, the Department cannot prevent embassies and consulates of other countries in the United States from issuing their passports to children who are also their nationals. You can, however, ask a foreign embassy or consulate not to issue a passport to your child. Send the embassy or consulate a written request, along with certified complete copies of any court orders addressing custody

338

or the overseas travel of your child you have. In your letter, inform them that you are sending a copy of this request to the U.S. Department of State. If your child is only a U.S. citizen, you can request that no visa for that country be issued in his or her U.S. passport. No international law requires compliance with such requests, but some countries will comply voluntarily.

PART II

WHAT THE STATE DEPARTMENT CAN AND CANNOT DO WHEN A CHILD IS ABDUCTED ABROAD

When a U.S. citizen child is abducted abroad, the State Department's Office of Children's Issues (CI) works with U.S. embassies and consulates abroad to assist the left-behind parent in a number of ways. There are, however, a number of things that we cannot do.

WHAT THE STATE DEPARTMENT CAN DO:

- **In cases where the Hague Convention** on the Civil Aspects of International Child Abduction applies (see Part IV), assist parents in filing an application with foreign authorities for return of the child;

- **In other cases,** attempt to locate, visit and report on the child's general welfare;

- Provide the left-behind parent with information on the country to which the child was abducted, including its legal system, family laws, and a list of attorneys there willing to accept American clients;

- **In all cases,** provide a point of contact for the left-behind parent at a difficult time;

- Monitor judicial or administrative proceedings overseas;

- Assist parents in contacting local officials in foreign countries or contact them on the parent's behalf;

- Provide information concerning the need for use of federal warrants against an abducting parent, passport revocation, and extradition from a foreign country to effect return of a child to the U.S.;

- Alert foreign authorities to any evidence of child abuse or neglect.

WHAT THE STATE DEPARTMENT CANNOT DO:

- Intervene in private legal matters between the parents;

- Enforce an American custody agreement overseas (U.S. custody decrees are not automatically enforceable outside of U.S. boundaries);

- Force another country to decide a custody case or enforce its laws in a particular way;

- Assist the left-behind parent in violating foreign laws or reabduction of a child to the United States;

- Pay legal or other expenses;

- Act as a lawyer or represent parents in court.

PART III

HOW TO SEARCH FOR A CHILD ABDUCTED ABROAD

[Note: If your child has been abducted to a country that is a party to the Hague Convention on International Child Abduction, see page 341 before you read further. As of January 1995, in addition to the United States, the following countries are party to the Convention:]

Argentina, Australia, Austria, Bahamas, Belize, Bosnia-Hercegovina, Burkina Faso, Canada, Chile, Croatia, Cyprus, Denmark, Ecuador, Ecuador, Finland, Former Yugoslav Rep. of Macedonia, France, Germany, Greece, Honduras, Hungary, Ireland, Israel, Luxembourg, Mauritius, Mexico, Mexico, Monaco, New Zealand, Norway, Panama, Poland, Portugal, Romania, Spain, Sweden, Switzerland, The Netherlands.

Where to Report Your Missing Child

1.   If your child has been abducted, file a missing person report with your local police department and request that your child's name and description be entered into the "missing person" section of the National Crime Information Center (NCIC) computer. This is provided for under the Missing Children's Act of 1982 (see page 349). The abductor does not have to be charged with a crime when you file a missing person report. In addition, through INTERPOL, the international criminal police organization,

your local police can request that a search for your child be conducted by the police in the country where you believe your child may have been taken. You may be able to achieve all of the above even if you do not have a custody decree.

2. Contact the National Center for Missing and Exploited Children (NCMEC) at 1-800-THE LOST/1-800-843-5678. With the searching parent's permission, the child's photograph and description may be circulated to the media in the country to which you believe the child may have been taken.

At the same time that you report your child missing, you should contact a lawyer to obtain a custody decree if you do not already have one. In many states, a parent can obtain a temporary custody decree if the other parent has taken their child.

3. Request information about a possible U.S. passport and have your child's name entered into the U.S. passport name check system (see page 338). A U.S. passport for a child under 18 years expires after 5 years. If you do not know where your child is, but information about the child is in the name check system, it may be possible to locate him or her through the passport application process. All U.S. passport agencies and almost all U.S. embassies and consulates are on-line with the name check system.

4. The Department of State, when requested to do so, conducts welfare and whereabouts searches for American citizens missing abroad. The Office of Children's Issues communicates such requests to the U.S. embassy or consulate responsible for the area to which you believe your child has been abducted. Call us on 202-736-7000 and have ready as much as you can of the following information on the child:

- full name (and any aliases),
- date and place of birth,
- passport number, date, and place of issuance;

and on the abductor:
- full name (and any aliases),
- date and place of birth,
-passport number, date, and place of issuance, occupation,

- probable date of departure,
- flight information,
- details of ties to a foreign country, such as the names, addresses, and telephone numbers of friends, relatives, place of employment, or business connections there.

A consular officer overseas, working with this information, will try to find your child. The consular officer may also request information from local officials on your child's entry or residence in the country. Unfortunately, not every country maintains such records in a retrievable form, and some countries may not release such information.

We may also ask you for photographs of both your child and the abducting parent because these are often helpful to foreign authorities trying to find a missing child.

The Search and Recovery a Basic Guide
It is possible that none of the institutions listed above (the police, the NCMEC, or the Department of State) will succeed in locating your child right away and you will need to carry out the search on your own. As you search, you should, however, ask these institutions informed of your actions and progress.

This booklet attempts to cover the international aspects of your search and recovery effort, but for other information, you should have a more basic guide. The Nation Center for Missing and Exploited Children publishes *Family Abduction: How to Prevent an Abduction and What to Do If Your Child Is Abducted*. For a copy, call 1-800-843-5678 (or 703-235-3900), or write the NCMEC at: 2101 Wilson Boulevard Suite 550; Arlington, VA 22201. This publication guides you through the U.S. legal system, helps you organize your search, and supplies a list of local support group. We have relied heavily on the NCMEC guide for the following list of suggestions.

Further Steps to Take in Your Search
- One of the best ways to find your child overseas is through establishing friendly contact with relatives and friends of the other parent, either here or abroad. Yo may have more influence with such persons than you suspect, and their interest in your child's welfare may lead them to cooperate with you.
Under the U.S. Department of Health and Human Services, the Office of Child Support Enforcement maintains the Federal Parent Locator Service (FPLS). The primary purpose of this service is to locate

340

parents who are delinquent in child support payments, but the service will also search for parental abductors when requested to do so by an authorized person. Generally speaking, an authorize person is a state court judge, police officer, prosecutor, or other state official seeking to enforce a child custody order.

- Using the abductor's social security number, the FPLS searches the records maintained by such federal agencies as the Internal Revenue Service, Veterans Administration, Social Security Administration, Department of Defense, and the National Personnel Records Center and Department of Labor records. An abductor who has had a connection with any of the above might, even from abroad, renew a connection with one of them. To learn how to access the services of the FPLS, contact your local or state Child Support Enforcement office. These offices are listed under government listing in our telephone director.

- To obtain information on requests that may have been made by the abductor to your child's school for the transfer of your child's records, you can contact the principal of the school. You will need to give the school a certified copy of your custody decree.

- You can find out from the National Center for Missing and Exploited Children how to prepare a poster on your child. A poster may assist foreign authorities in attempting to locate your child.

- You can ask your local prosecutor to contact the U.S. Postal Inspection Service to see if a 'mail cover' can be put on any address that you know of in the United States to which the abductor might write.

- You can ask local law enforcement authorities to obtain, by subpoena or search warrant, credit card records that may show where the abductor is making purchases. In the same manner, you can try to obtain copies of telephone company bills of the abductor's friends or relatives who may have received collect calls from the abductor.

PART IV

ONE POSSIBLE SOLUTION: THE HAGUE

CONVENTION

The most difficult and frustrating element for most parents whose child has been abducted abroad is that U.S. laws and court orders are not usually recognized in the foreign country and therefore are not directly enforceable abroad. Each sovereign country has jurisdiction within its own territory and over persons present within its borders, and no country can force another to decide cases or enforce laws within its confines in a particular way.

The increase in international marriages since World War II increased international child custody cases to the point where 23 nations, meeting at the Hague Conference on Private International Law in 1976, agreed to seek a treaty to deter international child abduction. Between 1976 and 1980, the United States was a major force in preparing and negotiating the Hague Convention on the Civil Aspects of International Child Abduction. The Convention came into force for the United States on July 1, 1988, and applies to abductions or wrongful retention between party countries that occurred on or after that date. In the United States, federal legislation, the International Child Abduction Remedies Act (P.L. 100-300), was enacted to implement the Convention in this country.

The United States actively encourages other countries to become party to the Convention. As of January 1995, the Convention is also in effect between the United States and (see following page):

Argentina, Australia, Austria, Bahamas, Belize, Bosnia-Hercegovina, Burkina Faso, Canada, Chile, Croatia, Cyprus, Denmark, Ecuador, Ecuador, Finland, Former Yugoslav Rep. of Macedonia, France, Germany, Greece, Honduras, Hungary, Ireland, Israel, Luxembourg, Mauritius, Mexico, Mexico, Monaco, New Zealand, Norway, Panama, Poland, Portugal, Romania, Spain, Sweden, Switzerland, The Netherlands.

Other countries are working toward ratification. Contact the Office of Children's
Issues-address on page 347) to learn if additional countries have joined.

If your child has been abducted to a country that is *not* party to the Convention,
page 343, *Legal Solutions in Countries Not Party to the Hague Convention.*

What Is Covered by the Convention
The countries that are parties to the Convention have agreed that, subject to certain limited exceptions and conditions outlined below, a child wh is habitually

resident in one country that is a party to the Convention and who is removed to or retained in another country that is party to the Convention in breach of the left-behind parent's custody rights shall be promptly returned to the country of habitual residence. The Convention also provides a means for helping parents to exercise visitation rights abroad.

There is a treaty obligation to return an abducted child below the age of 16 if application is made within one year from the date of the wrongful removal or retention. After one year, the court is still obligated to order the child returned unless the person resisting return demonstrates that the child is settled in the new environment. A court may refuse to order a child returned if there is a grave risk that the child would be exposed to physical or psychological harm or otherwise placed in an intolerable situation in his or her country of habitual residence. A court may also decline to return the child if the child objects to being returned and has reached an age and degree of maturity at which the court can take account of the child's views. Finally, the return of the child may be refused if the return would violate the fundamental principles of human rights and freedoms of the country where the child is being held. These exceptions have been interpreted narrowly by courts in the United States and the other countries art to the Convention.

How to Invoke the Hague Convention
You do not need to have a custody decree to invoke the Convention. However, to apply for the return of your child, you must have been actually exercising a "right of custody" at the time of the abduction, and you must not have given permission for the child to be removed or, in the case of a retention, to be retained beyond a specified, agreed-upon period of time. The Convention defines "rights of custody" as including "rights relating to the care of the person of the child and, in particular, the right to determine the child's place of residence." This "right of custody" may arise from operation of law as well as an order of custody. If there was no court order in effect at the date of the abduction, custodial rights are provided in the statutes of most states.

You may apply for the return of your child or the ability to exercise your visitation rights. You can also ask for assistance in locating your child and for information on your child's welfare.

Each country that is a party to the Convention has designated a Central Authority to carry out specialized duties under the Convention. You may submit an application either to the U.S. Central Authority or directly to the Central Authority of the country where the child is believed to be held. The Central Authority

for the United States is the Department of State's Office of Children's Issues (CI).

An application should be submitted as soon as possible after an abduction or wrongful retention has taken place. As stated above, there is a time factor of one year involved. If no custody decree exists for the left-behind parent, submit the application anyway. Detailed instructions to invoke the Hague Convention are found in Part VIII, page 349. Copies of the application form are at the end of this booklet.

The Role of the U.S. Central Authority
CI will review your application to ensure that it complies with the Convention. If it does, we will forward it to the foreign Central Authority and work with that authority until your case is resolved. If the abducting parent does not voluntarily agree to the return of your child, you may be required to retain an attorney abroad to present your case under the Hague Convention to the foreign court. If you need to retain an attorney abroad, see *Using the Civil Justice*

System-How to Proceed on page 343.
The Department of State cannot act as an agent or attorney in your case. We can, however, help in many other ways. We can give you information on the operating procedures of the Central Authority in the country where your child is believed to be located. We can help you obtain information concerning the wrongfulness of the abduction under the laws of the state in which the child resided prior to the abduction. At your request, we can ask for a status report six weeks after court action commences in the other country.

The Central Authority in the country where your child is located, however, has the primary responsibility of responding to your application. In the words of the Convention, that country has agreed to "ensure that rights of custody and access under the law of one Contracting State are effectively respected in the other Contracting State."

Good News Plus a Note of Caution for Applicants Under the Hague Convention
The Hague Convention on International Child Abduction is a success story. It has improved the likelihood and speed of return of abducted or wrongfully retained children from countries that are party to the Convention. In addition, the Convention has begun to influence some non-Hague countries where courts now look for guidance to the non-hostile pattern of resolution employed in Hague cases. The

Convention's increasing success is encouraging more countries to become party to the Convention. Twenty-seven countries have joined since the United States became the 10th country in July 1988. In addition, the reputation of the Hague Convention is such that, when an abducting or retaining parent learns that a Hague application has been filed, he or she may be more likely to return the child voluntarily. The majority of Hague cases still, however, require the applying parent to retain an attorney in the country where the child is located to petition that judiciary for return.

A note of caution: Criminal charges may have a distorting effect on the operation of the Hague Convention and may even prove counterproductive. With the Hague Convention, the emphasis is on the swift return of a child to his or her place of habitual residence where the custody dispute can then be resolved, if necessary, in the courts of that jurisdiction. As a rule, therefore, it is advisable to await the outcome of return proceedings under the Convention before deciding whether to initiate criminal proceedings against the other parent. Some courts have denied return of children solely because the taking parent would be arrested if they accompanied the child home. Many of these courts, U.S. and foreign, have held that the arrest of the parent would expose the child to psychological harm (Article 13(b)).

Children Abducted to the United States
The U.S. Central Authority also handles cases of children abducted to the U.S., provided the case meets the requirements of the Hague application and the child's country of habitual residence is a signatory to the Hague Convention.

PART V

LEGAL SOLUTIONS IN COUNTRIES NOT PARTY TO THE HAGUE CONVENTION
If your child has been abducted to a country that is *not* a party to the Hague Convention, you can seek legal remedies against the abductor, in the United States and abroad, from both the civil and criminal justice systems. The family court system from which you get your custody decree is part of the civil justice system. At the same time you are using that system, you can also use the criminal justice system consisting of the police, prosecutors, and the FBI. We will discuss each system in turn.

Using the Civil justice System

How To Proceed
After you obtain a custody decree in the United States, your next step is to use the civil justice system in the country to which your child has been abducted.

The Office of Children's Issues (CI) can provide information on the customs and the legal practices in the country where your child is. We can also give you general information on how to serve process abroad or obtain evidence from abroad, and on how to have documents authenticated for use in a foreign country. You may write or telephone CI for information sheets, such as: *Retaining a Foreign Attorney, and Authentication (or Legalization) of Documents in the United States for Use Abroad.*

To obtain authoritative advice on the laws of a foreign country or to take legal action in that country, you should retain an attorney there. U.S. consular and diplomatic officers are prohibited by law from performing legal services (22 C.F.R. 92.81). We can, however, provide you with a list of attorneys in a foreign country who speak English, who may be experienced in parental child abduction or family law, and who have expressed a willingness to represent Americans abroad. U.S. embassies and consulates abroad prepare these lists.

Cautionary note: Attorney fees can vary widely from country to country. The fee agreement that you make with your local attorney should be put into writing as soon as possible to avoid a potentially serious misunderstanding later.

Although officers at U.S. embassies and consulates cannot take legal action on behalf of U.S. citizens, consular officers can assist in communication problems with a foreign attorney. Consular officers may at times be able to inquire about the status of proceedings in the foreign court, and they will coordinate with your attorney to ensure that your rights as provided for by the laws of that foreign country are respected.

Once you retain a foreign attorney, send him or her a certified copy of your custody decree and/or state and federal warrants regarding the abducting parent. Also send copies of your state's laws on custody and parental kidnapping and the Federal Parental Kidnapping Prevention Act and copies of reported cases of your state's enforcement of foreign custody decrees under Section 23 of the Uniform Child Custody Jurisdiction Act. The National Center for Missing and Exploited Children can help you gather these materials (address on page 347).

What Are Your Chances of Enforcing Your U.S. Custody Order Abroad?
A custody decree issued by a court in the United States has no binding legal force abroad, although it may have

persuasive force in some countries. Foreign courts decide child custody cases on the basis of their own domestic relations law. This may give a "home court" advantage to a person who has abducted a child to the country of his or her origin. You could also be disadvantaged if the country has a cultural bias in favor of a mother or a father. A U.S. custody decree may, however, be considered by foreign courts and authorities as evidence and, in some cases, it may be recognized and enforced by them on the basis of comity (the voluntary recognition by courts of one jurisdiction of the laws and judicial decisions of another). Your chances of having your U.S. court order enforced depend, to a large degree, upon the tradition of comity that the legal system of the country in question has with the U.S. legal system. CI can give you some information on these traditions.

Using the Criminal Justice System: What Are the Risks?

Law enforcement authorities in the United States and abroad may be valuable sources of information. However, formal resort to the criminal justice system (filing of charges, issuance of an arrest warrant, transmission of an extradition request to a foreign government under an applicable treaty, and criminal prosecution) should be considered carefully. As noted on page 341, this is especially true if the other country concerned is a party to the Hague Convention. You should be aware that while you may have a degree of control over the ongoing civil procedures, you may not be able to effect the pursuit of criminal actions once charges are filed. Check with the prosecutor to determine if your wishes would be considered in the criminal action.

CI can obtain information on the criminal justice system of a particular country and on whether or not it is likely to cooperate in some form in parental child abduction cases. Your decision on whether or not to try to utilize the criminal justice system depends upon the circumstances of your case, but you should understand that you are likely to lose control of your case to a large extent when formal charges have been filed and an arrest warrant has been issued. You should also realize that extradition of the abductor to the United States is unlikely, and that neither extradition nor prosecution of the abductor guarantees the return of your child and may in some cases complicate, delay, or ultimately jeopardize return.

Presumably, your overriding interest is to obtain the return of your child. That is **not** the primary responsibility of the prosecutors. When the criminal justice system becomes involved in a case, there are several interests at stake, some of which are in conflict:

the interests of the child, the interests of each parent/guardian and other immediate family members, the interests of the civil justice system in a stable and workable custody arrangement, and the interests of the criminal justice system in apprehending, prosecuting, and punishing those who have violated criminal laws of their jurisdiction in connection with a parental child abduction.

Another factor to consider is the possible reaction of the abductor to the filing of criminal charges and the threat of ultimate prosecution and punishment. Although some individuals might be intimidated enough to return the child (with or without agreement by the prosecutors to the condition that the charges be dropped), others might go deeper into hiding, particularly if they are in a country where they have family or community support. If an abductor is ultimately brought to trial, how far are you willing to go in pursuing criminal prosecution? Unless you are prepared to testify in court against the abductor, you should not pursue criminal prosecution. A final factor to consider is the effect on the child of seeing the abducting parent prosecuted and perhaps incarcerated, with you playing an active role in that process.

The Steps To Take in Case You Decide to Use the Criminal Justice System
Once you have a custody decree and have decided to pursue criminal remedies, you or your attorney may contact your local prosecutor or law enforcement authorities to request that the abducting parent be criminally prosecuted and that an arrest warrant be issued, if provided for by your state law. In some states, parental child abduction or custodial interference is a misdemeanor; however, in most states it is a felony. If you are able to obtain a state warrant, the local prosecutor can contact the F.B.I. or your state's U.S. Attorney to request the issuance of a Federal Unlawful Flight to Avoid Prosecution (UFAP) warrant for the arrest of the abductor. The Federal Parental Kidnapping Prevention Act of 1980 provides for the issuance of this warrant (see page 349).

Furthermore, the International Parental Kidnapping Crime Act of 1993 (H.R. 3378) makes it an offense to remove a child from the United States or retain a child (who has been in the United States) outside the United States with intent to obstruct the law from exercise of parental rights (custody or visitation). An unlawful retention after the date of enactment could violate the statute, even though the actual removal of the child occurred before the date of enactment. Once a warrant has been issued for the abductor's arrest, ask local law enforcement authorities or the F.B.I. to enter the abductor's name in the "wanted persons" section of the

National Crime Information Center (NCIC) computer.

Prosecution of Agents or Accomplices of the Abductor
Find out if your state has laws that allow legal action to be taken against agents or accomplices to an abduction. Consider whether such actions would be useful in learning your child's whereabouts or compelling the return of your child.

Implications of an Arrest Warrant for a U.S. Citizen
If the abducting parent is a U.S. citizen and the subject of a federal arrest warrant, the F.B.I. or U.S. Attorney's office can ask the Department of State, Passport Services, to revoke the person's U.S. passport. This may or may not be a burden to an abducting parent who, as a dual national, may also carry a foreign passport. However, an abducting parent who is only a U.S. citizen becomes an undocumented alien in a foreign country if his or her U.S. passport is revoked. Some countries may deport undocumented aliens or at least make it difficult for them to remain in the country.

For a U.S. passport to be revoked, the F.B.I. or U.S. Attorney must send a request for such action and a copy of the Federal warrant to the Department of State's Office of Passport Policy and Advisory Services (telephone 202-955-0377). The regulatory basis for revocation of passports is found in the Code of Federal Regulations: 22 C.F.R. 51.70, et seq.

In certain circumstances you may decide that revoking the abducting parent's passport will not achieve the desired result. For example, if you know the location of the other parent, there is always the possibility of negotiation and a settlement or, at least, there is the possibility of communication with your child. Also, if the abducting parent is threatened with passport revocation, he or she might choose to flee with your child again.

Implications of a Warrant for a Non- U.S. Citizen
Even if the abductor is not a U.S. citizen, the existence of a Federal warrant is important. Such a warrant may encourage the abducting parent to return the child voluntarily, especially if he or she has business or other reasons to travel to the United States. The warrant also serves to inform the foreign government that the abduction of the child is a violation of U.S. law and that the abductor is a federal fugitive. An arrest warrant is also necessary if you wish to have authorities seek extradition of the abductor.

The Possibility of Extradition
Through INTERPOL and other international links, national law enforcement authorities in many countries regularly cooperate in the location and apprehension of international fugitives. Extradition, the surrender of a fugitive or prisoner by one jurisdiction for criminal prosecution or service of a sentence in another jurisdiction, is rarely a viable approach in international child abduction cases. Extradition is utilized only for criminal justice purposes in cases that local prosecutors believe can be successfully prosecuted due to the sufficiency of the evidence, which would presumably include your testimony. Moreover, it must be remembered that extradition does not apply to the abducted or wrongfully retained child, but only to the abductor. There is no guarantee that the child will be returned by foreign authorities in connection with extradition of the alleged wrongdoer. Threatened with impending extradition, abducting parents in other countries have hidden the child or children with a friend or relative in the foreign country.

Another reason that extradition is seldom useful is that the offenses of parental child abduction or custodial interference are covered by only a few of the extradition treaties now in force between the United States and more than 100 foreign countries. Most of these treaties contain a list of covered offenses and were negotiated before international parental child abduction became a widely recognized phenomenon. With respect to these older treaties, there was thus no intent on the part of the negotiators to cover such conduct, and it cannot therefore be validly argued that parental child abduction is a covered extraditable offense, even if the language used in the list of offenses covered by a given treaty appears somewhat broad (e.g., "abduction" or "kidnapping" or "abduction/kidnapping of minors").

In negotiating more modern extradition treaties, the United States has tried to substitute a "dual criminality" approach for a rigid list of extraditable offenses, or at least has tried to combine the two. Under an extradition treaty with a dual criminality provision, an offense is covered if it is a felony in both countries. Accordingly, if the *underlying conduct* involved in parental child abduction or custodial interference is a felony in both the U.S. and foreign jurisdictions involved, then that conduct is an extraditable offense under an extradition treaty based on dual criminality.

Despite the fact that parental child abduction may be covered by certain extradition treaties, you should be aware of potential difficulties in utilizing them, apart from the possible counterproductive effects already discussed. Specifically, nearly all civil law countries (in contrast with common law countries like the United States, United Kingdom, Canada, Australia) will not extradite their own nationals. Nearly all the nations of Latin America and Europe are civil law countries. Whatever the terms of any applicable extradition treaty, experience has also shown that foreign governments are generally reluctant at best (and often simply unwilling) to extradite anyone (their own citizens, U.S. citizens, or third country nationals) for parental child abduction.

For extradition to be possible, therefore,:

- your local prosecutor must decide to file charges and pursue the case, and you probably must be prepared to testify in any criminal trial;

- there must be an extradition treaty in force between the United States and the country in question;

- the treaty must cover the conduct entailed in parental child abduction or custodial interference;

- if the person sought is a national of the country in question, that country must be willing to extradite its own nationals; and,

-the country in question must be otherwise willing to extradite persons for parental child abduction/ Custodial interference (i.e., not refuse to do so for "humanitarian" or other policy reasons).

The Possibility of Prosecution of an Abductor in a Foreign Country

A final possibility in the area of criminal justice is prosecution of the abductor by the authorities of the foreign country where he or she is found. In many countries (not the United States), nationals of the country can be prosecuted for acts committed abroad under the "nationality" basis for criminal jurisdiction, if the same conduct would constitute a criminal offense under local law. U.S. law enforcement authorities can request such a prosecution and forward the evidence that would have been used in a U.S. prosecution. U.S. witnesses may, of course, have to appear and testify in the foreign proceeding. Like the courses of action discussed above, this approach may be counterproductive and will not necessarily result in the return of the child.

PART VI

OTHER SOLUTIONS: SETTLING OUT OF COURT

Promoting Communication Between Parents and Children

Legal procedures can be long and expensive. You may have greater success working in the area of negotiation

with the abducting parent. In some cases, friends or relatives of the abductor may be able to help you establish amicable relations with the abductor and may be willing to help mediate a compromise. A decrease in tension might bring about the return of your child, but, even if it does not, it can increase your chances of being able to visit the child and participate in some way in the child's upbringing. Sometimes compromise and some kind of reconciliation are the only solution.

Obtaining Information on Your Child's Welfare

If your child has been found, but cannot be recovered, you can request that a U.S. consular officer visit the child. If the consul succeeds in seeing your child, he or she will send you a report on your child's health, living conditions, schooling, and other information. Sometimes consular officers are also able to send you letters or photos from your child. If the abducting parent will not permit the consular officer to see your child, the U.S. embassy or consulate will request the assistance of local authorities, either to arrange for such a visit or to have a local social worker make a visit and provide a report on your child's health and welfare. Contact the Office of Children's Issues (CI) to request such a visit.

Working With Foreign Authorities

In child abduction cases, consular officers routinely maintain contact with local children welfare and law enforcement officers. If there is evidence of abuse or neglect of the child, the U.S. embassy or consulate will request that local authorities become involved to ensure the child is protected. This may mean removal of your child from the home for placement in local foster care.

The Question of Desperate Measures/Reabduction

Consular officers cannot take possession of a child abducted by a parent or aid parents attempting to act in violation of the laws of a foreign country. Consular officer must act in accordance with the laws of the country to which they are accredited.

The Department of State strongly discourages taking desperate and possible illegal measures to return your child to the United States. If you are contemplating such desperate measures, you should read the information available from the National Center for Missing and Exploited Children about the emotional trauma inflicted on child who is a victim of abduction and reabduction. The NCMEC advises against reabduction not only because it is illegal, but also because of possible psychological harm to the child.

Attempts to use self-help measures to bring an abducted child to the United States from a foreign country may endanger your child and others, prejudice any future judicial efforts you might wish to make in that country to stabilize the situation, an result in your arrest and imprisonment in that country. In imposing a sentence, the foreign court will not necessarily give weight to the fact that the would-be abductor was the custodial parent in the United States or otherwise had a valid claim under a U.S. court order (e.g., failure of the foreign parent to honor the terms of a joint custody order).

If you do succeed in leaving the foreign country with your child, you, and anyone who assisted you, may be the target of arrest warrants and extradition requests in the United States or any other country where you are found. Even if you are not ultimately extradited and prosecuted, an arrest followed by extradition proceedings can be very disruptive and disturbing for both you and your child.

Finally, there is no guarantee that the chain of abductions would end with the one committed by you. A parent who has reabducted a child may have to go to extraordinary lengths to conceal his or her whereabouts, living in permanent fear that the child may be reabducted again.

PART VII

REFERENCE Directory - Where to Go for Assistance Consular Assistance:

Office of Children's Issues (CI)
Overseas Citizens Services.
Department of State
2201 C Street, N.W., Room 4817
Washington, D.C. 20520-4818
202-736-7000; Fax 202-647-2835

U.S. Passport Restrictions:
Office of Passport Policy and Advisory Services
Passport Services, Suite 260
Department of State
1111 19th Street, N.W.
Washington, D.C. 20522-1705
202-955-0377; fax 202-955-0230

For General Technical Assistance:
National Center for Missing and Exploited Children (NCMEC)
2101 Wilson Boulevard, Suite 500
Arlington, VA 22201
703-235-3900

24-hour hot line for emergencies
1-800-843-5678; TTD 1-800-826-7653

For ABA Publications:

American Bar Association (ABA)
750 North Lake Shore Drive
Chicago, IL 60611
312-988-5555

Federal Parent Locator Service (FPLS):

Note: The FPLS can be accessed through local and state Child Support Enforcement offices. The names of those offices are available in telephone books and from the address below.

Department of Health and Human Services
Office of Child Support Enforcement
Federal Parent Locator Service (FPLS)
370 L'Enfant Promenade, S.W.
Washington, D.C. 20447
202-401-9267

Reading List
This list was compiled in January 1995. It is intended to give some idea of the relevant literature, but you should not regard it as complete or authoritative.

Atwood, "Child Custody Jurisdiction and Territoriality," 52 *Ohio St.* L.I. 369 (1991)

Charlow, "Jurisdictional Gerrymandering and the Parental Kidnapping Prevention Act," 25 *Fam.* L.Q. 299 (1991)

Copertino, "Hague Convention on the Civil Aspects of International Child Abduction: An Analysis of its Efficacy," 6 *Conn. I. Int'l* L. 715 (1991)

Crawford, "Habitual Residence of the Child as the Connecting Factor in Child Abduction Cases: Consideration of Recent Cases," 1992 *lurid. Rev. 177*

Crouch, "Use, Abuse, and Misuse of the UCCJA and PKPA," 6 Am. *1. Fam.* L. 147 (1992)

Davis, "The New Rules on International Child Abduction: Looking Forward to the Past," 3 *Aust'l J. Fam. L.* 31 (1990)

De Hart, *International Child Abduction: A Guide to Applying the 1988 Hague Convention, with Forms* (A publication of the Section of Family Law, American Bar Association) (1993)

Edwards, "The Child Abduction Agony," 140 *New L.J.* 59 (1990)

Evans, "International Child Abduction," 142 *Neiv L.J.* 232 (1992)

Frank, "American and International Responses to International Child Abductions," 16 *N.Y.U. J. Int L. & Pol.* 415 (1984)

Girdner, "Obstacles to the Recovery and Return of Parentally Abducted Children," 13 *Children's Legal Rts 1*. 2 (1992)

Greif, *When Parents Kidnap, The Families Behind the Headlines*

Hilton, "Handling a Hague Trial," 6 Am. *1. Fam. L.* 211 (1992)

Hoff, *Parental Kidnapping, How to Prevent an Abduction and What to Do If your Child Is Abducted* (A publication of the National Center for Missing and Exploited Children. To order, see page 340, no charge)

Kindall, "Treaties -. Hague Convention on Child Abduction - Wrongful Removal - Grave Risk or Harm to Child" 83 Am. *1. Int'l* L. 586 (1989)

Marks, "Fighting Back. The Attorney's Role in a Parental Kidnapping Case," 64 *Fla. B.J.* 23 (1990)

Murray, "One Child's Odyssey Through the Uniform Child Custody Jurisdiction and Parental Kidnapping Prevention Acts," 1993 *Wis. L. Rev.* 589

Oberdorfer, "Toward a Reasoned Response to Parental Kidnapping," 75 *Minn. L. Rev.* 1701 (1991)

Pfund, "The Hague Convention on International Child Abduction, the International Child Abduction Remedies Act, and the Need for Availability of Counsel for All Petitioners," 24 *Fam. L.Q.* 35 (1990)

Rutherford, "Removing the Tactical Advantages of International Parental Child Abductions under the 1980 Hague Convention on the Civil Aspects of International Child Abductions," 8 Ariz. *1. Int'l & Comp. L.* 149 (1991)

Sagatun, "Parental Child Abduction: The Law, Family Dynamics, and Legal System Responses," 18 Journal of Crim. Just. (1990)

Sharpless, "The Parental Kidnapping Prevention Act: jurisdictional Considerations Where There are Competing Child Custody Orders," 13 *1. Juv. L.* 54 (1992)

Shirman, "International Treatment of Child Abduction and the 1980 Hague Convention," 15 *Suffolk Transnat'l* L.J. 222 (1991)

Stotter, "The Light at the End of the Tunnel: The Hague Convention on International Child Abduction Has Reached Capitol Hill," 9 *Hastings Int'l and Comp. L. Rev.* 285 (1986)

Stranko, "International Child Abduction Remedies," *The Army Lazvyer* 28 (Department of the Army pamphlet 27-50-248, July 1993)

Family Advocate, A Practical Journal of the American Bar Association Family Law Section, Spring 1987. (Special issue on divorce law around the world and international parental child abduction.)

Family Advocate, A Practical Journal of the American Bar Association Family Law Section, Spring 1993. (Special issue on international family law.)

Family Law Quarterly,, Spring 1994. (Special issue on international family law.)

"The Hague International Child Abduction Convention and the International Child Abduction Remedies Act: Closing Doors to the Parent Abductor," 2 *Transnat'l Law* 589 (1989)

"The Hague Convention on International Child Abduction: A Practical Application," 10 *Loy. L.A. Int'l & Comp.* L.J. 163 (1988)

"International Child Abduction and the Hague Convention: Emerging Practice and Interpretation of the Discretionary Exception," 25 *Tex. Int'l L.J.* 287 (1990)

"International Parental Child Abduction: The Need for Recognition and Enforcement of Foreign Custody Decrees," 3 Emory *J. Int'l Dispute Resolution* 205 (1989)

"More Than Mere Child's Play: International Parental Abduction of Children," 6 *Dick. L. Rev.* 283 (1988)

"You Must Go Home Again: Friedrich v. Friedrich, The Hague Convention and the International Child Abduction Remedies Act," 18 *N.C. 1. Int'l L. & Com. Reg.* 743 (1993)

U.S. Government Documents on the Hague Convention
-Department of State notice in the *Federal Register* of March 26, 1986, pp. 10494-10516.
-Senate Treaty Doc. 99-11, 99th Congress, Ist Session.
-For the legislative history of the International Child Abduction Remedies Act, Public Law 100-300, see S.1347 and H.R. 2673, and H.R. 3971- 3972, 100th Congress, and related hearing reports.

Uniform State and Federal Laws on Custody, Parental Child Abduction, and Missing Children

The Uniform Child Custody Jurisdiction Act of 1968 (UCCJA) is now the law, with some variations, in ever state and the District of Columbia. The Act is intended to eliminate nationwide the legal incentives for interstate forum-shopping and child-snatching by parents, and to encourage communication, cooperation and assistance between state courts in the resolution of interstate child custody conflicts.

Section 23 of the UCCJA expressly provides that the general policies of the Act extend to the international arena. It further provides that custody decrees made in other countries by appropriate judicial or administrative authorities will be recognized and enforced in this country provided reasonable notice and opportunity to be heard were given to the affected persons.

The Parental Prevention Act of 1980 (PKPA) (P.L. 96-611; 28 U.S.C. 1738A, 1738A Note; 18 U.S.1073 Note; 42 U.S.C. 653-55, 663) requires the appropriate authorities of every state to enforce and not modi custody and visitation orders made by courts exercising jurisdiction consistent with standards set by the Ac authorizes the Federal Parental Locator Service to act on requests from authorized persons to locate the absconding parent and children who have been abducted or wrongfully retained; and expressly declares the intent of Congress that the Fugitive Felon Act applies to state felony cases involving parental kidnapping an interstate or international flight to avoid prosecutions. The state prosecutor may formally present a request the local U.S. Attorney for a Federal Unlawful Flight to Avoid Prosecution (UFAP) warrant.

The Missing Children's Act of 1982 (P.L. 97-292; 28 U.S.C. 534) provides for the entry of the names of missing children in the National Crime Information Center (NCIC). Since the enactment of P.L. 97-292, parents can ask their local police to enter their children's names into the NCIC computer and they can verify from the police or, if necessary, from the FBI that the names of their children are in the system.

The Missing Children's Assistance Act of 1984 (P.L. 98-473; 42 U.S.C. 5771 et. seq.) authorized the establishment of a national clearinghouse (now the National Center for Missing and Exploited Children) to:

- Provide technical assistance to local and state governments, public and private nonprofit agencies, and individuals in locating and recovering missing children;

- Coordinate public and private efforts to locate, recover, or reunite missing children with their legal custodians;

- Operate a national toll-free hotline through which individuals can report information on the location of missing children or request information on procedures for reuniting children with their legal custodians;

-Disseminate information on innovative and model missing children's programs, services, and legislation;

- Provide technical assistance to law enforcement agencies, state and local governments, elements of the criminal justice system, public and private nonprofit agencies, and individuals in the prevention, investigation, prosecution, and treatment of missing and exploited children's cases.

National Child Search Assistance Act (P.L. 101-647; 42 U.S.C. 5779, 5780) passed as part of the Crime Control Act of 1990, requires federal, state, and local law enforcement to enter reports of a missing child less than 18 and unidentified persons in the National Crime Information Center (NCIC). It provides for update of records with additional information within 60 days of the original entry, and it provides for close liaison between I enforcement and the National Center for Missing and Exploited Children for the exchange of information in technical assistance in missing children cases.

PART VIII

CHECKLIST FOR ASSISTANCE UNDER THE HAGUE CONVENTION

To invoke the Hague Convention, submit two completed forms (one original and one copy), plus two copies of your supporting documents. The application form may by photo-copied. Type or print all information. Furnish as much of the information called for as possible, using an additional sheet of paper if you need space. If you have further questions about the form, you may wish to refer to the text of the Convention. You may also call the Office of Children's Issues (CI) at 202-736-7000.

It is advisable to have some of the supporting documents translated into the official language of the requested country. Translations speed up the overall process. Foreign attorneys and judges act more favorably with such documents Ask CCS for more information about supporting documents.

You may fax your Hague application to CI fax number 202-647-2835. Send originals and supporting documents by mail, express mail, or courier service to: CA/OCS/CI Room 4811, Department of State, Washington, D.C. 20520-4818. **Be sure to sign the application.**

Check list and Instruction for Completing the Hague Application

Information Block	Details Needed

I. Identity of Child and Parents

Child's Name	-	The child's full name: last name, first, middle.
Date of Birth	-	Month/Date/Year
Place of Birth	-	City/State/Country.
Address	-	Child's address in the country of habitual residence **before** the abduction or removal.
U.S. Social Security No.	-	If known. A nine-digit number: 000-00-0000.
Passport/Identity Card	-	Issuing country and passport or I.D. number.
Nationality	-	Include all nationalities of the child.
Height	-	Feet and inches.
Weight (and Sex)	-	Pound. Please also include sex of child in this block.
Color of Hair Color of Eyes	-	Include color photo, if available

Father

Name	-	Full name of father, including alternative spellings of family names.
Date of Birth	-	of father.
Place of Birth	-	of father.
Nationality	-	of father. Include all nationalities.
Occupation	-	of father.
Passport/Identity Card	-	of father. Issuing country and number.
Current Address and Tel.	-	number of work and home.
U.S. Social Security No.	-	of father.
Country of Habitual Residence	-	of the father before the abduction or residence retention.

Mother

Name	-	Full name of mother of child, including maiden name.
Date of Birth	-	of mother.
Place of Birth	-	of mother.
Nationality	-	of mother. Include all nationalities.
Passport/Identity Card	-	of mother. Issuing country and number.
Current Address and Tel.	-	numbers of work and home.
Occupation	-	of mother.
U.S. Social Security No.	-	of mother.

350

Country of Habitual Residence	-	of the mother before the abduction or retention.
Date and Place of Marriage & Divorce	-	Indicate dates and location of marriage and divorce of the parents of the child. It is important to clearly state the marital status at the time of the abduction or retention.

II.   Requesting Individual or Institution

This section is for information concerning the person or institution applying for the return of the child to the United States.

Name	-	Provide the full name of the person or institution asking for the child to be returned.
Nationality	-	of the requester.
Occupation	-	of the requester (if a person).
Current Address and Tel.	-	of requester. Include home, work and fax number.
Passport/Identity Card	-	of requester (if a person).
Country of Habitual residence	-	of requester (if a person).
Relationship to Child	-	of requester.
Name, Address, and Tel.	-	Include zipcode as well as telephone of Legal Adviser, if Any and fax numbers.

III.   Information Concerning the Person Alleged to Have Wrongfully Removed or Retained Child

the information about the abducting parent in needed to assist in locating the child. Please provide all requested information and any additional facts that may help find the child.

Name	-	Full name of parent who has abducted or wrongfully retained the child.
Known Aliases	-	of the abductor. any other names the abductor may use.
Date of Birth	-	of the abductor
Place of Birth	-	of the abductor
Nationality	-	of the abductor. Include all nationalities
Occupation, Name and Address of Employer	-	of the abductor since the removal. Provide any employment information that may be helpful in locating the abductor, such as names, addresses and telephone numbers of relatives and or friends of the abducting parent who could help locate child (ren).
Passport/Identity Card	-	of the abductor. Country and number.
U.S. Social Security No.	-	of the abductor.
Current Location or Last Known Address	-	of the abductor in the country were the child was taken. Note: **NOT IN THE U.S.**
Height	-	of the abductor.
Weight	-	of the abductor.
Color of Hair	-	of the abductor.
Color of Eyes	-	of the abductor. Include photo, if available.
Other Persons With Possible Additional Information Relating to the Whereabouts of Child	-	Provide the name, address and telephone number of anyone in the country to which the child was taken who could give the Central Authority in that country information on the child's location.

IV.   Time, Place, Date, and Circumstances of the Removal or Retention

Provide the date, to the best of your knowledge, that the child left the U.S. or when the wrongful retention began. Include the place from which the child was taken. Describe the legal relationship existing between you and the abducting parent when the child was removed. What were the circumstances when the removal or retention occurred?

Did the other parent take the child during a scheduled visitation? Did the other parent take the child for what you believed would be a short visit and then inform you that they were staying? Did they purchase round-trip air tickets to show that they intended to return? Had you and your family moved to the other country, and then you decided to return to the U.S.?

Take this opportunity to tell your story. Try to anticipate what claims the other parent may make and provide your explanation.

[Do not limit yourself to the space provided on the form. Additional pages may be attached to fully narrate the circumstances. However, please be concise.]

V. Factual or Legal Grounds Justifying Request

Provide information and documentation establishing that you were exercising a right of custody under the Hague Convention at the time of the child's removal. Generally, a right of custody is created by a custody order, when parents are divorced, or by operation of state law, when parents are still married when the child is taken. As stated on page 341, the Convention defines "rights of custody" as including "rights relating to the care of the child and, in particular, the right to determine the child's place of residence." Thus, you may have a "right of custody" under the Convention even if you do not have joint or sole custody of the child.

If parents were married, please provide a copy of the state statue or case law that establishes your right of custody at the time of the child's removal. This provision is sometimes found in the estate and wills section of the state code. Remember, you are not attempting to show that you would have an equal right to obtain custody in a subsequent custody proceeding, but that you **had** and were exercising a right of custody when the child was taken.

[Do not wait to get a custody order before filing a Hague application.]

VI. Civil Proceeding in Progress, If Any

Indicate any civil action that may be pending (i.e.. custody, divorce). Name court and hearing dates.

VII. Child Is to Be Returned To:

Name - of person to whom child will be returned.
Date of Birth - of person to whom child will be returned.
Place of Birth - of person to whom child will be returned.
Address - of person to whom child will be returned.
Telephone Numbers (s)- of person to whom child will be returned.
Proposed Arrangements for Return Travel of Child- Provide exact means by which you propose that the child return to the return to the Child U.S., if this is ordered. Would you travel to pick up the child? Is the child old enough to travel by his or herself? Do you have someone who could return with the child? Be specific.

VIII. Other Remarks

State here whether you are applying for return or access under the Convention. You should include here any additional information that you believe may be pertinent to the Hague application.

XI Documents Attached

Check boxes of items enclosed. Original certified copies of documents are **NOT** needed to apply under the Hague Convention.

[Sign and date the application.]

PART IX

AFTER AN ABDUCTION--A CHECKLIST FOR PARENTS

Your situation is difficult, but there are things that you can do. This list assumes that you know, or strongly suspect, that your child has been abducted abroad to a country that is not a party to the Hague Convention on International Child Abduction (see page 341). If the country is a party to the Hague Convention, call the Office of Children's Issues (CI) to determine if your situation meets the requirements of the Convention.

1. EMERGENCY ACTION--WHAT TO DO RIGHT AWAY

■ If you do not know where your child is, have you filed a **missing person** report with your local police department? (see page 339)

■ Have you reported the abduction to the National Center for Missing and Exploited Children? (see page 339)

■ Have you obtained a decree of sole custody or one that prohibits your child from traveling without your permission? (see page 338) In most states you can obtain such a decree even after a child is abducted A custody decree in your favor is necessary for any legal action

■ Has your child's name been entered in the U.S. passport namecheck system? (see page 338)

■ If your child is a dual national, have the embassy and consulates of the foreign country been informed of your custody decree and asked not to issue a foreign passport to your child? (see page 338)

■ If your child is only a U S citizen but the other parent has close ties to a particular country, have the embassy and consulates of that country been informed of your custody decree and asked not to issue a visa to your child? (see page 338)

■ Have you asked the Department of State's Office of Citizens Consular Services (CCS) to initiate a welfare and whereabouts search for your child overseas? (see pages 339)

2. THE SEARCH

■ Have you obtained certified copies of your custody decree from the court that issued it? You may need to furnish proof of your custody rights at various stages in your search and recovery effort

■ Have you obtained a copy of the National Center for Missing and Exploited Children's publication, Parental Kidnapping How to Prevent an Abduction and What to Do If Your Child Is Abducted? (see page 340)

■ Have you tried to establish contact with relatives or friends of the abducting parent? (see page 340)

■ Have local law enforcement authorities asked the Federal Parent Locator Service to search for the abducting parent? (see page 340)

■ Have you contacted the principal of your child's school and asked to be informed of requests for transfer of your child's school records? (see page 340)

■ Have you prepared a poster of your child? see page 341)

■ Have you asked local law enforcement authorities to ask the US Postal Inspection Service to put a "mail cover" on addresses in the US to which the abductor might write? (see page 340)

■ Have you asked local law enforcement authorities to help you obtain information from telephone and credit card companies on the whereabouts of the abductor? (see page 340)

3. AFTER YOUR CHILD HAS BEEN LOCATED ABROAD

■ Have you retained the services of a foreign attorney? (see page 343)

■ Have you sent certified copies of the custody decree, court orders, state and federal warrants, copies of state custody and parental child abduction laws and the Federal Parental Kidnapping Prevention Act to the foreign attorney? (see page 343)

■ Have you read Part VI of this booklet, "Other Solutions"? (see page 346)

4. LEGAL PROCEEDINGS: POSSIBLE CRIMINAL REMEDIES

■ Is parental child abduction a crime in the state where your child resides or was abducted?

■ Has a state warrant been issued for the arrest of the abductor? (see page 344)

■ Has a Federal Unlawful Flight to Avoid Prosecution (UFAP) warrant been issued for the arrest of the abductor? (see page 344)

■ If a warrant has been issued, has the abductor's name been entered in the wanted persons section of the National Crime Information Center (NCIC) computer? (see page 344)

■ Is it possible or useful to take legal action against agents or accomplices to the abduction? (see page 345)

■ If the abductor is a U.S. citizen, have you considered seeking to have his or her passport revoked? (see pages 345)

■ Would extradition of the abductor, if possible, be effective in your case? (see page 345)

UNITED STATES DEPARTMENT OF STATE

APPLICATION FOR ASSISTANCE UNDER THE HAGUE CONVENTION ON CHILD ABDUCTION

SEE PRIVACY STATEMENT ON REVERSE

OMB NO. 1405-0076
EXPIRES: 6-9?
Estimated Burden – : hrs.

I. IDENTITY OF CHILD AND PARENTS

CHILD'S NAME (LAST, FIRST, MIDDLE)	DATE OF BIRTH	PLACE OF BIRTH	
ADDRESS (Before removal)	U.S. SOCIAL SECURITY NO.	PASSPORT/IDENTITY CARD COUNTRY: NO.:	NATIONALITY
HEIGHT	WEIGHT	COLOR OF HAIR	COLOR OF EYES

FATHER	MOTHER
NAME (Last, First, Middle)	NAME (Last, First, Middle)

DATE OF BIRTH	PLACE OF BIRTH	DATE OF BIRTH	PLACE OF BIRTH
NATIONALITY	OCCUPATION	PASSPORT/IDENTITY CARD COUNTRY: NO.:	NATIONALITY	OCCUPATION	PASSPORT/IDENTITY CARD COUNTRY: NO.:

CURRENT ADDRESS AND TELEPHONE NUMBER	CURRENT ADDRESS AND TELEPHONE NUMBER
U.S. SOCIAL SECURITY NO.	U.S. SOCIAL SECURITY NO.
COUNTRY OF HABITUAL RESIDENCE	COUNTRY OF HABITUAL RESIDENCE

DATE AND PLACE OF MARRIAGE AND DIVORCE, IF APPLICABLE

II. REQUESTING INDIVIDUAL OR INSTITUTION

NAME (Last, First, Middle)	NATIONALITY	OCCUPATION
CURRENT ADDRESS AND TELEPHONE NUMBER		PASSPORT/IDENTITY CARD COUNTRY: NO.:

COUNTRY OF HABITUAL RESIDENCE

RELATIONSHIP TO CHILD	NAME, ADDRESS, AND TELEPHONE NO. OF LEGAL ADVISER, IF ANY

III. INFORMATION CONCERNING THE PERSON ALLEGED TO HAVE WRONGFULLY REMOVED OR RETAINED CHILD

NAME (Last, First, Middle)	KNOWN ALIASES
DATE OF BIRTH	PLACE OF BIRTH	NATIONALITY

OCCUPATION. NAME AND ADDRESS OF EMPLOYER -	PASSPORT/IDENTITY CARD COUNTRY: NO.:	U.S. SOCIAL SECURITY NO.

CURRENT LOCATION OR LAST KNOWN ADDRESS IN THE U.S.

HEIGHT	WEIGHT	COLOR OF HAIR	COLOR OF EYES

FORM
6-88 DSP-105

354

OTHER PERSONS WITH POSSIBLE ADDITIONAL INFORMATION RELATING TO THE WHEREABOUTS OF CHILD
(Name, address, telephone number)

IV. TIME, PLACE, DATE, AND CIRCUMSTANCES OF THE WRONGFUL REMOVAL OR RETENTION

V. FACTUAL OR LEGAL GROUNDS JUSTIFYING THE REQUEST

VI. CIVIL PROCEEDINGS IN PROGRESS, IF ANY

VII. CHILD IS TO BE RETURNED TO:

NAME *(Last, First, Middle)*	DATE OF BIRTH	PLACE OF BIRTH
ADDRESS		TELEPHONE NUMBER

PROPOSED ARRANGEMENTS FOR RETURN TRAVEL OF CHILD

VIII. OTHER REMARKS

IX. DOCUMENTS ATTACHED (PREFERABLY CERTIFIED)

☐ DIVORCE DECREE   ☐ PHOTOGRAPH OF CHILD   ☐ OTHER _____

☐ CUSTODY DECREE   ☐ OTHER AGREEMENT CONCERNING CUSTODY _____

SIGNATURE OF APPLICANT AND/OR STAMP OF CENTRAL AUTHORITY	DATE	PLACE

PRIVACY ACT STATEMENT

Chapter 39

International Adoptions

[The information in this chapter is reprinted verbatim from a bulletin issued by the U.S. State Department, Office of Citizens Consular Services. It is intended to serve as advice to Americans at home and abroad.]

- - - -

SUMMARY

The subject of international adoptions has become an issue of considerable concern to the Department of State and its embassies and consulates abroad in recent years. There has been an increasing incidence of illicit activities in the area of international adoptions by intermediaries and adoption agencies both in the foreign countries involved and in the United States.

The Department considers adoptions to be private legal matters within the judicial sovereignty of the nation where the child resides. U.S. authorities, therefore, have no right to intervene on behalf of an individual American citizen with the courts in the country where the adoption takes place. However, while we cannot become directly involved in the adoption process, we do receive requests for assistance and information from American citizens who wish to adopt in foreign countries. Requests cover a broad range of subjects from the legal procedures involved to the expeditious issuance of immigrant visas to adopted children, or children being brought to the United States for the purpose of adoption. The information in this brochure is intended to provide a general overview of international adoptions and to warn prospective adoptive parents about problems they might encounter.

DEPARTMENT ASSISTANCE

The Department of State can offer assistance in several important ways. We can provide information on the details of the adoption process in the foreign country; make inquiries on behalf of adoptive parents regarding the status of their cases before foreign tribunals; assist in the clarification of documentary requirements; provide information on the U.S. visa application and issuance process; and endeavor to ensure that Americans are not discriminated against by foreign authorities and courts.

ANTICIPATING DIFFICULTIES

American citizens who desire to adopt foreign children should be aware of the numerous problems and pitfalls which may beset them in the natural course of the tedious process of foreign adoptions. Generally, adopting parents may expect to be temporarily frustrated by some of the vagaries of transnational bureaucracies, but in the long run adherence to procedures established by the laws and regulations of the country where the adoption is taking place and avoidance of short-cuts will save time, effort, and heartache.

One crucial fact which must be understood at the outset of any adoption is that the child is a national of the country of its origin (and remains so even after the adoption process is completed) and is subject to the jurisdiction of the foreign courts. Consequently, parents should be certain that the procedures they follow in arranging for such an adoption strictly comply with local (foreign) law. This is usually accomplished by dealing with a reputable, licensed international adoption agency which has experience in arranging adoptions in the particular foreign country, or, in the case of a private adoption, with a local attorney who has routinely handled successful adoptions.

Adopting parents should be wary of an agency or attorney who claims to be able to streamline established procedures. If it sounds too good to be true, it probably is. Procedural irregularities which sometimes result from an intermediary's desire to speed up the process can result in the foreign government's determination that the adoption is illegal and the refusal of that government to finalize the adoption.

GENERAL PROCEDURES

1. Foreign Adoption Practices and Procedures

The majority of countries require that the child who is placed for adoption be legally recognized as an orphan or, in the case where a parent is living, be legally and irrevocably released for adoption prior to any legal activity leading to final adoption of the child.

Nowadays, most countries have enacted legislation which requires the full scale adoption of the child through the foreign court after the child has been declared an orphan. Some countries do allow "simple" "adoption" which means that the adopting parent(s) are granted **guardianship** of the child by the foreign court, thus permitting the child to leave the foreign country **to be adopted in country of the adopting parent(s)' nationality.** Some countries may accept the properly authenticated home study of the prospective adoptive parent(s) on its face. Other countries may require the personal appearance of the adoptive parent(s) before the foreign court. This could involve a protracted stay in the foreign country until the court approves the adoption.

2. U.S. Immigration Requirements
In addition to the foreign adoption requirements, prospective adoptive parents must comply with U.S. immigration procedures. It is not possible, for example, to simply locate a child in a foreign country, then go to the U.S. embassy and obtain a visa for the child. Visa procedures in this area are complex, and designed with many safeguards to ensure that children adopted abroad or brought to this country for adoption are truly orphans and will go to healthy homes in the U.S. Contact the U.S. Immigration and Naturalization Service (INS) office having jurisdiction over your place of residence in the U.S. for information early in the process. One area which has been a source of confusion to prospective adoptive parents is whether a child identified in a foreign country actually meets the definition of orphan under U.S. immigration laws.

A. Does the Child Meet the Definition of Orphan?
Under Section 201(b) of the Immigration and Nationality Act (INA), foreign children may gain entry into the United States as "immediate relatives" of U.S. citizens. In this connection, the INA defines the term "orphan" as a "child under the age of 16 ... who is an orphan because of the death or disappearance of, abandonment or desertion by, or separation or loss from, both parents, or for whom the sole surviving parent is incapable of providing the proper care (proper care has been ruled as proper care according to the local (foreign) standard of living, not the U.S. standard of living) and has in writing irrevocably released the child for emigration and adoption." (8 U.S.C. 1101(b)(1)(F)). This means that a child who has been abandoned by both parents may meet the definition of orphan, for example, if the child has been unconditionally abandoned to an orphanage or legally documented as abandoned by a competent legal authority in the child's country of origin.

B. Orphan Petitions for U.S. Immigration
The procedures for adopting a child abroad or bringing a child to the U.S. for adoption must in all cases be initiated with INS. An orphan cannot be brought to the U.S. without a visa based on an INS approved petition (form I-600). If an adoptive parent(s) simply appears at a U.S. embassy or consulate asking for a visa for an adopted child with no prior processing and approval by INS, the visa cannot be issued immediately. The matter must be referred to INS. It could take a considerable period of time before INS could approve such a petition since a home study of the adoptive parent(s), fingerprint check, and any state pre adoptive requirements would have to be completed. We urge all prospective adoptive parents to contact INS and initiate the requisite procedures before going abroad to look for a child.

There are two separate procedures for the adjudication of orphan petitions.

(1) Specific Child Identified and I-600 Petition Fully Approved By INS
If the adoptive parent(s) has identified the child when beginning U.S. immigration processing, it is necessary to file petition form I-600 with the appropriate office of the U.S. Immigration and Naturalization Service (INS) in the United States. In that case, INS adjudicates all aspects of the I-600 petition -- the suitability of the adoptive parent(s), compliance with any state pre-adoption requirements (if the child is to be adopted after entry into the U.S.), and the qualification of the child as an orphan within the meaning of Section 101(b)(1)(F) of the Immigration and Nationality Act. INS will send the approved I-600 to the U.S. embassy or consulate in the country where the child will be adopted. If requested, INS will also send notification of their approval via telegram (the "visas 38" (adopted abroad) or "visas 39" (coming to the U.S. to be adopted) procedure) to help speed-up issuance of the U.S. visa.

In the case of a fully approved I-600 petition, the consular officer at a U.S. embassy or consular abroad must verify that the facts alleged about the child in the approved petition are correct. Information casting doubt upon the child's eligibility as an orphan or disclosing a medical consideration not identified in the approved petition requires return of the petition to the approving INS office for reconsideration.

(2) No Specific Child Identified and I-600A Approved by INS
If prospective adoptive parent(s) in the United States intend(s) to go abroad to locate a child for adoption the adoptive parent(s) should file an application on form I-600A for an advance determination of suitability as

adoptive parent(s). This application is filed at the appropriate INS office in the United States with jurisdiction over the adoptive parent(s) place of residence. INS will evaluate the suitability of the prospective adoptive parent(s) in the same manner as would be done if the parent(s) had filed an I-600 petition (see above) and will, if requested, forward the approved I-600A to the appropriate U.S. consular office or overseas office of INS. The INS office will, if requested, send notification of their approval via telegram (the visas 37' procedure) to help speed-up the issuance of the U.S. visa. This message will also state whether the adoptive parent(s) have fulfilled applicable pre-adoption procedures in their state of residence. Prospective adoptive parent(s) who file and have approved a form I-600A, once having located the child to be adopted, must file a petition I-600 with the appropriate U.S. consular officer or INS office abroad or with their local INS office in the United States if more convenient.

When prospective adoptive parent(s) file a petition form I-600 with a U.S. consular officer abroad after the approval of an I-600A application, the consular officer has the authority by delegation from INS to adjudicate the I-600, relying upon the approval of the I-600A for elements relating to the suitability of the parent(s) and establishing the eligibility of the child as an orphan, and compliance with any state pre-adoption requirements. If any doubt exists as to whether the petition may be approved, the consular officer must refer the petition to the appropriate overseas INS office for adjudication. A petition is clearly approvable only where primary documentation is presented which establishes the elements of eligibility. In orphan cases, there are certain possible circumstances which inherently cannot be documented by primary evidence. This could include issues such as the identity of the child, death of parent or parents, abandonment by parent or parents, disappearance or loss of, or separation from parent or parents and unconditional release by sole or surviving parent. A consular officer cannot approve an I-600 petition unless it is supported by primary evidence of all claimed elements of the eligibility of the child in question as an orphan within the meaning of section 101(b)(1)(F) of the Immigration and Nationality Act. An I-600 petition supported, in whole or in part, by secondary evidence must be referred by the U.S. consular officer to the appropriate overseas INS office for adjudication.

C. Child Who Does Not Meet the Definition of Orphan

If the child does not meet the definition of orphan under the INA, the child may qualify to enter the U.S. under section 101(b)(1)(E) of the INA based on an adoptive

relationship if the child was adopted before the age of 16 and if the child has been in the legal custody of, and has resided with, the adopting parent(s) for at least two years. The two year legal custody and residence period requirement may take place either before or after the adoption but must take place before issuance of a visa permitting the child to enter the U.S. This procedure should not be confused with the procedure for

orphan petitions which has completely different requirements .

D. "Proxy Adoptions"

There are no provisions in INS regulations for approving petitions signed by agents with powers of attorney. In addition, a petition cannot be approved if a married petitioner signs the I-600 on behalf of his/her spouse (even with a power of attorney). A signature on a blank I-600 later completed when the child is located abroad is invalid, and no such petition can be approved.

E. Procedures for Issuance of Immigrant Visa

Once petition procedures listed above have been completed and foreign adoption requirements taken care of, an immigrant visa application appointment will need to be scheduled by the U.S. consular officer at the U.S. embassy or consulate abroad. The officer will provide adoptive parent(s) with a list of visa requirements. Among other requirements, adopting parent(s) should be aware of the medical examination fee and the U.S. $200.00 immigrant visa fee (which must be paid either in local currency or U.S. dollars in cash or money order, cashiers check, or certified check).

VALIDITY OF FOREIGN ADOPTION IN UNITED STATES

In most cases the formal adoption of a child in a foreign court is accepted as lawful in the United States. In some instances, it will be necessary to re-adopt the child in the United States. For example, if the adoptive parent(s) did not see the child prior to or during the full adoption proceedings abroad, the child must be brought to the U.S. to be adopted here (IR-4) . In the case of a married couple, both parents must see the child before the U.S. visa can be issued if the child if to be considered "adopted abroad". Otherwise, the parent(s) must be able to meet the pre-adoption requirements of their state of residence in order for the child to qualify for a U.S. visa to come to U.S. to be adopted here. This is true even if a full final adoption decree has been issued in the foreign country. Adoptive parents should determine in advance the requirements of their own particular state of residence. Some states do not recognize foreign contracted adoptions, while others have a post-registration

359

requirement to confer legality on the adoption. The office of the state Attorney General in the state capital can provide such information. If no formal adoption is required by the country of the child's origin it will definitely be necessary for the child to be adopted in the state where the parents intend to reside with the child. Of course, a child brought to the U.S. for the purpose of being adopted here, rather than a child legally adopted abroad, must be adopted in accordance with state law.

ADOPTION FRAUD.

The Department of State refers to INS for investigation all petitions for children whose adoptions have been arranged through private or organizational "facilitators" motivated by undue personal gain or improper profit, or other irregular practices. This policy flows from our general obligation to respect host country laws and is based on a strong desire on the part of the United States not to promote abuse of adoption procedures ("baby-selling", kidnapping, etc.), and not to permit its officials to engage in conduct that might cause a host country to prohibit altogether further adoptions of host country children by U.S. citizens. To this end, the Department of State has consistently expressed its support for measures taken by foreign states to reduce adoption abuses.

Adoption fraud has recently been on the rise. Fraud can be perpetrated by the facilitator handling the adoption in the foreign country, especially if it is a private adoption, or by the facilitator or adoption agency in the United States. Unfortunately for adoptive parents, there exists a substantial black market trade in adoptive children. International adoptions have become a lucrative business in part because of the huge demand for adoptive infants in the United States.

The lack of state regulatory requirements for international adoption agencies has permitted unscrupulous individuals to set up businesses, often without prior experience or expertise in the area of adoptions. Exorbitant fees in the tens of thousands of dollars have been extorted from prospective adoptive parents desperate to adopt. Abuses perpetrated by these agencies and individuals have included offering for adoption a supposedly healthy child who is later found to be seriously ill, or obtaining prepayment for adoption of child who does not actually exist. (In some countries it is advisable to have a child considered for adoption examined by a doctor before completing adoption procedures.) Many states in the U.S. have experienced problems with such unscrupulous practitioners. Some states have moved to revoke licenses or prosecute individuals connected with these activities after receiving complaints from adoptive parents who have

been defrauded.

It should be noted, however, that by far, the majority adoption agencies practicing in the United States are legitimate professional organizations with a wealth of experience in domestic and international adoptions. It is the continuing rise of unscrupulous practitioners, who act in violation of regulatory requirements, which taints international adoptions.

Any problems experienced by American citizens in dealing with foreign attorneys or adoption agencies who employ these foreign attorneys should be reported to the American embassy or consulate or to the Office of Citizens Consular Services at the Department of State in Washington.

Any problems experienced with agencies or intermediaries in the United States should be reported immediately to the appropriate state authorities, i.e., Health and Human Services office, police, District Attorney, Better Business Bureau, or state Attorney General's office. The United States Immigration and Naturalization Service should also be notified of these activities.

FREQUENTLY ASKED QUESTIONS

- **What Can You Do To Avoid Adoption Problems?** Contact the local office of the Immigration and Naturalization Service early in the adoption process. Request a copy of the INS publication M-249Y (Revised, 1990) "The Immigration of Adopted and Prospective Adoptive Children.

Contact the Department of State, Office of Citizens Consular Services in Washington or the U.S. embassy or consulate in the country from which you desire to adopt to obtain information on adoption practices and procedures and ascertain if there are any particular problems of which you should be aware in connection with adoption from that country.

Demand an accounting of the services for which you are paying an agency or intermediary. Find out if adoption agencies/intermediaries must be licensed in your state, and if so, whether the one you are working with is licensed. You might also check with the Better Business Bureau, Consumer Affairs Office, or similar office of your District Attorney or Attorney General's office to obtain information about the past record of the agency/intermediary you have chosen to use.

- **What Can You Do About Problems Concerning an Orphan Petition for Immigration To the United States?**

If your problem concerns the adjudication of an orphan petition (I-600 or I-600A), discuss the matter with the INS examiner assigned to your case. If he/she is unable to assist you, ask to speak with the INS supervisory examiner. If the supervisor is unable to help, ask to speak with the next line supervisor/manager until you have reached the District Director or Officer-in-Charge. If the local INS office is unable to assist you, contact the Regional Office that has jurisdiction over the office handling your case.

• **Does an Adopted Child Automatically Acquire U.S. Citizenship?**

No. However, there does exist a mechanism by which the child can be expeditiously naturalized as a citizen of the United States. As of November 14, 1986, Section 341 of the Immigration and Nationality Act (INA) was amended to add subsections (b)(l) and (b)(2) which permit an adopting parent or parents to apply to the Attorney General of the United States for a Certificate of Citizenship for an a alien adopted child. Pursuant to Subsection (b)(l), the Attorney General shall issue a Certificate of Citizenship and the adopted child shall then automatically become a naturalized U.S. citizen if the following conditions have been established:

(1) the adopting parent (and spouse, if married) are U.S. citizens.

(2) the child meets the qualifications of Section 341(c)(2) of the INA. This Section defines "child" for the purposes of naturalization. The required criteria are (a) the child be under the age of 18, (b) the child was adopted before the age of 16 by a U.S. citizen parent, and (c) is residing in the United States in the custody of the adopting parent(s) pursuant to lawful admission for permanent residence.

(3) the child is in the United States.

How to Apply

The administrative process requires that INS Form N-643 Application for Certificate of Citizenship in behalf of an Adopted Child, be filed with the INS before the child is 18 years of age. The child is not a citizen until the Form N-643 is approved and the certificate of citizenship is issued. For information, contact the INS office nearest you.

• **Are There Any International Agreements on Adoption?**

The United States is not a signatory to any international agreement or convention relating to international adoptions. The only existing international agreement on adoption is the Hague Convention on Jurisdiction, Applicable Law and Recognition of Decrees to Adoption of November 15, 1965 which entered into force on October 10, 1978. It is only in force in the United Kingdom, Austria and Switzerland.

The Organization of American States (OAS) is in the process of drafting the Inter-American Convention on the Adoption of Minors. This draft provides in part that the courts of a nation in which the adopting parents are habitually resident may grant an adoption decree and that the adopted child's country of origin should not prevent the child from leaving the country after an adoption is granted in the absence of a public order or for police reasons. We do not expect the convention to be completed or in effect until well after 1992.

Forty nine countries, many of them countries from which children have been adopted, and ten international organizations, participated in the June 11-21, 1990 Hague Conference on Private International Law preliminary session in preparation for the drafting of a multilateral Convention on International Cooperation in Intercountry Adoptions. The June 1990 meeting was the first of four sessions aimed at adoption of the text of a convention for signature and ratification by States (countries) by spring 1993 .

• **From which Countries are Children available for adoption?**

The availability of children for adoption from particular countries can change very rapidly.

PROBLEMS

For information about procedures in specific countries, please contact the appropriate geographic division of the Department of State, Office of Citizens Consular Services:

Europe and Canada Division
(202) 647-3445
Inter-American Division
(202) 647-3712
East Asia and Pacific Division   (202) 647-3675
Near Eastern and South Asia Division   (2 0 2) 647-3926
Africa Division   (2 0 2) 647-4994

General recorded information about visa procedures is available from the Department of State's Visa Office at (202) 663-1225.

For questions about U.S. visa petition procedures, contact the nearest office of the U.S. Immigration and Naturalization Service located in the Federal Government section of your telephone book under Department of Justice.

PROSPECTIVE ADOPTING PARENTS

Notice to Prospective Adopting Parents

PLEASE TAKE NOTE
- The Immigration and Nationality Act allows for the immigration of two categories of adopted foreign children; they are orphans and non-orphans. Most foreign adopted children who immigrate to the United States are classified as orphans. As an individual considering **adopting a foreign child, you should remember that not all children adopted abroad qualify as orphans.** Non-orphan adopted children are **not** eligible to immediately immigrate to the United States

Under immigration law, the definition of orphan is broader than the common definition of orphan Under immigration law, a foreign child may be considered an orphan if his/her parents have died or disappeared; if they have unconditionally abandoned or deserted his/her; or if he/she is separated or lost from them. Normally, abandonment involves permanent placement of the child in an orphanage. If the natural parents exercise any parental control over the child, its placement or adoption, its support, or indicate an intent to reclaim the child in the future, a finding of abandonment cannot be made

A foreign child with one parent may be considered an orphan only if the sole or surviving parent is unable to provide proper care for the child and has, in writing, irrevocably released the child for emigration and adoption. The determination of proper care is based upon the local foreign conditions, that is, the parent must be impoverished by local standards The fact that the living standards of the country are below standards in the United States is not sufficient to satisfy this test

The definition of orphan guards against the splitting of intact, functioning foreign families. An orphan immigrant visa petition must be filed before the child is 16 years of age.

A non-orphan adopted child [who does not have to qualify as an orphan] is a child who has been **adopted under** the age of 16. **The child must have resided with, and been in the legal custody of, the adopting parent(s) for at least two years** prior to the filing of the immigrant visa petition .

Before you adopt a child abroad, whom you intend to bring to the United States under the orphan procedures, you should be certain that the child is an orphan under immigration law. If you have any questions, please address them to the U.S. Immigration and Naturalization Service In overseas locations where there is no Service office, you may address your questions to the nearest American Embassy or Consulate.

Please remember:
- Not all children adopted abroad qualify as orphans

- If you adopt a non-orphan, you will not be able to bring the child into the United States until he/she has resided abroad with you and has been in your legal custody for at least two years.

- Ask before you adopt a child who may be ineligible to accompany you home.

- Only a U S. citizen may petition for an orphan.

REFERENCES, PHONE NUMBERS AND ADDRESSES
The adoption process be it in the United States or abroad is a long, difficult, and expensive one. It is not possible to give one telephone number or person who will be able to help with the adoption. The following is a list of numbers you may find helpful in the process.

Local Government Agencies:
Check your local telephone directory for the addresses, phone numbers and location of these agencies of government. Inquire about adoption services and available brochures and information.

(1) Immigration and Naturalization Services (INS)

(2) State, Department of Social Services,
       Child Welfare Services Division

(3) County, Department of Social services
       Child welfare Division

Private Adoption Agencies and Services
The Barker Foundation
4114 River Road, NW
Washington, DC 20016
202-363-7751

Cradle of Hope Adoption Center
1815 H Street NW
Washington, DC 20006
202-296-4700
FAX 202-785-8131

The Datz Foundation
4545-42nd Street, NW, Suite 209
Washington, DC 20016

202-686-3400

FACE (Families Adopting Children Everywhere)
(An adoptive parents' support organization)

Maryland Chapter
    P.O. Box 28058
Baltimore, MD 21239
Helpline: 410-488-2656

Northern Virginia Chapter
    Lyndi Balven
    4629 North 35th Street
Arlington, VA 22207
703-536-6905

Family Liaison OfFice (M/FLO)
Room 1212A
Department of State
Washington, DC 20520-7310
202-647-1 076

Bureau of Consular Affairs (CA)
Office of Citizen Consular Services
Room 4817
Department of State
Washington, DC 20520
202-647-3444

International Social Services
95 Madison Avenue, 3rd floor
New York, NY 10016
212-532-5858

National Committee for Adoption
1930-17th Street, NVV
Washington, DC 20009-6207
202-328-1200

World Child, Inc.
4300-16th Street, NW
Washington, DC 20011
202-82g-5244

State Department Offices

Employee Consultation Service (ECS)
M/MED, Room 3243
U.S. Department of State
Washington, DC 20520
202-647-4929

BIBLIOGRAPHY

Klunder, Virgie L., *The Action Guide to Adoption Search,* Caraduim Publishing, Cape Coral Florida.

Melina, Lois Ruskai, *Making Sense of Adoption,* Harper and Row Publishers, Inc., New York, NY, 1989.

Melina, Lois Ruskai, *Raising Adopted Children,* Harper and Row Publishers, Inc., New York, NY, 1989.

Paul, Ellen, *Adoption Choices,* Visible Ink Press, Detroit, MI, 1991.

Paul, Ellen (ed), The Adoption Directory, Gale Research Inc, Detroit Michigan.

Posner, Julia L., *The Adoption Resource Guide,* Child Welfare League of America, Inc., Washington, DC, 1990.

Register, Cheri, *Are Those Kids Yours?,* Macmillan, Inc., New York, NY, 1991.

Chapter 40

Fly Rights: Your Rights and Responsibilities as an Air Traveler

[The information in this chapter is reprinted verbatim from a bulletin issued by the
U.S. Department of Transportation. It is intended to serve as advice
to Americans who travel by air.]

- - - -

INTRODUCTION

The elimination of government economic regulation of the airlines has resulted in lower fares and a wide variety of price/service options. In this new commercial environment, consumers have had to take a more active role in choosing their air service by learning to ask a number of questions.

- Am I more concerned with price or scheduling? Am I willing to fly at an odd hour if it means saving $25?

- Will the airline penalize me for changing my reservation?

- What will the airline do for me if it cancels my flight?

This booklet is designed to explain your rights and responsibilities as an air traveler. We hope it helps you become a resourceful consumer.

AIR FARES

Because of the emphasis on price competition, consumers may choose from a wide variety of air fares. Some airlines are trying a "back to basics" approach—offering flights at bargain basement prices with few extras.

For fare information, you can contact a travel agent, another ticket outlet or an airline serving the places you want to visit. Ask them to tell you the names of all airlines flying there. A travel agent can find virtually all airlines' fares in his or her computer. Or, if you prefer you can call each airline to ask about the fares they charge, particularly any special promotional fares they may be offering at the time. You can also pay attention to newspaper and radio ads, where airlines advertise many of the discount plans that apply to your city. Finally, be alert to new companies

Here are some tips to help you decide among air fares:

- Be flexible in your travel plans in order to get the lowest fare. The best deals may be limited to travel on certain days of the week or particular hours of the day. After you get a fare quote, ask the reservations agent if you could save even more by leaving a day earlier or later, or by taking a different flight on the same day.

- Plan as far ahead as you can. Some airlines set aside only a few seats on each flight at the lower rates. The real bargains often sell out very quickly. On the other hand, air carriers sometimes make more discount seats available later. If you had decided against a trip because the discount fare you wanted was not available on the desired date, try again, especially just before the advance-purchase deadline.

- Some airlines may have discounts that others don't offer. In a large metropolitan area, the fare could depend on which airport you use. Also, a connection (change of planes) or a one-stop flight is sometimes cheaper than a nonstop.

- Does the air fare include types of service that airlines have traditionally provided, such as meals or free baggage handling? If you have a connection involving two airlines, will your bags be transferred? Can you get advance seat assignments? If you are stranded, will the ticket be good on another carrier at no extra charge? Will the first airline pay for meals or hotel rooms during the wait?

- Many discount fares are non-refundable; if you buy one of these fares and later cancel your trip, you will not get your money back. Some fares also have a penalty for changing flights or dates even if you don't want a refund. You may also have to pay any difference in air fares if your fare is not available on the new flight.

- Some airlines will not increase the fare after the ticket is issued and paid for. (Simply holding a reservation without a ticket does not guarantee the fare.) Other airlines may reserve the right to collect more money from you if the fare that you had purchased goes up before departure time. Find out from the airline before you buy your ticket what its policy is on assessing fare increases after the ticket is purchased.

- After you buy your ticket, call the airline or travel agent once or twice before departure to check the fare. Fares change all the time, and if that same fare goes down before you fly, some airlines will refund the difference. But you have to ask.

Differences in air fares can be substantial. Careful comparison shopping among airlines does take time, but it can lead to real savings.

RESERVATIONS AND TICKETS

Once you decide when and where you want to go, and which airline you want to use, getting reservations and tickets is a fairly simple process. You can make all of your arrangements by telephone, at the airline's ticket office, or through a travel agent or other ticket outlet. There are a few potential pitfalls, however, and these pointers should help you avoid them.

- If your travel plans fall into a busy period call for reservations early. Flights for holidays may sell out weeks-sometimes months ahead of time. Don't buy a standby fare or an 'open return' ticket if you need to fly during a high demand period, especially the end of August. You could be stranded for a week or more before a seat becomes available.

- Ask the reservations agent to give you on-time performance code for any flight that you are considering. This is a one-digit code the reservations computer that shows how often the flight arrived on time (within 15 minutes) during the most recent reported month. For example, an "8" means that flight arrived within 15 minutes of the scheduled arrival time between 80% 89.9% of the time. you are deciding between two flights with similar schedules an fares, you

may want to choose the one with better on-time record. (Only the largest U.S. airlines are required to maintain these codes.) [Ask the reservations agent for your flight's on-time performance code]

- When you make a reservation, be sure the agent records the information accurately. Before you hang up or leave the ticket office review all of the essential information with the agent-the spelling of your name, the flight numbers and travel dates, and the cities you traveling between. If there is more than one airport at either city, be sure you check which one you' be using. It's also important to give the airline your home and work telephone numbers so they can I you know if there is any change in their schedule.

- Your ticket will show the flight number departure time, date, and status of your reservation for each flight of your itinerary. "status" box is important. "OK" means you' confirmed. Anything else means that reservation is not yet certain (e.g., waitlisted).

- A "direct" (or "through") flight can have one or more stops. Sometimes flights with only one flight number can even involve a change of planes. Ask about your exact routing.

- If you are flying to a small city and your flight number has four digits, you *may* be booked on a commuter airline that has agreement with the major carrier in whose name flight is held out. If you are unsure, ask reservations agent about the airline and the aircraft type; these flights are identified in the computer.

- When a reservations agent asks you to buy your tickets by a specific time or date, this is a deadline. And if you don't make the deadline, the airline may cancel your reservations without telling you.

- Try to have your tickets in hand before you go to the airport. This speeds your check-in and helps you avoid some of the tension you might otherwise feel if you had to wait in a slow-moving ticketing line and worry about missing your flight.

- If your reservations are booked far enough ahead of time, the airline may offer to mail your tickets to you. However, if you don't receive the tickets and the airline's records show that they mailed them, you may have to go through cumbersome lost-ticket procedures (see the end of this chapter). It is safer to check the telephone directory for a conveniently located travel agency or airline ticket office and buy your tickets there.

- As soon as you receive your ticket check to make sure all the information on it is correct, especially the airports (if any of the cities have more than one) and the flight dates. Have any necessary corrections made immediately.

- Bring a photo I.D. when you fly, and have your airline ticket issued using your name as it appears on that I.D. Many airlines are requesting such identification at check-in in order to reduce the re-selling of discount tickets. (Airlines don't permit tickets to be sold *or given* to other persons.) On international flights, make sure your name is the same on your ticket and your passport. If your name has recently changed and the name on your ticket and your I.D. are different, bring documentation of the change (e.g., a marriage certificate or court order).

- It's a good idea to reconfirm your reservations before you start your trip; flight schedules sometimes change. On international trips, most airlines require that you reconfirm your onward or return reservations at least 72 hours before each flight. If you don't, your reservations may be canceled.

- Check your ticket as you board each flight to ensure that only the correct coupon has been removed by the airline agent.

Paying for and refunding airline tickets
- If you plan to pay in person and with your own bank check, take at least two forms of identification with you like a driver's license, major credit card, or employee I.D. card. Particularly when you purchase tickets far from your home town, airlines, travel agencies and other ticket outlets will want to confirm your identity.

- If you paid for your ticket with cash and you have a refundable fare, you can often get an immediate refund from the issuing airline or travel agency. If you paid by personal check, the refund will generally have to be mailed to you.
- NOTE: In some cases tickets purchased overseas in foreign currency can only be refunded in that same currency and country, due to foreign government monetary restrictions. Keep this in mind if you are considering buying a ticket in a foreign country.
[Count your ticket coupons after checking in for each flight.]

- When you pay by credit card, your charge account is billed-whether you use your tickets or not. You won't receive credit unless the original unused tickets are returned to the airline. You usually can't get a cash refund for a credit card purchase.

- If you buy your tickets with a credit card and then change your flights, the ticket agent may want to credit the amount of the old tickets and issue another set with a second charge to your account. You may want to insist that the value of your old tickets be applied to the new ones, with the difference in price charged or credited to your account. While this creates a little extra work for the airlines, it prevents double-billing to your charge account.

Payment by credit card provides certain protections under federal credit laws. When a refund is due, the airline must forward a credit to your card company within seven business days after receiving a complete refund application. If you paid by credit card for a refundable fare and you have trouble getting a refund that you are due, report this *in writing* to your credit card company. If you write to them within 60 days from the time that they mailed your first monthly statement showing the charge for the airline ticket, the card company should credit your account even if the airline doesn't. This procedure is particularly useful if your airline ceases operations before your flight.
[Airline tickets should be treat like cash; lost tickets are not easy to refund]

Lost tickets
Airline tickets are similar to negotiable documents. Because of this, refunds can be difficult to obtain if tickets are lost or stolen. Many passengers believe that air tickets can be replaced as easily as travelers checks just because the reservation is in the computer, but that

is not the case.

Your ticket number may be shown on your credit card receipt or travel agency itinerary. If it is not, jot down the number on a sheet of paper and carry it separately from your ticket. Bring it with you on your trip. If the ticket does go astray, the airline can process your refunds application more quickly, and perhaps issue an on-the-spot replacement ticket, if you can give them this number.

You should report a lost ticket immediately to the airline that is shown as the issuing carrier at the top of the ticket. You may be required to repurchase a ticket in order to continue your trip. If you no longer meet all of the restrictions on your discount fare (e.g., seven-day advance purchase) the new ticket may cost more than the old one did. In that event, however, it is generally the higher fare that is eventually refunded, as long as you don't change any of the cities, flights or dates on your trip.

Once the airline establishes that you actually bought the ticket, they will begin processing your refund application. There is often a waiting period of two to six months. If anyone uses or cashes in your ticket while the refund is pending, the airline may refuse to give you your money back. Finally, there is a handling charge that the airline may deduct from the refund.

All in all, getting a refund or replacement for a lost ticket is a lot of trouble, and there's no guarantee you'll receive either one. So the best advice is-don't lose the ticket in the first place.

DELAYED AND CANCELED FLIGHTS

Airlines don't guarantee their schedules, and you should realize this when planning your trip. There are many things that can-and often do-make it impossible for flights to arrive on time. Some of these problems, like bad weather, air traffic delays, and mechanical repairs, are hard to predict and beyond the airlines' control.

If your flight is delayed, try to find out how late it will be. But keep in mind that it is sometimes difficult for airlines to estimate the total duration of a delay during its early stages. In so called "creeping delays," developments occur which were not anticipated when the carrier made its initial estimate of the length of the delay. Weather that had been forecast to improve can instead deteriorate, or a mechanical problem can turn out to be more complex than initially determined.

If the problem is with local weather or air traffic control, all flights will probably be late and there's not much you or the airline can do to speed up your

departure. If there's a mechanical problem with the plane for your particular flight or if the crew is delayed on an incoming flight, you might be better off trying to arrange another flight, as long as you don't have to pay a cancellation penalty or higher fare for changing your reservations. (It is sometimes easier to make such arrangements from a pay phone than at a ticket counter.) If you find a flight on another airline, ask the first airline to endorse your ticket to the new carrier; this could save you a fare increase. Remember, however, that there is no rule requiring them to do this.

If your flight is canceled, most airlines will rebook you on the first flight of theirs to your destination on which space is available, at no additional charge. If this involves a significant delay find out if another carrier has space, and ask the first airline to endorse your ticket. Finding extra seats may be difficult, however, especially over holidays and other peak travel times.

Each airline has its own policies about what it will do for delayed passengers waiting at the airport; there are no federal requirements. If you are delayed, ask the airline staff if they will pay for meals or a phone call. Some airlines, often those charging very low fares, do not provide any amenities to stranded passengers. Others may not offer amenities if the delay is caused by bad weather or something else beyond the airline's control.
[A departure early in the day is less likely to be delayed than a later flight.]

Contrary to popular belief, airlines are not required to compensate passengers whose flights are delayed or canceled. As discussed in the section on overbooking, compensation is required by law only when you are "bumped" from a flight that is oversold. Airlines almost always refuse to pay passengers for financial losses resulting from a delayed flight. If the purpose of your trip is to close a potentially lucrative business deal, to give a speech or lecture, to attend a family function, or to be present at any time-sensitive event, you might want to allow a little extra leeway and take an earlier flight. In other words, airline delays and cancellations aren't unusual, and defensive counter-planning is a good idea when time is your most important consideration.

When booking your flight remember that a departure early in the day is less likely to be delayed than a later flight, due to "ripple" effects throughout the day. Also, if an early flight does get delayed or canceled, you have more rerouting options. If you book the last flight of the day and it is canceled, you could get stuck overnight.

You may select a connection (change of planes) over a nonstop or direct flight because of the convenient departure time or lower fare. However, a change of planes always involves the possibility of a misconnection. If you have a choice of connections and the fares and service are equivalent, choose the one with the least-congested connecting airport, so it will be easier to get to your second flight. You may wish to take into consideration the potential for adverse weather if you have a choice of connecting cities. When making your reservation for a connection, always check the amount of time between flights. Ask yourself what will happen if the first flight is delayed; if you don't like the answer, pick another flight or ask the agent to "construct" a connection that allows more time.

OVERBOOKING

Overbooking is not illegal, and most airlines overbook their scheduled flights to a certain extent in order to compensate for "no-shows." Passengers are sometimes left behind or "bumped" as a result. When an oversale occurs, the Department of Transportation (DOT) requires airlines to ask people who aren't in a hurry to give up their seats voluntarily, in exchange for compensation. Those passengers bumped against their will are, with a few exceptions, entitled to compensation.

Voluntary bumping

Almost any group of airline passengers includes some people with urgent travel needs and others who may be more concerned about the cost of their tickets than about getting to their destination on time. Our rules require airlines to seek out people who are willing to give up their seats for some compensation before bumping anyone involuntarily. Here's how this works.

At the check-in or boarding area, airline employees will look for volunteers when it appears that the flight has been oversold. If you're not in a rush to arrive at your next destination, you can give your reservation back to the airline in exchange for compensation and a later flight.

But before you do this, you may want to get answers to these important questions:

- When is the next flight on which the airline can *confirm* your seat? The alternate flight may be just as acceptable to you. On the other hand, if they offer to put you on standby on another flight that's full, you could be stranded.

- Will the airline provide other amenities such as free meals, a hotel room, phone calls, or

ground transportation? If not, you might have to spend the money they offer you on food or lodging while you wait for the next flight.

DOT has not said how much the airline has to give volunteers. This means carriers may negotiate with their passengers for a mutually acceptable amount of money-or maybe a free trip or other benefits. Airlines give employees guidelines for bargaining with passengers, and they may select those volunteers willing to sell back their reservations for the lowest price.

If the airline offers you a free ticket, ask about restrictions. How long is the ticket good for? Is it "blacked out" during holiday periods when you might want to use it? Can it be used for international flights? Most importantly, can you make a reservation, and if so, how far before departure are you permitted to make it? .

Involuntary bumping

DOT requires each airline to give all passengers who are bumped involuntarily a written statement describing their rights and explaining how the carrier decides who gets on an oversold flight and who doesn't. Those travelers who don't get to fly are frequently entitled to an on-the-spot payment of denied boarding compensation. The amount depends on the price of their ticket and the length of the delay:

- If you are bumped involuntarily and the airline arranges substitute transportation that is scheduled to get you to your final destination (including later connections) within one hour of your original scheduled arrival time, there is no compensation.

- If the airline arranges substitute transportation that is scheduled to arrive at your destination between one and two hours after your original arrival time (between one and four hours on international flights), the airline must pay you an amount equal to your one-way fare to your final destination, with a $200 maximum.

[If the airline offers you a free ticket, ask about restrictions.]

- If the substitute transportation is scheduled to get you to your destination more than two hours later (four hours internationally), or if the airline does not make any substitute travel arrangements for you, the compensation doubles (200% of your fare, $400 maximum).

- You always get to keep your original ticket and use it on another flight. If you choose to make your own arrangements, you can request an "involuntary refund" for the ticket for the flight you were bumped from. The denied boarding compensation is essentially a payment for your inconvenience.

Like all rules, however, there are a few conditions and exceptions:

- To be eligible for compensation, you must have a confirmed reservation. An "OK" in the Status box of your ticket qualifies you in this regard even if the airline can't find your reservation in the computer, as long as you didn't cancel your reservation or miss a reconfirmation deadline.

- You must meet the airline's deadline for buying your ticket. Discount tickets must usually be purchased within a certain number of days after the reservation was made. Other tickets normally have to be picked up no later than 30 minutes before the flight.

- In addition to the ticketing deadline, each airline has a check-in deadline, which is the amount of time before scheduled departure that you must present yourself to the airline at the airport. For domestic flights most carriers have a deadline of 10 minutes before scheduled departure, but some can be an hour or longer. (Many airlines require passengers with advance seat assignments to check in 30 minutes before scheduled departure, even if they already have advance boarding passes. If you miss this deadline you may lose the specific seats you were promised, although not the reservation itself.) Check-in deadlines on international flights can be as much as three hours before scheduled departure time, due partially to security procedures. Some airlines may simply require you to be at the ticket/baggage counter by this time; most, however, require that you get all the way to the boarding area. If you miss the ticketing or check-in deadline, you may have lost your reservation and your right to compensation if the flight is oversold.

[You must appear at the gate at least 10 minutes before departure, even if you already have a boarding pass and seat assignment]

- As noted above, no compensation is due if the airline arranges substitute transportation which is scheduled to arrive at your destination within one hour of your originally scheduled arrival time.

- If the airline must substitute a smaller plane for the one it originally planned to use, the carrier isn't required to pay people who are bumped as a result.

- The rules do not apply to charter flights, or to scheduled flights operated with planes that hold 60 or fewer passengers. They don't apply to international flights inbound to the United States, although some airlines on these routes may follow them voluntarily. Also, if you are flying between two foreign cities-from Paris to Rome, for example-these rules will not apply. The European Community has a rule on bumpings that occur in an EC country; ask the airline for details, or contact DOT.

The most effective way to reduce the risk of being bumped is to get to the airport early. On oversold flights the last passengers to check in are usually the first to be bumped, even if they have met the check-in deadline. Allow extra time; assume that the airport access road is backed up, the parking lot is full, and there is a long line at the check-in counter. However, if you arrive so early that your airline has another flight to your destination leaving before the one that you are booked on, either switch to the earlier flight or don't check your bag until after the first flight leaves. If you check your bag right away, it might get put on the earlier flight and remain unattended at your destination airport for hours.

[The best way to avoid getting 'bumped' is to check in early]

Airlines may offer free transportation on future flights in place of a check for denied boarding compensation. However, if you are bumped involuntarily you have the right to insist on a check if that is your preference. Once you cash the check (or accept the free flight), you will probably lose the right to demand more money from the airline later on. However, if being bumped costs you more money than the airline will pay you at the airport, you can try to negotiate a higher settlement with their complaint department. If this doesn't work, you usually have 30 days from the date on the check to decide if you want to accept the amount of the check. You are always free to decline the check and take the airline to court to try to obtain more compensation. The government's denied boarding regulation spells out

370

the airlines' minimum obligation to people they bump involuntarily.

Finally, don't be a "no-show. " If you are holding confirmed reservations you don't plan to use, notify the airline. If you don't, they will cancel all onward or return reservations on your trip.

BAGGAGE

Between the time you check your luggage in and the time you claim it at your destination, it may have passed through a maze of conveyor belts and baggage carts; once airborne, baggage may tumble around the cargo compartment if the plane hits rough air. In all fairness to the airlines, however, relatively few bags are damaged or lost. With some common-sense packing and other precautions, your bags will probably be among the ones that arrive safely.

Packing

You can pack to avoid problems. Some items should never be put into a bag you plan to check into the cargo compartment:

- **Small valuables**. cash, credit cards, jewelry, cameras.

- **Critical items**. medicine, keys, passport, tour vouchers, business papers.

- **Irreplaceable items**. manuscript, heirlooms.

- **Fragile items**. eyeglasses, glass containers, liquids.

Things like this should be carried on your person or packed in a carry-on bag that will fit under the seat. Remember, the only way to be sure your valuables are not damaged or lost is to keep them with you.

Even if your bag is not lost, it could be delayed for a day or two. Don't put perishables ' in a checked bag; they may spoil if it is delayed. It is wise to put items that you will need during the first 24 hours in a carry-on bag (e.g. toiletries, a change of underwear).

Check with the airline for its limits on the size, weight, or number of carry-on pieces. (There is no single federal standard.) If you are using more than one airline, check on all of them. Inquire about your flight; different airplanes can have different limits. Don't assume that the flight will have unlimited closet space for carry-on garment bags; some may have to be checked. If you plan to go shopping at your destination and bring your purchases aboard as carry-on, keep the limits in mind. If you check these purchases, however, carry the receipts separately; they may be necessary for a claim if the merchandise is lost or damaged. Don't

put anything into a carry-on bag that could be considered a weapon (e.g. scissors, pen knife).

[Bring toiletries and a change of underwear in a carry-on bag, in case your checked luggage is delayed.]

Checked baggage is also subject to limits. On most domestic and international flights, it's two checked bags (three if you don't have any carry-on luggage). There can be an extra charge if you bring more, or if you exceed the airline's limits on the size of the bags.

On some flights between two foreign cities, your allowance may be based on the weight of the bags rather than the number of pieces. The same two bags that cost you nothing to check when you started your trip could result in expensive excess-baggage charges under a weight system. Ask the airlines about the limit for every segment of your international trip before you leave home, especially if you have a stopover of a day or two or if you are changing carriers.

The bags you check should be labeled inside and out-with your name, address and phone number. Add the name and address of a person to contact at your destination if it's practical to do so. Almost all of the bags that are misplaced by airlines do turn up sooner or later. With proper labeling, the bag and its owner can usually be reunited within a few hours.

Don't overpack a bag. This puts pressure on the latches, making it easier for them to pop open. Also, lock your bags. The locks aren't very effective against pilferage, but they help to keep the latches from springing.

If you plan to check any electrical equipment, glassware, small appliances, pottery, typewriters, musical instruments or other fragile items, they should be packed in a container specifically designed to survive rough handling preferably a factory-sealed carton or a padded hardshell carrying case.

Check-in

Don't check in at the last minute. Even if you make the flight, your bag may not. If you miss the airline's check-in deadline, the carrier might not assume liability for your bag if it is delayed or lost.

If you have a choice, select flights that minimize the potential for baggage disruption. The likelihood of a bag going astray increases from #1 to #4 below (i.e., #1 is safest):

1) nonstop flight
2) direct or 'through' flight (one or more stops, but no change of aircraft)

3) online connection (change of aircraft but not airlines)

4) interline connection (change of aircraft and airlines)

When you check in, remove straps and hooks from garment bags that you are sending as checked baggage. These can get caught in baggage processing machinery, causing damage to the bag.

The airline will put baggage destination tags on your luggage and give you the stubs to use as claim checks. Make sure you get a stub for every bag. Don't throw them away until after you get your bags back and you check the contents. Not only will you need them if a claim is necessary, but you may need to show them to security upon leaving the baggage-claim area.

Each tag has a three-letter code and flight number that show the baggage sorters on which plane and to which airport your luggage is supposed to go. Double-check the tag before your bags go down the conveyor belt. (The airline will be glad to tell you the code for your destination when you make reservations or buy your tickets.)

Your bags may only be checked to one of your intermediate stops rather than your destination city if you must clear Customs short of your final destination, or if you are taking a connection involving two airlines that don't have an interline agreement. Be sure all of the tags from previous trips are removed from your bag, since they may confuse busy baggage handlers.

Claiming your bags

Many bags look alike. After you pull what you think is your bag off the carousel, check the name tag or the bag tag number.

If your bag arrives open, unlocked or visibly damaged, check right away to see if any of the contents are missing or damaged. Report any problems to the airline before leaving the airport; insist on filling out a form. Open your suitcase immediately when you get to where you are staying. Any damage to the contents or any pilferage should be immediately re-ported to the airline by telephone. Make a note of the date and time of the call, and the name and telephone number of the person you spoke with. Follow up immediately with a *certified letter* to the airline.

[Remove straps and hooks from garment bags; they can get caught in the machinery.]

Damage

If your suitcase arrives smashed or torn, the airline will usually pay for repairs. If it can't be fixed, they will negotiate a settlement to pay you its depreciated value. The same holds true for belongings packed inside.

Airlines may decline to pay for damage caused by the fragile nature of the broken item or inadequate packing, rather than the airline's rough handling. Carriers may also refuse to give you money for your damaged items inside the bag when there's no evidence of external damage to the suitcase. But airlines generally don't disclaim liability for fragile merchandise packed in its original factory sealed carton, a cardboard mailing tube, or other container designed for shipping and packed with protective padding material.

When you check in, airline personnel should let you know if they think your suitcase or package may not survive the trip intact. Before accepting a questionable item, they will ask you to sign a statement in which you agree to check it at your own risk. But even if you do sign this form, the airline might be liable for damage if it is caused by its own negligence shown by external injury to the suitcase or package.

Delayed bags

If you and your suitcase don't connect at your destination, don't panic. The airlines have very sophisticated systems that track down about 98% of the bags they misplace and return them to their owners within hours. In many cases they will absorb reasonable expenses you incur while they look for your missing belongings. You and the airline may have different ideas of what's reasonable, however, and the amount they will pay is subject to negotiation.

If your bags don't come off the conveyor belt, report this to the airline before you leave the airport. Insist that they fill out a form and give you a copy, even if they say the bag will be in on the next flight. If the form doesn't contain the name of the person who filled it out, ask for it. Get an appropriate phone number for following up (not the Reservations number). Don't assume that the airline will deliver the bag without charge when it is found; ask them about this.

[If your delayed bag is declared lost, you will have to fill out a second form.]

Most carriers set guidelines for their airport employees that allow them to disburse some money at the airport for emergency purchases. The amount depends on whether or not you're away from home and how long it takes to track down your bags and return them to you.

If the airline does not provide you a cash advance, it may still reimburse you later for the purchase of necessities. Discuss with the carrier the types of articles that would be reimbursable, and keep all receipts.

If the airline misplaces sporting equipment, it will sometimes pay for the rental of replacements. For replacement clothing or other articles, the carrier might offer to absorb only a portion of the purchase cost, on the basis that you will be able to use the new items in the future. (The airline may agree to a higher reimbursement if you turn the articles over to them.)

When you've checked in fresh foods or any other perishable goods and they are ruined because their delivery is delayed, the airline won't reimburse you. Carriers may be liable if they *lose or damage* perishable items, but they won't accept responsibility for spoilage caused by a delay in delivery.

Airlines are liable for provable consequential damages up to the amount of their liability limit (see below) in connection with the delay. If you can't resolve the claim with the airline's airport staff, keep a record of the names of the employees with whom you dealt, and hold on to all travel documents and receipts for any money you spent in connection with the mishandling. (It's okay to surrender your baggage claim tags to the airline when you fill out a form at the airport, as long as you get a copy of the form and it notes that you gave up the tags.) Call or write the airline's consumer office when you get home.

Lost luggage

Once your bag is declared officially lost, you will have to submit a claim. This usually means you have to fill out a second, more detailed form. Check on this; failure to complete the second form when required could delay your claim. Missing the deadline for filing it could invalidate your claim altogether. The airline will usually refer your claim form to a central office, and the negotiations between you and the airline will begin. If your flight was a connection involving two carriers, the final carrier is normally the one responsible for processing your claim even if it appears that the first airline lost the bag.

Airlines don't automatically pay the full amount of every claim they receive. First, they will use the information on your form to estimate the value of your lost belongings. Like insurance companies, airlines consider the depreciated value of your possessions, not their original price or the replacement costs.

If you're tempted to exaggerate your claim, don't. Airlines may completely deny claims they feel are inflated or fraudulent. They often ask for sales receipts and other documentation to back up claims, especially

if a large amount of money is involved. If you don't keep extensive records, you can expect to dicker with the airline over the value of your goods.

Generally, it takes an airline anywhere from six weeks to three months to pay you for your lost luggage. When they tender a settlement, they may offer you the option of free tickets on future flights in a higher amount than the cash payment.

Ask about all restrictions on these tickets, such as "blackout" periods and how far before departure you are permitted to make a reservation.

Limits on liability

If your bags are delayed, lost or damaged on a domestic trip, the airline can invoke a ceiling of $1,250 per passengert on the amount of money they'll pay you. When your luggage and its contents are worth more than that, you may want to purchase excess valuation," if available, from the airline as you check in. This is not insurance, but it will increase the carrier's potential liability. The airline may refuse to sell excess valuation on some items that are especially valuable or breakable, such as antiques, musical instruments, jewelry, manuscripts, negotiable securities and cash.
[The airlines' domestic liability limit is generally $1250 per person.]

On international trips, the liability limit is set by a treaty called the Warsaw Convention. Unless you buy excess valuation, the liability limit is $9.07 per pound ($20 per kilo). In order to limit its liability to this amount, the airline must use one of the following procedures:

1)   The carrier weighs your bags at check-in and records this weight on your ticket. The airline's maximum liability to you is that weight multiplied by $9.07 (or by $20, if the weight was recorded in kilos).

2)   Instead of weighing your luggage, the carrier assumes that each of your bags weighs the maximum that it agrees to accept as checked baggage, usually 70 pounds (32 kilos). This yields a liability limit of about $640 per bag.

This international limit also applies to domestic segments of an international journey. This is the case even if the domestic and international flights are on separate tickets and you claim and re-check your bag between the two flights.

Keep in mind that the liability limits are *maximums*. If

the depreciated value of your property is worth less than the liability limit, this lower amount is what you will be offered. If the airline's settlement doesn't fully reimburse your loss, check your homeowner's or renter's insurance; it sometimes covers losses away from the residence. Some credit card companies and travel agencies offer optional or even automatic supplemental baggage coverage.

Hazardous Items
Except for toiletries and medicines totaling no more than 75 ounces, it is illegal *and extremely dangerous* to carry on board or check in your luggage any of the following hazardous materials:

Hazardous materials

Aerosols-Polishes, waxes, degreasers, cleaners, etc.

Corrosives-Acids, cleaners, wet cell batteries, etc.

Flammables-Paints, thinners, lighter fluid, liquid reservoir lighters, cleaners, adhesives, camp stoves or portable gas equipment with fuel, etc. Explosives-Fireworks, flares, signal devices, loaded firearms, gunpowder, etc. (Small arms ammunition for personal use may be transported in checked luggage if it is securely packed in material designed for that purpose. These may not be placed in carry-on baggage.)

Radioactives-Betascopes, radiopharmaceuticals, uninstalled pacemakers, etc.

Compressed gases-Tear gas or protective-type sprays, oxygen cylinders, divers' tanks (unless they're empty), etc.

Infectious substances

Poisonous materials-Rat poison, etc.

Matches (both 'strike anywhere' matches and safety or 'book' matches) may only be carried on your person.

If you must travel with any of these materials, check with the airline's air freight department to see if special arrangements can be made.

A violation of the hazardous materials restrictions can result in a civil penalty of up to $25,000 for each violation or a criminal penalty of up to $500,000 and/or up to 5 years in jail.

Smoking
Under U.S. government rules, smoking is prohibited on all domestic scheduled-service flights except for flights over six hours to or from Alaska or Hawaii. This ban applies to domestic segments of international flights, on both U.S. and foreign airlines (e.g., the Chicago / New York leg of a flight that operates Chicago/New York/London). The ban does not apply to nonstop international flights, even during the time that they are in U.S. airspace (e.g., a Chicago/London flight). The prohibition applies in the passenger cabin and lavatories, but not in the cockpit.

[On U.S. airlines, you are guaranteed a non-smoking seat worldwide.]

Smoking is also banned on other scheduled-service flights by U.S. airlines that are operated with planes seating fewer than 30 passengers (e.g., certain "commuter" flights to Canada, Mexico and the Caribbean). Cigar and pipe smoking is banned on all U.S.-carrier flights (scheduled and charter, domestic and international).

The following rules apply to U.S. airlines on flights where smoking is not banned (e.g. international flights, domestic charter flights). These regulations do not apply to foreign airlines; however, most of them provide non-smoking sections (although they may not guarantee seating there or expand the section).

- The airline must provide a seat in a non smoking section to every passenger who asks for one, as long as the passenger complies with the carrier's seat assignment deadline and procedures. (Standby passengers do not have this right.)

- If necessary, the airline must expand the non-smoking section to accommodate the passengers described above.

- The airline does not have to provide a non-smoking seat of the passenger's choice. It doesn't have to seat you with your traveling companion, and you don't have the right to specify a window or aisle non-smoking seat. Also, the airline is not required by this rule to provide advance seat assignments before the flight date in the non-smoking section, as long as they get you into the non-smoking section on the day of your flight.

- The flight crew must act to keep passengers from smoking in the non-smoking sections.

However, smoke that drifts from the smoking section into the non-smoking section does not constitute a violation.

- No smoking is allowed while an aircraft is on the ground or when the ventilation system is not fully functioning.

- Carriers are not required to have a smoking section. An airline is free to ban smoking on particular flight, or on all of its flights.

None of the regulations described in this chapter apply to charter flights performed with small aircraft by on-demand air taxi operators.

PASSENGERS WITH DISABILITIES

Over 40 million Americans have disabilities. Other Air Carrier Access Act and the DOT rule that implements it set out procedures designed to ensure that these individuals have the same opportunity as anyone else to enjoy a pleasant flight. Here are some of the major provisions of the rule.

- A person may not be refused transportation on the basis of disability or be required to have an attendant or produce a medical certificate, except in certain limited circumstances specified in the rule.

- Airlines must provide enplaning, deplaning and connecting assistance, including both personnel and equipment. (Some small commuter aircraft may not be accessible to passengers with severe mobility impairments. When making plans to fly to small cities, such passengers should check on the aircraft type and its accessibility.)

- Airport terminals and airline reservations centers must have TDD telephone devices for persons with hearing or speech impairments.

- Passengers with vision or hearing impairments must have timely access to the same information given to other passengers at the airport or on the plane concerning gate assignments, delayed flights, safety, etc.

- New widebody aircraft must have a wheelchair-accessible lavatory and an on-board wheelchair. Airlines must put an on-board wheelchair on most other flights upon a passenger's request (48 hours' notice required).

- Air carriers must accept wheelchairs as checked baggage, and cannot require passengers to sign liability waivers for them (except for pre-existing damage).

- Most new airplanes must have movable armrests on half the aisle seats, and on-board stowage for one folding passenger wheelchair.

- Carriers must allow service animals to accompany passengers in the cabin, as long as they don't block the aisle or other emergency evacuation route.

- FAA safety rules establish standards for passengers allowed to sit in emergency exit rows; such persons must be able to perform certain evacuation-related functions.

- FAA rules also prohibit passengers from bringing their own oxygen. Most airlines will provide aircraft-approved oxygen for a fee, but aren't required to.

- Airlines may not charge for services that are required by this rule.

- Airlines must make available a specially - trained Complaints Resolution Official if a dispute arises. There must be a copy of the DOT rule at every airport.

It's wise to call the airline again before your trip to reconfirm any assistance that you have requested. For additional details, see "Other Sources of Information" at the end of this pamphlet for information on ordering the booklet *New Horizons for the Air Traveler with a Disability*.

FREQUENT-FLYER PROGRAMS

Virtually all major U-S- airlines have a frequent flyer plan, and many foreign carriers are starting them. These programs allow you to earn free trips, upgrades (e.g., from Coach to First Class) or other awards based on how often you fly on that airline. In some programs you can earn credit by using specified hotels, rental car companies, credit cards, etc.

It doesn't cost anything to join a program, and you can enroll in the programs of any number of different airlines. However, it may not be to your advantage to "put all your eggs in one basket" with one plan by accumulating a high mile-age balance only to find out later that another carrier's program suits your needs better. Here are some things to look at when selecting a frequent-flyer program.

- Does the airline fly where you're likely to want to go?

- Are there tie-ins with other carriers, especially those with international routes? Is some of the airline's service provided by commuter-carrier "partners"? In both cases, can you earn credits and use awards on those other airlines?

- How many miles (or trips) are required for particular awards?

- Is there a minimum award per flight (e.g., you are only flying 200 miles but the airline always awards at least 500)?

- Is there a deadline for using accumulated miles?

- Carefully examine the number and length of any "blackout periods" during which awards cannot be used. On some carriers, the Thanksgiving blackout may last a week.

- If you are planning a big trip and are thinking about joining that airline's frequent-flyer program, enroll before you travel. Airlines usually won't credit mileage that was flown before you became a member.

- After you join a program, there are other things that you should know:

- Airlines reserve the right to make changes to their programs, sometimes on short notice. The number of miles required for particular awards might be raised, requiring you to use your old mileage (i.e., your current balance) under the more restrictive new rules. The airline may cease service on a route that you were particularly interested in-or it may drop the city you live in! The carrier may eliminate attractive frequent-flyer tie-ins with particular airlines or hotel chains. [Is there a deadline for using accumulated miles?]

- Cashing in your mileage frequently will limit your losses in case the carrier changes the rules, merges, or goes out of business. (Some private companies sell insurance covering some of these eventualities.) Accumulating a larger mileage balance will entitle you to bigger awards, however.

- Carriers often limit the number of seats on each flight for which frequent-flyer awards can be used. You may not be able to get reservations on your first- or second-choice dates or flights.

- Awards can often be issued in the name of immediate family members. However, if you sell or give an award to someone not named on the award or the travel document and the airline finds out, the recipient could have his or her ticket confiscated, and the carrier may penalize the program member's account balance.

- Ask the airline how mileage is registered; you will probably have to identify yourself as a program member when you book your flight or when you check in.

- Keep your boarding passes and the passenger coupon of your ticket until you receive a statement from the frequent-flyer program reflecting the correct mileage earnings for that trip. If a problem arises, get the names of the people you speak with and keep notes of your conversations.

CONTRACT TERM

Throughout this booklet, we have tried provide you general information about airline travel. It is important to realize, however, that airline has specific rules that make up your contract of carriage. These rules may differ among carrier. They include provisions such as check-in deadline refund procedures, responsibility for delay flights, and many other things.

Domestic Travel

For domestic travel, an airline may provide all of its contract terms on or with your ticket at the time you buy it. Many small "commuter" carriers use this system. Other airlines may elect to "incorporate terms by reference." This means that you are not given all the airline's rules with your ticket-most of them are contained in a separate document which you can inspect on request.

If an airline elects to "incorporate by reference" it must provide conspicuous written notice with each ticket that:

1)   it incorporates terms by reference, and

2)   these terms may include liability limitations,

claim-filing deadlines, check-in deadlines, and certain other key terms.

The airline must also:

- Ensure that passengers can receive an explanation of key terms identified on the ticket from any location where the carrier's tickets are sold, including travel agencies;

- Make available for inspection the full text of its contract of carriage at each of its own airport and city ticket offices;

- Mail a free copy of the full text of its contract of carriage upon request.

There are additional notice require for contract terms that affect your air fare. Airlines must provide a conspicuous written notice on with the ticket concerning any "incorporated" contract terms that:

· Restrict refunds;

· Impose monetary penalties; or

· Permit the airline to raise the price after you've bought the ticket.

If an airline incorporates contract terms by reference and fails to provide the required notice about a particular rule, the passenger will not be bound by that rule.

International Travel

Not all of the detailed requirements for disclosing domestic contract terms apply to international travel. Airlines file "tariff rules" with the government for this transportation. Passengers are generally bound by these rules whether or not they receive actual notice about them.

Every international airline must keep a copy of its tariff rules at its airport and city ticket offices. You have a right to examine these rules. The airline agents must answer your questions about information in the tariff, and they must help you locate specific tariff rules, if necessary. If the airline keeps its tariff in a computer rather than on paper, there are additional disclosure requirements which are similar to those for domestic contract terms.

The most important point to remember, whether your travel is domestic or international, is that you should not be afraid to ask questions about a carrier's rules. You have a right to know the terms of your contract of carriage. It is in your best interest, as well as that of the airline, for you to ask in advance about any matters of uncertainty.

'TRAVEL SCAMS'

Unlike most products, travel services usually have to be paid for before they are delivered. This creates opportunities for disreputable individuals and companies. Some travel packages turn out to be very different from what was presented or what the consumer expected. Some don't materialize at all!

If you receive an offer by phone or mail for a free or extremely low-priced vacation trip to a popular destination (often Hawaii or Florida), there are a few things you should look for:

- Does the price seem too good to be true? If so, it probably is.

- Are you asked to give your credit card number over the phone?

- Are you pressured to make an _immediate_ decision?

- Is the carrier simply identified as "a major airline," or does the representative offer a collection of airlines without being able to say which one you will be on?

- Is the representative unable or unwilling to give you a street address for the company?

- Are you told you can't leave for at least two months? (The deadline for disputing a credit card charge is 60 days, and most scam artists know this.)

- If you encounter any of these symptoms, proceed cautiously. Ask for written information to be sent to you; any legitimate travel company will be happy to oblige. If they don't have a brochure, ask for a day or two to think it over; most bona fide deals that are good today will still be good two days from now. If they say no to both requests, this probably isn't the trip for you. Some other advice:

- If you are told that you've won a free vacation, ask if you have to buy something else in order to get it. Some packages have promoted free air fare, as long as you buy expensive hotel arrangements. Others include a free hotel stay, but no air fare.

- If you are seriously considering the vacation offer and are confident you have established the full price you will pay, compare the offer to what you might obtain elsewhere. Frequently, the appeal of free air fare or free accommodations disguises the fact that the total price is still higher than that of a regular package tour.

- Get a confirmed departure date, in writing, before you pay anything. Eye skeptically any promises that an acceptable date will be arranged later. If the package involves standby or waitlist travel, or a reservation that can only be provided much later, ask if your payment is refundable if you want to cancel, and don't pay any money you can't afford to lose.

- If the destination is a beach resort, ask the seller how far the hotel is from the beach. Then ask the hotel.

- Determine the complete cost of the trip in dollars, including all service charges, taxes, processing fees, etc.

- If you decide to buy the trip after checking it out, paying by credit card gives you certain legal rights to pursue a chargeback (credit) - if promised services aren't delivered.

For further advice, see "Other Sources of Information" at the end of this brochure for details on how to order the Federal Trade Commission's pamphlet *Telemarketing Travel Fraud*.

TO YOUR HEALTH

Flying is a routine activity for millions of Americans, and raises no health considerations for the great majority of them. However, there are certain things you can do to ensure that your flight is as comfortable as possible.

Changes in pressure can temporarily block the Eustachian tube, causing your ears to 'pop' or to experience a sensation of fullness. To equalize the pressure, swallow frequently; chewing gum sometimes helps. Yawning is also effective. Avoid sleeping during descent; you may not swallow often enough to keep ahead of the pressure change.

If yawning or swallowing doesn't help, use the 'valsalva maneuver':

- Pinch your nostrils shut, then breathe in a mouthful of air.

- Using only your cheek and throat muscles, force air into the back of your nose as if you were trying to blow your thumb and finger off your nostrils.

- Be very gentle and blow in short successive attempts. When you hear or feel a pop in your ears, you have succeeded. Never force air from your lungs or abdomen (diaphragm); this can create pressures that are too intense.

Babies are especially troubled by these pressure changes during descent. Having them feed from a bottle or suck on a pacifier will often provide relief.

Avoid flying if you have recently had abdominal, eye or oral surgery, including a root canal. The pressure changes that occur during climb and descent can result in discomfort.

If you have an upper respiratory or sinus infection, you may also experience discomfort resulting from pressure changes. Postpone your trip if possible. (Check to see if your fare has cancellation or change penalties.)
A final tip on pressure changes: they cause your feet to swell. Try not to wear new or tight shoes while flying.

Alcohol and coffee both have a drying effect on the body. Airliner cabin air is relatively dry to begin with, and the combination can increase your chances of contracting a respiratory infection. If you wear *contact lenses,* the low cabin humidity and/or consumption of alcohol or coffee can reduce your tear volume, leading to discomfort if you don't blink often enough. Lens wearers should clean their lenses thoroughly before the flight, use lubricating eye drops during the flight, read in intervals, and take the lenses out if they nap. (This may not apply to extended wear lenses; consult your practitioner.)
[Airline air is dry; if you wear contact lenses, blink often and limit reading]

If you take *prescription medications, bring* enough to last through your trip. Take along a copy of the prescription, or your doctor's name and telephone number, in case the medication is lost or stolen. The medicine should be in the original prescription bottle in order to avoid questions at security or Customs inspections. Carry it in a pocket or a carry-on bag; don't pack it in a checked bag, in case the bag is lost.

You can minimize the effects of *jet lag* in several ways:

· Get several good nights' sleep before your trip.

· Try to take a flight that arrives at night, so you can go straight to bed.

· Sleep on the plane (although not during descent).

· During the flight do isometric exercises, eat lightly, and drink little or no alcohol.

Try to use a rest room in the airport terminal before departure. On some flights the cabin crew begins beverage service shortly after the "Fasten Seat Belts" sign is turned off, and the serving cart may block access to the lavatories.

AIRLINE SAFETY

Air travel is so safe you'll probably never have to use any of the advice we're about to give you. But if you ever do need it, this information could save your life. Airline passengers usually take safety for granted when they board an airplane. They tune out the crew's pre-flight announcements or reach for a magazine instead of the cards that show how to open the emergency exit and what to do if the oxygen mask drops down. Because of this, people are needlessly hurt or killed in accidents they could have survived.

Every time you board a plane, here are some things you should do:

Be reasonable about the amount of carry-on luggage that you bring. FAA rules require airlines to limit the amount of carry-on baggage, and if you try to carry too much with you, the crew may insist that you check in some items. (There is no universal limit; it depends on the aircraft type and the passenger load.) A bag that is not properly stowed could turn into an unguided missile in an accident or block the aisles during an evacuation.

- Be careful about what you put into the storage bins over your seat. Their doors may pop open during an accident or even a hard landing, spilling their contents. Also, passengers in aisle seats have been injured by heavy items falling out of these compartments when people are stowing or retrieving belongings at the beginning or end of a flight. Please be considerate of others and put hard, heavy items under the seat in front of you; save the overhead bins for coats, hats, and small, soft bags.

[Count the number of rows to the nearest emergency exit]

- As soon as you sit down, fasten and unfasten your seat belt, a couple of times. Watch how it works. There are several kinds of belts, and in an emergency you don't want to waste time fumbling with the buckle.

- Before take-off, there will be a briefing about safety procedures, pointing out emergency exits and explaining seat belts, life vests and oxygen masks. Listen carefully and if there's anything you don't understand ask the flight attendants for help.

- The plastic card in the seat pocket in front of you will review some of the safety information announced by the flight attendant. Read it. It also tells you about emergency exits and how to find and use emergency equipment such as oxygen masks.

As you're reading the card look for your closest emergency exit, and count the number of rows between yourself and this exit. Remember, the closest exit may be behind you. Have a second escape route planned in case the nearest exit is blocked. This is important because people sometimes head for the door they used to board the plane, usually in the front of the first class cabin. This wastes time and blocks the aisles.

Oxygen masks aren't the same on all planes. Sometimes they drop down in front of you. On some aircraft, however, you'll have to pull them out of a compartment in front of your seat. In either case, you must tug the plastic tube slightly to get the oxygen flowing. If you don't understand the instructions about how the mask works, ask a flight attendant to explain it to you.

When the plane is safely in the air and has reached its cruising level, the pilot usually turns off the "fasten seat belt" sign. He or she usually suggests that passengers keep their belts buckled anyway during the flight in case the plane hits rough air. Just as seat belts should always be worn in cars, they should always be fastened in airplanes.

If You are ever in an air accident, you should remember these things:

- Stay calm.

- Listen to the crew members and do what they say. The cabin crew's most important job is to help you leave safely.

379

- Before you try to open any emergency exit yourself, look outside the window. If you see a fire outside the door, don't open it or the flames may spread into the cabin. Try to use your alternate escape route.

- Remember, smoke rises. So try to stay down if there's smoke in the cabin. Follow the track of emergency lights embedded in the floor; they lead to an exit. If you have a cloth, put it over your nose and mouth.

After an air accident, the National Transportation Safety Board always talks to survivors to try to learn why they were able to make it through safely. They've discovered that, as a rule, it does help to be prepared. Avoiding serious injury or surviving an air accident isn't just a matter of luck; it's also a matter of being informed and thinking ahead.

Are you one of those people who jumps up as soon as the plane lands, gathers up coat, suitcase and briefcase, and gets ready to sprint while the plane is still moving? If so, resist the urge. Planes sometimes make sudden stops when they are taxiing to the airport gate, and passengers have been injured when they were thrown onto a seat back or the edge of a door to an overhead bin. Stay in your seat with your belt buckled until the plane comes to a complete halt and the 'fasten seat belt' sign is turned off.

Never smoke in airplane restrooms. Smoking was banned in all but the designated smoking sections after an accident killed 116 people in only 4 minutes, apparently because a careless smoker left a burning cigarette butt in the trash bin. There is a penalty of up to $2,000 for disabling a lavatory smoke detector. Also, don't smoke in the aisle. If there is a sudden bump you could stumble and bum yourself or another passenger. Lit cigarettes have also flown out of passengers' hands and rolled under seats.

COMPLAINING

When passengers comment on airline service, most airlines do listen. They analyze and keep track of the complaints and compliments they receive and use the information to determine what the public wants and to identify problem areas that need special attention. They also try to resolve individual complaints.

Like other businesses, airlines have a lot of discretion in how they respond to problems. While you do have some rights as a passenger, your demands for compensation will probably be subject to negotiation and the kind of action you get depends in large part on the way you go about complaining.

Start with the airline. Before you call or write to DOT or some other agency for help with an air travel problem, you should give the airline a chance to resolve it.

As a rule, airlines have trouble-shooters at the airports (they're usually called Customer Service Representatives) who can take care of many problems on the spot. They can arrange meals and hotel rooms for stranded passengers, write checks for denied boarding compensation, arrange luggage repairs and settle other routine claims or complaints that involve relatively small amounts of money.

If you can't resolve the problem at the airport and want to file a complaint, it's best to call or write the airline's consumer office at its corporate headquarters. Take notes at the time the incident occurs and jot down the names of the carrier employees with whom you dealt. Keep all of your travel documents (ticket receipts, baggage check stubs, boarding passes, etc.) as well as receipts for any out-of-pocket expenses that were incurred as a result of the mishandling. Here are some helpful tips should you choose to write a letter.

[A complaint letter should always include a daytime phone number.]

- Type the letter and, if at all possible, limit it to one page in length.

- Include your daytime telephone number (with area code).

- No matter how angry you might be, keep your letter businesslike in tone and don't exaggerate what happened. If the complaint sounds very vehement or sarcastic, you might wait a day and then consider rewriting it.

- Describe what happened, and give dates, cities, and flight numbers or flight times.

- Send copies, never the originals, of tickets and receipts or other documents that can back up your claim.

- Include the names of any employees who were rude or made things worse, as well as anyone who might have been especially helpful.

- Don't clutter up your complaint with petty gripes that can obscure what you're really angry about.

- Let the airline know if you've suffered any special inconvenience or monetary losses.

- Say just what you expect the carrier to do to make amends. An airline may offer to settle your claim with a check or some other kind of compensation, possibly free transportation. You might want a written apology from a rude employee or reimbursement for some loss you incurred-but the airline needs to know what you want before it can decide what action to take.

- Be reasonable. If your demands are way out of line, your letter might earn you a polite apology and a place in the airline's crank files.

If you follow these guidelines, the airlines will probably treat your complaint seriously. Your letter will help them to determine what caused your problem, as well as to suggest actions the company can take to keep the same thing from happening to other people.

Contacting the Department of Transportation

If you need assistance or want to put your complaint about an airline on record with DOT, call the Office of Consumer Affairs at (202) 3662220 or write:

Office of Consumer Affairs, I-25
U.S. Department of Transportation
400 7th Street, S.W.
Washington, D.C. 20590

If you choose to write, please be sure to include your return address and a daytime telephone number, with area code.

We can provide information about what rights you may or may not have under Federal laws. If your complaint was not properly handled by the airline, we will contact them and get back to you.

Letters from consumers help us spot problem areas and trends in the airline industry. We use our complaint files to document the need for changes in DOT's consumer protection regulations and, where warranted, as the basis for enforcement action. In addition, every month we publish a report with information about the number of complaints we receive about each airline and what problems people are having. You can write or call us for a free single copy of this *Air Travel Consumer Report*, which also has statistics that the airlines file with us on flight delays, oversales and mishandled baggage.

If your complaint is about something you feel is a safety or security hazard, write to the Federal Aviation Administration:

Community and Consumer Liaison
Division, APA-200
Federal Aviation Administration
800 Independence Avenue, S.W.
Washington, D.C. 20591

or call: (800) FAA-SURE. After office hours, if you want to report something that you believe is a serious safety hazard, call the Aviation Safety Hotline at 1-800-255-1111.

Local consumer help programs

In most communities there are consumer help groups that try to mediate complaints about businesses, including airlines and travel agencies.

- Most state governments have a special office that investigates consumer problems and complaints. Sometimes it is a separate division in the governor's or state attorney general's office. Check your telephone book under the state government's listing.

- Many cities and counties have consumer affairs departments that handle complaints. Often you can register your complaint and get information over the phone or in person.

- A number of newspapers and radio or TV stations operate "Hot Lines" or "Action Lines" where individual consumers can get help. Consumer reporters, with the help of volunteers, try to mediate complaints and may report the results as a news item. The possible publicity encourages companies to take fast action on consumer problems when they are referred by the media. Some Action Lines, however, may not be able to handle every complaint they receive. They often select the most severe problems or those that are most representative of the kinds of complaints they receive.

Your last resort

If nothing else works, small claims court might be the best way for you to help yourself. Many cities have these courts to settle disputes involving relatively small amounts of money and to reduce the red tape and expense that people generally fear when they sue someone. An airline can generally be sued in small claims court in any jurisdiction where it operates flights or does business.

You can usually get the details of how to use the small claims court in your community by contacting your city or county office of consumer affairs, or the clerk of the court. As a rule, small claims court costs are low, you don't need a lawyer, and the procedures are much less formal and intimidating than they are in most other types of courts.

See Other Sources of Information" at the end of this pamphlet for details on how to order

TELEMARKETING TRAVEL FRAUD

Have you ever been tempted to buy one of those bargain-priced travel packages sold over the telephone? Be careful. Your dream adventure may be a misadventure if you fall victim to one of the travel scams sold over the phone. While some of these travel opportunities are legitimate, many of them are scam operations that are defrauding consumers out of millions of dollars each month.

How the Scams Work

These schemes take many forms. Increasingly common is one that involves travel clubs. A consumer pays a membership fee from $50 to $400 to receive a travel package that includes round-trip air transportation for one person and lodging for two people for a week in Hawaii, London, or another vacation place. The catch? You must purchase a high-priced, round-trip ticket for the second person from the fraudulent travel operation. You may wind up paying two to three times what it would cost if you purchased your own tickets in advance or through an airline or reputable travel agency.

Another scam starts by sending you a postcard stating: "You have been specially selected to receive a free trip." The postcard instructs you to call a phone number, usually toll-free, for details about your trip. Once you call, you are told you must join their travel club to be eligible for the free trip. Sometimes, a credit card number is requested so that your account can be billed for the membership fee. Only after you join are you sent the vacation package with instructions on requesting reservations for your "prepaid trip." Usually, your reservation request must be accompanied by yet another fee. The catch here? New charges are being added at every step along the way. And, you never get your "free" trip because your reservations are not confirmed or you must comply with hard-to-meet hidden or expensive "conditions."

Telemarketing travel scams usually originate out of "boiler rooms." Skilled salespeople, often with years of experience selling dubious products and services over the phone, pitch travel packages that may sound legitimate, but often are not. These sales pitches usually have the following in common:

* *Oral Misrepresentations.* Whatever the particular scheme may be, telephone salespeople are likely to promise you a "deal" they cannot deliver. Unfortunately, you often do not realize this until after you have paid your money.

* *High Pressure/Time Pressure Tactics.* These scam operators are likely to tell you that they need your commitment to buy right away or that this special offer will not be available tomorrow. Often, they will brush aside your questions with vague answers.

* *'Affordable" Offers.* Unlike telephone fraud operators who try to persuade people to spend thousands of dollars on a particular investment scheme, travel scam operators usually pitch their offers in the $50 to $400 range. Because this amount is often in the price range of those planning vacations, the fraudulent scheme may appear to be a reasonably-priced package.

* *Contradictory Follow-up Material.* Some firms may agree to send you written confirmation of the deal. You usually will find, however, that the literature bears little resemblance to the offer you accepted. Often, the written materials will disclose additional terms, conditions, and costs.

How to Protect Yourself

No one wants unpleasant surprises on a vacation. Therefore, it pays to thoroughly investigate a travel package *before* you commit to a purchase. While it is sometimes difficult to tell a legitimate sales pitch from a fraudulent one, there are some things you can do to protect yourself.

· *Be wary of "great deals."* One tip-off to a scam is that the offer is very low-priced. Few legitimate businesses can afford to give away things of real value or to undercut substantially everyone else's price.

· *Do not be pressured into buying* - NOW Generally, a good offer today will remain a good offer tomorrow. Legitimate businesses do not expect you to make an instant decision.

· *Ask detailed questions.* Find out exactly

what the price covers - and does not cover. Ask if there are any additional charges later. Find out the names of the specific hotels, airports, airlines, and restaurants that your package includes. You may wish to contact these places yourself to double-check arrangements. Find out exact dates and times. Ask about cancellation policies and refunds. If the salesperson cannot give you detailed answers to these questions, this is not the deal for you.

· *Get all information in writing before you agree to buy.* Before purchasing a travel package, ask for detailed written information. Once you receive the information, make sure the written material confirms everything you were told by phone.

· *Do not give your credit card number over the phone.* One easy way for a scam operator to close a deal is to get your credit card number and then charge your account. Sometimes scam operators say they need the number for verification purposes only. Never give your credit or charge card numbers - or any other personal information (such as bank account numbers) - to unsolicited telephone salespeople.

· *Do not send money by messenger or overnight* mail. Instead of asking for your credit card number, some scam operators may ask you to send a check or money order right away -or offer to send a messenger to pick these up. ff you use money rather than a credit card in the transaction, you lose your right to dispute fraudulent charges under the Fair Credit Billing Act. (See section entitled "What To Do If You Have Problems.")

· *Check out the company.* Before purchasing any travel package, check first with various government and private organizations to see if any complaints have been lodged against the travel firm calling you. A list of some of these organizations is included at the end of this brochure. Be aware, however, that fraudulent firms change their names frequently to avoid detection.

· *If in doubt, say "no."* Sometimes an offer appears legitimate, but you still have doubts. In that case, it is usually better to turn down the offer and hang up the phone. Remember, if something goes wrong, the likelihood of your receiving all your money back is very slim.

What To Do If You Have Problems

If you have problems with a travel package, try resolving your disputes first with the company that sold you the package. If you are not satisfied, try contacting your local consumer protection agency, Better Business Bureau, or state Attorney General.

In addition, you may want to write to the American Society of Travel Agents (ASTA) at P.O. Box 23992, Washington, D.C. 20026-3992, which may be able to mediate your dispute. Or, write to the Federal Trade Commission at 6th and Pennsylvania Avenue, N.W., Washington, D.C. 20580. Although the FTC does not generally intervene in individual disputes, the information you provide may indicate a pattern of possible law violations requiring action by the Commission.

If you charged your trip to a credit card, you may dispute the charges by writing to your credit card issuer at the address provided for billing disputes. Try to do this as soon as you receive your statement, but no later than 60 days after the bill's statement date. Under some circumstances under the Fair Credit Billing Act, your credit card issuer may have to absorb the charges if the seller does not resolve your dispute. If you did not authorize the charge, you are not responsible for its payment.

For More Information

If you would like more information about travel issues, write to ASTA (see address above) for a list of its publications. In addition, for single free copies of factsheets on "Vacation Certificates," "Timeshare Tips," or "Fair Credit Billing" write: Public Reference, Federal Trade Commission, Washington, D.C. 20580.

Other Sources of Information

(Availability and prices subject to change)

U.S. Department of Transportation: Office of Consumer Affairs
Write to: Office of Consumer Affairs, 1-25
U.S. Department of Transportation
400 Seventh Street, S.W.
Washington, DC 20590

Plane Talk. A series of facts sheets on specialized topics. Free.
-Frequent Flyer Programs

-Tips on Avoiding Baggage Problems
-'Defensive Flying'
-Public Charter Flights
-Transporting Live Animals
-Passengers With Disabilities

Kids and Teens in Right. When children alone. Free.

Consumers Tell It to the Judge. Small Claims court. Free.

Air Travel Consumer Report. Single copies free. Statistics for the industry and for individual airlines on:
-Delayed and canceled flights
-Oversales
-Baggage problems
-Consumer complaints to DOT

U.S. Department of Transportation: Office of Regulatory Affairs
Write to: Office of Regulatory Affairs, P- 10
U.S. Department of Transportation
400 Seventh Street, S.W.
Washington, DC 20590
Or call (202) 366-4220.

New Horizons for the Air Traveler with Disability Free.

Federal Aviation Administration
Write to: Community and Consumer
Liaison Division, APA-200 Federal Aviation
Administration
800 Independence Ave. S.W.
Washington, DC 20591

Child/Infant Safety Seats Recommended for Use in Aircraft. Free.

Hazardous Material? Tips for Airline Passengers. Free.

Department of State

Write to: Superintendent of Documents U.S. Government Printing Office Washington, DC 20402

Your Trip Abroad. Customs, shots, insurance. $1.25.

A Safe Trip Abroad. Precautions against robbery, terrorism. $1.00.

Travel Tips for Older Americans. $ 1. 00.

For the following brochure, write to:
Consumer Information Center
Pueblo, CO 81009

Foreign Entry Requirements. Visa and other requirements for many foreign countries. 50 cents.

U.S. Customs Service
Write to: U.S. Customs Service
P.O. Box 7407
Washington, DC 20044

Know Before You Go. Customs advice for entering the U.S. Free.

Federal Trade Commission
Write to: Federal Trade Commission
6th & Pennsylvania Ave. N.W.,
Room 130
Washington, DC 20580

Telemarketing Travel Fraud. Travel scams marketed by phone. Free.

U.S. Office of Consumer Affairs Write to: Consumer Information Center Pueblo, CO 81009

Access Travel. Handicapped services at over 500 airports. Free.

U.S. Department of Agriculture
Write to: USDA/APHIS Public Information
6505 Belcrest Road, Room 613
Hyattsville, MD 20782

Travelers' Tips. Bringing plant and animal products into the U.S. Free.

Traveling By Air with your Pet. Free.

U.S. Public Health Service
Write to: Superintendent of Documents
U.S. Government Printing Office
Washington, DC 20402

Health Information for International Travelers $6.00 (182 pp.).

American Society for the Prevention of Cruelty to Animals
Write to: A.S.P.C.A. Education Dept.
424 E. 92nd St.
New York, NY 101 28

(Send a long self-addressed stamped envelope)

Air Travel Tips [for pets]. Free.
Airline Travel With Your Bird. Free

384

Aviation Consumer Action Project
Write to: Aviation Consumer Action Project
P.O. Box 19029
Washington, DC 20036

Facts and Advice for Airline Passengers. $2.00.

Better Business Bureau
Write to: Better Business Bureau
257 Park Ave. South
New York, NY 10010

Low-Cost Air and Ticket Consolidators $3.00 (4 pp.).

Consumer Information Center

A number of the federal government brochures listed above, as well as many others, are available from the Consumer Information Center. If you are thinking of ordering publications from several agencies, it may be more convenient to request a free CIC catalog by writing to Consumer Information Center, Pueblo, CO 81009. You may also call (719) 948-4000 (normal long-distance rates apply).

Chapter 41

Avoiding Jet Lag

- - - -

(The Traveler's Number 1 Complaint)

Jet lag has ruined more vacations, been the reason for more botched business meetings, and wreaked more general havoc on the air traveler than all the preflight or inflight irritations combined. Indeed, a term that four decades ago was an insider's expression used exclusively by an elite group of aviators, "jet lag" is now virtually a household word to 2.8 million passengers who have flown coast to coast in the United States, 2.1 million who have flown abroad from the United States, and more than 140 million people from around the globe who have flown through the world's international airports. Yet, despite the multitude of sufferers, only a handful of scientists specializing in chronobiology (the study of how time affects living organisms) and circadian regulatory biology (the study of how to control man's daily body rhythms) know its real cause, the true nature of its body-wide effect, and its simple cure.

The Phenomenon of East/West Flight

The biggest misconception that air travelers have is that jet lag is caused by being enclosed in a vehicle that is traveling at great speeds and at terrifically high altitudes. Somehow, air travelers correlate speed and altitude as key factors in jet lag. Yet the inflight velocity of the airplane and the distance traveled above the earth, per se, have absolutely nothing to do with jet lag. Nor do typical inflight symptoms of ear-popping, light-headedness, dehydration, irritability, motion sickness, and any other ailment about which air travelers might complain while en route to their destination. All these problems can be attributed to poor cabin pressure, drinking alcoholic beverages while in flight, and nerve-wracking engine noises-not jet lag. Jet lag is strictly, a phenomenon of long distance, east/west, too rapid travel to a new time frame. (caused primarily by the disruption of the sense of time, the sense of place and the sense of well being.)

The following is a list of jet lag symptoms that begin immediately upon deplaning.

Early and Late Jet Lag Symptoms

Early Symptoms	Late Symptoms
-fatigue	- constipation or diarrhea
-disorientation	-lack of sexual interest
-reduced physical ability	-limited peripheral vision
-reduced mental activity	-decreased muscle tone -
contusion	-impaired night vision upset appetite
	-reduced physical work capacity
	-off-schedule bowel and urinary movements
	-disrupted phases of body and functions onset of memory loss -
	-slowed response time to visual stimulation
	-reduced motor coordination and reflex time
	-interference with prescription drugs
	-insomnia
	-acute fatigue
	-loss of appetite
	-headache

AIR TRAVEL TIPS

Preflight

1. check with airlines to see if they will supply you with high-protein breakfasts and lunches, and high-carbohydrate suppers for those meals you will be eating on hometown time while en route, and those meals consumed on destination time while en route.

2. Try to pre-select your seat in the airplane so that you are physically removed from the area of the galley, lavatories, and bassinets (where lots of distracting activities and noises may interrupt your "rest" periods), try to arrange for plenty of leg room (near the emergency exits, in the front row of a section), and on the side of the plane opposite from where the sun will be when you are trying to sleep.

3. Pack the following items into a small bag to be carried onto the airplane: sleepshade, slipper socks, travel alarm, extra wristwatch (unless your normal wristwatch is of the type that can display two different time zones), toothbrush, toothpaste, razor, gum, lip balm, nasal and decongestant.

4. Pack a picnic basket of leftovers from the refrigerator in case meals served on the airplane do not correspond to the high-protein breakfast and lunch and high-carbohydrate supper program. Leftovers are also handy for light snacking inflight.

5. Wear loose clothing.

6. Do not let everything pile up until the last minute. Avoid tension, and get to the airport on schedule or with plenty of time to spare.

7. Try to avoid flying if you have a cold or ear problems. Remember that wine, sherry, or port contain histamines that can aggravate head congestion.

8. Check the weather at your destination and plan accordingly.

9. Consider using a small portable luggage cart as a "back-saving" device.

Inflight

10. Drink lots of fluids. The atmosphere in the airplane's cabin is literally as dry as the Gobi Desert.

11. If there are lots of empty seats on the airplane, make a quick move to a row of seats that can be converted into a quasi-bed for the "inactive" phase of the Jet Lag Program.

12. Reach for a pillow and blanket for the "inactive" phase of the Jet Lag Program. Covering yourself with a blanket helps keep you comfortable as your body temperature drops during inactivity. A pillow is a familiar psychological device that enhances your ability to sleep.

13. Loosen your clothing as an aid to circulation. Take off your shoes.

14. Avoid alcohol or limit it. Alcohol tends to add to the dehydration problem of poor cabin pressurization that pushes the humidity to as low as 5% or even 2%.

15. Eliminate or cut down on smoking. The carbon monoxide in cigarette smoke reduces the blood's ability to carry oxygen, and can cause headaches or slight dizziness while in flight.

16. If you wear contact lenses, consider removing them while in flight so that your eyes do not become irritated because of the extremely dry atmosphere in the cabin.

Postflight

17. Upon arrival, in your excitement at having landed at your destination, do not disregard the Postflight Steps of the Three-Step Jet Lag Program.

18. Remember to plan ahead for your next or return flight, and implement the Preflight Steps of the Jet Lag Program in plenty of time to assure the maximum benefits.

THE ARGONNE ANTI-JET-LAG DIET

How to avoid jet lag:

1. **DETERMINE BREAKFAST TIME** at destination on day of arrival.

2. **FEAST-FAST-FEAST-FAST** - Start four days before breakfast time in step 1. On day one, FEAST; eat heartily with high-protein breakfast and lunch and a high-carbohydrate supper. No coffee except between 3 and 5 p.m. On day two, FAST on light meals of salads, light soups, fruits and juices. Again, no coffee except between 3 and 5 p.m. On day three, FEAST again. On day four, FAST; if you drink caffeinated beverages, take them in morning when traveling west, or between 6 and 11 p.m. when traveling east.

3. **BREAK THE FINAL FAST** at destination breakfast time. No alcohol on the plane, if the flight is long enough, sleep until normal breakfast time at destination, but no later. Wake up and FEAST on a high-protein breakfast. Stay awake and active. Continue the day's meals according to mealtimes at

the destination.

FEAST on high-protein breakfasts and lunches to stimulate the body's active cycle. Suitable meals include steak, eggs, hamburgers, high-protein cereals, green beans.

FEAST on high-carbohydrate suppers to stimulate sleep. They include spaghetti and other pastas (but no meatballs), crepes (but no meat filling), potatoes, other starchy vegetables, and sweet desserts.

FAST days help deplete the liver's store of carbohydrates and prepare the body's clock for resetting. Suitable foods include fruit, light soups, broths, skimpy salads, unbuttered toast, half pieces of bread. Keep calories and carbohydrates to a minimum.

COUNTDOWN

	1 FEAST	2 FAST	3 FEAST	4 FAST	BREAK FINAL FAST
BRK.FAST	feast	fast	feast	fast	
LUNCH	feast	fast	feast	fast	
SUPPER	feast	fast	feast	fast	

Westbound: If you drink caffeinated beverages, take them morning before departure.
Eastbound: take them between 6 and 11 p.m. If flight is long enough, sleep until destination breakfast time. Wake up and FEAST, beginning with a high-protein breakfast. Lights on. Stay active.

Coffee, tea, cola, other caffeinated beverages allowed only between 3 and 5 p.m.

TIME ZONES AND MEDICINE--a confusing combination:[IL]

Whether you take a daily oral contraceptive, a twice-daily ulcer drug, or an every-four-hours cardiac medication, your routine is thrown off schedule when you travel out of your own time zone. Even coast-to-coast travel requires an adjustment. How can you make sure you are taking pills at the proper time when the time changes? There are several strategies.

For shorter trips (less than a week), many people keep their medication schedule on home time. But since that can mean waking up in the middle of the night to take a pill, this option isn't for everyone.

In these cases, you have to adjust your schedule and perhaps even your dosage. Unfortunately there is no simple formula to follow, so your doctor's advice is crucial. You may be told to skip one dose when you travel west to east, and your day is shortened. Or, you may be told to take an extra dose on the first day of your trip if you are going east to west. The specifics depend on how many time zones you are crossing and what type of medication you are taking.

According to pharmacist, Harold Silverman, author of **Travel Healthy** (Avon Books), drugs known to be affected by shifts in biological rhythm (including jet lag and time zone changes) are antihistamines, anti-inflammatory drugs, anabolic steroids, barbiturates, benzodiazepine tranquilizers and sedatives, (including chlordiazepoxide, diazepam, and flurazepam), corticasteroids, and narcotic pain relievers, such as morphine, meperidine, and codeine.

Two other medications that are greatly affected by time changes are oral contraceptives and insulin injections. Depending on the degree of time difference and the type of oral contraceptive, many women are able to stick to their regular schedules.   For instance, combination pills can still be taken at bedtime, no matter how great the time difference. But certain forms of birth control pills, such as progestin-only mini-pills, must be taken every 24 hours to be effective. If you are on this type of pill and will be for a considerable length of time, switch gradually so that you're taking a dose every 23 hours instead of every 24 until you are once again on a schedule that's convenient. The switch back should be just as gradual.(To be safe, check with your doctor.)

People with diabetes, also, should check with their physicians about altering insulin schedules when crossing two or more time zones, even if the insulin is taken in 24 hour dosages.   Recommendations will be based on the severity of the disease, the type of insulin, the direction of the journey, and the number of time zones being crossed.

In many cases, the general rule is to keep your watch set to home time while you are on the plane, and follow your usual eating schedule. (You can arrange with the airline in advance for a diabetic meal, and you can request that the meal be served at a specific time.) Then, when you arrive at your destination, adjust your watch to the new time and adjust your next dose of insulin according to your doctor's instructions. Throughout your trip, frequently test your blood sugar level; the symptoms of jet lag often mimic diabetic reactions.

For more information, send a self-addressed envelope to Becton Dickinson Consumer Products, 1 Becton Drive, Franklin Lakes, NJ 07417, Attention: Diabetes Health Care, with your request for Vacations, Travel, and Diabetes. Or write to Squibb Novo, 211 Carnegie Center, Princeton, 08540, for **"Traveling with Diabetes"**. The American Diabetes Association, 1660 Duke St., Alexandria, VA 22314, also provides information about how to cope while traveling with diabetes.

Chapter 42

Communicating To and From Overseas

- - - -

CALLING OVERSEAS FROM THE U.S.:

You can call over 170 countries from the U.S., easily and economically. Here's how:

NOTE: *To use the services described in these section you may be required to first become a subscriber or customer of a **Long Distance Carrier**. This can be accomplished by signing up (before you go,) with the long distance carrier of your choice or by signing up for the particular service being offered by the long distance carrier.*

A)   HOW TO PLACE INTERNATIONAL CALLS DIRECTLY FROM YOUR HOME OR OFFICE

Dial 011 + Country Code + City Code + Local Number
(A list of country codes is provided at the end of this chapter. Country and City Codes could also be found in Appendix 5E).

> For example: to call Tokyo in Japan simply call:
>
> **011   + 81 + 3 +   XXXXXX**
>
> | International Access Code | Country Code | City Code | Local Number |
> |---|---|---|---|

CALLING CANADA OR THE CARIBBEAN:

This procedure is even simpler since the dialing procedure is exactly the same as placing a long distance call from one U.S. state to another.

> | **1 +** | **XXX   +** | **XXXXXX** |
> |---|---|---|
> | Long distance Access Code | Area Code | Local Number |

INTERNATIONAL CALLING FROM YOUR HOTEL ROOM

Dialing procedure from a hotel room is the same as from your home or office, except that you start with a hotel access code.

Dial the hotel access code[1] and wait for a tone. Then dial the international access code + country code + city code + local number.

For example: to call Tokyo, simply dial

X   +   011   + 81 + 3 +   XXXXXX

Hotel Access	International Access Code	Country Code	City Code	Local Number

HOW TO PLACE INTERNATIONAL CALLS WITH OPERATOR ASSISTANCE

There are a few countries that cannot be direct-dialed. Most of these countries however, could still be accessed with an operator's assistance.

If direct-dialing is not available to the country you are calling simply dial any of the following numbers for an International Operator.

10 + AT&T   (If you need **AT&T** services or would like to use their calling card)

10333+0   (If you need **Sprint** services or would like to use their calling card)

10+222+0[2]   (If you need **MCI** services or would like to use their calling card)

10211+0   (if you need **Frontier** services or would like to use their calling card)

10488+0   (If you need MCC services or would like to use their calling card)

C) HOW TO PLACE INTERNATIONAL CALLS FROM THE U.S. USING A CALLING CARD:

TO CALL CANADA OR THE CARIBBEAN

(a) AT&T Calling CARDHOLDERS:
Dial **00+ Country Code + City Code + Local Number**.
Remember to dial "01" instead of "011" (if you do not hear "AT&T", hang up and dial: **01 + 288** before placing your call.

(b) Sprint (FONCARD) HOLDERS:

Dial 10333+01+Country Code, City Code and Local Number plus the "#" button. Listen for a recorded prompt (on rotary phones, wait for Sprint Operator). Dial the 14 digit FONCARD number (shown on your FONCARD)

If you do not hear "Welcome to Sprint":

Dial 1-800-877-8000. Listen for a computer tone. Dial:**01 + Country Code, City Code and Local Number plus the "#" button + # sign.** Listen for a computer tone. Dial the 14 digit FONCARD number.

If Calling the Caribbean (area Code 809) or Canada

Dial 10333+0+Area Code and Local Number. Listen for recorded prompt. Dial the 14 digit FONCARD number.

If you do not hear "Welcome to Sprint": Dial 1-800-877-8000.
Listen for a computer tone. Dial 0+Area Code and Local Number. Listen for computer tone. Dial the 14 digit FONCARD number.

(c) MCI CARDHOLDERS:

Dial: **9501022 + 01 + Country Code + City Code + Local Number (Wait for a dial Tone) + your 14 Digit Number.**

If dialing from an "809" Area Code, Dial 0 + **Area Code + Local Number**

(d) MCC CARDHOLDERS:

Dial: **1 + 800 + 275 + 1234 (Wait for a dial tone) + 01 + Country Code + City Code + Local Number + # sign (Wait for a dial tone) + your 14 digit Code.**

CALLING THE U.S. FROM OVERSEAS:[3]

You may have up to five choices:

a) **Using Special Services** of a U.S. International Telephone Carrier. e.g.: " AT&T USADirect Service(i)", " Sprint Express", MCI " Call USA", "Frontier Passport USA Service," and "Metromedia International Origination Service". These services allow you (when you dial a special number provided by your preferred carrier) to talk to that carriers operator in the U.S. who will then place your call.

b) **Using a Calling Card[4]** with U.S. Operators. e.g.: " AT&T Calling Card", Sprint "FONCARD", "Frontier Calling Card", MCI Card", or "Metromedia Calling Card".

To place a call, using your calling card simply dial the " In Country Local International Operator" who will then place your call. (A Chart listing International Operator Codes is provided at the end of this chapter).

C) **Using International Direct Dialing[5]**

This service may not be available from all countries and/at in all phones in the foreign country. Check with your long distance carrier before leaving.

To direct dial just get an outside line and use the proper access code for the country you are calling from. (See Chart at the end of this chapter for a list of International Direct Dialing Codes).

Here is for example how you'd dial Boston directly from Italy:

00 +	1 +	617 +	____
Direct U.S. Access Code	Country Code	Boston Area Code	Local Number

Calling the U.S. from Canada:

You can use your Calling Card in Canada as easily as you do in the States. Simply dial from any phone:
0 + Area Code + Number
The operator will ask for your regular Calling Card number or you may enter it at the sound of the tone.

How To Use Special Services:

AT&T USADirect Dial: Just dial the AT&T USA Direct Service Number++ for the country you are calling from. This will put you directly in touch with an AT&T operator in the U.S. who will then place your call.

MCI Call USA Service: Dial the Special MCI Toll Free Access Number++ for the country you are calling from.

392

This will put you in touch with an MCI operator in the U.S. who will then place your call.

SPRINT Express: Dial Sprint Express overseas Access Number:[++] This will put you in touch with a Sprint operator in the U.S., who will then place your call.

MCC: To use Direct Dial, Dial the MCC Access Number[++] for the country you are in + 488 + 14 digit code + # sign + 4 Security Code + 1 + area code + number. (Note: Use "0" instead of "1" for National calls. "1" is used for International calls.)

> [++] *[A list of AT&T Direct Service Numbers and Access Numbers for the major long distance carriers is provided at the end of this chapter. Contact your long distance carrier for additional listings.]*

CALLING IN AND BETWEEN INTERNATIONAL LOCATIONS [e.g from Venice (Italy) to Genoa (Italy) or from Venice (Italy) to Paris (France)

This service is not available for all countries or from all locations. Check with your long distance carrier before leaving.

MCC: For those using MCC services, this facility is presently available in over 26 locations. To use this Direct Dial service to place a call between locations within the same country (e.g. Venice (Italy) to Genoa (Italy) dial

1. Enter Direct Dial Access Number from the country you are   in
2. Enter 488 + 14 **Digit Code + # sign**
3. Enter 4 Digit Security Code
4. Press "0" For National Call + City Code + Phone   number + **# sign**
OR "1" for International Call + Country + City Code   +   Phone number + **# sign**

SHIP AND SEA SERVICES

AT&T HIGH SEAS SERVICE:

a) **Calling from U.S. Shores to Ships.**

> Use AT&T High Seas Service by dialing **1-800-SEA-CALL.** Give the operator the name of the ship and the person you wish to call. The operator will connect you once the contact is made.

b) **Calling from Ship to Shore.**

Before you go on your cruise, preregister your AT&T Calling Card number by calling **1-800-SEA-CALL.** Then, aboard ship, simply ask for AT&T High Seas Service, and the connection to a U.S. operator is made.

SPRINT INMARSAT/MCC MARSAT Services;

> Sprint customers can enjoy direct-dial services to ships at sea using this dialing pattern:
> DIAL **011 + Ocean Region Code + Ships Telephone Number**

The Ocean Region Code will vary depending on the ship's location:

INMARSAT Regions Ocean Codes

Atlantic Ocean Region (East)	871
Atlantic Ocean Region (West)	874
Indian Ocean Region	873
Pacific Ocean Region	872

FOR ADDITIONAL INFORMATION/CUSTOMER SERVICE CALL:

Frontier: 1-800-836-8080
MCI: 1-800-444-3333
MCC: 1-800-275-2273

To obtain an AT&T Calling Card:

1-800-CALL-ATT
1-800-874-4000
When outside the U.S., use AT&T USADirect Service and call (816) 654-6688, collect.

For further information on the AT&T USADirect service call 1-800-874-4000

~ ~ ENDNOTES ~ ~

1.   Check with the hotel operator for Hotel Access Code. The number is usually "8" or "9". Some hotels prefer to place International calls for their guests.

2.   This is true in most places in the

393

Northeast part of the United States except in large metropolitan areas. RCI however, will allow domestic <u>collect calls</u> in these areas.

3. To successfully use the services in this section, you must first become an approved customer of that carrier's calling service. In other words, you should not expect to just dial the access number and then place your calls. It is therefore, important to first inquire, and preferably, sign up with your long distance carrier before commencing on your trip.

4. Direct dialing is usually available from pay phones or specially marked phones in conjunction with your calling card.

In the absence of pay phones or specially marked phones, direct dialing will require going through a foreign operator for an outside line.

5. By using a calling card you avoid foreign surcharges. Furthermore, it allows you to have your calls billed to your card. This service however, may not be available in all foreign countries and/or at all phones in the foreign country. Check with your long distance carrier for availability before you go.

Country	In-Country Local Int'l. Operator	Int'l. Direct Dialing Code	AT&T USA Direct Service Number	MCI Toll Free Access Number	SPRINT Express Overseas Access Number	METROMEDIA Direct-Dial Access Number	Int'l. Country Codes
Algeria	16	00	na	na	na		213
Anguilla	na	1	1-800-872-2881	na	na		809
Argentina	300 or 953	800000	001-800-200-1111	001-800-777-1111	001-800-777-1111		54
Aruba	121	0c0	800-1011	na	na		297
Australia	0101	0011	0014-881-011	022-903-012	0014-881-877	0080-32-329	61
Austria+	09	900	022-903-011	0114-881-100	022-903-014		43
Bahamas	0	1	1-800-872-2881	1-800-624-1000	1-800-389-2111		809
Bahrain	151	0	800-001	800-002	na	808-808	973
Belgium+	1222	00	078-11-0010	078-11-00-12	078-11-0014	117-800	32
Belize	115	00	555	na	556		501
Bermuda	na	na	1-800-872-2881	1-800-623-0484	1-800-623-0877		809
Bolivia	35-67-00	00	na	na	0800-3333		591
Brazil	000-111	00	000-8010	000-8012	000-8016		55
Bulgaria	0123	na	na	na	na		359
Canada	0	1	na	na	na		01
Cayman Islands		na	na	1872	1-624	na	809
Chile+	122 & 123	00	00*-0312	00*0316	00*0317		56
China	115 Beijing	00	10811	na	108-13		86
Colombia	09	90	980-11-0010	980-16-0001	980-13-0010		57
Costa Rica	116	00	114	162	163		506
Cyprus	na	na	080-90010	080-90-000	na		357
Czech Republic		102 & 108	00	00-420-00101	na	na	42
Denmark+	0016	009	8001-0010	801-0022	8001-0877	8081-5123	45
Ecuador	116	00	119	na	171		593
Egypt	120	00	356-0020	355-5770	na		20
El Salvador	119	00	190	na	191		503
Finland+	09	990	9800-100-10	980-102-80	9800-1-0284	9800-3842	358
France+	19-3311	19	19*0011	19*-00-19	19*0087	05-020-800	33
Gambia	na	na	00111	na	na		220
Germany (xxx)		0010	00	0130-0010	0130-0012	0130-0013 0130-4749	
Great Britain	155	010	0800-89-0011	0800-89-0222	0800-89-0877	0800-181-158	
Greece	161	00	00-800-1311	00-800-1211	008-001-411		30
Grenada	na	1	872	na	na		809
Guam	013	011	018-872	950-1022	na		671
Guatemala	171	00	190	189	195		502
Haiti	09	001	001-800-872-2881	001-800-999-1234	na		509
Honduras	197	00	123	na	001-800-1212000		504

394

Country							
Hong Kong	011	001	008-1111	008-1121	008-1877	802-7555	852
Hungary	09	00	00*-36-0111	00-800-01411	00*800-01-877		36
Iceland	na	90	999-001	na	na		354
India	186 & 187	00	na	na	000-137		91
Indonesia	101	00	00-801-10	na	00-801-15		62
Iraq	105	00	na	00-801-11	na		964
Ireland	114	16	1-800-550-000	1-800-551-001	1-800-55-2001	1-800-626-800	353
Israel	18	00	177-100-2727	177-150-2727	177-102-2727		972
Italy+	170	00	172-1011	172-1022	172-1877	1678-77-360	39
Jamaica	na	00	0-800-872-2881	na	na		809
Japan+	0051	001	0039-111	0039-121	0039-131	0120-116-901	81
Jordan	10217	00	na	na	na		962
Kenya	0196	na	0800-10	na	na		254
Korea, South	007	001	009-11	na	009-16		82
Kuwait	102 & 104	00	800-288	na	800-777		965
Liberia	na	00	797-797	na	na		231
Libya	16	00	na	na	na		
Liechtenstein	na	na	155-00-11	155-0222	155-9777	155-1610	41
Luxembourg	0010	00	0800-0111	na	na	0800-2800	352
Macau	na	na	0800-111	na	0800-121		853
Malaysia	108	007	800-0011	800-0012	800-0016		60
Mexico	09	95	Designated	na	na		52
Monaco	na	19	19*0011	19*-00-19	19*0087	05-020-800	33
Montserrat	na	1	1-800-872-2881	na	na		809
Morocco	12	00	na	na	na		212
Netherlands, The+	0010	09	06-022-9111	06*-022-91-22	06*-022-9119	060-222-072	31
Netherlands Antilles	021	00	001-800-872-2881				599
New Zealand	0170	00	000-911	000-915	000-999	0800-800-064	64
Nicaragua	114/116	00	64 **	na	161 (Managua)		505
Nigeria	171	009	1881	na	na		234
Norway+	0115	095	050-12-011	050-12912	050-12-877	05-03-410-60	47
Oman	15 & 195	00	na	na	na	75-00-77	968
Pakistan	0102	00	na	na	na		92
Panama	106	00	109	108	115		507
Paraguay	0010	00	0081-800	na	008-12-800		595
Peru	108	00	191	special phones only	196		51
Philippines+	108	00	105-11	na	105-01		63
Poland	901 & 900	00	(0)-010-480-0111	na	0010-480-0115		48
Portugal	098	097	05017-1-288	05-017-1234	05017-1-877		351
Qatar	1 & 150	0	Designated	na	na		974
Romania	071	00	na	na	na		40
St. Kits	na	na	1-800-872-288	na	na		809
San Marino	na	na	na	172-1022	172-1877	1678-32-016	39
Saudi Arabia	900	00	1800-100	1-800-11	na		966
Singapore+	104	005	800-0011	800-0012	800-177-177	738-4567	65
So. Africa	090 & 093	09 or 091	na	na	na	900-11-10-11	27
Spain	005	07	900-99-0011	900-99-0014	900-99-0013	900-11-0011	34
Sweden+	018	009	020-795-611	020-795-922	020-799-011	020-880-000	46
Switzerland	114	00	155-00-11	155-0222	155-9777	155-1610	41
Taiwan	100	002	0080-10288-0	Airport phones only	0080-14-0877	080-231-831	886
Thailand	100	001	001-999-1111	na	001-999-13-877	001-800-66-1234	66
Tunisia	na	00	na	na	na		216
Turkey	528-23-03	99	919-8001-2277	99-8001-1177	99800-1-4477		90
United Arab Emirates	150 & 160	00		800-1-0010	800-1-0011	na	
Uruguay	007 & 02007	00	00-0410	000-412	000417		
U.S.A.	0	011	-	-	-		
Russia	339-62-66 &	810	na	na	na		7
Vahcau	271-90-20	na	na	na	na		
Vatican City	na	na	na	172-1022	172-1877	1678-32-016	na
Venezuela	122	00	Designated	na	800-1111-0	na	na
Yugoslavia	981	na	99-38-0011	na	na	na	na
Zambia	na	na	00-899	na	na	na	na
Zimbabwe	na	na	110-899	na	na	na	na

+	Public phones require deposit
*	Wait for second dial tone
**	Use 02-64 for locations outside Managua.
xxx	Access only for locations in the geographic area formerly known as West Germany.

Note:

New access numbers are continually being added by the long distance carriers mentioned in this chapter.
distance carriers.

For up-to-date information on available countries access numbers and rates, call their customer service at:

AT&T: 1-800-874-4000, when overseas call: (412) 553-7458, collect.
MCI: 1-800-275-0200
Sprint: 1-800-888-0800
METROMEDIA: 1-800-275-0200

[See Appedix 5E for a complete listing of country codes, including codes of major cities.]

Chapter 43

Climates of the World

[The Information in this chapter is reprinted verbatim from a bulletin issued by the
U.S. Department of Commerce, Environmental Science Services Administration, Environmental Data Service.]

- - - -

Temperature Distribution

The distribution of temperature over the world and its variations through the year depend primarily on the amount of distribution of the radiant energy received from the sun in different regions. This in turn depends mainly on latitude but is greatly modified by the distribution of continents and oceans, prevailing winds, oceanic circulation, topography, and other factors.

Maps showing average temperatures over the surface of the earth for January and for July are given in figures 1 and 2.

In the winter of the Northern Hemisphere, it will be noted, the poleward temperature gradient (that is, the rate of fall in temperature) north of latitude 15° is very steep over the interior of North America. This is shown by the fact that the lines indicating changes in temperature come very close together. The temperature gradient is also steep toward the cold pole over Asia-the area marked -50°. In western Europe, to the east of the Atlantic Ocean and the North Atlantic Drift, and in the region of prevailing westerly winds, the temperature gradient is much more gradual, as indicated by the fact that the isotherms, or lines of equal temperature, are far apart. In the winter of the Southern Hemisphere, as shown on the map for July (a winter month south of the Equator), the temperature gradient toward the South Pole is very gradual, and the isothermal deflections from the east-west direction (that is, the dipping of the isothermal lines) are of minor importance because continental effects are largely absent.

In the summers of the two hemispheres-July in the north and January in the south-the temperature gradients poleward are very much diminished as compared with those during the winter. This is especially marked over the middle and higher northern latitudes because of the greater warming of the extensive interiors of North America and Eurasia than of the smaller land areas in middle and higher southern latitudes.

Distribution of Precipitation

Whether precipitation (see the map, fig. 3) occurs as rain or snow or in the rarer forms of hail or sleet depends largely on the temperature climate, which may be influenced more by elevation than by latitude, as in the case of the perpetually snowcapped mountain peaks and glaciers on the Equator in both South America and Africa.

The quantity of precipitation is governed by the amount of water vapor in the air and the nature of the process that leads to its condensation into liquid or solid form through cooling. Air may ascend to great elevations through local convection, as in thunderstorms and in tropical regions generally; it may be forced up over topographical elevations across the prevailing wind direction, as on the southern or windward slopes of the Himalayas in the path of the southwest monsoon of India; or it may ascend more or less gradually in migratory low-pressure formations such as those that govern the main features of weather in the United States.

The areas of heaviest precipitation on the map (fig. 3) are generally located, as would be expected, in tropical regions, where because of the high temperature the greatest amount of water vapor may be present in the atmosphere and the greatest evaporation takes place-although only where conditions favor condensation can rainfall occur. Outstanding exceptions are certain regions in high latitudes, such as southern Alaska, western Norway, and southern Chile, where relatively warm, moist winds from the sea undergo forced ascent over considerable elevations.

In marked contrast to the rainy regions just named are the dry polar regions, where the water-vapor content of the air is always very low because of the low temperature and very limited evaporation. The dry areas in the subtropical belts of high atmospheric pressure (in the vicinity of latitude 30° on all continents, and especially from the extreme western Sahara
over a broad, somewhat broken belt to the Desert of Gobi) and the arid strips on the lee sides of mountains

on whose windward slopes precipitation is heavy to excessive, are caused by conditions which, even though the temperature may be high, are unfavorable to the condensation of whatever water vapor may be present in the atmosphere.

In the tables following are data on mean maximum and minimum temperatures for January, April, July, and October, with extremes recorded in the period of record, and monthly and annual precipitation for about 800 selected stations well distributed over the earth.

North America

North America is nearly all within middle and northern latitudes. Consequently it has a large central area in which the continental type of climate with marked seasonal temperature extremes is to be found.

Along the coasts of northern Alaska, western Canada, and the northwestern part of the United States, moderate midsummer temperatures are in marked contrast to those prevailing in the interior east of the mountains. (Note, for example, the great southward dip of the 60° isotherm along the west coast in fig. 2.) Again, the mild midwinter temperatures in the coastal areas stand out against the severe conditions to be found from the Great Lakes region northward and northwestward (fig. 1).

In the West Indian region, temperature conditions are subtropical; and in Mexico and Central America, climatic zones depend on elevation, ranging from subtropical to temperate in the higher levels.

The prevailing westerly wind movement carries the continental type of climate eastward over the United States, so that the region of maritime climate along the Atlantic Ocean is very narrow.

The northern areas are, of course, very cold; but the midwinter low temperatures fall far short of the records set in the cold-pole area of northeastern Siberia, where the vast extent of land becomes much colder than the partly ice-covered area of northern Canada.

From the Aleutian Peninsula to northern California west of the crests of the mountains, there is a narrow strip where annual precipitation is over 40 inches; it exceeds 100 inches locally on the coast of British Columbia (see fig. 3). East of this belt there is an abrupt fall-off in precipitation to less than 20 inches annually over the western half of the continent from Lower California northward, and to even less than 5 inches in parts of what used to be called the "Great American Desert," in the southwestern part of the United States.

In the eastern part of the continent-that is, from the southeastern part of the United States northeastward to Newfoundland-the average annual precipitation is more than 40 inches. Rainfall in the West Indies, southern Mexico, and Central America is generally abundant. It is very spotty, however, varying widely even within short distances, especially from the windward to the leeward sides of the mountains.

South America

A large part of South America lies within the Tropics and has a characteristically tropical climate. The remaining rather narrow southern portion is not subject to the extremes of heat and cold that are found where wide land areas give full sway to the continental type of climate with its hot summers and cold winters, as in North America and Asia. Temperature anomalies unusual for a given latitude are to be found mainly at the elevated levels of the Andean region stretching from the Isthmus of Panama to Cape Horn.

The Antarctic Current and its cool Humboldt branch skirting the western shores northward to the Equator, together with the prevailing on-shore winds, exert a strong cooling influence over the coastal regions of all the western countries of South America except Colombia. On the east the southerly moving Brazilian current from tropical waters has the opposite, or warming, effect except along southern Argentina.

In the northern countries of South America the sharply contrasted dry and wet seasons are related to the regime of the trade winds. In the dry season (corresponding to winter in the Northern Hemisphere) these winds sweep the entire region, while the wet season (corresponding to summer in the Northern Hemisphere) calms and variable winds prevail. In the basin of the Amazon River the rainfall is related to the equatorial belt of low pressure and to the trade winds, which give the maximum amounts of rainfall in the extreme west, where they ascend the Andean slopes.

The desert areas on the west coast of South America, extending from the Equator southward to the latitude of Santiago, are due primarily to the cold Humboldt or Peruvian Current and upwelling cold coastal water. The moist, cool ocean air is warmed in passing over the land, with a consequent decrease in relative humidity, so that the dew point is not reached and condensation of vapor does not occur until the incoming air has reached high elevations in the Andes, where temperatures are very much lower than along the coast.

In southern Chile the summer season has moderate rainfall, and winters are excessively wet. The conditions that prevail farther north are not present here, and condensation of moisture from the ocean progresses from the shores up to the crests of the Andes. By the time the air passes these elevations, however, the moisture has been so depleted that the winds on the leeward slopes are dry, becoming more and more so as they are warmed on reaching lower levels. The mountains can be looked upon as casting a great "rain shadow"-an area of little rain-over southern Argentina.

Europe

In Europe there is no extensive north-south mountain system such as is found in both of the Americas, and the general east-west direction of the ranges in the south allows the conditions in the maritime west to change rather gradually toward Asia. Generally rainfall is heaviest on the western coasts, where locally it exceeds 60 inches annually, and diminishes toward the east-except in the elevated Alpine and Caucasus regions-to less than 20 inches in eastern Russia. There is a well-defined rain shadow in Scandinavia, with over 60 inches of rain in western Norway and less than 20 inches in eastern Sweden.

Over much of Europe rainfall is both abundant and rather evenly distributed throughout the year. The chief feature of seasonal distribution of precipitation is the marked winter maximum and the extremely dry, even droughty, summers in most of the Mediterranean lands.

Isothermal lines have the general direction of the parallels of latitude except in winter, when the waters of the western ocean, warmed by the Gulf Stream, give them a north-south trend. Generally there are no marked dips in isotherms due to elevation and continental type of climate such as are found in North America. In Scandinavia, however, the winter map shows an abrupt fall in temperature from the western coast of Norway to the eastern coast of Sweden and thence a continued fall eastward, under a type of exposure more and more continental in contrast to the oceanic exposure on the west.

Asia

The vast extent of Asia gives full opportunity for continental conditions to develop a cold area of high barometric pressure in winter and a low-pressure, hot area in summer, the former northeast of the Himalayas and the latter stretching widely from west to east in the latitude of northern India. (See the area marked 90° on the map, fig. 2.) These distributions of pressure give to India the well-known monsoon seasons, during which the wind comes from one direction for several months, and also affect the yearly distribution of rainfall over eastern Asia.

In winter, the air circulation is outward over the land

from the cold pole, and precipitation is very light over the entire continent. In summer, on the contrary, there is an inflow of air from the oceans; even the southeast trade winds flow across the Equator and merge into the southwest monsoon which crosses India. This usually produces abundant rain over most of that country, with excessively heavy amounts when the air is forced to rise, even to moderate elevations, in its passage over the land. At Cherrapunji (4,455 feet), on the southern side of the Khasi Hills in Assam, the average rainfall in a winter month is about 1 inch, while in both June and July it is approximately 100 inches. However, this heavy summer rainfall meets an impassable barrier in the Himalaya Mountains, while the much lighter summer monsoon rainfall over Japan and eastern Asia does not extend far into China because of lesser elevations. Consequently, while the southeast quadrant of Asia, including the East Indies, also with monsoon winds, has heavy to excessive annual rainfall, the remainder of the continent is dry, with vast areas receiving less than 10 inches annually.

North of the Himalayas the low plains are excessively cold in winter and temperatures rise rather high in summer. At Verkhoyansk in the cold-pole area, and north of the Arctic Circle, the mean temperature in January is about -59°F, and in July approximately 64°; the extreme records are a maximum of 98°, from readings at 1 p.m., and a minimum of -90°.

In southwestern Asia the winter temperature control is still the interior high-pressure area, and temperatures are generally low, especially at high elevations; in summer at low elevations excessively high maxima are recorded, as, for example, in the Tigris-Euphrates Valley.

Africa

Africa, like South America, lies very largely within the Tropics. There too, temperature distribution is determined mainly by altitude. Moreover, along the southern portion of the western coast the cool Benguela Current moves northward, and on the eastern coast are the warm tropical currents of the Indian Ocean, which create conditions closely paralleling those found around the South American Continent. In the strictly tropical areas of Africa conditions are characterized by prevailing low barometric pressure, with convectional rainfall and alternate northward and southward movement of the heat equator, while in both the north and the south the ruling influences are the belts of high barometric pressure.

Except in the Atlas Mountains in the northwest where the considerable elevations set up a barrier in the path of trade winds and produce moderate rainfall, the desert conditions typified by the Sahara extend from the Atlantic to the Red Sea and from the Mediterranean southward well beyond the northern Tropic to about the latitude of southern Arabia.

South of the Sahara, rainfall increases rapidly, becoming abundant to heavy from the west coast to the central lakes, with annual maxima of over 80 inches in the regions bordering the eastern and western extremes of the Guinea coast. This marked increase in precipitation does not extend to the eastern portion of the middle region of the continent, where the annual amounts received are below 40 inches and decrease to less than 10 inches on the coasts of Somalia. Also to the south of the central rainy area there is a rapid fall in precipitation toward the arid regions of Southwest Africa, where conditions are similar to those in Somalia.

The heavy rainfall over sections of Ethiopia from June to October, when more than 40 inches fall and bring the overflowing of the otherwise arid Nile Valley, is one of the earth's outstanding features of seasonal distribution of rainfall.

Moist equatorial climate is typified by conditions in the Democratic Republic of the Congo; arid torrid climate by those of the United Arab Republic and the Sahara; and moderate plateau climate by those found in parts of Ethiopia, Kenya and Tanzania.

Australia

In the southern winter the high-pressure belt crosses the interior of Australia, and all except the southernmost parts of the continent are dry. In summer, on the other hand, this pressure belt has moved south of the continent, still giving dry conditions over the southern and western areas. Thus the total annual precipitation is less than 20 inches except in the extreme southwest and in a strip circling from southeast to northwest. The average annual precipitation is even less than 10 inches in a large south-central area.

In the south the winter precipitation is the cyclonic type; the heavy summer rains of the north are of monsoon origin; and those of the eastern borders are in large part orographic, owing to the presence of the highlands in the immediate vicinity of the coasts. In the outer border of the rainfall strip along the coastal region, the mean annual rainfall is over 40 inches and in many localities over 60 inches. This is true for the monsoon rains in the north.

Because of the location of Australia, on both sides of the southern Tropic, temperatures far below freezing are to be found only in a small part of the continent, in the south at high elevations. In the arid interior extreme maximum temperatures are very high, ranking with those of the hottest regions of the earth.

TEMPERATURE AND PRECIPITATION DATA FOR REPRESENTATIVE WORLD-WIDE STATIONS

Country and Station	Latitude	Longitude	Elevation (feet)	Length of record (yrs)	Jan max	Jan min	Apr max	Apr min	Jul max	Jul min	Oct max	Oct min	Extreme max	Extreme min	Length of record (yrs)	Jan	Feb	Mar	Apr	May	Jun	Jul	Aug	Sep	Oct	Nov	Dec	Year
United States (Conterminous):													**NORTH AMERICA**														
Albuquerque, N. Mex.	35 03N	106 37W	5,311	30	46	24	69	42	91	66	71	45	104	-16	30	0.4	0.4	0.5	0.5	0.8	0.6	1.2	1.3	1.0	0.8	0.4	0.5	8.4
Asheville, N.C.	35 26N	82 32W	2,140	30	48	28	67	42	84	61	68	45	99	-7	30	4.0	4.2	4.8	3.7	3.5	3.5	2.9	3.0	3.6	3.1	2.8	3.6	48.1
Atlanta, Ga.	33 39N	84 26W	1,010	30	52	37	70	50	87	71	74	52	103	-9	30	4.4	4.5	5.4	4.6	3.2	3.8	4.7	3.6	3.3	2.4	3.0	4.4	47.2
Austin, Tex.	30 18N	97 42W	597	30	60	41	78	57	95	74	82	60	109	-10	30	2.1	2.3	2.1	3.5	3.4	4.0	2.2	2.2	3.7	2.8	2.1	2.3	32.5
Birmingham, Ala.	33 34N	86 45W	620	30	57	36	78	52	93	71	79	53	107	-10	30	5.0	5.3	6.0	4.5	3.4	4.0	5.2	4.3	3.5	2.5	3.5	5.3	53.1
Bismarck, N. Dak.	46 46N	100 45W	1,647	30	20	0	58	34	85	58	59	34	114	-45	30	0.5	0.5	0.8	1.3	2.0	3.5	2.2	1.7	1.2	0.8	0.6	0.4	15.2
Bismarck, N. Dak.	46 46N	100 45W	1,647	30	22	2	55	31	85	58	59	34	114	-45	30	0.5	0.5	0.8	1.3	2.0	3.5	2.2	1.7	1.2	0.8	0.6	0.4	15.2
Boise, Idaho	43 34N	116 13W	2,838	30	36	21	63	37	91	59	65	38	112	-28	30	1.3	1.3	1.3	1.2	1.3	0.9	0.2	0.2	0.3	0.8	1.2	1.7	11.4
Boise, Idaho	43 34N	116 13W	2,838	30	36	22	63	36	91	59	65	38	111	-23	30	1.6	1.2	1.2	1.2	1.3	1.0	0.2	0.2	0.3	1.0	1.3	1.7	11.4
Brownsville, Tex.	25 54N	97 26W	16	30	70	51	82	67	93	76	85	67	106	16	30	1.3	1.3	1.0	1.6	2.5	2.9	1.8	2.8	5.0	3.5	1.3	1.0	26.9
Buffalo, N.Y.	42 56N	78 44W	705	30	31	18	53	34	80	59	60	43	99	-21	30	2.6	2.4	2.9	3.0	3.0	2.4	3.1	3.2	3.1	3.0	3.0	3.0	35.6
Cheyenne, Wyo.	41 09N	104 49W	6,126	30	37	14	55	30	84	55	63	32	100	-38	30	0.4	0.6	1.2	2.0	2.5	2.0	1.8	1.4	1.1	0.6	0.6	0.5	15.0
Chicago, Ill.	41 47N	87 45W	607	30	33	19	57	40	84	67	63	41	105	-27	30	1.9	1.6	2.7	3.0	3.7	3.9	3.4	3.2	3.2	2.8	2.2	1.8	33.2
Des Moines, Iowa	41 32N	93 39W	938	30	29	11	61	41	88	66	66	43	110	-30	30	1.2	1.2	2.1	2.5	4.1	4.7	3.1	3.7	3.2	2.1	1.8	1.1	30.5
Dodge City, Kans.	37 46N	99 58W	2,582	30	42	20	66	40	93	66	69	44	109	-26	30	0.4	0.7	1.2	1.8	3.2	3.0	3.1	2.4	2.6	1.4	0.6	0.5	19.2
El Paso, Tex.	31 48N	106 24W	3,918	30	56	29	78	49	95	69	79	50	109	-8	30	0.4	0.4	0.3	0.2	0.3	0.7	1.3	1.2	1.4	0.9	0.3	0.5	8.0
Indianapolis, Ind.	39 44N	86 17W	792	30	37	21	61	43	86	64	67	45	107	-25	30	3.0	2.7	3.5	3.6	4.0	4.0	3.1	2.4	2.6	2.6	3.1	2.7	39.2
Jacksonville, Fla.	30 30N	81 42W	742	30	67	45	80	58	92	72	79	62	105	10	30	2.9	3.5	3.6	3.5	3.5	6.3	6.9	6.9	7.7	5.2	1.7	2.6	54.2
Kansas City, Mo.	39 07N	94 36W	742	30	40	23	65	45	92	71	70	49	113	-22	30	1.4	1.4	2.5	3.4	4.4	5.0	3.2	3.8	4.1	3.0	1.7	1.2	34.2
Las Vegas, Nev.	36 05N	115 10W	2,162	30	56	33	78	51	104	76	80	53	117	8	30	0.5	0.4	0.3	0.2	0.1	0.1	0.5	0.5	0.3	0.2	0.4	0.4	3.8
Los Angeles, Calif.	33 56N	118 23W	97	30	66	45	68	52	83	62	76	57	110	23	30	2.7	2.4	1.8	1.1	0.1	*	2.4	3.0	2.6	2.3	1.1	2.4	12.8
Louisville, Ky.	38 11N	85 44W	477	30	44	27	66	45	89	67	70	46	107	-20	30	4.1	3.3	4.6	3.8	3.9	4.0	3.7	3.1	3.0	2.3	2.8	3.7	41.4
Miami, Fla.	25 48N	80 16W	7	30	76	58	83	66	89	75	85	71	100	28	30	2.0	2.0	1.9	3.1	6.1	9.0	6.8	7.0	9.5	8.2	2.8	1.8	59.9
Minneapolis, Minn.	44 53N	93 13W	834	30	22	8	56	33	84	61	61	37	108	-34	30	0.7	0.8	1.5	1.9	3.2	4.0	3.3	3.2	2.7	1.6	0.9	0.7	24.9
Missoula, Mont.	46 55N	114 05W	3,190	30	28	10	58	31	84	50	58	30	105	-33	30	1.1	0.9	0.5	1.0	1.7	1.9	0.7	0.9	1.1	1.0	1.1	1.4	12.9
Nashville, Tenn.	36 07N	86 41W	590	30	49	31	71	48	91	70	74	49	107	-15	30	5.3	4.2	5.3	3.9	3.8	3.3	3.7	3.5	2.3	2.3	3.3	4.2	45.2
New Orleans, La.	29 59N	90 15W	3	30	64	45	78	60	90	74	79	61	102	7	30	4.6	4.4	5.3	4.4	4.6	4.4	6.7	5.3	4.4	2.9	3.3	4.1	53.7
New York, N.Y.	40 47N	73 58W	132	30	40	27	60	43	85	68	66	50	106	-15	30	3.3	3.3	3.8	3.4	3.4	3.1	4.2	4.1	3.9	3.1	3.3	3.3	42.3
Oklahoma City, Okla.	35 24N	97 36W	1,285	30	48	28	71	49	93	72	74	51	113	-17	30	1.4	1.4	2.0	3.1	5.2	4.3	2.4	2.5	3.6	2.5	1.6	1.4	30.9
Phoenix, Ariz.	33 26N	112 01W	1,117	30	64	35	84	52	105	76	87	55	118	16	30	0.7	0.7	0.7	0.3	0.1	0.1	0.8	1.3	0.7	0.5	0.6	0.9	7.3
Pittsburgh, Pa.	40 27N	80 00W	747	30	40	25	62	42	85	64	66	45	103	-20	30	3.0	2.7	3.4	3.2	3.8	3.6	3.6	3.3	2.7	2.3	2.3	2.5	36.9
Portland, Maine	43 39N	70 19W	47	30	32	12	53	35	79	57	60	42	103	-39	30	4.1	4.2	4.3	3.7	3.5	3.0	2.8	2.5	3.5	3.6	5.3	4.4	42.9
Portland, Oreg.	45 36N	122 36W	21	30	44	34	62	44	79	56	64	46	107	-3	30	5.4	4.2	3.8	2.1	2.0	1.7	0.4	0.7	1.6	3.6	5.3	6.4	37.2
Reno, Nev.	39 30N	119 47W	4,404	30	45	16	64	30	91	46	70	30	105	-19	30	1.2	1.0	0.7	0.5	0.5	0.4	0.2	0.2	0.2	0.5	0.6	1.1	7.2
Salt Lake City, Utah	40 46N	111 58W	4,220	30	37	18	61	37	92	61	66	38	107	-30	30	1.3	1.2	1.6	2.1	1.4	1.0	0.7	0.7	0.5	1.2	1.3	1.3	14.1
San Francisco, Calif.	37 37N	122 23W	8	30	55	42	64	46	71	54	68	51	98	20	30	4.4	3.0	2.6	1.5	0.5	0.1	*	0.1	0.2	1.1	2.5	4.1	18.7
Sault Ste. Marie, Mich.	46 28N	84 22W	721	30	23	8	46	30	76	55	55	38	98	-37	30	1.8	1.5	1.8	2.2	2.8	3.3	2.5	2.9	3.8	2.8	3.4	2.3	31.3
Seattle, Wash.	47 27N	122 18W	400	30	44	33	58	40	76	54	60	45	100	0	30	4.2	3.0	2.4	1.6	1.6	1.6	0.8	0.9	2.1	4.0	5.4	6.3	39.0
Sheridan, Wyo.	44 46N	106 58W	3,964	30	33	9	58	31	87	56	62	33	106	-41	30	0.7	0.7	1.4	1.9	2.6	2.5	1.2	0.9	1.2	1.1	0.8	0.6	15.9
Spokane, Wash.	47 38N	117 32W	2,356	30	31	19	59	36	87	55	60	38	108	-30	30	2.4	1.9	1.4	0.9	1.2	1.4	0.4	0.6	0.8	1.6	2.4	2.4	17.2
Washington, D.C.	38 51N	77 03W	14	30	44	30	66	46	87	69	68	50	106	-15	30	3.0	3.0	3.7	3.2	4.1	3.2	4.2	4.9	3.8	3.1	2.8	2.8	40.8
Wilmington, N.C.	34 16N	77 55W	28	30	58	37	74	51	89	71	76	55	104	5	30	2.9	3.4	4.0	2.9	3.5	4.3	7.7	6.9	6.3	3.0	3.1	3.4	51.4

See footnotes at end of table.

TEMPERATURE AND PRECIPITATION DATA FOR REPRESENTATIVE WORLD-WIDE STATIONS

Country and Station	Latitude	Longitude	Elevation (feet)	Jan	Feb	Mar	Apr	May	June	July	Aug	Sept	Oct	Nov	Dec	Year
United States, Alaska:																
Anchorage	61 13N	149 52W	85	0.8	0.7	0.5	0.4	0.5	1.0	1.9	2.6	2.3	1.9	1.0	0.9	14.7
Annette	55 08N	131 34W	110	11.4	8.5	9.6	9.1	7.1	5.7	6.0	7.5	12.9	16.9	14.7	12.1	118.5
Barrow	71 18N	156 47W	31	0.2	0.2	0.1	0.1	0.1	0.4	0.8	0.9	0.6	0.5	0.2	0.2	4.3
Bethel	60 47N	161 48W	125	1.1	1.1	1.0	0.6	1.0	1.2	1.8	2.2	2.6	1.5	1.1	1.0	14.4
Cold Bay	55 12N	162 43W	96	2.3	3.2	1.8	1.3	2.3	2.0	1.8	4.3	4.3	4.6	3.8	2.6	34.5
Fairbanks	64 49N	147 52W	436	0.6	0.4	0.2	0.3	0.7	1.4	1.9	2.0	1.1	0.9	0.7	0.5	11.3
Juneau	58 22N	134 35W	12	4.0	3.3	3.3	2.9	3.2	3.4	4.5	5.0	6.7	8.3	5.1	4.2	54.7
King Salmon	58 41N	156 39W	49	1.0	1.0	0.9	0.8	0.7	0.9	2.3	3.8	3.2	1.7	1.3	1.0	19.4
Nome	64 30N	165 26W	13	0.9	0.9	0.8	0.7	0.6	1.0	2.3	3.1	2.4	1.2	1.1	1.0	17.9
St. Paul Island	57 09N	170 13W	30	2.2	2.1	2.0	1.0	1.0	1.2	1.5	2.0	2.1	2.8	2.3	2.1	23.8
Shemya	52 43N	174 06E	122	2.7	2.2	2.4	1.6	1.3	1.5	1.2	1.6	2.7	2.8	2.7	2.1	27.4
Yakutat	59 31N	139 40W	28	10.9	8.7	8.7	4.2	4.0	3.1	4.4	10.9	16.6	19.6	11.1	12.3	132.0
Canada:																
Aklavik, N.W.T.	68 14N	135 00W	30	0.5	0.4	0.4	0.5	0.5	0.8	1.4	1.1	0.9	0.9	0.8	0.4	9.0
Alert, N.W.T.	82 31N	62 20W	95	0.3	0.3	0.2	0.3	0.3	0.5	0.9	1.1	0.9	0.5	0.2	0.4	6.7
Calgary, Alta.	51 06N	114 01W	3,540	0.8	0.8	0.8	1.2	2.3	3.1	2.5	2.3	1.2	0.7	0.7	0.7	16.7
Charlottetown, P.E.I.	46 17N	63 08W	181	3.0	2.7	2.8	2.7	3.2	3.1	3.2	3.4	3.4	3.5	3.4	4.0	39.8
Chatham, N.B.	47 00N	65 27W	109	3.4	2.7	3.0	2.9	3.2	3.6	3.9	3.4	3.3	4.1	3.2	3.2	40.8
Churchill, Man.	58 45N	94 04W	94	0.6	0.6	0.9	0.9	0.9	1.8	2.2	2.7	2.3	1.4	1.0	0.7	18.0
Edmonton, Alta.	53 34N	113 31W	2,219	0.9	0.7	0.7	0.9	1.9	3.2	3.3	2.4	1.3	0.8	0.9	0.9	16.3
Fort Nelson, B.C.	58 50N	122 35W	1,253	0.9	0.8	0.7	0.7	1.4	2.2	2.4	2.0	1.8	1.1	1.2	1.2	16.3
Fort Simpson, N.W.T.	61 45N	121 14W	554	0.7	0.7	0.8	0.7	1.2	1.3	1.5	1.3	1.0	0.9	0.9	1.0	13.1
Frobisher Bay, N.W.T.	63 45N	68 33W	110	0.7	0.9	0.8	0.8	0.6	1.0	2.0	2.1	1.8	1.5	1.0	1.0	13.1
Gander, Nfld.	48 57N	54 34W	496	4.4	3.3	2.8	2.6	2.6	3.5	3.6	3.4	4.1	4.2	4.1	3.7	39.6
Halifax, N.S.	44 39N	63 34W	83	5.4	4.4	4.5	4.1	4.1	4.0	3.3	3.4	3.4	5.3	5.4	5.6	55.7
Kapuskasing, Ont.	49 25N	82 28W	743	2.0	1.9	1.6	1.6	2.6	3.3	3.2	3.4	3.7	2.4	2.4	1.9	27.5
Knob Lake, Que.	54 48N	66 49W	1,712	2.1	1.9	2.6	2.7	2.5	3.9	3.7	3.7	3.2	3.5	3.1	2.7	29.7
Montreal, Que.	45 30N	73 34W	187	3.8	3.3	3.3	3.0	3.1	3.2	3.6	3.4	3.4	3.6	3.4	3.6	40.8
North Bay, Ont.	46 21N	79 25W	1,216	2.1	1.8	2.4	2.4	2.5	3.1	3.3	2.7	3.7	3.2	3.1	2.1	30.8
Ottawa, Ont.	45 20N	75 40W	339	2.9	2.2	2.6	2.7	2.5	3.1	3.4	2.6	3.3	2.9	2.9	2.6	34.3
Penticton, B.C.	49 28N	119 36W	1,129	1.1	0.7	0.7	0.8	1.1	1.2	0.6	0.8	1.0	1.1	0.9	1.1	10.8
Port Arthur, Ont.	48 22N	89 19W	644	1.8	1.4	1.4	1.3	2.6	2.8	2.6	2.8	2.9	2.5	1.5	0.9	23.8
Prince George, B.C.	53 53N	122 41W	2,218	2.0	1.8	1.0	0.9	1.3	2.1	2.0	2.8	2.0	2.0	1.9	1.9	19.9
Prince Rupert, B.C.	54 17N	130 23W	170	9.8	8.6	6.7	5.8	4.6	3.7	4.0	4.4	7.0	12.0	13.3	11.2	95.3
Quebec, Que.	46 48N	71 23W	239	3.5	2.7	3.0	2.4	3.1	3.8	4.0	3.6	3.4	3.4	3.2	3.2	39.8
Regina, Sask.	50 26N	104 40W	1,884	0.5	0.5	0.7	0.9	1.9	2.5	2.4	1.9	1.3	0.7	0.6	0.6	14.7
Resolute, N.W.T.	74 43N	94 59W	119	0.1	0.1	0.2	0.2	0.3	0.3	0.9	0.9	0.8	0.5	0.2	0.1	3.5
St. John, N.B.	45 17N	66 04W	220	5.3	4.6	3.8	3.8	3.9	3.6	3.6	4.0	3.7	4.8	5.7	5.8	42.6
St. Johns, Nfld.	47 32N	52 44W	211	5.1	4.8	4.1	3.2	3.1	3.1	3.1	4.0	3.8	5.7	6.0	5.3	53.1
Saskatoon, Sask.	52 08N	106 38W	1,690	0.5	0.5	0.7	0.7	1.4	2.2	2.0	1.5	1.0	0.6	0.6	0.6	14.6
The Pas, Man.	53 49N	101 15W	890	0.5	0.5	0.6	0.8	1.4	2.2	2.7	2.4	2.0	1.2	1.0	1.0	15.5
Toronto, Ont.	43 40N	79 24W	379	2.7	2.5	2.7	2.5	2.8	2.9	3.0	2.7	2.9	2.4	2.6	2.6	32.2
Vancouver, B.C.	49 17N	123 05W	127	8.6	5.8	5.0	3.3	2.8	2.5	1.2	1.7	3.6	5.8	6.3	8.8	57.4

TEMPERATURE AND PRECIPITATION DATA FOR REPRESENTATIVE WORLD-WIDE STATIONS

Country and Station	Latitude	Longitude	Elevation (feet)	Extreme High (°F)	Extreme Low (°F)	Annual Precip. (in.)
Whitehorse, Y.T.	60 43N	135 04W	2,303	91	-62	10.6
Winnipeg, Man.	49 54N	97 14W	783	108	-54	21.2
Yellow Knife, N.W.T.	62 28N	114 27W	674	90	-60	10.8
Greenland:						
Angmagssalik	65 36N	37 33W	95	77	-26	31.1
Danmarkshavn	76 46N	19 00W	7	63	-54	
Eismitte	70 53N	40 42W	9,843	27	-85	4.3
Godthaab	64 10N	51 43W	66	86	-20	23.5
Ivigtut	61 12N	48 10W	98	77	-20	44.6
Jacobshavn	69 13N	51 02W	104	61	-46	8.9
Nord	81 36N	16 40W	118	61	-60	8.0
Scoresbysund	70 29N	21 58W	56	63	-42	4.9
Thule	76 31N	68 44W	251	63	-44	9.2
Upernivik	72 47N	56 07W	59	69	-35	9.2
Mexico:						
Acapulco	16 50N	99 56W	10	97	60	55.1
Chihuahua	28 42N	105 57W	4,429	102	12	15.4
Guadalajara	20 41N	103 20W	5,194	101	23	39.7
Guaymas	27 57N	110 55W	58	108	31	9.4
La Paz	24 07N	110 17W	65	108	34	5.7
Lerdo	25 30N	103 32W	3,740	103	11	10.2
Manzanillo	19 04N	104 20W	256	103	54	39.5
Mazatlan	23 11N	106 25W	72	93	40	30.2
Merida	20 58N	89 38W	72	106	52	36.5
Mexico City	19 26N	99 04W	7,340	93	24	23.0
Monterrey	25 40N	100 18W	1,732	107	25	22.9
Salina Cruz	16 12N	95 12W	184	98	34	38.5
Tampico	22 16N	97 51W	78	104	36	44.9
Vera Cruz	19 12N	96 00W	52	98	53	65.7
CENTRAL AMERICA						
British Honduras: Belize	17 31N	88 11W	17	97	49	74.4
Canal Zone: Balboa Heights	08 57N	79 33W	118	97	63	69.7
Cristobal	09 21N	79 54W	35	97	66	130.3
Costa Rica: San Jose	09 56N	84 08W	3,760	92	49	70.8
El Salvador: San Salvador	13 42N	89 13W	2,238	105	45	70.0
Guatemala: Guatemala City	14 37N	90 31W	4,855	90	41	51.8
Honduras: Tela	15 46N	87 27W	41	96	58	96.1
WEST INDIES						
Bridgetown, Barbados	13 08N	59 36W	181	95	61	50.3
Camp Jacob, Guadeloupe	16 01N	61 42W	1,750	92	54	140.4
Ciudad Trujillo, Dominican Rep.	18 29N	69 54W	57	98	56	55.8
Fort-de-France, Martinique	14 37N	61 05W	13	96	59	80.4
Hamilton, Bermuda	32 17N	64 46W	151	94	43	57.6
Havana, Cuba	23 08N	82 21W	80	104	49	48.2
Kingston, Jamaica	17 58N	76 48W	110	97	62	31.5
La Guerite, St. Christopher (St. Kitts)	17 20N	62 45W	157	91	61	50.9
Nassau, Bahamas	17 35N	77 21W	31	94	48	46.4
Port-au-Prince, Haiti	18 40N	72 20W	121	101	57	53.3
Saint Clair, Trinidad	10 40N	61 31W	67	92	63	64.2
Saint Thomas, Virgin Is.	18 20N	64 58W	57	94	63	43.7
San Juan, Puerto Rico	18 26N	66 00W	13	94	60	64.2

403

TEMPERATURE AND PRECIPITATION DATA FOR REPRESENTATIVE WORLD-WIDE STATIONS

SOUTH AMERICA

COUNTRY AND STATION	LATITUDE	LONGITUDE	ELEVATION (FEET)	PRECIPITATION YEAR
Argentina:				
Bahia Blanca	38 43S	62 16W	95	20.6
Buenos Aires	34 35S	58 29W	89	37.4
Cipolletti	38 57S	67 59W	889	6.4
Corrientes	27 28S	58 50W	177	46.4
La Quiaca	22 06S	65 36W	11,345	12.3
Mendoza	32 53S	68 49W	2,625	7.5
Parana	31 44S	60 31W	210	35.0
Puerto Madryn	42 47S	65 01W	33	7.0
Santa Cruz	50 01S	68 32W	39	5.3
Santiago del Estero	27 46S	64 18W	653	20.4
Ushuaia	54 50S	68 20W	26	19.9
Bolivia:				
Concepcion	16 15S	62 03W	1,607	38.6
La Paz	16 30S	68 08W	12,001	23.4
Sucre	19 03S	65 17W	9,344	27.8
Brazil:				
Barra do Corda	05 35S	45 22W	266	47.2
Bela Vista	22 06S	56 22W	525	52.2
Belem	01 27S	48 29W	42	96.0
Brasilia	15 51S	47 56W	3,481	54.0
Conceicao do Araguaia	08 15S	49 12W	53	66.2
Corumba	19 00S	57 39W	381	48.5
Florianopolis	27 35S	48 33W	96	53.1
Goias	15 58S	50 04W	1,706	64.8
Guarapuava	25 16S	51 30W	3,592	65.8
Manaus	03 08S	60 01W	144	71.3
Natal	05 46S	35 12W	52	54.2
Parana	12 26S	48 04W	853	62.1
Porto Alegre	30 02S	51 13W	33	49.6
Quixeramobim	05 12S	39 18W	653	29.4
Recife	08 03S	34 53W	97	42.6
Rio de Janeiro	22 55S	43 12W	201	74.8
Salvador (Bahia)	13 00S	38 30W	154	77.9
Santarem	02 30S	54 42W	66	57.3
Sao Paulo	23 33S	46 39W	2,628	81.2
Sena Madureira	09 03S	68 39W	443	105.4
Uruguaiana	29 45S	57 07W	246	46.6
Chile:				
Ancud	41 47S	73 52W	184	80.1
Antofagasta	23 42S	70 24W	308	0.5
Arica	18 28S	70 20W	95	*
Cabo Raper	46 50S	75 38W	131	87.1

TEMPERATURE AND PRECIPITATION DATA FOR REPRESENTATIVE WORLD-WIDE STATIONS

COUNTRY AND STATION	LATITUDE	LONGITUDE	ELEVATION (FEET)	TEMPERATURE — EXTREME / AVERAGE DAILY (JAN, APR, JUL, OCT)	AVERAGE PRECIPITATION (JAN–DEC, YEAR)
Los Evangelistas	52 23S	75 07W	190		
Potrerillos	26 30S	69 27W	9,350		
Puerto Aisen	42 24S	72 42W	33		
Punta Arenas	53 10S	70 54W	26		
Santiago	33 27S	70 42W	1,706		
Valdivia	39 48S	73 14W	16		
Valparaiso	33 01S	71 38W	135		
Colombia:					
Andagoya	05 06N	76 40W	197		
Bogota	04 42N	74 08W	8,355		
Cartagena	10 28N	75 30W	39		
Ipiales	00 50N	77 42W	9,680		
Tumaco	01 49N	78 45W	7		
Ecuador:					
Cuenca	02 53S	78 59W	8,301		
Guayaquil	02 10S	79 53W	20		
Quito	00 08S	78 29W	9,222		
French Guiana:					
Cayenne	04 56N	52 27W	20		
Guyana:					
Georgetown	06 50N	58 12W	6		
Lethem	03 24N	59 10W	270		
Paraguay:					
Asuncion	25 17S	57 30W	456		
Bahia Negra	20 14S	58 10W	318		
Peru:					
Arequipa	16 21S	71 34W	8,660		
Cajamarca	07 09S	78 30W	8,662		
Cuzco	13 33S	71 59W	10,966		
Iquitos	03 45S	73 03W	384		
Lima	12 05S	77 03W	394		
Mollendo	17 00S	72 07W	80		
Surinam:					
Paramaribo	05 49N	55 09W	12		
Uruguay:					
Artigas	30 24S	56 28W	384		
Montevideo	34 52S	56 12W	72		
Venezuela:					
Caracas	10 30N	66 56W	3,418		
Ciudad Bolivar	08 07N	63 32W	197		
Maracaibo	10 39N	71 36W	20		
Merida	08 36N	71 10W	5,293		
Santa Elena	04 36N	61 07W	2,976		
PACIFIC ISLANDS					
Easter Is. (Isla de Pascua)	27 10S	109 26W	98		
Mas a Tierra (Juan Fernandez)	33 37S	78 52W	20		
Seymour Is. (Galapagos Is.)	00 28S	90 18W	36		
ATLANTIC ISLANDS					
Fernando de Noronha	03 50S	32 25W	148		
Cumberland Bay, South Georgia	54 16S	36 30W	8		
Laurie Is., South Orkneys	60 44S	44 44W	13		
Stanley, Falkland Isles	51 42S	57 51W	6		

See footnotes at end of table.

405

TEMPERATURE AND PRECIPITATION DATA FOR REPRESENTATIVE WORLD-WIDE STATIONS

EUROPE

Country and Station	Latitude	Longitude	Elevation (feet)	Temp Jan (rec yr)	Jan max	Jan min	Apr max	Apr min	Jul max	Jul min	Oct max	Oct min	Extreme max	Extreme min	Rec length yr	Precip rec yr	Jan	Feb	Mar	Apr	May	Jun	Jul	Aug	Sep	Oct	Nov	Dec	Year
Albania: Durres	41 19N	19 28E	23	10	51	42	63	55	83	68	74	58	95	21	10	3.0	3.3	3.9	2.2	1.6	1.9	0.5	1.9	1.7	7.1	8.5	7.3	42.9
Andorra: Les Escaldes	42 30N	01 31E	3,543	5	43	29	59	39	78	55	61	42	91	0	9	1.5	1.7	2.9	2.4	4.7	3.1	2.2	3.4	3.1	3.5	3.3	2.5	34.3
Austria: Innsbruck	47 16N	11 24E	1,909	34	34	20	60	39	78	55	55	39	97	-16	35	2.1	1.8	1.5	2.2	2.9	4.1	5.1	4.5	3.1	2.4	2.2	1.9	33.8
Vienna (Wien)	48 15N	16 22E	664	50	34	26	57	41	75	59	55	44	98	-14	100	1.5	1.4	1.8	2.0	2.8	2.7	3.0	2.7	2.0	2.0	1.9	1.8	25.6
Bulgaria: Sofiya (Sofia)	42 42N	23 20E	1,805	30	34	22	62	42	82	62	63	42	99	-17	27	1.5	1.1	1.2	2.3	3.3	3.2	2.6	2.4	1.3	2.3	1.4	1.4	25.0
Varna	43 12N	27 55E	115	30	40	30	59	43	84	67	67	50	107	-12	20	1.3	0.9	1.1	2.0	1.8	2.6	1.9	1.2	1.5	1.5	2.0	2.0	19.6
Cyprus: Nicosia	35 09N	33 17E	716	40	58	50	74	50	97	69	81	50	116	23	64	2.9	2.0	1.3	0.8	1.1	0.4	*	*	0.2	0.9	1.7	3.0	14.6
Czechoslovakia: Praha (Prague)	50 05N	14 25E	662	40	34	25	55	40	74	58	54	44	98	-16	70	0.9	0.8	1.1	1.5	2.4	2.8	2.6	2.2	1.7	1.2	1.2	0.9	19.3
Presov	49 27N	17 27E	702	20	34	25	57	38	77	57	56	40	100	-23	21	1.3	1.1	1.1	2.0	2.6	3.5	3.2	2.2	2.0	1.5	1.5	1.4	24.8
Denmark: Copenhagen (Kobenhavn)	55 41N	12 33E	43	30	36	29	50	37	72	55	53	44	91	-3	30	1.6	1.3	1.2	1.7	1.7	2.1	2.2	3.2	2.1	2.1	2.2	2.1	23.3
Aarhus	56 08N	10 12E	161	21	35	27	51	37	70	54	53	44	87	-12	21	2.3	1.5	1.4	1.8	1.2	2.2	2.5	3.3	2.6	2.6	2.5	2.1	26.6
Finland: Helsinki	60 10N	24 57E	30	20	27	17	43	31	71	57	45	37	89	-23	50	2.2	1.7	1.7	1.1	1.9	2.0	2.0	3.3	2.8	2.9	2.7	2.4	27.6
Kuusamo	65 57N	29 12E	843	20	20	2	35	18	68	50	36	30	90	-40	20	1.7	1.1	1.1	1.1	1.4	2.3	2.3	3.0	2.1	2.1	2.1	1.1	20.8
Vaasa	63 05N	21 36E	13	18	26	16	41	28	69	53	44	36	89	-29	19	1.1	0.8	0.8	1.0	1.4	2.2	2.4	3.3	2.7	2.3	1.7	1.1	19.6
France: Ajaccio (Corsica)	41 52N	08 35E	243	66	56	44	66	48	83	64	72	55	103	23	86	2.2	2.3	2.6	2.2	1.9	0.9	2.8	0.7	2.8	3.8	4.4	3.1	29.1
Bordeaux	44 50N	00 43W	157	60	48	35	63	44	80	58	71	48	102	-7	45	2.7	2.8	2.9	2.5	2.5	2.3	2.0	1.9	2.3	3.0	3.9	3.1	32.1
Brest	48 39N	04 47W	56	49	49	40	57	40	70	56	61	49	91	-4	47	3.3	2.8	2.3	2.0	1.9	2.6	2.0	1.9	3.0	3.4	4.4	3.9	34.7
Cherbourg	49 39N	01 38W	36	40	47	40	54	43	67	57	58	50	92	0	40	3.3	2.9	2.7	1.8	1.9	1.8	1.9	2.0	2.6	3.6	5.1	4.4	37.3
Lille	50 34N	03 05W	141	40	42	33	57	38	73	55	57	45	94	-14	70	2.2	1.8	1.7	2.0	2.4	2.9	2.8	3.0	3.0	3.0	3.2	3.2	37.3
Lyon	45 42N	04 47E	938	72	41	31	61	42	80	58	58	43	105	-13	107	1.4	1.4	2.0	2.4	2.8	2.9	1.9	2.1	2.6	3.0	2.6	2.4	28.8
Marseille	43 18N	05 23E	246	72	53	38	64	46	78	63	66	53	101	1	102	1.5	1.0	1.8	2.0	1.9	0.6	0.6	0.9	2.0	3.7	2.6	1.9	23.2
Paris	48 49N	02 29E	164	66	42	32	60	41	76	55	59	44	105	-1	118	1.5	1.2	1.5	1.7	2.0	2.0	2.1	2.0	3.1	2.2	2.0	1.9	22.3
Strasbourg	48 35N	07 46E	465	20	40	31	59	40	76	57	58	43	101	-7	20	1.5	1.1	1.7	2.6	3.4	3.1	3.4	2.9	2.0	2.2	1.9	1.9	22.5
Toulouse	43 33N	01 23E	538	47	47	35	62	43	82	59	66	48	111	1	47	1.9	1.7	2.3	2.7	2.9	2.4	1.5	2.4	2.4	2.2	2.4	2.3	26.7
Germany: Berlin	52 27N	13 18E	187	50	35	26	55	38	74	55	55	41	96	-15	40	1.9	1.6	1.5	1.7	1.9	2.3	3.1	2.2	1.9	1.7	1.9	1.9	23.1
Bremen	53 05N	08 47E	52	37	37	29	53	38	71	55	56	43	94	-7	80	2.1	1.9	1.6	1.5	2.1	2.6	3.2	2.6	2.1	2.2	2.0	2.0	26.0
Frankfurt A/M	50 07N	08 40E	338	50	37	29	58	41	75	56	56	43	100	-4	80	1.7	1.3	1.6	2.0	2.0	2.5	2.8	2.6	2.1	2.1	2.1	2.0	26.1
Hamburg	53 33N	09 58E	66	50	35	28	52	37	69	55	54	43	92	-14	80	2.1	1.4	1.9	1.8	3.7	4.6	4.7	4.2	2.5	2.1	2.1	2.0	28.9
Munchen (Munich)	48 09N	11 34E	1,739	42	33	23	56	37	72	54	54	39	96	-17	80	2.6	1.9	1.9	2.7	3.3	3.3	3.3	4.2	2.4	2.7	1.9	2.4	34.1
Munster	51 58N	07 38E	207	50	35	29	56	38	73	56	55	43	99	-18	80	2.6	2.0	1.8	2.0	2.2	2.5	3.1	3.1	2.1	2.7	2.9	2.9	30.5
Nurnberg	49 27N	11 03E	1,050	50	35	26	56	38	74	55	55	41	99	-18	80	1.5	1.2	1.3	1.7	2.2	2.5	3.1	3.0	2.1	2.2	1.7	1.7	24.4
Gibraltar: Windmill Hill	36 06N	05 21W	400	12	58	50	64	55	77	70	66	61	97	35	12	4.6	3.4	3.7	2.5	1.4	0.2	*	0.1	0.8	3.5	4.1	5.4	29.7

TEMPERATURE AND PRECIPITATION DATA FOR REPRESENTATIVE WORLD-WIDE STATIONS

COUNTRY AND STATION	LATITUDE	LONGITUDE	ELEVATION (feet)	TEMPERATURE — AVERAGE DAILY JAN max	JAN min	APR max	APR min	JUL max	JUL min	OCT max	OCT min	EXTREME high	EXTREME low	LENGTH OF RECORD (years)	PRECIPITATION JAN	FEB	MAR	APR	MAY	JUN	JUL	AUG	SEP	OCT	NOV	DEC	YEAR
Greece:																										
Athinai (Athens)	37 58N	23 43E	351	54	42	67	52	90	72	74	60	109	20	80	2.2	1.6	1.4	0.8	0.8	0.6	0.4	0.4	0.7	1.7	2.8	2.8	15.8
Iraklion (Crete)	35 20N	25 08E	98	60	48	67	54	85	71	77	62	104	30	20	3.7	3.9	2.7	1.7	1.1	0.7	0.0	0.1	0.7	1.7	2.7	4.0	19.2
Rodhos (Rhodes)	36 26N	28 15E	289	59	51	67	57	83	74	76	68	106	32	6	5.7	3.9	2.6	1.7	1.3	0.3	0.0	0.0	0.4	2.4	5.2	6.7	28.5
Thessaloniki (Salonika)	40 37N	22 57E	78	49	37	66	49	92	66	69	49	107	15	15	1.5	1.5	2.0	2.0	2.1	1.7	0.9	0.7	1.2	1.4	2.1	1.9	19.0
Hungary:																										
Budapest	47 31N	19 02E	394	35	26	62	44	82	61	61	47	103	-10	50	1.5	1.3	1.7	2.0	2.7	2.6	2.0	1.9	1.8	2.1	2.4	2.0	24.2
Debrecen	47 36N	21 39E	430	33	21	61	39	81	57	57	44	102	-22	80	1.2	1.1	1.4	1.8	2.4	2.8	2.5	2.3	1.8	2.2	2.0	1.6	23.1
Iceland:																										
Akureyri	65 41N	18 05W	16	23	16	40	30	57	48	43	34	83	-8	26	1.7	1.3	1.3	0.6	0.6	0.9	1.3	1.6	1.8	1.9	1.9	2.0	18.6
Reykjavik	64 09N	21 56W	92	36	28	43	33	58	48	44	36	74	-4	30	4.0	3.0	3.1	1.6	1.6	1.7	2.0	2.6	3.1	3.4	3.6	3.7	33.9
Ireland:																										
Cork	51 54N	08 29W	56	48	38	53	41	68	53	58	44	85	13	35	3.6	2.7	2.6	2.9	2.1	2.0	2.9	3.1	2.9	3.9	4.5	4.7	41.3
Dublin	53 22N	06 21W	155	46	36	55	38	67	53	57	43	86	8	35	2.7	2.0	2.0	1.9	2.3	2.3	2.5	3.0	2.8	3.0	2.7	2.6	29.7
Shannon Airport	52 41N	08 55W	8	46	36	55	41	66	53	58	43	87	12	12	3.0	2.0	2.1	2.2	2.4	2.1	3.1	3.0	3.0	3.4	4.2	4.3	36.5
Italy:																										
Ancona	43 37N	13 32E	52	46	36	62	45	83	66	67	55	102	18	30	1.7	1.6	1.9	2.1	2.3	1.9	1.5	1.5	3.5	3.0	2.5	3.0	28.0
Cagliari (Sardinia)	39 15N	09 03E	23	58	43	66	50	86	65	72	58	102	23	9	2.7	2.3	2.2	1.5	1.2	0.4	0.1	0.4	1.0	3.0	1.8	4.1	17.0
Genova (Genoa)	44 24N	08 55E	318	50	40	65	51	82	70	73	60	113	18	14	4.0	3.3	3.4	4.6	3.2	2.4	1.5	3.6	4.7	5.1	7.2	4.5	46.6
Napoli (Naples)	40 51N	14 15E	82	54	40	65	47	86	64	75	58	114	24	11	3.9	3.4	2.4	1.9	1.1	0.9	0.6	0.7	2.8	3.7	4.5	4.5	35.2
Palermo (Sicily)	38 07N	13 19E	354	58	47	67	54	86	71	75	64	104	31	20	3.2	2.9	2.4	1.7	1.0	0.7	0.2	0.6	2.0	4.3	4.1	4.1	28.3
Roma	41 48N	12 36E	377	54	39	68	46	88	64	73	53	104	20	26	3.1	2.7	2.4	2.1	1.8	1.0	0.4	0.6	2.6	3.9	4.1	3.9	29.5
Taranto	40 28N	17 17E	56	55	43	59	49	82	68	68	59	108	26	11	1.9	1.9	1.3	1.7	1.0	0.7	0.4	0.6	1.0	2.3	1.8	1.9	14.2
Venezia (Venice)	45 26N	12 23E	82	43	33	63	49	82	67	63	49	97	11	23	3.0	3.2	2.8	3.2	3.0	3.3	1.5	2.6	2.0	2.7	3.5	2.6	33.4
Luxembourg:																										
Luxembourg	49 37N	06 03E	1,096	36	29	58	40	74	55	58	40	99	-10	7	2.3	2.0	1.9	2.4	2.4	2.5	2.8	2.6	2.4	2.7	2.8	2.8	29.2
Malta:																										
Valletta	35 54N	14 31E	233	59	51	66	56	84	72	76	66	105	34	90	3.3	2.3	1.5	0.8	0.4	0.1	*	0.2	1.3	2.7	3.6	3.9	20.3
Monaco:																										
Monaco	43 44N	07 25E	180	54	46	61	53	77	70	67	60	93	27	60	2.4	2.3	3.1	2.1	1.4	1.1	0.7	1.1	2.3	4.7	4.3	3.5	30.1
Netherlands:																										
Amsterdam	52 23N	04 55E	5	40	34	52	43	69	59	56	48	95	3	29	2.0	1.4	1.3	1.6	1.8	1.8	2.6	2.7	2.8	2.8	2.6	2.2	25.6
Norway:																										
Bergen	60 24N	05 19E	141	39	32	49	36	65	51	52	42	89	-14	75	7.9	6.0	5.4	4.4	3.9	4.8	5.2	7.3	9.2	9.2	8.0	8.1	78.8
Kristiansand	58 10N	07 59E	175	35	26	47	33	71	53	49	38	93	-21	56	3.7	3.2	3.6	2.5	2.5	2.5	3.1	6.4	6.2	5.7	5.2	6.4	52.0
Oslo	59 56N	10 44E	308	30	20	50	34	73	56	49	38	93	-21	56	1.7	1.5	1.4	1.6	1.8	2.4	2.9	3.8	2.9	2.9	2.3	2.3	26.9
Tromso	69 39N	18 57E	335	30	23	33	27	57	44	40	33	83	-1	65	3.9	3.2	3.2	2.1	2.1	2.1	2.0	3.8	4.5	4.5	2.3	4.0	40.1
Trondheim	63 25N	10 27E	417	30	20	42	30	64	51	46	36	95	-22	35	2.1	1.7	2.2	1.7	1.9	2.2	2.7	3.7	4.7	4.3	2.8	2.1	32.1
Vardo	70 22N	31 06E	43	27	19	34	26	53	44	38	32	80	-11	40	1.3	1.3	2.3	1.5	1.1	1.7	1.5	1.7	2.5	2.5	2.4	2.4	23.5
Poland:																										
Gdansk (Danzig)	54 24N	18 40E	36	36	23	49	35	70	56	53	42	94	-16	35	1.2	1.0	1.3	1.3	1.8	2.8	2.6	3.8	2.1	2.1	1.8	1.5	21.7
Krakow	50 04N	19 57E	723	36	21	55	36	76	56	56	41	97	-28	35	1.1	1.1	1.4	1.5	2.8	4.0	4.5	3.8	2.6	2.2	1.7	1.4	28.6
Warsaw	52 13N	21 02E	294	35	22	53	34	75	57	55	41	98	-22	40	1.1	1.1	1.5	1.6	2.4	2.7	3.4	2.7	1.9	1.5	1.5	1.5	22.0
Wroclaw (Breslau)	51 07N	17 05E	482	35	25	55	39	74	57	55	42	98	-26	42	1.0	1.1	1.5	1.8	2.4	2.7	3.4	2.7	1.8	1.4	1.5	1.5	23.2
Portugal:																										
Braganca	41 49N	06 47W	2,395	46	31	62	42	80	57	62	46	103	10	18	3.2	3.7	3.7	3.2	2.8	1.6	0.5	0.3	2.1	3.0	7.1	7.1	53.8
Lagos	37 06N	08 38W	46	61	47	64	52	83	64	69	57	107	28	10	2.4	1.4	2.4	0.8	0.2	*	0.1	0.1	0.4	1.5	2.8	2.8	18.3
Lisbon	38 43N	09 08W	313	56	46	64	53	79	63	69	58	103	29	75	3.3	3.0	3.1	2.4	1.7	0.7	0.2	0.2	1.3	3.1	4.2	3.6	27.0
Romania:																										
Bucuresti (Bucharest)	44 25N	26 06E	269	36	20	61	41	85	60	65	44	105	-18	20	1.1	1.6	1.6	1.8	2.4	3.4	2.3	2.1	1.5	1.6	1.5	1.1	22.8
Cluj	46 47N	23 40E	1,286	31	17	58	37	81	55	60	41	100	-24	26	1.9	1.8	1.9	2.4	3.3	3.3	2.8	2.3	2.0	2.0	1.0	1.8	24.0
Constanta	44 11N	28 39E	13	42	33	55	42	79	62	63	49	101	-13	27	1.1	0.9	1.1	1.1	1.5	1.3	0.4	0.5	1.1	1.4	1.2	1.3	15.1
Spain:																										
Almeria	36 51N	02 28W	213	61	48	69	55	85	69	73	62	76	24	20	1.1	0.9	0.7	0.8	0.1	0.1	*	0.1	0.6	0.9	1.5	1.1	8.6
Barcelona	41 24N	02 09E	312	56	42	64	49	81	69	69	58	98	22	30	1.6	1.5	1.8	1.9	2.1	1.3	0.8	1.4	3.4	3.4	2.7	1.8	23.5
Burgos	42 20N	03 42W	2,825	47	33	60	39	79	52	62	42	102	14	24	2.0	1.7	2.1	2.4	2.5	1.2	0.7	0.7	1.1	2.0	1.9	2.0	20.2
Madrid	40 25N	03 41W	2,188	47	33	64	44	87	62	66	48	102	12	30	1.5	2.1	1.7	1.5	1.5	1.3	0.4	0.3	1.1	2.6	1.9	2.0	16.5
Sevilla	37 25N	05 59W	98	58	41	73	51	96	67	78	57	117	20	27	2.2	2.5	2.3	1.5	1.2	0.5	0.1	0.1	1.2	2.6	2.7	2.8	23.3
Valencia	39 28N	00 23W	79	59	41	67	53	84	71	73	58	107	20	29	0.9	1.2	1.2	1.1	1.2	1.3	0.4	0.5	2.2	1.6	2.5	1.3	15.4
Sweden:																										
Abisko	68 21N	18 49E	1,273	20	6	33	19	61	45	35	24	82	-30	11	0.7	0.6	0.5	0.7	0.7	1.8	1.6	1.8	1.2	1.0	0.6	0.6	11.7

TEMPERATURE AND PRECIPITATION DATA FOR REPRESENTATIVE WORLD-WIDE STATIONS

COUNTRY AND STATION	LATITUDE	LONGITUDE	ELEVATION (FEET)	LENGTH OF RECORD (YEARS)	JAN low	JAN high	APR low	APR high	JUL low	JUL high	OCT low	OCT high	EXTREME high	EXTREME low	LENGTH OF RECORD (YEARS)	JANUARY	FEBRUARY	MARCH	APRIL	MAY	JUNE	JULY	AUGUST	SEPTEMBER	OCTOBER	NOVEMBER	DECEMBER	YEAR
Sweden cont'd:																												
Gotheborg	57 42N	11 58E	55	39	27	48	36	56	69	36	51	42	88	-13	61	2.5	2.0	2.0	1.7	1.9	2.2	2.8	3.7	3.1	3.1	2.7	2.8	30.5
Haparanda	65 50N	24 09E	30	20	10	28	23	38	71	32	39	30	89	-34	20	2.2	1.6	1.2	1.5	1.4	1.7	2.6	2.8	2.6	2.8	2.5	2.0	24.4
Karlstad	59 23N	13 30E	164	20	20	49	32	57	73	31	49	42	93	-21	20	1.9	1.2	0.9	1.4	1.9	1.9	2.6	3.1	2.9	2.4	2.4	1.9	24.8
Sarna	61 41N	13 07E	1,504	20	4	42	23	45	64	23	42	31	88	-51	30	1.6	0.8	0.8	1.2	1.6	1.9	2.8	2.8	2.6	2.1	1.9	1.8	24.3
Stockholm	59 21N	18 04E	146	30	23	42	33	45	70	33	48	41	97	-26	30	1.7	1.1	1.1	1.1	1.6	1.9	2.8	3.3	2.2	2.1	1.9	1.8	22.4
Visby (Gotland)	57 39N	18 18E	36	35	28	40	33	50	67	33	50	50	88	-1	30	1.7	1.1	1.2	1.5	1.6	1.9	2.7	2.7	1.7	2.3	2.0	2.0	20.3
Switzerland:																												
Berne	46 57N	07 26E	1,877	30	26	35	39	56	74	39	56	42	96	-9	77	1.9	2.0	2.6	2.3	3.7	4.4	4.4	4.3	3.4	3.5	2.7	2.3	38.5
Geneva (Geneva)	46 12N	06 09E	1,329	23	31	41	39	59	76	41	53	42	101	-13	125	1.9	1.8	2.2	2.5	3.0	3.1	2.9	3.1	2.9	3.8	3.1	2.4	33.9
Zurich	47 23N	08 33E	1,617	23	31	38	39	57	77	39	53	42	98	-12	23	3.0	2.9	2.9	3.4	4.0	5.0	4.6	4.6	3.3	3.2	2.9	2.9	40.9
Turkey:																												
Edirne (Adrianople)	41 39N	26 34E	154	18	28	44	38	66	88	44	70	49	107	-8	18	2.2	1.9	1.7	1.9	1.7	2.1	1.5	1.1	2.1	2.1	2.9	3.0	23.2
Istanbul (Constantinople)	40 58N	28 50E	59	45	36	45	45	61	81	45	67	54	100	17	32	3.7	2.3	2.6	1.4	1.3	1.3	1.7	1.5	2.3	3.8	4.1	4.9	31.5
United Kingdom:																												
Birmingham	54 35N	05 56W	57	7	34	42	38	53	65	38	55	47	91	14	30	4.2	2.8	2.1	2.4	2.3	2.8	2.9	3.5	3.4	3.8	3.6	3.9	38.7
Cardiff	52 29N	01 56W	535	30	35	44	40	54	69	40	57	45	92	11	30	2.8	2.1	1.7	2.3	2.3	1.9	2.2	3.2	2.3	2.5	2.6	2.6	29.7
Dublin	53 28N	03 10W	203	30	35	46	40	54	69	40	57	46	91	11	35	2.9	2.3	1.7	2.5	2.3	2.9	2.8	3.0	2.6	3.2	2.4	4.3	41.9
Edinburgh	55 55N	06 13W	441	30	36	45	38	53	66	37	57	43	86	-23	30	2.0	2.0	2.0	1.9	2.3	2.9	3.0	3.1	2.6	2.9	2.5	4.3	29.7
London	51 29N	00 00	149	30	35	44	40	55	73	41	58	50	99	-36	30	2.0	1.6	1.5	1.8	1.8	1.6	2.3	2.5	2.1	2.8	2.5	2.5	25.5
Liverpool	53 24N	03 04W	198	30	36	45	39	54	66	40	58	48	89	15	30	2.3	1.9	1.4	1.6	2.2	2.0	2.8	3.0	2.6	3.0	2.7	2.5	28.9
Perth	56 24N	03 27W	77	30	35	43	37	53	64	43	55	49	87	16	30	2.6	2.3	1.6	1.6	2.3	2.0	3.1	3.1	2.8	3.8	2.7	2.5	30.7
Plymouth	50 22N	04 07W	87	30	40	47	43	54	66	43	58	50	89	16	30	4.3	3.1	1.9	2.3	2.3	2.0	2.6	2.9	2.8	3.8	4.4	4.4	37.8
Wick	58 26N	03 05W	119	30	35	44	35	48	61	35	52	43	80	8	30	2.9	2.6	1.8	1.7	1.8	2.0	2.6	2.6	3.2	3.2	3.1	2.9	30.0
U.S.S.R.:																												
Arkhangelsk	64 33N	40 32E	22	23	2	36	14	57	64	23	31	36	91	-49	25	1.2	1.1	1.1	0.7	1.3	1.9	2.0	2.7	2.0	1.9	1.6	1.3	19.8
Astrakhan	46 21N	48 02E	45	18	14	26	40	57	85	40	62	57	99	-23	25	0.5	0.5	0.7	0.6	0.6	0.7	0.5	0.4	0.6	0.4	0.8	0.6	6.4
Dnepropetrovsk	48 27N	30 04E	259	16	16	28	34	56	82	31	56	40	101	-13	19	1.3	1.1	1.1	1.4	1.8	3.0	1.9	1.5	1.6	1.8	1.6	1.6	19.4
Kaunas	54 54N	23 53E	118	19	18	26	31	53	72	34	50	44	96	-26	20	1.4	1.3	1.3	1.4	1.8	2.5	3.0	3.2	2.4	2.0	1.6	1.6	25.0
Kirov	58 36N	49 41E	594	19	-2	18	27	47	74	27	47	34	91	-44	15	1.0	0.9	0.8	1.0	1.9	2.5	3.2	3.0	2.4	1.4	1.6	1.7	20.6
Leningrad	59 56N	30 16E	16	26	11	23	31	43	71	36	53	38	97	-30	30	1.0	0.9	1.1	1.5	1.5	2.3	2.6	2.8	2.1	2.1	1.4	1.1	19.2
Lvov	49 50N	24 01E	978	12	19	31	31	56	77	31	54	43	95	-30	21	1.3	1.2	1.2	2.0	2.8	3.2	4.1	3.8	2.4	1.8	1.4	1.6	28.2
Minsk	53 54N	27 33E	738	15	12	23	32	54	77	35	48	41	92	-30	23	1.4	1.0	1.1	1.3	2.3	2.9	3.0	2.9	1.9	1.6	1.4	1.6	19.2
Moskva (Moscow)	55 46N	37 40E	505	37	9	21	31	47	76	31	50	42	96	-27	30	1.5	1.3	1.3	1.5	1.8	2.1	3.0	2.9	2.1	1.9	1.8	1.6	22.9
Odessa	46 29N	30 44E	67	22	21	32	36	55	77	37	55	46	98	-4	63	1.0	1.0	1.0	1.0	1.4	2.4	1.9	1.4	1.4	1.5	1.6	1.5	24.8
Riga	56 57N	24 03E	197	14	18	26	31	49	71	35	50	41	91	-30	30	1.2	1.0	1.0	1.4	1.7	2.3	3.0	2.8	2.1	1.5	1.7	1.2	22.2
Saratov	51 33N	46 03E	75	17	8	19	32	53	82	32	57	43	102	-22	30	1.1	1.0	0.9	1.1	1.2	1.7	1.8	1.0	1.5	1.4	1.4	1.3	14.3
Sevastopol	44 37N	33 31E	36	20	29	39	42	54	76	42	64	49	95	-30	12	0.9	0.7	1.0	1.0	0.8	0.9	0.9	0.8	0.9	2.0	1.4	1.2	22.2
Stalingrad	48 02N	44 33E	1,086	13	3	17	35	51	83	32	57	41	97	-25	20	1.1	1.1	1.1	1.2	1.6	1.6	2.1	2.0	0.7	1.5	1.1	1.3	14.5
Stavropol	45 02N	41 58E	1,325	13	18	26	37	53	81	36	60	44	93	-30	41	1.1	1.1	1.1	1.5	2.1	2.7	2.0	2.7	2.3	1.9	1.4	1.2	22.9
Tallin	59 26N	24 48E	66	17	21	28	35	49	77	41	52	40	95	-19	63	1.4	0.9	0.8	1.3	1.7	2.4	3.1	3.0	1.9	1.9	1.4	1.2	20.9
Tbilisi	41 43N	44 48E	239	13	4	32	44	60	83	41	63	52	99	-67	10	0.7	0.8	1.1	2.4	3.6	3.1	2.1	1.7	2.1	2.0	1.5	2.0	22.4
Uas'tachagor	54 16N	37 34E	279	15	6	23	30	48	49	30	49	44	96	-42	23	1.4	1.2	0.9	1.6	1.6	2.4	2.6	2.2	1.9	2.1	1.2	3.2	21.4
Ufa	54 43N	55 56E	571	20	-3	17	30	44	75	30	58	44	99		23	1.6	1.3	1.2	0.9	1.6	2.4	2.6	2.2	1.8	2.3	2.2	2.3	22.5

TEMPERATURE AND PRECIPITATION DATA FOR REPRESENTATIVE WORLD-WIDE STATIONS

Country and Station	Latitude	Longitude	Elev. (feet)	Temp. Length of Record (yrs)	January Max	January Min	April Max	April Min	July Max	July Min	October Max	October Min	Extreme Max	Extreme Min	Precip. Length of Record (yrs)	Jan	Feb	Mar	Apr	May	Jun	Jul	Aug	Sep	Oct	Nov	Dec	Year
Yugoslavia:																												
Beograd (Belgrade)	44 48N	20 28E	453	16	37	26	64	45	84	61	65	47	107	-14	51	1.6	1.3	1.6	2.2	2.6	2.8	1.9	2.5	1.7	2.7	1.8	1.9	24.6
Skopje	41 59N	21 28E	787	10	40	26	67	42	88	50	65	43	105	-11	10	1.5	1.2	1.3	1.5	2.3	1.9	1.2	1.2	1.0	2.6	2.3	1.8	19.5
Split	43 31N	16 26E	420	14	51	29	65	50	87	68	69	55	100	17	51	3.1	2.5	3.2	3.0	2.5	2.1	1.2	1.6	2.9	4.4	4.2	4.4	35.1
OCEAN ISLANDS																												
Bjornoya, Bear Island	74 31N	19 01E	49	10	26	19	26	16	45	36	36	30	71	-25	25	1.6	1.4	1.3	0.9	0.8	0.7	1.8	1.2	1.8	1.7	1.4	1.6	15.1
Gronfjorden, Spitzbergen	78 02N	14 15E	23	19	10	4	17	2	42	33	25	17	60	-57	15	1.4	1.4	1.1	0.6	0.4	0.4	1.5	1.5	1.1	3.0	0.9	1.3	11.7
Horta, Azores	38 32N	28 38W	200	28	66	58	64	54	75	61	75	61	100	29	25	4.5	4.1	3.9	3.0	2.9	2.2	2.3	2.5	2.7	4.4	4.1	4.5	40.3
Jan Mayen	71 01N	08 28W	131	30	31	21	34	24	44	37	39	31	65	-18	15	2.1	1.7	1.6	1.4	0.9	0.9	1.4	1.8	2.5	4.3	2.2	2.2	21.2
Lerwick, Shetland Island	60 08N	01 11W	269	30	42	34	48	38	58	49	50	42	77	17	15	4.4	3.5	3.4	2.3	2.5	2.0	3.0	3.0	4.3	4.3	4.6	4.5	40.5
Matochkin Shar, Novaya Zemlya	73 16N	56 24E	61	9	-6	-13	18	8	47	36	30	21	68	-41	9	0.6	0.5	0.4	0.2	0.3	0.4	0.4	1.2	1.2	0.6	0.6	0.4	8.9
Ponta Delgada, Azores	37 45N	25 40W	118	30	62	55	64	55	76	64	71	61	85	38	30	3.6	2.9	2.8	2.5	2.1	1.5	1.5	1.9	2.7	3.6	3.0	3.3	32.6
Stornoway, Hebrides	58 11N	06 21W	34	30	44	37	49	38	61	51	53	44	84	13	50	6.4	4.6	3.4	2.5	2.5	2.4	3.0	3.5	4.6	6.2	4.6	5.5	49.1
Thorshavn, Faeroes	62 02N	06 45W	82	50	42	33	45	38	55	47	51	40	70	8	50	6.3	4.7	4.8	3.4	2.5	2.4	3.1	3.5	5.9	5.9	6.3	6.6	56.2
AFRICA																												
Algeria:																												
Adrar	27 52N	00 17W	938	15	69	39	92	60	115	82	92	70	124	25	15	*	*	0.1	0.2	0.1	0.0	0.0	*	*	0.2	0.2	*	0.6
Alger (Algiers)	36 46N	03 03E	194	25	59	49	68	54	83	70	74	61	107	32	25	4.4	3.3	2.9	1.6	1.8	0.6	*	0.3	1.6	3.1	5.1	5.4	30.0
Bone	36 54N	07 46E	66	26	59	44	67	52	83	65	75	61	107	32	25	5.6	4.1	3.0	2.2	1.5	0.6	0.1	0.6	1.7	3.0	5.2	5.2	31.0
El Golea	30 35N	02 53E	1,247	15	63	37	84	52	107	75	87	60	120	23	15	0.3	0.1	0.5	0.2	0.4	0.1	0.1	0.1	0.3	0.3	0.4	0.3	1.9
Fort Flatters	28 06N	06 42E	1,224	15	67	38	90	56	110	78	92	59	115	17	15	0.1	0.2	0.3	0.2	0.1	0.0	0.0	*	0.1	0.3	0.4	0.3	1.1
Tamanrasset	22 42N	05 31E	4,593	15	67	38	85	55	95	63	82	53	102	18	15	0.2	0.2	0.4	0.2	0.2	0.2	0.3	0.4	0.3	0.3	0.4	0.2	1.5
Touggourt	33 07N	06 04E	226	26	62	38	83	55	107	84	84	59	122	26	26	0.5	0.4	0.5	0.4	0.3	0.2	0.1	0.2	0.3	0.7	0.5	0.3	2.9
Angola:																												
Cangamba	13 41S	19 52E	4,331	6	84	62	89	62	82	46	87	63	109	20	7	8.9	7.4	6.8	1.8	0.1	0.0	0.0	0.0	0.9	7.0	7.4	8.5	40.6
Luanda	08 49S	13 13E	194	27	83	74	85	75	74	65	79	71	98	58	59	1.0	1.4	3.0	5.5	0.5	*	0.1	0.1	0.2	0.5	1.1	0.8	12.7
Mocamedes	15 12S	12 09E	10	10	75	68	77	68	68	61	71	61	102	49	11	0.1	0.4	0.7	0.5	0.4	0.4	0.1	0.2	0.2	0.2	0.1	0.1	2.1
Nova Lisboa	12 48S	15 45E	5,577	14	78	55	78	57	77	47	81	58	90	36	14	6.7	5.5	7.8	6.1	0.4	0.0	0.0	*	0.6	5.5	8.9	8.9	37.0
Botswana:																												
Francistown	21 13S	27 30E	3,294	24	87	63	83	58	75	41	85	57	107	24	24	4.3	3.1	2.8	0.7	0.2	0.1	0.0	*	0.9	1.3	1.9	3.4	17.7
Maun	19 59S	23 25E	3,091	20	90	66	87	60	77	42	91	59	110	24	20	4.3	3.8	3.5	1.3	0.2	0.1	0.0	0.1	0.5	0.7	2.3	2.8	18.2
Tsabong	26 03S	22 27E	3,156	20	94	65	85	57	71	34	84	47	109	21	20	3.1	3.8	2.9	1.3	0.2	0.4	0.0	*	0.5	0.7	1.3	1.5	11.5
Cameroon:																												
Ngaoundere	07 17N	13 19E	3,601	5	87	55	89	65	82	63	85	69	101	46	5	0.1	0.9	5.5	7.0	7.4	8.9	8.9	9.2	9.4	5.3	4.9	0.2	57.2
Yaounde	03 53N	11 32E	2,526	11	85	67	85	66	80	66	83	67	110	57	11	0.6	2.6	6.1	7.7	8.4	3.1	8.3	10.1	10.7	11.6	4.6	0.9	61.2
Central African Republic:																												
Bangui	04 22N	18 34E	1,270	3	90	68	91	68	85	69	89	70	100	63	3	1.0	1.7	5.0	4.5	7.3	7.9	7.8	8.1	9.2	5.3	4.9	0.2	60.8
Ndele	08 24N	20 17E	1,939	3	98	67	98	74	86	69	92	72	114	47	3	1.3	1.1	5.3	6.1	8.3	6.0	6.7	12.3	8.4	11.6	0.6	0.0	55.8
Chad:																												
Am Timan	11 02N	20 17E	1,430	3	98	56	105	74	89	70	96	72	113	43	3	0.0	0.0	0.1	1.2	2.9	7.3	10.6	12.3	5.8	1.2	0.0	0.0	37.2
Fort Lamy	12 07N	15 02E	968	14	93	57	107	75	92	74	97	76	114	47	14	0.0	0.0	0.1	0.1	2.9	6.7	13.2	12.6	5.6	1.4	0.0	0.0	29.3
Largeau (Faya)	18 00N	19 10E	837	5	84	54	104	69	109	76	103	72	121	37	5	0.0	0.0	0.2	0.0	0.0	0.0	0.0	0.0	*	0.0	0.0	0.0	0.7
Congo, Democratic Republic of the:																												
Albertville	05 54S	29 12E	2,693	15	87	67	85	67	82	58	87	67	98	50	18	6.3	4.7	6.3	8.4	4.3	0.3	0.1	0.8	2.8	4.7	7.9	6.3	45.4
Kinshasa (Leopoldville)	04 20S	15 18E	1,066	16	87	70	88	72	80	64	87	70	106	58	12	5.3	4.7	7.7	7.6	6.2	0.3	0.1	0.1	1.2	4.7	8.7	6.6	53.3
Luluabourg	05 54S	22 25E	2,198	7	85	67	86	68	85	62	86	67	94	51	14	5.4	5.6	7.0	6.2	3.4	0.5	0.0	0.3	5.2	6.5	7.1	8.9	62.3
Stanleyville	00 26N	25 14E	1,370	5	84	68	88	69	84	67	83	67	95	54	6	2.0	3.4	5.8	5.4	4.5	4.5	3.2	6.3	8.6	8.6	7.1	3.3	67.1
Congo, Republic of:																												
Brazzaville	04 15S	15 15E	1,063	15	88	71	89	71	79	60	89	69	100	53	15	5.4	4.3	7.0	4.3	0.6	0.0	0.0	0.0	0.6	4.7	9.0	5.4	58.0
Ouesso	01 37N	16 04E	1,132	6	87	68	88	68	82	68	85	68	106	54	6	2.2	3.2	4.6	6.4	6.4	3.9	3.7	10.0	10.2	8.1	8.7	2.4	58.6
Pointe Noire (Loango)	04 39S	11 46E	164	4	85	73	83	74	71	68	78	74	92	55	10	3.4	5.4	4.1	3.9	0.8	0.0	0.0	0.0	0.4	4.1	6.6	6.6	48.1
Dahomey:																												
Cotonou	06 21N	02 26E	23	5	88	74	83	78	78	74	78	74	95	65	10	1.3	1.3	4.6	4.9	10.0	14.4	3.5	2.6	5.3	2.6	2.3	0.5	32.4
Ethiopia:																												
Addis Ababa	09 20N	38 45E	8,038	15	75	43	77	50	69	50	75	45	94	32	37	0.5	1.5	2.6	3.4	3.4	5.4	11.0	11.8	7.5	0.8	0.6	0.2	48.7
Asmara	15 17N	38 55E	7,628	9	74	44	78	51	71	53	72	51	88	31	17	0.3	1.5	0.6	1.5	1.3	4.1	6.7	6.7	1.0	0.3	0.4	*	18.4

409

TEMPERATURE AND PRECIPITATION DATA FOR REPRESENTATIVE WORLD-WIDE STATIONS

COUNTRY AND STATION	LATITUDE	LONGITUDE	ELEVATION (FEET)	TEMP RECORD (YR)	JAN max	JAN min	APR max	APR min	JUL max	JUL min	OCT max	OCT min	EXTREME max	EXTREME min	PRECIP RECORD (YR)	JAN	FEB	MAR	APR	MAY	JUN	JUL	AUG	SEP	OCT	NOV	DEC	YEAR
Ethiopia cont'd:																												
Diredawa	09 02N	41 45E	3,937	8	81	58	91	69	90	68	89	68	100	49	8	0.8	0.8	3.3	3.0	2.8	1.5	4.3	3.8	2.2	0.5	0.3	0.8	24.1
Gambela	08 15N	34 35E	1,345	26	98	64	98	71	87	71	92	69	111	48	30	0.4	0.4	1.4	3.2	5.9	6.7	8.5	9.5	7.3	3.5	1.8	0.4	48.8
French Territory of Afars and Issas (F.T.A.I.):																												
Djibouti	11 36N	43 09E	23	16	84	73	90	79	106	87	92	80	117	63	46	0.4	0.5	1.0	0.5	0.2	*	0.1	0.3	0.3	0.4	0.9	0.5	>.1
Gabon:																												
Libreville	00 23N	09 26E	115	11	87	73	89	73	83	68	86	73	99	62	21	9.8	9.3	13.2	13.4	9.6	0.5	0.1	0.7	4.1	13.6	14.7	9.8	98.8
Mayoumba	03 25S	10 38E	200	8	84	73	86	73	68	68	86	69	91	60	8	6.5	9.3	10.2	10.2	2.3	*	0.0	2.3	2.3	9.3	10.7	4.6	62.0
Gambia:																												
Bathurst	13 21N	16 40W	90	9	88	59	91	65	86	74	89	74	106	45	9	0.1	0.1	*	0.4	0.4	2.3	11.1	19.7	12.2	4.3	0.7	0.1	51.0
Ghana:																												
Accra	05 33N	00 12W	88	17	87	73	88	76	81	73	85	73	96	59	65	0.6	1.3	2.2	3.2	5.6	7.0	1.8	0.6	1.4	2.5	1.4	0.9	28.5
Kumasi	06 40N	01 37W	942	10	88	66	89	71	82	70	86	70	100	51	10	0.8	2.3	5.7	3.1	7.5	7.9	4.3	3.1	6.8	7.1	3.7	0.8	55.2
Guinea:																												
Conakry	09 31N	13 43W	23	7	88	72	90	76	83	71	87	72	96	63	10	0.4	0.1	0.9	0.9	6.2	22.0	51.1	41.5	26.9	14.6	4.8	0.4	169.0
Kourousa	10 39N	09 53W	1,217	9	93	60	99	75	87	69	90	69	109	39	10	0.4	0.3	0.9	2.8	5.3	9.7	11.7	13.6	13.4	6.6	1.3	0.4	66.4
Ifni (now in Morocco):																												
Sidi Ifni	29 27N	10 11W	148	14	66	52	71	59	75	64	75	66	124	40	14	1.0	0.6	0.5	0.6	0.1	0.1	*	*	0.4	0.1	0.9	1.8	6.1
Ivory Coast:																												
Abidjan	05 19N	04 01W	65	13	89	73	90	75	83	72	85	73	96	59	10	1.6	2.1	3.9	14.2	24.2	19.5	8.4	2.1	2.8	6.6	7.9	3.1	77.1
Bouake	07 42N	05 00W	1,194	12	91	68	92	70	85	68	89	69	104	57	10	1.5	1.5	4.1	5.8	6.0	6.0	3.1	4.6	8.2	5.2	1.5	1.0	46.7
Kenya:																												
Mombasa	04 03S	39 39E	52	45	87	75	86	76	81	71	84	71	96	61	34	1.0	0.7	2.5	7.7	12.6	4.7	3.5	2.5	2.5	3.4	3.8	2.4	47.3
Nairobi	01 16S	36 48E	5,971	77	77	54	75	58	69	51	76	55	87	41	17	1.5	2.5	4.9	8.3	6.2	1.8	0.6	0.9	1.2	2.1	4.3	3.4	37.7
Liberia:																												
Monrovia	06 18N	10 48W	75	6	89	71	90	72	80	72	86	72	97	62	4	0.2	0.1	4.4	11.7	13.4	36.1	24.2	18.6	29.9	25.2	8.2	2.9	174.9
Libya:																												
Banghazi (Benghazi)	32 06N	20 04E	82	46	63	50	74	58	84	69	80	66	109	37	47	2.6	1.6	0.8	0.2	0.1	0.0	*	*	0.1	0.7	1.8	2.6	10.5
Oufra	24 12N	23 21E	1,276	3	69	43	90	58	101	75	90	64	122	34	4	*	0.0	0.0	0.0	0.1	0.0	0.0	0.0	0.0	0.0	0.0	*	0.3
Sabhah	27 01N	14 26E	1,457	4	64	41	89	60	102	76	91	65	122	33	10	3.2	1.8	1.1	0.4	0.2	0.1	0.0	0.0	0.4	1.6	2.6	3.7	15.1
Tarabulus (Tripoli)	32 54N	13 11E	72	47	61	47	72	57	85	71	80	65	114	23	56	3.2	1.8	1.1	0.4	0.2	0.1	0.0	0.0	0.4	1.6	2.6	3.7	15.1
Malagasy Republic:																												
Diego Suares	12 17S	49 17E	100	11	88	75	88	75	84	69	86	75	98	51	31	2.2	9.5	7.6	2.2	0.1	0.2	0.2	0.3	0.1	0.7	1.1	5.8	38.7
Tananarive	18 55S	47 33E	4,500	44	79	58	76	58	68	48	71	58	95	34	62	10.6	11.0	7.0	2.2	0.7	0.3	0.3	0.2	0.7	2.4	5.3	11.3	53.4
Tulear	23 20S	43 41E	20	27	92	72	89	64	81	53	86	58	108	33	15	3.1	3.2	1.4	0.3	0.2	0.3	0.2	0.2	0.0	0.7	1.4	1.7	13.5
Malawi:																												
Karonga	09 57S	33 56E	1,596	8	86	71	85	70	81	59	85	70	99	41	10	7.1	7.0	7.6	6.2	1.7	0.1	0.2	*	*	0.3	0.3	4.7	38.3
Zomba	15 23S	35 19E	3,141	27	80	65	78	62	72	53	78	64	99	41	10	12.1	9.9	7.4	2.7	0.7	0.4	0.3	0.3	0.2	1.0	4.3	10.9	52.9
Mali:																												
Araouane	18 54N	03 33W	935	8	81	48	110	67	111	79	103	79	37	—	10	*	*	0.0	0.0	0.1	0.4	0.3	0.3	0.6	0.1	0.1	*	1.7
Bamako	12 39N	07 59W	1,116	12	91	61	103	76	89	71	93	71	47	—	10	*	*	0.1	0.6	2.9	5.4	11.0	13.7	8.1	1.7	0.6	*	44.1
Gao	16 16N	00 03W	902	15	83	58	105	77	97	80	100	83	44	—	19	0.0	0.0	*	0.1	0.4	1.0	2.9	5.4	1.5	0.2	*	0.0	11.5

TEMPERATURE AND PRECIPITATION DATA FOR REPRESENTATIVE WORLD-WIDE STATIONS

Country and Station	Latitude	Longitude	Elevation (feet)	Temp. Length of Record (yrs)	Jan. avg max	Jan. avg min	Apr. avg max	Apr. avg min	Jul. avg max	Jul. avg min	Oct. avg max	Oct. avg min	Extreme max	Extreme min	Precip. Length of Record (yrs)	Jan	Feb	Mar	Apr	May	Jun	Jul	Aug	Sep	Oct	Nov	Dec	Year
Mauritania:																												
Atar	20 31N	13 04W	761	7	84	54	97	67	106	81	98	72	117	39	10	*	*	*	*	0.7	0.1	0.3	1.2	1.1	0.7	*	*	2.8
Nema	16 36N	07 16W	883	8	86	66	105	79	99	78	101	78	120	47	10	+	+	*	*	+	1.9	2.3	4.1	2.8	0.7	*	+	11.6
Nouakchott	18 07N	15 36W	69	5	85	57	90	71	89	76	91	74	115	44	10	0.1	0.1	0.1	*	+	+	0.5	4.1	0.9	0.4	0.1	*	6.2
Morocco:																												
Casablanca	33 35N	07 39W	164	48	63	45	69	52	79	65	78	57	110	31	40	2.6	2.1	2.2	1.4	0.9	0.1	0.0	*	0.3	1.5	2.6	2.8	15.9
Marrakech	31 36N	08 01W	1,509	35	63	40	79	52	101	67	83	57	120	27	29	1.1	1.0	1.1	1.7	0.6	0.1	0.1	0.1	0.4	1.1	1.2	1.2	9.4
Rabat	34 00N	06 50W	213	35	63	46	71	52	82	65	77	57	118	32	25	3.3	2.6	2.8	1.7	1.1	0.2	0.0	*	0.4	1.9	3.3	3.4	19.8
Tangier	35 46N	05 49W	239	47	65	47	67	51	80	64	71	51	114	35	51	5.4	4.8	3.9	2.4	1.7	0.6	0.1	0.2	1.2	3.9	5.8	5.4	35.3
Mozambique:																												
Beira	19 50S	34 51E	28	37	89	75	86	70	79	62	86	70	109	48	39	10.9	7.8	8.4	4.2	1.6	1.3	1.1	0.8	1.1	5.2	9.2	9.9	59.9
Chicoa	15 36S	32 21E	899	8	96	71	93	69	81	55	101	67	117	32	42	7.8	5.1	5.7	0.6	*	0.8	*	*	0.2	1.1	5.2	5.2	27.4
Lourenco Marques	25 58S	32 36E	194	42	86	71	83	66	76	55	82	64	114	45	42	4.9	4.4	4.9	2.1	1.1	0.8	1.1	0.5	*	2.2	3.8	2.9	29.9
Niger:																												
Agades	16 59N	07 59E	1,706	8	86	50	105	72	104	74	101	70	115	40	10	0.0	0.0	0.0	0.2	0.3	1.9	1.9	3.7	0.7	0.0	0.0	0.0	6.8
Bilma	18 41N	12 55E	1,171	9	81	45	101	74	108	77	101	74	116	29	10	0.0	0.0	*	*	*	0.1	0.1	0.5	0.1	0.1	0.0	0.0	0.9
Niamey	13 31N	02 06E	709	10	93	58	108	82	91	74	101	74	114	47	10	*	*	0.0	0.3	1.3	3.2	5.2	6.7	3.7	0.5	*	*	21.6
Nigeria:																												
Enugu	06 27N	07 29E	763	11	90	66	91	72	83	71	85	71	99	55	33	0.7	1.1	2.6	5.9	10.4	11.4	7.6	6.7	12.8	9.8	2.1	0.5	71.3
Kaduna	10 35N	06 29E	2,113	14	88	55	95	71	83	66	87	63	105	46	34	*	*	0.5	1.9	5.2	8.1	8.5	11.9	7.0	2.9	2.7	1.0	50.1
Lagos	06 27N	03 24E	10	32	88	74	89	76	82	74	85	73	104	60	47	1.1	1.8	4.0	5.9	10.6	18.1	11.0	2.5	5.5	8.1	2.7	1.0	72.3
Maiduguri	11 51N	13 05E	1,162	13	90	54	104	72	90	73	94	72	112	43	40	0.0	0.2	4.0	0.2	1.6	2.7	7.1	8.7	4.2	0.7	0.0	0.0	25.3
Portuguese Guinea:																												
Bolama	11 34N	15 29W	62	31	88	67	91	73	82	73	89	74	106	54	37	0.8	7.6	1.2	3.1	9.5	14.3	23.1	27.6	16.9	14.2	1.6	0.1	85.9
Rhodesia:																												
Bulawayo	20 09S	28 37E	4,405	15	81	61	81	56	70	44	85	59	99	28	50	5.6	4.3	3.3	0.7	0.4	*	*	*	0.2	1.5	3.2	4.8	23.4
Salisbury	17 50S	31 08E	4,831	15	78	60	78	55	70	44	83	59	95	32	50	7.7	7.0	4.6	1.1	0.5	0.1	0.1	0.1	0.3	1.5	3.8	6.4	32.6
Senegal:																												
Dakar	14 42N	17 29W	131	25	79	64	81	65	88	76	89	76	109	53	26	*	*	0.0	*	*	0.7	3.5	10.0	5.2	1.5	0.1	0.3	21.3
Kaolack	14 08N	16 04W	20	8	93	60	103	68	91	77	93	74	114	48	10	0.0	0.0	0.0	0.0	0.2	2.6	6.9	10.7	7.0	1.7	*	*	30.3
Sierra Leone:																												
Freetown/Lungi	08 37N	13 12W	92	8	87	73	88	76	82	73	85	72	98	62	8	0.4	0.2	1.2	3.1	9.5	14.3	29.2	36.1	22.3	14.2	5.5	1.2	137.6
Somali:																												
Berbera	10 26N	45 02E	45	30	84	68	89	77	107	88	88	77	117	58	30	0.3	0.5	0.7	0.5	0.3	*	*	*	*	0.1	0.2	0.2	2.0
Mogadiscio (Mogadiscio)	02 02N	45 21E	39	13	86	73	90	78	83	73	84	76	97	59	21	0.1	*	1.9	2.5	2.3	3.6	1.5	1.0	1.0	0.9	1.6	0.5	16.9
South Africa, Republic of:																												
Capetown	33 54S	18 32E	56	19	78	60	72	55	63	45	70	50	103	28	18	0.6	0.3	0.7	1.9	3.1	3.5	3.3	2.8	1.8	1.2	0.4	0.7	20.0
Durban	29 50S	31 02E	16	15	81	69	77	64	72	52	75	60	107	39	28	4.3	4.8	5.1	3.0	2.0	1.3	1.1	1.5	4.3	4.7	4.1	4.2	39.7
Kimberley	28 48S	24 46E	18	19	89	64	78	50	65	32	81	53	107	20	57	2.4	2.4	2.5	2.0	0.6	0.1	0.1	0.1	0.3	1.6	1.8	2.1	16.1
Port Elizabeth	33 59S	25 36E	190	14	78	61	73	57	64	45	70	53	104	31	84	1.2	1.3	1.9	2.4	2.4	1.8	2.0	2.3	2.2	4.3	1.6	1.0	22.7
Port Nolloth	29 14S	16 52E	23	13	68	57	66	53	62	47	66	50	101	31	61	0.1	0.1	0.1	0.1	0.3	0.3	0.3	0.2	0.1	0.1	0.1	0.1	2.3
Pretoria	25 45S	28 14E	4,491	13	81	60	77	53	67	41	77	57	104	24	14	5.0	4.3	4.5	1.7	0.9	0.3	0.2	0.6	0.8	2.2	5.2	5.2	30.9
Walvis Bay	22 56S	14 30E	24	20	67	59	65	56	62	47	67	55	112	25	20	0.1	0.2	0.1	*	*	*	*	*	*	0.2	0.1	0.2	0.9
Southwest Africa:																												
Keetmanshoop	26 35S	18 08E	3,295	17	95	65	85	57	70	42	87	55	108	26	45	0.8	1.1	1.4	0.6	0.2	*	*	*	*	0.2	0.3	0.4	5.2
Windhoek	22 34S	17 06E	5,669	30	85	63	82	59	73	43	85	60	97	25	60	3.0	3.0	3.1	1.6	0.3	*	*	*	*	0.4	0.9	1.9	14.3
Spanish Sahara:																												
Semara	26 46N	11 31W	1,509	6	73	47	88	58	96	65	88	60	121	37	6	0.1	*	0.0	*	*	*	0.0	*	*	*	1.0	0.4	1.5
Villa Cisneros	23 42N	15 52W	35	12	71	56	74	60	80	69	80	65	107	48	14	0.1	0.1	0.0	0.1	*	*	0.0	0.2	0.2	0.1	1.0	1.0	3.0
Sudan:																												
El Fasher	13 38N	25 21E	2,395	17	88	50	102	68	96	72	99	69	113	33	17	0.0	0.0	0.0	0.3	0.3	0.7	4.5	5.3	1.2	0.2	0.0	0.0	12.2
Khartoum	15 37N	32 33E	1,279	46	90	59	105	74	101	77	104	75	118	41	46	0.0	0.0	0.1	0.1	0.1	0.3	2.1	2.8	0.7	0.2	0.0	0.0	6.2
Port Sudan	19 37N	37 13E	18	30	81	68	98	78	106	83	95	80	117	50	40	0.2	0.1	0.3	0.3	0.1	*	*	*	0.3	0.4	1.7	0.9	3.7
Wadi Halfa	21 55N	31 20E	410	39	75	46	98	62	106	74	97	67	127	28	38	*	*	*	*	*	*	*	*	*	*	0.6	*	*
Wau	07 42N	28 03E	1,443	38	96	64	105	69	91	69	99	67	108	50	15	0.2	0.9	2.6	4.6	5.3	6.5	7.5	8.2	6.6	4.9	0.6	0.2	43.3
Tanzania:																												
Dar es Salaam	06 50S	39 18E	47	44	86	77	86	75	83	69	85	69	96	59	49	2.6	2.6	5.1	11.4	7.4	1.3	1.2	1.0	1.2	1.6	2.9	3.6	41.9
Iringa	07 47S	35 42E	5,330	14	75	59	75	57	73	49	80	55	90	42	29	4.8	5.1	5.9	3.5	1.7	0.2	0.2	0.2	0.7	1.9	3.5	5.3	29.3
Kigoma	04 53S	29 38E	2,903	26	80	67	81	67	82	63	84	69	100	53	18	4.8	5.0	5.9	3.1	1.7	*	0.2	0.2	0.7	1.9	5.6	5.3	36.5
Togo:																												
Lome	06 10N	01 15E	72	5	85	72	86	74	80	71	83	72	94	58	15	0.6	0.9	1.9	4.6	5.7	8.8	2.8	0.4	1.4	2.4	1.1	0.4	31.0

TEMPERATURE AND PRECIPITATION DATA FOR REPRESENTATIVE WORLD-WIDE STATIONS

Country and Station	Latitude	Longitude	Elevation (feet)	Annual Precip. (in)
Tunisia:				
Gabes	33 53N	10 07E	7	6.7
Tunis	36 47N	10 12E	217	16.5
Uganda:				
Kampala	00 20N	32 36E	4,304	46.2
Lira	02 15N	32 54E	3,560	60.7
United Arab Republic:				
Alexandria	31 12N	29 53E	105	7.0
Aswan	24 02N	32 53E	366	*
Cairo	29 52N	31 20E	381	1.1
Upper Volta:				
Bobo Dioulasso	11 10N	04 15W	1,411	46.4
Ouagadougou	12 22N	01 31W	991	35.2
Zambia:				
Balovale	13 34S	23 06E	3,577	38.3
Kasama	10 12S	31 11E	4,544	51.5
Lusaka	15 25S	28 19E	4,191	32.9
ATLANTIC ISLANDS:				
Funchal, Madeira Island	32 38N	16 55W	82	21.5
Georgetown, Ascension Island	07 56S	14 25W	55	5.2
Butte Gate, St. Helena	15 57S	05 40W	2,062	32.1
Las Palmas, Canary Islands	28 11N	15 28W	20	8.6
Porto da Praia, Cape Verde Is.	14 54N	23 31W	112	10.2
Santa Isabel, Fernando Po	03 46N	08 46E	----	74.9
Sao Tome, Sao Tome	00 20N	06 43E	16	38.0
Tristan da Cunha	37 03S	12 19W	75	66.1
INDIAN OCEAN ISLANDS:				
Agalega Island	10 26S	56 40E	10	84.7
Cocos (Keeling) Island	12 05S	96 53E	15	78.2
Heard Island	53 01S	73 23E	16	54.3
Hellburg, Reunion Island	04 37S	55 22E	3,070	90.5
Port Victoria, Seychelles	04 37S	55 27E	15	92.5
Royal Alfred Observatory, Mauritius	20 06S	57 32E	181	50.6
ASIA – FAR EAST				
China				
Canton	23 10N	113 20E	59	63.6
Chaoaha	28 15	112 58E	161	52.1
Chungking	29 30N	106 33E	855	42.9

Note: The full table also includes columns for Average Daily Temperature (January, April, July, October — max/min and length of record), Temperature Extremes (maximum, minimum, length of record), and monthly Average Precipitation (January through December, each with length of record).

TEMPERATURE AND PRECIPITATION DATA FOR REPRESENTATIVE WORLD-WIDE STATIONS

COUNTRY AND STATION
China cont'd:
Hankow
Harbin (Ha-erh-pin)
Kashgar
Kunming
Lanchow
Mukden (Shen-yang)
Shanghai
Tientsin
Urumchi
Hong Kong:
Japan:
Kushiro
Miyako
Nagasaki
Osaka
Tokyo
Korea:
Pusan
P'yongyang
Seoul
Mongolia:
Ulan Bator
Taiwan:
Tainan
Taipei
Union of Soviet Socialist Republics:
Alma-Ata
Chita (Tchita)
Dudinka
Irkutsk
Kazalinsk
Khabarovsk
Kirensk
Krasnoyarsk
Markovo
Naryn
Okhotsk
Omsk
Petropavlovsk
Samarkand
Semipalatinsk
Sverdlovsk
Tashkent
Verkhoyansk
Vladivostok
Yakutsk
Brunei:
Brunei
Burma:
Mandalay
Moulmein
Cambodia:
Phnom Penh
Indonesia:
Batavia (Jakarta)
Menokwari

ASIA — SOUTHEAST

TEMPERATURE AND PRECIPITATION DATA FOR REPRESENTATIVE WORLD-WIDE STATIONS

Temperature

COUNTRY AND STATION	LATITUDE	LONGITUDE	ELEVATION (FEET)	LENGTH OF RECORD (YEARS)	JANUARY max	JANUARY min	APRIL max	APRIL min	JULY max	JULY min	OCTOBER max	OCTOBER min	EXTREME max	EXTREME min	LENGTH OF RECORD
Indonesia cont'd:															
Mapanget	01 32N	124 55E	264	21	85	73	86	73	87	73	89	73	97	72	65
Penfui	10 10S	123 39E	335	21	87	72	89	72	88	70	92	72	101	72	58
Pontianak	00 00N	109 20E	13	20	87	74	89	74	89	74	89	74	96	75	68
Tabing	00 52S	100 21E	19	21	87	74	87	74	88	73	86	74	94	74	68
Tarakan	03 19N	117 33E	20	10	85	73	86	75	87	74	87	74	94	74	67
Laos:															
Vientiane	17 58N	102 34E	559	13	83	58	95	73	89	75	88	75	106	32	32
Malaya, Fed.:															
Kuala Lumpur	03 06N	101 42E	111	19	90	72	91	74	90	73	89	73	99	66	64
Singapore	01 18N	103 50E	33	39	86	73	88	75	88	75	87	75	97	66	64
North Borneo:															
Sanda Kan	05 54N	118 03E	38	45	85	74	89	76	89	76	88	75	99	70	70
Philippine Islands:															
Davao	07 07N	125 38E	88	15	87	72	91	73	88	73	88	73	99	65	65
Manila	14 31N	121 00E	49	61	86	69	93	75	88	75	88	74	101	58	58
Sarawak:															
Kuching	01 29N	110 20E	85	5	85	72	90	73	90	72	89	73	98	64	64
Thailand:															
Bangkok	13 44N	100 30E	53	10	89	67	95	78	90	76	88	76	104	50	50
Viet Nam:															
Hanoi	21 03N	105 52E	20	12	68	58	80	70	92	79	84	72	108	41	41
Saigon	10 49N	106 39E	33	31	89	70	95	76	88	75	88	74	104	57	57
ASIA – MIDDLE EAST															
Aden:															
Riyan	14 39N	49 19E	83	13	82	67	88	74	92	77	88	72	111	57	-
Afghanistan:															
Kabul	34 30N	69 13E	5,955	9	36	18	66	43	92	61	73	42	104	-6	-
Kandahar	31 36N	65 40E	3,462	7	56	31	86	50	102	66	85	44	111	14	-
Ceylon:															
Colombo	06 54N	79 52E	22	25	86	72	88	76	85	77	85	75	99	59	59
East Pakistan:															
Dacca	23 46N	90 23E	24	60	77	56	92	74	88	79	89	74	108	43	43
India:															
Ahmedabad	23 03N	72 37E	180	43	85	58	104	75	93	79	97	67	118	36	36
Bangalore	12 57N	77 40E	2,937	60	80	57	93	69	81	66	85	66	102	46	46
Bombay	19 58N	72 51E	21	68	88	62	88	76	85	77	89	76	110	49	46
Calcutta	22 32N	88 20E	21	60	80	55	97	76	90	79	89	74	111	44	44
Cherrapunji	25 15N	91 44E	4,309	46	60	46	73	59	73	65	71	61	87	33	33
Hyderabad	17 27N	78 28E	1,741	35	85	59	101	73	85	71	84	68	112	34	34
Jalpaiguri	26 32N	88 43E	272	30	76	47	88	71	92	80	87	70	119	36	36
Lucknow	26 45N	80 52E	400	60	77	47	101	71	92	80	92	70	119	34	34

Average Precipitation

COUNTRY AND STATION	LENGTH OF RECORD (YEARS)	JAN	FEB	MAR	APR	MAY	JUN	JUL	AUG	SEP	OCT	NOV	DEC	YEAR
Indonesia cont'd:														
Mapanget	63	18.6	13.8	12.2	8.0	6.4	6.5	4.8	4.0	3.3	4.9	8.9	14.7	106.1
Penfui	63	15.2	13.7	9.2	2.6	1.2	0.4	0.2	0.0	0.0	0.7	3.3	9.1	55.7
Pontianak	63	10.8	8.2	9.5	10.9	11.1	8.7	6.5	8.0	9.0	14.4	15.3	12.7	125.1
Tabing	63	13.7	10.1	12.8	14.5	13.5	12.8	11.7	16.2	20.1	20.5	19.2	175.4	
Tarakan	31	13.9	10.2	14.0	13.9	12.6	12.6	10.3	12.4	11.6	14.3	15.2	13.4	152.3
Laos:														
Vientiane	27	0.2	0.6	1.5	3.9	10.5	11.9	10.5	11.5	11.1	4.3	0.6	0.1	67.5
Malaya, Fed.:														
Kuala Lumpur	19	6.2	2.9	7.6	11.5	5.1	5.1	3.9	6.4	8.6	9.8	10.2	7.5	96.1
Singapore	39	9.9	7.9	7.6	6.8	6.8	6.8	6.7	7.7	7.0	8.2	10.1	9.9	95.0
North Borneo:														
Sanda Kan	46	19.0	10.9	8.6	4.5	6.2	7.4	6.7	7.9	9.3	10.2	14.5	8.5	123.7
Philippine Islands:														
Davao	34	3.4	4.5	5.2	5.8	9.2	9.1	6.5	6.5	6.7	7.9	5.3	6.1	77.6
Manila	75	0.9	0.5	0.7	1.3	5.1	10.0	17.0	16.6	14.0	7.6	5.7	2.6	82.0
Sarawak:														
Kuching	19	24.0	20.1	12.9	11.0	10.3	7.1	8.6	9.2	14.0	10.5	14.1	18.2	153.7
Thailand:														
Bangkok					2.3	5.2	6.0	6.9	9.2	14.0	9.9	3.5		57.8
Viet Nam:														
Hanoi	20	0.8	1.2	2.5	3.6	4.1	11.2	11.9	15.2	10.0	3.5	2.6	2.8	69.4
Saigon	33	0.6	0.1	0.5	1.7	8.7	13.0	12.4	10.6	13.2	10.6	4.5	2.2	78.1
ASIA – MIDDLE EAST														
Aden:														
Riyan	13	0.3	0.1	0.6	0.2	*	0.1	0.1	0.1	*	*	0.7	0.3	2.5
Afghanistan:														
Kabul	45	1.3	1.5	3.6	3.3	0.9	0.2	0.1	0.1	*	0.4	0.6	0.6	12.6
Kandahar	7	3.1	1.7	2.6	0.3	*	*	*	*	0.4	0.6	0.8	7.0
Ceylon:														
Colombo	40	3.5	2.7	5.8	8.8	12.4	13.0	5.3	4.3	6.3	13.7	12.4	5.8	92.3
East Pakistan:														
Dacca	61	0.3	1.2	2.4	5.4	9.6	13.0	13.3	13.3	9.8	5.3	1.0	0.2	73.9
India:														
Ahmedabad	45	*	0.1	0.1	*	0.4	3.7	12.2	8.1	4.2	1.0	0.4	*	29.3
Bangalore	60	0.2	0.3	0.4	1.6	4.2	2.9	3.9	5.0	6.7	5.9	2.7	0.4	34.2
Bombay	60	0.1	0.1	*	1.7	0.7	19.1	24.3	13.4	10.4	2.5	0.5	0.2	71.2
Calcutta	35	0.4	1.2	1.4	1.7	5.5	11.7	12.8	12.9	9.9	4.5	0.7	0.2	63.0
Cherrapunji	40	0.7	2.1	7.3	26.2	50.4	106.1	96.3	70.1	43.3	19.4	2.7	0.3	425.1
Hyderabad	45	0.4	0.3	0.5	1.1	1.1	4.4	6.0	5.3	5.1	2.5	1.1	0.5	29.6
Jalpaiguri	55	0.3	0.7	1.2	3.2	11.8	25.9	32.2	25.3	21.2	5.6	0.3	128.7
Lucknow	60	0.8	0.7	0.3	0.3	0.8	4.5	12.0	11.5	7.4	1.3	0.2	0.3	40.1

TEMPERATURE AND PRECIPITATION DATA FOR REPRESENTATIVE WORLD-WIDE STATIONS

COUNTRY AND STATION	LATITUDE	LONGITUDE	ELE-VATION (FEET)	TEMP LIMITS OF RECORD (YEAR)	JAN max	JAN min	APR max	APR min	JUL max	JUL min	OCT max	OCT min	EXTR max	EXTR min	PRECIP LIMITS OF RECORD (YEAR)	JAN	FEB	MAR	APR	MAY	JUN	JUL	AUG	SEP	OCT	NOV	DEC	YEAR
Madras	13 04N	80 15E	51	60	85	67	95	78	96	79	90	75	113	57	60	1.4	0.4	0.3	0.6	1.0	1.9	3.6	4.6	4.7	12.0	14.0	5.5	50.0
Mormugao	15 22N	73 49E	157	10	86	70	88	79	83	75	88	75	98	59	30	*	*		0.7	2.6	29.6	31.2	15.9	9.5	3.8	1.3	0.2	94.8
New Delhi	28 35N	77 12E	695	10	71	43	97	68	95	80	93	64	115	31	75	0.9	0.7	0.5	2.9	7.1	6.8	4.6	4.6	4.0	6.5	1.4	0.4	25.2
Silchar	24 49N	92 48E	95	60	78	52	88	69	90	77	88	72	103	41	53	0.8	2.1	7.9	14.3	15.6	21.7	19.7	19.7	14.4	6.5	1.4	0.4	124.5
Indian Ocean Islands:																												
Port Blair, Andaman Is.	11 40N	92 43E	261	60	84	72	89	75	84	75	84	74	97	62	60	1.8	1.1	1.1	2.4	15.1	21.7	15.4	16.3	17.4	12.5	10.5	7.9	123.2
Amini Divi, Laccadive Is.	11 07N	72 44E	13	29	86	74	92	80	86	77	86	77	99	65	30	0.7	*	*	1.5	3.7	14.3	12.0	7.7	6.3	5.8	2.6	1.3	56.0
Minicoy, Maldive Is.	08 18N	73 00E	9	20	85	73	87	80	85	76	85	76	98	63	50	1.8	0.7	0.9	2.3	7.0	11.6	8.9	7.8	6.3	7.3	5.5	3.4	63.5
Car Nicobar, Nicobar Is.	09 09N	92 49E	47	13	86	77	90	77	86	77	85	75	95	66	30	3.9	1.2	2.1	3.5	12.5	12.4	9.3	10.2	12.9	11.6	11.4	7.8	98.8
Iran:																												
Abadan	30 21N	48 13E	10	12	64	44	90	62	112	81	98	63	127	24	10	1.5	1.7	0.6	0.8	0.1	0.0	0.0	0.0	0.0	0.1	0.4	0.7	7.6
Esfahan (Isfahan)	32 37N	51 41E	5,238	45	47	25	72	46	98	67	78	47	108	- 4	45	0.7	0.6	0.8	0.6	0.3	*	0.1	*	*	0.4	2.0	2.4	4.4
Kermanshah	34 19N	47 07E	4,331	15	45	23	68	38	99	56	79	38	108	-13	15	2.6	2.3	2.8	1.6	*	*	*	*	*	*	1.6	1.4	16.4
Rezaiyeh	37 32N	45 05E	4,364	3	32	17	67	45	91	64	67	47	99	-11	3	1.9	2.3	2.0	1.7	1.2	0.5	*	0.1	0.2	1.5	0.8	1.6	13.8
Tehran	35 41N	51 19E	3,937	24	45	27	71	49	99	72	76	53	109	- 5	33	1.8	1.5	1.8	1.4	0.5	0.1	0.1	0.1	0.1	0.8	0.8	1.0	9.7
Iraq:																												
Baghdad	33 20N	44 24E	111	15	60	39	85	57	110	76	92	61	121	18	15	0.9	1.0	1.1	0.6	0.8	0.0	0.0	0.0	0.0	0.1	1.0	1.1	5.5
Basra	30 34N	47 47E	8	10	64	45	85	63	104	81	94	64	123	24	10	1.1	1.2	1.2	0.2	0.0	0.0	*	*	*	0.2	1.4	0.8	7.3
Mosul	36 19N	43 09E	730	26	54	35	77	49	109	72	88	51	124	12	29	2.8	3.1	2.1	1.9	0.7	*	*	*	*	0.4	1.9	2.4	15.2
Israel:																												
Haifa	32 48N	35 02E	23	16	65	49	77	58	88	75	85	68	112	27	30	6.9	4.3	1.6	1.0	0.2	*	*	*	0.1	1.0	3.7	7.3	26.2
Jerusalem	31 47N	35 13E	2,654	19	55	41	73	50	87	63	81	59	107	26	50	5.1	4.7	2.9	0.9	0.1	*	0.0	0.0	*	0.3	2.4	4.1	19.7
Tel Aviv	32 06N	34 46E	33	10	64	50	70	57	82	72	79	65	102	34	10	4.9	2.7	2.0	0.7	0.1	0.0	0.0	0.0	0.1	0.4	4.1	6.1	21.1
Jammu/Kashmir:																												
Srinagar	33 58N	74 46E	5,458	50	41	24	67	45	88	64	74	41	106	- 4	50	2.9	2.8	3.6	3.7	2.4	1.4	2.3	2.4	1.5	1.2	0.4	1.3	25.9
Jordan:																												
Amman	31 58N	35 59E	2,547	25	54	39	73	49	89	65	81	57	109	21	25	2.7	2.9	1.2	0.6	0.2	0.0	0.0	0.0	*	0.2	1.3	1.8	10.9
Kuwait:																												
Kuwait	29 21N	48 00E	16	14	61	49	83	68	103	86	91	73	119	33	10	0.9	0.9	1.1	0.2	*	0.0	0.0	0.0	0.0	0.1	0.6	1.1	5.1
Lebanon:																												
Beirut	33 54N	35 28E	111	62	62	51	72	58	87	73	81	69	107	30	71	7.5	6.2	3.7	2.2	0.7	0.1	*	*	0.2	2.0	5.2	7.3	35.1
Nepal:																												
Katmandu	27 42N	85 22E	4,423	27	65	36	84	53	84	69	80	56	99	27	9	0.6	1.6	0.9	2.3	4.8	9.7	14.7	13.6	6.1	1.5	0.3	0.1	56.2
Oman and Muscat:																												
Muscat	23 37N	58 35E	15	23	77	66	90	78	97	87	93	80	116	51	38	1.1	0.7	0.4	0.4	*	0.1	*	*	*	0.1	0.4	0.7	3.9
Pakistan (West):																												
Karachi	24 48N	66 59E	13	43	77	55	90	73	91	81	91	72	118	39	59	0.5	0.4	0.3	0.1	0.1	0.7	3.4	1.6	0.5	0.1	0.1	0.2	7.8
Multan	30 11N	71 25E	400	60	68	42	95	68	102	86	94	64	122	29	60	0.4	0.4	0.4	0.3	0.6	2.0	1.8	0.5	0.1	0.1	0.1	0.3	7.1
Rawalpindi	33 35N	73 03E	1,676	60	62	38	86	59	98	77	89	57	118	25	60	2.5	2.5	2.7	1.9	1.3	2.3	8.1	9.2	3.9	0.6	0.3	1.2	36.5
Saudi Arabia:																												
Dhahran	26 16N	50 10E	78	10	69	54	90	69	107	86	95	73	120	40	10	1.1	0.6	0.4	0.2	0.1	0.0	0.0	0.0	0.0	0.0	0.2	0.9	3.5
Jidda	21 28N	39 10E	20	5	84	66	91	70	99	79	95	73	117	49	5	0.2	*	*	*	0.0	0.0	0.0	0.0	0.0	*	1.0	1.2	2.5
Riyadh	24 39N	46 42E	1,938	3	70	46	89	64	107	78	94	61	113	19	3	0.1	0.8	0.9	1.0	0.4	*	0.0	0.0	0.0	*	*	0.0	3.2
Syria:																												
Deir Ez Zor	35 21N	40 09E	699	5	53	35	80	52	105	78	86	56	114	16	5	1.6	0.8	0.3	0.8	0.1	*	0.0	0.0	0.0	0.7	0.4	1.5	6.2
Dimashq (Damascus)	33 30N	36 20E	2,362	13	53	36	75	49	96	64	81	54	113	21	7	1.7	1.7	0.3	0.5	0.1	*	*	0.0	0.7	0.4	1.6	1.6	8.6
Halab (Aleppo)	36 14N	37 08E	1,280	8	50	34	75	48	97	69	81	54	117	9	10	3.5	2.5	1.5	1.1	0.3	0.1	0.0	*	*	1.0	2.2	3.3	15.5
Trucial Kingdoms:																												
Sharjah	25 20N	55 24E	18	11	74	54	86	65	100	82	92	71	118	37	12	0.9	0.9	0.4	0.2	0.0	0.0	0.0	0.0	0.0	0.0	0.4	1.4	4.2
Turkey:																												
Adana	36 59N	35 18E	82	21	57	39	74	51	93	71	84	58	109	19	31	4.3	4.0	2.5	1.6	2.0	0.7	0.2	0.2	0.7	1.9	2.4	3.8	24.3
Ankara	39 57N	32 53E	2,825	26	39	24	63	40	86	59	69	44	104	-13	24	1.3	1.2	1.3	1.3	1.9	1.0	0.5	0.4	0.7	0.9	1.2	1.9	13.6
Erzurum	39 54N	41 16E	6,402	16	24	8	50	32	78	53	59	37	93	-22	16	1.4	1.2	2.5	3.1	2.1	1.3	0.9	1.1	2.3	1.8	1.1	1.2	21.2
Izmir (Smyrna)	38 27N	27 15E	92	39	55	39	70	49	92	69	76	55	108	12	58	4.4	3.3	3.0	1.7	1.3	0.6	0.2	0.0	0.8	2.1	3.3	4.8	25.5
Samsun	41 17N	36 19E	131	24	50	38	59	45	79	65	69	56	103	20	27	2.9	2.6	2.7	2.3	1.8	1.5	1.5	1.3	2.4	3.2	3.5	2.4	29.1
Yemen:																												
Kamaran I.	15 20N	42 37E	20	26	82	74	89	79	98	85	93	82	105	66	21	0.2	0.2	0.1	0.1	0.1	*	0.5	0.7	0.1	0.1	0.4	0.9	3.4

See footnotes at end of table.

TEMPERATURE AND PRECIPITATION DATA FOR REPRESENTATIVE WORLD-WIDE STATIONS

AUSTRALIA & PACIFIC ISLANDS

Country and Station	Latitude	Longitude	Elevation (feet)	Annual Precipitation (in.)
Australia:				
Adelaide	34 57S	138 32E	20	21.1
Alice Springs	23 48S	133 53E	1,791	9.9
Bourke	30 05S	145 58E	361	13.2
Brisbane	27 25S	153 05E	137	44.7
Broome	17 57S	122 13E	56	22.9
Burketown	17 45S	139 33E	30	27.5
Canberra	35 18S	149 11E	1,886	23.0
Carnarvon	24 53S	113 40E	31	9.1
Cloncurry	20 40S	140 30E	622	18.0
Esperance	33 50S	121 55E	32	26.4
Laverton	28 40S	122 23E	14	8.8
Melbourne	37 49S	144 58E	96	25.7
Mundiwindi	23 52S	120 10E	1,510	10.1
Perth	31 56S	115 58E	115	34.7
Port Darwin	12 25S	130 52E	1,840	58.7
Sydney	33 52S	151 12E	64	46.5
Thursday Island	10 35S	144 44E	58	67.5
Townsville	19 15S	146 46E	62	45.7
William Creek	28 55S	136 21E	207	5.0
Wisdomah	25 26S	142 36E	18	11.4
Tasmania:				
Hobart	42 53S	147 20E	247	24.0
New Zealand:				
Auckland	37 00S	174 47E	390	49.1
Christchurch	43 29S	172 32E	177	25.1
Dunedin	45 55S	170 32E	23	36.9
Wellington	41 17S	174 46E	118	47.4
PACIFIC ISLANDS:				
Canton, Phoenix Is.	02 46S	171 43W	4	29.4
Guam, Marianas Is.	13 33N	144 50E	415	88.5
Honolulu, Hawaii	21 20N	157 55W	9	21.9
Iwo Jima, Bonin Is.	24 47N	141 19E	361	52.8
Madang, New Guinea	05 12S	145 47E	19	137.2
Midway Is.	28 13N	177 23W	12	40.7
Naha, Okinawa	26 12N	127 59E	96	82.8
Noumea, New Caledonia	22 16S	166 27E	29	43.5
Pago Pago, Samoa	14 19S	170 43W	2	193.6
Ponape, Caroline Is.	06 58N	158 13E	123	191.9
Port Moresby, New Guinea	09 29S	147 09E	126	39.8
Rabaul, New Guinea	04 13S	152 11E	28	88.8
Suva, Fiji Is.	18 08S	178 26E	19	117.1

416

TEMPERATURE AND PRECIPITATION DATA FOR REPRESENTATIVE WORLD-WIDE STATIONS

COUNTRY AND STATION	LATITUDE	LONGITUDE	ELE-VATION (FEET)	TEMPERATURE — LENGTH OF RECORD (years)	AVERAGE DAILY JANUARY (max/min)	APRIL (max/min)	JULY (max/min)	OCTOBER (max/min)	EXTREME (max/min)	PRECIP — LENGTH OF RECORD (years)	JANUARY	FEBRUARY	MARCH	APRIL	MAY	JUNE	JULY	AUGUST	SEPTEMBER	OCTOBER	NOVEMBER	DECEMBER	YEAR
Tahiti, Society Is.	17 33S	149 36W	7	23	89 / 72	89 / 72	86 / 68	87 / 70	93 / 61	27	13.2	11.5	6.5	6.8	4.9	3.2	2.6	1.9	2.3	3.4	6.5	11.9	74.7
Tulagi, Solomon Is.	09 05S	160 10E	8	20	88 / 76	88 / 76	86 / 76	87 / 76	96 / 68	37	14.3	14.6	15.0	10.0	8.1	6.8	7.6	8.7	8.0	8.7	10.0	10.4	123.4
Wake Is.	19 17N	166 39E	11	30	82 / 73	83 / 74	87 / 77	86 / 77	92 / 64	30	1.1	1.4	1.5	1.9	2.0	1.9	4.6	7.1	5.2	5.3	3.1	1.8	36.9
Yap, Caroline Is.	9 31N	138 08E	62	30	85 / 76	85 / 77	88 / 75	88 / 75	97 / 69	30	7.9	4.6	5.4	6.4	9.5	10.7	13.8	14.7	14.0	13.2	11.2	10.2	121.6
ANTARCTICA																							
Byrd Station	80 01S	119 32W	5,095	6	10 / -2	-11 / -30	-25 / -45	-15 / -33	31 / -82	6	0.4	0.4	0.2	0.3	0.4	0.5	0.7	0.7	0.3	0.7	0.0	0.3	4.9
Ellsworth	77 44S	41 07W	139	6	22 / 12	-10 / -25	-21 / -35	2 / -13	36 / -70	6	0.3	0.4	0.3	0.2	0.2	0.2	0.2	0.2	0.3	0.4	0.5	0.2	3.6
McMurdo Station	77 53S	166 48W	8	10	30 / 21	-1 / -13	-9 / -24	2 / -12	42 / -59	10	0.5	0.7	0.4	0.4	0.4	0.3	0.2	0.3	0.4	0.2	0.2	0.3	4.3
South Pole Station	89 59S	000 00W	9,186	5	-16 / -23	-66 / -79	-67 / -81	-55 / -64	6 / -107	5	*	*	0.0	0.0	0.0	0.0	1.3	0.0	0.0	*	0.8	0.3	0.1
Wilkes	66 16S	110 31E	31	7	34 / 28	17 / 9	8 / -3	16 / 6	46 / -35	7	0.5	0.4	1.7	1.1	1.4	1.2	0.8	0.8	1.5	1.2	0.0	0.3	12.2

NOTES

1. "Length of Record" refers to average daily maximum and minimum temperatures and precipitation. A standard period of the 30 years from 1931-1960 had been used for locations in the United States and some other countries. The length of record of extreme maximum and minimum temperatures includes all available years of data for a given location and is usually for a longer period.

2. * - Less than 0.05"

3. Except for Antarctica, amounts of solid precipitation such as snow or hail have been converted to their water equivalent. Because of the frequent occurrence of blowing snow, it has not been possible to determine the precise amount of precipitation actually falling in Antarctica. The values shown are the average amounts of solid snow accumulating in a given period as determined by snow markers. The liquid content of the accumulation is undetermined.

417

WORLDWIDE EXTREMES OF TEMPERATURE AND PRECIPITATION
RECORDED BY CONTINENTAL AREA

● Key numbers correspond to data entries on following page.

418

AVERAGE JANUARY TEMPERATURE (F°)

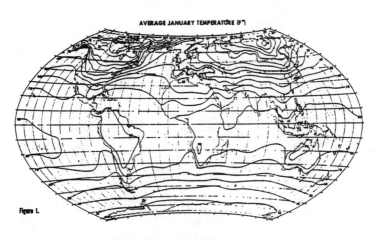

Figure 1.

AVERAGE JULY TEMPERATURE (F°)

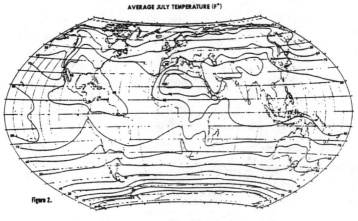

Figure 2.

GENERAL PATTERN OF ANNUAL WORLD PRECIPITATION (INCHES)

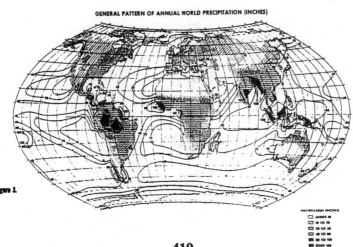

Figure 3.

419

TEMPERATURE EXTREMES

Key No.	Area	Highest °F	Place	Elevation Feet	Date
1	Africa	136	Azizia, Libya	380	Sep. 13, 1922
2	North America	134	Death Valley, Calif.	-178	July 10, 1913
3	Asia	129	Tirat Tsvi, Israel	-722	June 21, 1942
4	Australia	128	Cloncurry, Queensland	622	Jan. 16, 1889
5	Europe	122	Seville, Spain	26	Aug. 4, 1881
6	South America	120	Rivadavia, Argentina	676	Dec. 11, 1905
7	Oceania	108	Tuguegarao, Philippines	72	Apr. 29, 1912
8	Antarctica	58	Esperanza, Palmer Pen.	26	Oct. 20, 1956

Key No.	Area	Lowest °F	Place	Elevation Feet	Date
9	Antarctica	-127	Vostok	11,220	Aug. 24, 1960
10	Asia	- 90	Oymykon, U.S.S.R.	2,625	Feb. 6, 1933
11	Greenland	- 87	Northice	7,690	Jan. 9, 1954
12	North America	- 81	Snag, Yukon, Canada	1,925	Feb. 3, 1947
13	Europe	- 67	Ust'Shchugor, USSR	279	January +
14	South America	- 27	Sarmiento, Argentina	879	June 1, 1907
15	Africa	- 11	Ifrane, Morocco	5,364	Feb. 11, 1935
16	Australia	- 8	Charlotte Pass, N.S.W.	---	July 22, 1947*
17	Oceania	14	Haleakala Summit, Maui	9,750	Jan. 2, 1961

+ exact date unknown; lowest in 15-year period
* and earlier date
--- elevation unknown

EXTREMES OF AVERAGE ANNUAL PRECIPITATION

Key No.	Area	Greatest Amount Inches	Place	Elevation Feet	Years of Record
18	Oceania	460.0	Mt. Waialeale, Kauai, Hawaii	5,075	32
19	Asia	450.0	Cherrapunji, India	4,309	74
20	Africa	404.6	Debundscha, Cameroon	30	32
21	South America	353.9	Quibdo, Colombia	240	10-16
22	North America	262.1	Henderson Lake, B. C., Canada	12	14
23	Europe	182.8	Crkvica, Yugoslavia	3,337	22
24	Australia	179.3	Tully, Queensland	---	31

Key No.	Area	Least Amount Inches	Place	Elevation Feet	Years of Record
25	South America	0.03	Arica, Chile	95	59
26	Africa	<0.1	Wadi Halfa, Sudan	410	39
27	Antarctica	* 0.8	South Pole Station	9,186	10
28	North America	1.2	Batagues, Mexico	16	14
29	Asia	1.8	Aden, Arabia	22	50
30	Australia	4.05	Mulka, South Australia	---	34
31	Europe	6.4	Astrakhan, USSR	45	25
32	Oceania	8.93	Puako, Hawaii	5	13

* The value given is the average amount of solid snow accumulating in one year as indicated by snow markers. The liquid content of the snow is undetermined.

420

Chapter 44

UNDECIDED ON WHICH COUNTRY TO VISIT?

- - - -

Introduction

Choosing a suitable country to spend a vacation could at times be difficult and confusing, especially, for the non-experienced overseas vacationer. So if you are undecided on which country to spend that vacation you have always wanted, you are not alone. Several vacationers face the same dilemma.

To assist you in resolving this area of uncertainty, a list of the top twenty five countries that American citizens visit the most has been provided in this chapter. As you plan your trip, you may want to consider, as well, the quality of life in the country you are visiting.

Almost every traveler contemplating taking up a residence overseas or vacationing overseas, takes into consideration a variety of factors.

An effort to measure these factors for the countries of the world on a comparative basis is provided in the *quality of life index* published annually by Agora Inc. of Baltimore Maryland. And these are their findings and conclusions for 1995 based on a scored ranking system comprising seven different criteria.

(1) Cost of Living (2) Economic Prosperity (3) Recreation, Culture and Entertainment (4) Infrastructure (5) Health and Health Care (6) Freedom (7) Environment.

The Ranking System

Following are details on what factors are taken into account in each of our seven categories:

Cost of living. This is perhaps the most important category for anyone interested in visiting or retiring to another country. Our main source for this category is the U.S. Department of State Indexes of Living Costs Abroad, Quarters Allowances, and Hardship Differentials. This index is used to compute cost-of-living allowances according to a Western pattern of living. The lower the score, the higher the cost of living. This category is given a weight of 15% when we add up the scores and plays an important role in choosing our overall winner.

Economic prosperity. The economy of every country is given a weight of 35% more weight than any other category in our final tabulations. Considered are each country's gross national product (GNP) per capital average annual economic growth of the GNP, and overall economic diversity.

Recreation, culture, and entertainment. Considered in our culture category are the number of newspaper per 1,000 citizens, the number of museums and cinemas per capita the number of high school students per 10,000 citizens, the national literacy rate, and the variety of cultural offerings available. This is the category for which our Western bias is most evident.

Infrastructure. Considered are the number of cars and telephones per 1,000 citizens, the length of usable railroad track, the overall quality of the radio system in each country, and the availability of telecommunications.

Health and health care. Considered are the infant-mortality rate in each country, the number of physicians and hospital beds per capital, the available daily calories per capital (a determining statistic for the African nations in our survey), the cost of a doctor's visit, and the life expectancy in each country. We assume that a long life expectancy reflects a generally good health-care system.

Freedom. The freedom category is also one of the most important. It is based on the political rights and civil liberties granted to citizens in each country. This year, 26 countries received a perfect score in this category.

Environment. Our environmental category considers the population density in each country, the percentage of protected land, and each country's particular ecological problems, including pollution, deforestation, and desertification.

Our Sources.
To create the 1995 Quality of Life Index, we consulted the following references: the U.S. Department of State Indexes of Living Costs Abroad, Quarters Allowances, and Hardship Differentials: Freedom House's

December 1994 Freedom review; the New Book of World Rankings; Comparative World Data; A Statistical Handbook for Social Science; the Annual Report of the United Nations Development Programme; the World Bank Annual Report; and the 1994 Information Almanac. In addition, we consulted innumerable popular publications, as well as statistical publications available on specific world regions and states. We also relied upon the experience of our contributing editors around the world.

World's freest
The following countries are the freest countries are in the world this year and received a score of 100 in our freedom category.

Four countries are new to the list this year: Andorra, Kiribati, Norway, and San Marino.

Andorra
Australia
Austria
Barbados
Belgium
Belize
Canada
Cyprus
Denmark
Finland
Iceland
Kiribati
Liechtenstein
Luxembourg
Malta
Marshall Islands
Micronesia
Netherlands
New Zealand
Norway
Portugal
San Marino
Sweden
Switzerland
Tuvalu
United States

World's least free
The Freedom House survey from which we compiled this information points out that the vast majority of the world's people live in partly free or unfree regions. You'll notice that most of these restrictive countries are neo-Communists or post-Communist transitional societies or they are multi ethnic ones in which power is not held by a dominant ethic group. The following countries receive the worst ratings for political rights and civil liberties; their citizens enjoy almost no rights at all, Rwanda and Algeria joined this year because of increased violence in both countries.

Afghanistan
Algeria
Angola
Bhutan
Burma
China
Cuba
Equatorial Guinea
Iraq
Libya
Mauritania
North Korea
Rwanda
Saudi Arabia
Somalia
Sudan
Syria
Tajikistan
Turkmenistan
Uzbekistan
Vietnam

The Top Ten
Switzerland
United States
Canada
Germany
Iceland
Sweden
Austria
Liechtenstein
Luxembourg
Norway
New Zealand
Australia
Finland
Denmark

The Bottom Ten
Rwanda
Syria
Equatorial Guinea
Chad
Mauritania
Sierra Leone
Guinea
Afghanistan
Djibouti
Ethiopia

World's most affordable
Ecuador
Colombia
Venezuela
India
Guyana

Czech Republic
Bulgaria
Suriname
Dominica
Honduras
El Salvador
Pakistan
Kenya
Romania
Nauru

World's most expensive
Norway
Sweden
Finland
Denmark
France
Switzerland
Liechtenstein
Luxembourg
Japan
Norway
Zaire
Mali
Spain
Italy
Germany
Iceland

World's most cultural
United Kingdom
Italy
Canada
France
Germany
Australia
Spain
Greece
United States
New Zealand

World's least cultural
Somalia
Chad
Ethiopia
Burkina Faso
Afghanistan
Nigeria
Equatorial Guinea
Mali
Djibouti
Nauru

World's most ecological
Ecuador
Chile

Austria
New Zealand
Iceland
Costa Rica
Suriname
Botswana
Iceland
Namibia

World's least ecological
Hong Kong
Bahrain
Bangladesh
Singapore
Mauritius
Malta
Macao
Monaco
Bermuda

World's healthiest
Iceland
Ireland
New Zealand
Australia
Luxembourg
Spain
Monaco
Denmark
France
Belgium
Liechtenstein
Italy
Austria
Canada
Germany
Switzerland
Sweden

World's least healthy
Ethiopia
Guinea
Equatorial Guinea
Burkina Faso
Indonesia
Chad
Mozambique
Tuvalu
Mali
Namibia
Guinea-Bissau
Rwanda
Sierra Leone

World's best infrastructure
Germany

423

Monaco
Switzerland
San Marino
Liechtenstein
United States
Sweden
Canada
Andorra
Australia

World's worst infrastructure
Tuvalu
Kiribati
Bhutan
Central African Republic
Liberia
Burkina Faso
Rwanda
Bosnia-Herzegovina
Comoros
Guinea-Bissau
Papua New Guinea
Guinea
Burundi

World's most prosperous
Switzerland
Sweden
Luxembourg
Japan
Norway
Liechtenstein
United States
Iceland
Denmark
Belgium
Finland
United Arab Emirates
Germany

World's least prosperous
Malaysia
Palua
Tajikistan
Armenia
Congo
Georgia
Central African Republic
Equatorial Guinea
Kyrigistan
Senegal
Rwanda
Turkmenistan
Madagascar
Kazakhstan

TOP TWENTY-FIVE DESTINATIONS OF U.S. CITIZENS TRAVELING ABROAD

RANK**	COUNTRY	TRAVELERS (000)	
1	MEXICO	14,900	
2	CANADA	12,668	
3	U.K.	2,947	
4	GERMANY	1,879	
5	FRANCE	1,694	
6	ITALY	1,168	
7	BAHAMAS	1,012	
8	DOMINICAN REP.		1,006
9	JAPAN	1,105	
10	SWITZERLAND	752	
11	SPAIN	588	
12	S. KOREA	542	
13	HONG KONG	496	
14	JAMAICA	481	
15	AUSTRALIA	446	
16	NETHERLANDS	380	
17	BELGIUM	348	
18	NETH. ANTILLES		340
19	TAIWAN	306	
20	VENEZUELA	287	
21	ISRAEL	270	
22	COLUMBIA	244	
23	NEW ZEALAND	225	
24	SINGAPORE	211	
25	PHILIPPINES	210	

SOURCE: U.S. Travel and Tourism Administration Infight Survey.

** Rankings reflect 1990 statistics. The countries listed above have remained the top twenty since 1988, although not necessarily in the same ranking order. Mexico, Canada and the U.K., however, have consistently ranked numbers one, two and three since 1988.

Chapter 45

Additional Information, Tips and Advice

- - - -

Photocopy: Make 1-2 sets of photocopies of all of your documents including your passport, tickets, credit cards, travelers checks, drivers' license, and even prescriptions. Leave one or two sets with your family or friends at home,and carry one set with you in a separate place from the originals.

Purchases: Keep all original receipts of purchases. You may need them to satisfy U.S. Customs requirements, or in the event your luggage is lost or stolen.

Contents: Make an inventory of the contents of your check-in luggage before you leave. Such a list may become useful in the event they are lost or stolen.

Addresses: Make sure you have all the addresses and telephone numbers you may need while abroad, including those of your friends, and relatives at home and abroad, your physician, the nearest U.S. Embassy or consulate and the U.S. State Department.

Scheduling: Make sure you schedule to get your passport, visas and vaccination on time. An early start will save you a lot of heartaches. Similarly, do arrive at the airport on time, at least two hours early, and check in as early as you can. This way you will minimize the chances of being "bumped". It will, also, allow you time to make alternative plans in the event of a cancellation.

Research: No amount of information is too much for someone traveling to a foreign country, especially those dealing with the customs and laws of the foreign country, the people, the climate, transportation, food, etc. Learn as much as you can about the country from your local library, the U.S. Department of Tourism, the U.S. Department of State, the country's embassy, consulates and tourist offices, travel agencies and agents. And while you are abroad, brochures and newspapers often available in the large hotels and newsstands may be very helpful information sources.

Itinerary: A copy of your itinerary should be left with your family or friends at home. This will be handy in the event of an emergency. Travelers very concerned about their health may also leave a copy with their

physician just in case.

Getting Help: Abundant help and information are available to Americans traveling abroad. In addition to the enormous amount of information covered in this book, you could get general as well as country and region-specific travel information from the U.S. State Department, from the country's embassy, consulates and tourist offices in the U.S., and from travel agencies and travel consultants and advisors. Your local public library and bookstores should not be left out. While abroad the American Embassy and consulates will be one of your most important places to seek all forms of assistance.

Visas: Different countries have different visa requirements and may not allow you into the country without one. However, while some countries do not require visas from Americans, many others do. See Chapter 3 of this book for country by country visa and other entry requirements, including useful visa-related tips. Most countries charge a fee for their visas. Remember, visas are usually stamped in the passport, so you must have a valid passport before applying. You may, also, be denied a visa if your passport has a validity of less than six months and/or if other entry requirements have not been met.

In case you did not know, some countries do impose time restrictions on their visas, meaning that you may be required to use the visa by starting off your journey and/or entry to the country within a given time period (typically 90 days). In some cases, the visa period may also include the length of time you are allowed to stay in that country. Once the visa period has expired, you may have to re-apply.

Vaccination: Vaccination requirements vary from country to country, and some countries may deny you entry or subject you to vaccination at the airport before allowing you to enter. It will be very prudent to have your shots here in the U.S. before traveling. Make sure your shots are properly and officially documented on a yellow colored "International Vaccination Card" or the 'International Vaccination Certificate". For a list of countries and the recommended shots, see the Chapter on "Health Information for International Travel." You may also contact the Centers for Disease Control at (404) 329-3311 for additional diseases you should be aware of. As you go through the vaccination requirements for the various countries you plan to visit, do not overlook discussing with your physician about getting immunized for such diseases as hepatitis, polio, tetanus/diphtheria, typhoid and cholera. For those travelers who already had these shots, all that may be needed is just booster shots. A number of these shots are still controversial. Your physician however, should advise you appropriately. Whereas some of the shots you will need may be available free of charge in some places and with some health plans, in some cases you may be required to pay to get some or all of them. Contact your physician or your state or local health office on this matter. Remember, a number of these inoculations may require more than one dose of the shot and therefore, more than one visit. Some shots, may require up to several weeks apart. Furthermore, some shots have side-effects that could render you uncomfortable for several days. It is therefore, important to plan appropriately and give yourself reasonable amount of time.

Trouble: While abroad, should you find yourself in trouble (especially with local law enforcement officials) or with any other type of problem (stranded, sick, lost documents, emergency), immediately contact the nearest U.S. Embassy or consulate. When in trouble with the local law enforcement authorities, visit, or call, or request the presence of the U.S. Ambassador, consul or an official from the Embassy or consulate. While they might not help you resolve all of your problems, they are the best help available. It is recommended that you register with the nearest U.S. Embassy or consulate upon arrival. Check Appendix A for a list of U.S. Embassies and consulates all over the world.

Physician: Your travel plans should include a discussion and consultation with your physician. Your physician may be helpful in responding to your health problems while overseas, but equally important, in counseling you regarding how to maintain good health while abroad. He or she will be in a good position to advise you on what medications to carry, what to eat and drink and what to stay away from. Do not forget a trip to your dentist.

U.S. Customs: Familiarize yourself with the U.S. Customs Services, regulations and requirements. It could save you a lot in efforts, time and money. This is especially important for those travelers contemplating returning to the U.S. with food items, animal products and other merchandise purchased abroad or originating from certain countries. The U.S. Customs publications

referenced and reproduced in this book are a must read for those travelers.

Electricity: Electricity requirements vary from one country to another. In other words, appliances specifically designed for usage in the U.S. may not operate or be used in some other countries without risking disappointment, damage to the appliance, or even loss of life. For example, whereas U.S. appliances use 110 volts and 60 cycle, several countries require 220 volts and 50 cycles. Such appliances will be inappropriate and may not even function. To avoid this problem and still be able to use your 110 volt, 60 cycle American appliance, you will need a converter and an adapter plug. If your appliance is equipped with dual-voltage capability, all you may have to do in order to use it is to flip the switch accordingly. Even in the case of a dual-voltage appliance, you may still need an adapter plug with the right type of prong to fit into the wall outlet. Check your local department store or electronic shop for a converter and adapter. You may want to get a "universal adapter plug," since it has the advantage of having different size plugs which can be used when traveling to countries with different requirements. As in all cases with electrical appliances and devices, please read carefully the instructions before using them. If unsure, ask someone. Your hotel management will be of help. See appendix 4D for country by country electricity requirements.

Telephoning: Whereas the privilege of telephoning and telephones are taken for granted in the U.S., you must know that it is a luxury, especially in less developed countries. In other words, many countries' telephone facilities may not exist for some cities. If they do exist, they may not function properly or efficiently. In other cases, telephones may be hard to find or may be expensive. Considerable patience may be required on your part. You may have to explore alternative methods of sending messages, including telegram, cablegram, fax or telex. And while abroad you may save yourself a lot of worry by placing your overseas calls from a post office or from coin-operated phones as opposed to your hotel room. You may even benefit, through exchange rate differentials and billing procedures, if you use your credit card, calling card or call collect. See Chapter 42 for instructions on communicating to and from overseas.

Addressing Mail: In addressing mail to or from abroad, it is important to print as clearly as possible. This will minimize the chances of your mail not getting to its destination. If you are writing to a "foreign service post," remember to use the correct format. Check the table of contents for the section on "How to communicate with a Foreign Service Post.

Writing Dates: Whereas in the U. S. the month of the year is written before the day of the month, e.g. January 10, 1992, (1/10/92), in several countries it is customary when writing dates to write the day followed by the month and the year, e.g. 10 January 1992 (10/1/92).

Visa and Other Entry Requirements: Although a U.S. passport and/or visa may not be required for Americans traveling to some countries, it is required for travel to most countries in the world. And even for those countries not requiring visas, there may be other requirements that must be met. Each country has its own set of entry and exit requirements.

The U.S. Department of State publication, Foreign Entry Requirements, (reprinted in Chapter 3 of this book) gives basic information on entry requirements and tells where and how to apply for visas. The best authority on a country's visa and other requirements, however, is its embassy or consulate and it is recommended that you check with it before applying. Allow plenty of time to obtain the visas. An average of two weeks for each visa is recommended, but some countries may require at least a month. Do not forget that you may be able to get a second passport to travel on in the event your other passport is tied up with the visa application. When you make visa inquires, ask about the following:

*   Entry/Exit Visas
*   Visa price, length of validity, and number of entries.
*   Financial data required, proof of sufficient funds, proof of onward return ticket.
*   Immunizations required.
*   Currency regulations.
*   Import/export restrictions and limitations.
*   Departure tax. Be sure to keep enough local currency to depart as planned.
*   AIDS clearance certification. An increasing number of countries require certification that visitors are free from the AIDS virus.

As an international traveler, it is advisable to apply for a visa in person and at foreign consulates or embassies nearer you, especially considering that your presence may be needed for an interview. Furthermore, this will allow you to straighten things out as well as ensure that the visa has been issued properly. It is also advisable that you obtain your visa(s) before you leave home. If you decide to visit additional countries en route, it may be difficult or impossible to obtain visas. In several countries you may not be admitted into the country without a visa, and may be required to depart on the next plane if you arrive without one. This can be particularly inconvenient if the next plane does not arrive for several days, the airport hotel is full, and the airport has no other sleeping accommodations.

Should you decide to apply for your visa by mail remember to enclose the application form, the visa fee, your passport, photograph(s) and any other documents required. Should you chose to have your passport mailed to you, do enclose adequate postage money and request that it be returned to you by registered mail. Do not forget to find out what form of payments are acceptable since some embassies do not honor personal checks.

Remember, some countries require both entry and exit visas and depending on the country, you may be better off securing a multiple or double-entry visa before departure. Travelers with only a single entry visa may find it particularly difficult to leave the country in the event of an emergency. While planning your itinerary, be aware that some countries, mostly in Africa, will refuse to admit you if you have South African visas or entry and exit stamps on your passports. Similarly, some Arab countries will refuse to admit you if your passport shows any evidence of previous or expected travel to Israel. If you have such notations in your passport or plan to visit some of these countries in conjunction with a trip to other countries, contact a U.S. passport agency for guidance.

Adoption: For those Americans traveling abroad to attempt to adopt children, be aware that several countries prohibit adoptions by foreigners or have laws governing adoption by foreigners. In some cases, the law requires formal court adoption of the child in the country before the child is permitted to immigrate to the U.S. Because of scandals over the illegal activities of some adoption agencies and attorneys both in the U.S. and abroad, you should be ready to experience some difficulties. The more knowledgeable you are about the local laws and requirements, the less burdensome the process. Americans interested in adopting a child from a particular country should contact the U.S. embassy or consulate in that country or in the U.S. the Department of State's Office of Citizen Consular Services, (202) 647-3712, to obtain information on the adoption process in that country. See Chapter 39 for more information on International Adoptions. See Chapter 39 for additional information on foreign adoption.

Foreign Spouses: Americans traveling abroad with their foreign spouses and American children, should be aware of recent cases where the foreign spouse has prevented the children from returning to the U.S. In almost every one of those cases reported, the U.S. government, through various avenues, has continued their efforts for the safe return of the children. The results, have not always been successful, nor hopeful, due in part, to the laws and practices of those foreign countries. Remember, once overseas, you are subject to the laws and practices of the country you are in; United States laws cannot protect you. American women, in particular, should be aware that in some countries, either by law or by custom, a woman and/or her children may be required to get her husbands' permission in order to travel out of the country. If you or your children are planning to travel, be aware of the laws and customs of the places you visit. It is advisable not to visit or allow your children to visit, unless you are confident that you will be permitted to leave. Although this is not a common experience, you may want to give it some thought, as there may always be a chance of its happening. (See the Chapter on International Parental Child Abduction)

Shortages, High Prices and Other Problems: Consumer goods, gas and food are in short supply in some countries, and prices for these commodities may be high by U.S. standards. Shortages of hotel accommodations, also, exist, so confirm reservations well in advance. Some countries, especially in Africa, experience disruptions in electricity and water supply or in services, such as mail and telecommunications. Be informed, and be patient.

Tourists: Some countries, including Kuwait, Oman, Qatar and Saudi Arabia, do not permit tourism. All visitors must be sponsored either by a company in the country to be visited or by a relative or friend native to the country. Countries requiring visitors to be sponsored usually will require them to obtain exit permits from their sponsors, as well. It is advisable not to accept sponsorship to visit a country, unless you are sure you will also be able to obtain an exit permit.

Departure Tax: Some countries require all departing passengers to pay a departure tax or some type of tax or levy. You should, as part of your inquiry on entry requirements, verify if this applies and if so, keep enough local currency to ensure departure as planned.

Weather: As an international traveler, weather conditions in the countries you plan to visit should be an important consideration both as a guide to the type of clothing that you carry along and to your ability to have fun. Because weather and climatic conditions vary around the world, it is advisable to include this as part of your pre-trip plans and to verify what the conditions may be during the period of your intended travel. See Chapter 43 (Climates of the World) for a general guideline on world-wide temperature and precipitation. Remember, summer, winter, spring, and fall as

commonly used to describe seasons in the U.S. are not applicable or commonly used in many parts of the world. In some parts, you may find people referring to "dry' and "rainy" (wet) seasons. You may even find many people, totally lacking in knowledge about names we are so used to in the U.S. Incidentally, there are important differences as well as similarities in characteristics between rainy and dry seasons and the seasons in the U.S.

Political/Public Gathering: Always stay away from political gathering places and avoid public demonstrations. Americans have been arrested when local authorities have thought that they were participating in civil demonstrations. Remember, public gatherings are usually surrounded by security persons.

It is also prudent to avoid engaging in political discussions or making public political statements or announcements as this may get you arrested. If you are detained or arrested for these or any other reason(s), ask to speak with a U.S. Consular Officer.

In Your Person: As a foreign visitor and for safety purposes, always carry with you your traveling papers, such as your passport with visa, tourist card and any other documentation that you may be required to carry.

Overstaying: Overstaying the validity of your visa or tourist card is often a violation. If you think, you might overstay, it is advisable to contact the local immigration office to find out whether you could be allowed to go so and what the requirements may be. In some countries, you may be granted an extension after submitting a formal application. Usually, the sooner you make such determination and/or put in your application, the better.

Contraband: (Prohibited and restricted Items): Every country has a variety of goods that are prohibited for import or export, and for which violators may be subjected to heavy fines, or imprisonment, in addition to the goods being confiscated. Often a list of such products is available with the country's foreign mission (Embassy and Consulate) and Tourist Information Office. As part of your preparation to ensure a smooth trip to a foreign country, I suggest, requesting such a list. If in doubt, verify the import/export status of whatever object, or goods you plan to carry along with you. For example, whereas firearms are generally prohibited by many countries, some countries allow hunting guns and guns used in sporting activities. There might even be restrictions or a need to get a prior permit to import or use such gadgets as computers, and radio transmitter-receivers. Products commonly found on the list of import contraband for most countries include drugs (e.g. cocaine, heroin) pornographic materials, firearms, and certain wildlife products of endangered species.

Contraband goods for export purposes will often include some of those prohibited for import, such as drugs, pornographic materials, and wildlife products of endangered species. Other forms of contraband may prohibit the export of certain products by unauthorized or unlicensed exporters; e.g., precious metals and minerals, and certain artifacts. In some cases, the contraband may be limited to certain products or to products from certain countries or regions. The United States also prohibits and restricts the importation and exportation of a variety of items. See Chapters 7, and 31 .

<u>Consumer Protection</u>: One luxury that travelers do have in the U.S. as well as in several developed countries, is the existence of strict state and federal government rules, regulations and laws aimed at protecting them and insuring their safety and well being. These rules, regulations and laws covering such common travelers' concerns such as bumping, flight delays or cancellations, spell out your rights and privileges, thus, providing you with the legal backing for seeking redress if you feel your rights have been violated.

As an international traveler, you should be aware, however, that once you are outside the United States, you may not get the same level of protection as currently exists and is available to you in the United States. Although such protection may be provided on paper, it is not effective in many countries, particularly in less developed countries. Nevertheless, as an American traveling abroad you may still be able to take advantage of the protection provided you here at home by dealing with the U.S. offices of the airline or shipping lines, since their activities in the U.S. are, also, governed and subjected to U.S. laws.

Essentially, if you have complaints about an airline or if you feel you have not been treated fairly, you may contact the Customer Relations manager of the airline. Very often, it will make an effort to deal with your concerns. At other times, you may run into very uncooperative representatives or agents, in which case, you may consider contacting the office of Community and Consumer Affairs, U.S. Department of Transportation; 400 7th Street, S.W., Rm. 10405, Washington D.C. 20590 (202) 366-2220. Of course, your attorney is always at your disposal to take additional steps if necessary.

Before traveling, you may want to familiarize yourself with some of your rights, privileges and responsibilities as an air traveler. The U.S. Department of Transportation booklet entitled, <u>Fly Right</u>, is reprinted verbatim, elsewhere in this book and may be useful.

<u>Complaints</u>: As with many travelers, and long-haul travelers in particular, there is always a chance for cause to want to complain about one thing or the other. If such a situation should arise it is always advisable to do it immediately on the spot with the appropriate authorities or personnel. Later on, perhaps upon your return, follow up in writing. While you may at times have the urge to threaten and curse out loud, you may find a persistent, but polite approach more successful. In the event of damages, missing, or lost luggage, a verbal complaint may not be sufficient. (See Lost/Damaged Luggage).

<u>Lost/Damaged Luggage</u>: Losing luggage or finding your luggage damaged is a common experience among travelers, long and short haul travelers alike. Should you, upon disembarking at the airport, or seaport, train or bus station, find your luggage missing or damaged, immediately contact the appropriate personnel at the baggage area or at the lost luggage office to file your complaint. With airlines, you may have to complete a report form. Especially with missing luggage, insist on filing a written report (keep a copy) as this may become useful in the event your luggage is not found and you decide to seek legal recourse or compensation. Do not give up or release your luggage check ticket.

In addition, keep your ticket safely or any remaining portion of it. With regard to both lost or damaged luggage, you have the right to seek and receive some compensation. Rarely are you compensated fully. This right, however, does not extend to luggage misplaced elsewhere in the airport due to your negligence. In such cases, immediately contact the airport police or security, the Lost Property office, or the Information desk for assistance.

<u>Information Desk</u>: For any traveler, Information Desks, readily available and visible in almost every air and sea port as well as bus and train station, are your immediate sources for a variety of assistance and information ranging from locating post offices, police offices, banks, restrooms, dining places to finding connecting flights, taxi, bus, rail and limousine services. Information desks at most large hotels are, in addition, very useful in providing you with additional information on a variety of subjects that will help make your trip more enjoyable. Use them!

<u>Personal Appearance</u>: While relatively few travelers

ever get bothered or delayed just for their personal appearance, a tattered and weird appearance may attract an unwelcome attention and may subject you to avoidable scrutiny and or questioning by foreign immigration and security officers. A clean, smart and unsuspecting appearance and demeanor on the part of a foreigner in a foreign land, may after all, save you embarrassment and unnecessary delays.

Exchanging Your Currency: As an international traveler, knowing the host country's rules and requirements for exchanging your foreign currency is very important since the rules and requirements are different from country to country. While in some countries, the requirements are less stringent, or optional, in many other countries, especially Less Developed Countries, they may be quite strict. Obviously, if your interest is as, I will imagine, to safeguard your funds and stay out of trouble, then, follow strictly the government's requirements with regard to where to exchange foreign currency. While you might be used to using banks in the U.S., in many countries you might have the option of carrying out such transactions only at authorized banks, hotels, bureau de change and money changers. In most cases, you will be given a receipt (if not, ask for one) and/or the transaction may be endorsed in your passport. Hold on safely to your receipts and/or endorsement, since they may be requested of you, during departure.

Avoid having to exchange your money with unauthorized dealers or in the "black market" even though their higher rates of exchange are often tempting. Remember, with high expected return is always high risk, including the risk of getting counterfeit currency, the risk of robbery, and running into problems with the law. Some of these unauthorized dealers may be undercover officers of the law.

Currency Import/Export Requirements: As an international traveler, it is important to know that many countries do have restrictions on the import and export of both foreign and local currencies. Be aware, also, of U.S. Government currency requirement. Presently, there is no limit on the amount of money or negotiable instruments which can be brought into or taken out of the United States. However, any amount over $10,000 must be reported to U.S. Customs on Customs Form 4790 when you depart from or enter into the United States.

(a) Import of Foreign Currency: Most countries do not impose restrictions on the import of foreign currency. In several of these countries, however, there may be additional requirements, which often include

declaring the amount and/or exchanging your foreign currency only at approved or authorized offices or dealers. Declaration of currency usually takes place at the airport upon arrival. In all exchange transactions, ask for a copy of your receipt and keep it safe. You may need it on departure or in reclaiming or re-converting unused currency. Although not common with most countries, some do prohibit the import of certain amounts of the country's currency. In almost every country where the import of foreign currency is allowed, the usual assumption is that it is legal to export both the currency and the given amount from your country of departure. As you may expect, very large amounts of foreign currency, especially notes, will attract additional attention and questioning.

(b) Import of Local Currency: Most countries restrict and, in some cases, prohibit the import of local currency by both residents and non-residents, especially the latter. Where restrictions apply, they often take the form of a ceiling, above which it will be considered illegal or require that such monies be declared and even subject to visual inspection.

(c) Export of Local Currency: Like the import of local currency, most countries restrict or prohibit the export of local currency. Where restrictions apply, they often take the form of a ceiling above which it will be considered illegal or require that such monies be declared and even subject to visual inspection. Many countries, especially Less Developing Countries, are very strict with currency movement, particularly, the import or export of local currency. Even where some amount is allowable to non-residents, it is often a very small amount usually limited to local remembrance coins. Although developed countries are generally more generous with the import and export of local currency, it is a fact that no country will allow a large or unrestricted amount of import or export of its currency.

Because the rules and requirements dealing with the import and export of currency for many countries do change constantly, I suggest you verify with the country's embassy, consulates, Tourist Information Office or with your travel agents prior to traveling for the current list of requirements.

Duty Free Import Allowances: In almost every country, foreign travelers are allowed to import, duty free, some quantity of products or products up to a specified value for personal use. Expect to pay extra, for any quantity or value over what is specified. Some of the commonest products include liquor, spirit, alcohol, beer, wine, cigars, cigarettes, perfume, and cologne. The quantity of these products allowable as duty-free varies from one country to the other and changes from time to time for some countries. In fact, in some countries, the amount allowable may be determined by your country of departure. Other familiar products that may or may not be considered duty free, depending on the quantity, the value, intended purpose and perhaps country of origin will include such gadgets as cameras, tape recorders, video machines and tapes, sports equipment, TVs, faxes and radio transmitters. It is suggested for those travelers who may be planning to carry along some of these products to contact or verify with the country's embassy, consulates or with your travel agent prior to traveling for a more current list of requirements.

For those travelers, particularly, business travelers who plan to move certain items and gadgets back and forth, consider getting an ATA CARNET. This document which is described elsewhere in this Chapter will save you money and aggravation. Returning U.S. residents and U.S importers should also familiarize themselves with the list of duty-free imports as well as the other import requirements. Your import (which ordinarily will be subject to duty may even be duty-free) under the GSP program, just because you are importing it from one of the beneficiary countries. (See Chapters 7 and 34)

What To Take With You: There is always that urge and invariably the mistake to carry along as much as we can carry and often more than we will need or use. My advice is to travel lightly and do not carry anything you would hate to lose. Unnecessary credit cards and expensive jewelry should be left at home.

Money Belt: Use a money belt or concealed pouch for your passport, cash and other valuables.

Driving Abroad: Depending on the country you are visiting, driving abroad could be both exciting and safe or could be scary and risky. Whereas the road conditions and road infrastructure in many of the Developed Countries and some urban centers of Less Developed Countries are safe, good and properly maintained, the same may not be true for most of the developing countries. Travelers to European countries should expect about the same conditions as in the U.S. However, if you are traveling to a Less Developed Country, you must anticipate such conditions as narrower roads, untarred roads, muddy or dusty roads, poorly lighted roads, loose animals and livestock, poor or nonexistent shoulders, few road signs or traffic lights, as well as a limited number of restaurants, motels, gas stations or auto-repair shops. If you plan to drive, it is advisable to familiarize yourself with the route. As always, avoid excessive speed, and, if possible, avoid driving at night. In some countries local driving signals are prevalent. Familiarizing yourself with these signals will add to the pleasure of your driving.

In addition, you may want to familiarize yourself with driving automobiles with manual (stick) shift. Unlike in the U.S. where automatic transmissions and power accessories are plentiful, you will find more cars with manual transmissions in the rest of the world. Do not be surprised therefore, if that automatic shift car you reserved with your rental agency is not available, and you are offered instead, a car with stick shift.

Further, be aware that in some countries, European countries included, you may find cars with steering wheels on the right side of the car, and you might be required to drive on the left hand side of the road. Like in the U.S., you must be properly licensed to drive, and the car must be insured. Although some countries will accept a U.S driver's license, others may require that you have an International Driver's Permit. See Appendix M for information on how to obtain an International Drivers Permit. For those planning to use their U.S. automobiles abroad, remember you may be required to obtain a vehicle import permit. Furthermore, your U.S. automobile insurance plan and coverage may or may not be acceptable. Some countries may require that you have an International Green Insurance card or obtain such coverage from a local insurance company. Needless, to say, it is important to adhere to local traffic laws. Speeding and drunk driving may land you in jail, in addition to a financial penalty.

Foreign Jails: While it is never any traveler's wish to end up in a jail or a foreign prison, it is, nevertheless, a possibility and some travelers have had this experience. For would-be visitors, do not expect anything close to the condition of U.S. penal institutions. For most countries, especially in Less Developed Countries, it is worse. Reports of jail conditions have ranged from sheer physical abuse and torture, including beatings and sexual assault to outright deprivation of any rights or privileges. There have been reports of prisoners and even those awaiting trial of not being properly fed or fed at all, of poor lighting or no lights at all in their cells, and of poor sleeping conditions and toilet facilities. In many cases, you may have to sleep on a bare, dusty or muddy floor. American traveling abroad should make every effort to avoid having to face foreign jails and jail experiences.

Minors and Traveling Restrictions: For those travelers who may be traveling with minors, be aware that the definition of minor and the age of majority vary from country to country and, importantly, that many countries do impose restrictions on minor children who travel alone with only one parent or with someone who is not their parent. In many cases, some form of documentation or written authorization for travel from the absent parent, parents or legal guardian may be required. Check with your travel agent or with the country's embassy or consulate for requirements, if any.

Criminal Assault: Any U.S. citizen who is criminally assaulted should report the incident to the local police and to the nearest U.S. embassy or consulate.

At the Pool or Beach: Do not leave your belongings on the beach while swimming. Keep your passport and other valuables in a hotel safe.

On Public Transport: Be vigilant in bus and train stations and on public transport. Do not accept beverages from other passengers. There have been reports of tourists being drugged and robbed while they slept.

Sightseeing (getting around) on Foot: Avoid dark and isolated alleys, crowds and marginal areas. These are areas where you can easily be robbed and assaulted. Be aware that women and small children as well as men can be pickpockets or purse snatchers. Do not stop if you are approached on the street by strangers, including street vendors and beggars. Whenever possible do not travel alone. Avoid traveling at night. Keep your billfold in an inner front pocket; carry your purse tucked securely under your arm; and wear the shoulder strap of your camera or bag across your chest. To guard against thieves on motorcycles, walk away from the curb and carry your purse away from the street. A money belt or concealed money pouch would be helpful to safeguard your passport and other valuables.

Foreign Laws: Foreign laws, rules and regulations may be very different from those of the United States, and violators may be subject to different penalties. For a foreigner, these penalties may be even harsher. Tourists who commit illegal acts usually have no special privileges. It is, therefore, advisable before you travel and when you are abroad to learn as much of the country's do's and don'ts as possible, in particular those aspects which often get tourists in trouble with the law. In most cases, the same type of violations that will get you in trouble in the U.S. would more than likely, get you in trouble abroad; for example, those relating to drugs, firearms, traffic, public safety, theft and robbery. Remember that while traveling in a foreign country, you are subject to that country's laws, and not U.S. laws.

Drunkenness and Drunken Driving: Public drunkenness and drunken driving is against the law in several countries and should be avoided. These social nuisances often leads to fights, traffic accidents and even death. Arrests and jail terms are common for violators. In some countries drunken driving invites mandatory jail sentences.

Hotel Bills: Many countries consider it a fraud, if you fail to pay your hotel bills or pay for other services rendered. Those accused may be subject to arrest and conviction with stiff fines and jail sentences. Keep track of your expenditures and your resources. As usual, travel with sufficient funds including a little extra for a few days subsistence in case you are stranded.

Dealing with Merchants: Always avoid disputes with merchants as this may often lead to undesirable outcomes. Although haggling over prices is common with small independently owned shops; in others, it may be insulting and unwelcome. Learning as much as you can about the modus operandi in foreign market places will be very valuable. Avoiding disputes requires you to be a careful and informed shopper. Make sure the goods you buy are in good condition, since efforts to exchange or return the goods may be unsuccessful and may lead to disputes. As always, get a receipt for your transactions.

Green Backs: The U.S. dollar notes are as popular in several countries as U.S. tourists. You will find the U.S. dollar notes are readily accepted for transactions by local merchants. While the temptation will always be there, beware of local legal requirements concerning import and use of foreign currency, as this may get you into avoidable trouble. Equally, important is to beware of how you flash your dollar notes as this may invite or attract the attention of thieves and robbers. As an American, you are always associated with the dollar, and there is the tendency to think that you are carrying some U.S. dollars.

Photography: Be cautious when taking pictures. Some countries prohibit taking photographs of some facilities, buildings, places and events; e.g., airports, police stations, military locations, oil installations, harbors, mines, and bridges. Taking a photo of demonstrations or civil disturbances is usually prohibited. Violators have often had their films and/or cameras confiscated and, at times, have been beaten or detained. A safe rule is, when in doubt whether you can take a picture, ask first. Remember, when taking pictures of or including individuals to find out if it is OK with them. Some persons detest being photographed, and or may require some form of token compensation. Be courteous. Ask first.

Restricted Areas: Travelers abroad should be aware that some countries do have strict regulations prohibiting travel in certain areas or traveling without special permission. Contact the country's embassy or consulate in the U.S., or if you are abroad, contact the U.S. Embassy or the nearest U.S. consulate for a list of such places and what may be required.

Dress Code: Some countries, especially those in the Middle East and Moslem countries, expect foreigners to adhere to their dress codes. These codes may relate to and may be restricted to certain places, such as places of worship or to women, men or children. For example, some countries require women to have their hair covered when in public or covered when in places of worship, while some prohibit wearing of shorts and miniskirts in the public or sleeveless garments. Yet, in many other countries, such rules may not exist Check with your travel agent, the respective foreign embassy or the tourist office for the appropriate dress code in their country.

Travel Agencies/Agents: Travel Agencies and Agents can be very useful in providing answers to most of the common questions and concerns of foreign travelers and should be included as one of your important information sources. However, as in any other profession or trade, all travel agencies or agents do not possess the same degree of expertise or experience. It is important that you shop around for a reliable, reputable and competent one with experiences in foreign travels. Such agencies or agents must be committed to assisting you to have a successful and enjoyable trip by providing you with advice, answers, and other relevant information about the country or countries you plan to visit. Travel agencies and agents that are interested only in selling you a ticket, (remember they are sales persons and/or operate on commission) should be avoided. A real helpful agency or agent ought to be willing and able to provide you not only with the "best deal" cost-wise, but also with current information on such issues as relates to hotel reservations, car rentals, visas, passports, travel conditions in the country or region you are visiting and even some cultural **do's** and **don'ts**. While no formula exists for identifying the type of travel agencies and agents mentioned here, you may want to deal primarily with those travel agencies that are members of the American Society of Travel Agents (ASTA). Members usually will have the (ASTA) sign or seal clearly affixed to a visible place in the office. The strict membership requirements give their members an edge over non-members. Yet, I must caution that membership in ASTA or the lack of it, is not a guarantee that the agency or agent you choose will deliver. Shop around. Ask your traveled colleagues, friends, and neighbors for some references.

It'll be better than no reference. When you find one, seek his or her assistance. If you do not engage or ask them for assistance, all you may get from them for your money may be just a ticket, a handshake and nothing more. Interested in travel agents who are members of the Institute of Certified Travel Agents (ICTA)? These agents, upon certification, carry the title of Certified Travel Counselor (CTC). For additional information about these organizations, including members that may be in your area, write or call the American Society of Travel Agents (ASTA), 1101 King St., Alexandria, Virginia 22314. Tel: (703) 739-2782. Or the Institute of Certified Travel Agents (IGA), 148 Linden Street, Wellesley, Massachusetts 02181. Tel: (617) 237-0280.

Visa Services: (See Travel Counselors)

Travel Counselors/Travel Planners/Travel Advisors: (Also, see Travel Agencies). Travelers, in particular those planning an extensive trip, a trip for the first time or who may not have much time devoted to their travel plans, may consider using the services of a travel counselor, a travel advisor or travel planner for a fee. Although a good travel agency or agent should be able to provide you with valuable counseling and advice regarding your trip, you may find the services of a travel counselor more specialized, timely, personable and comprehensive. Remember, this is how they make their living; that is, consulting, advising and counseling you, not selling you a travel ticket or pass. A good travel counselor or travel planner, as they are sometimes referred to, should be respond and advise you on all these questions, every topic and every concern you may have regarding your trip including scheduling. How satisfied you are or how satisfactory the results are, will depend on how knowledgeable and how experienced the counselor. Some of your questions and concerns may require the counselor to do some research and, of course this means time and money. The more planning and research you do before or while using a counselor, the less costly for you and the less painful the outcome of a poor or insufficient consultation.

When looking for or researching a good travel agency or agent, you have to shop around for a reliable, reputable, knowledgeable and experienced travel counselor. Ask your colleagues, friends, and co-workers, for references. After all, levying a fee is not what makes one a good travel counselor. It is also advisable to engage the services of only those travel counselors who specialize in the country or region of the world you plan to visit or in certain aspects of travels such as ski-vacation, budget-tours, business travels, group and luxury travels. They are often more

433

helpful than the general practitioners. You may, moreover, consider using professionally certified travel counselors, such as those certified by the Institute of Certified Travel Agents (ICTA), a U.S. based nonprofit educational organization. Upon certification, their members carry the insignia and title of "Certified Travel Counselor (CTC). Look out for the ICTA and CTC logos. Although the eligibility requirements for members of these organization give them an edge over non-certified agents, being counseled by a member may not necessarily guarantee the best results; so shop around. Be careful and be selective. For information on ICTA certified travel counselors in your area, check your local telephone directory or write or call the Institute of Certified Travel Agents, 148 Linden Street, Wellesley, Massachusetts 02181. Tel: (617) 237-0280).

Visa and Passport Services: If you plan to travel abroad and do not have the time to process your application for a visa or passport, there are businesses out there whose primary service is to assist you in obtaining them. You can find additional listing of these businesses in your local telephone directory under the heading "Visa Services." A listing of some of the private visa and passport services has also been included in this book. See Appendix K.

Banking, Business and Shopping Hours: International travelers should be aware that banking, business and shopping hours vary from country to country and within a particular country. Sometimes, the hours of operation may change in response to changes between seasons. The typical differences that are likely to interest an American traveling abroad will include the fact that in some countries business is not transacted during some working days and/or during what we will generally consider as normal working hours by U.S. criteria. In some of these countries, banks, shops and offices may be closed either voluntarily or by law. In other countries you may find that government offices may be open during the weekend. Another likely observation in some countries is the "two-shift" type of operations, where banks, businesses and shops may close at mid-day for lunch, resume one to three hours later, and then close finally at night. Other than these striking differences, the others, for the most part, are merely differences in opening and closing hours. Since as an international traveler, you will inevitably be affected, I have included elsewhere in this book the banking, business and shopping hours of various countries. See Appendix 9I.

Weights and Measures: Most international travelers engage in some form of shopping while abroad. For these travelers, understanding the type of weights and measures used in the country will be beneficial at least in insuring that you do not end up buying something that may be cheaper in the U.S. The types and standards of weights and measures vary from country to country. Whereas, most countries use the metric system or are in the process of converting to metrication, several countries still use the imperial system or other local systems. In others, one or more of these systems of weights and measures are used. Even for those countries that have officially adopted either the metric or the imperial system, it is not uncommon to find transactions still being carried out using a different system. Understanding these differences will facilitate your shopping and may save you money. A list of countries and the type of system officially being used is provided elsewhere in this book. Provided, in addition, are conversion factor and tables of equivalent weights and measures in both metric and Imperial forms. See Appendices Z and 1A.

Clothing: If you are traveling abroad and you plan to go shopping for clothing, be aware that clothing such as shirts, pants, gowns, suits and shoes, may not carry the same size labels. Some countries employ labeling forms quite different from those used on U.S. made clothing. A table comparing the U.S. and two other labeling systems has been included elsewhere in this book. See Appendix Y.

Tipping: We, in America, are fond of and used to tipping in hotels, restaurants, saloons, and almost every time someone renders us some form of assistance. Well, if you are planning a trip abroad, you may want to know that, although the "rules" and expectations are the same for most countries, the amounts may be different. Importantly, in some countries, tipping may not be expected and may be officially prohibited.

Different countries have different rules and expectations regarding tipping and gratuities. In some countries, the practice is expected and clearly defined, whereas in some others, this may not be the case. For the International traveler to be confused in terms of whether to tip or not, or how much to tip, when, to whom and how is understandable. Since this could be a potential source of embarrassment, you should try to familiarize yourself with what the rules are in the country you plan to travel to. To assist you, a country by country guide to tipping has been provided in Appendix 2B. It is not comprehensive, but at least acquaints you with the country's official position as well as the expectations on tipping, particularly in hotels, restaurants, taxis and saloons. You may, also, contact that country's embassy or consulate or tourist bureau for advice. Your travel agent or advisor may also be of help.

Should you decide to tip wherever such practice is allowed do restrict your gratuities to services actually rendered. Do not forget that there are really no hard and fast rules as to how much you must tip. In other words, do not expect to be thrown in jail for not tipping. Generally, a tip, and the amount should reflect what you believe is "reasonable", and what you can afford. Sometimes, a handsome expression of appreciation (tip) may well make a difference in the quality of service you may subsequently receive, assuming you would still be around. A poor tip may be insulting and may even be worse than not giving at all. Finally, do not forget that your bill or fare may already include expected tips. The one way of knowing in most cases is to inquire.

Taboos: Travelers to foreign countries have often been embarrassed, humiliated and even isolated as a result of their inadvertently stumbling into actions and words considered as taboos. To many travelers, this could be very uncomfortable and could sour an otherwise exciting trip or relationship. Breaching a taboo in some societies could invite trouble and mean spirited treatment. It behooves the prospective foreign traveler to learn as much as possible about the cultural, and social **do's** and **don'ts**. Your local libraries and bookstores are excellent sources for general as well as country-specific books in this subject area. Also, check Chapter 46 for useful references on this subject.

Bribery and Corruption: This is a phenomenon that, admittedly, exists in every country, a phenomenon which is illegal in every country, yet, in practice, flourishes in different forms and with different degrees of impunity and tolerance. As you journey from one country to another, you may find yourself confronted with this moral dilemma. Although the effects on you for not abetting or complying may, in fact, be inconveniencing and time delaying, the consequences to you for bribing or attempting to bribe may get you into jail. For an international traveler, particularly in a foreign country or anywhere at all, your best bet is "do not attempt to give or accept a bribe." The cost for complying with the law always pays off favorably in the long run.

Clinical/Medical: For those travelers who are particularly concerned about their health and who feel, that during their trip abroad, they may have to seek some form of medical treatment, carrying along a copy of your medical records stating any special conditions, problems and suggested treatments may be a wise idea. A similar record or log of any type of problems encountered while overseas, including treatment should also be kept. It may be needed for reference by your physician upon return. You may consider investing in

a Medical Alert bracelet currently available from the Medical Alert Foundation. See Appendix 14N.

Medical Help Overseas: While no traveler wishes to be injured or ill while traveling overseas, it is a fact of life that travelers abroad do get injured and ill and may require medical attention. Americans traveling abroad may take solace in knowing that there are qualified physicians available world wide who are capable of providing them with the same level of quality treatment as is available at home. In several countries, especially in Europe and in urban centers of most developed countries, quality hospitals and medical facilities do exist. For the American traveler, the other important need may be for qualified physicians who understand and speak English. Well, for your consolation, you may want to take advantage of the services of the several international travel, medical assistance organizations listed in Appendix 14N.

While you contemplate on the topic of medical treatment abroad, you may, also, want to be aware of the fact that your medical treatment abroad, especially with private, independent physicians, may not be free of charge and you may be required to pay in advance, immediately, or initially, and/or in cash form. The cost to you may, also, be high. This is all the more reason that it is strongly recommended that before you travel abroad, that you take out some form of insurance that will cover all or most of your treatments or medical costs incurred abroad. You may, in other words, consider shopping around or delaying until you return home those routine, non-life threatening, non-essential, less urgent problems and treatments. It's really up to you.

As part of your pre-travel plans, you may want to find out the quality and status of medical facilities and treatment generally available to you in the country or countries you plan to visit, and whether as a foreign traveler, you may have to pay or not. It is always safer to think you may have to pay and make the necessary financial or payment plans. Should there be a need to be hospitalized, University affiliated hospitals may be worth considering. Besides the quality of treatments, chances are that you may run into American or Western trained doctors who may be fluent in English.

As always, taking the proper precautions through a careful preparation in consultation with your physician will save you a bundle and will make your trip abroad a healthy, safe and enjoyable one. For example, a medical emergency kit or first aid kit (with such items as bandages, cotton wool, swabs, and disinfectants), a little extra prescription medication, and extra eyeglasses, may be worth much more than any minor inconveniences taking them along may cause. Should you decide to carry with you a substantial quantity of needed medication or a controlled or prescription drug, you may also want to secure a special note or letter from your physician stating your care and need. Failure to do so may cause your medications to be taxed or confiscated. For additional health information, see Chapter 9. Although, you may find your medical needs abroad adequate for the most part, travelers to less developed countries and to rural parts of most countries must always take extra precautions. It is safer to be overly prepared than to be under prepared. Importantly, do not always expect the same level of quality medical treatment and facilities as may exist at home.

Insurance: Obtaining adequate insurance coverage must always be paramount in the minds of every international traveler. Coverage to be considered should include automobile, life, medical, trip interruptions and cancellations, bankruptcy, luggage and personal effects insurance. The need for insurance will vary from one traveler to another. Of course, if you don't plan to drive, you obviously do not need a car insurance. If you plan to take your own car as opposed to renting one, you may find that your existing insurance policy(ies) will not cover you in case of a loss. Whatever the case, should you plan to drive abroad, first ensure that you are comprehensively insured by a reputable company and that your insurance policy is valid and will be honored in the country you are visiting. A listing of International Automobile Rental and Leasing Agencies has been included in Appendix X While shopping for or evaluating your health insurance needs, remember that a good medical insurance should provide you with total coverage, including full coverage for hospital stay, medications and any medically related treatment you might incur, short or long-term. Health policies must, also, include the cost of transportation to the United States, in the event of emergencies and serious conditions, including that of a traveling companion.

Because damaged and lost luggage has become a common experience for many travelers, you may consider insuring these and other accompanying possessions and valuables, especially given the limited coverage, if any, provided to travelers by their carriers. Although you may not recover in full your losses, a good insurance coverage will inevitably minimize your loss. Time-conscious travelers who are concerned about the financial loss due to unscheduled trip cancellations or interruptions, may consider purchasing a trip cancellation or a trip-interruption policy.

There is, of course, life insurance, which is even more

important, while you are in transit or are abroad. Although you may already carry a life insurance policy, this may be another time to examine the adequacy of your existing policy.

All in all, your pre-travel plans, should include researching and getting the necessary insurance coverage. A good insurance broker should be able to help you, in avoiding duplication of policies and coverage. Your travel planner, advisor, travel agent and tour operators will be of assistance to you in this area. Also, check your existing automobile, medical and life insurance policies. You may already be partially or fully covered, and may or may not need additional coverage. You may, also, find that you are adequately covered by your credit card company (for those who may be charging their tickets). If you are not sure of what is covered or the extent of the coverage, contact your or credit card company. Also check with your travel agent, some of them now provide free flight insurance for their ticket clients.

Very often travelers overlook the fact that they may already be adequately covered, sometimes with double and triple indemnity clauses, for accidental death and/or dismemberment by the airline, the travel or auto clubs. Most major credit card companies for such cards as American Express, Mastercard, Visa Carte Blanche, Dinners Club and Discover automatically provide between $100,000 and $350000 for flight insurance (accident and life insurance) to cardholders who charge their trips to their cards. Cardholders desiring higher coverage can also buy them from these companies at a fairly reasonable rate. These card companies also provide insurance coverage for delayed or lost luggage; up to $500 for checked luggages and up to $1250 for carry-on baggages. It is important to also remember that in the event of an accident or death while riding as a passenger, International airlines are liable for up to $75000 if the ticket is bought in the U.S. The amount is different for tickets bought abroad.

When all is done do not forget to carry your insurance card and a photocopy of your policy with you, including the telephone numbers of your insurance company and agent, just in case a need arises. Be financially prepared as well, some insurance companies may require that you settle your expenses overseas and then apply for reimbursement. Some of the policies mentioned here can be easily purchased through your local insurance brokers. Remember, the more comprehensive the coverage (combination policies) the better. A list of some companies that provide travel-related insurance, including short-term policies is provided in Appendices 13M and 14N.

Value-Added Tax (VAT): Most foreign travelers to Western Europe are usually not knowledgeable about VAT. This is a tax, a sales tax of a sort, usually imposed on almost all goods sold in Western European countries. These taxes (ranging from 6% to 33% depending on the country) are usually included in the price of goods and services, and are levied on purchasers irrespective of the country of origin. The good news for the international traveler is that you may be able to get a refund. You must, however, ask for it, and meet the requirements.

To receive a refund, (a) you must shop at stores that are authorized to offer VAT refunds; (b) you must carry your purchases with you when you leave.

If you desire to request a refund of your VAT payments, do not forget to request the VAT form from your salesperson. The form should be signed by the salesperson. Upon departure, present the form and your receipt to the customs officers for final endorsement. Upon returning home, you may then mail the form to the store and a refund will be mailed to you.

Rail Passes: For the cost conscious international traveler, passes can be an important money saving investment. Rail passes, in particular, can be a source of a bargain for those travelers who plan to conduct a lot of their travel by train.

While some of the passes are limited to travel within the country, some do allow for travel across countries. The Eurailpass, for example, allows you to travel to all the 17 member European countries.

Rail passes and tourist cards are very popular in Europe. Similar arrangements and opportunities to travel at a discount are, also, available on other continents. Your travel agent should be able to assist you in this matter. You may, in addition, direct your inquiry to the country's tourist office in the U.S., the country's embassy, the consulate or railroad authority. A list of the most common European railroad passes, together with a directory of international railroads, is provided in Appendix V. A list of foreign government tourist offices and embassies in the U.S. is also provided. See Appendix L.

Further, children and older travelers, may take advantage of available opportunities. Several countries, especially in Europe, offer discounts of up to 50% in several areas, including rail and other travel passes. However, it is up to you to ask about the availability when making your reservation or purchasing your ticket or passes. Remember that the definition of "seniors" varies from country to country. While most countries restrict use to those 65 years and older, in some countries the definition might be different.

It is, furthermore, worth noting that despite the convenience of passes and the cost advantage, it may not be beneficial to everyone. The individual traveler should always compare the cost of a pass or tourist card with the total cost of alternative transportation, as the latter may turn out to be more convenient and/or cheaper especially, for those contemplating limited travel.

Like rail and bus passes, some airlines, also, sell limited air passes as well as other substantial discounts to older travelers. Contact your travel agent or the airlines.

Medical Emergency Kit: A good emergency medical kit should be an important carry-along item for an international traveler. This is particularly important for those traveling to Less Developed Countries, or to rural and remote parts of foreign countries. A timely attendance to a sudden, but minor, ailment by way of a first treatment may make a difference between enjoying your vacation, terminating it or finding yourself in a hospital. A good medical kit doesn't have to be bulky or heavy. Of more importance are the contents. A sample content of a medical kit is provided in this book. Check the table of contents for location. Remember even in the possession of the best of medical kits, it is always advisable to seek immediate professional medical attention in the event of any form of illness, even more so when you are in a foreign country. Being sick away from home is not something to take lightly, and you should not depend solely on a medical kit. See Appendix 15O for a sample Emergency Medical Kit.

Airport Facilities: Airports provide a variety of facilities aimed at providing safety and comfort to the traveler, and an increasing number of international airports are taking added steps to provide for the special needs of babies, young children and the disabled.

Most international airports are now equipped with special rooms where babies can be fed and changed, and some have short-term nursery and play facilities for young children.

Disabled travelers can also take advantage of various free services available to them. A disabled traveler is entitled to ask for an escort both in the aircraft and in the airport. Deaf passengers can request written announcements from the ground staff. Blind persons are entitled to take their guide dogs, but your dog may not be exempt from both the home and country quarantine laws.

For more traveling information and tips for the disabled, see the Table of Contents. It is worth remembering, however, that to take advantage of special airport facilities, you have to request them since most of them may only be available on demand. You are always better off making your requests early, especially for those facilities with limited availability or supplies.

For travelers to Less Developed Countries, especially African countries, you may want to keep in mind that the conditions of most of their international airports are comparatively poor and inadequate; hence, some of the facilities or services noted above may not be available. It is not uncommon to find unavailable even such facilities as clean toilets or toilets that are open or accessible. Should you have access to a toilet, you may be disappointed to find that there is no toilet paper. It is based on this experience, in particular, that I have since resolved and always carried a few rolls of toilet paper with me whenever I am traveling.

Comfort Hints on Flights: It is amazing how much we value comfort and strive to achieve it on flights, especially on long flights. The act of flying, in itself, can be discomforting, especially over time zones. However, as a frequent flyer and a long-haul traveler, you may take a few steps to minimize the source of discomfort, thus, making your trip less tiring and annoying. Among other factors, discomfort often results from inadequate leg room and noise. By properly choosing your seat, you may be able to reduce the level of discomfort. Aisle seats provide more legroom than window seats; seats directly behind the emergency exit doors provide even more additional legroom. Aisle seats are more convenient for those travelers who may have to use the restrooms frequently. Having secured an aisle seat, of course, you'll hope the other passengers on your row will not move frequently move in and out.

As for the noise, because most engines are situated at the back, the further away towards the front that you are seated, the lesser the noise effect. Besides, you are more likely to find excited and rowdy holiday groups toward the rear spectrum of the plane. Sitting just behind first class, may be your best choice, unless you are a first class passenger. You may, also, minimize on noise effect by sitting away from the toilet facilities. One area you may not have much pre-planning opportunity to affect are noisy neighbors. Even with that, a little politeness and smile may do the trick.

You can furthermore, minimize some of the discomforting feelings by being selective with what you eat and drink as well as what you wear. It is advisable to minimize on the intake of alcoholic and fizzy, carbonated drinks. Instead, drink non-alcoholic liquids, such as water and fruit juices. It is, also, advisable to wear loose-fitting clothes and shoes. Remember that feet tend to swell on long flights. Unless your shoes are sufficiently loose, you may find it difficult to put them back on.

Finally, you may consider periodically rotating your feet, ankles, and neck as an exercise or you may treat yourself to some sleep. Also, see the Chapter on Jet lag

Special Diets: One of the advantages of today's international travelers is the airlines' willingness to provide them with special diets. Whether you prefer vegetarian, fat-free, salt-free, infant, diabetic, Muslim or Jewish (Kosher and Kedassia) meals, there is a growing number of international airlines that will make an effort to get them for you. First class passengers may find their request for special meals more easily fulfilled. As with all special services, it is advisable to place your order with the airline well in advance. Remember, that not all airlines provide the wide ranges of special meals noted here. Whereas, the larger airlines are often good with providing this type of service, you may not have much luck or many choices with the smaller domestic airlines and with airlines of many Less Developed Countries. As a precaution, it is always a good idea to eat something before embarking on your flight and to take along a few of your favorite snacks.

Tickets: As a precaution, it is advisable to spend a few minutes making some sense out of your tickets, preferably right on the spot where they are being issued. You should be able to reconcile the information contained in your ticket with your travel plans. Many travelers have found, much to their disappointment and embarrassment, that the ticket they are carrying is deficient. Sometimes the tickets may contain schedules and clauses that are different, restricting and that may be expensive to rectify once you commence your trip. Double checking your ticket is, thus, essential and could save you money and time. In checking your ticket, take special note of the name of the airlines you will be traveling. The names of the airlines are usually identified by their respective two-letter codes. See the table of contents for these codes as well as the list of foreign and international airlines operating in the U.S. Your ticket check should also include reconciling the dates and times of departure and arrival, your class of ticket, the validity of your ticket and of the flight(s). Also check for the correct validation stamp or signature

438

of the issuer. Don't forget to read all other information both in the front and on the back of the ticket. You might find additional useful information.

<u>Air Sickness</u> (See the Chapter on Jet Lag).

<u>Hospitalization while Abroad:</u> Should there be a need to be hospitalized, University affiliated teaching hospitals may be worth considering. Besides the advantage of quality treatment, the chances are that you may run into American or Western trained doctors, who may also be fluent in English.

<u>Hold onto Your U.S. Passport</u>[IL]: A U.S. passport can cause you trouble in some regions of the world. But there are ways to get around that if you meet certain requirements. Children, sometimes grandchildren, of immigrants can obtain passports from the country of their parents' birth. In many countries, once you obtain a second passport, you, also, require a dual citizenship.

This is not as easy as it sounds. You must be careful not to unintentionally renounce your U.S. citizenship. The U.S. State Department recommends the following precautions:

* Do not accept a government job from an adopted government.
* Do not serve in another country's military.
* Do not suggest, to friends or anyone else, that you intend to renounce your U.S. citizenship.
* Write a statement of intent to retain your U.S. citizenship,and send it to a U.S. Embassy or consulate.
* File U.S. income tax forms.
* Vote in U.S. elections.
* Use your U.S. passport.

<u>Passport Scam</u>[IL]: In the classifieds, you'll see advertisements for private passport companies. Some of these advertisements are legitimate; others are not. Check the advertisement carefully. Does it list a telephone number? Does it list a complete address, not just a post office box somewhere in Malaysia? Does it list some ridiculously low or exorbitantly high amount of money? Does it ask for the money right away?

If the advertisement doesn't list a telephone number and doesn't have a legitimate-looking address, chances are the company is a hoax. If you are told to hand over the money right away, forget it. You'll never see your money again, especially if the sum the company is asking for is less than the cost of obtaining a passport from a passport agency. Valid companies usually charge you twice as much as a passport agency for their services.

Call the company and ask for more information. If you are turned down, drop the entire proposition. A legitimate company would be happy to send you more information.

If you must have your passport within a week or less, some countries can help you get a passport quickly and easily. (A list of private visa and passport services is provided elsewhere in this book. Check the table of contents).

<u>The Jet Lag Drag:</u>[IL] Your internal clock runs on a fairly regular schedule. But every time you fly into another time zone, you disrupt your internal rhythms-- and experience jet lag. (The medical term for jet lag is circadian dysynchronization.) Jet lag causes you to become overwhelmingly tired, groggy, and lightheaded. The following is a list of precautions to take:

* Before you leave, try to prepare your body for the new time zone. If you are going, for example, to London, which is five hours ahead of EST, start going to bed one hour early and getting up an hour earlier five days before your departure. By the time you depart, your body will have adjusted.

* A few days before you leave and during your flight, decrease your caffeine intake.

* Although many airline offer free alcoholic beverages, avoid them. You don't need the added impact of a hangover. If you do indulge, drink only wine. The alcohol content is lower in wine than in mixed drinks.

* Eat lightly during your flight. If you eat too heavily, you may feel nauseous.

* Try to sleep during your flight. This will reduce your exhaustion when you arrive.

* Once you land, take a few minutes to stretch. Do not go to your hotel to sleep if it is only 5 p.m. Stay awake

as long as possible, try to eat a light meal, and remain active. This will allow your body to adjust more quickly to the new timetable and reduce the effects of jet lag.

How to take the Kids:[IL] Yes, you can travel with your children and still enjoy the trip. The key is planning. Following are some tips:

*   Rent a car. Although public transportation is reliable and inexpensive, particularly in Europe, your children's schedules may not match those of the trains and buses. With your own car, you can come and go as you and children want, and you can carry around everything the children need. (A list of International Auto Rental Companies is provided in Appendix X).

*   Take your own car seat. Some car rental agencies also rent car seats, but most won't guarantee that one will be available when you pick up the car.

*   Contact the tourist bureau for the country you're planning to visit for help choosing your accommodations. Tourist bureaus (listed elsewhere in the appendix section of this book.) can tell you which hotels, pensions, and apartments welcome children, and are equipped with cribs, playrooms, and babysitting services.

*   Choose an airline that welcomes children. Ask if you can bring a car seat for your child to sit in during the flight. Ask if children's meals are available, and if training tables are provided.

*   Pack a backpack carrier, a stroller, and an attachable high chair. Take along your own baby wipes (those sold in Europe are heavier, rougher, and oilier than those sold in the United States), but buy disposable diapers on the road.

Do you need a helping hand in planning and arranging travels with your children? If you do you may consider using the services of this organization: Travel With Your Children (TWYCH), 80, Eighth Ave., New York, NY. (212) 206-0688.

Traveling with Pets:[IL] Veterinarians advise against traveling with your pet. But, some dogs and cats become so miserable when their owners are away that they literally starve themselves. And, if you are moving across the ocean, you probably will want to take your pet with you. As long as your pet has had its shots, it can travel with you freely throughout Europe--with the exception of Britain, Ireland, and Norway, which have quarantine systems because their areas are rabies-free. The only restriction usually is that you possess a yellow international vaccination certificate for your pet (similar to the paper people carry to show that they have been vaccinated for smallpox).

Most airlines will make arrangements for your pet--unless it is a boa constrictor, a ferret, or a bird (birds are particularly unwelcome on airlines, because they carry diseases).

In addition to the vaccination certificate, most European countries require a health certificate for any animal taken across borders. The certificate must be filled out by a veterinarian a limited number of days before you arrive in the country. You may be required to obtain a second certificate once inside Europe if you plan to cross additional borders--check with the consulates of the country you are visiting. (Also see chapter 32)

Choosing Your Flight: For trans-Atlantic passages, find out if your flight is direct or nonstop. Nonstop flights have no layovers or plane changes, but direct flights may stop four or five times en route, even though you don't have to change planes. The stops can be a strain on your pet.

Most airlines allow a limited number of pets per flight, so make arrangements early. Your pet will be issued its own ticket, and you will be billed at the rate for excess baggage (which can be an insult).

Even if you have a boarding pass, you are not guaranteed a seat until you are given a seat assignment. To avoid last-minute decisions to bump you because of your pet, try to get a seat assignment as soon as possible (usually you can get a seat assignment nearly a year before the flight, even if boarding passes are not available more than 30 days before the flight). If you are unable to get your seat assignment in advance, allow extra time to board with your pet.

Storing Your Pet on Board: Some airlines will allow you to bring your pet on board with you and to store it in a compartment under your seat. However, most airlines require that you use an approved airline carrier for your pet during the flight, which is stowed in the airplanes's cargo hold. You can get one of these carriers secondhand.

Your veterinarian can help your pet endure the flight by prescribing a tranquilizer. You should arrange for it to have water during the flight (remember how dehydrated you get while flying). One trick is to freeze water in the bowl that attaches to the carrier. That way you will avoid drips while transporting the carrier. (Also see chapter 32).

Tips on Shipping Pets:[IL]

* Ship your pet in a large, sturdy crate with a leak-proof bottom. Print on it your name, address, your pet's name and destination.

* A health certificate and a rabies inoculation and a rabies inoculation are recommended, along with distemper and hepatitis inoculations.

* Exercise pets well the day before the shipment.

* Feed the pet a light meal six hours before shipping.

* Don't give water to pets within two hours of shipping except on a very hot day. Provide a water dish for attendant's use.

* If the trip will be longer than 24 hours, provide food.

(Also see chapter 32)

Baggage Identification: Security concerns in many countries have led to a variety of practices and procedures in several international airports. One of these practices is a Baggage identification by owner-passengers, prior to embarkation. In other words, in some countries, especially in Africa, you may be required (long after checking in) to identify your baggage. Usually, upon physical identification, your baggage is immediately loaded onto a carriage or directly into the plane. Unidentified baggage are not loaded or carried, in which case you may arrive at your destination unaccompanied by your baggage. The worst of it is that such baggage left behind may end up being misplaced, tampered with and/or lost. To avoid this, take some time (before or after checking in) and verify with the airline or airport authority if such practices or procedures are in effect, and if so, when and where.

Emergency: Telephone codes used in summoning for help during emergencies vary from country to country. Most of us are used to dialing **911** during emergencies. While this may be the code for many parts of the U.S.

it may not be valid for other countries of the world. Travelers abroad should, upon arrival at their hotels, place of residence or destination, inquire and familiarize themselves with the local telephone system, particularly the correct emergency dialing code. Children accompanying parents should be included in this learning exercise. A country by country list of emergency numbers (codes) is provided in Appendix 24X.

Security Precautions: As a security protection, it is advisable for the International traveler to maintain always a low profile while in a foreign country. This is important, particularly for Americans and especially those visiting countries in the Middle East, Africa, Asia and South America. You can have a perfectly enjoyable vacation without revealing or showing off your citizenship or parading yourself as an American.

If contemporary or past events are indications to draw from, it is clear that not all countries nor all the citizens of a given country are friendly with Americans, nor with America as a country for a variety of reasons. Unfortunately, it is at times difficult to tell what country or countries, which individuals or communities as well as when and where this may be the case.

However, you can stay out of this area of controversy and uncertainty, and have yourself a safe and peaceful trip by minding what you say, when and where you say it, and what you do, how, when and where you do it and what you carry, how and where you carry it to. To improve your personal security (a) minimize stopover time you spend at airports, avoiding those airports that are known to have security problems; (b) try to book direct flights scheduling flights, preferably, on wide-body jets (two aisles) since they are more difficult for hijackers to take over and control; (c) request for window seats since passengers in aisle seats are more likely to be abused by hijackers, (d) try not to discuss your travel plans in public places, rather restrict information about your travel plans to those who need to know. For additional security-related information see Chapter 6 on security awareness overseas.

International Protocol Pointers:[RI] Whether traveling internationally for business or pleasure, here are some useful tips:

■ Don't "over-gesture" with your hands; it can be offensive.

■ Avoid American jargon and idioms.

■ Don't refuse food; taste a little of everything.

- Don't over schedule.

- In Arab countries, don't openly admire things.

- Arrange for your own translator. Relying on someone else's translator could be a mistake.

- Gift-giving is an art and a science. Study the science and perfect the art. Giving a clock in China is a bad idea.

- You may be expected to sing after a dinner in either Japan or Korea.

- Contact the State Department for travel advisories before embarking.

- Don't photograph religious statues.

The Best Seat on the Plane:[RI] Of course, the best seats on a plane are in first-class. But in coach, some are better than others. In terms of safety, experts agree that the midsection of the plan, close to the wings, is safest in case of disaster. And being close to an exit door should increase your chances for survival.

Should you specify an aisle, window, or center seat? The advantages of the aisle seat are:

1. It's easier to exit the plane.

2. Your shoulders and arms have more space.

3. You can see other passengers and have a more roomy feeling.

A problem with the aisle seat is that you might repeatedly get your side brushed or toes run over by the beverage cart if you don't stay out of the way of flight attendants.

The center seat has no advantages, except when you are sitting next to someone you know (or want to know). The window seat allows a view of the sky and ground, which can help if you tend to feel claustrophobic in flight.

The closer you are to the front, the less time you will wait in line to deplane. Engine noise will also be less pronounced toward the front. The first row after the coach bulkhead gives you a ride up front plus more storage space. On smoking flights (those over six hours), a seat toward the front means you are away from smoke.

All of the major airlines, except for Southwest, offer seat selection at least 30 days in advance. The sooner you choose your seat, the better the seat you'll get - if you specify what you want. Once you get on the plane, you may request a seat reassignment.

Seats over the wing provide the smoothest ride; those in the back, the bumpiest.

Minors Traveling Unaccompanied/Accompanied: Be aware that International Airlines may not fly children under 5 years who are unaccompanied. Some airlines, however, are willing to assist with an experienced personal hostess to take care of the child on its journey. Depending on the airline, this additional service may or may not require extra cost of a full adult fare.

For many International Airlines, children between 5 and 12 years, however, may travel unaccompanied provided certain conditions are met. The most common conditions are that (1) the unaccompanied child be brought to the airport of embarkation, and met at the airport of destination; (2) the parents or legal guardians sign a written authorization. This consent form is usually available at any of the airline offices; (3) overnight stays en route can only be included if the parents or legal guardian or representative provides an adult to accompany the child from arrival until departure the following day. Depending on the airline, and if the airlines involved allows it, two or more flights on the same day may be permitted.

For children between 5 and 12 years accompanied by a hostess, a full adult fare is often charged for the child, in addition to another full adult fare if a personal hostess is provided at a cost. Quite often no extra fare is charged if the personal hostess is an employee (hostess) of the airline.

For children over 12 years accompanied by hostess, a full adult fare is often charged, in addition to a percentage (about 50%) of the regular adult fare if the airline uses one of its own hostesses.

In all cases for children over 5 years accompanied by an independent, non-airline personal hostess a full adult fare is often charged to cover the hostess.

Because the rules and conditions vary from one airline to another, it is advisable to contact the airlines prior to departure date to find out more about their policy, cost, and conditions relating to traveling by minors. You may even be surprised to find out that the age limits differ from those discussed here.

Do remember to check visa requirements. Depending

on the country or countries the child is traveling to, visas may be required for the child, the paid independent personal hostess or for the both travelers.

Babies - On Board: Many reputable international airlines do carry on board a stock of baby food, diapers and useful accessories for the care of your baby. Some do, also, provide baby baskets for babies no more than about 27 inches in length. Because of the limited number of these baskets, it is advisable to give the airline an advance notice; and, to be on the safe side, to carry along some food for your baby. It is not unusual to run into international flights that do not provide any of these services.

Liability and Insurance: As an international or air travel, remember that the luggage you carry or check into the plane is not insured by the airline against loss or damage during air transportation. Under certain conditions, the liability of the airline is limited in value, and this liability is based in principle, on <u>weight</u> and <u>not on the value</u> of the contents. This is all the more reason that it is advisable to have your luggage insured.

Transport of Animals: The transport of animal is a normal service for most international airlines. Doing it does, however, require advance notice. Usually, domestic animals are carried in the cargo hold. The holds for animals are often pressurized, well ventilated, and maintained at a comfortable temperature.

Some airlines, however, do allow small domestic animals to travel in the cabinet. Some countries or airlines, by contrast, do not allow transportation of animals in the cabin.

This procedure is often subject to certain conditions. For most airlines, only a number of animals are allowed per cabin or class. Furthermore, the animals whether in the cabin or in the cargo hold are required to be carried, and must stay in a cage or container that must meet certain specifications: weight limit for cabin bound animals. For those travelers who may not have a suitable cage, you may want to contact the airline. Some of them do stock a limited number of these cabin for sale to their clients.

Regulations on Animal Transportation: As an international traveler, you should bear in mind that some countries do not permit either the import or the transit of animals. In certain countries, it is required that animals first spend some time in quarantine. This mandated period may last for a few days or even several weeks or months, and at a cost that may be considerably high. Most airlines would not fly pregnant animals or those under two months of age. International

airlines are generally willing to provide their customers with relevant information regarding the official and veterinary regulations in force at the place of embarkation, transit points, and destination. Regulations for the transportation of animals may vary from airline to airline.

Animal Transportation - Rates: The excess luggage tariff is often charged for the transportation of the animal. This tariff is based on the combined weight of the animal and the containers. The excess tariff rate applies, irrespective of whether or not you carry the full luggage allowance. If your pet flies as cargo, special cargo rates may apply. In this case, it is important to remember that checking and collection as frequently as is the case, may be carried out in the cargo building, rather than in the passenger terminal. Airlines generally transport guide dogs for blind or deaf passengers free of charge.

Reduced Fares For Children: International airlines generally charge lower fares to children. The rates charged, however, may vary from airline to airline, and so are the age limits. Some airlines will charge children under 2 years who do not require a seat of their own only 10% of the full fare, provided that they are accompanied by an adult. For each additional infant traveling with the same (one) accompanying adult, 50% of the corresponding fare is charged. These amounts are reduced only to 10% per child if there are two accompanying adults.

Most international airlines charge children between 2 and 12 years of age, 50% of the adult fare. In this case the children are entitled to seats of their own. Depending on the time, the country, the airline and the conditions, other opportunities for reduced fare for children and/or their traveling family members may be available. Check with your travel agent or the airline.

Expectant Mothers: Most airlines, generally, do allow expectant mothers, (who are in agreement with their physician) to fly until a specified period of their pregnancy. This period, however, varies from airline to airline. For a flight after this time, you may be denied boarding for obvious reasons. Check with your airline, after, of course, consulting with your physician.

Advanced Notice: To avoid any last minute disappointments, delay and/or embarrassment at the airport, it is essential to give advance notice to the airline for the following luggage:

■ Dangerous articles or articles subject to special conditions (see following paragraphs)

443

- Animals
- Heavy luggage (exceeding 32kg)
- Fragile objects
- Wheelchairs
- Bicycles
- Surfboards, delta gliders
- Baby baskets including accessories
- Voluminous luggage

Dangerous Goods/Articles: The following materials are often regarded by airlines and by law to be articles or goods subject to special conditions. They are generally not allowed to be carried on board airplanes. They are considered hazardous materials. Hazardous materials include many common items from the home, workshop, or garage which, because of their physical or chemical properties, can pose a danger when transported. The following is a partial list of common items that are hazardous materials forbidden in carry-on and checked luggage:

- Infectious substances (materials that may cause human disease)
- Explosives, munitions, fireworks and flares
- Compressed gases of any kind
- Magnetized materials
- Corrosive materials
- Radioactive substances
- Oxidizing materials and peroxides (e.g. lead powder)
- Toxic materials and irritants (e.g. tear gas)
- Readily flammable solids and liquids such as gasoline or matches
- Mace, tear gas, and other irritants
- Aerosols containing flammable material
- Loaded firearms
- Gunpowder
- Loose ammunition
- Gasoline, flammables
- Propane, butane cylinders or refills, lighter refills
- Wet-type batteries, e.g., as used in cars
- Any equipment containing fuel
- Scuba tanks if pressurized
- Fireworks, flares
- Safety or "strike-anywhere" matches
- Flammable paint and paint-related material
- Poisonous material
- Infectious substances

Many other hazardous materials are also prohibited. When in doubt, check with your airline.

[Violators of Federal hazardous materials regulations (49 CFR Parts 171-180) may be subject to a civil penalty of up to $25,00 for each violation and, in appropriate cases, a criminal penalty.]

Hazardous materials are prohibited in checked or carry-on luggage. However, there are certain exceptions for personal care, medical needs, sporting equipment, and items to support physically challenged travelers.

For example:

- **Toiletry and medicinal** articles containing hazardous material (e.g., flammable perfume) totaling no more than 75 ounces may be carried on board. Contents of each container may not exceed 16 fluid ounces or one pound.

- **Matches and lighters** may only be carried on your person. However, lighters with flammable liquid reservoirs and lighter fluid are forbidden. (Smoking is prohibited on scheduled air carrier flights of six hours or less within the 48 contiguous states, and between certain other locations.)

- **Carbon dioxide gas cylinders** worn by passengers to operate mechanical limbs, and spare cylinders of a similar size for the same purpose, are permitted in both carry-on and checked luggage.

- **Carrying firearms** on board aircraft is forbidden. Unloaded firearms can be transported in checked luggage if declared to the agent at check in and packed in a suitable container. Handguns must be in a locked container. Check with your airline representative for other restrictions concerning firearms.

- **Ammunition** may not be carried on board an aircraft. However, small arms ammunition may be transported in checked luggage, but must be secure packaged in material designed for the purpose. Amounts may vary depending on the airline. Check with your airline.

- **Dry ice** for packing perishables, in quantities not to exceed 4 pounds, may be carried on board an aircraft provided the package permits the release of carbon dioxide. Further restrictions apply to dry in checked luggage. Check with air

☐ **Electric wheelchairs** may only be transported as checked luggage. The airline may determine that the batter must be dismounted and packed in accordance with airline requirement. Check with airline representative.

[Some items however, can be shipped or transported as air cargo. Contact your airline representative for detailed instructions regarding the shipment of hazardous material.]

Safety from Thieves:[1] Tourists are often easy and lucrative marks for thieves. Special precautions will lessen the opportunities for thieves. Here's a list of things you can do:

■ Carry most of your money in traveler's checks insured for theft.

■ Never leave your belongings unattended in airports, hotels or restaurants.

■ Taxi drivers, also, can sometimes be thieves. If a taxi driver does not turn his meter on, ask him to turn it on or go get yourself another cab. Otherwise, he may take you to your destination, charge you a higher fee, and pocket it. If he tries to" rip you off," get his cab number and report him.

■ If you agree to let someone carry your luggage and load it into a taxi watch him closely. He could run off with your bag or pretend to load your bags into the taxi while holding some back. You may not realize you've been robbed until you reach the hotel.

■ When registering in hotels, do not put your brief case on the floor. That makes it a perfect target for a quick grab.

■ Keep your valuables in the hotel safe.

■ When you leave your hotel room, always lock your doors and windows, especially those leading to the balcony.

■ When eating in the hotel restaurant or lounge never leave your hotel key on the table. A thief can note the room number, go

to your room, and rob you when he knows you are out.

■ If you are in town for a convention, and are required to wear a name tag remove your name tag, when you are not in a meeting. Otherwise, thieves will notice your name, find out your room number from the desk clerk, and rob your room while you are out.

■ Never let a stranger into the hotel room even if he claims to be on the hotel staff. Call the desk to make sure the person is legitimate before you open the door.

■ In crowds, walk against the flow of traffic, even if you do get dirty looks. That makes a pickpocket's job much harder.

■ If someone jostles you in the crowd, turn around immediately while checking for your wallet. Pickpockets move fast.

■ Don't keep your passport and cash in the same place.

■ If you carry a purse, carry your money in a pocket. Cash should be kept in front pants pockets or skirt pockets. Pickpockets go for the purse and back pocket first. Money belts are even better, If they are well-attached, they are difficult to pick.

■ Try to get a **shadowed baggage tag**, so that thieves cannot easily memorize your name and address.

■ When shopping, do not put your package down on the ground to get your money out. Put them in front of you where you can see them or keep then in an over-the-shoulder bag. Keep your bag toward the front of your body while walking. If it's too far behind you, someone can reach in and take something out without your knowing it.

■ Sleazy clubs, topless bars, and strip joints are notorious for scams. Foreigners are easy prey. For example, if you buy a bottle of champagne for a "lady," the bartender, after she's had a few drinks, may exchange the bottle for a half-empty one. By the end of the night, you are charged an exorbitant price for six bottles, while you probably only drank one full bottle of champagne.

■ If you lose your checkbook and it is returned, make sure that no checks are missing.

Who Should not Fly?:[1L] A person who is undergoing severe emotional illness probably is not a good candidate for a long air trip unless absolutely necessary, and then a responsible traveling companion is essential.

In general, if good sense is used and proper consultation is made with a physician, most persons having an illness or a chronic disability, such as diabetes or epilepsy, can tolerate air travel and their disabilities will not be aggravated.

If you should have a disease that occasionally causes loss of consciousness, such as epilepsy or diabetes, carry a card in your wallet identifying the illness.

The Medic-Alert Company. has stainless-still bracelets or emblems with engraved serial numbers that, also, have key words such as **DIABETIC** written on them. The serial number enables the attending physician to call collect night or day for more specific information about the patient.

Carrying Parcels and Letters for Others: As hard as it may sometimes appear, avoid carrying parcels or letters on behalf of third persons whether or not such a person is traveling along with you in the same plane (or other means of transportation). It is highly dangerous to carry something, if you do not know its contents. Personally, if I must carry a parcel or letter for a very dear friend or relative, I insist on knowing the contents and on doing the actual packing. You can have your entire vacation or trip completely ruined by becoming a victim of a parcel or package with suspicious or illegal contents. Claiming ignorance or emphasizing your "Good Samaritan" spirit will not help you.

Credit Cards, Traveler's Checks and Personal Checks. Unless your trip abroad will entail only cash expenses, always inquire about the forms of payment widely accepted in the countries you plan to visit. If credit cards and travelers checks are acceptable, find out which ones are acceptable. This is particularly important for a variety of reasons: (a) In some countries, personal checks are not widely used and are looked upon with suspicion, especially, a check drawn on a far away foreign bank. (b) In some countries, credit cards are not widely used and in these countries, they are only gaining minimal recognition in a few select places. Even in those select places, not all types of major credit cards are readily acceptable. (c) In some countries travelers checks are not as popular as we may think. They may not be widely used and, therefore, will not be an acceptable form of payment. Like credit cards, the particular type of traveler's check may determine its acceptability. If you decide to carry travelers checks, you may consider using American Express or Thomas Cook traveler's checks. Although there are over seven brands of travelers checks world-wide, American Express and Thomas Cook traveler's checks are perhaps the most widely accepted. Their world-wide network of offices and service centers makes them easiest to replace.

It is appropriate to point out that most of the limitations noted above are more prevalent; largely in small, developing countries, in rural parts of some developed countries, and in small establishments (shops, hotels, etc.). Travelers to large metropolitan cities of most countries who plan to shop in large national boutiques or who plan to stay in large international hotels may hardly notice the limitations mentioned here. Nevertheless, it would not hurt to be quite certain and prepared. Questions regarding what forms of payments are widely acceptable in a particular country should be addressed to that country's embassy, consulate or tourist bureaus in the U.S. Your travel agent, credit card or travelers check company should assist you in this matter.

Currency Exchange: Make it a habit to find out precisely what the rules and regulations are with regard to exchanging your U.S. dollars, travelers checks and other currencies into local currency and vice versa and stick to them. In some countries, re-converting excess local currency back to U.S. dollars or other hard or convertible currency is not easy and may entail a substantial loss to you. Upon arrival, find out government authorized places for such transactions. Many travelers find themselves in trouble by failing to play by the rules either due to sheer ignorance, or taking actions on their part to short cut the regulations and procedures. The outcome for violators could spell disaster for your vacation. Do not be distracted or deceived by unauthorized entities wanting your U.S. dollars and offering you higher rates. Some of them turn out to be undercover government agents and plain clothes police. Although in many countries a large number of hotels serve as official currency exchange centers, not all of them are authorized. Personally, I restrict my currency transactions to banks; besides, they usually offer a much better rate as compared to other approved currency exchange centers. Keep in mind that coins are rarely accepted for conversion into local currency and that includes U.S. coins.

Hard Currencies Only!: In some poor, developing countries "hungry" for hard currency, non-residents and foreign visitors may be required to make virtually all of their purchases in hard or convertible currency, particularly in dollars. Beware, should your travels include some of these countries. For the most part, these are, in addition, the countries with strict rules regarding exchanging foreign currencies. They are also the countries where you might have your money confiscated with the slightest currency violations and where you might find it hard to re-convert your excess local currency to a convertible currency. Your best safeguards are (a) declare all of your currency upon arrival. This is especially important for all countries with currency restrictions. (b) Restrict your activities only to authorized currency exchange places. (c) Keep receipts of all of your currency transactions. (d) Even though the commissions may appear high, only exchange the amount you need to use in the country. To find out what the current rules and regulations are regarding currency transactions, contact that country's embassy or consulate in the U.S. or their tourist bureau in the U.S.

Customs Declaration: If in doubt, make it a habit to declare always to the customs and/or immigration anything you cannot afford to have confiscated, including all items of personal jewelry.

Records/Receipts: Make it a habit to keep all receipts of purchases and other financial transactions during your trip abroad. Arranging the receipts by country would facilitate your dealings with a host of law enforcement authorities abroad and even at home including the airlines, particularly in the case of loss or damage. The receipts you keep, in some cases, may very well prevent you from getting into trouble with the law or determine whether or not you will return home with those souvenirs you purchased abroad.

Validation on Passports: As an international traveler one observation you may not fail to see quite early is the number of times your travel documents, particularly your passport, will be requested by one authority or the other. The other observation is the number of times and accessions some form of sticker or stamp is placed or imprinted in your U.S. passport. This is not unusual. The important thing is that you should not hesitate to have any of these validations. In fact, in most cases you should ask whoever is requesting your passport if a validation by them is not required. The validations you

should always look out for and ask about include: (a) visas (entry and exit) unless they are not required, in which case you will be told and (b) all currency transactions.

Do remember, however, that in some countries, some of these validations may not necessarily be made directly into your passport. They may come in the form of a sheet of paper enclosed or attached to your passport or tourist card.

Surrendering Your Passport: While the importance of safeguarding your passport must be emphasized, do not panic if your hotel or designated tour guide should request to keep it during the period you are in their service. Although not a common practice in most countries of the world, you may encounter this practice in some Communist countries, developing countries, Middle East countries and in certain countries of the former Soviet Union.

In all cases, however, ask for an explanation, including when and under what conditions it will be returned to you. If you plan to travel to any of the regions cited above, you may want to contact the embassy, consulate, or tourist bureau of those regions here in the U.S. before leaving to find out if such practices are in effect. The U.S. Embassy in the country you plan to visit should, also, be able to advise you in this matter. You are better off getting the information here in the U.S. before departure.

Remember your passport will almost always be needed when cashing travelers checks and personal checks. You may want to carry out all necessary foreign exchange transactions before parting with your passport.

Medications/Prescription Drugs: Carry along with you any necessary medications and keep them in their original, labeled container in your hand luggage. Because of strict laws on narcotics, carry a letter from your physician explaining your need for any prescription drugs in your possession. Failure to do this may result in the confiscation of your medication and/or a fine and imprisonment.

Group Travel Versus Solo: There are advantages and disadvantages, to both group and solo traveling. These advantages and disadvantages not withstanding, an international traveler with adequate planning can always expect to have a perfectly enjoyable, exciting and successful trip abroad. Whether one plans to travel as part of a group or travel solo is really a matter of choice and personal preference, many times determined by such variables as cost (budget), age, foreign travel

447

experience, language, privacy, flexibility, timing, health conditions and familiarity with the foreign country.

By and large, traveling as part of a group can add to the overall security of your trip, and will facilitate some of the procedural requirements that accompany traveling to a foreign country. Without a doubt, group travelers attract and get faster attention, sometimes resulting in savings of time and/or money. Because your group travel may involve a tour guide, you probably will have the advantage of sampling the best sites in town on the usual congested schedule. As a member of a tour group, you must, however, be ready to sacrifice your need for complete privacy, flexibility and independence for a schedule that may not allow them. Ultimately, it is you, and only you, who must provide the verdict as to the success of your trip abroad.

Attitude: Success with your trip abroad may depend on your attitude, particularly your degree of tolerance, as well as on how much flexibility you build into it. What will become invariably clear to you is the strangeness of the environment which, in fact, is not dramatically different from a trip to another city back home. You can break these feelings and thoughts by maintaining a positive attitude, complete with unreserved tolerance and great flexibility, and by toning down your expectations. After all, this a foreign country, not really home. The folks you see could have come from some part of the United States with their weird looks, funny accents and "wild and crazy" attire.

Essentially, I must caution that in parts of some countries you might travel to, smiles may be rare and the faces you see may not be as inviting. Do not take these looks so seriously or pre-judge them as to feel, "Oh! I have come to the wrong place," for behind these sad looking and unpolished faces are truly peaceful and loving hearts just waiting to know and understand more about you. Even if you were to run into one or two of these faces with the "wrong heart" during your very first encounters, try not to jump to a quick generalization of how hostile and unfriendly the country and its people are/or get out of town with the next available plane. You may be cutting short what could have turned out to be a wonderful and exciting learning experience.

Coming across an unfriendly host or hostess or receiving unfriendly treatment is not an unusual experience of foreign travelers. You will more than likely come across this at one time or another during your overseas trips. But, this is not very different from the same incident you might experience in your city of residence in the U.S. While overseas, it is advisable to view these isolated incidents with more smiles than

something else. Unless you have done something particularly offensive, you may be sure that what you experience, and the faces you see are nothing more than expressions of momentary misunderstanding. They may, also, be, expressions of shyness, of inability to communicate appropriately, or of curiosity just waiting to be broken. And guess what will break it, **YOUR SMILES,** a product of your **ATTITUDE**, your willingness to be truly adventurous, tolerant, understanding and, above all, appreciative of cultural diversity.

CARNET:

What is an ATA Carnet ?

*   Carnet is an international customs document, a merchandise Passport.

*   Carnets facilitate **temporary** imports into foreign countries and are **valid for up to one year.**

What are the advantages of using an ATA Carnet?

*   **Reduces costs to the exporter.** Eliminates value-added taxes (VAT), duties, and the posting of security normally required at the time of importation.

*   **Simplifies Customs procedures.** Allows a temporary exporter to use a single document for all Customs transactions, make arrangements for many countries in advance, and do so at a predetermined cost.

*   **Facilitates reentry into the U.S.** Eliminates the need to register goods with Customs at the time of departure.

What merchandise is covered by the ATA Carnet ?

*   **Virtually all goods,** personal and professional, including commercial samples, professional equipment, and goods intended for use at trade shows and exhibitions.

*   **Ordinary goods** such as computers, tools, cameras and video equipment, industrial machinery, automobiles, gems and jewelry, and wearing apparel.

* **Extraordinary items,** for example, Van Gogh Self-portrait, Ringling Brothers tigers, Cessna jets, Paul McCartney's band, World Cup-class yachts, satellites, and the New York Philharmonic.

* **Carnets do not cover:** consumable goods (food and agricultural products) disposable items, or postal traffic.

Where can an ATA Carnet be used?

Currently, Carnets can be used in over 44 countries located in Europe, North America, Asia, and Africa. Additional countries are however, added periodically. To learn more about Carnets and how to apply for an ATA Carnet, contact the CARNET Headquarters at

U.S. Council for International Business:
1212 Avenue of the Americans
New York, New York 10036
(212) 354-4480 Fax: (212) 944-0012

* The U.S. Council for International Business was appointed by the Treasury Department in 1968 to manage the ATA Carnet System in the United States. Typically, the Council issues over 10,000 Carnets a year covering goods valued at over one billion dollars.

Extra Photographs: Carry with you additional passport-size photographs just in case. Six to eight will be adequate. It is not unusual to be confronted with situations requiring passport-size photographs. For example requests for certain types of permits and licenses or for extension of stay may require passport-size photographs. Having some handy will save you both time and money. Unlike in the U.S. where the requirements are less stringent, passport-size photographs you plan to use overseas should show both ears, not just one ear.

Facilities: Many of the services and gadgets that are customary in the U.S. are conspicuously missing or inadequate in many parts of the world. This is particularly true in developing countries but also occurs in rural areas and in some developed countries. Such amenities as a regular supply of heat, hot water, or air conditioning are rare in public as well as in private facilities.

In some areas even hotels lack these services. Medical services are often inadequate and transportation and telecommunications are often inefficient. Computers, color television sets and other modern gadgets remain luxury items in many parts of the world and are therefore not readily available. Even services as routine as dry cleaning may prove to be a challenge.

Essentially, you must be aware that many foreign countries are not as advanced, developed, rich, cultured and "blessed" as the U.S. and its citizens. Shortages abound and poverty and primitive technology are very much alive in several parts of the world. As an international traveler, you can avoid the failures, losses, disappointments and frustrations experienced by many overseas travelers through careful pre-travel research and planning. The more knowledgeable you are about the people, their culture and the level of development in the country you plan to visit, the better your chances of having an exciting and successful overseas trip.

Cash: Before you go abroad, exchange a small amount of your U.S. dollars into the local currency. This will be very handy and particularly useful in covering taxi fares, handling tips and other incidentals. It, also, assures that you have a ready supply of local currency and will save the cost of breaking larger bills into local currency that you may not need. Furthermore, it will eliminate the need to pay to re-convert currency. Furthermore, this can save you the cost of being "forced" to exchange your money with currency exchange centers whose rates, fees, and commissions may be much higher than those of banks.

Foreign (money) Exchange Centers: As an international traveler, you will have occasion to deal in foreign exchange. This will include: (a) buying travelers's checks, whether foreign currency denominated or denominated in U.S. dollars; (b) buying foreign currency (exchanging dollars for foreign currency); (c) exchanging excess foreign currency for U.S. dollars; (d) cashing foreign drafts and checks, including VAT refund checks; (e) wiring money to an account overseas. Some of these financial services can be provided directly by several large U.S. banks, however, a large number of smaller banks can only provide a limited number of these services at prices that may not be your best bargain.

Alternatively, you may consider dealing directly with specialized currency exchange firms, which provide direct currency exchange and transfer services. You are likely to get better rates from these services.

For a listing of companies specialized in providing exchange services, see Appendix 23W

In order to save money on currency exchange transactions, you will need keep abreast of current exchange rates, fees and commissions charged by the various institutions which engage in currency transactions. Exchange rates are subject to constant fluctuations With such fluctuations your savings will depend on what is happening to the U.S. dollar vis-a-vis the foreign currency. Generally, a stronger (appreciated) dollar, will favor your position in which case you will be able to get more for the same dollar than before the appreciation. Timing, therefore, is as important, as shopping around for financial institutions that charge lower commissions and fees. Did you know, for example, as a member of the Automobile Club of America that you can get American Express Traveler's checks free of commissions; and that you can also get Thomas Cook Traveler's Checks free if purchased through any of its travel agencies? Check with your bank and credit card issuer to discover if they provide currency exchange services or other including "freebie" services. A list of dollar-foreign currency exchange rates is often published in the financial sections of some local newspapers, and in a number of national and international financial newspapers. The Wall Street Journal, and the International Herald Tribune are two excellent sources of daily rates.

Hotel Phone Calls: Placing phone calls from your hotel room may be convenient but it may also cost you considerably. Before you make that call, check with the hotel desk clerk or hotel phone operator to ascertain charges for local, long distance and overseas calls. Surcharges of up to 200% are not unusual, the quality of the connection not withstanding.

There are various options and approaches you can use to reduce the cost of hotel phone calls. If you must make your call from the hotel, (a) Find out if the hotel has low rate calling periods, and if they do, place your calls during those times. (b) Remember, that most hotels have pay phones at the lobby. If those phones are programmed to handle long distance or international calls, use them. (c) Find out if the hotel has calling card facilities. By placing your calls with a calling card, you may end up paying in U.S. dollars when you return home. (d) Alternatively, make that first time sacrifice and use a call back approach. This allows you to provide your number to your calling party while asking the other party to call you back. (e) Explore collect calls if it is available. Remember, some of these approaches may only defer payments for your calls, but most will save you money.

Another option that will help to reduce telephone costs is to place your calls at the designated central telephone stations found at most airports and in some train stations. Specially marked public telephones which allow you to use your calling cards are springing up in several large cities overseas. Because you will need a calling card to access this service, you may want to request one by signing up with one of the major long distance carriers in the U.S. before you depart. For

information on these carriers and their services as well as detailed instructions on how to communicate by phone to and from abroad, see Chapter 42.

Receiving Mail overseas: Central Post Offices in several large cities do provide facilities that allow foreign travelers to receive mail while overseas. Poste Restante as it is often referred to, is a general delivery service which allows mail to be sent to someone overseas to the care of a particular post office. The mail is then held for pick up by the owner. Proper identification, such as a passport, is often required. Important points to remember about this facility are: (1) They may not be available in every country. It is important to find and use the exact address and phone number (2) Your letter may be held only for limited time period and can only picked up during designated hours. It is very important that you inquire about these things. (3) You may be charged a nominal fee for this service. (4) It is advisable for the sender to make an appropriate note on the envelope, for example: "Hold until Dec. 31, 1993". Additionally, it is advisable to call the post office before going to pick up your mail, in this way you will be sure the post office is open and that your letter is ready for pick-up.

You could also apply this same approach with mail sent to hotels. If appropriate, have the sender place note on the envelope, for example "Mail for a guest, Hold until Dec. 31, 1993" Another available would be to use the services of the American Express Company. Customers of American Express including American Express Cardholders and those using or subscribing to any of their services may have their letters sent to American Express Office nearest their destination. This service is provided free of charge. Some restrictions may apply, therefore it is important to inquire about these services before you leave. Decide on which services you wish to use and make appropriate inquiries.

Drunks: You will probably run into them in several places. Be aware not only of their presence, but the likelihood of their nuisance turning into confrontation. Some of these drunks will try to have a chat with you, will touch and fondle you, or even spit at you. Abusive and foul language is a common trade mark of drunks and you can deal with them relatively easily by simply ignoring them. The best way to handle them is to just walk away. Any attempt on your part to deal with their harassment is at best, a waste of time.

Do not forget, many tricksters, pickpockets and baggage thieves, sometimes go about their trade, pretending to be drunks.

Auto Rental/Leasing/Purchases: Renting or leasing an

450

automobile for use overseas may by a money-saving option, depending on your particular circumstance and travel plans. This might be an option worth considering if you are travelling with a large family or group, or plan an extended stay with travel to areas that are not accessible by public transportation. You could make your reservations upon arrival overseas or right here in the U.S. before you go. Booking your reservations in the U.S. can be done by contacting the rental agencies directly, or via several of the International Rental and Leasing Agencies listed in Appendix X.

Some travelers invest in used cars overseas and then sell them before returning to the U.S. Others buy cars in the U.S. for overseas delivery and use, or make arrangements to purchase new cars overseas which are, then, sold at the end of the stay abroad, or exported to the U.S. Several firms specialize in leasing and purchasing automobiles for overseas delivery. These firms are often knowledgeable about applicable foreign country regulations in these areas. See Appendix X. Companies specializing in overseas delivery will also be helpful in assisting you with shipping arrangements. Those travelers who contemplate importing or exporting foreign automobiles and pleasure boats must be well aware of U.S. Government regulations and procedures. See chapter 34 and 35.

If you plan to rent, lease or drive overseas you should be aware of the rules and requirements. Some countries have strict age requirements, not only for renting or leasing automobiles but also for driving. Because some of these requirements may differ from the U.S. it is prudent to familiarize yourself with those of the foreign country before you go. Useful information for driving overseas can be obtained from your local automobile association or from the American Automobile Association.

Freebies: Ever wondered what free services, products, and other bargains may be available to International Travelers? You may be surprised to know that there are a number of services and products, worth hundreds of dollars, for which you may already have qualify. You may automatically qualify for some, while you will have to shop around and apply for others. In some cases its a matter of just asking for them. Those who offer these freebies obviously will be delighted if you were only to ask or pay for their services without requesting any free offer they may have. A few will give them to you, nevertheless, or use them aggressively as a promotion device. While inquiring about the freebies, we should not forget the common adage which says: "There is no such thing as a free lunch". Keep in mind that a good number of offers are,

indeed, money-saving and worthwhile but there is the constant need to be cautious. It is advisable to comparative-shop and to read the fine print (if a contract or purchase is necessary) before you accept an offer for a "free" service or product. If you believe in real freebies as I do, you may consider the list of freebies and money-saving opportunities available to travelers listed in Appendix 25Y.

Making Business Contacts overseas: This can be particularly, taxing for businesses seeking new overseas markets for their products and sources for their raw materials. Business contacts in some countries become even more difficult for women. U.S. businesses in need of assistance in this area or in any activity relating to international trade may contact. The U.S. International Trade Commission in the Department of Commerce. This agency will, also, provide you with advice, references and resources on a variety of issues in international business, including sources of financial assistance for U.S. exporters. Furthermore, they will provide you with information on the domestic markets, including local business customs and practices. A listing of the Department of Commerce District Offices and the International Trade Information is provided in Appendix C and D, respectively. Other sources that should be explored are (1) the commercial section of the country's embassy or consulate in the U.S., (2) the U.S. Chamber of Commerce. A growing number of companies now have Chamber of Commerce in the U.S., (3) International Trade offices of City and State Governments, (4) Commercial attaches of American Embassies and Consulates Overseas, (5) International Business Clubs and Organization in the U.S.

Vehicle Precaution: If you plan to drive during your trip abroad, you should take safety precautions. Foreign travelers often become favored preys to local muggers and thieves. Incidentally, the same can be said of foreigners who visit the U.S. Incidents, ranging from car break-ins to car jacking, including physical assaults on the occupiers, have been reported by Americans travelers. The motives for these incidents vary, and the resultant impacts have, also, varied, and have sometimes been quite fatal. You can minimize the chances of becoming a victim by taking a few precautions, including:

- Drive the more common kinds of locally available cars; if there are not many American cars in use, don't insist on an American model.

- Make sure the car is in good repair.

- Keep car doors locked at all times.

- Wear seatbelts.

- Don't park your car on the street overnight if the hotel has a garage or secure area. If you must park it on the street, select a well-lit area.

- Don't leave valuables in the car.

- Never pick up hitchhikers.

- Don't get out of the car if there are suspicious individuals nearby. Drive away.

- If you are renting or leasing a car, request for one with a local tag as opposed to one with an international tag or clearly marked tourist tag. This way your car will not stand out.

- If you must stop to ask for directions, do so at a gas station or in a relatively populated and well lit area. In other words, avoid isolated areas when requesting services.

- If you are bumped, particularly repetitively, do not stop to check if you consider the area too isolated, or if you are suspicious of the motive. You might well be right. Instead, drive to a safe, populated, area.

- Although it may sound cruel, beware of situations that look like accidents. Some are staged just to attract your attention and sympathy. You could very well end up becoming a victim of one assault. This also include stopping to render help to, supposedly, a needy and helpless traveler or pedestrian, especially, in very isolated spots. Obviously, there are other ways besides having to stop, that you may be able to render help. If you must react to your need to help, drive to a safe area and place an emergency call on behalf of the accident or stranded victims. Remember, you are in a foreign country and environment, and may not totally understand how things work.

Need a Traveling Companion or Partner?: If you do, you are not alone. A growing number of travelers are doing just that for a variety of reasons: For some it is a way of curbing loneliness, others desire to reduce costs on accommodations by doubling up, and still others want to reduce the general risk of traveling alone. This can also create the opportunity for a new relationship. For those international travelers attracted

to this form of traveling you may find helpful resources in Appendix 22V useful.

Overseas Employment: If the purpose of your trip overseas is to take up a temporary or permanent job, you may consider exploring the services and resources provided in Appendix 20T.

Before considering employment overseas, you should familiarize yourself with the Internal Revenue Service rules regarding income earned abroad. Several rules and tests apply including the "foreign residence test" and the "physical presence test"; and so are exemptions and exclusions. You may avoid future confrontations with the IRS by checking the current rules and regulations. Check your local telephone directory for the IRS office nearest you.

As you embark on your search for employment overseas, I must caution you about the growing number of unscrupulous agents and agencies with bogus claims. Many of these so called "overseas employment agencies" are not reliable, but are out to con you out of your money. It is, therefore, advisable to think really hard and long before committing any monies to them. Alternatively, you should consider applying for overseas jobs directly with the overseas employer or an overseas employment agency (assuming the latter does not require for an up-front or advance-fee). A number of international newspapers and magazines, as well as foreign magazines circulated in the U.S. carry job announcements. A few of the large ones are listed in Appendix 20T. Other sources of information regarding overseas jobs may be obtained from the respective foreign embassies and consulates in the U.S. (See Appendix B).

Remember, an offer for a job overseas does not exempt you from the rules and regulations governing employment of foreigners in a particular foreign country, nor are you exempted from the necessary permits, including entry and exit visa, and other requirements of that country. Check with the respective embassies and consulates.

Discount Travel Opportunities: You can save a lot of money as I have, on your trips, and still enjoy the same treats as everyone else. This is true whether in the U.S. or abroad, if only, you know what it takes. And what does it take? It takes flexibility and willingness on your part to give up comfort and convenience, One must also be knowledgeable about these opportunities. The more of these you have, the greater potential for larger savings. Unfortunately, some of the opportunities for bargain fares carry risks and penalties, some of which may end up being costly, in both time and money. Hence, it is important to shop around for the least restrictive bargain opportunities.

Generally, the longer the planning period you have for your trip and the more time you will have to explore discount opportunities. This is particularly important, because there are several carriers from which to chose and the fact that fares change continually.

As you begin exploring opportunities for discount fares, you may want to bear these generalized observations in mind. (a) Tickets for flights during peak (high) seasons cost more than those for during off (low) seasons. Incidentally, this is also true for prices charged by hotels, theaters, etc.

As you will probably guess, summers are usually considered to be peak seasons as against winters. Airlines and cruise lines have actual months (cut-off dates) signaling the start and end of the various seasons. It is important to remember that the actual dates may vary from carrier to carrier and for travel to or from some parts of the world. It is advisable to shop around and to check with the various carriers. (b) Tickets for travel during early morning or night hours tend to be cheaper. Although this may not be true for international carriers, you may find such bargains with domestic flights. (c) Tickets for weekday and holiday travel tends to be more expensive than on weekends and non-holiday periods. (d) Depending on the class of ticket you buy, you may pay more or less, and still not notice (when on board), any significant difference in services provided the different classes of passengers. In the case of travel by air, depending on the airline, you will find as many as four classes of fares. These are, (in descending order of cost, beginning with the most expensive), first class, business class, coach class (sometimes called tourist or economy) and excursion or discount fares. There is also the "super first class" as one may categorize the fare on the Concord. In the majority of the international airlines you will find the four basic fares, in some, the numbers of fare classes may be less. To complicate things for the unsuspecting and amateur traveler, you may find slight variations between airlines in their definitions of these classes. It is not unusual to find some airlines selling different types of coach or economy tickets. From time to time new packages with new terms are added to the usual economy and excursions classes of fares. In recent years, these have included the advance purchase excursion (APEX) fare, and the Youth fare. These are all potentially bargain opportunities for international travelers. Exploring some of these special fares may be worth the effort.

You will readily notice, the lower the class, the cheaper the fare will be. (e) Standby fares are considerably lower than regular fares, and are potential money-savers for those who qualify. Standby opportunities are described elsewhere in this chapter. (f) Tickets for low-fare travel, generic airlines, such as Virgin Atlantic, Icelandair and several other small carriers, are generally much cheaper than tickets for the same flight, bought for travel with any of the large, regularly scheduled carriers.

Alternatively, you could save handsomely on your overseas trip by employing the services of charter operators, ticket rebators, air couriers, and bucket shops and consolidators. The services provided by these groups are explained elsewhere in this chapter. A listing is also provided in Appendix 21 U.

As you explore the various avenues to save on your trip expect some restrictions and learn to consider them before making any financial commitments. Read all fare permits. Some of the common conditions will include one or more of the following clauses: (a) advance reservation, (b) advance payment (purchase), (c) short notification of the traveler, (d) reconfirmation of reservation, (e) non-refundable payments, (f) no cancellations (except documented real emergency), (g) minimum and/or maximum stay (h) weekend sleep-overs (1) some stopovers/connections, (j) right to cancel on the part of the service provider.

You also have the option of booking or reserving a flight or cruise without making immediate payment. You can make reservations with more than one carrier, up to 6 or more months in advance. However, you may be required to pay and get your ticket within a few weeks before actual travel date. You could even make multiple reservations. But I must caution that carriers generally do not appreciate multiple reservations for the same traveler, since this ties up opportunities for others. Avoid booking your reservations with the airline and making a duplicate booking with a travel agency. Most airlines, once, they notice the duplication, will cancel both, and toss out your name.

Safe guarding your Camera Film: As an international traveler, you and your luggage will go through one or more airport x-Ray machines. This is a part of the security measures that are being taken worldwide. Some airline authorities have claimed that their X-ray machines will not damage camera films passing through them. This claim however, has been disputed, as some trusting passengers continue to notice the effects of X-ray exposure on their prints. Taking extra precautions to safeguard your films (including those inside the camera) will ensure that your hopes are not dashed. Imagine spending all that money, time and effort in taking the pictures just to lose them. One suggestion would be to politely ask the X-Ray operator or attending officer to pass the film through by hand, rather than through the machine. Make sure you do not open the film, as this will expose and render it useless. Let it stay in its original container (box) or wrapped in a plastic bag. Do the same with your camera, if it has film in it.

As you consider taking photographs overseas, you may also want to carry adequate film. Film is generally less expensive in the U.S. If you must buy your film overseas, expect to pay up to three times what they will cost in the U.S.

A Trip to Your Doctor: This is highly recommended for International Travelers, particularly, the elderly, the disabled and those with medical problems. To get more out of your visit, you should ask your physician to educate you on a host of health-related issues including the required vaccinations. Obviously you should be equally concerned about preventive measures. Because there are numerous diseases you may contract, and numerous related health problems that you may encounter when traveling abroad, it is fair to say, that the chances will very much depend on where you are traveling, the time of the year, and how much personal health precautions you have taken.

As you discuss these issues with your physician you may want to explore to the extent possible, what measures you can take to prevent and/or treat the following: diarrhea, blisters, stings bites (mosquitoes, dogs, and snakes, etc.), dysentery, ear aches, food poison, infections, (including fungal infections) sun burns, motion sickness, jet lag, hemorrhoids, giardia, exhaustion, tooth aches, rashes, anxiety, insomnia, and foreign objects in the eye. Discuss preventive measures for diseases such as malaria, yellow fever, hepatitis, typhoid, cholera, rabies, tetanus, AIDS, herpes syphilis, gonorrhea (STDs), measles, mumps, rubella, poliomyelities, diphtheria, pertussis, encephalitis, typhus fever, tuberculosis, schistosomiasis, trypanosomiasis (sleeping sickness) and leishmaniasis. As you will immediately notice the list can be quite extensive. The list however only includes the diseases and problems you are most likely to experience. Keep in mind that all of them may not be relevant or applicable to your destination. You will also be encouraged to know that you may already be immunized for some of these conditions and can make arrangements to be immunized against others. You may already be adequately knowledgeable about many of these conditions, but it will not hurt to make extra inquiries to protect yourself. Some of the diseases and health concerns mentioned here are discussed in detail in chapter 9.

Vegetarians: Surely, you are not left out. Most international airlines will honor your request for a special vegetarian diet. The only requirement is that you give them advance notice. Such notice is better done when booking your reservation, and again, when re-confirming your flight. Do not be surprised, however, if you suddenly find out while already on board, that they forgot to keep to their words. You can expect apologies when this happens, although that won't be of much help. It may not be a bad idea, therefore, to carry along some food or snacks, just in case. International airlines generally do a better job in meeting your dietary needs than do local or domestic airlines. In fact, do not expect much in this area from domestic airlines. So be prepared:

Similar to international flights, you may not have difficulties getting a decent vegetarian meal in the big, well-known hotels, where salad bars are equally popular. Travelers with alternative room and board arrangements should expect to be on their own as far as feasting on a good vegetarian meal. There are obviously other ways you can make up for these deficiencies, such as a trip to the local food market. This, however, is an alternative I will not recommend for an international traveler. Do not forget that you do not have to lodge in an expensive, big-time hotel to use or eat in their restaurants. Finally, do not be surprised, depending on what part of the world you are traveling to, if your host/hostess does not understand what a vegetarian meal is, and/or perhaps find it strange. To assist you in your travel plan, you may employ the assistance of the North American Vegetarian Society at P.O. Box 72, Dolgeville, NY. 13329 (518) 568-7970.

Tricksters: Perhaps, next to pickpockets, tricksters are another group determined at fowling up your trip. They will come in all shades and colors, some well dressed, knowledgeable and well spoken, and others just the opposite. They will prey upon in your confidence and desperation with promises to do wonders for you or to render services you never requested. Essentially, Beware! What they want is your money. You will probably find more tricksters in South Asian Countries than in other parts of the world. These individuals are nothing but con men, women and children who in a flash will render you penniless, as they disappear with your money and valuables. Just be on the look out for unsolicited assistance of any form or type. Besides, always be suspicious of unsolicited samaritans. Their motives are often unpredictable and "unsamaritan". Your best approach is to avoid them, and if approached, to simply say.: "No thanks" and walk away. Do not let them distract you or get you to participate (share) in their discussion.

Security and Hotel Rooms: Do not assume that your hotel room is always safe, whether, as relates to safe guarding your valuables or for personal safety. Important valuables should be carried with you at all times or locked up in the hotel safe. To get a safe deposit box, ask the desk clerk at the hotel. And for travelers lodging in facilities without safe deposit boxes, the choice should be obvious. Carry your valuables with you. You will be amazed at how fast an item of yours can disappear. Poverty is real in several parts of the world, and hotel employees are not exceptions. An item considered so unimportant by you might just be very valuable to a poor hotel employee.

Travel Guides: The following are the more popular travel guides and their publishers and/or distributors. Several of these guides are available in most bookstores and local public libraries. You may want to check with your library first before investing in these travel guides, although it is always better to have one of your own.

Remember, these travel guides vary in coverage and depth: Some are more broad and detailed, while some others are more specialized. One feature you will find common with the publishers listed below is that they each carry a line of country-specific or region specific guides as well some special-interest guides. Depending on how already knowledgeable or sophisticated a foreign traveler you are, you will find the information in these guides useful. Before you invest in them, it is better to scan through a few of these guides, including a look at their table of contents to see if they contain what you are looking for.

Newsletters: Other than the regular travel guides and books, some of which are listed in Chapter 46, newsletters and magazines for international travelers are available. The newsletters are particularly, common with travel clubs (Appendix U). Whereas the newsletters, which are almost all by subscription magazines, can be bought from general bookstores, travel book stores and newsstands. Most travel newsletters, however, tend to be specialized, targeting a particular country or region, or a particular group of travelers, such as singles, women, seniors, children, disabled and gays. A good number, however, is more general with a variety of information and tips that will benefit every international traveler. A listing of these newsletters, periodicals and magazines is provided in Appendix 17Q.

Emergencies and Restricted Reservations: We do not always expect them, but they do and can happen. I mean emergencies. And, sometimes the losses go beyond the actual emergency to include broken vacations or trips, and financial losses from restricted tickets. Certainly, airlines and other carriers and service providers are aware of such possibilities. It does not always, however, have to translate to a total loss. In other words, you can do something about it. Obviously, if you do not make the effort the loss may then become real. Remember the saying: "Nothing ventured nothing gained". Irrespective of the type of restrictions and penalties contained in your reservations and tickets, with proper and verifiable documentation and some luck, you may be able to recover. Proper documentation would include, for example, a note from your doctor in the case of illness, a copy of a newspaper release, or an obituary notice, in the case of death of a family member. Any convincing and verifiable document will help. If you are lucky you may not only be able to get some credit or refund, but you may even qualify for some discounts, such as the special bereavement fare offered by some airlines. Although these opportunities exist to minimize your loss in the event of an emergency, do not interpret this as an obligation on the part of the other party, unless specifically included in the contract. For the most part, it is a favor being rendered to you, and how you approach the other party is important. Be courteous.

Pickpockets and Baggage Thieves: These are two of the several types of menacing hosts and hostesses you will likely encounter during your trips abroad. They come in all forms and shades. They carry no name tags or special identifying features except that they are almost everywhere, but more in some places than in others, particularly at airports, train and bus stations and in crowded public gatherings. Many are well trained in the art, and operate as part of a gang, while some others may just be independent operating amateurs. Surely, you will like to be able to identify them, so as to stay away. Unfortunately, it may be difficult. It could be that 4 year old girl or boy hovering around you, that 16 year old offering to help carry one of your bags, that miserable-looking woman carrying a baby on one hand, with the other hand extended to you, or that well dressed and well spoken gentleman or woman, seemingly knowledgeable about everything around town, including your immediate need. However they are described, it should be clear that they are your worst enemies. They are capable of making you re-live all the problems faced by many travelers. Of course, pickpockets, baggage thieves and their derivatives can be found in every country, including the U.S., and their motives are the same: to take what is yours and get away with it by any means necessary. How you will deal with them in the U.S. is, therefore, no different from the approach you will use abroad? Well, not necessarily. As you journey from one country or community to another, you find that their **modus operandi** is different. Whereas, in some places, the law is there to protect you; in some countries you will find very little real help or consolation. You may even find blame for not being careful enough. Well, maybe the latter might make sense, at least to the extent that it motivates you to learn about the tricks and take necessary precautions.

Although pickpockets and baggage thieves occasionally operate overtly and with some degree of violence or force, most go about it in a subtle way. For the most part, their key strategy is DISTRACTION. Remember DISTRACTION. In other words, they will distract you by whatever means will work, and then rob you. There are numerous ways and techniques pickpockets and baggage thieves use in an effort to distract. There are stories of people using mustard or ketchup by "unintentionally" smearing it on your clothes. Some will create sudden situations and emotions such as pointing and looking to the sky for an unseen and unknown phenomenon, indirectly, encouraging you to do the same. Some even stage events and games that will attract the unsuspecting. Some will engage you in conversations long enough for you to loose your sense of where you are. There are, furthermore, the familiar forms of distractions used by pickpockets, including crowding you up, bumping you or into you, stepping on your toes, or cornering you, so tight that you can hardly feel differently or notice any serious picking taking place. Throughout your trip you have to bear in mind that many of these individuals are very smart, and they believe you can be distracted. And, of course, you help them by giving them the opportunity, the time, and the place. What can you do to minimize your becoming a victim.

(a) Avoid crowded areas and events (2) Stay away from dark alleys and poorly lit and isolated places, including train compartments with only very few people. Remember they tend to pick more on those who appears helpless and weak. (c) Avoid conversations with groups of unknown individuals, particularly during shopping (d) Refuse unsolicited assistance, and when you must do so, be careful. If you must need help with your luggage, do the approaching, and surrender the heavier and least valuable luggage definitely, not your wallet or hand bag, (e) Stay focused and keep walking to your destination. If you have any stains or whatever, you can certainly check it out somewhere else (for example, in your hotel) not on the street. (f) Carry your valuables in a secure and hidden place, where it is apparent that somebody must totally demobilize you to get into, without you at least noticing. A number of travelers

pouches, particularly money belts, are becoming very popular and many do provide better protection. (g) Do not make it a habit to tell people time when they ask. If it is so important, they can always ask some other person or invest in a cheap watch. (h) Do not make change for people. Certainly they can go to the bank. (i) Watch where you sit or stand even in trains and buses. Its better to back to the wall if you can. (j) Try to look like everyone around. Conspicuous looks and actions only expose you. You don't have to carry name tags and look like a tourist to be a tourist, or to display your valuables and money to appreciate why you must have them. (k) Do not ask strangers to watch your luggage or bags, no matter where, and no matter how short a time. (l) Be aware of your immediate environment and the people there. A careful look at faces and actions around you should be able to trigger an appropriate action on your part. A place with too many loiterers and strollers is not particularly an attractive place to be. It is often a fishing zone for pickpockets. (m) Avoid carrying your wallet or purse in a rear pocket. Carrying these items in front of you in clear view and crossed over with your arms is definitely better protection. Inside pockets are even much better, particularly, if they have zippers. Money belts (waist, leg and shoulder belts) have became popular with tourists. Every pickpocket-conscious traveler should consider getting one of these belts or making one for themselves.

And for those of you happy going travelers who, despite all the warnings and advice to the contrary, will get drunk, you are perhaps the most vulnerable.

<u>**Safety Precautions for Women Alone**[IL]</u> Unfortunately, women need to take special precautions when traveling abroad, especially when traveling alone. Attitudes toward women vary from country to country, but here are a few general precautions that women should take when traveling:

- If you're traveling solo, use public transportation whenever possible. The incidence of rape and robbery of lone women in cabs are alarmingly high. As an American, you are an even greater temptation.

- Do most of your traveling during the day. If you must go out at night, travel with an acquaintance, especially in southern Europe, where the men tend to be sexually aggressive toward women.

- The less you carry around with you,

the easier it will be to run if necessary. Do not overburden yourself with packages or luggage.

- Don't wear expensive jewelry or clothes, especially when you're alone.

- Men in Italy and Spain like to pinch. Stand with your back against the wall in elevators, and if you're traveling with a friend, ask him to walk behind you in crowds. If you figure out who's pinching you, turn around and say "Enough." That usually will put an end to it.

- Have your key ready before you reach your room so you won't be fumbling for it in the hallways.

- Don't flirt with men on the hotel staff - unless you're serious about it. They have a key to your room and may not be able to resist the invitation. If you hear anyone trying your door, call the front desk immediately. If you don't have a phone, be loud and aggressive. Yell. Threaten to notify the police.

- Ask for a hotel room near an elevator so that you won't be walking down long dim corridors alone at night.

- Try staying at a bed-and-breakfast instead of a hotel

Visa Vigilance: 14 tips to take the hassle out of traveling on a visa: Following are some useful tips to help you avoid problems when traveling to countries that require a visa:

- Don't travel on a passport that has less than six months validity. Countries that automatically extend visas for six months at a time will not give you a visa otherwise.

- Keep at least two clear pages in your passport. Many foreign consulates require both a left-and- a right-hand page for their visas. Renew your passport, whatever the expiration date, if you are running short of clear pages.

- It is sometimes possible to get a second passport to travel on while your other is tied up with visa applications.

- U.S. expatriates should avoid getting or renewing passports in their countries of residence. Foreign consulates frequently run time-consuming checks on visa applications from people with passports issued overseas.

- Apply in good time for all the visas you'll require for a trip. Don't rely on picking up a visa at the other end, even if it is possible (as in Egypt, for example).

- Be aware that certain countries impose a time limit from the date issue (typically three months) for using the visa. This in inclusive of the length of your stay.

- Whenever possible, apply for a visa at the foreign consulate nearest your home. You are always liable to be called for an interview.

- It is best to apply in person. You can often iron ut problems on the spot and check to be sure that the visa has been issued properly before you even leave the building.

- Visa authorities are looking for evidence of financial support and your clear intention to leave their country. Always remember this.

- Know in advance whether you need a tourist or a business visa. If in doubt, ask. In some countries, there is a crucial difference in formalities.

- Ask whether an international vaccination certificate is required with your visa application.

- Be sure you get a double - or multiple-entry visa to certain countries, such as India or Saudi Arabia. If you are on a business trip, you may need to return suddenly. This is impossible with a single-entry visa.

- Check whether you need an exit visa, especially for African countries, Belize, and Brazil.

457

- If you're going to Israel or South Africa, use a second passport or request that your visa and entry stamp be put on a separate sheet of paper. This can help avoid problems in the future when traveling to other countries.

Limitations To Airline Compensation For Lost Luggage: Contrary to what some travelers think, airlines rarely, and are not obligated to pay you an unlimited sum in compensation for lost or damaged luggage. The limit to an airline's obligation is clearly stated at the back of your ticket. Read it carefully. Even with all of your receipts in tact, you will be entitled to usually, no more than what is stated. Generally, how much you get, depends largely in part on the weight of your luggage as indicated on your ticket when you checked in, the contents, after being subject to depreciation and any additional insurance on the luggage. The value of the contents is not the primary determining criteria. Generally, for lost or damaged items, airlines may reimburse passengers for a maximum of $12.50 per passenger on domestic flights and $9.07 per pound for each piece of checked baggage on an International flights. The maximum reimbursement for unchecked baggage on International flight is $400. If the contents of your luggage(s) are over $800 dollars in value, and you are so concerned, get additional insurance just in case. A list of Travel Insurance providers is provided in Appendices 13N and 14M.

Alternatively, consider traveling light, and importantly, leaving at home, those pieces of personal item you cannot afford to loose. Unless you have to, expensive items such as jewelry, furs cameras, should be left safely at home; otherwise, you should consider having them insured. An additional floater into your existing policy may be all that you need to cover these items.

In the event your luggage is damaged or slightly damaged, you should request a replacement baggage to carry you through the
rest of your trip. Many airlines, particularly European Airlines, will often honor your request on the spot. Others may prefer to refer you elsewhere to have your luggage replaced or repaired. You may be requested to have you repaired elsewhere, of your choice, and then to send the bill for reimbursement. Because time is of essence to you, insist on immediate replacement. But, whatever your state of mind, do not forget to report immediately and document the loss or damage to the airline authorities in writing. Hold on to your copy of the report and to your ticket. Remember to not surrender your luggage tag unless you are provided with a signed letter stating that they are in possession of your luggage tag.

Road/Street Maps: Maps are very helpful tools, particularly in getting your way around town. They can save you time as well as add more thrills to your trip. Incidentally, they are one of those free items you can easily get if only you request them. Potential sources of free maps include the automobile clubs, tourist offices, travel agents, airlines, information centers and even your insurance company. Of course, if you do have money to spend, you can always purchase them from local bookstores or special travel bookstores listed in Appendix 16P.

Single and Companion Travelers:. With the diversity among today's travelers, there have sprung up a number of institutions and organizations, providing services to almost every special group of traveler. One such groups include single travelers, some of them looking for companions. If this fits your objective, you will find helpful the various single organizations and other resources listed in Appendix 22V.

Gay and Lesbian Travelers: A number of organizations and resources are available to gay and lesbian travelers. See Appendix 22V for a listing.

Protection Plans: As part of your overall travel insurance, do take advantage of any available services to minimize costly mistakes in planning your overseas trip. This will include ensuring that the travel planners, counselors, agents, agencies and tour operators you are dealing with are, competent, reputable and registered with their respective professional associations. In this regard, you may want to contact the Institute of Certified Travel Agents at (617)237-0280, the American Society of Travel Agents at (703) 739-2782 and the United States Tour Operators Association at (212) 944-5727. Some tour operators are part of ASTA Tour Protection Agreement, which protects clients from unscrupulous tour operators. Consider limiting your tour arrangements to these companies. To verify who is part of this plan and who is not, contact ASTA. A listing of other Associations you may likely come across or need before, during and after your trip abroad is provided in Appendix 23W.

Hitchhiking: Avoid the temptation, unless, of course, it is your normal way of life and your preferred means of transportation, in which case you are fully aware of the thrills as well as the risks that go with it. There are many personal safety considerations and risks to worry about in a foreign land, and you do not want to complicate them or add to the risks. Should you find yourself destitute or stranded, call or request assistance from the nearest police office and the U.S. consulate. Much better, plan well and avoid those things that may necessitate hitchhiking in the first place, such as carrying adequate funds, and emergency contact telephone numbers. Remember, hitchhiking may be frowned upon and may be illegal in some countries, or prohibited in certain areas. Despite the problems and risks inherent in hitchhiking, this practice appears relatively safer and more common in Europe than in other regions of the world.

Tickets/Passes and Reservations: Get as much of what you will need for your trip in the United States. These include your tickets, visas, insurance, medications, rail passes and reservations (hotel, airlines plane seat assignment, car rental). You can always re-confirm them, if need be, when overseas. By so doing, you will save considerable time, energy, and inconveniences. You may, also, save money. You may not be able to imagine these savings and the advantages of taking care of some of these aspects of your travel before you go, until you find yourself agonizing over your lack of foresight and foreknowledge. In several countries you may find yourself literally spending hours, days and weeks, and money, to succeed in obtaining the same information and services as are in the U.S. and that would have taken just a fraction of the time and cost to obtain. In other words, many of the things we take for granted here in the U.S. constitute luxuries in several countries. From transportation, to communication to speedy and courteous services, you will be amazed at the contrasts.

Other than for the above reasons, certain discount opportunities, such as some railway passes do have stipulations requiring the passes to be purchased in the United States, to qualify.

Warranties: Do not rely on them. Carry out your shopping on the assumption that there will be no reasons or cause for you to return the items for a refund or exchange, or to rely on the warrantee. Assume you never got one. Warranties and guarantees are not things you should take seriously when overseas. Surely, if you request a copy, you will get them, both, verbally and/or in writing, but often they are not worth much. In practice, you will have a hard time recovering on the strength of such warranties. This is not to say you should not ask for them or safeguard them, if you receive one. With every generalization, there are some exceptions. Your best approach is to examine thoroughly your agreements and purchases before you commit yourself or pay for them.

Automobile Accessories: If you plan to drive abroad, be aware that in several countries and regions, Europe included, certain accessories are standard, and are required in cars. Traffic police may stop you to check for these items. They include an emergency first-aid kit, and in some places, a jack, a spare tire, an emergency reflective triangular plate. Operating an automobile not equipped with these accessories may result in delays and/or fines. It is prudent, if you are going to drive overseas to find out the practices and requirements of that country. Your local Automobile Association should be able to assist you.

What to carry or pack: This is a subject that is not limited to international travelers. Most travelers, including seasoned travelers face the same issue. You are, therefore, not alone if you are concerned. And, to say that there is a universally accepted answer will be a joke. Obviously, you cannot carry more than what you have or can afford: While it will be up to you to decide really what is important to you, to have to carry, here are a few pointers and some things you must give careful consideration to: (a) You are only entitled to a certain number of free check-in luggages and each luggage limited to a specified weight, beyond, of which, you will be required to pay for the excess. Ask yourself, if you are within the limit and if not, if you can afford the extra cost of additional lugagges or over-weight luggages. (b) Traveling light is the ideal way to go, but in doing so, you should not sacrifice the convenience of having what you really need, or else you will have to deal with the risk and price of not taking the item(s) along with you. Remember, you are going to a foreign country, and perhaps to a location where finding even the most essential commodities and services might not be available or may be quite expensive, or, where finding those things you need might be very time-consuming, a hassle, or even impossible? But does this mean, then stuffing you baggage with every thing imaginable? Not necessarily. Traveling light after all has a lot of advantages. Besides cost considerations, it is less aggravating, less stressful and could be time-saving. It allows you the freedom you need to react quickly, walk faster, (if need be) keep an eye on your belongings, and catch up with late commitments.

For one, thing it gives you an edge for consideration when bargaining with hotels, airlines, and taxis. Of course, if your luggage is so small to qualify as a carry-on or hand luggage, you can kiss luggage insurance good bye.

All said and done, the real questions you should ask yourself as you consider any particular item for packing are: (1) Do I really need it? Is it essential? Will I use it?, (2) If yes, to question 1, is the item cheaper and readily available where I am going. Obviously if the

459

answer is yes and no, respectively, for the two questions, then go for it. If a lighter, but durable, form of the item is available take it, and if the item is versatile and with multiple uses, you have a must-take item for the trip. To facilitate your packing and to ensure that nothing important is left behind or left undone, a comprehensive final checklist has been provided to you elsewhere in this book. Remember, do not over do it. Research indicates many travelers do not get around to use many of the things they carry with them. And, please do not take what you cannot afford to lose.

Finally, your packing plan should include considerations for airline requirements. Some airlines restrict certain items in the cabin or in carry-on bags. There are the more familiar and perhaps obvious items generally prohibited by all airlines. These are listed elsewhere in this chapter. There are, of course, the not so familiar or obvious items such as battery-powered equipments, scissors and knives. The rules, however, from airline to airline. It is always advisable to check with the airlines.

Get The Name. As you make your plans to travel, you will, in more than one occasion have to deal with different individuals, including travel agents, travel counselors, ticket agents, airline personnel, hotel and automobile rental reservation clerks. Because some of the information they will be providing you may determine how your trip turns out, it is prudent that you make a note or log of the person(s) you speak to including the day and time. In the event of any mix-up, this will provide you with some basis to establish your case. It makes your story credible. Whenever possible, request a written confirmation of your reservations and any important agreements made between you and the other party.

Inventory: Maintain an inventory of your luggage and have the list in a separate place. A list of what is contained in each luggage would be very useful for identification and to establish a claim in the event of a loss. Similarly, keep a log of all purchases made, including the prices paid for each item. Also, note the form of payment, whether in local or hard currency.

Jokes: Avoid stupid and careless remarks particularly, around airport premises or in the plane. They could disrupt your trip and send you to jail. Statements or conversations about or relating to bombs, grenade, terrorists and terrorism, drugs, hijacking are usually sensitive to most travelers and law enforcement authorities. Some persons, particularly law enforcement officers may take it seriously, even when you consider it to be only a joke. The consequences can be painful

and could ruin your trip. Keep away from these words and lines of conversations that may employ their usage.

Checking and Boarding: Do it on time. You have spent weeks, perhaps months preparing for your trip; do not mess it up by being tardy. Tardiness could cause you, your trip and your luggage. It could even cause you your to loose money, especially, if you are traveling on a restricted ticket.

On the day of your trip whether to, or from your destination, allow yourself ample time. Try to get to the airport at least two to two and half hours before scheduled departure; and when boarding announcements are made proceed immediately to the departure gate. Arriving early will allow you time to check-in your luggage and get a seat assignment if you have not already done so.

Upon arrival at the airport, quickly check-in your luggage and get a seat assignment and boarding pass. Then, proceed to the appropriate boarding gate, or as soon as your are allowed to. In some countries, including the United States, getting to the airport, depending on the city, the day and hour of day, could be time consuming. Worst of it, in some countries, particularly developing countries, the time required to check-in and to go through various immigrations, customs and security formalities can be enormous and so is the risk of missing your flight and other scheduled connections. You can minimize this risk, including the chances of being bumped, by giving yourself ample time. The quicker you get through the formalities and into the boarding gate, the better. There are numerous experiences of travelers who make it through to their destination just to find out that their luggage did not, because they checked in late. Similarly, there are instances where the luggage makes it through to the destination, but the owners missed the flight because they were late in boarding.

Bumped: If you are denied boarding and bumped by an airline because of overbooking, in which case they have more passengers scheduled and ticketed for the flight than these are available seats, take heart. You may have recourse. Depending upon whether you are voluntarily or involuntarily bumped, you may be entitled to compensation by the airline. But, remember, the mere fact that you are booked and have a ticket for the flight does not automatically qualify or entitle you to fly, nor does it entitle you or to a compensation if you are bumped. Failure to confirm or re-confirm your flight within the time required (usually 72 hours), or to arrive and/or check-in on time as stipulated in your ticket, may result in forfeiture of your right to fly and to a seat on the plane. See Chapter 40 for additional information on bumping.

Re-Confirming Flights: The general rule with international airline tickets and reservations is that you re-confirm your flight within 72 hours. This could be done in person or over the phone. Do not take this for granted. You stand to loose your original reservation and seat in the plane, if you fail to confirm. Many airlines take it seriously, and will waste no time selling your seat. And, by the way, when you re-confirm your flight request, for confirmation number and the name of the airline personnel attending to you.

Canceled/Delayed Flights: Flight delays and cancellations are not unusual, and the effects on some travelers could be frustrating. This is all the more reason some travelers carry flight cancellation insurance coverage. The reasons for delays and cancellations vary, and may or may not entitle you to compensation, let alone, to special considerations. (See Chapter 40) It is very unlikely you can do much about it. In the instance of a protracted delay or cancellation, most airlines will often provide the travelers with alternative options and services, including meals, and lodging at no extra expense to the traveler. Sometimes, you may just have to request these services. And as upset as you may be, try not to loose your composure. In the event of flight cancellations or delays does the traveler have a legal recourse or is entitled to financial compensation? Maybe, maybe not. The rules governing flight delays and cancellations vary from country to country and, in some cases, among airlines. Unless your carrier is a U.S. based or U.S. registered airline, do not count your blessings. You may be just be wasting your time and money. In case you did not know, flight delays and cancellations are much more prevalent in developing countries. In may of these countries, do not even expect an explanation nor apologies, since none may be forthcoming. Nevertheless, do ask, and request for a substitute arrangement. If you have a suggestion on how you can be helped, make it. You may get what you ask for, especially, if your request is reasonable.

Valuables and Registration: If you plan to travel out with an item that may be subject to import duty by the U.S. Government, you may consider registering it with the U.S. Customs before you go. And if you do, retain your copy of the registration. You could have your valuables registered with the U.S. Customs at the airport, or you could check with the nearest customs office for a location. A list of U.S. Customs District Offices can be found in **Appendix E**. Remember, failure to register your valuables and other items of value may subject these items to duties when you return. One way you can eliminate the need to register with the customs at the time of departure is to obtain an ATA Carnet. See the section on Carnet in this chapter for additional information.

Dealing with foreign law enforcement authorities: Be smart, be alert and be polite. You need these virtues when dealing with foreign law enforcement personnel, including the police, customs and immigrations. On your trip, you will very likely make contact with customs and immigration officers. How you present yourself and interact with these officials are important and may very well determine how you start-off your first few hours or day in the foreign country. In dealing with customs and immigrations and all law enforcement officers try to (1) be polite; (2) speak clearly and coherently, particularly, in stating the purpose of your trip; (3) do not fraternize or flirt with foreign law enforcement officers. They are not a breed to be trusted with your secrets or jokes, besides, you may be risking your stay. (c) Stick only to the questions asked you and avoid volunteering information. (d) If you must "declare" what you are carrying, then, do so, and do not leave out any item. Describing the contents of your luggage as "personal items" will be subject to less scrutiny than if the contents are for sale or for business. (e) Avoid carrying any goods that may be considered as contraband or subject to quantity limitations. Most non-prescription drugs are likely to be illegal, and so are pornographic materials. The quantity of liquor, cigarettes, and tobacco products you may bring or carry into a country as duty-free may also be limited. Check with your travel agent for duty-free items, and limitations, for the countries you plan to visit..

Baggage Storage Facilities: Do not leave your luggage unattended or in the care of a stranger. Most international airports are equipped with baggage storage facilities, where, for a small fee, you can store your baggages. Although many of these facilities operate seven days a week, 24 hours a day there are variations from airport to airport. In some of these facilities you can leave your baggage with them for no minimum time, and for a maximum of up to several days. Obviously you do not want to leave your luggage in these places for too long. And please, take your valuables with you, including your passport, tickets, credit cards and travelers checks. Make sure the luggage left behind have locks and your identification tag. Collect a receipt and keep it safe. If you lose your receipt you may find it difficult to re-claim your luggage. Other than storage facilities at the airports, safety lockers could be found in train stations of large cities. Some of your excess luggages could be safely stored in these lockers for a very short period. Lockers found in Western Europe are safer than those in countries in Africa, South America and Asia.

461

Hotel Reservation from the Airport: For those who like to brave it by not making advance hotel reservations, you may want to know that at most international airports, there are often, specially marked or located telephones directly hooked up with the major hotels in the city. There is often, no cost to you in using these phones. All you have to do is lift up the phone and a hotel reservation clerk will be on the line to assist you. Most of these hotels also, operate free transportation to and from the airport. If you can not locate any of these phones, inquire at the information desk, located in every airport.

Finding Lodging: Finding a place to lodge is not usually difficult if you have the money to spend. However, if you are on a tight budget, you may have to do some comparison shopping, including toning down on the quality of services you expect from lodging facilities. Many large hotels in the U.S. have international subsidiaries or have reciprocal referral agreements, which makes it easier for international travelers in the U.S. to reserve accommodation overseas. All it may take is just a phone call. A list of international hotel chains and telephone numbers is provided in **Appendix W**. You could also make arrangements for lodging through your travel agents, and room-finding services provided by some international airlines tourist offices, student organizations, youth organizations, youth hostels, YMCAs, YWCAs.

Lastly, you could utilize travel guide and other publications.
Many of them list the names and addresses of a variety of foreign hotels, boarding houses or pensions, youth hostels and camps with detailed description and ranking, including price information. See Chapter 46 for a list of some of the popular travel guides, most of which are available in your local bookstore or public library. Do not forget, upon arrival in your destination, you can always, after the first night, find an alternative cheaper facility elsewhere, nearby. This is usually easier if you are located downtown, within the city, since you could literally do your search on foot as opposed to using a taxi. Do not get discouraged by signs saying "No Vacancy", go ahead an inquire, a room could be available right at that minute. Besides, it is not uncommon to find such signs, even when there are vacancies. Occasionally, management forgets to take down the "no-Vacancy" signs. You can save yourself a lot of money, if you conduct your own search for lodging than to rely on your travel agent. This is important, since most travel agents/agencies operate largely on commission basis, and many not commit the time and interest to finding you a real bargain. Remember, finding overseas accommodations for

travelers is not their specialty.

Lodging: A variety of lodging facilities and arrangements is available overseas. They include hotels (different sizes, types, and qualities) bread and breakfast, boarding houses, or pensions, villas, apartments, private homes, inns, youth hostels, student hotels, farm houses, camps, parks, road-side shelters, home exchange programs, and the Ys (YMCAs , YWCAs).

Addresses and telephone numbers of some of these facilities can be found in many special interest travel guides and from travel agents, foreign tourist offices and foreign embassies. You could, also, contact some of the organization specialized in one or more of the lodging types. See Appendix 18R for a listing of some U.S.-based organizations specialized in assisting you find affordable lodging overseas.

In planning and making reservations for your lodging, do not forget to discuss meal plans. Meal options vary, depending on the type of lodging or accommodation arrangements.

Some plans may include breakfast, while others may not. Similarly, meal plans alone, or as part of a package may include one, two or three meals a day, and may, or may not include weekends. Obviously, some comparison-shopping on your part may be a prudent thing to do, particularly, if you are looking for substantial savings. Do not forget, some packages that include room and board sometimes turn out to be cheaper, although this depends to a large extent, on the type of meal plans included. And when you make your reservation or sign the contracts, it is important not to forget to read the fine prints to ensure that what you pay or will pay for, is what you bargained.

Remember, with meal plans, there might be some restrictions which may, or may not include your favorite menu. As always the case, you do also have the choice of taking care of your food needs, outside any formal plans. In most large cities, particularly, in Europe and in other developed countries, you will have no problems, finding a wide variety of food houses, including several familiar American dishes and fast food restaurants.

Camping Carnet: If you plan to camp overseas, the international camping carnet could save you money. You can apply for a copy from the National Campers and Hikers Association at 7172 Transit Rd. Buffalo NY 14221 tel. (716) 634-5433.

U.S. Embassies Abroad and Holidays: Be aware that

462

U.S. Embassies and consulates abroad observe a number of holidays, and are, therefore, closed during those holidays. For the most part, they observe both U.S. holidays and public holidays of the host country. See Appendix 8H for a country by country list of commercial holidays.

What the U.S. Embassies and Consulates Can and Cannot Do: The U.S. embassies and consulates abroad provide a number of services to Americans. A list of these services is provided in Chapter 26. While you may be tempted, in desperation, to seek their assistance remember, that embassies and consulates do not engage in travel agency functions. Approaching them for assistance, for example, to change your itinerary, re-issue your ticket may yield you very little positive results. And, certainly, embassies and consulates will not be able to assist you in such things as recovering your lost or damaged luggage or cashing your checks. Although they may direct you to assistance elsewhere, they are much more concerned with emergency and life threatening issues affecting you and other American citizens.

Catching Local (domestic) Flights and Other Transportation: Talk of orderliness and timeliness? Do not expect to find that when taking domestic flights in many countries, particularly, in developing countries. Delays are rampant, planes are often overbooked and you may have to engage in some hustling if you really want to fly or travel from one point to another. This is true, even for other means of transportation. Do not be surprised to find fellow checked-in travelers surging, and running into the waiting plane. And even after all of this, do not be surprised to find someone occupying your seat, because it has been assigned to more than one person. It seems like a tradition in some environments. You may just have to learn and join them, at least in ensuring that you make the flight. In these type of environments, I usually put on my sneakers and travel light.

Vagabonds: In your trip around the world you will, from time to time, run into vagabonds. These individuals parade and roam around, inside and outside the airports, ticketing offices, ministries, and many other places where travelers and non-travelers alike go to apply for important documents. They are neither authorized nor employed by the respective agencies and offices, nor are their activities officially condoned. These vagabonds will often offer their services to you, promising to obtain for you in record time, whatever it is you need, be it boarding passes, visas, or just forms. And, they usually promise doing this for a reasonable price. Although many do in fact succeed in providing you with the requested services in real record time,

their activities are often illegal and frowned upon by the government. You will be taking a big risk dealing with them, and this could get you into trouble, including jail time. Besides, you can not be so sure, who the person you are contracting, really is. He or she may well be an undercover police officer. By supporting these vagabonds and patronizing their activities you, may end up losing, not only time and money, but also, any documents you might have advanced to them. If you plan appropriately, you will often succeed in getting legitimately, whatever it is you are applying for. Just give yourself more time.

Filing (standing) On Line: As civilized and rational as this practice may be, and as common as we find it here in the U.S., you may not always find it so in some countries. Corruption, lawlessness, favoritism and nepotism abound in may parts of the world, and you will likely find yourself a "victim". And many times, it is so blatant and overt as to make you really mad. Well, stay calm, that is all the more reason I am letting you know well in advance. It is advisable in such situations not to emulate them. Educate them instead, but do so politely and with integrity. Point out to the individual and attending official or clerk, your disapproval. Very likely, yours may be the only open incident you will witness before you are attended to. In most instances, the cost to you is time, and with proper planning, you will emerge, having your needs met.

Searches and Seizures: As your travel abroad and around the world, you will find a variety of practices which at best, could be frustrating, time wasting, and perhaps in your belief and opinion, uncalled for. Some of these practices will include road blocks, spot-checks, searches and seizures. Like many other travelers, you will hope you do not become a target. While such a feeling is OK, do anticipate them, and when confronted by these circumstances, it is in your best interest to cooperate. You will lose less time if you remain calm, and speak out politely, as opposed to acting confrontational, questioning the officer's authority, or showing signs of anger and disapproval. Law enforcement officers expect to be obeyed and respected. This is true in the U.S. and equally true of foreign law enforcement officers you will come across during your trip abroad.

Spot-checks are common in airports, but they could happen any where. A spot-check may just call for you to show or provide the officer with certain documents they normally will expect of you. Other times, they might lead to an elaborate search of your person, and your luggage. Female travelers should not expect much privacy as some foreign law enforcement officers can be especially malicious and "dirty".

Do not be surprised, if in the process the officer tells you that an item in your possession is a contraband and, therefore, will be confiscated. This is true even for such items that, in fact, are not prohibited. In other words, you may be unfortunate to come across an unscrupulous official who, in reality, would like to have your item, but figures the easiest way is to tell (scare) you that it is prohibited. When confronted with this type of situation, stay calm and polite. However, you can do one of two things. (1) Consider it a gift and let him or her have the item, particularly, if you can do without it. Besides, this may be all that the person wanted, and letting it go will likely be the end of the search or inspection. (2) Alternatively, request to speak to the boss. Chances are that the officer may, in a clever way, refuse to grant your request, but may turn around and let you keep your item. This may turn out to be the case, particularly if the original motive was suspect. On the other hand, you may have your request to see the higher in command, who may over rule the junior officer or who may reiterate the facts of the law to you.

As for road blocks, expect much more of these in developing countries of Africa, South America and in communist and police states. Routine road blocks often require checking of travel documents (passports, visas, inoculation certificate for required shots, purchase receipts); and if your are a resident or citizen, you tax receipts and voting registration. In some road blocks officers may inspect your travel luggage.

Unnecessary IDs: Before taking off on your trip, carefully go through your wallet and examine your identification cards (IDs). Remove those IDs you will not need, particularly those that could implicate and/or complicate your travels abroad. Implicating or "killer" IDs are those IDs that you do not need abroad and that may invite intense questioning by law enforcement officers. Included in this category are Federal, State and local government job IDs. IDs that indicate your title and position should also be left at home, more so, if you work in a "sensitive" industry, including weapon manufacturing nuclear laboratories, security and investigating agencies and law enforcement. Definitely, you may not need such IDs for any reason to justify the potential cost. You can, also, safely avoid using such titles as president, chairperson, director. Use instead,the common and simple titles such as Mr. Miss or Mrs., or Reverend. After all, you can have a perfectly nice time without these avoidable pieces of IDs and titles. Remember, you want to always keep a low profile when traveling abroad.

Stop-Over Flights: Unless it is necessary, always avoid stop-over flights and take direct flights instead.

By so doing, you will minimize the risk of flying (including landing and take-offs), as well as save time. You also avoid such inconveniences as having, is some cases, to subject yourself to security checks. Although transit travelers rarely go through this, it is not an uncommon practice in some countries.

Acceptable Credit Cards: Not all credit cards are widely accepted overseas. The best cards, and with the most world-wide recognition and acceptance are American Express, Visa, MasterCard, Dinners Clubs, and Carte Blanche. If you have other credit cards, you may consider leaving them at home. Department stores and oil companies cards are neither popular not acceptable.

Buying Prescription and Other Drugs Unless for very quick expiring medications, fill all of your prescriptions in the U.S. before you go. Because of the lack of rigid controls on drugs and other pharmaceutical products in certain countries, particularly, in developing countries, there have been numerous case of expired and adulterated drugs being sold. This is true, even among many of the supposedly, registered and professionally staffed chemists as they are sometimes referred to overseas. The proliferation of street-side drug vendors, unlicensed and non-professional pharmacists adds even more to the risk of endangering your life when you fill your prescriptions overseas.

An additional reason for getting your prescriptions in the U.S. is that you may not be able to find your favorite brand overseas. There is, of course, the likelihood that the nearest pharmacy may be several miles away and/or with limited operating hours. Finally, do not forget that in several countries, there is acute shortage of drugs. The drugs you need may therefore, may not be available, and if you do find them, they may command exorbitant price tags, perhaps turning out more expensive than the same drugs in the U.S.

It is for these reasons that you should seriously consider carrying along extra medications. This should include both prescription and non-prescription (over-the-counter) medications. On the other hand, if you must fill all, or some part of your medications abroad, do so only, at large, professionally attended drug stores. Do not forget to request generic prescription from your physician before you go, since names of drugs abroad may differ from those in the U.S.

Authentication Services: Foreigners engaged in some official businesses and transactions are occasionally required to submit only authenticated (not notarized) documents. These documents, most of which carry or require official seals, include birth certificate, marriage license, school transcripts and divorce papers. If you must submit documents to foreign governments, agencies or institutions, find out if notarized copies are acceptable or if they must be officially authenticated. To have your documents authenticated call or write: Authentication Service Foreign Affairs Center, Bureau of Administration, United States Department of state, 2201 C. St. NW Rm. 2815, Washington, D.C. 20520 tel: (202)647-7735.

Air Passes: This is another money-saving option, similar to rail passes. Air passes are particularly useful for those planning to engage in extensive traveling within a particular country or region. They often allow for multiple stops and unlimited mileage within the specific limitations of the particular pass. Air passes are common with European airlines. If you are interested in air passes, contact the respective airlines. Remember that air passes have their restrictions, and may not be cheaper or a money-saving alternative to every traveler. Your travel plans and the cost of alternative plans will help you determine the suitability of air passes.

Courier: If you have what it takes, you could fly for free or for a considerably cheaper cost as a courier. Good candidates for courier service are travelers who (1) are not inconvenienced traveling alone (i.e., can travel alone), (2) are flexible with their travel plans, (3) do not have baggages to check in since as a courier all you may carry is your carry-on bag. What the courier companies basically need from you is your checked baggage allowance. Of course, the courier company hopes you will deliver the baggage claim tags and the baggages to their agent on arrival. You can expect the courier company to check you in at the port of departure, and have their agent wait for you at the airport or at a designated location overseas. Courier services may be for one-way or round-trip travel. Remember as a courier you may have to subsidize part of the fare and/or be required to pay a nominal fee for the service, depending on the supply and demand for couriers. It may, also, depend on whether you are dealing with a broker or courier company. Of course you are expected to make arrangements for your visas and other entry requirements.

If you are interested in flying as a courier, you may want to contact any of the courier companies and other resources listed in Appendix 21U. Contacting these companies or brokers early enough is important, since it may take anytime up to four months to get you going.

Traveling Standby: This type of traveling can be a source of large savings, if, indeed, you can standby . To be able to take advantage of this service, you need

much flexibility with your travel schedule as well patience. Obviously, you must be willing to tolerate disappointments, especially those resulting from your not being able to make a particular flight. As a standby traveler, expect to purchase your standby ticket on a short notice. Beyond that, it is nothing more than engaging in the waiting game at the check-in counters of the airline, and praying for seat in the plane. Remember, once on board, you will enjoy the same privileges as any regular fare passenger. The problem is only with securing a seat on board. As a standby passenger, you will have less luck on weekends, holidays and other peak traveling periods. On the contrary, you may find better luck at night, off peak seasons and during the weekdays. Various airlines, however, have their definition and rules regarding standbys. Besides, standby arrangements may not always exist with every airline. For these reasons, it is advisable to check with the airlines first, and inquire if standby fares are in existence for your intended destination . If one is available, find out what the conditions are.

Alternatively, you may employ the services of some companies that, also, specialize in standby tickets. Most of the companies require registrations or service fee. See Appendix 21U. Cruise travelers should, furthermore, explore standby opportunities with the cruise lines. A listing is provided in Appendix S.

Frequent Flyers: The frequent flyer mileage program has become a growing phenomenon in the world of travels, and it will be unimaginable not to take advantage of it. Previously offered, only by the airlines, today, even credit card companies and automobile rental agencies and big hotels are getting involved one way or the other, offering frequent flyers and frequent users, opportunities for savings towards that future trip. Besides, as a frequent flyer, you may qualify for other complementary services offered by the airline such as upgrading to first class and use of special lounges at the airport. The problem, of course, is that most travelers who can benefit, because they happen to fly more frequently, do not sign up for these free services and/or do not take the time to register or maintain a good record of amount of air miles accumulated during their trips. On the other hand, there are many travelers who have accumulated frequent flyer miles (points), but are yet to utilize them. You may loose those points. Read the fine prints. To learn more about frequent flyers and similar programs, contact the respective airlines. Many U.S. and European carriers presently have frequent flyer programs. Some newsletters and magazines, in addition, have begun to emerge, focusing on the frequent flyer and mileage programs. See Appendix 21U.

465

Charters: Charter flights are increasing becoming very popular with budget-conscious travelers. Substantial savings can be accrued traveling on a chartered carrier. Although charter packages have been around for a long time, they are beginning to add new twists and incentives that appeal to today's sophisticated travelers. If you are considering traveling on a chartered flight either as part of a group as is often the case, or solo, you should be well aware of the characteristics and limitations of this form of travel arrangements. They include (1) advance reservation and payment, (2) sacrificing some of your comfort; (3) penalties, forfeiture of some or all of your payments in event you cancel; (4) possible postponement or cancellation of the trip by the charter operator. Generally, charters do not provide the type of flexibility as do regular flights. Some of the restrictions mentioned above may, additionally, turn out to be costly, when the time lost, and inconvenience are factored in. Of course, there are rules and regulations governing charter operators, such as those dealing with refunds, in event the operators cancel the charter. But, none of those regulations will adequately compensate you for a charter trip gone sour. It is, therefore, advisable to search around carefully for reputable and reliable specialized charter or tour operators, and compare cost. As you make your research, inquire further what services are included and what are excluded in the arrangements and the terms of the contract. The same level of prudence you apply when dealing with airlines must be applied when dealing with cruise line charters. If you are concerned about the reputation of a charter agency, check with the local Better Business Bureau. You may also check with the American Society of Travel Agents, or the National Association of Cruise only Agents listed in Appendix 26Z. For a list of charter operators, see Appendix 21U. A trip cancellation insurance is recommended for travelers on a charted carrier.

Rebators: Rebators, and rebator services are a growing phenomena in the travel industry. Rebators operate, more or less, like travel agents except that they may charge you a fee for their service in exchange for passing on to you some portion or all of the commissions traditionally available to travel agents. Depending on the amount of travel you plan to make, the savings could be substantial. Of course, rebators are not necessarily travel agents or agencies, and are not as organized as travel agents. Find out more about the particular rebator its charges and much better, get references, before committing your time and money. For a partial list of ticket rebators see Appendix 21U.

Bucket Shops and Discounted Tickets and Wholesalers: With careful researching you may be able to purchase air tickets at even a deeper discount

from the so called "discount travel agencies" or "bucket-shops", and/or from wholesalers, often called "consolidators". Due to a number of reasons, some of these "travel agents" are able to buy and/or obtain concessions from airlines, thus, allowing them to offer many times, an unusually sizable amount of discounts. If you are a traveler interested in this type of arrangements, you should expect certain restrictions on the tickets, including penalties for any deviation from the terms of the contract. Tickets bought from bucket shops and consolidators may carry non-refundable and non-endorsable clauses, and may require cash payments. Many reputable agencies will accept alternative means of payments, including credit cards. Be aware that not all travel agencies are bucket shops and that specialize in selling at deep discount. Importantly, most bucket shops are not registered travel agencies, as we know them. The same is true with consolidators, most of whom are just wholesalers, buying from the airline and selling to travel agencies or directly to the consumers. This means that great care and providence must be applied, should you chose to use their services. Certainly, there are a number of good and reputable ones, but the same is true for a number of flight-by-night agents and agencies. You may consider restricting your dealings with registered discount travel agencies. And like every opportunity to save a buck, do some shopping around, compare costs, risks terms of the contracts before letting go your money, and certainly check out the business before you go. A list of bucket shops and ticket wholesalers is provided in Appendix 21U. Additional lists can be found in the travel column of most big national and international dailies, and, further, in the advertisement sections of most travel magazines and newsletters.

Travel Clubs/Airline Clubs: Travelers interested in special treats should consider joining a travel club. Advantages accruing to club members could be wide ranged and does vary from club to club. Depending on the club, privileges often include opportunities for better services, at a bargain price. Airline clubs are becoming common with major air carriers, and the privileges members enjoy can better be appreciated when, for example, you suddenly find yourself hustling and bustling at the check-in counter or looking lost, helpless, or tired at the waiting area. During this time, club members are probably relaxing, and being provided with "free" entertainment in a private lounge, exclusive to members. Even an opportunity to take showers often exist in such lounges for club members. Its VIP treatment all the way. For the majority of travel clubs, however, benefits, in the form of savings (ticket, hotels, rentals) can be expected, including last minute reservations, some insurance coverage and regular newsletters and toll-free numbers to keep members informed of bargain opportunities. Membership in travel clubs for the most part requires an annual membership fee that could range from $30 to $200. Furthermore, some clubs charge a one time initiation fee. Lifetime membership opportunities do exist, and for a nominal fee benefits could be extended to spouses. Turn to Appendix U for a list of travel clubs. For inquiries on Airline Clubs, contact the respective airlines. A list is provided in Appendix P.

Time Zone Differential: Just as there is time variation, between cities in the U.S., depending on where you live, such variations, also, exist between countries. In the U.S. we have five time zones: Pacific, Mountain, Central, Eastern, and Atlantic. For example, Los Angeles, California is in the Pacific, Montana, in the Mountain, Texas and Illinois, in the Central, New York and Washington D.C., in the Eastern, and Maine in the Atlantic time zones. For example, when it is 12 noon in New York, it is 11 a.m. in Chicago because it is 1 hour behind (-1 hour) Eastern Standard Time, and it is 9 a.m. in Los Angeles because Los Angeles is 3 hours behind (-3 hours) Eastern Standard Time. Since these variations exist between countries, you should be well aware of them since they will invariably affect your flight time and schedule of appointments. The time difference between U.S. Eastern Standard Time and foreign countries is provided in Appendix 3C. Familiarize yourself with the time zone differential, and make appropriate adjustments.

Learning to Use Foreign Currencies: Before you go abroad, familiarize yourself with the foreign currencies you will soon be using. Check out money exchange services here in the U.S. and exchange a few of your dollars for the foreign currencies. Besides the obvious advantage of having a few foreign currency on hand, upon arrival you should make a deliberate effort to understand how they are used. This will save you time, and minimize the chances of short-changing yourself or being short-changed. Some travelers wait and only start learning how to use a foreign currency upon arrival, but only to quickly find out that it is not as simple as they had previously thought.

Cash Machines: Automatic Teller Machines, or ATMs, as they are called are becoming very popular overseas, particularly in Western Europe. With your ATM card, you may be able to access the cash machines in the same way, and with the same ease as you do in the states. As usual, a personal identification number or PIN, is required. And like in the U.S. you may only access machines at certain ATMs. Two ATM system with world-wide locations are the CIRRUS and the Plus System. Find out if your ATM is part of these systems. And if they are, find out if they are available

in the country and city you plan visiting. It is, also, important to check if your card and PIN number can be used at overseas locations. If not, your credit card company may issue a new access code or PIN valid for use overseas. To reach any of the two systems mentioned here, dial 1-800-THE-PLUS or 1-800 4-CIRRUS.

Place of Worship: Finding a place to worship while overseas is as simple as just asking. Your hotel desk clerk should be able to help you locate the nearest place of worship. Alternatively, the tourist information center or local phone book will do the same. As you journey around, however, remember that you may not necessarily find a denomination of your first choice. Just as some countries may be predominantly Christian, so too are some countries and regions dominated by non-Christian faith, such as Islam. In many countries you will find a mixture of minority and majority religious denominations and places of worship scattered here and there. There are, also, non-denominational houses of worship. The more flexible you are, the greater the chance of finding a place of worship or prayer center closer to where you may be staying. Further, there is the language issue. If your preference is for an English speaking place of worship, you may or may not be able to find one, but you can certainly enjoy the activities and recite your prayers even where the local language is the used in services.

Cruise Lines and Freighters: The difference between the two may be more of quality of service and trip completion time than any other factors. These differences are, also, reflected in the cost. Cruise lines are well specialized for providing an alternative, more romantic and equally comfortable means of traveling than by air or land, but at a longer time than by air. Freighters, on the other hand, take longer time than cruises liners for the same travel, carry fewer persons and of course charge considerable less. You may, in addition, have to be much more flexible with your travel schedule with freighters than with cruise lines. Long waits and frequent schedule changes are not uncommon. For an adventure by cruise line or by freighter, contact one of the carriers listed in Appendix S. For some reasons, foreign vessels, for the same quality of service, generally, tend to charge less than their U.S. counterparts. Apply the same level of prudence in dealing with cruise lines and freighters as you do in deciding what airline to fly with . Some shopping around and cost comparison are important. Ticket terms and conditions for travel with a sea vessel are different from those on your airline ticket. Read the dotted lines carefully before signing and, before letting go your money.

Your Ticket: Make it a habit to check your tickets and reservation confirmation slips once you receive them. Many of the tickets, particularly, your plane and rail tickets and passes have caveats and other details you must be clearly aware of before you go. You may ruin you entire trip, loose money and time, due in part, to information on your tickets and reservation slip you overlooked or did not know. Immediate and careful examination will give you ample time to correct mistakes, if any, as well request for clarifications, if you do not understand. Inquire about the meaning of any unfamiliar codes used, and any restrictions. Importantly, cross-check the information on the tickets with your intended itinerary.

Meal on Flight: Between international flights and domestic flights expect a wide range and variation in the quality of services provided. This is particularly true with meals. Meals on domestic flights are relatively poorer. When overseas, you may want to eat before boarding or carry some snacks with you. Do not be surprised, if no foods at all are served on journeys of reasonable distance. I have had to deal with this on more than one occasion during my trips in some African countries.

Travel Luggages: Specifications and Allowances: As you go shopping for your luggage and carry-on cases and bags, you should be aware that airlines do have specifications. Any luggage exceeding the required dimensions for check-in and carry-on luggages may be refused. Generally, the maximum total linear dimension for a check-in-luggage ranges between 45 and 62 inches (i.e. length and width and height). Luggage with sizes no more than 21 x 16 x 48" or 23 x 13 x 9" are ideal. For carry-on, each piece cannot exceed 45 inches in total linear dimension, and must fit in the overhead luggage compartment or underneath the seat.

Equally important are the weight and amount of luggage you are entitled to. Most international airlines allow two pieces of free check-in luggage and one carry-on, per passenger, with each piece of check-in luggage not exceeding 70 lbs. Some airlines give first-class passengers allowances of up to 80 lbs, while some limit the allowances to economy class passengers to only 50 lbs. If you must carry more than two pieces of check-in luggage expect to pay extra. For heavier or larger luggage, the airline may refuse to carry them or may levy additional charges. It is better not to count on the latter.

Incidentally, specifications vary from carrier to carrier. You are, therefore, better off checking with the carrier you intend to use. Furthermore, these specifications may differ from those on domestic travels within a

particular country, in which case, you may be asked have to pay extra. Again, check with your airline for guidelines on domestic flights regarding luggage requirements.

Language Barrier: Unless English is the language of conversation in the country you plan to visit, or you are quite fluent in the language of your host country, you will, as I have, occasionally ponder, on how much you may be missing or how much exciting and easier your trip would have turned out, if only you understood and spoke the language. Well, you are not alone in this territory. Depending on the length and purpose of your trip, and how much real interest and planning time you have, you could do something about it. Some travelers enroll in language courses offered by a number of national and local organizations and schools. Others engage in home study and self-tutoring, with the help of TVs videos, phrase books and cassette tapes. You could do any of these, or do nothing, and still have a perfectly exciting holiday. Yet, I must suggest that you familiarize yourself with a few conversational words and phrases of your host country. You will be amazed at the extra excitement and difference they will add to your trip. Check with your local colleges and libraries for basic language course offerings. Your local yellow pages and libraries would, also, have other resources, including names and addresses of foreign language institutes. There are, of course, the numerous books and other resources available in bookstores. (See Appendix 16P) Remember, the objective is not to be proficient in reading and writing the language, but in mastering a few important and common conversational phrases. Wouldn't you like to say "Thank you" to that cab driver, door man, waiter who just rendered you a magnificent service and in a language he or she understands?

Front Desk Service: Not sure of something, lost, confused or forgotten? Ask the clerk at the front desk. Every hotel you will find during your trip overseas will certainly have a service desk or an information desk, with a clerk ready to assist you use them. In most cases, these clerks will have answers to most of your questions regarding your host country. If they do not know, most front desk clerks will gladly direct you to the appropriate places to get answers. They may even have stamps to sell to you. Do not, therefore, hesitate to approach them practically, on any matters of concern to you. And, while at the front desk do ask, or look around for other items of information. Hotel lobbies are often stuffed with local newspapers, maps, and other publications that you will find very useful as you explore your new environment. You may want to familiarize yourself with the language(s) spoken in the country you plan to visit. A country by country listing of official and other major languages is provided in Appendix 11K.

Stray Animals: Afraid of animals, stray animals? Then, take precautions. In several parts of the world, particularly in rural communities of developing as well as some developed countries, animals, from dogs and cats, to pigs, goat, sheep and cows roam about freely. Do not be surprised also, finding yourself riding in a commercial vehicle next to these animals, or finding them in the company of local guests, or wandering around your place of residence. For the local inhabitants, these animals are, for the most part, not hostile nor a threat to them, and one will expect so for visitors. This, however, may not necessarily be true in all cases, particularly if your are not familiar with local signs and words used to communicate with these animals. Besides, some appear to be able to sense some strangeness in you in which case their reaction may be unfriendly, and unpredictable at best. My advice, is not to cuddle them, or try to play with them. Keep moving and mind your business. The last thing you want is a bite from an animal you may perceive as friendly. Remember, rabies from dogs, are alive in many developing countries. Beware!

Things Not to Buy Overseas: As you plan to go shopping overseas beware! You may buy things, but may not be able to import them into the United States. There are numerous commodities, items of seemingly, common and harmless use that are prohibited entry by the U.S. Government. These items range from certain birds, pets and wildlife, and products made from them to plants and animals. These are in addition, to many contraband items, considered dangerous and a threat to security. The latter may include unlicensed firearms, illegal drugs and pornographic materials. For a listing of prohibited items commonly considered by travelers, See chapters 31 and 33. Beside your concern for U.S. Government requirements, and lists of prohibited items, do not forget the requirements and lists of the host country. Every country has a list of items you cannot bring in, nor take out. If you are not sure, always check with that country's customs office.

Beware of Street-Side Vendors: Like in the United States, you will find them in almost every country, particularly in the large urban centers. You will find them trading in items ranging from ornaments, jewelry, radios, stereo sets, to cameras and watches. While some of the articles they sell may be legitimately acquired, some may not. Many turn out turn out to be stolen goods. It is advisable to stay away from these street-side vendors. While their prices may be unusually attractive and tempting, their activity may be illegal, and their products fake and defective, and with no guarantees. There is, of course, the danger that you may be dealing with an undercover police officer or being set-up for a robbery. Make things easy for yourself. Avoid buying or dealing with street vendors, whether they are registered or not.

Shopping Abroad: It is not always the case that you will find a better deal abroad. Those items you plan to buy may well turn out to be more expensive than at home. If you plan to buy any thing abroad, it is advisable to develop a list of those items, including their U.S. prices. And while you comparison shop abroad, you should consider the taxes and duties that will be assessed on those items. You may have to pay the cost of transporting them to the U.S. Furthermore, you should consider, the exchange rate of the dollar vis-a-vis that country's currency.

If your shopping abroad, including, shopping for articles of clothing (shoes, shirts, skirt, blouses), and precious stones, you should be aware that there are significant differences between American sizes, and the sizes, as used in other parts of the world. To assist you, a guide has been provided in Appendix Y. Similarly, you should be particularly careful as you shop around for precious stones. As you may already be aware of, fakes are common, and this is true, irrespective of the country of purchase. If you must shop for gems abroad, you may want to familiarize yourself with fake stones quite common in some countries. A shopper's guide is provided in Appendix 12L.

Stamps: Should you need local stamps while overseas you have a number of places to check, besides the post office. In some countries, stamps can be purchased from bookstores, department stores and stamp machines located at airports and railway stations. You may, also, be able to purchase stamps from shops located at the lobbies of hotels or from the front desk clerk. All you may need to do is ask.

Mail and Telephone Communication: Communication in several countries is slow and, sometimes, down right inefficient when compared to the United States. And, you need to communicate this reality to your friends and relatives at home, lest they panic for fear of not hearing from you. Expect mails, including express deliveries to take between 2 to 4 weeks to reach the U.S. instead of the few days often promised or stated. The actual time will, of course, vary depending on what country you may be writing from. Communication, whether by mail or by phone is faster and much more efficient in developing countries and in Western Europe than in other regions of the world. Developing countries tend to have the worst records. Not only do letters take long, telephone communication are either non-existent in most places, or do not function properly. Even reaching someone by phone from the U.S. may take you up to an hour, if you succeed. The circuits are often busy, or the connection at the other end is very poor. If you plan to write from overseas, then, keep this time frame in mind. And, if you chose to call, be prepared to spend time dialing and re-dialing, or perhaps spend time waiting on line in the central telephone office. Generally, the central telephone office or the post office provides the best chances to make calls or send telegrams. Even then, you may have to wait. Take time, therefore, to caution your loved ones here at home, before you go, not to have very high hopes of hearing from you as soon as you arrive and certainly not to panic as a result. To be sure, it is frustrating, but that is the way it is. Always send your letters by Airmail, just telling the postal officer that you would like to send your letter first class, may not be sufficient.

As an alternative, you may consider using the services of courier companies. Two well known International courier services are DHL and Federal Express. (Others are listed in Appendix R). Although they are a lot more expensive than other mail services, they appear to be faster and more reliable. Before going, find out the branch offices of these companies nearest your overseas destination. Faxes are becoming popular, and you will likely find private agencies providing this and regular telephone services. Incidentally, some of these agencies have better luck getting their calls and transmission through. Of course, if you plan to use fax, do not forget to carry along the fax number (in the U.S.) you plan to forward your messages.

Public Restrooms: In many countries, public toilets or restrooms are few and poorly maintained. If all you want is to relieve your bowels, you should have little or no problems. On the contrary, if you are particular about cleanliness and other services, you may be in for a surprise. With the exceptions of urban centers of Western Europe and some developing countries, public restrooms are not generally well taken care of. Unless you have a really strong will to use one, you may find yourself totally turned off and the urge disappear in the face of a seeming "disaster zone". Expect the following, hopefully it may not get worst than these: (1) the same facility may be used by both males and females, (2) broken toilets and sinks, (3) flooded toilets, (4) restrooms with urine and faeces on the floors, (5) restrooms with no flowing water, (6) maids cleaning the restrooms while you may be using it, and (7) restrooms without toilet papers or hand towels.

As you venture into the interiors of developing countries do not expect to find traditional toilets with water systems. Instead, you may find pits (both shallow and deep) or improvised gathering buckets, and open flat grounds for use by any one who so desires. I must add, the sight of some of these primitive toilet facilities can be frightening to use and aching to the legs. In several countries, you may also count out finding toilet tissues in their public toilets, including those at the airports and train stations. In some of these places, old newspapers and leaves substitute for toilet tissues. You can now see why I always travel with my own roll of toilet tissues.

Finally, remember that the word restroom is not universal; different names and signs are used to describe the same thing, including the equivalent of the word "toilet". If you are not sure ask. Besides, in some places the word "restroom" is used and understood literally, to represent the equivalent of a place to rest (eat, drink, or sleep). Do not be fooled or appear confused.

Water: In some parts of the world, water remains a scare resource. Potable water is scarce, and water for general purpose may not be readily available. Expect hotels without adequate water to shower, or with no hot water at all. This is true even in Europe. Of course, you may get some flimsy apologies and excuses from management, but the absence of water or hot water may be a regular occurrence rather than a sudden problem as they sometimes try to explain. Since your stay will very likely entail a hotel or similar lodging facility, find out from the reservation clerk if there is water available, and hot water, in particular, and if there are any limitations. This is important since there might be some rationing going on, in which case your room may be pre-programmed for just a few minutes of hot waters.

With regard to potable water, your best bet is to take the various precautions mentioned in Chapter 9. Not even the hotel clerks can truly guarantee the safety of the drinking water they serve you.

Beggars and Homeless Persons: As you journey round the globe, you will find beggars and homeless persons just as you will find them here in the U.S. This is common in large urban centers. It is uncertain, what to expect from these groups, as their mode of operation varies from country to country. Without a doubt, they can be a nuisance and a pest to travelers, and in some cases, a source of embarrassment. Its really up to you how you deal with them. In many countries, they will touch you, pull you, insult you, harass you and even rob you. Very often, a small token gift will satisfy them. Ironically, although they may complain of lack of food, most will not accept food, but will rather prefer money. However, you deal with this group of people,

470

be careful, not to lose sight of your valuables, as many are in fact <u>bona-fide</u> professional pickpockets, luggage thieves and muggers. Many of them, including women and young children, are in fact not what they claim to be, but rather part of a robbery or extortion ring or gang in disguise. Stories of parents actually training their children in the act of begging, as well as a way of life, are common. Also, common is the reality of poverty in several parts of the world, contributing in part to these illegal practices.

Places and Gestures to Avoid: As safety concerns, without a doubt, will be paramount in your mind during your trip abroad, you ought to be careful on what you do, how and where you do it. There are places that will certainly open you up to interrogation and other actions that may invite jail term for you even though, a citizen doing the same thing may go "scott-free".

1.   A partial list of <u>places</u> you should avoid include:
(a) military facilities; (b) facilities, that manufacture military or security products; (c) places where protests/political rallies are being staged

2. A partial list of <u>actions</u> to avoid include:
(a) Burning or de-facing the national flag;
(b) Sitting down (in public) when the National Anthem is being played, when everyone else is standing up; or not taking off your hat or head gear in the same instance, when everybody else is doing so. (c) Making negative or derogatory remarks about the head of state, the military or the country and government as a whole; (d) Participating in rallies, riots, protests and strikes; (e) Taking photographs of military installations; (f) Taking photographs in the airport, or of the airport; (g) Taking photographs of communication facilities; (h) Defecating or urinating in public (even though you may find the latter common with local inhabitants); (i) Fraternizing or flirting with local law enforcement authorities; (j) Engaging in political discussions; (k) Engaging in discussions about, or where such words as explosives, bombs, grenades, revolt, over throw, coup and the like are used; (l) Carrying in public SPY, CIA, FBI and/or reading books that may be perceived as a source for sensitive information and for dangerous ideas; (m) Drunkenness and public nuisance; (n) drunken driving; (o) cursing. Remember, equal rights and freedom of speech and expression may be inalienable rights of U.S. citizens, in the States, and central to the constitution of the U.S. but may be hardly so in practice in many countries abroad. Being careless and not watching what you say, and do, how and where you say and do things, may just be an invitation for trouble abroad. It does not take much to stay out of these given areas, but first you must be aware of them.

The Key to a Successful Trip Abroad: A sense of humor, a positive attitude, patience, tolerance, flexibility, alertness and a careful review of the information provided in this book will assure a successful trip. With these things, you can guarantee yourself a rich, safe, exciting and successful trip abroad.

471

Chapter 46

References and Resources for Overseas Travelers

- - - -

The following fourteen publications from the Department of State,(D.O.S.) Bureau of Consular Affairs (B.C.A) may be ordered for $1 each (unless, otherwise indicated) from the Superintendent of Documents, U.S. Government printing Office, Washington D.C. 20402; Tel. (202) 512-1800:

*Your Trip Abroad provides basic travel information - tips on passports, visas, immunizations, and more. It will help you prepare for your trip and make it as trouble - free as possible. (D.O.S. Publication # 9926, B.C.A. Revised February 1992)

*A Safe Trip Abroad gives travel security advice for any traveler, but particularly for those who plan trips to areas of high crime or terrorism. (D.O.S. Publication #10110, B.C.A. Revised September 1993)

*Tips for Americans Residing Abroad is prepared for the more than 2 million Americans who live in foreign countries. (D.O.S. Publication # 9745, B.C.A. Revised March 1990)

*Travel Tips for Older Americans provides health, safety, and travel information for older Americans (D.O.S. Publication, B.C.A. Revised October 1989)

*Tips for Travelers to Sub-Saharan Africa (D.O.S. Publication #10205, B.C.A. Revised October 1994), Price $1.50.

*Tips for Travelers to the Caribbean (D.O.S. Publication #10111, B.C.A. Revised September 1993)

*Tips for Travelers to Central and South America (D.O.S. Publication #9682, B.C.A. Released May 1989)

*Tips for Travelers to Mexico (D.O.S. Publication #9309 B.C.A Revised October 1989)

*Tips for Travelers to the Middle East and North Africa (D.O.S. Publication #10167, B.C.A. Revised October 1994), Price $1.50.

*Tips for Travelers to the People's Republic of China (D.O.S. Publication #9199, B.C.A. Revised December 1988)

*Tips for Travelers to South Asia (D.O.S. Publication #9601, B.C.A. Released September 1987)

* Tips for Travelers to Russia. (D.O.S. Publication #9971, B.C.A. Revised September 1992)

*Americans Abroad provides basic up to date information on passport, foreign laws, customs, personal safety and helpful travel tips. You may request for a free copy by writing to: Americans Abroad, Consumer Information Center, Pueblo, CO 81009. Multiple copies of 25 may be purchased from the Superintendent of Documents, U.S. Government Printing Office, Washington D.C. 20402; Tel: (202) 512-1800. (D.O.S. Publication #9739, Bureau of Diplomatic Security, Released June 1990)

*Foreign Entry Requirements lists visa and other entry requirements of foreign countries and tells you how to apply for visas and tourists cards. Updated Yearly. Order this publication for

50 cents from the Consumer Information Center, Dept. 438T, Pueblo, CO 81009. (D.O.S. Publication #10254, B.C.A. Revised March 1995)

Key Officers of Foreign Service Posts gives addresses and telephone, telex, and FAX numbers for all U.S. embassies and consulates abroad. **(NOTE: When writing to a U.S. embassies and consulates, address the envelope to the appropriate section, such as Consular Section, rather than to a specific individual.) This publication is updated 3 times a year and may be purchased from the Superintendent of Documents, U.S. Government Printing Office, Washington, D.C. 20402; Tel. (202) 783-3238. Single copy purchase price is $3.75 . One year subscription price is $5.

****Diplomatic List** lists the addresses, and telephone and fax numbers of foreign embassies and consulates in the U.S. including the names of key offices. This publication is updated quarterly and may be purchased from the Superintendent of Documents. U.S. Government Printing Office. (D.O.S. Publication #7894, B.C.A.), Price $4.75.

***Passports** provides information on where to apply, how to apply and the best time to apply for a U.S. Passport, including renewals; Everything you need to know about getting a passport- cost, requirements etc. (D.O.S. Publication #10049, B.C.A. Revised March 1993)

Background Notes are brief, factual pamphlets on each of 170 countries. They give current information on each country's people, culture, geography, history, government, economy, and political conditions. They also include a factual profile, brief travel notes, a country map, and a suggested reading list. To place orders or for information contact: Superintendent of Documents. U.S. Government Printing Office, Washington D.C. 20402: Tel. (202) 512-1800. Be sure to indicate the specific country or area you will be traveling to with your request.

***Consular Information Sheets** is part of the

U.S. State Department's travel advisory instruments. It covers such matters as location and telephone number of the nearest U.S. Embassy, health conditions, entry regulations, crime and security conditions that may affect travel, drug penalties and areas of instability. Consular Information Sheets are available for most countries. For a free copy of the Consular Information Sheet for the country you plan to visit write to the state Department, Bureau of Consular Affairs, Washington D.C. 20520.

Traveling Abroad More Safely - a 12-minute Department of State videotape, that provides practical advice to U.S. citizens traveling abroad. It is available from Video Transfer, Inc., 5710 Arundel Ave., Rockville, MD 20552, Tel: (301) 881-0270. Price: $12 for VHS or Beta 2, $27 for BetaCam.

***U.S. Consul Help Americans Abroad** explains some of the functions and services of U.S. Embassies and Consulates abroad. (D.O.S. Publication #10176 B.C.A. June 1994)

***Crises Abroad-What the State Department Does** available free of charge from Department of State, CA/PA Rm. 5807 Washington D.C. 20520. (D.O.S. Publication #9732, B.C.A.)

International Parental Child Abduction available free of charge. Write to Office of Citizens Consular Services, Bureau of Consular Affairs, Department of State, Rm.4817 Washington D.C. 20520. (D.O.S. Publication #10210 B.C.A. Revised January 1995)

***International Adoptions** discusses the issue of International Adoptions including valuable tips, guidelines and procedures. This circular (publication) is available free of charge from the Department of State, Overseas Citizens Services or call (202) 647-2688.

***Travel Warnings on Drugs Abroad** available free of charge from the Department of State, CA/PA Rm. 5807 Washington D.C. 20520. (D.O.S. Publication #9980 B.C.A. Revised August 1992)

***Travel advisories,** issued by the State Department, caution U.S. citizens about travel to specific countries or areas. If you are concerned about existing conditions in a given area, contact your travel agent or airline, the nearest passport agency or the Department of State's Citizens Emergency Center at (202) 647-5225.

Foreign Consular Offices in the U.S. lists all foreign diplomatic offices in the U.S. This booklet is available from the Superintendent of Documents, U.S. Government Printing Office, Washington D.C. 20402. Tel. (202) 512-1800. The cost is $6.50.

* **Security Awareness Overseas: An Overview** provides guidelines and tips on a variety of topics relating to personal safety and security while overseas.(D.O.S. Overseas Security Advisory Council, Bureau of Diplomatic Security). This pamphlet may be ordered from the Superintendent of Documents. U.S. Government Printing Office, Washington D.C. 20402. Tel: (202) 512-1800.

U.S. DEPARTMENT OF COMMERCE

* **Climates of the World** provides data on climatic conditions around the world, including temperatures and precipitations. This publication may be ordered from the Superintendent of Documents, U.S. Government Printing Office. (Department of Commerce, Environmental Science Services Administration, Environmental Data Service Publication).

DEPARTMENT OF TREASURY

***Know Before You Go, Customs Hints for Returning U.S. Residents** gives detailed information on U.S. Customs regulations, including duty rates. Single copies are available free from any local customs or by writing to the Department of the Treasury, U.S. Customs Service, P.O. Box 7407, Washington D.C. 20044. (U.S. Customs Publication #512. Revised April 1994)

***U.S. Customs: International Mail Imports** provides information on procedures and requirements pertaining to parcels mailed from abroad to the U.S. (U.S. Customs Publication No. 514, Revised March 1994).

***U.S. Customs: Importing a Car** provides essential information for persons importing a vehicle into the U.S. It also includes U.S. Custom requirements and those of other government agencies whose regulations are enforced by the U.S. Customs. (U.S. Customs Publication #520. Revised November 1992)

***Pleasure Boats** provides essential information for persons importing pleasure boats into the U.S. It includes requirements and charges. This publication is available free of charge from the Public Information Office, U.S. Customs Service, P.O. Box 7407, Washington D.C. 20044. (U.S. Customs Publication #544. Revised September 1993)

U.S. Customs: Highlights for Government Personnel provides information for returning U.S. Government civilian employees and military personnel. Subjects discussed in this pamphlet include, duties, gifts, personal and household effects, automobiles, restricted and prohibited goods. Available from Public Information Office, U.S. Customs: Department of Treasury, P.O. Box 7407, Washington D.C. 20044. Tel. (202) 927-2095. (U.S. Customs Publication #518. Revised April 1992)

***Pets, Wildlife: U.S. Customs** (U.S. Customs Publication #509. Revised September 1992)

***G.S.P. and the Traveler** provides basic information regarding the Generalized System of Preference which allows some products from certain countries to be brought into the U.S. duty-free. The leaflet only treats those non-commercial importations intended for personal use only. (U.S. Customs Publication #515. Revised August 1993)

U.S. DEPARTMENT OF AGRICULTURE

***Travelers Tips on Bringing Food, Plant, And Animal Products Into the United States** lists the regulations on bringing these items into the

United States from most parts of the world. Fresh fruits and vegetables, meat, potted plants, pet birds, and other items are prohibited or restricted. Obtain the publication free from the Animal and Plant Health Inspection Service, U.S. Department of Agriculture, 732 Federal Bldg., 6505 Belcrest Road, Hyattsville, Maryland 20782. Tel. (301) 734-7885. (Program Aid No. 1083. Revised December 1993).

*Shipping Foreign plants Home. Provides tips and guidelines. Obtain the publication free from the Animal and Plant Health Inspection Service, U.S. Department of Agriculture, 732 Federal Bldg., 6505 Belcrest Road, Hyattsville, Maryland 20782. Tel. (301) 734-7885. (Program Aid No. 1162. Revised September 1988)

*Travelers Tips on Prohibited Agriculture Products Free copies may be obtained from the address above.

U.S. DEPARTMENT OF HEALTH

*+Health Information for International Travel is a comprehensive listing of immunization requirements of foreign governments. In addition, it gives the U.S. Public Health Service's recommendations on immunizations and other health precautions for the international traveler. Copies are available for $7.00 from the Superintendent of Documents, U.S. Government Printing Office, Washington, D.C. 20402; Tel. (202) 512-1800. (H.H.S. Publication # C.D.C. 92-8280. June 1994)

DEPARTMENT OF INTERIOR

*Buyer Beware! tells about restrictions on importing wildlife and wildlife products. For a free copy, write to the Publications Unit, US Fish and Wildlife Service, Department of the interior, Washington D.C. 20240; (202) 343-5634.

ENVIRONMENTAL PROTECTION AGENCY

*Buying a Car Overseas? Beware! Free copies may be ordered from Publication Information Center PM-211B, 401 M Street S.W. Washington

DC 20460 (202) 260-7751. (U.S. Environmental Protection Agency, February 1988)

DEPARTMENT OF TRANSPORTATION

*Fly Rights explains your rights and responsibilities as an air traveler (U.S. Department of Transportation, Tenth Revised Edition, September 1994)

Although essential requirements are provided in the leaflets listed above and, all regulations cannot be covered in detail. If you have any questions, or are in doubt , write or call the specific agency or organization mentioned. Their addresses including the type of subject matter they might provide some assistance are noted below.

Agency/Source and Type of Inquiry/Assistance

U.S. Public Health Services
Centers for Disease Control
Division of Quarantine
Atlanta, Georgia 30333
Tel. (404) 539-2574

[On bringing food, plant and animal products into the U.S.]

Animal and Plant Health Inspection
U.S. Department of Agriculture
613 Federal Building
6505 Belcrest Road
Tel. (301) 734-7885,

[On bringing food, plant, and animal products into the U.S.]

U.S. Fish and Wildlife Service
Department of the Interior
Washington, D.C. 20240
Tel. (202) 343-9242,
(202) 343-5634

[Fish and Wildlife]

Department of the Treasury
U.S. Customs Service

P.O. Box 7407
Washington D.C. 20044
(202) 927-2095

[Imports and Exports, duties (tariffs) restricted and prohibited products]

Food and Drug Administration
Import Operations Unit
Room 12-8(HFC-131)
5600 Fishers Lane
Rockville, MD 20857

[Import of food and drugs into the U.S]

Office of Community and
Consumer Affairs
U.S. Department of Transportation
400 7th Street, S.W., Rm. 10405
Washington, D.C. 20590
(202) 366-2220

[To complain about an airline or cruise line or to check out the records of an airline or cruise line.]

Community and Consumer
Liaison Division
APA - 400
Federal Aviation Administration
800 Independence Avenue, S.W.
Washington, D.C. 20591
(202) 267-3481

[To complain about safety hazards.]

U.S. Environmental Protection Agency
Public Information Center
PM-211B, 401 M Street
S.W. Washington, D.C. 20460
(202) 382-2504

[Environmental issues dealing with imports of certain products or goods, including cars.]

TRAFFIC U.S.A.
World Wildlife Fund - U.S.
1250 24th Street
N.W. Washington, D.C. 20520

[On import of wildlife.]

U.S. Department of State
CA/PA Rm. 5807   Washington
,D.C. 20402
(202) 647 4000 or (202) 647 1488
[Citizen safety, whereabouts, and welfare abroad, passports, visas, U.S. embassies and consulates abroad, foreign embassies and consulates in the U.S.

Superintendent Of Documents
U.S. Government Printing Office
Washington, D.C. 20402
(202) 512-1800

[U.S. government publications, including publications of various agencies and departments of the Federal Government.]

Office Of Foreign Assets Control
Department Of The Treasury
Washington, D.C. 20220
(202) 566-2761

[Import of merchandise from foreign countries.]

Quarantines, USDA-APHIS-PPQ 6505 Belcrest
Rd. (301) 436-7472

[For permits and information on import of plants, meat products, livestock and poultry.]

Office Of Munitions Control
Department Of State
Washington, D.C. 20520

[Export/ import of weapons, ammunition and firearms.]

Bureau Of Alcohol, Tobacco and
Firearms
Department Of The Treasury
Washington, D.C. 20226

[Import of alcohol, tobacco and firearms.]

Office Of Vehicle Safety Compliance
(NEF 32)

Department Of Transportation
Washington, D.C. 20590

[Import of vehicles (standards).]

U.S. Information Agency
Washington, D.C.
(202) 619-4700

[Import/export of Cultural property.]

Consumer Information Center
Pueblo, Colorado 81009

[Publications of interest to the general public.]

TRAVEL GUIDES

FODOR's
Fordors Travel Publications, Inc. 201 E. 50th Street., New York, NY. 10022, (800) 800-3246

Frommer's
Frommer Books: published by Prentice Hall, 15 Columbus Circle, New York, NY 10023, (800) 223-2330, (212) 373-8500

Birnbaum's
Birnbaum Guides: Available from Harper Collins Publishers, 10 East 53rd St., New York, NY. 10022

Fielding's
Fielding Travel Books, c/o William Morrow and Company, Inc. 1350 Avenue of the America, New York, NY. 10019 (212) 889-3050

Baedeker
Baedeker Guides, published by Prentice-Hall 15 Columbus Circle, New York, NY. 10023, (800) 223-2330

Blue Guide
Blue Guides, published by WW Norton and Company, Inc. 500 Fifth Avenue, New York, NY 10110 (800) 233-4830, (212) 354- 5500

Manston's
Manston Guides, Travel Keys P.O. Box 160691

Sacramento, CA. 95816 (916) 452-5200

Insight Guides
APA Insight Guides, APA Publications Distributed by Prentice-Hall, 15 Columbus Circle, New York, NY 10023, (800) 223-2330, (212) 373-8500

Lonely Plant/Travel Survival Kit
Lonely Planet Guides, Lonely Planet Publications P.O. Box 2001A, Berkeley, CA. 94702

Let's Go
Lets Go Guides, written by Harvard Student Agencies, Inc. and published by St. Martins Press, 175 Fifth Ave, New York, NY 1001

RECOMMENDED READING

American Citizen Abroad: *A Handbook for Citizens Living Abroad,* Double Day Dell Publishing Group Inc. 666 5th Ave, New York, NY 10103.

Answers to the Most Asked Questions about Cruising available from the Cruise Lines International Association, New York, NY.

Antoinette De Land,(ed.) *Fodor's Cruises Everywhere,* David McKay Co., New York, 1978

Armond M. Noble, *International Travel News,* Martin Publications, Sacramento, CA.

Arthur Frommer's New World Of Travel. Prentice-Hall Trade Division, New York, NY

Charles F. Ehret and Lynne W. Scanlon, *Overcoming Jet Lag,* Berkley Books, New York

Dean Kaye, *The Traveling Woman,* Doubleday & Co., Garden City, New York, 1980

Douglas A.J. Mockett, *How To Travel For Free,* Phoenix Press, Box 3333, Manhattan Beach, CA

90266, 1979

Drs. Patrick Doyle and James Banta, *The New Traveler's Health Guide*, Acropolis Books Ltd. Herdon VA.

Edythe Syvertsen, *Travel Tips*, Tempo Books, Grosset & Dunlap, New York, 1976

Eleanor Adams Baxel, *A Guide For Solo Travel Abroad*, Berkshire Traveller Press, Stockbridge, MA, 1979

Elizabeth Devine and Nancy L. Braganti, *The Travelers' Guide to Middle Eastern and North African Customs and Manners*, St. Martins Press, 175 Fifth Ave, New York, NY. 10010.

Elizabeth Devine and Nancy L. Braganti, *European Customs and Manners*, Meadowbrook Press, Distributed by Simon and Schuster Inc., 1230 Ave. of the Americas, New York, NY 10020

Eric Kocher, *International Jobs*, Addison-Wesley Publishing Co., Reading, MA, 1979

Giuseppe Alberto Orefice, *Avon Five Language Dictionary*, Avon Books, New York, 1973

Greg Hayes and Joan Wright, *The Guide To Travel Guides*, The Harvard Common Press, Boston MA,

Hal Gieseking, *The Complete Handbook for Travelers*, Pocket Books, New York, NY. 1979

Holiday Magazine, *Holiday Guides*, Random House, New York, 1976

Ingrid Cranfield and Richard Harrington, *The International Traveler's Handbook*, Dial Press, New York, 1982

International Youth Hostel Handbook, International Youth Hostel Federation, 1332 "J" St, NW, Washington D.C.

International Cities The Wall Street Journal Guide to Business Travel, Fordor's Travel Publications Inc. 201 East 50th St. New York, 10022.

James Dearing, *Home Exchanging: A Complete Sourcebook for Travelers at Home and Abroad*, Globe Pequot Press CT.

Jane Walker & Mark Ambrose, *Business Traveller's Handbook, A Guide to Europe*, Facts on File, Inc., New York, 1981

John Whitman, *The Best European Travel Tips*, Meadowbrook Press, Wayzata, MN, 1981

Lee Baxandall, *World Guide To Nude Beaches & Recreation*, Stonehill Publishing Company, New York, 1980

Marian Cooper, *The World Best*, Agora Inc., 824 E. Baltimore, St. Baltimore, Md 21202

Marty Leshner, *Trouble Free Travel*, Franklin Watts, New York, 1980

Marvin L. Saltzman and Kathryn Saltzman Muileman Saltzman Companies, *Eurail Guide, How To Travel Europe And All The World By Train*, Malibu, CA, 1983

Mary Green and Stanley Gillmar, *How To Be An Importer And Pay For Your World Travel*, Celestial Arts, Milbrae, CA, 1979

Melissa Shales, *The Traveler's Handbook*, The Globe Pequot Press, Chester, CT. 1988

Nancy Meyer, *Traveler's Almanac*, Randy McNally, Bill Muster, Los Angeles, CA, 1977

Nancy Star, *The International Guide to Tipping* The Berkley Publishing Group, 200 Madison Avenue New York, NY 10016.

National Geographic Magazine, National Geographic Society, Washington, D.C.

Norman D. Ford, *Freighters Days...How To Travel By Freighter*, Harian Publications, Greenlawn, New York, 1973

Official Airline Guides, Official Airline Guides Inc., Clearwater Drive, Oak Brook, IL

Patricia Brooks & Lester Brooks, *How To Buy Property Abroad*, Doubleday & Company, Inc., Garden City, New York, 1974

Peter Savage, *The Safe Travel Book: A Guide For the International Traveler,* Lexington Books

Porter Sargent, *Schools Abroad of Interest To Americans,* 11 Beacon St., Boston, MA

Richard Dawood, *Travellers' Health: How to Stay Healthy Abroad,* Oxford University Press, 1989

Richard C. and Sheryl Levy, **Plane Talk:** *The Consumer's Air Travel Guide*, 1980

Robert Bradnock (ed) *South Asian Handbook,* Prentice Hall Travels, New York NY. 1992

Roger E. Axtell, *Do's and Taboos Around the World, A Guide to International Behavior*, 1985, The Parker Pen Co., P.O. Box 5100, Jamesville, WI. 53547-5100.

S.M. Hillman & R. S. Hillman, M.D., *Traveling Healthy*, Penguin Books, New York, 1980

The Worlds To Retirement Havens (1991), *The Traveler's Atlas* **(1988),** *Airline Passenger's Guerilla Handbook* **(1989),** *The World,s Best* **(1988)** and *Spa Finders Guide to Spa Vacations at Home and Abroad*, available from Agora, Inc. Baltimore, MD 1991

Thomas Cook World Travel/Pass Guide, Thomas Cook Publishing

Thomas cook Overseas **Timetable,** Thomas Cook Publishing

Thomas Cook Continental Timetable, Thomas Cook Publishing Co.

Travelers World Atlas and Guide, Rand McNally and Comp. Chicago.

Vivian Lewis, *The Traveler's Atlas*, Agora Inc., 824 E.Baltimore, St., Baltimore, Md. 21202.

----

*   Unless otherwise indicated, these publications have all been reprinted verbatim in this book. Check the Table of Contents.

*+   Some of the information in this booklet, better reserved and available through your personal physician have been left out.

**   Addresses, telephone, telex and fax numbers of all the U.S. Embassies and Consulates abroad; and the addresses, telephone,and fax numbers of all the Foreign Embassies in the U.S. can be found elsewhere in this book. Check the Table of Appendixes.

***   Sample copies of U.S. Department of State Travel Advisories have been provided elsewhere in this book. Check the Table of Contents.

( )   Citations in brackets denote the publication's number and the particular issue of the publications reprinted in this book. All editions of the publications included in this book were the latest available at the time this book went to press.

--   The prices quoted in this book were those in effect as of the time this book went to press. Since these prices are subject to change you are advised to contact the sources indicated for current prices.

A FINAL CHECKLIST

- - - -

☐ Addresses book.
☐ Addresses.
☐ Adhesive tape.
☐ Alarm clock.
☐ Alcohol pads
☐ Alcohol.
☐ Antacid.
☐ Anti-acid tablets
☐ Anti-diarrhea medication.
☐ Antibiotics.
☐ Aspirin.
☐ Athletes Foot medication.
☐ Auto repair kit
☐ Band Aids
☐ Bandage.
☐ Battery charger
☐ Belt.
☐ Binoculars/telescope
☐ Birth Certificate (copy)
☐ Birth Control Pills.
☐ Blank Personal Checks.
☐ Blood pressure kit
☐ Blouses
☐ Bottle Opener.
☐ Bra.
☐ Buttons (assorted).
☐ Calculator (pocket).
☐ Calling Card, telephone.
☐ Camera.
☐ Can Opener.
☐ Card (playing).
☐ Cash.
☐ Chapstick.
☐ Clothes line
☐ Coat (trench).
☐ Coat (overcoat).
☐ Coats.
☐ Cold tablets.
☐ Cologne.
☐ Comb.
☐ Compass.
☐ Condoms.
☐ cone remover.
☐ Contact lenses.
☐ Contact lens cleaning solution.
☐ Converter
☐ cotton swab.
☐ Credit Cards.
☐ Cufflinks.

☐ Curling Iron.
☐ Currency (Foreign)
☐ Currency (U.S)
☐ Customs registration Certificate
☐ Decongestant.
☐ Dental Floss.
☐ Dentures.
☐ Deodorant.
☐ Diary.
☐ Dress.
☐ Driver's License.
☐ Ear plugs.
☐ Ear drops
☐ Electric adapters and plugs.
☐ Emergency Kit.
☐ Envelopes.
☐ Extra batteries.
☐ Extra bag (collapsible).
☐ Extra Prescriptions.
☐ Eye drops.
☐ Films (camera).
☐ Flashlight.
☐ Flask.
☐ Foreign Language dictionary.
☐ Fur.
☐ Gifts (presents).
☐ Gloves.
☐ Glue
☐ Golf clubs.
☐ Guide books.
☐ Hair Conditioner.
☐ Hair Dryers.
☐ Hair Remover.
☐ Hair blower
☐ Hair Spray.
☐ Hair shaving blades
☐ Hairbrush.
☐ Hand luggage.
☐ Hangers.
☐ Hat.
☐ Head gear.
☐ Hearing aid.
☐ Hemorrhoidal cream.
☐ Hostel Card.
☐ Hydrocortisone cream.
☐ Immunizations.
☐ Insect Repellant.
☐ Insulin needles
☐ Insurance ID cards.
☐ Insurance claim forms.
☐ International Driver's Permit.

481

☐ International Vaccination certificate
☐ Iron.
☐ Jewelry.
☐ Knife.
☐ Language dictionary.
☐ Lint remover.
☐ Lipsticks.
☐ log book (diary).
☐ Lotion (suntan).
☐ Lotion (facial).
☐ Lotion (body).
☐ luggage keys (and extra set, put elsewhere).
☐ Luggage carts.
☐ Luggage (to be checked in).
☐ Magnifying glasses.
☐ Makeup Kit.
☐ Maps.
☐ Medic Alert bracelet.
☐ Medical/clinical records.
☐ Medication (prescription and non-prescription).
☐ Mirror (pocket-size).
☐ Money belt.
☐ Nail Polish.
☐ Neck Ties.
☐ Needle.
☐ Night Gown.
☐ Pajamas.
☐ Panties.
☐ Pants.
☐ Passport.
☐ Pen.
☐ Perfume.
☐ Personal checks.
☐ Photos:(passport-size).
☐ Phrase Book..
☐ Plastic bags.
☐ Plastic utensils
☐ Polish Remover.
☐ Prescription glasses(reading).
☐ Q-tips.
☐ Rain Coat.
☐ Raincoat
☐ Razor.
☐ Reading glasses carrying cases.
☐ Reservation slips.
☐ Rollers (hair).
☐ Safety pins.
☐ Sandals.
☐ Sanitary pads.
☐ Sanitary napkins.
☐ Scarves.
☐ Scissors (small).
☐ Sewing Kit
☐ Shampoo.
☐ Shaving cream/powder.

☐ Shaving blades.
☐ Shirts (dress).
☐ Shoe Polish.
☐ Shoe brush
☐ Shoe laces.
☐ Shoes.
☐ Shower cap.
☐ Ski-equipments.
☐ Ski-jacket.
☐ Skirt.
☐ Skis.
☐ Slacks.
☐ Sleeping bag.
☐ Sleeping pills.
☐ Slip (waist).
☐ Snacks, favorite.
☐ Sneakers.
☐ Soap (bathing).
☐ Soap (laundry).
☐ Socks.
☐ Souvenirs
☐ Spare glasses.
☐ Stain remover.
☐ Stockings
☐ Suit (bathing).
☐ Suit.
☐ Sun Glasses.
☐ T-shirts.
☐ Tape recorder
☐ Tape recorder
☐ Tape measure
☐ Tape (fiberglass).
☐ Thermal wear.
☐ Thermometer.
☐ Thread (assorted).
☐ Timetables
☐ Toilet tissue
☐ Toothbrush.
☐ Toothpaste.
☐ Toothpicks
☐ Tourist card.
☐ Towel.
☐ Tranquilizers
☐ Transformer
☐ Traveler's checks.
☐ Tweezers.
☐ Umbrella
☐ Underwear.
☐ Vaccination Card.
☐ Visas.
☐ Vitamins
☐ Walkman radio/cassette.
☐ Wallet.
☐ Washcloth.
☐ Watch.
☐ Water pills.

482

☐ Water heater
☐ Whistle
☐ Windbreaker.
☐ Writing pads.
☐ Zip lock plastic bags

HAVE YOU

☐ A copy of your medical report?

☐ Checked your credit card and bank account balances?

☐ Checked medications for clear labelling?

☐ Checked the dress code for the countries you are visiting?

☐ Checked currency requirements of host country?

☐ Checked medication for clear labelling?

☐ Checked your insurance coverage?

☐ Consulted with your physician?

☐ Consulted with your dentist?

☐ Discussed with your loved ones, key code words to use in case of an emergency?

☐ Familiarized yourself with a few conversational phrases of your host country?

☐ Had your shots?

☐ Jotted down addresses and phone number of the nearest U.S. embassy or consulate?

☐ Jotted down addresses and telephone numbers of overseas offices of traveler's checks issuing companies, in case of a refund or lost or stolen checks?

☐ Left a copy of your itinerary with relatives, friends?

☐ Made arrangements for money to be transferred to you in case of an emergency?

☐ Made a final telephone call to your host/hostess?

☐ Obtained a Carnet?

☐ Obtained a copy of your medical report?

☐ Obtained your ATM Card?

☐ Obtained your telephone dialing card?

☐ Picked up your prescriptions?

☐ Picked up letters of authorization/explanation from your doctor regarding drugs you are be carrying?

☐ Picked up a dialing card from your long distance telephone carrier?

☐ Picked up your travelers checks?

☐ Picked up your passport?

☐ Picked up your tickets?

☐ Placed tags on all of your luggage?

☐ Re-confirmed your flight/ reservations?

☐ Registered your valuables with the U.S. Customs?

☐ Requested your special diet with the airline/cruise line?

☐ Updated your insurance?

☐ Written down important, addresses, telephone and fax numbers?

APPENDIX A

U.S. EMBASSIES AND CONSULATES ABROAD

Note: APO/FPO addresses may only be used for mail originating in the United States. When you use an APO/FPO address, do not include the local street address. For more information See Appendix I. (List of abbreviations and symbols are provided and explained at the end of this appendix)

ALBANIA
Tirane (E), American Embassy Tirana Rruga E. Elbansanit 103; PSC 59, Box 100 (A), APO AE 09624; Tel 355-42-32875, 33520; FAX 355-42-32222

ALGERIA
Algiers (E), 4 Chemin Cheikh Bachir El-lbrahimi; B.P. Box 549 (Alger-Gare) 16000; Tel [213] (2) 69-11-86, 69-18-54, 69-38-75; Telex 66047; FAX [213] (2) 69-3979; COM Tel [213] (2) 69-23-17; COM FAX [213] (2) 69-18-63; USIS Tel [213] (2) 69-19-40; USIS FAX [213] (2) 69-14-88

ANGOLA
Luanda (E), 32 Rua Houari Bournedienne, Miramar, Luanda; International Mail: C.P. 6484, Luanda, Angola; Pouch: American Embassy Luanda, Dept. of State, Washington, D.C., 20521-2550; INMARSAT: Int'l Operator 873-151-7430; Tel: (244) (2) 346-418/345481; Embassy FAX [244] (2) 347-884; DAO FAX (244) (2) 347-217; Admin/Consulate Annex: Casa Inglesa, 132/135 Rua Major Kahangula, Luanda, Angola; Pouch: AmEmbassy Luanda, Dept. of State, Washington, D.C., 20521-2550; Tel: (Admin) (244) (2) 392498; (Con) (244) (2) 396-927; FAX (244) (2) 390-515

ANTIGUA AND BARBUDA
St. Johns (E). The post closed June 30,1994.

ARGENTINA
Buenos Aires (E), 4300 Colombia, 1425; Unit 4334; APO AA 34034; Tel [54] (1) 7774533 and 7774534; Telex 18156 AMEMBAR; FAX [54] (1) 777-0197; COM FAX [54] (1) 777-0673

ARMENIA
Yerevan (E), 18 Gen Bagramian; Tel 7-8852-151-144 or 7-8852-524-661; FAX 7-8852-151-138; Telex 243137 AMEMY

AUSTRALIA
Canberra (E), Moonah Pl., Canberra, A.C.T. 2600; APO AP 96549, Tel [61] (6) 270-5000; Telex 62104 USAEMB;

FAX [61] (6) 270-5970

Melbourne (CC), 553 St. Kilda Road, P.O. Box 6722 Melbourne, Victoria 3004; Unit 11011, APO AP 96551-0002; Tel [61] (3) 526-5900; FAX [61] (3) 510-4646; USIS Tel [61] (3) 526 5930; FAX [61] (3) 5104686; COM FAX [61] (3) 510-4660

Sydney (CG), 59th Fl., MLC Centre, 19-29 Martin Place, Sydney N.S.W. 2000; PSC 280 Unit 11026, APO AP 96554-0002; Tel [61] (2) 373-9200; ADMIN FAX [61] (2) 373-9125; COM FAX [61] (2) 221-0576; CON FAX [61] (2) 373-9184

Perth (CG), 13th Fl., 16 St. Georges Terr., Perth, WA 6000; Tel [61] (9) 231-9400; FAX [61] (9) 231-9444

Brisbane (C), 4th fl., 383 Wickham Terr., Brisbane, Queensland 4000; Tel [61] (7) 831-3330; FAX [61] (7) 832-6247

AUSTRIA
Vienna (E), Boltzmanngasse 16, A-1091, Vienna; Tel [43] (1) 313-39; FAX [43] (1) 3104682; Consular Section: Cartenbaupromenade 2, 4th Floor, A-1010 Vienna; Tel [43] (1)'313-39; FAX 1431 (1) 513-43-51; COM FAX [43] (1) 310-6917; to utilize the leased line toAmEmbass Viennaand/orUNVIE from the Department, lal Mission switchboard at 8-850-0000.

US Mission to International Organizations in Vienna (UNVIE), Obersteinergasse 11/1, A-1190 Vienna, Tel [43] (1) 36-31-52; afterhours [43] (1) 313 39, or FAX [431 (1) 36-9-1585

US Delegation to the Conference on Security and Cooperation in Europe (CSCE), Obersteinergasse 11/1, A-1190 Vienna; Tel [43] (1) 36-31-52; FAX [43] (1) 36-63-85; afterhours [43] (1) 313-39

Salzburg (CC). The post closed in September 1993.

AZERBAIJAN
Baku (E), Azadliq Prospect 83; Tel [7] (8922) 96-00-19 or [7] (8922) 93-64-80; WMARSAT 00-873-151-5447; or 171 (8922) 98-03-35; FAX [7] (8922) 98-37-55; Telex 142110 AMEMB SU

BAHAMAS, The
Nassau (E), Queen St.; P.O. Box N-8197; Tel (809)

3221181 and 328-2206; Telex 20-138 AMEMB NS138; FAX (809) 328-7838; Nonimmigrant Visa Section Tel (809) 328-3496; COM FAX (809) 328-3495

BAHRAIN
Manama (E), Building No. 979, Road 3119 (next to Al-Ahli Sports Club) Zinj District; FPO AE 09834-5100; International Mail: P.O. Box 26431; Switchboard Tel (973)273-300; afterhours Tel (973) 275-126; FAX (973)272-594; ECON/COM FAX (973) 256-717; USIS Tel (973) 276-180; USIS FAX (973) 270-547; US OMC Tel (973) 276-962; US OMC FAX (973) 276-046

BANGLADESH
Dhaka (E), Diplomatic Enclave, Madani Ave., Baridhara, C.P.O. Box 323 Dhaka 1212; Tel [880] (2) 884700-22; Telex 642319 AEDKA BJ; FAX [880] (2) 883-744; USIS Jiban Bima Bhaban, 5th floor, 10 Dilkusha C.A., Dhaka 1000; Tel [880] (2) 862550/4; FAX [880] (2) 833987

BARBADOS
Bridgetown (E), P.O. Box 302; FPO AA 34055; Tel (809) 436-4950; FAX (809) 429-5246; Telex 22.59 USEMB BGI WB; Marine Sec. Guard Tel (809) 436-8995; CON FAX (809) 431-0179; AID FAX (809) 429-4438; USIS FAX (809) 429-5316; MLO FAX (809) 427-1668; LEGAT FAX (809) 437-7772; Canadian Imperial Bank of Commerce Bldg., Broad Street

BELARUS
Minsk (E), Starovilenskaya #46; Tel 7-0172-34-65-37

BELGIUM
Brussels (E), 27 Boulevard du Regent; B-1000 Brussels, APO AE 09724; PSC 82, Box 002 Tel [32] (2) 513-3830; FAX [32] (2) 511-2725; COM FAX [32] (2) 512-6653

US Mission to the North Atlantic Treaty Organization (USNATO), Autoroute de Zaventem; B-1110 Brussels; APO AE 09724; Tel [32] (2) 7264580; FAX [32] (2) 726 4527; USIS FAX [32] (2) 7269368

US Mission to the European Union (USEU), 40 Blvd. du Regent, B-1000 Brussels, APO AE 09724; Tel [32] (2) 513-3830; FAX [32] (2) 511-2092; COMFAX [32] (2) 513-1228

European Logistical Support Office (ELSO Antwerp), Noorderlaan 147, Bus 12A, B-2030 .Antwerp; APO AE 09724; Tel [32] (03) 5424775; Telex 34964; FAX [32] (03) 542-6567

SHAPE (POLAD) B-7010, SHAPE, Belgium; APO AE 09705; Tel [32] (65) 445-000

EURMAC, 15 Klaverbladstraat, B-3560 Lurnmen, Belgium, APO AE 09724; Tel [32] (013) 531-071; FAX [32] (013) 531-315

BELIZE
Belize City (E), Gabourel Lane and Hutson St.; P.O. Box 286; APO: Unit 7401, APO AA 34025; Tel [501] (2) 77161 thru 63; ADM FAX (501) (2) 35321; ODA FAX [501] (2) 32795; DEA FAX [501] (2) 33856; PC FAX [501] (2) 303451; VOA [501] (7) 22127; MLO Tel [501] (2) 25-2009/2019; MLO FAX [501] (2) 25-2553; FAX [501] (2) 30802; USAID Tel [501] (2) 31067; USAID FAX [501] (2) 30215

BENIN
Cotonou (E), Rue Caporal Bernard Anani; B.P. 2012; Tel [229] 30-06-50, 30-05-13, 30-17-92; FAX [229] 41-15-22. workweek: Monday through Friday

BERMUDA
Hamilton (CG), Crown Hill, 16 Middle Road, Devonshire; P.O. Box HM325, Hamilton HMBX, Bermuda; PSC 1002, FPO AE 09727-1002; Tel (809) 295-1342; FAX (809) 295 1592

BOLIVIA
La Paz (E), Banco Popular Del Peru Bldg., corner of Calles Mercado and Colon; P.O. Box 425 La Paz; APO AA 34032; Tel [591] (2) 350251, 350120; Telex AMEMB BV 3268; FAX [591] (2) 359875; USAID Tel [591] (2) 786544; USAID FAX [591] (2) 782325

BRAZIL
Brasilia (E), Avenida das Nacoes, Lote 3; Unit 3500; APO AA 34030; Tel [55] (61) 321-7272; Telex [55] 61-1091 and 61-2318; FAX [55] (61) 225-9136; FCS FAX [55] (61) 225-3981; USIS FAX [55] (61) 321-2833; GSO FAX [55] (61) 226-2938

Rio de Janeiro (CG), Avenida Presidente Wilson, 147 Castelo, Rio de Janeiro-RJ 20030-020; AmConGen (Rio), Unit 3501, APO AA 34030; Tel [55] (21) 292-7117; FAX [55] (21) 220-0439; Telex 391-21-22831; USIS Telex [55] (21) 22831; USIS FAX [55] (21) 262-1820; COM FAX [55] (21) 240-9738

Sao Paulo (CG), Rua Padre Joao Manoel, 933, 01411; P.O. Box 8063; APO AA 34030; Tel [55] (11) 881-651 1; FAX [55] (11) 852-5154; Telex [55] (11) 31574; USIS Telex [55] (11) 862-1396; USIS FAX [55] (11) 852-1395

Commercial Office, Rua Estados Unidos, 1812, Sao Paulo, S.P. 01427-002; Tel (11) 853-2011/2411/2778; FAX (11) 853-2744; Telex 011-25274

Porto Alegre (C), Rua Coronel Genuino, 421 (9th Fl.), Unit 3504, APO AA 34030; Tel [55] (51) 2264288, 226-4177, 211-1666; Telex [55] (51) 2292; FAX [55] (51) 221-2213; USIS FAX [55] (51) 221-6212

485

Recife (C), Rua Goncalves Maia, 163; APO AA 34030; Tel [55] (81) 221-1412/1413; Telex [55] (81)-3206; FAX 55 (81) 231-1906; USIS FAX [55] (81) 231-5424

Belem (CA and FCS Branch), Rua Osvaldo Cruz 165, 66017-090 Belem Para, Brazil; Tel [55] (91) 223-0800 and 223-0613; Telex [55] (91) 1092; FAX [55] (91) 223-0413

Manaus (CA), Rua Recife 1010, Adrianopolis, CEP 69057-001, Manaus Amazonas, Brazil; Tel [55] (92) 234-4546; Telex [55] (92) 2183; FAX (81) 231-1906

Saalvador da Bahia (CA), Av. Antonio Carlos M galhaes S/N-Ed. Cidadella Center 1, Sala 410, 0275-440 Salvador, Bahia, Brazil; Tel [55] (71) 358-9166 or 9195; Telex [55] 71-2780 EEVA; FAX [55] (71) 351-0717

BRUNEI
Bandar Seri Begawan (E), Third Floor - Teck Guan Plaza, Jalan Sultan; AMEMB Box B, APO AP 96440; Tel [673] (2) 229-670; Telex BU 2609 AMEMB; FAX [673] (2) 225-293

BOSNIA-HERZEGOVINA
Sarajevo (E). This SEP post opened in November 1993 on the premises of the US Embassy in Vienna. International address: American Embassy Bosnia, c/o AmEmbassy Vienna Boltzmanngasse 16, A-1091, Vienna, Austria. APO address pouch: (Bosnia) Vienna, Department of State, Washington, D.C. 20521-9900. Tel [43] (1) 31-339; FAX [43] (1) 310-0682

BULGARIA

Sofia (E), 1 Saborna St., Unit 1335, APO AE 09213-1335; Tel [359] (2) 88-48-01 to 05; FAX [359] (2) 80-1977; GSO FAX [359] (2) 65-75-24; USIS FAX [359] (2) 80-0646; COM FAX [359] (2) 80-38-50; FAS FAX [359] (2) 65-00-59; AID FAX [359] (2) 54-31-11

BURKINA FASO
Ouagadougou (E), 01 B.P. 35; Tel [226] 30-67-23 thru 25; afterhours Tel (226) 31-26-60 and 31-27-07; Telex AMEMB 5290 BF; FAX [226] 31-23-68; USAID FAX [226] 30-89-03

BURMA
Rangoon (E), 581 Merchant St. (GPO 521); AMEMB Box B, APO AP 96546; Tel [95] (1) 82055, 82182; Telex 083-21230 AMBYGN BM; FAX [95] (1) 80409

BURUNDI
Bujumbura (E), B.P. 1720, Avenue des Etats-Unis; Tel [257] 22-34-54; FAX [257] 22-29-26; AID Tel [257] 22-59-51; AID FAX [257] 22-29-86

CAMBODIA

Phnom Penh (E), 27 EO Street 240; Mailing address: Box P, APO AP 96546; Tel (855) 23-26436 or (855) 23-26438; FAX (855) 23-26437

CAMEROON
Yaounde (E), Rue Nachtigal; B.P. 817; Tel [237] 23-4014; Pouch American Embassy DOS Wash, DC 20521-2520; Telex 8223 KN; FAX (237) 23-07-53

CANADA
Ottawa, Ontario (E), 100 Wellington St., KIP 5T1, P.O. Box 5000, Ogdensburg, NY 13669-0430; Tel (613) 238-5335 or (613) 238-4470; FAX (613) 238-5720; COM FAX (613) 233-8511

Calgary, Alberta (CG), Suite 1050, 615 Macleod Trail, S.E., Calgary, Alberta, Canada T2C 4T8; Tel (403) 266-8962; FAX (403) 264-6630; COM FAX (4033 264-6630

Halifax, Nova Scotia (CG), Suite 910, Cogswell Tower, Scotia Sq., Halifax, NS, Canada B3J 3K1; Tel (902) 429-2480; FAX (902) 423-6861; COM FAX (902) 423-6861

Montreal, Quebec (CG), P.O. Box 65, Postal Station Desiardins, H5B lGl; P.O. Box 847, Champlain, NY 129i9-0847; Tel (514) 398-9695; FAX (514) 398-0973, (514) 398-0711

US Mission to the International Civil Aviation Organization (ICAO), 1000 Sherbrooke St., West, Rm. 753, Montreal, Quebec; Box 847, Champlain, NY 12919; Tel (514) 285-8304; FAX (514) 285-8021

Quebec, Quebec (CG), 2 Place Terrasse Dufferin, C.P. 939, GIR 4T9; P.O. Box 1547 Champlain, NY 12919-1547; Tel (418) 692-2095; FAX (418) 692-4640

Toronto, Ontario (CG), 360 University Ave., M5C 1S4; P.O. Box 135, Lewiston, NY 14092-0135; Tel (416) 595-1700; FAX (416) 595-0051, (416) 595-5419; CON info FAX (416) 595-5466

Vancouver, British Columbia (CG), 1095 West Pender St., V6E 2M6, P.O. Box 5002, Point Roberts, WA 98281-5002; Tel (604) 685-4311; FAX (604) 6855285; COM FAX (604) 687-6095

REPUBLIC OF CAPE VERDE
Praia (E), Rua Abilio Macedo 81, C.P. 201; Tel [238] 61-56-16; FAX [238] 61-13-55

CENTRAL AFRICAN REPUBLIC
Bangui (E), Avenue David Dacko, B.P. 924; Tel [236] 61-02-00, 61-02-10, 61-25-78; Telex 5287 RC; FAX [236] 61A4-94

CHAD
N.Djamena (E), Ave. Felix Eboue, B.P. 413; Tel [235] (5i)-40-09, [235] (5l)-47-59, or [235] (5l)-62-18; Telex 5203 KD; FAX [235] (5l)-33-72 and [235] (5l)-56-54

CHILE
Santiago (E), Codina Bldg., Agustinas 1343, Unit 4127, APO AA 34033; Tel [561 (2) 232 2600; FAX [56] (2) 330-3710; COM FAX [56] (2) 330-3172; AID FAX [56] (2) 638-0931; FAS FAX [56] (2) 330-3203 FBO FAX [56] (2) 233-4108; CON [56] (2) 330-3719-

CHINA*
Beijing (E), Xiu Shui Bei Jie 3, 100600, PSC 461, Box 50; FPO AP 96521-0002; Tel [86] (1) 532-3831; Telex AMEMB CN 22701; Exec Con FAX [86] (1) 532-6422; POL/S&T/RSO FAX [86](1) 532-6423; ESO/MSG FAX [86] (1) 532-6421; CSO FAX [86] (1) 532-6057; HEALTH UNIT FAX [86] (1) 532-6424; AGR FAS FAX [86] (1) 532-2962; AGR FAX-ATO FAX [86] (1) 5054574; FAA FAX [86] (1) 513-0454; USIS FAX [86] (1) 532-2039; CON FAX [86] (1) 532-3178; FCS FAX [86] (1) 532-3297; USIS [86] (1) 532-2039 ADM/Travel FAX (86) (1) 532-2483; ATO Address 8-26 China World Tower, no. 1 Jianguomenwai Ave., Beijing, China 100004; Tel [86] (1) 505-4575, 4576; FAX [86] (1) 5054574; American Center for Educational Exchange (ACEE), Jing Juang Center, Tel [86] (1) 501-5247; Federal Aviation Administration (FAA); Jianguo Hotel, Rooms 128-130, No. 5 Jianguo Street, Tel [86] (1) 595-8093

Guangzhou (CC), No. 1 South Shamian Street, Shamian Island, Guangzhou 510133, PSC 461, Box 100, FPO AP 96521-0002; Tel [86] (20) 888-8911; FAX [86] (20) 886-2341; FCS FAX [861 (20) 666-6409; FAS FAX [86] (20) 666-0703; USIS FAX [86] (20) 335-4764

Shanghai (CG), 1469 Huai Hai Middle Road, Shanghai 200031, PSC 461, Box 200, FPO AP 965210002; Tel [86] (21) 433-6880; FAX [86] (21) 433-4122; COM FAX [86] (21) 433-1576; USIS FAX [86] (21) 431 - 7630; VISA/ACS FAX [86] (21) 437-5173

Shenyang (CG), 52,14th Wei Road, Heping Districf8t, 61 (110003, PSC 461, Box 45, FPO AP 96521-0002; Tel 24) 282-0068; FAX f861 (24) 282-0074; USIS FAX [861 (24) 282-0035

Chengdu (CC), 4 Lingshiquan Lu, Renmin Nan Lu Si Duan Chengdu 610041 PSC 461, Box 85; FPO AP 96521-0002; Tel [86] (28) 558-3992, [86] (28) 5589642; Telex 60128 ACCCH CH; FAX [86] (28) 5583520 and [86] (28) 558-3792

COLOMBIA
Bogota (E), Calle 38, No. 8-61; Apartado Aereo 3831; APO AA 34038; Tel [57] (1) 320 1300; FAX [57] (1) 288-5687; COM FAX [57] (1) 285-7945

Barranquilla (C), Calle 77 Carrera 68, Centro Comercial Mayorista; Apartado Aereo 51565; APO AA 34038; Tel [57] (58) 45-8480/9067; FAX [57] (58) 45-5216

COMOROS
Moroni (E). The post closed in September 1993. Port Louis is now responsible for Comoros.

REPUBLIC OF THE CONGO
Brazzaville (E), Avenue Amilcar Cabral, B.P. 1015; Tel (242) 83-20-70; Telex 5367 KG; FAX (242) 83-6338

COSTA RICA
San Jose (E), Pavas, San Jose; APO AA 34020; Tel (506) 220-3939; afterhours Tel (506) 220-3127; FAX (506) 220-2305; COM FAX (506) 231-4783

COTE D'IVOIRE
(formerly Ivory Coast)
Abidjan (E), 5 Rue Jesse Owens; 01 B.P. 1712; Tel (225) 21-09-79 or 2146-72; Telex 23660; FAX (225) 22-32-59

African Development Bank/Fund, Ave., Joseph Anoma; 01 B.P. 1387 Abidjan 01; Tel (225) 20-40-15; FAX (225) 33-14-34; COM'FAX (225) 22-24-37; Tel (225) 21-46-16

CROATIA
Zagreb (E), Andrije Hebranga 2, Unit 1345, APO AE 09213-1345; Tel [385] (41) 456000 ; afterhours Tel [3851 (41) 445-535; ADM FAX [385] (41) 458-585; USIS FAX [385] (41) 440-235; FAX [385] (41) 440-235; COM FAX [385] (41) 440-2351 CONS FAX (385) (41) 450-774 -
Havana (USIN-f), Swiss Embassy, Calzada Entre L Y M, Vedado; Tel 33-3551/9, 33-3543/7 ' and 333700; Telex 512206 EXEC OFF and Post 1 , afterhours - 33-3026; CON switchboard 33-3546/7; Telex 512206

CYPRUS
Nicosia (E), Metochiou and Ploutarchou Streets, Engomi, Nicosia, Cyprus; P.O. Box 4536 APO AE 09836; Tel [357] (2) 476100; Telex 4160 AMEMY CY; FAX [357] (2) 465944; CON FAX [357] (2) 465604; USIS Tel [357] (2) 473143; USIS FAX [357] (2) 454003

CZECH REPUBLIC
Prague (E), (Int'l) Trziste 15, 11801 Prague 1; Unit 1330; APO AE 09213-1330; Tel [42] (2) 2451-0847; COM Tel [42] (2) 2421-9844 or 2421-9846/7; ; afterhours Marine Post 1 Tel [42] (2) 531-200; FAX [42] (2) 2451-1001; ADM FAX [42] (2) 2451-1001; USIS and COM Address: Hybernska 7A, 117 16 Prague 1; USIS Tel: [42] (2) 2423-1685; USIS FAX [42] (2) 2422-0983; AID FAX [42] (2) 2451-0340; COM FAX [42] (2) 2421-9965; GSO FAX [42] (2) 2451-0742; ECON FAX [42] (2) 531-193; DAO FAX [42] (2)

487

532988

DENMARK
Copenhagen (E), Dag Hammarskjolds Alle 24; 2100 Copenhagen 0 or APO AE 09716; Tel [45] (31) 42-31 - 44; Telex 22216 AMEMB DK; FAX [45] (35)43-0223; USIS FAX [45] (31) 42-72-73; FAS FAX [45] (31) 43-02-78; USAF FAX [45] (31)25-5i-08; COM FAX [45] (31) 42-01-75

REPUBLIC OF DJIBOUTI
Djibouti (E), Plateau du Serpent, Blvd. Marechal Joffre, B.P. 185; Tel [253] 35-39-95; FAX [.253] 35-3940; afterhours [253] 35-13-43

DOMINICAN REPUBLIC
Santo Domingo (E), corner of Calle Cesar Nicolas Penson & Calle Leopoldo Navarro; Unit 5500, APO AA 34041; Tel (809) 5412171 and (809) 541-8100; Telex 3460013; FAX (809) 686-7437; COM FAX (809) 688-4838

ECUADOR
Auito (E), Avenida 12 de Octubrey Avenida Patria; PO AA 34039-3420; Tel [593] (25 562-890, 561-749, (night) 561-624; FAX [593] (2) 502-052; COM FAX [593] (2) 504-550

Guayaquil (CG), 9 de Octubre y Garcia Moreno; APO AA 34039; Tel [593] (4) 323-576; FAX [593] (4) 325-286; COM FAX [593] (4) 324-558

EGYPT (ARAB REPUBLIC OF)
Cairo (E), (North Cate) 8, Kamal El-Din Salah St., Carden City, APO AE 09839-4900; Tel [20] (2) 355-7371; Telex 93773 AMEMB UN, 23227 AMEMB UN FAX [20] (2) 357-3200; FAX ADM [20] (2) 355-4353; FAX CON f201 (2) 357-2472 ' ; FAX COM [20] (2) 3558368; FAX AID [20] (2) 357-2233; FAX USIS [20] (2) 357-3591; FAX DAO [20] (2) 357-3049; FAX FAS [20] (2) 356-3989; FAX LOC [20] (2) 356-0233; FAX FBO [20] (2) 356-2712; FAX OMC [20] (2) 357-2273; FAX POL/ECON [20] (2) 357-2181; FAX RSO [20] (2) 3572828; workweek: Sunday through Thursday

EL SALVADOR
San Salvador (E), Final Blvd. Station Antiguo 34023; Tel (503) 78-ID Tel (503) 98-1666; O/COM FAX (503) 79-03) 78-6012

EQUATORIAL GUINEA
Malabo (E), Calle de Los Ministros; P.O. Box 597; Tel Direct Dial [240] (9) 2185, 2406, 2507; FAX [240] (9) 2164

ERITREA
Asmara (E), 34 Zera Yacob St.; P.O. Box 211: Tel [291] (1) 12-00-04; FAX [291] (1) 12-75-84; USAID'Tel [291] (1) 12-18-95

ESTONIA
Tallinn (E), Kentmanni 20, EE 0001 Tel 011 [372] (6) 12-021 thru 024; Cellular tel 011 [372] 5-244-091; AX [372] (6) 312-025

FIJI
Suva (E), 31 Loftus St.; P.O. Box 218; Tel [679] 314-466; FAX [679] 300-081

FINLAND
Helsinki (E), Itainen Puistotie 14A, FIN-00140; APO AE 09723; Tel (358) (0) 171931; Telex 121644 USEMB SF, FAX [358] (0) 174681; COM FAX [358] (0) 635332; URSA [358] (0) 379359

Paris (E), 2 Avenue Gabriel, 75382 Paris Cedex 08, Jnit 21551, APO AE 09777; Tel [33] (1) 4296-12-02, 42-61-80-75; Telex 285319 and 285221 AMEMB; FAX [33] (1) 4266 9783; COM FAX [33] (1) 4266-4827

U.S. Mission to the Organization for Economic Cooperation and Development (USOECD),19 Rue de Franqueville, 75016 Paris; Unit 21551, APO AE 09777; Tel [33] (1) 45-24-74-77; Telex 643964 F; FAX [33] (1) 4524-7480; COM FAX [33] (1) 4524-7410

U.S Observer Mission to the United Nations Educational, Scientific, and Cultural Organization UNESCO), 2 Avenue Gabriel, 75382; Paris CEDEX 3; APO AE 09777; Tel [33] (1) 42-96-12-02, 42-61-805; FAX [33] (1) 42-66-97-83

Jordeaux (CG), 22 Cours du Marechal Foch, 33080 Bordeaux Cedex; Unit 21551, APO AE 09777; Tel [33] 56) 52-65-95; Telex 540918 USCSUL; FAX [33] (56))-1-60-42; COM FAX [33] (56) 51-60-42

Marseille (CG), 12 Boulevard Paul Peytral, 13286' Marseille Cedex 6; Paris Embassy (MAR) PSC 116; -%PO AE 09777; Tel [33] (91) 549-200; Telex 430597; :7AX [33] (91) 550-947; COM FAX [33] (91) 550-947

Strasbourg (CG), 15 Ave. D'Alsace; 67082 Strasbourg -EDEX or Unit 21551, APO AE 09777; Tel [33] (88) 15-31-04; FAX [33] (88) 24-06-95; Telex 870907 kMERCON; COM FAX [33](88) 24-0695

U.S. Commercial Office (Lyon), 45, Rue de la Bourse; Unit 21551, APO AE 09777; Tel [33] (16) 72-40-58, 7240-59-20; FAX [33] (16) 72-41-71-81

U.S. Commercial Office (Nice), Rue du Marechal'offre; c/o AMEMB Paris, Unit 21551, APO AE)9777; Tel [33] (16) 93-88-89-55; FAX [33] (16) 93-87-)7-38 'COM: The Commerce Department/Foreign Commercial Service operates separate American Business Centers in these locations.

FRENCH CARIBBEAN DEPARTMENT

488

Jartinique (CA). The post closed in August 1993.

GABON
Libreville (E), Blvd. de la Mer; B.P. 4000; Tel [241] 762003/4, 743492; Telex 5250 GO; FAX [241] 745507

GAMBIA, The
Banjul (E), Fajara, Kairaba Ave., P.M.B. 19, Banjul; Tel (220) 392-856, 392-858, 391-970, 391-971; FAX (220) 392-475

GEORGIA
Tbilisi (E), #91; Antoneli; SWBD 7-8832-989-967 or 7-8832-933-803; FAX 7-8832-933-759; Satellite (49) 5151-13057 Ext 165 (FAX) 166 Voice

FEDERAL REPUBLIC OF GERMANY
Bonn (E), Deichmanns Aue 29,53170 Bonn, Unit 21701; PSC 117, APO AE 09080; Tel [49] (228) 3391; FAX [49] (228) 339-2663; COM FAX (49) (228) 334649; (Tel ATO (49) (40) 341-207, and FAX (49) (40)

Berlin (BO), Neustaedtische Kirchstrasse 4-5, 10117 Berlin or Unit 26738, APO AE 09235-5500; Tel [49] 30-238-5174; FAX [49] (30) 238-6290; CON: Clayallee 170,14169 Berlin or Unit 26738, APO AE 092355500; Tel [49] (30) 819-7485; FAX [49] (30) 831-4926

US Commercial Office (Dusseldorf), Emanuel-Leutz Str. 1B 40547 Dusseldorf; c/o AMEMB Bonn, Unit 21701, Box 30, APO AE 09080; Tel [49] (211) 596-798; FAX [49] (211) 594-897

Frankfurt Am Main (CC), Siesmayerstrasse 21, 60323 Frankfurt, Unit 115, APO AE 09213-0115; Tel [49] (69) 7535-0; afterhours Tel [49] (69) 7535-3700; FAX [49] (69) 748 938; COM FAX [49] (69) 748-204

Hamburg (CG), Alsterufer 27/28, 20354 Hamburg; Tel [49] (40) 411710; afterhours [49] (40) 41171-211; FAX FBU [49] (40) 443-004; FAX ADM [49] (40) 4176-65; COM FAX [49](40) 410-6598; Tel USIS [49] (40) 450104-0; FAX USIS [49] (40) 444-705

Munich (CC), Koeniginstrasse 5, 80539 Muenchen, Unit 24718, APO AE-09178; Tel [49] (89) 28880; FAX [49] (89) 283-047 or [49] (89) 280-2317; CON FAX [49] (89) 280-5163; COM FAX [49] (89) 285-261; JUS/CIV FAX [49] (89) 282-230

Stuttgart (CG), Urbanstrasse 7, 70182 Stuttgart, Unit 30607, APO AE 09154-0001; Tel [49] (711) 2-10-0811; The CONGEN provides Emergency Citizen Services only. For nonemergency messages, leave a message on the CONGEN Stuttgart answering machine at (49) (71 1) 2-10-08-0; afterhours: [49] (69) 7535-3700 (the afterhours contact is through CONGEN Frankfurt; FAX [49] (711) 2-10-08-20; COM FAX [49] (711) 236-4350;

USIS Tel [49] (711) 22983-0; FAX [49] (711) 22983-39; POLAD (Vaihingen) Tel [49] (711) 680-4291; FAX [49] (711) 680-8166; POLAD (Heidelberg) Tel [49] (6221) 57-6651; FAX [49] (6221) 57-8097

Leipzig (CG), Wilhelm Seyfferth Strasse 4, 04107 LeIpVg; USEMB Berlin, Unit 26738 (CCL), APO AE 0923.' > -5500; Tel [49] (341) 213-840; FAX [49] (341) 213-8417; COM Tel [49] (341) 213-8440; COM FAX [49] (341) 213-8441; USIS FAX f 491 (341) 213-8432; USIS Tel [49] (341) 213-8420

GHANA
[**Accra** (E), Ring Road East; P.O. Box 194; Tel ChancerV 2331 (21) 775348/9, 775297/8; Tel Annex 776601/2, 776944; Telex 2579 EMBUSA GH; FAX [233] (21) 776008

GREECE
Athens (E), 91 Vasilissis Sophias Blvd., 10160 Athens or PSC 108, APO AE 09842; Tel [30] (1) 721-2951 or 721-8401; FAX [30](1)645-6282; COM FAX f301 (1) 721-8660; USIS FAX [30] (1) 723-7332

Thessaloniki (CG), 59 Leoforos Nikis, GR-546-22 Thessaloniki; PSC 108, Box 37 APO AE 09842; Tel [30] (31) 242905; FAX [30] (31) 242927, 242915

GRENADA
St. George's (E), P.O. Box 54, St. George's, Grenada, W.I.; Tel (809) 444-1173/8; FAX (809) 444-4820

GUATEMALA
Guatemala City (E), 7-01 Avenida de la Reforma, Zone 10; APO AA 34024; Tel [502] (2) 31-15-41; FAX [502] (2) 31-88-85; AID FAX [502] (2) 31-11-51; ROCAP FAX [502](2) 32-04-95; COM FAX [502] (2) 31-73-73

GUINEA
Conakry (E), 2d Blvd. and 9th Ave., B.P. 603; Tel [224] 41-15-20 thru 23; FAX [224] 41-15-22

GUINEA-BISSAU
Bissau (E), Bairro de Penha, Bissau, Guinea-Bissau, C.P. 297,1067 Codex, Bissau, Guinea-Bissau; Tel [245] 25-2273/6; FAX [245] 25-2282; Telex 240 Publico Bi; USAID Tel [245] 20-1809, 20-1810; FAX [245] 201808; Peace Corps Tel [245] 25-2127; FAX [245] 252132; Medical unit [245] 25-2133

GUYANA
Georgetown (E), 99-100 Young and Duke Sts., Kingston, Georgetown, Guyana; P.O. Box 10507; Tel [592] (2) 54900-9 and [592] (2) 57960-9; FAX [592] (2) 58497; USAID FAX [592] (2) 57969; USIS FAX [592] (2) 63636

HAITI
Port-au-Prince (E), Harry Truman Blvd., P.O. Box

1761; Tel [509] 22-0354, 22-0368, 22-0200, 22-0612; FAX [509] 231641

THE HOLY SEE
Vatican City (E), Via Delle Terme Deciane 26, Rome 00153; PSC 59, APO AE 09624; Tel [396] 46741; Telex 622322 AMBRMC; FAX [396] 638-0159

HONDURAS
Tegucigalpa (E), Avenida La Paz, Apartado Postal No 3453; AMEMB Honduras, APO AA 34022; Tel [5041 36-9320 or [504] 38-5114; FAX [504] 36-9037; COM FAX [504] 38-2888; USIS FAX [504] 36-9309; USAID FAX [504] 36-7776

HONG KONG
Hong Kong (CG), 26 Garden Rd.; PSC 464, Box 30, FPO AP 96522-0002; Tel [852] 523-9011; Telex 63141 USDOC HX; FAX [852] 845-4845 COM FAX [852] 8459800; ATO Address: 18th fl., St. John's Bldg., 33 Garden Rd.; Tel 841-2350; FAX 845-0943

HUNGARY
Budapest (E), V. Szabadsag Ter 12; Am Embassy, Unit 1320, APO AE 09213-1320; Tel [36] (1) 112-6450; FAX [36] (1) 132-8934; Telex 18048 224-222; Commercial Devel Ctr Telex 227136 USCDC H; USIS FAX [36] (1) 153-4274; COM FAX [36] (1) 142-2529

ICELAND
Reykjavik (E), Laufasvegur 21 Box 40; USEMB, PSC 1003, Box 40, FPO AE OD728 0340; Tel [354] (1) 629100; FAX [354] (1) 629139; USIS Tel [354] (1) 621020 and 621022; USIS FAX [354] (1) 29529

INDIA
New Delhi (E), Shanti Path, Chanakyapuri 110021; Tel [91] (11) 600651; Telex 031-82065 USEM IN; FAX [91] (11) 687-2028; COM FAX [91] (11) 687-2391; USIS Tel [91] (11) 331-6841 or 4251; USIS FAX [91] (11) 332-9499; USAID Tel [91] (11) 686-5301; USAID FAX

Bombay (CG), Lincoln House, 78 Bhulabhai Desai Rd. 400026; Tel [91] (22) 363-3611; Telex 011-75425 ACON IN; FAX [91] (22) 363-03501 COM FAX [91] (22) 262-3850

Calcutta (CG), 5/1 Ho Chi Minh Sarani, Calcutta 700071; Tel [91] (33) 242-3611 through 242-3615, 242-2336 through 242-2337; Telex 021-5982 ACON IN; FAX [91] (33) 242-2335; USIS FAX [91] (33) 245-1616

Madras (CG), 220 Mount Rd. 600006; Tel [91] (44) 827-3040/827-7542; FAX [91] (44) 825-0240; USIS FAX [91] (44) 826-3407; FCS Bangalore: W-202, 11 Floor, West Wing "Sunrise Chambers," 22 Ulsoor Road, Bangalore 560042; Tel [91] (080) 558-1452; FAX [91] (080) 558-3630

Surabaya (CC), Jalan Raya Dr. Sutorno 33; AMCONGEN, Box 1 Unft 8131, APO AP 96520-0002; Tel [62] (31) 582287 and 582288; Telex 34331 AMCOSB IA; FAX [62] (31) 574492; COM FAX [62] (31) 574-492

Baghdad (E), Opp. For. Ministry Club (Masbah Quarter); P.O. Box 2447 Alwiyah, Baghdad, Iraq; Tel [964] 1) 719-6138/9, 7181840, 719-3791; Telex 212287 USINT IK, 213966 USFCS IK; COM FAX [964] (1) 718-9297

Operations have been suspended temporarily.

IRELAND
Dublin (E), 42 Elgin Rd., Ballsbridge; Tel [353] (1) 6687122; ; afterhours Tel [353] (1) 6689612; FAX [353] (1) 6689946; COM FAX [353] (1) 682-840

INDONESIA
Jakarta (E), Medan Merdeka Selatan 5, Box 1, APO AP 96520; Tel [62] (21) 360-360; Telex 44218 AMEMB JKT; FAX [62] (21) 386-2259; USIS FAX [62] (21) 3810243; COM FAX [62] (21) 385-1632; AID FAX [62] (21) 380-6694; FAS FAX [62] (21) 380-1363; OMADP FAX [62] (21) 372-518

Medan (CG), Jalan Imam Bonjol 13; APO AP 96520; Tel [62] (61) 322200; Telex 51764; USIS Tel [62] (61) 515130; Telex 51737; FAX [62] (61) 518711; COM FAX [62] (61) 518-711

ISRAEL*

The Consulate General in Jerusalem is an independent US Mission, established in 1928, whose members are not accredited to a foreign government.

Tel Aviv (E), 71 Hayarkon St.; PSC 98, Box 100 APO AE 09830; Tel [972] (3) 517-4338; afterhours'['972] (3) 517-4347; FAX [972] (3) 663-449; USIS FAX [972] (3) 510-3830; ADM/GSO FAX [972] (3) 510-2444; FCS FAX [972] (3) 510-7215; FCS Tel [972] (3) 510-7212

Jerusalem (CC), 18 Agron Rd., Jerusalem 94190, P.O. Box 290; PSC 98, Box 100; APO AE 09830; Tel [972] (2) 253288 (via Israel); afterhours [972] (2) 253201; FAX [972] (2) 259270; Consular and USIS Sections: 27 Nablus Rd., P.O. Box 290, PSC 98, Box 100, APO AE 09830; CON Tel [972] (2) 894748/894113; afterhours 71 [972] (2) 253201; FAX [972] (2) 894198 (both offices via Israel); USIS Tel [972] (2) 895117; FAX [972] (2) 89471 1; USAID FAX [9721 (2) 259484

Rome (E), Via Veneto 119/A, 00187-Rome, PSC 59, Box 100, APO AE 09624; Tel [39] (6) 46741; Telex 622322 AMBRMA; USIS via Boncompagni 2, 00187 Rome; FAX [39] (6) 488-2672; COM FAX [39] (6) 46742113; FAX USIS [39] (6) 4674-2655.

US Mission to the United Nations Agencies for Food and Agriculture (FODAG), Annex, Via Sardegna 49,00187 Rome; or c/o US Embassy Rome, PSC 59 Box 100, APO AE 09624-0007; Tel [39] (6) 6394260; Telex 622322 AMBRMA; FAX [39] (6) 639-0027

ITALY

Milan (CC), Via Principe Amedeo, 2/10, 20121 Milano; c/o US Embassy, Box M; PSC 59, APO AE 09624; Tel [39] (2) 290-351; Telex 330208 USIMCI; FAX [39] (2) 29-00-11-65. Commercial Section: Centro Cooperazione Internazionale, Piazzale Giulio Cesare, 20145 Milan; Tel [39] (2) 498-2241/2/3; FAX [39] (2) 4982241/2/3; COM FAX [39] (2) 481-4161

US Information Service, Via Bigli 11/A, 20121 Milano; Tel [39] (2) 795051 2 3 4 5; FAX USIS [39] (2) 781-736

Naples (CG), Piazza della Repubblica 80122 Naples; Box 18, PSC 810, FPO AE 09619-0002; Tel [39] (81) 583-8111; FAX [39] (81) 761-1869; FAX USIS [39] (81) 664-207; COM Tel [39] (81) 761-1592; COM FAX [39] (81) 761-1869

Palermo (CA). The post closed in January 1994.

Florence (CG), Lungarno Amerigo Vespucci, 38, 50123 Firenze; APO AE 09613; Tel [39] (55) 2398276/7/8/9, 217-605; Telex 570577 AMCOFI 1; FAX [39] (55) 284-088; Commercial Section Tel [39] (55) 211-676; FAX COM [39] (55) 283-780; USIS Tel [39] (55) 216-531, 294-921; FAX [39] (55) 288-338

JAMAICA

Kingston (E), Jamaica Mutual Life Center, 2 Oxford Rd., 3d fl.; Tel (809) 929-4850 thru 9; FAX (809) 926-6743; USIS FAX (809) 929-4850, ext. 1042

JAPAN

Tokyo (E), 10-5, Akasaka 1-chorne, Minato-ku (107); Unit 45004, Box 258, APO AP 96337-0001; Tel [81] (3) 3224-5000; FAX [81] (3) 3505-1862; CPU [81] (3) 3224-5700; CPO [811 (3) 3224-5691; COM FAX [811 (3) 3589-4235; ATO Address: Tarneike Tokyu Bldg., 1-14 Akasaka 1-chome, Minato-Ku, Tokyo 107; Tel [811 (3) 3224-5115; Telex J29180 ATO Tokyo; FAX [81] (3) 3582-6429; USAID Tel (813) 3224-5015; FAX (813) 3224-5010

US Trade Center, 7th Fl., World Import Mart, 1-3 Higashi Ikebukuro 3-chorne, Toshima-ku, Tokyo 170; Tel [81] (3) 3987-2441; FAX [81] (3) 3987-2447; COM FAX [81] (3) 3987-2447

Naha, Okinawa (CG), 2564 Nishihara, Urasoe City, Okinawa 90121; PSC 556, Box 840, Unit 45, FPO AP 96372-0840; Tel [81] (98) 876-4211; FAX [81] (98) 8764243

Osaka-Kobe (CC), 11-5, Nishitenma 2-chome, Kita-Ku, Osaka 530; Unit 45004, Box 239; APO AP 96337-0002; Tel (81) (6) 315-5900; Telex 5233037 AMCONJ; FAX 81] (6) 361-5397; COM FAX [81] (6) 361-5978; CON FAX [81] (6) 315-5930; ATO Address: Shima Office Bldg., 3F, 1-18, Kitahama 3-chorne, Chuo-Ku, Osaka 541; Tel [81] (6) 208-0303; Telex 5233037; FAX [81] (6) 208-

Sapporo (CC), Kita 1-jo Nishi 28-chome, Chuo-ku, Sapporo 064; Unit 45004, Box 276, APO AP 96337-0003; Tel [81] (11) 641-1115/7; FAX [81] (11) 643-1283; COM FAX [81] (11) 643-0911

Fukuoka (C), 5-26 Chori 2-chome, Chuo-ku, Fukuoka-810 or Unit 45004, Box 242, APO AP 96337-0001; Tel [81] (92) 751-9331/4; Telex 725679; FAX [81] (92) 713-9222; COM FAX [81] (92) 713-922

Nagoya (C), Nishiki SIS Building 6F 10-33 Nishiki 3-chome Naka-ku, Nagoya 460; c/o AMEMB Tokyo, Unit 45004, Box 280, APO AP 96337-0001; Tel [81] (52) 2034011; COM Tel (direct) [81] (52) 203-4277 FAX [81] (52) 201-4612

Note: The Commerce Department/Foreign Commercial Service operates separate American Business Centers in these locations.

JORDAN

Amman (E), P.O. Box 354, Amman 11118 Jordan or APO AE 09892-0200; Tel [962] (6) 820-101; Direct line to Post 1 [962] (6) 820-148; USAID Office Tel [962] (6) 820-101; EXEC/POL FAX [962] (6) 820-159; ECON FAX [962] (6) 820-146; COM FAX [962] (6) 820-146 AID FAX [962] (6) 820-143; USIS FAX [962] (6) 820-121; MAP FAX [962] (6) 820-160

KAZAKHSTAN

Almaty (E), 99/97 Furmanova St.; Almaty, Republic of Kazakhstan 480012; Tel [7] (3272) 63-24-26; CPU and afterhours [7] (3272) 63-39-05, ext. 116; INMARSAT 02-00-873-151-2725; FAX [7] (3272) 63-38-83

KENYA

Nairobi (E), MOi/Haile Selassie Ave.; P.O. Box 30137, Unit 64100; APO AE 09831; Tel [254] (2) 334141; CPU STU-III 334122; Telex 22964; FAX [254] (2) 340838; COM FAX [254] (2) 216-648

Mombasa (C). The post closed in May 1993.

KOREA

Seoul (E), 82 Sejong-Ro; Chongro-ku; AMEMB, Unit 15550, APO AP 96205-0001; Tel [82] (2) 397-4114; FAX [82] (2) 738-8845; ATO Address: Room 303, Leerna Bldg, 146-1, Susong-dong, Chongro-ku; Tel [82] (2) 3974188; FAX [82] (2) 720-7921

US Export Development Office/US Trade Center, c\o US Embassy; Tel [82] (2) 397-4212; FAX [82] (2) 739-1628

KUWAIT
Kuwait (E) P.O. Box 77 SAFAT, 13001 SAFAT, Kuwait; Unit 69000 APO AE 09880 9000; Tel (9651 242-4151 thru 9; FAX [965] 244-2855; workweek: Saturday through Wednesday; Telex 2039 HILTELS KT; FCS FAX [965] 244-7692. GSO FAX [965] 2452490; OMC-K FAX [965] 242-4192

KYRGYZSTAN
Bishkek (E), Erkindik Prospekt #66, 720002; Tel 73312 22-29-20, 22-27-77; 22 2631, 22 2473; Telex 245133 AMEMB SU; FAX 7-3312 22-35-51; CSO FAX 7-3312 22-35-51; CON FAX 7-3312 22-32-10 emergencies; afterhours 7-3312 225358; 7-3312 223289

LAOS
Vientiane (E), Rue Bartholonie, B.P. 114; Mail to. AMEMB Vientiane Box V, APO AP 96546; Tel [856] (21) 212581, 212582, 212585; Duty Officer Emergency Cellular Tel [856] (21) 130-423; FAX [856] (21) 21,2854

LATVIA
Riga (E), Raina Boulevard 7, 226050; Tel [371] (2) 213-962; Cell. Tel [371] 882-0046; Cell FAX [371]-882-0047

LEBANON
Beirut (E), Antelias, P.O. Box 70-840, or PSC 815, Box 2- FPO AE 09836-0002; Tel [961] (1) 402-200, 403-300, 26-502, 426-183, 417-774; FAX [961] (1) 407-112; ADM FAX [961] (1) 403-313; ODA FAX [961] (1) 416-215

LESOTHO
Maseru (E), P.O. Box 333, Maseru 100 Lesotho; Tel [266] 312-666; FAX [266] 310-116; USAID Tel [266] 313-954; USAID Telex 4506 LO

LIBERIA
Monrovia (E), Ill United Nations Dr.; P.O. Box 100098, Mamba Point; Tel f2311 222-991 thru 4; FAX [231] 223-710

LITHUANIA
Vilnius (E), Akmenu 6,2600; APO AE 09723; Tel 370-2-223-031; FAX 370-2-222-779

LUXEMBOURG
Luxembourg (E), 22 Blvd. Ernmanuel-Servais, 2535 Luxembourg; PSC 11, APO AE 09132-5380; Tel [352] 460123; FAX [352] 46 14 01; official mail, name/office, American Embassy Luxembourg, Unit 1410; personal mail, name, American Embassy Luxernbourg PSC 9, Box 9500, APO AE 09123

MACEDONIA (the former Yugoslav Republic of)
Skopje (US LO), ul. 27 Mart No. 5, 91 00 Skopje, Pouch address USLO Skopje, Department of State, Washington, D.C. 20521-7120; Tel [389] (91) 118-311; FAX [389] (91) 117-103; Skopje (USLO), c/o USAID 26 Veljko Vlahovic, 9100 Skopje; APO address USLO Skopje c/o Embassy Sofia APO AE 09213-5740; Pouch address Embassy Sofia (USLO Skopje) Department of State, Washington, D.C. 20521-9900; Tel [389] (91) 117-2121; FAX [389] (91) 118-105

MADAGASCAR
Antananarivo (E), 14-16 Rue Rainitovo, Antsahavola; B.P. 620; Tel [261] (2) 212-57, 200-89 or 207-18; Telex USA EMB MG 22202, 101 Antananarivo; FAX [261] 234-539

MALAWI
Lilongwe (E), P.O. Box 30016 Lilongwe 3, Malawi; Tel [265] 783-166; Telex 44627; FAX [265] 780-471

MALAYSIA
Kuala Lumpur (E), 376 Jalan Tun Razak; 50400 Kuala Lumpur; P.O. Box No. 10035,50700 Kuala Lumpur, APO AP 96535-8152; Tel. [60] (3) 248-9011; FAX [60] (3) 242-2207; CCM/AGR FAX [60] (3) 2421866

MALI
Bamako (E), Rue Rochester NY and Rue Mohamed V, B.P. 34; Tel [223] 225470; Telex 2448 AMEMB MJ; FAX [223] 223712

MALTA
Valletta (E), 2d FL, Development House, St. Anne St., Floriana, Malta; P.O. Box 535, Valletta; Tel [356] 235960; FAX [356] 243229

MARSHALL ISLANDS
Majuro (E), P.O. Box 1379, Republic of the Marshall Islands, Tel (692) 247-4011; FAX (692) 247-4012;Pouch: Majuro, 20521-4380; via US Mail PO Box 680, Majuro, MH 96960-1379; No APO/FPO is available.

MAURITANIA
Nouakchott (E), B.P. 222; Tel [222] (2) 526-60 or 526) 515-92; 63; Telex AMEMB 5558 MTN; FAX [222] workweek: Sunday through Thursday

MAURITIUS
Port Louis (E), Rogers House Oth Fl.), John Kennedy St Tel [230] 208-9763 thru 7; FAX [230] 208-9534

MEXICO
Mexico City, D.F. (E), Paseo de la Reforma 305,06500 Mexico, Distrito Federal; Mail: P.O. Box 3087, Laredo,TX 78044-3087; Tel [52] (5) 211-0042; FAX [52] (5) 511-9980, 208-3373; COM FAX [52] (5) 207-8938 USDA/AGR Trade Office (ATO), Edificio Parque Virreyes, Month Pelvoux No. 220, Esquina. Prad; Sub,

11000 Mexico D.F.; Mail P.O. Box 3087, Laredo, Texas 788044-3087. Tel [52] (5) 202-0434, 202-0168, and 202-0212; FAX [52] (5) 202-0528

US Export Development Office, Liverpool 31, Colonia Benito Juarez, 06600 Mexico, DT .; Tel [52] (5) 591-0155; FAX [52] (5) 566-1115

US Travel and Tourism Office, Plaza Comermex, M. Avila Camacho 1-402,11560 Mexico, D.F.; Tel [52] (5) 520-2101; FAX [52] (5) 202-9231

Ciudad Juarez (CG), Chihuahua Avenue Lopez Mateos 924 N, 32000 Ciudad Juarez; Mail: Box 10545, El Paso, TX 79995-0545; Tel [52] (16) 113000- FAX [52] (16) 169056.

Guadalajara (CG), JAL; Progreso 175, 44100 Guadalajara, Jalisco, Mexico; Mail: Box 3088, Laredo, TX 78044-3088; Tel [52] (3) 825-29-98, 825-27-00; FAX [52](3) 626-6549

Monterrey (CG), Nuevo Leon; Avenida Constitucion 411 Poniente 64000 Monterrey, N.L.; Mail: Box 3098, Laredo, TX 78044-3098; Tel [52] (83) 45-2120; Telex 0382853 ACMYME; FAX [52] (83) 45-7748

Hermosillo (C), Sonora; Monterrey 141, 83260 Hermosillo, Sonara; Mail: Box 3598, Laredo, TX 78044-3598; Tel [52] (62) 17-2375; FAX [52] (62) 17-2578

Matamoros (C), Tamaulipas; Calle Primera 2002; Mail: Box 633; Brownsville, TX 78522-0633; Tel [52] (88) 12-44-02; FAX [52] (88) 12-21-71

Mazatlan The post closed in May 1993.

Merida (C), Yucatan; Paseo Montejo 453, 97000 Merida, Yucatan; Mail: Box 3087, Laredo, TX 780443087; Tel [52] (99) 25-5011; FAX [52] (99) 25-6219

Tijuana (CG), B.C.N.; Tapachula 96, 22420 Tijuana, Baja California Norte; Mail: P.O. Box 439039, San Diego, CA 92143-9039; Tel [52] (66) 81-7400; FAX [52] (66) 81-8016

Nuevo Laredo (C), Tamps.; Calle Allende 3330, Col. fardin; 88260 Nuevo Laredo, Tamps.; Mail: Drawer 3089, Laredo, TX 78044-3089; Tel [52] (871) 4-0512; FAX [521 (871)4-0512, x128

MICRONESIA
Kolonia (E), P.O. Box 1286, Pohnpei, Federated States of Micronesia 96941; Tel [6911 320-2187; FAX 691320-2186

MOLDOVA
Chisinau (E), Strada Alexei Mateevici, #103; Tel 373 '2) 23-37-72; Telex [6326] EMB SU; FAX 373 (2) 23 30 44; afterhours; 373 (2) 23 7345; ADM. 373 (2) 22 24 66

MONGOLIA
LJlaanbaatar (E), c/o American Embassy Beijing, Micro Region 11, Big Ring Road, PSC 461, Box 300, FPO AP 96521-0002; Tel [976] (1) 329095 or [976] (1) 329-606; FAX [976] (1) 320-776

MOROCCO
Rabat (E), 2 Ave. de Marrakech; PSC 74, Box 003 APO AE 09718; Tel [212] (7) 76 22 65; FAX [212] (7) 76 56 61; Telex 31005M; USAID FAX [212] (7) 70 79 30; USIS FAX [212] (7) 75 08 63; COM FAX [212] (7) 76 56 51

Casablanca (CC), 8 Blvd. Moulay Youssef; APO AE 09718 (CAS); Tel [212] (2)26-45-50; FAX [212] (2) 2041-27; COM FAX [212] (2) 22-02-59

MOZAMBIQUE
Maputo (E), Avenida Kenneth Kaunda 193; P.O. Box 783; Tel [258] (1) 49-27-97; Telex 6-143 AMEMB MO; FAX [258] (1) 49-01-14

NAMIBIA
Windhoek (E), Ausplan Building, 14 Lossen St.; Private Bag 12029 Ausspannplatz, Windhoek, Namibia; Tel [264] (61) 221-601; FAX [264] (61) 229792

NEPAL
Kathmandu (E), Pani Pokhari; Tel [977] (1) 411179; Telex 2381 AEKTM NP; FAX [977] (1) 419963; USAID FAX [977] (1) 272357

NETHERLANDS
The Hague (E), Lange Voorhout 102, 2514 EJ The Hague, PSC 71, Box 1000, APO AE 09715; Tel [31](70) 310-9209; FAX [31](70)361-4688; COM FAX [31] (70) 363-2985

Amsterdam (CG), Museumplein 19; 1071 DJ Amrsterclam; PSC 71, Box 1000, APO AE 09715; Tel [31] (20) 5755 309; FAX CC [31] (20) 5755 310; COM FAX [31] (20) 5755 350

NETHERLANDS ANTILLES
Curacao (CG), St. Anna Blvd. 19; P.O. Box 158, Willemstad, Curacao; Tel [599] (9) 613066; Duty Tel [599] (9) 601579; Telex 1062 AMCON NA; FAX [599] (9) 616489

NEW ZEALAND
Wellington (E), 29 Fitzherbert Terr., Thorndon, Wellington; P.O. Box 1190, Wellington; PSC 467, Box 1, FPO AP 96531-1001; Tel [64] (4) 472-2068; ADM FAX [64] (4) 471-2380; EXEC FAX [64] (4) 4723537

Auckland (CC), 4th fl., Yorkshire General Bldg., corner of Shortland and O'Connell Sts., Auckland; Private Bag, 92022, Auckland; PSC 467, Box 99, FPO AP 96531-1099; Tel [64] (9) 303-2724; FAX [64] (9) 366-0870; COM FAX [64] (9) 302-3156

NIGER
Niamey (E), Rue Des Ambassades; B.P. 11201; Tel [227] 72-26-61 thru 4; FAX [227] 73-31-67; Telex EMB NIA 5444 NI

NIGERIA
Lagos (E), 2 Eleke Crescent; P.O. Box 554; Tel [234] (1) 26Y-0097; Telex 23616 AMEMLA NG; FAX [234] (1) 261-0257; Consular Section FAX [234] (1) 261-2218; COM FAX [234] (1) 261-9856; DEA FAX [234] (1) 261-7874; USIS FAX [234] (1) 263-5397; AID FAX [234] (1) 261-4698; Family Health Serv. FAX [234] (1) 261-2815

Kaduna (CG), 9 Maska Road, P.O. Box 170; Tel [234] (62) 235990, 235991, 235992; Telex 71617 CC NG

Note: Kaduna State office closed in July 1994 and the BPAO is the only officer remaining at post.

Ibadan (USIS), Bodija Estate; Tel (022) 410-775, 410-836, and 412-802

Abuja (BO) 11 Mambilla, Maitama District; P.O. Box 5760, Carki District; Tel [234] (9) 523-0960; FAX [234] (9) 523-0353. Branch Office presently offers neither Commercial nor Consular Services. Consular Services will be available in Abuja in fall 1994.

NORWAY
Oslo (E), Drammensveien 18,0244 Oslo, or PSC 69, Box I 000, APO AE 09707; Tel f 47] 22-44-85-50; FAX [47] 22-44-33-63; ADMIN FAX (47) 22-43-07-77; FCS FAX [47] (22-55-88-03); POL/ECON (47) 22-55-43-13; USIS FAX f 471 (22-44-04-36).

OMAN
Muscat (E), P.O. Box 202, Code No. 115, Muscat switchboard: (968) 698-989; afterhours (968) 699-049; FAX: DAO 699-779; ECA 699-669; POL/ECON/COM 604-316; USAID 797-778; GSO 699-778; OMC 604327; USIS 699-771; Health Unit FAX: 699-088; workweek: Saturday through Wednesday, 7:304:00 (0330-1200 GMT)

PAKISTAN
Islamabad (E), Diplomatic Enclave, Ramna 5; P.O. Box 1048, PSC 1212, Box 2000, Unit 6220, APO AE 09812-2000; Tel [92] (51) 826161 thru 79; Telex 82-5864 AEISL PK; FAX [92] (51) 214222; workweek: Sunday through Thursday

Karachi (CG), 8 Abdullah Haroon Rd., PSC 1214, Box 2000, Unit 62400, APO AE 09814-6150; Tel [92] (21) 5685170 thru 79; Telex 82-21001ACGK PK; FAX [92] (21) 5683089 or 5680496; workweek: Sunday through Thursday

Lahore (CG), 50 Sharah-E-Bin Badees (50 Empress Rd.), Simla Hills Lahore K; Unit 62216, APO AE 09812-2216; Tel [921 6365530 through 6365539; FAX [92] (42)

6365177; workweek: Sunday through Thursday

Peshawar (C), 11 Hospital Road, Peshawar Cantt; AC Peshawar, Unit 62217, APO AE M12-2217; Tel [92] (521) 279801, 279802, 279803; Telex [92] 52364 AMCON PK; FAX [92] (521) 276712; workweek: Sunday through Thursday

REPUBLIC OF PALAU
Koror (USLO), P.O. Box 6028, Republic of Palau 06940 Tel (680) 488-2920; FAX 680-488-2911

PANAMA
Panama City (E), Apartado 6959, Panama 5, Rep. de Panama; AMEMB Panama, Unit 0945, APO AA 34002; Tel [507] 27-1777; FAX [507] 27-1964; afterhours and weekends [507] 27-1778; GSO/FBO [507] 27-2128; COM FAX [507] 27-1713

PAPUA NEW GUINEA
Port Moresby (E), Armit St.; P.O. Box 1492, APO AE 96553; Tel (675) 211-455/594/654; Telex 22189 USAEMB; FAX (675) 213423

PARAGUAY
Asuncion (E), 1776 Mariscal-Lopez Ave.; Casilla Postal 402; Unit 4711, APO AA34036-0001; Tel [595] (21) 213-715; FAX [595] (21) 213-728

PERU
Lima (E), corner Avenidas Inca Garcilaso de la Vega and Espana; P.O. Box 1995, Lima 1; or American Embassy (Lima), APO AA 34031; Tel [51] (14) 338000; afterhours [51] (14) 33-2442; FAX [51] (14) 316682; USEMB/ADM Section: Larrabure y Unanue 1 10, Lima 1, Tel [51] (14) 33-0555; (USEMBGSO) FAX [51] (14) 33-4588; Consular Section: Grimaldo del Solar 346, Miraflores, Lima 18; Tel [51] (14) 44-3621; FAX [51] (14) 47-1877; Commercial Section: Larrabure Y Unanue 110, Lima 1; Tel [51] (14) 33-0555; FAX [51] (14) 33-4887; USAID; Larrabure Y Unanue 110 Lima 1; Tel [51] (14) 33-3200; FAX [51] (14) 33-7034; Agriculture (FAS): Larrabure y Unanue 110, Lima 1, Tel [51] (14) 33-0555; FAX [51] (14) 33-4623; USIS: Larrabure Y Unanue 1 1 0, Lima 1; Tel [51] (14) 330555; FAX [51] (14) 33-4635

Manila (E), 1201 Roxas Blvd., Ermita Manila 1000; APO AP 96440; Tel (632) 521-7116; Telex 722-27366 AME PH; FAX (632) 522-4361; COM 395 Senator Gil J. Puyat Ave., Makati; Tel (632) 818-6674; Telex 22708 COSEC PH; COM FAX (632) 818-2684

Cebu (C), 3d FL, PCI Bank Building, Gorordo Avenue, Lahug Cebu City 6000; APO AP 96440; Tel [63] (32) 311-261; FAX [63] (32) 310-174

POLAND
Warsaw (E), Aleje Ujazdowskie 29/31; AmEmbassy

494

Warsaw, Box 5010, Unit 1340, APO AE 09213-1340; Tel [48] (2) 628-3041; Telex 817771 EMUSA PL; FAX [48] (2) 628-8298

Krakow (CG), Ulica Stolarska. 9, 31043 Krakow; Unit 25402, APO AE 09213; Tel [481 (12) 229764, 221400, 226040, "7793; Telex 325350 KRUSA PL; FAX [48] (12) 218292

Poznan (CG), Ulica Chopina 4, 61708 Poznan; Unit 25402, APO AE 09213; Tel [48] (61) 551088, 529587, 529874; Telex 413474 USA PL; FAX [48] (61) 530053

PORTUGAL
Lisbon (E), Avenida das Forcas Armadas, 1600 Lisbon; PSC 83, APO AE 09726; Tel [351] (1) 7266600, 726-6659, 726-8670, 726-8880; FAX [351] (11 726-9109; FCS FAX [351] (1) 726-8914; USIS FAX [351] (1) 726-8814

Ponta Delgada, Sao Miguel, Azores (C), Avenida D. Henrique; PSC 76, APO AE 09720-0002; Tel [351] (96) 22216/7/8/9; FAX [351] (96) 27216

American Business Center (Oporto), Praca Conde de Samodaes, 65, 4000 Porto, APO AE 09726; Tel [351] (2) 606-30-94 or 606-30-95; FAX [351] (2) 600-27-37

QATAR
Doha (E), 149 Ali Bin Ahmed St., Farig Bin Omran (opp. TV station); P.O. Box 2399; Tel (0974) 864701/2/3; USLO Tel (0974) 875140; Commercial Section Tel (0974) 867460; FAX (0974) 861669; USIS Tel (0974) 351279, 351207; FAX (0974) 321907

ROMANIA
Bucharest (E), Strada Tudor Arghezi 7-9, or AmConGen (Buch), Unit 1315, APO AE 09213-1315; Tel [40] (1) 210-4042, [40] (1) 210-0149; Telex 11416; FAX [40] (1) 210-0395; afterhours Tel [40] (1) 2106384; CON Tel [40] (1) 2104042; CON FAX [401 (1) 211-3360; US BO (CLUJ) [40] (64) 19-38-15; US Branch Office (CLUJ) FAX [40] (64) 19-38-68; AGR Tel [40] (1) 210-4042; FAX [40] (1) 210-0395; USIS [40] (1) 2104042; USIS FAX [40] (1) 210-0396; USIS Cultural Ctr. Tel [40] (1) 312-1688; 1761; 1821; FAX [40] (1) 2115659; ODA FAX [40] (1) 312-3360; GSO Tel [40] (1)

Cluj-Napoca (BO), International address US Branch Office, Universitatii 7-9, Etage 1, Cluj-Napoca, Romania 3400; APO address US Embassy Branch Office Cluj-Napoca, c/o American Embassy Bucharest Unit 1315 APO AE 09213-1315; Tel [40] (95) 19-38-15 (phone only); FAX and Tel [40] (95) 19-38-68.

RUSSIA
Moscow (E), Novinskiy Bul'var 19/23 or APCI/AE 09721; Tel [7] (095) 252-2451 thru 59; Telex 413160 USCSO SU; FAX [7] (095)-956-4261; afterhours Tel [7] (095) 230-2001/2610; USAID Tel [7] (095) 9564281; FAX [7] (095)

205-2813; USIS Tel [7] (095) 9564126/4246; FAX [7] (095) 255-9766

US Commercial Office (Moscow), Novinskjy Bul'var 15; Tel[7] (095) 956-4255, [7] (095) 2554848/4660 or [7] (502) 224-1105; FAX [7] (095) 2302101 or [7] (502) 224-1106

St. Petersburg (CC), Furshtadtskaya Ulitsa 15, St. Petersburg 191028; PSC 78 Box L, APO AE 09723; Tel (71 (812) 275-1701 or [71 (812) 850-4170; Telex 121527 AMCON SU; FAX [7] (812) 850-1473 or [7] (812) 110-7022; afterhours Tel [7] (812) 274-8692

US Foreign Commercial Service; American Consulate General, Bolshaya Morskaya Ulitsa 57, 190000 St. Petersburg, [7] (812) 110-6656 or f7] (812) 110-6727 or [71 (812) 850-1902; FAX [7] (812) 110-6479 or [7] (812) 850-1903; Mail from the US: Commercial Section, American Consulate General, PSC 78, Box L, APO AE 09723

USIS: US Cultural and Information Center: Millionnaya Ulitsa 5, 191065 St. Petersburg, [7] (812) 311-8905; FAX [7] (812) 119-8052

Vladivostok (CG), Ulitsa Mordovtseva 12; Tel [7] (4232) 268-458/554 or [7] (4232) 266-820; INMARSAT 011-7-50985-11011;Telex 213206 CGVLAD SU; FAX [7] (4232) 268-445; Con Tel [7] (4232) 266-734

Yekaterinburg (CC), P.O. BOX 400, 620151 Yekaterinburg; AmConGen Yekaterinburg, Dept. of State, Wash., D.C., 20521-5890; Tel (7) 3432) 601-143, FAX: (7) 3432) 601-181

RWANDA
Kigali (E), Blvd. de la Revolution, B.P. 28; Tel [250] 75601/2/3; FAX [250172128]; 7:30 am-5 pm; Amb.'s off.: 5 pm-6 pm 12501 72127; CPU [250] 72126; USAID Tel [250] 74719; USAID FAX [250] 74735; USIS after 5 pm [250] 76339; Peace Corps [250] 76339

SAUDI ARABIA
Riyadh (E), Collector Road M, Riyadh Diplomatic Quarter; AMEMB, Unit 61307, APO AE 09803-1307; International Mail: P.O. Box 94309, Riyadh 11693; Tel [966] (1) 488-3800; USIS P.O. Box 94310, Riyadh 11693; FAX POL/ECO [966] (1) 488-3278; FAX ADM and DPC [966] (1) 488-7360; FAX FCS [966] (1) 4883237; FAX USIS [966] (1) 488-3989; FAX GSO 488- 7939; FAX IRS [966] (1) 488-7531; ATO Tel [966] (1) 488-3800, ext. 560; Telex 401363 USFCS Sj; FAX ATO [966] (1) 482-4364 workweek: Saturday through Wednesday

Dhahran (CG), Between Aramco Hdqtrs and Dhahran Int'l Airport; P.O. Box 81, Dhahran Airport 31932 or APO Unit 66803, APO AE 09858-6803; Tel [966] (3) 891-3200;

EXEC FAX [966] (3) 891-0464; GSO FAX [966] (3) 891-3296; COM FAX [966] (3) 891-8332; afterhours [966] (3) 891-2203

Jeddah (CG), Palestine Rd., Ruwais; P.O. Box 149, jeddah 21411 or Unit 62112, APO AE 09811-2112; Tel [966] (2) 667-0080; COM Tel [966] (2) 667-0040; Telex 601459 USFCS SJ; COM FAX [966] (2) 665-8106; ATO Tel [966] (2) 667-0080, ext. 299; direct line 6612408; FAX [966] (2) 667-6196; USIS Tel [966] (2) 6606355; FAX [966] (2) 660-6367; JECOR Tel [966] (2) 640-0000, ext. 1398; workweek: Saturday through Wednesday

SENEGAL
Dakar (E), B.P. 49, Avenue jean XXIII; Tel [221] 23-42-96 or 23-34-24; USIS Tel [221] 23-59-28, 23-11-85; Telex 21793 AMEMB SC; FAX [221] 22-29-91

SERBIA-MONTENEGRO
Belgrade (E), American Embassy Belgrade, Unit 1310, APO AE 09213-1310; Tel [381] (11) 645-655; Telex 11529 AMEMBA YU; FAX [381] (11) 645-221; COM FAX [381] (11) 645-096; CON FAX [381] (11) 644-053

SEYCHELLES
Victoria (E), Box 148, Unit 62501, APO AE 098152501 or Victoria House, Box 251,Victoria, Mahe, Seychelles; Tel [248] 225256; FAX [248] 225189

SIERRA LEONE
Freetown (E), Corner of Walpole and Siaka Stevens Sts.; Tel (SWB) [232] (22) 226-481 through 226-485; AMB Tel [232] (22) 226-155; DCM'S OFC: [232] (22) 227-192; FAX [232] (22) 225471

SINGAPORE
Singapore (E), 30 Hill St.; Singapore 0617; FPO AP 96534; Tel (65) 338-0251; FAX (65) 338-4550

USIS/American Center MPH Building, Level 4, 7177 Stamford Road, Singapore 0617; Tel [65] 334-0910; FAX [65] 334-2780; Commercial Services and Library, I Colombo Court, Unit #05-16 Colombo Ct., Building, North Bridge Road, Singapore 0617; Tel [65] 338-9722; FAX [65] 338-5010; Telex RS25079 (SINCTC); FAX [65] 338-5010

ACRIATO OFF, 541 Orchard Road, Unit 08-04, Liat Towers Bldg., Singapore 0923; Tel [65] 737-1233; FAX [65] 732-8307; Telex RS55318

USAID/RIG/A, 111 North Bridge Road, No. 17-03 Peninsula Plaza, Singapore 0617; Tel [65].334-2766; FAX [65] 334-2541

FAA, Changi Airport Terminal 2, South Finger, 4th fl., Security Unit 048-002, International Area Office Director and Field Office Unit 048-006 Singapore 1781; Tel [65] 543-1466; (65) 545-5822; FAX (65) 543-1952 or (65) 545-

9722

SLOVAK REPUBLIC
Bratislava (E), (Int'l) Hviezdoslavovo Narnestie 4, 81102 Bratislava, Tel [42] (7) 330861 or (421 (7) 333338; FAX [42] (7) 330096; USIS FAX [42] (7) 335934; AID Tel [42] (7) 330667 or, 331588; AID FAX [42] (7) 334711

SLOVENIA
Ljubljana (E), Box 254, Prazakova 4, 61000 Ljubljana or AmEmbassy Ljubljana, Department of State, Washington, D.C. 20521-7140; Tel [386] (61) 301427/472/485; Tel [386] (61) 301-401; AID: Tel [386] (61) 131-5114; FAX [386] (61) 301-401; USIS: Cankarjeva 11 61000 Ljubljana; Tel [386] (61) 1258226 or 126-1169; FAX [3861 (61) 126-4284

SOLOMON ISLANDS
Honiara (E). The post closed in July 1993.

SOMALIA
Mogadishu (USLO). The US Liaison Office in Mogadishu reopened in March 1994. USLO Unit 64105, APO AE 09831-4105. Military personnel replace USLO with Unit Deployed Designator

SOUTH AFRICA
Pretoria (E), 877 Pretorius St., Arcadia 0083; P.O. Box 9536, Pretoria 0001; Tel [27] (12) 342-1048; FAX [271 (12) 342-2244; USIS Tel [27] (12) 342-3006; FAX [27] (12) 342-2090; AID Tel (27) (12); FAX [27] (12)

Cape Town (CG), Broadway Industries Centre, Heerengracht, Foreshore; Tel [27] (21) 214-280; FAX [27] (21) 25-4151; USIS Tel [27] (21) 419-4822; FAX [27](21)461-3603

Durban (CG), Durban Bay House, 29th Fl., 333 Smith St.; Tel [27] (31) 304-4737; FAX [27] (31) 301-8206; USIS FAX [27] (31) 304-2847; USIS Tel [27] (31) 305-5068

Johannesburg (CG), 11th Fl., Kine Center, Commissioner and Kruis Sts.; P.O. Box 2155; Tel [27] (11) 331-1681; FAX [27] (11) 331-1327; USIS Tel [27] (11) 838-2231; FAX [27] (11) 838-3920; COM Tel [27] (11) 331-3937; FAX [27] (11) 331-6178

SPAIN
Madrid (E), Serrano 75,28006 Madrid, or APO AE 09642; Tel [34] (1) 5774000; FAX [34] (1) 577-5735; FCS FAX [34] (1) 575-8655

Barcelona (CC), Reina Elisenda 23, 08034 Barcelona or PSC 61, Box 0005, APO AE 09642; Tel [34] (3) 2802227; FAX [34] (3) 205-5206; ADMIN FAX [34] (3) 2057764; USIS FAX [34] (3) 205-5857; FSC FAX [34] (3) 205-7705

Bilbao (C), Lehendakari Agirre 11-3,48014 Bilbao; PSC

496

61, Box 0006, APO AE 09642; Tel [34] (4) 4758300; Telex 32589 ACBIL E; FAX [34] (4) 476-1240

SRI LANKA

Colombo (E), 210 Calle Rd., Colombo 3; P.O. Box 106; Tel [94] (1) 448007; Telex 21305 AMEMB CE; FAX [94] (1) 437345; USAID: 356 Calle Rd., Colombo 3; Tel [94] (1) 574333; FAX [94] (1) 574264; USIS: 44 Calle Rd., Colombo 3; Tel [94](1) 421271; FAX: [94] (1) 449070; VOA: 228/1 Galle Rd., Colombo 4; Tel [94] (1) 589245; FAX [94] (1) 502675; Peace Corps: 75 1/1 Kynsey Rd., Colombo 8; Tel [94] (1) 687617

Khartoum (E), Sharia Ali Abdul Latif, P.O. Box 699; APO AE 09829 Tel 74700, 74611; Telex 22619 AMEMSD

SURINAME

Paramaribo (E), Dr. Sophie Redmondstraat 129; P.O. Box 1821; Tel [597] 4729001; 477881; 476459; FAX [597] 410025; USIS Tel [597] 475051; Telex 383 AMEMSU SN; USIS FAX [597] 410025, 479829, 420800; CPU Tel 476793

SWAZILAND

Mbabane (E), Central Bank Bldg, Warner Street; P.O. Box 199; Tel [268] 46441/5; FAX [268] 45959; U'SAID Telex 2016 WD; USAID FAX 44770

SWEDEN

Stockholm (E), Strandvagen 101, S-115 89 Stockholm; Tel [46] (8) 783-5300; FAX [46] (8) 661-1964; CON FAX [46] (8) 660-5879

SWITZERLAND

Bern (E), Jubilaeurnstrasse 93, 3005 Bern; Tel [41] (31) 357-7011; Telex (845) 912603; FAX [41] (31) 357-7344; CPU [41] (31) 357-7201; USIS FAX [41] (31) 357-7379; COM FAX [41] (31) 357-7336; FAS FAX [41] (31) 357-7363; ODA FAX [41] (31) 357-7381

US Mission to the European Office of the UN and Other International Organizations (Geneva), Mission Permanente Des Etats-Unis, Route de Pregny 11, 1292 Chambesy-Ceneva, Switzerland; Tel [41] (22) 749-4111; Telex 412865 USCV; FAX [41] (22) 7494880; COM FAX [41] (22) 7494885.

US Trade Representative (USTR), Botanic Bldg., 1-3 Avenue de la Paix, 1202 Geneva, Switzerland; Tel [41] (22) 749-4111; FAX [41] (22) 749-5308

US Delegation to the Conference on Disarmament(CD), Botanic Building, 1-3 Avenue De La Paix, 1202 Geneva; Tel [41] (22) 749-5355; FAX [41] (22) 749-5326

Zurich (CG) Zollikerstrasse 141, 8008 Zurich; Tel [41] (1) 422-25-66; Telex 0045-816830; FAX [41](1) 383-9814; COM FAX [41] (1) 382-26-55

SYRIA

Damascus (E), Abou Roumaneh, Al-Mansur St., No. 2; P.O. Box 29; Tel [963] (11) 333-2814, 714-108, 3330788; night contact number: 333-3232; FAX [963] (11) 224-7938; USIS Tel: 333-1878, 333-8413; Telex 411919 USDAMA SY; workweek: Sunday through Thursday.

TAJIKISTAN

Dushanbe (E), Interim Chancery, #39 Ainii Street; Oktyabrskaya Hotel; Tel: {7} (2772) 21-03-56

TANZANIA

Dar Es Salaam (E), 36 Laibon Rd. (off Bagamoyo Rd.) P.O. Box 9123; Tel [255] (51) 66010 thru 5; Telex 41250 USA TZ; FAX [255] (51) 66701

THAILAND

Bangkok (E), 95 Wireless Rd.; APO AP 96546; Tel [66] (2) 252-5040; FAX [66] (2) 254-2990; COM 3d fl., Diethelm Towers Bldg., Tower A, 93/1 Wireless Rd., 10330; Tel [66] (2) 255-4365 thru 7; COM FAX [66] (2) 255-2915

Chiang Mai (CG), Vidhayanond Rd., Box C, APO AP 96546; Tel [66] (53) 252--629; FAX [66] (53) 252-633

Udom (C), 35/6 Supakitianya Rd.; Box UD; APO AP 96546; Tel [66] (42) 244-'270-; FAX [66] (42') 244-273

TOGO

Lome (E), Rue Pelletier Caventou and Rue Vauban; B.P. 8,52; Tel f2281 21-77-17 and 21-29-91 thru 94; FAX [228] 21-79-52

TRINIDAD AND TOBAGO

Port-of-Spain (E), 15 Queen's Park West; P.O. Box 752; Tel (809) 622-6372/6, 6176; FAX (809) 628-5462;

TUNISIA

Tunis (E), 144 Ave. de la Liberte, 1002 Tunis-Belvedere; Tel [216] (1) 782-566; Telex 18379 AMTUNTN; FAX [216] (1) 789-719; Telex 14307 USATO; FAX [216] (1) 785-345

Istanbul (CC), '104-108 Mesrut - et Caddesi, Tepebasi, PSC 97, Box 0002, APO AE 09827-0002; Tel [90] (212) 251 36 02; Telex 24077 ATOT-TR; GSO FAX (90) (212) 251-2554; ADM FAX f901 (212) 251-3632; EXEC FAX [90] (212) 251-3218; COM FAX (90) (212) 252-2417; CON FAX [90] (212) 252-7851

TURKEY

Ankara (E), 110 Ataturk Blvd.; PSC 93, Box 5000, APO AE 09823; Tel [90] (312) 468-61 10 thru 6128; Tel USIS [90] (312) 468-6102 thru 6106; FAX EMB [90] (312) 467-0019; FAX GSO [90] (312) 467-0057; FAX FAS (90) (312) 467-0056; COM FAX [90] (312) 4671366; CON FAX [90] (312) 468-6131; FAX USIS [90] (312) 467-3624 (exec. off) and 468-6145

Adana (C), Ataturk Caddesi; PSC 94, APO AE 09824; Tel [90] (322) 453-9106, 545-2145, 454-3774; FAX [90] (322) 457-6591

TURKMENISTAN
Ashgabat (E), 6 Teheran Street, Yubilenaya Hotel; Tel [7] 3632 2449-25 or 24-49-22; FAX (7) 3632-255379; CPU After duty hours (7) 3632-240103

UGANDA
Kampala (E), Parliament Ave.; P.O. Box 7007; Tel [256] (41) 259792/3/5; FAX [2561 (41) 259794; Admin. Tel [256] (41) 259792; FAX [256] (41) 241863

UKRAINE
Kiev (E), 10 Yuria Kotsyubinskovo, 252053 Kiev 53; Tel [7] (044) 244-7349, 24 hr: [7] (044) 244-3745; Telex 131142 CGKIV SU; FAX [7] (044) 244-7350; COM FAX [7] (044) 279-1485

UNITED ARAB EMIRATES
Abu Dhabi (E), Al-Sudan St.; P.O. Box 4009; Pouch: AmEmbassy Abu Dhabi, Dept. of State, Washington, D.C. 20521-6010; Tel [971] (2) 436-691 or 436-692; afterhours [971] (2) 435-457; Chancery FAX [971] (2) 434-771; Admin. FAX (971) (2) 435-441; CONS FAX [971] (2) 435-786; USIS FAX [971] (2) 434-802; USLO FAX [971] (2) 434-604; COM Section: FCS: Blue Tower Bldg., 8th Fl., Shaikh Khalifa Bin Zayed St.; Tel (971) (2) 345-545; Telex 22229 AMEMBY EM; FAX [971] (2) 331-374; workweek: Saturday through Wednesday

Dubai (CG), Dubai International Trade Center, 21st fl.; P.O. Box 9343; Pouch: AMCONGEN Dubai, Dept. of State, Washington, D.C., 20521-6020; Tel [971] (4) 313-115; [971] (4) 314-043; COM-FCS: Tel [971] (4) 313-584; FAX [971] (4) 313-131; USIS Tel [971] (4) 314-882; USATO Tel [971] (4) 313-612/314-063; FAX (9714) 314-998; Navy Regional Contracting Office NRCC Tel [971] (4) 311-888; FAX [971] (4) 315-764; workweek: Saturday-Wednesday

UNITED KINGDOM
London, England (E), 24/31 Grosvenor Sq., W. 1A1AE; PSC 801, Box 40, FPO AE 09498-4040; Tel [44](71) 499-9000; FAX [44] (71) 409-1637; COM FAX [44] (71) 4914022 ATO Address Regent Arcade House, 19-25 Argyll St., London W1V 1AA; Tel [44] (71) 287-2624; FAX [44] (71) 287-2629

Belfast Northern Ireland (CG), Queen's House, 14 Queen St., BTI 6EQ- PSC 801 Box 40, APO AE 09498. 4040; Tel [44] (232) 328239; 'FAX [44] (23) 224-8482

Edinburgh Scotland (CG), 3 Regent Ter. EH7 513W; PSC 801 Box 40, FPO AE 09498-4040; Tel [44] (31) 556 8315 , FAX [44] (31) 557-6023

UNITED STATES

US Mission to the United Nations (USUN), 799 United Nations Plaza, New York, NY 10017-3505; Tel (212) 415-4050; afterhours Tel: (212) 415-4444; FAX (212) 415-4443; to utilize the]eased line to USUN from the Department, dial 4 and the four-digit extension; to utilize FTS to USUN from the Department, dial 8-667 and the four-digit office extension

US Mission to the Organization of American States (USOAS), Department of State, Washington, D.C. 20520; Tel (202) 647-9376; FAX (202) 647-0911

URUGUAY
Montevideo (E), Lauro Muller 1776; APO AA 34035;Tel [598] (2) 23-60-61 or 48-77-77; FAX [598] (2) 488611

UZBEKISTAN
Tashkent (E), 82 Chilanzarskaya; Tel [7] (3712) 77-14-07, 77-10-81; FAX [7] (3712) 77-69 ,532;-Telex (64) 116569 USA SU; USIS FAX 7-3712-89-l'

VENEZUELA
Caracas (E), Avenida Francisco de Miranda and Avenicla Principal de la Floresta; P.O. Box 62291, Caracas 1060-A or APO AA 34037; Tel [58] (2) 2852222; or [58] (2) 285-3111; Telex 25501 AMEMB VE; FAX (58) (2) 285-0366; US ATO Address Centro Plaza, Torre C, Piso 18, Los Palos Grandes, Caracas 1062; Tel [58] (2) 283-2353/Direct line 283-2521; FAX [58] (2) 284-5412

WESTERN SAMOA
Apia (E), 5th fl., Beach Rd., P.O. Box 3430, Apia; Tel (685) 21-631; Telex (779) 275 AMEMB SX; FAX (685) 22-030

REPUBLIC OF YEMEN
Sanaa (E), Dhahr Himyar Zone, Sheraton Hotel District, P.O. Box 22347, Sanaa, Republic of Yemen or Sanaa-Dept. of State, Washington, D.C. 20521-6330; Tel [9671 (1) 238-843/52; Telex 2697 EMBSAN YE; FAX [967] (1) 251-563; USIS Tel 19671 (1) 216-973 and 203-364; USPC Tel [967] (1) 275-504; USAID Tel [967] (1) 231-213/4 and 231-732; USPC Tel [967] (1) 275504; workweek: Saturday through Wednesday

ZAIRE
Kinshasa (E), 310 Avenue des Aviateurs, Unit 31550; APO 09828; Tel [243] (12) 21532, 21628; Telecel [243] (88) 43604/43608 Telex 21405 US EMB ZR; FAX [243] (12) 21534/5, ext. 2308 or [243] (88) 43805/43467

Lubumbashi (CC). The post closed in September 1993.

ZAMBIA
Lusaka (E), comer of Independence and United Nations Aves.; P.O. Box 31617; Tel [260] (1) 228-595, 228-601/2/3; Telex AMEMB ZA 41970; FAX [260] (1) 261-538; USIS Tel 227-993/4; FAX [260] (1) 226-523; USAID Tel [260] (1) 221-314, 229-327; FAX [260] (1) 225-741

ZIMBABWE
Harare (E), 172 Herbert Chitepo Ave., P.O. Box 3340; Tel [263] (4) 794-521; Commercial Section: 1st Fl., Century House West, 36 Baker Ave.; Tel [263] (4) 728-957; Telex 24591 USUSFCS ZW; FAX [263] (4) 796488

TAIWAN
Unofficial commercial and other relations with the people of Taiwan are conducted through an unofficial instrumentality, the American Institute in Taiwan, which has offices in Taipei and Kaohsiung. AIT Taipei operates an American Trade Center, located at the Taipei World Trade Center. The addresses of these offices are:

American Institute in Taiwan, #7 Lane 134, Hsin Yi Road Section 3 Taipei, Taiwan; Tel [886] (2) 709-2000; afterhours Tel [886] (2) 709-2013; FAX [886] (2) 702-7675

American Trade Center, Room 3207 International Trade Building, Taipei World Trade Center, 333 Keelung Road Section 1, Taipei 10548, Taiwan; Tel [886](2)720-1550; COM FAx [886] (2) 757-7162

American Institute in Taiwan, 5th fl., #2 Chung Cheng 3d Rd. Kaohsiung, Taiwan; Tel [886] (7) 2240154/7; FAX [886] (7) 223-8237

For further information, contact the Washington, D.C., office of the American Institute in Taiwan, 1700 N. Moore St. Suite 1700, Arlington, VA 22209-1996; Tel (703) 525-8474; FAX (703) 841-1385.

Note:

ACM	Assistant Chief of Mission
ADM	Administrative Section
ADV	Adviser
AGR	Agricultural Section (USDA/FAS)
AID	Agency for International Development
ALT	Alternate
AMB	Ambassador
AMB SEC	Ambassador's Secretary
APHIS	Animal and Plant Health Inspection Service Officer
APO	Army Post Office
ATO	Agricultural Trade Office (USDA/FAS)
BCAO	Branch Cultural Affairs Officer (USIS)
Bg	Brigadier General
BIB	Board for International Broadcasting
BO	Branch Office (of Embassy)
BOB/EUR	Board of Broadcasting, European Office
BPAO	Branch Public Affairs Officer (USIS)
B.P.	Boite Postale
C	Consulate
CA	Consular Agency/Agent
CAO	Cultural Affairs Officer (USIS0
Capt	Captain (USN)

CDC	Centers for Disease Control
Cdr	Commander
CEO	Cultural Exchange Officer (USIS)
CG SEC	Consul General's Secretary
CHG	Charge d' Affaires
CINCAFSOUTH	Commander-in Chief Allied Forces Southern Europe
CINCEUR	Commander-inChiefU.S. European Command
CINCUSAFE	Commander-in Chief U.S. Air Forces Europe
CINCUSAREUR	Commander-in Chief U.S. Army Europe
Col	Colonel
COM	Commercial Section (FCS)
CON	Consul, Consular Section
COUNS	Counselor
C.P.	Caixa Postal
CPO	Communications Program Officer
CUS	Customs Service (Treasury)
DAC	Development Assistance Committee
DCM	Deputy Chief of Mission
DEA	Drug Enforcement Agency
DEP	Deputy
DEP DIR	Deputy Director
DIR	Director
DOE	Department of Energy
DPAO	Deputy Public Affairs Officer (USIS)
DPO	Deputy Principal Officer
DSA	Defense Supply Adviser
E	Embassy
ECO	Economic Section
ECO/COM	Economic/Commercial Section
EDO	Export Development Officer
ERDA	Energy Research and Development Administration
EX-IM	Export-Import
FAA	Federal Aviation Administration
FIC/JSC	Finance Committee and Joint Support Committee
FIN	Financial Attache (Treasury)
FODAG	Food and Agriculture Organizations
FPO	Fleet Post Office
IAEA	International Atomic Energy Agency
IAGS	Inter-american Geodetic Survey
ICAO	International Civil Aviation Organization
IMO	Information Management Officer
IO	Information Officer (USIS)
IRM	International Resources Management
IRS	Internal Revenue Service
ISM	Information Systems Manager
JUS/CIV	Department of Justice, Civil Division
JUSMAG	Joint US Military Advisory Group
LAB	Labor Officer
LO	Liaison Officer
Ltc	Lieutenant Colonel
LEGAT	Legal Attache
M	Mission
Mg	Major General
MAAG	Military Assistance Advisory Group
MILGP	Military Group

MSG	Marine Security Guard
MIN	Minister
MLO	Military Liaison Office
MNL	Minerals Officer
NARC	Narcotics
NATO	North Atlantic Treaty Organization
NAU	Narcotics Assistance Unit
OAS	Organization of American States
ODA	Office of the Defense Attache
ODC	Office of Defense Cooperation
OIC	Office in Charge
OMC	Office of Military Cooperation
PAO	Public Affairs Officer (USIS)
PO	Principal Officer
PO SEC	Principal Officer's Secretary
POL	Political Section
POL/LAB	Political and Labor Section
POLAD	Political Adviser
POL/ECO	Political/Economic Section
Radm	Rear Admiral
REDSO	Regional Economic Development Services Office
REF	Refugee Coordinator
REP	Representative
RES	Resources
RHUDO Office	Regional Housing and Urban Development
ROCAP	Regional Officer for Central American Programs
RPSO	Regional Procurement and Support Office
RSO	Regional Security Officer
SAO	Security Assistance Office
SCI	Scientific Attache
SEC DEL	Secretary of Delegation
SHAPE	Supreme Headquarters Allied Powers Europe
SLG	State and Local Government
SR	Senior
STC	Security Trade Control
UNEP	United Nations Environment Program

UNESCO	United Nations Educational, Scientific, and Cultural Organizations
UNIDO	United Nations Industrial Development Organization
USA	United States Army
USAF	United States Air Force
USDA/APHIS	Animal and Plant Health Inspection Service
USEC	US Mission to European Communities
USGS	US Geological Survey
USINT	United State Interests Section
USIS	United States Information Service
USLO	United State Liaison Office
USMC	United States Marine Corps
USMTM	US Military Training Mission
USN	United State Navy
USNATO	US Mission to the North Atlantic Treaty Organization
USOAS	US Mission to the Organization of American States
USOECD	US Mission to the Organization for Economic Cooperation and Development
USTTA	US Travel and Tourism Agent
USUN	US Mission to the United Nations
VC	Vice Consul
VOA	Voice of America

APPENDIX B
FOREIGN EMBASSIES IN THE UNITED STATES

AFGHANISTAN
Embassy of Afghanistan
2341 Wyoming Ave. N.W.
Washington, DC 20008
(202) 234-3770/1
FAX (202) 328-3516

ALBANIA
Embassy of the Rep. of Albania
1150 18th Street N.W.
Washington DC 20036
(212) 249-4942

ALGERIA
Algeria, Democratic and Popular
Rep. of Algeria
2137 Wyoming Ave, NW
Washington, DC 20008
(202) 265-2800

ANGOLA
Ebassy of Angola
1899 L. Street N.W. 6th Flr.
Washington DC 20036
(202) 785-1156

ANGUILLA
Contact Embassy of
the United Kingdom
3100 Massachusetts Ave NW,
Washington, DC 20008
(202) 426-1340, FAX (202) 898-4255

ANTIGUA AND BARBUDA
Emabassy of Antigua and
Barbuda,
3400 International Drive, Suite 4M
Washington, DC 20008
(202) 362-5122/5166/5211

ARGENTINA
Embassy of Argentina
1600 New Hampshire Ave., NW
Washington, DC 20009
(202) 939-6400 to 6403

ARMENIA
Embassy of Armenia

122 C Street, NW,
Suite 360,
Washington DC 20001
(202) 393-5983

AUSTRALIA
Embassy of Australia
1601 Massachusetts Ave., NW
Washington, DC 20036
(202) 797-3000
FAX (202) 797-3168

AUSTRIA
Embassy of Austria
3524 International Court NW
Washington, DC 20008
(202) 895-6767

AZERBAIJAN
Embassy of Azerbaijan
927 15th Street NW, Suite 700
Washington D.C. 20005
(202) 842-0001

BAHAMAS
Embassy of The
Commonwealth of The Bahamas
2220 Massachusetts Ave., NW
Washington, DC 20008
(202) 319-2660
FAX (202) 319-2668

BAHRAIN
Embassy of Bahrain
3502 International Drive, NW.,
Washington, DC 20008
(202) 342-0741

BARBADOS
Embassy of Barbados
2144 Wyoming Ave., NW
Washington, DC 20008
(202) 939-9200

BANGLADESH
Embassy of Bangladesh
2201 Wisconsin Ave., NW
Washington, DC 20007
(202) 342-8373

BELARUS
Embassy of Belarus
1619 New Hampshire NW, Suite
619; Washington DC 20009
(202) 986-1604

BELGIUM
Embassy of Belgium
3330 Garfield St., NW
Washington, DC 20008
(202) 333-6900

BELIZE
Embassy of Belize
2535 Massachusetts Ave., N.W.
Washington, DC 20008
(202) 332-9636

BENIN
Embassy of Benin
2737 Cathedral Ave., NW
Washington, DC 20008
(202) 232-6656
FAX (202) 265-1996

BHUTAN
Kingdom of Bhutan
Mission to the United Nations
Two United Nations Plaza
New York, NY 10017
(212) 826-1919

BOLIVIA
Embassy of Bolivia
3014 Massachusetts Ave., NW
Washington, DC 20008
(202) 483-4410
Fax (202) 328-3712

BOTSWANA
Embassy of the Rep. of Botswana
3400 International Dr., NW, Ste.
7M
Washington, DC 20008
(202) 244-4990
FAX (202) 244-4164

BRITISH VIRGIN ISLANDS
Contact Embassy of the
United Kingdom

3100 Massachusetts Ave., NW
Washington, DC 20008
(202) 462-1340
FAX (202) 898-4255

BRAZIL
Embassy of Brazil
3009 Massachusetts Ave., NW
Washington, DC 20008
(202) 745-2828
FAX (202) 745-2827

BRUNEI
Embassy of the State
of Brunei Darussalam
2600 Virginia Ave., NW, Ste. 300
NW Washington, DC 20037
(202) 342-0159
FAX (202) 342-0158

BULGARIA
Embassy of the Rep. of Bulgaria
1621 - 22d St., NW
Washington, DC 20008
(202) 387-7969
FAX (202) 234-7973

BURKINA FASO
Embassy of Burkina Faso
2340 Massachusetts Ave., NW
Washington, DC 20008
(202) 332-5577

BURMA
(See Myanmar)

BURUNDI
Embassy of Burundi
2233 Wisconsin Ave., NW
Washington, DC 20007
(202) 342-2574

CAMEROON
Embassy of Cameroon
2349 Massachusetts Ave., NW
Washington, DC 20008
(202) 265-8790 to 8794

CANADA
Embassy of Canada
501 Pennsylvania Ave., NW
Washington, DC 20001
(202) 682-1740
FAX (202) 682-7726

Rep. OF CAPE VERDE
Embassy of Cape Verde
3415 Massachusetts Ave., NW
Washington, DC 20007

(202) 965-6820
FAX (202) 965-1207

CAYMAN ISLANDS
Contact Embassy of Jamaica
1850 K St. NW
Suite 355
Washington, DC 20006
(202) 452-0660

CENTRAL AFRICAN Rep.
Embassy of Cent. African Rep.
1618 - 22d St., NW
Washington, DC 20008
(202) 483-7800/1

CHAD
Embassy of Chad
2002 R St. NW
Washington, DC 20009
(202) 462-4009
FAX (202) 265-1937

CHILE
Embassy of Chile
1732 Massachusetts Ave., NW
Washington, DC 20036
(202) 785-1746
FAX (202) 887-5475

CHINA, PEOPLES Rep.
Embassy of the People's
Rep. of China
2300 Connecticut Ave., NW
Washington, DC 20008
(202) 328-328-2517

COLOMBIA
Embassy of Colombia
1825 Conn Ave. N.W.
Washington, DC 20009
(202) 3332-7476

COMOROS
Embassy of Comoros
336 E. 45th St.
2nd Floor
New York, NY 10017
(212) 972-8010
FAX (212) 983-4712

CONGO, PEOPLE'S Rep.
Embassy of Congo
4891 Colorado Ave., NW
Washington, DC 20011
(202) 726-5500/1

COSTA RICA
Embassy of Costa Rica

1825 Connecticut Ave., NW, Suite
211; Washington, DC 20009
(202) 328-6628

COTE D'IVOIRE
Embassy of Cote d'Ivoire
2424 Massachusetts Ave., NW
Washington, DC 20008
(202) 797-0300

CROATIA
Embassy of Croatia
236 Massachusetts Ave., NE,
Washington DC 20002
(202) 543-5580 or 5608

CUBA
Cuban Interest Section
Embassy of Czechoslovak
Socialist Rep.
2639 16th St., NW
Washington, DC 20009
(202) 797-8518

CYPRUS
Embassy of the Rep. of Cyprus
2211 R St., NW
Washington, DC 20008
(202) 462-5772

CZECH REPUBLIC
Embassy of the Czech Republic
3900 Spring of Freedom Street,
NW; Washington DC 20008
(202) 363-6315

DENMARK
Royal Danish Embassy
3200 Whitehaven St., NW
Washington, DC 20008
(202) 234-4300
FAX (202) 328-1470

Rep. OF DJIBOUTI
Embassy of the Rep. of Djibouti
1156 - 15th St., NW
Suite 515
Washington, DC 20005
(202) 331-0270
FAX (202) 331-0302

DOMINICA
Contact the Embassy of Barbados
2144 Wyoming Ave., NW
Washington, DC 20008
(202) 939-9200

DOMINICAN Rep.
Embassy of the Dominican Rep.

502

1715 - 22nd St., NW
Washington, DC 20008
(202) 332-6280
Fax (202) 265-8057

ECUADOR
Embassy of Ecuador
2535 15th St., NW
Washington, DC 20009
(202) 234-7166

EGYPT
Egypt, Arab Rep. of
2310 Decatur Place, NW
Washington, DC 20008
(202) 234-3903

EL SALVADOR
Embassy of El Salvador
1010 16th St., NW; 3rd Flr.
Washington, DC 20036
(202) 331-4032

EQUATORIAL GUINEA
Embassy of Equatorial Guinea
57 Magnolia Ave. (Temporary)
Mount Vernon, NY 10553
(914) 667-9664

ESTONIA
Embassy of the Republic of Estonia
9 Rockefeller Plaza, Suite J-1421
New York, NY 10020
(212) 247-1450

ETHIOPIA
Embassy of Ethiopia
2134 Kalorama Rd., NW
Washington, DC 20008
(202) 234-2281

FIJI
Embassy of the Rep. of Fiji
2233 Wisconsin Ave., Suite 240
Washington, DC 20007
(202) 337-8320
FAX (202) 337-1996

FINLAND
Embassy of Finland
3216 New Mexico Ave., NW
Washington, DC 20016
(202) 363-2430
FAX (202) 363-8233

FRANCE
Embassy of France
4101 Reservoir Rd., NW
Washington, DC 20007

(202) 944-6200/6215

FRENCH GUIANA
Contact Embassy of France
4101 Reservoir Rd., NW
Washington, DC 20007
(202) 944-6200/6215

GABON
Embassy of Gabon
2034 - 20th St., NW
Washington, DC 20009
(202) 797-1000

THE GAMBIA
Embassy of Gambia
1030 - 15th St., NW
Suite 720
Washinton, DC 20005
(202) 842-1356/1359
FAX (202) 842-2073

GEORGIA
Embassy of Georgia
1511 K St, N.W. Ste. 424
Washington D.C. 20005
(202) 393-6060

Fed. Rep. OF GERMANY
Embassy of the Fed.
Rep. of Germany
4645 Reservoir Rd., NW
Washington, DC 20007
(202) 298-4000

GHANA
Embassy of Ghana
3512 International Dr., NW
Washington, DC 20008
(202) 686-4520
FAX (202) 686-4527

GREECE
Embassy of Greece
2221 Massachusetts Ave., NW
Washington, DC 20008
(202) 232-8222

GRENADA
Embassy of Grenada
1701 New Hampshire Ave., NW
Washington, DC 20009
(202) 265-2561

GUADELOUPE
Contact the Embassy of France
2535 Belmont Rd., NW
Washinton, DC 20008
(202) 328-2600

GUATEMALA
Embassy of Guatemala
2220 R St., NW
Washington, DC 20008
(202) 745-4952
FAX (202) 745-1908

GUINEA
Embassy of Guinea
2112 Leroy Place, NW
Washington, DC 20008
(202) 483-9420

GUINEA-BISSAU
Embassy of the Rep.
of Guinea-Bissau
918 - 16th St., NW
Mezzanine Suite
Washington, DC 20006
(202) 872-4222
FAX (202) 872-4226

GUYANA
Embassy of Guyana
2490 Tracy Place NW
Washington, DC 20008
(202) 265-6900

HAITI
Embassy of Haiti
2311 Massachusetts Ave., NW
Washington, DC 20008
(202) 332-4090

HONDURAS
Embassy of Honduras
1612 K. St., NW
Washington, DC 20006
(202) 223-0285

HUNGARY
Embassy of the Rep. of Hungary
3910 Shoemaker St., NW
Washington, DC 20008
(202) 362-6730

ICELAND
Embassy of Iceland
2022 Connecticut Ave., NW
Washington, DC 20008
(202) 265-6653 to 6655
FAX (202) 265-6656

INDIA
Embassy of India
2536 Massachusetts Ave., NW
Washington, DC 20008
(202) 939-9839/9850

503

INDONESIA
Embassy of the Rep. of Indonesia
2020 Massachusetts Ave., NW
Washington, DC 20036
(202) 775-5200
FAX (202) 775-5365

IRAN
Iranian Interests Section
Embassy of Algeria
2209 Wisconsin Ave., NW
Washington, DC 20007
(202) 965-4990

IRELAND
Embassy of Ireland
2234 Massachusetts Ave., NW
Washington, DC 20008
(202) 462-3939

ISRAEL
Embassy of Israel
3514 International Dr., NW
Washington, DC 20008
(202) 364-5500
FAX (202) 364-5610

ITALY
Embassy of Italy
1601 Fuller St., NW
Washington, DC 20009
(202) 328-5500

JAMAICA
Embassy of Jamaica
1850 K St., NW
Suite 355
Washington, DC 20006
(202) 452-0660
FAX (202) 452-0081

JAPAN
Embassy of Japan
2520 Massachusetts Ave., NW
Washington, DC 20008
(202) 939-6800

JORDAN
Jordan, Hashemite Kingdom of
3504 International Dr., NW
Washington, DC 20008
(202) 966-2664
FAX (202) 966-3110

KAZAKHSTAN
Embassy of Kazakhstan
3421 Mass. Ave., NW
Washington D.C. 20007
(202) 333-4504/07

KENYA
Embassy of Kenya
2249 R. St., NW
Washington, DC 20008
(202) 387-6101

KOREA, SOUTH
Embassy of Korea
2600 Virginia Ave., NW, Ste.208
Washington, DC 20037
(202) 939-5660/63

KOREA, DEM. PEOPLE'S REP.
Contact the licensing Division,
Office of Foreign Assets Control,
Department of the Treasury, 1331
G St, NW, Washington DC 20220
(202) 622-2480

KUWAIT
Embassy of Kuwait
2940 Tilden St., NW
Washington, DC 20008
(202) 966-0702
FAX (202) 966-0517

LAOS
Embassy of the Lao People's
Democratic Republic,
2222 S St., NW,
Washington DC 20008
(202) 332-6416/7

LATVIA
Embassy of Latvia
4325 - 17th St., NW
Washington, DC 20011
(202) 726-8213/8214

LEBANON
Lebanon
2560 - 28th St., NW
Washington, DC 20008
(202) 939-6300
FAX (202) 939-6324

LESOTHO
Embassy of Lesotho
2511 Massachusetts Ave., NW
Washington, DC 20008
(202) 797-5533
FAX (202) 234-6815

LIBERIA
Embassy of Liberia
5201 - 16th St., NW
Washington, DC 20011
(202) 723-0437 t0 0440

LIBYA
Contact the Licensing Division,
Office of Foreign Assets Control,
Department of the Treasury, 1331
G St., NW Washington 20220
(202) 622-2480

LITHUANIA
Embassy of Lithuania
2622 - 16th St., NW
Washington, DC 20009
(202) 234-5860/2639
FAX (202) 328-0466

LUXEMBOURG
Embassy of Luxembourg
2200 Massachusetts Ave., NW
Washington, DC 20008
(202) 265-4171
FAX (202) 328-8270

MADAGASCAR
Embassy of Madagascar
2374 Massachusetts Ave., NW
Washington, DC 20008
(202) 265-5525/6

MALAWI
Embassy of Malawi
2408 Massachusetts Ave., NW
Washington, DC 20008
(202) 797-1007

MALAYSIA
Embassy of Malaysia
2401 Massachusetts Ave., NW
Washington, DC 20008
Annex: 1900 - 24th St., NW
Washington, DC 20008
(202) 328-2700
FAX (202) 483-7661

MALDIVES
Rep. of Maldives
Mission to the United Nations
820 Second Ave., Suite 800C
New York, NY 10017
(212) 599-6195

MALI
Embassy of Mali
2130 R. St., NW
Washington, DC 20008
(202) 332-2249

MALTA
Embassy of Malta
2017 Connecticut Ave., NW
Washington, DC 20008

(202) 462-3611/2
FAX (202) 387-5470

MARSHALL ISLANDS
Check Information with Rep.
Office
Suite 1004, 1901 Penn. Ave, NW
Washington DC 20006
(202) 234-5414
FAX (202) 232-3236

MARTINIQUE
Contact Embassy of France
4101 Reservoir Rd., NW
Washington, DC 2007
(202) 944-6000

MAURITANIA
Embassy of Mauritania
2129 Leroy Place, NW
Washington, DC 20008
(202) 232-5700/1

MAURITIUS
Embassy of Mauritius
4301 Connecticut Ave., NW
Suite 441
Washington, DC 20008
(202) 244-1491/2
FAX (202) 966-0983

MEXICO
Embassy of Mexico
2827 16th St. NW
Washington, DC 20009
(202) 736-1000

MICRONESIA
Embassy of the Federated States
of Micronesia
1725 N St., NW
Washington, DC 20036
(202) 223-4383
FAX (202) 223-4391

MOLDOVA
Contact Embassy of Russia
(202) 939-8907

MONGOLIA
Embassy of the Mongolian
2833 M Street, NW
Washington DC 20007
(202) 333-7117

MONTSERRAT
Contact the Embassy of
the United Kingdom
3100 Massachusetts Ave., NW

Washington, DC 20008
(202) 462-1340
FAX (202) 898-4255

MOROCCO
Morocco
1601 - 21st St., NW
Washington, DC 20009
(202) 462-7979
FAX (202) 265-0161

MOZAMBIQUE
Embassy of Mozambique
1990 M St., NW
Suite 570
Washington, DC 20036
(202) 293-7146
FAX (202) 235-0245

MYANMAR
Embassy of the Union of Myanmar
2300 S St., NW
Washington, DC 20008
(202) 332-9044/9045

NAMIBIA
Embassy of the Rep. of Namibia
1605 New Hampshire Ave., NW
Washington, DC 20009
(202) 986-0540
FAX (202) 986-0443

NEPAL
Embassy of Nepal
2131 Leroy Place, NW
Washington, DC 20008
(202) 667-4550

NETHERLANDS
Embassy of the Netherlands
4200 Linnean Ave., NW
Washington, DC 20008
(202) 244-5300 after 6pm 244-5304
FAX (202) 362-3430

NETHERLAND ANTILLES
Embassy of the Netherlands
4200 Linnean Ave., NW
Washington, DC 20008
(202) 244-5300
FAX (202) 362-3430

NEW ZEALAND
Embassy of New Zealand
37 Observatory Circle, NW
Washington, DC 20008
(202) 328-4800

NICARAGUA

Embassy of Nicaragua
1627 New Hampshire Ave., NW
Washington, DC 20009
(202) 939-6531 to 34

NIGER
Embassy of Niger
2204 R St., NW
Washington, DC 20008
(202) 483-4224 to 4227

NIGERIA
Embassy of Nigeria
2201 M St., NW
Washington, DC 20037
(202) 822-1500

NORWAY
Royal Norwegian Embassy
2720 - 34th St., NW
Washington, DC 20008
(202) 333-6000
FAX (202) 337-0870

OMAN
Oman, Sultanate of
2535 Belmont Rd., NW
Washington, DC 20008
(202) 387-1980-2

PAKISTAN
Embassy of Pakistan
2315 Massachusetts Ave., NW
Washington, DC 20008
(202) 939-6295

PANAMA
Embassy of Panama
2862 McGill Terrace, NW
Washington, DC 20008
(202) 483-1407

PAPUA NEW GUINEA
Embassy of Papua New Guinea
1615 New Hampshire Ave., NW,
Ste. 300; Washington, DC 20009
(202) 745-3680
FAX (202) 745-3679

PARAGUAY
Embassy of Paraguay
2400 Massachusetts Ave., NW
Washington, DC 20008
(202) 483-6960
FAX (202) 234-4508

PERU
Embassy of Peru
1700 Massachusetts Ave., NW

Washington, DC 20036
(202) 833-9860
FAX (202) 659-8124

PHILIPPINES
Embassy of the Philippines
1600 Massachusetts Ave., NW
Washington, DC 20036
(202) 467-9300

POLAND
Embassy of the Rep. of Poland
2224 Wyoming Ave. NW
Washington, DC 20008
(202) 232-4517

PORTUGAL
Embassy of Portugal
2125 Kalorama Rd., NW
Washington, DC 20008
(202) 328-8610

QATAR
Qatar
600 New Hampshire Ave., NW
Suite 1180
Washington, DC 20037
(202) 338-0111

ROMANIA
Embassy of Romania
1607 23rd St., NW
Washington, DC 20008
(202) 232-4747
FAX (202) 232-4748

RUSSIA
Embassy of Russia
1825 Phelps Pl., NW
Washington DC 20008
(202) 939-8907, 8911 or 8913

RWANDA
Embassy of Rwanda
1714 New Hampshire Ave., NW
Washington, DC 20009
(202) 232-2882
FAX (202) 232-4544

SAN MARINO
Embassy of San Marino
1899 L St., NW, Suite 500
Washington D.C. 20036
(202) 223-3517

SRI LANKA
Embassy of Sri Lanka
2148 Wyoming Ave., NW
Washington, DC 20008

(202) 483-4025

ST. KITTS and NEVIS
Embassy of St. Kitts and Nevis
2501 M St., NW,
Washington, DC 20037
(202) 833-3550
FAX (202) 833-3553

ST. LUCIA
Embassy of St. Lucia
2100 M St., NW, Ste. 309
Washington, DC 20037
(202) 463-7378
FAX (202) 887-5746

ST. MARTIN
Contact the Embassy of France
2535 Belmont Rd., NW
Washington, DC 20008
(202) 328-2600

SOA TOME AND PRINCIPE
c/o Permanent Mission to the UN
122 East 42nd Street, Ste. 1604;
New York, NY 10017
(212) 697-4211

ST. VINCENT and the GRENADINES
Embassy of St. Vincent and
the Grenadines
1717 Massachusetts Ave., NW,
Suite 102
Washington, DC 20036
(202) 462-7806/7846
FAX (202) 462-7807

SAUDI ARABIA
Saudi Arabia
601 New Hampshire Ave., NW
Washington, DC 20037
(202) 342-3800

SENEGAL
Embassy of Senegal
2112 Wyoming Ave., NW
Washington, DC 20008
(202) 234-0540/1

SERBIA AND MONTENEGRO
Contact the Licensing Division,
Office of Foreign Assets Control,
Department of the Treasury, 1331
G St., NW Washington 20220
(202) 622-2480

SEYCHELLES
Permanent Mission of Seychelles to

the United Nations
820 Second Ave., Ste. 203
New York, NY 10017
(212) 687-9766
FAX (212) 922-9177

SIERRA LEONE
Embassy of Sierra Leone
1701 - 19th St., NW
Washington, DC 20009
(202) 939-9261

SINGAPORE
Embassy of Singapore
1824 R St. NW
Washington, DC 20009
(202) 667-7555
FAX (202) 265-7915

SLOVAK REPUBLIC
Embassy of the Slovak Republic
2201 Wisconsin Ave. NW; Ste.
380; Washington DC 20008
(202) 965-5164

SLOVENIA
Embassy of Slovenia
1300 19th Street, NW
Washington DC 20036
(202) 828-1650

SOLOMON ISLANDS
Embassy of the Solomon Islands
c/o The Permanent Mission
of the Solomon Islands to the UN
820 Second Ave.,
Suite 800
New York, NY 10017
(212) 599-6193

SOMALIA
Embassy of Somalia
600 New Hampshire Ave., NW
Suite 710
Washington, DC 20037
(202) 333-5908

SOUTH AFRICA
Embassy of South Africa
3201 New Mexico Ave., NW
Washington, DC 20016
(202) 966-1650

SPAIN
Embassy of Spain
2700 15th St., NW
Washington, DC 20009
(202) 265-0190/1

SRI LANKA
Embassy of the Democratic
Socialist Rep. of Sri Lanka
2148 Wyoming Ave., NW
Washington, DC 20008
(202) 483-4025 to 4028
FAX (202) 232-7181

SUDAN
Embassy of Sudan
2210 Massachusetts Ave., NW
Washington, DC 20008
(202) 338-8565 to 8570
FAX (202) 667-2406

SURINAME
Embassy of Suriname
4301 Connecticut Ave., NW
Suite 108
Washington, DC 20008
(202) 244-7488
FAX (202) 244-5878

SWAZILAND
Embassy of the Kingdom
of Swaziland
3400 International Dr., NW,
Ste.3M; Washington, DC 20008
(202) 362-6683/6685
FAX (202) 244-8059

SWEDEN
Embassy of Sweden
600 New Hampshire Ave., NW
Suites 1200 and 715
Washington, DC 20037
(202) 944-5600
FAX (202) 342-1319

SWITZERLAND
Embassy of Switzerland
2900 Catherdral Ave., NW
Washington, DC 20008
(202) 745-7900
FAX (202) 387-2564

SYRIA
Syrian Arab Rep.
2215 Wyoming Ave., NW
Washington, DC 20008
(202) 232-6313
FAX (202) 234-9548

TAJIKISTAN
Contact Russian Embassy
(202) 939-8907

TANZANIA
Embassy of Tanzania

2139 R St., NW
Washington, DC 20008
(202) 939-6125
FAX (202) 797-7408

THAILAND
Embassy of Thailand
2300 Kalorama Rd., NW
Washington, DC 20008
(202) 234-5052

TOGO
Embassy of Togo
2208 Massachusetts Ave., NW
Washington, DC 20008
(202) 234-4212/3

TRINIDAD AND TOBAGO
Embassy of Trinidad & Tobago
1708 Massachusetts Ave., NW
Washington, DC 20036
(202) 467-6490
FAX (202) 785-3130

TUNISIA
Tunisia
1515 Massachusetts Ave., NW
Washington, DC 20005
(202) 862-1850

TURKEY
Embassy of the Rep. of Turkey
1714 Massachusetts Ave., NW
Washington, DC 20036
(202) 659-0742

TURKMENISTAN
Contact Russian Embassy
(202) 939-8907

TURKS AND CAICOS
Contact the Embassy of the
Bahamas
600 New Hampshire Ave, NW
Washington, DC 20037
(202) 338-3940

UGANDA
Embassy of Uganda
5909 - 16th St., NW
Washington, DC 20011
(202) 726-7100
FAX (202) 726-1727

UKRAINE
Embassy of Ukraine
3350 M St. NW,
Washington DC, 20007
(202) 333-7507

UNITED ARAB EMIRATES
United Arab Emirates
600 New Hampshire Ave., NW
Suite 740
Washington, DC 20037
(202) 338-6500

UNITED KINGDOM
Embassy of the United Kingdom
3100 Massachusetts Ave., NW
Washington, DC 20008
(202) 462-1340; (202)986-0205
FAX (202) 898-4255

URUGUAY
Embassy of Uruguay
1918 F St., NW
Washington, DC 20008
(202) 331-1313

UZBEKISTAN
Uzbekistan Consulate
866 United Nations Plaza, Ste. 326
New York, NY 10017
(212) 486-7570

VATICAN CITY
Apostolic Nunciature
3339 Massachusetts Ave., NW
Washington, DC 20008
(202) 333-7121

VENEZUELA
Embassy of Venezuela
1099 30th St., NW
Washington, DC 20007
(202) 342-2214

WESTERN SAMOA
Western Samoa Mission to the UN
820 2nd Avenue, Ste. 800
New York, NY 10017
(212) 599-6196

YEMEN, ARAB Rep.
Yemen Arab Rep.
2600 Virginia Ave., NW, Ste. 705
Washington DC 20037
(202) 965-4760

YEMEN, PEOPLE'S DEM. REP.
413 East 51st St.
New York, NY 10022
(212) 752-3066

YUGOSLAVIA
Embassy of the Socialist Fed.
Rep. of Yugoslavia
2410 California St., NW

507

Washington, DC 20089
(202) 462-6566

ZAIRE
Embassy of Zaire
1800 New Hampshire Ave., NW
Washington, DC 20009
(202) 234-7690/1

ZAMBIA
Embassy of Zambia
2419 Massachusetts Ave., NW
Washington, DC 20008
(202) 265-9717 to 9721

ZIMBABWE
Embassy of Zimbabwe
1608 New Hampshire Ave., NW
Washington, DC 20009
(202) 332-7100

APPENDIX C

DEPARTMENT OF COMMERCE DISTRICT OFFICES

ALABAMA
Birmingham - Medical Forum Building, 7th floor, 950 22nd Street North, 35203 (205) 731-1331, Fax: (202) 731-0076

ALASKA
Anchorage - Suite 319, World Trade Center Alaska 4201 Tudor Center Drive, 99508(907) 271-6237, Fax: (907) 271-6242

ARIZONA
Phoenix - Phoenix Plaza, Suite 970 2901 N. Central Avenue, 85012 (602) 640-2513, Fax: (602) 640-2518

ARKANSAS
Little Rock - TCBY Tower Building, Suite 700 425 West Capitol Avenue, 72201 501) 324-5794, Fax: (501) 324-7380

CALIFORNIA
Los Angeles - 11000 Wilshire Blvd, Room 9200, 90024 (310) 575-7104, Fax: (310)575-7220

*Newport Beach - 3300 Irvine Avenue, Suite 305, 92660 (714) 660-1688, Fax: (714) 660-8039

**Long Beach USEAC - One World Trade Center, Ste. 1670, 90831 (310) 980-4550, Fax: (310) 980-4561

San Diego - 6363 Greenwich Drive, Suite 230, 92122 (619) 557-5395, Fax: (619) 557-6176

San Francisco - 250 Montgomery St, 14th Floor, 94104 (415) 705-2300, Fax: (415) 705-2297

*Santa Clara - 5201 Great American Parkway, #456, 95054 (408) 291-7625, Fax: (408) 970-4618

COLORADO
Denver - 1625 Broadway, Suite 680, 80202 (303) 844-6622, Fax: (303) 844-5651

CONNECTICUT
Hartford - Room 610B, 450 Main Street, 06103 (203) 240-3530, Fax: (203) 240-3473

DELAWARE
Served by the Phildadelphia District Office

DISTRICT OF COLOMBIA
Served by the Gaithersburg Branch Office

FLORIDA
**Miami USEAC - Post Office Box 590570, 33159 5600 Northwest 36th Street, Ste. 617, 33166 (305) 526-7425, Fax: (305) 526-7434

*Clearwater - 128 North Osceola Avenue, 34615 (813) 461-0011, Fax: (813) 449-2889

*Orlando - Eola Park Centre, Suite 695 200 E. Robinso Street, 32801 (407) 648-6235, Fax: (407) 648-6756

*Tallahassee - 107 West Gaines Street, Room 366C, 32339 (904) 488-6469, Fax: (904)452-9105

GEORGIA
Atlanta - Plaza Square North, Suite 310 4360 Chamblee Dunwoody Road, 30341 (404) 452-9101, Fax: (404) 452-9105

Savannah - 120 Barnard Street, Room A-107, 31401 (912) 652-4204, Fax: (912) 652-4241

HAWAII
Honolulu - Post Office Box 50026 300 Ala Moana Blvd, Room 4106, 96850 (808) 541-1782, Fax: (808) 541-3435

IDAHO
*Boise - Portland District Office 700 West State Street, 83720 (208) 334-3857, Fax: (208) 334-2783

ILLINOIS
**Chicago USEAC - Stanley Bokota, US&FCS Dir. Xerox Center, 55 West Monroe Street, Suite 2440, 60603 (312)

*Wheaton -
353-8040, Fax: (312) 353-8098
c/o Illinois Institute of Technology
201 East Loop Road, 60187 (312)
353-4332, Fax: (312) 353-4336

*Rockford -
Post Office Box 1747
515 North Court Street, 61110
(815) 987-4347, Fax: (815) 987-8122

INDIANA
Indianapolis -
Penwood One, Suite 106
11405 N. Pennslyvania Street
Carmel, IN 46032
(317) 582-2300, Fax: (317) 582-2301

IOWA
Des Moines -
Room 817, Federal Building
210 Walnut Street, 50309
(515) 284-4222, Fax: (515) 284-4021

KANSAS
*Wichita -
Kansas City District Office
151 N. Volutsia, 67214
(316) 269-6160, Fax: (316) 683-7326

KENTUCKY
Louisville -
Marmaduke Building, 3rd Floor
520 South 4th Street, 40202
(502) 582-5066, Fax: (502) 582-6573

LOUISIANA
New Orleans -
Hale Boggs Federal Building
501 Magazine Street, Room 1043,
70130; (504) 589-6546, Fax: (504) 589-2337

MAINE
*Augusta -
Boston District Office
187 State Street, 04333
(207) 622-8249, Fax: (207) 626-9156

MARYLAND
**Baltimore USEAC -
World trade Center, Suite 2432
401 Pratt Street, 21202
(410) 962-4539, Fax: (410) 962-4529

*Gaithersburg -
c/o National Institute of Standards
& Technology
Room A102, Building 411, 20899
(301) 975-3904, Fax: (301) 948-4360

MASSACHUSETTS
Boston -
164 Northern Avenue

World Trade Center, Suite 307,
02210; (617) 424-5950, Fax: (617) 424-5992

MICHIGAN
Detroit -
1140 McNamara Building
477 Michigan Avenue, 48226
(313) 226-3650, Fax: (313) 226-3657

*Grand Rapids -
300 Monroe N.W., Room 409,
49503; (616) 456-2411, Fax: (313)456-2695

MINNESOTA
Minneapolis -
108 Federal Building
110 South 4th Street, 55401
(612) 348-1638, Fax: (612) 348-1650

MISSISSIPPI
Jackson -
201 W. Capitol Street, Suite 310,
39201; (601) 965-4388, Fax: (601) 965-5386

MISSOURI
St. Louis -
8182 Maryland Avenue, Suite 303,
63105; (314) 425-3302, Fax: (314) 425-3381

Kansas City -
601 East 12th Street, Room 635,
64106; (816) 426-3141, Fax: (816)426-3140

MONTANA
Served by the Boise Branch Office

NEBRASKA
Omaha -
Des Moines District Office
11133 "O" Street, 68137
(402) 221-3664, Fax: (402) 221-3668

NEVADA
Reno -
1755 East Plumb Lane, Room 152,
89502; (702) 784-5203, Fax: (702) 784-5343

NEW HAMPSHIRE
*Portsmouth -
Boston District Office
601 Spaulding Turnpike, Suite 29,
03801; (603) 334-6074, Fax: (603) 334-6110

NEW JERSEY
Trenton -
3131 Princeton Pike, Bldg. #6,
Suite 100, 08648

NEW MEXICO
*Santa Fe -
Dallas District Office
c/o New Mexico Dept. of Economic

Development, 1100 St. Francis Drive, 87503; (505) 827-0350, Fax: (505) 827-0263

NEW YORK

Buffalo -
1312 Federal Building
111 West Huron Street, 14202
(716) 846-4191, Fax: (716) 846-5290

*Rochester -
111 East Avenue, Suite 220, 14604
(716) 263-6480, Fax: (716) 325-6505

New York -
26 Federal Plaza, Room 3718,
10278; (212) 264-0634, Fax: (212) 264-1356

NORTH CAROLINA

Greensboro -
400 West Market Street, Suite 400,
27401; (910) 333-5345, Fax: (910) 333-5158

NORTH DAKOTA

Served by the Minneapolis District Office

OHIO

Cincinnati -
550 Main Street, Room 9504,
45202; (513) 684-2944, Fax: (513) 684-3200

Cleveland -
Bank One Center
600 Superior Avenue, Suite 700,
44114, (216) 522-4750, Fax: (216) 522-2235

OKLAHOMA

Oklahoma City -
6601 Broadway Extension, Room 200, 73116
(405) 231-5302, Fax: (405) 841-5245

*Tulsa -
440 South Houston Street, 74127
(918) 581-7650, Fax: (918) 581-2844

OREGON

Portland -
One World Trade Center, Suite 242
121 SW Salmon, 97204
(503) 326-3001, Fax: (503) 326-6351

PENNSLYVANIA

Philadelphia -
660 American Avenue, Suite 201
King of Prussia, PA 19406
(215) 962-4980, Fax: (215) 962-4989

Pittsburgh -
2002 Federal Building
1000 Liberty Avenue, 15222
(412) 644-2850, Fax: (412) 644-4875

PUERTO RICO

San Juan (Hato Rey)- Room G-55, Federal building
Chardon Avenue, 00918
(809) 766-5555, Fax: (809) 766-5692

RHODE ISLAND

*Providence -
Hartford District Office
7 Jackson Walkway, 02903
(401) 528-5104, Fax: (401) 528-5067

SOUTH CAROLINA

Columbia -
Strom Thurmond Federal Building,
Suite 172, 1835 Assembly Street,
29201; (803) 765-5345, Fax: (803) 253-3614

*Charleston -
c/o Charleston Trident Chamber of Commerce
Post Office Box 975, 29402, 81
Mary Street, 29402; (803) 727-4051, Fax: (803) 727-4052

SOUTH DAKOTA

*Sioux Falls -
Des Moines District Office
200 N. Phillips Avenue,
Commercial Control
Suite 302, 67102
(605) 330-4254, Fax: (605) 330-4266

TENNESSEE

Nashville -
Parkway Towers, Suite 114
404 James Robertson Parkway,
37219; (615) 736-5161, Fax: (615) 736-2454

*Memphis -
22 North Front Street, Suite 200,
38103; (901) 544-4137, Fax: (901) 575-3510

*Knoxville -
301 East Church Avenue, 37915
(615) 545-4637. Fax: (615) 523-2071

TEXAS

Dallas -
Post Office Box 58130
2050 N. Stemmons Fwy., Suite
170, 75258; (214) 767-0542, Fax: (214) 767-8240

*Austin -
Post Office Box 12728
410 E. 5th Street, Suite 414-A,
78711; (512) 482-5939, Fax: (512) 482-5940

Houston -
#1 Allen Center, Suite 1160
500 Dallas, 77002; (713) 229-2578,
Fax: (713) 229-2203

UTAH

Salt Lake City -
324 S. State Street, Suite 105,
84111; (801) 524-5116, Fax: (801)

524-5886

VERMONT
*Montpelier -   c/o Vermont Departmnet of
                        Economic Development
                        109 State Street, 05609; (802) 828-
                        4508, Fax: (802) 828-3258

VIRGINIA
Richmond-   8010 Fed. Bldg., 400 N. 8th St.,
                        23240; Tel (804) 771-2246; FAX
                        771-2390

WASHINGTON
Seattle-   Suite 290, 3131 Elliott Ave., 98121;
                        Tel (206) 553-5615; FAX 533-7253
*Tri-Cities-   320 North Johnson
Street, Ste.350,   Kennewick, WA 99336;
Tel: (509)   735-2751, FAX: (509)
735-9385

WEST VIRGINIA
Charleston-   Suite 809 405 Capitol St., 25301
                        Tel (304) 347-5123; FAX 347-5408

WISCONSIN
Milwaukee-   Room 606, Fed. Bldg. 517 E.
                        Wisconsin Ave., 53202; Tel (414)
                        297-3473; FAX 297-3470

WYOMING
Serviced by Denver District Office

REGIONAL OFFICES

***Region I, Philadelphia**
                        660 American Avenue, Suite 202
                        King of Prussia, PA 19406; Tel:
                        (215) 962-4990, Fax: (215) 962-
                        1326

***Region II, Atlanta**
                        Plaza Square North, Suite 405
                        4260 Chamblee Dunwood Road,
                        30341; Tel: (404) 455-7860, Fax:
                        (404) 45-7865

***Region III, Cincinnati**
9504 Federal Building
                        550 Main Street, 45202; Tel: (513)
                        684-2947, Fax: (513) 684-3200

***Region IV, St. Louis**
                        8182 Maryland Avenue, Suite 305,
                        63105; Tel: (314) 425-3300, Fax:
                        (314) 425-3375

***Region V, San Francisco**
                        250 Montgomery St., 14th Floor,

94104; Tel: (415) 705-2310, Fax:
(415) 705-2299

*   Denotes Trade Specialist at a Branch Office.

**   Denotes a U.S. Export Assistance Center
                ITA Trade Specialist at a Branch Office.

***   Office with managerial and administrative
                oversight responsibilities (offers no direct
                business counseling)

512

APPENDIX **D**

U.S INTERNATIONAL TRADE INFORMATION CENTER

The Trade Information Center is a "one-stop" source for information on all federal government export assistance programs. Located in the Department of Commerce, the Center is operated by the Trade Promotion Coordinating Committee (TPCC), an interagency group working to unify federal trade promotion activities.

The Center can provide information on:

- How to get started in exporting

- Foreign market research

- Export financing programs

- Locating overseas buyers

- Trade missions and fairs

- Local export seminars and conferences

- Where to find tariff rates and licensing requirements

> To reach the Center dial:
> **1-800-USA-TRADE**
> **(1-800-872-8723)**

Businesses can call the Trade Information Center Monday through Friday, 8:30 a.m. to 6:00 p.m. EST. The hearing-impaired can reach the Center by calling:
1-800-TDD-TRADE
(1-800-833-8723)

[See **Appendix C** for a listing of International Administration/US & FCS District Offices]

513

APPENDIX E

UNITED STATES CUSTOMS DISTRICT OFFICES

For Further Information

Every effort has been made to indicate essential requirements: however, all regulations of Customs and other agencies cannot be covered in full.

Customs offices will be glad to advise you of any changes in regulations which may have occurred since publication of this leaflet.

District Directors of Customs are located in the following cities:

Anchorage, Alaska 99501	907/271-2675
Baltimore, Md. 21202	301/962-2666
Boston, Mass. 02222-1059	617/565-6147
Buffalo, N.Y. 14202	716/846-4373
Charleston, S.C. 29402	803/724-4312
Charlotte Amalie	
St. Thomas-V.I. 00801	809/774-2510
Chicago, Ill. 60607	312/353-6100
Cleveland, Ohio 44114	216/891-3800
Dallas/Ft. Worth, Tex. 75261	214/574-2170
Detroit, Mich. 48226-2568	313/226-3177
Duluth, Minnesota 55802-1390	218/720-5201
El Paso, Texas 79925	915/540-5800
Great Falls, Montana 59405	406/453-7631
Honolulu, Hawaii 96806	808/541-1725
Houston, Texas 77029	713/671-1000
Laredo, Texas 78041-3130	512/726-2267
Los Angeles/Long Beach, Ca. 90731	213/514-6001
Miami, Florida 33102	305/876-6803
Milwaukee, Wisconsin 53237-0260	414/297-3925
Minneapolis, Minnesota 55401	612/348-1690
Mobile, Alabama 36602	205/441-5106
New Orleans, Louisiana 70130	504/589-6353
*New York, N.Y (Seaport) 10048	212/466-5817
*New York, NY (JFK),	718/917-1542
*Newark, New Jersey 07114	201/645-3760
Nogales, Arizona 85621	602/761-2010
Norfolk, Virginia 23510	804/441-6546
Ogdensburg, New York 13669	315/393-0660
Pembina, North Dakota 58271	701/825-6201
Philadelphia, Pennsylvania 19106	215/597-4605
Port Arthur, Texas 77642	409/724-0087
Portland, Maine 04112	207/780-3326
Portland, Oregon 97209	503/221-2865
Providence, Rhode Island 02905	401/528-5080
St. Albans, Vermont 05478	802/524-6527
St. Louis, Missouri 6134-3716	314/428-2662

San Diego, California 92188	619/557-5360
San Francisco, California 94126	415/465-4340
San Juan, Puerto Rico 00901	809/729-6950
Savannah, Georgia 31401	912/944-4256
Seattle, Washington 98104	206/442-0554
Tampa, Florida 33605	813/228-2381
Washington, D.C. 20166	703/318-5900
Washington Dulles Intl. Airport,	703/318-5900
Sterling, Va. 20166	703/318-5900

*Write to Area Director of Customs

514

APPENDIX F

UNITED STATES CUSTOMS SERVICE: FOREIGN OFFICES

Customs Assistance Abroad. Should you need Customs assistance while abroad, you can visit or telephone our representatives located at the American Embassy or consulate in . . .

Bangkok	662/252-5040
Beijing	86-1-532-3831
Bonn	49/228/339-2207
Caracas	58-2-285-0037
Central America (Miami)	305-596-6479
Dublin	353/1/688777
The Hague	31/703-924-651
Hermosillo	52/621-75258
Hong Kong	852/524-2267
London	44/71-493-4599
Merida	52/99/258235
Mexico City	(905) 211-0042
Milan	39/2/29-35-218
Monterrey	52/83/42-7972
Montevido	598/223-6061
Ottawa	(613) 230-12120
Panama City	507/257-562
Paris	33/1/4296-1202
Rome	39/6/4674-2475
Seoul	822/397-4644
Singapore	65/338-0251
Tokyo	81/3-3224-543
Vienna	43/1-310-5896

APPENDIX G

UNITED STATES CUSTOMS : INTERNATIONAL MAIL BRANCHES

The location and telephone numbers for Customs International Mail Branches are as follows:

Mail Branch	Location	Telephone Number
Anchorage Alaska	605 West Fourth Ave, Rm.205 Anchorage, AK 99501	(907) 248-3373
Atlanta, Georgia	Foreign Mail Division, PO Box 619050 Hapeville, GA 30320	(404) 763-7602
Boston, Massachusetts	U.S. Customs South Postal Annex, Room 1008,, G.M.F. Boston, Ma. 02205	(617) 565-8635
Buffalo, New York	1200 William Street Buffalo, NY 14206	(716) 846-4319
Charlotte, Amalie	Mail Branch Facility Sugar Estate Post Office Charlotte, Amalie VI 00801	(809) 774-1254
Chicago, Illinois	U.S. Customs Foreign Mail Unit 11600 West Irving Park Road A.M.F. O'Hare Chicago, IL 60666	(312) 353-6140
Dallas, Texas Dallas,	P.O. Box 619050 2300 West 22nd St. Dallas-Ft. Worth Airport, Dallas TX 75261	(214) 574-2128
Detroit, Michigan	Foreign Mail Section 1401 West Forest Street Room 226, G.M.F. Detroit, MI 48233	(313) 226-3137
Honolulu, Hawaii	3599 North Nimitz Highway Honolulu, HI 96818	(808) 422-9608 (808) 422-6522
Houston, Texas	Mail Facility, 2929 Air Freight Rd. Houston,TX 77032	(713) 233-3600
Los Angeles, California	300 N. Los Angeles St. Room B-202 Los Angeles, CA 90012-3391	(213) 894-4749
Miami, Florida	Foreign Mail Branch 1751 NW 79th Ave., Miami, FL 33152	(305) 536-4281

Minneapolis/ St. Paul Minnesota	180 East Kellogg Boulevard St. Paul, MN 55101	(612) 290-3639
Newark, New Jersey (NYBFMCE SURFACE) (SURFACE	U.S. Customs Foreign Mail Center 80 County Road Jersey City, NJ 07097	(201) 714-6371
New York, New York (AIR MAIL)	Mail Facility, Bldg. 250 J.F.K. Airport Jamaica, NY 11430	(718) 917-1446
Oakland, California	1675 7th Street Oakland, California 94615	(510) 273-7560)
Philadelphia, Pennsylvania	1000 Tinicum Island Rd. Philadelphia, PA 19153	(215) 937-5758
San Juan, Puerto Rico	G.P.O., Box 1280 San Juan, PR 00936	(809) 766-6006
Seattle, Washington (AMF)	16601 Air Cargo Rd. Seattle, WA 98158	(206) 553-5382
Washington, D.C.	44715 Prentice Drive Sterling, VA 20101-9998	(703) 406-6499

Preclearance Offices

Montreal 514/636-3859
Toronto. 416/676-3399
Winnipeg. 204/783-2206
Calgary. 403/221-1733
Edmonton 403/890-4514
Vancouver. 604/278-1825
Bermuda. 809/293-2560
Nassau 809/377-8461
Freeport 809/352-7256

517

APPENDIX H

KEY OFFICERS OF U.S. FOREIGN SERVICE POSTS

Guide for Business Representatives

The Key Officers Guide lists key officers at Foreign Service posts with whom American business representatives would most likely have contact. All embassies, missions, consulates general, and consulates are listed.

At the head of each U.S. diplomatic mission are the Chief of Mission (with the title of <u>Ambassador</u>, <u>Minister</u>, or <u>Charge d'Affairs</u>) and the Deputy Chief of Mission. These officers are responsible for all components of the U.S. Mission within a country, including consular posts.

<u>Commercial Officers</u> assist U.S. business through: arranging appointments with local business and government officials, providing counsel on local trade regulations, laws, and customs; identifying importers, buyers, agents, distributors, and joint venture partners for U.S. firms; and other business assistance. At larger posts, trade specialists of the US&FCS perform this function. At smaller posts, commercial interests are represented by economic/commercial officers from the Department of State.

<u>Commercial Officers for Tourism</u> implement marketing programs to expand inbound tourism, to increase the export competitiveness of U.S. travel companies, and to strengthen the international trade position of the United States. These officers are employees of the U.S. Travel and Tourism Administration (USTTA), an agency of the U.S. Department of Commerce with offices in various countries. Additional important markets in Europe, Asia, the Pacific, Latin America are covered by the Foreign Commercial Services and the private sector under USTTA leadership.

<u>Economic Officers</u> analyze and report on macroeconomic trends and trade policies and their implications for U.S. policies and programs.

<u>Financial Attaches</u> analyze and report on major financial developments.

<u>Political Officers</u> analyze and report on political developments and their potential impact on U.S. interests.

<u>Labor Officers</u> follow the activities of labor organizations and can supply information on wages, non-wage costs, social security regulations, labor attitudes toward American investments, etc.

<u>Consular Officers</u> extend to U.S. citizens and their property abroad the protection of the U.S. Government. They maintain lists of local attorneys, act as liaison with police and other officials, and have the authority to notarize documents. The Department recommends that business representatives residing overseas register with the consular officer; in troubled areas, even travelers are advised to register.

<u>The Administrative Officer</u> is responsible for the normal business operations of the post, including purchasing for the post and its commissary.

<u>Regional Security Officers</u> are responsible for providing physical, procedural, and personnel security services to U.S. diplomatic facilities and personnel; their responsibilities extend to providing in-country security briefings and threat assessments to business executives.

<u>Security Assistance Officers</u> are responsible for Defense Cooperation in Armaments and foreign military sales to include functioning as primary in-country point of contact for U.S. Defense Industry.

<u>Scientific Attaches</u> follow scientific and technological developments in the country.

<u>Agricultural Officers</u> promote the export of U.S. agricultural products and report on agricultural production and market developments in their area.

The Aid Mission Director is responsible for AID programs, including dollar and local currency loans, grants, and technical assistance.

The Public Affairs Officers is the post's press and cultural affairs specialist and maintains close contact with the local press.

The Legal Attache serves as a representative to the U.S. Department of Justice on criminal matters.

The Communications Program Officer is responsible for the telecommunications, telephone, radio, diplomatic pouches, and records management programs within the diplomatic mission. They maintain close contact with the host government's information/communications authorities on operational matters.

The Information Systems Manager is responsible for the post's unclassified information systems, database management, programming, and operational needs. They liaison with appropriate commercial contacts in the information field to enhance the post's systems integrity.

Business representatives planning a trip overseas should include in their preparations a visit or telephone call to the nearest U.S. Department of Commerce District Office. The District Office can provide extensive information and assistance as well as a current list of legal holidays in the countries to be visited. If desired, the District Officer can also provide advance notice to posts abroad of the representative's visit.

The Department of State, Bureau of Diplomatic Security, can also provide current data on the security situation to interested persons planning trips abroad. American business representatives desiring this information should contact the Diplomatic Security Service, Overseas Support Programs Division (202) 647-3122.

Some of the services jointly provided by the Departments of State and Commerce to U.S. business firms interested in establishing a market for their products or expanding sales abroad include:

-The Trade Opportunities Program (TOP) that provides specific export sales leads of U.S. products and services;

World Traders Data Report (WTDR) that provides detailed financial and commercial information on individual firms abroad upon request from U.S. companies;

-Agent Distributor Service (ADS) that helps U.S. firms find agents or distributors to represent their firms and market their products abroad; and

-Information about foreign markets for U.S. products and services and U.S.-sponsored exhibitions abroad in which American firms can participate and demonstrate their products to key foreign buyers.

-In all matters pertaining to foreign trade, the nearest U.S. Department of Commerce District Office should be your first point of contact. Foreign trade specialists at these facilities render valuable assistance to U.S. business representatives engaged in international commerce.

For additional information about Foreign Service assistance to American business overseas, or for specialized assistance with unusual commercial problems, you are invited to visit, telephone, or write the Office of Commercial, Legislative, and Public Affairs, Bureau of Economic and Business Affairs, U.S. Department of State, Washington, D.C. 20520-5816. Telephone (202) 647-1942.

519

APPENDIX I

HOW TO COMMUNICATE WITH A FOREIGN SERVICE POST

ADDRESSES ARE EXAMPLES ONLY
  EXAMPLES OF
  ACCEPTED FORMS FOR
  ADDRESSING MAIL

Posts with APO/FPO Numbers:

APO/FPO Address*

Name
Organization
PSC or Unit number, Box number
APO AE 09080 or APO AA 34038 or
APO AP 96337

International Address**

Name of Person/Section
American Embassy
P.O. Box 26431***
Manama, Bahrain

Posts without APO/FPO Numbers:

Diplomatic Pouch Address*

Name of Person/Section
Name of Post
Department of State
Washington, D.C. 20521-four digit add-on
(A list of 9-digit ZIP Codes and explanations is
provided below)

International Address*

Name of Person/Section
American Embassy
Jubilaeumstrasse 93***
3005 Bern, Switzerland

NOTE: Do not combine any of the above forms (e.g.,
international plus APO/FPO addresses). This will only
result in confusion and possible delays in delivery. Mail
sent to the Department for delivery through its pouch
system for posts with APO/FPO addresses cannot be
accepted and will be returned to the sender.

The Military Post Service Agency (MPSA) is in the
process of aligning APO/FPO numbers, according to
geographic location, that became effective July 15, 1991.
The APO/FPO and the U.S. Postal Service (USPS) will
provide service under both old and new APO/FPO
numbers until July 15, 1992.

Every person and organization overseas served by the
MPSA gets assigned a new address. For some, the change
includes a new ZIP Code, but for all, the structure of the
last two lines of the address changes. New York, San
Francisco, and Miami are no longer used with the ZIP
Code. AE, AP, and AA will be used. This change will
enable the MPSA mail to be processed on automated
equipment and will result in better mail service.

----
*Use domestic postage.
** Use international postage.
***Use street address only when P.O. box is not supplied.

STATE ZIP CODES

In conjunction with the U.S. Postal Service's new system
of 9-digit ZIP Codes, the Department of State has assigned
a unique 4-digit number to each Foreign Service post. All
mail sent through the Department's pouch system (for posts
without APO/FPO addresses) should add the 4-digit
number to the current ZIP Code 20521. For example, the
new ZIP Code for Abidjan would be 20521-2010; for Abu
Dhabi, 20521-6010. Refer to the following list for each
Foreign Service post's unique number.

Abidjan	2010
Abu Dhabi	6010
Accra	2020
Adana	5020
Addis Ababa	2030
Alexandria	6090
Algiers	6030
Alma-Ata	7030
Amman	6050
Amsterdam	5780
Ankara	7000
Antananarivo	2040
Antwerp	5240

Apia	4400	Dar Es Salaam	2140
Ashkhabad	7070	Dhahran	6310
Asmara	7170	Dhaka	6120
Asuncion	3020	Djibouti	2150
Athens	7100	Doha	6130
Auckland	4370	Douala	2530
Baghdad	6060	Dubai	6020
Baku	7050	Dublin	5290
Bamako	2050	Durban	2490
Bandar Seri Begawan	4020	Dushanbe	7090
Bangkok	7200	Edinburgh	5370
Bangui	2060	Florence	5670
Banjul	2070	Frankfurt	7900
Barcelona	5400	Freetown	2160
Barranquilla	3040	Fukuoka	4310
Beijing	7300	Gaborone	2170
Beirut	6070	Geneva (BO & M)	5120
Belfast	5360	Genoa	5680
Belgrade	5070	Georgetown	3170
Belize	3050	Goteborg	5760
Berlin	5090	Guadalajara	3280
Bern	5110	Guangzhou	4090
Bilbao	5410	Guatemala City	3190
Bishkek	7040	Guayaquil	3430
Bissau	2080	The Hague	5770
Bogota	3030	Halifax	5500
Bombay	6240	Hamburg	5180
Bonn	7400	Hamilton	5300
Bordeaux	5580	Harare	2180
Brasilia	7500	Havana	3200
Bratislava	5840	Helsinki	5310
Brazzaville	2090	Hermosillo	3290
Bridgetown	3120	Hong Kong	8000
Brisbane	4130	Honiara	4390
Brussels		Islamabad	8100
(USNATO - M)	5230	Istanbul	5030
Brussels (E)	7600	Izmir	5040
Bucharest	5260	Jakarta	8200
Budapest	5270	Jeddah	6320
Buenos Aires	3130	Jerusalem	6350
Bujumbura	2100	Johannesburg	2500
Cairo	7700	Kaduna	2260
Calcutta	6250	Kampala	2190
Calgary	5490	Karachi	6150
Canberra	7800	Kathmandu	6190
Cape Town	2480	Khartoum	2200
Caracas	3140	Kiev	5850
Casablanca	6280	Kigali	2210
Cebu	4230	Kingston	3210
Chengdu	4080	Kinshasa	2220
Chiang Mai	4040	Kolonia	4120
Ciudad Juarez	3270	Koror	4260
Colombo	6100	Krakow	5140
Conakry	2110	Kuala Lumpur	4210
Copenhagen	5280	Kuwait	6200
Cotonou	2120	Lagos	8300
Curacao	3160	Lahore	6160
Dakar	2130	La Paz	3220
Damascus	6110	Leipzig	5860

521

Libreville	2270	Panama City	9100
Lilongwe	2280	Paramaribo	3390
Lima	3230	Paris	9200
Lisbon	5320	Perth	4160
Ljubljana	7140	Peshawar	6170
Lome	2300	Phnom Penh	4540
London	8400	Ponta Delgada	5340
Luanda	2550	Port-au-Prince	3400
Lubumbashi	2230	Port Louis	2450
Lusaka	2310	Port Moresby	4240
Luxembourg	5380	Porto Alegre	3070
Lyon	5590	Port-of-Spain	3410
Madras	6260	Poznan	5050
Madrid	8500	Prague	5630
Majuro	4350	Praia	2460
Malabo	2320	Pretoria	9300
Managua	3240	Pusan	4270
Manama	6210	Quebec	5520
Manila	8600	Quito	3420
Maputo	2330	Rabat	9400
Maracaibo	3150	Rangoon	4250
Marseille	5600	Recife	3080
Martinique	3250	Riga	4520
Maseru	2340	Reykjavik	5640
Matamoros	3300	Riga	4520
Mazatlan	3310	Rio de Janeiro	3090
Mbabane	2350	Riyadh	6300
Medan	4190	Rome	9500
Melbourne	4140	St George's	3180
Merida	3320	St Johns	3010
Mexico City	8700	St. Petersburgh	5440
Milan	5690	Salzburg	5830
Minsk	7010	San Jose	3440
Mogadishu	2360	San Salvador	3450
Mombasa	2400	Sanaa	6330
Monrovia	8800	Santiago	3460
Monterrey	3330	Santo Domingo	3470
Montevideo	3360	Sao Paulo	3110
Montreal	5510	Sapporo	4340
Moroni	2380	Sarajevo	7130
Moscow	5430	Seoul	9600
Munich	5190	Shanghai	4100
Muscat	6220	Shenyang	4110
Naha	4320	Singapore	4280
Nairobi	8900	Sofia	5740
Naples	5700	Songkhla	4050
Nassau	3370	Stockholm	5750
N'Djamena	2410	Strasbourg	5620
New Delhi	9000	Stuttgart	5200
Niamey	2420	Surabaya	4200
Nicosia	5450	Suva	4290
Nouakchott	2430	Sydney	4150
Nuevo Laredo	3340	Tallinn	4530
Oran	6040	Tashkent	7110
Osaka-Kobe	4330	Tbilisi	7060
Oslo	5460	Tegucigalpa	3480
Ottawa	5480	Tel Aviv	9700
Ouagadougou	2440	Thessaloniki	5060
Palermo	5710	Tijuana	3350

Tirana	9510
Tokyo	9800
Toronto	5530
Tunis	6360
Udorn	4060
Ulaanbaatar	4410
Valletta	5800
Vancouver	5540
Vatican City	5660
Victoria	2510
Vienna	9900
Vientiane	4350
Vilnius	4510
Vladivostok	5880
Warsaw	5010
Wellington	4360
Windhoek	2540
Yaounde	2520
Yerevan	7020
Zagreb	5080
Zurich	5130

TELEPHONING A FOREIGN SERVICE POST

Below is the procedure for telephoning a Foreign Service post. American Embassy Canberra is used as an example.

Calling From a U.S. Government Agency:

Dial 9 + international access code + country code + city code + local number

Ex: 9 + 011 + [61] + (6) + 2705000

Others:
Dial international access code + country code + city code + local number

Ex: 011 + [61] + (6) + 2705000

NOTE: Some international calls will require operator assistance because the country is not an international dial country. The telephone listing for these countries will not be preceded by a country code and city code (always shown in brackets and parentheses).

Calls to certain points outside the continental U.S. can be dialed in the same manner as long distance. Simply dial the area code or country code and the local number. For these locations, no city code will appear with the telephone number.

APPENDIX J

U.S. GOVERNMENT PASSPORT AGENCIES

APPLY EARLY FOR YOUR PASSPORT!

Boston Passport Agency
Thomas P. O'Neill Fed. Bldg., Rm.247 10
Causeway Street Boston, Massachusetts 02222
*Recording: 617-565-6698
Public Inquiries: 617-565-6990

Chicago Passport Agency
Suite 380, Kluczynski Federal Bldg. 230 South
Dearborn Street Chicago, Illinois 60604-1564
*Recording: 312-353-5426
Public Inquiries: 312-353-7155 or 7163

Honolulu Passport Agency
Room C-106, New Federal Bldg. 300 Ala
Moana Blvd. Honolulu, Hawaii 96850
*Recording: 808-541-1918
Public Inquiries: 808-541-1918

Houston Passport Agency
Concord Towers 1919 Smith Street, Ste. 1100
Houston, Texas 77002
*Recording: 713-653-3159
Public Inquiries: 713-653-3153

Los Angeles Passport Agency
Room 13100, 11000 Wilshire Boulevard
Los Angeles, California 90024-3615
*Recording: 213-209-7070
Public Inquiries: 213-209-7075

Miami Passport Agency
3rd Floor, Federal Office Bldg.
51 Southwest First Avenue Miami, Florida
33130-1680
*Recording: 305-536-5395 (English)
305-536-4448 (Spanish)
Public Inquiries: 305-536-4681

New Orleans Passport Agency
Postal Services Building
701 Loyola Avenue, Room T-12005
New Orleans, Louisiana 70113-1931
*Recording: 504-589-6728
Public Inquiries: 504-589-6161
New York Passport Agency
Room 270, Rockefeller Center

630 Fifth Avenue, New York, New York
10111-0031
*Recording: 212-541-7700
Public inquiries: 212-541-7710

Philadelphia Passport Agency
Room 4426, Federal Bldg.
600 Arch Street, Philadelphia, Pennsylvania
19106-1684
*Recording: 215-597-7482
Public Inquiries: 215-597-7480

San Francisco Passport Agency
Suite 200, 525 Market Street
San Francisco, California 94105-2773
*Recording: 415-974-7972
Public Inquiries: 415-974-9941

Seattle Passport Agency
Room 992, Federal Office Bldg.
915 Second Avenue Seattle, Washington
98174-1091
*Recording: 206-553-7941
Public Inquiries: 206-553-7945

Stamford Passport Agency
One Landmark Square
Broad and Atlantic Streets
Stamford, Connecticut 06901-2767
*Recording: 203-325-4401
Public Inquiries: 203-325-3538, 3530

Washington Passport Agency
1425 K Street, N.W.
Washington, D.C. 20524-0002
*Recording: 202-647-0518
Public Inquiries: 202-647-0518

---

*   The 24-hour recording includes general passport information, passport agency location, and hours of operation and information regarding emergency passport services during non-working hours

**   For other questions, call Public Inquiries number.

APPENDIX K

VISA AND PASSPORT AGENCIES[OG]

ATLANTA, GA

International Visa Service, Inc., 278 Hilderbrand Dr. NE. Box 720715, Zip, 30328. TEL: 404/843-0005, Continental U.S. (except GA) 800 843-0050. Hours. 9 AM - 5,30 PM (Mon.-Wed., Fri.); 9 AM - 12 Noon (Sat.); 9 AM - 7:30 PM (Thurs.).

BALTIMORE, MD

Harbor City Visa Services, 1635 Eastern Ave., Zip, 21231. TEL: 301/342-8472. Hours, 1 PM - 5 PM (Mon.-Fri.).

Visa Adventure, Inc., 205 Hillendale Ave., Zip: 21227. TEL: 301/242-5602. Hours: 8:30 AM - 4 PM (Mon.-Fri.).

BOSTON, MA

Visa Service, Inc., 581 Boylston St., Zip: 02116. TEL: 617/266-7646. FAX, 617/262-9829. Hours, 9 AM - 5 PM (Mon.-Fri.).

CHICAGO, IL

Adventure Seekers Tours, 36 W. Randolph, Zip: 60601. TEL: 312/346-9100. Hours, 9:30 AM - 5:30 PM (Mon.-Fri.).

American Visa Service, Inc., 53 W. Jackson, Ste. 803, Zip: 60604. TEL: 312/922-8860. Hours, 9 AM - 5 PM (Mon.-Fri.).

Chicago Visa Service, 201 N. Wells, Rm. 430, Zip: 60606. TEL: 312/332-7211. Hours: 9 AM - 5 PM (Mon.-Fri.); 9 AM - 1 PM (Sat.).

Perry International Inc., 100 W. Monroe St., Zip: 60603. TEL: 312/372-2703. Hours: 9 AM - 5 PM (Mon.-Fri.).

DALLAS, TX

Dallas Visa Service, 2755 Valley View Lane, Ste. 103., Zip: 75234. TEL: 214/241-9900. Hours, 8:30 AM - 5 PM (Mon.-Fri.).

Passport and Visa Express, 2132 Willowbrook Way, Ste. 100, Zip: 75075. TEL: 214/867-7707. Continental U.S. 800-344-2810; FAX: 214/867-6006. Hours: 7 AM - 7 PM (Mon.-Fri.); 9 AM - 3 PM (sat.).

Wide World Visas, Greenville Bank Tower, 7515 Greenville Ave., Ste. 407, Zip: 75231. TEL: 214/739-5710. Hours: 8:30 AM - 5 PM (Mon.-Fri.).

DENVER, CO

International Passport Visas, Inc., 1325 S. Colorado Blvd., Ste. 604, Zip: 80222. 24 Hour Answering Service. TEL: 303/753-0424, Continental U.S., AK, HI 800-783-VISA. Hours: 9 AM - 5 PM (Mon.-Sun.).

FOUNTAIN VALLEY, CA

South Coast Visa & Passport Service, 18854 Brookhurst, Zip: 92708. TEL: 714/963-8464. Hours: 9 AM - 5 PM (Mon.-Fri.).

HOUSTON, TX

Visas & International Passports, 507 Dallas St., Ste. 304, Zip: 77002. TEL: 713/759-9119. Continental U.S. 800-876-VISA; FAX: 713/759-9589. Hours, 8 AM - 6 PM (Mon.-Fri.); 10 AM - 3 Pm (Sat.).

Wide World Visas, 1200 Smith St., Ste. 875, Zip: 77002. TEL: 713/655-9074, Continental U.S. (except TX), AK, HI 800-527-1861, TX 800-833-5423. Hours: 9 AM - 5 PM (Mon.-Fri.).

LAKEWOOD, OH

Adventure International Travel, 14305 Madison Ave., Zip: 44107. TEL: 216/228-7171. Hours. 9 AM - 6 PM (Mon.-Fri.); 9 AM - 2 PM (Sat.).

LOS ANGELES, CA

Consular Visa Assistance, 4276 Brunswick Ave, Zip: 90039. TEL: 818/241-4202. Hours:

8:30 AM - 5:30 PM (7 Days).

Intercontinental Visa Services, Los Angeles World Trade Center, 350 S. Figueroa, Ste. 185. Zip: 90071. TEL: 213/625-7175. Hours, 9 AM - 5 PM (Mon.-Fri.).

Visas International, 3169 Barbara Ct., Ste. F, Zip: 90068. TEL: 213/850-1192, Continental U.S. 800-638-1517. Hours. 9 AM - 12 PM 1:30 PM - 5 PM (Mon.-Fri.).

NEW YORK, NY

Foreign Visa Service, 18 E. 93rd St, Zip: 10128. TEL: 212/876-5890. Hours: 9 AM - 5 PM (Mon.-Fri.) & by appointment.

Mr. Visas Inc., 211 E. 43rd St, Zip: 10017. TEL: 212/682-3895. Hours: 9 AM - 7 PM (Mon.-Fri.); 10:30 AM - 2:30 PM (Sat.).

Passport Plus, 677 Fifth Ave., Zip: 10022. TEL: 212/759-5540, Continental U.S. (except NY) 800-367-1818. Hours: 9:30 AM - 5:30 PM (Mon.-Fri.).

Travel Agenda, Inc. (DBA "VISA PROS"), 119 W. 57th St. Zip: 10019. TEL: 212/265-7887, Continental U.S. 800-683-0119; FAX: 212/581-8144. Hours. 9:30 AM - 5:30 PM (Mon.-Fri.).

Visa Center, Inc., 507 Fifth Ave., Ste. 904, Zip: 10017. TEL: 212/986-0924. Hours. 9 AM - 4:45 PM (Mon.-Fri.).

ORANGE, CA

Orange County Visa & Passport Service, 309 N. Rampart, Zip: 92668. TEL: 714/385-2595. Hours. 8:30 AM - 5 PM (Mon.-Fri.).

Visa Consultants, 450 E. Chapman Ave., Ste. 102. Zip: 92666. TEL: 714/633 0839, Southern CA 800 441-VISA. Hours: 8:30 AM - 2:30 PM (Mon.-Fri.).

PHILADELPHIA, PA

New York Connection Visa Service, 1617 JFK Blvd., Ste. 630, Zip: 19103. TEL: 215/564 2300. Continental U.S., AK, HI 800-247-2300; FAX: 215/564-9927. Hours: 9 AM - 6 PM (Mon.-Fri.).

SALT LAKE CITY, UT

The Travel Broker-Express Visa & Passport, 1061 E. 2100 South, Zip: 84106. TEL: 801/486-7800. Hours: 9 AM - 5 PM (Mon.-Fri.).

SAN FRANCISCO, CA

Trans World Visa Service, 790 27th Ave., Box 22068, Zip: 94121. TEL: 415/752 6957, Continental U.S. (except CA) 800-848-9980; FAX: 415-752-0804. Hours: 9 AM - 5 PM (Mon.-Fri.).

Visa Aides, 870 Market St., Zip: 94102. TEL: 415/362-7137. Hours: 9 AM - 5 PM (Mon.-Fri.).

Visas Unlimited, 582 Market, Ste. 900, Zip: 94104. TEL, 415/421-7351. Hours: 9 AM - 5 PM (Mon.-Fri.).

Zierer Visa Service, 703 Market St., Ste. 802, Zip: 94103. TEL: 415/495-5216, Continental U.S. 800-843-9151; FAX: 415/495-4491. Hours: 7 AM - 5 PM (Mon.-Fri.).

SEATTLE, WA

Visa Services Northwest, Plaza 600 Bldg., Ste. 1900, Zip: 98101. TEL: 206/448 8400. Hours: 9 AM - 4:30 PM (Mon.-Fri.).

WASHINGTON, DC

Atlas Visa Service, Inc., 2341 Jefferson Davis Hwy., Ste, 116 (Arlington, VA), Zip: 22202. 24 Hour Answering Service. TEL: 703/418-0800. Hours: 8 AM - 6 PM (Mon.-Fri.).

Center For International Business & Travel, Inc., 2135 Wisconsin Ave. NW, Ste. 400, Zip: 20007. TEL: 202/333-5550, Continental U.S., AK, HI 800-424-2429. Hours: 8:30 AM - 6:30 PM (Mon.-Fri.).

Diran Visa & Translation Service, 1511 K St. NW, Ste. 309, Zip: 20005. TEL: 202/638-4328. Hours: 9 AM - 5 PM (Mon.-Fri.).

Express Visa, 150 Wisconsin Ave., Ste. 20, Zip: 20007. 24 Hour Answering Service. TEL: 202/337-2442. Hours: 9 AM - 6 PM (Mon.-Fri.).

Mercury Visa Service, 2004 17th St. NW, Zip: 20009. TEL: 202/939-8851, Continental U.S. 800-526-8456; FAX: 202/667-5303. Hours: 8:30 AM - 5 PM (Mon.-Fri.).

Nader Visa Service, Inc., 1325 18th St., NW, Ste. 104, Zip: 20036. TEL: 202/332-7797; 332-7650. Hours: 9 AM - 5 PM (Mon.-Fri.), 10 AM - 12 Noon (Sat.).

Passport & Visa Services, 1377 K St. NW, Zip: 20005. TEL: 202/293-6245, Continental U.S. (except DC) 800-237-3270. Hours: 8:30 AM - 5 PM (Mon.-Fri.); 10 AM - 1 PM (Sat.).

Trav-All Visa Service, 7311 Rockford Dr., Box 523 (Falls Church, VA), Zip: 22040. TEL: 703/698-1777. Hours: 9 AM - 5 PM (Mon.-Fri.).

Travel Document Systems, 734 15th St. NW, Ste. 400, Zip: 20005. TEL: 202/638-3800, Continental U.S. (except DC) 800-424-8472. Hours: 10 AM - 7 PM (Mon.-Fri.).

Travisa, Inc., 2122 P St. NW, Zip: 20037. TEL: 202/436-6166, Continental U.S. (except DC) 800-222-2589. Hours: 8:30 AM - 5:30 PM (Mon.-Fri.).

Visa Advisors, 1808 Swann St. NW, Zip: 20009. TEL: 202/797-7976. FAX: 202/667-6708. Hours: 9 AM - 5 PM (Mon.-Fri.).

Visa Fox International, 2020 Pennsylvania Ave. NW Ste, 123, Zip: 20006. TEL: 202/785-0787, Continental U.S., AK, HI 800-635-1047. Hours: 9 Am - 5 PM (Mon.-Fri.).

Visa Passport & Immigration Service, 815 15th St. NW, Ste. 537, Zip: 20005. TEL: 202/783-6290. Hours: 9 AM - 5:30 PM (Mon.-Fri.).

Visa Services, Inc., 1519 Connecticut Ave. NW, Ste. 300, Zip: 20036. TEL: 202/387-0300, Continental U.S. (except DC) AK, HI 800-222-VISA. Hours: 9 AM - 5:30 PM (Mon.-Fri.).

Washington Passport & Visa Service, Inc., 2318 18th St. NW, Zip: 20009. TEL: 202/234-7667, Continental U.S. (except DC) 800-272-7776; FAX: 202/462-2335. Hours: 9 AM - 5 PM (Mon.-Fri.).

Zierer Visa Service, 1521 New Hampshire Ave. NW, Ste. 100, Zip: 20036. TEL: 202/265-3007, Continental U.S. 800-421-6706, FAX: 202/265-3061. Hours: 9 AM - 5:30 PM (Mon.-Fri.).

CAUTION: *The listing of these companies (agencies) should not be interpreted as a recommendation from this author or publisher. As always, you must exercise prudence in dealing with any services of this type. Refer to the section in the book, entitled passport scam.*

APPENDIX L

FOREIGN GOVERNMENT TOURIST BOARDS AND OFFICES IN THE U.S.*

ANDORRA
Andorra Tourist Office
120 East 55th street
Nwe York, NY 10022
(212) 688-8681

AUSTRIA
Austrian Tourist
Information Office
P.O. Box 1142
New York, NY 10108
(212) 944-6880

ANGUILLA
Anguilla Tourist Office
c/o Medhurst & Assoc
271 Main St.
Northport, NY 11768
(516) 261-1234

ANDORRA
Andorra Tourist Office
120 East 55th Street
New York, NY 10022
(212) 688-8681

ANTIGUA AND BARBUDA
Antigua Dept. of Tourism
& Trade
610 5th Ave. Ste 311
New York, NY 10020
(212) 541-4117

ARGENTINA
Argentina Tourist
Information
12 W. 56th Street
New York, NY 10019
(212) 603-0443

ARMENIA
Armenian Tourism
122 C Street, NW
Washington, DC 20001
(202) 393-5983

AUSTRALIA
Australian Natl. Tourist
Office
489 Fifth Ave. 31st flr.
New York, NY 10017
(212) 687-6300

AUSTRIA
Austrian Natl. Tourist
Office
500 Fifth Ave. Ste.2009.
New York, NY 10110
(212) 944-6880

BAHAMAS
Bahamas Tourist Office
150 E. 52nd St
28th Floor, North
New York, NY 10022
(212) 758-2777

BARBADOS
Barbados Board of Tourism
800 2nd Ave. 17th Floor
New York, NY 10017
(212) 986-6516

BELGIUM
Belgian Tourist Office
780 Third Avenue # 1501
New York, NY 10017
(212) 758-8130

BELIZE
Belize Tourist Board
8 Haven Avenue,
Port Washington, NY
11050, 800-624-0686;
(516) 944-8554

BERMUDA
Bermuda Gov't. Travel
Info. Center
310 Madison Avenue
New York, NY 10017
(212) 818-9800

BOLIVIA
Bolivian Tourism
211 E. 43rd Street #702
New York, NY 10017
(212) 687-0530

BONAIRE
Bonaire Government
Tourist Office
275 7th Ave. 19th floor
New York, NY 10001-
6788 (212) 242-7707

BRAZIL
Brazil Tourism Office
551 5th Ave. Ste. 519
New York, NY 10176
(212) 286-9600

BRITISH VIRGIN ISLANDS
British Virgin Islands
Tourist Board
370 Lexington Ave.,
Ste.511
New York, NY 10017
(800) 835-8530

BULGARIA
Bulgarian Tourist Office
c\o Balkan Holidays
42nd Street, Suite 508
New York, NY 10017
(212) 573-5530

BHUTAN
Bhutan Travel Inc.
120 E. 56 Street, Ste. 1130
New York, NY 1022
(212) 838-6382

BURKINA FASO
Africa Travel Association
347 Fifth Ave. Suite 610
New York, NY 10036
(212) 447-1926

528

CAMEROON
Africa Travel Association
347 Fifth Ave. Suite 610
New York, NY 10036
(212) 447-1926

CANADA
Canadian Government -
Office of Tourism
1251 Ave. of the Americas
New York, NY 10020
(212) 581-2280

CAYMAN ISLANDS
Cayman Islands Dept of
Tourism
980 N. Michigan Ave.,
Suite 1260 Chicago, IL.
00611, (312) 944-5602

CHILE
Chilean National Tourist
Board
510 W. Sixth St. #1204
Los Angeles, CA 90014
(213) 627-4293

**CHINA, PEOPLES
REPUBLIC**
China Natl. Tourist Office
50 East 42nd St. Rm. 3126
New York, NY 10165
(212) 867-0271

CHINA, TAIWAN
Taiwan Visitors Assoc.
One World Trade Center,
Ste. 8855, New York, NY
10048

COLUMBIA
Columbian Government
Tourist Office
140 East 57th St. 2nd
Floor, New York, NY
10022, (212) 688-0151

COOK ISLAND
Cook Island Tourist
Authority
6033 W. century Blvd.
#690, Los Angeles, CA
90045 (310) 216-2872

CYPRUS
Cyprus Tourism Organ.
Cyprus Trade Center
13 E. 40th St.
New York, NY 10016

(212) 683-5280

CZECH REPUBLIC
Cedok Czechoslovakian
Travel Office
10 E. 40th. St.,Suite 3604
New York, NY 10016
(212) 689-9720

DENMARK
Danish Tourist Board
655 Third Ave.
New York, Ny 10017
(212) 949-2333

DOMINICANREPUBLIC
Dominican Rep. Tourist
Info. Center
485 Madison Avenue
New York, NY 10022
(212) 826-0750

EGYPT
Egyptian Government
Tourist Office
630 Fifth Avenue
New York, NY 10111
(212) 332-2570

EL SALVADOR
El Salvador Tourist Bureau
P.O. Box 818 Dept RB
Radio City, NY 10019

ESTONIA
Estonia Tourism
630 Fifth Avenue, Ste.
2415; New York, NY
10111 (212) 247-1450

FINLAND
Finnish Tourist Board
655 Third Avenue
New York, NY 10017
(212) 949-2333

FRANCE
French Government Tourist
Office
610 Fifth Avenue
New York, NY 10020
(212) 757-1125

GABON
Gabon Tourist Information
Office
347 Fifth Ave. Suite 1100
New York, NY 10016
(212) 447-6701

**FEDERAL REPUBLIC
OF GERMANY**
German Natl. Tourist
Office
122 E. 42nd St. 52nd Floor
New York, NY 10168
(212) 661-7200

GHANA
Ghana Trade & Investment
Office
19 E. 47th St.
New York, NY 10017
(212) 832-1300

GREAT BRITAIN
British Tourist Authority
551 5th Ave, 7th Flr.
New York, NY. 10176
(212) 986-2200, 800/462-
2748

GREECE
Greek Natl. Tourist Organ.
645 Fifth Avenue
New York, NY 10022
(212) 421-5777

GRENADA
Grenada Tourist Office
820 2nd Ave. Ste.900D
New York, NY 10017
(212) 687-9554

GUADELOUPE
French West Indies Tourist
Board
610 Fifth Ave.
New York, NY 10020
(212) 757-1125

GUATEMALA
Guatemala Tourist Office
299 Alhambra Circle #510
Coral Gables FL 33134
800-742-4529 (305) 442-
0651

HONG KONG
Hong Kong Tourist Assoc.
590 Fifth Avenue, 5th flr.
New York, NY 10036
(212) 869-5008

HONDURAS
c/o SAHSA Airlines
360 W. 31st Street, 4th fl.
New York, NY 10001
800-238-4043, 212-564-

0378

HUNGARY
Hungarian Travel Bureau
One Parker Plaza, Suite
1104 Fort Lee, NJ 07024
(201) 592-8585

ICELAND
Iceland Tourist Board
655 Third Ave.
New York, NY 10017
(212) 949-2333

INDIA
Government of India
Tourist Office
30 Rockefeller Plaza
New York, NY 10112
(212) 586-4901

INDONESIA
Indonesian Tourist
Promotion Office
5 E. 68th Street, New
York, NY 10021
(212) 879-0600

IRELAND
Irish Tourist Board
757 3rd Ave.; New York,
NY 10017; (212) 418-
0800, 800/223-6470

ISRAEL
Isreal Government Tourism
Office
350 Fifth Avenue
New York, NY 10118
(212) 560-0600

ITALY
Italian Government Travel
Office
630 Fifth Ave. Suite 1565
New York, NY 10111
(212) 245-4822

JAMAICA
Jamaica Tourist Board
801 2nd Ave 2oth flr.
New York, NY 10017
(212) 856-9727, 800/233-
4582

JAPAN
Japan Natl. Tourist Org.
630 Fifth Ave. Ste. 2101
New York, NY 10111

(212) 757-5640

JORDAN
Jordan Information Bureau
2319 Wyoming Avenue
NW.; Washington DC
20008; (202) 265-1606

KENYA
Kenya Tourist Office
424 Madison Avenue
New York, NY 10017
(212) 486-1300

KOREA
Korea Natl. Tourism Corp.
2 Executive Dr.
Fort Lee, N.J. 07024
(201) 585-0909

LATVIA
4325 17th Street NW
Washington DC 20011
(202) 726-6785

LESOTHO
Embassy of Lesotho,
Tourist Board
2511 Massachuettes Ave.
NW Washington, DC
20008 (202) 797-5533

LIECHTENSTEIN
Liechtenstein Natl. Tourist
Office
608 Fifth Ave.
New York, NY 10020
(212) 757-5944

LITHUANIA
Lithuania Tourism
2622 16th Street NW
Washington DC 20009
(202) 234-5860

LUXEMBURG
Luxemburg Natl. Tourist
Office
17 Beekman Place.
New York, NY 10022
(212) 935-8888

MACAU
Macau Tourit Info. Bureau
70A Greenwich Ave.
Ste.316, New York, NY
10011, (212) 206-6828

MALAYSIA

Malaysian Tourist Center
818 W Seventh St. # 804
Los Angeles, CA 90017
(213) 689-9702

MALAWI
Malawi Tourism
600 Third Ave.
New York, NY 10016
(212) 949-0180

MALDIVES
(See Sri Lanka)

MALTA
Malta Tourism Office
Consulate of Malta
249 E. 35th St.
New York, NY 10016
(212) 213-6686

MARTINIQUE
French West Indies Tourist
Board
610 Fifth Ave.
New York, NY 10020
(212) 757-1125

MAURITIUS
Mauritius Government
Tourist Office
40 J. Pask Associates Inc.
415 Seventh Ave.
New York, NY 10001
(212) 239-8350

MEXICO
Mexican Govt. Tourism
Office
405 Park Ave. Suite 1002
New York, NY 10022
(212) 755-7261

MONACO
Monaco Govt. Tourist
Office
845 Third Ave.
New York, NY 10022
(212) 759-5227

MOROCCO
Moroccan Tourist Board
20 E. 46th St.
New York, NY 10017
(212) 557-2520

MYANMAR (BURMA)
Myanmar Tourist Agency
10 E. 77th Street

530

New York, NY 10021
(212) 535-1310

NETHERLANDS
Netherlands Board of
Tourism Office
355 Lexington Ave.
New York, NY 10017
(212) 370-7367

**N E T H E R L A N D
ANTILLES**
Curacoa Tourist Board
400 Madison Ave. Suite
311 New York, NY 10017
(212) 751-8266

NEW ZEALAND
New Zealand Tourism
Office
510 Santa Monica Blvd.
#300, Los Angeles CA
90024
(310) 395-7480, 800/388-
5494

NIGERIA
Nigerian Info. Service
Center
828 Second Ave.
New York, NY 10017
(212) 808-0310

NORWAY
Norwegian Tourist Board
655 Third Ave.
New York, NY 10017
(212) 949-2333

PAKISTAN
Pakistan Tourism
12 E. 65th Street
New York,NY 10021
(212) 897-5800

PAPUA NEW GUINEA
Papua New Guinea
Information Office
c\o Air Niugini
5000 Birch St, Stew. 3000
Newport Beach, CA 92660
(714) 752-5440

PANAMA
Panama Government
Tourist Bureau
Airport Exec. Tower 2
7270 NW 12th St.
Coral Gables, FL 33134

PERU
Peru-FOPTUR
10629 N. Kendall Drive
Miami, FL 33176
800-854-0023, 305/279-
8494

PHILIPPINE
Philippine Dept. of
Tourism
556 Fifth Ave., New York,
NY. 10036; (212) 675-
7915

POLAND
Polish Natl. Tourist Office
275 Madison Avenue.
Ste.1711; New York, NY
10016 (212) 338-9412

PORTUGAL
Portuguese Natl. Tourist
Office
590 Fifth Ave. 4th fl.
New York, NY 10036
(212) 354-4403

ROMANIA
Romanian Natl. Tourist
Office
573 Third Avenue
New York, NY 10016
(212) 697-6971

SENEGAL
Senegal Tourist Office
888 Seventh Avenue, 27th
flr. New York, NY 10106
(212) 757-7115

SINGAPORE
Singapore Tourist Promo.
Board
590 Fifth Ave. 12th Flr.
Nwe York, NY 10036
(212) 302-4861

ST. KITTS-NEVIS
St. Kitts-Nevis Tourist
Office
414 E. 75th St.
New York, NY 10021
(212) 535-1234

ST. LUCIA
St. Lucia Tourist Board
820 2nd Ave. Suite 900
New York, NY 10017
(212) 867-2950

ST. MAARTEN
St. Maarten Tourist Office
275 7th Ave. 19th flr.
New York, NY 10017
(212) 989-0000

SEYCHELLES
Seychelles Tourist Office
820 Second Ave. Suite
900F New York, NY
10017; (212) 687-9766

SLOVENIA
Slovanian Tourist Office
122 E. 42nd Street, Ste.
3006; New York, NY
10168 (212) 682-5896

SOUTH AFRICA
South African Tourist
Board
500 Fifth Ave, 20th flr.
New York, NY 10110
(212) 730-2929

SPAIN
Spanish Government
Tourist Office
665 Fifth Ave.
New York, NY 10022
(212) 759-8822

SRI LANKA
Sri Lanka Tourist
Department
Embassy of Sri Lanka
2148 Wyoming Ave. NW
Washington, DC 20008
(202) 483-4025

SURINAM
Surinam Tourist Office
866 UN Plaza #320
New York, NY 10017
(212) 826-0660

SWEDEN
Swedish Tourist Board
655 Third Ave.
New York, NY 10017
(212) 949-2333

SWITZERLAND
Swiss Natl. Tourist Office
608 Fifth Ave.
New York, NY 10020
(212) 757-5944

TAHITI

Tahiti Tourism Board
300 N. Continental Blvd.
Ste. 180, El Segundo, CA
90245, (310) 414-8484

TAIWAN
Taiwan Visitors
Association
One World Trade Center,
Ste. 7953, New York, NY
10048, (212) 466-0692

TANZANIA
Tanzania Tourist Office
205 E. 42nd St.
13th flr. Rm. 1300
New York, NY 10017
(212) 972-9160

THAILAND
Thailand Tourism
Authority
5 World Trade Center, Ste.
3443, New York, NY
10048; (212) 432-0433

TOGO
Togo Info. Service
1706 R St. NW
Washington, DC 20009
(202) 667-8181

TRINIDAD AND TOBAGO
Trinidad & Tobago
Tourism Dev. Authority
25 W. 43rd St. Suite 1508
New York, NY 10036
(212) 719-0540

TURKEY
Turkish Government
Tourism Office
821 United Nations Plaza
New York, NY 10017
(212) 687-2194

UGANDA
Uganda Tourism
336 E. 45th Street
New York, NY 10017
(212) 949-0110

VANUATU
Vanuatu National Tourism
Office
520 Montery Drive, Dio
del Mar, Ca 95003, (408)
685-8901

VENEZUELA
Venezuelan Tourism
Organization
P.O. Box 3010, Sausalito,
CA 94966 (415)331-0100

ZAMBIA
Zambia Tourist Office
237 E. 52nd Street
New York, NY 10022

ZIMBABWE
Zimbabwe Tourist Office
1270 Avenue of the
Americas, ste. 412
New York, NY 10020
(212) 332-1090

NOTE:
Tourism information for
those countries not listed
here (basically countries
that do not have separate
touris offices) can be
obtained by calling their
respective embassies or
consulates.

APPENDIX M

HOW TO OBTAIN AN INTERNATIONAL DRIVER'S PERMIT

Although most countries no longer require an International Drivers Permit (IDP), it is advisable to verify in advance if such a permit is required or recommended for the country you plan to visit. Your travel agent, travel advisor, or the country's tourist bureau or Embassy should be able to provide you with that information. You may also contact your local automobile association or the American Automobile Association. One of the important advantages of the IDP is that it is written in nine different, major languages.

Here are the requirements to apply for an International Drivers Permit from the American Automobile Association (AAA).

Requirements:

    (1)   A completed application form;

    (2)   two recent signed passport size photograph not larger than 2 1/2" by 2 1/2";

    (3)   A $10 permit fee;

    (4)   Applicant must be 15 years or older;

    *(5)   Applicant must hold a valid U.S. or Territorial Driver's License.

You may request for an IDP by mail or in person. You are not required to be an AAA member to get and IDP from them. Check your telephone directories for an AAA office in your area you, or you may contact their headquarters at AAA Drive, Heathrow, Florida 32746-5063. Telephone: (407) 444-4000.

---

*Applicants with driving violations may be refused permit.

533

APPENDIX N

TO REPORT LOST OR STOLEN CREDIT/CHARGE CARD*
OR TO ARRANGE FOR CARD REPLACEMENT

CARD	IN U.S./CARIBBEAN	OUTSIDE U.S./OVERSEAS
VISA	800-336-8472	CALL COLLECT:(314) 275-6690
VISA GOLD	800-847-2911	CALL COLLECT:(314) 275-6690
MASTERCARD	800-826-2181	CALL COLLECT:(314) 275-6690
DINNERS CLUB	800-525-9135	CALL COLLECT:(303) 790-2433
AMERICAN EXPRESS*		
Personal Card (Green)	800-528-4800	CALL COLLECT:(919) 668-6668
Corporate Card	800-528-2122	CALL COLLECT:(602) 492-5450
Gold Card	800-528-2121	CALL COLLECT:(305) 476-2166
Platinum Card	800-525-3355	CALL COLLECT:(602) 492-5450
Optima Card	800-635-5955	CALL COLLECT:(602) 492-5450
Travelers Checks	800-221-7282	CALL COLLECT:(801) 964-6665
THOMAS COOK		
Travelers Checks	800-223-7373	CALL COLLECT:(609) 987-7300

---

*In the event of a stolen or lost Credit/Charge Card, it is advisable to quickly file a report with the local Police. Request a copy of the report for your file. American Express Cardholders are advised to call or visit the nearest American Express Travel Service Office immediately and/or call collect. Apply the same procedure as with cards, in the event your travelers checks are stolen or lost.

OFFICES OF CORPORATE CHARGE CARD ISSUERS

Air Travel Card
1301 Pennsylvania Ave., NW
Washington, DC 20004
(800) 222-4688, (202) 624-4224
Fax: (202) 626-4242

American Express Travel Management Services
World Financial Center
200 Vesey St.
New York, NY 10285
(800) 528-2122; (212) 640-2000
Fax: (312) 380-5483

Citicorp Diners Club
8430 W. Bryn Mawr Ave.

Chicago, IL 60631
(800) 2-DINERS; (312) 380-5467
Fax: (3112) 380-5483

Mastercard International
Seventh Ave.
New York, NY 10106
(800) 727-8825; (212) 649-5535
Fax: (212) 649-4772

VISA USA
P.O. Box 8999
San Francisco, CA 94128
(800) 847-2221; (415) 432-2076
Fax: (415) 432-8153

APPENDIX O

TO SEND MONEY/TELEX/TELEGRAM/CABLEGRAM (From the U.S.)

WIRING MONEY

WESTERN UNION   800-325-6000 or 800-257-4900

AMERICAN EXPRESS (MONEYGRAM)   800-543-4080.
From Abroad CALL COLLECT: (303) 980-3340

BANK OF AMERICA
(GLOBAL SELLERS NETWORK)   800-227-3460

CITIBANK   (212) 657-5161

BARCLAYS+   (212) 233-4200

TELEX/TELEGRAM/CABLEGRAM

WESTERN UNION   800-325-6000 or 800-257-4900

AT&T (EASYLINK)*   800-242-6005

---

* May be available only to subscribers.

+ Must have a Barclays account.

APPENDIX P

INTERNATIONAL AIRLINES

AER LINGUS
122 E. 42nd St.
New York, NY 10168
800-223-6537/6876

AEROFLOT-RUSSIAN AIRLINES
630 Fifth Ave. Ste. 1709
New York, NY 10111
800-535-9877,   800-995-5555

A E R O L I N E A S ARGENTINAS
6100 Blue Lagon Dr.
Ste.200, Miami, FL 331261
800-333-0276

AEROMEXICO
4900 Woodway, Ste 750
Houston, TX 77056
800-237-6639

AEROPERU
8181 NW 36th St., Ste 5
Miami, FL 33166,
or P.O. Box 523952
Miami FL 33152
800-777-7717

AIR INDIA
345 Park Ave.,
New York, NY 10154
800-223-7776

AIR NEW ZEALAND
9841 Airport Blvd., Ste. 1020
Los Angeles, CA 90045
800-262-1234

AIR UK
443 Park Ave S., Ste.1006
New York, NY 10016
800-249-2478

AIRLA
5933 W. Century Blvd., Ste 500, Los Angeles, CA

90045
800-933-5952

AIR FRANCE
125 W. 55th St.
New York, NY 10019
800-237-2747

AIR JAMAICA
92-95 Queens Blvd.
Rego Prk, New York, NY 11374; 800-523-5585

AIR ARUBA
760 NW 107th AVe.
Miami FL 33172
800882-7822

AIR NEW ZEALAND LTD.
1960 E. Grand Ave.
El Segundo, CA 90245
800-262-1234

AIR CANADA
1166 Ave. of the Americas,
New York, NY 10036
800-776-3000

AIR VANTAGE INC.
6201 34th Ave S.
Minneapolis, MN 5540
800-279-9383

AIRWAYS INTL. INC
P.O. Box 1244, Miami
Springs, FL 33266
305-526 1244

ALITALIA AIRLINES
666 Fifth Ave.
New York, NY 10019
800-223-5730

ALL NIPPON AIRWAYS
630 Fifht Ave., Ste 537
New York, NY 10111
800-2-FLYANA

ALM ANTILLEAN AIRLINES
1150 NW 72nd Ave.
Miami, FL 33166
800-327-7230

ALOHA AIRLINES, INC.
371 Aokea St.
Honolulu, HI 96819
800-367-5250

ASIANA AIRLINES
3530 Wilshire Blvd. Ste 145, Los Angeles, CA 90010; 800-2-ASIANA

AVIANCA
6 W. 49th St.
New York, NY 10020
800-284-2622

AUSTRALIANAIRLINES
360 Post Street 9th flr.
San Francisco, CA 94108
800-922-5122

AVENSA AIRLINES
800 Brickell Ave. Ste 1109
Miami, FL 33131; (305) 381-8706

AUSTRIAN AIRLINES
1 7 - 2 0   Whitestone
Expressway
Whitestone, NY 11357
800-937-8181

AVIATECA
6595 NW 36TH St. Ste. 100 Miami, FL 33166
800-327-9832

BAHAMASAIR
19495 Biscayne Blvd., Ste. 801, Aventura FL 33180
800-260-2699

BRITISH AIRWAYS
75-20 Astoria Blvd.

Jackson Heights, NY 11370
800-247-9297, 800-
AIRWAYS

BWIAINTERNATIONAL
6 W. 49th St. New York,
NY 10020; 800-260-2699

**CANADIAN AIRLINES
INTL.**
311 Convair Dr.
Mississanga, ON Canada
L5P IC2; 800-426-7000

**CATHEY PACIFIC
AIRWAYS**
300 N. Continental Blvd.
Ste 500,El Segando, CA
90245, 800-233-2742

CAYMAN AIRWAYS
250 Catalonia Ste 506
Coral Gables, FL 33134
800-422-9626

CHINA AIRLINES, LTD.
6053 West Century Blvd.
Ste. 800 Los Angeles, CA
90045; 800-227-5118

COMAIR
P.O. Box 75021
Cicinnati, OH 45275
800-354-9822

**CONTINENTAL
AIRLINES**
2929 Allen Parkway, 12th
Fl, Houston TX 77019
713-834-5000

**CZECHOSLAVAK
AIRLINES**
6033 W. Century Blvd, Los
Angeles, CA 90045
800-223-2365

DELTA AIRLINES, INC.
1030 Delta Blvd
Hartfield International
airport
Atlanta, GA 30320
800-221-1212

**DOMINICANA
AIRLINES**
1444 Biscayne Blvd.
Miami, FL 33132
800-327-7240

ECUATORIANA
Miami Internaional Airport
P.O. Box 522970
Miami, FL 33152
800-328-2367

EGYPTAIR
720 Fifth Ave. Ste. 5055
New York, NY 10019
800-334-6787

EVA AIR
260 W. Fifth ST, Ste. 200,
San Pedro, CA 90731
800-695-1188

**EL AL ISRAEL
AIRLINES**
120 W. 45th St.
New York, NY 10036
800-223-6700

FINNAIR
10 E. 40th St.
New York, NY 10016
800-950-5000

GARUDA INDONESIA
9841 Airport Blvd. STe 300
Los Angeles CA 90045
800-342-7832

GULF AIR
420 Lexington Ave., Ste
2044, New York, NY
10170; 800-553-2824

**GULFSTREAM INTL.
AIRLINES INC.**
P.O. Box 777, Miami
Springs, FL 33266
800-992-8532

GUYANA AIRWAYS
6555 NW 36th, Ste. 207
Miami, FL 33166
800-327-8680

HAITI TRANS AIR
7270 N.W. 12th St., Ste.
200
Miami, FL 33126
800-545-9949

HAWAIIAN AIRLINES
P.O. Box 30008
Honolulu, HI 96820
800-367-5320

HORIZON AIR
P.O. BOX 348309,
Seattle, WA 98148
900-523-1223

**IBERIA AIRLINES of
SPAIN**
6100 Blue Lagoon Dr
Miami FL 33126
800-521-9229

ICELANDAIR, INC.
5950 Symphony Woods Rd.
Ste. 410, Columbia MD
21044; 800-223-5500

**JAPAN AIR LINES,
LTD.**
655 Fifth Ave.
New York, NY 10022
800-525-3663

**K.L.M.-ROYAL DUTCH
AIRLINES**
565 Taxter Rd, Elmsford,
NY 10523; 800-374-7747

KOREAN AIRLINES
6101 W. Imperial Hwy.
Los Angeles, CA 90045
800-438-5000

KUWAIT AIR LINES
350 Park Ave. 24th Fl.
New York, NY 10022
800-458-9284; (212) 319-
1222

**LADECO CHILEAN
AIRLINES**
9500 S. Dadeland Blvd.
Ste. 510, Miami FL 33156
(800) 825-2332

LAN-CHILE AIRLINES
PENTHOUSE
9700 South Dixie Highway
Miami, FL 33126
800-735-5526, 800-SELL-
LAN

LACSA AIRLINE
1633 Bayshore Hwy. Ste.
206, Burlingame, CA
94010; 800-225-2272

LOT-POLISH AIRLINES
500 Fifth Ave., New York,
NY 10110; 800-223-0593

LUFTHANSA GERMAN AIRLINES
1640 Hempstead Turnpike
East Meadow, NY 11554
750 Lexington Ave.
New York, NY 10022
800-645-3880

MALAYSIAN AIRLINES
5933 W. Century Blvd.
Los Angeles, CA 90045
(800) 421-8641

MALEV HUNGARIAN AIRLINES
630 Fifth Ave., New York,
NY 1011, 800-223-6884

MEXICANA AIRLINES
55 E. Monroe Ste. 3220
Chicago, IL 60603-3220;
800-531-7923/7921

MIDWEST EXPRESS
4915 S. Howell Ave.
Milwaukee, WI 53207
800-452-2022

NORTHWEST AIRLINES
5101 North West Dr.
St. Paul, MN 55111
800-225-2525

OLYMPIC AIRWAYS
647 Fifth Ave.
New York, NY 10022
800-223-1226

PHILIPPINE AIRLINES
447 Sutter St.
San Francisco, CA 94108
800-435-9725

QANTAS AIRWAYS
360 Post St., San
Francisco, CA 94108
800-227-4500, 415-445-
1400

ROYAL AIR MAROC
55 East 59th St. Ste. 17b
New York, NY 10022
800-344-6726

ROYAL JORDANIAN AIRLINES
535 Fifth Ave, 18th flr.
New York, NY 10017
800-223-0470

SABENA-BELGIAN WORLD AIRLINES
1155 Northern Blvd.
Manhasset NY 11030
800-955-2000

SAUDI ARABIAN AIRLINES
2049 Century Park East,
Ste. 2000l; Los Angeles,
CA 90067; 800-472-8342

SCANDINAVIAN AIRLINES SYSTEM
9 Polito Ave, Lyndhurst,
NJ. 07071; 800-221-2350

SINGAPORE AIRLINES
5670 Wilshire Blvd
Los Angeles, CA 90036
800-742-3333

SURINAME AIRWAYS
5775 Blue Lagoon Dr. #320
Miami, FL 33126
800-327-6864

SWISSAIR
41 Pinelawn Rd. CS 8910
Melville, NY 11747
800-221-4750

SOUTH AFRICAN AIRWAYS
900 Third Ave, New York,
NY 10022; 800-722-9675

TACA INTERNATIONAL AIRLINES
New Orleans International
Airport
800 Airlines Highway
P.O. Box 20047
New Orleans, LA 70141
800-535-8780

TAP AIR PORTUGAL
399 Market St.
Newark, NJ 07105
800-221-7370

THAI AIRWAYS INTL.
222 N. Sepuveda Blvd.
El Segundo, CA 90245
800-426-5204

TOWER AIR
Hanger 17, JFK Intl.
Airport, Jamaica, NY

11430, 800-34-TOWER

TRANS WORLD AIRWAYS, INC.
1 City Center
515 N. sixth St., St. Louis,
MO 63101. 800-221-2000

TRANSBRASIL AIRLINE
500 Fifth Ave, New York,
NY 10110; 800-872-3153

TURKISH AIRLINES
821 United Nations Plaza
New York, NY 10017;
800-845-2161

TRINIDAD & TOBAGO AIRLINES
(See BIWA)

UNITED AIRLINES
P.O. Box 66100
Chicago, IL 60660
800-241-6522

USAIR
2345 Crystal Drive
Arlington, VA 22227
703-418-7167

UTA FRENCH AIRLINES
9841 Airport Blvd., Ste.
1000, Los Angeles, CA
90045, 800-282-4484

VARIG BRAZILIAN AIRLINES
622 Third Ave
New York, NY 10017
800-468-2744

VIASA-VENEZUELAN INTERNATIONAL AIRWAYS
1101 Brickell Ave., 6th flr.
Miami, FL 33131
800-327-5454

VIRGIN ATLANTIC AIRWAYS
96 Morton St., New York,
NY 10014, 800-VIRGIN-1

VIRGIN AIR
C/O Cyril King Airport
U.S. Virgin Islands 00803
800-522-3084

WORLD AIRWAYS, INC.
P.O. Box 2332
Oakland, CA 94614
415-577-2500

YUGOSLAV AIRLINES
630 Fifth Ave., Ste 3155
New York, NY 10111
800-334-5890

AIRLINES OPERATING WITHIN THE CARIBBEAN ZONE

AMERICAN EAGLE (A subsidiary of American Airlines)
(800) 433-7300

AIR BVI
(809) 774-6500

AIR ANGUILLA
(809) 497-2643

TYDEN AIR
(809) 497-2719

WINDWARD ISLANDS AIRWAYS
(809) 775-0183

APPENDIX Q

INTERNATIONAL AIRLINES TWO-LETTER CODES

Aer Lingus (Irish)	EI	Gulf Air	GF
Aermexico	AM	Guyana Airways	GY
Aeroflot-Russian Airlines	SU	Hawaiian Airlines	HA
Aerolineas Argentinas	AR	Hugfelag-Icelandair	FI
Aeroperu	PL	Iberia	IB
Air Canada	AC	Iraqi Airways	IA
Air New Zealand	NZ	Japan Airlines	JL
Air Jamaica	JM	Kenya Airways	KQ
Air Pacific	FJ	KLM-Royal Dutch Airlines	KL
Air China	CA	Korean Airlines	KE
Air Lanka	UL	Kuwait Airways	KU
Air Algerie	AH	LACSA-Lineas	LR
Air Afrique	RH	Lan-chile Airlines	LA
Air France	AF	LAP-Lineas Aereas Paraguayas	PZ
Air New Zealand-International	E	Lloyd Aero Boliviano	LB
Air India	AI	Lufthansa German Airlines	LH
ALIA-Royal Jordanian Airlines	RJ	Luxair-Luxembourg Airlines	LG
Alitalia	AZ	Malaysian Airline System	MH
All Nippon Airways	NH	Nigerian Airways	WT
Aloha airlines, Inc.	AQ	Olympic Airways	OA
American Airlines	AA	Pakistan International Airlines	PK
Ansett Airlines of Australia	AN	Phillipine Airlines	PR
Ansett Airlines of S. Australia	GJ	Quantas Airways	QF
Austrian Airlines	OS	Royal Nepal Airlines	RA
Avianca	AV	Royal Air Maroc	AT
Aviateca	GU	Sabena-Belgian World Airlines	SN
Bahamasair	UP	SAS-Scandinavian Airlines	SK
British Airways	BA	Saudi Arabian Airline	SV
Caribbean Airways	IQ	Singapore Airlines	SQ
Cathay Pacific Airways	CX	South African Airways	SA
China Airlines	CI	Suriname Airways	PY
Continental Airlines, Inc.	CO	Swissair	SR
CSA-ceslovenske Airline	OK	TACA International Airlines	TA
Delta Airlines	DL	TAP Air Portugal	TP
Dominicana Airlines	DO	Thai Airways International	TG
Eastern Airlines	EA	Trinidad and Tobago Airways(BWI)	
Ecuatoriana	EU	TWA-Trans World Airlines, Inc.	TW
Egyptair	MS	United Airlines	UA
El Al Israel Airlines	LY	UTA	UT
Empresa Ecuatoriana	EU	Varig, SA	RG
Finnair	AY	VIASA-Venezuelan	VA
Garuda Indonesian Airways	GA	Virgin Air	ZP
Ghana Airways	GH	Yugoslav Airlines	JU

APPENDIX R

AIR FREIGHT & PACKAGE EXPRESS SERVICES

AIR CANADA
800/422-6232

AIRBORNE
800/426-2323

AMERICAN AIRLINES INC.
800-334-7400 (U.S.)

CENTRAL AIR FREIGHT, INC.
800/982-3924 (U.S. except MI)
800/621-4377 (MI)

DELTA AIRLINES SMALL PACKAGE
PICKUP & DELIVERY SERVICE
800/638-7333 (U.S. except MD)

DHL
800/225-5345

DYNAMIC AIR FREIGHT INC.
800/631-3484 (U.S. except NJ)

EASTERN AIRLINE SPRINT DELIVERY
800/336-0336 (U.S.)

EMERY WORLDWIDE
800/443-6379 (U.S.)

FEDERAL EXPRESS
800/238-5355 (U.S.)

FIRST CLASS AIR SERVICES
800/422-7461 (U.S. except CA)

FRESH AIR COURIER
800/247-2329 (U.S. except NY)

INT'L. BONDED COURIERS
800/322-3067

MESSENGER AIR FREIGHT
800/421-0063 (U.S. except IL)

QUICKPAK   WORLDWIDE   SMALL
PACKAGE   PICKUP   &   DELIVERY
SERVICE
800/638-7237 (U.S.)

SEKO AIR FREIGHT
800/445-8298 (U.S. except MN)

SKYCAB
800/669-9998 (Cont'l U.S.)

TNT SKYPACK
800/544-1887

TWA   NEXT   FLIGHT   OUT   SMALL
PACKAGE SERVICE
800/638-7380 (U.S. except MD)
800/492-7363 (MD)

UNITED   AIRLINES   SMALL   PACKAGE
DISPATCH
800/241-6522 (U.S. except IL)

APPENDIX S

INTERNATIONAL CRUISES AND CRUISE LINES

Admiral Cruises, Inc.
1220 Biscayne Blvd.
Miami, FL 33132
(800) 327-0271

Adrift Adventures
378 N. Main St.
P.O. Box 577
Moab, UT 84532
(801) 259-8594 or (801)
485-5971, for reservations
only (800) 874-4483

Adventure Center
1311 63rd St. Suite 200
Emeryville, CA 94608
(510) 654-1879

Alpine Adventure Trails Tours
783 Cliffside Drive
Akron, OH 44313-5609
(212) 867-3771

Amazon Tours and Cruises
P.O. Box 39583
Los Angeles, CA 90039
(800) 423-2791

Ambassador Travel
3080 S. College Ave.
Fort Collins, CO 80525
(800) 453-7314

American Hawaii Cruise Line
550 Kearny St.
San Francisco, CA 94108
(800) 765-7000

American Canadian Caribbean Line
461 Water St. Warren, RI
02885 (401) 247-0955 or
(800) 556-7450

Cruise International
501 Front St,
Norfolk, VA. 23501

(800) 647-0009

Coral Bay Cruises
2631 E. Oakland Park,
Blvd. Fort Laudadale, FL

33306 (800) 433-7262

Asian Pacific Adventures
336 Westminster Ave.
Los Angeles, CA 90020
(213) 935-3156, (800) 825-1680

Archaeological Tours, Inc
30 E. 42nd St., Suite 1202
New York, NY 10017
(21.) 986-3504

Australian Pacific Tours
512 South Verdugo Drive,
Suit 200 Burbank, CA
91502 (800) 821-9513,
(800) 227-5401 or (818)
985-5616 in CA

Backroads International
6901 Pritchard Place, Suite
101 New Orleans, LA
70125 (504) 861-8593,
(800) 227-7889

Belize Promotions
720 Worthshire
Houston, TX 77008

Big Five Tour Expeditions, Ltd.
110 Walt Whitmen Rd.
South Huntington, N.Y
11746 (800) 541-2790,
(800) 445-7002

Carnival Cruise Lines
3655 N.W. 87th Ave.
Miami, FL 33178-2428
(305) 599-2200 or (800)
327-2058

Chandris Fantasy Cruises

900 Third Ave.
New York, NY 10022
(212) 223-3003

Clipper Cruise Line
7711 Bon Homme Ave.
St. Louis, MO 63105-1956
(800) 325-0010

Commodore and Crown Cruise Line
800 Douglas Road, Suite

600 Coral Gables, FL.
33134 (800) 327-5617

Costa Cruises, Inc.
World Trade Center
80 S.W. 8th St.
Miami, FL 33130-3097; or

P.O. Box 019614
Miami, FL 33101-9614
(305) 358-7325 or (800)
462-6782

Cruises, Inc.
5000 Campus Blv. Drive,
Pioneer Business Park
East Syracuse, NY 13057-9935
(315) 463-9695 or
(800)854-0500

The Cruise Line, Inc.
4770 Biscayne Blvd,
Penthouse 1-3
Miami, FL 33137
(800) 327-3021, (800)
777-0707 in Florida

Club Med-New York Boutique
3 E. 54th St.,
New York NY 10022
(800) CLUB-MED, (212)
750-1687

Costa Cruises

World Trade Center,
80 SW 8th St.
Maimi, FL 33130
(800) 462-6782

Cruise World
(800) 874-3220

Cunard Line
555 Fifth Ave
New York, NY 10017; or
P.O. Box 2935, Grand
Central Station
New York, NY 10163
(212) 880-7500 or (800)
528-6273
(800) 423-4264 in
California

**Delta Queen Steamboat
Co.**
P.O. Box 62787
New Orleans, LA 70162
(800) 543-1949

Discount Cruise Hotline
9495 Sunset Drive #B270
Miami, FL 33173
(800) 458-2840

Dolphin Cruise Lines
1007 North American Way
Miami, FL 33132
(800) 222-1003

Epirotiki Cruise Lines
551 Fifth Ave
New York, NY 10176
(212) 599-1750
(800) 221-2470

Eurocharters, Inc.
6765 South Tropical Trail
Merritt Island, FL 32952
(407) 632-5610 or (407)
453-4494

**Freighter World Cruises,
Inc.**
1805 Lake Ave., Suite 335
Pasadena, CA 91101
(818) 449-3106

German Rhine Line
(914) 948-3600

Glacier Raft Co.
P.O. Box 264A
West Glacier, MT 59936

(406) 888-5454

**Great American River
Cruises**
P.O. Box 276
Crystal Lake, IL 60014
(813) 262-6599 or
(800) 523-3716

**Hellenic Mediterranean
Lines**
(415) 989-7434

Holland America Lines
300 Elliot Ave. W.
Seattle, WA 98119
(206) 281-3535 or (800)
426-0327

**International Cruise
Center**
(800) 221-3245

Interworld Tours
(800) 845-6622
(800) 221-3882

Norwegian Cruise Line
95 Merrick Way
Coral Gables, FL 33134
(800) 327-7030

Horizon Cruises Ltd.
A Hemphill/Harris Co.
16000 Ventura Blvd., Suite
200 Encino, CA 91436

KD German Rhine Lines
(East) 170 Hamilton Ave.
White Plains, NY
10601-1788
(914) 948-3600; (West)
323 Geary St. San
Francisco, CA 94102-1860
(415) 392-8817

Ocean Cruise Lines
1510 S.E. 17th St.
Fort Lauderdale, FL 33316
(305) 764-3500 or (800)
556-8850

Pacific Sea-Fari Tours
2803 Emerson St.
San Diego, CA 92106
(619) 226-8224

Premier Cruise Lines
101 George King Blvd.

Cape Canaveral, FL 32920
(305) 783-5061 or (800)
327-7113

Princess Cruises
2029 Century Park East
Los Angeles, CA 90067
(213) 553-1770 or (800)
421-0522

Regency Cruises
260 Madison Ave.
New York, NY 10016
(212) 972-4499,
New York, (800) 547-5566
(elsewhere)

Royal Cruise Line
One Maritime Plaza, Suite
400. San Francisco, CA
94111
(415) 788-0610, (415) or
95 Merrick,
Coral Gables, FL 33134.
(800) 227-4534
or (305) 447-9660

**Royal Caribbean Cruise
Lines**
1050 Carribean Way
Miami, FL 33132
(305) 379-4731 or (800)
327-6700, (800) 327 0270

543

APPENDIX T

INTERNATIONAL TOURS AND TOUR OPERATORS

American Express Vacations
300 Pinnacle Way
Norcross GA 30093
(800) 241-1700

Bryan World Tour
1527 Fairlawn Road
P.O Box 4156
Topeka, KS 66604

China Advocates
1635 Irving St.
San Francisco, CA 94122
(415) 665-4505 or (800) 333-6474

CIE Tours International
122 E. 42nd St.
New York, NY 10168
(800)CIE-TOUR, or (212) 972-5600
Department of Antiquities

Ministry of Education and Culture
P.O Box 586 Jerusalem, Israel 91-004 tel. (972-2) 278-603, (972-2) 279-627, or (972-2)278-602

Earthwatch
680 Mount Auburn St.
P.O Box 403
Watertown, MA 02272
(672) 926-8200

Journeys
4011 Jackson Road
Ann Arbor, MI 48103
(313) 665-4407 or (800) 255-8755

Julie Steele's Fashion Tours
P.O. Box 3262
Aucklind, New Zealand
tel. (64-9) 397-442

The Kaye Group, Inc.
The Ajijic Adventures
Suite 17d, 5801 Sheridan Drive Chicago, IL 60660
(312) 794-3595

Kyrles Craft Tours,
Wilson Lake International
One Appian Way, Suite 704-8 South San Francisco, CA 94080
(415) 589-0352

Love Holidays/Uniworld
15315 Magnolia Blvd., Suite 110 Sherman Oaks, CA 91403
(800) HLO-LOVE, (213) 873-7991, or
(818) 501-6868

Magic Lands Travel Agency
528 Main St.
Vacaville, CA 95688
(707) 448-8456

Maupintour
1515 St. Andrews Drive
P.O. Box 807
Lawrence, KS 66044
(800) 382-6700; (913) 843-1211

Metropolitan Opera Guild

Members Travel Program
1865 Broadway
New York, NY 10023
(212) 582-7500
Milford Plaza Hotel
(212) 869-3600

Olson- Travelworld
970 W. 190th St., Suite 425
Torrence, CA 90502
(800) 421-2255

Mountain Travel
6420 Fairmont Ave.
El Cerrito, CA 94530
(800) 227-2384

Eastern Europe Tours
600 Stewart St. 19th Flr.
Seattle, WA 98101
(206) 441-1339 or(800) 441-1339

Big Five Tours and Expedition
110 Walt Whitman Rd.
South Huntington
New York, 11746
(800) 345-2445

Safaricentre
3201 N. Sepulveda Blvd.
Manhattan Beach, CA 90266
(213) 546-4411 or (800) 233-6043, (800) 624-5342 in California, (800) 233-6046 in Canada

Saga International Holidays, Ltd.
120 Boylston St.
Boston, MA 0211616
(800) 343-0273

Saskatchewan
1919 Saskatchewan Drive
Regina, Saskatchewan 54P 3V7, Canada
(800) 667-7191

Sierra Club
(415) 776-2211

Special Interest Tours and Travel
134 West 26th St., Suite 902
New York, NY 10001
(212) 645-6260

544

T-Rail Tours
15940 NE 19 Court,
Suite 4
North Miami Beach, FL
33162
(305) 940-TRIP

Trafalgar Tours
21 E. 26th St
New York, NY 10010
(800) 854-0103; (212) 689-
8977

Trains Unlimited Tours
235 West Pueblo St.
Reno, NV 89509
(702) 329-5590, (702)
329-5743, or
(800) 359-4870

TWA Getaway Vacations
(800) GETAWAY

**University Research
Expeditions Program**
University of California
Berkeley, CA 94720
(415) 642-6586

Volunteers for Israel
41 North St., Room 710
New York, NY 10013
(212) 608-4848

Wilderness Travel
801 Allston Way
Berkeley, CA 94710
(415) 548-0420, (800)
247-6700 outside California

**Worldwide Marketing
Associates**
909 W. Vista Way
Vista, CA 92083
(800) 624-0710 or (619)
758-8747

545

APPENDIX U

INTERNATIONAL TRAVEL CLUBS

ADCI/Club Costa
7701 College Blv., Suite 200A
Overland Park, KS 66210
(800) 225-0381

Adventures on Call
(301) 356-4080

Airhitch/Worldwide Destinations Unlimited
(212) 864-2000

CUC Travel Services
P.O. Box 1015,
Trumbell CT 06611-9938

Discount Travel International
Ives Building, 114 Forrest Ave., Suite 205
Narberth PA 19072
(800) 334 9294 (215) 668-7184

*Discount Club of America
133 Woodhaven Blvd
Rego Park, NY 11374
(718) 335-9612

Encore
4501 Forbes Blvd.,
Lanham MD, 20706
(800) 638-8976 or (301) 459-8020

*Hideaways International

Box 1270 Littleton
MA. 01460-9990
(800) 843-4433

*IN Good Taste (IGT) Services
1111 Lincoln Rd
Miami Beach, Fl. 33139
(800) 444-8872 or(305) 534-7900

*Official Airline Guide Travel Club
(OAG Travel Club)
2000 Clearwater Drive
Oak Brook, IL 60521
(800) 323-3537 or (312) 574-6000

First Travel Club
(312) 843-4433

Last Minute Travel Club
132 Brookline Ave.
Boston, MA 02215
(800) LAST-MIN or(617) 267-9800

Moments's Notice

425 Madison Ave.,
New York, NY 10017
(212) 486-0503

National Travel Club
Travel Building, 51 Atlantic Avenue
Floral Park, NY 11001
(516) 352-9700

Passport Club
(800) 433-1528 or
(206) 343-0128

*Sears Discount Travel Club
303 South Parker Rd., Suite 1000
Aurora, CO 80014
(800) 433-9383

Short Notice Go-Card
(212) 244-3562

Spur-of-the-Moment Tours and Cruises
10780 Jefferson Blvd.
Culiver City, CA 90230
(800)343-1991 or (213) 839-2418

The Good Sam Club
P.O. Box 500
Agoura, CA 91301
(800) 423-5061

Travel Guild
18210 Redmond Way,
Redmond WA 98052
(206) 885-1213

Travel World Leisure Club
225 W. 34th St. Ste. 2203
NY, NY 10122
(212) 239-4855, (800) 444-8952

Traveler's Advantage
3033 S. Parker Rd. Suite 900
Aurora, CO 80014
(800) 548-1116

*Vacations to Go
2411 Fountain View,
Houston, TX 77057
(800)338-4962; (713) 974-2121

*Worldwide Discount Travel Club
1674 Meridian Ave., Suite 300 Miami FL 33139
(305) 534-2082, (800) 622-2336

---

*   Discount Travel Clubs. Membership and annual fees or dues may be required.

** Do not forget to check with your local Automobile clubs. Many of them do provide other services (such as insurance, bail bonds, emergency funds), beneficial to the international traveler.

*** Two excellent sources for valuable information on budget and discount travel opportunities are <u>Consumer Reports Travel Letter</u> published by Consumer Union and <u>Travel Smart</u> published by Communication House. For subscription information, contact Consumer Reports Travel, P.O. Box 2886, Boulder CO 80322 (800) 234 1970; Communication House, 40 Beechdale Rd. Dobbs, NY 10522 (800) 327-3633.

APPENDIX V

INTERNATIONAL RAILROAD/RAIL PASSES INFORMATION**

AMTRAK
800/872-7245 (Cont'l U.S.)

AUSTRIAN FEDERAL RAILWAYS
(Austrian Networks Pass)
212/944-6880

BELGIAN NATIONAL RAILROADS
(Belgian Rail Pass)
212/758-8130

BRITRAIL (UNITED KINGDOM)
(Brit Rail Pass)
212/599-5400

BULGARIAN STATE RAILWAYS
212/573-5530

*DANISH RAILWAYS
312/427-8691

EAST JAPAN RAILWAY CO.
(Japan Railway Pass)
212/332-8688

EUROPEAN RAIL
(Eurail Pass)
202/659-9581
800/422-8426

*FINNISH STATE RAILWAYS
(Finnrail Pass)
212/949-2333

FRENCHRAIL INC.
(France Rail Pass)
212/582-2816
212/582-2110

FRENCH NATIONAL RAILROADS
See French Rail Inc.

GERMAN RAIL INC.

(The German Rail Tourist Card)
212/308-3100

GERMANRAIL
800/782-2424 (U.S.)

GERMAN FEDERAL RAILROADS
See German Rail Inc.

(GREECE) HELLENIC STATE RAILWAYS
212/421-5777

HUNGARIAN STATE RAILWAYS
314/442-6611

(IRELAND) CIE
(Rambler Pass)
800/243-7687

INDIA RAILWAY SYSTEM
(Indrail Pass)
212/957-9570 = -3000

INDONESIA RAILWAY
213/387-2078

ITALIAN STATE RAILWAYS
(Riglietto Turistico di Libera Circolazione)
212/274-0590, 800/223-7987

KOREAN NATIONAL RAILROADS
312/819-2560

LUXEMBOURG NATIONAL RAILWAYS
312/427-8691

MALAYAN RAILWAY
213/689-9702

NETHERLANDS RAILWAYS
212/370-7367

NEW ZEALAND RAILWAYS INTERCITY
(Travelpass)
213/395-7480

*NORWEGIAN STATE RAILWAYS
212/949-2333

POLISH STATE RAILWAYS
212/867-5011, or 312/236-9013

PORTUGUESE RAILROADS
312/427-8691

PHILIPPINE NATIONAL RAILWAYS
312/782-1707

***RAIL EUROPE INC.
914/682-2999, 800/4-EURAIL

RAILWAYS OF AUSTRALIA
800/423-2880 (U.S. except CA)
800/232-2121 (CA)

ROMANIAN STATE RAILWAYS
212/697-6971

RUSSIAN RAILWAYS
212/757-3884

548

SPANISH RAILWAY
(RENFE Tourist Card)
312/427-8691

*SWEDISH STATE RAILROADS
212/949-2333

SWISS FEDERAL RAILWAYS
(Swiss Holiday Card)
800/223-0448 (Cont'l U.S. except NY)

STATE RAILWAY OF THAILAND
213/382-2353

TAIWAN RAILWAY ADMINISTRATION
312/346-1037

TURKISH STATE RAILROADS
212/687-2194

VIA RAIL CANADA
800/665-0200 (Cont'l U.S.)
800/665-6830 (Canada)

YUGOSLAV STATE RAILWAYS
312/427-8691

---

* These countries also issue the Scandinavian Rail Pass. For information, call (212) 949-2333 or (800) 222-SCAN

** Some countries also offer rail and bus **combination** passes at no extra charge or at an additional charge.

***Sells a variety of rail passes such as Eurailpass, Austrian Rabbit Card, Scan Rail Pass, Brit Rail Pass, Benelux Tourail Pass, European, European East Pass, Nordturist and Rail Tickets. They also sell rail passes of most Western European countries.

549

APPENDIX W
HOTELS AND INTERNATIONAL RESERVATION INFORMATION

BEST WESTERN INT'L.
RESERVATION CENTER
800/528-1234 (U.S. &
Canada)

BRISTOL HOTELS
800/528-1234

CANADA PACIFIC
HOTELS
800/828-7447 (U.S.)

CIGA HOTELS/LANDIA
INT'L. SERVICES INC.
800/221-2340 (U.S.)

CLARION HOTELS &
RESORTS
800/252-7466 (U.S.)

CLIMAT DE FRANCE
800/237-2623 (U.S.)

COMFORT INNS
800/228-5150 (U.S.)

CONDO NETWORK
INC.
(U.S. Mexico &
Caribbean)
800/321-2525 (U.S. except
KS)

CONRAD
800/445-8667

CP HOTELS
800-268-4927

CREST
800/548-2323

DIAL BERLIN
800/237-5469
(Cont'l U.S. except TX)

DIAL AUSTRIA
INSTANT
RESERVATIONS

800/221-4980
(Cont'l U.S. except NY)

FIESTA AMERICANA
HOTELS
(Deluxe Hotels of Mexico)
800/223-2332

FOUR SEASONS
800/332-3442

FRIENDSHIP INNS
INT'L. INC.
800/453-4511 (Cont'l U.S.
& Canada)

GOLDEN TULIP
HOTELS AMERICA
800/344-1212

GRAND HOTELS INT'L.
800/323-7249 (Cont'l U.S.)

HELMSLEY HOTELS
800/221-4982 (U.S. &
Canada)

HILTON
RESERVATION
SERVICE
800/445-8667 (U.S.)

HOLIDAY INN -
WORLDWIDE
800/465-4329 (U.S.)

HUNGARY/HUNGARIA
N HOTELS
800/448-4321

HOTEL STOFITEL
800/221-4542

HOWARD JOHNSON
MOTORLODGES
800/654-2000

HYATT HOTELS
800/228-9000

INT'L. RESERVATION
SYSTEM
800/231-0404 (U.S. except
NY)

INTER-CONTINENTAL
800/332-4246

KEMPINSKI
800/426-3135

LATIN AMERICA
RESERVATION
CENTER
800/327-3573 (Cont'l
except FL)

LEADING HOTELS OF
THE WORLD
800/223-6800 (U.S. except
NY)

LOEWS
REPRESENTATION
INT'L.
800/223-0888 (Canada &
U.S. except NY)

MARRIOTT
800/228-9290

MERIDIEN
800/543-4300

MEXICO HOTEL &
TRAVEL
RESERVATION
800/252-0100 (Cont'l U.S.)

NOVOTEL
800/221-4542

NIKKO
800/645-5687

NEW OTANI
800/421-8795

OKURA
800/421-0000

550

OMNI
800/843-6664

PENTA
800-225-3456

PREFERRED HOTELS WORLDWIDE
800/323-7500
(U.S. except IL & Canada)

PRINCE HOTELS INT'L.
800/223-1818 (Cont'l U.S.)
800/442-8418 (NY)

PULLMAN
800/223-9862

QUALITY INNS
800/228-5151 (U.S.)

RADISSON HOTELS
800/333-3333

RAMADA INNS INC.
800/272-6332 (Cont'l U.S.)
800/228-2828

REGENT INT'L. HOTELS LTD.
800/545-4000 (U.S. & Canada)

SCANDINAVIAN RESERVATIONS & INFORMATION SERVICES
800/272-2626 (Cont'l U.S. except CA)

SCOTTISH INNS
800/251-1962 (Cont'l U.S. & Canada)

SHANGRI-LA
800/457-5050

SHERATON
800/325-3535

SONESTA INT'L. HOTELS
800/343-7170 (U.S.)

ST. CROIX HOTEL ASSOC. INC.
800/524-2026 (Cont'l U.S.)

TRAVELODGE INT'L. INC.
800/255-3050 (U.S. & Canada)

STOUFFERS HOTELS
800/468-3571

TAJ
800/458-8825

TRUSTHOUSE FORTE HOTELS
800/223-5672
(Cont'l U.S. & Canada)
800/225-5843 (U.S.)

UTELL INT'L. HOTEL RESERVATION SERVICE
800/448-8355

VISTA INT'L.
800/847-8232

VISTA
800/223-1146

WESTERN TRAVEL
800/423-2917
(Cont'l U.S. except CA)

WESTIN HOTELS
800/228-3000 (U.S., Canada, & Puerto Rico)

551

APPENDIX X

INTERNATIONAL AUTO RENTAL/LEASING AGENCIES

AUTOMOBILE RENTAL
AGENCIES

ALL ENGLAND/ALL IRELAND/ALL GERMANY CAR RENTALS
800/241-3228

AMERICAN INT'L.
800/527-0202

ANSA
800/527-0202

ATESA
800/223-6114

AUTO BRITAIN
800/343-0395
800/852-1000 (MA)

AUTO GLOBE
800/858-1515

AUTO EUROPE
800/223-5555
800/942-1309 (NY)

AUTO IRELAND
800/343-0395
(Cont'l U.S. except MA)
800/852-1000 (MA)

AVIS
800/331-1212

BRENDAN'S SELF DRIVE/NEW ZEALA
800/421-8446

BUDGET RENT A CAR
800/527-0700

"CONNEX INTERNATIONAL
800/333-3949

*'CORTELL INTERNATIONAL

800/228-2535

DOLLAR RENT-A-CAR
800/800-6000

*'EUROPEAN CAR RESERVATION
800/535-3303

EUROPCAR
800/227-7368 (U.S.)

EUROPE BY CAR
800/223-1516

FOREMOST
800/272-3299

HERTZ
800/654-3001

KEMWEL
800/678-0678

"MEIER'S WORLD TRAVEL
800/937-0700

NATIONAL
800/227-7368

THRIFTY
800/367-2277

TILDEN
800/227-7368

VAN WIJK CAR RENTAL/HOLLAND
800/255-2847

AUTOMOBILE
LEASING/PURCHASING

AUDI & PORSCHE
(800) 367-2834

BMW OF NORTH AMERICA, 114 Mayfield Ave., Edison, NY, 08837,

(800) 831-1117

*EUROPE AUTO TRAVELS, 9367 Wilshire Blvd., Beverly Hills, CA, 90210, (213) 273-4477

MERCEDES-BENZ OF NORTH AMERICA, One Mercedes Drive, Montvale, NJ, 07645, (201) 573-0600

PEUGEOT MOTORS OF AMERICA, One Peugeot Plaza, Lyndhurst, NJ, 07071, (201) 935-8400

RENAULT USA 499 Park Avenue, New York, NY, 10022, (800) 221-1052

SABB-SCANIA OF AMERICA, Saab Drive, P.O. Box 697, Orange, CA, 06477, (203) 795-5671

VOLVO OF AMERICA, 1 Volvo Drive, Rockleigh, NJ, 07647, (800) 248-6586

----

* These firms provide services covering several lines of automobiles, including, Volvo, Peugeot, Renault, Audi, Mercedes Benz, Saab, Posche and Volkswagon.

** These firms represent several car rental and leasing agencies and/or arranges overseas services for them.

552

APPENDIX Y

COMPARATIVE CLOTHING SIZES

Suits and Overcoats (men)

American	32	34	36	38	40	42	44	46
Continental	42	44	46	48	50	52	54	56
British	32	34	36	38	40	42	44	46

Dresses and Suits (women)

American		6	8	10	12	14	16	18
Continental		36	38	40	42	44	46	48
British		8	10	12	14	16	18	20

Shirts (men)

American	14	14.5	15	15.5	16	16.5	17	17.5
Continental	36	37	38	39	41	42	43	44
British	14	14.5	15	15.5	16	16.5	17	17.5

Women's Hosiery

American	8	8.5	9	9.5	10	10.5
Continental	0	1	2	3	4	5
British	8	8.5	9	9.5	10	10.5

Socks

American	8.5	9	9.5	10	10.5	11	11.5
Continental	36/37	37/38	38/39	39/40	40/41	41/42	42/43

British	8.5	9	9.5	10	10.5	11	11.5		

Shoes(Men)

American 7	8	8.5	9.5	10.5	11	11.5	12	13	
Contl.39.5	41	42	43	44	44.5	45	46	47	
British 6	7	7.5	8.5	9.5	10	10.5	11	12	

Shoes (women)

American	6	6.5	7	7.5	8	8.5	9
Continental	38	38	39	30	40	41	42
British	4.5	5	5.5	6	6.5	7	7.5

Children's Clothes

American	2	4	6	8	10	12	14
Continental Height (cm)	115	125	135	150	155	160	165
Age	5	7	9	12	13	14	15
British Height (in)	38	43	48	55	58	60	62
Age	2-3	4-5	6-7	9-10	11	12	13

Shoes (children)

American 1	2	3	4.5	5.5	6.5	8	9	10	11	12	13
Continental 32	33	34	36	37	38.5	24	25	27	28	29	30
British 13	1	2	3	4	5.5	7	8	9	10	11	12

APPENDIX Z

INTERNATIONAL WEIGHTS AND MEASURES

CONVERSION TABLES

DISTANCE

1 mile (Mi) = 1.609 Kilometers (Km)
1 kilometer (Km) = .6214 miles (Mi)

VOLUME (capacity)

IMPERIAL WEIGHT MEASURE

1 Imperial gallon = 4.5 liters (L)

1 liter (L) = .222 Imperial gallon (IGal)

Imperial gallons are larger than U.S. gallons
1mperial gallon = 1.2 U.S. gallons

TEMPERATURE

Degrees Fahrenheit (F°) = 9/5 x
Degrees Centigrade + 32
Degrees Centigrade/Celsuis (C°) =
(5/9 Degrees Fahrenheit - 32)

SPEED

1 Mile per hour (MPH) = 1.6
(KMH) 1 kilometer per hour
(KMH) = .625 (MPH)
1 inch = 2.54 centimeter (cm)
1 centimeter = .3937 inches (in)
1 foot = .3048 meters (m)
1 meter = 3.281 feet (ft)

WEIGHTS

1 ounce (oz) = 28.349 grams (gm)
1 gram (gm) = .0353 ounces (oz)
1 pound (lb) = .4536 Kilograms1Kg
Kilogram (Kg) = 2.205 pounds
(lb)

In	=	Cm
1	=	2.54
2	=	5.08
3	=	7.63
4	=	10.16
5	=	12.70
6	=	15.24
7	=	17.78
8	=	20.32
9	=	22.86
10	=	25.40
11	=	27.94
12	=	30.48

Cm	=	In
1	=	0.40
2	=	0.80
3	=	1.20
4	=	1.60
5	=	2.00
6	=	2.40
7	=	2.80
8	=	3.20
9	=	3.50
10	=	3.90
11	=	4.30
12	=	4.70

Lb	=	Kg
1	=	0.45
2	=	0.91
3	=	1.36
4	=	1.81
5	=	2.27
6	=	2.72
7	=	3.18
8	=	3.63
9	=	4.08
10	=	4.54
50	=	22.68
100	=	45.36

555

Kg	=	Lb
1	=	2.21
2	=	4.41
3	=	6.61
4	=	8.82
5	=	11.02
6	=	13.23
7	=	15.43
8	=	17.64
9	=	19.84
10	=	22.05
50	=	110.23
100	=	220.46

Mi	=	Km
1	=	1.61
2	=	3.22
3	=	4.83
4	=	6.44
5	=	8.05
6	=	9.66
7	=	11.27
8	=	12.88
9	=	14.48
10	=	16.09
50	=	80.47
100	=	160.90

Km	=	Mi
1	=	0.62
2	=	1.24
3	=	1.86
4	=	2.49
5	=	3.11
6	=	3.73
7	=	4.35
8	=	4.97
9	=	5.59
10	=	6.21
50	=	31.07
100	=	62.14

Gal	=	L
1	=	3.79
2	=	7.57
3	=	11.35
4	=	15.14
5	=	18.93
6	=	22.71
7	=	26.50
8	=	30.28
9	=	34.16
10	=	37.94
50	=	189.70
100	=	379.40

L	=	Gal
1	=	0.26
2	=	0.53
3	=	0.79
4	=	1.06
5	=	1.32
6	=	1.58
7	=	1.85
8	=	2.11
9	=	2.38
10	=	2.64
50	=	13.20
100	=	26.40

TEMPERATURE

F	=	C
32	=	0
40	=	5
50	=	10
60	=	15
70	=	20
75	=	25
85	=	30
105	=	40
140	=	60
175	=	80

SPEED

MPH	=	KMH
20	=	32
30	=	48
40	=	64
50	=	80
60	=	96
70	=	112
80	=	128
90	=	144
100	=	160

APPENDIX 1A

INTERNATIONAL SYSTEMS OF WEIGHTS & MEASURES

AFGHANISTAN	M	CZECH REP.	M	LAOS	M
ALBANIA	M	DENMARK	M	LATVIA	M
ANGOLA	M	DOMINICA	I*	LEBANON	M
ANGUILLA	M,I	DOMINICAN REP.	I*	LESOTHO	M
ANTIGUA &		ECUADOR	M	LIBERIA	I
BARBUDA	I*	EGYPT	M*	LIBYA	M
ARGENTINA	M	EL SALVADOR	M*	LIECHTENSTEIN	M
ARMENIA	M	EQUAT. GUINEA	M	LITUANIA	M
AUSTRALIA	M	ESTONIA	M	LUXEMBOURG	M
AUSTRIA	M	ETHIOPIA	M*	MADAGASCAR	M
AZERBAIJAN	M	FIJI	M	MALAWI	M
BAHAMAS	I	FINLAND	M	MALAYSIA	M*
BAHRAIN	M	FRANCE	M	MALI	M
BANGLADESH	I*	FRENCH GUIANA	M	MALTA	M
BARBADOS	M	FR. ANTILLES	M	MARTINIQUE	M
BELGIUM	M	FR. POLYNESIA	M	MAURITANIA	M
BELIZE	I	GABON	M	MAURITIUS	M
BERMUDA	M,I	GEORGIA	M	MEXICO	M
BHUTAN	M	GERMANY	M	MOLDOVA	M
BOLIVIA	M	GHANA	M	MONACO	M
BOTSWANA	M	GREECE	M	MONGOLIA	M
BRAZIL	M	GRENADA	M	MONTSERRAT	I*
BRITISH V.I.	I	GUADELOUPE	M	MOROCCO	M
BRUNEI	I**	GUATEMALA	M	MOZAMBIQUE	
BULGARIA	M	GUINEA	M	NAMIBIA	M
BURKINA FASO	M	GUINEA-BISSAU	M	NAURU	M
BURUNDI	M	GUYANA	M	NETHERLANDS	M
BYELARUS	M	HAITI	M	NETH. ANTILLES	M
CAMBODIA	M	HONDURAS	M*	NEW ZEALAND	M
CAMEROON	M	HONG KONG	M	NICARAGUA	M*
CANADA	M	HUNGARY	M	NIGER	M
CAYMAN IS	I	ICELAND	M	NIGERIA	M
CENTRAL		INDIA	M,I*	NORWAY	M
AFRICAN REP.	M	INDONESIA	M	OMAN	M,I*
CHAD	M	IRAN	M*	PAKISTAN	M,I*
CHILE	M	IRAQ	M*	PANAMA	M,I
CHINA,		IRELAND	I*	PAPUA	
PEOPLES REP.	M*	ISRAEL	M	NEW GUINEA	M
CHINA, TAIWAN	M	ITALY	M	PARAGUAY	M
COLOMBIA	M	JAMAICA	M,I	PERU	M
COMOROS	M	JAPAN	M	PHILIPPINES	M
CONGO,		JORDAN	M	PORTUGAL	M
PEOPLE'S REP.	M	KAZAKHSTAN	M	QATAR	M*
COSTA RICA	M	KENYA	M	REP. OF	
COTE D'IVOIRE	M	KOREA, NORTH	M	CAPE VERDE	M
CUBA	M	KOREA, SOUTH	M*	ROMANIA	M
CYPRUS	M*,I*	KUWAIT	M	RUSSIA	M
CZECHOSLO-		KYRGYZSTAN	M	RWANDA	M
				SAN MARINO	M

SAO TOME & PRINCIPE	M
SAUDI ARABIA	M
SENEGAL	M
SEYCHELLES	I*
SIERRA LEONE	M
SINGAPORE	M*
SOMALIA	M,I
SOUTH AFRICA	M
SPAIN	M
SRI LANKA	M*
ST. VINCENT	I
ST. KITTS	I
ST. LUCIA	I
ST.PIERRE & MIQUELON	M
SUDAN	I*
SURINAME	M
SWEDEN	M
SWITZERLAND	M
SYRIA	M
TAJIKISTAN	M
TANZANIA	M
THAILAND	M*
THE GAMBIA	I*
TOGO	M
TONGA	M
TRINIDAD & TOBAGO	I*
TUNISIA	M
TURKEY	M
TURKMENISTAN	M
TURKS & CAICOS	I
UGANDA	M
UKRAINE	M
UN. ARAB EMIRATES	I,M
U.K	I*
URUGUAY	M
UZBEKISTAN	M
VENEZUELA	M
VIETNAM	M
YEMEN, P.D.M.	I*
YUGOSLAVIA	M
ZAIRE	M
ZAMBIA	M
ZIMBABWE	M

I = Imperial system of Weights and Measures is in use.

I* = Imperial system of Weights and Measures is in use, however metrication program is being introduced.

I =** Imperial and /or local systems of Weights and Measures are being used.

M = Metric system of Weights and Measures is in use.

M* = Traditional systems of Weights and Measures is still in use.

M,I = Metric and Imperial systems of Weights and Measures are in use.

APPENDIX 2B

INTERNATIONAL GUIDE TO TIPPING*

	HOTELS	TAXIS	OTHERS
ANDORRA	10-20%	10%	YES
ANGUILLA	D	D	YES
ANTIGUA & BARBUDA	10%	D	YES
ARGENTINA	10-22%	10%	YES
ARMENIA	YES	OD	OD
AUSTRALIA	10%	D	YES
AUSTRIA	10-15%	10%	YES
AZERBAIJAN	YES	OD	OD
BAHAMAS	15%	15%	YES
BANGLADESH	5-10%	5-10%	YES
BARBADOS	10%	10%	YES
BELARUS	YES	OD	OD
BELGIUM	15%	D	YES
BELIZE	D 10%	D	YES
BENIN	D	D	D
BOLIVIA	10-23%	D	YES
BRAZIL	D	YES	
BURMA	10%	10%	YES
CAMEROON	10%	D	YES
CANADA	15-20%	15-20%	YES
CAYMAN IS	NC 10-15%	NC	YES
CHILE	10%	NC	YES
CHINA, PEOPLES REP.	F	F	F
CHINA, TAIWAN	D 10%	D 10%	YES
COLUMBIA	10%	NC	YES
COSTA RICA	10%	NC	YES
COTE D'IVOIRE	5-10%	5-10%	YES
CYPRUS	10%	NT	YES
CZECHOSLOVAKIA	OD 5-10%	5-10%	YES
DENMARK	15%	upto 15%	YES
DOMINICA	10%	D	YES
DOMINICAN REP.	10%		
ECUADOR	10%	NC	YES
EGYPT	10-12%	10%	YES
ETHIOPIA	5-10%	NC	YES
FIJI	D	D	YES
FINLAND	14-15%	NT	YES
FRANCE	upto 25%	15%	YES
FRENCH GUIANA	12 1/2%	NC	YES
GERMANY	10%	5%	YES
GHANA	YES	YES	YES
GIBRALTAR	10-12%	10%	YES
GREECE	10-15%	10%	YES
GRENADA	D	D	YES
GUADELOUPE	10-15%	YES	
GUATEMALA	10%	10%	YES

559

GUINEA	D	D	YES
GUYANA	10%	10%	YES
HAITI	NC 10%	D	YES
HONDURAS	10%	10%	YES
HONG KONG	10-15%	10%	YES
HUNGARY	OD 10-15%	YES	YES
ICELAND	NC	NC	NC
INDIA	10%	NC	YES
INDONESIA	NC 10%	NC 10%	YES
IRELAND	10-15%	YES	YES
ISRAEL	10%	NC	YES
ITALY	12-15%	15%	YES
JAMAICA	15%	10-20%	YES
JAPAN	NC 10-20%	NC	YES
JORDAN	10%	10%	YES
KAZAKHSTAN	OD	OD	OD
KENYA	10-15%	10%	YES
KOREA, SOUTH	NC 10%	NC 10-15%	YES
KUWAIT	10%	D	YES
KYRGYZSTAN	OD	OD	OD
LATVIA	NT	10-20%	YES
LIBERIA	10-15%	NC	YES
LIECHTENSTEIN	10-15%		
LITHUANIA	NC	NC	NC
LUXEMBOURG	NC 10-20%	15-20%	YES
MALAYSIA	NC 10%	NC 10%	YES
MALTA	10%	10%	YES
MARTINIQUE	10-15%	D	YES
MEXICO	7-15%	D	YES
MOLDOVA	OD	OD	OD
MONTSERRAT	10%	10%	YES
MOROCCO	10-15%	10-15%	YES
NEPAL			YES
NETHERLANDS	15%	10-15%	YES
NEW CALEDONIA		F	F
NEW ZEALAND	NC 10%	NC	
NICARAGUA	10%	NC	YES
NIGERIA	10%	D	YES
NORWAY	15%	D	YES
PAKISTAN	5-10%	D	YES
PANAMA	10-15%	NC	YES
PAPUA NEW GUINEA	NC	NC	NC
PARAGUAY	10%	5-12%	YES
PERU	5-10%	NC	YES
PHILIPPINES	10%	D 10%	YES
POLAND	10%	10%	YES
PORTUGAL	10-15%	15%	YES
ROMANIA	NC	NC	
RUSSIA	10-15%	10-15%	YES
SAUDI ARABIA	10-15%	NC	YES
SENEGAL	10%	D	YES
SEYCHELLES	10%	D	YES
SINGAPORE	OD	10%	OD
SOUTH AFRICA	10%	10%	YES
SPAIN	5-10%	10-15%	YES
SRI LANKA	10%	D	YES
ST. KITTS	D	D	YES
ST. LUCIA	10%	10%	YES
ST. VINCENT	10-15%	10-15%	YES

ST. MAARTEN	10%	10%	YES
SURINAME	10%	NC	YES
SWEDEN	12-15%	10-15%	YES
SWITZERLAND	12-15%	12-15%	YES
TAJIKISTAN	OD	OD	OD
TANZANIA	5%	(OD) D	YES
THAILAND	D 10%	NC	YES
TOGO	OD	OD	
TRINIDAD & TOBAGO	10%	10-15%	YES
TUNISIA	10%	10%	YES
TURKEY	10-15%	D	YES
TURKMENISTAN	OD	OD	OD
UKRAINE	OD	OD	OD
UNITED KINGDOM	12-15%	10-15%	YES
URUGUAY	10%	10%	YES
UZBEKISTAN	OD	OD	OD
VENEZUELA	10%	NC	YES
YUGOSLAVIA	10%	10%	YES
ZAIRE	10%	D	YES
ZAMBIA	10%	OD	YES

xxx		YES, persons who perform other services such as porters, luggage handlers, door persons, etc. may be tipped or may expect to be tipped. Tipping and amount of tip is at your discretion.
D	=	Tipping is expected. Amount of tip is at your discretion.
OF	=	Tipping is Officially Discouraged although privately welcome.
NC	=	Tipping is not customary, nevertheless welcome.
NT	=	Not usually tipped
F	=	Tipping is prohibited

APPENDIX 3C

INTERNATIONAL TIME ZONES

(TIME DIFFERENCE, IN HOURS, BETWEEN U.S.EASTERN STANDARD TIME AND FOREIGN CAPITAL CITIES)

COUNTRIES	HOURS
AFGHANISTAN	9.5
ALBANIA	6
ALGERIA**	6
AMERICAN SAMOA	6
ANDORRA	6
ANGUILLA	1
ANTIGUA & BARBUDA	1
ARGENTINA	2
ARMENIA	8
AUSTRALIA*	15
AUSTRIA	6
AZERBAIJAN	8
BAHAMAS	0
BAHRAIN	8
BANGLADESH	11
BARBADOS	1
BELGIUM	6
BELIZE	-1
BENIN	6
BERMUDA	1
BHUTAN	11
BOLIVIA	1
BOTSWANA	7
BRAZIL*	2
BRITISH VIRGIN IS	1
BRUNEI	1 3
BULGARIA	7
BURKINA FASO	5
BURMA	11.5
BURUNDI	7
BYELARUS	8
CAMBODIA	12
CAMEROON	6
CANADA*	0
CAYMAN IS	0
CENT. AFRICAN REP.	6
CHAD	6
CHILE**	1
CHINA, PEOPLES REPUBLIC.	13
CHINA, TAIWAN	3

(TIME DIFFERENCE, IN HOURS, BETWEEN U.S.EASTERN STANDARD TIME AND FOREIGN CAPITAL CITIES)

COUNTRY	HOURS
COLUMBIA	0
COMOROS	8
CONGO, PEOPLE'S REP	6
COSTA RICA	-1
COTE D'IVOIRE	5
CUBA**	0
CYPRUS	7
CZECH REP.	6
DENMARK	6
DOMINICA	1
DOMINICAN REP.	0
ECUADOR	0
EGYPT	7
EL SALVADOR	-1
ESTONIA	8
EQUAT. GUINEA	6
ETHIOPIA	8
FAEROW IS	5
FIJI	17
FINLAND	7
FRANCE	6
FR. POLYNESIA	-5
FR. ANTILLES	1
FRENCH GUIANA	2
GABON	6
GEORGIA	6
GHANA	5
GIBRALTAR	6
GREECE	7
GREENLAND	2
GRENADA	1
GUADELOUPE	1
GUAM	15
GUANTANAMO BAY	0
GUATEMALA	-1
GUINEA	5
GUINEA-BISSAU	5
GUYANA	2
HAITI	0
HONDURAS	-1
HONG KONG	13

(TIME DIFFERENCE, IN HOURS, BETWEEN U.S.EASTERN STANDARD TIME AND FOREIGN CAPITAL CITIES)

COUNTRY	HOURS
HUNGARY	6
ICELAND	5
INDIA	10.5
INDONESIA*	12
IRAN	8.5
IRAQ	8
IRELAND	5
ISRAEL	7
ITALY	6
JAMAICA**	0
JAPAN	14
JORDAN	7
KAZAKHSTAN	11
KENYA	8
KIRIBATI	-5
KOREA, SOUTH	14
KOREA, NORTH	14
KUWAIT	8
KYRGYZSTAN	11
LAOS	12
LATVIA	8
LEBANON	7
LESOTHO	7
LIBERIA	5
LIBYA	6
LIECHTENSTEIN	6
LITUANIA	8
LUXEMBOURG	6
MADAGASCAR	8
MALAWI	7
MALAYSIA*	13
MALDIVES	10
MALI	5
MALTA	6
MARSHALL IS	17
MAURITANIA	5
MAURITIUS	9
MAYOTTE IS	8
MEXICO*	1
MICRONESIA*	16
MOLDOVA	8
MONACO	6

MONGOLIA	13	SUDAN	7
MONTSERRAT	1	SURINAME	2
MOROCCO	5	SWAZILAND	7
MOZAMBIQUE	7	SWEDEN	6
MUSTIQUE	1	SWITZERLAND	6
NAMIBIA	7	SYRIA	7
NAURU	17	TAJIKISTAN	11
NEPAL	10.5	TANZANIA	8
NETHERLANDS	6	THAILAND	12
NETHERLANDS		THE GAMBIA	5
ANTILLES	1	TOGO	5
NEW CALEDONIA	16	TONGA	18
NEW ZEALAND**	17	TRANSKEI	7
NICARAGUA	-1	TRINIDAD &	
NIGER	6	TOBAGO	1
NIGERIA	6	TUNISIA	6
NORWAY	6	TURKEY	7
OMAN	9	TURKMENISTAN	10
PAKISTAN	10	TURKS &	
PANAMA	0	CAICOS	**0
PAPUA N. GUINEA	15	U.S.A.	0
PARAGUAY	2	UGANDA	8
PERU	0	UKRAINE	8
PHILIPPINES	13	UNION IS	1
POLAND	6	U.K**	5
PORTUGAL	5	UNITED ARAB	
PUERTO RICO	1	EMIRATES	9
QATAR	8	URUGUAY	2
REP. OF DJIBOUTI	8	UZBEKISTAN	11
REP. OF CAPE VERDE	4	VATICAN CITY	6
REUNION IS	9	VENEZUELA	1
ROMANIA	7	WESTERN SAMOA	-6
RUSSIA	8	YEMEN, .P.D.R.	8
RWANDA	7	YEMEN,	
SAIPAN	15	ARAB REP.	8
SAN MARINO	6	YUGOSLAVIA	6
SAO TOME &		ZAIRE*	6
PRINCIPE	5	ZAMBIA	7
SAUDI ARABIA	8	ZIMBABWE	7
SENEGAL	5		
SEYCHELLES	9		
SIERRA LEONE	5	*	Countries with multiple Time Zones. Hours indicated may be different depending on your location in these countries.
SINGAPORE	13		
SOLOMON IS	16		
SOMALIA	8		
SOUTH AFRICA	7		
SPAIN	6		
SRI LANKA	10.5		
ST. MARTIN	1		
ST. LUCIA	1	**	Countries with varying time, depending on the month.
ST. KITTS-NEVIS	1		
ST. PIERRE & MIQUELON	2		
ST. VINCENT	1		

APPENDIX 4D

INTERNATIONAL ELECTRICITY REQUIREMENTS

COUNTRIES	Volts/AC
AFGHANISTAN	20/50 AC
ALGERIA	110-115/50, 220/50 AC*
ANDORRA	125/50 AC
ANGUILLA	220
ANTIGUA	110/60 AC
ARGENTINA	220/60 AC
ARMENIA	220/50
AUSTRALIA	240 AC
AUSTRIA	220/50
AZERBAIJAN	220/50
BAHAMAS	120/60 AC
BAHRAIN	220/50 AC
BANGLADESH	220 AC
BARBADOS	110/50 AC
BELGIUM	220/50 AC
BELIZE	110/220/60 AC
BENIN	220/50
BERMUDA	110/60 AC
BHUTAN	110-220/50 AC*
BOTSWANA	220
BRAZIL+	110/60; 220/60, 127/60 AC*
BRITISH V.I	115-210/60 AC
BULGARIA	220/50 AC
BURKINA FASO	220/50
BURMA	220/50 AC
BURUNDI	220/50
BYELARUS	220/50
CAMEROON	110-220
CANADA	110/60 AC
CAYMAN ISLANDS	110/60 AC
CENTRAL AF. REP.	220
CHAD	220
CHILE+	220/50 AC
CHINA	110/50
CHINA, TAIWAN	110/60 AC
COLOMBIA	150/60 AC, 110/60**
COMOROS	220/50
CONGO, REP.	220/50
COSTA RICA	110/60 AC
COTE D'IVOIRE	220/50 AC
CUBA	110/60
CYPRUS++	240/50 AC
ZECH REP.	220/50 AC
DENMARK	220/50
DOMINICA	220-240/50 AC
DOMINICAN REP.	110/60 AC
ECUADOR	110/60 AC

COUNTRIES	Volts/AC
EGYPT	220/50, 110-120/50*
EL SALVADOR	110/60
ESTONIA	220/50
EQUAT. GUINEA	220/50
ETHIOPIA	220/60 AC
FIJI	240/50 AC
FINLAND	220/60 AC
FRANCE	220/50
FRENCH GUIANA	220 & 110/50 AC
GABON	220/240/50
GEORGIA	220/50
GERMANY	220/50 AC
GHANA	220-240/50 AC
GIBRALTAR	240-250/50 AC
GREECE+	220/50 AC
GRENADA	220-240/50 Ac
GUADELOUPE	220/50 AC
GUAM	120/60 AC
GUATEMALA	110/60 AC
GUINEA	220/50
GUYANA	110-120/60 AC
HAITI	110/60 AC
HONDURAS	110 or 220/60 AC*
HONG KONG++	200-220/60 AC
HUNGARY	220/50 AC
ICELAND	220/50 AC
INDIA+	220/50 AC
INDONESIA	220/50 AC
IRAN	220/50
IRAQ	220 DC
IRELAND	220/50 AC
ISRAEL	220/50 AC
ITALY	220/50, 110-127/50 AC*
JAMAICA	110/50 AC
JAPAN	110/50, 100/60 AC*
JORDAN	220/50 AC
KAZAKHSTAN	220/50
KENYA	220/50 AC
KOREA, SOUTH	110/60 AC
KUWAIT	240/50 AC
KYRGYZSTAN	220/50
LATVIA	220/50
LEBANON	110-220/50
LESOTHO	220 AC
LIBERIA	120/60 AC
LIBYA	220/50
LIECHTENSTEIN	220/50 AC
LITHUANIA	220/50

564

LUXEMBOURG	220/110	SWITZERLAND	220/50 AC
MADAGASCAR	220/50	TAJIKISTAN	220/50
MALAWI	220	TANZANIA	240/50/60 AC
MALAYSIA	220/50 AC	THAILAND	220/50 AC
MALI	220	TOGO	220/50 AC
MALTA	240/50 AC	TONGA	220 AC
MARTINIQUE	2 2 0 / 5 0 A C	TRINIDAD & TOB.	110/60 AC
MAURITANIA	220/50	TUNISIA	110-115/50, 220/50 AC*
MAURITIUS	220/230	TURKEY	220/50
MEXICO	110/60 AC	TURKMENISTAN	220/50
MICRONESIA	110/60 AC	TURKS & CAICOS	110/60
MOLDOVA	220/50	U.S.A	110-115/60 AC
MONTSERRAT	230/60 AC	UKRAINE	220/50
MOROCCO	110-120/50 AC	UNITED ARAB EM.	240/415 AC
MOZAMBIQUE	220/50	UNITED KINGDOM	220/50 AC
NAMIBIA	220/240/60	URUGUAY	220/50 AC
NEPAL	220/50 AC	UZBEKISTAN	220/50
NETHERLANDS		VENEZUELA	110/60 AC
ANTILLES.	110-130/50,120/60AC*	YEMEN, ARAB REP.	220/50 AC
NETHERLANDS	220/50 AC	YEMEN, P.D.R	220/240/50
NEW CALEDONIA	220/50 AC	YUGOSLAVIA	220/50 AC
NICARAGUA	110/60 AC	ZAIRE	220/50
NIGER	220-240/50	ZAMBIA	220/50 AC
NIGERIA++	220/50 AC	ZIMBABWE++	220/240/50
NORWAY	220/50 AC		
OMAN	220/240/50		
PAKISTAN	220/240/50 AC		
PANAMA	110/60 AC		
PAPUA NEW GUINEA	240 AC		
PARAGUAY+	220/50 AC		
PERU	220/60 AC		
PHILIPPINES	220/60 AC		
POLAND	220/50 AC		
PORTUGAL	210-220/50 AC		
PUERTO RICO	110-115/60 AC		
QATAR	220/50		
REP. OF DJIBOUTI	220/50		
CAPE VERDE	220/50		
ROMANIA	220/50		
RUSSIA	220/50		
RWANDA	220/50		
SAUDI ARABIA	110 & 120/60 AC		
SENEGAL	110 & 220/50 AC		
SEYCHELLES	240/50 AC		
SIERRA LEONE	220/50		
SINGAPORE++	230-250 AC		
SAO TOME & PRIN.	220/50		
SOMALIA	220/50		
SOUTH AFRICA	220-230/50 AC		
SPAIN	110-220/50 AC		
SRI LANKA	230-240/50 AC		
ST. KITTS	230/60 AC		
ST. LUCIA	220/50 AC		
ST. MARTIN	220/60 AC		
ST. VINCENT	220-230/50 AC		
SUDAN	240 AC		
SURINAME	110-115/60 AC		
SWAZILAND	240/50		
SWEDEN+	220/50 AC		

----

*   Electricity requirements vary in some parts of the country.

\+   Some parts of the country still use DC.

++   In some or most parts of the country, you may need three square pin plugs.

APPENDIX 5E

INTERNATIONAL TELEPHONE DIALING CODES

COUNTRY/COUNTRY CODE
City & Codes
Albania   355
Durres 52 plus 4 digits, Elbassan 545 plus 4 digits, Korce 824 plus 4 digits, Shkoder 224 plus 4 digits, Tirana 42 plus 5 digits

Algeria   213

City code not required.

American Samoa   684
City code not required.

Andorra   376
Use 628 for all cities.

Anguilla   809
Dial 1 + 809 + Local Number.

Antigua   809
Dial 1 + 809 + Local Number.

Argentina   54
Bahia Blanca 91. Buenos Aires 1, Cordoba 51, Corrientes 783, La Plata 21, Mar Del Plata 23, Mendoza 61, Merlo 220, Posadas 752, Resistencia 772, Rio Cuarto 586, Rosario 41, San Juan 64, San Rafael 627, Santa Fe 42, Tandil 293

Armenia   374
City codes not required

Aruba   297
Use 8 for all cities.

Ascension Island 247
City code not required.

Australia   61
Adelaide 8, Ballarat 53, Brisbane 7, Canberra 62, Darwin 89, Geelong 52, Gold Coast 75, Hobart 02, Launceston 03, Melbourne 3, Newcastle 49, Perth 9, Sydne 2, Toowoomba 76, Townsville 77, Wollongong 42

Austria   43
Bludenz 5552, Graz 316, Innsbruck 5222, Kitzbuhel 5356, Klagenfut 4222, Krems An Der Donau 2732, Linz Donau 732, Neunkirchen Niederosterreich 2635, Salzburg 662, St. Polten 2742, Vienna 1, Villach 4242, Wels 7242, Wiener

Neustadt 2622

Bahamas   809
Dial 1 + 809 + Local Number.

Bahrain   973
City code not required.

Bangladesh   880
Barisal 431, Bogra 51, Chittagong 31, Comilla 81, Dhaka 2, Khulna 41, Maulabi Bazar 861, Mymensingh 91, Rajshaki 721, Sylhet 821

Barbados   809
Dial 1 + 809 + Local Number.

Blarus   375
Loev 2347, Minsk 172, Mogilev 222

Belgium   32
Antwerp 3, Bruges 50, Brussels 2, Charleroi 71, Courtrai 56, Ghent 91, Hasselt 11, La Louviere 64, Leuven 16, Libramont 61, Liege 41, Malines 15, Mons 65, Namur 81, Ostend 59, Verviers 87

Belize   501
Belize City (City code not required), Belmopan 08, Benque Viejo Del Carmen 093, Corozal Town 04, Dangviga 05, Independence 06, Orange Walk 03, Punta Gorda 07, San Ignacio 092

Benin   229
City code not required.

Bermuda   809
Dial 1 + 809 + Local Number.

Bolivia   591
Cochabamba 42, Cotoga 388, Guayafamerin 47, La Belgica 923, La Paz 2, Mineros 984, Montero 92, Oruro 52, Portachuelo 924, Saavedra 924, Santa Cruz 33, Trinidad 46, Warnes 923

Bosnia-Herzegovina 387
Mostar 88, Sarajevo 71, Zenica 72

Botswana   267
Francistown 21, Gaborone 31, Jwaneng 38, Kanye 34, Lobatse 33, Mahalapye 41, Maun 26, Mochudi 37, Molepoloe 32, Orapa 27, Palapye 42, Ramotswana 39,

Selibe (Phikwe) 8, Serowe 43

Brazil   55
Belem 91, Belo Horizonte 31, Brasilia 61, Curitiba 41, Fortaleza 85, Goiania 62, Niteroi 21, Pelotas 532, Porto Alegre 512, Recife 81, Rio de Janeiro 21, Salvador 71, Santo Andre 11, Santos 132, Sao Paulo 11, Vitoria 27

British Virgin Islands   809
Dial 1 + 809 + Local Number in the following cities: Anegada, Camanoe Island, Guana Island, Josh Vah Dyke, Little Thatch, Marina Cay, Mosquito Island, North Sound, Peter Island, Salt Island, Tortola, Virgin Gorda.

Brunei   673
Bandar Seri Begawan 2, Kuala Belait 3, Mumong 3, Tutong 4

Bulgaria   359
Kardjali 361, Pazardjik 34, Plovdiv 32, Sofia 2, Varna 52

Burkina Faso   226
Bobo Dioulasso 9, Fada N'Gorma 7, Koudougou 4, Ouagadougou 3

Burma   95
Akyab 43, Bassein 42, Magwe 63, Mandalay 2, Meikila 64, Moulmein 32, Pegu 52, Prom 53, Rangoon 1

Cameroon   237
City code not required.

Canada   NPA's
Dial 1 + Area Code + Local Number.

Cape Verde Islands   238

City code not required.

Caymen Islands   809
Dial 1 + 809 + Local Number.

Chile   56
Chiquayante 41, Concepcion 41, Penco 41, Recreo 31, San Bernardo 2, Santiago 2, Talcahuano 41, Valparaiso 32, Vina del Mar 32

China   86
Beijing (Peking) 1, Fuzhou 591, Ghuangzhou (Canton) 20, Shanghai 21

Colombia   57
Armenia 60, Barranquilla 5, Bogota 1, Bucaramanga 73, Cali 3, Cartagena 59, Cartago 66, Cucuta 70, Giradot 832, Ibague 82, Manizales 69, Merdellin 42, Neiva 80, Palmira 31, Pereira 61, Santa Marta 56

Costa Rica   506
City code not required.

Croatia   387
Dubrovnik 20, Rijeka 51, Split 21, Zagreb 41.

Cyprus   357
Kythrea 2313, Lapithos 8218, Lamaca 41, Lefkonico 3313, Limassol 51, Moni 5615, Morphou 71, Nicosia 2, Paphos 61, Platres 54, Polis 63, Rizokarpaso 3613, Yialousa 3513. The following cities are handled by the Turkish Telephone Network. Use country code 90 for Turkey: Famagusta 536, Kyrenia 581, and Lefka 57817.

Czech Rep.   42
Brno 5, Havirov 6994, Ostrava 69, Prague (Praha) 2,

Denmark   45
City code not required.

Djibouti   253
City code not required.

Dominica   809
Dial 1 + 809 + Local Number.

Dominican Republic 809
Dial 1 + 809 + Local Number.

Ecuador   593
Ambato 2, Cayambe 2, Cuenca 7, Esmeraldas 2, Guayaquil 4, Ibarra 2; Loja 4, Machachi 2, Machala 4, Manta 4, Portoviejo 4, Quevedo 4, Quito 2, Salinas 4, Santa Domingo 2, Tulcan 2

Egypt   20
Alexandria 3, Answan 97, Asyut 88, Benha 13, Cairo 2, Damanhour 45, El Mahallah (El Kubra) 43, El Mansoura 50, Luxor 95, Port Said 66, Shebin El Kom 48, Sohag 93, Tanta 40

El Salvador   503
City code not required.

Estonia   372
Tallinn 2, Tartu 7.

Ethiopia   251
Addis Ababa 1, Akaki 1, Asmara 4, Assab 3, Awassa 6, Debre Zeit 1, Dessie 3, Dire Dawa 5, Harrar 5, Jimma 7, Makale 4, Massawa 4, Nazareth 2, Shashemene 6

Faeroe Islands   298
City code not required.

Fiji Islands   679
City code not required.

Finland   358
Epoo-Ebbo 15, Helsinki 0, Joensuu 73, Jyvaskyla 41, Kuopio 71, Lahti 18, Lappeenranta 53, Oulu 81, Port 39, Tammefors-Tampere 31, Turku 21, Uleaborg 81, Vaasa

61, Vanda-Vantaa 0

France   33
Aix-en-Provence 42, Bordeaux 56, Cannes 93, Chauvigny 49, Cherbourge 33, Grenoble 76, Le Havre 35, Lourdes 62, Lyon 7, Marseille 91, Nancy 8, Nice 93, Paris 1, Rouen 35, Toulouse 61, Tours 47

French Antilles   596
City code not required.

French Guiana   594
City code not required.

French Polynesia   689
City code not required.

Gabon Republic   241
City code not required.

Gambia   220
City code not required.

Georgia   7
Sukhumi 881, Tblisi 88

Germany, Fed. Rep. 49
Bad Homburg 6172, Berlin 30, Bonn 228, Bremen 421, Cologne (Koln) 221, Cottbus 355, Dresden 351, Dusseldorf 211, Erfurt 361, Essen 201, Frankfurt am Main (west) 69, Frankfurt an der Oder (east) 335, Gera 365, Halle 345, Hamburg 40, Heidellberg 6221, Karl-Stadt 9353, Koblenz 261, Leipzig 341, Magdeburg 391, Mannheim 621, Munich 89, Numberg 911, Postdam 331, Rostock 381, Saal 38223, Schwerin 385, Stuttgart 711, Wiesbaden 6121

Ghana   233
City code not required.

Gibraltar   350
City code not required.

Greece   30
Argos 751, Athens (Athinai) 1, Corinth 741, Iraklion (Kristis) 81, Kavala 51, Larissa 41, Patrai 61, Piraeus Pireefs 1, Rodos 241, Salonica (Thessaloniki) 31, Sparti 731, Thessaloniki 31, Tripolis 71, Volos 421, Zagora 426

Greenland   299
Goatham 2, Sondre Stromfjord 11, Thule 50

Grenada   809
Dial 1 + 809 + Local Number.

Guadeloupe   590
City code not required.

Guam   671
City code not required.

Guantanemo Bay   5399
City code not required.

Guatemala   502
Guatemala City 2. All other cities 9.

Guinea   224
City code not required.

Guyana   592
Anna Regina 71, Bartica 5, Beteryerwaging 20, Cove & John 29, Georgetown 2, Ituni 41, Linden 4, Mabaruma 77, Mahaica 28, Mahalcony 21, New Amsterdam 3, New Hope 66, Rosignol 30, Timehri 61, Vreed-En-Hoop 64, Whim 37

Haiti   509
Cap-Haitien 3, Cayes 5, Gonalve 2, Port au Prince 1

Honduras   504
City code not required.

Hong Kong   852
Castle Peak 0, Cheung Chau 5, Fan Ling 0, Hong Kong 5, Kowloon 3, Kwai Chung 0, Lamma 5, Lantau 5, Ma Wan 5, Peng Chau 5, Sek Kong 0, Sha Tin 0, Tai Po 0, Ting Kau 0, Tsun Wan 0

Hungary   36
Abasar 37, Balatonaliga 84, Budapest 1, Dorgicse 80, Fertoboz 99, Gyongyos 37, Kaposvar 82, Kazincbarcika 48, Komlo 72, Miskolc 46, Nagykaniza 93, Szekesfehervar 22, Szolnok 56, Varpalota 80, Veszprem 80, Zalaegerzeg 92

Iceland   354
Akureyi 6, Hafnafijorour 1, Husavik 6, Keflavik Naval Base 2, Rein 6, Reykjavik 1, Reyorarjorour 7, Sandgerol 2, Selfoss 9. Siglufijorour 6, Stokkseyri 9, Suoavik 4, Talknafijorour 4, Varma 1, Vik 9

India   91
Ahmedabad 272, Amritsar 183, Bangalore 812, Baroda 265, Bhopal 755, Bombay 22 Calcutta 33, Chandigarh 172, Hyderabad 842, Jaipur 141, Jullundur 181, Kanpur 512, Madras 44, New Dehli 11, Poona 212, Surat 261

Indonesia   62
Bandung 22, Cirebon 231, Denpasar (Bali) 361, Jakarta 21, Madiun 351, Malang 341, Medan 61, Padang 751, Palembang 711, Sekurang 778, Semarang 24, Solo 271, Surabaya 31, Tanjungkarang 721, Yogykarta 274

Iran   98
Abadan 631, Ahwaz 61, Arak 2621, Esfahan 31, Ghazvin 281, Ghome 251, Hamadan 261, Karadj 2221, Kerman 341, Mashad 51, Rasht 231, Rezaiyeh 441, Shiraz 71, Tabriz 41, Tehran 21

Iraq   964
Baghdad 1, Basiah 40, Diwanyia 36, Karbala 32, Kirkuk 50, Mosul 60, Nasryia 42

Ireland   353
Arklow 402, Cork 21, Dingle 66, Donegal 73, Drogheda 41, Dublin 1, Dundalk 42, Ennis 65, Galway 91, Kildare 45, Killamey 64, Sligo 71, Tipperary 62, Tralee 66, Tullamore 506, Waterford 51, Wexford 53

Israel   972
Afula 65, Ako 4, Ashkelon 51, Bat Iam 3, Beer Sheva 57, Dimona 57, Hadera 63, Haifa 4, Holon 3, Jerusalem 2, Nazareth 65, Netania 53, Rehovot 8, Tel Aviv 3, Tiberias 67, Tsefat 67

Italy   39
Bari 80, Bologna 51, Brindisi 831, Capri 81, Como 31, Florence 55, Genoa 10, Milan 2, Naples 81, Padova 49, Palermo 91, Pisa 50, Rome 6, Torino 11, Trieste 40, Venice 41, Verona 45

Ivory Coast   225
City code not required.

Jamaica   809
Dial 1 + 809 + Local Number.

Japan   81
Chiba 472, Fuchu (Tokyo) 423, Hiroshima 82, Kawasaki (Kanagawa) 44, Kobe 78, Kyoto 75, Nagasaki 958, Nagoya 52, Nahat (Okinawa) 988, Osaka 6, Sapporo 11, Sasebo 956, Tachikawa (Tokyo) 425, Tokyo 3, Yokohama 45, Yokosuka (Kanagawa) 468

Jordan   962
Amman 6, Aqaba 3, Irbid 2, Jerash 4, Karak 3, Maam 3, Mafruq 4, Ramtha 2, Sueeleh 6, Sult 5, Zerqa 9

Kazakhstan   7
Alma-Ata 3272, Chimkent 325, Guryev 312, Petropavlovsk 315.

Kenya   254
Anmer 154, Bamburi 11, Embakasi 2, Girgiri 2, Kabete 2, Karen 2882, Kiambu 154, Kikuyu 283, Kisumu 35, Langata 2, Mombasa 11, Nairobi 2, Nakuru 37, Shanzu 11, Thika 151, Uthiru 2

Kiribati   686
City code not required.

Korea   82
Chung Ju 431, Chuncheon 361, Icheon 336, Incheon 32, Kwangju (Gwangju) 62, Masan 551, Osan 339, Osan Military (333+414), Pohang 562, Pusan (Busan) 51, Seoul 2, Suwon (Suweon) 331, Taegu (Daegu) 53, Ulsan 552, Wonju (Weonju) 371

Kuwait   965
City code not required.

Kyrgyzstan   7
Osh 33222 plus 5 digits, Pishpek 3312

Latvia   371
Riga 0132

Lebanon   961
Beirut 1, Juniyah 9, Tripoli 6, Zahlah 8

Lesotho   266
City code not required.

Liberia   231

City code not required.

Libya   218

Agelat 282, Benghazi 61, Benina 63, Derma 81, Misuratha 51, Sabratha 24, Sebha 71, Taigura 26, Tripoli 21, Tripoli International Airport 22, Zawai 23, Zuara 25

Liechtenstein   41
Use 75 for all cities.

Lithuania   370
Kaunas 7, Klaipeda 6, Panevezys 54, Siauliai 1, Vilnius 2.

Luxembourg   352
City code not required.

Macao   853
City code not required.

Macedonia   389
Asamati 96, Bitola 97, Gostivar 94, Kicevo 95, Krusevo 98, Lozovo 92, Skopje 91.

Malawi   265
Domasi 531, Likuni 766, Luchenza 477, Makwasa 474, Mulanje 465, Namadzi 534, Njuli 664, Thondwe 533, Thornwood 486, Thyolo 467, Zomba 50, City code not required for other cities.

Malaysia   60
Alor Star 4, Baranang 3, Broga 3, Cheras 3, Dengil 3, Ipoh 5, Johor Bahru 7, Kajang 3, Kepala Batas 4, Kuala Lampur 3, Machang 97, Maran 95, Port Dickson 6, Semenyih 3, Seremban 6, Sungei Besi 3, Sungei Renggam 3

Maldives   960
City code not required.

Mali   223
City code not required.

Malta   **356**
City code not required.
Marshall Islands   **692**
Ebeye 871, Majuro 9

Mauritius   **230**
City code not required.

Mayotte Islands   **269**
City code not required.

Mexico   **52**
Acapulco 748, Cancun 988, Celaya 461, Chihuahua 14, Ciudad Juarez 16, Conzumel 987, Culiacan 671, Ensenda 667, Guadalajara 36, Hermosillo 621, La Paz 682, Mazatlan 678, Merida 99, Mexicali 65, Mexico City 5, Monterrey 83, Puebla 22, Puerto Vallarta 322, Rasarito 661, San Luis Potosi 481, Tampico 121, Tecate 665, Tijuana 66, Torreon 17, Veracruz 29

Micronesia   **691**
Kosrae 851, Ponape 9, Truk 8319, Yap 841

Moldova   **373**
Benderi 32, Kishinev 2

Monaco   **33**
Use 93 for all cities.

Mongolian People's Rep.   **976**
Ulan Bator 1

Montserrat   **809**
Dial 1 + 809 + Local Number.

Morocco   **212**
Agardir 8, Beni-Mellal 48, Berrechid 33, Casablanca (City code not required). El Jadida 34, Fes 6, Kenitra 16, Marrakech 4, Meknes 5, Mohammedia 32, Nador 60, Oujda 68, Rabat 7, Tanger (Tangiers) 9, Tetouan 96

Mustique   **809**
Dial 1 + 809 + Local Number.

Namibia   **264**
Gobabis 681, Grootfontein 673, Industria 61, Keetmanshoop 631, Luderitz 6331, Mariental 661, Okahandja 622, Olympia 61, Otjiwarongo 651, Pioneerspark 61, Swakopmund 641, Tsumeb 671, Windhoek 61, Windhoek Airport 626

Nauru Island   **674**
City code not required.

Nepal   **977**
City code not required.

Netherlands   **31**
Amsterdam 20, Arnhem 85, Eindhoven 40, Groningen 50, Haarlem 23, Heemstede 23, Hillegersberg 10, Hoensbraoek 45, Hoogkerk 50, Hoogvliet 10, Loosduinen 70, Nijmegen 80, Oud Zuilen 30, Rotterdam 10, The Hague 70, Utrecht 30

Netherlands Antilles   **599**
Bonaire 7, Curacao 9, Saba 4, Eustatius 3, St. Maarten 5

Nevis   **809**
Dial 1 + 809 + Local Number.

New Caledonia   **687**
City code not required.

New Zeland   **64**
Auckland 9, Christchurch 3, Dunedin 24, Hamilton 71, Hastings 70, Invercargill 21, Napier 70, Nelson 54, New Plymouth 67, Palmerston North 63, Rotorua 73, Tauranga 75, Timaru 56, Wanganui 64, Wellington 4, Whangarei 89

Nicaragua   **505**
Boaco 54, Chinandega 341, Diriamba 42, Esteli 71, Granada 55, Jinotepe 41, Leon 311, Managua 2, Masatepe 44, Masaya 52, Nandaime 45, Rivas 461, San Juan Del Sur 466, San Marcos 43, Tipitapa 53

Niger Republic   **227**
City code not required.

Nigeria   **234**
Lagos 1 (Only city direct dial)

Niue   **683**

Norfolk Island   **672**

Norway   **47**
Arendal 41, Bergen 5, Drammen 3, Fredrikstad 32, Haugesund 47, Kongsvinger 66, Kristiansund N. 73, Larvik 34, Moss 32, Narvik 82, Oslo 2, Sarpsborg 31, Skien 35, Stavanger 4, Svalbard 80, Tonsberg 33, Trondheim 7

Oman   **968**
City code not required.

Pakistan   **92**
Abbotabad 5921, Bahawalpur 621, Faisalabad 411, Gujtanwala 431, Hyderabad 221, Islamabad 51, Karachi 21, Lahore 42, Multan 61, Okara 442, Peshawar 521, Quetta 81, Sahiwal 441, Sargodha 451, Sialkot 432, Sukkur 71

Palm Island   **809**
Dial 1 + 809 + Local Number.

Panama   **507**
City code not required.

Papau New Guinea 675
City code not required.

Paragua 595
Asuncion 21, Ayolas 72, Capiata 28, Concepcion 31, Coronel Bogado 74, Coronel Oviedo 521, Encarnacion 71, Hermandarias 63, Ita 24, Pedro J. Caballero 36, Pilar 86, San Antonio 27, San Ignacio 82, Stroessner: Ciudad Pte. 61, Villarica 541, Villeta 25

Peru 51
Arequipa 54, Ayacucho 6491, Callao 14, Chiclayo 74, Chimbote 44, Cuzco 84, Huancavelica 6495, Huancayo 64, Ica 34, Iquitos 94, Lima 14, Piura 74, Tacna 54, Trujillo 44

Phillippines 63
Angeles 55, Bacolod 34, Baguio City 442, Cebu City 32, Clark Field (military) 52, Dagupan 48, Davao 35, Lloilo City 33, Lucena 42, Manila 2, San Fernando: La Union 46, San Fernando: Pampanga 45, San Pablo 43, Subic Bay Military Base 89, Subic Bay Residential Housing 89, Tarlac City 47

Poland 48
Bialystok 85, Bydgoszcz 52, Crakow (Krakow) 12, Gdansk 58, Gdynia 58, Katowice 32, Lodz 42, Lubin 81, Olsztyn 89, Poznan 48, Radom 48, Sopot 58, Torun 56, Warsaw 22

Portugal 351
Alamada 1, Angra Do Heroismo 95, Barreiro 1, Beja 84, Braga 53, Caldas Da Rainha 62, Coimbra 39, Estoril 1, Evora 66, Faro 89, Horta 92, Lajes AFB 95, Lisbon 1, Madalena 92, Madeira Islands 91, Montijo 1, Ponta Del Gada 96, Porto 2, Santa Cruz (Flores) 92, Santarem 43, Setubal 65, Velas 95, Vila Do Porto 96, Viseu 32

Qatar 974
City code not required.

Reunion Island 262
City code not required.

Romania 40
Arad 66, Bacau 31, Brasov 21, Bucharest 0, Cluj-Napoca 51, Constanta 16, Crajova 41, Galati 34, Lasi 81, Oradea 91, Pitesti 76, Ploiesti 71, Satu-Mare 97, Sibiu 24, Timisoara 61, Tirgu Mures 54

Russia 7
Magadan 413, Moscow 095, St. Petersburg 812

Rwanda 250
City code not required.

St. Kitts 809
Dial 1 + 809 + Local Number.

St. Lucia 809
Dial 1 + 809 + Local Number.

St. Pierre & Miquelon 508
City code not required.

St. Vincent 809
Dial 1 + 809 + Local Number.

Saipan 670
Capitol Hill 322, Rota Island 532, Susupe City 234, Tinian Island 433

San Marino 39
Use 541 for all cities.

Saudi Arabia 966
Abha 7, Abqaiq 3, Al Khobar 3, Al Markazi 2, Al Ulaya 1, Damman 3, Dhahran (Aramco) 3, Jeddah 2, Khamis Mushait 7, Makkah (Mecca) 2, Medina 4, Najran 7, Qatif 3, Riyadh 1, Taif 2, Yenbu 4

Senegal 221
City code not required.

Seychelles Islands 248
City code not required.

Sierra Leone 232
Freetown 22, Juba 24, Lungi 25, Wellington 23

Singapore 65
City code not required.

Solomon Island 677
City code not required.

Slovakia 42
Bratislava 7, Presov 91.

Slovenia 386
Ljubljana 61, Maribor 62

South Africa 27
Bloemfontein 51, Cape Town 21, De Aar 571, Durban 31, East London 431, Gordons Bay 24, Johannesburg 11, La Lucia 31, Pietermaritzburg 331, Port Elizabeth 41, Pretoria 12, Sasolburg 16, Somerset West 24, Uitenhage 422, Welkom 171

Spain 34
Barcelona 3, Bibao 4, Cadiz 56, Ceuta 56, Granada 58, Igualada 3, Las Palmas de Gran Canaria 28, Leon 87, Madrid 1, Malaga 52, Melilla 52, Palma De Mallorca 71, Pamplona 48, Santa Cruz de Tenerife 22, Santander 42, Seville 54, Torremolinos 52, Valencia 6

Sri Lanka 94
Ambalangoda 97, Colombo Central 1, Galle 9, Havelock

Town 1, Kandy 8, Katugastota 8, Kotte 1, Maradana 1, Matara 41, Negomgo 31, Panadura 46, Trincomalee 26

Suriname   597
City code not required.

Swaziland   268
City code not required.

Sweden   46
Alingsas 322, Boras 33, Eskilstuna 16, Gamleby 493, Goteborg 31, Helsinborg 42, Karlstad 54, Linkoping 13, Lund 46, Malmo 40, Norrkoping 11, Stockholm 8, Sundsvall 60, Trelleborg 410, Uppsala 18, Vasteras 21

Switzerland   41
Baden 56, Basel 61, Berne 31, Davos 83, Fribourg 37, Geneva 22, Interlaken 36, Lausanne 21, Lucerne 41, Lugano 91, Montreux 21, Neuchatel 38, St. Gallen 71, St. Moritz 82, Winterthur 52, Zurich 1

Taiwan   886
Changhua 47, Chunan 36, Chunghsing-Hsintsun 49, Chungli 34, Fengyuan 4, Hsiaying 6, Hualien 38, Kaohsiung 7, Keelung 2, Lotung 39, Pingtung 8, Taichung 4, Tainan 6, Taipei 2, Taitung 89, Taoyuan 33

Tajikistan   7
Dushanbe 3772

Tanzania   255
Dar Es Salaam 51, Dodoma 61, Mwanza 68, Tanga 53

Thailand   66
Bangkok 2, Burirum 44, Chanthaburi 39, Chien Mai 53, Cheingrai 54, Kamphaengphet 55, Lampang 54, Nakhon Sawan 56, Nong Khai 42, Pattani 73, Pattaya 38, Ratchaburi 32, Saraburi 36, Tak 55, Ubon Ratchathani 45

Togo   228
City code not required.

Tonga Islands   676
City code not required.

Trinidad & Tabago   809
Dial 1 + 809 + Local Number.

Tunisia   216
Agareb 4, Beja 8, Bizerte 2, Carthage 1, Chebba 4, Gabes 5, Gafsa 6, Haffouz 7, Hamman-Souse 3, Kairouan 7, Kef 8, Khenis 3, Medenine 5, Tabarka 8, Tozeur 6, Tunis 1

Turkey   90
Adana 711, Ankara 41, Antalya 311, Bursa 241, Eskisehir 221, Gazianter 851, Istanbul 1, Izmir 51, Izmit 211, Kayseri 351, Konya 331, Malatya 821, Mersin 741, Samsun 361

Turka & Caicos   809
Dial 1 + 809 + Local Number.

Turkmenistan   7
Ashkkhabad 3632, Chardzhou 378

Tuvalu   688

Ukraine   380
Kharkiv 572, Kiev 44, Lviv 322

Uganda   256
Entebbe 42, Jinja 43, Kampala 41, Kyambogo 41

Union Island   809
Dial 1 + 809 + Local Number.

United Arab Emirates   971
Abu Dhabi 2, Ajman 6, Al Ain 3, Aweer 58, Dhayd 6, Dibba 70, Dubai 4, Falaj-al-Moalla 6, Fujairah 70, Jebel Ali 84, Jebel Dhana 52, Khawanij 58, Ras-al-Khaimah 77, Sharjan 6, Tarif 53, Umm-al-Quwain 6

United Kingdom   44
Belfast 232, Birmingham 21, Bournemouth 202, Cardiff 222, Durham 385, Edinburgh 31, Glasgow 41, Gloucester 452, Ipswich 473, Liverpool 51, London (Inner) 71, London (Outer) 81, Manchester 61, Nottingham 602, Prestwick 292, Sheffield 742, Southampton 703

Uruguay   598
Atlantida 372, Colonia 522, Florida 352, La Paz 322, Las Piedras 322, Los Toscas 372, Maldonado 42, Mercedes 532, Minas 442, Montevideo 2, Parque De Plata 372, Paysandu 722, Punta Del Este 42, Salinas 372, San Jose 342,
San Jose De Carrasco 382

Uzbekistan   7
Karish 375, Samarkand 3662, Tashkent 3712

Vanuatu, Rep. of   678

Vatican City   39
Use 6 for all cities.

Venezuela   58
Barcelona 81, Barquisimeto 51, Cabimas 64, Caracas 2, Ciudad Bolivar 85, Coro 68, Cumana 93, Los Teques 32, Maiquetia 31, Maracaibo 61, Maracay 43, Maturin 91, Merida 74, Puerto Cabello 42, San Cristobal 76, Valencia 41

Vietnam   84
Hanoi 4, Ho Chi Minh City 8

Wallis & Futuna Islands   681

Western Samoa   685
City code not required.

Yeman (North)   967
Al Marawyah 3, Al Qaidah 4, Amran 2, Bayt Al Faquih 3,
Dhamar 2, Hodeidah 3, Ibb 4, Mabar 2, Rada 2, Rawda 2,
Sanaa 2, Taiz 4, Yarim 4, Zabid 3

Yugoslavia   38
Belgrade (Beograd) 11, Dubrovnik 50, Leskovac 16,
Ljubjana 61, Maribor 62, Mostar 88, Novi Sad 21, Pirot
10, Rijeka 51, Sarajevo 71, Skopje 91, Split 58, Titograd
81, Titovo-Uzice 31, Zagreb 41

Zaire   243
Kinshasa 12, Lubumbashi 222

Zambia   260
Chingola 2, Kitwe 2, Luanshya 2, Lusaka 1, Ndola 26

Zimbabwe   263
Bulawayo 9, Harare 0, Mutare 20

APPENDIX 6F

INTERNATIONAL TELEX CODES

AFGHANISTAN	930	COTE D'IVOIRE	969	JAPAN	781		
ALGERIA	936	CUBA	307	JORDAN	925		
AME. SAMOA	782	CYPRUS	826	KAZAKHSTAN	871		
ANDOA	833	CZECH REPUBLIC	849	KENYA	963		
ANGOLA	998	DENMARK	855	KIRIBATI	727		
ANGUILLA	317	DIEGO GARCIA IS	919	KOREA, SOUTH	787		
ANTIGUA & BARBUDA	306	DOMINICA	304	KOREA, NORTH	779		
ARGENTINA	390	DOMINICAN		KUWAIT	959		
ARMENIA	871	REP.	326, 346, 366	KYRGYZSTAN	871		
ARUBA	364, 384	ECUADOR	393	LAOS	715		
ASCENSION IS.	920	EGYPT	927	LATVIA	871		
AUSTRALIA	790	EL SALVADOR	301	LEBANON	923		
AUSTRIA	847	ELLICE IS	726	LESOTHO	990		
AZERBAIJAN	871	EQUAT GUINEA	939	LIBERIA	937		
AZORES	835	ESTONIA	871	LIBYA	929		
BAHRAIN	955	ETHIOPIA	976	LIECHTENSTEIN	845		
BALERIC IS	831	FAEROE IS	853	LITHUANIA	871		
BANGLADESH	950	FIJI	792	LUXEMBOURG	848		
BARBADOS	386	FINLAND	857	MADAGASCAR	983		
BELARUS	871	FRANCE	842	MALAWI	988		
BELGIUM	846	FR. POLYNESIA	711	MALAYSIA	784		
BELIZE	310	FRENCH GUIANA	313	MALDIVES	940		
BENIN	979	FR. ANTILLES	340	MALI	972		
BERMUDA	380	GABON	981	MALTA	838		
BHUTAN	733	GEORGIA	871	MARSHALL IS	730		
BOLIVIA	336, 355, 356, 376	GERMANY	841	MARTINIQUE	300		
BOTSWANA	991	GHANA	974	MAURITANIA	935		
BRAZIL	391	GIBRALTAR	837	MAURITIUS	996		
BRITISH V.I.	318	GREECE	863	MAYOTTE IS	942		
BRUNEI	799	GREENLAND	859	MEXICO	383		
BULGARIA	865	GRENADA	320	MICRONESIA	729		
BURKINA FASO	985	GUADELOUPE	340	MIDWAY IS	603		
BURMA	713	GUAM	721	MOLDOVA	871		
BURUNDI	977	GUANTANAMO BAY	606	MONACO	842		
CAMBODIA	720	GUATEMALA	305	MONGOLIA	719		
CAMEROON	978	GUINEA	995	MONTSERRAT	360		
CANADA	389	GUINEA-BISSAU	931	MOROCCO	933		
CANARY IS	966	GUYANA	312	MOZAMBIQUE	946		
CAYENNE	313	HAITI	349	NAMIBIA	964		
CAYMAN IS	309	HONDURAS	311	NAURU	739		
CENT. AFR.REP.	980	HONG KONG	780	NEPAL	947		
CHAD	984	HUNGARY	861	NETHERLANDS ANTILLES	384		
CHANNEL IS	851	ICELAND	858	NETHERLANDS	844		
CHILE	332, 352, 359, 392	INDIA	953	NEVIS	361		
CHINA, PEOPLES REP.	716	INDONESIA	796	NEW CALEDONIA	714		
CHINA, TAIWAN	785	IRAN	951	NEW ZEALAND	791		
COLOMBIA	396	IRAQ	943	NICARAGUA	388		
COMOROS	942	IRELAND	852	NIGER	982		
CONGO, PEOPLE'S REP.	971	ISRAEL	922	NIGERIA	961		
COOK IS	717	ITALY	843	NIUE	772		
COSTA RICA	303	JAMAICA	381	NORFOLK IS	756		

574

NORWAY	856		TOKELAU IS	731
OKINAWA	781, 789		TONGA	765
OMAN	926		TRINIDAD & TOBAGO	387
PAKISTAN	952		TUNISIA	934
PANAMA	328, 348, 368		TURKEY	821
PAPUA NEW GUINEA	798, 795		TURKMENISTAN	871
PARAGUAY	399		TURKS & CAICOS	315
PERU	334, 394		UGANDA	973
PHILIPPINES	712, 722, 732,		UKRAINE	871
	742, 762, 778		U.K	851
PITCAIRN IS	604		UNITED ARAB	
POLAND	867		EMIRATES	949, 958
PORTUGAL	832		URUGUAY	398
PUERTO RICO	324, 325, 345,		US. V.I.	327, 347,367
	365, 385		UZBEKISTAN	871
QATAR	957		VANUATU	718
REP. OF			VATICAN CITY	803
CAPE VERDE	938		VENEZUELA	395
REP. OF DJIBOUTI	9 9 4		VIETNAM	798
REUNION ISLAND	941		WESTERN SAMOA	793
RODRIGUEZ IS	996		YEMEN, PEOPLE'S DEM	
ROMANIA	864		REP.	956
RUSSIA	871		YEMEN, ARAB REP.	948
RWANDA	967		YUGOSLAVIA	862
SAIPAN	724, 783		ZAIRE	968
SAN MARINO	868		ZAMBIA	965
SAO TOME & PRINCIPE	916		ZIMBABWE	987
SAUDI ARABIA	928			
SENEGAL	962			
SEYCHELLES	997			
SIERRA LEONE	989			
SINGAPORE	786			
SOLOMON IS	769			
SOMALIA	999			
SOUTH AFRICA	960			
SPAIN	831			
SPANISH SAHARA	933			
SRI LANKA	954			
ST. THOMA IS	916			
ST. THOMAS	327, 347, 367			
ST. MARTEEN	384			
ST. MARTIN	340			
ST. PIERRE & MIQUELON	316			
ST. VINCENT	321			
ST. KITTS-NEVIS	361			
ST. LUCIA	341			
SUDAN	970			
SURINAME	397			
SWAZILAND	993			
SWEDEN	8 5 4			
SWITZERLAND	845			
SYRIA	924			
TAHITI	711			
TAJIKISTAN	8 7 1			
TANZANIA	975			
THAILAND	788			
THE GAMBIA	992			
TIBET	716			
TOGO	986			

575

APPENDIX 7G

CURRENCIES OF THE WORLD

COUNTRY	UNIT	Unit = 100
		Unless otherwise stated
AFGHANISTAN	Afghani	Puls
ALBANIA	Lek	Quintar
ALGERIA	Dinar	Centimes
ANGOLA	Kwanza	Lweis
ANGUILLA	E.C. Dollar	Cents
ARGENTINA	Peso	Centavos
ARMENIA	Luma	Dram
AUSTRALIA	Aust. Dollar	Cents
AUSTRIA	Schilling	Groschen
AZERBAIJAN	Manat/Rubles	Kopek
BAHAMAS	Bahamian Dollar	Cents
BAHRAIN	Bahrain Dinar	1000 Fils
BANGLADESH	Taka	Poisha
BARBADOS	Dollar	Cents
BELGIUM	Belgian Franc	Centimes
BELIZE	Dollar	Cents
BENIN	Franc (CFA)	---
BERMUDA	Dollar	Cents
BHUTAN	Ngultrum	
BOLIVIA	Boliviano	Centavos
BOTSWANA	Pula	Thebe
BOSNIA-HERZEGOVINA	Bosnian Dinar	
BRAZIL	Cruzeiro	Centavos
BRITISH V.I.	Dollar USC	Cents
BRUNEI	Brunei Dollar	Cents
BULGARIA	Lev	Stotinki
BURKINA FASO	Franc (CFA)	---
BURMA	Kyat	Pyas
BURUNDI	Burundi Franc	Centimes
BYELARUS	Rubles	Kopeks
CAMBODIA	Riel	
CAMEROON	Franc (CFA)	---
CANADA	Canadian Dollar	Cents
CAYMAN IS	Cayman Is. Dollar	Cents
CENTRAL A. REP.	Franc (CFA)	Centimes
CHAD	Franc (CFA)	Cents
CHILE	Chilean Peso	Centesimos
CHINA, P. REP.	Ren Min Bi	Fen
CHINA, TAIWAN	New Taiwan Dollar	
COLOMBIA	Colombian Peso	Centavos
COMOROS	Franc (CFA)	---
COSTA RICA	Colon	Cenavos
COTE D'IVOIRE	Franc (CFA)	---
CROATIA	Croatian Kuna	
CUBA	Peso	Centavos
CYPRUS	Cyprus Pound	1000 Mills

COUNTRY	UNIT	Unit = 100
		Unless otherwise stated
CZECH REPUBLIC	Koruna	Halers
DENMARK	Krone	Ore
DOMINICA	E.C. Dollar	Cents
DOMINICAN REP.	Peso	Centavos
ECUADOR	Sucre	Centavos
EGYPT	Egyptian Pound	Piastres
CONGO, P. REP.	Franc (CFA)	---
EL SALVADOR	Colon	Centavos
EQUAT. GUINEA	Ekuele	Centimos
ESTONIA	Kroon	
ETHIOPIA	Birr	Cents
FAEROE IS	Faeroese Krona	
FIJI	Fiji Dollar	Cents
FINLAND	Markka	Penni
FRANCE	French Franc	Centimes
FR. POLYNESIA	Franc	Centimes
FRENCH GUIANA	Franc	Centimes
GABON	Franc (CFA)	---
GEORGIA	Georgian Coupons	Kopek
GERMANY	Mark	Pfennig
GHANA	Cedi	Pesawas
GIBRALTAR	Pound	Pence
GREECE	Drachma	Lepta
GRENAD	E.C. Dollar	Cents
GUATEMALA	Quetzal	Centavos
GUINEA	Franc	Couris
GUINEA-BISSAU	Peso	Centavos
GUYANA	Guyana Dollar	Cents
HAITI	Gourde	Centimes
HONDURAS	Lempira	Centavos
HONG KONG	Hong Kong Dollar	Cents
HUNGARY	Forint	Fillers
ICELAND	Icelandic Krona	Aur
INDIA	Indian Rupee	Naya Paise
INDONESIA	Rupiah	Sen
IRAN	Iranian Rial	Dinars
IRAQ	Iraqi Dinar	1000 Fils
IRELAND	Irish Pound	Pence
ISRAEL	New Shekel	10 Agorot
ITALY	Lira	---
JAMAICA	Jamaican Dollar	Cents
JAPAN	Yen	---
JORDAN	Jordanian Dinar	1000 Fils
KAMPUCHEA	Riel	Centimes
KAZAKHSTAN	Ruble	
KENYA	Kenya Shilling	Cents

KIRIBATI	Australian Dollar Cents	SAUDI ARABIA	Saudi Riyal Hallalah
KOREA, NORTH	Won Jun	SENEGAL Franc (CFA) ---	
KOREA, SOUTH	Won Chon	SEYCHELLES	Seychelles Rupee Cents
KUWAIT	Kuwaiti Dinar 1000 Fils	SIERRA LEONE	Leone Cents
KYRGYZSTAN	Som Kopeks	SINGAPORE	Singapore Dollar Cents
LAOS	Kip Pot Po Centimes	SLOVAKIA	Slovak Crown Hellers
LATVIA	Latvian Lats Santimis	SLOVENIA	Slovene Tolar
LEBANON	Lebanese Pound Piastres	SOLOMON IS	Dollar Cents
LESOTHO	Loti Licente	SOMALIA	Somali Schilling Cents
LIBERIA	Liberian Dollar Cents	SOUTH AFRICA	Rand Cents
LIBYA	Libyan Dinar 1000 Dirham	SPAIN	Spanish Peseta Centimos
LIECHTENSTEIN	Franc	SRI LANKA	Sri Lanka Rupee Cents
LITHUANIA	Litas Cents	ST. KITTS-NEVIS	E.C. Dollar Cents
LUXEMBOURG	Luxembourg Franc Centimes	ST. VINCENT	E.C. Dollar Cents
MACEDONIA	Macedonia Deni Denars	ST. LUCIA	E.C. Dollar Cents
MADAGASCAR	Franc Centimes	SUDAN	Sudanese Pound Piastres
MALAWI	Kwacha Tambala	SURINAME	Surinam Guilder Cents
MALAYSIA	Ringgit Sen	SWAZILAND	Lilangeni Cents
MALDIVES	Rufiyaas Laree	SWEDEN	Swedish Kronor Ore
MALI	Mali Franc Centimes	SWITZERLAND	Franc Centimes
MALTA	Maltese Lira Cents	SYRIA	Syrian Pound Piastre
MAURITANIA	Ouguiya 5 Khoums	TAJIKISTAN	Ruble Kopeks
MAURITIUS	Mauritian Rupee Cents	TANZANIA	Tanzanian Shilling Cents
MEXICO	Mexican Peso Centavos	THAILAND	Baht Satang
MICRONESIA	U.S. Dollar Cents	THE GAMBIA	Dalasi Batut
MOLDOVA	Leu Bani	TOGO	Franc (CFA) ---
MONACO	Franc	TONGA	Pa'anga Seniti
MONGOLIA	Tugrik	TRINIDAD/TOBAGO	Dollar Cents
MONTSERRATE.	Caribbean Dollar Cents	TUNISIA Tunisian Dinar 1000 Millimes	
MOROCCO	Dirham Centimes	TURKEY	Turkish LiraKurus
MOZAMBIQUE	Metical Centavos	TURKMENISTAN	Ruble Kopeks
NAMIBIA	Rand	TURKS & CAICOS	U.S. Dollar Cents
NAURU	Australian Dollar	U.S.A	Dollar Cents
NEPAL	Nepalese Rupee Pice	UGANDA	Uganda Shilling Cents
NETH. ANTILLES	Guilder Cents	UKRAINE	Karbovanets
NETHERLANDS	Guilder Cents	UN.ARAB EMIRATE.	UAE Dirham Fils
NEW ZEALAND	N.Zealand Dollar Cents	UNITED KINGDOM Pound Sterling Pence	
NEW CALEDONIA	Franc Centimes	URUGUAY	New Uruguayan Peso Centimos
NICARAGUA	Cordoba Centavos	UZBEKISTAN	Ruble/Coupons Kopeks
NIGER	Franc (CFA) ---	VANUATU REP.	Vatu Centimes
NIGERIA	Naira Kobos	VENEZUELA	Bolivar Centimos
NORWAY	Norwegian Krone Ore	VIETNAM	Dong 10 Hao
OMAN	Rial 1000 Baizas	YEMEN, ARAB REP.	Yemeni Rial Fils
PAKISTAN	Pakistani Rupee Paisa	YEMEN, P.D.R.	Yemeni Dinar 1000 Fils
PANAMA	Balboa Cents	ZAIRE	Zaire Makutas
PAPUA N. GUINEA	Kina Toea	ZAMBIA	Zambian Kwacha Ngwee
PARAGUAY	Guaranie Centimos	ZIMBABWE	Zimbabwe Dollar Cents
PERU	Sol Centavos		
PHILIPPINES	Philippine Peso Centavos		
POLAND	Zloty Groszy	CFA =	Communaute Financiere Africaine
PORTUGAL	Potuguese Escudo Centavos		
PUERTO RICO	U.S. Dollar Cents	E.C. =	East Caribbean
QATAR	Qatar Riyal Dirhams		
REP. OF CAPE VERDE Escudo Centavos		* =	Several of the countries of the former Soviet Union
REP. OF DJIBOUTI	Franc Centimes		are in the process of introducing their own
REUNION ISLAND	Franc Centimes		currency. For now most are still using and
ROMANIA	Lei Bani		accepting the Soviet Ruble.
RUSSIA	Ruble Kopeks		
RWANDA	Rwandese Franc Centimes		
SAN MARINO	Lira		
SAO TOME	Dobra ---		

APPENDIX 8H

WORLD COMMERCIAL HOLIDAYS

Virtually every day in 1995 will be a holiday somewhere in the world with business and government offices closed while employees watch parades, pray, or perhaps enjoy a quiet holiday at home with their family. Seasoned business travelers build their schedules around these holidays, because the alternative can be a frustrating day wasted in a hotel room while the local people, from the top executives on down observe their traditional holiday rituals.

The following pages list alphabetically by country, the hundreds of commercial holidays around the world each year that will close business and government offices for a day or more. Major regional holidays that are observed in many countries are included, plus any other pertinent information.

In cases where holidays fall on Saturday or Sunday commercial establishments may be closed the preceding Friday or following Monday. For many countries, such as those in the Moslem world, holiday dates can be only approximated because the holidays are based on actual lunar observation and exact dates are announced only shortly before they occur. Note that references to the Moslem holidays often vary in spelling and dates, and that businesses in many Moslem countries are closed on Fridays.

Although U.S. holidays are not listed in this schedule, they should also be considered when appointments are made with U.S. and Foreign Commercial Service officers abroad. This calendar is intended as a working guide only. For some countries that have not yet announced holidays for 1995, the schedule was projected based on 1994 holidays. Corroboration of dates is suggested in final travel planning.

Algeria
March 13—Aid El Fitr; May 1—Labor Day; May 21—Aid El Adha; June 11—Awal Mouharem; June 19—Revolutionary Recovery Day; June 20—Achoura; July 5—Independence Day; August 20—El Moulid Ennaboui; November 1—Revolution Day.

Argentina
January 1—New Year's; April 1—Good Friday; May 1—Labor Day; May 25—Revolution (1810) Day; June 10—Sovereignty Day; June 20—Flag Day; July 9—Independence (1816) Day; August 17—Death of General J. de San Martin; October 12—Discovery of America; December 25—Christmas.

Australia
January 1—New Year's; January 26—Australia Day; April 14—Good Friday; April 17—Easter Monday; April 25—ANZAC Day; June 13—Queen's Birthday; December 26—Christmas; December 27—Boxing Day. [The preceding list is based on Australia's 1994 holiday schedule.]

Austria
January 1—New Year's; January 6—Epiphany; April 17—Easter Monday; May 1—Labor Day; May 25—Ascension; June 5—Whit Monday; June 6—Corpus Christi; August 15—Assumption; October 26—National Day; November 1—All Saint's; December 8—Immaculate Conception; December 25—Christmas; December 26—St. Stephen's Day.

Bahrain
January 1—New Year's; March 2-4—Eid Al Fitr; May 9-11—Eid Al Adha; May 29—Islamic New Year; June 8-9—Ashoora; August 7—Prophet's Birthday; December 16—National Day.

Bangladesh
February 21—Martyrs' Day; March 11—Shab-i-Qadr; March 13-14—Eid-ul-Fitr; March 26—Independence Day; April 14—Bangla New Year's Day; May 1—May Day; May 21-24—Eid-ul-Azha; June 20—Muharram (Ashura); August 29—Janmaausthami; November 7—Solidarity Day. (The Bangladesh Government announces holidays for the next year in late December. Muslim religious holidays vary with appearance of the moon. Religious holidays may move one or two days in either direction.)

Barbados
January 1—New Year's; January 21—Errol Barrow's Birthday; April 14—Good Friday; April 17—Easter Monday; May 1—May Day; June 5—Whit Monday; First Monday in August—Kadooment Day; First Monday in October—United Nation's Day; Last weekday of November—Independence Day; December 25—Christmas; December 26—Boxing Day.

Belgium
January 1—New Year's; April 17—Easter Monday; May 1—Belgian Labor Day; May 25—Ascension; June 5—Whit

Monday; July 21—Belgian Independence Day; August 15—Assumption; November 1—All Saints' Day; November 10-11—Veterans' Day; December 25—Christmas.

Brazil
January 1—New Year's; February 14-15—Carnival; April 14—Good Friday; April 21—Tiradentes' Day; June 2—Corpus Christi; September 7—Independence Day; October 12—N. Sra. Aparecida; November 2—All Souls; November 15—Proclamation of the Republic; December 25—Christmas; (The preceding list is based on Brazil's 1994 holiday schedule.)

Bulgaria
January 1—New Year's; March 3—Liberation from the Ottoman Yoke Day; May 1—Labor Day; First Monday after the Orthodox Easter—Easter Monday; May 24—Cyril and Methodius Day; December 25-26—Christmas.

Canada
January 1-2—New Year's; January 3—New Year's (Quebec only); February 20—Family Day (Alberta only); April 14—Good Friday; April 17—Easter Monday; May 22—Victoria Day; June 26—St. Jean Baptiste Day (Quebec only); July 3—Canada Day; August 7—Civic Holiday (most provinces); September 4—Labor Day; October 9—Thanksgiving; November 13—Remembrance Day; December 25—Christmas; December 26—Boxing Day.

Chile
January 1—New Year's; April 1—Good Friday; April 3—Easter Sunday; May 1—Labor Day; May 21—Commemoration of the Battle of Iquique; June 2—Corpus Christi; June 29—Saint Peter and Saint Paul; August 15—Assumption; September 11—Official Holiday; September 18—Independence Day; September 19—Day of the Army; October 12—Columbus Day; November 1—All Saints' Day; December 8—Immaculate Conception; December 25—Christmas.

China
February 10-12—Spring Festival; May 1—International Labor Day; October 1-2—Chinese National Day.

Colombia
January 1—New Year's; January 6—Epiphany*; March 19—St. Joseph's Day*; April 13—Holy Thursday; April 14—Good Friday; May 1—Labor Day; May 29—Ascension; June 19—Feast of the Sacred Heart; June 26—Corpus Christi; June 29—Saints Peter and Paul* (When holidays marked with an asterisk do not fall on Monday, they are transferred to the following Monday.)

Costa Rica
March 31—Holy Thursday; April 1—Good Friday; April 11—Juan Santamaria; June 2—Corpus Christi; June 29—Saint Peter and Saint Paul; July 25—Annexation of Guanacaste; August 2—Our Lady of Los Angeles; August

15—Assumption; September 15—Independence Day; October 12—Columbus Day; December 8—Immaculate Conception; December 26—Christmas.

Cote d'Ivoire
January 1—New Year's; March—End of Ramadan; April 17—Easter Monday; May 1—Labor Day; May 25—Ascension; May—Tabaski; June 5—Pentecost Monday; August 15—Assumption; August—Prophet Mohammed's Birthday; October—Houphouet Boigny's Birthday; November 1—All Saint's; November 15—National Peace Day; December 7—Independence Day; December 25—Christmas.

Czech Republic
January 1—New Year's; May 8—Liberation Day; July 5—Cyril & Methodius Day; July 6—Jan Hus Day; October 28—National Day; December 25—Christmas; December 26—St. Stephen's Day.

Denmark
January 1—New Year's; April 13—Maundy Thursday; April 14—Good Friday; April 17—Easter Monday; May 12—Prayer Day; May 23—Ascension; June 5—Whit Monday and Constitution Day; December 25—Christmas; December 26—Second Christmas Day.

Dominican Republic
January 1—New Year's; January 6—Epiphany; January 21—Our Lady of Grace; January 26—Duarte's Birthday; February 27—Dominican Independence; April 1—Good Friday; May 1—Dominican Labor Day; May 16—Dominican Election Day; June 2—Corpus Christi; August 16—Dominican Restoration Day; September 25—Our Lady of the Mercedes; December 25—Christmas.

Ecuador
April 1—Good Friday; May 24—Battle of Pichincha; July 25—Founding of Guayaquil (Guayaquil only); August 10—Independence Day; November 2—All Souls' Day; November 3—Independence of Cuenca; December 6—Founding of Quito (Quito only).

Egypt
January 1—New Year's; *March 13-15—Ramadan Bairam (End of Ramadan Fasting Month); April 25—Sinai Liberation Day; May 1—Labor Day; May 2—Sham El Nessim (Spring Day); *May 20-23—Kurban Bairam (Pilgrimage); *June 10—Islamic New Year; July 23—National Day; *August 19—Moulid El Nabi (Prophet's Birthday); [*Depends on Lunar Calendar; a difference of one day may occur.]

El Salvador
January 1—New Year's; January 16—Salvadoran Peace Day; April 14—Holy Thursday; April 15—Good Friday; May 1—Labor Day; June 30—Bank Holiday; August 3-6—San Salvador Feasts; September 15—Independence Day; October 12—Columbus Day; November 2—All

Souls' Day; November 5—Day of First Cry of Independence; December 25—Christmas.

Finland
January 1—New Year's; January 6—Epiphany; April 14—Good Friday; April 16—Easter; April 17—Easter Monday; May 1—May Day; May 25—Ascension; June 25—Mid-Summer Day; December 6—Independence Day; December 25-26—Christmas.

France
January 1—New Year's; April 17—Easter Monday; May 1—Labor Day; May 8—Veterans' Day (WWII); May 25—Ascension; June 5—Whit Monday; July 14—French National Day; August 15—AssumptionGabon; January 1—New Year's; April 17—Easter Monday; May 1—Labor Day; June 5—Pentecost Monday; August 15-17—Independence Day; November 1—All Saint's; December 25—Christmas; [Two muslim holidays—Id el Fitr and the Last Day of Ramadan—are; celebrated in Gabon, but their dates are known only at the last moment.]

Georgia
January 1—New Year's; January 7—Christmas; January 19—Baptism Day; March 3—Mother's Day; April 9—Memorial Day; May 2—Recollection of the Deceased; May 26—Independence Day; August 28—August Day of the Virgin; October 14—Svetitskhovloba; November 23—St. George's Day.

Germany
January 1—New Year's; April 14—Good Friday; April 17—Easter Monday; May 25—Ascension; June 5—Whit Monday; October 3—Day of German Unity; November 16—Repentance Day; December 25-26—Christmas; [The preceding list is based on Germany's 1994 holiday schedule.]

Greece
January 1—New Year; January 6—Epiphany; 49 days prior to Greek Easter Sunday—Kathara Deftera; March 25—Independence Day; Movable Holiday—Good Friday; Movable Holiday—Holy Saturday; Movable Holiday—Easter Sunday; Movable Holiday—Easter Monday; May 1—May Day; 50 days after Greek Easter Sunday—Whit Monday; August 15—Assumption; October 20—OXI Day; December 24—Christmas Eve; (half-day holiday, only shops open all day); December 25—Christmas Day; December 26—Boxing Day; December 31—New Year's Eve; (half-day holiday, only shops open all day); [Regional holidays: Liberation of Ioannina, February 20 (observed; in Ioannina only); Dodecanese Accession Day, March 7 (observed in; Dodecanese Islands only); Liberation of Xanthi, October 4 (observed; in Xanthi only); St. Demetrios Day, October 26 (observed in; Thessaloniki only); St. Andreas Day, November 30 (observed in; Patras only).]

Guatemala

January 1—New Year's; April 12 p.m.-April 15—Holy Week; May 1—Labor Day; June 30—Army Day; August 15—Feast of the Assumption; September 15—Independence Day; October 20—Revolution Day; November 1—All Saints'; December 24 (p.m. only)—Christmas Eve; December 25—Christmas; December 31 (p.m. only)—New Year's Eve; [In addition, the banking sector celebrates the following holidays: July 1—Bank Workers's Day, and October 12, Columbus Day. Business; travelers should avoid arriving in Guatemala on a holiday, if possible,; because of the unpredictability of transportation and other services,; especially during the Holy Week, when almost everything is shut down.]

Guinea
January 1—New Year's; Variable Holiday—end of Ramadan; (in 1994, it was celebrated March 19); April 3—Anniversary of the Second Republic; May 1—Labor Day; May 25—Anniversary of Organization of African Unity (OAU); Variable Holiday—Tabaski; (in 1994, it was celebrated June 8); August 25—Assumption; Variable Holiday—Prophet Mohammed's Birthday; (in 1993, it was observed September 23); October 2—Independence Day; December 25—Christmas.

Honduras
January 2—New Year's Day; April 13—Holy Thursday; April 14—Good Friday and Americas' Day; May 1—Labor Day; September 15—Honduran Independence Day; October 3—Francisco Morazan's Birthday; October 12—Discovery of America Day; October 21—Armed Forces' Day; December 25—Christmas.

Hong Kong
January 2—First Weekday after New Year's Day; January 31—Lunar New Year's Day; February 1—Second Day of Lunar New Year; February 2—Third Day of Lunar New Year; April 5—Ching Ming Festival; April 14—Good Friday; April 15—The day following Good Friday; April 17—Easter Monday; June 2—Dragon Boat Festival; August 26—The Saturday preceding the last Monday in August; August 28—Liberation Day; November 1—Chung Yeung Festival; December 25—Christmas; December 26—First Weekday after Christmas Day.

Hungary
January 1-2—New Year's; March 15—Revolution Day; April 17—Easter Monday; May 1—Labor Day; June 5—Whit Monday; August 20—National Day; October 23—Republic Day; December 25—Christmas; December 26—Boxing Day.

India
January 26—Republic Day; March 10—Mahashhivratri; March 14—Id'ul Fitr; April 14—Good Friday; April 20—Ramnavami; May 22—Bakrid; May 25—Buddha Purnima; June 20—Muharram; August 15—Independence Day; August 29—Janmashtami; October 13—Dussehra; November 3—Diwali; November 18—Guru Nanak's

Birthday; [The preceding list is based on India's 1994 holiday schedule.]

Indonesia
January 1-2—New Year's; January 10—Ascension of Mohammad; March 14-15—Idulfitri 1414H; April 14—Good Friday; May 1—Ascension of Christ; May 21—Idul Adha 1414H (Haj New Year); June 11—Moslem New Year 1415H; August 17—Independence Day; August 20—Mohammad's Birthday; December 25—Christmas; December 30—Ascension Day; [The preceding list is based on Indonesia's 1994 holiday schedule.]

Ireland
January 1—New Year's Day; March 17—Saint Patrick's Day; April 16—Easter Monday; First Monday in May—May Holiday; First Monday in June—June Holiday; First Monday in August—August Holiday; First Monday in October—October Holiday; December 25—Christmas; December 26—Saint Stephen's Day; [If New Year's Day, Saint Patrick's Day, Christmas Day, or; Saint Stephen's Day fall on a weekend, the following Monday is; a public holiday.; Most businesses close from December 24 through January 2 during; the Christmas festive period.; Certain other days are celebrated as holidays within local; jurisdictions.]

Israel
April 15—Passover (first day); April 21—Passover (last day); May 4—Independence Day; June 4—Shavuot (Pentecost); September 25—Rosh Hashana (New Year-first day); September 26—Rosh Hashana (New Year-second day); October 4—Yom Kippur (Day of Atonement); October 9—Succot (Feast of Tabernacles); October 16—Simhat Torah (Rejoicing of the Law); [Jewish holidays are determined according to lunar calendars, so their dates change from year to year.]

Italy
January 6—Epiphany; April 17—Easter Monday; April 25—Anniversary of the Liberation; May 1—Labor Day; August 15—Assumption; Patron Saint's Days are observed by the following cities: Florence, June 24, St. John's Day; Rome, June 29, St. Peter's and St. Paul's Day; Palermo, July 15, St. Rosalia's Day; Naples, September 19, St. Gennaro's Day; July and [August are poor months for conducting business in Italy; since most business firms are closed for vacation during this period. The same is true during the Christmas and New Year period. Certain; other days are celebrated as holidays within local jurisdictions. When; an Italian holiday falls on a Saturday, offices and stores are closed.]

Jamaica
January 1—New Year's; Variable—Ash Wednesday; Variable—Good Friday; Variable—Easter Monday; May 23—National Labor Day; August 5—Independence Day; October 21—National Heroes' Day; December 25—Christmas Day; December 26—Boxing Day.

Japan
January 1—New Year's; January 15—Adult's Day; February 11—National Foundation Day; March 21—Vernal Equinox Day; April 29—Greenery Day; May 3—Constitution Memorial Day; May 4—Declared Official Holiday; May 5—Children's Day; September 15—Respect-for-the-Aged; September 23—Autumnal Equinox Day; October 10—Health/Sports Day; November 3—Culture Day; November 23—Labor Thanksgiving Day; December 23—Emperor's Birthday; [If a national holiday falls on a Sunday, the following Monday is a compensatory day off. May 4 is also a national holiday, although; it has no specific title. In addition to the above public holidays, many Japanese companies and government offices traditionally close; for several days during the New Year's holiday season (December 28- January 3). Many also close during "Golden Week" (April 29-May 5); and the traditional "O-Bon" (Festival of Souls') period for several; days in mid-August (usually August 12-15).]

Korea
January 1-2—New Year's; January 30-; February 1—Lunar New Year Days; March 1—Independence Movement Day; April 5—Arbor Day; May 5—Children's Day; May 7—Buddha's Birthday; June 6—Memorial Day; July 17—Constitution Day; August 15—Independence Day; September 8-10—Korean Thanksgiving Days; October 3—National Foundation Day; December 25—Christmas.

Kuwait
January 1—New Year's; February 25—Kuwait National Day; February 26—Kuwait Liberation Day. [A number of variable Islamic holidays are also observed in Kuwait. Government offices operate with very limited business hours during the Holy Month of Ramadan (the dates of which vary from one year to the next). Appointments should not be scheduled on Thursdays and Fridays.]

Latvia
January 1—New Year's; April 14—Good Friday; May 1—Constitution Day; June 23-24—Midsummer Holiday; November 18—Proclamation Day; December 25-26—Christmas; December 31—New Year's Eve.

Lebanon
January 1—New Year's; February 9—St. Maron's Day; Variable—Feast of Ramadan; Variable—Good Friday Western Rite; May 1—Labor Day; Variable—Eastern Orthodox Good Friday; May 6—Martyr's Day; Variable—Feast of Al-Adha; Variable—Ashura; Variable—Moslem New Year; August 15—Assumption; Variable—Prophet's Birthday; November 1—All Saint's Day; November 22—Independence Day; December 25—Christmas.

Lesotho
March 12—Moshoeshoe Day; March 21—National Tree Planting Day; April 14—Good Friday; April 17—Easter

Monday; July 4—Ascension and Family Day; July 17—King's Birthday; October 4—Independence Day; December 26—Boxing Day.

Madagascar

January 1—New Year's; March 29—Day Commemorating Martyrs; April 14—Easter; April 17—Easter Monday; May 1—Labor Day; 6th Thursday after Easter—Ascension; 7th Sunday after Easter—Pentecost,; followed by Pentecost Monday; May 25—OAU Day; June 26—Independence Day; August 15—Assumption; November 1—All Saint's Day; December 25—Christmas.

Malawi

January 3—New Year's; March 3—Martyrs' Day; April 14—Good Friday; April 17—Easter Monday; May 16—Kamuzu Day; July 6—Republic Day; October 17—Mothers' Day; December 21—National Tree Planting Day; December 26—Boxing Day; December 27—Christmas observed.

Malaysia

January 1—New Year's; January 31-; February 1—Chinese New Year; February 1—Kuala Lumpur City Day; March 4 and 5 (variable, and subject to change); —Hari Raya Puasa May 1—Labor Day; May 12 (variable, and subject to change)—Hari Raya Haji; May 14—Wesak Day; May 31—Awal Muharam; June 3—Agong's Birthday; August 9—Prophet Mohammed's Birthday; August 31—National Day; October or November (variable)—Deepavali; December 25—Christmas.

Mali

January 1—New Year; January 20—Army Day; March 14 (approximate)—Ramadan; March 26—Day of Democracy; April 17 (approximate)—Easter Monday; May 1—International Labor Day; May 21 (approximate)—Tabaski; May 25—Day of Africa; August 21 (approximate)—Mawloud; August 28 (approximate)—Prophet's Baptism; September 22—Independence Day; December 25—Christmas; [Dates listed as approximate, other than Easter, are Muslim holidays; based on the lunar calendar and therefore subject to one or two days'; variation from the date given.]

Mexico

January 1—New Year's; February 5—Anniversary of Mexican Constitution; March 21—Benito Juarez' Birthday; April 14—Good Friday; May 1—Mexican Labor Day; May 5—Anniversary of Independence; September 16—Mexican Independence Day; November 2—All Soul's Day; November 20—Anniversary of the Mexican Revolution; December 25—Christmas; [The preceding list is a projection based on Mexican holidays in 1994.]

Morocco

March 3—Throne Day; March 30*—Aid El Fitr; May 1—Labor Day; May 23—National Holiday; June 5*—Aid El Adha; June 25*—Moslem New Year; July 9—King's Birthday; August 14—Saharan Province Day; September 5*—Prophet's Birthday; November 6—Green March Day; November 18—Independence Day. [Holidays marked with an asterisk are based on the lunar calendar; and change every year.]

Mozambique

January 1—New Year's; February 3—Mozambican Heroes' Day; April 7—Women's Day; May 1—Labor Day; June 25—Independence Day; September 7—Lusaka Agreement Day; September 25—Revolution Day; November 10—Maputo City day, a holiday only for Maputo; December 25—Christmas.

Netherlands

January 1—New Year's; April 14—Good Friday; April 17—Easter Monday; April 30—Queen's Birthday; May 5—Liberation Day; May 28—Ascension; December 25—Christmas; December 26—Second Christmas Day; [Certain other days are celebrated as holidays within; local jurisdictions.]

New Zealand

January 1-3—New Year's; January 23—Wellington Anniversary Day (Wellington only); January 30—Auckland Anniversary Day (Auckland only); February 6—Waitangi Day; April 14—Good Friday; April 17—Easter Monday; April 25—ANZAC Day; June 5—Queen's Birthday; October 23—Labor Day; November 6—Marlborough Anniversary (Blenheim only); November 10—Canterbury Anniversary (Christchurch only); December 25—Christmas; December 26—Boxing Day.

Nicaragua

January 1—New Year's Day; April 13—Holy Thursday; April 14—Good Friday; May 1—Labor Day; July 19—Sandinista Revolution Day; August 1—Festival of Santo Domingo; September 14—Battle of San Jacinto; September 15—Independence Day; December 8—Immaculate Conception; December 25—Christmas.

Nigeria

January 1—New Year's; April 1—Good Friday; April 4—Easter Monday; May 1—Labor Day; October 1—National Day; December 25—Christmas; December 26—Boxing Day.

Holidays falling on Saturdays are likely to be observed on the preceding Friday, while those falling on Sunday are likely to be observed on the following Monday.

[The Muslim holidays of Eid-El-Fitri and Eid-El-Kabir are usually celebrated for two consecutive work days. Their dates, as well as the date of Eid-El-Maulud, vary and are announced by the Ministry of Internal Affairs shortly before they occur.]

Norway

April 13—Holy Thursday; April 14—Good Friday; April 17—Easter Monday; May 1—Labor Day; May 17—Independence Day; May 25—Ascension; December

582

25—Christmas. [Some Norwegian manufacturing plants and major businesses are closed for three to four weeks for summer holidays from mid-July to mid-August. Easter (a 10-day holiday season for many Norwegians) also is a period of low business activity.]

Oman

March 1-2—Eid Al Fitr; May 9-10—Eid Al Adha; May 30—Islamic New Year; August 18—Birth of the Prophet; November 18-19—National Day; December 29—Ascension Day. [Most of these dates are approximations. The religious holidays are determined by locally observed phases of the moon. The actual date and duration of the National Day holiday is announced shortly before the holiday is to take place].

Pakistan

March 3-5*—Eid-ul-Fitr; March 23—Pakistan Day; May 1—May Day; May 12-13—Eid-ul-Azha; June 10-11*—9th and 10th of Muharram; August 10—Milad-An-Nabi; August 14—Independence Day; September 6—Defense of Pakistan Day; September 11—Death Anniversary of Quaid-i-Azam; November 9—Iqbal Day; December 25—Birthday of Quaid-i-Azam. [*Based on the Islamic lunar calendar and may differ by one or two days from the expected dates. In addition, there is often a one or two day discrepancy in timing among different parts of the country).

Panama

January 1—New Year's; January 9—Mourning Day; February 28—Carnival; April 14—Good Friday; May 1—Labor Day; November 3—Independence Day from Colombia; November 4—Flag Day; November 10—The Uprising of Los Santos; November 28—Independence Day from Spain; December 8—Mother's Day; December 25—Christmas.

Paraguay

January 1—New Year's; February 3—San Blas; March 1—Heroes' Day; April 14—Holy Thursday; April 15—Good Friday; May 1—Labor day; May 15—Independence Day; June 12—Chaco Armistice; August 15—Founding of Asuncion; December 8—Virgin of Caacupe Day; December 25—Christmas.

Philippines

January 1—New Year's; April 9—Bataan & Corregidor Day and Heroism Day; April 13—Maundy Thursday; April 14—Good Friday; May 1—Labor Day; June 12—Independence Day; August 28—National Heroes Day; November 1—All Saints' Day; November 30—Bonifacio Day; December 25—Christmas; December 30—Rizal Day. [June 24, Manila Day, is observed only in the City of Manila, and August 19, Quezon Day, is observed only in Quezon City. In addition, special public holidays such as Election Day and EDSA Revolution Day, may be declared by the President and are observed nationwide.]

Poland

January 1—New Year's; April 17—Easter Monday; May 1—Labor Day; May 3—Constitution DayLate; May or early; June—Corpus Christi; August 15—Assumption; November 1—All Saints' Day; November 11—Independence Day; December 25-26—Christmas. [One Saturday per month is by custom considered a working Saturday, but there is no consistency among institutions or exact observance as such.]

Qatar

February 22—Anniversary of the Accession of the Amir; September 3—Independence Day [Officially, Qatar uses the Gregorian calendar year for all purposes. The Hijra (Islamic) calendar is also widely used. Religious holidays vary from year to year. Eid Al-Fitr (four days) marks the end of the fasting month of Ramadan and Eid Al-Adha marks the conclusion of the pilgrimage (Haj) to Mecca.]

Romania

January 1-2—New Year's; April 23-24—Orthodox Easter; May 1-2—Labor Day; December 1—National Day; December 25—Christmas.

Russia

January 1-2—New Year's; January 7—Orthodox Christmas; March 8—International Women's Day; May 1—International Labor Day; May 2—Spring Day; May 9—Victory Day; June 12—Independence Day; November 7—Revolution Day. [When holidays occur on weekends, Russian authorities announce during the week prior to the holiday, if the day will be celebrated on the following Monday. It is likely that January 2 and 3 will be holidays in 1995 since January 1 is a Sunday.]

Saudi Arabia

Beginning about March 1—Eid al-Fitr; Beginning about May 9—Eid al-Adha; September 22—National Day. [There are two Islamic religious holidays around which most businesses in Saudi Arabia close for at least three working days. Eid al-Fitr occurs at the end of the holy month of Ramadan. Eid al-Adha celebrates the time of year when pilgrims arrive from around the world to perform the Haj. Their timing is governed by the Islamic lunar calendar and they fall approximately 11 days earlier in each successive year. In 1995, the Eid al-Fitr holiday will begin on or about March 1 and the Eid al-Adha holiday on or about May 9.]

Senegal

January 1—New Year's; April 4—Independence Day; 1st Monday in April—Easter Monday; May 1—International Labor Day; August 15—Assumption; November 1—All Saints' Day; December 25—Christmas. [The following holidays are moveable according to the religious calendar: Korite, Tabaski, Tamxarit, Mawlud, Ascension, and Pentecost (in May).]

South Africa
January 1-2—New Year's; April 6—Founders' Day; April 14—Good Friday; April 17—Family Day; May 1—Workers' Day; May 25—Ascension; May 31—Republic Day; October 10—Kruger Day; December 16—Day of the Vow; December 25—Christmas; December 26—Day of Goodwill.

Spain
January 1—New Year's; January 6—Epiphany; April 14—Good Friday; August 15—Assumption; October 12—National Day; November 1—All Saints' Day; December 6—Constitution Day; December 8—Immaculate Conception. [Regional holidays: April 13 (Holy Thursday), Bilbao/Madrid; April 17 (Easter Monday), Barcelona/Bilbao; May 2 (Labor Day), Madrid; May 16 (St. Isidro), Madrid; June 5 (Whit Monday), Barcelona; June 24 (St. John), Barcelona; July 25 (St. James), Bilbao/Madrid; September 24 (La Merced), Barcelona; November 9 (Our Lady of Almudena), Madrid; December 26, Barcelona/Madrid. The list of Spain's commercial holidays for 1995 is not available yet. It will not differ much from the preceding list for 1994.]

Sri Lanka
January 15—Thai Pongal; January 16—Duruthu Poya; February 4—National Day; February 14—Navam Poya; February 27—Maha Sivarathri; March 3—Ramazan Festival; March 16—Medin Poya; April 13—Day Prior to Sinhala and Tamil New Year; April 14—Sinhala and Tamil New Year Good Friday; April 15—Bak Poya; May 1—May Day; May 10—Hadji Festival; May 14—Vesak Poya; May 15—Day Following Vesak Poya; May 22—National Heroes' Day; June 12—Poson Poya; June 30—Special Bank Holiday; July 12—Esala Poya; August 10—Nikini Poya and Holy Prophet's Birthday; September 8—Binara Poya; October 8—Vap Poya; October 23—Deepavali Festival; November 6—Il Poya; December 6—Unduvap Poya; December 25—Christmas; December 31—Special Bank Holiday. [Sri Lankan holidays are connected with the country's four religions: Buddhism, Hinduism, Islam, and Christianity. Dates change from year to year. Holidays with fixed dates include National Day (February 4), National Heroes' Day (May 22), and Christmas (December 25). Each full moon is marked by a Poya Day holiday.]

Suriname
January 1—New Year's; About March 13—Holi Phagwa; About March 27—Ied Ul Fitr; April 14—Good Friday; April 17—Easter Monday; May 1—Labor Day; July 1—Emancipation Day; November 25—Independence Day; December 25—Christmas.

Swaziland
January 1—New Year's; April 14—Good Friday; April 17—Easter Monday; April 19—King Mswati III's Birthday; April 25—National Flag Day; May 12—Ascension; July 22—Public Holiday; August or September—Umhlanga (Reed Dance); September 6—Independence Day; December 25—Christmas; December 26—Boxing Day; December or January—Incwala. [The preceding list is a projection based on Swaziland holidays in 1994. Swaziland holidays falling on a Sunday are observed on the following Monday. Swaziland holidays falling on a Saturday are observed on that day unless an announcement to the contrary is made by the Government.]

Sweden
January 1—New Year's; January 6—Epiphany; April 14—Good Friday; April 17—Easter Monday; May 1—Swedish Labor Day; May 25—Ascension; June 5—Whit Monday; June 24—Midsummer Day; November 4—All Saints' Day; December 25-26—Christmas. [Offices are also closed on Mid-Summer Eve, Christmas Eve, and New Year's Eve. Government and many business offices generally close 1:00 p.m. on the day before major holidays.]

Switzerland
January 1—New Year's; January 2—Baerzelistag; April 14—Good Friday; April 17—Easter Monday; May 25—Ascension; June 5—Whit Monday; August 1—Swiss National Day; December 25—Christmas; December 26—St. Stephan's Day.

Syria
Jauary 1— New Year's; March 8—Revolution Day; March 13-15—Al-Fitr Holiday; March 21—Mothers' Day; April 3—Western Easter; April 10—Eastern Easter; April 17—In dependence Day; May 1—Labor Day; May 6—Martyrs' Day; May 22-25—Al-Adha Holiday; June 9—Muslim New Year; August 18—Prophet's Birthday; October 6—Tishree War; December 25—Christmas. [The Muslim religious holidays listed above are based on the lunar calendar; the exact dates are to be confirmed.]

Taiwan
January 1—Founding Day; Late January—Mid-February—Spring Festival; (Chinese New Year) March 29—Youth Day; April 4—Women and Children's Day; April 5—Tomb Sweeping Day and President Chiang Kai-Shek Day; Late May—Mid-June—Dragon Boat Festival September—Mid-Autumn Festival; September 28—Confucius' Birthday; October 10—Double Ten National Day; October 25—Taiwan Retrocession Day; October 31—President Chiang Kai-Shek's Birthday; November 12—Dr. Sun Yat-Sen's Birthday; December 25—Constitution Day. [There are 10 holidays and three festivals in Taiwan. Dates for the three festivals—which include Chinese Lunar New Year Day, Dragon Boat Festival, and Mid-Autumn (Moon) Festival—change with the lunar calendar.]

Tanzania
January 1—New Year; January 12—Zanzibar

584

Revolutionary Day; March 3-4*—Idd-El-Fitr; April 14—Good Friday; April 17—Easter Monday; April 26—Union Day; May 1—International Workers' Day; May 11*—Idd-El-Hajj; August 8—Peasants' Day; August 11—Maulid Day; December 9—Independence Day; December 25—Christmas; December 26—Boxing Day. [Holidays marked with an asterisk are subject to the sighting of the moon and may vary from the dates shown.]

Thailand

January 3—New Year's; February 9-10—Chinese New Year; February 25—Magha Puja Day; April 6—King Rama I Memorial and Chakri Day; April 12-14—Songkran Days; May 2—Labor Day; May 5—Coronation Day; May 24—Visakha Puja Day; July 25—Buddhist Lent Day; August 12—Her Majesty the Queen's Birthday; October 24—Chulalongkorn Day; December 5—His Majesty the King's Birthday; December 12—Constitution Day. [The preceding list is based on the list of Thailand holidays in 1994.]

Trinidad and Tobago

January 1—New Year's; April 14—Good Friday; April 17—Easter Monday; June 2—Corpus Christi; June 5—Whit Monday; June 19—Labor Day; August 1—Emancipation Day; August 31—Independence Day; September 24—Republic Day Date to be determined—Divali; December 25—Christmas; December 26—Boxing Day. [The dates for Carnival Monday and Tuesday (the Monday and Tuesday preceding Ash Wednesday) change from year to year. Carnival Monday and Tuesday are not official public holidays but most businesses are closed.]

Turkey

January 1—New Year's; March 2-5—Sugar Holiday; April 23—National Sovereignty and Children's Day; May 9-13—Sacrifice Holiday; May 19—Ataturk Memorial, Youth, and Sports Day; August 30—Zafer Bayrami (Victory Day); October 28-29—Turkish Independence Day.

Uganda

January 1—New Year's; January 26—Liberation Day; April 14—Good Friday; April 17—Easter Monday; March 8—International Women's Day; May 1—Labor Day; Date to be determined—Idd-el-Fitr; Date to be determined—Iddi Aduha; June 3—Uganda Martyrs' Day; June 9—National Heroes' Day; October 9—Independence Day; December 25—Christmas; December 26—Boxing Day.

United Arab Emirates

January 1—New Year's; January 19*—Ascension; March 2-4—Eid Al Fitr; May 9*—Waqfa; May 10-12*—Eid Al-Adha; May 31*—Islamic New Year; August 6—Shaykh Zayed Accession Day; August 8*—Prophet's Birthday; December 2-3—UAE National Day. [UAE religious holidays are marked with an asterisk and are dependent upon the sighting of the moon.]

United Kingdom

England and Wales: January 1—New Year's; April 14—Good Friday; April 17—Easter Monday; May 1—May Day; May 29—Spring Holiday-May; August 28—Summer Bank Holiday; December 25—Christmas; December 26—Boxing Day.

Scotland

Scotland observes the above except Easter Monday, Spring Holiday, and Summer Bank Holiday, and also observes the following: January 2—Bank Holiday; April 3—Spring Holiday; May 15—Victoria Day; August 7—Bank Holiday; September 18—Autumn Holiday.

Northern Ireland:

In addition to the U.K.-listed holidays, the following are observed: March 17—St. Patrick's Day; April 18—Easter Tuesday; July 12-13—Orangeman's Day.

Venezuela

February 27-28—Carnival; April 13—Good Thursday; April 14—Good Friday; April 19—Signing of Independence; May 1—Labor Day; July 5—Independence Day; July 24—Bolivar's Birthday.

Zambia

January 1—New Year's; March 12—Youth Day; April 14—Good Friday; April 17—Easter Monday; May 1—Labor Day; May 25—African Freedom Day; July 4—Heroes' Day; July 5—Unity Day; August 1—Farmers' Day; October 24—Independence Day; December 25—Christmas.

585

APPENDIX 9I

COUNTRIES: BANKING, BUSINESS AND SHOPPING HOURS

AFGHANISTAN
Business/Shopping Hours: 8:AM - 6:AM (Sun-Thur)Businesses are closed Thursday and Friday afternoons

ALGERIA
Banking Hours: 9:AM - 4:PM (Sun-Thur) Business Hours: 8:AM - 12:Noon, 1:PM - 5:PM (Sat-Wed) Businesses are closed Thursday and Friday

AMERICAN SAMOA
Banking Hours: 9:AM - 2:PM (Mon-Thur) 9:AM - 5:PM (Fri)

ANDORRA
Banking Hours: 9:AM - 1:PM; 3:PM - 7:PM Business Hours: 9:AM - 1:PM; 3:PM - 7:PM, Shopping Hours: 10:AM - 1:PM; 3:PM - 8:PM

ANGUILLA
Banking Hours: 8:AM - 12:00 Noon (Mon-Fri); 3:PM (Fri)Business Hours: 8:AM - 4:PM, Shopping Hours: 8:AM - 5:PM (Mon-Sat)

ANTIGUA AND BARBUDA
Banking Hours: 8:AM - 1:PM (Mon,Tue,Wed,Thur) 8:AM - 1:PM & 3:PM - 5:PM (Fri); Business Hours: 8:AM - 12:Noon & 1:PM - 4:PM (Mon-Fri) Shopping Hours: 8:AM - 12:Noon & 1:PM - 5:PM (Mon-Sat)

ARMENIA
Banking Hours: 9:AM - 6:PM
Business Hours: 9:AM - 6:PM
Shopping Hours: 8:AM - 9:PM

ARGENTINA
Banking Hours: 10:AM - 4:PM (Mon-Fri); Business Hours: 9:AM - 6:PM (Mon-Fri); Shopping Hours: 9:AM - 8:PM (Mon-Sat)

AUSTRALIA
Banking Hours: 10:AM - 3:PM (Mon-Thur); 10:AM - 5:PM (Fri)Banks are closed on Saturdays; Business/Shopping Hours: 9:AM - 5:30PM (Mon-Thur); 8:30AM - 12:Noon (Sat)

AUSTRIA
Banking Hours: 8:AM - 12:30 PM, 1:30 - 3:30 PM (Mon, Tue, Wed, Fri); 1:30 -5:30PM(Thur) Business Hours: 8:30 AM - 4:30 PM Shopping Hours: 8:AM - 6:PM (Mon - Fri); 8:AM -12:Noon (Sat)

AZERBAIJAN
Banking Hours: 9:AM - 6:PM; Business Hours: 9:AM - 6:PM; Shopping Hours: 8:AM - 9:PM

BAHAMAS
Banking Hours: 9:30AM - 3:PM (Mon-Thur); 9:30AM - 5:PM (Fri)

BAHRAIN
Banking Hours: 7:30AM - 12:Noon (Sat-Wed); 7:30AM - 11:AM Thur)

BARBADOS
Banking Hours: 8:AM - 3:PM (Mon-Thur); 8:AM - 1:PM & 3:PM - 5:PM (Fri); Business Hours: 8:30AM - 4:PM (Mon-Fri); Shopping Hours: 8:AM - 4:PM (Mon-Fri); 8:AM - 12:Noon (Sat)

BANGLADESH
Banking Hours: 9:30AM - 1:30PM (Mon-Thur); 9:AM - 11:AM (Fri- Sat); Business/Shopping Hours: 9:AM - 9:PM (Mon-Fri); 9:AM - 2:PM (Sat)

BELARUS
Banking Hours: 9:AM - 6:PM
Business Hours: 9:AM - 6:PM
Shopping Hours: 9:AM - 9:PM

BELGIUM
Banking Hours: 9:AM - 3:PM (Mon-Fri); Business Hours: 9:AM - 12:Noon & 2:PM - 5:30PM; Shopping Hours: 9:AM - 6:PM (Mon-Sat)

BELIZE
Banking Hours: 8:AM - 1:PM (Mon-Fri); 3:PM - 6:PM (Fri)Business Hours: 8:AM - 12:Noon; 1:PM - 5:PM (Mon-Fri)Shopping Hours: 8:AM - 4:PM (Mon-Sat)

BENIN
Banking Hours: 8:AM - 11:AM; 3:PM - 4:PM (Mon-Fri); Business Hours: 8:AM - 12:30PM; 3:PM - 6:30PM (Mon-Fri) Shopping Hours: 9:AM - 1:PM, 4:PM -7:PM (Mon-Sun)

BERMUDA
Business/Shopping: 9:AM - 5:PM (Mon-Sat)

BOLIVIA
Banking Hours: 9:AM - 12:Noon & 2:PM - 4:PM (Mon-Fri) Business Hours: 9:AM - 12:Noon & 2:30PM - 6:PM (Mon-Fri) Shopping Hours: 9:AM - 6:PM; 9:AM -

12:Noon (Sat)

BOSNIA HERZEGOVINA
Banking Hours: 7:AM - Noon or &:AM - 7:PM; Business Hours: 8:AM - 3:30 PM; Shopping Hours: 8:AM - 8:PM (Mon-Fri)

BOTSWANA
Banking Hours: 8:15 - 12:45PM (Mon-Fri), 8:15AM - 10:45 AM (Sat) Shopping Hours: 8:AM - 6:PM (Mon-Sat)

BRITISH VIRGIN ISLANDS
Banking Hours: 9:AM - 2:PM (Mon-Fri); Business Hours: 8:30AM - 2:00PM & 4:PM - 5:PM (Mon-Fri); Shopping Hours: 8:AM - 5:PM (Mon-Sat)

BRAZIL
Banking Hours 10:AM - 4:30PM (Mon-Fri) Shopping Hours: 9:AM - 6:30PM (Mon-Fri) & 9:AM - 1:PM (Sat)

BURKINA FASO
Business Hours: 7:AM - 12:Noon, 3:PM - 5:PM (Mon-Fri) Shopping Hours: 7:AM - 12:Noon, 2:PM - 7:PM (Mon-Sat)

BURMA
Banking Hours: 10:AM - 2:PM (Mon-Fri); 10:AM - 12:Noon (Sat) Bussiness/Shopping Hours: 9:30Am - 4:PM (Mon-Sat)

BURUNDI
Business Hours: 8:AM - 12:Noon (Mon-Fri); Shopping Hours: 8:AM - 6:PM (Mon-Sat)

CAMEROON
Banking Hours: French Speaking Part: 8:AM - 11:AM, 2:30PM - 4:PM (Mon-Fri)English Speaking Part: 8:AM - 2:PM (Mon-Fri) Business Hours: French Speaking Part: 7:30AM - 12: Noon, 2:30PM - 6:PM (Mon-Fri) English Speaking Part: 7:30AM - 2:30PM - (Mon-Fri), 7:30AM - 1:PM Shopping Hours: 8:AM - 12:30PM, 4:PM - 7:PM (Mon-Sat)

REPUBLIC OF CAPE VERDE
Banking Hours: 8:AM - 12: Noon (Mon-Fri); Business Hours: 8:AM - 12: Noon (Mon-Fri)

CAYMAN ISLANDS
Banking Hours: 9:AM - 2:30PM (Mon-Thur) & 9:AM - PM, :30PM -4:30PM (Fri) Business Hours: 8:30AM - 5:PM Shopping Hours: 8:30AM - 5:PM

CENTRAL AFRICAN REPUBLIC
Banking Hours: 8:AM - 11:30AM (Mon-Fri); Shopping Hours: 7:30AM - 9:PM (Mon-Sun)

CHAD
Banking Hours: 7:AM - 11:AM (Mon-Thur, Sat), 7:AM - 10:AM (Fri) Business Hours: 7:AM - 2:PM (Mon-Thur,

Sat), 7:AM -12: Noon (Fri)Shopping Hours: 8:AM - 1:PM, 4:PM - 6:PM (Mon-Sat)

CHILE
Banking Hours: 9:AM - 1:PM & 2:30PM - 6:PM (Mon-Fri); 9:AM -2:PM (Sat) Shopping Hours: 9:AM - 1:PM & 2:30PM - 6:PM (Mon-Fri)

CHINA, PEOPLES REPUBLIC
Banking Hours: varies (Mon-Sat)

CHINA, TAIWAN
Banking Hours: 9:AM - 3:30PM (Mon-Fri); 9:AM - 12:Noon (Sat)

COLUMBIA
Banking Hours: 9:AM - 3:PM (Mon-Thur); 9:AM - 3:30 (Fri); Business Hours: 8:30AM - 5:PM (Mon-Fri); Shopping Hours: 10:AM - 7:PM (Mon-Sat)

COMOROS ISLAND
Banking Hours: 9:AM - 12:30PM, 3:PM - 5:PM (Mon-Fri), 9:AM - 12:30PM (Sat); Shopping Hours: 8:AM - 8:PM (Mon-Sat)

CONGO, PEOPLE'S REPUBLIC
Banking Hours: 7:AM - 2:PM (Mon-Fri); Shopping Hours: 7:AM - 7:PM (Mon-Sat)

COSTA RICA
Banking Hours: 9:AM - 3:PM (Mon-Fri); Shopping Hours: 8:30AM - 11:30AM & 2:PM - 6:PM (Mon-Fri) 8:30AM - 11:30AM (Sat)

COTE D'IVOIRE
Banking Hours: 8:AM - 11:30AM, 2:30PM - 4:PM (Mon-Fri) Business Hours: 8:AM - 12:Noon, 2:30PM - 5:30PM (Mon-Fri) Shopping Hours: 8:30AM - 12:Noon, 2:30PM - 7:PM (Mon-Sat)

CUBA
Banking Hours: 9:AM - 3:PM (Mon-Fri); Business Hours: 8:30AM - 12:30PM & 1:30PM - 5:30PM (Mon - Fri) Shopping Hours: 9:AM - 5:PM (Mon-Fri); 9:AM - 12:Noon (Sat)

CYPRUS
Banking Hours: 8:30AM - 12: Noon (Mon-Sat); Business Hours: 8:AM - 1:PM, 2:30PM - 6:PM (Mon-Fri)8:AM - 1:PM (Sat)Shopping Hours: 8:AM - 1:PM; 4:PM - 7:PM (Mon-Fri) Closed Wednesday and Saturday afternoons.

CZECH REPUBLIC
Banking Hours: 8:AM - 4:PM (Mon-Fri); Business Hours: 8:30AM - 5:PM Shopping Hours: 9:AM - 6:PM (Mon-Fri), 9:AM - 1:PM (Sat)

DENMARK

Banking Hours: 9:30AM - 4:PM; (Mon,Tue,Wed, & Fri), 9:30AM -6:PM (Thur) Business Hours: 8:AM - 4:PM (Mon-Fri) Shopping Hours: 9/10:AM - 5:30/7:PM (Mon-Thur) 9/10:AM - 7/8:PM (Fri) 9/10:AM - 1/2:PM (Sat)

REPUBLIC OF DJIBOUTI
Banking Hours: 7:15AM - 11:45AM (Sun-Thur); Shopping Hours: 7:30AM - 12:Noon, 3:30PM - 7:30PM (Sat-Thur)

DOMINICA
Banking Hours: 8:AM - 1:PM (Mon-Fri); 3:PM - 5:PM (Fri) Business Hours: 8:AM - 1:PM & 2:PM - 4:PM (Mon-Fri); 8:AM - 1:PM (Sat) Shopping Hours: 8:AM - 1:PM & 2:PM - 4:PM (Mon-Fri); 8:AM- 1:PM (Sat)

DOMINICAN REPUBLIC
Banking Hours: 8:AM - 12:Noon (Mon-Fri); Business Hours: 9:AM - 6:PM (Mon-Fri) & 9:AM -12:Noon (Sat); Shopping Hours: 8:30AM - 12:Noon & 2:30PM - 6:PM (Mon-Fri); 8:30AM - 1:PM (Sat)

ECUADOR
Banking Hours: 9:AM - 1:30PM (Mon-Fri); Shopping Hours: 8:30AM - 12:30PM (Mon-Sat) & 3:30PM - 7:PM (Mon-Sat)

EGYPT
Banking Hours: 8:30AM - 1:PM (Mon-Thur, Sat), 10:AM - 12:Noon (Sat) Shopping Hours: 10:AM - 7:PM (Tue-Sat), 10:AM - 8:PM (Mon - Thur)

EL SALVADOR
Banking Hours: 8:AM - 12:Noon & 2:PM - 4:PM (Mon-Fri); Shopping Hours: 8:AM - 12:Noon & 2:30PM - 6:PM (Mon-Sat)

EQUATORIAL GUINEA
Banking Hours: 8:AM - 3:PM (Mon-Fri), 8:AM - 1:PM(Sat) Business Hours; 8:AM - 3:PM (Mon-Fri), 8:AM - 1:PM (Sat) Shopping Hours: 8:AM -3:PM, 5:PM - 7:PM (Mon-Sat)

ESTONIA
Banking Hours: 9:AM - 3:PM
Business Hours: 9:AM - 6PM
Shopping Hours: 9:am - 9:PM (Mon-Sat)

ETHIOPIA
Banking Hours: 9:AM - 5:PM (Mon-Fri); Business Hour: 8:AM - 12:Noon, 1:PM - 4:PM (Mon-Fri);Banks close for 3 hours for lunch

FIJI
Banking Hours: 10:AM - 3:PM (Mon-Thur); 10:AM - 4:PM (Fri); Business/Shopping Hours: 8:AM - 5:PM

FINLAND
Banking Hours: 9:15AM - 4:15PM (Mon-Fri); Business

Hours: 8:30AM - 4:PM (Mon-Fri);Shopping Hours: 9:AM - 5/6:PM (Mon-Fri), 9:AM - 2/3:PM (Sat)

FRANCE
Banking Hours: 9:AM - 4:30PM (Mon-Fri); Business Hours: 9:AM - 12:Noon; 2:PM - 6:PM (Mon-Fri), 9:AM - 12:Noon (Sat); Shopping Hours: 9:AM -6:30PM (Tue-Sat)

FRENCH GUIANA
Banking Hours: 7:15AM - 11:45AM (Mon,Tue,Thur, Fri); 7:AM -12:Noon (Wed)

GABON
Banking Hours: 7:AM - 12:Noon (Mon-Fri); Business Hours: 8:AM - 12:Noon, 3:PM - 6:PM (Mon-Fri); Shopping Hours: 8:AM - 12:Noon, 4:PM - 7:PM (Mon-Sat)

GEORGIA
Shopping Hours: 9:AM - 7:PM

THE GAMBIA
Banking Hours: 8:AM - 1:PM (Mon-Fri); 8:AM - 11:AM (Sat); Business/Shopping Hours: 8:AM - 5:PM (Mon-Fri); 8:AM -12:Noon (Sat)

FEDERAL REPUBLIC OF GERMANY
Banking Hours: 8:30AM - 12:30PM; 1:45PM - 3:45PM (Mon-Fri), Thur- 5:45PM Business Hours: 8:AM - 5:PM Shopping Hours: 8:AM - 6:30PM (Mon-Fri), 8:AM - 2:PM (Sat)

GHANA
Banking Hours: 8:30AM - 2:PM (Mon-Fri); Business Hours: 8:30AM - 5:PM (Mon-Fri); Shopping Hours: 8:30AM - 5:PM (Mon-Sat)

GIBRALTAR
Banking Hours: 9:AM - 3:30PM (Mon-Fri), 4:30PM - 6:PM (Fri) Business Hours: 9:AM -6:PM; Shopping Hours: 9:AM - 1:PM & 3:30PM - 7:PM (Mon-Fri), 9:-1:PM (Sat)

GREECE
Banking Hours: 8:AM - 2:PM (Mon-Fri); Business Hours: 8:30AM - 1:30PM, 4:PM - 7:30PM; Shopping Hours: 8:AM - 2:30PM (Mon, Wed, Sat), 8:AM - 1:30PM, 5:PM- 8:PM (Tue, Thur, Fri)

GRENADA
Banking Hours: 8:AM - 12:Noon (Mon-Fri) & 2:30 PM - 5:PM (Fri) Business Hours: 8:AM -4:PM (Mon-Fri) 8:AM - 11:45 AM (Sat) Shopping Hours: 8:AM -4:PM (Mon-Fri); 8:AM - 11:45 AM (Sat)

GUADELOUPE
Banking Hours: 8:AM - 12:Noon & 2:PM - 4:PM; Shopping Hours: 9:AM - 1:PM & 3:PM - 6:PM (Mon-

Fri); Sat mornings

GUATEMALA
Banking Hours: 9:AM - 3:PM (Mon-Fri); Shopping Hours: 9:AM - 7:PM (Mon-Sat)

GUINEA, REPUBLIC
Banking Hours: 7:30AM - 3:PM (Mon-Sat); Business Hours: 7:30 - 3:PM (Mon-Sat); Shopping Hours: 8:AM - 6:PM (Mon-Sun)

GUYANA
Banking Hours: 8:AM - 12:30PM (Mon-Fri); Business Hours: 8:AM - 4:PM (Mon-Fri); Shopping Hours: 8:AM - 12:Noon; 2:PM - 4:PM

HAITI
Banking Hours: 9:AM - 1:PM (Mon-Fri); Business Hours: 8:AM - 5:PM (Mon-Fri); 8:AM - 12:Noon (Sat) Shopping Hours: 8:AM - 5:PM (Mon-Fri); 8:AM - 12:Noon (Sat)

HONDURAS
Banking Hours: 9:AM - 3:30PM (Mon-Fri); Shopping Hours: 8:AM - 6:30PM (Mon-Sat)

HONG KONG
Banking Hours: 10:AM - 3:PM (Mon-Fri); 9:AM - 12:Noon (Sat) Business/Shopping Hours: 9:AM - 5:PM; 9:AM - 1:Pm (Sat)

HUNGARY
Banking Hours: 8:30AM - 3:PM (Mon-Sat); Business Hours: 8:30AM - 5:PM Shopping Hours: 10:AM - 6:PM (Mon-Fri); 10:AM - 2:PM (Sat)

ICELAND
Banking Hours: 9:15AM - 4:PM (Mon-Fri); Business Hours: 9:AM - 5:PM (Mon-Fri); Shopping Hours: 9:AM - 6:PM (Mon-Fri); 9:AM - 12:Noon (Sat)

INDIA
Banking Hours: 10:30AM - 2:30PM (Mon-Fri); 10:30AM - 12:30PM (Sat); Business/Shopping Hours:Government Offices: 10:AM - 1:PM; 2:PM - 5:PM (Mon-Sat); Non-Gov't Offices: 9:30AM - 1:PM; 2:PM - 5:PM (Mon-Sat)

INDONESIA
Banking Hours: 10:AM - 3:PM (Mon-Fri); 9:AM - 12:Noon (Sat)

IRAN
Banking Hours: 8:AM - 1:PM; 4:PM - 6:PM (Sat-Thur); Business/Shopping Hours:Gov't Office: 8:AM - 4:30PM (Sat-Wed) Non-Gov't. Offices: 8:AM - 4:30PM (Sat-Thur) Offices closed on Friday

IRELAND
Banking Hours: 10:AM - 12:30PM; 1:30PM - 3:PM (Mon-Fri); Business Hours: 9:AM - 1:PM, 2:PM - 5:PM;

Shopping Hours: 9:AM - 5:30PM (Mon-Sat)

ISRAEL
Banking Hours: 8:30AM - 12:30PM; 4:PM - 5:30PM (Sun-Tue,Thur) 8:30AM -12:30PM (Wed); 8:30AM - 12:Noon (Fri)Business Hours: Non-Gov't Office: 8:AM - 4:PM (Mon-Fri) Offices close early on Friday

ITALY
Banking Hours: 8:35AM - 1:35PM; 3:PM - 4:PM (Mon-Fri) Business Hours: 8:30AM - 12:30PM, 3:30PM-7:30PM Shopping Hours: 9:AM - 1:PM, 3:30/4:PM - 7:30/8:PM

JAMAICA
Banking Hours: 9:AM - 2:PM (Mon - Thur); 9:AM - 12:Noon & 2:PM- 5:PM (Fri) Business Hours: 8:AM - 4:PM Shopping Hours: 8:30AM - 4:30PM

JAPAN
Banking Hours: 9:AM - 3:PM (Mon-Fri); 9:AM - 12:Noon (Sat) Business/Shopping: 9:AM - 5:PM (Mon-Fri); 9:AM - 12:Noon (Sat)

JORDAN
Banking Hours: 8:AM - 12:30PM (Sat-Thur) Business/Shopping Hours: 8:AM - 6:PM (Sat-Thur)

KENYA
Banking Hours: 9:AM - 2:PM (Mon - Fri); 9:AM - 11;AM (1st & last saturday of month) Business Hours: 8:30AM - 4:30PM (Mon -Fri), 8:30 - 12:Noon (Sat) Shopping Hours: 8:30AM - 12:30PM, 2:PM - 5:PM (Mon - Sat)

KOREA, SOUTH
Banking Hours: 9:30AM - 4:30PM (Mon-Fri); 9:30AM - 11:PM (Sat) Business/Shopping Hours: 9:AM - 5:PM (Mon-Fri): 9:AM - 1:PM (Sat)

KUWAIT
Banking Hours: Mostly in the morning ;Business/Shopping Hours: Gov't Offices: 7:30AM - 1:30PM Non-Gov't Offices: 7:30AM - 2:30PM (Sat-Wed);7:AM - 1:PM; 5:PM - 8:PM

KYRGYZSTAN
Banking Hours: 9:AM - 6:PM
Business Hours: 9:AM - 6:PM
Shopping Hours: 8:AM - 9:PM

LATVIA
Banking Hours: 9:AM - 12:Noon
Business Hours: 9:AM - 6:PM
Shopping Hours: 8:Am - 10:PM

LEBANON
Banking Hours: 8:30AM - 12:30PM (Mon-Fri); 8:30AM - 12:Noon (Sat)

589

LESOTHO
Banking Hours: 8:30AM - 1:PM (Mon-Fri); 9:AM - 11:AM (Sat) Business Hours: 8:AM - 4:30PM (Mon-Fri) Shopping Hours: 8:AM - 4:30PM (Mon-Fri); 8:AM - 1:PM (Sat)

LIBERIA
Banking Hours: 9:AM - 5:PM (Mon-Sat); Business Hours: 9:AM - 6:PM (Mon-Sat)

LIBYA
Banking Hours: 8:AM - 4:PM (Sat-Thur); Business Hours: 8:AM - 4:PM (Sat-Thur)

LIECHTENSTEIN
Banking Hours: 8:30AM - 12:Noon, 1:30 - 4:30PM (Mon-Fri) Business Hours: 8:AM - 12:Noon, 2:30PM - 6:PM; Shopping Hours: 8:AM - 12:15PM, 2:PM - 6:30PM (Mon-Fri), 8:AM - 4:PM (Sat)

LITHUANIA
Banking Hours: 9:AM - 12:Noon; Business Hours: 9:AM - 1:PM, 2:PM - 6:PM (Mon-Sat)

LUXEMBOURG
Banking Hours: 9:AM - 12:Noon; 2:PM - 5:PM (Mon-Sat); Business Hours: 9:AM - 12:Noon, 2:PM - 5:30PM; Shopping Hours: 8:AM - 12:Noon, 2:PM - 6:PM (Mon-Sat)

MADAGASCAR
Banking Hours: 8:AM - 11:AM, 2:PM -4:PM (Mon-Fri); Shopping Hours: 9:AM - 6:PM (Mon-Sat); Business Hours: 8:AM - 12:Noon, 2:PM - 6:PM (Mon-Fri)

MALAWI
Banking Hours: 8:AM - 1:PM (Mon-Fri); Business Hours: 7:30AM - 5:PM (Mon-Fri); Shopping Hours: 8:AM - 6:PM

MALAYSIA
Business/Shopping Hours: 8:30/9:AM - 1:PM, 2:30PM - 4:30PM (Mon-Fri); 9:AM - 1:PM (Sat) Gov't Offices: 9:AM - 4:30Pm (Mon-Fri); 9:AM -1:PM (Sat)
MALI
Banking Hours: 8:AM - 12:Noon, 2:PM - 4:PM (Mon-Fri); Business Hours: 7:30AM - 2:30PM (Mon-Sat), 7:30AM -12:30PM (Fri)Shopping Hours: 9:AM - 8:PM (Mon-Sat)

MALTA
Banking Hours: 8:30AM - 12:30PM (Mon-Fri), 8:30AM - 11:30AM (Sat) Business Hours: 8:30AM - 5:30PM (Mon-Fri), 8:30AM - 1:PM (Sat) Shopping Hours: 9:AM - 1:PM, 4:PM - 7:PM (Mon-Fri), 9:AM -1:PM, 4:PM - 8:PM (Sat)

MARTINIQUE
Banking Hours: 7:30AM - 4:PM (Mon-Fri); Shopping Hours: 8:30AM - 6:PM (Mon-Fri); 8:30AM - 1:PM (Sat)

MAURITANIA
Banking Hours: 8:AM - 3:PM (Sun-Thur);Business Hours: 8:AM - 3:PM (Sun-Thur); Shopping Hours: 8:AM - 1:PM, 3:PM - 6:PM (Sun-Thur)

MAURITIUS
Banking Hours: 10:AM - 2:PM (Mon - Fri), 9:30AM - 11:30AM (Sat) Shopping Hours: (Varies) 9:AM - 5:PM (Mon-Fri), 9:AM -12:Noon (Sat, Sun)

MEXICO
Banking Hours: 9:AM - 1:30PM (Mon-Fri); Business Hours: 9:AM - 6:PM (Mon-Fri) Shopping Hours: 10:AM - 5:PM (Mon-Fri); 10:AM 8:/9:PM

MICRONESIA
Banking Hours: 9:30Am - 2:30PM (Mon-Fri)

MONACO
Banking Hours: 9:AM - 12:Noon, 2:PM - 4:PM (Mon-Fri); Business Hours: 8:30AM - 6:PM Shopping Hours: 9:AM - 12:Noon, 2:PM - 7:PM (Mon-Sat)

MONTSERRAT
Banking Hours: 8:AM - 1:PM (Mon-Thur); Business Hours: 8:AM - 4:PM; Shopping Hours: 8:AM - 4:PM

MOROCCO
Banking Hours: 8:30AM - 11:30AM, 3:PM - 5:30PM (Mon-Fri) Business Hours: 8:30AM - 12:Noon, 2:30PM - 6:30PM (Mon-Fri), 8:30AM - 12:Noon (Sat) Shopping Hours: 8:30AM - 12:Noon, 2:PM - 6:30PM (Mon-Sat)

MOZAMBIQUE
Banking Hours: 7:30 -12:Noon, 2:PM - 5:PM (Mon-Fri), 7:30AM - 12:Noon (Sat) Business Hours: 7:30AM - 12:Noon, 2:PM - 5:PM (Mon-Fri), 7:30AM - 12:Noon (Sat)

NAMIBIA
Banking Hours: 9:AM - 3:30PM (Mon-Fri), 8:30AM - 11:AM (Sat) Business Hours: 8:30AM - 5:PM (Mon-Fri) Shopping Hours: 8:30AM - 5:30PM (Mon-Fri) 9:AM - 1:PM (Sat)

NEPAL
Banking Hours: 10:AM - 3:PM (Sat-Thur);10:AM - 12:Noon (Sat)

NETHERLANDS
Banking Hours: 9:AM - 4/5:PM (Mon-Fri); Business Hours: 8:30 - 5:30PM; Shopping Hours: 8:30/9:AM - 5:30/6:PM (Mon-Fri)

NETHERLANDS ANTILLES
Banking Hours: 8:30AM - 11:AM; 2:PM - 4:PM (Mon-

Fri) Business/Shopping Hours: 8:AM - 12:Noon; 2:PM - 6:PM (Mon-Sat)

NEW CALEDONIA
Banking Hours: 7:AM - 10:30AM; 1:30PM - 3:30PM (Mon-Fri); 7:30 - 11:AM (Sat)

NEW ZEALAND
Banking Hours: 10:AM - 4:PM (Mon-Fri); Business/Shopping Hours: 9:AM - 5:PM (Mon-Fri)

NIGARAGUA
Banking Hours: 8:30AM - 12:Noon; 2:PM - 4:PM (Mon-Fri); 8:30AM - 11:30AM (Sat); Business/Shopping Hours: 8:AM - 5:30PM (Mon-Sat)

NIGER
Banking Hours: 7:30AM - 12:30PM, 3:30PM - 5:PM; Business Hours: 7:30AM - 12:30:PM, 3:30PM - 6:30PM; Shopping Hours: 7:30AM - 12:30PM, 3:30PM - 6:30PM

NIGERIA
Banking Hours: 8:AM - 3:PM (Mon), 8:AM - 1:30PM (Tues-Fri):Business Hours: Gov't Offices: 7:30AM - 3:30PM (Mon-Fri) Private Firms: 8:AM - 5:PM (Mon-Fri)

NORWAY
Banking Hours: 8:15AM - 3:30PM (Mon, Tue, Wed, Fri); 8:15AM - 5:PM (Thur); Business Hours: 9:AM - 4:PM; Shopping Hours: 9:AM - 5:PM (Mon-Fri); 9:AM - 6/7:PM (Thur); 9:AM- 1/2:PM (Sat)

PAKISTAN
Banking Hours: 9:AM - 1:PM (Mon-Thur); 9:AM - 11:30AM (Sat) Business/Shopping Hours: 9:30AM - 1:PM (Mon-Thur); 9:AM -10:30AM (Sat)

PANAMA
Banking Hours: 8:30AM - 1:PM (Mon-Fri); Business Hours: 8:30AM - 12:30PM & 1:30PM - 4:PM (Mon-Fri); Shopping Hours: 8:30AM - 6:PM (Mon-Sat)

PARAGUAY
Banking Hours: 7:AM - 12:Noon (Mon-Fri); Shopping Hours: 7:AM - 12:Noon & 3:PM - 7:PM

PERU
Banking Hours: 9:AM - 1:PM (Mon-Fri); Business Hours: 9:AM - 5:PM (Mon-Fri);Shopping Hours: 9:AM - 7:PM (Mon-Sat)

PHILIPPINES
Banking Hours: 9:AM - 6:PM (Mon-Fri); 9:AM - 12:30 (Sat)

POLAND
Banking Hours: 8:AM - 1:PM; Business Hours: 8:30AM - 3:30PM; Shopping Hours: 9:AM - 8:PM

PORTUGAL
Banking Hours: 8:AM - 3:PM (Mon-Fri) Business Hours: 10:AM - 6:PM Shopping Hours: 9:AM - 1:PM, 3:PM - 7:PM (Mon-Fri), 9:AM -12:Noon (Some Shops)

PUERTO RICO
Banking Hours: 9:AM - 5:PM (Mon-Fri); Business Hours: 8:AM - 5:PM (Mon-Fri); Shopping Hours: 9:AM - 6:PM (Mon-Sat)

QATAR
Banking Hours: 7:30AM - 11:30AM (Sat-Thur)

REUNION ISLAND
Business/Shopping Hours: 8:AM - 12:Noon; 2:PM - 6:PM

ROMANIA
Banking Hours: 8:30 - 11:30AM Business Hours: 8:AM - 4:PM (Mon-Fri), 8:AM - 12:30PM (Sat); Shopping Hours: 9:AM - 1:PM, 4:PM-6/8:PM

RUSSIA
Banking Hours: 9:AM - 6:PM; Business Hours: 9:AM - 6:PM; Shopping Hours: 9:AM - 9:PM (Mon-Sat)

RWANDA
Banking Hours: 8:AM - 11:AM, 2:PM - 5:PM (Mon-Fri), 8:AM -1:PM (Sat) Business Hours: 7:AM - 12:Noon, 2:PM - 6:PM (Mon-Fri) Shopping Hours: 8:AM - 6:PM (Mon-Fri), 11:AM - 6:PM (Sat)

SRI LANKA
Banking Hours: 9:AM - 1:PM (Mon-Fri); 9:am - 11:AM (Sat)

ST. KITTS & NEVIS
Banking Hours: 8:AM - 1:PM (Mon-Fri); 8:AM - 1:PM; 3:PM -5:PM (Fri) Business Hours: 8:AM - 12:Noon, 1:PM - 4:30PM (Mon, Tues); 8:AM - 12:Noon; 1:PM - 4:PM (Wed Thur, Fri) Shopping Hours: 8:AM - 12:Noon, 1:PM -4:PM Shops closed on Thursday afterNoons

ST. LUCIA
Banking Hours: 8:AM - 12:30PM (Mon-Thur); 8:AM - 12:Noon & 3:PM - 5:PM (Fri) ; Shopping Hours: 8:AM - 4:30PM (Mon-Fri); 8:AM - 1:PM (Sat)

SAN MARINO
Banking Hours: 8:30AM - 12:Noon, 2:30PM -3:15PM; Business Hours: 8:AM - 12:Noon, 2:PM - 6:PM; Shopping Hours: 8:AM - 12:Noon 3:PM - 7:PM

ST. MAARTEN
Banking Hours: 8:30AM - 1:PM (Mon-Thur); 8:30AM - 1:PM & 4:PM - 5:PM (Fri); Business Hours: 8:AM - 12:Noon & 2:PM - 6:PM; Shopping Hours: 8:AM - 12:Noon & 2:PM - 6:PM

ST. MARTIN

591

Banking Hours: 9:AM - 12:Noon & 2:PM - 3:PM (Mon-Fri); Shopping Hours: 9:AM - 12/12:30 & 2:PM - 6:PM (Mon-Sat)

SAO TOME AND PRINCIPE
Banking Hours: 7:30AM - 12:30PM, 2:30PM -4:30PM (Mon-Fri); Businss Hours: 7:30AM - 12:30PM, 2:30PM - 4:30PM (Mon-Fri); Shopping Hours: 9:AM - 12:30PM, 2:30PM - 6:PM (Mon-Sat)

ST. VINCENT & THE GRENADINES
Banking Hours: 8:AM - 12/1:PM (Mon - Thur); 8:AM - 12:/1:PM & 2:/3:PM -5:PM (Fri) Business Hours: 8:AM - 12:Noon & 1:PM - 4:PM (Mon - Fri); 8:AM- 12:Noon (Sat)

SAUDI ARABIA
Banking Hours: 7/8:AM - 2:30PM (Sat-Thur); Business Hours: Gov't Offices: In Winter 8:AM - 4:PM (Sat-Wed); In Summer 7:AM - 3:PM; During Ramadan 8:AM - 2:PM Others: 8:30AM- 1:30PM; 4:30AM -8PM (Sat-Thur) closed Friday

SENEGAL
Banking Hours: 8:AM - 11:AM, 2:30PM - 4:30PM (Mon-Fri) Business Hours: 8:AM - 12:Noon, 3:PM - 6:PM (Mon-Fri), 8:AM - 12:Noon (Sat) Shopping Hours: 8:AM - 7:PM (Mon-Sat)

SEYCHELLES
Banking Hours: 8:30AM - 1:30PM (Mon-Sat) Business Hours: 8:AM - 12:Noon, 1:PM - 4:PM (Mon-Fri) Shopping Hours: 8:AM - 5:PM (Mon-Fri), 8:AM - 1:PM (Sat)

SIERRA LEONE
Banking Hours: 9:AM - 2:PM (Mon-Fri); Business Hours: 9:AM - 2:PM (Mon-Fri); Shopping Hours: 9:AM - 6:PM (Mon-Sat)

SINGAPORE
Banking Hours: 10:AM - 3:PM (Mon-Fri); 9:30AM - 11:30AM (Sat) Business Hours: Gov't: 9:AM - 4:30PM (Mon-Fri); 9:AM - 1:PM (Sat) Shopping Hours: 9:AM - 6:PM (Mon-Sat)

SOUTH AFRICA
Banking Hours: 9:AM - 3:PM (Mon,Tue,Thur,Fri); 9:AM - 1:PM (Wed); 9:AM -11:AM (Sat) Business/Shopping Hours: 8:30AM - 5:PM (Mon-Fri); 8:30AM - 12:Noon (Sat) Some stores

SPAIN
Banking Hours: 9:AM - 2:PM (Mon-Fri), 9:AM - 1: PM (Sat)Business Hours: 9:AM - 2:PM, 4:PM - 7:PM Shopping Hours: 9:AM - 1:PM, 4:PM - 8:PM

SUDAN

Banking Hours: 8:30AM - 12:Noon (Sat-Thur); Business/Shopping Hours: 8:AM - 1:PM; 5:PM - 8:PM (Sat-Thur)

SURINAME
Banking Hours: 8:AM - 3:PM (Mon-Fri); Business Hours: 7:AM - 3:PM (Mon-Fri); Shopping Hours: 7:30AM - 4:PM (Mon-Fri)

SWEDEN
Banking Hours: 9:30AM - 3:PM (Mon,Tue,Wed,Fri), 9:30AM -3:PM, 4:PM - 5:30PM (Thur) Business Hours: 8:AM - 5:PM Shopping Hours: 9:30AM - 6:PM (Mon-Fri), 9:30AM - 1:PM (Sat), Noon - 4:PM (Sun)

SWITZERLAND
Banking Hours: 8:30AM - 4:30PM (Mon-Fri); Business Hours: 8:AM - 12:Noon; 2:PM - 6:PM; Shopping Hours: 8:AM - 12:15PM, 1:30PM - 6:30AM (Mon-Fri); 8:AM - 4:PM (Sat)

SYRIA
Banking Hours: 8:AM - 12:30PM (Sat-Thur); Business Hours: 8:AM - 1:30PM; 4:30PM - 9:PM (Sat-Thur)

TANZANIA
Business/Shopping Hours: 8:AM - 5/6:PM (Mon-Sat)

TAJIKISTAN
Bankng Hours: 9:AM - 6:PM; Business Hours: 9:AM - 6:PM; Shopping Hours: 8:AM - 9:PM

THAILAND
Business/Shopping Hours: 8:30AM - 7/8:PM

TOGO
Banking Hours: 7:30AM - 11:30AM; 1:30 - 3:30PM (Mon-Fri); Business/Shopping Hours: 8:AM - 6:PM (Mon-Fri); Sat morning

TONGA
Banking Hours: 9:30AM - 4:30PM (Mon-Fri)

TRINIDAD AND TOBAGO
Banking Hours: 9:AM - 2:PM (Mon-Thur) & 9:AM - 12:Noon; 3:PM -5:PM (Fri); Shopping Hours: 8:AM - 4:PM (Mon-Fri); 8:AM - 12:Noon (Sat)

TUNISIA
Banking Hours: 8:AM - 11:AM; 2:PM - 4:PM (Mon-Fri)

TURKEY
Banking Hours: 8:30AM - 12:Noon, 1:30 - 5:PM (Mon-Fri) Business Hours: 8:30AM - 12:30PM, 1:30PM - 5:30PM Shopping Hours: 9:AM - 1:PM, 2:PM - 7:PM (Mon-Sat)

TURKMENISTAN
Banking Hours: 9:AM - 6:PM

Business Hours: 9:AM - 6:PM
Shopping Hours: 8:AM - 9:PM

TURKS AND CAICOS
Banking Hours: 8:30AM - 3:30PM
Business Hours: 8:30AM - 5:PM
Shopping Hours: 9:AM - 7:PM

UKRAINE
Banking Hours: 9:AM - 6:PM
Business Hours: 9:AM - 6:PM
Shopping Hours: 8:AM - 9:PM

UNITED KINGDOM
Banking Hours: (Varies) England & Wales: 9:AM - 3:PM (Mon-Fri) Scotland: 9:30 - 12:30PM, 1:30 - 3:30PM (Mon - Wed), 9:30AM -12:30PM, 1:30 - 3:30PM, 3:30PM - 4:30PM-6PM (Thur) 9:30AM - 3:30PM (Fri), North Ireland: 10:AM - 3:30PM (Mon - Fri) Business Hours: 9:AM - 5:PM Shopping Hours: 9:AM - 5:30PM

UZBEKISTAN
Banking Hours: 9:AM - 6:PM
Business Hours: 9:AM - 6:PM
Shopping Hours: 8:AM - 9:PM

URUGUAY
Banking Hours: 1:PM - 5:PM (Mon-Fri)
Business Hours: 7:AM - 1:30PM (Mon-Fri) Summer & 12:30 - 7:PM (Mon-Fri) Winter Shopping Hours: 10:AM - 7:PM (Mon-Sat)

VENEZUELA
Banking Hours: 9:AM - 12:Noon & 3:PM - 5:PM (Mon-Fri) Business Hours: 8:AM - 12:Noon & 2:PM - 5:PM (Mon-Fri) Shopping Hours: 9:AM - 12:Noon & 2:PM - 5:PM (Mon-Sat)

VIETNAM
Banking Hours: 8:AM - 11:30AM; 2:PM - 4:PM (Mon-Fri); 8:AM - 11:AM (Sat)

WESTERN SAMOA
Banking Hours: 9:30AM - 3:PM (Mon-Fri); 9:30AM - 11:30AM (Sat)

YUGOSLAVIA
Banking Hours: 7:AM - 12:Noon or 7:AM - 7:PM; Business Hours: 8:AM - 12:30PM Shopping Hours: 8:AM - 12:Noon, 4:PM - 8:PM or 8:AM - 8:PM (Mon-Fri) 8:AM - 3:PM (Sat)

ZAIRE
Banking Hours: 8:AM - 11:30 (Mon-Fri); Business/Shopping Hours: 8:AM - 12:Noon; 3:PM - 6:PM (Mon- Sat)

ZAMBIA
Banking Hours: 8:AM - 1:PM (Mon-Fri); 8:AM - 11:AM (Sat) Business/Shopping Hours: 8:AM - 5:PM (Mon-Fri); 8:AM - 3:PM (Sat)

ZIMBABWE
Banking Hours: 8:30AM - 2:PM (Mon,Tue, Thur, Fri); 8:30AM -12:Noon (Wed); 8:30AM - 11:AM (Sat)Business/Shopping Hours: 8:AM - 5:PM

APPENDIX 10J

DIRECT FLIGHT TIME FROM THE U.S.++
(Time is expressed in Hours)

Country	Hours		Country	Hours
ALGERIA	9		KUWAIT	13
ANTIGUA & BARBUDA	3.5		LIBERIA	8.75
ARGENTINA	10.25		LUXEMBOURG	9
AUSTRIA	8.5		MALAYSIA	18**
BAHAMAS	2.5		MALTA	9
BARBADOS	4.25		MARTINIQUE	5.5
BELGIUM	7.5		MEXICO	5.75
BELIZE	4.75		MONTSERRAT	5
BERMUDA	2		MOROCCO	8
BOLIVIA	9.25		NEPAL	18
BRITISH VIRGIN IS	3.75		NETHERLANDS	7
BULGARIA	10		NEW CALEDONIA	14.75*
CAYMAN IS	3.5		NICARAGUA	7
CHINA, TAIWAN	13**		NIGERIA	11.25
COLOMBIA	5.5		NORWAY	7.75
COSTA RICA	6.25		PANAMA	5.5
COTE D'IVOIRE	10.75		PARAGUAY	9.5
CZECH REPUBLIC	10		PERU	7.5
DENMARK	8		PHILIPPINES	14.5**
DOMINICAN REP.	3.75		POLAND	9
ECUADOR	6		PORTUGAL	6.5
EGYPT	11.25		PUERTO RICO	4
ETHIOPIA	16		ROMANIA	10
FINLAND	8		RUSSIA	11
FRANCE	7		ST. KITTS	4
FRENCH GUIANA	7		ST. LUCIA	5.5
FED. REP. OF GERMANY	7.5		ST. VINCENT	4.75
GHANA	10.5		SAUDI ARABIA	12
GIBRALTAR	7.5		SENEGAL	7
GREECE	10		SEYCHELLES	19.5
GRENADA	4.5		SINGAPORE	17.25**
GUATEMALA	4.75		SPAIN	6
GUINEA	8.75		SURINAME	4.5
GUYANA	5.25		SWEDEN	9
HAITI	3.75		TANZANIA	18
HONDURAS	6		THAILAND	22*
HONG KONG	14**		TONGA	18.75
HUNGARY	8.25		TRINIDAD AND TOBAGO	4.75
ICELAND	6		TUNISIA	9
INDIA	16.75		UNITED KINGDOM	6.75
INDONESIA	18.25**		URUGUAY	11.25
IRELAND	6		VENEZUELA	4.5
ISRAEL	10.5		YUGOSLAVIA	9
ITALY	8.25		ZAIRE	18
JAMAICA	3.5		ZAMBIA	18.5
JORDAN	11.5			
KENYA	16.5			
KOREA, SOUTH	11.75**			

++These are approximate flight time from New York to the country's Capital City or the nearest airport to the Capital City, usually not more than 25 miles away. Countries omitted are those without direct flights from New York and /or may require 1-2 connecting flights. They also include countries with International Airports located in cities other than the capital and over 25 miles away.

* From Los Angeles, California

** From San Francisco, California

APPENDIX 11K

COUNTRIES AND OFFICIAL LANGUAGES

COUNTRY	OFFICIAL LANGUAGE	OTHER LANGUAGES
AFGHANISTAN	Dari, pashto	Uzbek, Turkmen
ALBANIA	Albanian	Greek
ALGERIA	Arabic	Berber, French
ANDORRA	Catalan	Spanish, French
ANGOLA	Portuguese	
ANTIGUA & BARBUDA	English	
ARGENTINA	Spanish	English, Italian, German
ARMENIA	Armenian	Azerbaijani, Russian
AUSTRALIA	English	
AUSTRIA	German	
AZERBAIJAN	Azeerbaijani	Russian , Armenian
BAHAMAS	English	Creole
BAHRAIN	Arabic	English, Farsi, Urdu
BANGLADESH	Bangla (Bengali)	English
BARBADOS	English	
BELARUS	Byelorussian	Russian
BELGIUM	Dutch (Flemish)	French, German
BELIZE	English	Spanish, Garifuna, Mayart
BENIN	French	Fon, Adja,
BERMUDA	English	
BHUTAN	Dzongkha	Tibeatan & Nepalese
BOLIVIA	Spanish	Quechua, Aymara
BOSNIA-HERCEGORVINA	Serb, Croat, Albanian	
BOTSWANA	English	Tswana
BRAZIL	Portuguese	Spanish, English
BRITISH VIRGIN IS.	English	
BRUNEI	Malay	English, Chinese
BULGARIA	Bulgarian	
BURKINA FASO	French	
BURMA	Burmese	
BURUNDI	French, Kirundi	Swahili
CAMBODIA	Cambodian (Khmer)	French
CAMEROON	English, French	
CANADA	English, French	
CENTRAL AFRICAN REP.	French	Sango, Arabic,
CHAD	French	Arabic
CHILE	Spanish	
CHINA, PEOPLES REP.	Chinese	
CHINA, TAIWAN	Chinese	
COLUMBIA	Spanish	
COMOROS	French	Abrabic, Shaafi Islam
CONGO, PEOPLE'S REP.	French	
COSTA RICA	Spanish	
COTE D'IVOIRE	French	
CROATIA	Croat	Serb
CUBA	Spanish	
CYPRUS	Greek, Turkish, English	
CZECH REP.	Czech & Slovak	Hungarian

DENMARK	Danish	
DOMINICA	English	
DOMINICAN REP.	Spanish	
ECUADOR	Spanish	Quechua
EGYPT	Arabic	
EL SALVADOR	Spanish	Nahua
EQUATORIAL GUINEA	Spanish	
ESTONIA	Estonian	Russian
ETHIOPIA	Amharic	Tigrinya, Orominga, Arabic
FAEROW ISLANDS	Danish, Faroese	
FIJI	English	Fiji
FINLAND	Finnish	Swedish
FRANCE	French	
FRENCH POLYNESIA	French	Tahitian, Chinese
FRENCH GUIANA	French	
FRENCH ANTILLES	French	
GABON	French	Fang
GEORGIA	Georgian	Russian, Armenian
GERMANY	German	
GHANA	English	Akan
GIBRALTAR	English	Spanish
GREECE	Greek	
GREENLAND	Danish	Greenlandic, Inuit
GRENADA	English	
GUADELOUPE	French	Creole
GUAM	English	Chamorro, Tagalog
GUATEMALA	Spanish	
GUINEA	French	
GUINEA-BISSAU	Portuguese	Crioulo
GUYANA	English	
HAITI	French	Creole
HONDURAS	Spanish	
HONG KONG	Chinese (Cantonese)	English
HUNGARY	Magyar	
ICELAND	Icelandic	
INDIA	Hindi	English
INDONESIA	Indonesian	Javanese, Sundanese
IRAN	Farsi	Turkish, Kurdish, Arabic
IRAQ	Arabic	Kurdish, Assyrian, Armenian
IRELAND	English, Gaelic	Irish
ISRAEL	Hebrew, Arabic	Yiddish, English
ITALY	Italian	
JAMAICA	English	Creole
JAPAN	Japanese	
JORDAN	Arabic	
KAZAKHSTAN	Kazakh	Russian, German, Ukraine
KENYA	English	Swahili
KIRIBATI	English	Gilbertese
KOREA, SOUTH	Korean	
KOREA, NORTH	Korean	
KUWAIT	Arabic	English
KYRGYZSTAN	Kirghiz	Russian, Uzbek
LAOS	Lao	French, Tai
LATVIA	Latvian	Russian
LEBANON	Arabic	French, Armenian, English
LESOTHO	English	Sesotho, Zulu, Xhosa
LIBERIA	English	
LIBYA	Arabic	
LIECHTENSTEIN	German	

LITHUANIA	Lithuanian	Russian, Polish
LUXEMBOURG	French, German	Luxembourgish
MADAGASCAR	Malagasy, French	
MALAWI	Chichewa, English	Tombuka
MALAYSIA	Malay	Chinese, English, tamil
MALDIVES	Divehi	
MALI	French	Bambara
MALTA	English, Maltese	
MARSHALL ISLANDS	English	Malay-Polynesian, Japanese
MARTINIQUE	French	Creole
MAURITANIA	Arabic, French	
MAURITIUS	English	Creole, Bhohpuri, Hindi
MAYOTTE ISLANDS	French	Swahili
MEXICO	Spanish	
MICRONESIA	English	Malay-Polynesian
MOLDOVA	Moldavian	Russian, Ukrainian
MONACO	French	English, Italian, Monegasque
MONGOLIA	Khalkha Mongol	Kazakh, Russian, Chinese
MONTSERRAT	English	
MOROCCO	Arabic	Berber, FRench
MOZAMBIQUE	Portuguese	
NAURU	Nauruan	English
NEPAL	Nepali	Maithali, Bhojpuri
NETH. ANTILLES	Dutch	Papiamento, English
NETHERLANDS	Dutch	
NEW CALEDONIA	French	
NEW ZEALAND	English	Maori
NICARAGUA	Spanish	English
NIGER	French	Hausa, Ndjerma
NIGERIA	English	Hausa, Yoruba, Ibo
NORWAY	Norwegian	Lapp
OMAN	Arabic	English, Baluchi, Urdu
PAKISTAN	Urdu	English, Punjab, Pashto, Sindhi, Saraiki
PANAMA	Spanish	English
PAPUA NEW GUINEA	English	Motu, Pidgin
PARAGUAY	Spanish	Guarani
PERU	Spanish, Quechua	Aymara
PHILIPPINES	English, Philipino	Tagalog
POLAND	Polish	
PORTUGAL	Portuguese	
QATAR	Arabic	English
REP. OF DJIBOUTI	Arabic	French, Somali, Afar
REP. OF CAPE VERDE	Portuguese, Crioulo	
REP. OF PALAU	Paluan, English	
REUNION ISLAND	French	Creole
ROMANIA	Romanian	Hungarian, German
RUSSIA	Russian	Tatar, Ukrainian
RWANDA	French, Kinyarwanda	
SAN MARINO	Italian	
SAU TOME & PRINCIPE	Portuguese	Fang
SAUDI ARABIA	Arabic	
SENEGAL	French	
SEYCHELLES	English, French	Creole
SIERRA LEONE	English	Krio
SINGAPORE	Chinese, English,	Malay, Tamil
SLOVAK REP.	Slovak, Czech	Hungarian
SLOVANIA	Slovene	
SOLOMON ISLANDS	English	
SOMALIA	Somali	Arabic, English, Italian

SOUTH AFRICA	Afrikaans, English	Zulu, Xhosa
SPAIN	Spanish (Castilian)	Catalan, Galician, Basque
SRI LANKA	Sinhala, Tamil	English
ST. KITTS & NEVIS	English	
ST. LUCIA	English	French
ST. PIERRE & MIQUELON	French	
ST. VINCENT	English	French
SUDAN	Sudan	English
SURINAME	Dutch	Sranan, Tongo, English, Hindustani, Javanese
SWAZILAND	English, Siswati	
SWEDEN	Swedish	
SWITZERLAND	German, French, Italian	Romansch
SYRIA	Arabic	Kurdish, Armenian, Aramaic, Circassian
TAJIKISTAN	Tajik	Uzbek, Russian
TANZANIA	English, Swahili	
THAILAND	Thai	
THE GAMBIA	English	Malinke, Wolof, Fula
TOGO	French	
TONGA	Tongan	English
TRINIDAD & TOBAGO	English	Hindi, French, Spanish
TUNISIA	Arabic	French
TURKEY	Turkish	Kurdish, Arabic
TURKMENISTAN	Turkmen	Russian, Uzbek, Kazakh
TURKS & CAICOS	English	
UGANDA	English	Luganda, Swahili
UKRAINE	Ukrainian	Russian
UNITED KINGDOM	English	Welsh, Gaelic
UNITED ARAB EMIRATES	Arabic	English, Fashi, Hindi, Urdu
URUGUAY	Spanish	
UZBEKISTAN	Uzbek	Russian, Kazakh, Tajik
VATICAN CITY	none	Italian, Latin
VENEZUELA	Spanish	
VIETNAM	Vietnamese	French, Chinese, Khmer
WESTERN SAMOA	Samoan, English	
YEMEN, ARAB REP.	Arabic	
YEMEN, P.D. REP.	Arabic	
YUGOSLAVIA	Macedonian, Serbo-Croatian	Slovene, Albanian, Hungarian
ZAIRE	French	Kikongo, Lingala, Swahili, Tshiluba
ZAMBIA	English	Tonga, Lozi
ZIMBABWE	English	ChiShona, SiNdebele

598

APPENDIX 12L

WHERE TO FIND THOSE GEMS (PRECIOUS STONES)[IL]

Country:	Gems Indigenous to the area:	Practices to beware:
Australia & New Zealand	opal, emerald, sapphire, & jade	dyed jades, synthetic emeralds and sap-phires, and doublet opals
Brazil	amethyst, aquamarine, emerald, garnet, topaz, tourmaline, citrine, and diamond (uncut)	misleading names, synthetic emeralds and amethysts, color alteration, and stone substitutes
Colombia	emerald	look-alikes and synthetics
Egypt	turquoise and camelian	plastic or imitation turquoise and dyed stones
Hong Kong	jade and pearl	Simulated pearls, misleading names, dyed opaque stones,synthetics, and high prices
India	fine Kashmit sapphire, ruby	poor quality, star ruby, and garnet synthetic

rubies and sapphires, color alteration, and look-alike substitutes |
Israel	diamond	poor quality, flaw concealment, color alterations, and look-alike substitutes
Japan	pearl, coral, & jade	simulated pearls, premature pearls that chip easily, and dyed jades and corals
Mexico	jelly, water, fire & cherry opal; moss, fire, & plume agate; and turquoise	plastic and simulated turquoise, color alterations, synthetics, and doublets
South Africa	diamond, emerald, green garnet, & semi-precious colored is a vorite stone	misleading names, synthetics, substitutions, and color alteration
Sri Lanka	fine and star sapphire, precious cats-eye (chrysobery), alexandrite and moonstone	synthetics, doublets, and pink rubies; sapphires and rubies said to be flawless should be looked upon with suspicion

599

Tahiti	fine and black pearl	simulated and dyed and coral pearls and corals
Thailand	ruby, sapphire, and zircon stone	synthetics, substitutions, mis-misleading names, and dark sapphires

APPENDIX 13M

TRAVEL INSURANCE PROVIDERS\AIR AMBULANCE SERVICE

Some companies and organizations specialize in providing a variety of insurance coverage and travel related services to domestic as well as international travelers including coverage for medical expenses, accidental injury and sickness, medical assistance, baggage loss, trip cancellation or trip interruption. Check with your travel agent/agency, broker, or travel advisor for reputable insurers in your area. Members of travel clubs and automobile clubs may also check with their associations for availability of such policies.

Here are a few companies widely known in the country to provide travel-related insurance coverage. These companies also sell short-term policies.

ACCFM AMERICA, INC.
P.O. Box 90310
Richmond, VA 23230-9310

AIR-EVAC INTERNATIONAL
8665 Gibbs Dr. Suite 202
San Diego, CA 92123
800-854-2569

ALLSTATE provides insurance covering off-premises losses, including those due to theft. Check your local telephone directory for the nearest ALLSTATE insurance agent.

Carefree Travel Insurance
120 Mineola Blvd.,
P.O.Box 310, Mineola NY 11501
(800) 323-3149 or (516) 294-0220

Edmund A Cocco/Globalcare Travel Insurance
220 Broadway, #201,
Lynnfield MA 01940
(800) 821-2488

GATEWAY
Seasbury & Smith
1255 23rd St., N. W.
Washington. DC 20037
800-282-4495/202-457-7707

HEALTHCARE ABROAD
243 Church St.. N.W.. Suite 100-D
Vienna, VA 22180
800-237-6615/703-281-9500

INTERNATIONAL S0S ASSISTANCE
1 Nesharminy Interplex
Suite 310; Trevose, PA 19047
800-523-8930/215-244-1500

Mutual of Omaha/Tele-Trip
Mutual of Omaha Plaza
Box 31685, 3201 Farnam St.
Omaha, Nebraska 68175
(800) 228-7669 or (800) 228-9792

NEAR, INC.
450 Prairie Ave., Suite 101
Calumet City. IL 60409
800-654-6700

Safeware provides insurance coverage for computers. You should consider this since other travel policies do not often cover equipments such as computers. Safeware could be reached at 2929 North High Street, Columbus Ohio, 43202. (800) 848-3469; (614) 262-0559.

Travel Insurance Programs Corporation
243 Church St.
West Vienna, VA 22180
(703) 448-2472

Travel Pak
The Travelers Insurance Co.
One Tower Square, 15NB
Hartford, CT 06115
(800) 243-3174; (203) 277-0111

Travel Guard International
1100 Centerpoint Drive,
Stevens Point Wisconsin 54481
(800) 782-5151 or (715) 345-0505

TRAVEL ASSISTANCE INTERNATIONAL
1133 15th Street, N.W., Suite 400
Washington, DC 20005
800-821-2828/202-331-1609

TRAVMED
P.O. Box 10623
Baltimore, MD 21235-0623
800-732-5309

WORLD CARE TRAVEL ASSISTANCE
1150 S. Olive St.
Ste. T-2233
Los Angeles. CA 90015
800-253-1877

[** Some of the insurance coverage mentioned here are
also available from several travel assistance organizations
listed in Appendix 14N.]

APPENDIX 14N

MEDICAL ASSISTANCE ORGANIZATIONS

ACCESS AMERICA offers 24-hour emergency medical assistance for the traveler. One call to their hotline center, staffed by multilingual coordinators, connects travelers to a worldwide network of professionals able to offer specialized help in reaching the nearest physician or hospital. Services include medical consultation and monitoring of travelers by hot line center physicians, medical transportation and on-site hospital payments. For further information call: Toll Free: 800-284-8300 or write: P.O. Box 11188, Richmond, VA 23230.

AMERICAN INTERNATIONAL ASSISTANCE SERVICES, INC., a member company of American Int'l Group (AIG), provides information for medical treatments to be considered prior to departure; makes arrangements for special medical care enroute, arranges facsimile or courier transfer of medical records and when allowed, for shipment of prescribed drugs & medical equipment. Provides assistance in medical emergencies such as help in obtaining local medical care, monitoring the care of a hospital patient, maintaining contact between the attending physician and the family physician at home. Arranges medical evacuation and repatriation and when necessary, will arrange transportation and escort home of unaccompanied minors. For further information call: 713/267-2500, FAX: 713/952-3619 or write to: 675 Bering Dr., Ste. 100, Houston, TX 77057.

ASSIST-CARD INTERNATIONAL
1001 S. Bayshore Dr. Miami Florida 33131. (800) 221-4564 or (305) 381-9969

CAREFREE TRAVEL INSURANCE
Carefree provides health, emergency health evacuation, baggage and trip cancellation insurance. They are located at 100 Garden City Plaza, P.O. Box 9366, Garden City NY 11530. (800) 323-3149 or (516) 294-0220.

EMERGENCY DATA BUREAU OF AMERICA INC., an international company, provides a complete Emergency Medical Identification System. The laminated membership card contains medical and personal history on four microfilm chit)s sufficient for Emergency Room use for informed treatment. Information includes treatment and surgical authorizations, and authorization to treat minor children if parents or guardian cannot be reached. EKG and other charts or records can be included on microfilm at no additional cost. EMERGENCY DATA BUREAU can be called without charge worldwide 24 hours a day if microfilm viewer is not readily available. Special decals

are furnished to each member so that emergency personnel know the card is being carried. Membership cards can be easily updated. Individual memberships are $45 annually; spouse may be included for $22.50, children for $11 each. Special group and corporate rates are available. For information write to P.O. Box 4187 Mesa, AZ. 85201 or call 602/833-2583.

WALLACH & CO., Health Care Abroad
provides medical assistance for insured travelers. Their policies cover hospitalization, prescriptions, doctor's office visits, medical evacuations to the U.S. For more information, 243 Church Street West Vienna, VA 22180. (703) 591-9800. 703/281-9500

I.T.C. TRAVELLERS ASSISTANCE LTD. is an international assistance service with coordination centers in 174 countries. Trained, local, multilingual personnel provide free medical aid 24 hours a day. Worldwide membership includes: free telephone access to any of eight ITC Emergency Control Centers, afl required medical assistance (ambulatory, hospitalization, prescribed medication, transportation); repatriation, free return tickets for children left unattended because of the Member's hospitalization. Individual or family membership is available for any length of trip, up to 180 days. Membership to ITC Medical Data and Referral Bank is also available. This service records member's medical history, making it readily available to emergency treating personnel and provides member access to a worldwide network of English speaking doctors. For additional information call 403/228-4685, or Fax 403/228-6271, or write, POB 73008, RPO Woodbine, Calgary, Alberta, Canada T2W 6E4.

IAMAT (International Association for Medical Assistance to Travelers) is a nonprofit tax-exempt Foundation financed by donations from its members. The purpose of the Foundation is to assist travelers in need of medical attention while traveling outside of their country of residence, and to advise them of the sanitary and health conditions in different parts of the world. Upon joining @T, members receive a Directory which lists IAMAT centers in 450 cities in 120 countries, along with the names and addresses of individual English-speaking physicians associated with IAMAT and a schedule of agreed upon fees. Membership also includes a Traveler's Clinical Record, various charts and brochures with information pertaining to climate, clothing, food, water conditions, immunizations and other Health related recommendations for travel to Foreign countries. Contact IAMAT at 417 Center St., Lewiston, NY 14092 or at 40 Regal Rd., Guelph, ON, Canada NIK IB5.

INTERMEDIC INC.,
777 Third Avenue, New York, NY 10017. (212) 486-8900

INTERNATIONAL HEALTH CARE SERVICE
440 East 69th Street, New York, NY 10021. (212) 472-4284.

INTERNATIONAL SOS ASSISTANCE, INC. A network of offices in 40 countries, including 15 multilingual SOS Alarm Centers, offers worldwide emergency medical services ranging from referrals to one of their 2,500 English-speaking doctors, to a complex aeromedical evacuation. SOS coordinates and provides for all aspects of an aeromedical evacuation and/or repatriation including selection of appropriate aircraft, the medical team, medical equipment and pharmacy needs, ground ambulance transportation and hospital admission arrangements. For further information call Toll Free 800-523-8930, 215/244-1500, FAX: 215-244-2227 at P.O. Box 11568 Philadelphia, PA 19116.

LIFE EXTENSION INSTITUTE'S Primary Care Center, is open to the public for the administration of immunization required for travel abroad. For further information call 212/415-4747; or write to 437 Madison Ave., 14th Flr., New York, NY 10022.

MEDEX/TravMed--a worldwide travelers' assistance program that provides prompt access to medical and related assistance services 24 hours a day 7 days a week. By calling the nearest MEDEX Assistance Center, a multilingual specialist will immediately assist you in locating quality medical providers and services and assist you in overcoming language barriers by directing you to English speaking doctors/translators. MEDEX will coordinate and establish contact with your family, personal physician and employer and monitor your progress during treatment and recovery and will make direct immediate payment of your medical bills. When necessary, arrangements can be made for emergency medical evacuation and repatriation. For TravMed information call Toll-free: U.S. 800-732-5309 or write: I.T.A.A. P.O. Box 5375 Timonium Maryland 21094-5375.

MEDICAL ALERT FOUNDATION INTERNATIONAL a nonprofit and charitable foundation that has since 1956 offered a lifetime emergency medical ID service--an alerting bracelet individually engraved with patient information and a 24 hour hotline phone number, so that physician and family can be contacted in emergency, plus an annually updated wallet card with medical and personal information. There is a one-time fee of $35.50 for all services; medically indigent patients are enrolled without charge at the request of physicians. Each year a new wallet card is issued and members' computer data can be

updated with any change in medical or personal information whenever necessary for a small fee of $7.00. For additional information, write to Medic Alert Foundation International, 2323 Colorado Ave., Turlock, CA 95380. Tel. 800-344-3226.

MEDIC ALERT Foundation International is a nonprofit and charitable foundation that has since 1956 offered a lifetime emergency medical ID service - an alerting bracelet individually engraved with patient information and a 24 hour hotline phone number, so that physician and family can be contacted in emergency, plus an annually updated wallet card with medical and personal information. There is a one-time fee of $35 and up for all services; medically indigent patients are enrolled without charge at the request of physicians. Each year a new wallet card is issued and members' computer data can be updated with any change in medical or personal information whenever necessary for a small fee of $7.00. For additional information, write to Medic Alert Foundation International, 2323 Colorado Ave., Turlock, CA 95380. Or call Toll Free 800-344-3226.

MEDJET ASSISTANCE, a division of MEDjet International, provides aeromedical evacuation and repatriation anywhere in the world. Each jet is a fully equipped intensive care unit staffed with a physician, an ICU nurse and any other medical staff necessary to provide bedside to bedside care. MEDjet Assistance is on call 24 hours a day and will aid members travelling abroad with English speaking physicians, treatment facilities and interpreters. For information call Toll Free 800/356-2161 or 2051592-4460, FAX: 205/592-4556 at 4900 69th St. North, Birmingham, AL 35206.

PATRIOT INTERNATIONAL, provided by IMG/International Medical Group, has a staff physician and medical support staff available 24 hours a day for responding to medical emergencies worldwide. Provides assistance in finding access to international medical facilities, emergency evacuation, emergency reunion, and if necessary, repatriation. For further information, contact International Medical Group, Inc.; 135 N. Pennsylvania, Suite 1700; Indianapolis, IN 46204. Or call 317/636-4721, Toll-Free: 800-628-4664, Fax: 317/687-9272.

TRAVEL GUARD INTERNATIONAL
1145 Clork St. Stevens Point, Wisconsin 54481, (800) 782-5151 or (715) 345-0505.

TRAVEL CARE INTERNATIONAL, INC. provides assistance or evacuation in the event of a medical emergency (or non-emergency) anywhere in the world, 24 hours a day, 7 days a week; communicates with the patient's physician; provides appropriate medical crew, flight escorts and necessary medical equipment; arranges medical ground clearance on an ends, ground transportation at every landing and coordinates all the

604

logistics of the repatriation. Coordinators provide language translators. Bedside to bedside services offered. For information contact Travel Care International, Inc., Eagle River Airport, P.O. Box 846, Eagle River, WI 54521. Or call 715/479-8881, Toll Free 800-5 AIR-MED.

TRAVELER'S AID INTERNATIONAL provides medical and legal assistance, and a number of other services such as theft and illness. TAI can be reached at 918 16th St. NW Washington DC 20006. (202) 659-9468.

US Assist offers Corporate Assist, a Program that provides medical and other travel assistance services through a worldwide network of hospitals, physicians, agents, and translators in over 210 countries. Arranges for transportation to the nearest medical facility capable of providing treatment, shipment of medications and blood, evacuation or repatriation, necessary medical payments, obtains and translates necessary documents, and monitoring the care and condition of the traveller. For more information please contact US Assist at 301/214-8449; Toll Free: 800/756-5900; FAX: 301/214-8205 or mail to 6903 Rockledge Dr., Ste. 800, Bethesda, MD 20817.

WORLDWIDE ASSISTANCE SERVICES, INC. provides comprehensive medical and personal emergency assistance 24 hours a day, 365 days a year through agent offices in 211 nations and territories. TAI emergency services include medical referral, On-The-Spot payment for medical expenses, unlimited transportation expenses for medical evacuations, medical monitoring and follow-up, shipment of medication worldwide, repatriation of a child under the age of 16 if left unattended due to your hospitalization, payment for a friend or family member to visit if hospital more than 10 days and payment of added travel expenses for a traveling companion. For further information call Toll Free 800-821-2828 or FAX 202/331-1588, or write to: 1133 15th Street, N.W., Suite 400, Washington D.C. 20005.

AIR AMBULANCE SERVICE

AIR AMBULANCE INC.
Hayward, CA
800-982-5806/510-786-1592

AERO AMBULANCE INTERNATIONAL
FL Lauderdale, FL
800 443-8042/305-776-6800

AIR AMBULANCE NETWORK
Miami, FL
300-327-1966/305-387-1708

AIR MEDIC - AIR-AMBULANCE OF AMERICA
Washington, PA
800-321-4444/412-228-8000

CARE FLIGHT - AIR CRITICAL CARE INT'L
Clearwater, FL
900-282-6879 813-530-7972

NATIONAL AIR AMBULANCE
FL Lauderdale, FL
800-327-3710/305-525-5538

INTERNATIONAL MEDIVAC TRANSPORT
Phoenix AZ
800-468-1911/602-678-4444

INTERNATIONAL SOS ASSISTANCE
Philadelphia, PA
800-523-8930/215-244-1500

MERCY MEDICAL AIRLIFT
Manassas, VA
800-296-1217/703-361-1191

(Service area: Caribbean and Canada only. If necessary will meet commercial incoming patients at JFK, Mia and other airports.)

PUBLISHED MEDICAL INFORMATION

DIABETES TRAVEL SERVICES, INC.
39 East 52nd Street
New York, NY 10022
Worldwide information on diabetic treatments and physicians.

IAMAT
International Association for Medical Assistance to Travelers
736 Center Street
Lewiston, NY 14002
716-754-4883
A medical directory, clinical record, and a malaria risk chart are sent without charge; however, a contribution is requested for World Climate Charts.

IMMUNIZATION ALERT
P.O. Box 406
Storrs, CT 06268
203-487-0611
For $25 a traveler is provided with an up-to-date, detailed and personalized health report on up to 6 countries to be visited. It will tell you what diseases are prevalent and what precautions are recommended or Advisable.

Emergency Medical Payment/Information Services
Available to American Express CARDHOLDERS ONLY:
1)   A directory of "U.S. Certified Doctors Abroad" (Price. $3.00)
2)   A health insurance plan is available through the Firemens Fund Life Insurance Company, 1600 Los Gamos Rd., San Raphael, CA 94911, Attention: American Express Card Service.

**STUDENTS, TEACHERS, and YOUTHS may want to also contact the COUNCIL ON INTERNATIONAL EDUCATION EXCHANGE (CIEE) at 205 East 42nd Street, New York, NY 10017. (212) 661-1414. CIEE offers very affordable short term policies called "Trip Safe" to holders of the International Student Identification Card (ISIC), International Teachers Identification Card (ITIC) or the International Youth Card (IYC). These cards are issued by CIEE and can be easily obtained from them.

606

APPENDIX 150

MEDICAL EMERGENCY KIT

Listed below are some items you may wish to include in your medical emergency kit. These items are readily available (in various brands) in your local pharmacy. Consult your physician for advice on other useful items and health matters.

Aspirin, 5 gr., or Tylenol, 325 mg.
Aluminum Hydroxide with Magnesium Trisilicate Tablets
Milk of Magnesia Tablets
Chlorpheniramine Tablets
Antihistamine Nasal Spray
Antimicrobial Skin Ointment
Calamine Lotion
Liquid Surgical Soap
Tweezers
Antifungal Skin Ointment
Zinc Undecylenate Foot Powder
Vitamin Mineral Tablets
Oil of Clove and Benzocaine Mixture
Opthalmic Ointment
Throat Lozenges
Kaolin Pectin Mixture, Tablets or Liquid
Paregoric or Lomotil
Adhesive Bandages
3-inch Wide Elastic Bandage
2-foot-by-19-Yard Gauze Bandage
4-inch by 4-inch Gauze Pad
Adhesive Medical Tape
Medium-Size Safety Pins
Thermometer
Insect Repellent
Sleeping Pills
Small Pack of Cotton Wool
Tampons
Tissues
A Pair of Scissors

APPENDIX 16P

TRAVEL BOOKSTORES

*AAA TRAVEL STORE, 330 Sixth Ave, N.Seattle, WA. 98109

AMERICAN YOUTH HOSTELS DISCOUNT STOREROOM, 1108 "K" Street, NW (lower level), Washington, D.C., 20005, Tel. (202) 783-4943

AROUND AND ABOUT TRAVEL, 931 Shoreline Drive, San Mateo, CA 94404, Tel. (415) 573-7998

BERLITZ, 40 W. 51st St. New York, NY, 10020, Tel. (212) 765-1000

*BOOK PASSAGE, 51 Tamal Vista Blvd. Corte Madera, CA, 94925, Tel. (800) 321-9785 or Tel. (415) 927-0960

BRITISH TRAVEL BOOKSHOP, 551 5th Ave. New York, NY, 10176, Tel. (212) 490-6688.

COMPLETE TRAVELLER BOOKSTORE, 199 Madison Avenue, New York, NY, 10016, Tel. (212) 685-9007

*FORSYTH TRAVEL LIBRARY, 9154 W. 57th St. P.O. Box 2975, Shawnee Mission, KS 66201, Tel. (913) 384-3440; Tel. (800) 367-7984

GEOGRAPHIA MAP AND TRAVEL BOOK STORE, 4000 Riverside Drive, Burbank, CA, 91505, Tel. (818) 848-1414

GLOBE CORNER BOOKSTORE, 1 School St., Boston, MA, 02108, Tel. (617) 523-6658

GOING PLACES TRAVEL BOOKSTORE, 2860 University Ave, Madison WI. 53705

HAGSTROM MAP AND TRAVEL CENTER 57 West 43rd St. New York, NY 10036, Tel. (212) 398-1222

KAPMANN NATIONAL BOOK NETWORK

226 W. 26th St., New York, NY 10001

MAP CENTRE, 2611 University Avenue, San Diego, CA, 92104, Tel. (619) 291-3830

CHESLER BOOKS P.O. Box 399 Kittredge, CO 80457, Tel. (800) 654-8502, Tel. (303) 670-0093

MICHELIN TRAVEL PUBLICATIONS, p.o. bOX 3305 Spartanburg SC 29304 Tel. (800) 423-0485

PACIFIC TRAVELLERS SUPPLY, 529 State St., Santa Barbara, CA. 93101

SANDMEYER'S BOOKSTORE, 714 S. Dearborn St., Chicago, IL, 60605, Tel. (312) 922-2104

TATTERED COVER 1536 Wynko, Denver CO 80202 or 2995 E. First Avenue, Denver CO 80206, Tel. (800) 833-9327, Tel. (303) 322-7727

THE TRAVEL ACCESSORIES MARKET, P.O. Box 19791, Seattle, WA. 98109

THE TRAVEL SUPPLIES, 1876 North Tustin, Orange, CA. 92665

THOMAS BROTHERS MAPS AND TRAVEL BOOKS 603 W. 7th St., Los Angeles, CA 90017, Tel. (213) 627-4018

*TRAVEL BOOKS AND LANGUAGE CENTERS 4931 Cordell Ave., Bethesda, MD

20814, Tel. (800) 220-Book, Tel. (301) 951-8533

*TRAVELLER'S BOOKSTORE, 22 W. 52nd St. New York, NY 10019 Tel. (212) 664-0995

*TRAVELLING BOOKS, P.O. Box 77114 Seattle WA 98177, Tel. (206) 367-5848

TRAVEL BOOK NOOK, 2409 Main St. Vancouver, WA. 98660

TRAVEL BOOKS PLUS, P.O. Box 3767, Santa Clara, CA. 95055

TRAVEL EMPORIUM, 19810 Ventura Boulevard, Woodland, Hills, CA. 91364

TRAVEL SHOP, 56 1/2 N. Santa Cruz Ave. Los Gatos, CA 95030

TRAVEL BOOKCASE, 8375 West 3rd St. Los Angeles, CA. 90048

TRAVEL BOOKS AND LANGUAGE CENTER, 4931 Cordell Ave, Bethesda, MD, 20814, Tel. (301) 951-8533

TRIP SMITH, 434 Main Street, Glen Ellyn, IL, 60137, Tel. (312) 858-7810

WAYFARER BOOKS, P.O. Box 1121, Davenport, IA, 52805

WIDE WORLD BOOKSHOP, Dept. M, 401 NE 45th Street, Seattle, WA, 98105, Tel. (206) 634-3453

WIDEWORLD BOOKS AND MAPS, 401 N.E. 45th St., Seattle, WA, 98105, Tel. (206) 634-3453

---

* These bookstores also operate Mail order Catalog services. Write for a catalog.

APPENDIX 17Q

INTERNATIONAL TRAVEL NEWSLETTERS, PERIODICALS AND MAGAZINES*

ANDREW HARPER'S HIDEAWAY REPORT, Harper Associates Inc. P.O. Box 50 Sun Valley, ID 83353, Tel. (208) 622-3193

BUSINESSTRAVELERINTERNATIONAL, 41 E. 42nd St. Ste. 1512 New York, NY. 10017

BUSINESS TRAVEL NEWS, 600 Community Dr. Manhasset, NY. 11030

CORPORATE TRAVEL, 1515 Broadway, New York, NY. 10036

CNN TRAVEL GUIDE, P.O. Box. 105366-Atlanta, GA. 30348-5366

CONSUMER REPORTS TRAVEL NEWSLETTER P.O. Box 53629, Boulder CO 80322, Tel. (800) 234-1970, Tel. (303) 447-9330

CRUISE VIEWS, 60 E. 42nd St. Suite 905, New York, NY. 10165

CRUISE WORLD, 5 John Clarke, Rd. Newport RI. 02840

CRUISE INDUSTRY NEWS, 441 Lexington Ave, 1209-A, New York, NY 10017

EMBARKATIONS, (specializes in cruise news), Landry and Kling, 1390 S. Dixie Highway, Coral Gables, FL 33146, Tel. (800) 431-4007or (305)661-1880

ENTREE P.O. Box 5148, Santa Barbara, CA 93150, Tel. (805) 969-5848

FAMILY TRAVEL TIMES, 80 Eighth Ave, New York, NY. 10011, Tel. (212) 206-0686

TRAVEL PUBLICITY LEADS P.O. Box. 88 West Redding CT. 06896

TRAVEL AGENTS MARKET PLACE, 1515 Broadway, New York, NY. 10036- 5703

TRAVEL TIPS, 300 East 40th St. #3H, New York, NY. 10016

TRAVEL WORLD NEWS, 624 S. Grand Ave. #1210, Los Angeles, CA. 90017

TRAVEL NEWS, P.O. Box. 8097, Portland, OR. 97207

TRAVEL WEEKLY, New York, NY. 10016

TRAVEL DIGEST, 1654 SW. 28th Ave. Ft. Lauderdale, FL. 33312

TRAVEL COMPANIONS P.O. Box 833, Amityville, NY 11701, Tel. (516) 454-0880

TRAVEL AND LEISURE 1120 Ave. of the Americas, New York, NY 10036, Tel. (212) 382-5600

TRAVEL WEEKLY, P.O. Box 7664, Riverton N.J. 08077, Tel. (201) 902-1500

TRAVEL SMART, Communications House, Inc. 40 Beechdale Road, Dobbs Ferry, NY, 10522, Tel. (914) 693-8300

TRAVEL-HOLIDAY, (212) 366-8700

TRAVELERS HOTLINE NEWSLETTER, P.O. Box 80966, San Diego, CA 92138-0966

TRAVEL MARGAZINE, 333 Main Ave; Knoxville, TN 37902

TRAVELORE REPORT, 225 South 15th Street, Philadelphia, PA, 19102, Tel. (215) 545-0616

YANKEE TRAVELLER NEWSLETTER, P.O. Box 523, Doublin, NH. 03444

---

*   Write and request sample copies of newsletter or magazine.

610

APPENDIX 18R

OVERSEAS ACCOMMODATIONS/ RENTALS AND HOME EXCHANGE SERVICES

Big Ben Apartment Rentals, 1333 Columbus Ave., San Francisco, CA, 94133, Tel. (415) 922-8145

American Youth Hostels (Travel Store) P.O. Box 37613, Washington, D.C. 20013 Tel. (202) 783-4943 or (202) 783-6161

At Home Abroad Inc. 405 East 56th Street, #6H New York, NY 10022

Council on International Education Exchange 205 E. 42nd St. New York, NY. 10007 Tel. (212) 661-1414 (800) 800-8222

Elder Hostel 75 Federal St., 3rd fl., Boston MA.02110 Tel. (617) 426-7788 or Tel. (617) 426-8056

Hideaways International, 15 Goldsmith, P.O. Box 1270 Littleton, MA 01460, (800) 843-4433

InterHostel University of New Hampshire, Division of Continuing Education, 6 Garrison Ave, Durham, NH 03824, Tel. (608) 862-1147

'International Home Exchange Box 190070 San Francisco, CA 94119 Tel. (415) 435-3497

Loan-a-Home 2 Park lane, 6E, Mount Vernon, N.Y. 10552, Tel. (914) 664-7640

RAVE 5000 Triangle Building, Rochester, NY 14604

STA Travel 17 East 45th St., New York, NY 10017 Tel. (800) 777-0112 or Tel. (212) 986-9470

'Vacation Exchange Club 12006 111TH Ave. Suite 12, Youngstown AZ 85363, Tel. (602)972-2186

Villas and Apartments Abroad 420 Madison Avenue, Rm. 1105, New York, N.Y. 10017, Tel. (212) 759-1025

Villas International Ltd.., 605 Market Street, Suite 510, San Francisco, CA, Tel. (800) 221-2260.

YMCA 101 North Wacker Drive, Chicago, Il 60606 (or check with your local branch)

YWCA 726 Broadway New York, NY 10003 (or check with your local branch)

Other Resources:

Home Exchange: A complete source book for Travelers at home and abroad. Available from Globe Perquot Press, Tel. (800) 243-0495

----

* Home Exchange Clubs/Agencies

** Also contact Foreign Tourist Offices. See listing in Appendix L). Be careful of fraudulent operators. Make inquiries first and ask for references before commiting any funds.

APPENDIX 19S

EDUCATIONAL SERVICES

American Institute of Foreign Study, 102 Greenwich Ave., Greenwich CT 06830, Tel. (800) 727-2437 or (203) 869-9090

Council on International Education Exchange, 205 East 42nd St., New York, NY, 10017, Tel. (800) 800-8222 or (212) 883-8200

European Studies Association (ESA), 780 Monterey Blvd. Ste. 203, San Francisco, CA, 94127, Tel. (415) 641-5502

Experiment in International Living, P.O. Box 676, Kipling Rd., Brattleboro, VT. 05302, Tel: (800) 451-4465 or (802) 257-7751

Institute of International Education, 809 United Nations Plaza, New York, NY 10017, Tel. (212) 883-8200.

** Several institutions in the U.S. have Study Abroad programs. Your college or university may have such programs. Check with your institution.

APPENDIX 20T

RESOURCES FOR OVERSEAS EMPLOYMENT*

<u>Organizations/Agencies:**</u>

Council on International Education Exchange, 205 E. 42nd St., New York, NY 10017, Tel. (212) 661-1414.

Experiment in International Living, P.O. Box 676, Kipling Rd., Brattleboro, VT 05302, Tel. (800) 257-7751 or (800) 451-4465.

International Employment Hotline, P.O. Box 3030, Oakton, VA 22124, tel. (703) 620-1972.

Volunteers for Peace International Work Camps, 43 Tiffany Rd., Belmont VT 05730, Tel. (802) 259-2759.

<u>Publications:</u>

Directory of Overseas Summer Jobs by David Woodworth, available from Petersons Guides Inc., 202 Carnegie Center, Princeton, P.O. Box 2123, N.J. 08543, Tel. (800) 338-3282.

The Directory of Jobs and Careers Abroad, The International Directory of Voluntary Work, Teaching English abroad, The Directory of Work and Study in Developing Countries and Directory of Summer Jobs Abroad are all available from Peterson's Guides Inc.,Tel. (800) 338-3282.

Summer Jobs in Britain, edited (annually) by Emily Hatchwell

Directory of American Firms Operating in Foreign Countries, available from World Trade Academy Press, 50 East 42nd St., New York, NY 10017, Tel. (212) 697-4999.

<u>Foreign/International Newspapers Listing Jobs and Employment Agencies:***</u>

- The Asian Wall Street Journal
- The International Herald Tribune
- The London Times (Great Britain), the Guardian (Great Britain)
- The Hong Kong Standard
- The Australian (Australia), the Sydney Morning Herald (Australia)

----

*   Be careful of fraudulent overseas employment agencies and brokers. Make inquiries first and ask for references before committing any funds.

**   Also check with embassies and consulates of foreign countries for work opportunities in their countries. A listing of these embassies is provided in Appendix B.

***   Some of these newspapers may be available in your local public or university libraries.

APPENDIX 21U

RESOURCES FOR THE BUDGET TRAVELER

Air Courier Services and Resources

Companies*:

Halbart Express, 147-05 176th Street, Jamaica, NY. 11434. Tel. (718) 656-8189

Discount Travel International, 152 W. 72nd St., Suite 223, New York, NY. 10023. Tel. (212) 362-3636

Now Voyager Freelance Couriers, 74 Varick Street, Suite 307, New York, NY. 10013 Tel. (212) 431-1616

Courier Travel Service, 530 Central Ave, Cedarhurst, NY. 11516, Tel. (516) 763-6898

Excaliber International Courier c/o Way to Go Travel, 3317 Barham Blvd. Hollywood, CA 90068, Tel. (213) 851-2572

Publications:

Fly there for less, 70 strategies to save money flying worldwide. by Bob Martin, Teak Wood Press, 160 Fiesta Drive, Kissimmee Fl. 32743

A Simple Guide to Courier Travel by Jesse L. Riddle, Published by the Carriage Group P.O. Box 2394, Lake Oswego OR 97035.

Travel Secrets P.O.Box 2325, New York, NY 10108, Tel. (212) 245-8703

Travel Unlimited, P.O. Box 1058, Allston, MA 02134-1058

World Courier News P.O. Box 77471, San Francisco, CA 94107

Flying Standby*

Airhitch, 2790 Broadway, Suite 100, New York, NY 10025, Tel. (212) 864-2000

Frequent Flyer Program

Publications:

Frequent Flyers, Tel. (a magazine) P.O. Box 58543, Boulder, CO 80322 Tel. (800) 323-3537, Tel. (719) 597-8889

Inside Flyer. (a newsletter) Inside Flyer Publications 4715 - C Town Center, Dr. Colorado Springs, Co. 80916 Tel. (800) 333-5937

The Frequent Flyer Guide by Kris Hammond. Available from 1988 Guide, 1220 Third St., Spearfish SD 57783.

Charter Operators

Martinair Tel. (800) 366-4655; Tel. (516) 627-8711

Travac Tours and Charters 989 6th Ave, New York, NY. 10018, Tel. (800) TRAV-800, Tel. (212) 563-3303

Sceptre Charters Tel. (800) 221-0924; Tel. (718) 738-9400

Homeric Tours Tel. (800) 223-5570; Tel. (212) 753-1100

Schwaven Charters Tel. (800) 457-0009

C.I.E.E. (Council Charter) 205 East 42nd St., New York, N.Y. 10017; Tel. (800) 800-8222, Tel. (212) 661-0311.

Ticket Rebators**

The Smart Traveller, 3111 S.W. 27th Avenue, Miami, FL. 33133 Tel. (800) 448-3338; Tel. (305) 448-3338

Travel Avenue, 641 West Lake Street, Suite 201, Chicago, IL 60606, Tel. (800) 333-3335; Tel. (312) 876-1116

Bucket Shops and Consolidators

Council Charter 205 E. 42nd Str., New York, NY. 10017; Tel. (800) 800-8222 or Tel. (212) 661-0311

614

Council Travels 3300 "M" St. NW, 2nd Flr. Washington DC 20007 (202) 337-6464

Euro Asia Express 475 El Camino Real, Millbrae, CA, 94030; Tel. (800) 782-9625 or Tel. (415) 692-9966

International Adventures, 60 E. 42nd St., Rm. #763 New York, NY, 10165; Tel. (212) 599-0577

Maharaja/Consumer Wholesale 34 33rd ST. Rm 1014, New York, NY, 10001; Tel. (212) 695-8435

TFI Tours International 34W. 37th St. 12th Floor, New York, NY, 10001; Tel. (212) 736-1140, (800) 745-8000

Travac Tours and Charters, 989 Sixth Ave., New York, NY, 10018, Tel. (212) 563-3303

Unitravel 117 N. Warson Rd., St. Louis, MO. 63132; Tel. (314) 569-0900

25 Cruises, 2490 Coral Way, Miami, FL 33145; (800) 925-0250

FREQUENT FLYER TRACKING

Competetive Technologies Inc.
2901 Wilcrest, Ste. 600, Houston, TX 70042, (713) 954-2900

Frequent Flyers Services
Ran Decisions 4715-C Town Center Drive,Colorado Springs, CO 80916. Tel: (800) 333-5937, (719) 597-8880

IVI Business Travel International
400 Skokie Blvd, Northbrook, Il 60062; (708) 480-8400

TRAVELWARE
2964 West 4700 South, Ste. 201, Salt Lake City, UT 84118. TEL: (800) 892-5577, (801) 965-1800

---

*   Also check the classified section of your local telephone directories or the travel section of your local newspapers and travel magazines.

**   These are fee-based travel agencies. Travelers are expected to research their trip plans and itinerary.

APPENDIX 22V

ASSISTANCE AND RESOURCES FOR SPECIAL TRAVELERS

WOMEN TRAVELERS

Publications:

Handbook for Women Travellers by Maggie and Gemma Ross, (Piatkus Books, 5 Windmill St., London WIP 1 HF. (071) 631-0710

In Another Dimension: A Guide for Women Who Live Overseas by Nancy J. Piet-Pelon and Barbara Hornby, (Intercultural Press, 1985)

The Women's Guide to Business Travel, published by Penelope Naylor, (Hearst Books, 1981)

The Business Women's Travel Guide and *Have a Safe Trip.* These two brochures are published by American Express

Ferari's Places for Women, published by Ferrari Publications, P.O. Box 37887, Phoenix AZ 85069, Tel. (602) 863-2408

SINGLE/COMPANION TRAVELERS/MATCHMAKERS

Club Med, 40 West 57th Street, New York, NY 10019, Tel. (800) 258-2633 or (212) 977-2100

Contiki Holidays, 1432 East Katella Ave., Anaheim CA 92805 Tel. (800) 466-0610

Mesa Travel Singles Registry, P.O. Box 2235, Costa Mesa, CA 92628, Tel. (714) 546-8181.

Partners-in-Travel, 491145 Los Angeles CA 90049, Tel. (213) 476-4869

Singleworld Cruises and Tours, 401 Theodore Freund Ave., Rye NY 10580, Tel. (800) 223-6490 or (914) 967-3334.

Society of single Travelers, (Travelcare) 3000 Ocean Park Boulevard, Suite 1004, Santa Monica CA, Tel. (310) 450-8510 or (310) 473-4185

Travel Companion Exchange, P.O. Box 833, Amityville, NY 11701, Tel. (516) 454-0880

TravelMatch, P.O.Box 6991, Orange CA, 92667, Tel. (714) 997-5273.

Travel Share International, P.O. Box 30365, santa Barbara, CA 93130, Tel. (805) 965-4955

VEGETARIAN TRAVELERS

Organization:

Vegetarian Resource Group, P.O.Box 1463, Baltimore, Maryland, 21203, Tel (410) 366-8343.

North American Vegetarian Society, P.O. Box 72, Dolgeville, NY 13329, Tel. (518) 568- 7970.

Publications:

International Vegetarian Guide, available from Vegetarian Times Bookshelf, P.O. Box 446 Mount Morris, IL 61054. Tel. (800) 435-9610.

GAY AND LESBIAN TRAVELERS

Organizations:

International Gay Travel Association, P.O. Box 18247 Denver, CO. (303) 860-9105

Homosexual Information Center, 115 Monroe, Bossier City, LA 71111, Tel. (318) 742-4709.

Renaissance Home, P.O. Box 533, Village Station, New York, NY 10014, Tel. (212) 674-01220.

Publications/Bookstores:

Spartacus International Gay Guide, available from Gmunder Publishing.

Ferrari's International Place for Men, Ferrari's International Places for Women, Ferrari's Places of Interest, and Inn Places: U.S. and Worldwide Gay Accommodations are all available from Ferrai Publication, P.O. Box 37887, Phoenix AZ, 85069, Tel. (602) 863-2408. Fax. (602) 439-3952.

CHILDREN:

Organizations:

Travel With Your Children (TWYCH), 45 W. 18th St., New York, NY 10011, Tel. (212) 206-0688.

Publications:

Travel With Your Children by Mureen Wheeler, available from Lonely Planet publications, 112 Linden St., Oakland CA 94607, (800) 229-0122. or (415) 893-8555.

The Family Travel guide Catalog, Carousal Press, P.O. Box 6061, Albany CA 94706, Tel. (510) 527-5849

Great Vacations with Your Kids by Dorothy Jordan and Majorie Cohen, available from E.P. Dutton, 2 Park Ave., New York, NY 10016 Tel. (212) 725-1818.

How to Take Great Trips with Your Kids by Sanford Portnoy and Joan Portnoy, Harvard Common Press, 535 Albany St., Boston MA 02118, Tel (617) 423-5803.

Kids and Teens in Flight, free from U.S. Department of Transportation, Tel. (202) 366-2220

Family Travel Times Newsletter, available by subscription from Travel with Your Children, 80 eight Ave., New York, NY 10011, Tel. (212) 206-0688

When Kids Fly, free from Massport Port Authorities, Public Affairs Department, 10 Park Plaza, Boston, MA 02116, Tel. (617) 973-5600.

617

APPENDIX 23W

CURRENCY EXCHANGE SERVICES

Thomas Cook, 1800 K Street, N.W. Washington D.C. 20006, Tel. (800) 368-5683

Ruesch International, 1350 I Street, N.W. Washington D.C. 20005, Tel. (800) 424-2923

American Express Travel Services*, Salt Lake City Utah, 84184 Tel. (800) 221-7282

Citibank*, Foreign Currency Dept., 55 Water Street, 47th Flr., New York, NY. 10043, Tel. (800) 285-3000, or (212) 308-7863

----

*   These firms provide limited currency services.

** See Appendix O for information on how to send money.

APPENDIX 24X

INTERNATIONAL EMERGENCY CODES

Country	Emergency #	Ambulance #	Police #
Algeria			17
Andorra		182-0020	21222
Andorra	11/15	20020	
Anguilla	999		
Antigua	999		20045/20125
Argentina			101
Austria		144	133
Bahamas		3222221	3224444
Barbados			112/60800
Belgium	900/901	906	101
Belize			2222
Bermuda			22222
Bolivia	118		110
Brazil	2321234		2436716
Columbia			12
Costa Rica	2158888		117
Cyprus	999		
Czech Republic	155		
Denmark	000		
Dominican Republic			6823000
Egypt			912644
Ethiopia			91
Fiji Islands	000		
Finland	000	002/003	
France	17	12/17	
French Guiana			18
Germany	110		
Gibraltar	199		
Great Britain	999		
Greece	100		171
Guyana	999		
Haiti	0		
Hong Kong	999		
Hungary	04		
Iceland			
(Reykavik)	11100	11166	
(elsewhere dial 02 for the operator who will then place the call)			
India		102	100
Ireland	999		
Israel			100
Italy		113	112
Jamaica		110	119
Japan		119	100
Jordan	19		
Kenya	999		
Liechtenstein		144	117
Luxembourg	012		

Country			
Malaysia	0		
Malta	99		
Maltese Island		196	191
Monaco		933-01945	17
Morocco			19
Nepal	11999		
Netherlands			
Amsterdam	559-9111	5555555	222222
(elsewhere dial 008 for the operator who will then place the call)			
New Zealand	111		
Norway		003	110011
Pakistan	222222		
Papua New Guinea			255555
Paraguay			49116
Peru	05		
Phillipines			599011
Poland		999	997
Portugal	115		
San Marino	113		
Singapore	999		
Spain	091		
Sri Lanka			26941/21111
St. Vincent			71121
St. Kitts & Nevis	999		
St. Lucia	95		99
Suriname	99933		711111/77777
Sweden	90000		
Switzerland		144	117
Tanzania	999		
Thailand			2810372/2815051
Tunisia			243000
U.S. Virgin Is.		922	915
Uruguay	401111		890
Venezuela			169/160
Yugoslavia	94		92

APPENDIX 25Y

FREEBIES/MONEY-SAVERS FOR TRAVELERS

Toll - Free (800) Numbers: A number of travel agencies organizations, and transportation firms in the U.S. presently have toll-free numbers. Request these numbers and use them. You can reach an 800 number operator by dialing 1-800 -555-1212.

Traveler's Checks: No fee traveler's checks are available through American Express and Thomas Cook to travelers who use their services. It is also good to check with your local banks and credit card issuers.

Insurance: Major credit card companies automatically provide you with some insurance coverage if your trip is charged to their card. Similarly, a growing number of travel agencies providing some insurance coverage to their clients.

Free Import Duties: You can enjoy free import duties if you import certain products from some countries under the U.S. Generalized System of Preferences (GSP).

Help for the Disabled: This service is available at several travel organizations, airlines, cruise lines, and port authorities. You must, however, make the request.

Maps: Free maps are available (upon request) from travel agencies, insurance companies, auto clubs, hotel lobbies, tourist offices and visitor information desks.

Reservations: Upon request, some tourist offices, airlines, travel agencies and travel organizations will handle your reservations (including hotel and auto rental) at no extra cost.

Transportation: Several major hotel chains and airlines will provide you, upon request, free shuttle service and ground transportation to and from the airport.

Inoculations: Several public or community health centers will (upon request) provide you with some of the shots you need for free or at a substantially reduced cost.

Special Diet: This is available on most International Flights with advance request.

Front Desk Service and Information Boot Clerks: They will, at no cost to you, provide answers to some of your questions.

Frequent Flyer Miles: This will entitle you to a number of free services, including free tickets. You must be registered and you must log your miles.

Free Drinks on Flight (all drinks): This service is available in some international flights.

Lounge Facility: You may be entitled to free use of airline lounge at the airport depending on the class or type of ticket you have. Check with your airline.

Hotel Accommodation: Upon request many International Airlines will provide you with free lodging and/or meals during an overnight stopover. This service may also be available to transit passengers, those passengers who must wait for six or more hours between connections. Certain restrictions apply, as this service depends on the type of ticket you have. Passengers holding discounted tickets, often, do not qualify.

Meals: (See Hotel Accommodation).

Senior ID Cards: These are available, upon request from several organizations and agencies catering to older citizens.

Student, Teacher and Youth ID Cards: I cards are available upon request from a number of academic institutions and travel organizations such as the Council on International Education Exchange.

621

International Association for Medical Assistant to Travelers (IAMAT) Cards: Available upon request from IAMAT.

APO/FPO Mailing Addresses: This service will save you money if you are sending letters to an overseas military base or any U.S. government office such as the American Embassy. It allows you to pay local rates, instead of the usual rates paid for overseas-bound mail.

Travel Publications: Several travel publications are available for free or for a nominal cost from the U.S. government. Most are available upon request from various agencies and departments of the government, the superintendent of Documents, U.S. government printing office, and from the Consumer Information Center, Pueblo Colorado.

Travel Advisories: This service is available, 24 hours, 7 days a week and is offered free of charge by the U.S. Government, Citizens Emergency Center.

Extreme Emergencies Abroad: Free assistance is available through the U.S. Government (State Department) in the case of extreme emergencies abroad.

Collect Calls: Most major credit card companies will accept overseas collect calls from their customers.

Mail Transfer: Some credit card, traveler's checks, airlines, hotel chains and auto rental firms will transfer as well as receive mail for their clients. Some post offices overseas with the poste restante services will do the same for International Travelers.

Bumped: If you are bumped through no fault of yours, you may be entitled to compensation including a complementary ticket from the carrier.

Couriers Service: Travelers who do not mind some restrictions and inconveniences can travel as air couriers for free, or at a substantial saving.

Note: Except in a few cases where you automatically qualify by virtue of using the services of the provider, most of the freebies and money - saving opportunities listed here require the traveler to initiate the request. Because some conditions and restrictions may apply, it would be wise to ask questions to be fully informed and avoid any surprises or misunderstandings.

622

APPENDIX 26Z

ORGANIZATIONS THAT PROVIDE SERVICES TO INTERNATIONAL TRAVELERS

Academic Travel Abroad, 3210 Grace St., N.W. 1st flr. Washington, D.C. 20007, Tel. (202) 333-3355

Airline passenger of America, 4212 King St., Alexandria, VA 22302, Tel. (703) 824-0505

Airport Operators Council International, Inc., 1220 19th St. NW, Suite 200, Washington DC, 20036, Fax. (202) 331-1362.

American Council for International Studies, 19 Bay State, Road, Boston, MA. 02215, Tel. (617) 236-2051

American Automobile Association (AAA), AAA Drive, Heathrow, Florida 32746 (404) 444-4000

American Youth Hostels, P.O. Box 37613 Washington DC 20013, Tel. (202) 783-4943.

American Association of Retired Persons (AARP), 1909 K-Street, NW Washington DC 20049 Tel. (800) 441-7575 or (800) 927-0111.

American Society of Travel Agents (ASTA), 1101 King St., Alexandria, VA 22314, Tel. (703) 739-2782

Association of Group Travel Executives, c/o Arnold H. Light A.H. Light Co., Inc. 424 Madison Ave., Suite 705, New York, NY. 10017 Tel. (212) 486-4300

Association of Corporate Travel Executives, P.O. Box 5394, Parsippany, N.J. 07054, Tel. (201) 537-4614

Citizens Emergency Center, Bureau of Consular Affairs, Rm 4811, N.S. U.S. Department of State, Washington DC 20520, Tel. (202) 647-5225.

Council on International Education Exchange (CIEE), 205 E. 42nd St., New York, NY 10017 (212) 661-1414.

Council on International Education Exchange (CIEE), 205 E. 42nd St., New York, NY 10017 Tel. (212) 661-1414.

Cruise Lines International Association, 500 Fifth Ave, Suite 407, New York, NY. 10110, Tel. (212) 921-0066

Fly Without Fear (FWF), 310 Madison Ave., New York, NY 10017, Tel. (212) 697-7666

Freighter Travel Club of America (FTC), P.O. Box 12693, Salem OR, 97309, Tel. (503) 399-8567

Hideaways International, 15 Goldsmith St., P.O. Box 1270, Littleton, MA 01460, Tel. (508) 486-8955, (800) 843-4433

Institute of Certified Travel Agents (ICTA), P.O. Box, 8256, 148 Linden St., Wellesley, MA. 02181 Tel. (617) 237-0280

Interexchange, 356 W. 34th St., 2nd flr. New York, NY., 10001 Tel. (212) 947-9533

International Gay Travel Association, P.O. Box 18247, Denver, CO. 80218, Tel. (303) 467-7117

International Federations of Women's Travel Organizations, 4545 N. 36th St., Suite 126, Phoenix, AZ, 85018 Tel. (602) 956-7175

International Association for Medical Assistance to Travellers (IAMAT), 417 Center St. Lewiston, NY. 14092 Tel. (716) 754-4883

International Airline Passengers Association (IAPA), 4341 Lindburg Dr., Dallas, TX, 75244, Tel. (214) 404-9980

International Association of Tour Managers, 1646 Chapel St., New Haven, CT. 06511, Tel. (203) 777-5994

International Cruise Passengers Association (ICPA), Box 886 F.D. R. Station, New York, NY 10150, Tel. (212) 486-8482

International Visitors Information Service, 733 15th Street, NW Suite 300, Washington DC 20005, Tel. (202) 783-6540.

International Bicycle Tours, Champlin Square, Box 754 Essex, CT 06426 Tel. (203) 767-7005

National Association of Cruise Only Agents, (NACOA) P.O. Box 7209, Freeport, NY. 11520

National Campers and Hikers Association, 4804 Transit Rd., Building 2, Depend, NY 1404, Tel. (716) 668-6242.

North American Vegetarian Society, P.O. Box 72, Dolgeville, NY 1339, Tel. (518) 568-7970.

SCI International Voluntary Service, Innisfree Village, Rt.2, BOX 506 Crozet, VA 22932, Tel. (804) 823-1826.

Share-A-Ride International (SARI), 100 Park Ave. Rockville, Maryland, Tel. (301) 217-0871

Society of Incentive Travel Executives, 347 Fifth Ave., Suite 610, New York, NY. 10016, Tel. (212) 725-8253

Society for the Advancement of Travel for the Handicapped (SATH), 347 Fifth Ave., Suite 610, New York, NY 10016 Tel. (212) 447-7284. 858-5483

Travel Information Service (TIS), Moss Rehabilitation Hospital , 12th St., and Tabor Rd, Philadelphia, PA. 19141, Tel. (215) 456-9600

U.S. Department of Commerce, International Trade Information Center, Tel (800) 872-8723.

U.S. Department of Transportation, Office of General Counsel, 400 7th St. SW, Rm. 10422, Washington DC 20590, Tel. (202) 366-9306 (voice), (202) 755-7687 (TDD)

U.S. Public Health Services, Centers for Disease Control, Atlanta Georgia, Tel. (404) 539-2574.

Volunteers for Peace International Work Camps, 43 Tiffany Rd., Belmont VTY 05730, Tel. (802) 259-2759.

World Ocean and Cruise Liner Society, P.O. Box 92, Stamford, CT. 06904, Tel. (203) 329-2787

Institute of Certified Travel Agents (ICTA), 148 Linden St., P.O. Box, 812059, (800) 542, 4282.

International Air Passenger Association (IAPA), P.O. Box 870188, Dallas TX. 75287, (800) 821-4274.

International Air Transport Association (IATA), 2000 Peel St., Montreal, QC Canada, H3A 2R4, (514) 844-6311.

International Airlines Travel Agent Network (IATAN), 300 Garden City Plaza, Ste. 342, Garden City, NY. 11530, (7516) 747-4716.

International Association for Medical Assistance to Travelers (IAMAT), 417 Center St., Lewiston, NY. 14092, (716) 754-4883

International Association of Convention and Visitor Bureaus (IACVB), 2000 L. St., NW., Ste. 702, Washington, D.C. 20036, (202) 296-7888.

International Civil Aviation Organization (ICAO), 1000 Sherbrooke West, Montreal, QC Canada H3A 2R2, (514) 285-8219.

National Business travel Association (NBTA), 1650 King St., STe. 301, Alexandria, VA. 22314, (703) 684-0836.

Society of Incentive Travel Executives (SITE), 21 W. 38th St., 10th Fl., New York, 10018, (212) 575-0910.

Society of Travel Agents in Government (STAG), 6935 Wisconsin Ave, Bethesda, MD. 20815, (301) 654-8595.

Travel and Tourism Government Affairs Council, 1100 New York Ave., NW., Ste. 450, Washington, DC. 20005, (202) 408-9600.

Travel and Tourism Research Association, 10200 W. 44th Ave., Ste. 304, Wheat ridge, CO. 80033, (303) 940-6557.

Travel Industry Association of America (TIA), 1100 New York AVe. NW. Ste. 450, Washington, D.C. 20005, (202) 408-8422.

U.S. Travel Data Center, 1100 New York Ave, NW., Ste. 450, Washington, D.C. 20005, (202) 408-1832.

World Travel & Tourism Council, Chaussee de La Hulpe 181, Box 10, 1170 Brussels, Belgium, (32-2) 660 20 67.

INDEX

628

629

630

LIBRARY RECOMMENDATION FORM

(This form should be hand delivered to your local
Head Librarian or Reference Librarian)

Sir/Madam,

I regularly use the book entitled **"AMERICANS TRAVELING ABROAD: WHAT YOU SHOULD KNOW BEFORE YOU GO** (published by World Travel Institute Press, 647 pages, $39.99, ISBN 0-9623820-7-8.) Your records indicate that the library does not carry this valuable and comprehensive travel reference book. Could you please place an order for this book for our library? Thanks for your considerations.

Name of Recommender:---

Address:---

Phone:--

LIBRARY RECOMMENDATION FORM

(This form should be hand delivered to your local
Head Librarian or Reference Librarian)

Sir/Madam,

I regularly use the book entitled **"AMERICANS TRAVELING ABROAD: WHAT YOU SHOULD KNOW BEFORE YOU GO** (published by World Travel Institute Press, 647 pages, $39.99, ISBN 0-9623820-7-8.) Your records indicate that the

library does not carry this valuable and comprehensive travel reference book. Could you please place an order for this book for our library? Thanks for your considerations.

Name of Recommender:---

Address:---

Phone:--

NOTES

ORDER FORM

[This book would save you **money, time,** embarrassment and above all, your **life.**]

Telephone Orders: Call toll-free 1-800-345-0096
        Have Your Credit Card ready. Order any time,
        day or night, 7 days a week, 24 hours a day.

Fax Orders: 410-922-8115 (Send this form)

Postal Orders: World Travel Institute
        P.O. Box 32674-1A, Baltimore
        Maryland 21208-8674 U.S.A.
        {tel: (410) 922-4903}
        Make check payable to WTI.

Ship to:--
Firm Name:--
Your Name:--
Address:---
City:------------------------------**State:**----------------------------**Zip:**-----------------------

Yes! Please send me --------copies of your book
at $39.99 per book <u>plus</u>
Shipping Cost per book
        [First Class $4.00 Takes up to 7 working days]
        [Book Rate $3.00 Takes up to 3 weeks]
Sales Tax: (Maryland Residents Only) Add 5%

Enclosed is my Payment of $---------------**By**

  ☐ Check   ☐ Money Order   ☐ Credit Card

  ☐ VISA   ☐ MASTERCARD

Card Number:--
Card Holder Name:--
Expiration Date:--
Card Holder Signature:---

No Cash or C.O.D.s please. Prices subject to change
without notice. <u>Quantity discounts available upon request.</u>

Inquiries: *All inquiries regarding your order or this book should be directed to our headquarters at the address and phone number shown above. The toll-free number is for orders only. No inquiries will be accepted at that number.*

NOTES

ORDER FORM

The Best Gift you could ever give that special person or client traveling abroad is a gift of this book. It is indeed a gift for all seasons.

A gift of this book would save your relative, friend or colleague lots of **money, time, embarrassment** and above all, their **life.**

I AM GIVING A GIFT

My name is :---
Please send the gift to:--
Name:--
Address:---
City:----------------------State:------Zip:---

Price Per Book: $39.99
Shipping Cost per book
      [First Class $4.00 Takes up to 7 working days]
      [Book Rate $3.00 Takes up to 3 weeks]
Sales Tax: (Maryland Residents Only) Add 5%

Enclosed is my Payment of $————————**By**
  □ Check   □ Money Order   □ Credit Card

  □ VISA   □ MASTERCARD
Card Number:---
Card Holder:---
Expiration Date:--
Card Holder Signature:---

Telephone Orders: Call toll-free 1-800-345-0096
      Have Your Credit Card ready. Order any time,
      day or night, 7 days a week, 24 hours a day.

Fax Orders: 410-922-8115 (Send this form)

Postal Orders: World Travel Institute
      P.O. Box 32674-1A, Baltimore
      Maryland 21208-8674 U.S.A.
      {tel: (410) 922-4903}
      Make check payable to WTI. No C.O.D.s

Inquiries: *All inquiries regarding your order or this book should be directed to our headquarters at the address and phone number shown above. The toll-free number is for orders only. No inquiries will be accepted at that number.*

COMMENT FORM

YOUR OPINION MEANS A LOT TO US

(Please use this postcard to tell us how you feel about this book. We may quote you and/or use your comments, testimonials or suggestions in our promotions and future editions)

Institution--
Address---
City, State & Zip---
Attention--
Name/Title/Department
  Phone (   )---

( ) Check here if we may quote you. Signature....................................Date:...........

[Mail your comments to WTI, P.O. Box 32674 Baltimore MD. 21208]

COMMENT FORM

YOUR OPINION MEANS A LOT TO US

(Please use this postcard to tell us how you feel about this book. We may quote you and/or use your comments, testimonials or suggestions in our promotions and future editions)

Institution--
Address---
City, State & Zip---
Attention---
Name/Title/Department
 Phone (   )---

( ) Check here if we may quote you. Signature....................................Date:...........

[Mail your comments to WTI, P.O. Box 32674 Baltimore MD. 21208]

ABOUT THE AUTHOR

Dr. Gladson I. Nwanna (Ph.D) is a university professor, a former consultant to the World Bank, and a veteran traveler. He has over the past 15 years traveled to several countries of the world, logging thousands of miles in the process.

WHAT OTHERS ARE SAYING ABOUT

AMERICANS TRAVELING ABROAD

This is one publication that truly lives up to its description. It should be read at least in part, if not in its entirety, by anyone embarking on foreign travel for the first time. Even seasoned travelers would benefit from it...this book will be a most welcome addition to any travel reference collection. *ALA BOOKLIST, December 15, 1993.*

"Nwanna provides an extremely comprehensive and well-researched resource guide for the American traveler abroad....A traveler would be hard pressed to find information not included in this volume. Its excellent table of contents and index make it easy to use. Well recommended." *Library Journal, September 1993.*

"This all-in-one guide packs in details on everything from health and safety to money tips, terrorism, funds replacement, driving and visa requirements, making it the most comprehensive handbook in print on international travel. A "must" for any who frequently go overseas." *The Midwest Book Review (BOOKWATCH), January 1994.*

"'Americans Traveling Abroad: What You Should Know Before You Go' is a nice big book filled with helpful information. It is excellent for the first timer or the experienced business traveler or tourist. Travel agents should invest in a copy of this and keep it handy." *The press Tribune, Dec. 1993.*

"The Americans Traveling Abroad Resource Guide is without a doubt the most complete compilation of information I believe I have ever seen in one publication. There isn't anything that I am aware of that has been left out. An excellent resource guide." *Robert W. Whitley, President United States Tour Operators Association.*

"...a very thorough compilation of travel information which should be helpful to Americans traveling abroad." *H. Wayne Berens, Chairman, Institute of Certified Travel Agents.*

"Every American traveling abroad should buy a copy of this ultimate guide. It's a definitive international traveler's resource covering everything from abduction to vaccinations. This remarkable tome sets a new standard for world travel and tourism. No inexperienced traveler should leave home without it." *Andrew S. Linick, Ph.D, Chairman/CEO, Travel, Tourism, Transportation and Hospitality Adviceline. Bestselling Author of Guide to Trouble-Free Travel.*

"Terrific! It's great to have all the necessary international travel information at your finger tips rather than trying to find the one single publication. A great asset for Human Resource departments that are responsible for relocating employees and their families overseas." *John H. Hintz, President National Business Travel Association.*

"This is an extremely useful compilation of information, much of which would not be available in small libraries, and useful in large libraries with U.S. Documents because it compiles the wealth of information in one easy source." *Harriet C. Jenkins, Librarian, Enoch Pratt Free Library, Baltimore, MD.*

"Americans Traveling Abroad is very detailed, it contains everything from what to do if you are held hostage to how to obtain visas. This book would be an excellent addition as a reference work for libraries, travel agents and companies doing business abroad." *Christopher J.J. Thiry, Map Librarian, New York Public Library.*

"A very unique complete book. Contains much useful information... The nitty gritty of traveling that looks deeper than the usual tourist attractions. A must for the frequent traveler or public library collection." *Jean Alexander, Regional Administrator, County of Los Angeles, Public Library.*

"Anything that promotes the goal of traveler safety and security must be applauded. Your effort to compile and organize a comprehensive anthology of information on the subject is a positive and useful step toward this goal." *Edward R. Book, President, Travel Industry Association of America.*

"Information is relevant, reliable, and easy to use. This resource delivers on all it promises. It is a great book! Very highly recommended." *American Reference Book Annual, 1995.*